Commentary on
PSALMS

Commentary on
PSALMS

JOSEPH A. ALEXANDER

KREGEL PUBLICATIONS
Grand Rapids, Michigan 49501

Commentary on the Psalms, by Joseph Addison Alexander. © 1991
by Kregel Publications, a division of Kregel, Inc., P. O. Box 2607,
Grand Rapids, MI 49501. All rights reserved.

Library of Congress Cataloging-in-Publication Data

Alexander, Joseph Addison, 1809-1860.
   [Psalms translated and explained]
   Commentary on the Psalms / by Joseph Addison Alexander.
     p.   cm.
   Reprint. Originally published: The Psalms translated and
explained. Edinburgh: A. Elliot and J. Thin, 1864.

   1. Bible O. T. Psalms — Commentaries.   I. Title.

BS1430.A3   1991   223'.2077—dc20   89-2563
                                                           CIP
ISBN 0-8254-2140-3 (paperback)
ISBN 0-8254-2141-1 (deluxe hardback)

1 2 3 4 5 Printing/Year 95 94 93 92 91

CONTENTS

6 *Contents*

FOREWORD

The book of *Psalms* was the hymnal and prayer book of the Jews composed by many different authors over a long period of time. These hymns and prayers were collected and used by the people of Israel in their worship gatherings. Eventually this collection was included in their scriptures.

These religious poems represent many different forms. There are hymns of praise and worship of God; many take the form of prayers for help, protection, and salvation; and others are pleas for forgiveness. They may be songs of thanksgiving for God's blessing or petitions for the punishment of enemies. The prayers are both personal and national. They portray the most intimate feelings of one individual or are the expression of many. Some of the Psalms represent the needs and feelings of all the people of God.

The Psalms were quoted by Jesus, cited by the writers of the New Testament, and became the treasured book of worship of the early Christian church, from its very beginning.

The Hebrew name for *Psalms* was "The Book of Praises." The present name derives from the Latin Vulgate, which followed the Septuagint (the Greek translation of the Old Testament). It is the second of three Old Testament books considered poetical: Job, Psalms, and Proverbs. These three were also called "books of truth." Some scholars feel the final editing probably took place in the time of Ezra. Thus the dates when the individual Psalms were written must range through many centuries.

The *Psalter* was closely associated with the Pentateuch. The repeated reading of the Psalter led to the use of certain Psalms on specific occasions and festivals such as the Feast of Booths. Thus, scholars believe that the Psalms were used liturgically in Hebrew worship, just as they have been in the life of the church.

Seventy-three of the Psalms were written by David. A number were contributed by the Levitical singing clans of Asaph and Korah. Forty-nine have anonymous authorship.

The 150 Psalms are organized into five books, which represent four collections added to the first worship book. Book 1 (Psalms 1-

41) is Davidic, compiled before his death. The collection is largely personal psalms which reflect David's own experiences. Book 2 (Psalms 42-72) was probably added in the days of Solomon. Books 3 and 4 (73-89, 90-106) are collections from the days of the exile, while the final book 5 (Psalms 107-150), is strongly liturgical and probably was organized around the time of Ezra the scribe after the return from Babylonian captivity. It is probable that many Psalms were used by the Hebrew people even before their official compilation in these five books.

Dr. Cyril Barber describes J.A. Alexander's classic commentary on the *Psalms* as having: ". . . genuine scholarship and evangelical warmth." He goes on to mention that such scholarship and warmth are singularly missing from many commentaries today. Another commentary reviewer, David W. Brookman, says that Alexander's work on the Psalms ". . . is a valuable classic. . . . soundly scholarly and warmly evangelical...." The eminent C.H. Spurgeon said that this commentary ". . . occupies first place among expositions. . . . (it is) a clear and judicious exposition of the text (that) cannot be dispensed with."

Kregel Publications is honored to make this classic *Commentary on the Psalms* available to a new generation of Bible students.

THE PUBLISHERS

PREFACE

THE present publication owes its origin to Hengstenberg's Commentary on the Psalms. The original design was to make that work, by abridgment and other unessential changes, more acceptable and useful to the English reader than it could be in the form of an exact translation. It was soon found, however, that by far the most important part of such a book would be a literal version of the Hebrew text, and that this was precisely what could not be obtained at second hand, by the awkward and unsatisfying process of translating a translation, but must be derived directly from an independent scrutiny of the original. In attempting this, the deviations from Hengstenberg, continually in form and not unfrequently in substance, rendered it wholly inexpedient and improper to make him responsible for what was really a new translation. The only course remaining therefore was to make this general acknowledgment, that his work is the basis of the one now offered to the public, and that more has been directly drawn from that source than from all others put together. The present writer has so freely availed himself of Hengstenberg's translations, exegetical suggestions, and illustrative citations, in preparing his own version and explanatory comments, that nothing could have led him to forego the advantage of inserting that distinguised name upon his title-page, except a natural unwillingness to make it answerable for the good or evil which is really his own. At the same time, he considers it by no means the least merit of the book, that it presents, in a smaller compass and a more familiar dress, the most valuable results of so masterly an exposition.

In justice to his work and to himself, the author wishes it to be distinctly understood, that he has aimed exclusively at *explanation*, the discovery and statement of the meaning. To this he has confined himself for several reasons: first, because a wider plan would have required a larger book than was consistent with his general purpose; then, because this is really the point in which assistance is most needed by the readers of the Psalter; and lastly, because he had especially in view the wants of ministers, who are better able than himself to erect a doctrinal, devotional, or practical superstructure on the exegetical basis which he has endeavoured here to furnish. It follows of course, that the book is not designed to supersede the admirable works in common use, except so far as it may be found to correct their occasional errors of translation or verbal exposition.

It may be thought that, in order to accomplish this design, the author might have satisfied himself with a bare translation. But experience has more and more convinced him, that the meaning of an author cannot be fully given in another language by the use of exact equivalents, which are in fact so few, that the deficiency can only be supplied by the addition of synonymous expressions or by explanatory paraphrase, or by exegetical remark directly added to the text, or by the use of all these means together. The idea which he has endeavoured here to realize is that of an amplified translation. In the version properly so called, he has endeavoured to preserve, not only the strength but the peculiar form of the original, which is often lost in the English Bible, by substituting literal for figurative and general for specific terms, as well as by a needless deviation from the order of the words in Hebrew, upon which the emphasis, if not the sense, is frequently dependent, and which has here been carefully restored wherever the difference of idiom would suffer it, and sometimes, it may possibly be thought, without regard to it. Another gratuitous departure from the form of the original, which has been perhaps too scrupulously shunned, but not, it is believed, without advantage to the general character of the translation, arises from the habit of confounding the tenses, or merging the future and the past in a jejune and inexpressive present. The instances where this rule has been pushed to a rigorous extreme may be readily detected, but will not perhaps be thought to outweigh the advantage of preserving one of the most marked and striking features of the Hebrew language.

The plan of the book, as already defined, has excluded not only all devotional and practical remark, but all attempt to give the history of the interpretation, or to enumerate the advocates and authors of conflicting expositions. This, although necessary to a complete exegetical work, would rather have defeated the design of this one, both by adding to its bulk and by repelling a large class of readers. It has therefore been thought better to exclude it, or rather to reserve it for a kindred work upon a larger scale, if such should hereafter be demanded by the public. The same course has been taken with respect to a great mass of materials, relating to those topics which would naturally find their place in a Critical Introduction. Many of these, and such as are particularly necessary to the exposition, have been noticed incidentally as they occur. But synoptical summaries of these, and full discussions of the various questions, as to the age and authors of the several psalms, the origin and principle of their arrangement, the best mode of classification, and the principles on which they ought to be interpreted, would fill a volume by themselves, without materially promoting the main object of the present publication. As the topics thus necessarily excluded will probably constitute a principal subject of the author's private and professional studies for some time to come, he is not without the hope of being able to bring something of this kind before the public, either in a separate work upon the Psalms, or in a general Introduction to the Scriptures.

The difficulty of discussing these preliminary matters within reasonable compass, although great in the case of any important part of Scripture, is aggravated by the peculiar structure of the Psalter, the most miscellaneous of the sacred books, containing a hundred and fifty compositions, each complete in itself, and varying in length, from two sentences (Ps. cxvii.) to a hundred and seventy-six (Ps. cxix.), as well as in subject, style, and tone, the work of many authors, and of different ages; so that a superficial reader might be tempted to regard it as a random or fortuitous collection of unconnected and incongruous materials.

A closer inspection shews, however, that this heterogeneous mass is not without a bond of union; that these hundred and fifty independent pieces, different as they are, have this in common, that they are all poetical, not merely imaginative and expressive of feeling, but stamped externally with that peculiar character of parallelism, which distinguishes the higher style of Hebrew composition from ordinary prose. A still more marked resemblance is that they are all not only poetical but lyrical, *i. e.* songs, poems intended to be sung, and with a musical accompaniment. Thirdly, they are all religious lyrics, even those which seem at first sight the most secular in theme and spirit, but which are all found on inquiry to be strongly expressive of religious feeling. In the fourth place, they are all ecclesiastical lyrics, psalms or hymns, intended to be permanently used in public worship, not excepting those which bear the clearest impress of original connection with the social, domestic, or personal relations and experience of the writers.

The book being thus invested with a certain unity of spirit, form, and purpose, we are naturally led to seek for something in the psalms themselves, which may determine more definitely their relation to each other. The first thing of this kind that presents itself is the existence, in a very large proportion, of an ancient title or inscription, varying in length and fulness; sometimes simply describing the composition, as a psalm, a song, a prayer, &c.; sometimes stating the subject or historical occasion, either in plain or enigmatical expressions; sometimes directing the performance, by indicating the accompanying instrument, by specifying the appropriate key or mode, or by naming the particular performer: these various intimations occurring sometimes singly, but frequently in combination.

The strenuous attempts which have been made by modern writers to discredit these inscriptions, as spurious additions of a later date, containing groundless and erroneous conjectures, often at variance with the terms and substance of the psalm itself, are defeated by the fact that they are found in the Hebrew text, as far as we can trace its history, not as addenda, but as integral parts of the composition; that such indications of the author and the subject, at the commencement of a composition, are familiar both to classical and oriental usage; and that the truth of these inscriptions may in every case be vindicated, and in none more successfully than those which seem at first sight least defensible, and which have therefore been appealed to, with most confidence, as proofs of spuriousness and recent date.

The details included in this general statement will be pointed out as they occur, but are here referred to by anticipation, to explain and vindicate the constant treatment of the titles in this volume as an integral part of the sacred text, which in some editions of the Bible has been mutilated by omitting them, and in others dislocated or confused, for purposes of reference, by passing them over in the numeration of the verses. As this last arrangement is familiar to all readers of the English Bible, an attempt has been made in the following exposition to consult their convenience, by adding the numbers of the English to those of the Hebrew text, wherever they are different.

Another point of contact and resemblance between these apparently detached and independent compositions is the frequent recurrence of set phrases and of certain forms extending to the structure of whole psalms, such as the alphabetical arrangement, in which the successive sentences or paragraphs begin with the letters of the Hebrew alphabet. This is the more remarkable, because these alphabetic psalms have all a common character, distinguishing them from the rest, to wit, that instead of a progression of ideas, they consist of variations on a theme propounded at the outset, whether this be regarded as the cause or the effect of the peculiar form itself.

The same inquiries which have led to these conclusions also shew that the arrangement of the psalms in the collection is by no means so unmeaning and fortuitous as may at first sight seem to be the case, but that in many instances at least, a reason may be found for the juxtaposition, in resemblance or identity of subject or historical occasion, or in some remarkable coincidence of general form or of particular expressions. If in some cases it is difficult to trace the reason of the collocation, there are others in which two psalms bear so intimate and obvious a mutual relation, that they seem to constitute a pair or double psalm, either because they were originally meant to match each other, or because one has been subsequently added for the purpose. Sometimes, particularly in the latter part of the collection, we may trace not only pairs but trilogies, and even more extensive systems of connected psalms, each independent of the rest, and yet together forming beautiful and striking combinations, particularly when the nucleus or the basis of the series is an ancient psalm ; for instance one of David's, to which others have been added, in the way of variation or of imitation, at a later period, such as that of the Captivity.

Although the facts just mentioned are sufficient to evince that the Book of Psalms was not thrown together at random, but adjusted by a careful hand, the principle of the arrangement is not always so apparent, or of such a nature as to repress the wish to classify the psalms and reduce them to some systematic order. The most obvious arrangement would be that by authors, if the data were sufficient. But although the titles ascribe one to Moses, seventy-two to David, two to Solomon, twelve to Asaph, one to Ethan, and eleven to the Sons of Korah, it is doubtful in some of the cases, more particularly those last mentioned, whether the title was designed to indicate the author or the musical performer, and more than fifty are anonymous. In some of these the hand of David may be still distinctly traced, but as to most, we are abandoned to conjecture, which of course affords no solid basis for a satisfactory or useful distribution.

Another principle of classification is the internal character, the subject, style, and manner of the psalms. This was applied by the older writers, in accordance with the forms of artificial rhetoric, and with endless variety in the result. But the best application of the principle is that proposed by Hengstenberg, and founded on the tone of pious feeling which the psalm expresses : whether joyous, as in the general psalms of praise, and more especially in those of thanksgiving ; or sad, as in the querulous and penitential psalms ; or calm, as in most of the prophetic and didactic psalms. All these, however, are arrangements which the reader can make best to please himself, and which are rather the results of exposition than preliminary aids to it.

Apart from these attempts at systematic distribution and arrangement, there is also a question with respect to the division of the Psalter as it stands. There is an ancient division into five parts, corresponding, as the Rabbins say, to the five books of Moses, and indicated by doxologies at the close of Ps. xli., lxxii., lxxxix., cvi., while Ps. cl. is itself a doxology, winding up the whole. The modern critics, more especially in Germany, have tasked their ingenuity to prove that these are distinct collections, contemporaneous or successive, of detached compositions, afterwards combined to form the present Psalter. But they never have been able to account, with any plausibility or show of truth, for the remarkable position which the psalms of David occupy in all parts of the book. A much more probable hypothesis, though coupled with a theory, to say the least, extremely dubious, is that of Hengstenberg, who looks upon the actual arrangement as the work of Ezra, or some other skilful and authoritative hand, and accounts for the division into five books as follows. The first book (Ps. i.–xli.) contains only psalms of David, in which the use of the divine name Jehovah is predominant. The second (Ps. xlii.–lxxii.) contains psalms of David and his contemporaries, *i. e.*, Solomon, Asaph, and the Sons of Korah, in which the predominant divine name is Elohim. The third (Ps. lxxiii.–lxxxix.) contains psalms of Asaph and the Sons of Korah, in which the name Jehovah is predominant. The fourth (Ps. xc.–cvi.) and fifth (cvii.–cl.) contain, for the most part, psalms of later date, the principal exceptions being one by Moses (Ps. xc.), and several of David's, to which others in the same strain have been added, in the way already mentioned.

However ingenious this hypothesis may be, it will be seen at once that it contributes very little to the just appreciation or correct interpretation of the several psalms, except by enabling us, in certain cases, to derive illustration from a more extended context, as the reader will find stated in its proper place. Even granting, therefore, the historical assumption upon which it rests, and the favourite doctrine as to the divine names, with which it is to some extent identified, it will be sufficient for our present purpose to have stated it in outline, leaving the reader to compare it with the facts as they successively present themselves, and reserving a more full investigation of the general question to another time and place.

The best arrangement for the ordinary student of the Psalter is the actual arrangement of the book itself : first, because we have no better, and the efforts to invent a better have proved fruitless ; then, because, as we have seen, there are sufficient indications of a principle or purpose in this actual arrangement, whether we can always trace it there or not ; and lastly, because uniform tradition and analogy agree in representing it as highly probable that this arrangement was the work of Ezra, the inspired collector and *rédacteur* of the canon, so that even if nothing more should ever be discovered, with respect to his particular design or plan, we have still the satisfaction of relying, not on chance, but on a competent or rather an infallible authority, as well as the advantage of studying the psalms in a connection and an order which may possibly throw light upon them, even when it seems to us most fortuitous or arbitrary.

If any subdivision of the book is needed, as a basis or a means of more convenient exposition, it may be obtained by taking, as the central column of this splendid fabric, its most ancient portion, the sublime and affecting Prayer of Moses, known from time immemorial as the Ninetieth Psalm, and suffering this, as a dividing line, to separate the whole into two great parts, the first composed entirely of psalms belonging to the times of David, the other of a few such, with a much greater number of later compositions, founded on them and connected with them.

This simple distribution seems to secure all the substantial advantages of Hengstenberg's hypothesis, without its complexity or doubtful points. Among the latter may be reckoned the extraordinary stress laid by this eminent interpreter on what may be called Symbolical Arithmetic, or the significance ascribed to the number of verses, of Selahs, of Jehovahs, of Elohims, used in any given psalm. Setting out from the unquestionable fact, that certain numbers are symbolically used in the Old Testament ; that seven is the symbol of the covenant, twelve of the theocracy, ten of completeness or perfection, five of the reverse, &c., he attempts to trace the application of this principle throughout the psalms, and not, as might have been expected, without many palpable failures to establish his favourite and foregone conclusion. The effect which this singular prepossession might have had upon his exposition is prevented by his happily restricting it entirely to form and structure, and putting it precisely on a level with the alphabetical arrangement of the Hebrews, and with rhyme as used by other nations. There is still, however, reason to regret the space allotted to this subject in his volumes, and good ground for excluding it from works of an humbler and more popular description. As all the views of such a mind, however, are at least entitled to consideration, this subject may appropriately take its place among the topics of a Critical Introduction.

With respect to the historical relations of the Psalter and its bearings on the other parts of Scripture, it will be sufficient to remind the reader, that the Mosaic system reached its culminating point and full development in the reign of David, when the land of promise was in full possession, the provisions of the law for the first time fully carried out, and a permanent sanctuary secured, and, we may even say, prospectively erected. The chain of Messianic promises, which for ages had been broken, or concealed beneath the prophetic ritual, was now renewed by the addition of a new link, in the great Messianic promise made to David (2 Sam. vii.) of perpetual succession in his family. As the head of this royal race from which the Messiah was to spring, and as the great theocratical model of succeeding ages, who is mentioned more frequently in prophecy and gospel than all his natural descendants put together, he was inspired to originate a new kind of sacred composition, that of Psalmody, or rather to educe from the germ which Moses had planted an abundant harvest of religious poetry, not for his own private use, but for that of the Church, in the new form of public service which he added by divine command to the Mosaic ritual. As an inspired psalmist, as the founder and director of the temple-music. and as a model and exemplar to those after him, David's position is unique in sacred history. As his military prowess had been necessary to complete the conquest of the land, so his poetical and musical genius was necessary to secure his influence upon the church for ever. The result is, that no part of the Bible has been so long, so constantly, and so extensively familiar, both to Jews and Christians, as the PSALMS OF DAVID. This *denominatio a potiori* is entirely correct, as all the other writers of the psalms, excepting Moses, merely carry out and vary what had been already done by David ; and as if to guard the system from deterioration, the further we proceed the more direct and obvious is this dependence upon David, as "the man raised up on high, the anointed of the God of Jacob, and the sweet psalmist of Israel" (2 Sam. xxiii. 1), the master and the model of all other psalmists, from the days of Solomon to those of Ezra.

The interesting questions which have so often been discussed, as to the theology and ethics of the Psalter, and especially in reference to the doctrine of a Messiah and a future state, and to the so-called imprecations of the psalms, can be satisfactorily settled only by detailed interpretation of the passages concerned, and any summary anticipation of the general result may here be spared, although it would be highly appropriate in a Critical Introduction.

After this brief statement of preliminary points which might be fully treated in an Introduction, it only remains to add, in explanation of the plan adopted in the work itself, that the reader is constantly supposed to be familiar with the Hebrew text and with the authorised version, but that, in order to make the exposition accessible to a larger class of educated readers, the original words have been introduced but sparingly, and only for the purpose of saving space and avoiding an awkward circumlocution. The translation of the text is printed in italic type as prose, partly for a reason just assigned, to save room; partly because it is really prose, and not verse, according to the common acceptation of those terms; partly because the effect of the poetical element, so far as it exists, is weakened rather than enhanced when printed as irregular blank verse: but especially because the version is not meant to stand by itself, or to be continuously read, but to be part and parcel of the exposition, and to be qualified by the accompanying paraphrase and comments.

The religious uses of the Psalms, both doctrinal and practical, though not directly aimed at in these volumes, are so far from being undervalued by the author, and indeed so essential to his ultimate design, that any effect which the book may have, however humble or remote, in the promotion of this end, will be esteemed by him as its most flattering success, and the most acceptable reward of his exertions.

NOTE TO THE READER

Because of the unfamiliarity of most of us today with the Roman numeral system used throughout this book, the following conversion table may offer welcome assistance to many readers:

i	1	xxii	22
ii	2	xxiii	23
iii	3	xxiv	24
iv	4	xxv	25
v	5	xxvi	26
vi	6	xxvii	27
vii	7	xxviii	28
viii	8	xxix	29
ix	9	xxx	30
x	10	xl	40
xi	11	l	50
xii	12	lx	60
xiii	13	lxx	70
xiv	14	lxxx	80
xv	15	xc	90
xvi	16	c	100
xvii	17	cx	110
xviii	18	cxx	120
xvix	19	cxxx	130
xx	20	cxl	140
xxi	21	cl	150

THE PSALMS

Psalm 1

THE book opens with an exquisite picture of the truly Happy Man, as seen from the highest ground of the old dispensation. He is described both literally and figuratively, positively and negatively, directly and by contrast, with respect both to his character and his condition, here and hereafter. The compression of all this into so short a composition, without confusion or obscurity, and with a high degree of graphic vividness, shews what the psalm is in a rhetorical or literary point of view, apart from its religious import and divine authority. Its moral design is both didactic and consolatory. There is no trace of any particular historical occasion or allusion. The terms employed are general, and admit of an easy application to all times and places where the word of God is known. The psalm indeed contains a summary of the doctrine taught in this book and in the Scriptures generally, as to the connection between happiness and goodness. It is well placed, therefore, as an introduction to the whole collection, and although anonymous, was probably composed by David. It is altogether worthy of this origin, and corresponds, in form and substance, to the next psalm, which is certainly by David. The two seem indeed to form a pair or double psalm, of which arrangement there are several other instances. The structure of the first psalm is symmetrical but simple, and the style removed from that of elevated prose by nothing but the use of strong and lively figures.

1. The Happy Man is first described in literal but negative expressions, *i. e.* by stating what he does not habitually do. The description opens with a kind of admiring exclamation. (*Oh*) *the blessedness of the man!* The plural form of the original (*felicities* or *happinesses*), if anything more than a grammatical idiom like *ashes, means,* &c., in our language, may denote fulness and variety of happiness, as if he had said, *How completely happy is the man!* The negative description follows. *Happy the man who has not walked*, a common figure for the course of life or the habitual conduct, which is furthermore suggested by the use of the past tense, but without excluding the present, who has not walked and does not walk, *in the counsel, i. e.* live after the manner, on the principles, or according to the plans, *of wicked* (*men*), *and in the way of sinners has not stood.* The word translated *sinners* properly denotes those who fall short of the standard of duty, as the word translated *wicked* denotes those who positively violate a rule by disorderly

conduct.   Together they express the whole idea of ungodly or unrighteous
men.   *And in the seat*, not the chair, but the company, or the place where
men convene and sit together, *of scorners*, scoffers, those who treat religion
with contempt, *has not sat*.   The three verbs denote the three acts or postures of a waking man, namely, walking, standing, sitting, and are therefore well adapted to express the whole course of life or conduct.   It is also
possible that a climax was intended, so that walking, standing, and sitting
in the company of sinners will denote successive stages of deterioration, first
occasional conformity, then fixed association, then established residence
among the wicked, not as a mere spectator or companion, but as one of
themselves.   The same kind of negative description reappears in Psalm
xxvi. 4, 5, and in Jer. xv. 17.   It is of course implied that no one, of whom
any of these things can be affirmed, is entitled to the character of a Happy
Man.

2. A positive trait is now added to the picture.   Having shewn what the
truly happy man does not, the Psalmist shews us what he does.   *But*, on
the contrary, in contrast with the previous description, *in the law of Jehovah*,
i. e. the written revelation of his will, and more especially the Pentateuch
or Law of Moses, which lay at the foundation of the Hebrew Scriptures, (*is*)
his delight, not merely his employment, or his trust, but his pleasure, his
happiness.   *And in his law he will meditate, i. e.* he does so and will do so
still, not merely as a theme of speculation or study, but as a cherished
object of affection, a favourite subject of the thoughts, *day and night, i. e.*
at all times, in every interval of other duties, nay in the midst of other
duties, this is the theme to which his mind spontaneously reverts.   The
cordial attachment to an unfinished revelation, here implicitly enjoined,
shews clearly what is due to the completed word of God which we possess.

3. The literal description of the Happy Man, both in its negative and
positive form, is followed by a beautiful comparison, expressive of his character and his condition.   *And he is*, or he shall be; the present and the future
insensibly run into each other, so as to suggest the idea of continuous or
permanent condition, like the past and present in the first verse.   *And
he is*, or shall be, *like a tree*, a lively emblem of vitality and fruitfulness.
He is not, however, like a tree growing wild, but *like a tree planted*, in the
most favourable situation, *on* or *over, i. e.* overhanging, *streams of water*.
The original words properly denote canals or channels, as customary means
of artificial irrigation.   Hence the single tree is said to overhang more than
one, because surrounded by them.   The image presented is that of a highly
cultivated spot, and implies security and care, such as could not be enjoyed
in the most luxuriant wilderness or forest.   The divine culture thus experienced is the cause of the effect represented by the rest of the comparison.
Which (tree) will give, or yield, *its fruit in its season, and its leaf shall not
wither;* it shall lose neither its utility nor beauty.   This is then expressed
in a more positive and prosaic form.   *And all*, or every thing, *which he*,
the man represented by the verdant fruitful tree, *shall do, he shall make to
prosper*, or do prosperously, with good success.   This pleasing image is in
perfect keeping with the scope of the psalm, which is not to describe the
righteous man, as such, but the truly happy man, with whom the righteous
man is afterwards identified.   The neglect of this peculiar feature of the
composition impairs its moral as well as its rhetorical effect, by making it
an austere declaration of what will be expected from a good man, rather
than a joyous exhibition of his happy lot.   That the common experience,
even of the best men, falls short of this description, is because their cha-

racter and life fall short of that presented in the two preceding verses. The whole description is not so much a picture drawn from real life, as an ideal standard or model, by striving to attain which our aims and our attainments will be elevated, though imperfect after all.

4. *Not so the wicked.* The direct description of the Happy Man is heightened and completed by comparison with others. *Not so the wicked, i. e.* neither in condition nor in character. The dependence of the one upon the other is suggested by describing them as wicked, rather than unhappy. *Not so, i. e.* not thus happy, *(are) the wicked*, because they are wicked, and are therefore destitute of all that constitutes the happiness before described. The immediate reference, in the phrase *not so*, is to the beautiful, well-watered, green, and thriving tree of the preceding verse. To this delightful emblem of a healthful happy state the Psalmist now opposes one drawn likewise from the vegetable world, but as totally unlike the first as possible. Thé wicked are not represented by a tree, not even by a barren tree, a dead tree, a prostrate tree, a shrub, a weed, all which are figures not unfrequent in the Scriptures. But all these are more or less associated with the natural condition of a living plant, and therefore insufficient to present the necessary contrast. This is finely done by a comparison with *chaff*, which, though a vegetable substance, and connected in its origin with one of the most valuable products of the earth, is itself neither living, fruitful, nor nutritious, but only fit to be removed and scattered by the wind, in the ancient and oriental mode of winnowing. There is a double fitness in the emblem here presented, as suggesting the idea of intrinsic worthlessness, and at the same time that of contrast with the useful grain, with which it came into existence, and from which it shall be separated only to be blown away or burned. *Not so the wicked, but like the chaff, which the wind drives away.* The same comparison is used in Psalm xxxv. 5, Isa. xvii. 13, xxix. 5, Hos. xiii. 3, Zeph. ii. 2, Job xxi. 18, and by John the Baptist in Mat. iii. 12, with obvious allusion to this psalm, but with a new figure, that of burning, which seems to be intended to denote final and complete destruction, while in all the other cases, the idea suggested by the chaff being blown away is that of violent and rapid disappearance.

5. *Therefore*, because they are unlike a living tree, and like the worthless chaff, fit only to be scattered by the wind, *wicked (men) shall not stand, i. e.* stand their ground or be able to sustain themselves, *in the judgment, i. e.* at the bar of God. This includes two ideas, that of God's unerring estimation of all creatures at their real value, and that of his corresponding action towards them. The wicked shall neither be approved by God, nor, as a necessary consequence, continue to enjoy his favour, even in appearance. Whatever providential inequalities may now exist will all be rectified hereafter. The wicked shall not always be confounded with their betters. *They shall not stand in the judgment*, either present intermediate judgments, or the final judgment of the great day. *And sinners*, the same persons under another name, as in ver. 1 *(shall not stand) in the congregation*, or assembly, *of righteous (men)*. They shall not continue intermingled with them in society as now, and, what is more important, they shall not for ever seem to form part of the church or chosen people, to which the word translated *congregation* is constantly applied in the Old Testament. Whatever doubt may now exist, the time is coming when the wicked are to take their proper place and to be seen in their true character, as totally unlike the righteous.

6. The certainty of this event is secured by God's omniscience, from

which his power and his justice are inseparable. However men may be deceived in their prognostications, he is not. *The Lord*, Jehovah, the God of Revelation, the covenant God of Israel, *knows*, literally (*is*) *knowing*, *i. e.* habitually knows, or knows from the beginning to the end, *the way of right-eous* (*men*), *i. e.* the tendency and issue of their character and conduct. As if he had said, the Lord knows whither they are going and where they will arrive at last. This is a clear though indirect assertion of their safety, here and hereafter. The figure of a *way* is often used to express the character and conduct itself; but this idea is here implied or comprehended in that of destiny, as determined by the character and conduct. There is no need, there-fore, of taking the verb *know* in any other than its usual and proper sense. The verse is an appeal to divine omniscience for the truth of the implied assertion, that the righteous are safe and will be happy, as well as for that of the express assertion, with which the whole psalm closes. *The way of wicked* (*men*), in the same sense as before, *shall perish*, *i. e.* end in ruin. The apparent solecism of making a way perish only brings out in more prominent relief the truth really asserted, namely, the perdition of those who travel it. This completes the contrast, and sums up the description of the truly Happy Man, as one whose delight is in the law and his happi-ness in the favour of Jehovah, and whose strongest negative characteristic is his total want of moral likeness here to those from whom he is to dwell apart hereafter.

Psalm 2

A SUBLIME vision of the nations in revolt against Jehovah and his Anointed, with a declaration of the divine purpose to maintain his King's authority, and a warning to the world that it must bow to him or perish. The structure of this psalm is extremely regular. It naturally falls into four stanzas of three verses each. In the first, the conduct of the rebel-lious nations is described. In the second, God replies to them by word and deed. In the third, the Messiah or Anointed One declares the divine decree in relation to himself. In the fourth, the Psalmist exhorts the rulers of the nations to submission, with a threatening of divine wrath to the dis-obedient, and a closing benediction on believers. The several sentences are also very regular in form, exhibiting parallelisms of great uniformity. Little as this psalm may, at first sight, seem to resemble that before it, there is really a very strong affinity between them. Even in form they are related to each other. The number of verses and of stanzas is just double in the second, which moreover begins, as the first ends, with a threatening, and ends, as the first begins, with a beatitude. There is also a resemblance in their subject and contents. The contrast indicated in the first is carried out and rendered more distinct in the second. The first is in fact an intro-duction to the second, and the second to what follows. And as the psalms which follow bear the name of David, there is the strongest reason to believe that these two are his likewise, a conclusion confirmed by the authority of Acts iv. 25, as well as by the internal character of the psalm itself. The imagery of the scene presented is evidently borrowed from the warlike and eventful times of David. He cannot, however, be himself the subject of the composition, the terms of which are wholly inappropriate to any king but the Messiah, to whom they are applied by the oldest Jewish writers, and again and again in the New Testament. This is the first of those prophetic psalms, in which the promise made to David, with respect to the Messiah (2 Sam. vii. 16, 1 Chron. xvii. 11–14), is wrought into the lyrical devotions of the ancient church. The supposition of a double reference to David, or some one of his successors, and to Christ, is not only needless and gratuitous, but hurtful to the sense by the confusion which it introduces, and forbidden by the utter inappropriateness of some of the expressions used to any lower subject. The style of this psalm, although not less pure and simple, is livelier than that of the first, a difference arising partly from the nature of the subject, but still more from the dramatic structure of the composition.

1. This psalm opens, like the first, with an exclamation, here expressive of astonishment and indignation at the wickedness and folly of the scene presented to the psalmist's view. *Why do nations make a noise,* tumultuate, or rage? The Hebrew verb is not expressive of an internal feeling, but of the outward agitation which denotes it. There may be an allusion to the rolling and roaring of the sea, often used as an emblem of popular commotion, both in the Scriptures and the classics. The past tense of this verb (*why have they raged?*) refers to the commotion as already begun, while the future in the next clause expresses its continuance. *And peoples,* not *people,* in the collective sense of persons, but in the proper plural sense of nations, races, *will imagine, i.e.* are imagining and will continue to imagine, *vanity,* a vain thing, something hopeless and impossible. The interrogation in this verse implies that no rational solution of the strange sight could be given, for reasons assigned in the remainder of the psalm. This implied charge of irrationality is equally well founded in all cases where the same kind of opposition exists, though secretly, and on the smallest scale.

2. The confused scene presented in the first verse now becomes more distinct, by a nearer view of the contending parties. (*Why will*) *the kings of earth set themselves,* or, without repeating the interrogation, *the kings of earth will set themselves,* or take their stand, *and rulers consult together,* literally sit together, but with special reference to taking counsel, as in Ps. xxxi. 14 (13), *against Jehovah and against his Anointed,* or *Messiah,* which is only a modified form of the Hebrew word here used, as *Christ* is a like modification of the corresponding term in Greek. External unction or anointing is a sign, in the Old Testament, of the gifts of the Holy Spirit, and especially of those conferred on prophets, priests, and kings, as ministers of the theocracy, and representatives of Christ himself. To kings particularly, as the highest and most comprehensive order, and peculiar types of Christ in his supremacy as Head of the church, the sacred history applies the title of *the Lord's Anointed.* The rite of unction is explicitly recorded in the case of Saul, David, and Solomon, and was probably repeated at the coronation of their successors. From the verse before us, and from Dan. ix. 26, the name *Messiah* had, before the Advent, come into use among the Jews as a common designation of the great Deliverer and King whom they expected. (Compare John i. 41 with ver. 49 of the same chapter, and with Mark xv. 32.) The intimate relation of the Anointed One to God himself is indicated even here by making them the common object of attack, or rather of revolt. In Acts iv. 25–27, this description is applied to the combination of Herod and Pilate, Jews and Gentiles, against Jesus Christ, not as the sole event predicted, but as that in which the gradual fulfilment reached its culmination. From that quotation, and indeed from the terms of the prophecy itself, we learn that *nations* here does not mean *Gentiles* or *heathen,* as opposed to *Jews,* but whole com-

munities or masses of mankind, as distinguished from mere personal or insulated cases of resistance and rebellion.

3. Having described the conduct of the disaffected nations and their chiefs, he now introduces them as speaking. In the preceding verse they were seen, as it were, at a distance, taking counsel. Here they are brought so near to us, or we to them, that we can overhear their consultations. *Let us break their bands*, *i.e.* the bands of the Lord and his Anointed, the restraints imposed by their authority. The form of the Hebrew verb may be expressive either of a proposition or of a fixed determination. *We will break their bands*, we are resolved to do it. This is, in fact, involved in the other version, where *let us break* must not be understood as a faint or dubious suggestion, but as a summons to the execution of a formed and settled purpose. The same idea is expressed, with a slight modification, in the other clause. *And we will cast*, or *let us cast away from us their cords*, twisted ropes, a stronger term than *bands*. The verb, too, while it really implies the act of breaking, suggests the additional idea of contemptuous facility, as if they had said, Let us fling away from us with scorn these feeble bands by which we have been hitherto confined. The application of this passage to the revolt of the Ammonites and other conquered nations against David, or to any similar rebellion against any of the later Jewish kings, as the principal subject of this grand description, makes it quite ridiculous, if not profane, and cannot therefore be consistent with the principles of sound interpretation. The utmost that can be conceded is that David borrowed the scenery of this dramatic exhibition from the wars and insurrections of his own eventful reign. The language of the rebels in the verse before us is a genuine expression of the feelings entertained, not only in the hearts of individual sinners, but by the masses of mankind, so far as they have been brought into collision with the sovereignty of God and Christ, not only at the time of his appearance upon earth, but in the ages both before and after that event, in which the prophecy, as we have seen, attained its height, but was not finally exhausted or fulfilled, since the same rash and hopeless opposition to the Lord and his anointed still continues, and is likely to continue until the kingdoms of this world are become the kingdoms of our Lord and of his Christ (Rev. xi. 15), an expression borrowed from this very passage.

4. As the first strophe or stanza of three verses is descriptive of the conduct of the rebels, so the next describes the corresponding action of their sovereign, in precisely the same order, telling first what he does (in ver. 4, 5), and then what he says (in ver. 6), so that these two stanzas are not only regular in their internal structure, but exactly fitted to each other. This symmetrical adjustment is entitled to attention, as that feature of the Hebrew poetry which fills the place of rhythm and metre in the poetry of other nations. At the same time, it facilitates interpretation, when allowed to speak for itself without artificial or unnatural straining, by exhibiting the salient points of the passage in their true relation. The transition here is a sublime one, from the noise and agitation of earth to the safety and tranquillity of heaven. No shifting of the scene could be more dramatic in effect or form. While the nations and their kings exhort each other to cast off their allegiance to Jehovah, and thereby virtually to dethrone him, he reposes far above them, and beyond their reach. *Sitting in the heavens*, *i.e.* resident and reigning there, *he laughs*, or will laugh. This figure, strong and almost startling as it is, cannot possibly be misunderstood by any reader, as a vivid expression of contemptuous

security on God's part, and of impotent folly on the part of men. *At them* may be supplied from Ps. xxxvii. 13, and lix. 9 (8) ; but it is not necessary, and the picture is perhaps more perfect, if we understand the laughter here to be simply expressive of contempt, and the idea of directly *laughing at them* to be first suggested in the other clause. *The Lord,* not *Jehovah,* as in ver. 2, but *Adhonai,* the Hebrew word properly denoting *Lord* or *Sovereign* as a divine title, *the Lord shall mock them,* or *mock at them,* as the strongest possible expression of contempt. This verse conveys in the most vivid manner, one indeed that would be inadmissible in any uninspired writer, the fatuity of all rebellious opposition to God's will. That such is often suffered to proceed long with impunity is only, in the figurative language of this passage, because God first laughs at human folly, and then smites it. "Who thought," says Luther, "when Christ suffered, and the Jews triumphed, that God was laughing all the time?" Beneath this bold anthropomorphism there is hidden a profound truth, namely, that to all superior beings, and above all, to God himself, there is something in sin not only odious but absurd, something which cannot possibly escape the contempt of higher, much less of the highest, intelligence.

5. This contemptuous repose and seeming indifference shall not last for ever. *Then,* after having thus derided them, *then,* as the next stage in this fearful process, *he will speak to them,* as they, after rising up against him, spoke to one another in ver. 3. *And in his heat, i. e.* his hot displeasure, the wrath to which the laughter of ver. 4 was but a prelude, *he will agitate them,* terrify them, make them quake with fear, not as a separate act from that described in the first clause, but by the very act of speaking to them in his anger, the words spoken being given in the following verse.

6. The divine address begins, as it were, in the middle of a sentence ; but the clause suppressed is easily supplied, being tacitly involved in what precedes. As if he had said, you renounce your allegiance and assert your independence, *and I,* on my part, the pronoun when expressed in Hebrew being commonly emphatic, and here in strong antithesis to those who are addressed. *You* pursue your course *and I* mine. The translation *yet,* though inexact and arbitrary, brings out the antithesis correctly in a different form from that of the original. *And I have constituted,* or created, with allusion in the Hebrew to the casting of an image, or as some less probably suppose to unction, *1 have constituted my King,* not simply *a king,* nor even *the king,* neither of which expressions would be adequate, but *my king,* one who is to reign for me and in indissoluble union with me, so that his reigning is identical with mine. This brings out still more clearly the intimate relation of the Anointed to Jehovah, which had been indicated less distinctly in ver. 2, and thus prepares us for the full disclosure of their mutual relation in ver. 7. *And I have constituted my King upon Zion, my hill of holiness,* or holy hill, *i. e.* consecrated, set apart, distinguished from all other hills and other places, as the seat of the theocracy, the royal residence, the capital city, of the Lord and of his Christ, from the time that David took up his abode, and deposited the ark there. The translation *over Zion* would convey the false idea, that Zion was itself the kingdom over which this sovereign was to reign, whereas it was only the visible and temporary centre of a kingdom coextensive with the earth, as we expressly read it, ver. 8, below. This shews that the application of the verse before us to David himself, although intrinsically possible, is utterly at variance with the context and the whole scope of the composition.

7. We have here another of those changes which impart to this whole

psalm a highly dramatic character. A third personage is introduced as
speaking without any formal intimation in the text. As the first stanza
(ver. 1–3) closes with the words of the insurgents, and the second (ver. 4–6)
with the words of the Lord, so the third (ver. 7–9) contains the language
of the king described in the preceding verse, announcing with his own lips
the law or constitution of his kingdom. *I will declare,* or *let me declare,*
the same form of the verb as in ver. 3, *the decree,* the statute, the organic
law or constitution of my kingdom. The Hebrew verb is followed by a
preposition, which may be expressed in English, without any change of
sense, by rendering the clause, *I will declare,* or make a declaration, *i. e.*
a public, formal announcement (*as*) *to the law* or constitution of my kingdom.
This announcement is then made in a historical form, by reciting what had
been said to the king at his inauguration or induction into office. *Jehovah
said to me, My son* (*art*) *thou, this day have I begotten thee.* Whether this
be regarded as a part of the decree or law itself, or as a mere preamble to
it, the relation here described is evidently one which carried with it universal dominion as a necessary consequence, as well as one which justifies
the use of the expression *my King* in ver. 6. It must be something more,
then, than a figure for intense love or peculiar favour, something more than
the filial relation which the theocratic kings, and Israel as a nation, bore to
God. (Exod. iv. 22 ; Deut. xiv. 1, 2, xxxii. 6 ; Isa. lxiii. 16 ; Hos. xi. 1 ;
Mal. i. 6 ; Rom ix. 4.) Nor will any explanation of the terms fully meet
the requisitions of the context except one which supposes the relation here
described as manifest in time to rest on one essential and eternal. This
alone accounts for the identification of the persons as possessing a common
interest, and reigning with and in each other. This profound sense of the
passage is no more excluded by the phrase *this day,* implying something
recent, than the universality of Christ's dominion is excluded by the local
reference to Zion. The point of time, like the point of space, is the finite
centre of an infinite circle. Besides, the mere form of the declaration is a
part of the dramatic scenery or costume with which the truth is here
invested. The ideas of a king, a coronation, a hereditary succession, are
all drawn from human and temporal associations. *This day have I begotten
thee* may be considered, therefore, as referring only to the coronation of
Messiah, which is an ideal one. The essential meaning of the phrase *I
have begotten thee* is simply this, *I am thy father.* The antithesis is perfectly identical with that in 2 Sam. vii. 14, "I will be his father, and he
shall be my son." Had the same form of expression been used here, *this
day am I thy father,* no reader would have understood *this day* as limiting
the mutual relation of the parties, however it might limit to a certain point
of time the formal recognition of it. It must also be observed, that even
if *this day* be referred to the inception of the filial relation, it is thrown
indefinitely back by the form of reminiscence or narration in the first clause
of the verse. *Jehovah said to me,* but when ? If understood to mean from
everlasting or eternity, the form of expression would be perfectly in keeping
with the other figurative forms by which the Scriptures represent things
really ineffable in human language. The opinion that this passage is applied
by Paul, in Acts xiii. 33, to Christ's resurrection, rests upon a misapprehension of the verb *raised up,* which has this specific meaning only when
determined by the context or the addition of the words *from the dead,* as in
the next verse of the same chapter, which is so far from requiring the more
general expressions of the preceding verse to be taken in the same sense,
that it rather forbids such a construction, and shews that the two verses

speak of different stages in the same great process : first, the raising up of Jesus in the same sense in which God is said to have raised him up in Acts ii. 30, iii. 22, 26, vii. 36, *i. e.* bringing him into being as a man; and then the raising up from the dead, which the apostle himself introduces as another topic in Acts xiii. 34. There is nothing, therefore, inconsistent with the statement that the psalmist here speaks of eternal sonship, either in the passage just referred to, or in Heb. v. 5, where the words are only cited to prove the solemn recognition of Christ's sonship, and his consequent authority, by God himself. This recognition was repeated, and, as it were, realised at our Saviour's baptism and transfiguration (Mat. iii. 17, xvii. 5), when a voice from heaven said, " This is my beloved Son, in whom I am well pleased, hear ye him ! "

8. The recital of Jehovah's declaration to his Son is still continued. *Ask of me, and I will give nations (as) thy heritage,* i. e. thy portion as my Son, *and (as) thy (permanent) possession,* from a verb denoting to hold fast, *the ends of the earth,* a common Old Testament expression for the whole earth, the remotest bounds and all that lies between them. The phrase is never applied to 'a particular country, and cannot therefore be explained of Palestine or David's conquests, without violently changing the sublime to the ridiculous. The only subject, who can be assumed and carried through without absurdity, is the Messiah, who, as the Son and heir of God, had a right to ask this vast inheritance. That he had asked it and received it, is implied in the dominion claimed for him in ver. 2 and 3, where the nations are represented in revolt against him as their rightful sovereign. It was to justify this claim that the divine decree is here recited, the constitution of Messiah's kingdom, in which its limits are defined as co-extensive with the earth.

9. This extensive grant had been accompanied by that of power adequate to hold it. That power was to be exercised in wrath as well as mercy. The former is here rendered prominent, because the previous context has respect to audacious rebels, over whom Messiah is invested with the necessary power of punishment, and even of destruction. *Thou shalt break them with a rod* (or *sceptre*) *of iron,* as the hardest metal, and therefore the best suited to the use in question. By a slight change of pointing in the Hebrew, it may be made to mean, *thou shalt feed them* (as a shepherd) *with a rod of iron,* which is the sense expressed in several of the ancient versions, and to which there may be an ironical allusion, as the figure is a common one to represent the exercise of regal power. (See for example 2 Sam. vii. 7, and Micah vii. 14.) *Like a potter's vessel thou shalt shiver them,* or dash them in pieces, which last, however, weakens the expression by multiplying the words. The idea suggested by the last comparison is that of easy and immediate destruction, perhaps with an implication of worthlessness in the object. This view of the Messiah as a destroyer is in perfect keeping with the New Testament doctrine, that those who reject Christ will incur an aggravated doom, and that Christ himself is in some sense the destroyer of those who will not let him be their Saviour, or, to borrow terms from one of his own parables, in strict agreement with the scene presented by the psalm before us, " those mine enemies which would not that I should reign over them, bring hither and slay them before me" (Luke xix. 27). That false view of the divine nature which regards God as delighting in the death of the sinner, is more revolting, but not more dangerous than that which looks upon his justice as extinguished by his mercy, and supposes that the death of Christ has rendered

perdition impossible, even to those who will not believe in him. The terms of this verse are repeatedly applied to Christ in the Book of Revelation (ii. 27, xii. 5, xix. 15).

10. The description having reached its height in the preceding verse, there is here a sudden change of manner, a transition to the tone of earnest admonition, still addressed, however, to the characters originally brought upon the scene. *And now (O) kings*, after all that you have seen and heard, after this demonstration that you cannot escape from the dominion of Messiah, and that if you persist in your rebellion he will certainly destroy you, *be wise*, act wisely ; *be warned*, be admonished of your danger and your duty, *(O) judges of the earth !* A specific function of the regal office is here used as an equivalent or parallel to *kings* in the first clause, just as *rulers* is employed for the same purpose in ver. 2. The change of tone in this last strophe shews that the previous exhibition of Messiah as invested with destroying power was, as it usually is in Scripture, only introductory to another aspect of the same great object, which becomes more clear and bright to the conclusion of the psalm. At the same time the original dramatic structure is maintained ; for the speaker, in this closing stanza, is the Psalmist himself.

11. *Serve the Lord*, Jehovah, in the way that he requires, by acknowledging his Anointed as your rightful sovereign. *Serve the Lord with fear*, religious awe, not only on account of his tremendous majesty, but also in view of his vindicatory justice and destroying power. *And shout*, as a customary recognition of a present sovereign, *with trembling*, an external sign of fear, employed as an equivalent or parallel to fear itself. The word translated *shout* may also mean *rejoice*, as joy is often publicly expressed by acclamation. The sense will then be, *and rejoice with trembling, i.e.* exercise those mingled feelings which are suited to your present situation, in full view of God's wrath on one side, and his mercy on the other. This explanation agrees well with the transition, in these verses, from the tone of terrible denunciation to that of friendly admonition and encouragement.

12. Lest the exhortation in the preceding verse should seem to have respect to Jehovah as an absolute sovereign, without reference to any other person, the attention is again called to his King, his Anointed, and his Son, as the sovereign to whom homage must be paid, in order to escape destruction. *Kiss the Son*, an ancient mode of doing homage or allegiance to a king (1 Sam. x. 1), sometimes applied to the dress, and sometimes to the person, either of the sovereign or the subject himself. Even in modern European courts the kissing of the hand has this significance. In the case before us there may possibly be an allusion to the kiss as a religious act among the heathen (1 Kings xix. 18; Hos. xiii. 2; Job xxxi. 27). *Kiss the Son*, the Son of God, the Messiah, so called by the Jews in Christ's time (John i. 50; Matt. xxvi. 63; Mark xiv. 61; Luke xxii. 70): do him homage, own him as your sovereign, *lest he be angry, and ye lose the way, i.e.* the way to happiness and heaven, as in Ps. i. 6, or *perish from the way*, which is the same thing in another form, or *perish by the way, i.e.* before you reach your destination. All these ideas are suggested by the Hebrew phrase, which is unusual. The necessity of prompt as well as humble submission is then urged. *For his wrath will soon burn, or be kindled.* The translation, "when his wrath is kindled but a little," does not yield so good a meaning, and requires two of the original expressions to be taken in a doubtful and unusual sense. The same view of the Messiah as a judge and an avenger, which appeared in ver. 9, is again

presented here, but only for a moment, and as a prelude to the closing beatitude or benediction. *Blessed (are) all*, oh the felicities of all, *those trusting him*, believing on him, and confiding in him. This delightful contrast of salvation and perdition, at one and the same view, is characteristic of the Scriptures, and should teach us not to look ourselves, and not to turn the eyes of others, towards either of these objects without due regard to the other also. The resemblance in the language of this verse to that of Ps. i. 1 and 6, brings the two into connection, as parts of one harmonious composition, or at least as kindred and contemporaneous products of a single mind, under the influence of one and the same Spirit.

Psalm 3

THIS Psalm contains a strong description of the enemies and dangers by which the writer was surrounded, and an equally strong expression of confidence that God would extricate him from them, with particular reference to former deliverances of the same kind. Its place in the collection does not seem to be fortuitous or arbitrary. It was probably among the first of David's lyrical compositions, the two which now precede it having been afterwards prefixed to the collection. In these three psalms there is a sensible gradation or progressive development of one great idea. The general contrast, which the first exhibits, of the righteous and the wicked, is reproduced, in the second, as a war against the Lord and his Anointed. In the third it is still further individualised as a conflict between David, the great historical type of the Messiah, and his enemies. At the same time, the expressions are so chosen as to make the psalm appropriate to its main design, that of furnishing a vehicle of pious feeling to the church at large, and to its individual members in their own emergencies. The structure of the psalm is regular, consisting of four double verses, besides the title.

1. *A Psalm of David*, literally *(belonging) to David*, *i.e.* as the author. This is not a mere inscription, but a part of the text and inseparable from it, so far as we can trace its history. It was an ancient usage, both among classical and oriental writers, for the author to introduce his own name into the first sentence of his composition. The titles of the psalms ought, therefore, not to have been printed in a different type, or as something added to the text, which has led some editors to omit them altogether. In all Hebrew manuscripts they bear the same relation to the body of the psalm, that the inscriptions in the prophet's or in Paul's epistles bear to the substance of the composition. In the case before us, as in every other, the inscription is in perfect keeping with the psalm itself, as well as with the parallel history. Besides the author's name, it here states the historical occasion of the composition. *A Psalm of David, in his fleeing*, when he fled, *from the face*, from the presence, or before, *Absalom, his son* (see 2 Sam. xv. 14, 17, 30). Such a psalm might well be conceived, and even composed, if not actually written, in the midst of the dangers and distresses which occasioned it. There is no need therefore of supposing the reference to be merely retrospective. That the terms used are so general, is because the psalm, though first suggested by the writer's personal experience, was intended for more general use.

2 (1). *O Lord*, Jehovah, the name of God as self-existent and eternal, and also as the covenant God of Israel, *how many*, or *how multiplied, are*

my foes, my oppressors or tormentors ! This is not a question, but an exclamation of surprise and grief. *Many rising up against me.* The sentence may either be completed thus : many (are they) that rise up against me ; or the construction of the other clause may be continued. *(How) many (are there) rising up against me !* The same periphrasis for *enemies* is used by Moses, Deut. xxviii. 7. What is here said of the multitude of enemies agrees well with the historical statement in 2 Sam. xv. 13, xvi. 18.

3 (2). *(There are) many saying,* or, *(how) many (are there) saying to my soul, i. e.* so as to affect my heart, though really said of him, not directly addressed to him. (Compare Ps. xxxv. 3 ; Isa. li. 23.) *There is no salvation,* deliverance from evil, whether temporal, spiritual, or eternal. *There is no salvation for him,* the sufferer, and primarily the psalmist himself, *in God, i. e.* in his power, or his purpose, implying either that God does not concern himself about such things, Ps. x. 11, or that he has cast the sufferer off, Ps. xlii. 4, 11 (3, 10), lxxi. 11, xxii. 8, 9, (7, 8) ; Matt. xxvii. 43. This is the language, not of despondent friends, but of malignant enemies, and is really the worst that even such could say of him. For, as Luther well says, all the temptations in the world, and in hell too, melted together into one, are nothing when compared with the temptation to despair of God's mercy. The first stanza, or double verse, closes, like the second and fourth, with the word *Selah.* This term occurs seventy-three times in the Psalms, and three times in the prophecy of Habakkuk. It corresponds to *rest,* either as a noun or verb, and like it is properly a musical term, but generally indicates a pause in the sense as well as the performance. See below, on Ps. ix. 17 (16). Like the titles, it invariably forms part of the text, and its omission by some editors and translators is a mutilation of the word of God. In the case before us, it serves as a kind of pious ejaculation to express the writer's feelings, and, at the same time, warns the reader to reflect on what he reads, just as our Saviour was accustomed to say : He that hath ears to hear let him hear.

4 (3). From his earthly enemies and dangers he looks up to God, the source of his honours and his tried protector. The connection is similar to that between the fifth and sixth verses of the second psalm. The *and* (not *but*) has reference to a tacit comparison or contrast. This is my treatment at the hands of men, *and thou,* on the other hand, *O Lord,* Jehovah, *(art) a shield about me,* or around me, *i. e.* covering my whole body, not merely a part of it, as ordinary shields do. This is a favourite metaphor with David ; see Ps. vii. 11 (10), xviii. 3 (2), xxviii. 7. It occurs, however, more than once in the Pentateuch ; see Gen. xv. 1 ; Deut. xxxiii. 29. *My honour, i. e.* the source of the honours I enjoy, with particular reference, no doubt, to his royal dignity, not as a secular distinction merely, but in connection with the honour put upon him as a type and representative of Christ. The honour thus bestowed by God he might well be expected to protect. *My honour, and the (one) raising my head, i. e.* making me look up from my despondency. The whole verse is an appeal to the psalmist's previous experience of God's goodness as a ground for the confidence afterwards expressed.

5 (4). *(With) my voice to the Lord,* Jehovah, *I will call,* or *cry.* The future form of the verb is probably intended to express continued or habitual action, as in Ps. i. 2. I cry and will cry still. *And he hears me,* or, *then he hears me, i. e.* when I call. The original construction shews, in a peculiar manner, the dependence of the last verb on the first, which can hardly be conveyed by an exact translation. The second verb is not the

usual verb to hear, but one especially appropriated to the gracious hearing or answering of prayer. *And he hears* (or *answers*) *me from his hill of holiness,* or *holy hill.* This, as we learn from Ps. ii. 6, is Zion, the seat and centre of the old theocracy, the place where God visibly dwelt among his people. This designation of a certain spot as the earthly residence of God, was superseded by the incarnation of his Son, whose person thenceforth took the place of the old sanctuary. It was, therefore, no play upon words or fanciful allusion, when our Saviour " spake of the temple of his body " (John ii. 21), but a disclosure of the true sense of the sanctuary under the old system, as designed to teach the doctrine of God's dwelling with his people. The same confidence with which the Christian now looks to God in Christ the old believer felt towards the holy hill of Zion. Here again the strophe ends with a devout and meditative pause, denoted as before by *Selah.*

6 (5.) *I,* even I, whose case you regarded as so desperate, *have lain down, and slept,* (and) *awaked,* notwithstanding all these dangers, *for the Lord,* Jehovah, *will sustain me,* and I therefore have no fears to rob me of my sleep. This last clause is not a reason for the safety he enjoys, which would require the past tense, but for his freedom from anxiety, in reference to which the future is entirely appropriate. This construction, the only one which gives the Hebrew words their strict and full sense, forbids the supposition that the psalm before us was an evening song, composed on the night of David's flight from Jerusalem. If any such distinctions be admissible or necessary, it may be regarded as a morning rather than an evening hymn.

7 (6). The fearlessness implied in the preceding verse is here expressed. *I will not be afraid of myriads,* or *multitudes,* the Hebrew word being used both in a definite and vague sense. It also contains an allusion to the first verb in ver. 2 (1), of which it is a derivative. *I will not be afraid of myriads of people,* either in the sense of persons, men, or by a poetic licence for *the people, i. e.* Israel, the great mass of whom had now revolted. *Whom they,* my enemies, *have set,* or posted, *round about against me.* This is a simpler and more accurate construction than the reflexive one, *who have set* (*themselves*) *against me round about,* although the essential meaning still remains the same. The sum of the whole verse is, that the same courage which enabled him to sleep without disturbance in the midst of enemies and dangers, still sustained him when those enemies and dangers were presented to his waking senses.

8 (7). That this courage was not founded upon self-reliance, he now shews by asking God for that which he before expressed his sure hope of obtaining. *Arise, O Lord,* Jehovah ! This is a common scriptural mode of calling upon God to manifest his presence and his power, either in wrath or favour. By a natural anthropomorphism, it describes the intervals of such manifestations as periods of inaction or of slumber, out of which he is besought to rouse himself. *Save me,* even me, of whom they say there is no help for him in God. See above, ver. 3 (2). *Save me, O my God,* mine by covenant and mutual engagement, to whom I therefore have a right to look for deliverance and protection. This confidence is warranted, moreover, by experience. *For thou hast,* in former exigencies, *smitten all my enemies,* without exception, (*on the*) *cheek* or *jaw,* an act at once violent and insulting. See 1 Kings xxii. 24; Micah iv. 14; v. 1; Lam. iii. 30. *The teeth of the wicked,* here identified with his enemies, because he was the champion and representative of God's cause, *thou hast broken,* and thus

rendered harmless. The image present to his mind seems to be that of wild beasts eager to devour him, under which form his enemies are represented in Ps. xxvii. 2.

9 (8). *To the Lord*, Jehovah, *the salvation*, which I need and hope for, is or belongs, as to its only author and dispenser. To him, therefore, he appeals for the bestowment of it, not on himself alone, but on the church of which he was the visible and temporary head. *On thy people (be) thy blessing !* This earnest and disinterested intercession for God's people forms a noble close or winding up of the whole psalm, and is therefore preferable to the version, *on thy people (is) thy blessing*, which, though equally grammatical, is less significant, and indeed little more than a repetition of the fact asserted in the first clause, whereas this is really an importunate petition founded on it. The whole closes, like the first and second stanzas, with a solemn and devout pause. SELAH.

Psalm 4

THE Psalmist prays God to deliver him from present as from past distresses, ver. 2 (1). He assures the haters of his regal dignity that God bestowed it, and will certainly protect it, ver. 3, 4 (2, 3). He exhorts them to quiet submission, righteousness, and trust in God, ver. 5, 6 (4, 5). He contrasts his own satisfaction, springing from such trust, with the hopeless disquietude of others, even in the midst of their enjoyments, ver. 7, 8 (6, 7). He closes with an exquisite proof of his tranquillity by falling asleep, as it were, before us, under the divine protection, ver. 9 (8). The resemblance of the last verse to ver. 6 (5) of the preceding psalm, together with the general similarity of structure, shews that, like the first and second, they were meant to form a pair, or double psalm. For the reasons given in explaining Ps. iii. 6 (5), the third may be described as a morning, and the fourth as an evening psalm. The historical occasion is of course the same in both, though mentioned only in the title of the third, while the musical directions are given in the title of the fourth. The absence of personal and local allusions is explained by the object of the composition, which was not to express private feelings merely, but to furnish a vehicle of pious sentiment for other sufferers, and the church at large.

1. *To the chief musician*, literally the *overseer* or *superintendent*, of any work or labour (2 Chron. ii. 1, 17, xxxiv. 12), and of the temple music in particular (1 Chron. xv. 21). The psalm is described as *belonging to him*, as the performer, or as intended *for him*, to be given *to him*. This shews that it was written for the use of the ancient church, and not for any merely private purpose. That this direction was not added by a later hand is clear from the fact that it never appears in the latest psalms. The same formula occurs at the beginning of fifty-three psalms, and at the close of the one in the third chapter of Habakkuk. A more specific musical direction follows. *In, on,* or *with stringed instruments*. This may either qualify *chief musician*, as denoting the leader in that particular style of performance, or direct him to perform this particular psalm with that kind of accompaniment. *A psalm to David, i.e.* belonging to him as the author, just as it belonged *to the chief musician*, as the performer. The original expression is the same in both cases. *Of David* conveys the sense correctly, but is rather a paraphrase than a translation.

2 (1). The psalm opens with a prayer for deliverance founded on pre-

vious experience of God's mercy. *In my calling*, when I call, *hear me*, in the pregnant sense of hearing favourably, hear and answer me, grant me what I ask. *O my God of righteousness*, my righteous God! Compare *my hill of holiness*, Ps. ii. 6, and *his hill of holiness*, Ps. iii. 5 (4). The appeal to God, as a God of righteousness, implies the justice of the Psalmist's cause, and shews that he asks nothing inconsistent with God's holiness. The same rule should govern all our prayers, which must be impious if they ask God to deny himself. The mercy here asked is no new or untried favour. It is because he has experienced it before that he dares to ask it now. *In the pressure*, or confinement, a common figure for distress, which I have heretofore experienced, *thou hast widened*, or made room *for me*, the corresponding figure for relief. All he asks is that this may be repeated. *Have mercy upon me*, or *be gracious unto me*, now as in former times, *and hear my prayer*. This appeal to former mercies, as a ground for claiming new ones, is characteristic of the Bible and of true religion. Among men past favours may forbid all further expectations; but no such rule applies to the divine compassions. The more we draw from this source, the more copious and exhaustless it becomes.

3 (2). *Sons of man!* In Hebrew, as in Greek, Latin, and German, there are two words answering to *man*, one generic and the other specific. When placed in opposition to each other, they denote men of high and low degree, as in Ps. xlix. 3 (2), lxii. 10 (9), Prov. viii. 4. It seems better, therefore, to give the phrase here used its emphatic sense, as signifying men of note or eminence, rather than the vague one of men in general or human beings. This agrees, moreover, with the probable occasion of this psalm, viz., the rebellion of Absalom, in which the leading men of Israel were involved. *To what (time)*, *i.e.* how long, or *to what (point)*, degree of wickedness; most probably the former. *How long (shall) my honour*, not merely personal, but official, *(be) for shame*, *i.e.* be so accounted, or *(be converted) into shame*, by my humiliation? David never loses sight of his religious dignity as a theocratical king and a type of the Messiah, or of the insults offered to the latter in his person. The question, *how long?*. implies that it had lasted long enough, nay, too long, even when it first began; in other words, that it was wrong from the beginning. *(How long) will ye love vanity*, or a vain thing, in the sense both of a foolish, hopeless undertaking, and of something morally defective or worthless. The same word is used above in reference to the insurrection of the nations against God and Christ (Ps. ii. 1). *(How long) will ye seek a lie*, *i.e.* seek to realise a vain imagination, or to verify a false pretension, with particular reference perhaps to the deceitful policy of Absalom (2 Sam. xv. 4, 7). As the *love* of the first clause denotes the bent of their affections, so the *seek* of this clause signifies the acting out of their internal dispositions. Compare Ps. xxxiv. 15 (14), and Zeph. ii. 3. The feeling of indignant surprise implied in the interrogation is expressed still further by a solemn pause. *Selah*. See above, on Ps. iii. 3 (2). The position of this word, here and in ver. 5 (4) below, seems to forbid the division of the psalm into strophes or stanzas of equal length.

4 (3). The pause at the close of the preceding verse expresses feeling. The connection of the verses, as to sense, is as intimate as possible. The *and* at the beginning of the verse before us has reference to the exhortation implied in the foregoing question. (See above, on Ps. ii. 6.) Cease to love vanity and seek a lie, *and know*, be assured, *that the Lord*, Jehovah, *hath set apart*, the same verb used to signify the segregation of Israel from

the rest of men (Ex. viii. 18, ix. 4, xi. 7, xxxiii. 16), here applied to the designation of an individual to the highest theocratical dignity. *The Lord hath set apart for himself*, for his own service, the execution of his own plans, and the promotion of his own honour. It was not, therefore, an attack on David, but on God himself and the Messiah whom he represented. The Hebrew word חָסִיד, derived from חֶסֶד, love to God or man, may either signify an object of the divine mercy, or one actuated by religious love. If both ideas are included, which is altogether probable, neither *godly* nor any other single word in English is an adequate translation. The predominant idea seems to be the passive one, so that the words are not so much descriptive of religious character as of divine choice: and know that the Lord hath set apart for the accomplishment of his own purpose one selected in his sovereign mercy for that purpose. This is mentioned as a proof that their hostility was vain, and that the prayer of verse 2 (1) would certainly be heard and answered. This followed as a necessary consequence from the relation which the Psalmist bore to God, not only as a godly man, but as a theocratic sovereign. *The Lord*, Jehovah, *will hear, in my calling*, when I call, *unto him*. The terms of the opening petition are here studiously repeated, so as to connect the prayer itself with the expression of assured hope that it will be answered.

5 (4). The address to his enemies is still continued, but merely as a vehicle of truth and his own feelings. *Rage and sin not, i.e.* do not sin by raging, as you have done, against me, the Lord's Anointed, and indirectly therefore against himself. This construction of the Hebrew words, though not the most obvious or agreeable to usage, agrees best with the context and with the Septuagint version, adopted by Paul in Ephesians iv. 26, where the precept, *Be ye angry and sin not*, seems to be a positive prohibition of anger, *i.e.*, of its wilful continuance, as appears from what the apostle adds, perhaps in allusion to the last clause of the verse before us. Some, it is true, have understood Paul as meaning, Be angry upon just occasions, but be careful not to sin by groundless anger or excess. But even if this be the sense of the words there, it is entirely inappropriate here, where the anger of the enemies was altogether sinful, and they could not therefore be exhorted to indulge it. There is still another meaning which the Hebrew words will bear. The verb strictly means to be violently moved with any passion or emotion, whether anger (Prov. xxix. 9), grief (2 Sam. xviii. 33), or fear (Isa. xxxii. 11). It might therefore be translated here, *tremble*, stand in awe, *and sin not*. But this, although it yields a good sense, cuts off all connection between David's words and those of Paul, and makes the explanation of the latter still more difficult. The English word *rage* not only conveys the sense of the original correctly, but is probably connected with it in its etymology. The command to cease from raging against God and his Anointed, is still further carried out in the next clause. *Say in your heart*, to yourselves, and not aloud, much less with clamour, what you have to say. The Hebrew verb does not mean to *speak* but to *say*, and, like this English word, is always followed by the words spoken, except in a few cases where they can be instantly supplied from the context. *E.g.* Exod. xix. 25, "So Moses went unto the people and *said* (not *spake*) to them" what God had just commanded him. Gen. iv. 8, "And Cain *said to* Abel his brother (not *talked with* him)," let us go into the field, as appears from what immediately follows. Compare 2 Chron. ii. 10 (11). It might here be rendered, *say (so) in your heart, i.e.* say we will no longer sin by raging

against David; but the other is more natural, and agrees better with what follows. *Say* (what you do say) *in your heart, upon your bed, i. e.* in the silence of the night, often spoken of in Scripture as the season of 'reflection (Eph. iv. 26), *and be still*, be silent, implying repentance and submission to authority. The effect of this exhortation to be still is beautifully strengthened by a pause in the performance. *Selah.*

6 (5). Before his enemies can be successful they must have a fear of God and a faith, of which they are entirely destitute. This confirmation of the Psalmist's hopes is clothed in the form of an exhortation to his enemies. *Offer offerings*, or sacrifice sacrifices, *of righteousness, i. e.* righteous sacrifices, prompted by a right motive, and implying a correct view of the divine nature. There may be an allusion to the hypocritical services of Absalom, and especially his pretended vow (2 Sam. xv. 7, 8). The form of expression here is borrowed from Deut. xxxiii. 19. As an indispensable prerequisite to such a service, he particularly mentions faith. *And trust in the Lord*, Jehovah, not in any human help or temporal advantages.

7 (6). *Many (there are) saying, Who will shew us good?* This may be in allusion to the anxious fears of his companions in misfortune, but is more probably a picture of the disquiet and unsatisfied desire arising from the want of faith and righteousness described in the foregoing verse. Of all who do not trust in God it may be said, that they are continually asking *Who will shew us good*, who will shew us wherein happiness consists, and how we may obtain it? In contrast with this restlessness of hope or of despair, he shews his own acquaintance with the true source of tranquillity by a petition founded on the ancient and authoritative form in which the High Priest was required to bless the people (Num. vi. 24–26). "The Lord bless thee and keep thee; the Lord make his face shine upon thee and be gracious unto thee; the Lord lift up his countenance upon thee and give thee peace." Two of these solemn benedictions are here mingled in a prayer. *Lift upon us the light of thy countenance, O Lord*, Jehovah! The light of the countenance is a favourite figure in the Psalms, for a favourable aspect or expression. See Ps. xxxi. 17 (16), xliv. 4 (3), lxxx. 4 (3). The lifting up may have reference to the rising of the sun, or be put in opposition to the act of looking down or away from any object, as a token of aversion or displeasure. *Upon us* extends the prayer to his companions in misfortune, or to all God's people, or to men in general, as if he had said, This is the only hope of our lost race. The plural form may be compared with those in the Lord's Prayer, as indicating the expansive comprehensive spirit of true piety.

8 (7). The faith, of which his enemies were destitute, he possessed in such a measure, that the mere anticipation of God's favour made him happier, in the midst of his distresses, than his foes in the actual possession of their temporal advantages. *Thou hast given gladness in my heart*, not to my heart, but to me in my heart, *i. e.* a real, inward, heartfelt gladness, *more than the time*, or more than when, *i. e.* more than they ever enjoyed when *their corn and their wine abounded*, or increased. The original nouns properly denote the new corn and wine of the passing year, the fresh fruits of the field and vineyard. The reference may be either to the proverbial joy of harvest and of vintage, or to the abundant stores of David's enemies contrasted with his own condition when dependent on a faithful servant for subsistence (2 Sam. xvi. 1, 2).

9 (8). With this faith in the divine protection, he has nothing even to disturb his rest. *In peace*, tranquillity, composure, *at once*, or at the same

time, by the same act, *I will lie down and will sleep*, or rather go to sleep,
fall asleep, which is the meaning of the Hebrew verb in Gen. ii. 21, xli. 5,
1 Kings xix. 5, and elsewhere.   Nothing could be more natural and beautiful, as a description of complete tranquillity, than this trait borrowed from
the physical habits of the young, the healthy, and those free from all
anxiety, to whom the act of lying down and that of sleeping are almost
coincident.   The ground of this security is given in the last clause.   *For
thou, Lord,* Jehovah, *alone in safety*, or security, *wilt make me dwell*.   The
future form, though not exclusive of the present (see above, on Ps. i. 2),
should be retained because it indicates the Psalmist's assured hope of
something not yet realised, and is thus in perfect keeping with ver. 8 (7).
Alone may be connected with what goes before : for thou Lord, and no
other, thou, even though all other friends and advantages should fail me, art
sufficient to protect and provide for me.   Or it may be connected with
what follows : *alone, in safety, thou wilt make me dwell*.   There is then an
allusion to the repeated application of the same Hebrew word to Israel as
dwelling apart from other nations under God's protection and in the enjoyment of his favour.   See Num. xxiii. 9, Duet. xxxiii. 28, 29, and compare Micah vii. 14, Jer. xlix. 31, Deut. iv. 7, 8, 2 Sam. vii. 23.   What
was originally said of the people is then transferred, as in ver. 4 (3)
above, to David, not as a private member of the ancient church, however
excellent, but as its theocratic head and representative, in whom, as afterwards more perfectly in Christ, the promises to Israel were verified and
realised.   This last interpretation of *alone* is so striking, and agrees so
well with the other allusions in this context to the Pentateuch, *e. g.* to Lev.
xxv. 18, 19, and Deut. xxxiii. 12 in this verse, and to Num. vi. 24—26 in
ver. 7 (6), that some combine the two constructions, and suppose *alone* to
have a kind of double sense, as if he had said, Thou alone wilt make me
dwell alone.   Although the form of this verse has respect to the particular
historical occasion of the psalm, the sentiment is so expressed as to admit
of an unforced application to the case of every suffering believer, and to the
distresses of the church at large, for whose use it was not only left on
record but originally written.

Psalm 5

THE Psalmist prays for the divine help, ver. 2 (1), on the ground that
Jehovah is his King and his God, ver. 3 (2), that he early and constantly
invokes his aid, ver. 4 (3), that the enemies, from whom he seeks to be delivered, are the enemies of God, ver. 5, 6 (4, 5), and as such must inevitably perish, ver. 7 (6), while he, as the representative of God's friends, must
be rescued, ver. 8 (7).   He then goes over the same ground afresh, asking
again to be protected from his enemies, ver. 9 (8), again describing them as
desperately wicked, ver. 10 (9), again appealing to God's justice to destroy
them, ver. 11 (10), and again anticipating certain triumph, ver. 12 (11),
on the ground of God's habitual and uniform dealing with the righteous,
ver. 13 (12).   As the two preceding psalms appear to constitute a pair, so
this one seems to contain such a pair or double psalm within itself.   It is
also obvious that this is but a further variation of the theme which runs
through the preceding psalms, and therefore an additional proof that their
arrangement in the book is not fortuitous or arbitrary.   If ver. 4 (3) of
this psalm be supposed to mark it as a morning hymn, its affinity to the
two before it becomes still more close and striking.

1. *To* (or *for*) *the Chief Musician.* See above on Ps. iv. 1. *To* (or *for*) *Nehiloth.* This, though undoubtedly a part of the original inscription, is obscure and enigmatical. Its very obscurity indeed may be regarded as a proof of its antiquity and genuineness. Some understand it to mean *flutes* or wind-instruments in general, as *Neginoth*, in the title of the fourth psalm, means stringed instruments. The sense would then be : (to be sung) to (an accompaniment of) flutes or wind-instruments. But as the Hebrew word is nowhere else used in this sense, and the preposition here employed is not the one prefixed to names of instruments, and flutes are nowhere mentioned as a part of the temple music, others make *Nehiloth* the name of a tune, or of another song to the melody of which this was to be adapted : (to be sung) to (the air of) Nehiloth. Others follow the ancient version in making it refer, not to the musical performance, but the subject of the psalm : (as) to inheritances, lots, or destinies, viz. those of the righteous and the wicked. This is favoured by the circumstance, that most of the other enigmatical inscriptions of the psalms may be more probably explained as having reference to their theme or subject than in any other manner. The title closes, as in the foregoing psalm, by ascribing it to *David* as its author. Nor is there anything, as we shall see, to militate against the truth of this inscription.

2 (1). *To my words, O Lord,* Jehovah, *give ear, perceive my thought.* Attend not only to my vocal and audible petitions, but to my unexpressed desires, to those " groanings which cannot be uttered," but are no less significant to God than language (Rom. viii. 26, 27). The second verb suggests the idea of attention, as well as that of simple apprehension.

3 (2). *Hearken to the voice of my crying,* or my cry for help, to which the Hebrew word is always specially applied. *My king and my God,* not as a mere creator and providential ruler, but as the covenant God and king of Israel, whom David represented. As he was himself the king of Israel, so God was his king, the lord paramount or sovereign, in whose right he reigned. This address involves a reason why his prayer must be heard. God, as the king of his people, could not deny them his protection, and they asked no other. *For to thee,* and thee only, *will I pray.* As if he had said, It is in this capacity that I invoke thee, and I therefore must be heard. This is a specimen of that παῤῥησία, or freedom of speech towards God, which is recognised as an effect and evidence of faith, in the New as well as the Old Testament, Heb. iv. 16, x. 19, 35 ; 1 John ii. 28, iii. 21, iv. 17, v. 14.

4 (3). *O Lord,* Jehovah, (*in*) *the morning thou shalt hear my voice.* This is not so much a request to be heard as a resolution to persist in prayer. The reference may be either to stated hours of prayer or to early devotion as a proof of earnestness and faith. See Ps. lv. 18 (17), lxxxviii. 14 (13.) (*In*) *the morning I will set* (my prayer) *in order,* to (or *for*) *thee.* There is here a beautiful allusion to the Mosaic ritual, which is unavoidably lost in a translation. The Hebrew verb is the technical term used in the Old Testament to signify the act of arranging the wood upon the altar (Gen. xxii. 9, Lev. i. 7, 1 Kings xviii. 33), and the shewbread on the table (Exod. xl. 23, Lev. xxiv. 6, 8). It would therefore necessarily suggest the idea of prayer as an oblation, here described as a kind of morning sacrifice to God. *And I will look out,* or watch, for an answer to my prayers. The image presented is that of one looking from a wall or tower in anxious expectation of approaching succour. A similar use of the same verb occurs in Hab. ii. 1, and Micah vii. 7. True faith is not contented

with the act of supplication, but displays itself in eager expectation of an answer.

5 (4). Here, as elsewhere, the Psalmist identifies his cause with God's, and anticipates the downfall of his enemies because they are sinners and therefore odious in God's sight. *For not a God delighting in wickedness (art) thou*, as might appear to be the case if these should go unpunished. It is necessary, therefore, for the divine honour, that they should not go unpunished. *Not with thee*, as thy guest or friend, *shall evil*, or *the bad (man)*, *dwell*. For an opposite use of the same figure, see below, Ps. xv. 1, lxi. 5 (4). It is still implied, that the impunity of sinners would appear as if God harboured and abetted them, and therefore must be inconsistent with his honour as a holy God.

6 (5). What was said in the preceding verse of sin is here, to prevent misapprehension, said of sinners. *They shall not stand, the proud*, or *insolent*, here put for wicked men in general and for the Psalmist's enemies in particular, *before thine eyes*. Thou canst not bear the presence of thy moral opposites. Sin is not only opposed to God's will, but repugnant to his nature. By ceasing to hate it, he would cease to be holy, cease to be perfect, cease to be God. This idea is expressed more directly in the other clause. *Thou hast hated*, and must still hate, *all doers of iniquity*. This last word is originally a negative, meaning inanity or nonentity, but like several other negatives in Hebrew, is employed as a strong term to denote moral deficiency and worthlessness.

7 (6). As the preceding verse extends what was said of sin in the abstract to personal offenders, so here what was said of the divine dispositions is applied to divine acts. That which God hates he must destroy. Particular classes of transgressors are here put, as before, by way of specimen or sample, for the whole; with special reference, however, to the sins of David's enemies. *Thou wilt destroy speakers of falsehood;* see above, on Ps. iv. 3 (2.) *A man of blood*, literally *bloods*, the plural form being commonly used where there is reference to blood-guiltiness or murder. See Gen. iv. 10, 11; Ps. li. 16 (14). *A man of blood and fraud*, a bloody and deceitful man, *the Lord*, Jehovah, *will abhor;* he must and will shew his abhorrence by the punishment of such offenders. This confident anticipation of God's righteous retributions really involves a prayer for the deliverance of the Psalmist from his enemies.

8 (7). For the same reason he is equally confident in the anticipation of his own deliverance. Since his enemies must perish as the enemies of God, he must escape, not on account of his own merit, nor simply as an object of God's favour, but as the champion of his cause, his earthly vicegerent, the type and representative of his Messiah. *And I*, as distinguished from these sinners, *in the abundance of thy mercy*, which excludes all reliance on his own strength or goodness, *will come to thy house*, the tabernacle set up on Mount Zion by David. *I will worship*, literally prostrate or bow myself, *towards thy temple of holiness*, thy holy temple, or rather palace, so called as the residence of Israel's divine King, and therefore no less applicable to the tabernacle than the temple. See 1 Sam. i. 9, iii. 3, Ps. xxvii. 4, xxviii. 2. *Towards*, not *in*, because the worshippers did not go into the sanctuary itself, but worshipped in the court, with their faces turned towards the place of God's manifested presence. Such usages are now superseded by the advent of the true sanctuary. See above, on Ps. iii. 5 (4). *In thy fear*, the reverence engendered even by the view and the experience of God's mercy. There may be an allusion in this verse to David's painful sense of

his exclusion from the house of God (2 Sam. xv. 25); but it cannot be merely an anticipation of renewed access to the sanctuary, which was equally open to all others, and could not therefore be used to indicate the contrast between his condition and that of others. The verse is rather an engagement to acknowledge God's delivering mercy in the customary manner. See below, Ps. lxvi. 13. As if he had said, While my enemies perish by the hand of God, I shall be brought by his mercy to give thanks for my deliverance at his sanctuary.

9 (8). The Psalmist here begins his prayer and argument anew, pursuing the same order as before. *O Lord*, Jehovah, *lead me*, guide me safely, *in thy righteousness, i. e.* in the exercise of that same justice which destroys my enemies, *on account of my enemies*, that they may not triumph ; *make straight before my face thy way, i. e.* mark out a safe and easy path for me to tread. The explanation of the *way* as that of duty and obedience, although not at variance with scriptural usage, is less suited to the context here, in which the prayer throughout is for protection and deliverance.

10 (9). The same reason as before is now assigned for his deliverance from his enemies, viz. because they were the enemies of God, and they were such because they were atrocious sinners. *For there is nothing in his mouth, i. e.* the mouth of any one of them, or of all concentrated in one ideal person, *sure* or *certain, i. e.* true. *Their inside*, their heart; their real disposition, as distinguished from the outward appearance, *(is) mischiefs*, injuries, or crimes, consists of nothing else. *A grave opened*, to receive the victim, *(is) their throat*, like that of a devouring monster. Or the throat may be mentioned as an organ of speech, as in Ps. cxlix. 6, cxv. 7, and compared with the grave as a receptacle of corruption or a place of destruction. *Their tongue they smooth*, or *make smooth*, by hypocrisy or flattery, as the wicked woman is said to *make her words smooth*, Prov. ii. 16, vii. 5. The Septuagint version of this clause is quoted by Paul (Rom. iii. 13), with several other passages from the Old Testament, as a strong description of human depravity. The last words are rendered in that version, "with their tongues they have used craft or deceit," an idea really included in the literal translation.

11 (10). *Condemn them*, literally *make them guilty, i. e.* recognise and treat them as such, *O God ! They shall fall, i. e.* they must, they cannot but fall, a common figure for destruction (Ps. xxxvi. 13, cxli. 10), *from their plans, i. e.*, before they can accomplish them, or in consequence, by means of them. (Compare Hos. xi. 6). *In the fulness*, or abundance, *of their sins, thrust them forth*, cast them out from thy presence, and down from their present exaltation. *For they have rebelled against thee*, not me, or against me only as thy instrument and representative. Or the opposition may be between rebelling against God and simply sinning against man. The imperative and future forms, in this verse, both express the certainty of the event, with an implication of approving acquiescence. Such expressions, in the Psalms, have never really excited or encouraged a spirit of revenge in any reader, and are no more fitted to have that effect than the act of a judge who condemns a criminal to death, or of the officer who executes the sentence. The objections often urged against such passages are not natural, but spring from over-refinement and a false view of the Psalms as expressions of mere personal feeling. See below, on Ps. vii. 13 (12).

12 (11). The transition and contrast are the same as in ver. 8 (7) above. While the wicked perish, the righteous shall have cause for everlasting joy.

And all (those) trusting in thee, making thee their refuge, *shall be glad ; for ever shall they shout* (or *sing*) *for joy, and* (not without cause, for) *thou wilt cover over* (or *protect*) *them ; and in thee*, in thy presence and thy favour, *shall exult*, or triumph, (*the*) *lovers of thy name*, *i. e.* of thy manifested excellence, which is the usual sense of this expression in the Old Testament. The believers and lovers of God's name, here spoken of, are not merely friends of the psalmist who rejoice in his deliverance, but the great congregation of God's people, to which he belonged, and of which he was the representative, so that his deliverance was theirs, and a rational occasion of their joy, not only on his account but on their own.

13 (12). The confident hope expressed in the foregoing verse was not a groundless or capricious one, but founded on the nature of God and the uniform tenor of his dispensations. The psalmist knows what God will do in this case, because he knows what he does and will do still in general. *For thou wilt bless*, and art wont to bless, *the righteous*, the opposite of those described in ver. 5–7 (4–6) and 10, 11 (9, 10), *O Lord*, Jehovah! *Like the shield*, as the shield protects the soldier (*so with*) *favour thou wilt surround him*, or *enclose him*, still referring to the righteous ; see the same comparison in Ps. iii. 4 (3.) The confident assertion that God will do so, implies that he has done so, and is wont to do so, to the righteous as a class. And this affords a reasonable ground for the belief, expressed in the preceding verse, that he will do so also in the present case.

Psalm 6

THE psalmist prays for the removal of God's chastisements, ver. 2 (1), because they have already brought him very low, ver. 3, 4 (2, 3), because the divine glory will be promoted by his rescue, ver. 5 (4), and obscured by his destruction, ver. 6 (5), and because, unless speedily relieved, he can no longer bear up under his sufferings, ver. 7, 8 (6, 7). He is nevertheless sure of the divine compassion, ver. 9 (8). His prayer is heard and will be answered, ver. 10 (9), in the defeat and disappointment of his enemies, by whose malignant opposition his distress was caused, ver. 11 (10). This reference to his enemies constitutes the link of connection between this psalm and the foregoing series, and maintains the contrast, running through that series, between two great classes of mankind, the righteous and the wicked, the subjects of Messiah and the rebels against him, the friends and foes of the theocracy, the friends and foes of David, as an individual, a sovereign, and a type of the Messiah. At the same time, this psalm differs wholly from the others in its tone of querulous but humble grief, which has caused it to be reckoned as the first of the Penitential psalms. This tone is suddenly exchanged, in ver. 9 (8), for one of confident assurance, perfectly in keeping with what goes before, and true to nature.

1. *For the Chief Musician,* (to be sung) *with stringed instruments upon the eighth.* This last word corresponds exactly to our *octave ;* but its precise application in the ancient music we have now no means of ascertaining. An instrument of eight strings, which some suppose to be the sense, could hardly be described by the ordinal number *eighth.* We probably lose little by our incapacity to understand these technical expressions, while, at the same time, their very obscurity may serve to confirm our faith in their antiquity and **genuineness, as parts of the** original composition. This

psalm, like the three which immediately precede it, describes itself as *a psalm of* (or *by*) David, belonging *to David,* as its author. The correctness of this statement there is as little reason to dispute in this as in either of the other cases.

2 (1). *O Lord,* Jehovah, *do not in thine anger rebuke me, and do not in thy heat,* or hot displeasure, *chasten me.* Both the original verbs properly denote the conviction and reproof of an offender in words, but are here, as often elsewhere, applied to providential chastisements, in which God speaks with a reproving voice. This is not a prayer for the mitigation of the punishment, like that in Jer. x. 24, but for its removal, as appears from the account of the answer in ver. 9–11 (8–10). Such a petition, while it indicates a strong faith, at the same time recognises the connection between suffering and sin. In the very act of asking for relief, the psalmist owns that he is justly punished. This may serve to teach us how far the confident tone of the preceding psalms is from betraying a self-righteous spirit, or excluding the consciousness of personal unworthiness and ill-desert. The boldness there displayed is not that of self-reliance, but of faith.

3 (2). *Have mercy upon me,* or *be gracious unto me,* O Lord, Jehovah, *for drooping,* languishing, *am I.* The original construction is, *for I am* (*one who*) *droops* or withers, like a blighted plant. Like a child complaining to a parent, he describes the greatness of his suffering as a reason for relieving him. *Heal me, O Lord,* Jehovah, *for shaken,* agitated with distress and terror, *are my bones,* here mentioned as the strength and framework of the body. This might seem to indicate corporeal disease as the whole from which he prays to be delivered. But the absence of any such allusion in the latter part of the psalm, and the explicit mention there of enemies as the occasion of his sufferings, shews that the pain of body here described was that arising from distress of mind, and which could only be relieved by the removal of the cause. To regard the bodily distress as a mere figure for internal anguish, would be wholly arbitrary and destructive of all sure interpretation. The physical effect here ascribed to moral causes is entirely natural and confirmed by all experience.

4 (3). The Psalmist himself guards against the error of supposing that his worst distresses were corporeal. *And my soul,* as well as my body, or more than my body, which merely sympathizes with it, *is greatly agitated,* terror-stricken, the same word that was applied to the bones in the preceding verse. The description of his suffering is then interrupted by another apostrophe to God. *And thou, O Lord,* Jehovah, *until when,* how long ? The sentence is left to be completed by the reader: how long wilt thou leave me thus to suffer ? how long before thou wilt appear for my deliverance ? This question, in its Latin form, *Domine quousque,* was Calvin's favourite ejaculation in his times of suffering, and especially of painful sickness.

5 (4). The expostulatory question is now followed by direct petition. *Return, O Lord,* Jehovah, *deliver my soul,* my life, my self, from this impending death. As God seems to be absent when his people suffer, so relief is constantly described as his return to them. (*Oh*) *save me,* a still more comprehensive term than that used in the first clause, *for the sake of thy mercy,* not merely according to it, as a rule or measure, but to vindicate it from reproach, and do it honour, as a worthy end to be desired and accomplished.

6 (5). As a further reason for his rescue, he now urges that without it God will lose the honour, and himself the happiness, of his praises and

thanksgivings. *For there is not in death*, or the state of the dead, *thy remembrance*, any remembrance of thee. *In Sheol*, the grave, as a general receptacle, here parallel to *death*, and, like it, meaning the unseen world or state of the dead, *who will acknowledge*, or give thanks, *to thee?* The Hebrew verb denotes that kind of praise called forth by the experience of goodness. The question in the last clause is equivalent to the negative proposition in the first. This verse does not prove that David had no belief or expectation of a future state, nor that the intermediate state is an unconscious one, but only that in this emergency he looks no further than the close of life, as the appointed term of thanksgiving and praise. Whatever might eventually follow, it was certain that his death would put an end to the praise of God, in that form and those circumstances to which he had been accustomed. See below, on Ps. xxx. 10 (9); lxxxviii. 11–13 (10–12), cxv. 17, 18, and compare Isa. xxxviii. 18. So far is the argument here urged from being weakened by our clearer knowledge of the future state, that it is greatly strengthened by the substitution of the second or eternal death.

7 (6). *I am weary in* (or *of*) *my groaning*, I have become wearied with it, and unless I am relieved, *I shall* (still as hitherto) *make my bed swim every night, my couch with tears I shall dissolve*, or make to flow. The uniform translation of the verbs as presents does not bring out their full meaning, or express the idea, suggested in the Hebrew by the change of tense, that the grief which had already become wearisome must still continue without mitigation, unless God should interpose for his deliverance. Thus understood, the verse is not a mere description, but a disguised prayer.

8 (7). *Mine eye has failed*, grown dim, a common symptom both of mental and bodily distress, *from vexation*, not mere grief, but grief mixed with indignation at my enemies. *It has grown old*, dim like the eye of an old man, a still stronger expression of the same idea, *in* (the midst of) *all my enemies*, or *in* (consequence of) *all my enemies*, *i. e.* of their vexatious conduct. Compare Ps. xxxi. 10 (9). In these two verses he resumes the description of his own distress, in order to shew that the argument in ver. 6 (5) was appropriate to his case, as that of one drawing near to death, and therefore likely soon to lose the capacity and opportunity of praising God.

9 (8). Here the key abruptly changes from the tone of sorrowful complaint to that of joyful confidence. No gradual transition could have so successfully conveyed the idea that the prayer of the psalmist has been heard, and will be answered. The effect is like that of a whisper in the sufferer's ear, while still engrossed with his distresses, to assure him that they are about to terminate. This he announces by a direct and bold address to his persecuting enemies. *Depart from me, all ye doers of iniquity*, the same phrase that occurs in Ps. v. 6 (5). The sense is not that he will testify his gratitude by abjuring all communion with the wicked, but that his assurance of divine protection relieves him from all fear of his wicked foes. When God arises, then his enemies are scattered. This sense is required by the last clause of ver. 8 (7), and confirmed by a comparison with ver. 11 (10), *For the Lord*, Jehovah, *hath heard the voice of my weeping*, or my weeping voice. The infrequency of silent grief is said to be characteristic of the orientals, and the same thing may be observed in Homer's pictures of heroic manners.

10 (9). *Jehovah hath heard my supplication.* The assurance of this fact relieves all fear as to the future. *Jehovah my prayer will receive.* The change of tense is not unmeaning or fortuitous. The combination of the

past and future represents the acceptance as complete and final, as already begun, and certain to continue. The particular petition thus accepted is the one expressed or implied in the next verse.

11 (10). *Ashamed and confounded, i.e.* disappointed and struck with terror, *shall be all my enemies.* The desire that they may be is not expressed, but involved in the confident anticipation that they will be. In the second verb there is an obvious allusion to its use in ver. 3, 4 (2, 3). As he had been terror-stricken, so shall they be. As they filled him with consternation, so shall God fill them. *They shall return,* turn back from their assault repulsed ; *they shall be ashamed,* filled with shame at their defeat ; and that not hereafter, *(in) a moment,* instantaneously.

Psalm 7

THE Psalmist still prays for deliverance from his enemies, ver. 2, 3 (1, 2), on the ground that he is innocent of that wherewith they charge him, ver. 4-6 (3-5). He prays for justice to himself and on his enemies, as a part of that great judicial process which belongs to God as the universal judge, ver. 7-10 (6-9). He trusts in the divine discrimination between innocence and guilt, ver. 11, 12 (10, 11). He anticipates God's vengeance on impenitent offenders, ver. 13, 14 (12, 13). He sees them forced to act as self-destroyers, ver. 15-17 (14-16). At the same time he rejoices in God's mercy to himself, and to the whole class whom he represents, ver. 18 (17).

The penitential tone, which predominated in the sixth psalm, here gives way again to that of self-justification, perhaps because the Psalmist here speaks no longer as an individual, but as the representative of the righteous or God's people. The two views which he thus takes of himself are perfectly consistent, and should be suffered to interpret one another.

1. *Shiggaion, i.e.* wandering, error. The noun occurs only here, and in the plural form, Hab. iii. 1, but the verb from which it is derived is not uncommon, and is applied by Saul to his own errors with respect to David (1 Sam. xxvi. 21). See also Ps. cxix. 10, 118. Hence some explain the word here as denoting moral error, sin, and make it descriptive of the subject of the psalm. See above on Ps. v. 1. Still more in accordance with the literal meaning of the root is the opinion that it here denotes the wandering of David at the period when the psalm was probably conceived. In either case, it means a song of wandering or error, *which he sang,* in the literal sense, or in the secondary one of poetical composition, as Virgil says, I sing the man and arms, *i.e.* they are the subject of my poem. *To the Lord,* Jehovah, to whom a large part of the psalm is really addressed. *Concerning* (or *because of*) *the words of Cush the Benjamite.* It is clear from ver. 4-6 (3-5), that *the words* referred to were calumnious reports or accusations. These may have been uttered by one Cush, a Benjamite, who nowhere else appears in history. But as this very circumstance makes it improbable that he would have been singled out, as the occasion of this psalm, from among so many slanderers, some suppose Cush to be Shimei, who cursed David when he fled from Absalom (2 Sam. xvi. 5-13). As the psalm, however, seems much better suited to the times of Saul, some suppose *Cush,* which is properly the Hebrew name of Ethiopia, to be here an enigmatical name applied to Saul himself, in reference to the blackness of his heart, and perhaps to his incorrigible wickedness. See Jer. xiii. 23, and Amos ix. 7. The description *Benjamite,* is equally

appropriate to Saul (1 Sam. ix. 1, 2 ; xvi. 5, 11) and Shimei, who, indeed, were kinsmen. This explanation of the word *Cush* is less forced than it might otherwise appear, because enigmatical descriptions of the theme are not unfrequent in the titles of the Psalms. See above, on Ps. v. 1, and below, on Ps. ix. 1 ; xxii. 1 ; liii. 1 ; lvii. 1 ; lx. 1.

2 (1). The psalm opens with an expression of strong confidence in God, and a prayer founded on it. *O Lord,* Jehovah, *my God,* not merely by creation, but by special covenant, *in thee,* as such, and therefore in no other, *I have trusted,* and do still trust. This relation and this trust entitle him to audience and deliverance. *Save me from all my persecutors,* or pursuers, a term frequently employed in David's history. See 1 Sam. xxiv. 15 (14) ; xxvi. 20. By these we are here to understand the whole class of worldly and ungodly men, of which Saul was the type and representative. The *all* suggests the urgency of the necessity, as a motive to immediate interposition. *And extricate me,* or deliver me. The primary idea of the verb translated *save* is that of making room, enlarging. See above, on Ps. iv. 2 (1).

3 (2). *Lest he tear, like a lion, my soul.* The singular form, following the plural in the foregoing verse, may have particular reference to Saul, or to the class of which he was a type, personified as an ideal individual. The imagery of the verse is borrowed from the habits of wild beasts, with which David was familiar from a child. See 1 Sam. xvii. 34–37. The soul or life is mentioned as the real object of attack, and not as a mere periphrasis for the personal pronoun, as if *my soul* were equivalent to *me. Rending,* or *breaking* the bones, *and there is none delivering,* or with none to deliver.

4 (3.) He proceeds upon the principle that God will not hear the prayer of the wicked, and that he must hear that of the righteous. He proceeds, therefore, to assert his innocence, not his freedom from all sin, but from that particular offence with which he had been charged. *O Lord,* Jehovah, *my God,* as in ver. 2 (1), *if I have done this,* which follows, or this of which I am accused, referring to " the words of Cush," the calumnies, which gave occasion to the psalm itself. *If there is,* with emphasis on the verb, which might have been omitted in Hebrew, and is therefore emphatic, *if there is indeed,* as my accusers say, *perverseness,* iniquity, *in my palms,* in the palms of my hands, here mentioned as instruments of evil. The apodosis of the sentence is contained in ver. 6 (5) below.

5 (4). *If I have repaid my friend,* one at peace with me, *evil, and spoiled,* plundered, *(one) distressing me,* acting as my enemy, *without a cause.* There seems to be an allusion here to the two periods of David's connection with Saul, that of their friendly intercourse, and that of their open enmity. During neither of these had David been guilty of the sins charged upon him. He had not conspired against Saul while in his service (1 Sam. xxii. 7, 8), and when persecuted by him he had spared his life (1 Sam. xxiv. 10, 11). Some suppose this last fact to be here referred to, and translate the second clause, *yea, I have delivered him that without cause is mine enemy.* The Hebrew verb is certainly used elsewhere in this sense (2 Sam. xxii. 20, Ps. vi. 5), but its primary meaning seems to be that of stripping or spoiling a conquered enemy. The first construction above given is moreover much more natural, and agrees better with the grammatical dependence of the second verb upon the first.

6 (5). His consciousness of innocence is expressed in the strongest manner by invoking the divine displeasure if the charge can be established. *An enemy,* or by poetic licence, *the enemy,* whether Saul or the ideal enemy

referred to in verse 3 (2), *shall pursue*, or *may pursue*, which is equivalent
to saying, *Let the enemy pursue my soul*, the figure being still the same as in
verse 3 (2) above, but carried out with more minuteness, *and overtake (it)*,
and trample to the earth my life, and my honour in the dust make dwell, i.e.
completely prostrate and degrade. Some regard *honour* as equivalent to
soul and *life*, the intelligent and vital part, which is the glory of man's constitution. But the analogy of Ps. iii. 4 (3) and iv. 3 (2) makes it more
probable that in this case also there is reference to the Psalmist's personal
and official honour. The allusion, however, is not so much to posthumous
disgrace as to present humiliation. All this he imprecates upon himself if
really guilty of the charges calumniously brought against him. The solemnity of this appeal to God, as a witness and a judge, is enhanced by the
usual pause. *Selah.*

7 (6). Upon this protestation of his innocence he founds a fresh prayer
for protection and deliverance. *Arise*, arouse thyself, *O Lord*, Jehovah.
See above, on Ps. iii. 8 (7). *Arise in thine anger, raise thyself*, or *be exalted,
in, i.e.* amidst, *the ragings of my enemies.* The idea *because of my enemies* is
rather implied than expressed. The sense directly intended seems to be
that, as his enemies are raging, it is time for God to arise in anger too. As
they rage against him, he calls upon God to rise in anger against them.
And awake, a still stronger figure than *arise*, because implying sleep as well
as inactivity. *Awake unto me*, at my call and for my benefit. *Judgment
hast thou commanded*, or ordained. Let that judgment now be executed.
He appeals to the general administration of God's justice, as a ground for
expecting it in this one case. As it was part of the divine plan or purpose to do justice, both on friends and foes, here was an opportunity to
put it into execution.

8 (7). *And the congregation of nations shall surround thee*, which in this
connection is equivalent to saying, *let it surround thee.* The most probable
sense of these obscure words is, appear in the midst of the nations as their
judge. The same connection between God's judicial government in general
and his judicial acts in a particular case, that is implied in the preceding
verse, is here embodied in the figure of an oriental king dispensing justice
to his subjects in a popular assembly. *And above it*, the assembly, *to the
high place*, or *the height, return thou.* This may either mean, return to
heaven when the judgment is concluded, or, which seems more natural,
Resume thy seat as judge above this great ideal congregation. *Above it*,
thus assembled to receive thee, *to the high place*, or the judgment-seat, *return thou*, after so long an absence, previously intimated by the summons to
arise and awake. Inaction, sleep, and absence from the judgment-seat, are all
bold metaphors for God's delay to save his people and destroy their enemies.

9 (8). The same thing is now expressed in a direct and formal manner.
Jehovah will judge, is to judge, *the nations.* This is laid down as a certain
general proposition, from which the Psalmist draws a special inference in
the shape of a petition. *Judge me, O Lord*, Jehovah! If it be true that
God will judge the world, redress all wrong, and punish all iniquity, let him
begin with me. Let me share now in the justice which is to be universally
administered. *Judge me, O Lord, according to my right*, and *my completeness*, or perfection, *over me, i.e.* according to my innocence which covers and
protects me. All such expressions must be qualified and explained by the
confession of unworthiness in Ps. vi. and elsewhere, which sufficiently demonstrates that the Psalmist here makes no claim to absolute perfection and
innocence, nor to any whatever that is independent of God's sovereign mercy.

10 (9). *Let cease, I pray, the badness of wicked* (*men*). The future has an optative meaning given to it by the Hebrew particle (נָא), which is often rendered *now*, not as an adverb of time, but of entreaty. Between man and man, it is frequently equivalent to *if you please* in modern parlance. When addressed to God, it scarcely admits of any other version than *I pray*. The assonance or paronomasia in the common version, *wickedness of the wicked*, is not found in the original, where two words, not akin to one another, are employed. The plural form of *wicked* is also lost or left ambiguous in the common version. *And thou wilt confirm*, or establish, *a righteous* (*man*), *and a trier of hearts and reins*, constantly used in Scripture for the internal dispositions, (*is the*) *righteous God*, or (*art thou*) *O righteous God*, which last agrees best with the direct address to God in the preceding clauses. This does not merely mean that God is omniscient, and therefore able thus to try the hearts and reins, but that he actually does it. Here he is specially appealed to, as a judge or umpire between Saul, or "the wicked" whom he represented, and "the righteous," of whom David was the type and champion.

11 (10). *My shield* (*is*) *upon God*. My protection or defence depends on him alone. The figure is the same as in Ps. iii. 4 (3) and v. 13 (12). Here again the hope of personal deliverance is founded on a general truth, as to the course of the divine administration. *My shield* (*is*) *upon God, saving*, or *who saves*, the Saviour of *the upright*, straightforward, or sincere *in heart*. This is a new indirect assertion of his own integrity and innocence.

12 (11). The second word in the original of this verse may be either a participle or a noun, so that the clause admits of two translations, *God* (*is*) *a righteous judge*, and, *God is judging*, i. e. *judges, the righteous*. The first would be a repetition of the general truth taught in ver. 9 (8) above, but here applied to the punishment of the wicked, as it is there to the salvation of the innocent. According to the other construction, the verse before us presents both ideas : *God judges the righteous*, i. e. does him justice, and *God is angry every day*. The object of this anger, although not expressed, is obvious, and is even rendered more conspicuous by this omission. As if he had said, "God, who does justice to the righteous, has likewise objects for his indignation."

13 (12). *If he*, the sinner at whom God is angry, *will not turn*, i. e. turn back from his impious and rebellious undertakings, *his sword he will whet*, i. e. with a natural though sudden change of subject, God will whet his sword, often referred to as an instrument of vengeance. *His bow he has trodden on*, alluding to the ancient mode of bending the large and heavy bows used in battle, *and made it ready*. The bow and the sword were the most common weapons used in ancient warfare. The past tense of these verbs implies that the instruments of vengeance are prepared already, and not merely viewed as something future.

14 (13). *And at him* (the wicked enemy) *he has aimed*, or directed, *the instruments of death*, his deadly weapons. This is still another step in advance. The weapons are not only ready for him, but aimed at him. *His arrows to* (*be*) *burning he will make*, i. e. he will make his arrows burning arrows, in allusion to the ancient military custom of shooting ignited darts or arrows into besieged towns, for the purpose of setting them on fire, as well as that of personal injury. The figurative terms in these two verses all express the certainty and promptness of the divine judgments on incorrigible sinners. For even these denunciations are not absolute,

but suspended on the enemy's repentance or persistency in evil. That significant phrase, *if he will not turn*, may be tacitly supplied as qualifying every threatening in the book, however strong and unconditional in its expressions.

15 (14). *Behold, he*, the wicked man, *will writhe*, or travail (*with*) *iniquity*, (towards others), *and conceive mischief* (to himself), *and bring forth falsehood*, self-deception, disappointment. The meaning seems to be, that while bringing his malignant schemes to maturity, he will unconsciously conceive and bring forth ruin to himself.

16 (15) The same idea is then expressed by other figures, borrowed perhaps from certain ancient modes of hunting. *A well he has digged*, *i.e.* a pitfall for his enemy, *and hollowed it*, or made it deep, *and fallen into the pit he is making*, or about to make. The change from the past tense to the future seems to place the catastrophe between the inception and completion of the plan. The translation of the last verb as a simple preterite is entirely ungrammatical.

17 (16). Still a third variation of the same theme. *His mischief shall return upon his own head*, literally into it, like a falling body which not only rests upon an object, but sinks and is imbedded in it. *And on his own crown his violence*, including the ideas of injustice and cruelty, *shall come down*.

18 (17). While the wicked enemy of God and his people is thus made to execute the sentence on himself, the Psalmist already exults in the experience of God's saving mercy. *I will praise the Lord*, Jehovah, *i.e.* acknowledge his favours. See above, on Ps. vi. 6 (5). *According to his right*, desert, or due, as in ver. 9 (8) above. Or *according to his righteousness*, his justice, *i.e.* the praise shall correspond to the display just made of this attribute, as well in the deliverance of the Psalmist as in the destruction of his enemies. *And I will sing praise*, praise by singing, praise in song, *the name*, the manifested excellence (see above, on Ps. v. 12 (11),) *of the Lord*, Jehovah, *High* or *Most High*. He will praise the Lord in this exalted character as manifested by his dealings in the case which gave occasion to the psalm. The resolution thus expressed may be considered as fulfilled in the psalm itself, so confident is he that it cannot be performed before his prayer is answered. Or the words may be understood as engaging to continue these acknowledgments hereafter.

Psalm 8

THIS psalm begins and ends with an admiring recognition of God's manifested excellence, ver. 2 (1) and 10 (9). In the intermediate verses the manifestation is traced, first in the inanimate creation, ver. 3, 4 (2, 3 , and then in animated nature, vers. 5–9 (4–8), with particular reference to man's superiority. This is indeed the main subject of the psalm, the glory of God in nature being only introduced to heighten his goodness to mankind. We have here, therefore, a description of the dignity of human nature, as it was at first, and as it is to be restored in Christ, to whom the descriptive terms may therefore be applied, without forced or fanciful accommodation on the one hand, and without denying the primary generic import of the composition on the other.

1. *To the Chief Musician, on* (or *according to*) *the Gittith*. This word, which reappears in the titles of two other psalms (the eighty-first and

eighty-fourth), would seem, from its form, to be the feminine of *Gitti*,
which always means a Gittite or inhabitant of Gath. See Josh. xiii. 3;
2 Sam. vi. 10, xv. 18. As David once resided there, and had afterwards
much intercourse with the inhabitants, the word may naturally here denote
an instrument there invented or in use, or an air, or a style of performance,
borrowed from that city. Some prefer, however, to derive it from the
primary sense of *Gath* in Hebrew, which is *wine-press*, and apply it either
to an instrument of that shape, or to a melody or style which usage had
connected with the joy of vintage or the pressing of the grapes. Either of
these explanations is more probable than that which derives *Gittith* from
the same root with *Neginoth* in the titles of Ps. iv. and vi., and gives it
the same sense, viz. stringed instruments, or the music of stringed instruments. Besides the dubious etymology on which this explanation rests, it
is improbable that two such technical terms would have been used to
signify precisely the same thing. The only further observation to be made
upon this title is, that all the psalms to which it is prefixed are of a joyous
character, which agrees well with the supposition that it signifies an air or
style of musical performance. The ascription of this *Psalm to David*, as
its author, is fully confirmed by its internal character.

2 (1). *Jehovah, our Lord,* not of the Psalmist only, but of all men, and
especially all Israel, *how glorious (is) thy name,* thy manifested excellence
(see above, Ps. v. 11, vii. 17), *in all the earth, which gave thy glory, i. e.*
which glory of thine give or place, *above the heavens.* The verbal form here
used is, in every other place where it occurs, an imperative, and should not
therefore, without necessity, be otherwise translated. Thus understood,
the clause contains a prayer or wish, that the divine glory may be made
still more conspicuous. To give or place glory on an object is an idiomatic
phrase repeatedly used elsewhere, to denote the conferring of honour on an inferior. See Num. xxvii. 20; 1 Chron. xxix. 25; Dan. xi. 21. It here implies
that the glory belonging to the frame of nature is not inherent but derivative.

3 (2.) *From the mouth of babes and sucklings thou hast founded strength.*
The instinctive admiration of thy works, even by the youngest children, is
a strong defence against those who would question thy being or obscure
thy glory. The Septuagint version of the last words in this clause, thou
hast prepared (or provided) praise, conveys the same idea with a change of
form, since it is really the praise or admiration of the child that is described in the original as strength. This version is adopted by Matthew,
in his record of our Lord's reply to the Pharisees, when they complained of
the hosannas uttered by the children in the temple (Mat. xxi. 16). That
allusion does not prove that Christ was the primary subject of this psalm,
but only that the truth expressed in the words quoted was exemplified in
that case. If the Scriptures had already taught that even the unconscious
admiration of the infant is a tribute to God's glory, how much more might
children of maturer age be suffered to join in acclamations to his Son. The
sense thus put upon the words of David agrees better with the context than
the one preferred by some interpreters, viz., that the defence in question is
afforded by the structure and progress of the child itself. If this had been
intended, he would hardly have said *from the mouth*, or have confined his
subsequent allusions to the splendour of the firmament.—The effect, or rather
the legitimate tendency of this spontaneous testimony is *to silence enemy
and avenger, i. e.* to stop the mouths of all malignant railers against God,
whose cavils and sophisms are put to shame by the instinctive recognition
of God's being and his glory by the youngest children.

4 (3). *When I see thy heavens, the work of thy fingers,* an expression borrowed from the habits of men, to whom the fingers are natural organs of contrivance and construction, *the moon and the stars which thou hast fixed,* or settled in their several spheres. As we constantly associate the sky and sun together, the latter, although not expressly mentioned, may be considered as included in the subject of the first clause. Or the mention of the moon and stars without the sun may be understood to mark this as an evening hymn. There is no ground, however, for referring this psalm to the pastoral period of David's life, or for doubting that it was composed when he was king.

5 (4). The sentence begun in the preceding verse is here completed. When I see thy heavens, &c., *what is man,* frail man, as the original word signifies, *that thou shouldst remember him,* think of him, attend to him, *and (any) son of man,* or *the son of man,* as a generic designation of the race, *that thou shouldst visit him,* i. e. according to the usage of this figure, manifest thyself to him, either in wrath or mercy. See Gen. xviii. 14, xxi. 1, Ruth i. 6, &c. Here of course the latter is intended. The scriptural idea of a divine visitation is of something which reveals God's special presence and activity, whether as a friend or foe. The interrogation in this verse implies a strong negation of man's worthiness to be thus honoured, not in comparison with the material universe, to which he is in truth superior, but with the God whose glory the whole frame of nature was intended to display and does display, even to the least matured and cultivated minds. It was with a view to this comparison, and not for its own sake, or as the main subject of the psalm, that the glory of creation was referred to the foregoing verse.

6 (5). *And remove him little from divinity,* i. e. from a divine and heavenly, or at least a superhuman state. The Hebrew noun is the common one for *God,* but being plural in its form, is sometimes used in a more vague and abstract sense, for all conditions of existence higher than our own. 1 Sam. xxviii. 13, Zech. ix. 7. Hence it is sometimes rendered *angels* in the Septuagint, which version, although inexact, is retained in the New Testament (Heb. ii. 7), because it sufficiently expresses the idea which was essential to the writer's argument. The verb in this clause strictly means to make or let one want, to leave deficient. Eccles. iv. 8, vi. 2. The form here used (that of the future with vav conversive), connects it in the closest manner with the verb of the preceding verse, a construction which may be imperfectly conveyed by the omission of the auxiliary verbs in English. " What is man, that thou shouldst remember him, and visit him, and make him want but little of divinity, and crown him with honour and glory?" The Hebrew order of the last clause is, *and (with) honour and glory crown him.* These nouns are elsewhere put together to express royal dignity. Ps. xxi. 1, 6 (5), xlv. 4 (3), Jer. xxii. 18, 1 Chron. xxix. 25. There is an obvious allusion to man's being made in the image of God, with dominion over the inferior creation. Gen. i. 26, 28 ; ix. 2. This is predicated not of the individual but of the race, which lost its perfection in Adam and recovers it in Christ. Hence the description is pre-eminently true of him, and the application of the words in Heb. ii. 7, is entirely legitimate, although it does not make him the exclusive subject of the psalm itself.

7 (6). The same construction is continued through the first clause of this verse. *Make him rule,* i. e. what is man that thou shouldst make him rule, *in,* among, and by implication *over, the works,* the other and

inferior creatures, *of thy hands*. The use of the future form in Hebrew up to this point is dependent on the question and contingent particle (*what is man that*) in ver. 5 (4). The question being now exhausted or exchanged for a direct affirmation, the past tense is resumed. *All*, everything, *hast thou put under his feet*, *i. e.* subjected to his power. The application of these terms to Christ (1 Cor. xv. 27, Eph. i. 22), as the ideal representative of human nature in its restored perfection, is precisely similar to that of the expressions used in the preceding verse.

8 (7). This verse contains a mere specification of the general term *all* in the verse before it. *Sheep*, or rather *flocks*, including sheep and goats, *and oxen*, as a generic term for larger cattle, *and also*, not only these domesticated animals, but also, *beasts of the field*, which always means in Scripture wild beasts (Gen. ii. 20, iii. 14, 1 Sam. xvii. 44, Joel i. 20), field being used in such connections to denote, not the cultivated land, but the open, unenclosed, and wilder portions of the country. The whole verse is a general description of all quadrupeds or beasts, whether tame or wild.

9 (8). To complete the cycle of animated nature, the inhabitants of the air and water are now added to those of the earth. *Bird of heaven*, a collective phrase, denoting the birds of the sky, *i. e.* those which fly across the visible heavens. The common version, " fowl of the air," is descriptive of the same objects, but is not a strict translation. *And fishes of the sea, and* (*every thing*) *passing in*, or *through, the paths of the sea*. Some read without supplying anything, *fishes of the sea passing through the paths of the sea*. But this weakens the expression, and is also at variance with the form of the original, where *passing* is a singular. Others construe it with man, who is then described as passing over the sea and ruling its inhabitants. But neither the syntax nor the sense is, on the whole, so natural as that proposed above, which makes this a residuary comprehensive clause, intended to embrace whatever might not be included in the more specific terms by which it is preceded. The dominion thus ascribed to man, as a part of his original prerogative, is not to be confounded with the coercive rule which he still exercises over the inferior creation (Gen. ix. 2, James iii. 7), although this is really a relic of his pristine state, and at the same time an earnest of his future restoration.

10 (9). *Jehovah, our Lord, how glorious is thy name in all the earth*, not only made so by the splendour of the skies, but by God's condescending goodness to mankind. With this new evidence and clearer view of the divine perfection, the Psalmist here comes back to the point from which he started, and closes with a solemn repetition of the theme propounded in the opening sentence.

Psalm 9

THIS psalm expresses, in a series of natural and striking alternations, gratitude for past deliverances, trust in God's · power and disposition to repeat them, and direct and earnest prayer for such repetition. We have first the acknowledgment of former mercies, ver. 2–7 (1–6) ; then the expression of trust for the future, ver. 8–13 (7–12) ; then the petition founded on it, ver. 14, 15 (13, 14). The same succession of ideas is repeated : recollection of the past, ver. 16, 17 (15, 16) ; anticipation of the future, ver. 18, 19 (17, 18) ; prayer for present and immediate help, ver. 20, 21 (19, 20). This parallelism of the parts makes the structure of the psalm remarkably like that of the seventh. The composition was intentionally so framed as to be a vehicle of pious feeling to the church at any period of strife and persecution. The form is that of the Old Testament; but the substance and the spirit are common to both dispensations.

1. *To the Chief Musician, Al-muth-labben.* This enigmatical title has been variously explained. Some understand it as descriptive of the subject, and make *labben* an anagram of *Nabal*, the name of one of David's enemies, and, at the same time, an appellative denoting *fool*, in which sense it is frequently applied to the wicked ; see, for example, Ps. xiv. 1. The whole would then mean *on the death of the fool, i. e.* the sinner. Such enigmatical changes are supposed to occur in Jer. xxv. 26, li. 1, 41 ; Zech. ix. 1. Others, by a change of pointing in the Hebrew, for *al-muth* read *alamoth*, a musical term occurring in the title of Ps. xlvi., or a cognate form *almuth*, and explain *labben* to mean *for Ben*, or *the (children of) Ben*, one of the Levitical singers mentioned in 1 Chron. xv. 18. Neither of these explanations seem so natural as a third, which supposes *muth-labben* to be the title, or the first words, or a prominent expression of some other poem, in the style, or to the air of which, this psalm was composed. *After the manner*, or *to the air*, of (the song or poem) *Death to the son*, or the death of the son. Compare 2 Sam. i. 18, where David's elegy on Saul appears to be called *Kesheth* or the *Bow*, because that word is a prominent expression in the composition. As it cannot be supposed that the expression was originally without meaning, the obscurity, in this and many similar cases, is rather a proof of antiquity than of the opposite.

·2 (1). *I will thank Jehovah*, praise him for his benefits, *with all my heart*, sincerely, cordially, and with a just appreciation of the greatness of his favours. *I will recount all thy wonders*, the wonderful things done by thee, with special reference to those attested by his own experience. The change from the third to the second person is entirely natural, as if the Psalmist's warmth of feeling would not suffer him to speak any longer merely of God, as one absent, but compelled him to turn to him, as the immediate object of address. There is no need, therefore, of supplying *thee* in the first clause, and construing *Jehovah* as a vocative.

3 (2). *I will joy and triumph in thee*, not merely in thy presence, or because of thee, *i. e.* because of what thou hast done, but in communion with thee, and because of my personal interest in thee. The form of the verbs, both here and in the last clause of the preceding verse, expresses strong desire and fixed determination ; see above, on Ps. ii. 3. *I will praise*, or *celebrate in song ;* see above, on Ps. vii. 18 (17). *Thy name*, thy manifested excellence ; see above, on Ps. v. 12 (11). *(Thou) Highest*, or *Most High!* see above, on Ps. vii. 18 (17). Here again there is special reference to the proofs of God's supremacy afforded by his recent dealings with the Psalmist and his enemies.

4 (3). *In the turning of my enemies back, i. e.* from their assault on me, which is equivalent to saying, in their retreat, their defeat, their disappointment. This may either be connected with what goes before, and understood as a statement of the reason or occasion of the praise there promised : " I will celebrate thy name when (or because) my enemies turn back ;" or it may begin a new sentence, and ascribe their defeat to the agency of God himself : " When my enemies turn back (it is because) *they are to stumble, and perish from thy presence*, from before thee, or *at thy presence, i. e.* as soon as thou appearest." The Hebrew preposition has both a causative and local meaning. The form of the verbs does not necessarily imply

that the deliverance acknowledged was still future, but only that it might occur again, and that in any such case, whether past or yet to come, Jehovah was and would be the true author of the victory achieved. The act of stumbling implies that of falling as its natural consequence, and is often used in Scripture as a figure for complete and ruinous failure.

5 (4). This was not a matter of precarious expectation, but of certain experience. *For thou hast made,* done, executed, wrought out, and thereby maintained, *my cause and my right.* This phrase is always used elsewhere in a favourable sense, and never in the vague one of simply doing justice, whether to the innocent or guilty. See Deut. x. 18; 1 Kings viii. 45, 49; Ps. cxl. 12; and compare Isa. x. 2. And this defence was not merely that of an advocate, but that of a judge, or rather of a sovereign in the exercise of those judicial functions which belong to royalty. See Prov. xx. 8. *Thou hast sat,* and sittest, *on a throne,* the throne of universal sovereignty, *judging right, i. e.* rightly, or *a judge of righteousness,* a righteous judge. See above, on Ps. vii. 12 (11). In this august character the Psalmist had already seen Jehovah, and he therefore gives it as a reason for expecting him to act in accordance with it now.

6 (5). The forensic terms of the preceding verse are now explained as denoting the destruction of God's enemies. *Thou hast rebuked nations,* not merely individuals, but nations. God's chastisements are often called rebukes, because in them he speaks by act as clearly as he could by word. *Thou hast destroyed a wicked (one), i. e.* many a wicked enemy, in former times, in other cases, and that not with a partial ruin, but with complete extermination even of their memory. *Their name,* that by which men are distinguished and remembered, thou hast *blotted out,* erased, effaced, obliterated, *to perpetuity and eternity,* an idiomatic combination, coincident in sense, though not in form, with the English phrase, *for ever and ever.* This verse does not refer exclusively to any one manifestation of God's power and wrath, but to the general course of his dealings with his enemies, and especially to their invariable issue, the destruction of the adverse party.

7 (6). *The enemy,* or *as to the enemy,* a nominative absolute placed at the beginning of the sentence for the sake of emphasis—*finished,* completed, *are (his) ruins,* desolations, *for ever, i. e.* he is ruined or made desolate for ever. The construction of the first word as a vocative—*O enemy, ended are (thy) desolations for ever, i. e.* the desolations caused by thee—affords a good sense, but is neither so agreeable to usage nor to the context as the one first given. Still less so are the other versions which have been given of this difficult clause. *E. g.* The enemies are completely desolate for ever; —the enemies are consumed, (there are) ruins (or desolations) for ever, &c. The address is still to Jehovah, as in the preceding verse. *And (their) cities,* viz. those of the enemy, *hast thou destroyed.* According to the second construction above given, this would mean, *thou* (O enemy) *hast destroyed cities,* but art now destroyed thyself. The same reasons as before require us to prefer Jehovah as the object of address. *Gone,* perish, *is their very memory.* The idiomatic form of the original in this clause cannot be retained in a translation. The nearest approach to it would be, *gone is their memory, themselves.* This may either mean *their memory,* viz. (*that of*) *themselves, i. e.* their own; or, *perished is their memory (and) themselves (with it).* There seems to be an obvious allusion to the threatenings against Amalek in the books of Moses (Exod. xvii. 14; Num. xxiv. 20; Deut. xxv. 19), which received their literal fulfilment in the conquests of Saul and David (1 Sam. xv. 3, 7, xxvii. 8, 9, xxx. 1, 17; 2 Sam. viii. 12;

1 Chron. iv. 43). But this is evidently here presented merely as a sample of other conquests over the surrounding nations (2 Sam. viii. 11–14), and even these as only samples of the wonders wrought by God for his own people, and celebrated in ver. 2 (1) above.

8 (7). *And Jehovah to eternity,* for ever, *will sit,* as he sits now, upon the throne and judgment-seat. *He has set up for judgment,* for the purpose of acting as a judge, *his throne.* It is not as an absolute or arbitrary ruler, but as a just judge, that Jehovah reigns. This recognition of God's judicial character and office as perpetual is intended to prepare the way for an appeal to his righteous intervention in the present case.

9 (8). *And he,* himself, with emphasis upon the pronoun, *is to judge the world,* the fruitful and cultivated earth, as the Hebrew word properly denotes, here put for its inhabitants, *in justice,* or righteousness, *i. e.* in the exercise of this divine perfection. *He will judge,* a different Hebrew verb, to which we have no equivalent, *he will judge nations,* peoples, races, not mere individuals, *in equities,* in equity, the plural form denoting fulness or completeness, as in Ps. i. 1. As the preceding verse describes Jehovah's kingship as judicial, so the verse before us represents him in the actual exercise of his judicial functions.

10 (9). *And (so) will Jehovah be a high place,* out of reach of danger, hence a refuge, *for the oppressed,* literally the bruised or broken in pieces, *a high place,* refuge, *in times of distress,* literally *at times in distress,* i. e. *at times* (when men are) *in distress.* God's judicial sovereignty is exercised so as to relieve the sufferer and deliver those in danger.

11 (10). *And in thee will trust,* as now so in all times to come, *the knowers of thy name,* those who know the former exhibitions of thy greatness and thy goodness, all which are included in the *name* of God. See ver. 3 (2), and Ps. viii. 2 (1), vii. 18 (17), ver. 12 (11). *For thou hast not forsaken thy seekers,* or *(those) seeking thee, O Lord,* Jehovah, *i. e.* seeking thy favour in general, and thy protection against their enemies in particular. The certain knowledge of this fact is laid as the foundation of the confidence expressed in the first clause.

12 (11). *Sing,* make music, give praise by song or music, *to Jehovah,* as the God of Israel, *inhabiting Zion,* i. e. the sanctuary there established. Or the words may mean *sitting,* as a king, enthroned, *(in) Zion,* which agrees well with the use of the same verbs in ver. 5, 8 (4, 7) above, although the other version is favoured by the obvious allusion to the symbolical import of the sanctuary under the Mosaic law, as teaching the great doctrine of God's dwelling among men. See above, on Ps. iii. 5 (4), v. 8 (7). Zion is here represented as the centre of a circle reaching far beyond the house of Israel, and indeed co-extensive with the earth. *Tell,* declare, make known, *in,* among, *the nations, his exploits,* his noble deeds, the *wonders* mentioned in ver. 2 (1). We have here, in his inspired formula of worship, a clear proof that the ancient church believed and understood the great truth, that the law was to go forth from Zion, and the word of the Lord from Jerusalem, Isa. ii. 3, Mic. iv. 2.

13 (12). *For seeking blood,* or *as an inquisitor of blood, he has remembered,* he remembers, *it, i. e.* the blood; *he has not forgotten the cry of the distressed.* God is here revealed in the character which he assumes in Gen. ix. 5, where the same verb and noun are used in the first clause of the verse before us. The word translated *blood* is in the plural form. See above, on Ps. v. 7 (6). Hence the literal translation of the next word is, *he has remembered them, i. e.* the bloods or murders. The cry meant is

the cry of suffering and complaint, with particular reference to Gen. iv. 10. According to another reading of the last clause, the cry is that of the meek or humble, not of the distressed. But the common text affords a better sense, and really includes the other, as the innocence of the sufferers is implied, though not expressed. The general import of the verse is that God's judgments, though deferred, are not abandoned, that he does not forget even what he seems to disregard, and that sooner or later he will certainly appear as an avenger. Murder is here put as the highest crime against the person, for all others, and indeed for wickedness in general.

14 (13). *Have mercy upon me,* or be gracious to me, *O Jehovah, see my suffering from my haters, raising me from the gates of death.* The view previously taken of God's faithfulness and justice is now made the ground of an importunate petition for deliverance from present dangers and distress. *My haters,* those who hate me. *From my haters* may be taken as a pregnant construction, meaning, see my suffering (and free me) from my enemies. Thus in 2 Sam. xviii. 19, " Jehovah hath judged him from the hand of his enemies," means " hath done him justice (and so freed him) from the power of his enemies." See a similar expression in Ps. xxii. 22 (21) below. It seems more natural and obvious, however, in the case before us, to give *from* a causal meaning. " See my distress (arising) from, or caused by, those who hate me." *Raising me* does not denote an accompanying act, as if he had said, see my distress, and at the same time lift me up, &c. It is rather descriptive of a certain divine character or habit, and agrees with the pronoun of the second person understood. " Thou that liftest me up," that art accustomed so to do, that has done so in other cases, with an implied prayer, do so now. The *gates of death* may have reference to the image of a subterranean dungeon, from which no prisoner can free himself; or it may be simply a poetical expression for the *entrance* to the grave or the state of the dead. Compare Isa. xxxviii. 10, and Mat. xvi. 18.

15 (14). *That I may recount all thy praise in the gates of the daughter of Zion, may joy in thy salvation.* This is one important end for which he asks to be delivered, namely, that God may have the praise of his deliverance. There is a trace, in the Hebrew text, of an original plural form, *praises,* which might then denote praiseworthy deeds, actions worthy to be celebrated. But the singular form occurs with *all* in Ps. cvi. 2 below. The gates here mentioned are contrasted with those of the preceding verse. The God who saves him from the gates of death shall be praised for this deliverance in the gates of the daughter of Zion. This last expression is supposed by some to be a personification of the people inhabiting Zion or Jerusalem, who are then put for Israel at large, as the church or chosen people. Others regard the genitive construction as equivalent to a simple apposition, as in *river of Euphrates,* or in our familiar phrase, *the city of Jerusalem.* The personification is then that of the city itself, considered as an ideal virgin, and on that account called *daughter,* by a usage similar to that of the corresponding word in French. In either case, there is an obvious reference to the ancient church, as the scene or the witness of the Psalmist's praises. The verb in the last clause may be made to depend upon the particle at the beginning of the verse, *(that) I may exult;* or it may be still more emphatically construed as an independent proposition, *I will exult in thy salvation.* The form of the verb is the same as in Ps. ii. 3 above. The second verb itself occurs in ver. 11 of that psalm, and as in that case, may either denote an inward emotion or the outward expression of it, *I will*

shout. *In thy salvation, i. e.* in the possession or experience of it, and in acknowledgment of having thus experienced or possessed it.

16 (15). *Sunk are nations in a pit they made; in a net which they hid, taken is their foot.* This may be either a confident anticipation of the future as if already past, or a further reference to previous deliverance, as a ground of hope for others yet to come. *Nations,* whole nations, when opposed to God. Compare Ps. ii. 1. The accessory idea of *Gentiles, heathen,* would be necessarily suggested at the same time to a Hebrew reader. Most versions have the definite forms, *the pit, the net;* but the indefinite form of the original is equally intelligible in English, and therefore preferable as a more exact translation. The ellipsis of the relative, *a pit* (which) *they made,* is common to the Hebrew idiom and our own. The figures are borrowed from ancient modes of hunting. See above, on Ps. vii. 16 (15). *Their foot,* their own foot, not that of the victim whose destruction they intended.

17 (16). *Known is Jehovah,* or has made himself known. *Justice has he done,* or judgment has he executed. *In the work of his (own) hands ensnared is a wicked (man). Higgaion,* meditation. *Selah,* pause. God has revealed himself as present and attentive, notwithstanding his apparent oblivion and inaction, by doing justice on his enemies, or rather by making them do justice on themselves, converting their devices against others into means of self-destruction. In view of this most striking attestation of God's providential government, the reader is summoned to reflect, and enabled so to do by a significant and solemn pause. The sense of meditation or reflection is clear from Ps. xix. 15 (14), and Lam. iii. 62. See below, on Ps. xcii. 4 (3). The addition of *Higgaion* to *Selah* here confirms the explanation already given of the latter word. See above, on Ps. iii. 3 (2). With this understanding of the terms, we may well say, to ourselves or others, in view of every signal providential retribution, especially where sin is conspicuously made its own avenger, *Higgaion Selah!*

18 (17). *The wicked shall turn back even to hell,* to death, or to the grave, *all nations forgetfu. of God.* The enemies of God and of his people shall be not only thwarted and repulsed, but driven to destruction; and that not merely individuals, but nations. For the meaning of *Sheol* see above, on Ps. vi. 6 (5). The figure of turning back, retreating, failing, is the same as in ver. 4 (3) above. The idea expressed is not that of being turned directly into hell, but that of turning back, first to one's original position, and then beyond it, to the grave or hell. In the last clause there is an allusion to the implied charge of forgetfulness on God's part in ver. 13 (12) above. He had not forgotten the "poor innocents," as they feared, and as their enemies believed; but these very enemies had forgotten him, and must now abide the consequences of their own forgetfulness. The future forms of this verse may have reference to the same things mentioned in the verse preceding as already past. It seems more natural, however, to explain them as a confident anticipation of results precisely similar to those which had already been produced by the same causes. As Jehovah had already caused the heathen to become their own destroyers, so he might be expected to renew the same judicial process in another case.

19 (18). *For not for ever shall the poor be forgotten,* (and) *the hope of the humble perish to eternity.* However long God may appear to be forgetful of his suffering people, even this seeming oblivion is to have an end. Still another allusion to the charge or imputation of forgetfulness implied in ver. 13 (12) above. The difference between the readings *humble* and *afflicted*

(עָנִים and עָנִיִּים) is not essential, as the context shews that the humble
meant are humble sufferers.

20 (19). *Arise, Jehovah! Let not man*, frail man, *be strong. Let nations*, or the heathen, *be judged*, and as a necessary consequence condemned,
before thy face, in thy presence, at thy bar. Here again, as in ver. 13, 14
(12, 13), the expression of strong confidence is made the occasion of an
earnest prayer. So far is an implicit trust from leading men to cast off
fear and restrain prayer before God. On the exhortation to arise, as from a
state of previous inaction, see above, Ps. iii. 7 (6). For the full sense of the
word translated *man*, see above, on Ps. viii. 5 (4). *Let him not be strong*,
i.e. let him not so appear, or so esteem himself. Let him have no occasion,
by indulgence or prolonged impunity, to cherish this delusion, or to practise this imposture. The absurdity of making man the stronger party in
this strife with God is so preposterous, that God is summoned to arise for
the purpose of exploding it. To be judged, in the case of the wicked, is of
course to be condemned. To be judged in God's presence, or at his tribunal, is of course to be condemned without appeal.

21 (20). *Set*, place, or join, *O Jehovah, fear to them. Let nations know*,
or then shall nations know, *(that) man*, not God, *(are) they. Selah.* God
is entreated so to frighten them, that they may become conscious of their
own insignificance and weakness. The word translated *fear* is elsewhere
used to signify a *razor*. Hence some would render the first clause, *apply
the razor to them*, *i.e.* shave them, in allusion to the oriental feeling with
respect to the beard. But this seems far-fetched, and the masoretic reading yields a better sense. The precise import of the first phrase seems to
be, set fear as a guard over them (Ps. cxli. 3), or join it to them as a constant companion. The word translated *man* is still the same as in the
foregoing verse, and was therefore intended to suggest the idea of human
frailty, as contrasted with divine omnipotence.

Psalm 10

THE Psalmist complains of God's neglect, and of the malice of his enemies, ver. 1–11. He prays that both these subjects of complaint may be
removed, ver. 12–15. He expresses the most confident assurance that
his prayer will be heard and answered, ver. 16–18.

The Septuagint and Vulgate unite this with the ninth psalm as a single
composition. But each is complete in itself, and the remarkable coincidences even of expression only shew that both were meant to form a pair
or double psalm like the first and second, third and fourth, &c. From the
same facts it is clear, that this psalm, though anonymous, is, like the ninth,
the work of David, and that both were probably composed about the same
time.

1. *For what (cause)*, why, *O Jehovah, wilt thou stand afar, wilt thou hide
at times* (when we are) *in trouble?* The question really propounded is,
how this inaction can be reconciled with what was said of God in Ps. ix.
10 (9).—To *stand afar off*, is to act as an indifferent, or, at the most, a
curious spectator. *Wilt thou hide*, *i.e.* thyself or thine eyes, by refusing to
see, as in Lev. xx. 4, 1 Sam. xii. 3. The futures imply present action
and the prospect of continuance hereafter. The question is not merely why
he does so, but why he still persists in doing so. The singular phrase, *at
times in trouble*, occurs only here and in Ps. ix. 10 (9), a strong proof of the

intimate connection of the two psalms, and perhaps of their contemporary composition. This expostulation betrays no defect either of reverence or faith, but, on the contrary, indicates a firm belief that God is able, and must be willing, to deliver his own people. Such demands are never uttered either by scepticism or despair.

2. *In the pride of the wicked burns the sufferer ; they are caught in devices which they have contrived.* This very obscure verse admits of several different constructions. The first verb sometimes means to persecute, literally to *burn after*, or pursue hotly. Gen. xxxi. 36 ; 1 Sam. xvii. 53. In one case it seems to have this meaning even without the preposition *after*. Lam. iv. 19. The sense would then be, *in the pride of the wicked he will persecute*, &c. But the collocation of the words seems to point out עָנִי as the subject, not the object, of the verb. The sufferer's burning may denote either anger or anguish, or a mixed feeling of indignant sorrow.— The adjective עָנִי means afflicted, suffering, whether from poverty or pain.

Poor is therefore too specific a translation. In the Psalms this word is commonly applied to innocent sufferers, and especially to the people of God, as objects of malignant persecution. It thus suggests the accessory idea, which it does not formally express, of righteousness or piety.—In the last clause there is some doubt as to the subject of the first verb. If referred to the wicked, the sense will be, that they are taken in their own devices. If to the poor, that they are caught in the devices of the wicked. The first is favoured by the analogy of Ps. vii. 15–17 (14–16), and Ps. ix. 16, 17 (15, 16). But the other agrees better with the context, as a description of successful wickedness.

3. *For a wicked (man) boasts of* (or simply *praises*) *the desire of his soul, and winning* (i. e. when he wins), *blesses, despises Jehovah.* This seems to be a description of the last stage of corruption, in which men openly defend or applaud their own vices, and impiously thank God for their dishonest gains and other iniquitous successes.—The preterite forms, *has praised*, &c., denote that it always has been so, as a matter of familiar experience. *The desire of his soul* means his natural selfish inclination, his heart's lust. *And winning,* i. e. when he wins or gains his end, with special reference to increase of wealth. Hence the word is sometimes used to signify the covetous or avaricious grasper after wealth by fraud or force. The same participle, joined with a cognate noun, is rendered "greedy of gain" in Prov. i. 19, xv. 27, and "given to covetousness" in Jer. vi. 3, viii. 10. See also Hab. ii. 9, where the true sense is given in the margin of the English Bible.—He who gains an evil gain *blesses* (and) *despises Jehovah,* i. e. expresses his contempt of him by thanking him, whether in jest or earnest, for his own success. He blesses God, and thereby shews that he despises him. An illustrative parallel is Zech. xi. 4, 5. "Thus saith the Lord my God, Feed the flock of the slaughter, whose possessors slay them and hold themselves not guilty, and they that sell them say, Blessed is the Lord, for I am rich." This parallel, moreover, shews that *blesses,* in the verse before us, does not mean *blesses himself,* as some suppose, but *blesses God.*

4. *A wicked (man), according to his pride, will not seek. There is no God* (are) *all his thoughts.* Pride is here expressed by one of its outward indications, loftiness of look, or as some suppose the Hebrew phrase to signify originally, elevation of the nose.—*Will not seek,* i. e. seek God in prayer (Ps. xxxiv. 4), or in the wider sense of worship (Ps. xiv. 2), or in

that of inquiring the divine will (Gen. xxv. 22), all which religious acts are
at variance with the pride of the human heart.—*All his thoughts*, not merely
his opinions, but his plans, his purposes, which is the proper meaning of
the Hebrew word. The language of his life is, that there is no God.—Another
construction of the first clause is as follows. *The wicked, according to his
pride* (*says*), *He*, i. e. *God will not require*, judicially investigate and punish,
as in Ps. ix. 13 (12), and in ver. 13 below, where there seems to be a reference to the words before us, as uttered by the wicked man himself.—A
third construction thus avoids the necessity of supplying *says*.—' As to the
wicked in his pride—He will not require, there is no God—are all his
thoughts." This may be transferred into our idiom as follows: All the
thoughts of the wicked in his pride are, that God will not require, or rather
that there is no God. In favour of the first construction given is the fact
that it requires nothing to be supplied like the second, and does not disturb
the parallelism of the clauses like the third. Common to all is the imputation of proud self-confidence and practical atheism to the sinner.

5. *His ways are firm*, or will be firm, *in all time*, always. *A height*, or
high thing, (*are*) *thy judgments from before him*, away from him, out of his
sight. (*As for*) *his enemies he will puff* at them, as a natural expression of
contempt, or *he will blow upon them*, *i. e.* blow them away, scatter them,
with ease. This describes the prosperity and success of sinners, not only
as a fact already familiar, but as something which is likely to continue.
Hence the future forms, which indicate continuance hereafter, just as the
preterites in ver. 3 indicate actual experience.—The only other sense which
can be put upon the first clause is, *his ways are twisted*, *i. e.* his actions are
perverse. But the Chaldee paraphrase, the cognate dialects, and the analogy of Job xx. 21, are in favour of the rendering, *his ways are strong*, *i. e.*
his fortunes are secure, his life is prosperous, which moreover agrees best
with the remainder of the verse, as a description of the sinner's outward
state. Thus understood, the second clause describes him as untouched or
unaffected by God's providential judgments, and the third as easily ridding
himself of all his human adversaries. Both together represent him as impregnable on all sides, in appearance equally beyond the reach of God and
man. (Compare Luke xviii. 2, 4.) As this immunity from danger, strictly
understood, could exist only in appearance, the whole verse may be regarded
as an expression of the sinner's own opinion rather than his true condition.

6. *He hath said in his heart, I shall not be moved; to generation and
generation*, (I am one) *who* (shall) *not* (be) *in evil*, or as the same Hebrew
phrase is rendered in the English version of Exod. v. 19, *in evil case*, *i. e.*
in trouble, in distress. This is a natural expression of the proud security
engendered in the natural man by great prosperity. *He hath said*, implying
that the cause has already been in operation long enough to shew its natural
effect. *In his heart*, to himself, in a spirit of self-gratulation and self-
confidence. *To age and age*, throughout all ages or all generations. The
strength of this expression shews that the speaker is not a real person, but
the ideal type of a whole class. The sinner, who thus says in his heart, is
not the sinner of one period or country, but the sinner of all times and
places, one who never disappears, or ceases thus to feel and act.—The form
of the last clause in Hebrew is peculiar and emphatic. He does not simply
say, I shall never be in evil or adversity, but I am he, I am the man, who
shall never be in evil, as if the very supposition of such a contingency,
however justified by general experience, would be not only groundless but
absurd in this one case. (Compare Isaiah xlvii. 8–10.) There could

scarcely be a stronger expression of the self-relying spirit of the sinner, as contrasted with the saints' implicit confidence in God's will and power, not only to preserve him from falling, but to raise him when he does fall.

7. (*Of*) *cursing his mouth is full, and deceits, and oppression. Under his tongue* (*are*) *trouble and iniquity.* He now gives a more particular description of the wicked man, beginning with his sins against his neighbour, and among these, with his sins of word or speech. If this be a correct view of the whole verse, the *cursing*, mentioned in the first clause, is most probably false swearing, or the invocation of God's name, and imprecation of his wrath upon one's self, in attestation of a falsehood. This kind of cursing is closely connected with the fraud and violence which follow. The Hebrew word תֹּךְ, to which the older writers gave the sense of *fraud*, is now commonly explained to mean *oppression* ; so that with the noun preceding, it denotes injustice, injury to others, both by fraud and violence.—*Under the tongue* may have reference to the poison of serpents, or to the use of the tongue for speaking, as in Ps. lxvi. 17, where the same phrase occurs in the original, though not in the common version.—*Toil*, labour, trouble, endured by others as the consequence of his deceits and violence.—For the meaning of the last word in the verse, see above, on Ps. v. 6 (5).—*Oppression* is here reckoned among sins of speech, because the latter may be made the means of violent injustice, by tyrannical command, by unjust judgment, or by instigating others to deprive the victim of his rights. If only fraud had been referred to, this description of the sins committed with the tongue would have been palpably defective.

8. *He will sit in the lurking-place of villages ; in the secret places he will slay the innocent ; his eyes for the sufferer will hide*, watch secretly, or lie in wait. From sins of word he now proceeds to those of deed or outward action. The wicked enemy is here represented as a robber. The futures, as in ver. 5, imply that what is now is likely to continue. *Sitting* implies patient waiting for his prey or victim. *The lurking-place*, the place where murderers and robbers usually lurk or lie in wait. Where such crimes are habitually practised, there is commonly some spot especially associated with them, either as the scene of the iniquity itself, or as a place of refuge and resort to those who perpetrate it.—The mention of *villages* is no proof that the psalm relates to any specific case of lawless violence, but only that the Psalmist gives individuality to his description by traits directly drawn from real life. A slight change in the form of expression would convert it into a poetic simile. ' As the robber sits in the lurking-place of villages,' &c. The verb *hide* has the same sense as in Prov. i. 11, 18.—The word translated *sufferer* (חֵלְכָה for חֵילֵךְ) is peculiar to this psalm, and was not improbably coined for the occasion, as a kind of enigmatical description, in which David seems to have delighted. A Jewish tradition makes it mean *thy host, i.e.* the church of God ; but this, besides being forced in itself, is forbidden by the use of the plural in ver. 10 below. Others derive it from an Arabic root, meaning to be black, dark, gloomy, sad, unhappy. A third hypothesis explains it as a compound of two Hebrew words, one meaning weak or sick, the other sad or sorrowful, and both together representing the object of the enemy's malice, in the strongest light, as a sufferer both in mind and body.

9. *He will lurk in the hiding-place as a lion in his den ; he will lurk* (or *lie in wait*) *to catch the sufferer ; he will catch the sufferer by drawing him into his net*, or *in drawing him* (*towards him*) *with his net.* That the pre-

ceding verse contains a simile, and not a description of the enemy as an
actual robber, is here rendered evident by the addition of two new comparisons, applied to the same object.   In the first clause he is compared to a
lion, in the second to a hunter.   See above, on Ps. vii. 16 (15), ix. 16 (15),
and below, on Ps. xxxv. 7, lvii. 7 (6).   The force of the futures is the same
as in the foregoing verse.—*His den*, his shelter, covert, hiding-place.   The
Hebrew word is commonly applied to any temporary shed or booth, composed of leaves and branches.   He lies in wait to seize the prey, and he
succeeds, he accomplishes his purpose.   A third possible construction of
the last clause is, *in his drawing* (*i.e. when he draws*) *his net*.   The whole
verse, with the one before it, represents the wicked as employing craft no
less than force for the destruction of the righteous.

10. *And bruised he will sink; and by* (or *in, i.e.* into the power of*) *his
strong ones fall the sufferers*, the victims.   These are represented, in the
first clause, by a collective singular, and in the second by a plural proper,
that of the unusual word used in ver. 8 above.   Its peculiar etymology and
form might be imitated in an English compound, such as *sick-sad, weak-sad,*
or the like.   By *his strong ones* some would understand the strong parts of
the lion, teeth, claws, &c.; others the same parts personified as warriors.
But even in the foregoing verse, the figure of a lion is exchanged for that of
a hunter; and this again gives place here to that of a military leader or a
chief of robbers, thus insensibly returning to the imagery of ver. 8.   These
numerous and rapid changes, although not in accordance with the rules of
artificial rhetoric, add greatly to the life of the description, and are not
without their exegetical importance, as evincing that the whole is metaphorical, a varied tropical exhibition of one and the same object, the combined
craft and cruelty of wicked men, considered as the enemies of God and of
his people.   According to this view of the passage, by *his strong ones* we
may understand the followers of the hostile chief, those who help him and
execute his orders, or the ideal enemy himself, before considered as an individual, but now resolved into the many individuals, of whom the class which
he represents is really composed.

11. *He hath said in his heart, God hath forgotten, he hath hidden his
face, he hath* not *seen*, doth not see, and will not see, *for ever*.   The opening
words are the same, and have the same sense, as in ver. 6 above.   The three
parallel clauses which follow all express the same idea, namely, that God
takes no note of human offences.   This is first expressed by the figure of
forgetfulness; then by that of deliberately refusing to see, as in ver. 1 above;
then by a literal and direct affirmation that he does not see, either the sufferings of his people or the malice of their enemies; and that this is not a
transient or occasional neglect, but one likely to continue for ever.

12. *Arise, Jehovah!   Almighty* (*God*)*, raise thy hand!   Forget not
sufferers* (or *the wretched*)*!*   The impious incredulity, expressed in the preceding verse, is now made the ground of an importunate petition.   God is
besought to do away with the appearance of inaction and indifference.   See
above, on Ps. vii. 7 (6).   *Raise thy hand*, exert thy power.   The second
name by which God is addressed (אֵל) is one expressive of omnipotence,
and may be correctly rendered by our phrase, *Almighty God*.   As the name
Jehovah appeals to his covenant relation to his people, as a reason for
granting their requests, so this invokes his power as necessary to their
deliverance and the vindication of his own honour from the imputation of
forgetfulness cast upon him by his enemies.   This imputation he is entreated,

in the last clause, to wipe off by shewing that he does remember. *Forget not* is, in this connection, tantamount to saying, shew that thou dost not forget. Here, as in Ps. ix. 13 (12), the margin of the Hebrew Bible reads (עֲנָוִים) *meek* or *humble*, while the text has (עֲנִיִּים) *suffering* or *afflicted*. The *Kethib*, or textual reading, is regarded by the highest critical authorities as the more ancient, and therefore, except in some rare cases, entitled to the preference.

13. *On what (ground) has the wicked contemned God, has he said in his heart, Thou wilt not require?* · The question implies the sin and folly of the conduct described. The past tense suggests the inquiry why it has been suffered to go on so long. *Contemned, i. e.* treated with contempt. The reference is not to inward feeling merely, but to its external manifestation. The second clause shews how the feeling has been manifested. *Said in his heart*, is here repeated for the third time in this psalm. See ver. 6, 11, above.. The direct address to God in the last clause is peculiarly emphatic. The wicked man not only speaks irreverently of him, but insults him to his face. *Thou wilt not require.* The Hebrew verb includes the ideas of investigation and exaction. Thou wilt not *inquire* into my conduct, or *require* an account of it. See ver. 4 above, and compare Ps. ix. 13 (12). The whole verse contains an indirect expostulation or complaint of the divine forbearance towards such high-handed and incorrigible sinners.

14. *Thou hast seen* (this particular instance of iniquity); *for trouble,* the suffering occasioned by such sins, *and provocation,* that afforded by such sins, *thou wilt behold,* it is thy purpose and thy habit to behold it, *to give with thy hand* a becoming recompence, or *to give into thy hand, i. e.* to lay it up there in reserve, as something to be recompensed hereafter. *Upon thee the sufferer will leave* (his burden), will rely. *An orphan,* here put for the whole class of innocent and helpless sufferers, *thou hast been helping ;* God has ever been a helper of the friendless, and may therefore be expected to do likewise now. The whole verse is an argument drawn from the general course of the divine administration. Hence the preterite and future forms. Thou *hast seen* in this case, for thou always *wilt see* in such cases. For the meaning of *trouble* and *provocation,* see above, on Ps. vi. 8 (7), vii. 15 (14).

15. *Break thou the arm,* destroy the power, *of the wicked, and the bad (man),* or as to the bad man, *thou wilt seek for his wickedness* (and) *not find it.* This may either mean, thou wilt utterly destroy him and his wickedness, so that when sought for it cannot be found (Ps. xxxvii. 36), or thou wilt judicially investigate his guilt, and punish it till nothing more is left to punish. The Hebrew verb (דָּרַשׁ) has then the same sense as in ver. 4, 13, above, and there is a direct allusion to the sinner's boast that God will not inquire into men's acts or require an account of them. There may be a latent irony or sarcasm, as if he had said, Thou wilt find nothing, as he boasts, but in a very different sense ; not because there is nothing worthy of punishment, but because there will be nothing left unpunished.

16. *Jehovah (is) king!* He is not dethroned, as his enemies imagine ; he is still king, and will so remain, *perpetuity and eternity,* for ever and ever. *Lost,* perished, *are nations,* the heathen, *i. e.* hostile nations, *from,* out of, *his land,* the Holy Land, the Land of Israel, the land of which he is the king in a peculiar sense, distinct from that of providential ruler. The Psalmist sees Jehovah still enthroned, not only as the sovereign of the world, but as the sovereign of his people. (See Num. xxiii. 21, Deut. xxxiii. 5). The *nations* or *heathen* of this verse may be either literal or spiritual gentiles

(Jer. ix. 25, Ezek. xvi. 3). The psalm is so framed as to express the feelings of God's people in various emergencies. The preterite tense in the last clause represents the destruction of God's enemies as already past, not only on account of its absolute certainty, but because the process of destruction, although not completed, is begun and will infallibly continue. Here, as often elsewhere, earnest prayer is followed by the strongest expression of confidence and hope.

17. *The desire of the meek* (or *humble*) *thou hast heard, Jehovah!* Their desire is already accomplished. And this not merely once for all. *Thou wilt settle* (or *confirm*) *their heart, i. e.* dispel their fears and give them courage, by new assurances of favour and repeated answers to their prayers. *Thou wilt incline thine ear*, or make it attentive, cause it to listen, to their future no less than their past petitions. The figure of a fixed or settled heart recurs more than once below. See Ps. li. 12 (10), lvii. 8 (7), cxii. 7. The essential idea is that of a firm resolution, as opposed to timid doubt and vacillation.

18. *To judge*, or do justice to, *the orphan and the bruised*, or oppressed. See above, on Ps. ix. 10 (9). This clause seems properly to form a part of the preceding verse; thou wilt incline thine ear to judge, &c. The remainder of the verse is a distinct proposition. *He shall not add* (or continue) *any longer to resist*, or defy, *i. e.* to set God at defiance. The subject of these verbs is placed last for the sake of greater emphasis. *Man*, frail man, *from the earth*, springing from it, and belonging to it; see Gen. iii. 19. For the full sense of the word translated *man*, see above, on Ps. viii. 5 (4), ix. 20 (19), and compare the whole prayer in the latter passage with the one before us. The sense here is, that weak and short-lived man shall not continue to insult and defy Almighty God. It implies a wish or prayer, but is in form a strong expression of the Psalmist's confident assurance that it will be so, and in connection with the similar expressions of the two preceding verses, forms a worthy and appropriate close of the entire composition. The original of this verse is commonly supposed to exhibit an example of the figure called paronomasia, an intentional resemblance, both in form and sound, between two words of very different meaning. The words supposed to be so related here are those translated *to defy* (ערץ) and *earth* (ארץ). This peculiarity of form, if really designed and significant, is one which cannot be completely reproduced in any version. There is reason to suspect, however, that in this, as in many other cases, the resemblance is fortuitous, like that which frequently occurs in a translation, without anything to match it in the original; *e. g.* in the Vulgate version of Gen. viii. 22, *æstus* and *æstas*, and in that of Gen. xii. 16, *oves et boves*.

Psalm 11

THE Psalmist is advised, by friends or foes, to escape by flight from the inextricable difficulties in which he finds himself involved, ver. 1–3. This he refuses to do, as inconsistent with his faith in the righteousness and grace of God, ver. 4–7. The logical relation of these parts makes the form of the whole somewhat dramatic, although this peculiarity is much less marked than in the second psalm. The language is not so much that of an historical person as of an ideal sufferer, representing the whole class of persecuted innocents. There is no specific reference to any incidents in David's life, although some of the images were probably suggested by his recollections, both of Saul's persecution and of Absalom's rebellion. The general resemblance of this psalm to that before it, and the special resemblance of ver. 2 to Ps. x. 8, 9, may account for its position in the Psalter. The very difficulties of this psalm are proofs of its antiquity and strong corroborations of the title, which ascribes it to David.

1. *To the chief musician,* belonging to him as the performer, and *to David,* as the author. *In Jehovah I have trusted,* and do still trust. *How will* (or *can*) *ye say to my soul, Flee* (*to*) *your mountain* (*as*) *a bird?* The profession of confidence in God at the beginning is the ground of the following interrogation, which implies wonder and disapprobation. How can ye say so ? really means, ye should not say so. The question seems to be addressed to timid or desponding friends, rather than to taunting and exulting enemies, as some suppose.—*To my soul* does not simply mean *to me,* but so as to affect my feelings. See above, on Ps. iii. 3 (2). In the genuine text the verb *flee* is plural, because addressed to the whole class represented by the ideal sufferer in this case. Hence the frequent change of number throughout the psalm. See above, on Ps. x. 10. The exhortation to flee must be understood as implying that there is no longer any hope of safety.—*To your mountain,* as a customary place of refuge, not for birds, but for persecuted men. The comparison with a bird has no particular connection with this clause, but is a kind of after-thought, suggesting the idea of a solitary helpless fugitive. (Compare 1 Sam. xxvi. 20, and Lam. iii. 52). There may be an allusion to the words of the angel in Gen. xix. 17, as there certainly is to one or both these places in our Lord's exhortation to his followers, Matt. xxiv. 16.

2. *For lo, the wicked will tread* (i. e. bend) *the bow ; they have fixed their arrow on the string, to shoot in darkness at the straightforward* (upright) *of heart.* These are still the words of the advisers introduced in the preceding verse, assigning a reason for the advice there given.—*Tread the bow ;* see above, on Ps. vii. 13 (12). *Will tread,* are about to tread, are treading. The preterite which follows refers to a later point of time. The speakers are supposed to describe what they see actually passing. " They are bending the bow, (and now) they have fixed the arrow on the string." The graphic vividness of the description is impaired, if not destroyed, by giving both the verbs a present form.—*Fixed, i. e.* in its proper place. The same verb occurs above, in Ps. vii. 13 (12). *Make ready* is too vague in the case before us.—*In darkness,* in the dark, in secret, treacherously. See above, Ps. x. 8. 9.—*The straight of heart,* the upright and sincere. We do not use the adjective in this sense ; but we have the cognate substantive, *rectitude,* which properly means straightness.

3. *For the pillars* (or *foundations*) *will be* (are about to be) *destroyed : what has the righteous done, i. e.* accomplished? The pillars or foundations are those of social order or society itself. These are said to be destroyed, when truth and righteousness prevail no longer, but the intercourse of men is governed by mere selfishness. The question in the last clause implies that the righteous has effected nothing, in opposition to the prevalent iniquity. The past tense represents this as a matter of actual experience, but as one which still continues. The substitution of any other form in the translation is gratuitous and ungrammatical. The true relation of the tenses is correctly given in the Prayer Book Version. *For the foundations will be cast down, and what hath the righteous done ?*

4. *Jehovah* (*is*) *in his palace* (or *temple*) *of holiness ; Jehovah* (or *as to Jehovah*), *in the heavens* (*is*) *his throne. His eyes behold, his eyelids prove*

the sons of men. He is so exalted that he can see, and so holy that he must see and judge the conduct of his creatures. By an equally gramma-tical but less natural construction, the whole verse may be thrown into a single proposition. "Jehovah in his holy temple, Jehovah whose throne is in heaven, his eyes," &c.—For the meaning of the word translated *temple*, see above on Ps. v. 8 (7).—*Eyelids* are mentioned as a poetical parallel to *eyes*, being the nearest equivalent afforded by the language.—*Try or prove*, as if by seeing through them. With the whole verse compare Ps. cii. 20 (19).

5. *Jehovah the righteous will prove*, will prove the righteous, *and the wicked and the lover of violence his soul hates.* The sentence might also be divided thus : *Jehovah will prove the righteous and the wicked, and the lover of violence his soul hates.* Different from both is the masoretic interpunction, which seems, however to be rather musical than grammatical or logical.— The divine proof or trial of the righteous implies favour and approval like the knowledge spoken of in Ps. i. 6 ; but in neither case is it expressed. *Violence*, including the ideas of injustice and cruelty. See above, on Ps. vii. 17 (16). *His soul has hated* and still hates. This is not simply equiva-lent to *he hates*, but denotes a cordial hatred. *Odit ex animo.* He hates with all his heart.

6. *He will rain on wicked (men) snares, fire and brimstone, and a raging wind, the portion of their cup.* The mixed metaphors shew that the whole description is a tropical one, in which the strongest figures elsewhere used, to signify destruction as an effect of the divine wrath, are combined. *Rain* is a natural and common figure for any copious communication *from* above, whether of good or evil. *Snares* are a favourite metaphor of David for inextricable difficulties. See above, vii. 16 (15), ix. 16 (15), x. 9.—*Fire and brimstone* are familiar types of sudden and complete destruction, with constant reference to the great historical example of Sodom and Gomorrah. See Gen. xix. 24, and compare Ezek. xxxviii. 22, Job xviii. 15.—*Raging wind*, literally *wind* (or *blast*) *of furies*, is another natural but independent emblem of sudden irresistible inflictions. The second Hebrew word is elsewhere used for strong indignation (Ps. cxix. 53), and is once applied to the *ragings* (or *ravages*) *of famine*. (Lam. v. 10.)—*The portion of their cup*, or their cup-portion, something measured out for them to drink, according to the frequent Scriptural representation, both of God's wrath and favour, as a draught, or as the cup containing it. Compare Ps. xvi. 5, xxiii. 5, with Mat. xx. 22, 23, xxvi. 39. The meaning of the whole verse is that, notwithstanding the present security of the ungodly, they shall, sooner or later, be abundantly visited with every variety of destructive judgment.

7. *For righteous (is) Jehovah ; righteousness he loves ; the upright (man) shall his face behold.* The *for* suggests the intimate connection between God's judgment on the wicked and his favour to the righteous. The second clause is a necessary inference from the first. The nature of God determines his judgments and his acts. He who is righteous in himself cannot but approve of righteousness in others. The righteousness of others is in fact nothing more than conformity to his will and nature. Nor does he merely approve of righteousness in the abstract ; he rewards it in the person of the righteous man. This idea is expressed in the last clause, which admits of several constructions. It may mean that *the upright shall behold his face, i. e.* enjoy his favourable presence, as in Ps. xvii. 15. But the collocation of the singular noun and the plural verb, with the analogy of ver. 4 above, is in favour of a different construction : *his face shall behold* (or *does behold*)

the righteous, i. e. view them with favour and affection. Because the original expression is not properly *his face*, but *their face* or *faces*, Luther explains this as a reason why God loves the righteous, to wit, because *their faces look upon (the) right*, or that which is right. Another construction, founded on the same fact, is, *the righteous shall behold* (it with) *their faces.* It is better, however, to regard this as an instance of that remarkable idiom in Hebrew, which applies to the One True God, verbs, nouns, and pronouns in the plural, and which some explain as a *pluralis majestaticus*, like that employed by kings at present, and others as a form of speech transferred from polytheism to the true religion. Most probably, however, it was intended to express the fulness of perfection in the divine nature, not without a mystical allusion to the personal distinction in the Godhead. The most remarkable examples of this usage may be found in Gen. i. 26, iii. 22, xi. 7, Job. xxxv. 10, Ps. lviii. 12, Eccles. xii. 1, Isa. vi. 8, liv. 5.—The *face* is here, like the *eyelids* in ver. 4, a poetical equivalent to *eyes*, and the same parallelism reappears in Ps. xxxiv. 16, 17 (15, 16): " the *eyes* of Jehovah (are) towards the righteous ;" " the *face* of Jehovah (is) against evil-doers."

Psalm 12

THIS psalm consists of two parts easily distinguished : a complaint with an expression of desire, and a promise with an expression of confidence and hope. The Psalmist laments the waning number of good men, ver. 2 (1), and the abounding of iniquity, ver. 3 (2), to which he desires and expects that God will put an end, ver. 4, 5 (3, 4). In answer to this prayer, he receives an assurance of protection and deliverance for the righteous, ver. 6 (5), on which he rests as infallibly certain, ver. 7 (6), and consoles himself under present trials, ver. 8 (7).

There seems to be no specific reference to the persecution of the Jews by the Gentiles, or of David by Absalom or Saul. The contrast exhibited is rather that between the righteous and the wicked as a class, and the psalm seems designed to be a permanent vehicle of pious sentiment for the church or chosen people under persecution by malignant enemies. It contains an unusual number of difficult expressions in proportion to its length ; but these are not of such a nature as to make its general import doubtful or obscure.

1. *To the Chief Musician, on the eighth* (or *octave*), *a Psalm of David.* This title is identical with that of the sixth psalm, except that *Neginoth* is here omitted.

2 (1). *Save, Jehovah, for the merciful* (or the object of divine mercy) *ceaseth, for the faithful fail from (among) the sons of men.* The adjective הָסִיד, whether taken in an active or a passive sense, is descriptive of the pious or godly man ; see above, on Ps. iv. 4 (3). The preterite form of the verbs (has ceased, have failed) represents the fearful process as already begun. The word rendered *faithful* in the last clause may also have the abstract sense of truth, fidelity ; see below, Ps. xxxi. 24 (23), and compare Isa. xxvi. 2. In either case, the whole verse is a strong hyperbolical description of the small number of good men left in the community, and their consequent exposure to the malice of the wicked. Such expressions, as Luther well suggests, are too familiar in the dialect of common life to be mistaken or produce perplexity.

3 (2). *Vanity, i. e.* falsehood, *they will speak;* as they now do, so will they persist in doing; *(each) man with his neighbour*, not merely with another man, but with his friend, his brother, towards whom he was particularly bound to act sincerely; compare Eph. iv. 25. *A lip of smoothness,* or *of smooth things, i. e.* flattering; see above, on Ps. v. 10 (9). This may be connected either with what goes before or with what follows : " They speak falsehood, each to his neighbour, with a flattering lip ;" or, " (with) a flattering lip (and) with a double heart will they speak." *A heart and a heart, i. e.* a double heart, as *a stone and a stone* means " divers weights." Deut. xxv. 13. By a double heart we are probably to understand, not mere dissimulation or hypocrisy, but inconsistency and instability of temper, which leads men to entertain opposite feelings towards the same object. Compare the description of the " double-minded man" in James i. 8.

4 (3.) *May Jehovah destroy all lips of smoothness*, flattering lips, *(and every) tongue speaking great things, i. e.* speaking proudly, boasting. The form of the Hebrew verb is one commonly employed to express an optative meaning ; but as this form is often poetically used for the future proper, it might be rendered here, *Jehovah will destroy.* There is no inconsistency between the flattering lips and the boastful tongue, because the subject of the boasting, as appears from what follows, is the flattery or deceit itself. As if he had said, Jehovah will destroy all flattering lips, and every tongue that boasts of their possession or use. For an example of such boasting, see Isa. xxviii. 15.

5 (4). *Who have said, By our tongues will we do mightily; our lips (are) with us: who is lord to us*, or over us ? This is an amplified specification of the phrase *speaking great things* in the preceding verse. *By our tongues,* literally, as to, with respect to our tongues. The idea of agency or instrumentality is suggested by the context. *Do mightily,* exercise power, shew ourselves to be strong. *Our lips are with us* may either mean they are our own, at our disposal, or, they are on our side. The idea of the whole verse is, by our own lips and our tongues we can accomplish what we will.

6 (5). *From the desolation of the wretched, from the sighing of the poor, now will I arise, shall Jehovah say, I will place in safety him that shall pant for it.* The preposition *from* has a causal meaning, because of, on account of. *The wretched*, afflicted, sufferers ; see above, on Ps. ix. 13 (12). *I will arise ;* see above, on Ps. iii. 8 (7). The future, *shall Jehovah say,* implies that the promise is not yet uttered, much less fulfilled. An analogous use of the same form of the same verb runs through some of the prophecies, and especially the later chapters of Isaiah.—The last clause is obscure, and may also be translated, " from him that puffeth at him,"— " him at whom they puff,"—" him whom they would blow away," &c. The most probable meaning is the one first given, according to which the verse contains a promise of deliverance to those who especially desire and need it.

7 (6). *The sayings of Jehovah are pure sayings, silver purged in a furnace of earth, refined seven times.* The Psalmist does not use the term commonly translated *words*, but one derived from the verb to *say*, with obvious allusion to the use of the verb itself in the preceding verse. What Jehovah there says, the promises there given, are here declared to be true, without any mixture of mistake or falsehood. This is expressed by the favourite figure of pure metallic ore. The idea of extreme or perfect purity is conveyed by the idiomatic phrase, *purified seven times, i. e.* repeatedly, or *sevenfold, i. e.* completely. Compare Dan. iii. 19. The general meaning of the verse is clear, but it contains one phrase which is among the

most doubtful and disputed in the whole book. This is the phrase בַעֲלִיל
לָאָרֶץ. To the common version above given, *in a furnace of earth,* and to
another somewhat like it, *purged in a furnace as to* (i. e. *from*) *the earth,* or
earthy particles, it has been objected, that אֶרֶץ never means earth as a
material. Some avoid this difficulty by translating, *in a furnace on the
earth* (or *ground*), or, *in the workshop* (laboratory) *of the earth, i. e.* the
mine; but this is not the place where ores are purified. It is further
objected to all these translations, that they attach a supposititious meaning
to the noun עֲלִיל. It is therefore explained by some as a variation of בַעַל,
lord or master, and the whole clause made to mean, *purified silver of a lord
of the earth, i. e.* refined not for ordinary use, but for that of some great
prince or noble. The obscurity which overhangs the meaning of this clause
is less to be regretted, as the main idea must, on any supposition, still be
that of unusual and perfect purity.

8 (7). *Thou, Jehovah, wilt keep them ; thou wilt guard him from this
generation to eternity, i. e.* for ever. In the first clause, though not in the
second, the pronoun *thou* is expressed in Hebrew, and may therefore be
regarded as emphatic; see above, on Ps. ii. 6, iii. 4 (3). Thou, and no
other, or, thou without the aid of others, wilt preserve them. The plural
pronoun in the first clause, and the singular in the second, refer to the
same persons, viz., the sufferers mentioned in ver. 7 (6). By a licence
common in the Psalms, they are first spoken of as a plurality, and then as
an ideal person; see above, on Ps. x. 10. *This generation,* this contemporary race of wicked men, with reference perhaps to the description, in
ver 2 (1), of the disproportion between these and the righteous. *For ever,*
as long as the necessity or danger lasts, so long shall the injured innocent
experience the divine protection.

9 (8). *Round about will the wicked walk.* This may either mean that
they shall walk at liberty and have full licence, or that they shall encompass
and surround the righteous. Compare Ps. iii. 7 (6). The other clause is
one of the most doubtful and disputed in the whole book. The particle כ
may denote either time or resemblance, and the noun זֻלּוּת, which occurs no-

where else, has been variously explained to mean, a storm, an earthquake,
vileness or contempt, &c. Among the different senses put upon the whole
phrase are the following : " When the vileness (or vilest) of men is exalted."
" Like the rising of a storm upon the sons of men." " When they rise (or
are exalted) there is shame (or disgrace) to the sons of men." " When
disgrace arises to the sons of men." " Like exaltation is disgrace to the
sons of man." In favour of this last it has been urged, that it gives to each
word its most natural and obvious sense, and that it closes with a prospect
of relief, and not with an unmitigated threatening, which would be at variance with the usage of the Psalms. The meaning of the verse is then, that
although the wicked are now in the ascendant, and the righteous treated
with contempt, this disgrace is really an exaltation, because only external
and in man's judgment, not in God's, who will abundantly indemnify his
people for the dishonour which is put upon them. The unusual and almost
unintelligible form in which this idea is expressed, is supposed to agree
well with David's fondness for obscure and enigmatical expressions; see
above, on Ps. v. 1 and vii. 1.

Psalm 13

THIS psalm consists of a complaint, ver. 2, 3 (1, 2), a prayer for deliverance, vers. 4, 5 (3, 4), and an expression of strong confidence that God will grant it, ver. 6 (5, 6).

There is no trace of a specific reference to any particular period in the life of David, or to any persecution of the ancient Israel by heathen enemies. The psalm appears to be intended as a vehicle of pious sentiment, for the church at large and individual believers, under any affliction of the sort here described, namely, that arising from the spiteful hostility of wicked men. The tone, as in several of the foregoing psalms, varies from that of deep depression to that of an assured hope, connected, as in actual experience, by one of strong desire and fervent supplication.

1. *To the Chief Musician, a Psalm of David.* This title differs from that of the fourth psalm, as the title of the twelfth does from that of the sixth, to wit, by the omission of בנגינות.

2 (1). *Until when,* how long, *Jehovah, wilt thou forget me for ever ? Until when wilt thou hide thy face from me ?* The refusal or delay of the divine help is here, as often elsewhere, represented by the figures of forgetfulness and an averted countenance. See above, on Ps. ix. 13, 19 (12, 18), x. 11, 12. The apparent solecism of combining *how long* with *for ever* may be avoided by supposing two interrogations, *how long ? for ever ?* It may also be avoided by giving to נֶצַח the sense of continuously, uninterruptedly.

But even the obvious construction, which is more agreeable to usage and the masoretic interpunction of the sentence, may be justified as a strong but natural expression of the conflict between sense and faith. To the eye of sense and reason, the abandonment seemed final ; but faith still prompted the inquiry, *how long,* which implies that it was not to last for ever. As if he had said, How long wilt thou persist in the purpose of forgetting me for ever ?

3 (2). *Till when,* how long, *shall I place* (or *lay up*) *counsels,* plans, *in my soul, grief in my heart by day ? Till when shall my enemy be high above me ?* The idea in the first clause seems to be that of accumulating methods or expedients of escape, as in a storehouse, without finding any that will answer the purpose. The same figure may be continued in the second clause : (how long shall I lay up) sorrow in my heart ? The sense is then that the multiplication of devices only multiplies his sorrows. Or the figure of laying up may be confined to the first clause, and the noun *grief* governed by a verb understood : (how long shall I feel) sorrow in my heart ? The common version, *having sorrow,* conveys the same idea, but supplies a verb unknown to the Hebrew and its cognate languages.—*By day* is elsewhere put in opposition to *by night,* as for instance in Ps. i. 2 above. Here it may possibly mean *all day,* but more probably means *every day, daily,* as in Ezek. xxx. 16.—*Be high :* the original expression is a verb alone. How long shall my enemy soar or tower above me, *i.e.* be superior, prevail ? This clause determines the precise form of suffering complained of, namely, that occasioned by the malice of a powerful persecutor or oppressor. In all such cases, Saul was no doubt present to the mind of David, but only as a specimen or type of the whole class to which the psalm relates.

4 (3). *Look, hear me, Jehovah, my God, lighten my eyes, lest I sleep the death.* The complaint is now followed by a corresponding prayer. In

allusion to the hiding of the face in ver. 2 (1), he now beseeches God to look towards him, or upon him, to shew by his acts that he has not lost sight of him. As he before complained of God's forgetting him, so here he prays that he will hear and answer him. See above, on Ps. iii. 5 (4). The idea of Jehovah as a God in covenant with his people, is brought out still more fully by the phrase *my God, i.e.* one on whom I have a right to call, with a well-founded hope of being heard. See above on Ps. iii. 8 (7).— *Enlighten my eyes,* or make them shine, is by some understood to mean, Dispel my doubts, and extricate me out of my perplexities, with reference to the plans or counsels mentioned in the preceding verse. Others, with more probability, suppose an allusion to the dimness of the eyes produced by extreme weakness or approaching death, and understand the prayer as one for restoration and deliverance from imminent destruction. Compare 1 Sam. xiv. 27, 29, where the relief of Jonathan's debility, occasioned by long fasting, is described by saying that his eyes were enlightened.—*Lest I sleep (in) death,* or *lest I sleep the (sleep of) death,* as in the common version. Compare the beautiful description of death as a *sleep of perpetuity,* a perpetual or everlasting sleep, in Jer. li. 39, 57.

5 (4). *Lest my enemy say, I have overpowered him (and) my adversaries shout when I am shaken,* or *because I shall be shaken.*—The verb יכלתי strictly means, *I have been able.* The unusual construction with a pronoun (יכלתיו) cannot be literally rendered into English, but the meaning evidently is, I have been able (to subdue) him, or, I have been strong (in comparison with) him. As to the combination of the singular and plural (*enemy* and *adversaries*), see above, on Ps. x. 11 (10).—*Shout, i.e.* for joy, or in a single word, *triumph.* See above, on Ps. ii. 11.—The last verb (אמּוֹט) has the same sense as in Ps. x. 6, viz., that of being moved or cast down from one's firm position.

6 (5, 6). *And I in thy mercy have trusted ; let my heart exult in thy salvation ; I will sing to Jehovah, for he hath done me good,* or acted kindly towards me. The transition indicated by the phrase *and I,* is the same as in Ps. ii. 6 above. Such are the enemies and dangers which environ me, *and (yet) I have trusted in thy mercy.* The past tense of the verb describes the trust, not as something to be felt hereafter, or as just beginning to be felt at present, but as already entertained and cherished, and therefore likely to be still continued. I have trusted, and do still trust, and will trust hereafter.—There is a beautiful gradation in the clauses of this verse. First, a fact is stated : ' I have trusted in thy mercy ;' then a desire is expressed : ' let my heart rejoice in thy salvation ;' then a fixed purpose is announced : ' I will sing unto Jehovah.' The reason annexed to this determination or engagement, implies an assured expectation of a favourable issue. As if he had said, I know the Lord will treat me kindly, and I am resolved to praise him for so doing.—*In thy salvation,* not merely on account of it, but in the contemplation, the possession, the enjoyment of it. See above, Ps. v. 12 (11), ix. 3 (2). The verb גָּמַל, which occurs above in Ps. vii. 5 (4), corresponds most nearly to the English *treat,* in the sense of dealing with or acting towards ; but when absolutely used, as here, almost invariably has a good sense, and specifically means to treat well or deal kindly with a person. The idea of requital or reward, which is frequently attached to it in the English version, is suggested, if at all, not by the word itself, but by the context.

The Septuagint has an additional clause, which is retained in the Prayer Book version, and thus rendered : *Yea, I will praise the name of the Lord most Highest.* The words are not found in any Hebrew manuscript.

Psalm 14

WE have first a description of human depravity as universal, ver. 1–3; then a confident anticipation of destructive judgments on the incorrigibly wicked, ver. 4–6; and an earnest wish for the speedy deliverance of God's elect from the evils of their natural condition and from the malice of their unconverted enemies, ver. 7.

There seems to be no reference to any particular historical occasion. The psalm was, no doubt, originally written to express the feelings of God's people, in all times and places, with respect to the original depravity of all men, and the obstinate persistency in evil of the greater number. The points of resemblance and of difference between this psalm and the fifty-third will be considered in the exposition of the latter.

1. *To the Chief Musician, by David. The fool hath said in his heart, There is no God. They have done corruptly, they have done abominably* (in) *deed* (or *act*); *there is none doing good.* Sin is constantly held up to view in Scripture as the height of folly, and the sinner as the fool by way of eminence. See Gen. xxxiv, 7, Josh. vii. 15, Ps. xxxix. 9 (8). The term is here collective and applied to the whole race, as appears from the plurals which follow, and the negative statement in the last clause. The preterites include the present, but suggest the additional idea, that the truth here asserted is the result of all previous experience and observations.—*In his heart*, to himself, if not to others, as above, in Ps. x. 11. That the error is one of the affections, and not merely of the understanding, is supposed by some to be implied in the use of the word *heart*, which is often used, however, to denote the mind or soul in general.—אֵין is properly a noun, and means nonentity or non-existence : " nothing of God," or " no such thing as God." It cannot be explained as a wish—" No God! " *i. e.* Oh that there were no God!—because אֵין in usage always includes the substantive verb, and denies the existence, or at least the presence, of the person or thing to which it is prefixed. This is also clear from the use of the same word in the last clause, where its sense is unambiguous.—The addition of the word *act* or *deed* shews that the atheism described is not merely theoretical but practical.—There is obvious allusion in this verse to the description of the general antediluvian corruption in Gen. vi. 12. This makes it the more certain that the description here was not intended either for Jews or Gentiles, as such, but for wicked men of either class, and that Paul's application of the words, in Rom. iii. 10, 12, is perfectly legitimate, and not a mere accommodation of the Psalmist's language to another purpose.

2. *Jehovah from heaven has looked down on the sons of man, to see if there were* (one) *acting wisely, seeking God.* While the fool denies the being of a God, Jehovah's eye is on him and his fellow-men. Yet even that omniscient eye can discern no exception to the general depravity and folly. The earnestness of the inspection is suggested by the verb in the first clause, which originally means to lean or bend over, and is peculiarly appropriate to the act of one gazing intently down upon a lower object. The force of

the preterite tense is the same as in the preceding verse. The inquiry has been made already, and proved fruitless. It is no longer a doubtful question, but one definitively settled.—*Acting wisely*, in contrast to the atheistical folly mentioned in ver. 1. The test of wisdom is in seeking God, whether in the general religious sense of seeking his favour and communion with him, or in the special sense of seeking proofs of his existence. As if he had said, Even those who think there is no God, if they were wise, would seek one ; but these fools take pleasure in the hideous negation. The image presented in this verse may be compared with that in Gen. vi. 12, xi. 5, xviii. 21. See also Ps. xxxiii. 13, 14.

3. *The whole has apostatised ; together they have putrefied ; there is none doing good ; there is not even one.* Total and universal corruption could not be more clearly expressed than by this accumulation of the strongest terms, in which, as Luther well observes, the Psalmist, not content with saying *all*, adds *together*, and then negatively, *no not one*. It is plain that he had no limitation or exception in his mind, but intended to describe the natural condition of *all men*, in the widest and most unrestricted sense. *The whole*, not merely *all* the individuals as such, but the entire race as a totality or ideal person.—*The whole (race) has departed*, not merely from the right way, but from God, instead of seeking him, as intimated in ver. 4. *Together*, not merely altogether or without exception, but in union and by one decisive act or event. The etymological import of the verb נֶאֱלָחוּ is to turn sour, to spoil. It is applied to moral depravation not only here, but in Job xv. 16. The Septuagint version of these words is quoted by Paul in Rom. iii. 12, as a part of his scriptural description of human depravity, the rest of which is taken from Ps. v. 10 (9), x. 7, xxxvi. 2 (1), cxl. 4, Isa. lix. 7, 8. Under the false impression that he meant to quote a single passage, some early Christian copyist appears to have introduced the whole into the Septuagint version of this psalm, where it is still found in the Codex Vaticanus, as well as in the Vulgate, and even in one or two Hebrew manuscripts of later date. The interpolation is also retained in the Anglican Psalter. It is evident, however, that the apostle's argument is strengthened by the fact of his proofs being drawn, not from one, but several parts of the Old Testament.

4. *Do they not know, all (these) workers of iniquity, eating my people (as) they eat bread, (and) on Jehovah call not ?* The question is elliptical : the object of the verb must be supplied from the context. Do they not know that they are thus corrupt and estranged from God, and therefore objects of his wrath ? Is it because they do not know this or believe it, that they thus presume to oppress and persecute his people ? The figure of devouring occurs often elsewhere, *e.g.* Prov. xxx. 14, Mic. iii. 3, Hab. iii. 14. See below, on Ps. xxvii. 2 (1). *As they eat bread* may either mean for their support—living on the plunder and oppression of my people ; or for pleasure—feeding on them with delight ; or with indifference and as little sense of guilt as when they take their ordinary fond.—*Call not on Jehovah*, do not worship him, as they were before said not to seek him, nor even to acknowledge his existence, all which are periphrastical descriptions of the wicked as a class. The general description of their wickedness is here exchanged for a specific charge, that of persecuting the righteous. The mention of two classes here is not at variance with the universal terms of the preceding context, nor does it render any limitation of those terms necessary. All men are alike " children of wrath," but some are elected to be " vessels of mercy," and thereby become objects of hatred to the un-

converted mass who still represent the race in its apostasy from God.—*My people* does not make it necessary to regard these as the words of God himself, who is nowhere introduced as speaking in this psalm, and is spoken of in the third person in the very next clause. The Psalmist, as a member of the body, calls it his, and the same form of expression occurs elsewhere. See 1 Sam. v. 10, Isa. iii. 12, liii. 8, Micah iii. 3.—For the meaning of the phrase, *workers of iniquity*, see above, on Ps. v. 6 (5).

5. *There have they feared a fear, for God (is) in the righteous generation.* A later period is now present to his view. They who seemed incapable of fear have now begun to be afraid at last. *There*, without any change of place or outward situation. Where they before denied the being of a God, even there they have begun to fear. See below, on Ps. xxxvi. 13 (12). The reason is given in the next clause. God, though denied by them, exists and is present, and will manifest his presence by the protection and deliverance of his people. *Feared a fear*, is a common Hebrew idiom for greatly feared, were sore afraid. *Generation*, contemporary race, as in Ps. xii. 8 (7).

6. *The plàn* (or *counsel*) *of the sufferer* (the afflicted) *ye will shame, because Jehovah is his refuge.* The workers of iniquity are here addressed directly. The sufferer is the persecuted innocent. *Poor* is too restricted a translation. See above, on Ps. ix. 13, 19 (12, 18). The plan or counsel is described in the last clause, to wit, that of trusting in Jehovah. This very trust is an object of contempt to the wicked. Until they are made to fear by the manifestation of God's presence with his people, they will continue to despise it. The Psalmist here seems to revert to the interval which should precede the divine interposition. As if he had said, You will one day be made to fear, but in the mean time you will shame the counsel of the poor. Some, however, give תביש its usual sense of putting to shame, disappointing, and understand the clause as an ironical concession : you may shame his counsel if you can.

7. *Who will give out of Zion salvation to Israel, in Jehovah's returning the captivity of his people ? Let Jacob exult, let Israel joy!* The phrase *who will give* is an idiomatic optative in Hebrew, equivalent to *Oh that* with a verb, and *Oh for* with a noun in English. *Oh for the salvation of Israel!* Or, *Oh that the salvation of Israel* (might come) *out of Zion*, as the earthly residence of God and seat of the theocracy. The same local designation is connected with the prayer or promise of divine help, in Ps. iii. 5 (4), xx. 3 (2), cxxviii. 5, cxxxiv. 3. (Compare Ps. xxviii. 2). This shews that the psalm does not belong to the period of the Babylonish exile, and that the captivity referred to is not literal, but a metaphorical description of distress, as in the case of Job (xlii. 10). The same idea is elsewhere expressed by the figure of confinement and incarceration (Ps. cxlii. 8, Isa. xlii. 7, xlix. 9). The sense remains essentially the same in this case, whether the verb *return* be transitive or intransitive. Most interpreters prefer the former sense, and understand the clause to mean, " in Jehovah's *bringing back* the captivity of his people." But as שוב in every other combination means to *come back*, and, like other verbs of motion, often governs a noun of place directly (Exod. iv. 19, 20, Num. x. 36), it is better to understand the words as meaning that the salvation wished for would consist in God's revisiting his captive or afflicted people. The sense is also admissible, if not necessary, in such places as Deut. xxx. 3, Ps. lxxxv. 5 (4), Isa. lii. 8, Hos. vi. 11, Nah. ii. 3 (2). *Let Jacob shout (for joy)!* This is both an exhortation and a wish, but the latter is the prominent idea, as

the parallelism of the clauses shews. *Oh that the salvation of Israel were come!* corresponds exactly to, *May Jacob exult, may Israel be glad!* The common version is forbidden by the optative form (יָגֵל) of the Hebrew verb, and by the masoretic interpunction, which connects *in the Lord's returning, &c.*, not with what follows as a specification of time, but with what goes before as an explanatory clause. The whole may be paraphrased as follows: " Oh that Jehovah, from his throne in Zion, would grant salvation to his people, by revisiting them in their captive and forsaken state, and that occasion of rejoicing might be thus afforded to the church ! " Or more closely thus : " Oh may Israel's salvation (soon) come forth from Zion, in Jehovah's return to the captivity of his people ! (In such a restoration) may Jacob (soon have reason to) exult and Israel (to) triumph ! "

Psalm 15

THIS psalm teaches the necessity of moral purity as a condition of the divine protection. It first propounds the question who shall be admitted to God's household, and the privileges of its inmates, ver. 1. This is answered positively, ver. 2, and negatively, ver. 3; then positively again, ver. 4, and negatively, ver. 5. The last clause of the last verse winds up by declaring, that the character just described shall experience the protection tacitly referred to in the first verse. As the contrast exhibited in this psalm and the fourteenth may account for its position in the Psalter, so its obvious resemblance to the twenty-fourth makes it not improbable that their historical occasion was identical.

1. *A Psalm by David. Jehovah, who shall sojourn in thy tent? who shall dwell in thy hill of holiness?* The holy hill is Zion, as in Ps. ii. 6 ; the tent is the tabernacle which David pitched there for the ark, when he removed it from Gibeon (2 Sam. vi. 17, 1 Chron. xv. 1, xvi. 1, 39, 2 Chron. i. 3–5). Both together signify the earthly residence of God ; see above on Ps. iii. 5 (4). The idea is not that of frequenting Zion as a place of worship, but of dwelling there, as a guest or as an inmate of God's family. The same figure for intimate communion with Jehovah, and participation of his favour, reappears in Ps. xxiii. 6, xxvii. 4, 5, xxiv. 3, lxi. 5, lxv. 5 (4), lxxxiv. 5 (4). So too, in Eph. ii. 19, believers are described as members of God's family (οἰκεῖοι τοῦ Θεοῦ).

2. *Walking perfect, and doing right, and speaking truth, in his heart.* The Psalmist, speaking in behalf of God, here answers his own question. The only person who can be admitted to domestic intercourse with God is one walking perfect, &c. *Walking* is put for the habitual course of life (see above, on Ps. i. 1). *Perfect*, complete, as to all essential features of the character, without necessarily implying perfection in degree. The form of expression seems to be borrowed from Gen. xvii. 1. A remarkably analogous expression is that used by Horace : *integer vitae scelerisque purus.* The next phrase, *doing right*, practising rectitude, may be either a synonymous parallel to the first, or a specification under it, parallel to *speaking truth*. The general idea of walking perfect is then resolved into the two particular ideas of doing right and speaking truth. *In his heart, i. e.* sincerely, as opposed to outward show or hypocritical profession. This phrase seems to qualify not merely what precedes, *speaking truth*, but the whole description, as of one who sincerely and internally, as well as outwardly, leads a blameless life by doing right and speaking truth.

3. *(Who) hath not slandered with his tongue, (who) hath not done his neighbour harm, and a scandal hath not taken up against his neighbour.* The positive description of the foregoing verse is now followed by a negative one. (Compare Ps. i. 1, 2). The social virtues are insisted on, and their opposites excluded, because they are apt to be neglected by hypocrites, against whom this psalm is directed. The past tense of the verbs denotes a character already marked and determined by the previous course of life. The verb רָגַל seems strictly to denote the act of busy or officious tale-bearing. There seems to be an allusion to Lev. xix. 16. *With his tongue,* literally *on his tongue,* as we say to *live on, i. e.* by means of anything, an idiom which occurs in Gen. xxvii. 40. (Compare Isa. xxxviii. 16.) The next clause adds deed to word, as in the foregoing verse. *Scandal,* reproach, defamatory accusation. The verb נָשָׂא is by some explained as meaning to take up upon the lips (Ps. xvi. 4), and then to utter or pronounce. Others give it the same sense as in Gen. xxxi. 17, where נָשָׂא עַל means to lift up upon, *i. e.* to burden. The idea then is, that he has not helped to load his neighbour with reproach. *Friend and neighbour* does not mean any other man, but one sustaining a peculiarly intimate relation, such as that of the members of the chosen people to each other. See above, on Ps. xii. 3 (2).

4. *Despised in his eyes (is) a reprobate, and the fearers of Jehovah he will honour; he hath sworn to his own hurt, and will not change* The Chaldee Paraphrase, followed by the Prayer Book version, makes the first clause descriptive of humility. He is despised in his own eyes (and) rejected. But the parallelism with the next clause shews that a contrast was designed between his estimation of two opposite classes, and as one of these is *those who fear Jehovah,* the other must be represented by נִמְאָס, *rejected, i. e.* by Jehovah, reprobate. The future form, as usual, suggests the idea of a present act repeated or continued in the future. He honours, and will still persist in honouring, the fearers of Jehovah. The Septuagint and Vulgate explain לְהָרַע *to the neighbour,* and some modern versions *to the bad (man).* But the sense is determined by the obvious allusion to Lev. v. 4: "if a soul swear to do evil (לְהָרַע) or to do good," *i. e.* whether to his own advantage or the contrary. So here the phrase must mean "he hath sworn to injure (himself)" not designedly, but so as to produce that effect. *He will not change,* literally, exchange, *i. e.* substitute something else for what he has promised.

5. *His silver he hath not given for usury, and a bribe against a guiltless (person) hath not taken. Doing these (things), he shall not be moved for ever.* In Hebrew as in French, silver is put for money in general. There is obvious allusion to the frequent prohibition in the Mosaic law, not of lending money upon interest for commercial purposes, a practice then unknown, but of usurious lending to the poor, and especially to poor Israelites. See Exod. xxii. 24, Lev. xxv. 37, Deut. xxiii. 20, and compare Prov. xxviii. 8, Ezek. xviii. 8. The taking of judicial bribes is also expressly forbidden in Exod. xxiii. 8, Deut. xvi. 19, xxvii. 25. The masoretic interpunction of this sentence seems to be merely rhythmical or musical, as in Ps. xi. 5. The words *doing these* cannot be separated from what follows without destroying the sense. This last clause is an answer to the question in ver. 1, but with a change of form, implying that admission to God's household was itself security against all danger. Compare Ps. lv. 23 (22). For the sense of אִמּוֹט, see above, on Ps. x. 6, xiii. 5.

Psalm 16

A SUFFERER in imminent danger of death, expresses his strong confidence in God, ver. 1, as the sole source and author of his happiness, ver. 2, and at the same time his attachment to God's people, ver. 3, his abhorrence of all other gods, ver. 4, his acquiescence in God's dealings with him, ver. 5, 6, and his assured hope of future safety and blessedness, ver. 7–11.

The psalm is appropriate to the whole class of pious sufferers, of which Christ is the most illustrious representative. It is only in him, therefore, that some parts of it can be said to have received their highest and complete fulfilment. This will be shewn more fully in the exposition of the ninth and tenth verses.

1. *Michtam of David. Preserve me, O God: for I have trusted in thee.* Some explain *Michtam* as a compound term; but it is most probably a simple derivative of a verb meaning to *hide*, and signifies a mystery or secret. The similar word *Michtab* in the title of Hezekiah's psalm (Isa. xxxviii. 9) is probably an imitation of the form here used, or at least involves an allusion to it. It seems to be substituted for the usual terms *song, psalm*, &c., not only here but in the titles of Ps. lv.–lx. It probably indicates the depth of doctrinal and spiritual import in these sacred compositions. The derivation from a noun meaning *gold* is much less probable. This verse may be said to contain the sum and substance of the whole psalm, and is merely amplified in what follows. The prayer, *Keep, save*, or *preserve me*, implies actual suffering or imminent danger, while the last clause, *I have trusted in thee*, states the ground of his assured hope and confident petition. The verb used is one that seems especially appropriate to the act of seeking shelter under some overshadowing object. See Judges ix. 15, Isa. xxx. 2, Ps. lvii. 2 (1), lxi. 5 (4). The preterite form implies that this is no new or sudden act, but one performed already. He not only *trusts* in God at present, but *has trusted* him before. Compare Ps. vii. 2 (1), xi. 1.

2. *Thou hast said to Jehovah, The Lord (art) thou; my good (is) not besides thee* (or *beyond thee*). The verb in the first clause has the form of a second person feminine, which some regard as an abbreviation of the first person, אָמַרְתְּ for אָמַרְתִּי and translate accordingly, *I have said*. But this neither agrees so well with usage, nor affords so good a sense as the old construction, which supplies as the object of address the same that is expressed in Ps. xlii. 6 (5), 12 (11), xliii. 5, Jer. iv. 19, Lam. iii. 24, 25. A similar ellipsis is assumed by some in 1 Sam. xxiv. 11, and 2 Sam. xiii. 39. By this peculiar form of speech the Psalmist calls upon himself to remember his own solemn acknowledgment of Jehovah as THE LORD or Supreme God.—The obscure clause which follows has been very variously explained. Some understand by *good* moral goodness, merit, and explain the whole to mean, "My goodness is not such as to entitle me to thy regard." Most interpreters, however, give to *good* its usual sense of good fortune, happiness (see Ps. cvi. 5, Job ix. 25), and make the whole clause mean, "My happiness is not obligatory or incumbent on thee, thou art not bound to provide for it;" or "My happiness is not above thee; I have no higher happiness than thee." The true sense is probably afforded by a modification of this last: "My happiness is not beside thee, independent of, or separable from thee," with allusion to the form of expression in the Hebrew of the first commandment (Exod. xx. 3). The verse, then, contains a twofold acknow-

ledgment of God, as the universal sovereign, and as the only source of individual enjoyment. Compare Ps. lxxiii. 25. That this recognition was not a mere momentary act, but a habitual affection of the mind, seems to be indicated by the Psalmist's appeal to his own soul as having made the acknowledgment already, hitherto or heretofore.

3. *To* (or *with*) *the saints who* (*are*) *in the land, and the nobles in whom* (*is*) *all my delight.* The construction of the first clause, and its connection with the preceding verse, are very obscure. Some make *to* synonymous with *as to.* " As to the saints who are in the land, and the nobles, in them is all my delight." Or, "as to the saints who are in the land, they are the nobles in whom is all my delight." Others understand *to the saints* and *to Jehovah* as correlative expressions. " To Jehovah I have said thus; to the saints thus." Or, as the English Bible has it, " My goodness extendeth not to thee, but to the saints," &c. The least violent construction seems to be that which takes the preposition in its usual sense, that of *belonging to,* as in the phrases, *to David, to the chief Musician,* and in 1 Kings xv. 27. The meaning then is that the Psalmist's recognition of Jehovah as The Lord, and as the only source of happiness, is not peculiar to himself, but common to the whole body of the *saints* or *holy ones.* This epithet denotes personal character, not as its primary meaning, but as the effect of a peculiar relation to God, as the objects of his choice, set apart from the rest of men for this very purpose ; see Exod. xix. 6, Deut. vii. 6, Ps. xxxiv. 10 (9), Dan. vii. 21, viii. 24, 1 Pet. ii. 9. The pre-eminence of these over others, as the fruit of the divine election, is expressed by the word *nobles,* which, like *saints,* denotes moral character only in an indirect and secondary manner. The construction in this part of the verse is strongly idiomatic ; the literal translation is, *the nobles of all my delight in them.* Under the old dispensation, the nobles or elect of God had their local habitation in the land of promise. Hence they are here described as the " saints or consecrated ones who are in the land," not *in the earth,* which would be too indefinite and not so well suited to the context. As thus explained, the whole verse may be paraphrased as follows : " This profession of my trust in God I make, not merely as an individual believer, but as one belonging to the great body of the saints or consecrated ones, the nobles of the human race, not such by any original or natural pre-eminence, but by the sovereign and distinguishing favour of Jehovah, whom they trust as I do, and are therefore the rightful objects of my warmest love."

4. *Many* (or *multiplied*) *shall be their sorrows—another they have purchased—I will not pour their drink-offering of blood, and will not take their names upon my lips.* With the happiness of those who like himself trust the Lord, he contrasts the wretchedness of those who have chosen any other object of supreme affection. The relative construction in the English version, " their sorrows shall be multiplied that hasten," &c., gives the sense correctly, but with more variation from the Hebrew idiom, which conveys the same idea by means of short independent propositions. In the word translated *their sorrows,* (עַצְּבוֹתָם), there seems to be an allusion to a very similar form, which would mean *their idols* (עֲצַבֵּיהֶם), as if to suggest that false gods are

mere troubles and vexations. *Another* means *another god,* in opposition to the one true God, Jehovah, as in Isa. xlii. 8, xlviii. 11. The contrast which is there expressed is here to be supplied from ver. 2 and 5, and from the general antithesis, running through the context, between God and gods,

not idols merely, but any created object of supreme affection. The verb
מָהַר in its derived form means to *hasten*, and is so translated here by the
English and some other versions. But in the only other place where the
primitive verb occurs (Exod. xxii. 15), it means to *endow* a wife, or secure
her by the payment of a dowry, according to the ancient oriental custom.
The same usage of the verb exists in several of the cognate dialects. It
seems here to have the general sense of purchasing, by costly sacrifice or
self-denial, but with particular allusion to the conjugal relation which is
constantly described in Scripture as existing between worshippers and their
gods; see Hos. iii. 2, and viii. 9, Ezek. xvi. 33, 34. In the last clause he
abjures all communion with such idolaters. He will not join in their
impious services, nor even name the names of their divinities. *Drink-offer-
ings of blood*, libations no less loathsome than if composed of human blood,
perhaps with an allusion to the frequent poetical description of wine as the
blood of the grape; see Gen. xlix. 11, Deut. xxxii. 14, Isa. lxiii. 3. To
take the name upon the lips is to stain or pollute them by pronouncing it.
Both here and in Hos. ii. 19, there is an obvious allusion to the solemn
prohibition of the law (Exod. xxiii. 13): "Make no mention of the name of
other gods, neither let it be heard out of thy mouth." The pronoun *their*,
in this whole clause, refers not to the worshippers but to their divinities, as
comprehended under the collective term *another*.

5. *Jehovah (is) my allotted portion and my cup; thou wilt enlarge my lot.*
The other side of the contrast is again exhibited. The idea is, that in the
Lord the Psalmist has all that he can wish or hope for. The figures are
borrowed from the regular supply of food and drink. Compare Ps. xi. 6,
xxiii. 5. There may also be allusions to the language of the Pentateuch
in reference to the tribe of Levi, Deut. x. 9, xviii. 1, 2. The common
version of the last clause, *thou upholdest my lot*, is neither so grammatical
nor yields so good a sense as that above given, where *enlarge* implies both
honour and abundance, and the future form expresses confident assurance
that the favour now experienced will be continued.

6. *The lines are fallen to me in pleasant things* (or *pleasant places*); *yea,
my heritage is goodly.* The *lines* here spoken of are those used in measuring and dividing land. *Fallen, i. e.* assigned, with or without allusion to
the lot, as the means of distribution. Compare Num. xxxiv. 2, Judges
xviii. 1. The idea of *places* is suggested by the context, or the plural adjective may have the abstract sense of pleasure, pleasures, like the cognate
form in Job xxxvi. 11. The particle (אַף) which introduces the last clause
is more emphatic than the simple copulative *and*. It properly means *also*,
and implies that this clause contains something more than that before it.
The original construction of the last clause is, *a heritage is goodly to me* or
upon me, with allusion to the natural and common image of gifts or favours
as descending from above. The heritage or portion thus described is God
himself, but considered as including all desirable possessions.

7. *I will bless Jehovah, who hath counselled me; also by night have my
reins prompted me.* He praises God for having counselled or persuaded
him to choose this goodly heritage in preference to every other portion.
The second clause begins with *yea* or *also*, as in the preceding verse. It
here implies that, under the divine control just mentioned, his own habitual
dispositions tended to the same point. *By night*, literally *nights*, an idiom
not unknown in vulgar English. The plural may in this case be emphatic,

meaning whole nights, all night long.   The night is mentioned, both as a
time naturally favourable to reflection, and as shewing that the same subject occupied his thoughts by night as well as by day; see above on Ps. i. 2.
The *reins* are figuratively put like the *heart, bowels,* &c., for the affections; see above on Ps. vii. 10 (9).   *My reins have taught me*, warned me,
prompted me, to utter the praise mentioned in the first clause, or to make
the choice described in ver. 1, 2, 5.

8. *I have set Jehovah before me always: because (he is) at my right hand,
I shall not be moved.*   I have set him before me, *i. e.* I recognise his presence and confide in his protection.   The actual expression of this confidence
is given in the other clause.   The right hand is here mentioned, not as a
post of honour, but as that of a guard or defender.   See below, on Ps. cix.
31, cx. 5, cxxi. 5.—*I shall not be moved* from my secure position.   See
above, on Ps. x. 6, xv. 5.   The whole verse is a varied repetition and
amplification of the last clause of ver. 1, *I have trusted* (or *sheltered myself*)
in thee.—The Septuagint version of this sentence is quoted in Acts ii. 25,
with an express recognition of David as the author of the psalm.

9. *Therefore has rejoiced my heart and exulted my glory ; yea, my flesh
shall dwell in security (or confidence).*—Therefore, because God is my ever
present helper.   *Glory* seems here to mean his nobler part, his soul, but
not as wholly separate from the body, as appears from what follows.   See
above, on Ps. vii. 6 (5).—*Flesh* may either mean the body, as distinguished
from the soul, or the whole person as including both.   Compare Ps. lxiii.
2 (1), lxxxiv. 3 (2).—The idea of dwelling in security or confidence of safety
is borrowed from the Pentateuch.   See Deut. xxxiii. 12, 28, and compare
Judges xviii. 7, Jer. xxiii. 6, xxxiii. 16.   A similar allusion has been found
already in Ps. iv. 9 (8).   The Septuagint version of the sentence, although
it substitutes *tongue* for *glory*, is substantially correct, and therefore retained
in Acts ii. 26.—The second clause is not simply parallel and equivalent
to the first, but is rather an actual performance of the duty there described.
Having there said that his heart did triumph in the certainty of God's
protection, he here proves the truth of his assertion, by professing his
assured hope that his whole person, not excepting his material part, shall
dwell in safety under that protection.   This is applicable both to preservation from death and preservation in death, and may therefore without
violence be understood, in a lower sense, of David, who did die and see
corruption, but whose body is to rise again, as well as in a higher sense
of Christ, whose body, though it died, was raised again before it saw corruption.

10. *For thou wilt not leave my soul to Hell ; thou wilt not give thy Holy
One to see corruption.*   He now assigns the ground or reason of the confidence expressed in the preceding verse.   "I am sure my soul and body
will be safe, because thou canst not, without ceasing to be God and my
God, give me up to the destroyer."   He does not say *leave in* but *to, i. e.*
abandon to, give up to the dominion or possession of another.   The same
Hebrew phrase occurs, with the same sense, in Lev. xix. 10, Job xxxix. 14,
and in Ps. xlix. 11 (10) below.—*Hell* is here to be taken in its wide old
English sense, as corresponding to the Hebrew *Sheol* and the Greek *Hades*,
the invisible world or state of the dead.   See above on Ps. vi. 6 (5), and
ix. 18 (17).—*Give, i. e.* permit, or more emphatically, give up, abandon,
which makes the parallelism of the clauses more exact.   *Thy Holy One,* or
more exactly, thy favourite, the object of thy special favour.   See above, on
Ps. iv. 4 (3).   The textual reading is a plural form (חסידיך), the singular

(חֲסִידֶךָ) being a marginal correction or *keri*. The Jews contend for the former, and most Christians for the latter, which is favoured by the oldest versions and retained in the New Testament. The essential difference between the two is less than it may seem at first sight, since even the singular is really collective, and includes the whole class of God's chosen and favoured ones, of whom Christ is the head and representative. —*To see, i. e.* to experience or undergo *corruption.* Compare the phrase to *see death,* Luke ii. 26.—It has been disputed whether שַׁחַת is derived from שׁוּחַ, and means a pit, or from שָׁחַת, and means corruption. Both allegations are probably true, the antecedent improbability of such a double sense and derivation being counterbalanced by the clear analogy of נַחַת, which is of a different sense and gender, as derived from נָחַת and נוּחַ. The use of this equivocal expression may have been intentional, in order to make it applicable both to David and to Christ. (See above, on the preceding verse.) To both, the words contain a promise of deliverance from death, but in the case of Christ with a specific reference to his actual escape from the corruption which is otherwise inseparable from dissolution. Believers in general are saved from the perpetual dominion of death, but Christ was saved even from the first approach of putrefaction. In this peculiar and most pregnant sense the words are applied to Christ exclusively by two apostles, and in that sense declared to be inapplicable to David. (Acts ii. 29–31, xiii. 35–37.) Their reasoning would utterly forbid the application to any lower subject, were it not for the ambiguity or twofold meaning of the Hebrew word, which cannot therefore be explained away without embarrassing the interpretation of this signal prophecy.

11. *Thou wilt teach me the way of life, fulness of joy with thy face* (or *presence*), *pleasures in thy right hand for ever.* He trusts God not only for deliverance from death, but for guidance in the way to life, or blessed immortality. (Compare Prov. ii. 19.) The Hebrew verb is causative, and means *thou wilt make me know,* point out, or shew to me. *Fulness,* satiety, or rather satisfaction, in its strongest sense, including the ideas of contentment and abundance. The plural, *joys,* denotes not only richness but variety. The next phrase may simply mean before thy face or in thy presence. But it will also bear a stronger sense, and represent God's presence or the sight of him, not merely as the place, but the source of enjoyment. See above, on Ps. iv. 7 (6), and compare Ps. xvii. 15, lxxx. 4 (3). So in the last clause, the idea is not merely *at thy right hand* as a place of honour and of safety, but *in thy right hand* as the depository of eternal joys, or *with thy right hand,* as the instrument by which they are dispensed. See below, on Ps. xvii. 7.—This last clause is omitted in Peter's citation of the passage, Acts ii. 27, no doubt because it is a mere poetical reiteration of the one before it, which is itself only added to complete the period, and not because it was essential to the apostle's purpose. That purpose was accomplished by applying the two preceding verses to our Saviour, not exclusively indeed, but by way of eminence and in a peculiar sense, which we learn, however, from Acts ii. 30, 31, was actually present to the mind of the inspired Psalmist. The same argumentative interpretation of the prophecy is given by Paul in Acts xiii. 35–37.

Psalm 17

A SUFFERER, in imminent danger, professes his sincere conformity to God's will, and invokes his favour and protection, ver. 1–5. This petition is enforced by an appeal to former mercies, ver. 6, 7, and a description of the wickedness of his enemies, ver. 8–12, whose character and spirit he contrasts with his own, ver. 13–15.

The position of this psalm in the collection seems to have been determined by the resemblance of its subject, tone, and diction, to those of the sixteenth, with which it may be said to form a pair or double psalm, like the first and second, third and fourth, ninth and tenth, &c.

1. *A Prayer. By David. Hear, O Jehovah, the right, hearken to my cry, give ear to my prayer not with lips of deceit.* This psalm is called a prayer because petition is its burden, its characteristic feature, its essential element. *By David,* literally, *to David, i. e.* belonging to him as its author. —*The right,* righteousness or justice in the abstract, here put for a just cause, or perhaps for one who is in the right, who has justice on his side. The prayer that God will hear the right implies that no appeal is made to partiality or privilege, but merely to the merits of the case. The righteousness claimed is not merely that of the cause but that of the person, not inherent but derived from the imputed righteousness of faith according to the doctrine of the Old as well as the New Testament. The quality alleged is not that of sinless perfection but that of sincere conformity to the divine will. The last clause, *not with lips of deceit,* applies to all that goes before, and represents sincerity as necessary to acceptance. The original expression is still stronger, and conveys much more than a negative. It does not merely say, *not with deceitful lips,* but more positively *with lips not deceitful.*

2. *From before thee my judgment shall come forth; thine eyes shall behold equities.* This sentence really involves a prayer, but in form it is the expression of a confident hope. *From before thee,* from thy presence, thy tribunal. *My judgment,* my acquittal, vindication; or *my justice, i.e.* my just cause, my cause considered as a just one. *Shall come forth,* to the view of others, shall be seen and recognised in its true character, as being what it is. The reason is, because God's judgments are infallible. His eyes cannot fail to see innocence or righteousness where it exists. The plural, *rectitudes* or *equities,* is an emphatic abstract. See above, on the parallel passage, Ps. xi. 7.

3. *Thou hast tried my heart, hast visited (me) by night, hast assayed me; thou wilt not find; my mouth shall not exceed my thought.* He still appeals to God as the judge and witness of his own sincerity. The preterites represent the process as no new one, although still continued in the present. *Visited* for the purpose of examination or inspection, in which specific sense the English verb is often used. *By night,* as the time when men's thoughts are least under restraint, and when the evil, if there be any, is most certain of detection. *Purged me,* as the purity of metals is tested by fire, to which process the Hebrew word is specially applied. *Thou shalt not find* any thing at variance with the sincerity of this profession.—The future form implies that the investigation is to be continued, but without any change in the result.—The last clause is doubtful and obscure. The common version, *I am purposed (that) my mouth shall not trangress,* agrees well enough with the form of the words, but is forbidden by the accents. The reversed construction, *my thoughts shall not exceed my mouth (or speech),*

is ungrammatical; nor does either of theseconstructions suit the context so well as the first, which makes the clause a renewed profession of sincerity.

4. (*As*) *to the works of man, by the word of thy lips I have kept the paths of the violent* (*trangressor.*) The works of man are the sinful courses to which man is naturally prone. The generic term *man* (אָדָם) is often used in reference to the sinful infirmities of human nature. See 1 Sam. xxiv. 10 (9), Hos. vi. 7, Job xxxi. 33. The word of God's lips is the word uttered by him, with particular reference to his precepts or commands, but including his entire revelation. *By this word*, by means of it as an instrument, and in reliance on it as an authority.—The verb (שָׁמַר) translated *kept* properly means *watched*, and is elsewhere applied to the observance of a rule, but in this place seems to mean *watched* for the purpose of avoiding, as we say in English to *keep away from* or *keep out of* danger.—From the verb (פָּרַץ) to break forth, elsewhere applied to gross iniquities (Hos. iv. 2.) comes the adjective (פָּרִיץ) violent, outrageous, here used as an epithet of the flagrant sinner.

5. *My steps have laid hold of thy paths, my feet have not swerved.* His profession of integrity is still continued. The first verb is in the infinitive form, but determined by the preterites before and after. The English language does not furnish equivalents to the parallel terms in Hebrew, both which denote footsteps. The common version violates the context by converting the first clause into a prayer, which would here be out of place.

6. *I have invoked thee because thou wilt answer me, O God! Incline thine ear to me, hear my speech.* The alternation of the tenses is significant. ' I have invoked thee heretofore, and do so still, because I know that thou wilt hear me.'' It is needless to observe how much the sentence is enfeebled by the change of either to the present.—*Thou wilt hear me*, in the pregnant sense of hearing graciously or answering a prayer. See above, on Ps. iii. 5 (4).—*O* (*mighty*) *God!* The divine name here used is the one denoting God's omnipotence. See above, Ps. v. 5 (4), vii. 12 (11), x. 11, 12. xvi. 1. —*My speech*, what I say, אִמְרָה from אָמַר to say.

7. *Distinguish thy mercies,* (*O thou*) *saving those trusting, from those rising up, with thy right hand.* The first verb is the same that occurs in Ps. iv. 4 (3.) Here, as there, it means to set apart, or single out, but with particular reference to extraordinary favours, implying an unusual necessity. Such mercy is described as perfectly in keeping with the divine mode of action in such cases.—*Trusting*, seeking refuge, *i. e.* in God. See above, on Ps. xvi. 1. The same ellipsis may be assumed after *rising up*, or we may supply *against them*.—With thy right hand, as the instrument of deliverance. Compare Ps. xvi. 11. These words must be connected in construction with *saving*.

8. *Keep me as the apple of the eye, in the shadow of thy wings thou wilt hide me.* The first verb means to watch over, guard, preserve with care. See above, on ver. 4, where it occurs in a figurative application. The pupil or apple of the eye is a proverbial type of that which is most precious and most easily injured, and which therefore has a double claim to sedulous protection. The original phrase is strongly idiomatic, exhibiting what seems to be a singular confusion of the genders. Its literal meaning is, supplying the articles omitted by poetic licence, *the man* (or *the little man*, or *the manlike part*) *the daughter of the eye.* The first word has reference to the image

reflected in the pupil, which is then described as belonging to the eye, by an oriental idiom which uses personal relations, son, daughter, &c., to denote the mutual relations even of inanimate objects. The comparison is borrowed from Deut. xxxii. 10, where it is followed by another with the eagle's treatment of her young, to which there seems to be allusion in the last clause of the verse before us. The imperative form of the first verb is no reason for departing from the future form of the other, which is much more expressive. What he asks in one clause he expresses his assured hope of obtaining in the other.

9. *From the face of the wicked who have wasted me; mine enemies to the soul will surround me.* The preceding sentence is continued, with a more particular description of the objects of his dread. "Thou wilt hide me from the face, sight, or presence of the wicked." *Wasted*, desolated, destroyed, with allusion perhaps to the siege of a town or the invasion of a country. The same term is applied to a dead man in Judges v. 27. The *enemies* of the last clause are identical with the *wicked* of the first. *Enemies in soul* may mean cordial haters, or enemies who seek the soul or life, called *deadly enemies* in the English version. Or בְּנֶפֶשׁ may be construed with the verb : surround me eagerly (with craving appetite); or surround me against my soul or life, *i.e.* with a view to take it.—The future form suggests that the danger which the first clause had described as past, was still present, and likely to continue. As if he had said, "from my wicked foes who have already wasted me, and will no doubt still continue to surround me." In this description present danger is included, whereas if we substitute the present form, we lose the obvious allusion to the future and the past.

10. *Their fat they have closed; (with) their mouth they have spoken in pride.* The first clause, though not exactly rendered, is correctly paraphrased in the English Bible; *they are enclosed in their own fat.* This is no uncommon metaphor in Scripture for moral and spiritual insensibility ; see Deut. xxxii. 15, Job xv. 27, Ps. lxxiii. 7, cxix. 70. The literal sense of the expressions derives some illustration from Judg. iii. 22. Some give to *fat* the specific sense of *heart*, which is said to have in Arabic, "their heart they have closed." But the other explanation yields the same sense in a more emphatic form, and with closer conformity to Hebrew usage.

11. *In our footsteps now have they surrounded us; their eyes they will set, to go astray in the land.* The meaning of the first words, *in our footsteps*, seems to be, wherever we go. Compare Ps. cxxxix. 3, 5. For the masoretic reading *us*, the text has *me*, which, although harsher, amounts to the same thing, as the sufferer is an ideal person respecting many real ones. The parallel clauses exhibit the usual combination of the preterite and future forms, implying that what had been done was likely to be still continued. *They fix their eyes,* upon this as the end at which they aim. *To go astray* or turn aside, *i. e.* from the way of God's commandments, to which the Psalmist, in ver. 5, had declared his own adherence. The translations *bowing down* and *casting down* are less in accordance with the context and with the usage of the Hebrew verb, which is constantly employed to express departure from God and aberration from the path of duty; see 1 Kings xi. 9, Job xxxi. 7, Ps. xliv. 19 (18), cxix. 51, 157. *To the earth*, or *in the earth*, although grammatical, affords a less appropriate sense than *in the land, i. e.* the holy land or land of promise, the local habitation of God's people under the old economy ; see above on Ps. xvi. 3, and compare Isaiah xxvi. 10.

12. *His likeness (is) as a lion; he is craving to tear; and as a young*

lion sitting in secret places. The singular suffix refers to the enemy as an ideal person. The future (כְסוֹף) means that he is just about to feel or gratify the appetite for blood. *To tear* in pieces, as a wild beast does his prey before devouring it.—*Sitting,* lurking, lying in wait, with special reference to the patient promptness of the wild beast in such cases.—The comparison is the same as in Ps. x. 8–10.

13. *Arise, Jehovah, go before his face, make him bow, save my soul from the wicked (with) thy sword.* On the meaning of the prayer that God would *arise,* see above on Ps. iii. 8 (7).—*Go before his face :* the same Hebrew phrase occurs below (Ps. xcv. 2), in the sense of coming into one's presence. Here the context gives it the more emphatic sense of meeting, encountering, withstanding. *Make him bend* or *bow,* as the conquered bows beneath the conqueror.—The construction of *thy sword* seems to be the same with that of *their mouth* in ver. 10. The Septuagint puts *thy sword* in apposition with *my soul,* the Vulgate with the word immediately preceding, *men (who are) thy sword,* as the Assyrian is said to be the rod in God's hand (Isa. x. 5). But such a representation of the enemy as God's chosen instruments, instead of enforcing, would enfeeble the petition. The verb translated *save* is a causative strictly meaning *make to escape.*

14. *From men (with) thy hand, from the world; their portion is in (this) life, and with thy hoard thou wilt fill their belly ; they shall have enough of sons, and leave their residue to their babes.* All the parts of this obscure verse have been variously explained. As in the preceding verse, some here read *men (which are) thy hand, i. e.* the instrument of thy wrath. The difficult expression מֵחֶלֶד is by some understood as a description of their character and spirit—*men of the world*—men who belong to it, and whose hearts are set upon it. Others give חֶלֶד its primary meaning of *duration,* and make the phrase descriptive of prosperity—*men of duration* or perpetuity—who not only prosper now, but have long done so, and seem likely to continue. The simplest construction is that given in the prayer-book version, which takes the proposition in the same sense before both nouns—"*from* the men, I say, and *from* the evil world." " *World* is then simply a collective equivalent to the plural *men.* This translation of the former word is justified by the analogy of Ps. xlix. 2 (1).—*Life* is by some understood to mean a life of ease or pleasure; but this is far less natural than the obvious sense of *this life,* this present state as distinguished from futurity. The rest of the verse shews that their desires have not been disappointed. To the eye of sense God sometimes seems to have reserved his choichest gifts for the ungodly. *Thy hidden (treasure), i. e.* hoarded, carefully secreted. *Fill their belly,* satisfy their appetite. The future form implies that the state of things described is likely to continue.—The next clause may be also rendered : *(their) sons shall be satisfied, and leave their residue to their babes.* This would be a strong description of prosperity continued from generation to generation. According to the version before given, the men of the world are represented as having their largest wishes gratified, not only in the number but the prosperous condition of their children ; see Ps. cxxvii. 3, cxxviii. 3, 4, Job xxi. 11. The whole is only a description of things as they seem to man, before God's judgments interpose to change them.

15. *I in righteousness shall see thy face ; I shall be satisfied in awaking with thy appearance.* The pronoun expressed at the beginning of the sentence is emphatic. I, in opposition to the men described in the preceding

verse. "They may rejoice in richer providential gifts, and be satisfied with
what they thus possess.   But I enjoy what they do not, the sense of acceptance in thy sight, righteousness, justification, recognition as a righteous
person."   The ambiguity of construction in the last clause is the same both
in Hebrew and in English.   The preposition *with* may connect what follows
either with *awaking* or with *satisfied*.   Thus the prayer-book version reads,
"And when I awake up after thy likeness, I shall be satisfied with it;" but
the authorised version: "I shall be satisfied, when I awake, with thy likeness."   The latter construction is the one required by the accents, and preferred by most interpreters, the rather as the last word does not mean *resemblance* in the abstract, but form, shape, or visible appearance, Exod. xx. 4,
Num. xii. 8, Deut. iv. 16, 23, 25, Job iv. 16.   The idea here suggested is
the sight of thee, exactly corresponding to *behold thy face*, in the parallel
clause.—*In awaking*, or *when I shall awake*, is understood by some to
mean, when I awake to-morrow, and from this expression they infer that the
psalm was originally composed, and intended to be used, as an evening-song
or prayer.   See above on Ps. iii. 6 (5), iv. 9 (8), v. 4 (3).   Others give
the phrase the same sense but a wider application; *in awaking, i. e.* whenever I awake.   As if he had said, while the men of the world think day and
night of their possessions and their pleasures, I rejoice, whenever I awake,
in the sight of God's reconciled countenance and the consciousness of friendship with him.   A third interpretation puts a still higher sense upon the
phrase as referring to the act of awaking from the sleep of death.   But
this excludes too much from view the enjoyment of God's favour and protection even here, which is the burden of the whole prayer.   If the hope of
future blessedness had been enough, the previous petitions would have been
superfluous.   The utmost that can be conceded to this view of the passage
is that, by a natural association, what is here said of awaking out of sleep
in this life may be extended to that great awaking which awaits us all hereafter.   The same state of mind and heart which enables a man now to be
contented with the partial views which he enjoys of God will prepare him
to be satisfied hereafter with the beatific vision through eternity.

Psalm 18

THIS psalm consists of five unequal parts.   In the first, David announces
his desire to praise God for his wonderful deliverances, ver. 2–4 (1–3).
In the second, these are described, not in historical form, but by the use of
the strongest poetical figures, ver. 5–20 (4–19).   In the third, he declares
them to have been acts of righteousness as well as mercy, and in strict
accordance with the general laws of the divine administration, ver. 21–28
(20–27).   In the fourth, he goes again into particulars, but less in the way
of recollection than of anticipation, founded both on what he has experienced
and on what God has promised, ver. 29–46 (28–45).   In the fifth, this
change of form is accounted for by summing up the promises referred
to, and applying them not merely to David as an individual, but to his
posterity for ever, thus including Christ, and shewing the whole composition
to be one of those Messianic psalms, in which he is the principal subject of
the prophecy, though not the only one, nor even the one nearest to the eye
of the observer, ver. 46–51 (45–50).

1. *To the Chief Musician.   By a Servant of Jehovah.   By David, who
spake unto Jehovah the words of this song, in the day Jehovah freed him*

from the hand of all his foes and from the hand of Saul. The first clause of the title shews, in this as in other cases, that the composition was designed from the beginning to be used in the public worship of the ancient church, and has reference therefore to the experience of the writer, not as a private person, but as an eminent *servant of the Lord, i. e.* one entrusted with the execution of his purposes, as an instrument or agent. The expressions, *spake unto Jehovah,* &c., are borrowed from Exod. xv. 1, and Deut. xxxi. 30. This is the more observable, because the psalm contains obvious allusions to the song of Moses in Deut. ch. xxxii. An analogous case is found in 2 Sam. xxiii. 1, where the form of expression is evidently borrowed from Num. xxiv. 3.—The repetition of *hand* is not found in the original, where the first word (כַּף) properly denotes the *palm* or inside of the hand, but is poetically used as an equivalent to יָד. The hand is a common figure for power and possession. This whole clause bears a strong analogy to Exod. xviii. 10, where " out of the hand of the Egyptians and out of the hand of Pharaoh" corresponds exactly to " out of the hand of all his foes and out of the hand of Saul," *i. e.* and especially of Saul. Compare " Judah and Jerusalem," Isa. i. 1; "the land and Jericho," Josh. ii. 1. This form of expression does not imply that Saul was the last of his enemies, but rather that he was the first, both in time and in importance, so that he might be considered equal to all the others put together. And accordingly we find their idea carried out in the structure of this psalm, one half of which seems to relate especially to Saul, and the remainder to his other enemies. The general expressions of this title shew that the psalm was not occasioned by any particular event, but by a retrospect of all the deliverances from persecution which the writer had experienced.

2 (1). *And said, I will love thee, Jehovah, my strength !* The sentence is continued from the foregoing verse, *who sang unto the Lord . . . and said.* The future form, *I will love,* represents it as a permanent affection, and expresses a fixed purpose. I not only love thee now, but am resolved to do so for ever. The verb itself occurs nowhere else in its primitive form, but often in one of its derived forms, to express the compassionate regard of a superior to an inferior. The simple form is here used to denote the reciprocal affection of the inferior party. From its etymology the verb seems to express the strongest and most intimate attachment, being properly expressive of στοργή, or parental love. The noun translated *strength* is also peculiar to this passage, though its root and cognate forms are very common. Combined with one of the divine names, it constitutes the name *Hezekiah,* which may have been suggested by the verse before us. *My strength, i. e.* the giver of my strength or the supplier of its deficiencies, the substitute for my strength, my protector and deliverer.

3 (2). *Jehovah (is) my rock, and my fortress, and my deliverer ; my (is) my rock, I will trust in him ; my shield and my horn of salvation, my height* (or *high place*). By this accumulation of descriptive epithets, the Psalmist represents God as the object of his trust and his protector. The first two figures, *my rock* and *my fortress,* contain an allusion to the physical structure of the Holy Land, as well as to David's personal experience. The caves and fissures of the rocks, with which the land abounded, had often afforded him shelter and concealment when pursued by Saul. See Judges vi. 2, 1 Sam. xxiv. 3, 2 Sam. v. 7. The literal expression, *my deliverer,* seems to be added as an explanation of the figures which precede. *My God* may also be explained as one of the descriptive terms ; but it seems

more natural to make it the subject of a new proposition, equivalent and parallel to that in the first clause. Here again we are obliged to use the same English word as a translation of two different words in Hebrew. As the *rock* (סֶלַע) of the first clause suggests the idea of concealment and security, so the *rock* (צוּר) of the second clause suggests that of strength and immobility. The figure is borrowed from Deut. xxxii. 4, and reappears in Ps. xcii. 16 (15). Compare Isaiah's phrase, *a rock of ages* (Isa. xxvi. 4), and Jacob's phrase, *the stone of Israel* (Gen. xlix. 24), where *stone*, like *rock* in the clause before us, denotes not the place but the material, not *a stone*, but *stone*, as one of the hardest and least mutable substances with which we are acquainted, and therefore an appropriate figure for combined immutability and strength. For the figurative use of *shield* in such connections, see above on Ps. iii. 4 (3). The next phrase has allusion to the defensive habits of horned animals. The figure seems to be borrowed from Deut xxxiii. 17. (Compare 1 Sam. ii. 10, Job. xvi. 15.) *My horn of salvation* may be understood to mean, *my horn, to wit, my salvation*, so that the second noun is explanatory of the first. More probably, however, the expression means *the horn that saves me*, by repelling or destroying all my enemies. In Luke i. 69, the same phrase is applied to Christ by Zacharias. The last term in the description belongs to the same class with the first, and was probably suggested by the Psalmist's early wanderings among the rocks and caverns of Judea. The Hebrew word properly denotes a place so high as to be beyond the reach of danger. See above, on Ps. ix. 10 (9), where the same word is twice used in the same sense and figurative application.

4 (3). *To be praised I will call Jehovah, and from my enemies I shall be saved.* "I will invoke God as a being worthy of all praise." The first Hebrew word, which has the force of a future passive participle, is a standing epithet of Jehovah in the lyrical style of the Old Testament. See Ps. xlviii. 2 (1), xcvi. 4, cxiii. 3, cxlv. 3, 1 Chron. xvi. 25. The connection of the clauses is, that the believing invocation of Jehovah in his true character, and with a just appreciation of his excellence, must needs be followed by the experience of his favour. They who cry and are not heard, as we read in ver. 42 (41) below, cry indeed to Jehovah, but they do not invoke him as the one to be praised, they do not see him as he is, and cannot pray to him as they ought. They ask and receive not, because they ask amiss (James iv. 3).

5 (4). *The bands of death have enclosed me, and the streams of worthlessness* (or *Belial*) *will* (*still*) *affright me* From the general acknowledgment contained in ver. 1–4, he proceeds to a more particular description of his danger. By *bands* we are probably to understand the cordage of a net, such as fowlers spread for birds. This is a favourite metaphor with David to denote dangers, and particularly those of an insidious and complicated kind. See below, Ps. cxvi. 3. The word *Belial* properly means *worthless, good for nothing*. The reference is here to wicked men, whose number and violence are indicated by the figure of torrents, overflowing streams. The use of the future in the last clause shews that the writer, as in many other cases, takes his position in the midst of the event, and views it as partly past and partly future. This bold assumption of an ideal situation greatly adds to the life and vividness of the description.

6 (5). *The bands of hell surrounded me, the snares of death encountered me.* This verse merely repeats and amplifies the first clause of the fifth,

Hell, in the wide old English sense, is a poetical equivalent to *death*. See above, on Ps. vi. 6 (5). The explicit mention of *snares* in the last clause confirms the explanation before given of *bands*. *Encountered*, met me, crossed my path. The sense *prevented* or *anticipated* does not suit the context, and that of *surprised* is not sufficiently justified by usage. See above, on Ps. xvii. 13.

7 (6). *In my distress I will invoke Jehovah, and to my God will cry ; he will hear from his palace my voice, and my prayer before him will come, into his ears.* The verbs are·in the future, because they express the feelings not of one looking back upon the danger as already past, but of one actually implicated in it. See above, on ver. 5 (4). The literal meaning of the words is, *in distress to me.* Compare the phrase, *at times in distress*, Ps. ix. 10 (9), x. 1. *My God* implies a covenant relation and a hope of audience founded on it. The verb translated *cry* is specially appropriated to a cry for help. *His palace* here means heaven, as God's royal residence. See above, on Ps. xi. 4. *Into his ears* is a kind of after-thought, designed to strengthen the preceding expression. It shall not only reach his presence, but, as it were, shall penetrate his ears. The whole expresses an assured hope of being heard, and is really tantamount to an assertion that he was heard.

8 (7). *Then did the earth shake and quake, and the foundations of the mountains trembled and were shaken because he was angry.* The idea of succession expressed by the English *then* is conveyed in Hebrew by the form of the verb. The resemblance, in form and sound, of *shake* and *quake*, corresponds to that of the original verbs (וַתִּגְעַשׁ וַתִּרְעַשׁ). A reflexive or emphatic passive form of the first verb appears in the second clause. The closing words of this clause strictly mean *because it was inflamed (or enkindled) to him* with an ellipsis of the noun (אַף) *anger.* The full construction may be found in Deut. vi. 15, and Ps. cxxiv. 3. The phrase *foundations of the mountains* is copied from Deut. xxxii. 22.

9 (8). *There went up smoke in his wrath, and fire from his mouth devours : coals are kindled from it.* Smoke and fire are mentioned as natural concomitants and parallel figures, both denoting anger, and suggested by the phrase *it was inflamed to him* in the preceding verse. Compare Deut. xxxii. 22, xxix. 19 (20), Ps. xxiv. 1. The translation *nostrils* rests on a confusion of two collateral derivatives from the verb to breathe. (See my note on Isa. xlviii. 9.) Nor is this sense required by the parallelism, unless *mouth* and *nose* must always go together. There seems to be some allusion to the fire and smoke at Sinai, Exod. xix. 18. *From it* may have reference to *fire ;* but the nearest antecedent is *his mouth.* Compare Job xli. 11–13 (19–21). There is no need of supplying any object with *devours ;* the idea is that of a *devouring fire, i. e.* one capable of consuming whatever combustible material it may meet with.

10 (9). *So he bowed the heavens and came down, and gloom (was) under his feet.* The scene seems here to be transferred from heaven to earth, where the psalmist sees not only the divine operation but the personal presence of Jehovah. The word *so*, familiarly employed in English to continue a narrative, here represents the vau conversive of the Hebrew. The word translated *gloom* is not the usual term for darkness, but a poetical expression specially applied to dense clouds and vapours. The expression seems to be derived from Deut. v. 22. Compare with this clause, Exod. xix. 16, and with the first, Isa. lxiii. 19 (lxiv. 1).

11 (10). *And he rode on a cherub and flew, and soared on the wings of a wind.* The cherubim of the Mosaic system were visible representations of the whole class of creatures superior to man. The singular form *cherub* seems to be used here to convey the indefinite idea of a superhuman but created being. The whole verse is a poetical description of God's intervention, as a scene presented to the senses. As earthly kings are carried by inferior animals, so the heavenly king is here described as borne through the air in his descent by beings intermediate between himself and man. The word *soared*, in the second clause, is used to represent a poetical term in the original borrowed from Deut. xxviii. 49. With the whole verse compare Ps. lxviii. 18 (17), and civ. 3.

12 (11). *(And) set darkness (as) his covert about him, his shelter, darkness of waters, clouds of the skies,* This concealment suggests the idea of a brightness insupportable by mortal sight. Compare Deut. iv. 11, Job xxxvi. 29, Ps. xcvii. 2. *Darkness of waters* does not mean dark waters, but watery darkness, a beautiful description of clouds charged with rain. The two nouns in the last clause both mean clouds, but the second is used only in the plural, and seems properly to designate the whole body of vapours constituting the visible heavens or sky. A somewhat similar combination occurs in Exod. xix. 9.

13 (12). *From the blaze before him his clouds passed—hail und coals of fire.* The dark clouds which enveloped him are now described as penetrated by the light within. *Passed, i. e.* passed away, were dispelled. The last clause may be construed as an exclamation such as an eye-witness might have uttered. The combination is borrowed from Exod. ix. 24. (Compare Ps. lxxviii. 47, 48.) Hail, as an instrument of the divine vengeance, is also mentioned in Josh. x. 11.

14 (13). *Then thundered in the heavens Jehovah, and the Highest gave his voice—hail and coals of fire.* The second clause is a poetical repetition of the first. " The Most High gave his voice," means in this connection neither more nor less than that he " thundered in the heavens." Though visibly present upon earth he is described as still in heaven. Compare Gen. xi. 5, 7 ; xviii. 21 ; John iii. 13. The last clause may be construed as in ver. 13, or made dependent on the verb *gave*, as in Exod. ix. 23 : " Jehovah gave thunder and hail." This clause is repeated because the hail and lightning were not merely terrific circumstances, but appointed instruments of vengeance and weapons of destruction.

15 (14). *Then sent he his arrows and scattered them, and shot forth lightnings and confounded them.* The lightnings of the last clause may be understood as explaining the arrows of the first. Instead of *shot forth lightnings* some translate *and lightnings much, i. e.* many, in which sense the Hebrew word (רַב) occurs sometimes elsewhere (Exod. xix. 21, 1 Sam. xiv. 6, Num. xxvi. 54). In several other places it seems to mean *enough* or *too much* (Gen. xlv. 28, Exod. ix. 28, Num. xvi. 3, 7, Deut. i. 6). If either of these constructions is adopted, the verb *sent* must be repeated from the other clause. The version first given, *shot*, is justified by the analogy of Gen. xlix. 23. The last verb in the sentence is a military term denoting the confusion of an army produced by a surprise or sudden panic; see Exod. xiv. 24, xxiii. 27, Josh. x. 10, and with the whole verse compare Ps. cxliv. 6.

16 (15). *Then were seen the channels of water and uncovered the foundations of the world, at thy rebuke, Jehovah, at the blast of the breath of thy wrath.* The idea meant to be conveyed by this poetical description is that of sudden and complete subversion, the turning of the whole earth upside down. The language is not designed to be exactly expressive of any real physical change whatever. *From*, or *at thy rebuke, i. e.* after it and in consequence of it. *The breath of thy wrath*, thy angry breath, might also be rendered, *the wind of thy wrath*, thy angry or tempestuous wind. That the Hebrew words do not mean *thy nose* or *nostrils*, see above, on ver. 9 (8). Some suppose an allusion, in the figures of this verse, to the *floods of worthlessness* in ver 5 (4), and the *bands of hell* in ver. 6 (5).

17 (16). *He will send from above, he will take me, he will draw me out of many waters.* Here again the writer seems to take his stand between the inception and the consummation of the great deliverance, and to speak just as he might have spoken while it was in progress. " All this he has done in preparation, and now he is about to send," &c. This seems to be a more satisfactory explanation of the future forms than to make them simple presents, and still more than to make them preterites, which is wholly arbitrary and ungrammatical, although the acts described by these futures were in fact past at the time of composition. *To send from above* in our idiom means to send a messenger; but in Hebrew this verb is the one used with *hand*, where we say *stretch out, e. g.* in the parallel passage Ps. cxliv. 7. (See also Gen. viii. 9, xlviii. 14). The noun, however, is sometimes omitted, and the verb used absolutely to express the sense of the whole phrase, as in 2 Sam. vi. 6, Ps. lvii. 4 (3). *From above*, from on high, from the height or high place, *i. e.* heaven, the place of God's manifested presence. There is peculiar beauty in the word translated *draw*, which is the root of the name *Moses*, and occurs, besides the place before us, only in the explanation of that name recorded by himself, Exod. ii. 10. The choice of this unusual expression here involves an obvious allusion both to the historical fact and the typical meaning of the deliverance of Moses, and a kind of claim upon the part of David to be regarded as another Moses.

18 (17). *He will free me from my enemy* (because he is) *strong, and from my haters, because they are mightier than I.* The futures are to be explained as in the verse preceding. The enemy here mentioned is an ideal person, representing a whole class, of whom Saul was the chief representative. The idiomatic phrase, *my enemy strong*, may be understood as simply meaning *my strong enemy*; but the true construction seems to be indicated by the parallelism. His own weakness and the power of his enemies is given as a reason for the divine interposition.

19 (18). *They will encounter me in the day of my calamity ; and Jehovah has been for a stay to me.* The first clause seems to express a belief that his trials from this quarter are not ended, while the other apppeals to past deliverances as a ground of confidence that God will still sustain him. Most interpreters, however, make the future and preterite forms of this verse perfectly equivalent. " They encountered me in the day of my calamity, and the Lord was for a stay to me." As to the meaning of the first verb, see above, on ver. 6 (5). It is not improbable that David here alludes to his sufferings in early life when fleeing before Saul; see above on ver. 3 (2).

20 (19). *And brought me out into the wide place ; he will save me because he delights in me.* The construction is continued from the foregoing sentence. As confinement or pressure is a common figure for distress, so relief from it is often represented as enlargement, or as coming forth into an open space. See above, on Ps. iv. 2 (1). Here, as in the preceding verse, most interpreters make no distinction between preterite and future. The mean-

ing may, however, be that he expects the same deliverance hereafter which he has experienced already.

21 (20). *Jehovah will treat me according to my righteousness; according to the cleanness of my hands will he repay me.* The future verbs have reference to the condition of the Psalmist under his afflictions, and the hopes which even then he was enabled to cherish. At the same time they make this the announcement of a general and perpetual truth, a law by which God's dispensations are to be controlled for ever. The hands are mentioned as organs or instruments of action. Compare Isa. i. 15, Job ix. 30, xxii. 30. The righteousness here claimed is not an absolute perfection or entire exemption from all sinful infirmity, but what Paul calls submission to the righteousness of God (Rom. x. 3), including faith in his mercy and a sincere governing desire to do his will. This is a higher and more comprehensive sense than innocence of some particular charge, or innocence in reference to man, though not in reference to God.

22 (21). *For I have kept the ways of Jehovah, and have not apostatised from my God.* The Lord's ways are the ways which he marks out for us to walk in, the ways of duty and of safety. To *keep* them is to keep one's self in them, to observe them so as to adhere to them and follow them. The last clause strictly means, *I have not been wicked* (or *guilty*) *from my God;* a combination of the verb and proposition which shews clearly that the essential idea in the writer's mind was that of apostasy or total abjuration of God's service. It is of this mortal sin, and not of all particular transgressions, that the Psalmist here professes himself innocent.

23 (22). *For all his judgments* (are) *before me, and his statutes I will not put from me.* Judicial decisions and permanent enactments are here used as equivalent expressions for all God's requisitions. To have these before one is to observe them, and the opposite of putting them away or out of sight. The terms of this profession have been evidently chosen in allusion to such dicta of the law itself as Deut. v. 29, xvii. 11. From the past tense of the foregoing verse he here insensibly slides into the present and the future, so as to make his profession of sincerity include his former life, his actual dispositions, and his settled purpose for all time to come.

24 (23). *And I have been perfect with him, and have kept myself from my iniquity.* He not only will be faithful, but he has been so already, in the sense before explained. There is evident reference in the first clause to the requisition of the Law, " thou shalt be perfect with the Lord thy God," Deut. xviii. 13. (Compare Gen. xvii. 1.) *With* means not merely in his presence, or his sight, as distinguished from men's estimate of moral objects, but "in my intercourse and dealing with him." Compare 1 Kings xi. 4, and the description of David in 1 Kings xiv. 8, xv. 5. In the last clause some see an allusion to David's adventure in the cave, when his conscience smote him for meditating violence against Saul. See 1 Sam. xxiv. 6, and compare 1 Sam. xxvi. 23, 24. But whether this be so or not, the clause undoubtedly contains a confession of corruption. *My iniquity* can only mean that to which I am naturally prone and subject. We have here, then, a further proof that the perfection claimed in the first clause is not an absolute immunity from sin, but an upright purpose and desire to serve God.

25 (24). *And Jehovah has requited me according to my righteousness, according to the cleanness of my hands before his eyes.* This verse shews clearly that the futures in ver. 21 (20) must be strictly understood. What he there represents himself as confidently hoping, he here professes to have really experienced. In the intervening verses he shews how he had

done his part, and now acknowledges that God had faithfully performed his own.

26, 27 (25, 26). *With the gracious thou wilt shew thyself gracious ; with the perfect man thou wilt shew thyself perfect; with the purified thou wilt shew thyself pure ; and with the crooked thou wilt shew thyself perverse.* What he had previously mentioned as the method of God's dealings towards himself, he now describes as a general law of the divine administration. The essential idea is that God is, in a certain sense, to men precisely what they are to him. The particular qualities specified are only given as examples, and might have been exchanged for others without altering the general sense. The form of expression is extremely strong and bold, but scarcely liable to misapprehension, even in ver. 27 (26). No one is in danger of imagining that God can act perversely even to the most perverse. But the same course of proceeding which would be perverse in itself or towards a righteous person, when pursued towards a sinner becomes a mere act of vindicatory justice. In the first clause of ver. 26 (25), the ambiguous word *gracious* has been chosen to represent the similar term חָסִיד, for the comprehensive use of which we see above, on Ps. iv. 4 (3), xii. 2 (1). *Perfect* has the same sense as in ver. 23 (22), namely, that of freedom from hypocrisy and malice. The verbs are all of the reflexive form and might be rendered, *thou wilt make thyself gracious, thou wilt act the gracious,* or simply *thou wilt be gracious,* &c., but the common version approaches nearest to the force of the original expression. The first verb of ver. 27 (26) occurs once elsewhere (Dan. xii. 10), the rest only here. The forms may have been coined for the occasion, to express the bold conception of the writer. The resemblance of the last clause of ver. 27 (26) to Lev. xxvi. 23, 24, makes it highly probable that the whole form of this singular dictum was suggested by that passage, the rather as this Psalm abounds in allusions to the Pentateuch and imitations of it.

28 (27). *For thou wilt save the afflicted people, and lofty eyes thou wilt bring down.* Another general description of God's dealings with mankind, repeated more than once in the New Testament. See Mat. xxiii. 12, Luke xiv. 11, xviii. 14. *High looks* or *lofty eyes* is a common Old Testament expression for pride and haughtiness. See below, on Ps. ci. 5, cxxxi. 1, and compare Prov. xxi. 4, xxx. 13, Isa. x. 12, xxxvii. 23. *The afflicted people* means the people of God when in affliction, or considered as sufferers. *Thou* is emphatic : "however men may despise and maltreat thy afflicted people, I know that *thou* wilt save them."

29 (28). *For thou wilt light my lamp ; Jehovah, my God, will illuminate my darkness.* Having ascended from particulars to generals, he now reverses the process. On his own experience, as described in ver. 4–25 (3–24), he had founded a general declaration of God's mode of dealing with men, which statement he proceeds now to illustrate by recurring to his own experience. In this second part there is reason to believe that he has reference to the other cases of deliverance in his history, besides those from Saul's persecutions which had furnished the theme of his thanksgiving in the first part of the psalm. In accordance with this difference of subject, it has been observed that in this second part he appears more active, and not merely as an object but an instrument of God's delivering mercy. As to the form of expression in this part, it has been determined by the writer's assuming his position at the close of the Sauline persecution, and describing his subsequent deliverances as still prospective. This was the more con-

venient, as he wished to express a confident assurance of God's goodness, not only to himself individually but to his posterity. A lamp or candle in the house is a common Hebrew figure for prosperity, and its extinction for distress. See Job xviii. 5, 6, xxi. 17, Prov. xxiv. 20. The first clause may also be translated, *thou wilt make my light shine*. The verb in the parallel clause is from another root, and there is consequently no such assonance as in the English version (*light, enlighten*). The pronoun in the first clause is again emphatic. " Whatever I may suffer at the hands of others, THOU at least wilt light my candle." The emphasis is sustained in the last clause by a sudden change of person and introduction of the divine name.

30 (29). *For in thee I shall run* (through or over) *a troop, and in my God I shall leap a wall.* From his ideal post of observation he foresees the military triumphs which awaited him, and which were actually past at the time of composition. The *for*, as in the two preceding verses, connects the illustration with the general proposition in ver. 27–29 (26–28). "This is certainly God's mode of dealing, *for* I know that he will deal thus with me." *In thee*, and *in my God, i. e.* in intimate union with him and possession of him, a much stronger sense than that of mere assistance (*by thee*), which however, is included. See below, on Ps. xliv. 6 (5).—The ellipsis of the preposition, with which the verbs are usually construed, belongs to the licence of poetical style. Even in prose, however, we can say, to walk the streets, to leap a wall. To *run a troop* may either mean to run *against* or *through* it ; the phrase may therefore be completed so as to have either an offensive or defensive sense. In like manner, leaping a wall may either mean escaping from an enemy or storming his defences. Most interpreters prefer the stronger meaning of attack, which is certainly entitled to the preference, unless the writer be supposed to have selected his expressions with a view to the suggestion of both these ideas, which together comprehend all possible varieties of success in war. As if he had said, " Weak though I be in myself, I am sure that in conjunction with thee, neither armies nor fortifications shall be able to subdue or even to resist me." With David's tone of triumphant confidence in this verse, compare Paul's in 2 Cor. ii. 14, and Philip. iv. 13.

31 (30). *The Almighty—perfect is his way—the word of Jehovah is tried —a shield* (*is*) *he to all those trusting in him.* The first clause seems to be an amplification of *my God* in the preceding verse. *In my God, the Mighty* (*God*), *whose way is perfect, i. e.* his mode of dealing, as before described, is free from all taint of injustice. This explanation suggests a further description of Jehovah as a sure protector. *His word* here means especially his promise, perhaps with specific allusion to the seventh chapter of 2 Samuel. *Tried*, as metals are tried by fire, and thus proved to be genuine ; see above, on Ps. xii. 7 (6). *A shield ;* see above, on Ps. iii. 4 (3). *Trusting in him ;* see above, on Ps. ii. 12.

32 (31). *For who is God save Jehovah ? And who is a rock besides our God ?* The *for* shews that this verse gives the ground of the strong assurances contained in that before it. " I affirm all this because I recognise Jehovah as the only true God." *Rock* has the same sense as in ver. 3 (2). The whole verse bears a strong resemblance to 2 Sam. vii. 22.

33 (32). *The Almighty girding me with strength, and* (*who*) *has given* (*or rendered*) *my way perfect.* The connection of the verses is the same as that between ver. 31 (30) and 32 (31). The *our God* of the preceding verse is here described as *the Almighty girding me*, &c. For the true

sense of the divine name here and in ver. 32 (31), see above, on Ps. v. 5 (4). vii. 12, (11), x. 11, 12, xvi. 1, xvii. 6. The imparting of a quality or bestowing of a gift is in various languages described as clothing. Thus the English words *endue* and *invest* have almost lost their original meaning. The figure of girding is peculiarly significant, because in the oriental dress the girdle is essential to all free and active motion. Compare Ps. lxv. 13 (12), as translated in the margin of the English Bible, and Isa. xi. 5. The last clause may either mean, " who is faultless in the way by which he leads me," *i. e.* whose dispensations towards me are free from all injustice ; or, " who gives my conduct the perfection which belongs to it." The first construction gives the words the same sense as in ver. 31 (30), but the other is by far the simplest and most natural, and as such entitled to the preference.

34 (33). *Making my feet like hinds, and on my heights he makes me stand.* The first word properly means equalling, assimilating, the idea of resemblance being expressed in Hebrew both by the verb and by the particle of comparison. The female animal is supposed by some to be mentioned because it was regarded as more fleet, and accordingly we find it used in the Egyptian hieroglyphics as a symbol of swiftness. The name, however, may be used generally, as in English we apply either the masculine or feminine pronoun to some whole species. *My heights*, those which are to be mine by right of conquest and by divine gift. The heights may be either the natural highlands of the country or the artificial heights of its fortified places. It has been disputed whether the swiftness mentioned in the first clause has reference to attack or flight. Most probably both were meant to be included, as in ver. 30 (29) above. For both reasons swiftness of foot was prized in the heroic age, as appears from Homer's standing description of Achilles. See 2 Sam. ii. 18, 1 Chron. xii. 8.

35 (34). *Teaching my hands to war, and my arms have bent a bow of brass.* The construction is continued from the preceding verse, all the participles having reference to the name of God in ver. 33 (32). The last clause is a strong expression for extraordinary strength, which is mentioned merely as a heroic quality. The translation *broken* rests on what is now regarded as a false etymology. Brass was used before iron in Egypt and other ancient countries as a material for arms.

36 (35). *And hast given me a shield, thy salvation; and thy right hand is to hold me up, and thy condescension is to make me great.* In the first clause we may also read *the shield of thy salvation*, or thy shield of salvation, *i. e.* thy saving shield, without material variation of the sense. The futures have reference to the point from which he is surveying things past as still future. The noun in the last clause means *humility*, as an attribute of human character (Prov. xv. 33), but when applied to God, benignant self-abasement, condescending kindness to inferiors. Compare Ps. viii. 5 (4), Isai. lxvi. 1, 2.

37 (36). *Thou wilt enlarge my steps under me, and my ankles shall not swerve.* To enlarge the steps is to afford ample room for walking freely without hindrance. The opposite figure is that of confined steps. See Prov. iv. 12, Job xviii. 7. The meaning of the whole verse is, thou wilt guide me safely.

38 (37). *I am to pursue my enemies and overtake them, and not to turn back until I destroy them.* This is not a threat of vengeance, but a confident anticipation of perpetual triumphs, either in his own person or in that of his descendants. The form of expression in the first clause is borrowed

from the Song of Moses, Exod. xv. 9.   See above on Ps. vii. 6 (5), where
the same two verbs are combined.   The reference of all these future forms
to past time would be not only gratuitous but ungrammatical.

39 (38). *I shall smite them and they cannot rise, they shall fall beneath
my feet.* This simply carries out the idea of successful pursuit in the preceding verse.

40 (39). *And thou hast girded me with strength for the war* (or *battle*),
thou wilt bow down my assailants under me. He returns to God as the
author of his triumphs and successes.   The first clause blends the ideas
expressed in the corresponding clauses of ver. 33, 36 (32, 35).—*My
assailants,* literally, *my insurgents,* those rising up against me.   See ver.
49 below, and compare Ps. xliv. 6 (5), lix. 2 (1), Job xxvii. 7.   Here
again the spirit of the Psalmist is not that of an ambitious conqueror, but
of a willing instrument in God's hand, to be used for the promotion of his
sovereign purpose.

41 (40). *And my enemies—thou hast given to me the back—and my
haters—I will destroy them.* Each clause begins with an absolute nominative which might be rendered, *as to my enemies, as to my haters.*   The
remainder of the first clause is highly idiomatic in its form, and scarcely
admits of an exact translation.   The word translated *back* properly means
the back of the neck, but is frequently used in such connections.   The
meaning of the whole phrase is, thou hast given me their back, *i. e.* made
them to turn it towards me by putting them to flight.   This is also a
Mosaic form of speech.   See Exod. xxiii. 27, and compare Josh. vii. 8,
2 Chron. xxix. 6. Ps. xxi. 13 (12).

42 (41), *They shall call for help, and there is no deliverer—upon Jehovah,
and he hears them not.* Because they have no covenant relation to him, as
the Psalmist had.   Their calling on Jéhovah does not exclude all reference
to heathen foes, as appears from Jonah i. 14.—*Hear,* in the pregnant sense
of hearing favourably, granting, answering a prayer.   See above, on Ps.
iii. 5 (4).

43 (42). *And I shall beat them small as dust before the wind, as dirt in
the streets I will pour them out.* The comparisons in this verse are intended
to express the Psalmist's superiority to his enemies, his consequent contempt for them, and the facility with which he will destroy them.   Similar
images are not unfrequent in the Old Testament.   See for example Isa. x. 6,
Zeph. i. 17. Zech. x. 5.

44 (43). *Thou wilt save me from the strifes of the people ; thou wilt place
me at the head* (or *for a chief*) *of nations ; a people I have not known shall
serve me.* He was not only to be freed from the internal strifes of his own
people, but by that deliverance enabled to subdue other nations.   The
closing words of the psalm, and its obvious connection with the promises in
2 Sam. vii., shew that this anticipation was not limited to David's personal
triumphs, either at home or abroad, but meant to comprehend the victories
of his successors, and especially of him in whom the royal line was at once
to end and be perpetuated.   It may, therefore, be affirmed with truth that
this prediction had its complete fulfilment only in Christ.

45, 46 (44, 45). *At the hearing of the ear they will obey me, the sons of
outland will lie to me; the sons of outland will decay, and tremble out of
their enclosures.* The meaning of the first words of this verse is clear from
Job xlii. 5, where the hearing of the ear is put in opposition to the sight of
the eye, report or hearsay to personal and ocular inspection.   The verb
translated *will obey*, whenever it occurs elsewhere, is a simple passive of the

verb to *hear*, and accordingly some render it here, they who have only been heard of by the hearing of the ear, *i. e.* those whom I have only heard of, but have never seen, will feign obedience. But as the corresponding form of the verb to *lie* (יְכַחֲשׁוּ) is used by Moses actively in Deut. xxxiii. 29, to which place there is an obvious allusion here, the first translation above given is entitled to the preference, and the sense is, that as soon as foreign nations hear of him they will lie to him, *i. e.* yield a feigned obedience through the influence of fear, in which sense another form of the same verb is used, not only in the passage of the Pentateuch just cited, but in Ps. lxvi. 3, lxxxi. 16 (15).—The old word *outland*, which may still be traced in its derivative adjective *outlandish*, has been here employed to represent a Hebrew word for which we have no equivalent in modern English, and which means *foreign parts* indefinitely or collectively. The marginal version in the English Bible (*sons of the stranger*) is only an inexact approximation to the form of the original. The verb *decay*, which properly denotes the withering of plants (see above, Ps. i. 3), is applied to the wasting of the human subject, and indeed of whole communities, in Exod. xviii. 18. To *tremble from*, or *out of*, is a pregnant phrase, involving the idea of a verb of motion, and meaning to come forth with fear. The same form of expression may be found in Micah vii. 17, and analogous ones in 1 Sam. xvi. 4, Hosea xi. 11.—*Their enclosures*, their retreats or refuges, perhaps with special reference to military enclosures, such as fortresses and camps.

47 (46). *Jehovah lives, and blessed be my rock, and high shall be the God of my salvation.* The first phrase, (חַי יְהֹוָה) which is elsewhere always used as a formula of swearing (*as the Lord liveth*, *i. e.* as certainly as God exists), is by some interpreters confounded with a kindred phrase (יְחִי הַמֶּלֶךְ) *vive le roi*, (*long*) *live the king*, and regarded as a kind of acclamation, similar to those which were uttered at the coronation of the Jewish kings (1 Sam. x. 24, 1 Kings i. 25, 39, 2 Kings xi. 12). But besides the difference of form in Hebrew, such a wish is inappropriate to any but a mortal. There may, however, be an intentional allusion to the custom in question, as well as to the practice of swearing by the life of Jehovah, both of which would naturally be suggested to a Hebrew reader. Jehovah is described as the *living God*, in contrast to dead idols, or imaginary deities, which, as Paul says (1 Cor. viii. 4), are nothing in the world. *Blessed be my rock*, the foundation of my hope, my refuge and protector; see above, on ver. 3 (2). The word translated *blessed* does not mean *happy*, but *praised*, and may here have the peculiar sense of *worthy to be praised*, like מְהֻלָּל in ver. 4 (3) above. It may be rendered as an affirmation: My rock (is) worthy to be praised. Or it may be taken as a wish: Praised (be) my rock, to which there is the less objection, as the preceding proposition is, in fact though not in form, a doxology, *i. e.* a declaration of what God is in himself, and of that to which he is in consequence entitled. The third phrase, *he shall be high*, may be understood to mean, not only he shall still be glorious, but he shall be magnified as such, exalted by the praises of his creatures. *The God of my salvation*, or, *my God of salvation*, does not merely mean *the God who saves me*, but *my God who is a Saviour*, of whom this is one essential character. Compare Luke i. 47. This epithet is common in the Psalms, and occurs once or twice in the Prophets. Isa. xvii. 10, Mic. vii. 7, Hab. iii. 18.

48 (47). *The Mighty (God) who gives revenges to me and has subdued nations under me.* The construction is the same as in ver. 31, 33 (30, 32) above. This verse contains a further description of the God of his salvation, and at the same time justifies the affirmations of the preceding verse. What the Psalmist here rejoices in is not vengeance wreaked upon his personal enemies, but punishment inflicted on the enemies of God through himself as a mere instrument. Not to rejoice in this would have proved him unworthy of his high vocation. With the last clause compare Ps. xlvii. 4 (3), cxliv. 2.

49 (48). *Saving me from my enemies; yea, from my assailants (or insurgents) thou wilt raise me high; from the man of violence thou wilt deliver me.* Here again the construction changes from the participle to the finite verb, but with a further change to the second person, which adds greatly to the life and energy of the expression. The *yea* may be taken as a simple copulative, and *assailants* as a mere equivalent to *enemies.* Some prefer, however, to assume a climax, and to understand the verse as meaning that he had not only been delivered from external foes, but from the more dangerous assaults of domestic treason or rebellion. There would then seem to be an allusion to Absalom's conspiracy. *Thou wilt raise me*, set me up on high, beyond the reach of all my enemies. For a similar expression see below, Ps. lix. 2 (1), as translated in the margin of the English Bible. *The man of violence* has, no doubt, reference to Saul, but only as the type of a whole class. Compare Ps. cxl. 2, 5 (1, 4).

50 (49). *Therefore I will thank thee among the nations, O Jehovah, and to thy name will sing.* The first word has reference not merely to the fact of his deliverance and promotion, but to the character in which he had experienced these blessings, and the extent of the divine purpose in bestowing them. "Therefore—because it is God who has done and is to do all this for me, and because it is in execution of a purpose comprehending the whole race—I will not confine my praises and thanksgiving to my own people, but extend them to all nations." The performance of this vow has been going on for ages, and is still in progress wherever this and other psalms of David are now sung or read. The verse before us is legitimately used by Paul, together with Deut. xxxii. 43, Isa. xi. 1, 10, and Ps. cxvii. 1, to prove that, even under the restrictive institutions of the old economy, God was not the God of the Jews only, but of the Gentiles also. (Rom. iii. 29, xv. 9–12).—The verb in the first clause strictly means *I will confess* or *acknowledge,* but is specially applied to the acknowledgment of gifts received or benefits experienced, and then corresponds almost exactly to our *thank.* The corresponding verb in the last clause means to praise by music. See above, on Ps. vii. 18 (17), ix. 3, 12 (2, 11).

51 (50). *Making great the salvations of his King, and doing kindness to his Anointed, to David, and to his seed unto eternity.* We have here another instance of the favourite construction which connects a sentence with the foregoing context by means of a participle agreeing with the subject of a previous sentence; see above, ver. 31 (30), 32 (31), 33 (32), 34 (33), 49 (48). *Making great salvations,* saving often and signally. The plural form conveys the idea of fulness and completeness. As the phrase *His Anointed* might have seemed to designate David exclusively, he shews its comprehensive import by expressly adding *David and his seed,* from which it clearly follows that the *Messiah* or *Anointed One* here mentioned is a complex or ideal person, and that Jesus Christ, far from being excluded, is, in fact, the principal person comprehended, as the last and greatest of the royal line of

David, to whom the promises were especially given, in whom alone they are completely verified, and of whom alone the last words of this psalm could be uttered, in their true and strongest sense, without a falsehood or without absurdity. In this conclusion, as in other portions of the psalm, there is a clear though tacit reference to the promise in 2 Sam. vii. 12–16, 25, 26, where several of the very same expressions are employed. Compare also Ps. xxviii. 8, lxxxiv. 10 (9), and Ps. lxxxix, *passim.*

Another copy of this psalm is found recorded near the close of David's history (2 Sam. ch. xxii.), which confirms the intimation in the title, that it was not composed in reference to any particular occasion, but in a general retrospection of the miseries of his whole life. The two texts often differ, both in form and substance, which has led some to suppose, that one is an erroneous transcript of the other. But this conclusion is forbidden by the uniform consistency of each considered in itself, as well as by the obvious indications of design in the particular variations, which may be best explained by supposing, that David himself, for reasons not recorded, prepared a twofold form of this sublime composition, which is the less improbable, as there are other unambiguous traces of the same process in the Old Testament, and in the writings of David himself. See below, the exposition of Ps. liii., and compare that of Isaiah, ch. xxxvi.–xxxix. If this be a correct hypothesis, the two forms of the eighteenth psalm may be treated as distinct and independent compositions ; and it has therefore been thought most advisable, both for the purpose of saving room and of avoiding the confusion which a parallel interpretation might have caused, to confine the exposition in this volume to that form of the psalm, which was preserved in the Psalter for permanent use in public worship, and which exhibits strong internal proofs of being the original or first conception, although both are equally authentic and inspired.

Psalm 19

THIS psalm consists of three parts. The subject of the first is God's revelation of himself in his material works, ver. 2–7 (1–6). That of the second is the still more glorious revelation of himself in his law, ver. 8–11 (7–10). The third shews the bearing of these truths upon the personal character and interest of the writer, and of all who are partakers of his faith, ver. 12–15 (11–14).

The object of the psalm is not to contrast the moral and material revelations, but rather to identify their author and their subject. The doctrinal sum of the whole composition is, that the same God who reared the frame of nature is the giver of a law, and that this law is in all respects worthy of its author.

1. *To the Chief Musician, a Psalm by David.* The form of this inscription is the same as that of Ps. xiii. Its historical correctness is attested by its position in the Psalter, its resemblance to Ps. viii., and its peculiar style and spirit.

2 (1). *The heavens (are) telling the glory of God, and the work of his hands (is) the firmament declaring.* The participles are expressive of continued action. The *glory of God* is the sum of his revealed perfections (compare Ps. xxiv. 7–10, xxix. 3, Rom. i. 20. The *expanse* or *firmament* is used as an equivalent to *heaven,* even in the history of the creation, Gen. i. 8. To

dec'are the work of his hands is to shew what he can do and has actually done. The common version *handywork* means nothing more than *hand-work ;* to take *handy* as an epithet of praise is a vulgar error.

3 (2). *Day to day shall pour out speech, and night to night shall utter knowledge.* Both verbs are peculiar to the poetical dialect and books of the Old Testament. *Pour out*, in a copious ever-gushing stream. As the participles of ver. 2 (1) express constant action, so the futures here imply continuance in all time to come. *Speech* means the declaration of God's glory, and *knowledge* the knowledge of the same great object. The idea of perpetual testimony is conveyed by the figure of one day and night following another as witnesses in unbroken succession.

4 (3). *There is no speech, and there are no words ; not at all is their voice heard.* As the first clause might have seemed to contradict the first clause of ver. 3 (2), the Psalmist adds *no words*, to shew that he here uses *speech* in the strict sense of articulate language.—The first word of the last clause is properly a noun, meaning cessation or defect, non-entity, and here used as a more emphatic negative, expressed in the translation by the phrase *not at all.*—*Their voice* might either be referred exclusively to the *heaven* and *firmament* of ver. 2 (1), or extended to the *day* and *night* of ver. 3 (2). But the first is the true construction, as appears from the next verse. The absence of articulate language, far from weakening the testimony, makes it stronger. Even without speech or words, the heavens testify of God to all men. This construction of the sentence is much simpler, as well as more exact, than the ancient one, retained in the common version, " there is no speech nor language where their voice is not heard," or that preferred by others, " it is not a speech or language whose voice is not heard." The true sense is given in the margin of the English Bible.

5 (4.) *In all the earth has gone out their line, and in the end of the world* (*are*) *their words. For the sun he has pitched a tent in them.* The word rendered *line* always means a measuring line, and in Jer. xxxi. 39 is combined in that sense with the same verb as here. The idea is, that their province or domain is co-extensive with the earth, and that they speak with authority even in its remotest parts.—*Words* may also be construed with the verb of the first clause, but it will then be necessary to translate the preposition *to.* The explanation of *line* as meaning the string of a musical instrument, and then the sound which it produces, although favoured by the ancient versions, is entirely at variance with Hebrew usage. The subject of the verb in the last clause is the name of God expressed in ver. 2 (1) above.—*Pitched a tent*, provided a dwelling, or without a figure, assigned a place. *In them* must refer to *the heavens* mentioned in ver. 2 (1), which makes it probable that all the plural pronouns in the intervening clauses have the same antecedent. The sun is introduced in this sentence probably because his apparent course is a measure of the wide domain described in the first clause. It must be co-extensive with the earth, because the sun which visits the whole earth has his habitation in the sky. The boundless extension of the heavens and their testimony is used by Paul (Rom. x. 18) to signify the general diffusion of the gospel, and the same thing might have taught the earlier Jews that their exclusive privileges were granted only for a time, and as a means to a more glorious end.

6 (5). *And he* (*is*) *as a bridegroom coming out of his chamber; he rejoices as a mighty man to run a race.* The second simile has reference to the sun's daily course, the first to his vigorous and cheerful reappearance after the darkness of the night. By a fine transition, the general idea of a tent or

dwelling is here exchanged for the specific one of a nuptial couch or chamber. *Rejoices*, literally *will rejoice*, for ever as he now does.

7 (6). *From the end of the heavens (is) his outgoing, and his circuit even to the ends of them, and there is none (or nothing) hidden from his heat.* What is said in ver. 5 (4) of the heavens is here said of the sun, to wit, that his domain is coextensive with the earth or habitable world. The last clause is added to shew that it is not an ineffective presence, but one to be felt as well as seen. The sun's heat is méntioned, not in contrast with his light, but as its inseparable adjunct.—The plural *ends* seems to be added to the singular in order to exhaust the meaning, or at least to strengthen the expression. The word translated *circuit* includes the.idea of return to a starting-point. The Hebrew preposition properly means *up to* (or *down to*) their very extremity.

8 (7). *The law of Jehovah is perfect, restoring the soul ; the testimony of Jehovah is sure, making wise the simple.* The God, whose glory is thus shewn forth by the material creation, is the author of a spiritual law, which the Psalmist now describes in the next three verses, by six characteristic names, six qualifying epithets, and six moral effects produced by it. In the verse before us, besides the usual term *law*, it is called God's *testimony*, *i. e.* the testimony which he bears for truth and against iniquity. It is described as *perfect*, *i. e.* free from all defect or blemish, and as sure, *i. e.* definite, decided, and infallible. Its two effects, mentioned in this verse. are, first, that of *restoring the soul, i. e.* the life and spirits exhausted by calamity. See below, on Ps. xxiii. 3, and compare Ruth. iv. 15, Lam. i. 11, 16. The effect of *converting the soul* would not have been attributed to the law in this connection, where the writer is describing the affections cherished towards the law by men already converted, which removes all apparent inconsistency with Paul's representation of the law as working death, and at the same time the necessity of making the law mean the gospel, or in any other way departing from the obvious and usual import of the Hebrew word. The other effect ascribed to the law is that of *making wise the simple*, not the foolish, in the strong sense in which that term is applied to the ungodly—see above, on Ps. xiv. 1—but those imperfectly enlightened and still needing spiritual guidance, a description applicable, more or less, to all believers. It is a singular fact, that while this usage of the Hebrew word is peculiar to David, Solomon constantly applies it to the culpable simplicity of unconverted men. (See Ps. cxvi. 6, cxix. 130, Prov. i. 22, vii. 7, ix. 4, xiv. 15, &c.)—In like manner Paul describes the " sacred scriptures " as *able to make wise unto salvation*, 2 Tim. iii. 15.

9 (8). *The statutes of Jehovah (are) right, rejoicing the heart ; the commandment of Jehovah is pure, enlightening the eyes.* The words translated *statute* and *commandment* differ very slightly from each other, the one expressing more distinctly the idea of a charge or commission, the other that of a prescription or direction. There is also no great difference between the epithets applied in this verse to the law of God, which is *right*, as being an exact expression of his rectitude, and *pure*, as being free from all taint of injustice or iniquity. The first effect described is that of *rejoicing the heart*, to wit, the heart loving righteousness, and consequently desirous of knowing what is right by knowing what is acceptable to God, and what is required by him. The other effect, *enlightening the eyes*, is understood by some of intellectual illumination with respect to spiritual things. But it is more agreeable to Hebrew usage to suppose an allusion to the dimness of the eyes produced by extreme weakness and approaching death, recovery

from which is figuratively represented as an enlightening of the eyes. See
above, on Ps. xiii. 4 (3), and compare Ps. xxxiv. 6 (5). The figure,
thus explained, bears a strong resemblance to *restoring the soul* in the
preceding verse, the one referring rather to the sense, and the other to
the life itself.

10 (9). *The fear of Jehovah is clean, standing for ever ; the judgments of
Jehovah are truth, they are righteous altogether.* As the fear of Jehovah, in
its proper sense, would here be out of place, and as the law was designed to
teach men how to fear the Lord (Deut. xvii. 19), the phrase may here
be understood as a description of the law viewed in reference to this peculiar
purpose, the *fear of the Lord* being put for that which leads or teaches
men to fear him, a sense which the expression is supposed to have in several
other places. See Ps. xxxiv. 12 (11), Prov. i. 29, ii. 5, xv. 33.—*Standing
for ever*, of perpetual obligation. Even Christ came not to destroy, but to
fulfil. See Mat. v. 17, 18. With the form of expression here compare
Ps. xxxiii. 11, cxii. 3.—*Judgments* are properly judicial decisions, but
are here put, as in Ps. xviii. 23 (22), for all God's requisitions. *They are
truth* (*itself*) may be a strong expression, meaning they are perfectly and
absolutely true ; but as this would make the last clause little more than a
tautology, the first phrase may be understood to mean that they are really
that which they purport and claim to be, and therefore must be *righteous
altogether, i. e.* all, without exception, righteous, which is tantamount, in
fact, though not in form, to *wholly* or *completely righteous.*

11 (10). (*Judgments*) *to be desired more than gold, and much fine gold;
and sweeter than honey and the dropping of the combs.* The description of
the law of God is wound up by comparing it to the costliest and sweetest
substance in common use. The sense of the passive participle is like that
in Ps. xviii. 4 (3). Its plural form, and the article prefixed to it in Hebrew,
shew that it is to be construed with *judgments*, and that the sentence
is continued from the foregoing verse, as in Ps. xviii. 31 (30), 33 (32), 34
(33), 35 (34), 48 (47), 51 (50).—The Hebrew answering to *fine gold* is a
single word (פָּז), not used in prose, and by some supposed to mean solid
or massive gold, but according to a more probable etymology denoting
purified or fine gold. The combination here used is found also in Ps. cxix.
127. See also Prov. viii. 19, and compare Ps. xxi. 4 (3), below. To
make the resemblance of the clauses perfect, the usual word for *honey* is
followed by a beautiful periphrasis, denoting that kind which was most
highly valued, The ideas expressed by both comparisons are those of
value and delightfulness.—As the preceding verses describe what the law
is in itself and in its general effects, so this seems to express what it is to
the Psalmist's apprehensions and affections, thus affording a transition
from the comprehensive doctrines of the foregoing context to the practical
and personal approbation of those doctrines, which now follows and concludes the psalm.

12 (11). *Moreover, thy servant is enlightened by them ; in keeping them
there is much reward.* The verb in the first clause is used with special
reference to admonition and warning against danger. See Eccles. iv. 13,
Exod. xxxiii. 4, 5, 6, Eccles. xii. 12. The plural suffixes have reference to
judgments in ver. 10 (9) above.—*Reward* is here used not to signify a
recompence earned in strict justice, but a gratuity bestowed. The spirit of
the passage is the same as in 1 Cor. xv. 19, 1 Tim. iv. 8. The phrase

thy servant brings the general doctrines of the foregoing context into personal application to the writer.

13 (12). *Errors who shall understand? Clear thou me from hidden ones!* The word translated *errors* is akin to one sometimes used in the Law to denote sins of inadvertence, error, or infirmity, as distinguished from deliberate, wilful, and high-handed sins, such as are deprecated in the next verse. See Lev. iv. 2–27, Num. xv. 27. Against such sins no wisdom or vigilance can wholly guard.—The word translated *clear* is also borrowed from the Law, and means not so much to cleanse by renovation of the heart, as to acquit by a judicial sentence. See Exod. xxxiv. 7, Num. xiv. 18. Such an acquittal, in the case of sinners against God, involves the idea of a free forgiveness.

14 (13). *Also from presumptuous (ones) withhold thy servant; then shall I be perfect and be clear from much transgression.* As he prays 'for the forgiveness of his inadvertent sins, so he prays for the prevention of deliberate ones. The Hebrew word (זֵדִים) properly denotes proud men, but seems to be here applied to sins by a strong personification. The use of the verbal root and its derivatives in the Old Testament may be seen by comparing Exod. xxi. 14, Deut. xvii. 12, xviii. 22, 1 Sam. xvii. 28.—To be perfect has the same sense as in Ps. xviii. 24–26 (23–25). That it does not there mean sinless perfection is confirmed by the language of the verse before us.—*The great transgression*, as if referring to some one particular offence, is not the true sense of the Hebrew phrase, which is indefinite and perfectly analogous to that rendered *much* (or *great*) *reward* in ver. 12 (11) above.

15 (14). *(Then) shall be for acceptance* (or *acceptable*) *the sayings of my mouth, and the thought of my heart before thee, Jehovah, my rock and my redeemer.* The simplest and most obvious construction of the Hebrew sentence makes it a direct continuation of the last clause of ver. 14 (13), and like it an anticipation of the happy effects to be expected from an answer to the foregoing prayers. If his sins of ignorance could be forgiven, and the deliberate sins, to which his natural corruption prompts him, hindered by divine grace, he might hope not only to avoid much guilt but to be the object of God's favour. As this confident anticipation really involves a wish that it may be fulfilled, there is little real difference between the construction above given and the common version: *let the words of my mouth and the meditation of my heart be acceptable, &c.* It is much more natural, however, to connect the words *before thee* with *my meditation*, which immediately precedes, than with the first words of the verse as in the English Bible. *What I think in thy presence* is then joined with *the words of my mouth*, to express all prayer, whether clothed in words or not. See above, on Ps. v. 2 (1). The prayer or expectation of acceptance in this clause derives peculiar beauty from the obvious allusion to the frequent use of the same Hebrew phrase (לְרָצוֹן) in the law of Moses, to denote the acceptance of the sacrificial offerings, or rather the acceptance of the offerer on account of them. See Exod. xxviii. 38, Lev. xix. 5, 7, xxii. 19, 20, 29, xxiii. 11, Isa. lvi. 7, lx. 7, Rom. xii. 1. This allusion also serves to suggest the idea, not conveyed by a translation, of atonement, expiation, as the ground of the acceptance which the Psalmist hopes or prays for.

Psalm 20

A PRAYER for the use of the ancient church in time of war. Addressing her visible head, she wishes him divine assistance and success, ver. 2-6 (1–5), and expresses a strong confidence that God will answer her petition, ver. 7–9 (6–8), which she then repeats and sums up in conclusion, ver. 10 (9).

There is no trace of this psalm having been composed with reference to any particular occasion, its contents being perfectly appropriate to every case in which the chosen people under their theocratic head, engaged in war against the enemies of God and Israel.

To the Chief Musician. Written for his use and entrusted to him for execution. As in all other cases, this inscription shews the psalm to have been written, not for the expression of mere personal feelings, but to be a vehicle of pious sentiment to the collective body of God's people.—*A Psalm by David.* The correctness of this statement is not only free from any positive objection, but confirmed by the whole tone and style of the performance, as well as by its intimate connection with the next psalm. See below, on Ps. xxi. 1.

2 (1). *Jehovah hear thee in the day of trouble! The name of Jacob's God exalt thee!* The name of God, the revelation of his nature in his acts. " May those divine attributes, which have been so often manifested in the experience of the chosen people, be exercised for thy protection. See above, on Ps. v. 12 (11).—*The God of Jacob*, of the patriarch so called, and of his seed. See Mat. xxii. 32.—*Exalt thee*, raise thee beyond the reach of danger. See above, on Ps. ix. 10 (9), xviii. 3, 49 (2, 48).

3 (2). *(May Jehovah) send thee help from (his) sanctuary, and from Zion sustain thee.* The mention of Zion and the sanctuary shews that Jehovah is appealed to as the king of his people, and as such not only able but bound by covenant to afford them aid. See below, on ver. 10 (9.) *Sustain thee*, hold thee up, the same verb that is used in Ps. xviii. 36 (35). Both verbs may also be translated as simple futures, *will send, will sustain;* but see below.

4 (3). *(May Jehovah) remember all thy gifts and accept thy offering. Selah.* The word *remember* in the first clause seems to involve an allusion to the *memorial* (אַזְכָּרָה), a name given in the sacrificial ritual to that part of the vegetable offering which was burnt upon the altar. See Lev. ii. 2, vi. 8 (15).—The word translated *gifts*, although properly generic, is specially used to denote the vegetable offerings of the law, while the word translated *offering* is the technical name of the principal animal sacrifice. They are put together to describe these two species of obligation. Compare Ps. xl. 7 (6), Jer. xvii. 26, Dan. ix. 27.—The verb translated *accept* means elsewhere to make fat (Ps. xxiii. 5), or to remove the ashes of the altar. (Exod. xxvii. 3, Num. iv. 13). Some give it here the sense of turning into ashes or consuming, others that of pronouncing fat, and therefore fit for sacrifice. In either case acceptance is implied. The optative form of the verb in the original seems to confirm the sense already put upon the foregoing futures. From this verse it has been inferred, with some probability, that the whole psalm was specially intended to be used at the sacrifice offered by the Israelites before a campaign or a battle. (See 1 Sam. xiii. 9, 10). To this some add the supposition, that the *selah*, in the verse be-

fore us, marks the pause in the performance of the psalm, during which the sacrifice was actually offered. See above, on Ps. iii. 3 (2).

5 (4). *(May he) give thee according to thy heart, and all thy counsel* (or *design) fulfil.* This is not a vague wish for success in general, but a prayer for success on the particular occasion when the psalm was to be used.— *Thy heart,* thy desire. *Thy counsel,* the plan which thou hast formed and undertaken to execute in God's name, and for the protection or deliverance of his people.

6 (5). *May we rejoice in thy deliverance, and in the name of our God display a banner! May Jehovah fulfil all thy petitions!* The phrase *thy deliverance* may mean that wrought or that experienced by thee. In all probability both ideas are included. *In the name of our God,* and therefore not as a mere secular triumph. The second verb (נִדְגֹּל) seems to be connected with a noun (דֶּגֶל) used by Moses to denote the banners under which the four great divisions of the host marched through the wilderness (Num. i. 52, ii. 2, 3, 10, 18, 25, x. 14). Hence the conjectural translation, " may we set up (or display) a banner." But as the participle of the same verb seems, in the only other place where it occurs (Song of Sol. v. 10), to signify *distinguished* or *exalted,* others follow the Septuagint and Vulgate in translating, *may we be lifted up* or *magnified.*—The last clause is a comprehensive prayer, equivalent in meaning to ver. 5 (4) above, and including not merely what had been expressly specified, but all that the theocratic sovereign might desire or attempt in conformity with God's will, whether known to the whole body of his followers or not. This clause concludes the first division of the psalm by recurring to the theme with which it opens, and with which again the whole psalm closes. See below, on ver. 10 (9).

7 (6). *Now I know that Jehovah has saved his Anointed—he will hear him from his holy heavens—with the saving strength of his right hand.* What was asked in the foregoing context is here said to be already granted. Hence some imagine that a battle or other decisive event must be supposed to intervene. But this, besides being highly improbable and forced in so brief a composition, is forbidden by the immediate recurrence to the future form, *he will hear.* A far more natural solution is, that this verse expresses a sudden conviction or assurance that the preceding prayers are to be answered. As if he had said: "Such are my requests, and I know that Jehovah has already granted them, so that in his purpose and to the eye of faith, his Anointed is already safe, and has already triumphed." The change to the first person singular does not indicate a different speaker, but merely puts what follows into the mouth of each individual believer, or of the whole body viewed as an ideal person.

The second member of the sentence may be best explained as a parenthesis, leaving the third to be construed directly with the first, as in the version above given. In this verse we have two examples of a common Hebrew idiom, one of them a very strong one. The phrase translated *from his holy heavens* might seem to mean *the heavens of his holiness;* but the true construction is *his heavens of holiness, i. e.* the heavens where the Holy One resides, and from which his assistance must proceed. See above, on Ps. ii. 6, xi. 4. The attribute of holiness is mentioned to exalt still further the divine and sacred nature of the warfare and the victory to which the psalm relates. Another example of the Hebrew idiom before referred to is *the saving strength of his right hand,* which literally rendered is *the strengths*

of the salvation of his right hand. The plural *strengths* may either be intensive, or refer to the various exertions of the power here described. The
right hand has the same sense as in Ps. xviii. 36 (35). Here, as in Ps.
xviii. 51 (50), *His Messiah or Anointed One* includes the whole succession
of genuine theocratic kings, not excepting him whose representatives they
were, and in whom the royal line was at the same time closed and made
perpetual.

8 (7). *These in chariots and these in horses, and we in the name of Jehovah
our God, will glory.* All the objects are connected by the same preposition with the same verb, namely, that at the end of the sentence. In
order to retain the preposition, which must otherwise be varied, and thereby
obscure the structure of the sentence, the verb *glory*, which is construed
with the preposition *in*, has been substituted for the strict sense of the
verb, *we will cause to be remembered, i. e.* mention or commemorate. See
Exod. xxiii. 13, Amos vi. 10, Isa. xlviii. 1, lxiii. 7. The insertion of the
verb *trust*, in the English versions of the first clause, is entirely gratuitous.
These and these is the Hebrew idiom for *some and others.* Compare *this to
this*, in Exod. xiv. 20, Isa. vi. 3.—The verb, in the case before us, may
have been selected in allusion to the cognate form in ver. 4 (3) above.
" As God has remembered thy offerings, so we will cause his name to be
remembered."—*Our God* is again emphatic and significant, as shewing that
the whole psalm has reference to the covenant relation between God and
his people represented by their theocratic sovereign. With the contrast
in this verse compare 1 Sam. xvii. 45, Isa. xxxi. 3, Ps. xxxiii. 16, 17.

9 (8). *They have bowed and fallen, and we have risen and stood upright.*
Here, as in ver. 7 (6), the past tense expresses the certainty of the event,
or rather the confidence with which it is expected. The emphatic *they* at
the beginning means the enemies and oppressors of God's people. *We have
arisen* seems to imply a previous prostration and subjection.—The last verb
occurs only here in this form, which is properly reflexive, and may be explained to mean, *we have straightened ourselves up.*

10 (9). *Jehovah, save! Let the King hear us in the day we call*, or still
more closely, *in the day of our calling.* The Septuagint and Vulgate make
the king a part of the first clause: " Jehovah, save the king " (*Domine
salvum fac regem*). But this not only violates the masoretic accents, which,
though not ultimately binding, are entitled to respect as a traditional
authority, but separates the verb in the last clause from its subject, so that
both the ancient versions just referred to have been under the necessity of
changing the third into the second person (*hear us*). The first clause is
besides more expressive and emphatic without *the king* than with it. Nothing could be more pregnant or sonorous than the laconic prayer, *Jehovah,
save!* The object is, of course, to be supplied from ver 7 (6), and from the
tenor of the whole psalm. The other construction, it is true, enables us to
make *the King* of this verse the same person with *the Anointed* of ver. 7 (6).
But far from any disadvantage, there is great force and beauty, in referring the
expected blessing to the true King of Israel, whom David and his followers
only represented. See Deut. xxxiii. 5, Ps. xlviii. 3 (2), Mat. v. 35.—By
taking the last verb as a future proper (*the King will hear us*) the psalm may
be made to close with a promise, or rather with a confident anticipation of
God's blessing. Most interpreters, however, prefer to make it optative,
and thus to let the psalm conclude as it began, with an expression of intense
desire.

Psalm 21

As in the eighteenth psalm, David publicly thanks God for the promises contained in 2 Sam. vii., so here he puts a similar thanksgiving into the mouth of the church or chosen people. In ver. 2–7 (1–6), the address is to Jehovah, and the king is spoken of in the third person. In ver. 8 (7) this form of speech is used in reference to both. In ver. 9–13 (8–12) the address is to the king. In ver. 14 (13) it returns to Jehovah. As to the substance or contents of these successive parts, the first praises God for what he has bestowed upon the king, ver. 2–7 (1–6). In the second, there is a transition to another theme, ver. 8 (7). The third congratulates the king on what he is to do and to enjoy through the divine mercy, ver. 9–13 (8–12). The fourth returns to the point from which the whole set out, ver. 14 (13). The opinion that this psalm relates to the fulfilment of the prayer in that before it, seems to be inconsistent with its structure and contents as just described. They are rather parallel than consecutive, the principal difference being this, that while the twentieth psalm relates to the specific case of assistance and, success in war, the twenty-first has reference to the whole circle of divine gifts bestowed upon the Lord's Anointed.

1. *To the Chief Musician. A Psalm by David.* The correctness of the first inscription is apparent from the structure of the psalm, throughout which the speaker is the ancient church. The correctness of the other may be argued from the general resemblance of the style to that of the Davidic psalms, from numerous coincidences of expression with the same, and from the tone of lively hope which seems to indicate the recent date of the divine communication, especially when compared with psalms which otherwise resemble it, such as the eighty-ninth. The particular resemblance between this psalm and the twentieth makes them mutually testify to one another's genuineness and authenticity.

2 (1). *Jehovah, in'thy strength shall the king rejoice, and in thy salvation how shall he exult!* This verse commences the description of God's favour to the king with a general statement, afterwards amplified in ver. 3–7 (2–6). *Thy strength,* as imparted to him, or as exercised in his deliverance, which last agrees best with the parallel expression, *thy salvation, i.e.* thy deliverance of him from the evils which he felt or feared. *In thy strength and salvation, i.e.* in the contemplation and experience of it. The future verbs shew that the gift has not yet been consummated, without excluding the idea of it as begun already.

3 (2). *The desire of his heart thou hast given unto him, and the quest of his lips hast not withholden. Selah.* The occasion of the joy and exultation mentioned in the preceding verse is now more particularly set forth. It is easy to imagine, although not recorded, that the great promise in the seventh chapter of 2 Samuel was in answer to the fervent and long-continued prayers of David for a succession in his own family.—The word translated *quest* occurs only here, but its sense is determined by the parallelism and the Arabic analogy. The combination of the positive and negative expressions of the same idea (*given* and *not withholden*) is a favourite Hebrew idiom.

4 (3). *For thou wilt come before him with blessings of goodness, thou wilt set upon his head a crown of gold.* This, as Luther observes, is an answer to the question what he had desired. The *for* connects it with the state-

ment in the foregoing verse, which is here explained and justified. As the
preterites in ver. 3 (2) shew that his request was granted in the divine purpose, so the futures here shew how it was to be fulfilled in fact. *Come
before*, come to meet in a friendly manner. See above, on Ps. xvii. 13,
xviii. 6 (5), and compare Deut. xxiii. 5 (4).—*Blessings of good*, not blessings
prompted by the divine goodness, but conferring, or consisting in, good
fortune, happiness. See above, on Ps. xvi. 2.—The reference in the last
clause is not to David's literal coronation at the beginning of his reign, nor
to the golden crown which he took from the Ammonitish king of Rabbah
(2 Sam. xii. 30), but to his ideal coronation by the granting of these glorious
favours to himself and his successors. The divine communication in the
seventh of 2 Samuel seems to be here viewed, as the only real coronation
of David as a theocratic sovereign. The last word in the sentence is the
same that was translated *pure gold* when contrasted with the ordinary word
for gold, Ps. xix. 11 (10).

5 (4). *Life he asked of thee, thou hast given (it) to him, length of days,
perpetuity and eternity.* By disregarding the masoretic interpunction, the
construction may be simplified without a change of sense. " Life he asked
of thee, thou hast given him length of days," &c. The last words of the
verse are often used adverbially to mean *for ever and ever ;* but as they are
both nouns, it is best to put them here in apposition with the same part of
speech which immediately precedes. This last clause shews that the life
which David prayed for was not personal longevity, but the indefinite continuation of his race, an honour which was granted to him, even beyond
his hopes and wishes, in the person of our Saviour. Compare 2 Sam. vii.
13, 16. Ps. lxxxix. 5 (4), cxxxii. 12.

6 (5). *Great shall be his majesty in thy salvation ; glory and honour thou
wilt put upon him.* His personal experience of God's saving grace, and his
connection with the great scheme of salvation for mankind, would raise him
to a dignity far beyond that of any other monarch, and completely justifying
even the most exalted terms used in Scripture, from the charge of adulation
or extravagance.

7 (6). *For thou wilt make him a blessing to eternity ; thou wilt gladden
him with joy by thy countenance* (or *presence*). He shall not only be blessed
himself, but a blessing to others, the idea and expression being both derived
from the promise to Abraham in Gen. xii. 2, an allusion which serves also
to connect the Davidic with the Abrahamic covenant, and thus to preserve
unbroken the great chain of Messianic prophecies. *Make him a blessing,*
literally, *place him for* (or *constitute him*) *blessing.* The plural form suggests
variety and fulness, as in Ps. xviii. 51 (50), xx. 7 (6). *By thy countenance,*
or *with thy face, i. e.* by looking on him graciously, not merely in thy presence or before thee, as the place of the enjoyment, but by the sight of thee,
as its cause or source. See above, on Ps. xvi. 11.

8 (7). *For the king (is) trusting in Jehovah, and in the grace of the Most
High he shall not be moved.* The consummation of this glorious promise
was indeed far distant, but to the eye of faith distinctly visible. *In the grace*
seems to mean something more than *through the grace* (or *favour*) *of the
Most High*, as the ground of his assurance, or the source of his security.
The words appear to qualify the verb itself, and to denote that he shall not
be shaken from his present standing in God's favour. The use of the third
person in this verse, with reference both to God and the king, makes it a
kind of connecting link between the direct address to God in the first part
of the psalm, and the direct address to the king in the second.

9 (8). *Thy hand shall find out all thine enemies; thy right hand shall find (those) hating thee.* Having shewn what God would do for his Anointed, the psalm now describes what the latter shall accomplish through divine assistance. Corresponding to this variation in the subject, is that in the object of address, which has been already noticed. By a kind of climax in the form of expression, *hand* is followed by *right hand*, a still more emphatic sign of active strength. To *find*, in this connection, includes the ideas of detecting and reaching. Compare 1 Sam. xxiii. 17, Isa. x. 10; in the latter of which places the verb is construed with a preposition (ל), as it is in the first clause of the verse before us, whereas in the other clause it governs the noun directly. If any difference of meaning was intended, it is probably not greater than that between *find* and *find out* in English.

10 (9). *Thou shalt make them like a fiery furnace at the time of thy presence; Jehovah in his wrath shall swallow them up, and fire shall devour them.* The ascription of this destroying agency to God in the last clause serves to shew that the king acts merely as his instrument. *Thou shalt make*, literally *set* or *place, i. e.* put them in such or such a situation. *A fiery furnace*, literally *a furnace* (or *oven*) *of fire.* To make them like a furnace here means, not to make them the destroyers of others, but, by a natural abbreviation, to make them as if they were in a fiery furnace. *At the time of thy presence*, literally *thy face*, which may be understood to mean, *when thou lookest at them.*

11 (10). *Their fruit shalt thou make to perish from the earth, and their seed from (among) the sons of man* (or *Adam*). This extends the threatened destruction of the enemies to all their generations. The same figurative use of *fruit* occurs in Hos. ix. 16.

12 (11). *For they stretched out evil over thee; they devised a plot; they shall not be able* (to effect it). The figure of the first clause is the same as in 1 Chron. xxi. 10. (Compare 2 Sam. xxiv. 12.) The idea here is that they threatened to bring evil on thee. As the verb to *be able* is sometimes used absolutely, it is translated, *they shall not prevail.*

13 (12). *For thou shalt make them turn their back; with thy (bow) strings shalt make ready against their face.* The common version of the first word (*therefore*) is not only contrary to usage, but disturbs the sense by obscuring the connection with the foregoing verse, which is this: " they shall not prevail, *because* thou shalt make them turn their back." This last phrase, in Hebrew, is so strongly idiomatic that it scarcely admits of an exact translation. *Thou shalt make* (or *place*) *them shoulder.* See above, on Ps. xviii 41 (40), where a similar idiom occurs. In the verse before us, the chronological succession is reversed; it was by shooting at their face that he should make them turn their back. The true relation of the clauses is denoted, in the English Bible, by supplying a particle of time: " thou shalt make them turn their back (when) thou shalt make ready (thine arrows) upon thy strings against the face of them." The version *make ready* is also a correct one, although some translate the phrase *take aim*, which is really expressed by another form of the same verb. The true sense of the one here used is clear from Ps. xi. 2, and the distinctive use of both from Ps. vii. 13, 14 (12, 13).

14 (13). *Be high, Jehovah, in thy strength; we will sing and celebrate thy power.* Here the psalm returns to God as its great theme, and gives him all the glory. *Be high*, exalted, both in thyself and in the praises of thy people. See above, on Ps. xviii. 47 (46). *Thy strength and power*, as

displayed in the strength given to thine anointed. *Celebrate* by music, as
the Hebrew verb always means. There is a beautiful antithesis in this
verse, as if he had said : thou hast only to deserve praise, we will give it.

Psalm 22

THE subject of this Psalm is the deliverance of a righteous sufferer
from his enemies, and the effect of this deliverance on others. It is so
framed as to be applied without violence to any case belonging to the class
described, yet so that it was fully verified only in Christ, the head and representative of the class in question. The immediate speaker in the psalm is an
ideal person, the righteous servant of Jehovah, but his words may, to a
certain extent, be appropriated by any suffering believer, and by the whole
suffering church, as they have been in all ages.

The psalm may be divided into three nearly equal parts. The first
pleads the necessity of God's interposition, arising from his covenant relation to the sufferer, ver. 2–11 (1–10). The second argues the same
thing from the imminence of the danger, ver. 12–22 (11–21). The
third declares the glorious effects which must follow from an answer to the
foregoing prayer, ver. 23–32 (22–31). Ver. 12 (11) and 22 (21) form
connecting links between the first and second, second and third parts.

1. *To the Chief Musician. On the hind of the morning. A Psalm by
David.* Designed for the permanent use of the church, and therefore not
relating to mere individual or private interests. The second clause of the
inscription is one of those enigmatical titles in which David seems to have
delighted. See above, on Ps. v. 1, vii. 1, ix. 1, xvi. 1. The opinion
that it refers to the melody or subject of some other poem, is less probable
than that it describes the theme of this. The *hind* may then be a poetical
figure for persecuted innocence, and the *morning*, or rather *dawn*, for deliverance after long distress. Compare 2 Sam. i. 19, Prov. vi. 5, Isa.
xiii. 14, with Isa. viii. 20, xlvii. 11, lviii. 8, 10, Hos. vi. 3, x. 15. The
use of such emblems here is less surprising, as this psalm abounds in
figures drawn from the animal kingdom. See below, ver. 13 (12), 14
(13), 17 (16), 21 (20), 22 (21).

2 (1). *My God, my God, why hast thou forsaken me, far from my deliverance, the words of my roaring ?* In this verse and the next we have the
sufferer's complaint, the summary description of his danger and distress,
the highest point of which is here described as the sense of desertion or
abandonment on God's part. " Why hast thou left me so to suffer, that I
cannot but consider myself finally deserted ? " The use of these words by
our Saviour on the cross, with a slight variation from the Hebrew (Mat.
xxvii. 46, Mark xv. 34), shews how eminently true the whole description is
of him, but does not make him the exclusive subject. The divine name
here used is the one descriptive of God's power (אֵל), and may therefore be
considered as including the idea of *my strength*. " Why hast thou, whom
I regarded as my strength, my support, and my protector, thus forsaken
me in this extremity?" The last clause admits of several constructions.
" Far from my deliverance (are) the words of my roaring," *i. e.* they are
far from having the effect of saving me. Or the question may be repeated :
(Why art thou) far from my help and the words of my roaring ?" Or the
same idea may be expressed by a simple affirmation : " (Thou art) far from

my help," &c. But the simplest construction is to put these words into apposition with the object of address in the first clause, and throw the whole into one sentence. " Why hast thou forsaken me, (standing or remaining) far from my help, *i. e.* too far off to help and save me, or even to hear the words of my roaring ? " This last combination shews that although the figure of roaring is borrowed from the habits of the lower animals, the subject to which it is applied must be a human one, and as such capable of articulate speech. The roaring of the psalmist was not the mere instinctive utterance of physical distress, but the complaint of an intelligent and moral agent. Compare Isaiah xxxviii. 14.

3 (2). *My God, I call by day and thou wilt not answer, and by night and there is no silence to me.* The divine name here used is the common Hebrew word for *God*, denoting an object of religious worship. *I call*, literally *I shall call*, implying a sorrowful conviction that his cries will still be vain. *Thou wilt not hear* or *answer :* the original expression is a verb specifically appropriated to the favourable reception of a prayer. See above, on Ps. iii. 5 (4). *Day and night, i. e.* without intermission. See above, on Ps. i. 2. *No silence* implies *no answer*, and the parallelism is therefore an exact one.

4 (3). *And thou (art) holy, inhabiting the praises of Israel.* Here begins his statement of the grounds on which he might claim to be heard, and all which may be summed up in this, that Jehovah was the covenant God of Israel. The word translated *holy*, in its widest sense, includes all that distinguishes God from creatures, not excepting what are usually termed his natural perfections. Hence the epithet is often found connected with descriptions of his power, eternity, &c. See Isa. vi. 3 ; xl. 25, 26 ; lvii. 15 ; Hab. iii. 3 ; Ps. cxi. 9. The primary meaning of the verb appears to be that of separation, which may here be alluded to, in reference to Jehovah's peculiar relation to the chosen people. Or it may be taken in its wider and higher sense, leaving the other to be expressed in the last clause. " Thou art the glorious and perfect God who inhabitest the praises of Israel," *i. e.* dwellest among those praises, and art constantly surrounded by them. Some prefer, however, to retain the primary meaning of the Hebrew verb, *sitting (enthroned upon) the praises of Israel.*

5 (4). *In thee trusted our fathers ; they trusted and thou savedst them.* Not only was Jehovah the covenant God of Israel, and as such bound to help his people, but he had actually helped them in time past. This is urged as a reason why he should not refuse to help the sufferer in this case. The plural form, *our fathers*, makes the prayer appropriate to the whole church, without rendering it less so to the case of Christ, or to that of the individual believer.

6 (5.) *To thee they cried and were delivered ; in thee they trusted, and were not ashamed.* This last word is continually used in Scripture for the disappointment and frustration of the hopes. The argument of this verse lies in the tacit contrast between the case referred to and that of the sufferer himself. As if he had said, " How is it then that I cry and am not delivered, I trust and am confounded or ashamed?"

7 (6). *And I (am) a worm, and not a man; a reproach of men, and despised of the people.* The pronoun expressed at the beginning is emphatic. *I*, as contrasted with my fathers. Our idiom would here require an adversative particle, *but I*, the use of which is much less frequent in Hebrew. See above, on Ps. ii. 6. The insignificance and meanness of mankind in general are elsewhere denoted by the figure of a worm (Job xxv. 6). But

even in comparison with these, the sufferer is a worm, *i. e.* an object of contemptuous pity, because apparently forsaken of God, and reduced to a desperate extremity. (Compare Isa. xli. 14, and 1 Sam. xxiv. 15.) *A reproach of mankind*, despised by them, and disgraceful to them.—*The people*, not a single person or a few, but the community at large.

8 (7). *All seeing me mock at me; they pout with the lip; they shake the head.* This is an amplification of the last clause of the verse preceding. The verb in the second member of the sentence is of doubtful meaning. It may either mean to stretch the mouth, or to part the lips with a derisive grin. (See Ps. xxxv. 21, Job xvi. 10.) The shaking of the head may be either a vague gesture of contempt, or the usual expression of negation, by a lateral or horizontal motion, equivalent to saying " No, no ! " *i. e.* there is no hope for him. Either of these explanations is more probable than that which applies the words to a vertical movement of the head or nodding, in token of assent, and acquiescence in the sufferings of the sufferer, as just and right. The peculiar gesture here described is expressly attributed by the evangelists to the spectators of our Saviour's crucifixion (Mat. xxvii. 39, Mark xv. 29). It is one of those minor coincidences, which, although they do not constitute the main subject of the prophecy, draw attention to it, and help us to identify it.

9 (8). *Trust in Jehovah ! He will deliver him, he will save him, for he delights in him.* The literal meaning of the first clause is, *roll to* (or *on*) *Jehovah*, which would be unintelligible but for the parallel expressions in Ps. xxxvii. 5, *roll thy way upon Jehovah*, and in Prov. xvi. 3, *roll thy work upon Jehovah*, where the idea is evidently that of a burden cast upon another by one who is unable to sustain it himself. This burden, in the first case, is his *way, i. e.* his course of life, his fortune, his destiny, and in the other case, his *work, i. e.* his business, his affairs, his interest. In evident allusion to these places, the apostle Peter says, *casting all your care upon him, for he careth for you* (1 Pet. v. 7). By these three parallels light is thrown on the elliptical expression now before us, *roll, i. e.* thy burden or thy care *upon Jehovah.*—A further difficulty is occasioned by the form of the original, which, according to usage, must be either the infinitive construct or the second person of the imperative. But as these seem out of place in such a context, some arbitrarily explain it as an absolute infinitive, or a third person imperative, or change the form to that of a preterite. This last is the construction in the Septuagint version retained in the New Testament (Mat. xxvii. 43), and really included in the Hebrew, but by no means an exact representation of its form. Perhaps the best solution of the syntax is to make this clause a quotation, or derisive repetition of the sufferer's own words, as if they had said, " This is he who was so fond of repeating the precept, Trust in Jehovah ! Let him now try its virtue in his own case. He in whom he has trusted, and exhorted others to trust also, will no doubt deliver him." The next two verbs are ironical futures, not imperatives, and should be so translated.—The last words of the verse (חָפֵץ בּוֹ) are always applied elsewhere to God's complacency in man, and not to man's reciprocal delight in God. The Septuagint version, retained in the New Testament, *if he will* (*have*) *him*, or *if he will* (*deliver*) *him*, although not incorrect, is much inferior in strength to the original.—By appropriating these words, the spectators of our Lord's sufferings identified themselves with the wicked persecutors, by whom they are here supposed to be originally uttered.

10 (9). *For thou didst draw me from the womb, making me trust upon the*

breasts of my mother. The argument from past time is here pushed still further. God had not only shewn himself to be the God of the sufferer's forefathers, but of the sufferer himself in early life. The *for* connects this verse with the last clause of the one preceding. What his enemies ironically said was seriously true. God had indeed delighted in him once, for it was he that brought him into life, and through the perils of infancy. *Thou didst draw me,* literally, *thou (art or wast) my breaking forth, i. e.* the cause of it, as God is said to be the light, joy, strength of the believer, *i.e.* the source or the dispenser of these blessings.—*Made me trust,* does not refer to the literal exercise of confidence in God, which could not be asserted of a suckling, but means *gave me cause to trust* or feel secure, in other words, secured me, kept me safe. The original construction is, *making me trust,* but the Hebrew infinitive and participle used in these two clauses may be here represented by the past tense of the English verb.—As applied to the whole church or chosen people, this verse may be considered as descriptive of God's dealings with them at the exodus from Egypt, which is elsewhere metaphorically represented as a birth. The direct and obvious reference, however, is to individual birth and infancy.

11 (10). *Upon thee was I cast from the womb; from the bowels of my mother, my God (art) thou.* Into thy arms I was at first received, as into those of an affectionate parent. See Ruth iv. 16, and compare the opposite use of the same figure in Ezek. xvi. 5. In the last clause we are brought back to the point from which we set out, the sufferer having, in the mean time, as it were, established his right to say, *my God, my God, why hast thou forsaken me?*

12 (11). *Be not far from me, for distress is near, for there is no helper.* Having shewn that he was justified in expecting that God would not forsake him in extremity, he now shews that the extremity exists. The first clause constitutes the link of connection between the first and second subdivisions of the psalm. "Since, then, thou art my God, and as such must be near in my distress, Oh be not far from me now, for my distress is near, and there is no one else to help me."—*Near* is not put in opposition to proximity or actual contact, but to distance. The particular form of expression was suggested by the prayer in the first clause. It was no time for God to be afar off, when trouble was so near, so close upon the sufferer.—The second *for* may be subordinated to the first, and introduce a reason for declaring that distress was near. But it is much more natural to make the two co-relative, and understand the second as suggesting an additional reason for the prayer, *be not far from me.*

13 (12). *Many bulls have compassed me, strong bulls of Bashan have surrounded me.* He now proceeds to amplify the last clause of the foregoing verse, by shewing that trouble was indeed at hand. The strength and fierceness of his persecutors are expressed by comparing them to cattle fed in the rich and solitary pastures of Bashan, where the absence of men would of course increase their wildness. Corresponding to the noun in the first clause is an epithet frequently applied to it in Hebrew.

14 (13). *They have opened upon me their mouth, a lion tearing and roaring.* The tropical nature of the language is evinced by the entire change of figure in this verse. The same persons who before were bulls of Bashan now appear as a ravening and roaring lion. There is no need of supplying a particle of comparison, the absence of which in both these verses, by substituting metaphor for simile, adds greatly to the life of the description.

15 (14). *Like water I am poured out, and all my bones are parted; my*

heart has become like wax, melted in the midst of my bowels. Similar terms
are used in Josh. vii. 5, Lam. ii. 19, to describe dismay and fear; but in
the case before us they seem rather descriptive of extreme weakness. See
Ps. lviii. 8 (7), 2 Sam. xiv. 14, and compare the symbolical action in 1 Sam.
vii. 6. The comparison with water is applied to moral weakness also in
Gen. xlix. 4. The parting of the bones may either denote dislocation or
extreme emaciation, making the bones prominent. In either case the essential idea is still that of desperate exhaustion and debility.

16 (15). *Dried like the potsherd (is) my strength, and my tongue fastened
to my jaws, and to the dust of death thou wilt reduce me.* The description
of debility is still continued. He is as destitute of vigour as a broken piece
of earthenware is of sap or moisture.—*Fastened*, literally, made to cleave
or stick, through dryness.—*The dust of death, i.e.* the grave, the place of
burial, or more generally, the debased, humiliated state of the dead.—*Thou
wilt place me in* it, or *reduce me to* it. The translation of this future as a
preterite is not only ungrammatical, but hurtful to the sense, as the idea
evidently is, that this is something not experienced already, but the end to
which his sufferings are tending. The direct address to God recognises
him as the sovereign disposer, and men only as his instruments.

17 (16). *For dogs have surrounded me, a crowd of evil-doers have beset
me, piercing my hands and my feet.* He now resumes the description of
his persecutors, under figures borrowed from the animal kingdom. The
comparison with dogs is much less forcible to us than to an oriental reader,
because dogs in the east are less domesticated, more gregarious, wilder,
and objects not of affection, but abhorrence, as peculiarly unclean. In the
next clause the figurative dress is thrown aside, and the dogs described as
an assembly of malefactors. The first noun seems intended to suggest the
idea of a whole community or organised body as engaged in the persecution. See above, on *people*, in ver. 7 (6). This makes the passage specially appropriate to the sufferings of our Saviour at the hands both of the
mob and of the government. The Hebrew word is one of those applied in
the Old Testament to the whole congregation of Israel. (See above, on
Ps. i. 5, and compare Exod. xii. 3, xvi. 1, 2, 9, Num. xxvii. 17, Lev. iv. 15.)
The last clause, as above translated, contains a striking reference to our
Saviour's crucifixion, which some have striven to expunge, by denying that
the ancients nailed the feet as well as the hands to the cross. But although
there is a singular absence of explicit declaration on the subject, both in
the classical and sacred writers, the old opinion, that the feet were pierced,
may be considered as completely verified by modern investigation and dis-
cussion. So far, therefore, as the question of usage is concerned, we can
have no difficulty in referring this clause to our Saviour's crucifixion, and
regarding it as one of those remarkable coincidences, some of which have
been already noticed, all designed and actually tending to identify our Lord
as the most prominent subject of the prophecy. It is very remarkable, however, that no citation or application of the clause occurs in any of the gos-
pels. It is also worthy of remark that the clause, thus explained, although
highly appropriate to one part of our Saviour's passion, is, unlike the rest
of the description, hardly applicable, even in a figurative sense, to the case
of any other sufferer. Even supposing the essential idea to be merely that
of wounds inflicted on the body, it seems strange that it should be expressed
in the specific and unusual form of piercing the hands and the feet. On
further inspection it appears that, in order to obtain this meaning, we must
either change the text (כָּאֲרוּ or כָּאֲרִי for כָּאֲרִי) or assume a plural form

so rare that some grammarians deny its existence altogether (כָּאֲרִי for
כָּאֲרִים), and an equally rare form of the participle (כָּאֲרִים for כָּרִים),
and a meaning of the verb itself which nowhere else occurs, but must be
borrowed from a cognate root (כּוּר for כָּרָה) ; an accumulation of grammatical and lexicographical anomalies, which cannot be assumed without the
strongest exegetical necessity, and this can exist only if the words admit of
no other explanation more in accordance with analogy and usage. Now
the very same form in Isa. xxxviii. 13, is unquestionably used to mean *like
the lion*, and a slight modification of the same, in Num. xxiv. 9, Ezek.
xxii. 25, *like a lion.* This idea would be here the more appropriate, because
the psalm abounds in such allusions, and because the lion is expressly
mentioned both before and afterwards. See above, ver. 14 (13), and below,
ver. 22 (21). The sense would then be : " they surround my hands and
my feet, as they would a lion," or, " as a lion would," *i. e.* with the strength
and fierceness of a lion. The hands and feet may be mentioned as the
parts used in defence and flight. That the mention of these parts, after
all, in connection with the lion is not altogether natural, cannot fairly be
denied, and this objection should have all the weight to which it is entitled.
But whether it can outweigh the grammatical difficulties that attend the
other construction, is a serious question, which ought not to be embarrassed
by any supposed conflict with New Testament authority, since no citation of
the clause occurs there. It may even be possible to reconcile the two interpretations by supplying a verb and giving כָּאֲרִי its usual meaning. " Like
the lion (they have wounded) my hands and my feet." The point of comparison would then be the infliction of sharp wounds in those parts of the
body, an idea common to the habits of the lion, and to the usages of crucifixion.

18 (17). *I tell all my bones (while) they look and stare upon me.* The
pronoun of the last clause is expressed in Hebrew, which removes the
ambiguity of the construction, by shewing that the subject of the following
verbs is not the *bones* of the preceding clause, but something more remote,
namely, the sufferer's enemies and persecutors. The ambiguity of the
English word *tell* corresponds to that of the Hebrew (אֲסַפֵּר), which means
both to number and to relate, to count and to recount. Some suppose,
not improbably, that this verse presents the sufferer as stripped by his
enemies, and looking with grief and wonder at his own emaciation, while
they gaze at it with delight, as the Hebrew phrase implies. See below, on
Ps. xxvii. 13.

19 (18). *They (are about to) divide my garments for themselves, and on
my clothing they (are ready to) cast lots.* This is the last stroke necessary
to complete the picture. Having stripped him, nothing more is left but to
appropriate his garments, whether from cupidity or in derision   The futures
intimate that things can go no further without actual loss of life, and that
the case is therefore an extreme one. The providential realisation of this
ideal scene in our Lord's history is expressly mentioned by all the four
evangelists (Mat. xxvii. 35, Mark xv. 24, Luke xxiii. 34, John xix. 23, 24).
This makes their silence as to ver. 17 (16) the more remarkable.

20 (19). *And thou, Jehovah, be not far ; my strength ! to my assistance
hasten.* The pronoun in the first clause is emphatic. " Such is the conduct of my enemies ; but as for thee, O Lord, be not far from me." The
word translated *strength* is used in this place only, and apparently in refer-

ence to the name of God with which the psalm begins (אֵלִי) and to the word *hind* (אַיֶּלֶת) in the title, both which are akin to it in etymology.

21 (20). *Free from the sword my life* (or *soul*), *from the hand of the dog my lonely one* (or *only one*). The sword is a general expression for life-destroying agents. See 2 Sam. xi. 24, 25, where it is applied to archery. —*My life, my soul, i. e.* myself considered as a living person.—The apparent solecism, *hand of the dog*, shews that both terms are figurative, or as one has quaintly expressed it, that the dog meant is a dog with hands. See above, on ver. 17 (16), where the plural *dogs* is co-extensive in its meaning with the ideal or collective singular in this place.—*My only* (*life*), the only one I have to lose, is a good sense in itself, both here and in Ps. xxxv. 17 ; but the analogy of Ps. xxv. 16, and lxviii. 7 (6), recommends the sense of *solitary, lonely,* which is admissible in all the places.

22 (21). *Save me from the mouth of the lion, and from the horns of the unicorns thou hast heard* (or *answered*) *me.* The petition in the first clause is directly followed by an expression of confident assurance that his prayer will be answered, or rather that it is already heard, corresponding to the figurative expression in ver. 3 (2), *thou wilt not hear* (or *answer*), where the same Hebrew verb is used.—*From the horns* denotes of course the place from which the prayer proceeded, not the answer. The figure is a strong one for the midst of danger. The name of any wild horned animal would be appropriate. The precise sense of the Hebrew word (רֵמִים) is

therefore comparatively unimportant. The common version *unicorns* rests on the authority of the Septuagint ; but although the unicorn, long regarded as a fabulous animal, has now been proved to be a real one, we have no reason to believe that it was ever known in Palestine, or to dissent from the common judgment of the learned, that the Hebrew word denotes the wild bull or a species of the antelope, most probably the former.

23 (22). *I will declare thy name to my brethren, in the midst of the assembly I will praise thee.* His certainty of audience and acceptance is further expressed by declaring his intention to give thanks for it.—To declare God's name, in Scripture usage, is to celebrate the acts by which he has manifested his perfections. See above, on Ps. v. 12 (11).—*The assembly,* or congregation of Israel, to which the Hebrew word is constantly applied (Lev. xvi. 17, Deut. xxxi. 30), whether present in person or by their repre-sentatives (2 Chron. xx. 13–15). The same sense of the word occurs below, Ps. xxxv. 18, xl. 10 (9). The idea here is that his praise shall not be merely private or domestic, but public.

24 (23). *Fearers of Jehovah, praise him ! All the seed of Jacob, glorify him ! And be afraid of him, all the seed of Israel!* These words are uttered, as it were, in the midst of the ideal congregation mentioned in the verse preceding. That the call, though formally addressed to the whole race, was really intended for the spiritual Israel, excluding wicked Israelites and including the righteous of whatever name or nation, is indicated by the words of the first clause, while the last shews that the praise required is not familiar, but in the highest degree reverential.

25 (24). *For he has not despised and not abhorred the suffering of the sufferer, and has not hid his face from him, and, in his crying to him, heard.* This is the ground on which the fearers of the Lord are called upon to praise him, namely, the faithful execution of his promise to the sufferer in this case, and the pledge thereby afforded of like faithfulness in every other.

26 (25). *From thee* (*shall be*) *my praise in* (*the*) *great congregation ; my*

vows I will pay before his fearers, those who fear him. *From thee* is something more than *of thee*. It does not merely indicate the theme or subject, but the source or cause of his thanksgiving. " It is thou who givest me occasion thus to praise thee." In the last clause there seems to be a reference to the sacrificial feasts connected with the fulfilment of vows made in distress or danger. (See Deut. xii. 18, xvi. 11.) These were occasions of festivity, not only to the offerer and his nearest friends, but to a wide circle of invited guests, which makes the metaphor peculiarly appropriate in this place. The essential idea is the same as in ver. 23 (22).—*His fearers*, worshippers, the true Israel, as distinguished from the mere natural descendants of the patriarch.

27 (26). (Then) *shall eat* (thereof) *the humble, and be satisfied ;* (then) *shall praise Jehovah those who seek him. May your heart live for ever !* The adverb *then* is here supplied in the translation, in order to retain the Hebrew order of the sentence. The word *thereof* is introduced to remove all ambiguity of syntax, and to connect the act of eating with the sacrificial feast of the foregoing verse.—*To seek God*, in the dialect of Scripture, is to seek to know him, and also to seek his favour, not only by specific acts of prayer, but by the whole course of the life. See above, on Ps. xiv. 2.— The concluding wish, *your heart live for ever*, comprehends an assurance that it shall live. The heart is said to die, in cases of extreme grief and distress. See 1 Sam. xxv. 37, and compare Ps. cix. 22. The objects of address are those who seek and praise God. The sudden change of person is analogous to that in ver. 26 (25), which begins *from thee*, and ends with *fearing him*. That this is not an inadvertent irregularity, appears from its recurrence in the next verse.—The *humble* and the *seekers of Jehovah* are parallel descriptions of the same class, namely, true believers, those who are elsewhere called *the righteous.*

28 (27). *Remember and return to Jehovah shall all the ends of the earth, and worship before thee all the kindreds of the nations.* As the joyful effects of this deliverance were not to be restricted to himself or his domestic circle, but extended to the *great congregation* of God's people, so too we now read that they shall not be confined to any one race, but made to embrace all. *The ends of the earth*, here put for the remotest nations. See above, on Ps. ii. 8. These are named as the least likely to be comprehended in the promise, but of course without excluding those less distant. As if he had said, the ends of the earth and all that is between them. In the other clause, accordingly, we find as a parallel expression, not the furthest, but all nations. *They shall remember* this deliverance, this exhibition of God's faithfulness and might, and *shall turn unto Jehovah*, be converted to his worship and his service. Some suppose an allusion to the great original apostasy, or to the temporary casting off of the Gentiles : *they shall remember* their original condition, *and return unto the Lord*, from whom they have revolted. But this, though true and really implied, is not the strict sense of the words, which would then have no perceptible connection with the general subject of the psalm, and the immediate occasion of the praise which it contains.—*Worship*, literally *prostrate themselves*, the accustomed oriental indication both of civil and religious worship.—The form of expression in the last clause is evidently borrowed from the patriarchal promise. Compare Gen. xii. 3, xxviii. 14.

29 (28). *For unto Jehovah is the kingdom, and (he is) governor among the nations.* This will not be a gratuitous extension to the Gentiles of what properly belongs to Israel alone, but a restoration of God's mercies, after

ages of restriction, to their original and proper scope. *For* Jehovah is not
the king of Israel only, but of all mankind. See Rom. iii. 29.—*The kingdom, i. e.* general ecumenical dominion.—*Governor,* properly a participle,
ruling, the use of which may be intended to suggest that as he has always
been their governor *de jure,* so now he begins to govern them *de facto,* not
with a providential sway, which is invariable as well as universal, but with
a spiritual sway, which is hereafter to be co-extensive with the earth itself.
Compare the similar expressions, Obad. 21, Zech. xiv. 9, and the still closer
parallels, Ps. xcvi. 10, xcvii. 1, xcix. 1.

30 (29). *They have eaten and worshipped—all the fat (ones) of the earth
—before him shall bend all going down (to) the dust, and (he who) his own
soul did not save alive.* The distinction of ranks shall be as little regarded
at this feast as that of nations.—*Eaten and worshipped,* partaken of the
sacrificial feast in honour of this great salvation. *Fat,* a common oriental
figure for the prosperous, and especially the rich. These are particularly
mentioned to exhibit a peculiar feature of the feast in question, which was
not, like the sacrificial feasts of the Mosaic law, designed expressly for the
poor, though these are not excluded, as appears from the parallel clause.—
Going down to the dust, i. e. the dust of death, as in ver. 16 (15) above.
Compare the analogous expressions used in Ps. xxviii. 1, 4, 10 (3, 9), lxxxviii.
5 (4), cxv. 17, cxliii. 7. The idea is, that this enjoyment shall be common
to the rich and those who are ready to perish, or as it is expressed in the
last clause, *he who cannot keep his soul* (or *himself*) *alive,* a strong expression
for the extreme of destitution. He who before, or a little while ago, no
longer kept himself alive, but was just about to perish, is now seen kneeling
at the sacrificial feast in honour of this great salvation.

31 (30). *Posterity shall serve him; it shall be related of the Lord to the*
(next) *generation.* The last restriction to be done away is that of time.
The effects of this salvation shall no more be confined to the present generation than to the higher classes of society, or the natural descendants of the
patriarchs.—*A seed, i. e.* posterity, the seed of those who witness or first
hear of the event.—*Shall serve him, i. e.* worship and obey Jehovah, the
same thing that is expressed by eating and bowing down in ver. 30 (29)
above. The means of this conversion shall be the perpetuated knowledge
of what God has done.—*Generation* is used absolutely, as in Ps. lxxi. 18,
where it means not *this generation,* but the next. The complete phrase
(דור אחרון) occurs below, Ps. xlviii. 14 (13), lxxviii. 4. *The Lord.* The
original is not *Jehovah,* but *Adhonai,* the divine name properly denoting
sovereignty. See above, on Ps. ii. 4, xxi. 2. The exposition above given
of the verse before us is equally agreeable to usage, and much better suited
to the context, than the one which makes it mean that *a seed shall be reckoned by the Lord* (as belonging) *to the generation, i. e.* to the generation of
his people. (See below, on Ps. xxiv. 6.) It is highly improbable that the
passive verb (יְסֻפַּר) has a meaning wholly different from that of the corresponding active form (אֲסַפְּרָה) in ver. 23 (22) above.

32 (31). *They shall come and shall declare his righteousness to a people
born, that he hath done (it).* The subjects of the first verbs are the *seed*
and *generation* of the preceding verse. *They shall come* into existence, shall
appear upon the scene. But even they shall not monopolise the knowledge
thus imparted, but communicate it to a people now unborn, but then born,
i. e. to their own successors. The construction of the participle as a future
is unnecessary, although not unauthorised by usage. See above, on Ps.

xviii. 4 (3). Compare with this verse the beautiful figures of Ps. xix. 3 (2).
—*His righteousness*, including the faithful execution of his gracious promise. The last clause gives the substance of the declaration to be made,
to wit, that *he has done* what forms the subject of the whole psalm. A
similar ellipsis of the object, where the context readily supplies it, may be
found above in ver. 27, 28, 30 (26, 27, 29). To these words it is supposed
by some that our Lord alluded in his dying exclamation, IT IS FINISHED !
(John xix. 30). The allusion, though not obvious, is interesting, as it brings
the beginning and the end of this remarkable psalm into connection with
each other and with that affecting scene to which there are so many clear
and pointed references in the whole composition ; thus completing, as it
were, the proof, already strong enough, that Christ is the great subject of
the psalm, as being the great type and representative of that whole class to
whom it ostensibly relates, but of whom some parts, and especially the last
five verses, are true only in a modified and lower sense.

Psalm 23

AN exquisite description of God's care over his people under the figure
of a shepherd and his flock, no doubt suggested by the writer's recollections
of his own pastoral experience, although probably composed at a much later
period of his life. The idea of the whole psalm is contained in ver. 1, carried
out and amplified in ver. 2–5, and again summed up, without continuing
the metaphor, in ver. 6. The psalm is so constructed as at the same time
to express the feelings of the Psalmist, and to serve as a vehicle for those
of every individual believer and of the whole body of God's people for
whose use it was intended.

1. *A Psalm of David. Jehovah (is) my shepherd, I shall not want.*
This is the general theme or idea of the whole psalm, that the believer's
relation to Jehovah carries with it necessarily the full supply of all his
wants. Spiritual gifts are neither excluded nor exclusively intended. No
nice distinction between these and temporal advantages is here made for
us, and none need be made by us. The comparison of God's care to that
of a shepherd is first used by Jacob, (Gen. xlviii. 15, xlix. 24), then by
Moses (Deut. xxxii. 6–12, compared with Ps. lxxviii. 52), both of whom,
like David, had themselves lived a pastoral life. From these the figure is
frequently borrowed by the later writers of the Old Testament. See Isa.
xl. 11, Ezek. xxxiv. 12, Micah vii. 14, Ps. lxxx. 2 (1), xcv. 7. This
endearing relation of Jehovah to his people was exercised under the old
dispensation by the agency of human or angelic messengers, but under the
new by Christ, of whom these were only types and representatives (Zech.
xiii. 7), and to whom the figure is expressly applied by himself (John x. 11),
and his apostles (1 Peter ii. 25, v. 4, Heb. xiii. 20). From him again, on
the principle of delegated representation, is derived the pastoral character
of Christian ministers (Eph. iv. 11). The future form, *I shall not want*,
includes the present, *I do not want*, with an additional assurance that the
provision will be still continued. The form of expression is derived from
Deut ii. 7, viii. 9, and recurs below, Ps. xxxiv. 11 (10).

2. *In pastures of verdure he will make me lie down ; by waters of rest*
(or *repose*) *he will lead me.* Here begins the amplification of the general
proposition in the foregoing verse. The first specification is, that he shall
not want healthful and delightful rest. This is expressed by figures bor-

rowed from the exquisite enjoyment of a flock in verdant and well-watered pastures. The allusion, in the first clause, is not to the supply of food, which is mentioned afterwards in ver. 5, but to the refreshing rest and coolness of green meadows. The first noun properly means *dwellings*, but is applied specifically to the dwellings of flocks, *i. e.* their pasture-grounds. See below, Ps. lxv. 13 (12), and compare Amos i. 2, Jer. ix. 9 (10), xxv. 37. The next word in Hebrew means the fresh tender grass, here referred to, not as food, but in allusion to its cooling effect upon the eye and the skin. This explanation is confirmed by the fact, that the act expressed by the verb is not that of eating but of lying down. The verb itself is one which specially denotes the lying down of animals (Gen. xxix. 2, Num. xxii. 27, Isa. xi. 6), but is sometimes transferred to the human subject (Isa. xiv. 30, Job. xi. 19), or to other objects (Gen. xlix. 25, Deut. xxix. 19). *By waters*, not simply *to* them, but *along* them, which is one of the senses of the Hebrew preposition, and affords a much more pleasing image. *By waters of rest* we are not to understand *still* or *quiet waters*, a sense which the Hebrew word has nowhere else, and which would here suggest the idea of stagnation, or at least that of silence, which is far less agreeable than that of an audible flow. The idea really conveyed is that of waters, by or at which rest may be enjoyed. The repose is not that of the waters themselves, but of the flocks reclining near them. The last verb sometimes means to nourish, or more generally to provide for (Gen. xlvii. 17, 2 Chron. xxxii. 22), and the Septuagint version so explains it here. The idea would then be that the shepherd *takes care* of his flock, or *tends* it, by the waters of repose. But a more specific act is described, and therefore a more vivid image presented, by retaining the common version, *leadeth*, which is fully sustained by the use of the same Hebrew verb in Exod. xv. 13, 2 Chron. xxviii. 15. The form, however, should be future, as in the preceding verse.

3. *My soul he will restore ; he will lead me in paths of right* (or *rectitude*) *for his name's sake.* To restore the soul, here as in Ps. xix. 8 (7), is to vivify or quicken the exhausted spirit. *Paths of right* may either mean *right paths*, as opposed to those which are devious and dangerous, or *paths of righteousness*, not man's but God's, not ways of upright conduct on the Psalmist's part, but ways of faithfulness on God's part. The righteousness of God, so often appealed to by the ancient saints, includes his covenanted mercy, the exercise of which, according to his promise, was ensured by his essential rectitude. *For his name's sake*, not merely *for his own sake*, nor *for his own glory*, but for the sake of what he has already done, the previous display of his perfections, which would be dishonoured by a failure to fulfil his promises. See above, on Ps. xxii. 23 (22).

4. *Also when I walk into* (or *through*) *the valley of death-shade, I will not fear evil, for thou* (*wilt be*) *with me ; thy rod and thy staff, they will comfort me.* He is sure, not only of repose, restoration, and guidance, but of protection. The *also* shews that something new is to be added ; not only this which I have said, but more. The common version (*yea, though I walk*) is too indefinite and hypothetical. The situation is not spoken of as possible, but certain, though still future.—*Death-shade* is a strong poetical expression for the profoundest darkness. See below, Ps. xliv. 20 (19). The common version, *shadow of death*, conveys more than the original, and fails to reproduce its compound form. The effect is heightened by the mention of a valley, as a deep place, often overhung with woods, and naturally darker than a plain or mountain. There may be some allusion to the

dread of darkness on the part of sheep and other timid animals.—The rod and the staff are mentioned, not as weapons of defence, but as badges of the shepherd and as tokens of his presence.

5. *Thou wilt spread before me a table in the presence of my adversaries ; thou hast anointed with oil my head ; my cup (is) overflowing.* To the negative benefits before enumerated, he now adds the positive advantage of abundant sustenance. Instead of retaining the image of a sheep and its pasture, the Psalmist substitutes that of a table furnished for a human guest. The connection, however, is so close and the metaphors so near akin, that the general impression remains undisturbed.—*In the presence of my enemies* implies *in spite of them ;* they are forced to witness my enjoyment without being able to disturb it.—*Anointed,* literally *fattened,* in allusion to the richness and abundance of the unction. This was a familiar part of an ancient festal entertainment, and is therefore frequently employed in Scripture as a symbol of joy. See below, on Ps. xlv. 8 (7).—*My cup,* my beverage, which, with food, makes up the supply of necessary nutriment, but with the additional suggestion of exhilaration. See above, on Ps. xvi. 5. —*Overflowing,* literally *overflow,* or abundant drink. The change of tense is significant and expressive. What he had just before confidently foreseen, he now describes as actually realised.

6. *Only goodness and mercy shall follow me all the days of my life, and I shall dwell in the house of Jehovah to length of days.* The specifications of the four preceding verses are followed by another summary expression of the general idea propounded in the first verse, but with a change of form. The Hebrew particle at the beginning has its usual and proper sense of *only* or exclusively. The favour which he shall experience is so great that he regards it as unmixed, or the exceptions as unworthy of consideration.— The word translated *goodness* may be understood to mean good fortune, good experienced, as a cognate form does in Ps. xvi. 2 ; but the other version agrees better with the parallel expression, *mercy.* The verb to *follow* or *pursue* seems to be chosen in allusion to the persecution of his enemies, and as a strong expression for an unbroken series or succession of divine benefactions. Dwelling in the house of Jehovah does not mean frequenting his sanctuary, but being a member of his household and an inmate of his family, enjoying his protection, holding communion with him, and subsisting on his bounty. See above, on Ps. xv. 1.

Psalm 24

This psalm consists of two distinct and, it may seem at first sight, unconnected parts. The first praises God as the universal sovereign by right of creation, ver. 1, 2, and describes the moral requisites to intimate communion with him, ver. 3–6. The second represents him, .in a striking figurative form, as entering some place provided for his residence, ver. 7–10. The idea common to both parts is the supremacy of God, both in holiness and majesty. There is no historical occasion to which such a composition would seem more appropriate than the removal of the ark to mount Zion by David, as described in 2 Sam. vi. and 1 Chron. xv. And as the first part of this psalm carries out the idea of dwelling in God's house, expressed at the close of Ps. xxiii., it is not an improbable conjecture, though by no means a necessary supposition, that the two psalms were designed to form a pair, and to be sung upon the same occasion; the first, it may be, as the ark left its former resting-place, the second as it drew near to its new one. The resemblance of ver. 3–6 to Ps. xv. make it not improbable that that psalm also was composed for use on a similar if not the same occasion. The supposition of alternate choirs in the case before us appears to be a useless and gratuitous refinement. The sanctuary of the old economy, both in its permanent and temporary forms, was intended to symbolise the doctrine of God's special presence and residence among his people ; and as this was realised in the advent of Christ, the psalm before us has a permanent interest and use, and in a certain sense may be described as Messianic.

1. *To David, i.e.* belonging to him as its author. See above, on Ps. iii. 1, iv. 1, v. 1. *A Psalm. To Jehovah* (belongs) *the earth and its fulness, the world and* (*those*) *dwelling in it.* Its fulness, that which fills it, its contents. The word translated *world* is a poetical equivalent to *earth*, denoting specially, according to its etymology, the productive portion of the earth, and thus corresponding indirectly to the Greek οἰκουμένη, or inhabited earth. This assertion of Jehovah's sovereign propriety is intended to shew that he was not the God of Israel only, but of the whole world, and thereby entitled to be served with reverence and purity, an idea more distinctly brought out afterwards.

2. *For He above the seas has settled it, and above the streams has fixed it.* The pronoun is emphatic ; He and no one else. See below, Ps. c. 3. He has made the earth what it is, and is therefore the sovereign, both of it and its inhabitants. The idea is not that of subterraneous waters bearing up the land, but simply that of the habitable earth, raised above the surface of the waters which surround it. The use of the Hebrew preposition (עַל) is the same as in Ps. i. 3. There is obvious allusion to the rescue of the dry land from the universal prevalence of water, as described in the Mosaic cosmogony, Gen. i. 9, 10. The sense of the two verses, taken in connection, is that since Jehovah is the God who collected the waters, and caused the dry land to appear, he is the rightful sovereign of the habitable earth, and of those whom it sustains.

3. *Who shall go up into the mountain of Jehovah, and who shall stand in his holy place ?* Since he is thus, by right of creation, the universal sovereign, which of his creatures shall enjoy the happiness and honour of appearing in his presence ! The *hill of the Lord*, or *mountain of Jehovah*, is mount Zion, henceforth to be hallowed as his earthly dwelling-place. The verb in the last clause does not simply mean to *stand*, but to *stand fast*, to maintain one's ground. See above, on Ps. i. 5. It may, therefore, be implied, that some who gain a bodily access to the consecrated place shall not be suffered to remain there. It is indeed implied in the whole interrogation that mere bodily presence on mount Zion might be wholly unconnected with spiritual access to the holy place.

4. *The clean of hands and pure of heart, who has not lifted up his soul to vanity, and has not sworn to fraud* (or *falsehood*). This is the answer to the foregoing question, given by the Psalmist himself. There is no more need of supposing two speakers than in the rhetorical interrogations which are so abundant in Demosthenes and other animated writers. All moral purity is here referred to the hands, the tongue, and the heart, as the organs of external action, speech, and feeling. The same distribution may be made in the commandments of the decalogue. The second clause is very obscure. The form of expression is directly borrowed from the third commandment (Exod. xx. 7), where the common version (*take in vain*) is neither intelli-

gible in itself nor an exact copy of the original. The precise construction) (נָשָׂא לַשָּׁוְא) is found in these two places only; but a cognate one (נָשָׂא אֶל) occurs repeatedly in the sense of setting the heart or the desires on something (See Deut. xxiv. 15, Prov. xix. 18, Ps. xxv. 1, lxxxvi. 4, cxliii. 8). The only two plausible interpretations of the former phrase are that which makes לַשָּׁוְא a mere poetical variation of אֶל הַשָּׁוְא and that which gives נָשָׂא לַשָּׁוְא, in both places, the sense of *carrying to vanity, i. e.* bringing the name of God or the soul of man into connection with a falsehood, whether this be taken in its strict sense, or as meaning an unlawful or unsatisfying object of affection. It seems more natural, however, to explain the case before us, not by the single one in which the combination נָשָׂא ל occurs, but by the many in which the same verb is connected with the same noun although by a different preposition. The meaning of the clause will then be, *who has not set his heart on falsehood*, or on any false and sinful object. That false swearing is particularly mentioned in the last clause cannot prove that it is exclusively intended here, as parallel clauses very seldom say precisely the same thing.—*Sworn to falsehood, i.e.* made a false oath, or *sworn for deceit, i.e.* with a fraudulent design.

5. *He shall carry away a blessing from Jehovah, and righteousness from the God of his salvation.* The first verb (יִשָּׂא) seems to have been chosen with some reference to its use in the foregoing verse, but not so as to require us to take it in precisely the same sense. A blessing from Jehovah, not merely from man, with allusion, as some think, to David's blessing the people, 2 Sam. vi. 18.—*Righteousness* may either mean a practical justification, an attestation of his innocence afforded by his experience of God's favour; or the gift of righteousness itself, the highest and most precious of all gifts, and one which always follows upon justification.—*The God of his salvation, i. e.* God his Saviour, or his God who is a Saviour. See above, on Ps. xviii. 47 (46).

6. *This is the generation seeking him; the seekers of thy face (are) Jacob, i. e.* the true Jacob, the true Israel. *This* refers to the description in ver. 6.—*Seeking him* (in the singular) is the reading in the text; the marginal reading is *those seeking him*, which amounts to the same thing. *To seek God* and *to seek his face, i. e.*, his countenance or presence, are common phrases for the earnest endeavour to secure his favour, Ps. xxvii. 8, cv. 4, Hos. v. 15, 2 Sam. xxi. 1. Our language does not furnish equivalents to the two Hebrew verbs employed to express this idea in the verse before us.—The connection of the last word with the rest of the sentence is obscure. Some make it a vocative : " who seek thy face, O Jacob!" *i. e.* who seek the countenance and friendship of God's people. Or, " who seek thy face, O (God of) Jacob!" a very harsh ellipsis, which could only be justified by exegetical necessity. The best sense is yielded by the construction first proposed, or by another, which differs from it only in dispensing with a verb and throwing all into one sentence " This is the generation seeking thee, those seeking thy face (O Jehovah), (the true) Israel." The sudden apostrophe to God himself makes the sentence more impressive without making it obscure.—The distinction here made between the nominal and real Israel was peculiarly necessary on occasions which were suited to flatter the natural pride of the chosen people, such as that of Jehovah's solemn entrance into Zion, as the peculiar God of Israel. To

correct this abuse of their extraordinary privileges, two great doctrines are here set forth; that their God was the God of the whole earth; and, secondly, that he was holy, and required holiness as a term of admission to his presence. The idea of a true and false Israel reappears in the New Testament, and is propounded with peculiar distinctness and emphasis by Paul in Rom. ix. 6, 7.

7. *Lift up, O gates, your heads, and be lifted up, ye doors of perpetuity! And in will come the king of glory!* The procession is now commonly supposed to have arrived at the entrance of the citadel or walled town of Zion, the acropolis of Jerusalem. The gates of this acropolis are those personified in this fine apostrophe. They are called *perpetual* or *everlasting* on account of their antiquity, and not in mere anticipation of their subsequent duration, as in 1 Kings viii. 13. They are called upon to raise their heads, that he who is about to enter may not debase himself by stooping to pass through them. The connection of the clauses is correctly given, but in a form much more agreeable to the English than the Hebrew idiom, by translating the future as a subjunctive tense, *that the king of glory may come in.* The king of glory is a phrase analogous to *hill of holiness, strength of salvation,* &c., and means *glorious king.*

8. *Who is this, the king of glory?* Jehovah *strong and mighty, Jehovah mighty in battle* (or *a mighty warrior*). The supposition of alternate or responsive choirs is as unnecessary here as in ver. 4 above. It is the case, so common in all animated speech and composition, of a speaker asking a question simply for the purpose of answering it himself. As if he had said, "Do you ask who this king of glory is? It is the Lord," &c. The common version, *Who is this king of glory?* does not fully convey the force of the original, the sense of which is, "who is this (of whom you speak as) the king of glory?" The word translated *mighty,* although properly an adjective, is continually used as a noun substantive, and is the nearest equivalent in Hebrew to the classical term *hero.* But the simple majesty of David's language would be marred in a translation by the use of this word, and still more by that of the combination, *martial* or *military hero,* in the other clause. The idea, both in this and other places, is borrowed from the Song of Moses, Exod. xv. 3.

9. *Lift up, O gates, your heads, and lift (them) up, ye doors of perpetuity, and in will come the king of glory.* In order to conclude with an emphatic repetition of the epithets in ver. 8, it was necessary that the question in that verse should be repeated likewise; and in order to this the summons in ver. 7 is repeated here, but, as in most like cases, with a variation, which, though slight, relieves the repetition from entire sameness. The variation here consists in the exchange of the passive form, *be lifted up,* for the corresponding active, *lift up,* so *your heads,* the object being readily suggested by the other clause.

10. *Who is this, the king of glory?* Jehovah *(God) of Hosts, he is the king of glory. Selah.* Between the question here and in ver. 8 the only variation is one which cannot well be imitated in translation. For the simple Hebrew phrase (מִי־זֶה) *Who is this?* we have here the fuller form (מִי הוּא זֶה), in which the personal pronoun is interposed between the interrogative and demonstrative, so as to suggest the two forms, *Who is he?* and *Who is this?* though really constituting but a single question, as the personal pronoun (הוּא), in Hebrew usage, often serves as an index of the substantive when not expressed.—There is a more material variation in the answer,

where, instead of the two phrases, *Jehovah strong and mighty, Jehovah mighty in battle*, the Psalmist substitutes the single but still more expressive title, *Jehovah Zebaoth*, or *of Hosts*. In Exodus xii. 41, Israel is called *the hosts of Jehovah;* but a much more frequent designation is *the host* or *hosts of heaven*, sometimes applied to the heavenly bodies, especially as objects of idolatrous worship (Deut. iv. 19, xvii. 3, 2 Kings xvii. 16, Isa. xxxiv. 4, Jer. xxxiii. 22, Zeph. i. 5, Dan. viii. 10), and sometimes to the angels (Jos. v. 14, 15, 1 Kings xxii. 19, 2 Chron. xviii. 18, Ps. ciii. 21, cxlviii. 2). In both these senses God may be described as the God of Hosts, *i. e.* as the sovereign both of the material heavens and of their inhabitants. From the use of *hosts* in Gen. ii. 1, some would extend it to the earth as well as the heavens, and explain the compound title as denoting *Lord of the Universe*, as Mohammed in the Koran speaks of Allah as the *Lord of Worlds*. But this explanation, even supposing it to be correct as to the single place on which it rests, derives no countenance from usage elsewhere. Still less admissible is that which makes it simply mean the God of Battles or the God of War, a name and an idea much less scriptural than heathenish. The phrase *Jehovah Zebaoth* does not occur in the Pentateuch, Joshua or Judges, from which some have inferred that it was afterwards introduced in opposition to the worship of the heavenly bodies, and of the spirits which were supposed to govern and inhabit them. According to the usage of the Hebrew language, *Jehovah*, as a proper name, cannot be construed with a genitive directly, nor is it ever so connected with any other noun. The anomaly can only be removed by making *Zebaoth* itself a proper name, or by supplying the word *God* between it and *Jehovah*. The first solution may appear to be favoured by the σαβαώθ of the Septuagint, retained in Rom. ix. 29 and James v. 4. But the other is proved to be the true one by such passages as Hos. xii. 6 (5), Amos iv. 13, where we have the full form, *Jehovah God of Hosts*. Compare Ps. lix. 6 (5), lxxx. 5 (4), lxxxiv. 9 (8).—This description of Jehovah as the God of heaven no less than of earth, while it sensibly strengthens the expressions of ver. 8, and thus removes the appearance of a mere tautological reiteration, at the same time brings us back in the conclusion to the point from which we set out in ver. 1, to wit, the universal sovereignty of God. The whole psalm is then brought to a solemn and sonorous close by making the answer echo the terms of the interrogation, *He is the king of glory!* These points of difference between ver. 8 and 10 impart a beautiful variety to the repeated sentence, without impairing in the least the rhetorical or musical effect of the repetition itself, which is followed only by the customary indication of a pause, both in the sense and the performance. See above, on Ps. iii. 3 (2).

Psalm 25

THE first of the alphabetical psalms, in which the verses begin with the different Hebrew letters in their order, an arrangement peculiar to those psalms, in which a single theme or idea is repeated under various forms, and, as it were, in a series of aphorisms. Now and then, in order to complete the expression of the thought, the series of the letters is neglected, either by repeating or omitting one. In this psalm, for example, two successive verses begin with א, and two with ר, while ו and ק are left out. The first verse, however, does not properly belong to the alphabetical series, but constitutes one sentence with the short verse at the end, which is added after the completion of the alphabet. The theme which runs through this psalm is deliverance from enemies, occasionally blended with a prayer for the divine forgiveness.

1. *By David. Unto thee, Jehovah, my soul will I lift up*, or as some explain it, *bring* or *carry*. All agree, however, that the essential idea is that of confident desire. See above, on Ps. xxiv. 4, and compare Ps. lxxxvi. 4, cxliii. 8, below, where the phrase occurs again. The sentiment expressed is that of settled confidence in God, to the exclusion of all other helpers.

2. *My God, in thee have I trusted, let me not be ashamed; let not my enemies triumph over me*, or more exactly, *with respect to me*. As the future verb of the preceding verse implies a fixed determination to confide in God hereafter, so the preterite in this verse indicates that such trust has been exercised already. The present is included under both forms.—*Ashamed*, disappointed, defeated in my plans and expectations. See above, on Ps. xxii. 6 (5).—The last clause shews that suffering from enemies was in the Psalmist's mind throughout.

3. *Likewise all (those) waiting for thee shall not be ashamed, ashamed shall be the traitors without cause*. He does not ask for any special dispensation in his own behalf, but merely for a fair participation in God's customary mode of dealing with the whole class of which he is a member, here described as those *waiting for God, i. e.* hoping in him, awaiting the fulfilment of his promises. The modern English sense of *waiting on* is too restricted, though the phrase once exactly corresponded to the Hebrew.—The position of the verbs, at the end and the beginning of successive clauses, gives a peculiar turn to the sentence, which is lost in some translations.—*Without cause* qualifies the word immediately preceding, and describes the enemy not only as perfidious, but as acting so gratuitously, and without provocation. See above, on Ps. vii. 5 (4), and below, on Ps. xxxv. 19, xxxviii. 20 (19), lxix. 5 (4).

4. *Thy ways, Jehovah, make me know; thy paths teach me*. As the ways of God, throughout this psalm, are the same as in Deut. xxxii. 4, namely his dispensations towards his people, the way in which he orders their condition and disposes of their lot, the teaching prayed for must be that of experience. "Let me know in my own case what it is to be guided and protected and provided for by God himself." This meaning suits the context better than that of moral guidance, which however is implied, if not expressed.

5. *Make me walk in thy truth and teach me, for thou (art) the God of my salvation; for thee have I waited all the day*. The obvious meaning of this verse, interpreted according to New Testament and modern usage, would be that of a prayer for divine instruction in religious truth or doctrine. But the usage of the Psalms, and the preceding context, are in favour of explaining *truth* to mean the veracity of God, or the faithful performance of his promises. See Ps. xxx. 10 (9), lxxi. 22, xci. 4. The teaching asked is then experimental teaching, or the actual experience of God's faithfulness.—*The God of my salvation*, or my Saviour God. See above, on Ps. xviii. 47 (46).—*I have waited*. This is no new or untried exercise of faith, to be attempted for the first time, but one with which I have been long familiar.—*All the day*, continually, always.

6. *Remember thy mercies, O Jehovah, and thy favours, for from eternity are they*. The prayer for future favours is here founded upon those experi-

enced already.—*Of old* is an inadequate translation of מֵעוֹלָם, and even in the stronger form, *ever of old*, less exact and expressive than the literal translation *from eternity*, to which there is the less objection here, as the words relate not merely to God's acts but to his attributes.

7. *The sins of my youth and my transgressions* (*O*) *remember not; according to thy mercy remember thou me, for the sake of thy goodness, O Jehovah!* Among the mercies which he craves, the most important is the pardon of his sins, not only in itself considered, but as that without which all the others must be worthless. The sins of his youth are mentioned as the earliest in date, and probably as those committed with the least restraint, at an age when reflection is subordinate to passion. Compare Job xiii. 26, 2 Tim. ii. 22. Besides the obvious reference to the youthful sins of individuals, there may be also an allusion to the national iniquities of Israel, committed in the period of their childhood as a people, namely, that of their sojourn in the wilderness. See below, on ver. 22, and compare Deut. ix. 7.

8. *Good and upright* (*is*) *Jehovah; therefore will he guide sinners in the way.* Not only the goodness, but the rectitude of the divine nature requires the exercise of covenanted mercy. The second epithet is borrowed from Deut xxxii. 4.—The *way* meant in the last clause is the way of safety or salvation. What is meant may be either that God guides sinners *into* it by converting them, or that he guides those sinners *in* it who are still his people, as the same person claims to be both righteous and a sinner in Ps. xli. 5, 13, (4, 12). Hence perhaps he uses the indefinite term *sinners*, not the distinctive phrase *the sinners*, or the more emphatic epithet, *the wicked*.

9. *He will guide humble* (sinners) *in justice, and teach humble* (sinners) *his way.* The common version of עֲנָוִים, *meek*, is too restricted and descriptive of mere temper. The Hebrew word is the nearest equivalent to *humble* in its strong religious sense. The omission of the article may be explained as a poetic licence, and the word translated *the humble*, so as to include the whole class. But the intimate connection between this verse and the one before it, makes it more natural to take עֲנָוִים as a description of the sinners mentioned in ver. 8, who are then of course to be regarded as penitent believing sinners, *i. e.* as true converts. *In justice, i. e.* in the exercise of justice, as before explained. The *way* and the *teaching* are the same as in the foregoing context, namely, those of Providence.

10. *All the paths of Jehovah* (are) *mercy and truth to the keepers of his covenant and his testimonies.* The paths of Jehovah are the paths in which he walks himself, in other words, the ways in which he deals with his creatures.—*Truth*, veracity, fidelity. See above, on ver. 5. A similar combination occurs, John i. 14. The last clause shews that the preceding promises are limited to those who are in covenant with God.—*Keepers*, observers, those obeying.—*His covenant*, the commands to which his promise is annexed. The same are called *his testimonies* against sin and in behalf of holiness. See above, on Ps. xix. 8 (7).

11. *For the sake of thy name* (wilt thou do this), *and wilt pardon my iniquity because it is great.* The form of the verb (וְסָלַחְתָּ) is one that is commonly preceded by a future, which may here be readily supplied, so as to make the first clause refer to the preceding promises. *For thy name's sake*, for the honour of thy nature and thy attributes, as heretofore revealed in act. See above on Ps. xxiii. 3. The emphatic pronoun at the end (רַב־הוּא) may possibly refer to the remoter antecedent, as in Ps. xxii.

18 (17). The sense will then be, "and forgive my iniquity because that name is great." (Compare Mal. i. 11.) There is nothing ungrammatical, however, in the usual construction, which also agrees better with the usage of the adjective (רַב), as denoting rather quantity than elevation, and with the parallel phrase, *much transgression* (פֶּשַׁע רַב), in Ps. xix. 14 (13).

12. *Who (is) the man fearing Jehovah ?   He will guide him in the way he shall choose.* In the first clause the form of the original is highly idiomatic; who (is) this, the man, a fearer of Jehovah? See above, on Ps. xxiv. 8.—The ellipsis of the relative in the last clause is common to both idioms.—*He guides him*, and will guide him. There is not only an affirmation, but a promise. The *way*, as in the foregoing context, is the providential way in which God directs the course of a man's life. His *choosing* it implies not only sovereign authority, but a gracious regard to the interests of his servant.

13. *His soul in good shall lodge, and his seed shall possess the land.* The parallelism between *soul* and *seed* seems to shew that by *his soul* we are to understand *himself*, for which the Hebrew has no appropriate expression. The promise, then, includes both himself and his posterity. To *lodge*, to be at home, to dwell at ease, and by implication, to abide or continue undisturbed. *In good*, not goodness, but good fortune or prosperity. The verb, translated *shall possess*, denotes specifically to *inherit*, or possess as an inheritance, *i. e.* from generation to generation, in perpetual succession. *The land*, to wit, the land of Canaan; and as this was the standing promise of the law, uttered even in the decalogue (Exod. xx. 12), it became a formula for all the blessings implicitly embraced in the promise of Canaan to the ancient Israel, and is so used even by our Lord himself, (Mat. v. 5.)

14. *The friendship of Jehovah is to (those) fearing him, and his covenant to make them know.* The word translated *friendship* means originally a company of persons sitting together, Ps. cxi. 1 ; then familiar conversation, Ps. lv. 15 (14); then confidential intercourse, intimacy, friendship, Prov. iii. 32 ; then a confidence or secret, Prov. xi. 13. The last sense is commonly preferred in the English version, even when one of the others would be more appropriate, as in this case, where the sense of intimacy, friendship, seems required by the context. The last clause is ambiguous, and may either mean, his covenant is designed to be known by them, or his covenant is designed to make them know, *i. e.* his way ; or in general, to give them knowledge. *To make them know his covenant* is a forced construction, and forbidden by the collocation of the Hebrew words. The meaning of the whole verse seems to be, that Jehovah condescends to hold familiar intercourse with those who fear him, and enters into covenant relation with them, for the purpose of making them know all that they need know for his service or their own advantage.

15. *My eyes (are) always towards Jehovah ; for he will bring out from the net my feet.* The first clause expresses settled trust and constant expectation. The figure of a net is a favourite one for dangers arising from the craft and spite of enemies. See above, on Ps. ix. 16 (15), x. 9.

16. *Turn thee unto me, and have mercy upon me, for lonely and distressed (am) I.* The prayer to turn implies that his face was before averted, a common figure in the Psalms for the suspension or withholding of God's favour. See above, on Ps. iv. 7 (6).—The word translated *lonely* is the same that occurs above, Ps. xxii. 21 (20).

17. *The troubles of my heart have they enlarged ; from my distresses do*

thou bring me out. The plural of the first clause is indefinite, equivalent to a passive construction in English, *are enlarged.* (Compare the common version of Luke xii. 20.) It does not refer even to his enemies specifically, but to all others, as distinguished from his lonely self, and from his sole deliverer.

18. *See my affliction and my trouble, and forgive all my sins.* So long as God leaves him to endure, he is conceived of as not seeing his condition. The prayer that he will see includes the prayer that he will save. The renewed prayer for forgiveness in the last clause seems again to recall to mind the intimate connection between suffering and sin.

19. *See my enemies, for they are many, and (with) hatred of violence have hated me.* The agency of wicked foes in causing his distresses, which had been referred to in ver. 2, 15, 17, is here again brought into view. The word translated *violence* is very strong, including the ideas of injustice and cruelty. See above, on Ps. xi. 6 (5), xviii. 49 (48).—The past tense represents the enmity as something of long standing.

20. *(O) keep my soul and deliver me ; let me not be ashamed, for I have trusted in thee.* To *keep* is here to keep in safety, to preserve.—*Ashamed*, confounded, disappointed. See above, on ver. 2. The word translated *trusted* is not that employed in ver. 2, but the one which occurs in Ps. ii. 12, and which originally means to seek a refuge or a hiding-place. See above, on Ps. xi. 2 (1).

21. *Integrity and rectitude shall preserve me, because I have waited for thee.* The first word means completeness or perfection (*integritas*), *i. e.* freedom from essential defect. See above, on Ps. xviii. 21, 24 (20, 23). Here, however, it may signify the perfect rectitude of God, which will not suffer him to cast off or forsake those who *wait for him, i. e.* trustfully expect the fulfilment of his promises.

22. *Redeem, O God, Israel out of all his troubles !* As the psalm was designed, from the first, to be a vehicle of pious feeling and desire for the whole church, it is here wound up with a petition shewing this extent of purpose. The Psalmist prays no longer for himself, but for all Israel. The peculiar name, *Jehovah*, which had hitherto been used exclusively, is here exchanged for the generic name of *God*, perhaps in opposition to the human adversaries of the Psalmist, and his total destitution of all human help. This verse forms no part of the alphabetical series, but begins with the same letter as ver. 16. Like the first verse, it consists of a single clause, as if the two together were designed to constitute one sentence.

Psalm 26

An appeal to God's justice and omniscience, ver. 1–3, enforced by a disavowal of all sympathy and communion with the wicked, ver. 4–6, and a profession of devotion to God's service, ver. 7, 8, with an earnest prayer to be delivered from the death of those whose life he abhors, ver. 9, 10, and an expression of strong confidence that God will hear his prayer, ver. 11, 12. There is a certain similarity of form between this psalm and the foregoing, which, together with their collocation in the Psalter, makes it not improbable that they were designed to constitute a pair or double psalm.

1. *By David. Judge me, Jehovah, for I in my integrity have walked, and in Jehovah I have trusted ; I shall not swerve (or slip).* The correctness of the title is confirmed by the resemblance of the psalm itself to

several, the authorship of which is undisputed, more especially Ps. xv. xvii. xviii. xxiv.—*Judge me*, do me justice, vindicate or clear me. See above, on Ps. xvii. 1, 2.—*In my integrity* of purpose and of principle. To this is added its inseparable adjunct, trust in God.—*Walked*, lived, pursued a certain course of conduct. See above, on Ps. i. 1. The last clause is by some explained as the expression of a wish, *let me not be moved*. But there is no reason for departing from the strict sense of the future, as expressing a confident anticipation. *Swerve*, as in Ps. xviii. 37 (36), xxxvii. 31.

2. *Try me, Jehovah, and prove me; assay my reins and my heart.* The first verb is supposed by etymologists to signify originally trial by touch, the second by smell, and the third by fire. In usage, however, the second is constantly applied to moral trial or temptation, while the other two are frequently applied to the testing of metals by the touchstone or the furnace. This is indeed the predominant usage of the third verb, which may therefore be represented by the technical metallurgic term, *assay*. See above, on Ps. xvii. 3, where two of the same verbs occur.—*Reins* and *heart* are joined, as seats of the affections. See above, on Ps. vii. 10 (9).—The prayer of this verse is an appeal to God's omniscience for the psalmist's integrity of purpose, which agrees much better with the context than the explanation of צרופה as a participle, and of the last clause as an affirmation, *purified* (or *purged*) *are my reins and my heart*.

3. *For thy mercy (is) before my eyes, and I have walked in thy truth.* This verse assigns a reason for his confident persuasion that he shall not slide, to wit, because God's mercy is before his eyes, literally, *in front* of them, *i. e.* constantly in view, as an object of memory and ground of hope. He is also encouraged by his previous experience of God's *truth* or faithfulness. See above, on Ps. xxv. 5. The verb translated *walked* is an intensive form of that used in ver. 1 above, and ver. 11 below. It means properly to walk about or to and fro, and expresses more distinctly than the primitive verb, the idea of continuous habitual action. " My constant experience of thy mercy and thy faithfulness assure me that I shall not fall away hereafter."

4. *I have not sat with men of falsehood, and with hidden (men) I will not go.* He is further encouraged to believe that he will be sustained because he has not hitherto espoused the cause of those who hate God.—*Men of falsehood*, liars or deceivers, which appears to suit the context better than the wider sense of *vain men, i. e.* destitute of all moral goodness, good for nothing, worthless. See above, on Ps. v. 7 (6), xxiv. 4. The same class of persons are described in the last clause as masked, disguised, or hypocritical.—*Sat*, not merely in their company, but in their councils, taking part in their unlawful machinations. The change of tense is anything rather than unmeaning. " I have not sat with them in time past, and I will not go with them in time to come." The form of expression is borrowed from Gen. xlix. 6.

6. *I will wash in innocence my hands, and will compass thy altar, O Jehovah !* To the negative professions of the two preceding verses he now adds a positive declaration of his purpose. Not content with abstaining from all share in the counsels of the wicked, he is fully resolved to adhere to the service of the Lord. He will cleanse himself from all that would unfit him for that service, and then cleave to the sanctuary where God dwells. The expression in the first clause seems to be copied from Gen. xx. 5, and the symbol or emblem from Deut. xxi. 6. (Compare Mat.

xxvii. 24.) Whether *compassing* the altar be explained to mean going round it in procession, or embracing it, the idea expressed is still that of close adherence and devoted attachment.

7. *To make known with a voice of thanksgiving, and to recount all thy wondrous works.* The object of the acts described in the preceding verse was to promote's God's glory. *To make known*, literally *to cause to hear* or *to be heard.* The clause admits of several constructions. 1. To publish thanksgivings with the voice. 2. To publish with a thankful voice, without expressing what. 3. To publish and recount all thy wondrous works with a voice of thanksgiving. The last is on the whole entitled to the preference. —The last word in the verse is a passive participle, meaning *wonderfully made or done.* The plural feminine is used indefinitely like the neuter in Greek and Latin, to mean *things done wonderfully*, which is also the idea of the common version, *wondrous works.*

8. *Jehovah, I have loved the habitation of thy house, and the place of the dwelling of thy glory.* This verse expresses more directly and literally the idea of ver. 6 above, and shews that his compassing the altar was intended to denote his love for the earthly residence of God, the altar being there put for the whole sanctuary, which is here distinctly mentioned. *The habitation of thy house* might be understood to mean a residence in it ; but the usage of the first noun and the parallelism shew that it rather means *the place where thy house dwells*, perhaps in allusion to the migratory movements of the ark and its appendages before the time of David. So too in the last clause, Hebrew usage would admit of the translation, *thy glorious dwelling-place*, as in Ps. xx. 7 (6) ; but the use of כָּבוֹד, in the Pentateuch, to signify the visible presence of Jehovah (Exod. xxiv. 16, xl. 34, 35), seems decisive in favour of explaining it *the place where thy glory dwells*, *i. e.* where the glorious God is pleased to manifest his presence.

9. *Take not away my soul with sinners, and with men of blood my life.* The primary meaning of the first verb is to *gather*, as a harvest or as fruit, a figure not unfrequently applied in various languages to death, here described as the taking away of the life or soul. This verse and the next contain a prayer that he may die as he has lived ; that since he has had no community of interest or feeling with ungodly men in life, he may not be united with them in his death.—*Men of blood*, literally *bloods*, *i. e.* murderers, either in the strict sense or by metonymy for sinners of the worst class. See above, on Ps. v. 7 (6). Another idiomatic plural in this sentence is the word *lives* at the end, which is used as an abstract simply equivalent to *life* in English.

10. *In whose hands is crime, and their right hand is filled with a bribe.* The first clause exhibits the peculiar construction of the relative in Hebrew with the personal pronoun expressed, of which it is the substitute in other languages. *Who* (or *as to whom*)—in *their hands* (is) *crime.* This last word (זִמָּה) is a very strong one, used *in* the Law to denote specifically acts of gross impurity, but signifying really any wicked act or purpose· The common version, *mischief*, is too weak. The last word in the verse denotes especially a judicial bribe (Ps. xv. 5), and may be intended to suggest that the whole description has reference to unrighteous rulers, or to wicked men in public office.

11. *And I in my integrity will walk ; redeem me and be merciful to me.* The use of the conjunction and emphatic pronoun is the same as in Ps. ii. 6 above. Our idiom would require an adversative conjunction, *but I*, in

opposition to the sinners just described, *but as for me*, I will still walk as I have done in sincerity and simplicity of purpose. The obvious contrast of the tenses here and in ver. 1, may serve to shew how seldom they are used promiscuously or confounded.—That the Psalmist's *perfection* or *integrity* was neither absolute nor inherent, is clear from the petition of the last clause. He expects still to be perfect, not because he is without sin, but because he hopes to be *redeemed* from its dominion through the *mercy* of Jehovah.

12. *My foot stands in an even place ; in the assemblies will I bless Jehovah.* As a state of danger and distress might be compared to a precipitous and rugged path, so one of ease and safety is denoted by a smooth or level path. *My foot* (now) *stands*, or *has* (at last) *stood*, found a resting-place, implying previous wanderings and hardships.—The *assemblies* primarily meant are no doubt the stated congregations at the sanctuary. The determination to praise God implies a strong assurance that the occasion for so doing will be granted. See above, on Ps. v. 8 (7). The whole verse indeed is an expression of confident belief that God will hear and answer the foregoing prayers, and thus, as in many other psalms, we are brought back at the conclusion to the starting-point. Compare the last clause of ver. 1.

Psalm 27

A SUFFERER, surrounded by enemies intent on his destruction, and deprived of human help, implores divine assistance and expresses his assured hope of obtaining it. The expression of confidence occurs at the beginning and the end, the description of the danger and the prayer for deliverance in the body of the psalm. If God be for him, and admit him to his household, he is satisfied and safe, ver. 1–6. With this persuasion he implores that God will interpose for his deliverance from present danger, ver. 7–12. If he did not believe that God would grant his request he must despair; but as he does believe it, he encourages himself to wait for it, ver. 13, 14. There is no apparent reference to any particular historical occasion, but an obvious intention to provide a vehicle of pious sentiment for all God's people under the form of trial here described.

1. *By David. Jehovah (is) my light and my salvation ; of whom shall I be afraid ? Jehovah (is) the stronghold of my life; of whom shall I be in dread ?* As darkness is a common figure for distress, and light for relief from it, the same idea is here twice expressed, first in a figurative form as light, and then more literally as *salvation*. These terms are applied to God, by a natural and common figure of speech, as the source or dispenser of light and salvation. Compare Micah vii. 8. The interrogations imply negation of the strongest kind. The form of expression is imitated in Rom. viii. 31–35.—The noun מָעוֹז is sometimes used as an abstract, *strength ;* but its proper meaning, as its very form denotes, is local. The *stronghold* or *fortress of my life*, that which makes my life as safe as walls and fortifications. The variation of the verbs in the two clauses is merely rhetorical, without any change in the idea.

2. *In the drawing near against me of evil-doers, to devour my flesh,* (in the drawing near of) *my adversaries and my enemies to me,* (it is) *they'(that) have stumbled and fallen.* Even in the most imminent dangers which have hitherto befallen me, the divine protection has enabled me to see those who

sought to overwhelm me overwhelmed themselves. *Evil-doers,* not only against me, but in general. It was not because they were his enemies merely, but because they were the enemies of God, that he so easily subdued them.—*To eat my flesh,* a figure borrowed from the habits of wild beasts. Compare Job xix. 22, Ps. xiv. 4, xxxv. 1.—*To me* is to be construed not with *enemies,* but with the verb, as in Job xxxiii. 22. See below, on Ps. lv. 19. The pronoun expressed in the last clause is emphatic, " They themselves, not I, as they expected, fell."

3. *If there encamp against me an encampment, my heart shall not fear; if there arise against me war,* (even) *in this* (case) *I* (am) *confident.* With the sentiment of this verse compare Ps. iii. 7 (6). The primary meaning of the noun in the first clause is retained in the translation for the sake of its assonance with the verb, which is lost in the common version, although marked in the original. *By encampment,* however, must be understood the men encamped, the host, the army.—*In this,* even in this extremity. Compare Lev. xxvi. 27, Job i. 22. The common version, *in this will I be confident,* although ambiguous, appears to mean, " I will confide in this, *i.e.* in the fact that Jehovah is my light and my salvation." This construction is grammatical, and yields a good sense, but the other is more pointed and emphatic, and the absolute use of בּוֹטֵחַ in the sense of *safe, secure,* is justified by Judges xviii. 27, Jer. xii. 5, Prov. xi. 15.

4. *One* (thing) *have I asked from Jehovah,* (and) *that will I* (still) *seek, that I may dwell in the house of Jehovah, to gaze at the beauty of Jehovah, and to inquire in his temple.* To dwell in the house of the Lord is not merely to frequent his sanctuary as a place of worship, but to be a member of his household, and as such in intimate communion with him. See above, on Ps. xv. 1, xxiii. 6.—*Beauty,* loveliness, desirableness, all that makes God an object of affection and desire to the believer. See below, on Ps. xc. 17. Some take the last verb in the secondary sense of meditating; but the proper one of inquiring is entirely appropriate.—*Temple,* properly palace, the earthly residence of the great King, and therefore equally appropriate to the temple and the tabernacle. See above, on Ps. v. 8 (7).

5. *For he will hide me in his covert in the day of evil; he will secrete me in the secrecy of his tent; on a rock he will set me high.* This verse assigns his reason for wishing to be still a member of Jehovah's household, namely, because there he is sure of effectual protection.—The word translated *covert* means a booth or shelter made of leaves and branches, such as the Jews used at the feast of tabernacles (Lev. xxiii. 42). It is here used as a figure for secure protection *in the day of evil, i.e.* of suffering or danger.—*Secrete* and *secrecy* are used in the translation to represent the cognate verb and noun in Hebrew.—*By his tent,* as appears from the preceding verse, we are to understand the tabernacle, not considered merely as a place of public worship, but as Jehovah's earthly residence, his mansion. In the last clause the idea of protection is conveyed by an entirely different figure, that of a person placed upon a high rock beyond the reach of danger. See above, on Ps. ix. 14 (13), xviii. 49 (48).

6. *And now shall my head be high above my enemies around me, and I will sacrifice in his tabernacle sacrifices of joyful noise; I will sing and make music to Jehovah. And now* may either be a formula of logical resumption, as in Ps. ii. 10, xxxix. 8 (7), or be taken in its strict sense, as denoting that he not only hopes for future safety, but is ready in the mean time, *even now,* to thank him publicly for his protection as already realised. The first clause merely amplifies the last of the preceding verse. The next adds

the promise of a thank-offering at the tabernacle, which implies an assured hope of deliverance and prosperity. By *a joyful noise* some understand the blowing of trumpets which accompanied certain offerings (Num. x. 10, xxix. 1); but as this is never mentioned in connection with private sacrifices, it seems more advisable to rest in the general sense of the expression.

7. *Hear, O Jehovah ! (with) my voice I will call, and do thou have mercy on me and answer me.* The Psalmist here descends from the tone of confident assurance to that of strong desire, prompted by a sense of urgent need.—*With my voice*, not merely with my mind, but audibly, aloud. See above, on Ps. iii. 5 (4).

8. *To thee hath said my heart—Seek ye my face—thy face, Jehovah, will I seek.* The general meaning of this verse is obvious enough, although its syntax is exceedingly obscure. The best solution is to take " seek ye my face " as a citation of God's own words. " My heart has said to thee —(whenever thou hast said) Seek ye my face,—thy face," &c. Or, " my heart has said to thee—(in answer to thy words) Seek ye my face—thy face," &c.—*My heart hath said, i. e.* I have said with or from the heart. See above, on Ps. xi. 1. There may be an allusion to Deut. iv. 29, from which the expression *seek God* (2 Sam. xii. 16, 2 Chron. xx. 4), and *seek his face* (Ps. xxiv. 6, cv. 4) seems to be derived. The idea is that of seeking admission to his presence for the purpose of asking a favour. See above, on Ps. xxiv. 6.

9. *Hide not thy face from me, put not away in wrath thy servant; my help thou hast been; forsake me not, and leave me not, (O) God of my salvation!* The first petition is that God will not withhold from him the manifestation of his love or favour. See above, on Ps. iv. 7 (6).—*Put not away*, or thrust aside, as one unworthy to be noticed.—*Thy servant*, and as such entitled to thy kind regard.—*My help, i. e.* the source and author of my help, my helper. *Thou hast been ;* the past tense is here essential : what thou *hast been*, continue to be still.—*God of my salvation*, my Saviour God, or God my Saviour ; see above, on Ps xviii. 47 (46).

10. *For my father and my mother have left me, and Jehovah will take me in.* Parents are here put for the nearest friends, whose loss or desertion is frequently complained of in the Psalms as one of the most painful signs of desolation. See Ps. xxxi. 12 (11), xxxviii. 12 (11), lxix. 9 (8), lxxxviii. 9 (8), and compare Job xix. 13. The first clause may also be translated, *when my father and my mother have left me, then the Lord will take me in.* —The last expression is applied to the compassionate reception of strangers or wanderers into one's house. See Josh. xx. 4, Judges xix. 15, and compare Mat. xxv. 35, 43. The case described is an ideal one, and may be thus expressed in paraphrase : " The kindness of the nearest earthly friends may cease by death or desertion (for the verb to *leave* may comprehend both) ; but the Lord's compassions cannot fail."

11. *Guide me, Jehovah, (in) thy way, and lead me in a straight (or level) path, because of my adversaries.* The way in which he here desires to be led, is not the way of duty but of providence, which he calls a straight or smooth path, as distinguished from the rough or crooked ways of adversity. See above, on Ps. xxv. 4, xxvi. 12.—*Because of my enemies*, that they may have no occasion to exult or triumph. Of the many Hebrew words applied to enemies, the one here used is supposed by some to signify malignant *watchers* for the errors or calamities of others. The one used in the next verse means oppressors or causers of distress.—With this clause compare Ps. xxvi. 12.

12. *Give me not up to the will of my enemies ; for risen up against me are witnesses of falsehood, and a breather forth of cruelty.* The word translated *will* properly means *soul*, and is here used for the ruling wish or heart's desire, as in Ps. xxxv. 25. The second clause assigns the ground or reason of this prayer. As if he had said, I have reason to ask this, *for* there have risen up, &c.—*One breathing violence* or *cruelty*, a strong but natural expression for a person, all whose thoughts and feelings are engrossed by a favourite purpose or employment, so that he cannot live or breathe without it. Compare the description of Saul's persecuting zeal in Acts ix. 1, and the Latin phrases, *spirare minas, anhelare scelus.*

13. *Unless I believed* (or fully expected) *to look upon the goodness of Jehovah in the land of life.* This is an instance of the figure called aposiopesis, in which the conclusion of the sentence is suppressed, either from excitement and hurried feeling, or because of some unwillingness to utter what is necessary to complete it. Thus in this case the apodosis would probably have been, *I would despair*, or *I must have perished.* (Compare Ps. cxix. 92.) Of the other cases usually cited, that in Gen. xxxi. 42 especially resembles this, because the sentence opens with a similar conditional expression.—*To look upon*, not merely to *behold*, but to *gaze at* with delight. See above on Ps. xxii. 18 (17).—*The land of life*, as opposed to that of darkness and the shadow of death (Job x. 21), seems to be a more correct translation than the common one, *land of the living.*

14. *Wait thou for Jehovah ; be firm, and may he strengthen thy heart ; and wait thou for Jehovah !* Instead of finishing the inauspicious sentence which he had begun, he interrupts himself with an earnest exhortation to await the fulfilment of God's promises, to hope in him. See above, on Ps. xxv. 3.—The optative and causative senses of the third verb (יְאַמֵּץ) are both determined by its form, which equally forbids the versions, *let thy heart be strong*, and *he will strengthen it.*—The repetition, *wait for the Lord, and wait for the Lord*, implies that this is all he has to enjoin upon himself or others, and is more impressive, in its native simplicity, than the correct but paraphrastic version of the last clause in the English Bible, *wait, I say, upon the Lord.*

Psalm 28

As in the preceding psalm, a righteous sufferer prays that he may not be confounded with the wicked whom his soul abhors, so here a like prayer is offered by the Anointed of Jehovah. He first prays in general for audience and acceptance, without which he must quickly perish, ver. 1, 2. He then asks to be distinguished from the wicked in the infliction of God's judgments, ver. 3–5. He then gives thanks for the anticipated answer to his prayer, ver. 6–8, and implores an extension of the blessing to all God's people at all times, ver. 9. The collocation of the psalm is clearly not fortuitous, but founded on its close resemblance to the one before it.

1. *By David. Unto thee, Jehovah, will I call ; my rock, be not silent from me, lest thou hold thy peace from me, and I be made like to those going down (into) the pit.* My rock, the immoveable foundation of my hope and object of my trust. See above, on Ps. xviii. 3, 32 (2, 31), xix. 15 (14). That God is such affords a sufficient reason for the importunate demands which follow. It is inconsistent with the relation he sustains to those who trust him, that he should be silent when they pray, *i. e.* refuse to answer. The ideas of distance and estrangement are really implied in being silent, and suggested by the pregnant construction *silent from.* The meaning of the last clause is correctly given, with a change of idiom, in the English version, *lest, if thou be silent,* &c. The passive verb does not merely mean to be like, but to be made like, assimilated, confounded. *The pit,* the grave, both in its narrower and wider sense. (Compare Isa. xiv. 15, 19.) *Those going down into the pit* is a common description of the dead. See Ps. xxx. 4 (3), lxxxviii. 5 (4), and compare Ps. xxii. 30 (29).

2. *Hear the voice of my supplications, in my crying unto thee* (for help) ; *in my lifting up my hands to thy holy oracle.* In my crying, in my lifting, *i. e.* at the time of my so doing, when I am in the very act. The lifting up of the hands is a natural symbol of the raising of the heart or the desires to God, and is therefore often mentioned in connection with the act of prayer. Exod. ix. 29, xvii. 11, 12, 1 Kings viii. 22, 54, Lam. ii. 19, iii. 41, Ps. lxiii. 5 (4).—The word translated *oracle* is derived from the verb to speak, and seems to mean a place of speaking or conversation, like the English *parlour* from the French *parler.* Now we learn from Exod. xxv. 22, Num. vii. 89, that the place whence God talked with Moses was the inner apartment of the tabernacle ; and from 1 Kings vi. 19, that the corresponding part of the temple bore the name here used. To this, as the depository of the ark and the earthly residence of God, the ancient saints looked as we look now to Christ, in whom the idea of the Mosaic sanctuary has been realised. See above, on Ps. v. 8 (7).

3. *Draw me not away with wicked* (men), *and with workers of iniquity, speaking peace with their neighbours, and evil* (is) *in their heart.* This is the prayer for which he bespeaks audience and acceptance in the foregoing verse. *Draw me not away, i. e.* to punishment or out of life. Compare Ps. xxvi. 9, where the parallel expression is *gather me not.* In both cases he prays that he may not be confounded in his death with those whose life he abhors. The last clause exhibits a particular trait in the character of the *wicked men* and *evil doers* of the other clause. This trait is hypocritical dissimulation, the pretence of friendship as a mask to hatred. The simple construction with the copulative *and* is equivalent to our expressions, *but, though, while,* &c.

4. *Give to them according to their act, and according to the evil of their deeds, according to the work of their hands give thou to them ; return their treatment to them.* Having prayed that he may not share the destruction of the wicked, he now prays that they may not escape it. But as this is merely asking God to act as a just and holy being must act, the charge of vindictive cruelty is not merely groundless, but absurd.—The *evil of their* deeds is a phrase borrowed from Moses (Deut. xxviii. 20), and often repeated by Jeremiah (iv. 4, xxi. 12, xxiii. 2, 22, xxvi. 3, xliv. 22). The same prophet has combined two of the phrases here employed in Jer. xxv. 14, and Lam. iii. 64. The word translated *treatment* is a participle meaning that which is done by one person to another, whether good or evil. See above, on Ps. vii. 5 (4).

5. *Because they will not attend to the acts of Jehovah and to the doing of his hands, he will pull them down and will not build them up.* Having appealed to the divine justice for a righteous recompence of these offenders, he now shews what they have deserved and must experience, by shewing what they have done, or rather not done. The acts of Jehovah and the works of his hands are common expressions for his penal judgments. See

Ps. lxiv. 10 (9), xcii. 5 (4), Isa. v. 12, xxviii. 21, xxix. 23.—*Pull down and not build up*, is an idiomatic combination of positive and negative terms to express the same idea.—*Build*, therefore, does not mean *rebuild*, but is simply the negative or opposite of *pull down*. The form of expression is copied repeatedly by Jeremiah (xxxi. 28, xlii. 10, xlv. 4.) See also Job xii. 14.

6. *Blessed (be) Jehovah, because he hath heard the voice of my supplications.* What he asked in ver. 2 he has now obtained, or at least the assurance of a favourable answer, in the confident anticipation of which he begins already to bless God. The word translated *supplications* means, according to its etymology, prayers for grace or mercy.

7. *Jehovah, my strength and my shield! In him has my heart trusted, and I have been helped, and my heart shall exult, and by my song I will thank* (or *praise*) *him.* The construction of the first clause as a proposition, by supplying the substantive verb, *Jehovah* (is) *my strength and my shield*, is unnecessary, and neither so simple nor so strong as that which makes it a grateful and admiring exclamation.—*My heart* is twice used in this sentence to express the deep and cordial nature of the exercises which he is describing. The same heart that trusted now rejoices. As .he believed with all his heart, so now he rejoices in like manner.—*By my song*, literally *from* or *out of it*, as the source and the occasion of his praise. Compare Ps. xxii. 26 (25).

8. *Jehovah (is) strength to them, and a stronghold of salvation (to) his Anointed (is) He.* The Psalmist having spoken hitherto not only for himself but for the people, here insensibly substitutes the third person plural for the first person singular. In the last clause he reverts to himself, but with the use of an expression which discloses his relation to the people, of which he was not only a member but the delegated head, the *Anointed* of Jehovah. See above, on Ps. ii. 2. *A stronghold.* See above on Ps. xxvii. 1.—*Salvations*, full salvation. See above on Ps. xviii. 51 (50). The personal pronoun at the end of the sentence is emphatic, and intended to concentrate the attention upon one great object.

9. *Oh save thy people, and bless thy heritage, and feed them, and carry* (or *exalt them*) *even to eternity!* The whole psalm closes with a prayer that the relation now subsisting between God and his people may continue for ever. *Thy heritage*, thy peculiar people, whom thou dost preserve and treat as such from generation to generation. The idea and expression are Mosaic. See Deut. ix. 29, and compare Ps. xxxiii. 12, lxviii. 10 (9), xciv. 5. The image then merges into that of a shepherd and his flock, a favourite one with David and throughout the later scriptures. See above, on Ps. xxiii. 1. —*Feed them*, not only in the strict sense, but in that of doing the whole duty of a shepherd. The next verb is by some translated *carry them*, in which sense the primitive is elsewhere used in speaking of a shepherd (Isa. xl. 11), and this very form appears to have the same sense in Isa. lxiii. 9, while in 2 Sam. v. 12 it is applied to the exaltation of David himself as a theocratic sovereign.

Psalm 29

THE essential idea in this psalm is the same as in the twenty-eighth, to wit, that God is the strength of his people, but clothed in a different costume, the divine power being proved or exemplified by its exertion in the elements, and then applied, in the close, to the believer's consolation. The Psalmist first invokes the heavenly host to celebrate their sovereign's honour, ver. 1, 2. He then describes Jehovah's voice as producing the most striking physical effects, ver. 3–9, and represents it as belonging to the same God who presided at the deluge, and who now protects and will continue to protect and bless his people, ver 10, 11. The superficial notion that this psalm is merely a description of a thunderstorm, or of Jehovah as the God of thunder, may be corrected by observing that the last verse gives the key-note of the whole composition.

1. *A psalm by David. Give to Jehovah, ye sons of the mighty, give to Jehovah honour and strength.* To give in such connections, is to recognise something as belonging to another, to ascribe it to him. The form of expression is derived from Deut. xxxii. 3, and is found not only elsewhere in the the Psalms (xcvi. 7, 8), but with a slight modification in the New Testament (Rev. iv. 11, v. 12, xix. 1, 1 Peter v. 11).—The word translated *mighty* is the plural form of one of the names (אֵל) which describe God as omnipotent. See above, on Ps. v. 5 (4), vii. 12 (11), x. 11, 12, xvi. 1, xvii. 6 (5), xviii. 3, 31, 33, 48 (2, 30, 32, 47), xix. 2 (1), xxii. 2 (1). The plural form may here arise from assimilation, both parts of the compound phrase being put into the plural, *son of God, sons of Gods.* Compare *words of deceits*, Ps xxxv. 20. But a much more probable solution is that אֵלִים is here used as אֱלֹהִים is elsewhere, by a kind of ellipsis for אֵל אֵלִים, Dan. xi. 36, *the God of Gods*, or the Supreme God. Compare Deut. x. 17.— *The sons of God* are the beings intermediate between God and man, sometimes called *angels*, in reference to their office. The same application of the same phrase occurs in Ps. lxxxix. 7 (6).

2. *Give to Jehovah the honour of his name; bow to Jehovah in beauty of holiness.* The honour of his name is that belonging to it, due to it. His name is his manifested nature. See above, on Ps. v. 12 (11). The verb in the last clause strictly means, bow down or prostrate yourselves in worship.— *The beauty of holiness* is by many understood to mean holy or consecrated garments, such as were put on in the place of ordinary dress, as a token of reverence, by the priests when they approached unto the presence of Jehovah. See 2 Chron. xx. 21. But neither here nor in Ps. xcvi. 9, cx. 3, is there any valid objection to the obvious but spiritual sense of ornament produced by or consisting in holiness, such decoration as became the peculiar people of Jehovah. Compare 1 Peter iii. 3–5.

3. *The voice of Jehovah on the waters! The God of glory thundered. The voice of Jehovah* (was) *on many waters.* The invocation to the heavenly host in the two preceding verses is now justified by an appeal to one particular manifestation of God's majesty, to wit, that afforded by the tempestuous strife of elements.—The first clause may be construed as an exclamation, or the substantive verb may be supplied, either in the past or present tense. The preterite form of the original does not relate to any specific point of past time, but merely shews that the phenomena described have been heretofore witnessed, and though grand are nothing new. Our present tense gives the sense correctly, but with a departure from the idiomatic form of the original.—*The God of glory* contains an allusion to ver. 1, 2. Compare Ps. xxiv. 7-10.—*On* (or *above*) *the waters, i. e.* the clouds charged with rain. See above, on Ps. xviii. 12 (11), and compare Jer. x. 13.

4. *The voice of Jehovah in power ! The voice of Jehovah in majesty !* The exclamations, as in ver. 3, may be converted into propositions by supplying either the past or present tense of the verb *to be.* ' The voice of Jehovah *is* (or *was*) in power.' In power, in majesty, *i. e.* invested with those attributes, a stronger expression than the corresponding adjectives *strong* and *majestic*, would be, and certainly more natural and consonant to usage than the construction which makes *in* a mere sign of that in which something else consists. It is, indeed, little short of nonsense to affirm that the voice of God consists in power, consists in majesty, whereas there is truth as well as beauty in describing it as clothed or invested with those qualities.

5. *The voice of Jehovah* (*is*) *breaking cedars, and Jehovah has broken the cedars of Lebanon.* In the powerful working of the elements the Psalmist hears the voice of God. That this expression always denotes thunder (Exod. ix. 28) is a perfectly gratuitous assumption.—Cedars are mentioned as the loftiest forest trees, and those of Lebanon as the loftiest of the species. Between the verbs of the two clauses there is a twofold variation which appears to be significant. The first is the primitive verb which simply means to break ; the other an intensive form, implying an extraordinary violence. See above, Ps. iii. 8 (7). This distinction can be reproduced in English only by a change of verb (*break* and *crush*), or by some qualifying addition (*break* and *break in pieces*), But besides this variation, the first word is an active participle (*breaking*), and the second a finite tense denoting past time (*broke* or *has broken*), which together may indicate progression (*it is breaking* and now *he has broken*), or express the same idea, namely, that he habitually breaks, or has often broken, the cedars of Lebanon.

6. *And made them skip like a calf, Lebanon and Sirion like the young of the unicorns* (*antelopes* or *wild bulls*). The pronoun in the first clause may refer to *cedars*, or by anticipation to *Lebanon and Sirion.* This last is the Sidonian name of Hermon (Deut. iii. 9), the principal summit in the range of Anti-libanus, here mentioned simply as a parallel to *Lebanon*, without any special local reference. By a similar rhetorical specification, the natural vivacity of young animals is specially ascribed to a particular species, well known to the writer and his readers as remarkable for wildness and agility. See above, on Ps. xxii. 22 (21).

7. *The voice of Jehovah* (*is*) *hewing flames* (or *with flames*) *of fire.* The reference to lightning in this verse is universally admitted, some even seeing an allusion to the brief and sudden flash in the single clause of which the sentence is composed. Interpreters are not agreed, however, with respect to the specific image here presented. Some understand the act described to be that of *cleaving* or *dividing*, in allusion to the forked appearance of a flash of lightning ; others that of *hewing out, extracting flames ;* and others that of *hewing with* them, *i. e.* using them as weapons of warfare or instruments of vengeance. This last construction is a common one in Hebrew, and is favoured here by the analogy of Isa. li. 9, Hos. vi. 5, where the same verb is applied to God's penal judgments.—The voice of God must here mean his authority or order, as it could not be said without absurdity, that the thunder either hews the lightning, or hews with it.

8. *The voice of Jehovah is about to shake the wilderness ; Jehovah will shake wilderness of Kadesh.* This is equivalent to saying that he can do so, the Hebrew verb having no distinct potential form. The verb translated *shake* is stronger, meaning properly to *cause to tremble.* Having spoken of

God's power as exerted on the mountains, he now says the same thing of
the desert; and as the mountains which he specified were on the northern
frontier, so the wilderness which he selects is that which bounded Palestine
upon the south, the northern portion of the great Arabian desert, with
which the Israelites had many strong associations, founded partly in their
personal experience, but still 'more in their national history. See Deut.
i. 19, viii. 15, xxxii. 10.   It is in this point of view, and not simply as a
plain, which it is not in its whole extent, that the wilderness of Kadesh is
here added to Mount Lebanon.

9. *The voice of Jehovah can make hinds bring forth, and strip forests;
and in his temple, all of it says, Glory !*   The use of the futures is the same
as in the foregoing verse.   As if to shew that the divine control extends to
things both small and great, the Psalmist passes suddenly from lofty mountains and vast deserts to the weakest animals, in whom the terror of his
presence hastens the throes of parturition.   See Job xxxix. 1–3, and compare 1 Sam. iv. 19.   He then returns to more imposing natural phenomena,
such as the stripping of the leaves and branches from whole forests by a
mighty wind, which, no less than the thunder, is to be regarded as the voice
of God.—The temple or palace mentioned in the last clause is not the
temple at Jerusalem, nor any earthly structure, but heaven, or the whole
frame of nature, considered as God's royal residence.   See above, on Ps.
v. 8 (7).   Throughout this palace, *all of it,* i. e. all its parts, its contents,
or its inhabitants—with special reference, perhaps, to the angelic hosts
invoked in ver. 1, who are then described as doing what he there invites
them to do—not merely *speaks of his glory,* as the English version has it,
but *says "glory ! "* as their constant and involuntary exclamation.   As to
the true sense of the verb אָמַר, see above, on Ps. iv. 5 (4).

10. *Jehovah at the flood sat (enthroned), and Jehovah sits (as) King to
eternity.*   There are only two ways in which this verse can be understood.
It must either be explained as introducing a new trait in the description of
a tempest, namely, that of a flood or inundation—or referred to the universal deluge, as the grandest instance of the natural changes which had
been described.   In favour of the latter explanation may be urged the intrinsic grandeur of the image which it calls up, its better agreement with the
solemn declaration in the last clause, the peculiar fitness of a great historical
example just in this place, and the invariable usage of הַמַּבּוּל to mean
Noah's flood.   The sense of the whole verse may be thus expressed in
paraphrase.   The God whose voice now produces these effects is the God
who sat enthroned upon the deluge, and this same God is still reigning over
nature and the elements, and will be able to control them for ever.

11. *Jehovah strength to his people will give; Jehovah will bless his people
(with) peace.*   This is the application of the whole psalm, clearly shewing
that the description of external changes was not given for its own sake, or
for mere poetical effect, but as a source of consolation and a ground of
hope to true believers, who are here assured, in a pregnant summary of
all that goes before, that the God who is thus visible and audible in nature,
who presided at the flood and is to reign for ever, is pledged to exercise the
power thus displayed for the protection and well-being of his people.

Psalm 30

AFTER a title, giving the historical occasion of the psalm, ver. 1, the writer praises God for a signal deliverance from destruction, ver. 2–4 (1–3), and calls upon God's people to join in the praise of the divine compassion, ver. 5, 6 (4, 5). He then reverts to the cause of his affliction, ver. 7, 8 (6, 7), and recounts the means which he employed for its removal, ver. 9–11 (8–10), and for the success of which he vows eternal thankfulness, ver. 12 (13), 11 (12). The occasion and design of the psalm will be considered in the exposition of the title or inscription, which constitutes the first verse of the Hebrew text.

1. *A Psalm. A Song of Dedication (for) the House. By David.* The construction *house of David*, although not ungrammatical, is forced, as that idea would, according to usage, have been otherwise expressed in Hebrew. This construction has moreover given rise to the false notion, that the psalm has reference to the dedication of the king's own dwelling, whereas *the house*, as an absoulte phrase, can only mean the house of God. The historical occasion of the psalm is furnished by the narrative in 2 Sam. xxiv. and 1 Chron. xxi. David's presumption in numbering the people had been punished by a pestilence, which raged until the destroying angel had, in answer to the king's prayer, been required to sheathe his sword. The spot where this indication of God's mercy had been given, was immediately purchased by David, and consecrated by the erection of an altar, upon which he offered sacrifices and received the divine approbation in the gift of fire from heaven (1 Chron. xxi. 26). This place the king expressly calls the house of God (1 Chron. xxii. 1), either in the wide sense of the patriarchal *Bethel* (Gen. xxviii. 17, 22), or as the designated site of the temple, for which he immediately commenced his preparations (1 Chron. xxii. 2), and in reference to which this psalm might well be called a *song of dedication*, although naturally more full of the pestilence, and the sin which caused it, than of the sanctuary yet to be erected,

2 (1). *I will exalt thee, O Jehovah, because thou hast raised me up, and hast not let my enemies rejoice respecting me.* In the first clause there is an antithesis of thought, though not of form. " I will raise thee because thou hast raised me." The second verb is a modified form of one meaning to draw water from a well (Exod ii. 16, 19), and may therefore have been chosen for the purpose of suggesting the idea of a person drawn up from some depth in which he had been sunk, a figure not unfrequent elsewhere. See particularly Ps. xl. 3 (2), below.—*Hast not caused or permitted to rejoice* by abandoning me to them.— לְ does not properly mean *over me*, but *as to me*. The specific idea of *rejoicing over* is suggested by the context.

3 (2.) *Jehovah, my God, I cried to thee (for help) and thou didst heal me.* The address, *my God*, is never unmeaning or superfluous, but always intimates a covenant relation as the ground of confidence. Any severe suffering is represented in Scripture under the figure of disease, and relief from it as healing. See above, on Ps. vi. 3 (2), and compare Ps. xli. 5 (4), cvii. 20, Jer. xiv. 19, xv. 18, xvii. 14, xxx. 17. The healing here meant is identical with the help in ver. 4 (3) and the joy in ver. 12 (11,) and proves nothing therefore as to literal sickness in the Psalmist's case. It is altogether natural, however, to suppose that David may himself have been affected by the prevalent disorder.

4 (3.) *Jehovah, thou hast brought up out of hell my soul, thou hast made*

me alive from (among those) *going down* (into the) *pit.* The extremity of
his danger is described in the strongest terms afforded by the language.
The essential meaning of both clauses is, that God had saved him from what
seemed to be inevitable and irrecoverable ruin.—*Hell,* sheol, the state of
the dead. See above, on Ps. vi. 6 (5).—*Going down into the pit, i.e.* dying.
See above, on Ps. xxii. 30 (29).—*Made me alive from them, i.e.* separated me
from them by restoring or preserving my life, so that I no longer can be
numbered with them.

5 (4.) *Make music to Jehovah, ye his gracious ones, and give thanks to
the memory of his holiness.* The exhortation in the first clause is to praise
God by song with instrumental accompaniment. See above, on Ps. vii.
18 (17), ix. 3, (2, 11). *His gracious ones,* the objects of his mercy, and
themselves endowed with the same attribute. See above, on Ps. iv. 4 (3).—
Memory, in this connection, does not mean the power or the act of remembering, but that which is remembered when we think of God, to wit, his glorious
perfections, which are summed up in *his holiness,* as to the comprehensive
sense of which, see above, on Ps. xxii. 4 (3). See also Hos. xii. 6 (5),
where the *memory* of God is particularly coupled with his mercy, and
Exod. iii. 15, Isa. xxvi. 8, Ps. cxxxv. 13, where *memory* and *name* are used
as parallel expressions.

6 (5). *For a moment in his wrath, life in his favour; in the evening
shall lodge weeping, and at the morning shouting* (or *singing*). Some understand the contrast in the first clause to be one of duration; there is only
a moment in his wrath, but a lifetime in his favour. It is simpler, however, and more agreeable to the usage of the word translated *life,* to read
the clause without an antithesis ; his wrath endures but a moment, and then
his favour restores life, in its wide sense, as including all that makes existence desirable. The same idea is expressed in the last clause by a beautiful figure. Sorrow is only a sojourner, a stranger lodging for the night, to
be succeeded, at the break of day, by a very different inmate. This,
though primarily referring to the joys and sorrows of the present state,
admits of a striking application to the contrast between this life and the
next. See above, on Ps. xvii. 15.

7 (6). *And I said in my security, I shall not be moved for ever.* The
pronoun is emphatic : it was I that said.—*Security.* The Hebrew word
includes the ideas of prosperity, and of that self-confidence which it produces. Compare Deut. viii. 11–18, xxxii. 15, Hos. xiii. 6, 2 Chron. xxxii.
25.—*Moved,* disturbed in my enjoyment, shaken from my present firm
position. See above, on Ps. x. 6, xvi. 8, and compare Ps. xiii. 5 (4),
xv. 5, xxi. 8 (7).

8 (7). *Jehovah, in thy favour thou didst establish to my mountain strength;
thou didst hide thy face, I was confounded.* It was only through God's
mercy that his power was established.—*Thou didst confirm strength* (literally, make it stand) *to my mountain,* a common figure for royal power, and
especially for that of the theocracy, the central point of which was mount
Zion. See 2 Sam. v. 9, 12, Neh. iii. 15, Micah iv. 8, Isa. ii. 3. The idea
of personal prosperity in general, though not expressed directly, is suggested
by the special case of David's official eminence.—*Thou didst hide thy face,*
withdraw the tokens of thy presence and thy favour. See above, on Ps.
xiii. 2 (1).—*I was confounded,* agitated, terrified, perplexed. See above,
on Ps. vi. 3, 4, 11 (2, 3, 10), and compare Ps. ii. 5. The common version,
troubled, is too weak.

9 (8). *Unto thee, Jehovah, will I call, and to Jehovah I will cry for mercy.*

This was the resolution formed at the time when God concealed his face and he was troubled. The insertion of the words *then said I*, at the beginning of the verse, would render the connection clear, but is unnecessary. The translation of the futures as past tenses is a licence which could only be justified by extreme exegetical necessity, certainly not by the trivial circumstance, that the last clause speaks of Jehovah in the third person, which is not more surprising in a prayer than the second person of the first clause would be in a narrative. The sudden change of person is, of course, the same in either case.

10 (9). *What profit* (is there) *in my blood, in my descending to corruption* (or *the grave*)? *Will dust praise* (or *thank*) *thee? Will it tell thy truth?* This argument in favour of his being heard and rescued is the same as that in Ps. vi. 6 (5), and reappears in Ps. lxxxviii. 11–13 (10–12), and in Hezekiah's psalm, Isa. xxxviii. 18, 19, both of which are obvious imitations of David. For the twofold etymology and sense of שַׁחַת, either of which is here appropriate, see above, on Ps. xvi. 10.—*Dust*, the lifeless and disorganised remains of the body.—*Tell thy truth*, attest the truth of thy promises by reciting their fulfilment, and so bear witness to the divine veracity and faithfulness. The questions of course imply negation. " My destruction can be no advantage to the divine glory, but must rather involve a loss of praise."

11 (10). *Hear, Jehovah, and have mercy on me; Jehovah, be a helper for* (or *to*) *me.* This petition is an indirect conclusion from the reasoning of the preceding verse. The logical connection may be made clear by a change of form. " Since thy glory will not be promoted by my death, I am entitled to deliverance, not for my sake but thy own." This last idea is suggested by his appealing to the divine *mercy*, as the ground on which he asked God to become his helper.

12 (11). *Thou hast turned my lament into a dance for me ; thou hast opened my sackcloth and hast girded me* (*with*) *joy.* To his prayer he now adds the account of its fulfilment. The relief of his distress is described as an exchange of his *lament* or funeral song for a joyful dance. Compare Jer. xxxi. 13, Lam. v. 15. In further allusion to the mourning customs of the east, he represents his mourning dress, made of the coarsest hair-cloth, as now *opened*, *i. e.* loosened, unfastened, for the purpose of removal, to be replaced not merely by a gay or festive dress, but by joy itself, poetically represented as a garment. See above, on Ps. xviii. 33, 40 (32, 39), and compare Isa. lxi. 3.

13 (12). *In order that glory may make music to thee and not be dumb, Jehovah, my God, I will praise thee* (or *give thanks to thee*) *for ever.* This verse describes not only the effect but the design of the deliverance asked for, and so furnishes a counterpart to the argument in ver. 10 (9). As the death of the Psalmist would deprive God of praise, so his deliverance is intended to ensure it.—The use of *glory* in the first clause is obscure. Some understand by it the tongue or voice, which is entirely arbitrary ; others the soul, the nobler part of man, as in Ps. xvi. 9, lvii. 9, cviii. 2 (1). But as the form in all these cases is *my glory*, it seems better to take *glory* here without the pronoun in the wide sense of *every thing glorious*, including the worshipper's highest powers, and perhaps his regal dignity, as in Ps. vii. 6 (5) As in God's temple every thing says " Glory !" (Ps. xxix. 9), so every thing glorious among his works is bound to praise him.—*Not be dumb*, a stronger phrase than *not be silent*.—With the last clause compare the words of Hezekiah, Isa. xxxviii. 20.

Psalm 31

THE Psalmist first prays in general for deliverance from his sufferings and his enemies, on the ground of his confidence in God and previous experience of his mercy, ver. 2–9 (1–8). He then prays more particularly for deliverance from his present danger, with a description of the same, ver. 10–14 (9–13). In the remainder of the psalm, the tone of supplication and complaint is gradually exchanged for that of thankful assurance, ver. 15–23 (14–22), and the whole is wound up with an application of the lesson furnished by the Psalmist's experience to the case of all God's people, ver. 24, 25 (23, 24).

1. *To the Chief Musician. A Psalm by David.* Here we meet again with the inscription, *to the chief musician*, which has not appeared before since the title of Ps. xxii. As in all other cases, it explicitly describes the psalm as intended for musical performance in the public worship of the ancient church. As this, however, was the case with all the psalms, the fact that it is mentioned only in some may be explained by supposing, that in them there was something which might otherwise have caused them to be looked upon as mere expressions of personal feeling.—The correctness of the other clause—*a Psalm of David*—is fully attested by internal evidence. The idea that Jeremiah wrote it rests entirely on the imitation of the first clause of ver. 14 (13) in Jer. xx. 10, which is in perfect keeping with the practice of that prophet.

2 (1). *In thee, Jehovah, have I trusted. Let me not be shamed for ever. In thy righteousness deliver me* (or *help me to escape*). The first clause contains the ground of the petitions following, which ground is the same that is often urged elsewhere, namely, that a just God cannot destroy those who trust him. See above, Ps. vii. 2 (1), xi. 1.—The prayer in the next clause may be either that his present shame may not endure *for ever*, or that he may *never* be put to shame, which last idea could not well be otherwise expressed in Hebrew. *Shamed, i. e.* utterly confounded, disappointed, and frustrated in his hopes. See above, on Ps. vi. 11 (10), xxii. 6 (5), xxv. 2, 20. He appeals to God's righteousness or justice, in the strict sense, upon which trust or faith creates a claim, even on the part of the unworthy, not by virtue of any intrinsic merit, but of God's gracious constitution. See, above, on Ps. xvii. 1, 2, xviii. 21–25 (20–24), xxv. 21. xxvi. 1. This verse and the two following reappear, without material variation, in Ps. lxxi. 1–3.

3 (2). *Incline unto me thine ear; (in) haste deliver me; be to me for a rock of strength for a house of defences to save me.* The prayer for speedy deliverance implies extreme necessity and danger. For the meaning of the figures, *rock of strength and house of defences* or fortress, see above, on Ps. xviii. 3 (2), and as to the plural form, on Ps. xviii. 51 (50), xx. 7 (6).—The petition of the first clause seems to imply that God had hitherto appeared to turn a deaf ear to his prayers. It may perhaps have been intended to suggest the additional idea, that his cry was feeble, so that it had hitherto escaped the ear of him to whom it was addressed, and who is now implored to bow down or incline his ear, that the distant sound may reach him.

4 (3). *For my rock and my fortress (art) thou, and for thy name's sake thou wilt lead me and conduct me* (or *provide for me*). What he asks in the preceding verse he here asserts, to wit, that God is his protector, and must therefore, of necessity, protect him, not only for the sufferer's sake, but for

the honour of his own name or manifested nature. See above, Ps. xxiii. 3, for the meaning of this phrase, and on the second verse of the same psalm, for that of the last verb.—The futures in the second clause suggest the idea of necessity, and might perhaps be correctly rendered by the use of our auxiliary *must*.

5 (4). *Thou wilt bring me out from the net which they have hid for me; for thou (art) my strength* (or *my stronghold*). "By thee I confidently hope to be delivered from the craft and malice of my enemies, for my defence and safety are in thee alone." With the first clause compare Ps. xxv. 15, and with the last Ps. xxvii. 1. The change of figure in the last clause shews the whole verse to be highly metaphorical.

6 (5). *Into thy hand I will commit my spirit ; thou hast redeemed me, (O) Jehovah, God of truth.* The verb in the first clause means to entrust or deposit anything of value. By *my spirit* we may either understand my *my life* or *myself*, but not *my soul*, as distinguished from *my body*.—The preterite *thou hast redeemed*, expresses, in the strongest manner, his assured hope, and the certainty of the event.—*God of truth*, veracity or faithfulness. See above, on Ps. xxv. 5, and compare Jer. x. 10. The words of the first clause of this verse were quoted or imitated by our Saviour on the cross, Luke xxiii. 46, which only proves that he considered himself one of those to whom the psalm might be applied, but without excluding others ; and accordingly John Huss, while on his way to the stake, repeatedly quoted this whole verse, as the expression of his own emotions.

7 (6). *I have hated those regarding vanities of falsehood, and I* (for my part) *in Jehovah have confided.* The present is included in the preterite of the first clause. "I have hated them, and hate them still." "I hate them, and have done so heretofore." See above, Ps. xvi. 4, xxvi. 5.—*Regarding*, religiously observing, waiting upon, watching with respect and trust. Compare Hos. iv. 10, Zech. xi. 11, Jonah ii. 9 (8). This last place contains also the word *vanities* here used, and even in the Law applied to idols, as no gods, and as "nothing in the world" (1 Cor. viii. 4). See Deut. xxxii. 21, and compare Jer. ii. 5, x. 15, xiv. 22, xvi. 19, xviii. 15. The words here combined are highly contemptuous, denoting *vanities of emptiness*, or *nothings of nonentity*, presented in contrast to *Jehovah, God of truth*, in whom the Psalmist has confided. *And I*, as opposed to them. See above, on Ps. ii. 6.

8 (7). *I will triumph and joy in thy mercy, thou who hast seen my affliction, hast known the pangs of my soul.* In the strength of his faith he sees deliverance already present.—*Hast known in the pangs of my soul, i.e.* in the time of my distress hast been aware of it, which seems to be the meaning of this verb and preposition elsewhere (Gen. xix. 33, 35, Job xxxv. 15). Luther and others give a different construction, *hast known my soul in distress*, but the other is favoured by the occurrence of the phrase *distress* (or *agonies*) *of soul* in Gen. xlii. 21, and Ps. xxv. 17. The sight and knowledge here applied to God imply a corresponding action. "Thou hast seen and known my state, and dealt with me accordingly." With the first clause compare Ps. ix. 3 (2).

9 (8). *And hast not shut me up in the hand of a foe*, (but) *hast made to stand in the wide place my feet.* To shut up in the hand of any one is to abandon to his power. The expression is a figurative one, but occurs in prose, and even in the history of David. See 1 Sam. xxiii. 11, xxvi. 8. The figure of the last clause is a favourite with David. See above, on Ps. iv. 2 (1), xviii. 20, 37 (19, 36).

10 (9). *Have mercy upon me, O Jehovah, for distress is to me ; sunken through grief is my eye, my soul, and my belly.* Having thus professed his confidence of ultimate deliverance, he reverts to his actual condition, and prays for the divine interposition, on the ground of what he has already suffered. On the sinking or falling of the eye, as a sign of extreme grief and weakness, see above, on Ps. vi. 8 (7). Having mentioned this as a specific symptom, he then uses the generic terms, *soul* and *belly, i. e. body.*— For the true sense of the word translated *grief,* see above, on Ps. x. 14.

11 (10). *For wasted with grief* (or *indignation*) *is my life, and my years with sighing ; my strength totters because of my iniquity, and my bones are decayed.* Wasted, consumed before the time.—*Life* and *years, grief* and *sighing,* are correlative expressions. Life is made up of years ; grief is expressed by sighs and groans.—To *totter* or *stumble* is a verb applied elsewhere to the parts of the body—as the knees in Ps. cix. 24—here metaphorically to the strength itself.—*Because of my iniquity* or *guilt* is not inconsistent with the appeal to God's righteousness in ver. 2 (1), but only proves that the Psalmist lays no claim to a sinless perfection. See above, on Ps. xviii. 24 (23).—The *bones* are mentioned as the seat of strength, the solid frame-work of the body.—*Decayed,* grown old, worn out. See below, on Ps. xxxii. 3.

12 (11). *By means of* (or *because of*) *all my adversaries I was a reproach, and to my neighbours very* (*much*), *and a fear to my acquaintances ; seeing me in the street they fled from me* (or *those seeing me in the street fled from me*). The first word properly means *from* or *out of.* It was from his enemies, both as the cause and the occasion, that his disgrace proceeded. *A reproach,* despised by others, and considered a disgrace to them. See above, on Ps. xxii. 7 (6). In the second clause there is an obvious progression. He was so esteemed, not only by his fellow-men indefinitely, but by his neighbours, and that greatly (מְאֹד), which seems equivalent to saying, " and to none more than my neighbours," or, " above all to my neighbours." In the last clause the climax is completed. Not only were his neighbours ashamed of him ; his acquaintances were afraid of him. See below, Ps. xxxviii. 12 (11), lxix. 9 (8), lxxxviii. 19 (18), and compare Job xix. 13, 14.

13 (12). *I was forgotten as a dead man out of mind ; I was like a broken vessel* (or *a vessel perishing*). The next stage of his calamity was that of contemptuous oblivion, which usually follows the acute one of disgust and shame described in the foregoing verse.—*From the heart, i. e.* the memory ; the expression seems to correspond exactly to the second member of the English proverb, *Out of sight, out of mind.*—The comparison with an earthen vessel, at best of little value, easily broken, and when broken, worthless, only fit to be contemptuously thrown aside, is a favourite with Jeremiah, who appears to have derived it, with some other favourite ideas and expressions, from the psalm before us. See Jer. xix. 11, xxii. 28, xxv. 34, xlviii. 38, and compare Hos. viii. 8.

14 (13). *For I heard the slander of many—terror* (was) *all around—in their consulting together against me, to take my soul* (or *my life*) *they plotted.* The *for* connects what follows not so much with what immediately precedes as with the general description of his urgent need in ver. 10 (9). *Have mercy upon me, for distress is to me,* of which he is about to give another proof or instance. The first clause is closely copied in Jer. xx. 10, and the phrase *magor missabib* (fear round about) is a favourite with that prophet. See Jer. vi. 25, xx. 3, xlvi, 5, xlix. 29, and compare Lam. ii. 22. —The term used for *consulting* is akin to that in Ps. ii. 2.—The connection between the slander of the first clause and the plotting of the second seems to be, that the former was regarded as a necessary means to the successful execution of the latter.

15 (14). *And I on thee did trust, Jehovah ; I said, my God* (art) *thou !* " Amidst these distresses, and in spite of them, I still confided in Jehovah, and expressed my confidence by solemnly avouching him to be my God, and therefore bound by covenant to save me, as I am no less bound by covenant to trust him." It is worthy of remark how constantly the ancient saints make trust in God essential to all spiritual safety.—With the last clause of this verse compare Ps. xvi. 1.

16 (15). *In thy hand* (are) *my times; set me free from the hand of my foes and from my persecutors.* By *times* we are to understand the current of events or the vicissitudes of life, as when we speak familiarly of good times, hard times, and the like. There may be also an allusion to the turning-points or critical junctures of his history. The first clause presents the ground or reason of the second. " Since the events of my life are at thy disposal, set me free," &c. Freeing from the hand is the opposite of shutting up in it. See above, on ver. 9 (8).—*Foes* and *persecutors*, not as distinct classes, but as different descriptions of the same.

17 (16). *Let thy face shine on thy servant; save me in thy mercy.* The first clause contains an allusion to the sacerdotal benediction recorded in Num. vi. 25. See above, on Ps. iv. 7 (6), where we have a similar allusion to that passage. " Grant me a sensible assurance of thy favour." This he asks because he is his servant, a relation implying the necessity of God's interposition in his favour. While God is God, he cannot leave his faithful servants to perish. Even here, however, his appeal is to God's mercy, as the only source or means of safety.

18 (17). *Jehovah, let me not be shamed, for I have called* (upon thee). *Let the wicked be shamed, be silenced, in hell.* He distinguishes himself, as one who calls upon God, from the wicked who do not, and appeals to the righteousness of God as requiring that defeat, and disappointment, and frustration of the hopes, should fall, not upon the class to which he belongs and of which he is the representative, but upon that represented by his enemies, of whom it has been well said, that they are not reckoned sinners because they are his enemies, but enemies because they are sinners, or in other words, enemies to him because they are the enemies of God.— *Silenced* in reference to their present loud and angry contests with the righteous.—*In hell*, or in the grave, *i. e.* in death.

19 (18). *Struck dumb be the lips of lying, the (lips) speaking against a righteous (man), insolently in pride and scorn.* This wish has special reference to the slanders mentioned in ver. 14 (13).—*Insolently*, literally *insolent*, that which is insolent, or as an abstract, insolence, audacity.

20 (19). *How great is thy goodness which thou hast hidden for those fearing thee,* (and) *wrought for* (those) *trusting in thee before the Son of man* (or *mankind*) *!* Some suppose an antithesis between what God does secretly for those who trust him openly, or publicly profess their faith. Compare Mat. vi. 4. But usage and the masoretic accents are in favour of a different construction, which connects *before the sons of man* with *wrought*, and supposes the antithesis to be between the two successive stages of God's dispensations towards believers, first what he does in secret, and then what he does in public. " How great is thy goodness which thou hast first treasured up, and then wrought openly before the sons of men for those who trust thee."

21 (20). *Thou wilt secrete them in the secret of thy face* (or *presence*) *from the leagues of man ; thou wilt hide them in a covert from the strife of tongues.* A particular manifestation of this goodness is now specified, to wit, the protection of its objects from the craft and malice of their fellow-men. The figures are the same as in the first clause of Ps. xxvii. 5, except that the presence of God is substituted for his dwelling, which indeed derives its power of protection solely from that presence. The *leagues* or *plots of man* are those mentioned in ver. 14 (13), and the *strife of tongues* the *slander* there referred to ; not the strife of tongues in mutual dispute among his enemies, but the united strife of all their tongues against himself.

22 (21). *Blessed* (be) *Jehovah, for he hath made his mercy wonderful to me in a city of defence* (or *fortified city*). What he had just asserted to be generally true of all believers, he now declares to have been verified in his own experience.—*Has made his mercy wonderful*, has exercised surprising mercy, or in modern phrase, has been wonderfully gracious.—*In a fenced city* is by some understood to mean *as* such a city, a comparison which really occurs in other places. For another supposed instance of the same construction, see above, on Ps. xxix. 4. In this case, however, as in that, the strict sense of the particle may be retained, not only without injury but with advantage to the sense, which will then be, that Jehovah had exercised extraordinary mercy towards the psalmist, by bringing him into a position where he was as safe from the evils which he felt or feared, as he would have been from mere corporeal perils in a walled town or a fortress.

23 (22). *And* (yet it was) *I* (that) *said in my terror, I am cut off from before thine eyes. Nevertheless, thou didst hear the voice of my prayers* (for mercy) *in my crying unto thee* (for help). The full force of the emphatic pronoun can be represented only by a paraphrase. The meaning is that this very person who experiences this wonderful protection was the same who, but a little while before, had given himself up for lost.—*In my haste.* The Hebrew word denotes the hurried flight of one escaping panic-struck from his pursuers. See the literal application of the verb, in historical prose, to the case of David himself, 1 Sam. xxiii. 26, and compare Ps. xlviii. 6 (5), civ. 7. Our idiom absolutely requires an adversative particle at the beginning of the second clause, although the Hebrew word is properly a particle of affirmation, meaning *certainly* or *surely*. Notwithstanding his despondency and unbelief, Jehovah heard and answered his prayers for mercy and his cries for help, both which ideas are suggested in the original.

24 (23) *Love Jehovah, ye his gracious ones* (or *favoured ones*); *faith-keeping* (is) *Jehovah, and repaying in plenty* (the man) *working pride* (or *acting proudly*). In this and the remaining verse, he makes a further application of the truth, which he had just attested from his own experience, to the case of all God's saints or gracious ones, at once the subjects and the objects of benignant dispositions, those who are merciful because they obtain mercy (Mat. v. 7). See above, on Ps. iv. 4 (3).—The next words admit of two interpretations : *keeping* (preserving) *the faithful*, and *keeping faith*, literally *fidelities*, the plural being often used in Hebrew as an abstract. The predominant usage of אמונים is in favour of this last construction. See above, on Ps. xii. 2 (1). *Keeping faith* of course means with those who are faithful to himself, so that we still have the antithesis between them and the man *doing, exercising pride*, a form of speech much stronger than its English equivalent, acting proudly.—*Abundantly*, or literally, *in plenty*.

25 (24). *Be strong, and let him confirm your heart, all ye that wait for Jehovah* (or *hope in him*). The idea and the form of expression are the same as in Ps. xxvii. 14, except that what the Psalmist there says to himself, or to his own soul, he here says to all that hope in God, or wait for the fulfilment of his promises. See the same description of God's people in Ps. xxxiii. 18, below.—*Be strong* in purpose and desire, and he will make you strong in fact. This promise is conveyed under the form of a wish, *may he strengthen* (or *confirm*) *your heart.* See above, on Ps. xxvii. 14.

Psalm 32

THE Psalm opens with a general assertion of the blessedness arising from the pardon of sin, ver. 1, 2, which is then exemplified by a statement of the Psalmist's own experience, ver. 3–6, and extended to the case of others also, ver, 7–9, the whole ending, as it began, with an assertion of the misery of sinners and the happiness of the righteous, ver. 10, 11.

1. *By David. Maschil. Happy* (*he whose*) *transgression* (*is*) *taken away, covered* (*his*) *sin.* The ascription of the psalm to David is not only free from all improbability, and recognised in the New Testament (Rom. iv. 6), but confirmed by its resemblance to his other compositions, and by a seeming reference to a signal incident in David's life, described as unique in the history itself (1 Kings xv. 5), and the same which gave occasion to the fifty-first psalm. The feelings here described bear a striking analogy to those recorded in the narrative, 2 Sam. xii., as will be more distinctly pointed out below. But although there is reason to believe that this psalm was connected, in its origin, with a peculiar and most painful passage of the writer's own experience, it was not intended to express his personal emotions merely, nor even those of other saints in precisely the same situation, but to draw from this one case a general lesson, as to the misery of impenitent dissimulation, and the happiness arising from confession and forgiveness. And lest this wide scope of the psalm should be lost sight of in the contemplation of the circumstances which produced it, it is described in the inscription as a *maschil*, an instructive or didactic psalm, a designation which, in the case of many other psalms, would be superfluous, and which is actually found, for the most part, only where the didactic purpose of the composition is for some cause less obvious than usual. (Compare the introduction to Ps. xxxiv. below.) That the *maschil* was prefixed by David himself, is rendered still more probable by the allusion to it in the body of the psalm. See below, on ver. 8.—*Taken away*, put out of sight, the same idea that is expressed in the other clause by *covered.* This verse is explained by Paul, in Rom. iv. 6, as relating to justification " without works " and " by faith."

2. *Happy man — Jehovah will not impute to him iniquity — and there is not in his spirit guile.* The peculiar form of the construction may be thus resolved into our idiom: happy the man to whom the Lord, &c. The phrase at the beginning, *Oh the happinesses of the man*, is substantially the same as in Ps. i. 1.—*Impute*, reckon or charge to his account, and deal with him accordingly. The whole phrase occurs in 2 Sam. xix. 20 (19). The threefold designation, *sin, transgression*, and *iniquity*, seems to be borrowed from Exod. xxxiv. 7, where the doctrine of forgiveness is first fully and explicitly propounded.—*Guile*, deceit, including self-deception as to one's own character and dissimulation in the sight of God, the attempt

to palliate or conceal sin instead of freely confessing it, which is an indispensable condition of forgiveness, according to the doctrine of both testaments (Prov. xxviii. 13, 1 John i. 8–10).

3. *For I kept silence (and) my bones decayed, in my roaring all the day.* The sentence admits of several different constructions—'because I kept silence my bones decayed'—'when I kept silence,' &c. But the simplest is that which gives the כִּי its usual and proper meaning, and supposes it to introduce the Psalmist's proof of the preceding proposition drawn from his own experience. "I know this happiness, *for* I was once in a different condition and have been delivered."—*Kept silence*, refrained from acknowledging my sins to God. The bones are here put for the framework of the body, in which the strength resides, and the decay of which implies extreme debilitation. The verb translated *decayed* is especially applied to the weakening effect of time ; they grew old, or wore out.—*In* denotes both time and cause—'while I roared,' and 'because I roared.' The figure is borrowed from the habits of inferior animals, and means loud or passionate complaint. See above, on Ps. xxii. 2 (1).

4. *For day and night thy hand weighs upon me; changed is my moisture in* (or *into*) *droughts of summer. Selah.* The *for* at the beginning shews the connection of this verse with that before it, as assigning the cause of the decay there mentioned. "My bones waxed old *because* thy hand," &c.—The future in the first clause cannot, without arbitrary violence, be taken as a preterite. It seems to have been used for the purpose of describing his condition as it seemed to him at the time, when the hand of God not only weighed upon him but seemed likely still to do so. See above, on Ps. xviii. 17 (16). The word translated *moisture, i. e.* vital juice, analogous to the sap of plants, is so explained from an Arabic analogy ; but some think this sense inappropriate in the only other case where the Hebrew word occurs (Num. xi. 8), and infer from Ps. cii. 5 (4), that it is an unusual expression for the heart. His inward agonies are represented as intense and parching heats.

5. *My sin I will make known to thee, and my guilt I did not conceal. I said, I will make confession of my transgressions to Jehovah. And thou didst take away the guilt of my sin. Selah.* Most interpreters explain the future verb of the first clause as a preterite, because all the other verbs are preterites ; but this only renders the future form of the first verb more remarkable, and makes it harder to explain why a past tense was not used in this, as in all the other cases, if the writer intended to express past time. The only consistent method of solution is to understand the first clause as a reminiscence of the Psalmist's resolution in the time of his distress, repeated in the second clause, and, in both cases, followed by a recital of the execution of his purpose. (I said) my sin I will make known to thee, and my guilt I (accordingly) did not conceal. I said, I will make confession to Jehovah, and thou didst take away the guilt of my sin. See above, on Ps. xxx. 9 (8).

6. *For this shall every gracious one make supplication to thee at the (right) time (for) finding (thee); surely at the overflow of many waters, unto him they shall not reach.* The first words are equally ambiguous in Hebrew and in English. At first sight, both may seem to mean, for this grace, this forgiveness, every godly man shall pray to thee. But although this construction yields a good sense, it is less consistent with the usage of the Hebrew verb and preposition than another which explains the phrase to mean *for this cause*, or on this account, to wit, because I have experienced

the blessedness of penitent confession and the pardon which invariably follows it. For the true sense of חָסִיר, see above, on Ps. xxxi. 24 (23).—

Shall pray is not a mere prediction or anticipation, but a jussive future, such as is constantly employed in laws. The sense might therefore be conveyed by rendering it, *let every pious person pray.*—The *time of finding* is the time when God is to be found. See Isa. lv. 6, and compare Deut. iv. 29, Jer. xxix. 12–14. In this case there may be a particular allusion to the interval between the sin and punishment, during which the penitent confessions and importunate petitions of the sinner,—*i. e.* the offending saint, to whom alone the Psalmist here refers—may avail to avert the judgments which must otherwise inevitably follow. This effect is described in the last clause by the figure of a flood, which is not suffered to extend to him. The word translated *surely* means in strictness *only*; *i. e.* the effect of such a prayer will be only this, or, as we say, neither more nor less.

7. *Thou* (*art*) *a hiding-place for me; from distress thou wilt preserve me; with songs* (or *shouts*) *of deliverance thou wilt surround me. Selah.* This is not, as some suppose, the prayer itself, which the believer is exhorted, in ver. 6, to offer, but a confirmation of the truth of the assurance that the prayer will prove effectual, derived from the psalmist's own experience, or rather from the feelings which it has produced. As if he had said, "Every gracious soul may try this method without fear of disappointment, for I have tried it, and the effect is that, at this very moment, God is my refuge and protector, and I feel a strong assurance that he has the joy of his salvation in reserve for me." The solemnity and truth of this profession are then indicated by a meditative pause, denoted in the usual manner.

8. *I will instruct thee, and will guide thee, in the way which thou shalt go; I will counsel thee, my eye* (shall be) *upon thee.* Some regard these as the words of God to David; but besides the gratuitous assumption of two different speakers in the two successive verses, without anything to indicate a change, the obvious allusion in the first word (אַשְׂכִּילְךָ) to the laconic title of the psalm (מַשְׂכִּיל)—as if the instruction there promised was about to be imparted—makes it altogether probable that David is here speaking in his own person and fulfilling the vow recorded in another place, that when forgiven and restored to communion with God, he would teach transgressors his ways. See Ps. li. 15 (13). He may therefore be considered as addressing another like himself—to wit, a godly person (חָסִיד) overtaken in transgression or exposed to strong temptation—and offering to point out to him the path of safety. The construction of the latter clause which some prefer—*I will counsel for thee* (*with*) *my eye*—is much less natural and simple than the one above given, where the phrase, *my eye is* (or *shall be*) *upon thee*, adds to the idea of advice that of friendly watchfulness and supervision.

9. *Be ye not as a horse* (or) *as a mule* (in which) *there is no understanding—in bridle and bit* (consists) *its ornament, to muzzle it,* (because of its) *not approaching to thee.* The counsel or advice, which was promised in the previous verse, is here imparted. The plural form does not imply a change in the object of instruction, but merely shews that the individual addressed in ver. 8 was the representative of a whole class, namely, that described by the collective phrase, *every gracious* (*person*), in ver. 6.—The mule is, among various nations, a proverbial type of stubborn persistency in evil, and we find analogous allusions to the horse in Jer. v. 8, viii. 6.

The reason for using a comparison with brutes is intimated in the second clause, to wit, that the debased irrationality of sin might be distinctly brought into view. The analogy is carried out with no small subtilty by representing that what seems to be the trappings or mere decoration of these brutes is really intended to coerce them, just as that in which men pride themselves may be, and if necessary will be used by God for their restraint and subjugation. The common version of the last clause—*lest they come near unto thee*—would be suitable enough in speaking of a wild beast, but in reference to a mule or horse the words can only mean, because they will not follow or obey thee of their own accord, they must be constantly coerced, in the way both of compulsion and restraint.

10. *Many pains* (are) *to the wicked; and* (as to) *the* (man) *trusting in Jehovah, mercy shall encompass him*, or, *he will encompass him* (with) *mercy*. In this and the remaining verse the psalmist loses sight, not only of the horse and mule, to which he had compared the stubborn sinner, but of the particular case which had occasioned the comparison, and closes with the statement of a general truth, founded in necessity and verified by all experience, that sin produces misery and trust in God salvation. It is implied though not expressed in the first clause, that the sufferings of the wicked, while he still continues such, are hopeless and incurable, while those to which the righteous is subjected, are salutary in effect and temporary in duration. See below, Ps. xxxiv. 20 (19). Here again, as in Ps. xxxi. 15 (14) above, we may observe that the antithesis is not between the wicked and the absolutely righteous, but between the wicked and the man trusting in Jehovah, and that the effect ascribed to this trust is not the recognition of the man's inherent righteousness, but his experience of God's mercy, which implies that he is guilty and unworthy in himself, and can only be delivered from the necessary consequences of his sin, by simply trusting in the mercy of the very Being whom he has offended.—Of the two constructions given in the version of the closing words, the last is recommended by the analogy of ver. 7, where the same verb governs two accusatives.

11. *Rejoice in Jehovah, and exult, ye righteous, and shout* (or *sing*), *all ye upright in heart!* This is the practical use to be made of the preceding doctrine; for, if that be true, it follows that the righteous have abundant cause for exultation, not in themselves but in Jehovah, *i. e.* in their knowledge and possession and enjoyment of him.—*The righteous*, as opposed to the *wicked;* not the absolutely perfect, but those trusting in the mercy of Jehovah for deliverance both from punishment and sin. The verb of the second clause is properly a causative, and means to make others shout or sing for joy. See Deut. xxxii. 43, Ps. lxv. 9 (8), Job xxix. 13. In one place, however, Ps. lxxxi. 2 (1), it appears to be intransitive, and such may be the case here, where the other verbs mean simply to rejoice.

Psalm 33

A SONG of praise, intended to excite and to express the confidence of Israel in Jehovah, and closely connected with the didactic psalm before it, the closing sentiment of which is here carried out. This intimate relation of the two psalms may account for the absence of a title in the one before us, as in the case of the ninth and tenth. See above, p. 46.

After a general invitation to praise God, ver. 1–3, the reasons are assigned, to wit, his truth, faithfulness, and mercy, ver. 4–6, his creative power, ver-

7–9, and his control of human agents, not only individuals but whole nations, making them subservient to his own designs, ver. 10, 11, from all which is inferred the happy lot of his peculiar people, ver. 12. The Psalmist then continues his praise of God, as omniscient, ver. 13, 14, and contrasts the insufficiency of all created help, ver. 15, 16, with the security of those whom he protects, ver. 17, 18, and the whole concludes with an expression of strong confidence in him, on the part of all his people, ver. 19-21.

1. *Exult, ye righteous, in Jehovah! To the upright suitable* (is) *praise.* The Hebrew verb, according to the etymologists, originally means to dance for joy, and is therefore a very strong expression for the liveliest exultation. *In Jehovah, i. e.* in the knowledge and possession of him, with particular reference to the covenant relation between him and his peculiar people, who are here called the *righteous* and the *upright*, by way of eminence, as in Num. xxiii. 10, not because they were all actually so, but because they ought to have been so, as this was the idea or, so to speak, the theory of a chosen people, and those natural descendants of Israel who were not of this character were not entitled to the privileges of the church, which, on the contrary, to the true Israel, were legitimate occasion of rejoicing, and made praise peculiarly *comely* or *suitable* to them.

2. *Give thanks to Jehovah with a harp ; with a lyre of ten* (strings) *make music to him.* The first verb means to acknowledge, either sins or favours; in the first case, it answers to *confess*, Ps. xxxii. 5, in the other to *thank*, Ps. vii. 18 (17). See also Ps. xxviii. 7, xxx. 10 (9). The common version, *praise*, is too indefinite, though this idea is undoubtedly included. The mention of the instruments does not exclude vocal praise, but merely gives it an accompaniment and support, as if the voice were too weak by itself to utter the divine praise. The precise form of the instruments here named is now unknown and wholly unimportant. The ten strings of the second are mentioned, either to identify it by a similar circumstance, or, as some suppose, because the number had a mystical significance. The same combination reappears below in Ps. cxliv. 9, while in Ps. xcii. 4 (3) the two words are separately used, as if denoting different instruments.

3. *Sing unto him a new song ; play well with joyful noise!* A new song implies the continual recurrence of fresh reasons and occasions for the praise of God, and also the spontaneous ebullition of devout and thankful feelings in the hearts of those by whom the praise is offered. This is the first instance of the expression, but it frequently reappears in later psalms— Ps. xl. 4 (3), xcvi. 1, xcviii. 1—and once or twice in the New Testament, Rev. v. 9, xiv. 3.—*Play well*, literally *do well to play* or *in playing.* This peculiar idiom occurs in the history of David, 1 Sam. xvi. 17.—*Joyful noise*, see above, on Ps. xxvii. 6, in which place, as in this, there is no certain or necessary reference to sacrifice, but only to an audible and lively expression of religious feeling.

4. *For right is the word of Jehovah, and all his work is* (done) *in faithfulness.* The *word* here meant is the word of promise, and the *work* is its performance or fulfilment. The *word* is right or upright, *i. e.* uttered in sincerity and with a full determination to redeem it. *In faithfulness*, executed faithfully. Compare Num. xxiii. 19, Ps. cv. 42.

5. *Loving righteousness and justice*—(with) *the mercy of Jehovah is the earth filled.* He is loving, *i. e.* he habitually loves. The last clause represents God's mercy as a matter of notorious and universal observation, and the whole verse exhibits his justice and his mercy as in harmony with one another, and equally consolatory to his people.

6. *By the word of Jehovah were the heavens made, and by the breath of his mouth all their host.* Having set forth the righteousness, fidelity, and mercy of Jehovah, as displayed on earth, the Psalmist now demonstrates his ability to deliver and protect his people, by exhibiting his almighty power in the creation and sustentation of the universe. There is obvious allusion to the history of the creation in Genesis. This is especially apparent in the closing words, *all their host*, which are borrowed from Gen. ii. 1. *Breath* is a poetical equivalent to *word,* 'and conveys still more strongly the idea of the ease with which a God could make a world. At the same time, it is not a mere fortuitous coincidence, that these two words are used in Scripture to designate the second and third persons of the Godhead. Compare Gen. i. 2, Job xxvii. 3, xxxiii. 4, Ps. civ. 29, 30, Isa. xi. 4.

7. *Gathering as a heap the waters of the sea, putting in storehouses the depths.* The participle represents it is an act still continued, and affording a perpetual evidence of God's almighty power, which is just as necessary now as on the first day of creation, to prevent the earth from being totally submerged.—*As a heap.* Dealing with fluids as if they were solids, with an obvious allusion to Exod. xv. 8. See also Josh. iii. 13–16, Ps. lxxviii. 13. —*Putting*, literally *giving*, storing, depositing.—*Depths*, masses of water. The main point of the description is God's handling these vast liquid masses, as men handle solid substances of moderate dimensions, heaping the waves up and storing them away, as men might do with stones or wheat.

8. *Let them be afraid of Jehovah—all the earth ; let them stand in awe of him—all the dwellers in the world.* The position of the verbs at the beginning of the clauses adds greatly to the strength of the expression. The parallelism is exact, the terms being nearly synonymous. That the earth of the first clause means its rational inhabitants, is implied in the plural verb, and expressed in the parallel clause. For the precise sense of the word translated *world*, see above, on Ps. xxiv. 1. The remoter inference suggested is, that this omnipotent creator and preserver of the universe is able to protect his people, and entitled to their confidence.

9. *For* (it was) *He* (that) *said* (Be), *and it was;* (it was) *He* (that) *commanded, and it stood.* The whole form of the sentence here is modelled upon that of the cosmogony in Genesis, where these two verbs repeatedly alternate. The common version, *he spake and it was done*, is liable to three exceptions. The first is, that the emphatic pronoun of the Hebrew is not fairly represented ; the second, that the phrase *it was done* is much less striking than *it was;* the third, that the Hebrew verb (אָמַר) does not mean to *speak* but to *say.* See above, on Ps. iv. 5 (4). What was said, every reader could supply from recollection of the narrative in Genesis.—*Stood*, appeared, came into existence. Compare Ps. cxix. 90, 91.

10. *Jehovah has annulled the counsel of nations ; he has frustrated the plans of the peoples.* What he has done he can do, although this is not explicitly affirmed. He who created and sustains the universe can frustrate, as he pleases, the designs of his own creatures, whether individuals or nations, from whom, therefore, his own people can have nothing to fear.

11. *The counsel of Jehovah to eternity shall stand ; the thoughts of his heart to generation and generation.* This is the converse of the proposition. For the same reason that no purpose of his creatures can succeed against his will, no opposition of the creature can affect the execution of his own designs.—*Counsel*, plan, purpose.—*Thoughts of his heart*, conceptions or intentions of his mind.—*To generation and generation*, a common idiomatic phrase meaning one generation after another, or indefinitely, all generations.

12. *Happy the nation whose God (is) Jehovah, the people he hath chosen for a heritage for him.* This is the centre of the whole psalm, the conclusion from what goes before, and the text or theme of all that follows. Under the general proposition is included a particular felicitation of Israel as the actual choice and heritage of God, *i.e.* chosen to be his, in a peculiar sense, by hereditary succession, through a course of ages.

13. *From heaven looked Jehovah; he saw all the sons of man* (or *Adam*). He looked not at any one time merely, but at all times ; he has always looked upon them since he first created them. As his omnipotence is constantly exerted to sustain them in existence, so his omniscience is continually exercised in the same inspection as at first.

14. *From the place of his dwelling he gazed at all the dwellers on the earth.* From his own residence without and above the earth, he has continued still to look intently upon its inhabitants. The verb is a poetical one, stronger than the ordinary *look.* See Song Sol. ii. 9, Isa. xiv. 16.

15. *The (God) forming all their hearts, the (God) attending to all their deeds.* The article agrees with the subject of the verb understood, and this construction it is necessary to retain, in order to connect the sentence as closely with the one before it as in the original. *Forming* implies *knowing*, which is more distinctly expressed, in reference to their outward conduct, in the other clause. God is also described as the creator of the human soul in Zech. xii. 1. Compare Num. xvi. 22, xxvii. 16. His control of it is expressly affirmed in reference to kings, Prov. xxi. 1.

16. *Not at all is the king saved by greatness of force ; a mighty (man) shall not be freed by greatness of strength.* It shall not be, because it is not so, nor ever has been. The future therefore really includes a universal present. The negation is of course to be limited by what precedes, the saving power of mere human strength being only denied as it stands opposed to God, or affects to be independent of him. The Psalmist here begins a contrast between God's perfection and all created helps, considered as objects of confidence. *The king* is a generic term, describing a whole class, more strongly than our indefinite phrase, *a king.*

17. *A lie* (is) *the horse for salvation, and by the greatness of his strength he shall not deliver.* This is a mere specification of the general statement in the sixteenth verse. The *horse* meant is the war-horse, and is singled out as one of the elements of military strength in which the ancients were especially disposed to trust. See above, on Ps. xx. 8 (7), and compare Isa. xxxi. 1–3. *A lie*, a falsehood, *i.e.* something which deceives and disappoints the confidence reposed in it. The deliverance and salvation here referred to are deliverance and salvation from the perils of war.

18. *Lo, the eye of Jehovah* (is) *towards his fearers, to those waiting for his mercy.* While the material strength of other men fails to secure them, those who fear the Lord, and hope in his mercy, are secure beneath his vigilant inspection. That this is intended for their good, is more distinctly stated in the next verse.

19. *To deliver from death their soul, and to keep them alive in the famine.* The sentence is continued from the foregoing verse. His eye is towards them for the very purpose of interposing when he sees it to be necessary, for the rescue of *their soul*, their life, *from death* in general, to which is added one specific form of danger well known to the ancient Hebrews. *The famine* is a similar expression to *the king* in ver. 16, and to our common phrase *the pestilence*, when used in a generic sense, and not in reference to any particular disease or visitation.

20. *Our soul has hoped* (or *waited*) *for Jehovah ; our help and our shield (is) He.* In the remainder of the psalm, the people of God express their trust in him, and pray that he will deal with them according to their faith. The preterite expresses a habit already formed and fixed, and therefore really including a description of the present. In the terms of this verse, there appears to be a reference to the language of the Pentateuch in several places. See Gen. xv. 1, xlix. 18, Deut. xxxiii. 29. The figure of a shield occurs above, in Ps. iii. 4 (3), xviii. 3, 31, 36 (2, 30, 35). The position of the pronoun is emphatic and significant. Our safety and protection are in him, and him alone.

21. *For in him shall our heart rejoice, for in his holy name have we trusted.* The consecution of the tenses is not unmeaning or fortuitous. The Psalmist's assurance of the future is derived from the possession of a faith already tried and proved to be truly in existence. It is because he has trusted that he knows he shall rejoice. The exchange of both these tenses for a present is at once enfeebling to the sense and ungrammatical.— *His holy name*, in the wide sense which the epithet so often has in this book, nearly corresponding to *his glorious, his divine name*. See above on Ps. xxii. 4 (3). To trust in this name is to build one's hopes on the manifestation of God's attributes in previous acts ; to believe that what he [has heretofore shewn himself to be, he will be still in the experience of his people.

22. *Be thy mercy, Jehovah, upon us, as we have waited for thee.* The faith implied in this hope being the sole condition of God's mercy, its possession constitutes a claim upon that mercy, which is here urged as the sum of all the previous petitions. What is thus waited for cannot but be realised. A merciful and righteous God cannot, without denial of himself, withhold that which his people thus expect. Any appearance of a meritorious claim is excluded by the doctrine sufficiently implied here and abundantly taught elsewhere, that the condition is as much the gift of God as that which is suspended on it. The claim in reality amounts to a petition that as God had given the desire he would fulfil it.—*As*, according as, not merely since, because, in proportion to our faith, so deal with us. Compare Mat. ix. 29.

Psalm 34

AFTER the title containing the historical occasion, ver. 1, the Psalmist expresses his determination to praise God for his goodness as experienced already, ver. 2, 3, (1, 2), and invites others to unite with him in so doing, ver. 4 (3). He then briefly states his own experience, ver. 5–7 (4–6), and founds upon it the general doctrine of God's care for his own people, ver. 8–11 (7–10). Assuming then the tone of an instructor, he lays down rules for the securing of this great advantage, ver. 12–15 (11–14), and contrasts, in the remainder of the psalm, the safety of the righteous, even when afflicted, with the certain ruin of the wicked, ver. 16–23 (15–22).

The psalm is so evidently a didactic one, or *maschil*, that an express designation of this character was not required. See above, on Ps. xxxii. 1.

As to its form, this is the second instance of an alphabetical psalm, approaching very nearly to perfect regularity, the only letter omitted being ו. It is very remarkable that here, as in Ps. xxv., the last verse begins with פ, like ver. 16, and seems to be added to the alphabetic series.

1. *By David, in* (the time of) *his changing* (disguising) *his reason before Abimelech, and he drove him away, and he went.* The incident referred to is recorded in 1 Sam. xxi. David, having fled from Saul into the land of the Philistines, was brought into the presence of Achish king of Gath, from whom he had reason to expect retaliation for injuries formerly received, and therefore pretended to be mad, an expedient which, in spite of its dubious morality, it pleased God to allow to be successful. In grateful recollection of this undeserved deliverance, not without some compunction with respect to the means by which he had secured it, David seems, at a later period of his life, to have composed this psalm for popular instruction, to which it is peculiarly adapted by its clearness and simplicity, as well as by its alphabetic form, which is a valuable aid to the memory.—*In his changing* does not necessarily designate the date of composition, but only that of the event which gave occasion to it. The common version, *behaviour*, is inconsistent with the usage of the Hebrew word, which means taste, judgment, understanding, reason.—*Abimelech*, king's father, hereditary sovereign, was the traditional title of the king. See Gen. xx. 2, xxvi. 1. His personal name was Achish, 1 Sam. xxi. 10, 11, 12, 14.

2 (1). *I will bless Jehovah at every time: always his praise* (shall be) *in my mouth.* The promise of unceasing praise suggests the idea of extraordinary benefits to call it forth.—*In all time*, in every variety of situation, even the most discouraging, he is resolved to bear in mind what God has done for him in times past.

3 (2). *In Jehovah shall glory my soul; the humble shall hear and rejoice.* The first verb is strictly a reflective form, and means to *praise one's self*, *i. e.* to boast, or, as denoting a more permanent affection of the mind, to *glory*, *i. e.* to exult in the possession and enjoyment of some admired and beloved object. The act of glorying is ascribed to the soul, in order to describe it as done cordially, *ex animo*.—*The humble*, as opposed to the proud and the presumptuous, is a general description of God's people, who are naturally interested in the good experienced by the Psalmist, both for his sake and their own. See above, on Ps. xxii. 27 (26), xxv. 9.

4 (3). *Magnify* (praise) *to Jehovah with me, and let us exalt his name together.* In Ps. lxix. 31 (30), the verb to *magnify* is construed directly with its object, but in this case with a dative, *to Jehovah*, which may either be regarded as a poetical equivalent to the accusative, or connected with the noun *praise* understood, or with *name*, supplied from the other clause.

5 (4). *I sought Jehovah, and he answered me, and from all my fears delivered me.* He here begins to assign a reason why he and others should praise God. He had delivered him from all his fears by removing the occasions of them. The same plural form occurs Isa. lxvi. 4.

6 (5). *They looked unto him and brightened, and let not their faces blush.* The plural *they* refers to the whole class of which the Psalmist was the representative.—*Brightened*, or as we say in English, *brightened up*, is a natural expression of relief and renewed cheerfulness. In the last clause the optative form is substituted for that of simple affirmation, so as to increase the emphasis. The wish, *let not their faces blush*, implies that there is danger of their doing so, and need of divine grace to prevent it.

7 (6). *This sufferer called, and Jehovah heard, and from all his distresses saved him.* From the general expressions of the preceding verse, he now recurs to his own case in particular. *This sufferer*, or afflicted one, meaning himself, as we say in modern phrase, the speaker or the writer, as a periphrasis for the personal pronoun.

8 (7). *Encamping* (is) *the angel of Jehovah round about his fearers—and* (now) *he has rescued them.* The angel, not only in the collective sense of angels, but in its specific sense, as denoting the Angel of the Lord by way of eminence, the angel of the covenant and of the divine presence (Isa. lxiii. 9), in whom the manifestation of the Godhead took place under the Old Testament. As this angel was the captain of the Lord's host (Josh. v. 14, 1 Kings xxii. 19), his presence implies that of many others, and the word *encamp* is therefore perfectly appropriate. The conversive future represents the act denoted by the last verb as consequent upon the other. This grammatical relation can only be imperfectly expressed in a translation, though the general idea is sufficiently clear.

9 (8). *Taste ye and see that Jehovah is good; happy the man who will trust in him.* The only proof is furnished by experience. The exhortation seems to imply that the provision is already made and only waiting for the guests. Compare Luke xiv. 17, and see above, on Ps. ii. 12.

10 (9). *Fear Jehovah, ye his saints, for there is no want to his fearers.* The fear of God is here put, as in several other places, for the whole of piety or genuine religion, which must ever rest upon the basis of profound awe and veneration. See Ps. ii. 11, Prov. i. 7, ix. 10. *His saints*, those set apart and consecrated to his service, and as such bound to be holy in the strict sense. See above, on Ps. xvi. 3. The last clause represents this as no less the interest than the duty of God's people. They are called upon to fear him, not only because fear is due to him, but because it is the surest method of securing their own safety and supplying their own wants.

11 (10). *Young lions have lacked and hungered, and the seekers of Jehovah shall not want all* (or *any*) *good.* The first verb properly means *grown poor* or *become impoverished*, and is therefore strictly applicable only to a human subject, a sufficient proof that such a subject is really referred to here under the figure of a lion, which is frequently used elsewhere to denote men of strength and violence. See Job iv. 10, 11, and compare Ps. lvii. 5 (4), Nahum ii. 12–14 (11–13), Ezek. xix. 2, 3, xxxviii. 13. The sentiment then is, that while the most powerful and least scrupulous of men may be reduced to want, the people of God shall be abundantly and constantly provided for. The contrast is analogous to that presented in Isa. xl. 30, 31.

12 (11). *Come, sons, hearken to me; the fear of Jehovah I will teach you.* As one experienced in the ways of God, he now addresses those less enlightened, and invites them to avail themselves of his instructions. *Sons* or *children* is a natural and common designation of the pupil as related to the teacher. Compare Prov. i. 8, 10, 15. To teach men the fear of the Lord is to teach them how and why they should fear him. And accordingly we find in the ensuing verses a practical argument in favour of true piety derived from its beneficent effects on those who cherish it and practise it.

13 (12). *Who* (is) *the man, the* (one) *desiring life, loving days* (in which) *to see good?* The interrogation is equivalent to saying, *whosoever desires life*, i. e. desires to live, not in the sense of mere existence but of genuine enjoyment, which is distinctly expressed in the last clause by the words *loving days*, i. e. desiring many days or long life, not for its own sake, but as a time of happiness. Whoever does desire this—and the wish must of course be universal—let him observe the following precepts. *To see good* is to know it by experience, to possess it and enjoy it. See above, on Ps. iv. 7 (6).

14 (13). *Keep thy tongue from evil and thy lips from speaking guile.*

The man who was inquired for in ver. 13 (12), is here directly addressed. Whoever thou art, if thou desire thus to live, *keep*, watch, guard, *thy tongue from speaking evil*, a comprehensive phrase, for which the last clause substitutes one more specific, namely, *speaking guile*, uttering deceit, or lying. The stress here laid upon this sin is so remarkable, when viewed in connection with the means by which David escaped from Achish, as suggested in the title, that it can only be explained by supposing that he looked on the success of his deception as a most unmerited forbearance upon God's part, which, far from recommending the same course in other cases, made it incumbent on the Psalmist to dissuade others from it.

15 (14). *Depart from evil and do good ; seek peace and pursue it.* Not only in relation to this one sin, but to all, if thou desire to enjoy life, *depart from evil*, break off the practice and abjure the love of it ; and since this is neither practicable nor sufficient as a mere negation, effect it by a positive performance of its opposite, *do good.* Compare the exhortation in Isa. i. 16, 17, *Cease to do evil, learn to do good.* The last clause may be explained as a return from generals to particulars, hostility and hatred being singled out as falsehood and deceit were in the preceding verse. Compare Rom. xii. 18, 2 Cor. xiii. 11. Or *peace* may be understood as comprehending peace with God and the enjoyment of his favour.—In either of these senses, or in both, if thou desire to enjoy life, *seek peace*, not in an indolent and listless manner, but *pursue it*, chase it, hunt for it, and eagerly endeavour to attain it. The command implies that the object is both worthy of pursuit and liable to be lost.

16 (15). *The eyes of Jehovah* (are) *towards the righteous, and his ears towards their cry.* The inducement to comply with the foregoing precepts is that God will protect his servants from those dangers against which neither violence nor craft can secure them. They have no need neither to speak guile or break the peace, in order to be safe from injury. Another watches over them, whose vigilance cannot be eluded or exhausted. *The eyes of the Lord are to the righteous, i. e.* open to them, or turned towards them, so that he continually sees their true condition, and *his ears* are directed *to their cry*, or open to receive it. This, without a figure, means, that he is constantly apprised of their necessities and ready to receive their prayers, in which assurance that of safety and abundance is fully comprehended.

17 (16). *The face of Jehovah* (is) *with evil-doers, to destroy from the earth their memory.* The same unsleeping vigilance is exercised towards others also, but for a very different purpose. *The face of the Lord is with evil-doers, i. e.* visible or present to them, no less than to good men. The preposition before *evil-doers* is not the same that occurs twice in the verse preceding, and which properly denotes direction, but another meaning *in* or *with*. The unfavourable sense, *against*, which it may seem to have both here and elsewhere (*e. g.* Jer. xxi. 10, xliv. 11), is suggested by the context. In all these cases some interpreters suppose the sense to be that the eyes or face of God penetrate, as it were, and rest in the object.—The design with which Jehovah watches evil-doers is not to interpose for their deliverance or relief, but *to destroy from the earth their* very *memory*, a strong expression for entire extirpation. Compare Exod. xvii. 14, Deut. xxv. 19, Isa. xxvi. 14, and see above, on Ps. ix. 6, 7 (5, 6).

18 (17). *They cried and Jehovah heard, and from all their distresses delivered them.* This may at first sight seem to have respect to the evil-doers of the preceding verse, who are then represented as obtaining relief from

deserved judgments by humble prayer to God. But as the wicked are, in
this whole passage, mentioned only incidentally, and as a kind of foil or
contrast to the righteous, it seems better on the whole, to make the first
verb here indefinite, *men cry for help,* but with special reference to the
righteous of ver. 16 (15). God watches over the righteous to protect them
—as he does over the wicked to destroy them—and whenever they cry to
him for help, he saves them. This parenthetical construction of ver. 17
(16) is the more admissible because it contains no finite verb, whereas ver.
18 (17) contains three.

19 (18). *Near (is) Jehovah to the broken in heart, and the crushed in
spirit he will save.* These figurative terms are always used in a good sense
and applied to humble penitents. See Ps. li. 19 (17), Isa. lvii. 15, lxi. 1,
lxvi. 2. They are descriptive of the contrition wrought by divine grace in
the hearts of sinners. To such the Lord is always *near, i. e.* ready to
deliver and protect. See above, on Ps. xxii. 12 (11).

20 (19). *Many evils* (befall) *the righteous, and from them all will Jehovah
deliver him.* The preceding promise might have seemed to imply exemption from all suffering; but this can only be enjoyed in connection with exemption from all sin. While sin continues to exist, sorrow must coexist
with it, even in the case of true believers or the righteous, who are never
described in this book as absolutely sinless. See above, Ps. xix. 13 (12),
xxv. 7. While the sufferings of the righteous shew them to be sinners,
their deliverance illustrates the divine compassion. The relation of the
clauses would in our idiom require a *but* instead of the simple copulative,
which the Hebrew writers commonly employ in such connection.

21 (20). *Keeping all his bones—not one of them is broken.* The sentence
may be completed by supplying the substantive verb : (*he is*) *keeping, i. e.*
habitually keeps ; but it is simpler and better to regard this and the verse
before it as one sentence, and the participle as agreeing regularly with
Jehovah.—*Keeping,* in the pregnant sense of watching and preserving.—
His bones, his frame, his body. See above, Ps. xxxii. 3, and below, Ps.
xxxv. 10.—The literal translation of the last clause, *one of them is not
broken,* would be equivocal in English. The original expression occurs
also in Isa. xxxiv. 16. The doctrine or promise of this verse is analogous
to that in Mat. x. 30.

22 (21.) *Evil shall slay the wicked, and the haters of the righteous shall
be guilty.* While the sufferings of which the righteous man is a partaker
are but temporary, those of the wicked shall be ultimately fatal. See above,
on Ps. xxxii. 10. *Evil* must have the same sense in both cases, namely,
that of physical evil, suffering or misfortune. The result here described is
not fortuitous, but brought about by moral causes. They must be destroyed because they are found *guilty, i.e.* of rebellion against God, one
conclusive proof of which is afforded by their hatred of his people. They
shall be guilty, i.e. recognised and known as such and treated accordingly.
" The sufferings of the wicked man, unlike those of the righteous, tend to
death, because the hatred of the former to the latter proves himself to be
worthy of destruction."

23 (22.) *Jehovah redeems the soul of his servants, and guilty shall none be
(of) those trusting in him.* The precise form of the first clause in Hebrew
is, *Jehovah redeeming the soul of his servants,* which seems to mean that he
is doing so now, and that he habitually does so. The soul or vital principle
is named because the case was one of life and death. None of those trusting in him shall be recognised and treated as guilty, the opposite of that

which had been just asserted of the wicked. The condition and ground of this immunity is faith or trust in God, without which, according to the doctrine of both testaments, there can be no escape from guilt or punishment.

Psalm 35

WE have here another of those psalms, in which two great parties, the righteous and the wicked, are exhibited in contrast and in an attitude of mutual hostility. The psalm may be divided into three parts, parallel to one another, in all of which the elements combined are complaint, prayer, and the promise of thanksgiving for anticipated deliverance. The first division is occupied with an invocation of divine judgments on God's enemies, ending with an expression of triumph in God's favour, ver. 1-9. The second contains a more particular description of these enemies, as oppressors, false accusers, unthankful renderers of evil for good, and malignant scoffers, with a prayer for the divine interposition, and a pledge of public thanksgiving, ver. 10-18. The third renews briefly the description of the enemy, but is chiefly filled with prayer to be delivered from them, and closes, like the others, with a promise of perpetual thanksgiving, ver. 19-28.

1. *By David. Oppose, Jehovah, my opposers ; devour my devourers.* The correctness of the title is confirmed by the appearance of allusion to 1 Sam. xxiv. 16 (15), the incident recorded in which place may have been present to the Psalmist's mind although we have no reason to believe that he wrote it with exclusive reference to that time or to himself, but for the use of pious sufferers in general.—*Strive with my strivers*, or *contend with my contenders.* The original verb is one specifically used to denote judicial contest, litigation, in which sense a cognate noun is used below, ver. 23, and the English Bible thus translates the verse before us: *plead (my cause) with them that strive against me ; fight against them that fight against me.* It is only in the passive form, however, that לחם means to fight; its primary sense is to devour. The application of this metaphor to warfare is not uncommon. See below, Ps. lvi. 2, 3 (1, 2), and compare Num. xiv. 9, xxiv. 8, Deut. vii. 16.

2. *Lay hold of shield and buckler ; and stand up in my defence* (or *for my help*). The manifestation of God's saving and protecting power is described in Scripture under various figures corresponding to the form of the particular suffering or danger. Against injustice he appears as an advocate or judge (see ver. 23 below); against violence as a warrior (see Deut. xxxii. 41, 42). In this character the Psalmist here entreats him to appear, and for that end to *seize*, grasp, or lay hold of his weapons of defence. The *shield* and *buckler* seem to have been different in size (1 Kings x. 16, 17), though not in use.—*Arise*, address thyself to action. See above, on Ps. iii. 8 (7).—*In my help* is by some explained to mean *as my help*, *i. e. my helper ;* but the Hebrew idiom seems to be identical with our phrase *in my defence.*

3. *And draw out the spear, and stop* (the way) *against my pursuers ; say to my soul, Thy salvation (am) I.* The first verb properly means *empty*, *pour out*, and then *draw out.* Some suppose the expression to be strictly applicable only to the sword, but to be here applied by a kind of poetic licence to the spear. Others suppose it to be strictly used, but in relation to the drawing of it out of its repository or concealment. Some explain

סֻגֹּר as a foreign word, identical with the Scythian σάγαρις, or battle-axe.

But no such word occurs in Hebrew elsewhere, and the meaning of the verb סָגַר is entirely appropriate, to *close* or stop the way against another.

Against, or literally *to meet*, in a hostile or military sense which the word has in Deut. i. 44, Josh. viii. 14, and elsewhere.—*To my soul;* see above, on Ps. xi. 1.—*Thy salvation*, see below, Ps. xxxviii. 23 (22).

4. *Shamed and confounded be the seekers of my soul; turned back and made to blush the devisers of my hurt.* Entirely disappointed in their hopes and efforts. The optative meaning of the futures is determined by the unambiguous form יְהִי in ver. 6 below. *The seekers of my soul* or *life, i. e.* such as seek it to destroy it. Compare Mat. ii. 13, 20. *Turned back*, disgracefully repulsed and defeated. See above, on Ps. ix. 18 (17). *Made to blush:* the form of the verb in Hebrew is not causative, but simply means to blush or be confused. The causative form is here employed in order to give uniformity to the English sentence.—*My hurt*, literally *my evil, i. e.* evil fortune, calamity, or injury.—*Devisers*, literally *thinkers, i. e.* such as meditate or purpose my destruction.

5. *Let them be as chaff before a wind, and the angel of Jehovah smiting.* Under the influence of inspiration, the Psalmist sees the natural and righteous consequences of their wickedness, and viewing the case merely in itself, apart from personal feeling, speaks of this effect as desirable. The wish expressed is, to all intents and purposes, equivalent to a prediction or the affirmation of a general truth. The Psalmist desires the destruction of these sinners precisely as God wills it; nor is it any harder to reconcile such wishes with the highest degree of human goodness than it is to reconcile the certain fact that God allows some men to perish with his infinite benevolence. The figure of *chaff before the wind* suggests the idea of intrinsic worthlessness with that of easy and complete destruction. Compare Ps. i. 4. The participle at the close means *striking (them) down*, so that they cannot rise. Compare Ps. xxxvi. 13 (12). The *angel of Jehovah*, his appointed instrument of vengeance. See above, on Ps. xxxiv. 8 (7).

6. *Let their way be dark and slippery, and the angel of Jehovah chasing them.* The optative form of the verb at the beginning determines the sense of those which go before, and which otherwise might be ambiguous.—*Dark and slippery*, literally *darkness and smoothnesses*, an emphatic substitution of the abstract for the concrete. The fearful image thus suggested of men driven, like chaff before the wind, along a dark and slippery path, is rendered more terrific by the additional idea of their being hotly pursued by the destroying angel. The construction of the last clause, both in this verse and the one before it, is: (let) the angel of Jehovah (be) pursuing them.

7. *For without cause they hid for me their pit-fall; without cause they digged for my soul.* This verse assigns the reason of the imprecations or denunciations which precede.—*Without cause*, wantonly, gratuitously, unprovoked, and therefore prompted by mere malice. See below, ver. 19.— *The pit of their net* is an idiomatic phrase like *the hill of my holiness.* See above, on Ps. ii. 6. The true sense of the phrase appears to be *their net-pit, i. e.* their pit covered with a net, a figure borrowed from the ancient modes of hunting. See above, on Ps. vii. 16 (15), ix. 16 (15). In the last clause we may either supply a relative, as in the common version, *which they digged*, or take the verb in the absolute sense of making a pit or ditch.

8. *Let ruin come* (upon) *him* (when) *he does not know ; and his net which he hid—let it take him—with ruin* (to his ruin) *let him fall into it.* The first noun properly denotes a *crash*, as of a falling house, and then a *ruin*, both in the narrower and wider sense. *When he does not know*, unawares, unexpectedly, as in Isa. xlvii. 11, Job. ix. 5. The last clause may also be translated, *into ruin let him fall into it, i. e.* as the common version has it, *into that very ruin.* But it is simpler to let בְּשׁוֹאָה qualify the verb ; let him fall with ruin, *i. e.* ruinously to his own destruction.

9. *And my soul shall exult in Jehovah, shall joy in his salvation.* Our idiom would require *so* or *then* at the beginning of the sentence, to make the connection of the verses clear.—*In Jehovah*, not merely on account of him, but in union with him and possession of him, as the parallel phrase, *in his salvation*, means in the experience and enjoyment of it. This is a kind of promise that the favour asked shall not be unrequited by thanksgiving, and the same idea is still further carried out in the next verse.

10. *All my bones shall say, Jehovah, who is like thee, delivering the sufferer from* (one) *stronger than himself, and the sufferer and the needy from his spoiler?* The bones, the frame, the person, are here put for the whole man. See above, on Ps. xxxii. 3. The interrogative form implies negation. " There is no such saviour besides God." The apparent tautology may be relieved in English by translating *even the sufferer*, &c. But such repetitions are entirely congenial to the Hebrew idiom. With the second clause compare Jer. xxxi. 11, and with the third Ps. x. 2.

11. *There rise up witnesses of violence;* (as to) *that which I have not known they ask me.* The future verbs describe the acts as still in progress, and as likely to be long continued. *They are rising* or *about to rise, asking* or *about to ask.* The word translated *violence* is one of very frequent occurrence in the psalms, and includes the ideas of injustice and cruelty. See above, on Ps. vii. 17 (16), xi. 5, xviii. 49 (48), xxv. 19, xxvii. 12. " They endeavour to draw from me the acknowledgment of crimes which I have not committed, and of which I have no knowledge."

12. *They repay me evil for good—bereavement to my soul.* " If given up to them, I have nothing to expect but a continued recompence of evil for good, extending even to the loss of what is most essential to my being and well-being." The word translated *bereavement* commonly means loss of children, but is here used metaphorically for the most extreme and lamentable destitution.

13. *And I—in their sickness my clothing* (was) *sackcloth ; I humbled with fasting my soul—and my prayer into my bosom shall return.* The general idea is that he displayed the deepest sympathy with their distresses. This idea is expressed by figures borrowed from the oriental mourning usages. Sackcloth, fasting, and prayer are here particularly mentioned. To *humble the soul* (or *one's self*), or as some explain it, to *mortify the appetite*, is the phrase by which fasting is described in the Law of Moses (Lev. xvi. 31, xxiii. 27, 32, Num. xxix. 7), and which is here combined with the later word צוּם.—The last clause is obscure, and is by some understood to signify the constancy of supplication, coming back and going out again without cessation. Others explain it as a mere description of the attitude of prayer with the head bowed upon the bosom, as if he had said, I was continually pouring prayer into my bosom. But neither of these explanations is so probable as the traditional one of the Jews, according to which he desires that the prayer which he offered for them might redound to his own advantage. Or the clause may be still more simply construed as a prediction :

" My prayer shall not be lost, it shall return in blessings to the heart which prompted it."

14. *As* (if it had been) *a friend, a brother to me, I went on* (or *went about*); *as a mourner for a mother, squalid I bowed down.* He not only mourned in their calamity, but with the deepest grief, as for a friend, a brother, or a parent, which terms are so arranged as to produce a beautiful and striking climax.—The verb in the first clause corresponds very nearly to the familiar English phrase *went on*, in the sense of lived or habitually acted. See above, on Ps. i. 1.—The Hebrew word קָדַר means *squalid*, dirty, in allusion to the ancient oriental practice of neglecting the appearance, and even covering the dress and person with dust and ashes, as a token of extreme grief. The bowing down is also to be taken as a part of the same usage.

15. *And* (yet) *in my limping they rejoiced, and were gathered together; there were gathered together against me cripples, and I did not know* (it): *they did tear and were not silent.* With his behaviour to them in their affliction he contrasts theirs to him. As disease in general is a common figure for distress, so lameness in particular is so used here and in Ps. xxxviii. 18 (17), Jer. xx. 10. They assembled not to comfort but to mock him and revile him.—The obscure word נֵכִים has been variously explained to mean *smiters* with the tongue (Jer. xviii. 18), *i. e.* slanderers—*whipped* (Job xxx. 8), *i. e.* degraded criminals—and *smitten* (Isa. liii. 4), *i. e.* afflicted. But Luther's explanation, which connects the word with the cognate form נְכֵה רַגְלָיִם (2 Sam. iv. 4, ix. 3), *smitten in the feet*, lame, crippled, not only yields a good sense, but agrees best with the figure of the first clause. ' When I limped cripples mocked at me '—*i. e.* those who were themselves contemptible treated me with contempt. *I did not know it.* It was done behind my back, and while I was entirely unsuspicious. See above, on ver. 8. This is a more natural construction than *whom I did not know*, which is, moreover, inconsistent with what goes before.—*They rent* or *tore* me by their slanders.

16. *With worthless mockers for bread—gnashing against me their teeth.* This they did in the company of impious, reprobate, or worthless scoffers, who calumniate others for the sake of gaining favour with their wicked patrons. Hence they are called *bread* or *cake scoffers*, those who earn their food by spiteful mockery of others. The form of the whole verse is extremely idiomatic, and scarcely admits of an exact translation. The literal meaning of the first clause is *with the worthless of mockers of bread*, and in the second the verb *gnash* is an infinitive, which can only be rendered in intelligible English by a participle or a finite verb, *they gnashed*, or *gnashing*. This is always expressive of malignant rage, and shews that what is here described is not mere raillery but spiteful defamation.

17. *Lord, how long wilt thou look on? Restore my soul from their ruins* (or *ruinous plots*), *from the young lions my lonely one.* The first Hebrew word is not *Jehovah* but *Adhonai*, properly expressive of dominion or sovereignty. See above, on Ps. xvi. 2—*How long?* The Hebrew phrase usually means *how much*, ¦but is here specially applied to time; *how much time? how long? Wilt thou see* what treatment I receive, and merely see it, as an indifferent spectator ?—*Restore my soul* has not the same sense as in Ps. xix. 8 (7), xxiii. 3, but the strict one of *bringing back* from the dangerous extreme to which he had been brought by the *ruins* or *ruinous devices—i. e.* designed to ruin others—of his enemies. Lions are mentioned

as the strongest and fiercest of wild beasts, and young lions as the most active of their species. See above, on Ps. xxxiv. 11 (10).—*My lonely*, solitary *soul*. See above, on Ps. xxii. 21 (20).

18. *I will thank thee in the great assembly, in* (the midst of the) *mighty people I will praise thee* On the supposition that his prayer will be heard and answered, he engages to give public thanks, *in the great congregation* or assembly of God's people. See above, on Ps. xxii. 23, 26 (22, 25).— *Strong people*, strong in numbers, a poetical equivalent to *great congregation*.—The verb in the last clause means to *praise* in general; that in the first to praise for benefits received, to acknowledge favours, in other words to *thank*. See above, on Ps. xxxiii. 2.

19. *Let them not rejoice respecting me, my enemies of falsehood*, (and let not) *my haters without cause wink the eye*. Respecting me, at my expense, or, in this and similar connections, *over me*, although this idea is not so much expressed in the text as suggested by the context. See above, Ps. xxv. 2, and below, ver. 24, Ps. xxxviii. 17 (16). *Let them not rejoice*, let them have no occasion so to do.—*My enemies of falsehood*, my false enemies, who gratify their spite by calumny and slander.—*My haters without cause*, those who hate me gratuitously, out of sheer spite, without any reasonable ground or even colourable pretext. This is a favourite description of the enemies of the righteous—see above, on Ps. vii. 5 (4), xxv. 3—and was pre-eminently true of the enemies of Christ, to whom it is applied in the New Testament (John xv. 25). The negation of the first clause is to be repeated in the other, as in Ps. ix. 19 (18). Winking is here referred to as a gesture of mutual congratulation among accomplices in guilt. Compare Prov. vi. 13, x. 10.

20. *For not peace will they speak, and against the quiet of the land words of deceits will they devise.* The *for* assigns a reason why they ought not to be suffered to rejoice in the success of their designs. The reason is, because their designs are evil, tending not to *peace*—in the strict sense, as opposed to strife, or in the wide sense, as opposed to trouble and calamity —but to the disturbance of those who are peacefully inclined, *the quiet* (or *tranquil*) *of the land, i. e.* the land of promise, considered as the home of God's chosen people, who, as its rightful proprietors, are characteristically peaceful, and averse from all strife and disorder. Compare Mat. v. 5. To disturb these, the wicked devise *words of deceits*, in which phrase *words* is not an idiomatic pleonasm,—compare xli. 9 (8), lxv. 4 (3),—but a substantive expression, meaning *false* (or *lying*) *words*, and more specifically slanders—see below, Ps. xxxvi. 4 (3)—the utterers of which are called *lying enemies* in ver. 19. The futures of this verse include the present: they do so now and will do so still. Some connect *not peace* as an emphatic compound, meaning just the opposite of peace. Compare Isa. x. 15.

21. *And have widened against me their mouth; they have said, Aha, aha, our eye has seen.* "They have mocked at my distress with contemptuous grimaces, and rejoiced in the fulfilment of their spiteful wishes." With the first clause compare Ps. xxii. 8 (7) above. The Hebrew interjection in the last clause (הֶאָח) seems to be a natural expression of joyful surprise.

Their success was almost too great to be real, yet attested by their senses. The verse ends with a kind of aposiopesis : " our own eyes have seen "— what we could not have believed on the report of another, to wit, the gratification of our warmest wishes. See below, ver. 25.

22. *Thou hast seen, Jehovah, be not silent ; Lord, be not far from me.*

" But they are not the only witnesses of my distress, for thou, Lord, likewise seest and hast long seen it.   Seeing it, therefore, be no longer silent;
refrain no longer from interposing in my favour; speak in my behalf; be
near me in this time of peril."   The connection of the verses is like that
in Ps. x. 13, 14, and the prayer in the last clause not unlike that with
which the same psalm opens.   With the other petition, *be not silent*, compare that at the beginning of Ps. xxviii.; and with the first words, *thou hast
seen*, those of ver. 17 above.

23. *Arouse* (thee) *and awake for my right* (or *judgment*), *my God and
my Lord, for my cause*.   " Put an end to this inaction and apparent indifference, and manifest thy presence, as my sovereign and my covenant-
keeping God, for the vindication of my innocence against false accusers and
unrighteous judges."   The same petition, clothed in nearly the same words,
occurs above in Ps. vii. 7, 9 (6, 8).   See also Ps. ix. 5 (4), xvii.

24. *Judge me according to thy righteousness, Jehovah, my God, and let
them not rejoice respecting me*.   " Do me justice, clear me from aspersion,
grant an attestation of my innocence, in the exercise and exhibition of thine
own essential rectitude, and in accordance with that covenant relation
which exists between us; and thus, in the most effectual manner, take away
from my malignant enemies all pretext and occasion for exulting in my
overthrow, or otherwise triumphing at my expense."   With the last clause
compare Ps. xxx. 2 (1) above, where he thanks God for the very favour
which he here asks.   The verb in this clause may be referred to men in
general, or with still greater probability to the enemies described in the
preceding context.

25. *Let them not say in their heart, Aha, our soul* (or *our heart's desire*)!
Let them not say, We have swallowed him up! In their heart, not secretly,
but cordially, not as opposed to saying so to others, but to mere profession.
—*Our heart's desire!* an abbreviated exclamation prompted by strong feeling.
" This is precisely what we have so long and so intensely wished for !"   See
above, on Ps. xxvii. 12.   *Let them not say*, let them not have occasion so to
say; let not the events which befall me justify them in so saying.—*Swallowed
him up*, utterly destroyed him.   See above, on Ps. xxi. 10 (9), and compare Lam. ii. 16, where the form of expression is no doubt copied from the
verse before us.

26. *Let them be ashamed and blush together—the rejoicers in my evil; let
them put on shame and contempt the* (men) *magnifying against me* (their
words, or their deeds, or themselves)!   The relative construction, *who
rejoice in my hurt, who magnify against me*, gives the sense, but in an English
rather than a Hebrew form.—*Ashamed*, disappointed and defeated.   See
above, on ver. 4.—*Blush*, be confused or confounded.—*My evil, i. e.* evil
fortune, injury, including the idea of injustice, as the antithetical term in
ver. 27 is *righteousness* or justification.—*Put on*, as a dress, and wear it, or
be covered with it.   See below, on Ps. cix. 18 (17), and compare Job viii.
22.—*Contempt*, disgrace, ignominy.—*Making great*, &c., their mouth or
words, *i. e.* speaking proudly, Obad. 12, Ezek. xxxv. 13 ; or still more probably and agreeably to usage, *acting proudly*, as in Ps. lv. 13 (12), and
elsewhere.   The complete expression may be that used in Joel ii. 20.

27. *Let them shout* (or *sing*) *and rejoice—the desirers of my righteousness
—and let them always say, Great is* (or *be*) *Jehovah, the* (God) *willing* (or
desiring) *the peace of his servant!*   The sentence may be brought into closer
conformity to our idiom by adopting a relative construction.   " Let them
rejoice who desire my righteousness," *i. e.* my justification, who desire to

see me practically justified by God's providential dealings with me.—*Let them always say*, *i. e.* always have occasion so to do, which is virtually wishing that the peace or prosperity of Jehovah's servant may be perpetual. The verbal adjective in both these clauses means *desiring*, with a strong implication of complacency or satisfaction in the object, and therefore really includes the two ideas of *desire* and *delight*.—The *righteousness* or *justification* of the first clause is an obvious antithesis to the *evil, hurt*, or *injury* of ver. 26, and no less obviously identical, or at least coincident, with the *peace* or *welfare* of the last clause here.

28. *And my tongue shall utter thy righteousness—all the day* (long) *thy praise*. The *and* connects the verse with what precedes, as the effect with its occasion or its cause. This connection may be made clear in our idiom by the use of a more definite particle, such as *then* or *so*.—The verb used in this verse is applied elsewhere both to articulate and inarticulate animal sounds. The nearest equivalent in English is to *utter*. For a secondary or derived sense of the same verb, see above, on Ps. i. 2.—*All the day long*, or *every day*, common expressions for continually, always.—The *righteousness* of the first clause is the object of the *praise* in the second. The righteousness of God here mentioned has reference to the Psalmist's righteousness in ver. 27. By vindicating this, the divine justice or fidelity acquires, as it were, a new claim to the praises of the justified sinner, which he here declares himself resolved to pay.

Psalm 36

THIS remarkable psalm consists of three distinguishable parts, besides the title, ver. 1. The first contains a strong description of human depravity, ver. 2–5 (1–4). The second contrasts with this the divine excellence, ver. 6–10 (5–9). In the third, the Psalmist prays to be delivered from the first, and made a partaker of the second, with a strong assurance that his desire will be fulfilled, ver. 11–13 (10–12).

The first part differs from the rest, in form as well as substance, being much more obscure and difficult.

1. *To the Chief Musician. By a Servant of Jehovah. By David.* This peculiar collocation of the words, which occurs only here and in the title of the eighteenth psalm, seems to imply something more than would have been conveyed by the description, *David, a servant of Jehovah*. The difference intended may be this, that *servant of Jehovah* is not added to the name as a descriptive epithet, but is itself the salient point of the inscription, the name being added merely to identify the person. This would seem to shew that, for some reason founded in the psalm itself, it is important that it be regarded as the work of a servant of Jehovah, one inspired by him, perhaps in opposition to the inspiration of depravity referred to in the next verse.

2 (1). *Thus saith depravity to the wicked (one) in the midst of my heart, there is no fear of God before his eyes.* This is one of the most difficult and doubtful verses in the whole book of Psalms. The first word in Hebrew (נְאֻם) is a passive participle used as a noun, like the Latin *dictum*, and employed as a standing formula in prophecy to indicate the person speaking. The usual combination is (נְאֻם יְהוָֹה) *a dictum of Jehovah*, commonly translated in our Bible, *saith* (or *thus saith*) *the Lord*. Instead of the divine name, that of David is substituted in 2 Sam. xxiii. 1 (נְאֻם דָּוִד) and *the man*

there and also in Prov. xxx. 1 (נְאֻם הַגֶּבֶר), both which appear to be copied
from the words of Balaam in Num. xxiv. 15. The constant use of this
formula to introduce prophetic *dicta* seems to require an analogous interpretation of it here, as meaning something more than the mere act of speaking, and suggesting the idea of an authoritative dictum or oracular response,
proceeding not from God nor from his prophets, but from sin (פֶּשַׁע), which
here supplies their place. *A dictum of depravity*, or, copying the paraphrastic but familiar version of נְאֻם יְהוָֹה in the English Bible, *thus saith
transgression* or *corruption*.—The meaning of the next phrase (לָרָשָׁע) is
determined by the analogy of Ps. cx. 1, where the same preposition, after
נְאֻם יְהוָֹה, can only indicate the object of address, *the saying of Jehovah*
(or *thus saith Jehovah*) *to my Lord*. So here, the true construction is not,
the transgression of the wicked, which indeed is ungrammatical, but *thus saith
transgression to the wicked*. The only possible modification of this syntax,
at all justified by usage, is to make לָרָשָׁע denote the subject, not the object
of the dictum—*thus saith depravity (as) to the wicked*—this is the testimony
which it bears against him. This explanation, although not supported by
Ps. cx. 1, is consistent with the frequent use of לְ to denote the subject, and
affords a good sense, namely, that depravity itself bore witness against the
wicked, in the Psalmist's mind, that there was no fear of God before his
eyes. If, on the other hand, לָרָשָׁע indicates the object of address, the
first clause may be the words of the wicked man himself, and the last clause
the comment of the Psalmist on them. " *Thus saith depravity to* (me) *the
wicked man, in the midst of my heart.*" *There is no fear of God before his
eyes.* That is to say, the wicked man makes sin his god, and its suggestions
his prophetic oracles, and thereby shews that there is no fear of God before
his eyes. By a different interpunction, this sense may be put upon the
sentence. *Thus saith depravity to the wicked man : " In the midst of my
heart there is no fear of God before his eyes,*" or even in his presence. But
as this interpretation would make sin speak of its own heart in addressing
the sinner, and as the reference of *his eyes* to God is somewhat forced, the
choice seems to lie between the other two constructions before stated, one
of which yields the same sense that appears to be intended in the common
version, *the transgression of the wicked saith within my heart that there is
no fear of God before his eyes*, and that of the Prayer Book, *my heart sheweth
me the wickedness of the ungodly that there is*, &c. Amidst these various
and doubtful explanations, one thing is certain, that the wicked man is here
described as one who fears not God, just as the fear of God is elsewhere
put for godliness or piety.

3 (2). *For he has flattered himself in his own eyes, as to* (God's) *finding
his iniquity* (and) *hating* (it). The obscurity of the original may be shewn
by a bald translation. *For he has made smooth to him in his eyes, to find
his iniquity to hate.* To make smooth, here and in Prov. xxix. 5, is an
elliptical expression for making smooth the words or the actions, *i. e.*
speaking or acting in a flattering manner. See above, on Ps. v. 10 (9).
As there is no reflexive pronoun in Hebrew, the personal pronouns are
occasionally so used, *him* for *himself*, *his* for *his own*, &c. In this case,
however, it is possible to give them their strict meaning by referring them
to God. *He* (the wicked man) *has made* (his words or actions) *smooth to
him* (*i. e.* to God), *in his eyes* (the eyes of God). In other words he has

endeavoured to deceive him by a specious appearance. But this construction is less natural, because it makes the phrase *in his eyes* still more redundant; because it represents the sinner as a hypocrite, rather than a bold, self-confident transgressor; and because it makes the last clause more obscure and difficult. *To find iniquity*, i. e. to detect and punish it, is an expression borrowed from Gen. xliv. 16. The unfavourable meaning of the phrase is determined by the addition of the words *to hate*. The reference of this clause to the sinner's own feelings is at variance with usage. With the whole verse compare Deut. xxix. 18 (19), and see above, on Ps. x. 6.

4 (3). *The words of his mouth (are) falsehood and fraud, he has ceased to act wisely, to act well.* The use of the abstract for the concrete, *falsehood* and *deceit* for *false* and *deceitful*, adds to the strength of the expression. What he says is not merely false, but falsity itself. For the precise meaning of the Hebrew words, see above, on Ps. v. 6, 7 (5, 6). The verbs of the last clause are in the causative form, which always has an active meaning. *To be wise* is therefore an inadequate translation, and *to do good* an ambiguous one, as this English phrase is specially applied to acts of beneficence or practical utility. The true sense of the last verb is *to do well* or *right*, in opposition to doing wrong. See below, on Ps. xxxvii. 3. Instead of ceasing from his sins, the sinner has abandoned even the appearance of well-doing. The form of expression is like that in Isa. i. 16.

5 (4). *Falsehood he will meditate upon his bed; he will take his stand upon a way not good; evil he will not abjure.* The first word (אָוֶן), both in this and the preceding verse, does not mean mere false speaking, but a false character, one not according to the truth, of which the divine will is the standard. It is therefore nearly equivalent to wickedness. The futures express present habit and a settled purpose of continuance. While he continues what he is, he will continue thus to act. *On his bed*, by night, the natural season of reflection. Or the idea may be, that instead of sleeping he spends the hours of rest in meditating evil, or contriving mischief.—The verb to *set himself*, or *take his stand*, is the snme that occurred before in Ps. ii. 2, and implies both a settled purpose and the commencement of its execution.—*A way not good* is an example of the figure called *meiosis*, in which more is meant than is expressed, although suggested by the context. The idea really conveyed to every reader is that of an extremely bad way, or the worst way possible.—The last verb means to reject or renounce with contempt and abhorrence. See above, on Ps. xv. 4.

6 (5). *O Jehovah, in the heavens (is) thy mercy, and thy faithfulness unto the clouds.* From the odious image of the sinner just presented he now turns away to contemplate the divine perfections. The parallelism of the clauses seems to shew that *in the heavens* means in heaven as well as on earth, i. e. reaching from the one to the other, which idea is then literally expressed, *as far as*, even to, or up to, *the clouds*, which last is simply an equivalent to *heavens*.—*Mercy and faithfulness* are also parallels, the latter meaning God's fidelity or truth in the fulfilment of his promises, even to the undeserving. See below, on Ps. xxxvii. 3.

7 (6). *Thy righteousness (is) like the hills of the Almighty; thy judgments (are) a great deep; man and beast thou wilt save, (O) Jehovah!* Righteousness here means rectitude in its widest sense, including the veracity and faithfulness mentioned in the foregoing verse. *Judgments* is an idiomatic synonyme, the plural being either used to give it an abstract meaning, as in (הַיִּים) *life*, or to denote particular acts of righteousness. This attribute

is here described as infinite, by a comparison with natural emblems of immensity. The first mentioned are *the mountains of God*, or *of the mighty (God)*, the divine name here used being that which properly denotes omnipotence. See above, on Ps. v. 5 (4). By explaining this word as an abstract, we obtain the sense, *mountains of strength, i. e.* strong mountains ; but the constant usage of the term as a divine name seems decisive in favour of the sense, hills produced by the almighty power of God and therefore proving it.—The *great deep*, the ocean, as in Gen. vii. 11. (Compare Gen. i. 2). The idea conveyed is not so much that of depth and mystery as that of vastness and immensity. The comprehensiveness of God's protecting care is further indicated by the combination *man and beast* (or *brute*). To *save* includes the acts of helping, protecting and providing.

8 (7). *How precious (is) thy mercy, (O) God, and the sons of man in the shadow of thy wings may trust* (or *take refuge*). The richness of God's mercy is apparent from the very fact that it affords protection to mankind, meaning of course only those to whom it has been promised. The figure of overspreading wings is carried out more fully in Deut. xxxii. 11, and Mat. xxiii. 37.—For the meaning of the verb used in this verse, see above, on Ps. ii. 12.

9 (8). *They shall be drenched with the abundance of thy house ; (with) the stream of thy pleasures thou wilt water them* (or *give them drink*). They, *i. e.* such of the children of men as are permitted to take refuge under God's protection.—*Shall drink abundantly*, or to satiety, be soaked or drenched. The derivative noun occurs above, in Ps. xxiii. 5.—*Abundance*, literally fat or fatness, put for the richest food. *Thy house*, thy household, with or without allusion to the tabernacle, not as a place of worship merely, but as the earthly residence of God. See above, on Ps. xxiii. 6, xxvii. 4. In the second clause there is a beautiful allusion to the river which watered the garden of Eden (Gen. ii. 10). This allusion, although lost in a translation, is marked in the original by the use of the word *eden* in the plural number to mean pleasures or delights. The verb to *water* or *make drink* is also the one used in Gen. ii. 10, which shews that it is not a mere fortuitous coincidence.

10 (9). *For with thee is a fountain of life ; in thy light shall we see light.* They shall derive all this from thee, because in thee alone is the exhaustless source of all these blessings.—*With thee*, in thy presence, in union and communion with thee.—The well-spring, fountain-head, or source of life, a summary expression for all enjoyments and advantages. The same idea is then clothed in another figurative dress. *In thy light we shall see light.* It is only by the light of God's countenance that man can see any good. It is only in God's favour that he can be happy. The only bliss attainable or desirable is that which is bestowed by God and resides in him. See above, on Ps. iv. 7 (6).

11 (10). *Continue thy mercy to those knowing thee, and thy righteousness to the upright in heart.* To his glowing description of the blessedness resident in God and flowing from his favour, he now adds a prayer that it may be extended to the class, of which he claims to be a member. The first verb literally means to *draw out* or *protract*, and is the same that is used in different applications in Ps. x. 9, xxviii. 3, above.—*Those knowing thee*, and as a necessary consequence loving thee, since genuine knowledge of the true God is inseparable from right affections towards him.—*Thy righteousness*, thy true and faithful dealings with those trusting in thy mercy,

here and often elsewhere represented as the *upright* or straightforward *in heart* as well as in behaviour.

12 (11). *Suffer not to come (upon) me foot of pride, and let not hand of wicked ones expel me.* What he had just asked for the upright in general, he now asks for himself in particular, plainly implying that the view which he had taken of human depravity in ver. 2–5 (1–4), was suggested by his own sufferings, or fear of suffering, at the hand of wicked enemies.—The verb in the first clause does not merely mean to *come against,* invade or threaten, but to *come upon,* implying actual and violent assault. See above, Ps. xxxv. 8. The mention of the *foot* suggests the ideas of spurning trampling, and crushing ; that of the *hand* the more general idea of exerted strength or violence. The last verb is a causative, and strictly means to put to flight, cause to wander, or send into exile. Compare its use in 2 Kings xxi. 8. The general idea of the verse is, do not give me up to the power of my enemies.

13 (12). *There are the doers of iniquity fallen ; they are struck down and cannot rise* (or *stand*). The prayer is followed by a sudden assurance of its being answered, in the strength of which the Psalmist speaks of his desire as already accomplished. See above, on Ps. xx. 7 (6).—*There* has very much the same sense as in common parlance, when uttered as a sudden exclamation. *There ! they have fallen* (*already*). Strictly explained, it means on the very spot and in the very midst of their anticipated triumph. See above, on Ps. xiv. 5, where the same use of the particle occurs, and compare Ps. cxxxii. 17, and Judges v. 11, in all which places it is better to retain the local sense of *there* than to exchange it for the supposititious one of *then,* which never occurs elsewhere.—*Iniquity,* vanity or falsehood, in the sense explained above, on ver. 5 (4).—*Struck,* or *smitten down,* a stronger phrase than *cast down.* See above, Ps. xxxv. 5.—The last words may either mean, they cannot stand their ground, save themselves from falling, or they cannot rise again when fallen. See above, Ps. i. 5, xviii. 39 (38), and compare Prov. xxiv. 16.

Psalm 37

THIS is an alphabetical psalm, and, like others of the same kind (see above, on Ps. xxv.), consists of variations on the theme propounded in the two first verses, namely, the idea, that the sinner is a self-destroyer, and therefore not an object of envy or revenge to the righteous, who may safely leave the punishment of his enemies, and the vindication of his own cause, in the hands of God. The whole psalm seems to have reference to David's own experience in the case of Saul, Nabal, Absalom, Ahithophel, and others. See especially 1 Sam. xxv. 39. The psalm, from its aphoristic form, bears a very strong resemblance to the book of Proverbs, and may have been the model on which it was constructed. The alphabetical arrangement, as in other cases of the same kind, is not perfect. Most of the letters have two verses each, but one has three, three have only one, and the letter ‫ע‬ is omitted.

1. *Fret not thyself at evil-doers ; be not envious at workers of iniquity.* The first Hebrew verb is a reflexive form, and strictly means to *heat one's self* with anger. It occurs only here and in Prov. xxiv. 19, where there is obvious allusion to this verse, as there is also in ver. 1 of the same chapter, and in chap. iii. 31, xxiii. 17 of the same book.—*Be not envious at,* do not

envy, the original verb being almost always construed with a preposition.
Evil-doers in the Hebrew is a participle, and literally means those *making
evil, i. e.* making their own conduct so. *Workers*, or more simply, *doers
of iniquity.* The last noun, according to its etymology, denotes perversion,
depravation, or depravity.

2. *For like the grass (in) haste shall they be mown, and like the green
herb shall they fade (or wither).* This verse assigns the reason of the
exhortation in the one before it. Why should we vex ourselves or indulge
an envious feeling towards that which is so soon to perish, and is therefore
rather an object of compassion? These two verses contain the theme, of
which the rest is a protracted variation.—*In haste*, soon, quickly. The
preposition is expressed before the same noun in Eccles. iv. 12, but suppressed as here, in many other places, *e. g.* Num. xvii. 11, (xvi. 46), Deut.
xi. 17.—*The green herb*, literally *greenness of herbage*, the second noun
denoting the young tender grass, or the first growth of other plants. See
above, on Ps. xxiii. 2. The verb at the end of the sentence is the same
with that in Ps. i. 3.

3. *Trust in Jehovah and do good; inhabit the land and feed (on) truth.*
The leading verb of each clause suggests the idea of security, the first
sometimes meaning to be safe (Prov. xi. 15), and the second to repose
(Deut. xxxiii. 20, Ps. lv. 7). *Trust securely, dwell at ease* or in safety.
To *do good* is not merely to perform acts of kindness and promote the
happiness of others, but in a wider sense, to do what is morally good or
right. See above, on Ps. xxxvi. 4 (3). *The land* is the land of promise,
a secure abode in which is often used as a comprehensive expression for
all the covenanted blessings of the chosen people. See Prov. ii. 21, x. 30.
The verb *feed*, in Hebrew as in English, is used both transitively, and intransitively, to denote the act of the shepherd and his flock respectively.
Here it means to feed upon anything with delight, as in Hosea xii. 2 (1),
Isa. xliv. 20. The *truth* thus fed upon is God's truth and faithfulness in
the performance of his promise. See above, on Ps. xxxvi. 6 (5). This
last clause has the force, though not the form, of a promise, and is so
paraphrased in many versions. A less excusable departure from the form
of the original is the explanation of אֱמוּנָה as an adverb (*verily*), thus
depriving the verb of its object and the clause of its chief emphasis, which
lies in representing the veracity of God, or the certain fulfilment of his
promise, as the very food by which the believer is sustained and his hope
nourished.

4. *And delight thyself in Jehovah, and he will give thee the requests of
thy heart.* Here too the command implies a promise, which is afterwards
expressed. *Delight thyself*, seek and find thy happiness, *in Jehovah*, literally
upon him, the form of expression suggesting the idea of dependence and
reliance, as well as that of union and communion. *Requests*, not mere
desires, but *askings*, prayers. Compare Ps. xx. 6 (5), xxi. 3 (2).

5. *Roll upon Jehovah thy way, and trust upon him, and he will do (it).*
This last expression shews that the *way* is something to be done, and
accordingly we find in Prov. xvi. 3, the explanatory variation, *roll to (or on)
the Lord thy works, i. e.* what thou hast to do but canst not do it, metaphorically represented as a burden too heavy for the person bearing it, and
therefore rolled upon the shoulders of another. See above, on Ps. xxii. 9 (8),
and below, on Ps. lv. 23 (22), and compare 1 Peter v. 7.—*Trust upon him*,
a phrase more suggestive of dependence than *trust in him.* See above, on

ver. 4.—*He will do* what thou canst not do, or whatever must be done. See above, on Ps. xxii. 32 (31).

6. *And (will) bring out thy right like the light, and thy cause like the noon.* He will espouse thy cause, and make it triumph in the sight of all men. The figure of light suggests the double idea of relief from suffering and clear revelation after long concealment. Compare Job xi. 17, Isa. lviii. 8, Mic. vii. 9.—The Hebrew word for *noon* is of the dual form, and properly denotes twofold or double light, *i. e.* the brightest, the most intense.

7. *Be silent to Jehovah*, await in silence what he is about to do, without impatient clamour or presumptuous interference. Compare Exod. xiv. 13, 2 Chron. xx. 17. *And wait for him*, allow him time to act, instead of attempting to act for him. *Fret not thyself*, as in ver. 1, heat not thyself with anger, *at (one) prospering his way*, making his way prosperous, *i. e.* succeeding in his course of life. See above, on Ps. i. 1, 3. *At a man doing, i. e.* practising or executing, *plans* or *plots*, as the Hebrew word has constantly a bad sense. Let no success or prosperity of sinners tempt thee to anticipate God's righteous judgments.

8. *Cease from anger, and forsake wrath; fret not thyself only to do evil.* Do not indulge a passion which can only make thee a partaker in the guilt of those who are its objects.

9. *For evil-doers shall be cut off.* This is a twofold reason for obeying the injunction of the preceding verse : first, because the certain destruction of the wicked made such anger unnecessary as well as uncharitable ; secondly, because the same destruction would befall the servant of the Lord, if he indulged an anger tending only to evil. *And (those) waiting for Jehovah*, patiently expecting the fulfilment of his promises and threatenings. As for them, *they*, with emphasis on the pronoun, *shall inherit the land*, the land of promise, the common formula for covenanted blessings. See above, on ver. 3, and on Ps. xxv 13.

10. *And yet a little, i. e.* ere long, soon—bear and forbear a little longer —*and the wicked is not*, or there is no wicked, there is no such person as the wicked man who seemed so prosperous—*and thou shalt gaze*, or look attentively, *upon his place*, the place which he now occupies, *and it is not*, his very place has disappeared—or referring the pronoun to the person, *he is not*, he is no more. Why then be discomposed, and even tempted into sin, by the sight of what is so soon to vanish ?

11. *And the humble*, or, as we should say in our idiom, *but the humble*, on the other hand, on their part, as contrasted both with the presumptuous sinner and the impatient querulous believer. *The humble*, here put for the whole class of submissive waiters upon God. For the true meaning of the Hebrew word, see above, on Ps. ix. 13 (12).—*Shall inherit the land*, possess it by a filial right, be heirs to all the blessings of the covenant. See above, on ver. 3, 9.—*And delight themselves*, enjoy themselves, be happy, as in ver. 4, above.—*In abundance*, or increase, the infinitive of a verb which means to be increased or multiplied, and which occurs above, in Ps. iii. 2 (1).—*Of peace*, in the wide sense of prosperity, well-being, as opposed to want and suffering, and not merely of repose or quiet, as opposed to strife and perturbation.

12. *Plotting*, habitually meditating evil, *(is the) wicked (man), as to* (or *against) the righteous, and gnashing at him* (or *upon him) with his teeth*, gnashing his teeth at him, as a natural token of bestial malignity. This is a kind of concession, that the wicked man deserves no forbearance on

the part of the righteous, who is not, however, therefore at liberty to anticipate God's judgments, for the reason given in the next verse.

13. *The Lord,* the sovereign of the universe, as well as the protector of
his people, *laughs,* or will laugh, *at him,* with derisive pity. See above,
on Ps. ii. 4.—*For,* because, *he sees,* he has already seen, as something
fixed and certain, *that his day,* his own appointed day of vengeance, or
more probably, the sinner's day of punishment, *will come,* is coming.
However long it may be put off, God knows that it will come at last, a
fearful intimation of the certainty of future retribution. Compare Eccles.
viii. 11, 2 Pet. iii. 4, Heb. x. 37.

14. *The sword,* put for all offensive weapons, and indeed for all destructive agents. See above, on Ps. xxii. 21 (20).—*They have opened, i. e.*
loosened or uncovered, drawn.—*The wicked,* the whole class of evil-doers,
whose destruction he had just foretold.—*And have trodden, i. e.* bent by
treading on it. See above, on Ps. vii. 13 (12).—*Their bow,* often coupled
with the sword, both in prose, as being literally the other most familiar
implement of ancient warfare, and in poetry, as a parallel figure for destructive hostility.—*To make fall,* cast down, overthrow, *the sufferer,* the afflicted.
See above, on Ps. ix. 13 (12).—*And the poor,* the destitute or needy one,
a more specific term, often added to the generic one, which here precedes
it. In all such cases, it is implied that the sufferers are the suffering
righteous, the afflicted people of Jehovah.—*To slay,* or slaughter. The
original expression is a very strong one, being properly applied to the
slaughtering of cattle. See Exod. xxi. 37, xxii. 1, 1 Sam. xxv. 11. So
in English a sanguinary battle is described as a great slaughter.—*The
straight,* straightforward, upright, or sincere, (*in*) *way,* a common figure
for the course of life or the habitual conduct. See above, on Ps. i. 1.
The mention of this moral quality confirms the explanation just given of
the *suffering and needy,* not as such considered, but as sufferers in the cause
of truth and righteousness, as suffering for God and from the malice of his
enemies.

15. *Their sword,* the sword of these malignant foes, *shall go into their
heart,* their own heart. They shall be destroyed by the very means which
they prepared for the destruction of their betters. This idea of a providential *lex talionis'* is one repeatedly expressed under various figurative
forms. See above, Ps. vii. 16, 17 (15, 16), ix. 16, 17 (15, 16), and below,
Ps. lvii. 7 (6), and compare the imitation in Prov. xxvi. 27, and the historical example afforded by the case of Haman, Esther vii. 10.—*And their bows,*
the parallel expression, as in ver. 14, for their implements of warfare and
destruction, *shall be broken,* rendered useless. The substitution of the
plural for the singular, and of a single verb for the expected repetition of
the first clause, adds greatly to the force and beauty of the passage.

16. *Good is a little to the righteous,* which, in our idiom, means, *better
is a little that the righteous has.* This clause exemplifies two remarkable
deficiencies of the Hebrew language, the want of a distinct form for the
comparative degree, which can only be suggested by construction or the
context, and the want of the verb *have,* which is common to the whole
Semitic family of languages.—*Than the noise,* tumult, turmoil, which attends
the acquisition and the care of great possessions. That the Hebrew word
(המון) denotes this incident of wealth rather than wealth itself, may be
inferred, not only from its etymology and its use in 1 Sam. iv. 14, xiv. 19,
1 Kings xviii. 41, &c., but from the analogy of Ps. xxxix. 7 (6), and Prov.
xv. 16.—*Of many wicked,* whose noisy and vexatious wealth is here con-

trasted with the quiet enjoyment of one righteous man, not only with respect
to present ease of mind, but also to their future destiny, as stated in the
next verse.

17. *For the arms of the wicked shall be broken.* The ambiguity of our
word *arms* has nothing corresponding to it in the Hebrew, where the only
possible sense is that of *arms* as members of the body. Not only their
weapons, but their arms, not only their implements of death, but the
strength with which they wielded them, is broken, weakened, rendered useless.—*And*, or, as our idiom requires an adversative in such connections,
but sustaining the righteous, their habitual supporter, (*is*) *Jehovah*, the
divine name being placed emphatically at the close, a feature copied in the
ancient versions, but obliterated in most modern ones.

18. *Knowing*, habitually, always knowing, (*is*) *Jehovah*, *i.e.* Jehovah
knows.—*The days*, the life, including both duration and events. Compare
Ps. xxxi. 16 (15).—*Of perfect* (*men*), those free from essential defect or
obliquity of character. See above, on Ps. xviii. 24 (23). The epithet is
evidently used as an equivalent to *the righteous* in ver. 17. God knows
their days, how long they are to live, and what is to befall them, with an
implication that he knows they will be numerous and good days. See
above, on Ps. i. 6. The same idea is then stated more distinctly in the
last clause. *And their heritage*, their portion, their condition, as God's
heirs, *to eternity shall be*, or shall continue. While this expression would
perhaps suggest to a contemporary reader nothing more than an undisturbed
possession, on the part of the righteous, as contrasted with the short-lived
prosperity of sinners, it necessarily conveys to our minds the idea of a literally everlasting, indefeasible inheritance. See 1 Pet. i. 4.

19. *They shall not be ashamed*, disappointed, or deceived in their expectations. See above, on Ps. vi. 11 (10), xxii. 6 (5).—*In an evil time*, or,
in a time of evil, *i.e.* of calamity or danger. See above, on Ps. ix. 10 (9),
x. 1. At such a time, their expectation of deliverance and safety shall not
be frustrated.—*And in days of famine*, a specification of the general description, *evil time*, or *time of evil*, not unlike that of the general term, *suffering*
or *afflicted*, by the specific one, *poor* or *needy*, in ver 14 above.—*They shall
be satisfied*, or *filled*, but only in a good sense, without any implication of
satiety or surfeit. Compare Mat. v. 6, Luke vi. 21. The promise of this
clause is not only specific but positive, whereas that of the first is both
generic and negative. Compare Ps. xxxiii. 19.

20. This verse shews how the truth of the foregoing promises can be
consistent with the actual prosperity of wicked men. Do not doubt the
truth of these assurances because the wicked now seem happy, or because
they now prevent your being so, by their oppressions and hostilities. *For*
all this is soon to cease. *The wicked shall perish*, are to perish, *and the
enemies of Jehovah*, another description of the same class, shewing that
these judgments awaited them, not merely as the foes of the Psalmist, or of
righteous men in general, but of God himself. See above, on Ps. v. 5 (4).
—*Like the precious* (part) *of lambs*, *i.e.* the sacrificial fat, which was burnt
upon the altar, *they have consumed ; in smoke*, or *into smoke, they have consumed* (or *vanished*). The preterite form of the verb represents the predicted consummation as already past in the perceptions of the writer. Some
understand by יְקַר בָּרִים *the delight of lambs*, *i.e.* their pasture, and suppose an allusion to the short-lived verdure of the fields, a common figure for
the brevity of human life, which occurs near the beginning of this very

psalm (ver. 2). Others obtain the same sense by explaining כָּרִים itself to mean *pastures*, as it seems to do in Isa. xxx. 23, and perhaps in Ps. lxv. 14 (13). It is best, however, to retain the usual and certain sense of *lambs*, whether the reference be to their *pasture* or their *fat*, which last is recommended by the mention of *smoke* in the same connection. This may indeed be an independent figure, but it is much more natural to connect it with the lambs, and understand it to denote the smoke ascending from the altar upon which they were consumed in sacrifice. In either case, however, and on any exegetical hypothesis whatever, the essential meaning of the figures is the same, to wit, that the prosperity of sinners is but short-lived, and that they themselves will vanish speedily and wholly, and are therefore in the mean time not a proper object of envious dissatisfaction or a legitimate occasion of sceptical misgiving to the righteous.

21. *Borrowing*, a habitual borrower, (*is*) *the wicked, and he will not pay*, *i. e.* he cannot, because he is reduced to poverty, whereas *the righteous*, under the divine blessing on his outward condition, is continually *shewing mercy*, doing acts of kindness, and particularly *giving*, supplying the necessities of others. This description of the difference between the two conditions is derived from the promise in the Law to the true Israel. ' " For the Lord thy God hath blessed thee as he said to thee, and thou shalt lend to many nations and thou shalt not borrow, and thou shalt rule over many nations, and over thee they shall not rule." Deut. xv. 6, xxviii. 12, 44. Compare Prov. xxii. 7. This proverbial use of borrowing and lending as a sign of poverty and wealth, shews that the verse before us does not relate to willingness but to ability to lend or give. It is not the moral but the material difference of the two men, or the classes which they represent, that is here brought directly into view, although the one is really dependent on the other, as appears from the next verse.

22. *For his blessed ones*, those blessed by him, *i. e.* by God, *shall inherit the land*, in the same sense as before, and so be able not only to lend but to give away, *and*, on the other hand, or *but, his cursed ones*, those cursed by him, shall not only be unable to do either and dependent on the charity of others, but *shall be cut off*, destroyed, exterminated, with allusion no doubt to the use of the same Hebrew verb in reference to excision from the communion and the privileges of the chosen people. See Gen. xvii. 14, Exod. xii. 15, Lev. vii. 20, 21 ; Num. xv. 30, &c., but especially Lev. xvii. 14, xx. 17, where the verb is absolutely used in this sense as in the case before us. Thus understood, the verse assigns the blessing and the curse of God as a reason for the difference of condition mentioned in the verse preceding, whereas no such reason could be given for the difference of moral character, and the *for* in that case would be either out of place or unmeaning.

23. *From Jehovah*, by him, or by a power proceeding from him, the *steps of a man*, his course of life, all that befalls him, *have been settled*, fixed, or ordered, *and in his way*, a parallel expression to *his steps, will he delight*, *i. e.* he will delight to execute the plan thus formed. Although this is in form a general proposition, it is obviously meant to be applied specifically to the righteous as the objects of God's favour, and to account for their superior prosperity, if not at present, yet hereafter.

24. *For he will fall ;* in this life fluctuations and reverses are to be expected, and it forms no part of the divine plan to prevent them. (But) *he shall not be thrown down*, prostrated wholly or for ever. The contrast of a mere fall and a permanent prostration is intended to express that between

occasional misfortunes and utter ruin. This clause may also be translated, *when* (or *if*) *he falls he shall not be thrown down ;* but the construction is less simple, and the sense given to the particle more doubtful and unusual. And although the essential meaning of the sentence is the same in either case, it is weakened by losing the concession, that even the righteous must expect to suffer, but not to perish like the wicked. *For Jehovah* (*is*) *holding up his hand,* or holding him up by his hand. See below, on Ps. lxxiii. 23. The participle, as usual, denotes continued action. God not only sustains him in particular emergencies, but is his habitual upholder. See above, on ver. 12, 18, 21.

25. *A boy,* a child, or more indefinitely, *young have I been ; I have also been old,* am now become old ; and yet, throughout this long life, *I have not seen a righteous* (*man*) *forsaken* (*of God*), *i. e.* finally and utterly, *and his seed,* his children or his more remote descendants, *begging bread,* subsisting on the charity of others. This is not to be absolutely understood, but as a general proposition, and with due regard to the peculiar state of things under the law of Moses, which made ample provision for the temporal comfort of every individual who acknowledged its authority and obeyed its precepts, so that entire destitution might more justly be regarded as a token of divine displeasure than it can be among us.

26. On the contrary, he has enough, not only for himself, but for his poorer neighbours. *All the day* (long), *i. e.* continually, as a habitual employment, (*he is*) *shewing mercy,* doing acts of kindness, *and lending,* as an act of charity, not as a commercial operation, which was unknown among the ancient Hebrews. See above, on Ps. xv. 5.—*And his seed* (*is*) *for a blessing, i. e.* happy themselves and a source of happiness to others. The form of expression seems to be borrowed from the promise to Abraham in Gen. xii. 2.

27. *Depart from evil, and do good, and dwell for evermore.* This is the practical application of the foregoing lessons. *Evil* and *good* are correlative and coextensive terms. As *evil* includes all that is morally wrong, *good* includes all that is morally right, and to *do good* is to do well or act rightly. See above, on ver. 3.—*Dwell, i. e.* dwell securely, as in ver. 3, where as here the exhortation or command involves a promise. *For ever,* literally *to eternity* or *perpetuity.* As to the idea which these expressions would convey to Jewish and to Christian readers, see above, on ver. 18.

28. *For Jehovah* (*is*) *loving,* he habitually loves, *judgment, i. e.* justice actually exercised, the doing of justice. The *for* assigns a reason for the strong assurance at the close of the preceding verse. No one need fear to lay hold of the promise in its widest sense; for it is not an arbitrary one, but a spontaneous expression of God's natural essential love of moral rectitude. *And,* as a necessary consequence of this, *he will not forsake his gracious ones,* the objects of his grace or favour. For the true sense of the Hebrew word, see above, on Ps. iv. 4 (3), xii. 2 (1), xviii. 26 (25), xxx. 5 (4), xxxi. 24 (23.) Those whom he once favours he will not forsake. *For ever,* to eternity, *they are kept,* kept safe, preserved. The past tense of the verb is peculiarly appropriate to describe their preservation as already secured. So certain is it, that he seems to look back upon the future as already past, and says, *they have been kept for ever.* Here again, although a Jewish reader might have been inclined to put a lower sense upon *for ever,* as denoting nothing more than permanency in contrast with the fluctuations of secular prosperity, it is neither right nor possible for us to give it any but its strongest and its most extensive application. (See above, on ver. 18,

and compare 1 Peter i. 5.—Equally certain is the fate of the ungodly. *And the seed of wicked men (is) cut off*, has already been cut off, in the divine prescience and purpose, from all participation in the blessings of the righteous. See above, on ver. 22.

29. *The righteous shall inherit the land*, possess the land of promise by a filial right, *and dwell*, securely and in peace, *for ever*, to eternity, *upon it.* See the same expressions used and explained above, on ver. 3, 9, 18, 22.

30. *The mouth of the righteous will utter wisdom.* Lest the foregoing promises should be appropriated by the wicked, he lays down a test of character by which the righteous man may be distinguished. He is one whose mouth utters wisdom, in the high religious sense. For the meaning of the verb, see above, on Ps. xxxv. 28.—*And his tongue will speak judgment*, *i. e.* justice, rectitude, here used as an equivalent to wisdom, both denoting true religion, in its intellectual and moral aspects, with particular reference to its effects upon the speech or conversation of its subjects.

31. *The Law of his God is in his heart*, not merely on his lips, and may therefore be expected to keep him in the right way. *His steps shall not swerve* from the straight path, or *waver* in it. See above, on Ps. xvii. 37 (36).

32. *Watching*, ever watching, *(is) the wicked for the righteous*, for means and opportunities of injury, *and seeking to kill him.* The enemies of God, as all the wicked are, must needs be the enemies of his people also.

33. *Jehovah will not leave him in his hand*, will not abandon the righteous to the power of the wicked, *and will not make him guilty*, a forensic term of the Mosaic Law, meaning to regard or treat as guilty, to condemn (Exod. xxii. 8, 9, Deut. xxv. 1), *in his being judged*, when he is tried. The image here presented may be that of a judicial process between the righteous and the wicked at the bar of God, who will not and cannot condemn the innocent.

34. *Wait thou for Jehovah*, for the manifestation of his presence and his will, as in ver. 7 above. *And keep his way*, adhere to the path which he has marked out for thee. *And he will raise thee*, lift thee up, exalt thee, from thy present low condition *to inherit the land*, to enjoy the benefits and blessings of his covenant. See above on ver. 3, 9, 11, 30. *In the excision of the wicked*, when the wicked are cut off from all connection with God's people and participation in their privileges, *thou shalt see (it).* Or as the verb to *see*, when construed with this preposition (ב), often means to see with pleasure, this clause may be translated, *at the excision of the wicked thou shalt gaze*, as a pleased and wondering spectator.

35. *I saw a wicked (man).* The issue just predicted is now made the subject of a picture, as if present to the senses. The Hebrew word which follows (עָרִיץ) means terrible, especially from one's extraordinary strength or power, with an implication sometimes of its violent exertion. *I saw* (such) *a wicked man, a terrible one, and spreading himself like a native (tree)* *i. e.* one which has never been transplanted, *green* and flourishing. The word translated *native* is always elsewhere used of human subjects, but is here applied, by a bold personification, to a vigorous tree, rooted in its native soil, and seemingly immoveable

36. *And he passed (away), and lo !* an expression always implying something unexpected, *he was not*, he was no more, there was no longer such a person. See above, on ver. 10. *And I sought him.* I looked round as if to see what was become of him, *and he was not found*, or as we might say, *to be found.* This verse may be referred to the tree, *it* passed away, I looked for *it*, and *it* could not be found. But as the tree is only

introduced in the preceding verse as a comparison, it is better to regard the wicked man as the subject of both sentences.

37. *Mark the perfect (man)*, observe him closely, *and behold the upright,* or straightforward. He appeals to general experience and calls upon his hearers or readers to judge for themselves. *For an end,* a future state, and by implication a happy one, *(is) to the man of peace,* who instead of undertaking to avenge himself, patiently waits for the divine interposition. The common version *(for the end of that man is peace)* is forbidden not only by the accents, but by the impossibility of making לְאִישׁ mean *of that man,* without a violation of all usage and analogy.

38. *And the rebels* against God, those who revolt from his authority, and cast off their allegiance to their rightful sovereign, a common scriptural description of the wicked, *are destroyed together,* or *at once.* See the use of the same adverb in Ps. iv. 9 (8). This certain issue is referred to, as already past or present. See above, on ver. 28. *The end,* futurity, or hope, *of the wicked is cut off.* The futurity meant is one of happiness, as in ver. 37, the true sense of which is thus determined. The contrast presented is, that one has an end or a futurity, the other none.

39. *And the salvation of the righteous,* far from being wrought out by themselves, *(is) from Jehovah,* comes from him as its author and source. See above, on Ps. iii. 9 (8). (He is) *their strength,* or stronghold, fortress, place of refuge and defence, as in Ps. xxvii. 1, xxviii. 8, xxxi. 3, 5 (2, 4). *In time of trouble,* or distress. See above, on Ps. ix. 10 (9), x. 1.

40. *And Jehovah has helped them.* It is not in name or in profession merely that he is their stronghold and protector. *Jehovah has helped them and delivered them.* And what he has done he will still do. *He will deliver them from the wicked.* The mention of this specific evil brings us back to the point from which we started, the temptation to repine at the prosperity of sinners and resent their evil treatment. But the true wisdom of the righteous is to wait, to wait for God. *He will deliver them from the wicked, and will save them* from all evil, as this verb when absolutely used imports, not because of any merit upon their part, but *because they have trusted,* taken refuge, sought for shelter, *in him,* not only under his protection, but in intimate union and communion with him. See above, on Ps. ii. 12, v. 12 (11), vii. 2 (1), xxv. 20, xxxi. 2 (1).

Psalm 38

A SUFFERER, in sore distress of mind and body, aggravated by the neglect of friends and the spite of wicked enemies, acknowledges all to be the fruit of his own sins, and prays that the effect may cease by the removal of the cause.

The psalm contains three distinct complaints, or descriptions of his suffering, separated by two appeals to God, with a prayer at the beginning and the end of the whole Psalm. After the title, ver. 1, comes the first prayer, ver. 2 (1); then the first complaint, ver. 3–9 (2–8); then an appeal to the divine omniscience, ver. 10 (9); then the second complaint, ver. 11–15 (10–14); then an expression of hope and confidence in God, ver. 16 (15); then the third complaint, ver. 17–21 (16–20); and then the closing prayer, ver. 22, 23 (21, 22).

1. *A Psalm. By David. To remind,* or bring to remembrance, *i. e.*

to remind God of the sufferer, whom he seems to have forgotten, with
allusion no doubt to the frequent use of the same verb in reference to
penitent self-recollection on the part of sinners.   See 1 Kings xvii. 18, Ezek.
xxi. 29 (24), xxix. 16, Num. v. 15.

2 (1). *Jehovah, do not, in thy wrath, rebuke me, and in thy heat* (or *hot
displeasure*) *chasten me*.   The force of the negative extends to both clauses.
Rebuke, not in word merely, but in deed, corresponding to *chasten,* chastise,
punish, in the other clause.   He does not pray, as some suppose, for moderate punishment, or for loving as opposed to angry chastisement, but for
deliverance from any punishment whatever, which is always indicative of
God's displeasure.   See above, on Ps. vi. 2 (1).

3 (2). *For thine arrows are sunk into me, and thy hand has sunk upon me.*
This verse assigns the reason of the prayer in that before it.   *Arrows,* sharp
inflictions, as in Deut. xxxii. 23, Job vi. 4.   The verbs of the two clauses
are active and passive forms from the same root.   *Sunk into,* penetrated,
and by implication, *stuck fast,* although this specific idea is not expressed.
Sunk upon, heavily descended, or, as the English version has it, *presseth
me sore.*   Compare Ps. xxxii. 4, xxxix. 11 (10).

4 (3). *There is no sound place in my flesh because of thine anger; there is
no peace in my bones because of my sin.*   Here begins a more particular description of the sufferings indicated by the general terms of the preceding
verse.   The first thing mentioned is his bodily suffering, as a token of God's
wrath and an effect of his own sin, by which that wrath had been provoked.
Flesh and *bones* are put for the whole bodily frame.   The word translated
sound place is a local noun, as indicated by its form, and not an abstract
(*soundness*).   It occurs only in this passage and in Isaiah's imitation of it
(Isa. i. 6).   There, as here, the body is represented as one bruise, in which
there is *no sound place, i. e.* no spot free from pain or soreness.—*Because of,*
literally from the face of, from the presence of, from before, the phrase being
primarily used to denote fear or flight before an enemy.   *Peace* may be
taken in the wide sense of well-being, good condition, health (see above, on
Ps. xxxvii. 11); but it more probably denotes peace in the strict sense, *i. e.*
rest or freedom from the disquietude produced by pain.

5 (4). *For my iniquities are gone over my head; as a heavy burden, they
are too heavy for me.*   This is an amplification of the last words of the
verse preceding.   "I say my sin, because the sensé of my iniquities has now
become intolerable."   *Gone over,* literally *passed, i. e.* surpassed, exceeded,
or transcended.   *Too heavy for me,* or *heavier than I, i. e.* heavier than I
can bear.   The reference is not merely to the effects of sin, but to the sense
of sin itself, the consciousness of guilt, which he now associates with all his
sufferings.   As the preterite of the first clause represents the overwhelming
sense of guilt as something experienced already, so the future of the second
speaks of its excessive weight as something likely to continue.

6 (5). *My stripes have putrefied and are corrupted because of my foolishness.*   The first noun does not denote *wounds* in general, but the swelling
produced by stripes.   Compare Isa. i. 6.   The two verbs both denote sup-
puration, the first in reference to the offensive smell, the second to the
running or discharge of matter.   This may be literally understood as denoting a particular form of bodily distress; but it seems more natural to explain
it as a figurative representation of extreme suffering, not unmingled with
disgrace.   All this he refers to his own *foolishness* or folly, in the strong
sense of criminal blindness and irrationality.   See above, on Ps. xiv. 1.

7 (6). *I have writhed, I have bowed down greatly; all the day mourning I*

have gone. The first word is a passive, meaning strictly to be twisted or distorted, elsewhere metaphorically applied to moral obliquity or perverseness (Prov. xii. 8, 1 Sam. xx. 30), but here used in its proper sense to signify the distortion of the body by extreme pain, as in Isa. xxi. 3. The bowing or bending down may be from the same cause, or as a customary sign of grief. Indeed, the two ideas of sorrow and bodily pain run into each other throughout this passage. The word translated *mourning* properly means *black*, or more specifically, black with dirt, begrimmed, or squalid, in allusion to the ancient oriental custom of sitting in the dust and putting ashes on the head, as signs of mourning. See above, on Ps. xxxv. 14. *Greatly.* The Hebrew phrase means *until very much*, or unto extremity. מְאֹד is originally a noun meaning *strength*, but except in the formula, *with all thy strength*, is generally used as an adverb answering to *very*, greatly, or exceedingly, in English. *I have gone.* The Hebrew verb is an intensive form, nearly equivalent to *gone about* in English. For a still stronger intensive from the same root, see above, on Ps. xxvi. 3, xxxv. 14, in the last of which places we have also the words here translated *bowed down* and *mourning.*

8 (7). *For my loins are filled with parching, and there is no sound place in my flesh.* The loins, instead of being covered with fat (Job xv. 27), are filled with dryness, literally *(something) parched* or *dried up* with extreme heat. To a Hebrew reader this word would necessarily suggest the additional idea of *despised, contemptible*, which the same form often conveys elsewhere (*e. g.* 1 Sam. xviii. 23, Prov. xii. 9, Isa. iii. 5). Indeed, it may be doubted whether this is not the only sense intended here, as that of *parched* is always expressed elsewhere by a different participial form (Lev. ii. 14, Josh. v. 11). On either supposition, the meaning given in the English version (*a loathsome disease*) is implied, if not expressed. The repetition in the last clause from ver. 4 (3) above brings him back to the point from which he started.

9 (8). *I am benumbed and bruised exceedingly : I have roared from the murmur of my heart.* *Benumbed*, especially from cold, chilled, frozen, torpid. *Bruised* or broken. The same verb is used to express contrition or brokenness of heart in Ps. li. 18 (17) below ; but here it has its proper sense, and is descriptive of a bodily condition. See above, on Ps. x. 10.— *Exceedingly*, the same phrase as in ver. 7 (6) above. In the last clause two words are employed, both denoting animal sounds, and nearly corresponding to our *roar* and *growl*. In Isa. v. 29, both verbs are applied to the lion, and both translated *roar* in the English Bible. For the use of such figures, see above, on Ps. xxii. 2 (1). The idea here is that his audible complaints are not expressions of mere bodily distress, but of mental and spiritual anguish. The roaring of his voice is but an echo of the murmur in his heart.

10 (9). *Lord, before thee* (*is*) *all my desire, and my sighing* (or *groaning*) *from thee is not hid.* This is at once an asseveration that his account of his own sufferings was not exaggerated or fictitious, and a reason why it need not be continued. "Thou knowest, O Lord, what I ask and what I need, the depth of my necessities and the intensity of my desires."

11 (10). *My heart pants* (or *palpitates*) *; my strength has left* (or *failed*) *me ; and the light of my eyes—even they are not with me.* Here begins his second complaint or compassionate description of his sufferings, in which those arising from the conduct of others are made prominent. In this introductory verse, however, he describes the effect upon his own feelings,

before proceeding to declare the cause. The palpitation of the heart,
denoting violent agitation, is combined with loss of strength and that dimness of the eyes, so often mentioned as a sign of extreme weakness. See
above, on Ps. xiii. 4 (3), and compare Ps. vi. 8 (7), xxxi. 10 (9), xl. 13 (12).
The last clause admits of two grammatical constructions. 1. " My strength
has failed me, and (so has) the light of my eyes; even they are not with
me." 2. " (As to) the light of my eyes, even they are not with me." The
first agrees best with our idiom, and the last with the masoretic interpunction, which separates *the light of my eyes* from the preceding verb and noun
by a pause accent.—*Even they*, literally, *they too.*—"Not only is my
strength gone, but my eye-sight likewise, but my very eyes."—*Not with me*,
not in my possession, not at my command, gone from me. For a similar
expression, see above, on Ps. xii. 5 (4).—The preterites in the first clause
represent the palpitation and debility as something of long standing, or at
least as fully experienced already.

12 (11). *My lovers and my friends away from my stroke will stand, and
my neighbours afar off have stood.* He now gives expression to the anguish
caused by human unkindness, and first, by that of such as he believed to
be his friends. These are represented as *standing aloof*, literally *from
before, i. e.* out of sight, as in Gen. xxi. 16, and Isa. i. 16, not *over against*,
as implying opposition or hostility. What he here complains of is indifference and neglect, as appears from the parallel expression, *far off*, literally
from afar, according to a common Hebrew idiom which expresses the position of an object in terms strictly denoting motion or direction. See for
example Gen. ii. 8, where *eastward* is in Hebrew *from the east*, and the
familiar phrase *from the right* or *left hand*, where we say *at* or *on* it. This
usage renders it unnecessary, although not inadmissible, in the case before
us, to supply a word, " they stand (looking) from afar." The word translated *neighhours* means those near one, either in local habitation or affinity,
and may therefore be considered as including the idea expressed in the
English Version, *kinsmen*. Unless the variation of the tenses in this sentence is entirely unmeaning, which is highly improbable, both in itself and
from analogy, the last clause may be understood to state as an actual reality,
what is only apprehended in the first as probable or certain but still future.
As if he had said, " My friends will no doubt stand aloof from this affliction ;
nay, they are already afar off."—*Stroke* is here put for a providential or
divine infliction in general, not for sickness exclusively, much less for a
particular disease, such as the leprosy, which Jerome actually introduces
into his translation. See below, on Ps. xxxix. 11 (10), and compare Job
xix. 21, Isa. liii. 4. Some· suppose that there is an allusion to this verse
in the statement made by one of the evangelists, that the women who had
followed Christ from Galilee, and *all his acquaintances*, stood afar off, gazing
at his crucifixion. See Luke xxiii. 49, and compare Mark xv. 40, 41.

13 (12). *And those seeking my soul* (or *life*) *have laid wait* (or *laid
snares) for me, and those seeking my hurt have spoken mischiefs, and deceits
all the day will they utter* (or *devise*). While his friends and neighbours
stand aloof, his enemies are busy in attempting to destroy him. *Seeking
my life*, as in Ps. xxxv. 4, and Exod. iv. 19. This phrase is particularly
frequent in the history of David's persecutions. See 1 Sam. xx. 1. xxii. 23,
xxiii. 15, 2 Sam. iv. 8, xvi. 11. The idea of *seeking* is expressed by two
entirely different verbs in Hebrew. With the first clause compare Ps.
xxxvii. 32.—*Mischiefs*, or still more strongly, *crimes*. See above, on Ps.
v. 10 (9). The reference may be either to malicious consultation, or to

slander, or to both. The last verb may be taken in either of its senses
(see above, on Ps. i. 2, ii. 1, xxxvii. 30), both which are appropriate in
this connection. *All the day* (long), continually. See above, on Ps.
xxxvii. 26.

14 (13). *And I, as a deaf (man), will not hear, and as a dumb (man)
will not open his mouth.* This is at the same time an aggravation of his
sufferings and a declaration of his patience under them. He is obliged to
hear their calumnies and blasphemies as though he heard them not, being
neither able to silence them nor willing to dispute them. The same two
Hebrew words for *deaf* and *dumb* are used together in Exod. iv. 11. Not
only the idea, but the form of expression in this sentence, is copied by
Isaiah in his prophetical description of Christ's sufferings (Isa. liii. 7), and
seems to have been present to our Saviour's own mind when he " held his
peace" before the High Priest (Mat. xxvi. 62, 63), and " gave no answer"
to the Roman Governor (John xix. 9).

15 (14). *And I was as a man who does not hear, and there are not in his
mouth replies* (or *arguments*). The same thing is repeated, to make still
more prominent the patience and forbearance of the sufferer. *Does not
hear*, literally (is) *not hearing*. In our idiom the last clause would have
been, *in whose mouth there are no replies.* The meaning *reproofs* is a
secondary one, derived from that of *proofs* or arguments. See Job xiii. 6,
xxiii. 4.—The idea in both verses is, that he endured the evil speaking of
his enemies, as one who had nothing to say for himself or in reply to their
reproaches. This, while it mortified his pride, and thereby added to his
pain, was at the same time an evidence of faith and patience, and thus
prepares the way for the profession in the next verse.

16 (15). *Because for thee I waited; thou wilt answer, Lord, my God!*
His silence and forbearance, though a part of his sore trial, did not spring
from weakness, but from faith in God, and submission to his precept.
(See above, Ps. xxxvii. 7.) " I retorted not their calumnies and taunts,
because I waited for thee to vindicate my cause, and so thou wilt, thou
wilt certainly answer." The last verb does not mean *shalt answer for me,*
as the Prayer-Book version has it, but as in other cases, *hear* or *answer* my
petition for relief and vindication, whether silent or expressed. See above,
on Ps. v. 2 (1), and compare Ps. iii. 5 (4), iv. 2 (1), xiii. 4 (3), xvii. 6,
xviii. 42 (41), xx. 10 (9), xxii. 3 (2), xxvii. 7, xxxiv. 5 (4).—*Lord*, not
Jehovah, but *Adhonai*, the divine name which properly means *Lord* or
Sovereign. See above, Ps. ii. 4, xxii. 31 (30), xxxv. 17, 22, 23, xxxvii. 13.
—*My God*, and as such bound by covenant to hear me.

17 (16). *For I said, Lest they rejoice respecting me; in the slipping of
my foot they have* (already) *magnified* (themselves) *against me.* His tranquillity did not arise from insensibility to danger, but from confidence in
God. He was not without fear that his enemies might triumph over him,
as they were already disposed to do, when he merely stumbled, but did
not actually fall.

18 (17). *Because I for limping (am) ready, and my grief is before me
always.* This verse assigns a reason for the triumph of his enemies, to
wit, that he was really in danger. *Ready to halt* or *limp, i. e.* constantly
liable to some interruption of his even prosperous course. See above, on
Ps. xxxv. 15. The form of expression does not exclude the idea of his
actually halting, but rather suggests it. As if he had said, " The slightest
occasion makes me halt or limp." *Grief* or *sorrow* seems to be put here
for that which causes it. I am always in full view of my worst distress.

19 (18). *For my iniquity I will declare, I will be anxious on account of my sin.* In our idiom this is tantamount to saying, I must confess that I am guilty; I have reason to be anxious on account of my sin.

20 (19). *And my deadly enemies are strong, and multiplied are those hating me falsely* (or *without a cause*). Instead of *deadly* some find the opposite idea, *lively*, here expressed. *My enemies* (are) *living* (or *alive*), *they are strong.* Or, *my living enemies are strong.* But חַיִּים is the common Hebrew word for *life*, and as שֹׂנְאַי שֶׁקֶר means *my enemies of falsehood*, אֹיְבֵי חַיִּים may mean *my enemies of life*, those who hate my life and would deprive me of it. Compare אֹיְבַי בְּנֶפֶשׁ in Ps. xvii. 9 above.— *Hating me falsely.* Compare Ps. xxxv. 19, lxix. 5 (4).

21 (20). *And* (those) *repaying evil for good—they will oppose me for pursuing good.* The first clause seems to belong to the preceding sentence, and to complete the description of his enemies, "those hating me without cause, and repaying evil for good." Compare Ps. xxxv. 12–16. *Oppose me*, be my enemies. The Hebrew verb is the root of the name *Satan*, the enemy or adversary of God and man. From its etymology, the verb would seem to denote specifically treacherous hostility.—The preposition in the last clause properly means *under*, then *instead of*, and more rarely *in return for*, which is the sense here. *In return for my pursuing good, i. e.* earnestly and eagerly endeavouring to be good and to do right. This was of itself sufficient to provoke their enmity.

22 (21). *Leave me not* (O) *Jehovah!* (O) *my God, be not far from me!* Having twice described his urgent need, he now resumes the tone of complaint with which the psalm began. The petition in this verse is one of frequent occurrence in the Psalms. See above, Ps. x. 1, xiii. 2 (1), xxii. 2 (1), xxxv. 22. The most striking parallel, however, is Ps. xxii. 20 (19).

23 (22). *Hasten to help me,* (O) *Lord, my salvation!* The literal meaning of the first clause is *hasten to* (or *for*) *my help.* The same words form the last clause of Ps. xxii. 20 (19). *My salvation*, my deliverer, my saviour. This form of address bears a strong resemblance to the prayer in Ps. xxxv. 3: *Say unto my soul, I am thy salvation.*

Psalm 39

THIS psalm consists of two parts, in the first of which the Psalmist describes his feelings and his conduct at a former period, in relation to God's providential dealings, ver. 2–7 (1–6), while in the second he expresses what he now feels and believes in reference to the same subject, closing with an earnest appeal to the divine compassion, ver. 8–14 (7–13).

If this view of the structure of the psalm is just, the first part ought not to be quoted as an expression of pious feeling, but as an acknowledgment of sin and error. Some interpreters have gone so far as to affirm this of the whole psalm; but there seems to be an obvious change of tone and spirit in ver. 8 (7). There is no impropriety or danger in admitting that the Psalms contain expressions of unhallowed feeling, if the admission be restricted to those cases where the fact is indicated in the psalm itself, and not left to the discretion or caprice of the interpreter.

1. *For the Chief Musician. For Jeduthun* (or *Jedithun*). *A psalm. By David.* The masoretic punctuation requires the first name to be read

Jeduthun, while the text itself presents the form *Jedithun*. The same diversity appears in Ps. lxxvii. 1, 1 Chron. xvi. 38, Neh. xi. 17. The first form stands alone in 1 Chron. xvi. 41, 42, xxv. 1, 3, 2 Chron. v. 12. In all these places, it is the name of one of David's chief musicians or levitical singers, whose descendants held the same employment, as appears from Neh. xi. 17. The personal name is here added to the official title, perhaps for the purpose of doing honour to the individual, by connecting his name with this inspired composition, as in modern dedications and inscriptions.

2 (1). *I said, I will keep my way, from sinning with my tongue; I will keep for my mouth a muzzle, while the wicked (is) before me.* Here begins the account of his former experience, but without any intimation of the time which had elapsed before he wrote. The two states of mind here described may have followed one another in immediate succession. *I said* to myself, implying a resolution, although this is not the meaning of the verb itself, as some allege. The idea of a fixed determination is moreover suggested by the form of the next verb, which is that of the paragogic future. *I will keep*, guard, preserve. *Take heed to*, although not incorrect, is an inadequate expression of the meaning. *My ways*, my course of conduct, my habitual behaviour. See above, on Ps. i. 1. *From sinning*, so as not to sin, that I may not sin, a form in which this idea is frequently expressed in Hebrew. The word translated *muzzle* occurs only here, but its verbal root is used in Deut. xxv. 4, *thou shalt not muzzle the ox when he treadeth out the corn*, and in Ezek. xxxix. 11, where it evidently means to *stop*, either the nose or the way. The noun therefore must mean a stopper or a muzzle rather than a curb or bridle, by which some explain it. *While the wicked is before me*, or more literally, *in the wicked's (being) still before me.* If this referred merely to his personal presence, the verse would contain a resolution to avoid unguarded speeches in his company or hearing. But this is not the sin to which the Psalmist afterwards pleads guilty, and the true sense of the clause appears to be, while the prosperity of wicked men is still before my eyes, instead of vanishing at once as I expected. See above, Ps. xxxvii. 10, 36.—*For my mouth, i. e.* in reserve for it, or *to my mouth, i. e.* in actual contact with it.

3 (2). *I was silenced (with) dumbness; I held my peace from good, and my sorrow was stirred.* The first clause is highly idiomatic, but the sense is clear, to wit, that he enjoined the strictest silence on himself, in reference to the providential mysteries which excited his envious discontent. The silence meant is abstinence from murmurs and repining against God. The second clause is obscure. *From good* is understood by some to mean *from every thing*, because that idea is elsewhere expressed by the idiomatic combination, *good or evil*. See Gen. xxxi. 24, 29, 2 Sam. xiii. 22. But the antithesis in all such cases is essential, and the omission of one term destroys the meaning. Others give *from* a negative or privative sense, *away from good, without good, i.e.* without any good effect. But the simplest construction is the one given in the English Bible, *even from good*, or more fully in the Prayer-Book version, *yea, even from good words*. The meaning then is, that in his anxiety to avoid the language of complaint against God, he was silent altogether, and suppressed even what he might have said without sin, or was in duty bound to say. The natural effect was that his inward grief, instead of being soothed, was roused, excited, and exasperated.

4 (3). *Hot was my heart within me; while I muse the fire is kindling;* (then) *spake I with my tongue.* His compulsory silence only rendered more intense the feelings which it was intended to conceal. The less he said the

more he thought and felt, until at last it burst forth with more violence than if expressed at first. *My heart glowed*, or *was hot*, with angry discontent and envious repining. *Within me*, literally *in my inner part*, or *inside*, an emphatic phrase referring to the studied absence of all outward indications. Without, all seemed calm and cool; within, his heart was in a glow on fire. *While I muse*, literally *in my meditation*. See above, on Ps. v. 2 (1). The future verb in this clause marks a transition. *The fire will burn*, or is about to burn, is kindling. The gradation is completed by the laconic phrase, *I spake*. "I did what I had fully resolved not to do." The reference to ver. 2 is made more obvious by the additional words, *with my tongue*, which would else be unmeaning and superfluous. "That very tongue, with which I had determined not to sin, I nevertheless spake with, in an unadvised and unbecoming manner."

5 (4). *Make me to know, (O) Jehovah, my end, and the measure of my days, what it is; let me know when I shall cease.* According to the view already taken of the first part of the psalm, this is not a prayer to be made duly sensible of the brevity of life, which would have been superfluous, but an impatient wish to know how soon its sufferings are to cease. The same sentiment is amplified in Job vi. 8–12, vii. 7, xiv. 13, xvi. 21, 22. The last clause may also be translated, *let me know how ceasing, i. e.* frail or short-lived, *I (am)*. But the general drift of the passage favours the construction, *let me know (at) what (point)*, or *(at) what (time) I (am) ceasing*, or about to cease. The indefinite pronoun (מָה) has then the same sense as in the compound phrase (עַד־מָה) *until what (point)*, until when, how long? The verbal adjective (חָדֵל), as in other cases, is only a less usual participial form.

6 (5). *Lo (by) spans*, or *(as) hand-breadths, hast thou given my days, and my life (is) as nothing before me. Only all vanity is every man constituted. Selah.* The idea of the first clause is, that God had dealt out life to him in the scantiest measure. Hence the verb *given* must be taken in its proper sense, and not in that of *placed* or *made*, which it sometimes has. See above, on Ps. viii. 2 (1), xxxiii. 7. The *lo* or *behold*, at the beginning, is expressive of surprise, not unmixed with indignation. As if he had said, "See how short a space thou hast allotted me."—The word rendered *life* is not the common one, but that employed in Ps. xvii. 14, and here used in its primary sense of *duration* or continued existence. *As nothing*, or more strictly, non-existence, nonentity. See above, on Ps. xiv. 1. "My duration is so short that I seem scarcely to exist at all." *Before thee*, not merely in thy estimation, but by thine authority or sovereign constitution. "I only appear in thy presence long enough to disappear." *Only all vanity*, consisting or composed of nothing else. The word translated *vanity* means primarily *breath*, but is transferred, by a natural figure, to anything impalpable and evanescent. The whole phrase means a *mere breath*. *Every man*, or taking the Hebrew noun as a collective, *all mankind*. The participle at the end means fixed, established, constituted, ordained, and describes the brevity of life as something not fortuitous but comprehended in the divine purpose. The melancholy nature of the fact alleged, and perhaps the reasonableness of the complaint founded on it, are indicated by a meditative pause.

7 (6). *Only in an image does a man walk; only (for) a breath do they make a noise; he hoards up and he knows not who will gather them.* So short and transient is man's life, that what he does, and what befalls him,

seems to be not so much a reality as a show, a picture, a phantasma, an ideal scene, in which he *walks about*, as one of the imaginary actors. *For a breath, i. e.* the time spent in a single respiration, an instant, a moment. Or *as a breath, i. e.* something intangible and momentary. Or *as vanity*, vainly, in vain, without use or effect. This last agrees best with the previous use of חֶבֶל, and its frequent usage elsewhere, in the sense of *vanity*.

What is said in the first clause of the individual is said in the second of the species, as indicated by the plural verb. The noise referred to is the bustling clamorous activity with which men seek for pleasure and especially for wealth. Hence the derivative noun, which properly means *noise*, has frequently the secondary sense of *wealth*. See above, on Ps. xxxvii. 16. *Disquieted* is too weak, as denoting passive uneasiness rather than tumultuous exertion. In the last clause the plural is again exchanged for the singular, a clear proof that they both relate to the same subject. The first verb in this clause is applied elsewhere to the heaping up of earth (Hab. i. 10), the storing away of corn (Gen. xli. 35), and the hoarding of treasures (Job xxvii. 16), which is its sense here. *Who will gather them, i. e.* the hoarded treasures, not accumulate them, which is done already, but take them to himself, enjoy, or use them. The future verbs describe this as a process which may be expected to continue, and perhaps to last for ever.

8 (7). *And now what have I waited for? Lord, my hope is in thee.* The conclusion, to which the previous complaints seemed to tend, was that he would wait no longer, but abandon the hope of divine favour in despair. But this result did not ensue, and he asks, as if in wonder at his own inconsistency, how it is that he has waited after all, or still waits, for the good which seemed, a little while ago, so desperate. The answer is given in the other clause. His hope was, from the first, in God, and although sorely tried, was not extinct. At this point it revives, and recovers its ascendancy, and from this point he takes a new and more believing view of those very inequalities and riddles, which before so severely exercised his faith. This may, therefore, be regarded as the turning-point of the whole psalm, the transition from a worse to a better state of feeling. *And now* may be strictly understood, in opposition to past time and to a previous state of mind. At the same time, it serves as a term of logical resumption and connection, as in Ps. ii. 10. *Now, i. e.* since this is the case. *In thee*, literally *to* (or *as to*) *thee*, the Hebrew particle denoting relation in the widest sense; the particular relation is suggested by the context. See above, on Ps. xxx. 2 (1). The divine name, *Adhonai*, Lord, seems to belong more naturally to the second clause, although the masoretic interpunction joins it with the first. *And now, what wait I for, O Lord?* The emphatic pronoun at the end of the sentence cannot well be imitated in translation. (*As for*) *my hope, in thee* (*is*) *it.*

9 (8). *From all my transgressions free me ; the reproach of the fool do not make me.* The first clause contains an implicit acknowledgment that his error was a sinful one. *Transgressions*, treasons, or apostasies, committed against God. The Hebrew word is much stronger than its English equivalent. In asking to be freed from his transgressions, he asks to be delivered from their consequences, one of which is then particularly mentioned. *A reproach*, an object of derision and contempt. See above, on Ps. xxii. 7 (6). *The fool*, by way of eminence, the impious unbeliever. See above, on Ps. xiv. 1. *Do not make me*, literally *place* (or *put*) *me, i. e.* set me up, exhibit, or expose me, as a mark for their invective or their ridicule.

10 (9). *I am silenced, I will not open my mouth, because thou hast done* (*it*). This is far from being a reiteration of the statement in ver. 3 (2) above. The common version of the second verb (*I opened not*) is altogether arbitrary, and even the first, although a preterite, does not mean *I was dumb, i. e.* at some former time, but *I have been silenced* or *am dumb,* at present. There is obvious allusion to the similar expressions of ver. 3 (2), but rather in the way of contrast than of repetition. As before he was kept silent by an obstinate suppression of the rebellious feelings which he really experienced, so now he is kept silent by a filial submission to his father's chastisements. *I will not open my mouth*, to murmur or give utterance to undutiful complaints. *Thou hast done* the very thing at which I was tempted to repine. See above, on Ps. xxii. 32 (31). The pronoun is emphatic : (*it is*) *thou* (*who*) *hast done* (*it*), and no other. See above, on Ps. xxx. 7 (6), xxxiii. 9.

11 (10). *Remove from upon me thy stroke ; from the strife of thy hand I have wasted away* (or *consumed*). The silence vowed in the preceding verse had reference merely to repining and undutiful complaint, not to prayer, which he immediately subjoins. *Remove*, or retaining the form of the original, *cause to remove*, make to depart, take away, withdraw, not merely *from me*, but *from upon me*, implying previous pressure. *Thy stroke*, thy chastisement, thy punishment. See above, on Ps. xxxviii. 12 (11). The same thing is intended by *the strife of thy hand*, the judgments of God being sometimes represented as a controversy or contention between him and the afflicted person. See Isa. lxvi. 16, Ezek. xxxviii. 22. The last verb is not a passive but a neuter, as in Ps. xxxvii. 20. Here again the pronoun is emphatic. *I, even I*, and not merely men in general, know this by experience.

12 (11). *With rebukes for iniquity thou dost chasten man, and waste like the moth what he desires. Only vanity is every man* (or *all mankind*). *Selah*. He here presents his new and more correct view of God's providential strokes which he has now learned to regard as the punishment of sin. The emphasis of the sentence rests upon the first clause. It is not with cruel and vindictive strokes, it is not with random and unmeaning blows, but with penal visitations, *with rebukes* (or *chastisements*) *for sin,* that thou dost chasten man. The past tense of the verb implies that what he suffers is but one link in a long chain of consistent uniform experiences. He is looking not at what has happened once or for the first time, but at something which has always been so. It is God's accustomed mode of dealing with his sinful creatures. The deduction of meanings in תֻרְכַּחַת is first argument, then conviction, then condemnation, then punishment. See above, on Ps. xxxviii. 15 (14).—*Waste*, literally cause to melt away. The same verb is used above, Ps. vi. 7 (6), and below, Ps. cxlvii. 18.—*Like the moth*, not as the moth decays, but as the moth consumes. See Job iv. 19, xiii. 28.—*What he desires*, literally *his desired* or *desirable*, whatever he delights in. *Beauty* is too specific and confined a sense. The last clause, with the *selah* at the close, announces that the Psalmist has come back to the point from which he started, but, as we have seen, with an extraordinary change of views and feelings.

13 (12). *Hear my prayer, O Jehovah, and to my cry* (for help) *give ear ; to my weeping be not silent, for a stranger* (am) *I with thee, a sojourner like all my fathers*. The word translated *weeping* properly means *tear*, but is always used collectively for *tears*. *Be not silent*, as an expression of indifference or hostility, not to be moved even by the sight of tears. *A stranger,* and by implication homeless and friendless, wholly dependent on thy hospitable bounty. To a Hebrew, familiar with the law of Moses, which continually joins the stranger with the widow and the orphan, as legitimate objects of compassionate regard, this description must have been peculiarly affecting. *With thee*, under thy roof, at thy fireside, or in Scripture phrase, *within thy gates*, (Ex. xx. 10), *i. e.* at thy mercy, and dependent on thee. The parallel term (תּוֹשָׁב) means one who has no land of his own, but is settled upon that of another, as a tenant, a vassal, or a beneficiary. The same description is applied by Abraham to himself (Gen. xxiii. 4), by Moses to all Israel, considered as the feudal subjects and dependents of Jehovah (Lev. xxv. 23), and by David to himself and his contemporaries (1 Chron. xxix. 15), on a different occasion from the one before us, and in a different connection, thus affording a striking incidental confirmation of the truth of the inscription which makes him the author of the psalm. See above, on ver. 1. In both cases, the expression *like our fathers* shews the relation which the words describe to be not merely personal but national. Another interesting parallel is 1 Kings xix. 4, where Elijah, in a state of feeling not unlike the one recorded in the first part of this psalm, " requested for himself that he might die, and said, It is enough ; now, O Lord, take away my life, for I am not better than my fathers."

14 (13). *Look away from me, and let me cheer up before I go* (hence), *and am no more.* Both Hebrew words are causatives, and seem to govern *face* understood. " Cause thy face, thy angry countenance, to look away from me, and let me cheer up or exhilarate my own face." The last clause in Hebrew is exceedingly laconic ; the literal translation is, *before I go and am not.* It has been justly represented as remarkable, that all the words and phrases of this verse occur in different places of the book of Job. How long wilt thou not look away from me ? (Job vii. 19). Look away from him and let him cease (Job xiv. 6). Are not my days few? Cease then and let me alone, that I may cheer up a little before I go (hence) and return no more (Job. x. 20, 21). Thine eyes are upon me, and I am not . . . thou shalt seek me in the morning and I am not, or I shall not be (Job vii. 8, 21). These repeated coincidences, not in common but comparatively rare expressions, together with the analogies already mentioned in the explanation of ver. 6 (5) above, seem to shew, not only that the writer of that book was acquainted with the psalm before us, but that the germ or seminal idea of the book itself is really included in this psalm. We have seen already that the thirty-seventh psalm sustains a similar relation to the Book of Proverbs. See above, p. 159. Thus the Psalter, and especially the Psalms of David, furnished themes and models to the inspired writers of a later date, while at the same time they abound themselves with allusions to the Pentateuch and imitations of it. This was the more natural, and even unavoidable, because the books of Moses and the Psalms were especially familiar to all pious Jews from their incessant use in public worship. That the Book of Job is not, in this case, the original, is clear from the number and dispersion of the passages in which this one psalm is alluded to or copied.

Psalm 40

THE Psalmist celebrates delivering grace, already experienced by himself and others, ver. 2-6 (1-5). He declares his resolution to attest his grati-

tude, by deed as well as word, ver. 7–14 (6–13).   He prays that God will
grant him new occasion of thanksgiving, by delivering him from present
troubles, ver. 15–18 (14–17).   This psalm, like the sixteenth, twenty-
second, and some others, seems to be so constructed that it may be applied
generically to the whole class of pious sufferers, but specifically to its head
and representative, the Messiah.

The reappearance of the last part of this psalm in the seventieth will be
considered in the exposition of the latter.

1. *For the Chief Musician.   By David.   A Psalm.*   This title, with a
slight transposition, is the same with that of Ps. xiii. xix. xx. xxi. xxxi.   It
shews that the psalm was not, as might have been supposed from its contents, a mere expression of personal feeling, but designed for permanent and
public use.

2 (1). *I waited, waited for Jehovah, and he bowed* (or *inclined*) *unto me,
and heard my cry.*   The psalm opens with the narrative of what the writer,
or ideal speaker, had himself experienced.   The emphatic repetition of the
verb implies patient perseverance, and is perhaps exclusive of all other
means.   " I simply waited ; I did nothing but wait."   *Bowed himself*, or
the heavens, as in Ps. xviii. 10 (9), or his ear, as in Ps. xvii. 6, xxxi. 3 (2),
most probably the last.   The image then presented is that of one leaning
forward to catch a faint or distant sound.   *My cry* for help.   See above,
on Ps. v. 3 (2), xviii. 7 (6), xxxix. 13 (12).

3 (2). *And brought me up from a pit of noise, and from the miry clay,
and made my feet stand on a rock ; he fixed my steps.*   The first verb in
Hebrew is a causative, *he caused me to ascend.*   The noise referred to seems
to be that of water in a deep place.   *Miry clay*, literally *clay of mire*, in
which there can be no firm foothold, as there is upon the *rock*, with which
it is contrasted.   *Fixed*, established, rendered firm.

4 (3). *And put in my mouth a new song, praise to our God ; many shall
see and shall fear, and shall trust in Jehovah.*   In this, as in ver. 3 (2), the
construction is continued from the foregoing sentence.   *Put*, literally *gave*,
gave (to me) in my mouth.   See above, on Ps. iv. 8 (7).   *A new song*,
implying a new subject or occasion.   See above, on Ps. xxxiii. 3.   By the
new song, we are not to understand this psalm exclusively, but *fresh praise*,
of which this psalm is an instance or particular expression.   *Our God*, the
God of Israel, a further proof that this is not an expression of mere personal
feeling, but a permanent formula of public praise.   The effect of it, anticipated in the last clause, is the same as in Ps. xxii. 26–32 (25–31).   The
original exhibits a paronomasia, which is lost in the translation, arising from
the close resemblance of the verbs *see* and *fear* (יִרְאוּ and יִירָאוּ).   The *fear*
meant is that religious awe or reverence, which always accompanies true
faith or trust in God.

5 (4). *Happy the man who has made Jehovah his trust, and has not looked
to proud (men) and (those) swerving to falsehood.*   From his own experience
he draws a general conclusion, as to the safety and prosperity of those who
trust in God.   The first phrase is properly an exclamation, *Oh the happinesses of the man*, as in Ps. i. 1, ii. 12, xxxii. 1, 2, xxxiii. 12.   The next
words in Hebrew have properly a local sense.   *Who has set Jehovah (as) his
place of security*, the form of the noun being one which has commonly a
local meaning.   See above, on Ps. xxvii. 1.   The verb translated *looked*
means strictly *turned round* towards an object for the purpose of looking at
it.   It may here imply confidence or trust, as cognate verbs do in Isaiah
xvii. 7, 8.   Or it may convey the additional idea of taking sides, espousing

the cause, joining the party, of those *swerving*, turning aside, apostatising, from the way of truth and duty, or from God himself. See above, on Ps. xiv. 3, xviii. 22 (21).

6 (5). *Many (things) hast thou done, Jehovah, my God ; thy wonders and thy thoughts to us it is not* (possible) *to state unto thee ; I would declare and speak* (them ; but) *they are too many to be numbered.* This is not the only instance of the kind, but one of a great multitude. *Many things, i. e.* many such things. *My God,* as well as *our God, i. e.* in personal covenant with me, as well as in national covenant with Israel. See above, on ver. 3 (2). The combination of the two divine names suggests that Jehovah was not the God of Israel only, but the Supreme God. The word translated *wonders* is properly a passive participle, meaning (*things*) *made wonderful* or *wonderfully done,* and therefore constantly used absolutely as a noun in the sense of *wondrous deeds* or *wonderful works.* See above, Ps. ix. 2 (1), xxvi. 7. *Thoughts,* purposes, and in this connection, purposes of mercy. *To us,* towards us, respecting us, and for our benefit. The next words may also mean, *there is no resemblance* (or *comparison*) *to thee, i. e.* none to be compared with thee. See below, Ps. lxxxix. 7 (6), and compare Isa. xl. 18, Job xxviii. 17, 19. This use of the Hebrew word is founded on its primary sense of arranging, putting in order, with particular reference to the arrangement of the offerings and other sacred objects under the Mosaic law. Then it was used to signify the act of putting things together, side by side, and so comparing them. See above, on Ps. v. 4 (3), where it is figuratively applied to the presentation of a prayer, and compare its similar use in Isa. xliv. 7, Job xxxvii. 19, xxxii. 14, in the last of which places we have the phrase to *order* or *present words.* As this is a more frequent sense than that of resembling or comparing, and in this case agrees better with the words immediately before and after, it is safer to retain it. *I would declare,* literally *I will declare,* the form of the verb being that of the paragogic future, which expresses in the first person strong resolution. This is more expressive than the hypothetical proposition, " I would declare them, if I did not know it to be impossible." The idea conveyed by the original expression is that of an actual attempt and failure. As if he had said : " Yes, I will declare and tell thy wondrous works ; but no, they are too many to be numbered or recounted." For the meaning of the last verb, see above, on Ps. ii. 7, ix. 2, 15 (1, 14), xix. 2 (1), xxii. 18, 23 (17, 22), xxvi. 7.

7 (6). *Sacrifice and offering thou hast not desired ; my ears thou hast pierced. Burnt-offering and sin-offering thou hast not asked.* Here begins his account of the way in which his gratitude should be expressed. This is first negatively stated—not by mere oblations or other ceremonial rites. To express this idea he combines four technical expressions of the Law. The first two are the usual descriptions of animal and vegetable offerings. The first means anything slaughtered for a sacrificial purpose. The second means originally any gift, but is appropriated, in the Law, to those secondary offerings of corn, oil, wine, and incense, which accompanied the animal oblations. In the English version of the Pentateuch it is rendered *meat-offering,* a version which no longer conveys the correct meaning to the common reader, since these were precisely the offerings from which *meat,* in the modern sense of *flesh,* was entirely excluded. In this case, however, the Hebrew word is joined with that before it to describe the two great kinds of offering, animal and vegetable. The parallel terms in the last clause are those denoting the general expiatory sacrifice statedly offered, and the spe-

cial sacrifice in reference to particular offences. The last words of the first
clause are exceedingly obscure. The Hebrew verb elsewhere means *to dig*,
and is so used in Ps. vii. 16 (15) above. It may be naturally used, however, to denote the act of piercing, perforating. Some suppose it to mean
opening the ear or causing one to hear, and understand the whole phrase
as meaning, " thou hast told me so, or hast revealed it to me." This is
favoured by the use of cognate phrases to express the same idea, such as
opening, uncovering, awakening, the ear, &c. See Isa. l. 4, 5 ; 1 Sam.
ix. 15, xx. 2, 12 ; xxii. 8. It is more probable, however, that the strong
expression here used was intended to suggest the additional idea of obeying
or rendering obedient, which is often expressed even by the simple verb to
hear. The peculiar figurative form in which the thought is clothed may be
accounted for, by supposing an allusion to the ceremony of boring a slave's
ear with an awl, as a symbol of perpetual obedience. See Exod. xxi. 6.
The whole verse may then be paraphrased as follows :—" Thou hast not
required ceremonial services, but obedience, and hast pierced my ear, as a
sign that I will hear thee and obey thee for ever." The Septuagint version
of this clause (*a body hast thou prepared me*) is retained in the New Testament as an unimportant variation, *i. e.* in reference to the writer's purpose
in making the quotation, and perhaps as suggesting that the incarnation of
the Son was a prerequisite to his obedience. The contrast intended is
between ceremonial rites in themselves considered, and the obedience, of
which they only formed a part, and from which they could not be severed
without rendering them worthless. There is obvious allusion to 1 Sam.
xv. 22, not only here but in the parallel passages, Ps. li. 18, 19 (16, 17),
Hos. vi. 6, Isa. i. 12, Jer. vii. 22–24.

8 (7). *Then I said, Lo, I come, in the volume of the book it is written of
me.* The first word refers not so much to time as to other circumstances.
Then, in these circumstances, this being the case. Seeing and knowing
that mere ceremonial services are worthless, *I come*, I bring myself, all that
I have and am, as a rational or spiritual service. (Rom. xii. 1.) *The
volume of the book*, or *the roll of scripture*. The second noun is the one used
in Hebrew to denote the written revelation of God's will, and the first to
describe the form of an ancient oriental book, not unlike that of a modern
map, and still retained in the manuscripts used in the synagogue worship.
The reference is here to the Law of Moses. *Written of me* is by some referred
to prophecy, by others to the requisitions of the law. The literal meaning
of the Hebrew words is *written upon me, i. e.* prescribed to me, the *upon*
suggesting the idea of an incumbent obligation. " Enjoined upon me by a
written precept." This is clearly the meaning of the same phrase in
2 Kings xxii. 13. Thus understood, the clause before us may be paraphrased as follows :—" Since the ceremonies of the Law are worthless, when
divorced from habitual obedience, instead of offering mere sacrifice I offer
myself, to do whatever is prescribed to me in the written revelation of thy
will." This is the spirit of every true believer, and is therefore perfectly
appropriate to the whole class to whom this psalm relates, and for whom it
was intended. It is peculiarly significant, however, when applied to Christ:
first, because he alone possessed this spirit in perfection ; secondly, because
he sustained a peculiar relation to the rites, and more especially the sacrifices, of the Law. David, or any other individual believer under the old
economy, was bound to bring himself as an oblation, in completion or in
lieu of his external gifts ; but such self-devotion was peculiarly important
upon Christ's part, as the real sacrifice, of which those rites were only

figures. The failure of any individual to render this essential offering insured his own destruction. But if Christ had failed to do the same, all his followers must have perished. It is not, therefore, an accommodation of the passage to a subject altogether different, but an exposition of it in its highest application, that is given in Heb. x. 5–10. The limitation of the words to Christ, as an exclusive Messianic prophecy, has the twofold inconvenience of forbidding its use by the large class of godly sufferers, for whom it seems so admirably suited, and of requiring us to understand even the confession of sins as uttered in his person. See below, on ver. 13 (12).

9 (8). *To do thy will, my God, I have delighted* (or *desired*) *and thy law (is) in the midst of my bowels.* The self-devotion, just professed, is now described as a cordial and spontaneous act, because the law requiring it is not regarded as a mere external rule, but as existing in the heart and coinciding with the will. This, which is true, in measure, of all genuine obedience, is pre-eminently true of that obedience unto death, by which Christ magnified the law and honoured it, proved his own zeal for God and deference to his will, and wrought out that salvation which alone can render similar obedience upon man's part possible. With the last clause compare Ps. xxxvii. 31, Deut. xx. 14, Prov. iii. 3, vii. 3, Isa. li. 7. This verse, together with the one before it, on which it is a kind of comment, holds up to view the sincere obedience of the true believer, including the observance of commanded rites, in contrast with the formal hypocritical observance of the rites alone, and at the same time the perfect obedience and self-sacrifice of Christ in contrast with the types by which they were prefigured.

10 (9). *I have proclaimed righteousness in a great assembly. Lo, my lips I will not restrain ; Jehovah, thou knowest* (or *hast known*). The first verb is the nearest Hebrew equivalent to the Greek εὐαγγελίζομαι, to announce good news, to proclaim glad tidings. The *righteousness* meant is that of God. The *great congregation* or *assembly* is his church or people. *Restrain, i. e.* from still proclaiming it. The past tense, in the first clause, shews this to be, not a mere engagement or a promise, but a statement of what has been already done. The future following completes the statement, by providing also for the time to come. The return to the preterite in the last clause appeals to God's omniscience for the truth of what was first alleged, as well as of the promise just recorded. " Thou hast already been a witness of my zeal in the annunciation of thy righteousness, and art a witness, at this moment, of the sincerity with which I vow that it shall be continued."

11 (10). *Thy righteousness I have not hid in the midst of my heart ; thy faithfulness and thy salvation I have uttered ; I have not concealed thy mercy and thy truth from the great congregation* (or *assembly*). The same idea is again expressed, but with a pointed allusion to the last clause of ver. 9 (8), as if to guard against a misconstruction of its language. In opposition to a mere external formal service, he had there said that the Law of God was in his heart. But now he hastens, as it were, to add that it was not confined there. He was not contented with his own impressions of God's righteousness, derived both from his word and from his providence. He considered himself bound to make it known to the whole body of God's people, for the twofold purpose of comforting and edifying them, and of promoting the divine glory. The expression of the same thing, both in negative and positive form, is a natural method of enforcing what is said, which is common to all languages, although particularly frequent in the Hebrew.

12 (11). *Thou, Jehovah, wilt not withhold thy compassions from me ;
thy mercy and thy truth will always preserve me.* This is not a prayer, as
it seems to be in the common version, but an expression of strong confidence, like that in Ps. xxiii. 6. As if he had said, "I am sure that thou
wilt not withhold," &c. Here, again, there is an obvious allusion to a previous expression. As he had said in ver. 10 (9), *my lips I will not restrain,*
so now he says, *and thou, O Lord* (on thy part), *wilt not restrain thy mercies from me.* The phrase supplied, *on thy part,* is really included in the
pronoun *thou,* which, being unnecessary to the sense, must be emphatic.
See above, on Ps. ii. 6. *Thy compassions,* tender mercies, warm affections.
See above, on Ps. xxv. 6, and compare Ps. xviii. 2 (1). *Truth* means the
veracity of God's engagements, as in the preceding verse, where it is joined
with *faithfulness,* fidelity. *Preserve me* from distresses, dangers, enemies.
See above, Ps. xii. 8 (7), xxxi. 24 (23), xxxii. 7.

13 (12.) *For upon me have gathered evils till there is no number ; my
sins have overtaken me, and I am not able to see ; they are more than the
hairs of my head, and my heart has failed me.* The original expression in the
first clause, to *surround upon,* is a strong one, to denote an accumulation
of evils from all quarters. This is intended to account for the necessity of
protection and deliverance, implied in the last clause of the verse preceding. It introduces the prayer for relief from present troubles, founded on
previous experience of God's mercy, and forming the conclusion of the psalm.
Sins, not punishments, although the experience here described is that of
their effects. *Overtaken,* reached after long delay and hope of escape. See
Deut. xxviii. 15. The common version, *cannot look up,* gives a meaning
which the Hebrew phrase never has elsewhere. It always denotes dimness
or failure of sight, arising from distress, weakness, or old age. See 1 Sam.
iii. 2, iv. 15, 1 Kings xiv. 4, and compare Ps. vi. 8 (7), xiii. 4 (3), xxxi.
10 (9), xxxviii. 11 (10). *More than the hairs of my head.* See below,
Ps. lxix. 5 (4). *My heart has failed me,* literally *left me.* See above, on
Ps. xxxviii. 11 (10), where the same thing is said of his *strength.* This
picture of complicated sufferings, produced by his own sins, is inapplicable
to the Saviour, who neither in prophecy nor history ever calls the sins for
which he suffered *my sins.*

14 (13). *Be pleased,* (O) *Jehovah, to deliver me ;* (O) *Jehovah, to my help
make haste !* The first clause contains an implied acknowledgment of dependence on God's mercy. In the second, the form of expression is the
same as in Ps. xxii. 20 (19).

15 (14). *Ashamed and confounded together shall be* (those) *seeking my soul
to destroy it ; turned back and disgraced shall be* (those) *desiring* (or *delighting in*) *my hurt.* Strictly speaking, this is not so much the expression of
a wish as of a confident expectation. See above, on ver. 12 (11). But
its intimate connection with the foregoing prayer seems to give it the force
of an optative. The wish implied is precisely the same as in Ps. xxxv. 4, 26.

16 (15). *They shall be desolate on account of their shame—those saying
to me, Aha, aha !* The common version, *for a reward of their shame,* seems
to make their shame the crime for which they were to be punished. The
Hebrew word (עֵקֶב) sometimes means wages or reward, as the *consequence*
of labour. See Ps. xix. 12 (11), Prov. xxii. 4. But the general meaning
of the phrase, *in consequence,* is admissible, and quite sufficient here. For
the meaning of the last clause, see above, on Ps. xxxv. 21, 25.

17 (16). *They shall rejoice and be glad in thee—all* (those) *seeking thee.
They shall say always, Great be Jehovah—*(those) *loving thy salvation.* The

structure of the clauses is alike, each beginning with the action, and ending with a description of the agent. The joy and praise are represented as the fruit of the deliverance here prayed for. *In thee*, in communion with thee, in the enjoyment of thy favour. *Seeking thee*, seeking that communion and that favour. *Great is Jehovah*, or *the Lord be magnified, i.e.* recognised as great and glorious. *Loving thy salvation*, not merely desiring it for themselves, but rejoicing in it as bestowed on others. See above, Ps. xxxv. 27, and compare xxii. 24 (23), lxix. 33 (32).

18 (17) *And I* (am) *afflicted and poor, and the Lord will think of me* (or *for me*). *My help and my deliverer* (art) *thou. O my God, do not delay.* The connection is the same as in Ps. ii. 6, above. " And (yet) I am a sufferer, and poor ; and (yet) the Lord will think," &c. The Hebrew phrase (יחשב לי) may either mean, *will think respecting* (or *concerning*) *me, i.e.* remember me, attend to me—or *will think for me, i.e.* plan, provide, for me. *My help art thou*, and therefore canst not fail to help me ; *my deliverer*, and therefore must deliver me. See above, on Ps. iii. 4 (3). The same thing is implied in the address, *my God.* See above, on ver. 4, 6 (3, 5). *Do not tarry*, linger, or delay to grant this prayer.

Psalm 41

1. *To the Chief Musician. A Psalm by David.* This psalm, though intended, like all the rest, for permanent and public use, exhibits very strong marks of the personal experience of the author. He first states a general rule of the divine dispensations, namely, that the merciful shall obtain mercy, ver. 2–4 (1–3). He then claims the benefit of this law in his own case, which is described as one of great suffering from sickness and the spite of wicked enemies, ver. 5–10 (4–9). He concludes with an earnest prayer to God for succour, and expresses a strong confidence that he shall receive it, ver. 11–14 (10–13).

The juxtaposition of this psalm with that before it is not fortuitous, but founded on their common resemblance to the thirty-fifth, and on their mutual resemblance as generic descriptions of the sufferings of the righteous, with specific reference to those of the Messiah, as the head and representative of the whole class. In this, as in the fortieth psalm, the exclusive reference to Christ is forbidden, by its obvious adaptation to a whole class, and by the explicit confession of sin in ver. 6 (5).

2 (1). *Happy* (the man) *acting wisely towards the poor* (man) ; *in the day of evil Jehovah will deliver him.* The form of expression at the beginning is the same as in Ps. i. 1, xl. 5 (4). As the first verb sometimes has the sense of *attending* or *attentively considering*, some understand it to mean here *considering* (or *attending to*) *the poor.* But its proper import of *acting prudently* (or *wisely*) is entirely appropriate, and therefore entitled to the preference. See above, on Ps. ii. 10, xiv. 2. What is meant by *acting wisely towards the poor*, may be gathered from the parallel passage, Ps. xxxv. 13, 14. The principle assumed is that expressed by our Saviour in Mat. v. 7. See above, on Ps. xxxvii. 28. *The poor*, in the wide sense of the English word, corresponding very nearly to that of the Hebrew דָּל, which means poor in flesh (Gen. xli. 19), and poor in strength (2 Sam. iii. 1), as well as poor in point of property and social standing (Exod. xxiii. 3). It here includes all forms of want and suffering, and might be translated *wretched.* This is not a mere reflection on the unkindness of his

own acquaintances, but an indirect assertion of his own benevolence. " Happy the man acting wisely towards the poor—*as I have done*. In the day of evil, of his own misfortune, when his own turn comes to suffer, the Lord will deliver him—*as I desire and expect to be delivered*."

3 (2.) *Jehovah will keep him and save him alive; he shall be prospered in the land; and do not thou give him up to the will of his enemies.* What he has done for others the Lord will do for him. *Save him alive :* the same verb occurs above in Ps. xxii. 30 (29). *Prospered:* the Hebrew verb (יאשר) orignally means *led straight*, or in a straight path. See above, on Ps. xxiii. 3. But here it has the same sense as in Prov. iii. 18. The marginal reading in the Hebrew Bible (ואשר) only differs from the text by introducing the conjunction *and*. *In the land, i. e.* the land of promise. See above, on Ps. xxv. 13, xxxvii. 3, 9, 11, 22 29, 34. These are generally propositions, but are evidently meant to be applied specifically to himself. His solicitude respecting the event is betrayed by his sudden transition from prediction to petition. *Give him up to the will,* literally *into the soul,* here put for the desire or appetite. See above, on Ps. xxvii. 12, and compare Ps. xvii. 9.

4 (3.) *Jehovah will support him on the couch of languor; all his bed hast thou turned in his sickness.* The images are borrowed from the usages of real life. The first is that of holding a sufferer up, sustaining him, in pain and weakness; the other that of changing, making, or adjusting his bed. The parallelism favours this interpretation of the second clause much more than that which makes it mean " thou has converted all his sickness into health." The words translated *couch* and *languor* are unusual equivalents to *bed* and *sickness* in the other clause.

5 (4). *I have said, Jehovah, have mercy upon me ; heal my soul, for I have sinned against thee.* The pronoun at the beginning is emphatic. He is here applying to himself the doctrine which he had before laid down in general terms. " Knowing this to be the rule of the divine administration, I myself have claimed the benefit of it; I myself have said," &c. There is no need of diluting the past tense into a present. The use of the preterite implies that it is not an act yet to be performed, but one that has been done already. The same emphasis, though not required by the form of the original, may be supposed to rest upon the *me* and the *my*. The prayer for the healing of his soul may be considered as including that for the removal of his bodily disease, which seems to be referred to in this psalm as a mere consequence of inward agony. And this is itself referred to sin as its occasion in the last clause of the verse. The intimate connection between sin and suffering is continually recognised by David. See above, Ps. xxxi. 11 (10), xxxii. 5, xxxviii. 4, 5, 19 (3, 4, 18), xl. 13 (12). *Against thee,* literally *to thee, as to thee.* The idea of direct opposition is suggested by the context. See above, on Ps. xxx. 2 (1), xxxv. 19, 24, xxxviii. 17 (16).

6 (5.) *My enemies will say evil to* (or *as to*) *me: when shall he die and his name perish?* The word translated *evil* is constantly applied to moral evil, and here means spite or malice. ˙The ambiguous phrase *to me* seems to include the two ideas of speaking of him and in his hearing, or as we say in familiar English, *talking at him.* See above, on Ps. iii. 3 (2), xi. 1. The question in the second clause implies impatience. With the last phrase compare Ps. ix. 7 (6).

7 (6.) *And if he come to see me, falsehood he will speak; (in) his heart he is gathering mischief; he will go out, to the street* (or *out of doors*) *he will speak* (or *tell it*). The subject of the sentence is his enemy viewed as an

ideal person. Compare the alternation of the singular and plural forms in ver. 6 (5) and 12 (11). *If he come*, literally *has come*, at any former time ; or still better, if he has come now, if he is now here, the scene being then described as actually present to the writer's senses, which adds greatly to its graphic vividness and beauty. *To see*, not merely *to see me*, in the usual sense of *visiting*, which is rather an English than a Hebrew idiom, but *to see for himself*, to observe, to play the spy, to watch the progress of the malady, and judge how soon a fatal termination may be looked for. *Falsehood*, vanity, in the strong scriptural sense of emptiness, hypocrisy, false professions (in this case) of sympathy and friendly interest. *He will speak:* I am sure that he will do so ; I know him too well to doubt it for a moment. The idea thus suggested by the future is entirely lost by exchanging it for the present, which it really includes, but something in addition. The construction, *his heart gathereth*, is at variance with the Masoretic accents, and does not yield so good a sense as that which makes *his heart* an adverbial phrase, a Hebrew idiom of perpetual occurence. In our idiom it will then mean *in* (or *as to*) *his heart*, as opposed to the outward appearance of benevolence and friendship. The second future (יִקְבָּץ) may be either construed like the first, he (certainly) *will gather*, (I know that) *he will gather;* or understood to signify an action which has been begun but is not finished, *he is gathering*. To gather mischief is, in this connection, to collect materials for calumnious reports. *He will go out, he will speak*, or as we should say in English, *when he goes out he will speak*. The Hebrew verb itself (יֵצֵא) means to *go out*. The additional phrase means strictly *to the street*, or *to the outside* of the house. It might be grammatically construed with the verb before it, *he will go out to the street*. But the accents connect it with the verb that follows, *to the street he will tell* (*it*), or *to the outside, i. e.* to those without, who are perhaps to be conceived of, as impatiently awaiting his report.

8 (7). *Together against me they will whisper all* (*those*) *hating me; against me they will meditate—injury to me*. The collocation in the first clause is like that in Ps. xl. 15–17, (14–16), the action being first described, and then the actors. The future has the same force as in the first clause of ver. 6, 7 (5, 6). They will certainly persist in doing as they now do. The substitution of the present in translation conveys only half of this idea. The last word in Hebrew (לִי) is omitted in most versions, though expressed in the margin of the English Bible. It defines the *evil* meditated, not as evil in the abstract or in general, but as evil to the sufferer, *i. e.* injury, which is the usual meaning of the Hebrew word (רָעָה), a modified form of (רַע), the one used in ver. 6 (5) to denote moral evil. The last words are a kind of after-thought.—*Against me they will meditate* or *plot*, is a complete proposition in itself, which is then made more explicit by mentioning the object of their plots, *namely, evil* (or *injury*) *to me*. This form of the sentence may have been adopted to render the resemblance in the structure of the clauses more complete.

9 (8). *A word of Belial is poured into him, and he who lies* (there) *shall arise no more*. These are the words of his malignant visitors, either uttered in his presence, or to their companions after leaving him. The literal translation of the first clause is given, to shew its obscurity, and enable the reader to understand the different explanations of it which have been proposed. Some give *word* its not unfrequent idiomatic sense or *thing, affair* (1 Sam. x. 2, 2 Sam. xi. 18, 19, Ps. cv. 27), and *Belial* that

of *ruin* or *destruction*, which they suppose it to have in Nah. i. 11, and
Ps. xviii. 5 (4) above. But there, as elsewhere, it is better to retain its
primary meaning, *good for nothing, worthless*, or as an abstract, *worthlessness*, a strong though negative expression for depravity. The whole phrase
will then mean a *wicked matter*, a *depraved affair*. By this again some
understand the disease with which he was afflicted, and which is then
described as the result of his own wickedness; others the plan or plot
devised by the speakers for the ruin of the sufferer. But this would hardly
be described by themselves as a depraved affair. None of these explanations seem so natural or so exact, as that which gives to both words their
customary meaning, and understands by a *word of Belial* a disgraceful
charge or infamous reproach, which is then represented as the cause of his
distress and his approaching death. The next phrase may either mean
poured into his mind or soul, as a moral poison, producing agony and
death; or *poured upon* him, so as to submerge or overwhelm him. In
Job xli. 15, 16 (23, 24), the same participle (יָצוּק) seems to be thrice used
in the sense of poured out, melted, soldered, firmly fastened. So here the
English Bible renders it *cleaveth fast unto him*, and the same meaning is
assumed by some who understand by the preceding words a wicked plot or
a destructive visitation, which is then described as cleaving fast to him so
that he cannot shake it off or otherwise escape from it. The common version of the next words, *now that he lieth*, is extremely forced. The only
natural construction of the relative is that which refers it to the sufferer
himself. *He who has lain down shall not add to rise*, the common Hebrew
method of expressing a continued or repeated action. See above, on Ps.
x. 18. The expression becomes still more graphic if we understand it to
mean *he who is lying* (here before you), or *he who lies there*, *i. e.* in yonder
house or chamber.

10 (9). *Even the man of my peace—whom I confided in—eating my
bread—has lifted against me the heel.* The first word properly means *also*.
Not only foes, but *also* friends; not only strangers, but *likewise* they of my
own household. *The man of my peace*, or *my man of peace*, is a strong
idiomatic expression for the man with whom I was at peace. As to the
construction, see above, on Ps. ii. 6. *Eating my bread*, not merely as a
guest, but as a dependent. Such must have been the current usage of the
phrase in David's time. See 2 Sam. ix. 11, 13, xix. 29 (28), and compare
1 Kings xviii. 19. *Lifted*, literally *magnified* or made great. See above,
on Ps. xxxv. 26, xxxviii. 17 (16). The act described seems to be one of
contemptuous violence, but probably with an implicit allusion to supplant-
ing as an act of treachery. Our Lord applies this verse expressly to himself and Judas (John xiii. 18), which shews that he was really included in
the class to which the psalm relates. It is remarkable, however, that he
only quotes the second of the three descriptive phrases, *eating my bread*,
enjoying my society and subsisting on my bounty, while he omits the other
two, because these would have represented Judas as his friend, and one in
whom he trusted. But he knew from the beginning who it was that should
betray him (John vi. 64). This accurate distinction seems to confirm the
assumption that the psalm has a generic meaning, and is only applicable
to our Saviour as the most illustrious representative of the class which it
describes. The allusion to Judas would be still more striking if, as some
suppose, the phrase *man of my peace* had reference to the customary use
of the word *peace* in salutation. He who was wont to wish me peace or to

say, Peace be with thee. Compare Mat. xxvi. 49. But this, although
ingenious, is by no means an obvious or natural interpretation.

11 (10). *And thou, Jehovah, have mercy upon me, and cause me to arise,
and I will repay them.* The connection between this verse and the one
before it can be fully expressed in English only by a *but* at the beginning
of the sentence. The pronoun is emphatic, *thou*, on thy part, as distinguished from these spiteful enemies. He here resumes the prayer begun
in ver. 5 (4), and interrupted by the description of the malice of his enemies.
Make me to rise, help me up from this bed of weakness and suffering, with
obvious allusion to their having said that he would never rise again, ver. 9
(8). " O Lord, do what they pronounce impossible." The last words of
this verse seem at first sight inconsistent with the Christian doctrine of
forgiveness, as laid down in Mat. v. 39, 40, Rom. xii. 19. (Compare
1 Pet. ii. 23.) But as this is also an Old Testament doctrine (see Prov.
xx. 22), as David himself recognised the principle, Ps. vii. 5 (4), and acted
on it, as appears from 2 Sam. xix. 24 (23), the disagreement can be only
an apparent one. It may be partially removed by observing that the
speaker here is neither Christ nor David in his proper person, but an ideal
character, representing the whole class of righteous sufferers, so that what is
here said really amounts to little more than a prediction that the malignant
persecutors of this class shall be requited. In the next place, let it be
observed that it is not said how he will repay them, whether by punishment or by heaping coals of fire upon their heads, according to Solomon's
and Paul's directions. (Prov. xxv. 21, 22, Rom. xii. 20, 21.) Lastly,
the rule laid down by Christ himself admits of righteous retribution, not
only on the part of magistrates and rulers, but of private persons, where
the means employed are lawful in themselves, and where their use is
prompted, not by selfish pride or a revengeful malice, but by a desire to
prevent a greater evil, to assert God's honour, and even to benefit the
offender himself.

12 (11). *By this have I known that thou hast delighted in me, because
my enemy is not to triumph over me.* This implies a previous divine assurance that his enemy should not so triumph. For a similar intimation, see
above, Ps. xx. 7 (6). The certainty thus afforded is expressed by the past
tenses of the two first verbs. " Since thou hast assured me that my
enemy is not to triumph over me, I know already that thou hast even heretofore regarded me with favour." The original expression is a very strong
one, and denotes not only preference but warm and tender affection. See
Gen. xxxiv. 19, where it first occurs. The last verb means properly to
shout or make a noise as a sign of exultation, more especially in war.
See 1 Sam. xvii. 20.

13 (12). *And as for me—in my integrity thou hast held me, and hast
made me stand before thy face for ever.* The first phrase literally means
and I, as if agreeing with some verb suppressed, or as if the construction
had been suddenly changed from *I have been held* to *thou hast held me*.
The integrity here claimed is not absolute or sinless perfection, as appears
from the confession in ver. 5 (4), but freedom from essential or fatal defect.
See above, on Ps. xviii. 21–25 (20–24). *In my integrity*, not simply *on
account of it*, which is rather implied than expressed, but in the possession
and exercise of it. *Thou hast held* may either mean *held fast* or *held up*,
but the first seems to be the essential meaning of the verb, and really involves
or at least suggests the other. " Thou hast so held me fast as to hold
me up. By retaining thy hold upon me thou hast sustained me." *Setting*

before the face seems here to mean making one the object of attention. keeping constantly in view. The reciprocal act of man towards God is spoken of in Ps. xvi. 8. As man sets God before him as an object of trust, so God sets man before him as an object of protection. That this is not to be a transient but a permanent relation, is implied in the future form of the verb, and expressed in the adverbial phrase *for ever*.

14 (13). *Blessed (be) Jehovah, the God of Israel, from everlasting and to everlasting. Amen and Amen.* In such connections, *blessed* is nearly synonymous with *praised* or *glorified*. In the sense of *happy*, the Hebrew word can only be applied to creatures. *From the perpetuity* (already past) *and even to the perpetuity* (to come), is a paradoxical but strong expression for unlimited duration. *Amen* is a Hebrew verbal adjective meaning *firm, sure, certain, true*. It is used as an expression of assent, just as we use *right, good*, and *true* itself, for the same purpose. It was uttered by the people as an audible response, not only in the time of Moses (Num. v. 22, Deut. xxvii. 15–26), and of David (1 Chron. xvi. 36), but after the return from exile (Neh. v. 13, viii. 6), and under the New Testament (1 Cor. xiv. 16). Its repetition here and elsewhere simply makes it more emphatic and expressive of a stronger and more cordial acquiescence. The doxology before us marks the close of the first of the five books into which the Psalter is divided. See below, on Ps. lxxii. 19, lxxxix. 53 (52), cvi. 48.

Psalm 42

1. *To the Chief Musician. Maschil. To the Sons of Korah.* The obvious reference to personal experience and feelings in this psalm made it the more necessary to designate it as a *maschil* or didactic psalm, intended for permanent and public use. See above, on Ps. xxxii. 1. The experience described is evidently that of David, and most probably at the time of his exclusion from the sanctuary in consequence of Absalom's rebellion. See 2 Sam. xv. 25. The only doubt is whether the psalm was composed by him or by the Sons of Korah. These were a Levitical family of singers, 1 Chron. vi. 1, 7, 16 (16, 22, 31), ix. 19, xxvi. 1, who still continued that employment in the reign of Jehoshaphat, as appears from 2 Chron. xx. 19. This being their office, it would seem more natural to regard them as the performers rather than the authors of the psalm. It seems improbable, moreover, that the composition should be ascribed to a whole class or family. On the other hand, the *Sons of Korah* are here separated from the *Chief Musician*, and occupy precisely that place where we usually find the author's name. It is also remarkable that we never find the *Sons of Korah* named with David or any other individual author except Heman, who was probably one of themselves. See below, on Ps. lxxxviii. 1. If he, or any other of the *Sons of Korah*, be regarded as the author of the psalm before us, he must be supposed to have composed it in the person of David, *i. e.* to express David's feelings at a particular juncture of his history. It is, of course, a much more obvious supposition, that David himself wrote it for this purpose. Nor can the intrinsic probability of this supposition be destroyed, although it may undoubtedly be weakened, by the difficulty of accounting for the fact, that David's name is never mentioned in the titles of any of the eleven psalms inscribed to the *Sons of Korah*. The psalm before us is divided by its structure into two parts, marked by the burden or *refrain* in ver. 6, 12 (5, 11). In the first, he laments his exclusion from

God's presence, ver. 2, 3 (1, 2), aggravated by the taunts of his enemies, and the recollection of his former privileges, ver. 4 (3), but confidently anticipates their restoration, and calls upon his soul to hope and trust in God, ver. 5, 6 (4, 5). In the second, he goes over the same ground, though not in the same words, ver. 7, 11 (6, 10), and closes with the same expression of confidence as before, ver. 12 (11).

2 (1). *As a hart panteth after streams of water, so panteth my soul for thee, (O) God.* The first noun is masculine but the verb feminine, so that we may either read *hart* or *hind*. The verb occurs only here and in Joel i. 20, which is evidently copied from the verse before us. The allusion may be either to the exhaustion caused by flight, or to the natural effects of drought. See below, on Ps. lxiii. 2 (1). The essential idea is that of intense desire and an overwhelming sense of want. *Streams of water,* waterbrooks. See above, on Ps. xviii. 16 (15).

3 (2). *Thirsted has my soul for God, for the living God. When shall I come and appear before God?* The past tense of the first verb shews that he is not expressing a desire just conceived for the first time, but one with which he is already familiar. Of the two divine names here used, one (Elohim) describes God as an object of religious worship, the other (El) as a Being of infinite power. He is Living and Mighty, as distinguished from imaginary deities, and from impotent and lifeless, idols. *When shall I come?* implies a local, bodily approach, and this agrees with the following phrase, *appear before God,* which is the technical expression in the Law for stated appearance at the sanctuary, except that the divine name Jehovah is exchanged for Elohim, which occurs ten times in this psalm, and Jehovah only once.

4 (3). *My tears have been my bread day and night, in (their) saying to me all the day, Where (is) thy God?* The word translated *tears* is the collective term used in Ps. xxxix 13 (12). The Hebrew verb is in the singular. " My weeping has been my bread," *i. e.* my food. " Instead of eating I have wept." See below, Ps. cii. 5 (4), and compare 1 Sam. i. 7, Job iii. 24. *Day and night, all the day,* are strong but common phrases for continually, constantly. See above, on Ps. i. 2. *In saying, i. e.* in the time of saying, while it is said. Or a pronoun may be supplied, *in (their) saying,* while they say, *i. e.* his enemies. *Where is thy God?* The very question is an indirect assertion that God had forsaken him. See above, Ps. iii. 3 (2), xxii. 9 (8), and below, Ps. lxxi. 11, cxv. 2, and compare Joel ii. 17. The words of Shimei may have been present to the mind of David. See 2 Sam. xvi. 7, 8.

5 (4). *These (things) I will remember and will pour out upon me my soul, when I pass in the crowd, (when) I march (with) them up to the house of God, with the voice of joy and praise, with festive noise (or tumult).* This is the only construction of the sentence which gives the future forms their proper force instead of converting them into past tenses, which is wholly arbitrary, and therefore ungrammatical. If the last clause contained a reminiscence of his former privileges, there was nothing whatever to prevent the use of the preterite forms. *These things,* not his former enjoyments, but his present sufferings. *I will remember,* I am determined so to do, this idea being suggested by the very form of the Hebrew verb. If the verse related only to the past, this strong expression would be out of place. The act of reflection or self-introversion is expressed by the stong figure of pouring out his soul upon himself, which at the same time suggests the idea of lively emotion ; not necessarily of grief, as in Job. xxx. 16, but of

mingled joy and sadness in the recollection of past sufferings and deliverances, just as we might speak of a man's heart being melted, either with
sorrow or gratitude, or both.   *When I pass*, or still more literally, *for I
shall pass*, which in that case expresses the confident expectation of a favourable issue.   *Pass, i. e.* pass along in solemn procession.   *The crowd*, or
throng, the Hebrew word suggesting, by its etymological affinities, the idea
of a thicket, and then of a confused mass.   The verb translated *march*
occurs only here and in Isa. xxxviii. 15, where it seems to be borrowed
from the place before us.   Its construction is like that of the English *march*,
which, though commonly intransitive, in some cases governs the noun
directly.   If we render it here, *I shall march them*, it conveys the additional
idea of conducting as well as joining the procession.   *Up to*, a stronger
expression than *to*, implying actual arrival at the place in question.   The
use of music in the processions to the temple may be inferred from 2 Sam.
vi. 5.   The word translated *noise* or *tumult* may also mean the *multitude*
by whom it is produced.   See above, on Ps. xxxvii. 16, xxxix. 7 (6).   But
the other is the primary meaning and agrees best with the parallel expressions.   The last word in Hebrew means originally *dancing* (1 Sam. xxx. 16),
but with special reference to its ceremonial use, as an expression of religious
joy (2 Sam. vi. 14).

6 (5). *Why art thou cast down, (O) my soul, and why art thou disquieted within me? Wait thou for God, for I shall yet thank him (for) the
salvations of his face* (or *presence*).   The Psalmist's faith addresses his unbelieving fear, as if it were another person.   The question involves a
reproof, as if he had said, thou hast no reason to be thus dejected.   *Why*,
literally *what, i. e.* for what cause, or on what account.   *Art thou*, literally
wilt thou be?   Why wilt thou persevere in this extreme and gratuitous dejection?   The form of the Hebrew verb is reflexive, *why wilt thou deject
thyself*, implying, still more strongly than before, that the dejection was a
voluntary one, and therefore culpable.   *Disquieted*, the same verb that is
used in Ps. xxxix. 7 (6), and the root of the noun meaning *noise* or *multitude*
in ver. 5 (4) above.   Here, as elsewhere, it denotes, not mere uneasiness,
but violent agitation, and is sometimes applied to the commotion of the sea.
See below, on Ps. xlvi. 4 (3), and compare Jer. v. 22.   *Within me*, literally
upon me, as in the foregoing verse.   *Wait for God, i. e.* for the fulfilment
of his promises, implying confidence and hope.   The verb translated *thank*
means strictly to *acknowledge*, and is applied both to the confession of sin
and to the thankful acknowledgment of benefits received.   See above, on
Ps. xxx. 5 (4), xxxii. 5.   *Salvations*, frequent or complete deliverance.   See
above, on Ps. xviii. 51 (50).   *His face*, his propitious countenance or aspect,
with allusion to the benediction in Num. vi. 25, 26.   See above, on Ps.
iv. 7 (6), xvi. 11, xvii. 15, xxxi. 17 (16).   The determination to thank
God for his goodness implies a confident expectation that it will be exercised.
See above, on Ps. v. 8 (7).

7 (6). *My God, upon me is my soul cast down.   Therefore I will remember thee from the land of Jordan and the Hermons, from the hill Mizar.*   In
spite of his expostulations, his dejection still continues, and can only be removed or mitigated by a more direct recollection of what God is, and has
done for him, and of the mutual relation still subsisting between them.
Upon me, as in the two preceding verses.   Here perhaps the phrase may
be intended to suggest, that reliance on himself only deepened his dejection,
and compelled him to repose his trust on some other and more sure foundation.   *Is cast down*, will be so, unless and until thou lift it up.   *From the*

land implies that he was there excluded from God's presence by exclusion from his sanctuary. The indefinite expression, *land of Jordan, i. e.* the tract through which it flows, as we say the valley of the Mississippi, is referred specially to the eastern side by the mention of the *Hermons, i. e.* as some suppose mount Hermon, and the other mountains upon that side of the river, just as *Baalim* means Baal, and other idols worshipped with him (1 Kings xviii. 18), or more probably mount Hermon, considered not as a single eminence, but a chain or range like the Alps, the Alleghanies, &c. In either case it is put for the whole region east of Jordan, which did not properly belong to Canaan or the Holy Land. (See Josh. xxii. 11). In this wide sense the expression might be used by David, even in reference to his abode at Mahanaim, north of the Jabbok, on the borders of Gad and Manasseh (2 Sam. xvii. 24, 27, 1 Kings ii. 8). *Mizar*, little or littleness. Whether this be taken as a proper name, of which there is no trace elsewhere, or as a descriptive epithet, it seems to be contemptuous.

8 (7). *Deep unto deep* (*is*) *calling at the voice of thy waterspouts; all thy billows and thy waves over me have passed.* The first word in Hebrew seems to denote strictly a great body of water, and in that sense is applied to the ocean—see above, on Ps. xxxvi. 7 (6)—and also to its waves. It may here mean either a wave of a flood. The participle (*calling*) represents the scene as actually passing. The idea may be simply, that they respond to one another's noise, or more emphatically, that each wave invites or summons another to succeed it. For a somewhat similar expression see above, Ps. xix. 3 (2). *Voice, i. e.* sound or noise. The Hebrew word is less restricted in its application than the English, so that it is not necessary even to assume a personification. The next word, in the only other place where it occurs (2 Sam. v. 8), has the literal meaning of a water-spout or gutter. It may here denote the continued streams of rain poured upon the earth. The sense of water-falls or cataracts, although supported by the ancient versions, has no foundation in etymology or usage. The idea that David here alludes to the water-falls of Lebanon, by which he was surrounded, rests on a false interpretation of ver. 7 (6), which, as we have seen, contains a general description of the country east of Jordan, called in later times Perea. *Billows and waves*, literally *breakers and rollers, i. e.* masses of water rolling towards the shore and broken on it. Throughout this verse there is an obvious allusion to the universal deluge, as there is in Ps. xxix. 11 (10), xxxii. 6, and often elsewhere.

9 (8). *By day will Jehovah command his mercy, and by night his song with me, a prayer to the God of my life.* Notwithstanding his distresses he is still convinced that God has not forsaken him. By *day* and *night* some understand prosperity and adversity; but they are probably put together to denote all time, the opposition between song and prayer being merely rhythmical, *i. e.* occasioned by the parallelism. Compare Ps. xcii. 3 (2). *Command his mercy, i. e.* exercise it authoritatively, or as a sovereign. *His song*, a song of praise to him, implying the experience of his goodness, even in a season of distress. Compare Job xxxv. 10. These words may be governed by the verb of the first clause, *he will command his song* (*to be*) *with me*, he will give me occasion to sing his praise, or construed with the substantive verb understood, *his song* (*shall be*) *with me*. The *God of my life* may be explained to mean *my God of life, i. e.* my living God. Compare *the hill of my holiness*—my hill of holiness—my holy hill, Ps. ii. 6. It is more natural, however, to understand by *the God of my life* the God to whom my life belongs, upon whom it depends, and who is bound to protect it. " A prayer

to him who is by creation the author, and by covenant the preserver of my life."

10 (9). *I will say to God, my rock, why hast thou forgotten me ? Why go I mourning in the oppression of the enemy ?* This expostulation may be regarded as a part or a sample of the *prayer* which God enabled him to offer, even in the midst of his afflictions. The divine name here used is (אֵל) the one significant of strength. *My rock*, my refuge, my protector, and the foundation of my hope. See above, on Ps. xviii. 3 (2). *Why go I ?* more exactly, why shall or must I go ? *Mourning*, literally squalid, dirty. See above, on Ps. xxxv. 14, xxxviii. 7 (6). *In the oppression*, may either mean during its continuance, or in consequence of it, or rather both ideas are included.

11 (10). *With murder in my bones, my enemies have taunted me, in their saying to me all the day, where is thy God ?* The strong expression in the first clause is intended to denote excruciating pain. *My enemies*, oppressors, or persecutors, as the Hebrew word denotes. *Taunted me*, a stronger expression than *reproach* or *reviled me*, implying scorn as well as anger and hatred. *In their saying*, i. e. by their saying and while they say, as in the foregoing verse. *All the day*, continually. See above, on ver. 9 (8). *Where is thy God ?* See above, on ver. 4 (3).

12 (11). *Why art thou cast down, (O) my soul, and why art thou disquieted within me. Hope thou in God, for I shall yet thank him (as) the help of my countenance and my God.* As usual in such cases, there is a slight variation in the burden or *refrain* from that in ver. 6 (5). See above on Ps. xxiv. 7–10. Instead of the *salvations of his face* we have here the *salvations of my face*. The attempt to assimilate the two expressions, by an emendation of the text, is not only destitute of all authority and evidence, but forbidden by the general practice of the sacred writers in repeating the expressions either of themselves or others. *The salvations of my face* is a bold and unusual expression, which appears to mean such deliverances or such abundant help as clears up and illuminates the countenance before clouded and dejected. *And my God* is not an unmeaning or gratuitous addition, but has reference to the taunting question in the preceding verse, *Where is thy God ?* As if he had said, "Behold him, he is here. My God is he who dissipates my clouds and animates my hopes, and raises me superior to the sneers as well as to the fury of my enemies." While this variation relieves the repetition from entire sameness, the repetition itself brings the second strophe and the whole psalm to a striking and symmetrical conclusion.

Psalm 43

A SUFFERER prays to be delivered from unjust and treacherous enemies, ver. 1–3, expresses a confident assurance that his request will be granted, ver. 4, and upbraids himself for his despondency and unbelief, ver. 5.

As the last verse is identical with that of the preceding psalm, and the last clause of ver. 2 nearly so with that of Ps. xlii. 10 (9), some have inferred that this is really the third stanza or strophe of that psalm, separated from it by mistake. But the difficulty of accounting for such a mistake, a difficulty aggravated by the resemblance of the compositions, together with a very perceptible difference in the general tone of the two psalms, makes it far more probable that it is a supplementary psalm, composed by the same person, or in imitation of him, on a different occasion. The union of the two in more than thirty Hebrew manuscripts, only shews that their transcribers drew the same hasty conclusion that has since been drawn by many interpreters, and is much more easily explained than the division of the psalms in all the other copies, on the contrary hypothesis. Their juxtaposition in the Psalter is owing not merely to their mutual resemblance, but to the fact that one was actually written as an appendix or continuation of the other. The same hypothesis sufficiently accounts for the absence of a title or inscription in the psalm before us.

1. *Judge me, (O) God, i. e.* do me justice, vindicate my innocence, exercise thy righteousness in my behalf. See above, on Ps. x. 18, xxvi. 1. *And plead my cause,* literally *strive my strife,* but with particular allusion to litigious or forensic contest. See above, on Ps. xxxv. 1. *Against an ungodly nation,* literally *from* one ; the idea of deliverance, as the necessary consequence of God's being his advocate, is here implied, and afterwards expressed. The word *nations* (גּוֹיִם) being constantly applied to the gentiles or heathen, the use of the singular in reference to Israel always conveys an idea of reproach. Compare Isa. i. 4. *Ungodly,* more exactly *not merciful,* the Hebrew word denoting both the object and the subject of benignant pity. See above, on Ps. xxxvii. 28. *From a man of fraud.* See above, on Ps. v. 7 (6). *And iniquity,* or more precisely, perverseness, moral obliquity. *Thou wilt deliver me.* This is strictly an expression of strong confidence, but really includes the prayer, *deliver thou me.*

2. *For thou art the God of my strength.* The last word means properly *my place of strength,* my stronghold, or my fortress. See above on Ps. xxvii. 1. *For what (cause) hast thou cast me off,* renounced, rejected me ? The original expression is a very strong one, and implies disgust or loathing. Compare Rev. iii. 16. *(Why) do I go,* or more exactly, *shall I, must I go, i. e.* go about, in different directions. The verb is an intensive form of that used in Ps. xlii. 10 (9), and occurs above, in Ps. xxxv. 14, in the same connection as here. *Mourning,* with special reference to the neglect of neatness, both in dress and person, as a customary sign of grief. See above, on Ps. xxxv. 14, xxxviii. 7 (6), xlii. 10 (9). *In (i. e.* during and because of) *the oppression* (persecution) *of the enemy.* All this is indirectly represented as inconsistent with the covenant relation he sustains to God.

3. *Send, i. e.* send forth out from thy presence. See above, on Ps. xiv. 7, xx. 3 (2). *Thy light,* the light of thy countenance, thy favourable aspect, as in Ps. iv. 7 (6), or more generally, *light,* as the opposite of darkness, and a figure for relief from that of which darkness is the emblem, to wit, danger and distress. *And thy truth,* thy veracity, thy faithfulness, the certain fulfilment of thy promises. See above, on Ps. xxv. 5, xxvi. 3, xxx. 10 (9). To send it out is to exercise this attribute, to manifest it in act, by performing his engagements. *They,* with emphasis on the pronoun, which is otherwise superfluous in Hebrew, they and no other, nothing else. See above, on Ps. xxiii. 4. *Shall guide* (conduct or lead) *me,* or giving the future an optative meaning, which is certainly implied in this connection, *let them lead me. They shall cause me to come* (or *let them bring me) to thy hill of holiness (thy holy hill) and to thy dwellings,* or *thy tabernacles,* as the Hebrew word is specially applied to the Mosaic sanctuary (Ex. xxv. 9, Num. i. 50). This petition seems to imply a previous exclusion from it, and thereby shews that the historical occasion of the psalm, if not the same, was similar to that of the forty-second. The form of expression

seems to be borrowed from Exod. xv. 13. The mention of the tabernacle
and the holy hill, *i. e.* mount Zion, shews that the psalm is neither earlier
nor later than the times of David and Solomon, before whom there was no
holy hill, and after whom there was no tabernacle. This strengthens the
presumption that David was himself the author of both psalms.

4. *And I shall come*, as an expression of strong confidence that God will
save him from his present troubles, or *I will come*, as the expression of a
purpose, amounting to a vow or solemn promise. Both these ideas, though
requiring a slight variation of expression in our idiom, would be necessarily
suggested to a Hebrew reader by the original verb, the paragogic form of
which, however, shews that the second is the primary idea. See above, on
Ps. xlii. 5 (4). *To the altar of God* (*Elohim*), as the place of sacrifice
here put for the whole sanctuary. *To God* (*El*) *the gladness of my joy*, my
joyous gladness, the author and the object of my highest exultation. *And
I will thank thee*, praise thee for thy benefits, *with a harp* (כִּנּוֹר), the instrument on which David's history describes him as excelling. See above, on
Ps. xxxiii. 2, and compare 1 Sam. xvi. 16, 23. What he here vows is not
mere private praise, but participation in the public praises of the sanctuary.
God, my God. Not merely God in general, but my God in particular.
Either expression by itself would have been insufficient to express the whole
idea, *God* being too vague, *my God* too restricted, whereas the combination
of the two implies that his God was not a personal, domestic, or national
divinity, but the supreme God.

5. *Why art thou cast down*, literally *why wilt thou deject thyself*, implying
self-rebuke for an unreasonable and untimely sadness. (*O*) *my soul*, which
is really equivalent to *myself.* *And why art thou disquieted*, why wilt thou
be agitated by these anxious doubts and groundless fears ? See above, on
Ps. xlii. 6 (5). *Within me*, literally *upon me*, as if his unbelieving fears
weighed upon him as a heavy burden. *Hope thou in God*, or more exactly,
wait thou for him, for his appearance, for his help, for the fulfilment of his
promise. This, he is confident, will come at last. *For I shall yet praise
him*, thank him, or acknowledge his kindness. (*As*) *the health of my countenance*, or more exactly, *the salvations of my face*, the salvations which are
yet to cheer my clouded aspect and lift up my dejected countenance. The
exact coincidence of this verse with the last of the preceding psalm, so far
from proving it to be a part of it, rather proves the contrary, for reasons
which have been already stated in the exposition of Ps. xlii. 12 (11).

Psalm 44

1. *To the Chief Musician. To the Sons of Korah. Maschil.* The same
question here arises as in Ps. xlii., as to the sense in which the psalm is
ascribed to the Sons of Korah. For the reasons there assigned, it is, on
the whole, most probable that David is the author, however difficult it may
be to account for the omission of his name in the inscription, and the appearance of the sons of Korah in the place which it usually occupies. See above,
on Ps. xlii. 1. The addition of *Maschil*, *i. e.* a didactic psalm, is meant to
shew that though occasioned by a particular event, perhaps the same as in
Ps. lx., it was composed and left on record for the permanent use and edifi-
cation of God's people. See above, on Ps. xxxii. 1. The train of thought
is marked with unusual distinctness. God was, in ancient times, the protector and deliverer of Israel, ver. 2–5 (1–4). He is still their national

and covenanted God, ver. 6–10 (5–9). But he seems to have given them up to their enemies, ver. 11–18 (10–17). Yet Israel still cleaves to him and suffers for his sake, ver. 19–23 (18–22). He is therefore importuned to reappear for their deliverance, ver. 24–27 (23–26). The state of things described and the sentiments expressed in this psalm, do not afford the slightest reason for referring it to any later period than that of David, when the same occasions of complaint and importunity were in existence, although not to so great an extent as afterwards.

2 (1). *O God, with our ears have we heard, our fathers have recounted to us, the work thou didst work in their days, in the days of old.* What they had heard with their ears is tacitly contrasted with the very different things which they had seen with their eyes. See below, Ps. xlviii. 9 (8), and compare Judges vi. 13, 2 Chron. xx. 7, Hab. iii. 2. *Our fathers have told us,* as enjoined or predicted in Exod. x. 2. The verb means properly to *count*, and then to *recount* or relate, with particular reference to the detailed enumeration of particulars. See above, on Ps. ii. 7. The last clause may be construed as a separate proposition. *A work thou didst work,* &c. But this leaves the active verbs of the first clause without a grammatical object. The emphatic combination of the verb and its derivative noun is greatly weakened in the English Bible, *what work thou didst*, and still more in the Prayer-book version, *what thou hast done.* The particular work meant, as appears from what follows, is the conquest of Canaan and the settlement of Israel in it.

3 (2). *Thou (with) thy hand didst nations dispossess and plant them, didst crush peoples and extend them.* This, though a literal translation, is obscure in English, because the pronoun *them* in both clauses refers to Israel. In the second clause it might indeed have reference to the Canaanites, and the verb be taken in the sense of sending out, expelling, as in Gen. iii. 23, 1 Kings ix. 7, Isa. l. 1. But as it is also used to signify the sending out of shoots or branches by a tree or vine, Ps. lxxx. 12 (11), Jer. xvii. 8, Ezek. xvii. 6, 7, xxxi. 5, the parallelism seems decisive in favour of that meaning here. The verb translated *dispossess* means properly to cause to inherit, but is sometimes applied to the substitution of one heir or possessor for another. See Exod. xxxiv. 24, Num. xxxii. 21, xxxiii. 52, Deut. iv. 38. The verb translated *crush* may simply mean to *injure;* but the stronger sense is here entitled to the preference.

4 (3). *For not with their sword did they possess the land, and their* (own) *arm did not save them; for* (it was) *thy right hand, and thy arm, and the light of thy countenance; for thou didst favour them.* The *for* at the beginning introduces the proof or amplification of the general statement in the preceding verse, that it was God who planted and settled them. *Save them,* literally *to* or *for them. i. e.* did not bring deliverance to them, or work out deliverance for them. The translation of the second כִּי by *but* gives the sense but not the form of the original, as the use of the particle, in its strict sense, just before and after, forbids our taking the intermediate one in any other. With the first clause compare Josh. xxiv. 12 with the last clause, Ps. iv. 7 (6).

5 (4). *Thou art He, my King, (O) God! Command deliverances for Jacob.* The form of expression in the first clause is highly idiomatic and somewhat obscure. It may either mean, "Thou who hast done all this art still my king," or "Thou art he who is my king," which last may be thus resolved into the English idiom, "It is thou who art my king." Compare 2 Sam. vii. 28, 1 Chron. xxi. 17. The church here claims the same

relation to Jehovah that was sustained by the former generations of his
people.　The last clause may also be translated, *order the salvations of Jacob,*
i. e. cause them to take place and regulate them by thy providence.　The
personal name of the patriarch is poetically substituted for his official title
as the father of the chosen people.　See above, on Ps. xxiv. 6.

6 (5).　*In thee our adversaries will we push; in thy name will we trample*
our assailants.　The hopes of Israel still rely upon that power which expelled
the Canaanites.　The word translated *adversaries* properly means those who
press, oppress, or persecute.　See above, on Ps. iii. 2 (1), and compare Ps.
xiii. 5 (4), xxvii. 2, 12.　Our *assailants,* literally our risers up, those
rising up against us.　See above, on Ps. xviii. 40 (39), and compare Deut.
xxxiii. 11.　The verb in the first clause means specifically to push with the
horns, to toss, or gore.　See Exod. xxi. 28–32, and compare Deut. xxxiii.
17, 1 Kings xxii. 11.　*In thy name,* not merely by thy authority, or as thy
representatives, but in thyself, in union and communion with thee.　See
above, on Ps. v. 12 (11), xviii. 30 (29).　The meaning of the future verbs
in this connection is, that they will triumph, if at all, in this way.　They
must prevail thus or be vanquished.

7 (6).　*For not in my bow will I trust, and my sword will* (or *can*) *not*
save me.　" What was true of my fathers is equally true of me.　As they
did not prevail by their own strength, neither can I hope to prevail by
mine."

8 (7).　*In God have we praised all the day, and thy name unto eternity*
will we acknowledge.　Selah.　The construction in the first clause, although
foreign from our idiom, is more expressive than the simple phrase, *we have*
praised God.　It names God first, as the object *in* which the occasion and
the theme of praise had been sought and found.　" It is in God that we
find the subject of our praises."　The common version (*boasted*) confounds
the verb here used with another derivative of the same root.　*Thy name,*
thy manifested nature.　See above, on Ps. v. 12 (11).　*To eternity,* or
perpetuity, for ever.　*All the day* (*long*), *i. e.* always.　See above, on Ps.
xxv. 5, xlii. 11 (10).　*Acknowledge, i. e.* gratefully give thanks.　See above,
on Ps. vi. 6 (5).

9 (8).　*For thou hast saved us from our adversaries, and our haters* (or
those hating us) *hast shamed.*　The preterites in this verse are explanatory
of the futures in the one before it.　" We will not rely upon ourselves
hereafter, because it is thou who hast helped us heretofore."　This logical
relation of the verses is destroyed by confounding the preterites and futures
with each other, or explaining both as presents.　*Shamed, i. e.* defeated,
disappointed.　See above, on Ps. vi. 11 (10), xiv. 6.

10 (9).　*Nay, thou hast rejected and disgraced us, and thou wilt not go*
forth with our hosts.　The particle at the beginning (אַף) implies something
more than a negation of the favours just described.　" But now thou dost
not so deal with us ; *nay more,* thou hast rejected us."　This Hebrew verb
implies disgust and abhorrence.　See above; on Ps. xliii. 2.　The other
verb means to put to shame, to cover with disgrace, as in Ps. xxxv. 4, xl.
15 (14).　The past tense of the first verbs implies that the rejection was
already manifest ; the future following implies an apprehension that it would
continue.　*Go out with our hosts,* as a guide, a commander, and an ally.
Compare 2 Sam. v. 24.

11 (10).　*Thou wilt make us turn back from the adversary, and* (already)
those hating us have plundered for them, i. e. for themselves.　Two of the
most unwelcome incidents of warfare are here specified, flight and spolia-

tion. *Spoiled for themselves,* not merely for their own advantage, but at their own will and discretion. Compare 1 Sam. xiv. 48, xxiii. 1.

12 (11). *Thou wilt give us as sheep (for) food, and among the nations hast scattered us,* The consecution of the tenses is the same as in the preceding verse. *Sheep for food,* or *flocks of food, i. e.* intended and accustomed to be eaten. *Give* may either mean place, render, constitute, or give up, abandon. The last clause has by some been understood to refer to the Babylonish exile, and regarded as a proof of later date. But in every war with the surrounding countries, there were partial deportations and dispersions. See Joel iv. 2, Amos i. 6, 9, and compare 1 Kings viii. 46.

13 (12). *Thou wilt sell thy people without gain, and hast not increased by their price.* They seemed to be gratuitously given up, *i. e.* without necessity or profit. *Without gain,* literally wealth or riches, as a product or equivalent. The same noun may be repeated in the next clause, *thou hast not increased (thy wealth),* just as the verb *gain* is absolutely used in English. *Their price,* literally *their prices,* perhaps with reference to the individual captives, or to repeated sales of the kind here mentioned. Another possible but far less natural construction, treats the preposition as a mere connective, and reads, *thou hast not enhanced their price, i. e.* set a high price upon them, implying that he had, on the contrary, sold them for too little, or rather given them away for nothing. Compare Jer. xv. 13.

14 (13). *Thou wilt make us a reproach to our neighbours, a scoff and a jest to those around us.* If this state of things continues, such will be the necessary issue. *Make us,* literally *place us,* set us up, expose us. See above, on Ps. xxxix. 9 (8), and with the whole verse compare Ps. lxxix. 4, lxxxix. 42 (41).

15 (14). *Thou wilt make us a byword among the nations, a shaking of the head among the peoples.* A byword, literally a likeness or comparison, a case that may be cited as a memorable instance or example. The expression is borrowed from Deut. xxviii. 37. *A shaking of the head, i. e.* an object at which men will shake their heads, as an expression of contemptuous pity. See above, on Ps. xxii. 8 (7).

16 (15). *All the day my disgrace is before me, and shame my face has covered.* It is before me so that I cannot fail to see it or lose sight of it. See above, Ps. xxxviii. 18 (17). Shame is here represented as a covering, as in Jer. iii. 25, but perhaps with special reference to the suffusion of the face with blushes, as in Ps. lxix. 8 (7).

17 (16). *From the voice of slanderer and reviler, from the face of enemy and avenger.* The preposition indicates the source or the occasion of the shame described in the preceding verse. *Face* may here mean either presence or the expression of the countenance. The last word is properly a participle, and means *taking vengeance* or *avenging one's self.* Here, as in Ps. viii. 3 (2), it denotes a spiteful and revengeful enemy.

18 (17). *All this has come upon us, and we have not forgotten thee, and have not been false to thy covenant.* With the first clause compare Judges vi. 13. *Come upon us :* the construction is the same as in Ps. xxxv. 8. *We have not been false,* or *acted falsely.* The same verb with the same preposition, in Lev. xix. 11, has the sense of lying, or acting fraudulentiy, towards another. See also Ps. lxxxix. 34 (33). What is here professed is not entire exemption from all acts of infidelity, but freedom from the deadly sin of total oblivion and apostasy. In spite of his unfaithfulness, Israel still claimed to be and was the chosen people of Jehovah.

19 (18). *Our heart has not turned back and our steps declined from thy*

path. The force of the negative extends to both clauses, as in Ps. ix. 19 (18). *Heart* and *steps* are put for inward affection and its fruit, external action. *Turned back* and *turned aside* are natural and common figures for moral delinquency. *Thy path*, the way of thy commandments.

20 (19). *That thou hast crushed us in a place of dragons, and hast covered over us with deathshade.* The construction is continued from the preceding sentence. The connection may be thus made plain in our idiom. " We have been guilty of no such infidelity or total apostasy, that thou shouldest deal with us in this way." *Crushed*, bruised, or broken in pieces. See above, on Ps. x. 10, and below, on Ps. li. 9 (8). *Dragons* may here be understood as meaning wild beasts or lonely animals in general. Whether the Hebrew word specifically signifies wild-cats, wolves, or jackals, is a question of little exegetical importance. The essential meaning of the whole phrase is a place inhabited by lonely creatures, *i. e.* a wilderness or desert. Compare Isa. xiii. 22, xxxiv. 13, xliii. 20, Jer. ix. 10 (11), x. 22, xlix. 33, Ps. lxiii. 11 (10). *Covered over, i.e.* covered up, completely covered, a stronger expression than the simple verb. *Deathshade*, or the shadow of death, a strong poetical expression for the profoundest darkness. See above, on Ps. xxiii. 4.

21 (20). *If we have forgotten the name of our God, and spread our hands to a strange God.* Some regard this as the common elliptical formula of swearing. "(God do so to us and more also) if we have forgotten," which is equivalent to saying, " we have not forgotten." Another method of supplying the ellipsis is exemplified in Josh. xxii. 22. But since the verse, conditionally understood, yields a good sense in connection with the next verse, this, as being the more obvious construction, is entitled to the preference. The act of holding up or stretching out the hands is often mentioned as a natural gesture of entreaty. See Exod. ix. 29, 33, 1 Kings viii. 38, Isa. i. 15. The word *God* in the version represents two different divine names in Hebrew, *Elohim* and *El.* See above, on Ps. xliii. 4. *A strange God*, or *a God (who is) a stranger, i.e.* to Jehovah and his people. The Hebrew word is applied by Moses both to men (Exod. xxx. 33) and idols (Deut. xxxii. 16),

22 (21). *Shall not God search this out? For he knoweth the secrets of the heart.* This is the apodosis of the sentence begun in the preceding verse. " If we have done thus, must not God know it ?" The primary meaning of the verb translated *search out* is to *dig*, to bring to light what is hidden under ground. Thence, by a natural transition, it denotes the investigation and disclosure of all secrets. The interrogation is an indirect but strong affirmation of the fact in question. The *for*, at the beginning of the last clause, does not indicate the reason of the question, but of the affirmative answer which is tacitly implied. *He (is) knowing*, a form of expression which denotes continued and habitual knowledge. See above, on Ps. i. 6, and with the sentiment compare that of Ps. vii. 10 (9).

23 (22). *Because for thee have we been killed all the day ; we have been reckoned as sheep for slaughter.* The causal particle at the beginning does not refer to what immediately precedes, but to the remoter context, and adduces a proof of the assertion, that the church had not forgotten or forsaken God. This proof is afforded by the fact that their very sufferings were on his account. *For thee*, for thy sake, literally *on thee, on (account of) thee*, on thy account. The preterite form, *we have been killed*, includes the present, *we are killed*, but with the additional idea that the sufferings in question were not new or altogether recent, but had long been experi-

enced. *Reckoned,* counted, estimated, *i. e.* by our enemies, who set no higher value on our lives than on those of *sheep for the slaughter,* literally *a flock of slaughter, i. e.* one destined or accustomed to be slaughtered. This expression corresponds exactly to *sheep for food,* or *flock of food,* in ver. 12 (11) above. The whole verse is a strong poetical description of severe persecution or distress arising from the spite of enemies, and as such is applied by Paul to the sufferings of the church of Christ, in which the ancient Israel continues to exist. See Rom. viii. 36.

24 (23). *Arouse thee! Why wilt thou sleep, O Lord? Awake, do not cast off for ever.* This bold apostrophe implies strong faith, as well as warm affection. Such an address would not be made to an inanimate object, or an imaginary being. The idea is the same as in Ps. iii. 8 (7), to wit, that the withholding of God's help, or of his sensible presence, may be figuratively described as a state of inaction or of sleep, from which he awakes and arises when he once more manifests his presence and affords his aid. Compare Ps. cxxi. 4, Mat. viii. 25. The verse is therefore really nothing more than an importunate petition for divine assistance. *Cast off,* reject with loathing and contempt, the same strong expression that occurs in ver. 10 (9), above. *For ever,* literally *to perpetuity.* The Hebrew phrase is not the same, however, that occurs in ver. 9 (8). above.

25 (24). *Why wilt thou hide thy face, wilt thou forget our suffering and our persecution* (or *oppression*)? The same thing which had just been represented by the figure of sleep is here described as a refusal to see and to remember. Both figures are employed in Ps. xiii. 2 (1), above, in reference to precisely the same subject. These anthropomorphisms, which would be unlawful in an uninspired writer, are perfectly intelligible, and exceedingly expressive. The word translated *suffering* (or *affliction*) is generic, and includes all forms of physical evil, one of which is then specified, to wit, the suffering caused by powerful and spiteful enemies. The same word denotes *oppression* or *persecution* at the hand of wicked men, in Ps. xlii. 10 (9), xliii. 2. *Why wilt thou forget* is evidently more than *why dost thou forget,* for it conveys the additional idea, " Why wilt thou persist in doing as thou hast done heretofore, and art doing now?"

26 (25). *For bowed* (or *sunk*) *to the dust is our soul, fixed to the earth is our belly.* Both Hebrew verbs are active, and literally mean, our soul has bowed down, our belly has adhered. *Belly* may either have the sense of *body,* as opposed to *soul,* as in Ps. xxxi. 10 (9), above, or be taken in its proper sense, in which case the whole clause is descriptive of the deepest degradation, a grovelling on the earth, without the capacity or wish to rise, a state like that of the lowest reptiles, or the one denounced upon the serpent in Gen. iii. 14. Whatever the image here presented may be, it is evidently meant to represent a state of deep depression and debasement.

27 (26). *Rise, a help for us, and redeem us for the sake of thy mercy!* This is the conclusion of his arguments, and the sum of his petitions. *Arise,* from this state of apparent inaction, and exert thy power. Not merely *for our help,* as in Ps. xxxviii. 23 (22), but *as our help,* thou who art thyself our help, its source, its author, a much stronger expression than *our helper,* though essentially synonymous. See above, Ps. xl. 18 (17), and below, Ps. lxiii. 8 (7). *Because of thy mercy,* as a ground or reason; *according to thy mercy,* as a rule or measure ; *for the sake of thy mercy, i. e.* for its honour, as a motive and an end to be accomplished.

Psalm 45

THE intimate relation of the Messiah to the chosen people, and eventually to the other nations, is described in this psalm as the union of a mighty king with foreign princesses, among whom one is represented as the queen. This kind of allegory is a common one in Scripture, but appears to have derived its peculiar form in this case from the court and household of Solomon. After a title, ver. 1, the Psalmist announces his design to sing the praises of the King, ver. 2 (1), whom he then describes as full of beauty, grace, and the divine blessing, ver. 3 (2), as a conquering hero in the cause of truth and righteousness, ver. 4-6 (3-5), as a divine, perpetual, and righteous sovereign, ver. 7 (6), and as such invested with peculiar honours and enjoyments, ver. 8 (7), clothed in royal, festal, and nuptial garments, ver. 9 (8), surrounded by kings' daughters, with a queen at his right hand, ver. 10 (9). The Psalmist then addresses her directly in the language of congratulation and admonition, ver. 11-13 (10-12), and describes her apparel and her marriage procession, ver. 14–16 (13-15). In conclusion, the king is again addressed, with the assurance of a numerous posterity, ver. 17 (16), and endless fame, ver. 18 (17). The attempt to explain this as a mere epithalamium in honour of Solomon, or Ahab, or some later king, Jewish or Persian, has always been defeated by the difficulty of determining the subject, and the impossibility of accounting for the reception of such a poem into a collection of devotional songs, intended for the permanent use of the ancient church. The absence of any analogous example is admitted upon all hands. The allegorical or Messianic sense is given by the oldest interpreters, both Jewish and Christian. The allegorical idea of this psalm is carried out in the Song of Solomon, to which it bears the same relation as Ps. xxxvii. to the Book of Proverbs, and Ps. xxxix. to the Book of Job.

1. *To the Chief Musician.   Upon lilies.   To the Sons of Korah.   Maschil   A song of loved (ones).*   The unusual accumulation of descriptive titles in this verse suggests at once that the psalm is one of deep and solemn import, and thus raises a presumption against its being a mere epithalamium, or a secular poem of any kind. This presumption is confirmed by the inscription *to the Chief Musician,* implying that the psalm was designed for permanent and public use. See above, on Ps. iv. 1. This description, it is true, might be applied to all the psalms without exception ; but it was particularly needed in the case of those which seem, at first sight, to be mere expressions of individual feeling, and still more in the case of those which, to a superficial reader, seem to be entirely secular in theme and spirit. The same thing is true, in substance, of the next term, *maschil, instruction.* The psalm before us is among the last which would have been selected by a modern critic as didactic in its character. But since it is so, this very fact affords a cogent reason for so designating it. This designation, at the same time, corroborates the previous presumption, that the psalm is allegorical, because an amatory nuptial song could not, in any sense, be called a *maschil.* The same thing is rendered still more certain by the ascription *to the Sons of Korah,* whether as authors or performers, since in either character their function was a sacred one ; they were not profane bards or minstrels, but Levitical precentors in the temple worship. See above, on Ps. xlii. 1. As this employment was continued in the family for many generations, there is no difficulty in assum-

ing that the Sons of Korah here meant were contemporaries of Solomon, to whose regal and domestic habits the psalm contains so many obvious allusions. The other two expressions in the title are more dubious. *Upon lilies* is supposed by some to mean on instruments of that shape. See above, on Ps. viii. 1. Others suppose it to denote a mode of execution, or an air, or another composition upon which this was modelled. Others more plausibly maintain that this and all analogous inscriptions have respect to the subject or contents, and that *lilies* are a natural emblem of female beauty, the plural form implying a plurality of persons, such as we meet with in the psalm itself. See below, ver. 10, 11, 16 (9, 10, 15). *A song of loves* would seem to mean either a *love-song* or a *lovely song*. But the usage of the Hebrew word requires it to be taken in the concrete sense of *loved* or *beloved*, the plural feminine form serving to identify the person thus described with the *lilies* of the other clause. These two phrases, taken together, represent the subject of the psalm to be lovely and beloved women, while the other terms of the description, which have been explained already, shew that the love and marriage here referred to are not natural, but spiritual, to wit, the union of Messiah with his people, or of Christ with his church, an idea running through both testaments. Compare Isa. liv. 5, lxii. 4, 5, Jer. iii. 1, Ezek. xvi. and xxiii., Mat. ix. 15, xxii. 2, xxv. 1, John iii. 29, Rom. vii. 4, 2 Cor. xi. 2, Eph. v. 25–32, Rev. xix. 7, xxi. 2, xxii. 17. The allegory is more fully carried out in the first three chapters of Hosea, but in these and all other passages referred to, the essential idea is borrowed from the Law, in which the national unfaithfulness to Jehovah is constantly described as a spiritual adultery, implying a conjugal relation between him and his people. See Exod. xxxiv. 15, 16, Lev. xvii. 7, xx. 5, 6, Num. xiv. 33. On the whole, then, this psalm appears to be a description of Messiah in his conjugal relation both to Israel and other nations, composed either by or for the sons of Korah in the reign of Solomon, from which the imagery seems to be borrowed, and designed for the permanent instruction of the church, by being used as a vehicle of pious feeling in her public worship.

2 (1). *My heart has overflowed—a good word (am) I saying—my works for the king—my tongue the pen of a rapid writer.* The whole verse is a strong metaphorical description of the way in which his thoughts were engrossed, and his words suggested, by one great theme. The first word properly denotes ebullition, the agitation and effervescence of a boiling liquid, or the similar phenomena presented by the bubbling up of water in a fountain. It is here used to express the spontaneous gush of feeling, thought, and word, in the inspired writer. This first clause may also be connected with the next, as indicated by the accents. *My heart is over-flowing (with) a good word* (or *goodly speech*), *i. e.* the subject upon which he is about to speak. The next words may then be rendered, *I am saying*, (or *I say*), *my works to the king*, *i. e.* they belong to him, or as an exclamation, "let them be his!" *My works*, all that I do, including the praise here offered. The king meant is the ideal and expected king of Israel, the Messiah. The last clause may also be an exclamation. (*Be*) *my tongue the pen of a rapid writer! i. e.* let it skilfully and promptly give expression to my thoughts and feelings. It is probably in allusion to this passage that Ezra is described as a *ready scribe* or *rapid writer* (Ezra vii. 6). Although particular expressions in this verse may be obscure, its general import is entirely unambiguous, as an animated declaration of the writer's purpose, and a preface to his praise of the Messiah.

3 (2). *Beautiful, beautiful, art thou above the sons of man ; grace is poured into thy lips ; therefore God hath blessed thee to eternity.* The first word in Hebrew is a reduplicated form, expressing the idea with intensity and emphasis. He is not praised as the fairest or most beautiful of men, but as fair or beautiful beyond all human standard or comparison. This general ascription of all loveliness is followed by the specification of a single charm, that of delightful captivating speech. *Grace*, in Hebrew as in English, denotes both a cause and an effect ; in this case, grace or beauty of expression, produced by the divine grace or favour, and reciprocally tending to increase it. On any hypothesis, except the Messianic one, this verse is unintelligible. If the first clause were intended to describe a mere corporeal beauty, how could this be followed up by commending the grace of the lips, or either be recognised as the ground of an eternal blessing ? It is only by supposing that the person here meant is the chief among ten thousand and altogether lovely, that the beauty predicated of him includes every moral and spiritual attraction, and that the grace of his lips has reference to his prophetic character and office, that the sentence can be made to seem coherent, and the promise at its close appropriate. The type, in this allegorical description, may have been furnished by him, of whom the queen of Sheba said (1 Kings x. 8), "Happy thy men, happy these thy servants who stand before thee always, who hear thy wisdom." But the glorious antitype was He, to whom " all bare witness, and wondered at the WORDS OF GRACE proceeding out of his mouth" (Luke iv. 22).

4 (3). *Gird thy sword on thy thigh, Mighty (One), thy honour and thy majesty.* Arm thyself for battle and for conquest. Compare 1 Sam. xxv. 13. As the act of girding is applied both to weapons and to clothing, the mention of the one here suggests the other. " Arm thyself with strength and clothe thyself with majesty." The two words at the end of the sentence are constantly employed to denote the divine majesty (Ps. xcvi. 6, civ. 1, cxi. 3), as distinguished from that of mortals (Job xl. 10), or as bestowed upon them by a special divine favour (Ps. xxi. 6). The first of the two is separately used to signify specifically royal dignity (1 Chron. xxix. 25, Dan. xi. 21). The use of these expressions, together with the epithet of Mighty or Hero, which is one of the characteristic titles of Messiah in prophecy (Isa. ix. 6), confirms the previous conclusion that he is here the object of address. As to the sword, see Rev. i. 16, ii. 12, xx. 15, 21 ; and with the whole verse compare Ps. cx. 5–7.

5 (4). *And (in) thy majesty, pass on, ride forth, for the sake of truth and humble right ; and thy right hand shall guide thee (to) terrible deeds.* The first words may also be explained, without supplying *in*, as an emphatic repetition of what goes before. *And thy majesty (I say).* The first verb may be rendered *prosper*, as in Isa. liii. 10 ; but it seems best to retain its primary sense, which is to pass by or over, to advance, or as we say familiarly, to go ahead. By *riding* we may understand the act of riding in a chariot of war, which was customary with the ancient kings. See the same verb so used in 2 Kings ix. 16, and compare 1 Kings xxii. 34, 35. *For the sake*, literally *on the word*, which may possibly denote that on which the conqueror rides, to wit, the *word of truth*. But this figure would not be very intelligible, and in almost every other case where the Hebrew phrase occurs, it is evident that *word* is used precisely as the English words *account* and *sake* are in the familiar combinations, *on account of, for the sake of*. See above on Ps. xviii. 1. Thus understood, it here points out the object of Messiah's conquests, to wit, the vindication of *truth, i. e.*

veracity, as opposed to fraud, and *humble right,* as opposed to proud iniquity. In this last phrase both the Hebrew words are nouns, but rather in apposition than regimen, so that the literal translation would be *humility-righteousness,* right asserted in humility against a wrong maintained by pride and selfishness. *Thy right hand,* as the seat of martial strength, and the organ of aggressive action. *Shall guide,* or point the way, the proper meaning of the Hebrew verb, which, like other verbs expressing or implying motion, may be followed directly by a noun, where our idiom would require an intervening preposition. *Terrible (things), fearful (deeds),* literally *dreaded;* but the Hebrew passive participle frequently includes the idea of a future passive participle in Latin. The insensible transition from the imperative to the future shews that the former was really prophetic, and that the prayer of this and the preceding verse is only a disguised prediction of Messiah's triumphs, as one going forth conquering and to conquer.

6 (5). *Thine arrows are sharp—nations under thee shall fall—in the heart of the king's enemies.* The word translated *sharp* is properly a participle meaning *sharpened,* like *acutus* from *acuo,* and may here have the same sense as in Isa. v. 28, *whose arrows are sharpened and all his bows bent, i. e.* all his weapons of war ready for immediate use. *Nations,* not merely individuals, nor even armies, but whole nations, a description peculiarly, though not exclusively, appropriate to a superhuman conqueror. In order to remove the apparent incoherence of the second and third members of the sentence, some give *heart* the local sense of *midst.* " Nations shall fall under thee in the midst of the king's enemies." But this explanation of *heart* is not justified by usage, and the *king's enemies* are evidently the *nations* themselves. Others make the second clause a vocative—*thou under whom the nations fall*—or a mere parenthesis, with a verb supplied after it—*thy sharp arrows (nations fall under thee) shall penetrate into the heart of the king's enemies.* But these are forced if not ungrammatical constructions, and by far the simplest solution is to repeat the first clause before the third—*thine arrows are sharp—nations fall under thee—(thine arrows are sharp) in the heart of the king's enemies.* This is the more natural, as the falling of the nations is supposed to be produced by the arrows. " Thine arrows are sharpened, and ready for the conquest of the nations ; yes, thine arrows are already sharp in the heart of the king's enemies." This last expression does not refer to a different person from the one addressed, but is merely a more emphatic way of saying, " thine enemies, O king !"

7 (6). *Thy throne, (O) God, (is) for ever and ever ; a sceptre of rectitude (is) the sceptre of thy kingdom.* To avoid the obvious ascription of divinity contained in the first clause, two very forced constructions have been proposed. 1. Thy throne (is the throne of) God for ever and ever. 2. Thy God-throne (or divine throne) is for ever. But even admitting, what is very doubtful, that a few examples of this syntax occur elsewhere, the sense thus obtained is unsatisfactory and obscure, and this is still more true of that afforded by the only obvious or natural construction besides the one first given, namely, *thy throne is God for ever and ever.* The explanation of *God* as a vocative is not only the most obvious, and sustained by the analogy of Ps. xliii. 1, xliv. 5 (4), xlviii. 10, 11 (9, 10), &c., but is found in all the ancient versions and adopted in the New Testament (Heb. i. 8), and was admitted even by the anti-Messianic interpreters, until they were obliged to abandon the position that *Elohim* might be taken in a lower

sense. *For ever and ever*, literally *eternity and perpetuity*. See above, on Ps. v. 12 (11), ix. 6 (5). The same perpetuity is asserted of Jehovah's reign in Ps. x. 16. It is also promised to the royal line of David, ending and eternised in Messiah. See the original promise in 2 Sam. vii. 13, 16, and its varied repetition in Ps. xxi. 5 (4), xviii. 51 (50), lxxii. 5, lxxxix. 5, 37, 38 (4, 36, 37), cx. 4, cxxxii. 12 (11), Isa. ix. 6 (7). *A sceptre*, properly a staff or rod, particularly as a badge of office and especially of royal dignity. See above, on Ps. xxiii. 4. *Rectitude*, in a moral or figurative sense, derived from the physical and proper one of straightness, whether linear or superficial. See below, Ps. lxvii. 5 (4), and compare Isa. xi. 4. *Kingdom*, or as an abstract, *royalty*, in which sense it may qualify the noun before it, so that the whole phrase will express the idea *royal sceptre*.

8 (7). *Thou hast loved righteousness and hated wickedness ; therefore God, thy God, hath anointed thee (with) oil of joy above thy fellows.* The moral excellency of the person here addressed is represented as the meritorious ground of the divine favours by which he was distinguished. In an epithalamium, or an amatory poem, this would be ridiculous. The past tenses represent the moral qualities ascribed to him as already manifested and familiar. The substitution of the present greatly weakens the expression. Here, as in the verse preceding, *God* may be a vocative. *Thy God, O God, hath anointed thee, &c.* Compare Ps. xliii. 4, li. 15 (14). But the more obvious construction above given is favoured by the collocation of the words and the analogy of Ps. l. 7. *Oil of joy* (or *gladness*) is a figure borrowed from the ancient oriental usage of anointing the head on festive occasions. See above, on Ps. xxiii. 5. The expression is copied in Isa. lxi. 3. *Above thy fellows*, more than thy companions, *i. e.* other men, or more specifically, other kings. Compare what is said of Solomon, 1 Kings iii. 12, 13, 2 Chron. i. 12.

9 (8). *Myrrh and aloes (and) cassia (are) all thy garments, from palaces of ivory, from (thence) have they gladdened thee.* The figure of unction in the close of the preceding verse suggests the idea of perfumes and aromatic substances, several of which are specified, as samples of the whole class, which makes it comparatively unimportant, though by no means difficult, to identify the species. His dress is described as so impregnated with these odours, that it may be poetically said to be composed of them. By another natural association, these perfumed garments, which were not usually worn, suggest the idea of some rare festivity, and especially of that which is most joyous in all countries. It is from marriage feasts in splendid palaces that these sweet odours and these joyful feelings have been brought away. Why more than one such celebration is referred to, will appear below. *Palaces of ivory, i. e.* adorned with it, like that of Ahab in 1 Kings xxii. 39, and that of Menelaus in the Odyssey. That this kind of luxury was not unknown in real life, may also be inferred from Amos iii. 15, vi. 4, Song of Sol. vii. 5 (4). The next word (מִנִּי) is by some explained as a contraction of (מִנִּים), a word meaning strings, and then stringed instruments (Ps. cl. 4). *From palaces of ivory stringed instruments have gladdened thee.* But as this breaks the connection between verses 8 and 10 (7 and 9), others make מִנִּי the poetical form of the preposition מִן, as it is in Ps. xliv. 11, 19 (10, 18), lxviii. 32 (31). See also Judges v. 14, and Isa. xlvi. 3. The repetition of the particle without the noun is similar to that in Isa. lix. 18, *according to their deeds, according to (them) will he repay.* So here, *from palaces of ivory, from them* (or *thence*)

have they gladdened thee. The plural verb may be construed indefinitely, as tantamount to saying, *thou hast been gladdened,* or referred to a more definite subject, namely, that presented in the next verse.

10 (9). *Daughters of kings (are) among thy precious (ones); stationed is the queen at thy right hand, in gold of Ophir.* The idea of a marriage-feast, suggested in the foregoing verse, is here carried out by a description of the bride or brides. These are represented as being of the highest rank and splendid in appearance. *Precious,* dear, not in the sense of *beloved,* which the Hebrew word never has, but in that of *costly,* valuable, which it always has. *Stationed,* not simply *stands,* but *placed* there, as the post of honour. Compare 1 Kings ii. 19. The word translated *queen* means properly a *spouse* or *consort,* but is specially applied to the wives of kings, particularly those of Babylonia (Dan. v. 2) and Persia (Neh. ii. 6). It is here used as a poetical expression, which is also the case with the word translated *gold,* and derived from a verb meaning to *conceal;* it may therefore denote *ore,* as hidden in the mine, or hoarded treasure. Here, and in Isa. xiii. 12, it is combined with Ophir, one of the places to which Solomon's ships traded with the Phenicians (1 Kings ix. 28, x. 11, 2 Chron. viii. 18, ix. 10). Its situation is disputed, and of no exegetical importance in the case before us. Whether it was in India, Arabia, or Africa, it is here mentioned only as an El Dorado, with the very name of which the idea of gold was associated in the mind of every Israelite, as it is in ours with the name of California. *In gold* means, of course, in garments decked with gold, or golden jewels. The image here presented of a queen surrounded by inferior princesses was probably borrowed from the court of Solomon (1 Kings xi. 1), but employed to represent the chosen people as the bride of the Messiah, and as such pre-eminent among the nations. This kind of personification is not uncommon. See, for example, Isa. xlvii. 1, liv. 1, Jer. xlvi. 11.

11 (10). *Hear, daughter, and see, and bend thine ear, and forget thy people and the house of thy father.* The Psalmist, in view of the ideal scene which he has brought before us, utters a kind of nuptial exhortation to the queen or chief bride of Messiah. *Hear* what I have to say; *see,* with the mind's eye, what I set before thee, look at it, consider it. *Incline thine ear,* lean forward as a sign of attention, so that nothing shall escape thee. See above, on Ps. xvii. 6, xxxi. 3 (2). This preliminary summons to attend implies that something of serious moment is to follow. The word *daughter* may be simply used, as *son* is elsewhere, to suggest the relation of a junior to a senior, or of a pupil to a teacher. See above, on Ps. xxxiv. 12 (11), and compare Prov. i. 8, ii. 1, iii.1, iv. 1, &c. Or the Psalmist may be understood as speaking in the person of the bride's father, when about to part with her ; but this is less natural, since the father is referred to, in the last clause, as a third person. Some suppose a specific reference to the *daughter of Zion* as the real object of address, while others understand by *daughter* a king's daughter, a royal princess, or suppose her to be here addressed as one who was no longer to be treated as a daughter, but as a wife and mother. As if he had said, " Hitherto thou hast been a daughter, but now thou must forget thy father's house." All these ideas may have been present to the writer's mind, as they are all spontaneously suggested to the reader's. *Forget thy people, &c.,* is a strong but natural and perfectly intelligible mode of saying, form new relations, or accommodate thyself to them when formed. There is obvious allusion to the law of marriage in Gen. ii. 24, and to the calling of Abraham in Gen. xii. 1. What the

patriarch was there required to do is here enjoined upon his children in the person of their ideal representative. The ancient church or chosen people is required to come out from the world and be exclusively devoted to Jehovah. The exhortation becomes still more pointed and significant when taken in connection with the fact, that Solomon's wives, who seem to have supplied the figures for this striking allegorical tableau, instead of acting on the principle here laid down, by adopting the religion of their husband, " turned away his heart after other gods" (1 Kings xi. 4).

12 (11). *And let the king desire thy beauty ; for he is thy Lord, and* (therefore) *bow thyself to him.* The common version (*so shall the king desire, &c.*) is inconsistent with the form of the Hebrew verb, which is one used to express a command or wish. The verse must be read in close connection with the one before it. " Forget thy father's house and be entirely devoted to thy husband, so that his affection may be fixed upon thee, without anything to hinder or impair it, such as a lingering desire for thy previous condition." This is enjoined as a duty springing from the very nature of the conjugal relation, in which the husband is the head by divine right. Compare Gen. iii. 16, xviii. 12, 1 Pet. iii. 5, 6. In recognition of this obligation, she is called upon to bow down or prostrate herself (1 Sam. xxv. 41, 1 Kings i. 16, 31), a gesture both of civil and religious homage, and therefore peculiarly appropriate here, where the ideal king and husband represents the real object of religious worship.

13 (12). *And the daughter of Tyre with a gift thy face shall soften—the rich of the people.* In the Hebrew idiom *the daughter of Tyre*, or *the daughter (i. e. the virgin) Tyre* denotes the city, or the population of the city, personified as a woman. See above, on Ps. ix. 15 (14). It has been proposed, indeed, to take this as a vocative (*and O daughter of Tyre, the rich of the people shall, &c.*) addressed to Jezebel, in honour of whose marriage with Ahab (1 Kings xvi. 31) the psalm is then supposed to have been written. But besides the harsh construction of the first words, and the constant usage of the phrase and others like it in the sense explained above, it is inconceivable that a poem in celebration of the marriage between a wicked king of Israel and a heathen princess could have been composed by the sons of Korah for permanent religious use in the kingdom of Judah. And yet this is the only hypothesis, except the Messianic one, on which the reference to Tyre can be explained. In the time of Solomon, the Tyrians were the most commercial nation in the world, and the one with which the Israelites had most commercial intercourse. It was natural, therefore, to use Tyre as a type for the wealth and commerce of the world, and the same mode of representation is employed by later writers. (See especially Isa. xxiii. 18.) Thus understood, the promise that the daughter of Tyre should seek, by means of gifts, to conciliate the favour of the queen, is a prediction that the richest of the nations should seek union and communion with the chosen people. See below, Ps. xlvii. 10 (9), lxxii. 10, lxxxvii. 4, in the last of which places Tyre is particularly mentioned. See also Isa. lx. 6, Hag. ii. 7, 8, Zech. ix. 10. That the daughter of Tyre is here an ideal person, comprehending many individuals, is clear from the plural verb with which it is construed, and from the epexegetical clause, *the rich (i. e. the richest) of the people*, whether this be understood to mean the richest of that people, or the richest of the nations. In either case it is an apposition with *daughter of Tyre*, and in some way explanatory of it. " The daughter of Tyre, that richest of the nations (or the daughter of Tyre, even the richest of that nation), shall entreat thy favour." This last

idea is conveyed by a highly idiomatic phrase, meaning, as some suppose, to stroke or soothe the face, and then, by a natural transition, to conciliate, to flatter. Others obtain nearly the same sense by making it mean to weaken, soften, or subdue the face, *i. e.* the opposition which the face expresses.

14 (13). *All glorious (is) the king's daughter within ; of gold embroidery (is) her vesture.* The second word in Hebrew may be either an adjective, as in Ezek. xxiii. 41, or a substantive, as in Judges xviii. 21. *All (i. e. altogether) splendid,* or *all splendour, i. e.* containing nothing else, as the king's garments are said, in ver. 9 (8) above, to be *all perfume,* and mankind in Ps. xxxix. 6 (5), to be *only all vanity.* The local adverb in the first clause means *within doors,* in the house (Lev. x. 18, 1 Kings vi. 18, 2 Kings vii. 11), and describes the bride as still awaiting her removal from her father's to her husband's house. *Gold embroidery,* or *network of gold.* The common version (*wrought gold*) conveys the false idea of a dress entirely metallic, whereas the Hebrew phrase denotes some kind of artificial texture or tissue, in which gold is interwoven.

15 (14). *With* (or *on*) *variegated cloths shall she be conducted to the king; virgins behind her, her companions, brought unto thee.* The lively picture of an oriental wedding is now completed by a view of the procession to the bridegroom's house. The customary train of female friends is not forgotten, but with this peculiar feature added, that the bridesmaids are themselves described as brides, *being brought* (or *made to come*) *to the king,* precisely as the queen was. This departure from the usages of real life, which would have been revolting in a mere epithalamium, is peculiarly appropriate to the design of the allegory, as it enables the writer to include in his description a striking figurative representation of the eventful accession of the Gentiles to the spiritual privileges and prerogatives which for ages were confined to Israel. The ancient church or peculiar people is the chief bride or queen of the Messiah, chosen from among the nations ; but these very nations are *the virgins, her companions,* not her servants or attendants merely, who are brought to the king afterwards as she was brought before, to be united with him in an honourable marriage, not as the inferiors but the equals of his first and chosen consort. The noun at the beginning of the verse has been variously explained as meaning *needle-work, embroidery,* and *variegated stuffs;* but the essential idea is sufficiently clear, to wit, that of rich and highly ornamented fabrics. As the dress of the bride has been twice described already, in ver. 10, 14 (9, 13), some suppose that these words have allusion to the practice of spreading rich and costly cloths or carpets on the ground where royal personages walk. (Compare Mat. xxi. 8.) Others refer the clause to the embroidered coverings of the nuptial couch. The preposition here used is the one denoting relation in the most indefinite manner, and may be translated *in, upon,* or *to,* according to these different hypotheses respectively. See above, on Ps. xxx. 2 (1), xxxv. 19, 24, xxxviii. 17 (16). *Conducted,* or escorted in procession, as the Hebrew word denotes, being applied both to nuptial and funeral pomps. Compare Job x. 19, xxi. 32. The king is first mentioned in the third person, and then in the second, by which insensible transition the way is prepared for the direct address with which the psalm concludes, although the third person is resumed for a moment in the next verse.

16 (15). *They shall be conducted with rejoicings and mirth ; they shall come into the palace of the king.* The first clause exhibits the procession,

as it were, in motion, while the second brings it to its destination. As if he had said, "I see the joyous train advancing, to the sound of merry music, towards the palace; and now they reach it and are entered in." This brings the description of the marriage to a close, and leaves nothing to be added but the joyful anticipations expressed in the concluding verses.

17 (16). *Instead of thy fathers shall be thy sons; thou shalt set them for princes in all the earth.* In the translation, this might seem to be a renewed address to the bride, consoling her, in her separation from her father's family, by the hope of having one herself. The antithesis, however, is not between *parents* and *children* in general, but between *fathers* and *sons* in particular. Nor does the ambiguity of the translation exist in the original, at least in the masoretic text, where the pointing of the suffixed pronouns shews them to be masculine, so that the object of address must be the king himself, as it is in ver. 3–11 (2–10). We have here another allusion to the marriage customs of the ancient orientals, among whom it was usual to wish the newly married pair a numerous and distinguished offspring. See Gen. xxiv. 60, Ruth iv. 11, 12. This wish is here replaced by a positive prediction, that the king's descendants shall be more illustrious than his progenitors. Such a comparison would have but little force, however, unless he were himself descended from a long line of royal ancestors, a sufficient proof that the king here glorified was neither Solomon nor Ahab. At the same time there is obvious allusion to the state of things under the reign of Solomon, who divided his kingdom into twelve viceroyalties (1 Kings iv. 7), and that of David, who made his own sons viceroys (2 Sam. viii. 18), a policy which seems to have been still pursued by Rehoboam (2 Chron. xi. 23). What they did on a small scale, the Messiah is to do upon a large one. As they made their sons princes in Israel, so he shall make his to be rulers over the whole earth. Some, indeed, translate the last words *all the land;* but this is inconsistent with the conquests promised in ver. 5–7 (4–6), with the mention of Tyre in ver. 14 (13), and with that of *nations* in ver. 18 (17). The *sons* of Messiah are his spiritual seed (Isa. liii. 10), to *set* whom *for princes* is to constitute or make them such, to give them places suited to their royal rank. The universal reign here predicted is also promised in Ps. ii. 8 above and Ps. lxxii. 11, below. Compare Zech. ix. 10.

18 (17). *I will make thy name to be remembered in all generations; therefore shall nations acknowledge thee for ever and ever.* The Psalmist speaks as one in the long series of inspired heralds, and in behalf of all. The form of the first verb implies fixed determination, and involves a pledge. *Thy name,* as the expression of thy nature. See above, on Ps. v. 12 (11), xliv. 21 (20). *In all generations,* literally in every generation and generation. *For ever and ever,* literally to eternity and perpetuity. See above, on Ps. xliv. 9, 24 (8, 23). *Therefore,* not merely because I celebrate his name, but because his name itself is glorious. *Acknowledge thee* to be what thou art, involving therefore the ideas of praise in general and thanksgiving in particular. See above, on Ps. vi. 6 (5), xliv. 9 (8).

Psalm 46

THE Church is safe under divine protection. This theme is amplified in three strophes, the close of which is indicated by the *selahs* in ver. 4 (3), 8 (7), 12 (11). If the psalm owed its origin to any particular historical occasion, of which there seem to be some traces in the last part, there is none to which it would be more appropriate than the miraculous destruction of the Assyrian host in the reign of Hezekiah (2 Kings xix. 35, Isa. xxxvii. 36), as this was a signal instance of divine interposition for the deliverance of the chosen people, and peculiarly adapted to exalt the God of Israel among the nations.

1. *To the Chief Musician. To the Sons of Korah. Upon Alamoth. A song.* The Sons of Korah may here be mentioned either as the authors or performers of the psalm. (See above, on Ps. xlii. 1, xlv. 1). In either case, we are perhaps to understand the Sons of Korah in the reign of Hezekiah. Some have ascribed the psalm to Isaiah; but of this there is no evidence. *Alamoth* means *virgins* or young women, and is here used as a technical expression of the Hebrew music, to denote soprano or treble voices. See above, on Ps. iv. 1, vi. 1.

2 (1). *God (is) for us a refuge and strength; a help in distresses he has proved—exceedingly.* The first clause states the general theme or proposition of the psalm; the last asserts it to have been established by experience. *A refuge,* a hiding-place, a place where men seek shelter and security from impending danger. The original expression is a local noun derived from a verb, the primary sense of which is to take refuge. (See above, on Ps. ii. 12, xvi. 1). A different word is so translated in ver. 8, 12 (7, 11), below. In this connection, *strength* may mean a stronghold or fortified place, which figure is expressly used in Ps. xviii. 3 (2), xxvii. 1, and elsewhere. Or it may simply mean the source or author of strength, as in Ps. xxviii. 8, and elsewhere. *In distresses :* the plural form may involve a reference to various occasions, or to complex and aggravated troubles in some one case. *He has proved,* literally *been found, i. e.* by us, in our experience. The common version (*a present help*) is scarcely justified by the occasional use of the original expression in the sense of being present or forthcoming. The last word, *very* or *exceedingly,* appears to have been added to qualify the whole clause or proposition, as one eminently and emphatically true.

3 (2). *Therefore we will not fear in the changing of the earth, and in the moving of mountains in the heart of seas.* The simple idea expressed by these strong figures is, in the midst of the most violent changes and commotions. By the *changing* or *exchanging of the earth* (see above, on Ps. xv. 4), we may understand either its change of place, violent removal, or more probably a change of face and aspect or condition, as the effect of mighty revolutions. *In its changing, i. e.* when it changes and because it changes. See above, on Ps. xlii. 4 (3). The mountains, as appears from ver. 7 (6) below, are emblems of great kingdoms and powerful states. See above, on Ps. xxx. 8 (7), and compare Isa. xxxvii. 24, Rev. viii. 8. The sea may be mentioned only as the place to which the mountains are transplanted (Luke xvii. 6), or in which they are shaken ; but it may also be a specific emblem of the world, continually moved and agitated by the strife of human passions. See Isa. lvii. 20, and compare Isa. xxvii. 1, Dan. vii. 2, 3. This description is peculiarly appropriate to the commotions necessarily produced by the extensive conquests of the great empires of the ancient world, perhaps with special reference in this case to Assyria.

4 (3). *Let its waters roar and foam, let mountains tremble in its swelling. Selah.* The singular pronoun refers to the sea, which is only poetically plural in the preceding verse. The verb translated *roar* occurs above in Ps. xxxix. 7 (6). The one translated *foam* means strictly to ferment or effervesce. As the word rendered *swelling* is also used elsewhere in the figura-

tive sense of *pride*, it is peculiarly appropriate to the commotions of the
world, occasioned by the pride of man.   The verbs in this verse may also
be explained as proper futures.   *Its waters shall* (indeed) *roar and foam,
the hills shall tremble at its swelling;* but the people of God shall still be
safe, as promised in the next verse.   The *selah*, as usual, indicates a pause
in the performance, and at the same time marks the close of the first stanza
or strophe.

5 (4). (*There is*) *a river—its streams shall gladden the city of God, the
holy* (*place*) *of the dwellings of the Highest.*   In contrast with the turbulent
and threatening sea, he now presents a peaceful and abundant river.   This
emblem of God's favour, which is frequent in the Scriptures, seems to have
been borrowed by the later writers from the river of Eden, Gen. ii. 10.   See
above, on Ps. xxxvi. 9 (8), and compare Ezek. xlvii. 1, Joel iv. (iii.) 18,
Zech. xiv. 8, Rev. xxii. 1.   *The city of God, i. e.* Jerusalem, his earthly
residence, and ꞌthe centre of the theocracy.   See below, Ps. xlviii. 2, 3
(1, 2).   *The holy* (*place*) may either mean the same thing, or be a more specific
designation of the temple.   See below, Ps. lxv. 5 (4), and compare Exod.
xxix. 31, Lev. vi. 9, 19 (16, 26).   The place rendered holy by the presence
of God's earthly residence.   *The Highest* or *Most High*, the divine name
which denotes God's infinite superiority to other beings.   See above, Ps.
vii. 18 (17), ix. 3 (2), xxi. 8 (7).   The mention of *streams* in the plural
indicates variety and fulness of divine favour.

6 (5). *God* (*is*) *in the midst of her, she shall not be moved ; God will help
her at the turning of the morning.*   This last idiomatic phrase seems to mean,
at the point when the day turns to come back, after reaching its greatest
distance.   See Exod. xiv. 27, Judges xix. 26, and compare Deut. xxiii.
12 (11).   The idea is that of a critical transition from grief to joy.   See
Ps. xxx. 6 (5), xlix. 15 (14), xc. 14, cx. 8.   The terms of this verse become still more significant and striking, if we suppose a specific reference to
the night in which Sennacherib's host was smitten, and the sight which was
disclosed at break of day.   See Isa. xxxvii. 36, and compare Isa. xvii. 14.

7 (6). *Nations roared, kingdoms quaked ; he has uttered his voice, the
earth will melt.*   There is here an allusion to the roaring, foaming sea of
ver. 4 (3).   *Uttered*, literally *gave* (a sound) *with his voice*, just as we may
speak of giving a groan or a shriek.   Compare Ps. lxviii. 34 (33), Jer.
xii. 8.   This voice is not represented as assuaging the commotion, but increasing it, by making the very earth dissolve.   As in many other instances,
the psalmist takes his stand between the inception and the consummation
of the. event which he describes.   Hence the transition from the past tense
to the future.   See above, on Ps. xviii. 7 (6).   With the last clause compare Ps. lxxv. 4 (3), Amos ix. 6.   God is represented as the ultimate author
of these mighty changes.   See Haggai ii. 21, 22.

8 (7). *Jehovah of Hosts* (*is*) *with us ; a refuge for us* (*is*) *the God of
Jacob.   Selah.*   Notwithstanding these commotions and dangers, the
divine protection makes us perfectly secure.   *Jehovah of Hosts*, the God of
the Universe, and especially of heaven.   See above, on Ps. xxiv. 10, and
below, on Ps. xlviii. 9 (8).   *With us.*   Compare the name *Immanuel*, Isa.
viii. 8.   *A refuge*, literally a high place, a place beyond the reach of enemies and dangers.   See above, on Ps. ix. 10 (9), xviii. 3 (2).   *God of
Jacob.*   See above, oh Ps. xxiv. 6.

9 (8). *Come, see the doings of Jehovah, who hath put desolations in the
earth.*   The first word properly means *go*, but is constantly used in summoning and inviting others.   See above, Ps. xxxiv. 12 (11).   *The doings,*

what he has been doing. The common version, *what desolations he hath made*, is not so natural as that above given, which takes the relative in its proper sense, and refers it to the nearest antecedent. *Put* (or *placed*) *desolations, i. e.* produced, occasioned, caused them to exist. *In the earth*, because the ruling power of the world was smitten ; or *in the land, i. e.* the Holy Land, as the immediate scene of God's retributive judgments, which all men are invited now to witness. The use of the name *Jehovah* intimates that the God who thus controls the world is identical with the God of Israel.

10 (9). *Silencing wars to the end of the earth ; the bow he will break, and cut the spear, and the chariots will burn in the fire.* The participle, followed by the future, shews that the process is not finished, but still going on. *Silencing*, making to cease. *To the end.* The original expression is a stronger one, and means *up to the end*, or *to the very end*. The bow, spear, and chariots, are named as necessary instruments of warfare. See above, on Ps. vii. 13 (12), and with the whole verse compare Isa. ii. 4, Mic. iv. 3, Josh. xi. 9, Ezek. xxxix. 9.

11 (10). *Leave off, and know that I (am) God ; I will be exalted in the nations, I will be exalted in the earth.* These words are addressed to the discomfited foes of Jehovah and his people. " Cease from your vain attacks upon my people ; learn from what you have already seen and felt that their protector is divine, and that he is resolved to be acknowledged as supreme, not only by his chosen people, but by all the nations and throughout the earth." This general recognition of Jehovah as the true and the supreme God, would of course be promoted by such a signal overthrow as that experienced by Sennacherib. Compare Isa. xxxvii. 20.

12 (11). *Jehovah of Hosts (is) with us ; a refuge for us (is) the God of Jacob. Selah.* This repetition of the burden or refrain in ver. 8 (7), brings us back not only to the close of the second stanza, but to the beginning of the first, where the same idea is expressed in other words.

Psalm 47

1. *To the Chief Musician. To the Sons of Korah. A Psalm.* A song of triumph, in celebration of a signal victory gained by the chosen people over certain confederated nations. In the first stanza, ver. 2–5 (1–4), Jehovah is celebrated as the conqueror of the nations ; in the second, ver. 6–10 (5–9), as their rightful sovereign ; in both, as the tutelary God of Israel. Another difference of form between the two parts seems to be, that in the first, the exhortation to praise God is addressed directly to the Gentiles ; in the second, to Israel or the ancient church. The psalm has every appearance of having been composed in reference to some particular event ; but as this is not indicated in the psalm itself, it can only be conjectured. Of the various suppositions which have been suggested, the most probable is, that it was written to commemorate the victory of Jehoshaphat over the Ammonites and Edomites, recorded in the twentieth chapter of Second Chronicles. Besides the general appropriateness of the composition to the juncture there described, it is, to say the least, a very singular coincidence, that the history records the presence, upon that occasion, not only of Levites in general, but of the Korhites (sons of Korah) in particular (2 Chron. xx. 19). We read too that singers went before the army (ver. 21), and that on the fourth day they assembled in a valley which they

called *Berachah* (blessing), because there there they blessed the Lord (ver. 26).
There is also something in the simple, animated, flowing style of the psalm
before us which agrees very well with the supposition of its being an inspired impromptu, a psalm composed upon the spur of the occasion, either
by some anonymous prophet who accompanied the army, or by the Sons of
Korah themselves. See above, on Ps. xlii. 1. This conjecture, as to the
historical occasion of the psalm before us, is corroborated by the apparent
relation of the next psalm to the same event. See below, on Ps. xlviii. 1.

2 (1). *All nations, clap the hand ! shout unto God with a voice of
triumph !* The clapping of the hands is a natural gesture both of triumph
and applause. See Nah. iii. 19, and compare Ps. xcviii. 8, Isa. lv. 12. The
last word in the verse does not denote a feeling, but the audible expression
of joy and exultation, by song or shout. See above, on Ps. v. 12 (11).
The nations addressed are not the particular nations which had just been
conquered, but the whole gentile world, the nations collectively, who are
summoned to rejoice in the proof just afforded, that Jehovah is their
rightful sovereign. See above, on Ps. xviii. 50 (49), and below, on Ps.
lxvi. 4 (3), cxvii. 1, and compare the original expression upon which this
is modelled, Deut. xxxii. 43.

3 (2). *For Jehovah, Most High, is terrible, a great king over all the
earth.* He is not, as the heathen were disposed to imagine, a mere local
deity, the God of the Hebrews only, but the God of the whole earth, the
Universal Sovereign, and an object of fear to its inhabitants. See the
same epithet applied to him in Ps. lxviii. 36 (35).

4 (3). *He will subdue nations under us, and peoples under our feet.* This
is a proof both of his covenant relation to his people, and of his sovereign
power over other nations. What he has done is but an earnest of what he
will do. Compare Ps. xviii. 39 (38), 48 (47). This, though not a matter
of rejoicing to the nations immediately concerned, may well be represented
as a matter of rejoicing to the world at large, because it involves a promise that the Gentiles shall one day be included among the subjects of this
divine protector, and partakers of his favour.

5 (4). *He will choose for us our heritage, the pride of Jacob whom he loved.
Selah.* By defeating the enemies who sought to expel Israel from the land
of promise (2 Chron. xx. 11), God might be poetically said to settle them
again therein, and, as at first, to choose their inheritance for them. *The
pride of Jacob,* that of which he is proud, in which he glories, whether this
be understood specifically of the Holy Land, or generically of all the privileges and distinctions which belonged to them as the peculiar people of
Jehovah. *Pride,* exaltation, or distinction, as in Nah. ii. 3 (2), Amos
vi. 8. In Amos viii. 7, God himself is so described. *Jacob,* as in Ps.
xxiv. 6, xlvi. 8 (7), 12 (11). *Whom he loved.* See Mal. i. 2, and compare
Ps. lxxviii. 68.

6 (5). *God has gone up with shouting, Jehovah with sound of trumpet.*
He is here described as returning to heaven after the conquest of his enemies
and the rescue of his people, as in Ps. vii. 8 (7), he does the same, after
sitting in judgment on the nations, and asserting the right of his own
people. See Ps. lxviii. 19 (18), and compare Gen. xvii. 22, Judges xiii. 20.
The shouting and sound of the trumpet represents the ascension as a public
and triumphant one. The ideal scene is typical of the actual ascension of
our Saviour. See below, on Ps. lxviii. 19 (18).

7 (6). *Sing praises (to) God, sing praises! Sing praises to our King,
sing praises !* The Hebrew corresponding to *sing praises* is a single word

(זַמְּרוּ), which means to praise musically, both with voice and instrument. See above, on Ps. ix. 3, (2). God, who is first mentioned as the object of the praise, is then described as *our King*, the actual King of Israel and the rightful King of all the earth.

8 (7). *For King of all the earth (is) God. Perform a maschil, i.e.* sing and play a didactic psalm. See above, on Ps. xxxii. 1, xlii. 1, xliv. 1, xlv. 1. The *maschil* here meant is the psalm itself. The designation may have been omitted in the title for the very reason that it is contained in the body of the composition. The doctrine taught is that of Jehovah's universal sovereignty, and of the ultimate subjection of all nations to his peaceful sway. This idea is realised in the reign of the Messiah, so that the psalm is, in a wide sense, Messianic. The peculiar import of this last clause is lost in the common version (*sing ye praises with understanding*), which is also that of the Septuagint (ψάλατε συνετῶς), the Vulgate (*psallite sapienter*), and Jerome (*canite erudite*).

9 (8). *God hath reigned over the nations, God hath sat down on his throne of holiness.* He has begun to reign, has become a king, and as such has ascended the throne of universal empire. This and the next verse may be specially regarded as constituting the *maschil* mentioned in ver. 8 (7). *The throne of his holiness*, his holy throne, *i.e.* his divine throne, his throne unlike and above all others. See above, on Ps. xxii. 4 (3), and below, on Ps. ciii. 19, and compare Isa. vi. 1, lxvi. 1.

10 (9). *Princes of nations are assembled—the people of the God of Abraham; for unto God belong the shields of the earth; he is greatly exalted.* The first word properly means *willing*, and especially spontaneous givers; then by a natural deduction, liberal, generous, noble, and as a substantive, nobles, princes. They are here named as the representatives of the nations, gathered in the presence of God, to do him homage and acknowledge his supremacy. The next phrase may mean either *as, with,* or *to the people of God*, most probably the first. *The God of Abraham*, their founder and progenitor, with whom the covenant was made, not only for himself but for his children. See the same phrase, Gen. xxxi. 42, Exod. iii. 6, Mat. xxii. 32. *The shields of the earth*, its protectors, here put for protection in the abstract, or for the *princes* mentioned in the foregoing clause. Compare Hos. iv. 18. It is not till all the principalities and powers of earth acknowledge their subjection to Jehovah, that he can be duly and sufficiently exalted. See above, on Ps. xxii. '29 (28).

Psalm 48

1. *A Psalm. A Song. To the Sons of Korah.* The generic term *psalm* (*mizmôr*) is rendered more specific by the addition of *song* (*shir*), which commonly denotes a song of praise. See above, on Ps. xlii. 9 (8). It is further described as (*belonging*) *to the Sons of Korah*, either as authors or performers. See above, on Ps. xlii. 1. The psalm before us celebrates Jehovah, and Jerusalem as his residence, ver. 2–4 (1–3), with particular reference to a recent deliverance from certain confederate kings, ver. 5–9 (4–8), which is recognised as a subject of perpetual praise, ver. 10–15 (9–14). The most probable conjecture as to the historical occasion of the psalm is, that it has reference to the same event that is commemorated in the one before it. This is the more probable, as we learn from 2 Chron. xx. 19, 27, that Jehoshaphat and his followers first praised God for their

deliverance on or near the field of battle, and then again in the temple after
their return to Jerusalem.   The psalm before us was probably written for
the latter purpose.

2 (1). *Great (is) Jehovah, and to be praised exceedingly, in the city of
our God, his holy mountain.*   This verse propounds, as the theme of the
whole psalm, the glory of Jehovah as revealed to his own people.   *To be
praised :* see above, on Ps. xviii. 4 (3).   The paronomasia, *great and greatly
to be praised*, is not in the original, where the words translated *great* and
greatly in the English Bible, are entirely different both in form and etymology.   *The city of our God :* see above, on Ps. xlvi. 5 (4).   The parallel
expression, *the mountain of his holiness, his mountain of holiness, his holy
mountain*, is intended to convey the same idea, Jerusalem in general and
Zion in particular being here referred to as the seat of the theocracy, the
place where God resided in the midst of his peculiar people, as their king
and their tutelary deity, and where the duty of praising him was therefore
peculiarly incumbent.

3 (2). *Beautiful for elevation, the joy of the whole earth, Mount Zion, (on)
the sides of the north, the city of the great king.*   The common version,
situation, although not erroneous, is too vague.   The reference is to the
lofty site of Jerusalem, as seen from the surrounding country.   It is called
the joy of the whole earth, as a source of spiritual blessings to all nations.
The *sides of the north* may mean the northern division of the city, and be
joined with Zion, which was in the southern part, in order to express the
whole.   Or as the word here rendered *sides* always denotes the extreme
edge or frontier, it may here be used to describe the appearance of the
Holy City, as it rose upon the view of the army returning from the south.
Either of these is a more natural interpretation than the modern one, which
supposes an allusion to the heathen notion of a mountain in the extreme
north, where the gods resided, to which belief there is supposed to be a
reference in Isa. xiii. 14.

4 (3). *God in her palaces is known for a refuge.*   In this, his chosen
seat, he has revealed himself already, as the protector of his people.   See
below, on Ps. lxxvi. 2 (1).

5 (4). *For lo, the kings met—they passed away together.*   They had no
sooner come together than they disappeared together.   *Lo* or *behold*, as
usual, indicates something unexpected.   The definite expression, *the kings*,
seems to refer to something recent and well-known.   The kings originally
meant were those of Moab and Edom.   The word translated *met* means to
come together by appointment or agreement, and here implies a combination against Judea.   Compare Ps. lxxxiii. 4–6 (3–5).   *Passed away*, fled
or disappeared.

6 (5). *(As) they saw, so they wondered, were struck with terror, were put
to flight.*   This verse explains what was meant by their *passing* in the one
before it.   The *as*, corresponding to *so*, which is expressed in ver. 9 (8),
seems to be here omitted, as in Isa. lv. 9.   *As soon as they saw* the holy
city, or the tokens of divine protection.   The last two verbs are passives.
For the meaning of the first, see above, on Ps. ii. 5, and for that of the
second, on Ps. xxxi. 23 (22).   The whole verse is descriptive of a panic
leading to a disorderly retreat or flight.

7 (6). *Trembling seized them there, pain as of a travailing (woman).*
There, *i. e.* on the very spot of their anticipated triumph.   See above, on
Ps. xiv. 5.   Or on the spot from which they first obtained a sight of Jeru-
salem.   This may have been Tekoa (2 Chron. xx. 20), the lofty site of

which commands an extensive prospect. See Robinson's Palestine, ii. 182. The comparison in the last clause is a common one in Scripture, to denote intense but transient pain. Compare Isa. xiii. 8, xxi. 3, xlii. 14.

8 (7). *With an east wind thou wilt break ships of Tarshish.* It is an interesting coincidence that such a disaster did befall the navy of Jehoshaphat himself. See 1 Kings xxii. 49 (48), 2 Chron. xx. 36, 37. Some suppose this to be specifically meant in the case before us, while others understand it as a figurative description of God's sovereign control over all inferior agents. The east wind seems to be mentioned as the one most to be dreaded in the neighbouring seas. The trade to Tarshish and Ophir was almost the only maritime commerce known to the contemporary Hebrews. See 2 Chron. ix. 21, and compare Isa. ii. 16, xxiii. 1, 14 ; lx. 9.

9 (8). *As we have heard, so have we seen, in the city of Jehovah of Hosts, in the city of our God. God will confirm it to eternity. Selah.* What they had heard of as occurring elsewhere or in ancient times, they had now witnessed for themselves. See above, on Ps. xliv. 2 (1), and compare Job xlii. 5. *Jehovah of Hosts ;* see above, on Ps. xxiv. 10. *God will confirm it,* or *establish her, i. e.* Jerusalem, the city of our God. He will secure it against all such assaults as it has just escaped. As Jerusalem is here regarded not as a mere town, but as the seat of the theocracy, the earthly residence of God, the promise is still valid, in its strongest sense, with respect to the church, of which the ancient Zion was the constituted type and local centre.

10 (9). *We have compared, O God, thy mercy in the midst of thy temple.* The verb in this verse sometimes means to *meditate,* but scarcely ever, if at all, without some reference to its primary sense of likening or comparing. It may here denote the act of comparing what they saw with what they had previously heard, as in the foregoing verse. *In the midst* of (*i. e.* within) *thy temple,* literally *thy palace,* a term applied both to the tabernacle and the temple, as the royal residence of Jehovah. See above, on Ps. v. 8 (7), xi. 4, xviii. 7 (6), xxvii. 4, xxix. 9. This expression agrees well with the supposition, that this psalm was intended to be sung at the temple after the return of the army. See 2 Chron. xx. 27.

11 (10). *As thy name, O God, so is thy praise, to the ends of the earth ; (of) righteousness full is thy right hand.* The most obvious meaning of the first clause would seem to be that wherever God is known he is praised. Some, however, understand by *name* the previous manifestations of God's nature, and by *praise* the glory due to his most recent interposition in behalf of his people. The sense will then be still the same as in ver. 9 (8), namely, that what the contemporary Israelites had heard of God's wonderful works in time past they had now seen and felt in their own experience. *To the ends of the earth,* literally *on* or *over* them, which may be a poetical hyperbole describing the fame of these events as already gone beyond the boundaries of earth. See below on ver. 15 (14). *Righteousness,* that of God, as manifested in the destruction of his enemies and the rescue of his people. See above, on Ps. xxxv. 28. This is said to fill his right hand, *i. e.* to be abundantly displayed in the exercise of his almighty power. See above, on Ps. xvi. 11.

12 (11). *Rejoice shall Mount Zion, exult shall the daughters of Judah, because of thy judgments.* According to a very ancient usage, which is found even in the prose of technical geography (Josh. xv. 45, 47), the *daughters of Judah* may be the minor towns dependent on Jerusalem. The more obvious sense is that of female inhabitants, who, as the weaker sex,

had particular occasion to rejoice in the deliverance of the country from its barbarous invaders. The verbs may be understood as expressive of a wish or prayer (*let mount Zion rejoice, &c.*). But the proper future sense agrees better with what immediately precedes, as the declaration of the glory, which has already redounded to the name of God from this exhibition of his power and faithfulness, is then followed up by a declaration, that the same effect shall be continued. *For the sake* (or *on account*) *of thy judgments*, these experimental proofs of thy righteousness, afforded by its actual exercise.

13 (12). *Surround Zion and encircle her ; count her towers.* The verbs in the first clause mean to *walk* (or *go*) *around.* They are twice used together in the history of the taking of Jericho (Josh. vi. 3, 11). The second occurs above in Ps. xvii. 9, xxii. 17 (16). The object of the walk here proposed is to survey the perfect state of her defences, as untouched by the recent dangers. Compare Isa. xxxiii. 20. *Count her towers*, to see if any of them have been demolished.

14 (13). *Set your heart to her rampart, examine her palaces, that you may recount* (*it*) *to a generation following.* The meaning of the first phrase is, *apply your mind*, give attention, observe closely. The word translated *rampart* seems to denote the exterior circumvallation, here contrasted with the *palaces* which it surrounded. *Recount it, i. e.* the result of your inspection, or the sound state of the defences, both as a reminiscence of this particular deliverance, and as a type or emblem of the safety which the church enjoys under divine protection, and therefore entitled to perpetual remembrance. The last word in Hebrew is not a participle but an adjective, strictly meaning *later* or *latter*, subsequent or future.

15 (14). *For this God* (*is*) *our God for ever and ever ; he will guide us unto death.* The *for* assigns a reason for representing this event as one to be remembered, namely, because it is an instance of the favour of Jehovah, who is our perpetual defender. The whole may be thrown into a single sentence, without supplying *is* in the first clause. *For this God, our God, for ever and ever, he will guide, &c.* Or still more in accordance with the usual construction of the pronoun (זֶה), *this is our God for ever and ever, i. e.* he who has done this is and is to be our God. According to the other and more usual construction, *this God* means the God who has performed these wonders. *For ever and ever*, literally *eternity and perpetuity.* See above, on Ps. ix. 6 (5), x. 16, xxi. 5 (4), xlv. 7 (6). *Unto death*, or as some explain it, *at death, i. e.* he will save us from it ; others, *over death*, beyond it. But the most obvious explanation, and the one most agreeable to usage, is that which makes the phrase mean even to the end of life, or as long as we live. The idea of a future state, though not expressed, is not excluded. See above, on Ps. xvii. 15.

Psalm 49

1. *To the Chief Musician. To the Sons of Korah. A Psalm.* This psalm, like the thirty-seventh, is intended to console the righteous under the trials arising from the prosperity and enmity of wicked men, by shewing these to be but temporary, and by the prospect of a speedy change in the relative position of the parties. It consists of a short introductory stanza, inviting general attention to the subject, ver. 2–5 (1–4), followed by two

longer stanzas, the close of which is marked by the recurrence of a burden
or *refrain* in ver. 13 (12) and 21 (20). In the first of these two divisions,
the prominent idea is the fallacy of all merely secular advantages and hopes,
ver. 6–13 (5–12). In the other, these advantages and hopes are directly
contrasted with those of the believer, ver. 14–21 (13–20). There is nothing
in the psalm to determine its date or historical occasion. The inscription
to the Sons of Korah is consistent with any date from the time of David to
that of Ezra. See above, on Ps. xlii. 1, xliv. 1, xlv. 1, xlvi. 1, xlvii. 1,
xlviii. 1. In favour of an earlier date, however, may be urged the obscurity
and difficulty of the style.

2 (1). *Hear this, all the nations; give ear, all inhabitants of the world!*
This general invocation implies that the doctrine to be taught is one of
universal interest. The form of expression is similar to that in Micah i. 2
and 1 Kings xxii. 28, and may be borrowed, in all these cases, from the
still stronger one in Deut. xxxii. 1. See below; Ps. l. 1, and compare Isa.
i. 2. The word translated *world* means primarily *duration* or continued
existence ; then more specifically, human *life*, the present state of things ;
and by a natural transition, the *world*, as the place where it is spent. See
above, on Ps. xvii. 14, xxxix. 6 (5), and below, on Ps. lxxxix. 48 (47).

3 (2). *Both low and high together, rich and poor* This is the conclusion
of the sentence begun in the preceding verse. The first clause is highly
idiomatic in its form, and cannot be literally rendered into intelligible
English. *Likewise sons of man, likewise sons of man.* The word *man* here
corresponds to two distinct Hebrew words which, when placed in opposition,
denote men of high and low degree. See above, on Ps. v. 3 (2), and below,
on Ps. lxii. 10 (9), and compare Prov. viii. 4. The same antithesis is presented in a different form, Ps. xxii. 30 (29). The rich are here summoned
to receive reproof and warning, the poor consolation and encouragement.

4 (3). *My mouth shall speak wisdom, and the meditation of my heart (is)
understanding.* This is no self-praise, as he is only to communicate what he
has received. *Shall speak*, is speaking or about to speak. *Wisdom* and
understanding are both plural in the Hebrew, that form denoting fulness or
variety. See above, on Ps. xviii. 51 (50). The plural of the first word is
also applied to the personification of the highest wisdom, in Prov. ix. 1.
The speech mentioned in the first clause is the outward expression of the
thought or meditation in the second. See the same combination above,
Ps. v. 2 (1), xix. 15 (14).

5 (4). *I will incline to a parable my ear, and open with a harp my riddle.*
I will hear what God says, and impart it to others. *To incline* (or *bend*)
the ear is to lean forward as a sign or gesture of attention. See above, on
Ps. xvii. 6, xxxi. 3 (2), xl. 2 (1). *Parable*, literally likeness or comparison ;
then any figurative, tropical expression. See above, on Ps. xliv. 15 (14).
The parallel word here means an enigma, something hard to understand.
To *open* it is not to begin it, but either to utter it or to explain it, probably
the latter. What he hears from God he will open or expound to man.
With the harp indicates the form in which his exposition is to be presented,
namely, that of a lyrical composition, intended to be sung with an instrumental accompaniment. See above, on Ps. xxxiii. 2, xliii. 4.

6 (5). *Why should I fear in days of evil, (when) the iniquity of my oppressors* (or *supplanters*) *shall surround me ?* The theme of the whole psalm is
the negative proposition involved in this interrogation, namely, that the
righteous has no cause to fear, even when surrounded by powerful and
spiteful enemies. *Days of evil, i. e.* of misfortune or distress. The word

translated *oppressors* commonly means *heels;* but as this yields no good sense here, it may be taken as a verbal noun, meaning either *treaders*, tramplers, oppressors, or supplanters, traitors, in a sense akin to which the verbal root is used, Gen. xxvii. 36, Hos. xii. 4 (3). In either case, it is clearly a description of his enemies, as practising violence or fraud against him.

7 (6). *Those relying on their strength, and in the abundance of their wealth they glory.* A further description of the oppressors and supplanters. The Hebrew word translated *strength* is applied, in different cases, to bodily, pecuniary, military, and moral strength. The parallelism here would seem to indicate a reference to the power which naturally springs from great possessions. The word translated *abundance* may also mean *increase*. For the use of the verbal root, see above, on Ps. iii. 2 (1). *Glory*, boast, or praise themselves, which last is the exact sense of the reflexive verb here used.

8 (7). *A brother can not* (or *he shall not*) *even redeem ; a man can not give to God his ransom.* In the first clause, *brother* may be either the subject or the object of the verb; the rich man cannot redeem his brother, or, his brother cannot redeem him. The former agrees better with the obvious design to shew the worthlessness of mere wealth, which does not enable a man to redeem a brother, *i.e.* save another's life. The *even* in this version is intended to express the emphatic repetition of the verb in Hebrew. It cannot do that which is most essential, and without which other advantages are worthless. Unless the last clause be regarded as a mere reiteration of the same idea in other words, it must be understood to mean that as the rich man cannot redeem his brother from the inevitable stroke of death, much less can he redeem himself, or pay to God his own ransom. This construction of the last words is the less unnatural, because there is properly no reflexive pronoun in the Hebrew language. See above, on Ps. xxxvi. 3 (2).

9 (8). *And costly is the ransom of their soul, and he* (or *it*) *ceases for ever.* This obscure verse admits of several constructions. *Their soul* refers most probably to the rich man and his brother. The soul or life of both requires so much to ransom it, that neither can redeem the other. The verb in the last clause may mean *ceases to live*, perishes, and agree with either or with each of the subjects previously mentioned. The ransom of their life is so costly, that neither can be saved. Or the verb may agree with *ransom*, as in the English Bible; it is too costly to be paid, and therefore *ceases*, or remains unpaid, for ever. The same sense substantially may be obtained by making *cease* mean cease (or fail) to pay, and construing it with one of the preceding nouns. The ransom is so costly that he fails to pay it, or ceases to attempt it, for ever. Upon any of these various suppositions, the essential idea is that the ransom of their life is too expensive to be paid.

10 (9). *That he should still live for ever, and not see corruption.* The form of the first verb in Hebrew shews that this is a dependent sentence, to be immediately connected, as some think, with the ninth verse: " he cannot even redeem a brother, a man cannot pay to God a ransom, so as to live for ever and not see corruption." The tenth verse is then a parenthetical amplification of the ninth. Others connect the ninth and tenth directly, by taking *cease* to mean that he cannot bring to pass. The redemption of their soul is too costly; he can never so contrive it, that he shall live for ever and not see corruption.

11 (10). *For he shall see* (*it*); *wise* (*men*) *must die; likewise the fool and*

brute must perish, and leave to others their substance. The usual construction of the first words—*when he sees* (or *for he sees*) *that wise men die*—is neither so simple in itself, nor so well suited to the context, as that which gives the verb the same sense, and the same object, as in the preceding verse. Wealth cannot ransom its possessor, so that he shall live for ever and not see corruption, *for he shall see it,* as all others do. Even the wisest men must die, much more the fool and brutish person. These are the terms so frequently used in the Book of Proverbs to describe the sinner as irrational. See above, on Ps. xiv. 1, and compare Prov. i. 32, x. 1, xii. 1, xxx. 2, Eccles. ii. 16. In the use of the verbs *die* and *perish,* there may be an intentional allusion to the different destiny of the wise and foolish. *Likewise,* or more literally *together,* at the same time. See above, Ps. iv. 9 (8), and compare Isa. i. 28. *Substance,* strength, pecuniary strength, the same word that is used in ver 7 (6) above.

12 (11). *Their inward thought* (is that) *their houses* (shall continue) *for ever, their dwellings to generation and generation : they call their lands by their own names.* This is substantially the common version, which is here retained because it yields a good sense, and is as probable as any other explanation of this very obscure verse. The first word in Hebrew strictly means the *inside* of anything, and especially of man, *i.e.* his mind or heart, particularly as distinguished from his words or outward conduct. See above, on Ps. v. 10 (9), and below, on Ps. lxiv. 7 (6). The plural form at the end of the sentence occurs nowhere else, but corresponds to our word *grounds,* when applied to cultivated lands. As the singular, however, though it commonly means *ground,* seems occasionally to denote *a land* or *country,* some understand the clause to mean that *they* (*i. e.* men indefinitely) *proclaim* (or *celebrate*) *their names over lands, i. e.* throughout various countries. Another possible, though not a probable construction, makes the last two words mean *upon earth,* the form of the Hebrew noun being assimilated to that of the particle before it. Amidst these various constructions the essential meaning still remains unchanged, to wit, that the rich fools of the foregoing context imagine their prosperity to be perpetual.

13 (12). *And man in honour shall not lodge ; he is made like to the brutes ; they are destroyed.* The *and* at the beginning is equivalent to *and yet,* or to the simple adversative *but.* It introduces the contrast of man's real frailty with his imaginary permanence. As if he had said, " Such are the dreams of the rich fool, and (yet) man really," &c. The word translated *honour* properly means *value,* price, but is applied precisely like the corresponding Greek word (τιμή). It here includes all that makes the condition of the rich fool seem desirable, either to his own conceit, or to the envious admiration of his neighbours. In this position *he is not to lodge, i. e.* remain permanently, or with closer adherence to the strict sense of the verb, continue even for a night, implying that he is to perish before morning. This passage seems to have been present to our Lord's mind, when he uttered the parable of the Rich Fool. Compare especially with the verse before us, Luke xii. 20. *Made like,* assimilated, not in his origin, but in his end. The point of comparison seems to be their blindness and irrational destitution of all foresight. The word translated *brutes* may be still more closely rendered *beasts,* being properly descriptive of the larger quadrupeds. It might even seem in this case to denote specifically *cattle* or domesticated animals, as those which men are especially accustomed to see suddenly deprived of life. But this limitation of the term is peculiar to prose style, whereas in poetry, when used distinctively, it rather signifies

wild beasts. It is better, therefore, to give it here its wider sense of beasts
in general, and to explain even these as mere representatives or samples of
the whole class, brutes or irrational animals, like whom the rich fool is cut
off suddenly and unawares. *They are destroyed,* or as the word seems to
signify originally, *silenced,* brought to silence, *i. e.* stilled or hushed in death.
By assuming an enallage or sudden change of number, we may construe
this verb with the human subject. *He* (the rich fool) *is treated like the
brutes; (like these) they* (the rich fools) *are destroyed.* A less emphatic but
more obvious construction is that which refers it to the brutes themselves.
He is made like to the beasts (which) *are destroyed* (before they are aware).

14 (13). *This (is) their course; (such is) their folly; and (yet) after
them (men) will delight in what they say. Selah.* Their *way* or course
means not only their behaviour, but their fate or destiny. See above, on
Ps. i. 6. *Such is their folly;* literally *folly (is) to them,* they have folly,
they are fools. The noun means originally *hope* or expectation; then an
overweening confidence, a fond or foolish hope; then *folly,* but not without a special reference to this specific form of it. The term is peculiarly
appropriate to those who had just been described as confidently looking for
a permanent enjoyment of their present pleasures, when about to be deprived of them for ever. *After them* may refer to those who follow them
in time, their successors or descendants. But as a similar expression elsewhere denotes those who follow in the sense of imitating or adhering to a
leader (Exod. xxiii. 2, 2 Sam. ii. 10), it is best to retain this meaning in
the case before us. *They who follow them,* their imitators, their adherents,
will delight in their mouth, approve of what they say, adopt their principles,
and act upon their maxims. The general meaning of the verse, as thus
explained, is that notwithstanding the gross folly of such sinners, as proved
by the end to which it brings them, they will still find some to walk in
their footsteps, and to share their ruin. Against this propagated and perpetuated folly there is a tacit but emphatic protest in the meditative pause
which follows, and in the *Selah* which denotes it.

15 (14). *Like a flock to the grave they drive; death is their shepherd; and
the righteous shall rule over them in the morning; and their form the grave
(is) to consume; from* (their) *home to him (they go* or *they belong).* This
is one of the most obscure and difficult verses in the book, although its
general meaning is obvious enough. *Like sheep,* or like a flock, *i. e.* blindly,
in confusion, and without choice or foresight of their own. See above, on
ver. 13 (12). *Hell,* in the wide old English sense of the grave or the
state of the dead. See above, on Ps. vi. 6 (5), ix. 18 (17), xvi. 10, xviii.
6 (5), xxx. 4 (3), xxxi. 18 (17). *They drive;* the Hebrew verb, like the
English one, is active in form, but really involves a passive meaning, *they
are driven,* literally *put* or *placed.* See above, on Ps. xii. 6 (5). The
figure of a flock is carried out by representing Death as the shepherd, by
whom they are led or driven. The literal meaning of the words is, *Death
shall feed them,* but the Hebrew verb means to feed as a shepherd; or
rather to perform the whole office of a shepherd. To this word and its
synonyme in greek (ποιμαίνω) we have no exact equivalent in English.
The bald translation, *death shall feed them,* seems to imply that the prominent idea is that of nourishment, whereas it is that of guidance or direction. The common version, *death shall feed on them,* although not ungrammatical, is entirely at variance with the figure of a flock and a shepherd,
which immediately precedes. The verb translated *rule* seems originally to
denote the act of treading on or trampling, in which sense it is supposed

to be used by Joel, iv. 13 (iii. 13). If this sense be adopted here, the idea may be either that of treading on a grave, or on the neck of a conquered enemy. As the Hebrew verb, however, in every other case, means to *rule over*, and especially when followed by the same preposition as in this place, it is better to adhere to the established usage, which affords a perfectly good sense, namely, that the righteous shall soon triumph over their once prosperous oppressors. *At break of day*, or in the morning, *i. e.* very soon, to-morrow, with allusion, no doubt, to the form of expression in ver. 13 (12), above, and to the general use of night and morning, as figures for distress and relief from it. See above, on Ps. xxx. 6 (5). *Their form*, shape, figure, perhaps with an implication of beauty, which is expressed in the English version. *Consume*, literally make old, wear out, waste away. See above, on Ps. xxxii. 3. *Is to consume*, will do so, or is about to do so. The last clause is even more obscure than what precedes. The last word in Hebrew means *to him* (or *it*), which most interpreters exchange, by an enallage of number, into *them*. It may, however, be referred directly to the nearest antecedent, *hell*, the grave, or to death, personified in the first clause. *From* (their) *dwelling*, *i. e.* driven from it, (they descend or they belong) *to him*. However harsh the ellipsis here assumed may seem, it is really less so than to omit the preposition with some writers, or the pronoun with others, or with one to understand *from dwelling* to mean a dwelling which is not a dwelling, or, as we might say, an *undwelling*. Apart from these minute verbal difficulties, the general idea of the verse is plain, to wit, that they who are now an object of envy or congratulation are soon to be deprived by death of all their coveted and boasted advantages.

16 (15). *Only God will redeem my soul from the hand of Hell, for he will take me.   Selah.* The Hebrew particle at the beginning of the sentence always denotes a limitation or exception. See above, on Ps. xxxvii. 8, xxxix. 12 (11). It may here mean either that his own case is excepted from the destruction which he has been describing, and which might seem to be described as universal; or that God alone can afford that safety which the rich fool hopes to derive from his secular advantages. *Redeem*, in allusion to ver. 8, 9 (7, 8), above. The *hand* is a common emblem of power, but it may here belong to a personification of *Sheol*, the grave, or hell, like that of death in ver. 15 (14). *For he will take me*, *i. e.*, as some suppose, will take me to himself, accept me. But as the verb is nowhere absolutely used in this sense, it is better to explain it as a parallel expression to *redeem*. " He will redeem me from the hand of Sheol, for he will take me (out of it)." Either of these constructions is more natural than that which makes Sheol the subject of the last verb. " He will redeem me from the hand of Sheol, when it seizes (or would seize) me." The hostile sense thus put upon the verb may be justified by the analogy of Isa. xxviii. 19; but the change of subject and the less usual meaning of the particle (כִּי) are not to be assumed without necessity.

17 (16). *Be not thou afraid because a man grows rich, because the glory of his house increases.* Here begins the application or practical conclusion of the foregoing meditations. It is marked by a change of form, the Psalmist now no longer speaking of himself, but to himself, or to another, as the person most directly interested in his subject. See a similar transition in Ps. xxxii. 8, and compare the parental or authoritative tone of the address with that in Ps. xxxiv. 12 (11). *Fear not*, be not apprehensive or solicitous, not merely for thyself, but for the cause of truth and goodness.

See above, on Ps. xxxvii. 1. The conjunction in the first clause may also be translated *when* or *though.* But the proper causal meaning of the particle should always be preferred when admissible, and especially in cases like the present, where it yields not only a good sense but the best sense, since the increasing wealth and honour of the wicked is certainly assigned as the cause or occasion of the anxious apprehensions here forbidden. The use of the English present tense in the translation of this verse is merely idiomatic, since in such connections it is really a future. The verb of the first clause is a causative, and strictly means to *enrich* or *make rich*. The transition to the neuter or intransitive sense is precisely similar to that of the English verb *increase*, which strictly means to *make greater*, but in this very sentence has the intransitive sense of *growing* (or *becoming*) *greater*. There is no other clear example of the first Hebrew verb being so used. Dan. xi. 2, and Prov. x. 4, are at least ambiguous. *A man* cannot of itself denote a *bad man*, but that idea is suggested by the context, and especially by the use of the word *man* in ver. 8 (7), 13 (12). *Glory* or *honour* here includes all the sensible effects of riches, as a source of admiration and applause. *House*, in the wide sense, common to both languages, including both the dwelling and the family, the house and household. See Gen vii. 1, xviii. 19, xxxv. 2, l. 4.

18 (17.) *For not in his death will he take the whole ; not down will go after him his glory*. The form of the original is here retained as far as possible, in order to exhibit its highly idiomatic character. The position of the negative in both clauses makes it far more emphatic than in our English collocation. *At his death*, in his dying, when he dies. *The whole :* this word is usually rendered *all*, but it is invariably a substantive in Hebrew, and is here determined to be such by the definite article prefixed. *Not the whole*, however, or *not all*, is by no means so significant a phrase in English as in Hebrew, where the absence of indefinite pronouns makes this the only way of saying *not anything*, *i. e.* nothing While the words therefore certainly mean that *he shall not take all*, they likewise mean that *he shall not take any* of his secular possessions with him ; and this stronger sense is here required by the context. *His glory*, as in the preceding verse, his wealth and the honours or distinctions springing from it. *Descend after him*, not in the moral or legal sense of a hereditary descent to his heirs, but in the local sense of a descent into the grave or the unseen world. The whole verse assigns a reason for not envying the wealthy sinner, namely, because he will be soon obliged to leave his wealth behind him.

19 (18). *For his soul in his life he will bless, and* (others) *will praise thee because thou doest good to thyself*. There is no need of giving כִּי the

sence of *but, though*, or any other than its proper causal sense of *for, because*. See above, on ver. 17 (16). This verse assigns the reason of the fact alleged in the one before it. The wealthy sinner is to carry nothing with him when he dies, because he is to have his " good things" in the present life. This is God's appointment in accordance with his own free choice. *In his life* (or *lifetime*), as long as he lives, *he is to bless his soul* (or *himself*), *i. e.* to reckon himself happy, and to be so esteemed by others. In the last clause, the third person is abruptly exchanged for the second, and the wealthy sinner, of whom the Psalmist had been speaking to himself or his disciple, is directly addressed, as if personally present. This application of the figure called apostrophe is made with great skill and rhetorical effect. The plural verb is indefinite, as in ver. 14 (13) above. *They, i. e.* men in general, or *others*, as distinguished from himself. The verb itself means strictly to *acknowledge* or confess ; then more specifically, to acknowledge benefits received, to *thank ;* and then to *praise* in general. See above, on Ps. vi. 6 (5). The primary meaning may be here still kept in view, by understanding him to mean, *they will recognise thee* (or *take knowledge of thee) that thou doest good* (or *as one doing good) to thyself.* There is no need of substituting either a present or a past tense for the futures, which are perfectly appropriate in speaking of a course of conduct yet to be acted out, the wealthy sinner being represented as still living, both in this verse and the one before it. There is pungent sarcasm in the close of this verse : they will praise thee because thou doest good—*to thyself.* Or, because thou doest well—*for thyself.* The addition of this last phrase serves to characterise vividly, not only the rich sinner but his flatterers. There can be little doubt that our Saviour tacitly alluded to the first clause of this verse, when he made Abraham say to Dives, " Son, remember that thou in thy lifetime receivedst thy good things, and likewise Lazarus evil things ; but now he is comforted, and thou art tormented" (Luke xvi. 25). This is indeed a most instructive commentary on the passage now before us, as exhibiting the future revolution in the relative position of the parties, as a reason for not envying the wealthy sinner now. It is equally certain, that the Rich Fool's address to his own soul, in Luke xii. 19, was suggested by the same clause of the psalm before us, *in his lifetime he will bless his soul.* Indeed, the whole conception of the Rich Man in the one case, and the Rich Fool in the other, may be said to be borrowed from this psalm, and may therefore derive instructive and interesting illustration from it.

20 (19). *It shall go* (or *thou shalt go) to the generation of his fathers; for ever they shall not see light.* The first verb may be either a third person feminine, agreeing with *soul,* or a second person masculine, addressed directly to the wealthy sinner. In the latter case, we must suppose an immediate change to the third person, in order to account for the expression *his fathers.* In either case, the idea is that *he shall go,* though this would not be a correct translation of the Hebrew words. The whole clause has reference to the frequent description of death in the Old Testament, as a man's sleeping with his fathers, or being gathered to his fathers. *Generation* may be taken as a collective term, denoting the successive generations of his fathers, either natural or spiritual, *i. e.* either his literal progenitors, or his predecessors in the same way of thinking and the same course of life. There is no absurdity indeed in supposing the two senses to be here coincident. *To perpetuity they shall not see,* in our idiom, *they shall never see. The light,* i. e. *the light of life,* or *the light of the living,* an expression used by David, Ps. lvi. 14 (13). The meaning of the whole verse is, that the wealthy sinner is to die as his fathers died before him, and continue dead like them, without returning to revisit, much less to repossess, the riches and honours which he once imagined were to last for ever. This completes the proof that these advantages are not legitimate or even rational occasions of envious dissatisfaction to the righteous.

21 (20). *Man* (that is) *in honour and understandeth not is likened to the beasts* (that) *are destroyed.* The first verb in this verse and the first verb in ver. 13 (12) differ only in a single letter (יבין and ילין), in consequence of which they are confounded by the ancient Greek and Syriac translators, and some modern critics have proposed to amend one of the places by assimilation to the other. But the prevalent practice of the Hebrew writers, where the same burden or *refrain* recurs, is not to repeat it slavishly, but with some slight variation in the form, which not unfrequently suggests

a new idea, or modifies the one before expressed. See above, on Ps.
xxiv. 10, xlii. 12 (11). So here, at the close of the first strophe, the rich
fool is compared to the brutes that perish, with respect to the uncertainty
of his enjoyments; and again at the close of the second, with respect to his
irrationality, the points of comparison being distinct but inseparable. No
wonder that the sinner is cut off unawares like the brutes, when in fact he
is equally irrational. By tampering with the text of either passage, therefore, we take from the psalm one of its moral lessons, as well as one of its
rhetorical beauties.

Psalm 50

UNDER the figure of a great judicial process, God himself is introduced,
exposing and condemning the hypocrisy of formalists, and expounding the
true nature of his law. After a striking introduction, ver. 1–6, he reproves
the perversion, and exhibits the true meaning, of the first table of the law,
ver. 7–15, and then of the second, ver. 16–21, and closes with a solemn
warning and a gracious promise, ver. 22–23.

1. *A Psalm. By Asaph. The Almighty, God, Jehovah, speaks, and
calls the earth, from the rising of the sun unto the going down thereof.*
Asaph was one of David's chief musicians (1 Chron. xv. 17, 19), and
also an inspired psalmist (1 Chron. xxv. 2, 2 Chron. xxix. 30). In
both these capacities the psalm might be ascribed to him, nor is it possible either to prove or disprove that it was composed by him. *Mighty* or
Almighty is not an adjective agreeing with the next word (*the Mighty God*),
but a substantive in apposition with it. Three divine names are put together in a kind of climax, *El, Elohim, Jehovah*. The first represents God
as almighty, the second as the only proper object of worship and (by its
plural form) as perfect, the third as self-existent and eternal, and at the
same time as the peculiar God of Israel. The same combination occurs in
Josh. xxii. 22. It is here intended to enhance the grandeur of the scene
by setting forth the titles of the judge or sovereign. *Speaks*, or more exactly
spoke, has spoken, by which, however, we may understand an act just past.
The same remark applies to the word *calls*, which is here used in the sense
of summoning or citing. From sunrise to sunset, or from east to west, is
a natural description of the earth in its whole extent, including its remotest
bounds but not excluding that which lies between them. See above, on
Ps. ii. 8.

2. *Out of Zion, the perfection of beauty, God hath shined.* He comes
forth, in a splendid and imposing manner, from his royal residence, the
seat of the theocracy, which is described as perfectly beautiful, not only in
a moral and spiritual sense, but in reference also to its lofty situation, celebrated in Ps. xlviii. 3 (2) above. The Hebrew verb is borrowed from the
sublime theophany in Deut. xxxiii. 2; see also Ps. lxxx. 2 (1), xciv. 1.

3. *Our God shall come—and let him not be silent—fire before him shall
devour, and around him it shall be tempestuous exceedingly.* The future in
the first clause may be rendered *he is coming*, as if the sound of his voice
and the light of his glory had preceded his actual appearance. The imagery
is borrowed from the giving of the law at Sinai, Exod. xix. 16, xx. 18.
Consuming fire is a common emblem of God's vindicatory justice (Deut.
xxxii. 22, 2 Thess. i. 8), and of God himself considered as a righteous God
(Deut. iv. 24, ix. 3, Heb. xii. 29).

4. *He will call to the heavens above and to the earth, to judge his people.* The future, as before, describes an act just about to be performed. It might even be translated, *he is calling.* The compound preposition, *from over*, is used adverbially in the sense of *above.* See for example Gen. i. 7. The strict sense, *from above*, would here be inappropriate, since God is represented not as speaking from heaven, much less from above it, but as appearing upon earth, and visibly coming out of Zion. In our idiom these words would naturally mean that he summons heaven and earth to sit in judgment on his people. But according to Hebrew usage, the last clause may refer to the remoter antecedent, the subject of the principal verb, and be translated, *so that he may judge his people.* The heavens and earth, put for the whole creation, are summoned not as judges but as witnesses, as appears from ver. 6 below. See Deut. iv. 26, xxx. 19, xxxi. 28, and compare Isa. i. 2.

5. *Gather for me my saints, ratifying my covenant over sacrifice.* The judge here addresses, as it were, the ministerial officers of justice. Compare Mat. xxiv. 31. *For me*, as my messengers, acting in my behalf, or *to me, i. e.* to the place where I am, here, around me. *My saints*, the objects of my mercy, those whom I have called and specially distinguished. See above, on Ps. iv. 4 (3). The term is here descriptive of a relation, not of an intrinsic quality. *Ratifying*, literally *cutting*, striking, perhaps in allusion to the practice of slaying and dividing victims as a religious rite accompanying solemn compacts. See Gen. xv. 10, 18. The same usage may be referred to in the following words, *over sacrifice, i. e.* standing over it, or *on sacrifice, i. e.* founding the engagement on a previous appeal to God. There is probably allusion to the great covenant transaction recorded in Exod. xxiv. 4–8. This reference to sacrifice shews clearly that what follows was not intended to discredit or repudiate that essential symbol of the typical or ceremonial system.

6. *And* (now) *the heavens have declared his righteousness, for God* (is) *judge himself. Selah.* The heavens are witnesses of God's judicial rectitude, *for he himself* (and not a delegated man or angel) *is the judge* (on this occasion). Or the last words may be rendered, *he is judging, i. e.* acting as a judge. The parties and the witnesses having been summoned, the judicial process now begins. The pause, denoted by the *Selah*, is one indicative of awe, excited by the dread solemnity of these proceedings.

7. *Hear, my people, and let me speak, and let me testify against thee. God, thy God, am I.* The introductory description being ended, the divine judgment now begins. *Let me speak*, or *I will speak*, the peculiar form of the Hebrew verb, sometimes expressing strong desire and sometimes fixed determination. See above, on Ps. ii. 3. God is himself the witness against Israel, by whom the charge is to be proved, the heavens and the earth being only witnesses of the judicial scene or spectacle. I am not only *God*, but *thy God*, bound to thee by covenant, and reciprocally claiming thy allegiance. This may be added as a reason why he has a right to testify against them ; or it may be the beginning of the testimony itself. " Let me testify against thee as thy God," or, " I will testify against thee, that I am thy God," although I am not so regarded or so treated.

8. *Not for thy sacrifices will I reprove thee, and thy burnt-offerings before me always.* The insertion of the words *to have been*, in the common version, seems to make the clause mean, that although they had neglected this external rite, it was of no importance, whereas the simple meaning of the Hebrew sentence is, that they were not chargeable with this neglect, im-

plying that the observance was obligatory, which is in perfect keeping with the tenor of the psalm. "I do not charge thee with withholding the material offerings to which I am entitled, for in truth they are ever before me." To the generic term *sacrifices*, animal oblations, he adds the more specific one, *burnt-offering*, the usual English version of a Hebrew term, denoting the principal and ordinary expiatory offering of the Mosaic ritual. See above, on Ps. xx. 4 (3), xl. 7 (6).

9. *I will not take from thy house a bullock, (nor) from thy folds he-goats.* Here begins the correction of the false and foolish notion, extensively prevalent among the heathen, and not unknown among the ancient Jews, especially in times of great corruption, that the sacrifices were designed to satisfy some physical necessity on God's part, whether in the way of food or otherwise. In opposition to this impious absurdity, it is argued that, even if God needed such supplies, he would not be dependent on the worshipper, who is here addressed directly as an individual, with great advantage to the liveliness and force of the whole passage. "If I needed bulls and goats, as you imagine, I would not be under the necessity of seeking them at your hands."

10. *For to me* (belongs) *every beast of the forest, the cattle in hills of a thousand.* This last idiomatic phrase may either mean a thousand hills, or hills where the cattle rove by thousands, with probable allusion to the hilly grounds of Bashan beyond Jordan. See above, on Ps. xxii. 13 (12). According to etymology, the noun in the first clause means an *animal*, and that in the second *beasts* or *brutes* in general. See above, on Ps. xlix. 13 (12). But when placed in antithesis, the first denotes a wild beast, and the second domesticated animals or cattle. Both words were necessary to express God's sovereign propriety in the whole animal creation. Thus understood, the verse assigns a reason for the negative assertion in the one before it. Even if God could stand in need of animal oblations, for his own sake, or for their sake, he would not be under the necessity of coming to man for them, since the whole animal creation is his property and perfectly at his disposal.

11. *I know every bird of the hills, and the population of the field* (is) *with me, i. e.* in my presence, under my inspection, and within my reach. The past tense of the verb suggests not merely that it is so now, but that it has been so from the beginning. This is no newly acquired knowledge or authority, but such as are involved in the very relation between creature and creator. *Population*, literally movement, motion, *i. e.* animal motion, and by a natural metonymy that which lives and moves.

12. *If I were hungry, I would not say* (so) *to thee ; for to me* (belongs) *the world and its fulness*, that which fills it, its contents and its inhabitants. See above, on Ps. xxiv. 1. The first clause may be rendered, with a closer adherence to the form of the original, *if I am hungry, I will not say* (so) *to thee.* All this is said upon the supposition, that God may, in some sense, need supplies of this kind, although even then he would be wholly independent of man's bounty or fidelity in furnishing them. But the supposition is of course a false one, and is so represented in the next verse.

13. *Will I eat the flesh of bulls and drink the blood of goats?* The future of the Hebrew verb is very expressive, suggesting the ideas of possibility, necessity, and desire. Do I desire the flesh and blood of beasts for my refreshment? Do I need them for my sustenance? Or is it even possible for me to use them in the way that you imagine? The negative

answer, which is obviously expected to these questions, presupposes the great doctrine that Jehovah is a spirit, and as such exempt from all corporeal necessities. This, then, is another refutation of the gross and impious error that he needed their oblations. If they were necessary in themselves, he could obtain them elsewhere; and that they are not necessary follows, as an inevitable consequence, from the spirituality of the divine nature. This is not the language of dry and formal ratiocination, which, on such a subject and in such a connection, would be not only misplaced but revolting. It is rather the language of impassioned and indignant expostulation, holding up the absurdities, to which the error of the formal worshipper inevitably tended, as a refutation of the error itself.

14. *Sacrifice to God thanksgiving, and* (so) *pay unto the Most High thy vows.* The first word means something more than *offer*, and contains a distinct allusion to the animal sacrifices mentioned in ver. 8 above. This is not an exhortaton to offer thanks or praise *instead* of material sacrifices, which would be inconsistent with the express requisition of the latter, but to offer them as expressions of thanksgiving, or in other words, to offer these as they were intended to be offered, not as a meritorious operation, nor as gross attempts to feed the Deity, but as symbolical expressions of devout affection, repentance, faith, and love, all which we may suppose to be represented, or at least suggested, by the single act of praise or thanksgiving, here explicitly enjoined. The imperative in the last clause may, according to a very common Hebrew idiom, be resolved into a future, and the whole verse paraphrased as follows : " If you offer your material sacrifices, not merely as such, but as the prescribed expression of inward spiritual exercises, you will thereby really discharge your obligations to the being whom you worship."

15. *And call upon me in a day of distress ; I will free thee and thou shalt honour me.* The imperative in the first clause, is dependent upon that in the preceding verse. The connection may be rendered clearer by substituting *then* for *and.* Offer such sacrifices, and you will really discharge your obligations ; then, when you call upon me, I will hear you. *Thou shalt honour me*, thou shalt have occasion to renew thy praises and thanksgivings for new benefits received. With this encouraging assurance closes the divine exposition of the sacrificial system.

16. *And to the wicked God saith, What hast thou* (to do) *to declare my statutes, and take thy covenant into thy mouth?* Thus far the doctrine of the psalm has had respect to the formal worshipper, whose rites are mere external services, expressive of no inward faith or love. But now it is applied to him who actually violates the law which he professes to acknowledge. *The wicked*, the man of vicious life, who is afterwards described with more particularity. He is not necessarily distinct in real life from the formalist of the foregoing context. The description is not of two individuals, but of two classes, to which one and the same person may belong, or two characters, which one and the same person may exhibit. *Saith*, said, or hath said, on the same ideal occasion. *What* (*is*) *to thee*, the only Hebrew mode of saying, *what hast thou*, *i. e.* what right or reason hast thou ? *To declare*, either by profession of one's own faith, or by authoritative teaching of others. There may perhaps be some allusion to the primary meaning of the Hebrew verb, which is to count or number. See above, on Ps. xl. ·6 (5). To count off or reckon up God's statutes is a very natural expression for censorious or ostentatious iteration, especially in this connection, where an obvious reference to the ten commandments

follows. *My covenant*, my law considered as conditional, or as involving reciprocal engagements upon my part. See above, on ver. 5. To *take into the mouth*, or more literally, to *take up on the mouth*, is a strong idiomatic phrase for uttering, pronouncing. See above, on Ps. xvi. 4.

17. *And thou hast hated instruction, and hast cast my words behind thee.* The very person who enforces the law, in all its rigour, upon others, refuses to submit to it himself, and treats its precepts not only with neglect but with contempt. This passage seems to have been present to the mind of Paul, in that remarkable series of interrogations, "Thou therefore which teachest another teachest thou not thyself," &c. Rom. ii. 21–23.

18. *If thou sawest a thief, thou consentedst with him, and with adulterers* (has been) *thy portion.* The first clause conveys far more than the simple idea of consent. The expression *if thou sawest* implies great eagerness and an instinctive drawing towards the thief as a congenial spirit. The second verb in Hebrew denotes a cordial and complacent acquiescence. *Thy portion* or participation, common interest, communion. These particular sins are mentioned with reference to their prohibition in the seventh and eighth commandments (Exod. xx. 14, 15).

19. *Thy mouth thou hast given up to evil, and thy tongue will weave* (or *frame*) *deceit.* The ninth commandment is now added to the other two, as being habitually violated by the person here addressed. *Given up to,* literally *sent out with* (or *into*) *evil.* The first clause is descriptive of mere evil speaking, the second of more artificial and ingenious lying. Both verbs include present time, but the first with the additional idea of an early habit, formed and settled in time past, the other with that of an inveterate habit, not likely to be broken or reformed hereafter.

20. *Thou wilt sit (and) against thy brother speak ; at the son of thy mother thou wilt aim a blow.* To the general charge of falsehood is now added the specific one of slander, not against strangers, but his nearest friends. The idea suggested by the future is that such behaviour may be confidently looked for on the part of such a character. *Thou wilt sit,* in the company of others, or more specifically of the wicked, or of other wicked slanderers, as one of them. See above, on ver. 18. As *brother* might be understood as meaning merely any other man, it is determined by the unambiguous phrase, *thy mother's* son. This is mentioned merely as an extreme case, not as excluding other relations and friends, but rather comprehending them. *Aim a blow*, literally *give a thrust*, so as to cast him down. The blow meant is a stroke of the tongue. Compare Jer. xviii. 18.

21. *These things hast thou done, and I have held my peace; thou hast imagined I was just like thyself. I will reprove thee, and array* (thy sins) *before thine eyes.* God is described as silent when he does not interpose with his reproofs or manifest his displeasure. See above, on Ps. xxviii. 1. *Imagined;* the Hebrew verb originally means to liken or compare, and another of the same form to be silent, so that it is peculiarly appropriate in this place, where the mention of God's silence immediately precedes, and the imagining referred to was a false assimilation of the Most High to the sinner himself. *Just like,* or exactly like, the intensive adverb corresponding to the emphatic repetition of the verb in Hebrew. In our idiom, an adversative particle is almost indispensable between the clauses; but the more abrupt transition is congenial with the spirit and usage of the Hebrew language. *Array*, arrange, set in order, so that none shall be omitted or overlooked. See above, on Ps. v. 4 (3). *Before thine eyes,* literally to thine eyes, or to thy face, again implying that the sight of them

is not to be avoided. This declaration of severe fidelity forms an appropriate conclusion to the second lesson of the psalm, or that in which the mask is stripped off from the vicious hypocrite, who professes to serve God while he lives in the grossest violation of his precepts, as in the first part (ver. 7–15) it was torn from the formal hypocrite, who satisfies himself with a mere outward aud mechanical performance of rites designed to be significant of spiritual and devout affections.

22. *Oh consider this, forgetters of God, lest I rend and there be no deliverer.* To both the argumentative invectives which precede there is added in conclusion a solemn exhortation, including both a warning or admonitory threatening and a promise. This verse contains the warning. The Hebrew particle of entreaty (נָא) is not so well expressed by the *now* of the English Bible as by the *Oh* of the Prayer Book version. The image presented in the last clause is that of a ravenous beast, and more especially a lion. See above, on Ps. xxii. 14 (13). *No deliverer*, or more literally *none delivering.* The description of those addressed, as *forgetting* (or *forgetters of*) *God*, suggests that both forms of hypocrisy exhibited in this psalm owe their origin to ignorance, mistaken notions, or oblivion, of God's attributes and purposes and former acts.

23. (The man) *sacrificing praise shall honour me, and prepare a way that I may shew him the salvation of God*, that of which he is the author. See above, on Ps. iv. 9 (8). This phrase is used instead of *my salvation*, for the sake of a more sonorous close. The common version of the first clause makes it an identical preposition : *whoso offereth praise glorifieth me.* At the same time it greatly weakens the expression by the use of the ambiguous term *offer.* The words are all borrowed fiom ver. 14, 15, to which there is therefore a direct allusion, and by which the clause must be interpreted. It is really a promise that he whose offerings are genuine expressions of thanksgiving shall have cause or occasion to praise God for his mercies. The rest of the sentence is more doubtful. According to the construction above given, which seems to be required by the accents, the meaning is, that he who offers the right kind of sacrifice, as before explained, prepares the way, literally *sets* or *lays* a way, by which he shall himself attain to the experience of salvation. But as this confines the promise to the observance of the first great lesson taught in the psalm, we may give it a wider application, and the sentence a more regular form, by rendering the last clause thus, *and* (the man) *ordering* (*his*) *way, I will shew the salvation of God.* The man ordering his way, *i. e.* placing it, defining it, marking it out, is then contrasted with such as turn aside unto their crooked ways (Ps. cxxv. 5). The precise form of the construction is, (*as to the man*) *ordering* (*his*) *way, I will shew him the salvation of God.* This clause then has reference to the second lesson of the psalm (ver. 16–21), as the other to the first (ver. 7–15). The preposition before *salvation* in Hebrew often gives the verb *to see* the pregnant sense of gazing at or viewing with delight. See above, on Ps. xxii. 18 (17), xxxvii. 34.

Psalm 51

1, 2. *To the Chief Musician. A Psalm. By David. When Nathan the Prophet came unto him, as he (i. e. David) had come unto Bathsheba.*

The first inscription was particularly necessary here, to shew that the psalm was designed for permanent and public use, since it might otherwise have been regarded as expressive of mere personal emotions. It has reference to the one great crime of David's life, noted as such in the inspired history itself (1 Kings xv. 5), and involving the guilt of both adultery and murder. See 2 Sam. xi. and xii. The significant repetition of the phrase *came unto* in ver 2 is lost in the English and most other versions. *As* is not a mere particle of time, simply equivalent to *when*, but suggests the ideas of analogy, proportion, and retaliation. The psalm consists of two parts, a prayer and a vow. In the first, he prays to be forgiven and restored to the divine favour, ver. 3–14 (1–12). In the second, he shews how he means to testify his gratitude, ver. 15–21 (13–19).

3 (1). *Be gracious to me, (O) God, according to thy mercy; according to the abundance of thy compassions, blot out my transgressions.* In this verse and the next, he presents the petition which constitutes the theme or burden of the psalm. The appeal to the divine grace, mercy, and compassion, involves a confession of his own guilt and the justice of his condemnation. *According to*, literally *like thy mercy, i. e.* in accordance with it, in proportion to it. Here again there is a tacit admission of the greatness of his guilt, as requiring infinite mercy to forgive it. *Abundance*, increase, multitude. See above, on Ps. v. 8 (7). *Compassions*, tender mercies, a term expressive of the warmest and tenderest affections. See above, on Ps. xviii. 2 (1). *Blot out*, erase, from thy remembrance. The allusion is probably to a record or register of crimes, or to the cancelling of accounts, although the former seems to agree better with ancient and oriental usage. Compare Num. v. 23. *Transgressions*, or with closer adherence to the primary etymological import of the term, *revolts, apostasies*. See above, on Ps. xix. 14 (13), xxxii. 1.

4 (2). *Thoroughly wash me from my iniquity, and from my sin cleanse me.* The first word in Hebrew is the infinitive or imperative of a verb meaning to increase or multiply, but often used adverbially in the sense of plentifully, abundantly. The verb in the first clause properly denotes the act of washing the garments, as distinguished from that of bathing the body. See Num. xix. 19. The image here presented, therefore, is the same as in Jude ver. 23, sin being represented as a stain, and the grace of God as purifying water.

5 (3). *For my transgressions I know, and my sin (is) before me always.* His consciousness of guilt is urged, not only as a reason why he should ask forgiveness, but as a reason why God should grant it. As no one is forgiven unless convinced of sin, so this conviction constitutes a kind of claim to pardon, not as being meritorious or intrinsically efficacious, but as an indication of God's merciful intentions, since conviction and forgiveness are alike his gift. The same mutual connection of the two things is uniformly recognised in Scripture. See above, on Ps. xxxii. 5, and compare 2 Sam. xii. 13, Prov. xxviii. 13, 1 John i. 9. The future in the first clause is significant. I know it and shall know it ; I can never henceforth lose the sense or knowledge of it.

6 (4). *To thee, thee only, have I sinned, and done the evil in thine eyes, to the intent that thou mayest be just in thy speaking, and be clear in thy judging.* The particle at the beginning denotes general relation, *as to*, or *respecting*. The precise relation meant must be determined by the context. See above, on Ps. xxxv. 19, 24, xxxviii. 17 (16). It does not, therefore, directly and explicitly substitute God for man as the injured party, which

is the only sense that can be put upon the English phrase *against thee.*
This idea, however, is undoubtedly implied, as well as perfectly consistent
with the usage of the Scriptures in describing all sin as committed against
God. Even murder, the highest crime that can be committed against man,
is condemned and punished as the violation of God's image (Gen. ix. 6).
It is also possible to understand *thee, thee only,* as opposed not to other
objects, but to the sinner himself, as one of two contending parties. As if
he had said, thou hast not sinned against me, but I have sinned against
thee, thee only. *The evil,* not *this evil,* which restricts the acknowledgment
too much, but *that which is evil,* meaning sin in general. *To the intent
that* may have reference to the divine purpose in permitting David's sin to
take this aggravated form, so that there could be neither doubt nor transfer
nor participation of his guilt, and so that when God spoke in condemnation
of it, he might not only be, but appear to be, entirely just. There is no
need, therefore, of adopting the weaker meaning, *so that,* denoting a mere
consequence but not a purpose, or of supposing the intention indicated to
be merely that of the confession, " I acknowledge this, that thou mayest be
just, &c. *Speaking, i. e.* speaking as a judge, deciding, or more definitely
still, condemning. It is therefore substantially equivalent to the parallel
term *judging.*

7 (5). *Lo, in iniquity I was born, and in sin did my mother conceive me.*
The meaning of the first verb is determined by its use in Job xv. 7, Prov.
viii. 24, 25, and that of the corresponding active form in Job xxxix. 1.
The iniquity and sin meant are not those of his mother, but his own.
Having just before confessed his actual transgressions, he now acknowledges
the corruption of his nature. This has always been regarded as the *locus
classicus* of the Old Testament, in reference to the doctrine of original sin.

8 (6). *Lo, truth thou hast desired in the inward* (or *secret*) *parts, and in
the hidden (part) wisdom thou wilt make me know.* The repetition of *behold*
or *lo,* at the beginning of the sentence, seems to indicate a close connection
with the preceding verse. That connection is most probably as follows :—
" Since I am corrupted in my very nature, and thou canst be satisfied with
nothing short of inward sincerity, thou must bestow what thou requirest,
by imparting to me heavenly wisdom." *Truth,* sincerity, reality, as opposed
to hypocritical profession or pretence. The first verb means not merely to
desire, but to *will,* as in Job xxxiii. 32. The past tense implies that it has
always been so, that the requisition is no sudden or capricious one, but an
eternal law founded in God's very nature. The inward and hidden parts
are mentioned as opposed to the mere outside. *Wisdom,* divine illumination, without which no correct view either of sin or holiness is possible.
Thou wilt make me know, involves a prayer, although in form it is an expression of strong confidence.

9 (7). *Thou wilt purge me with hyssop, and I shall be clean ; thou wilt
wash me, and I shall be whiter than snow.* What he asked in ver. 4 (2) he
here anticipates with confidence. The verb translated *purge* is very expressive, being a derivative of that which means to *sin* in ver. 6 (4) above. It
denotes specifically, therefore, purification from the stain of sin, either by
actual payment of the penalty (Gen. xxxi. 39), or by vicarious satisfaction
(Num. xix. 19). *Hyssop* is mentioned as a plant much used in the Levitical purgations, either as a convenient instrument of sprinkling (Exod. xii.
22), or as an emblem of the divine condescension, viewed in contrast with the
divine majesty (Isa. lxvi. 1, 2), as represented by the cedar, with which the
hyssop is perpetually joined. See Num xix. 18, and compare 1 Kings v. 13.

iv. 33.　In either case, to *purge with hyssop* necessarily suggests the idea of
a purification founded on atonement, as the hyssop was employed to sprinkle
purifying substances, and sometimes mingled with them (Exod. xii. 22,
Num. xix. 6, 18).　The second future in each clause expresses both consent
and expectation.　*Whiter than snow* is a natural hyperbole denoting perfect
purity.　See the sames image applied to the same subject in Isa. i. 18.　The
last verb answers to the English *whiten*, being properly a causative, but
sometimes used intransitively, just as we may say, that blushing *reddens* the
face, or that the face *reddens* in the act of blushing.　" Wash me, and I
shall whiten (become white) from (away from, as distinguished from, and
by implication more than) snow."

10 (8.)　*Thou wilt make to hear joy and gladness;* (then) *shall rejoice
the bones* (which) *thou hast broken* (*bruised*, or *crushed*).　What is formally
expressed is still a confident expectation or assured hope, under which,
however, an intense desire is implicitly contained.　The *joy* here anticipated is that of pardoned sin.　See above, on Ps. xxxii. 1.　He expects
to *hear* it, as communicated or announced by God.　The word *then* is introduced in the translation for the sake of retaining the original arrangement of the sentence, closing, as it does in Hebrew, with the emphatic
figure, *crushed* or *broken*, which expresses, in a very lively manner, the disorder and distress produced by consciousness of aggravated and unexpiated
guilt.　The change from this condition to a sense of safety and reconciliation with God, is not too strongly represented by the bold but most expressive figure of broken bones rejoicing.　The ellipsis of the relative in
this clause is common to both idioms.

11 (9.)　*Hide thy face from my sins, and all my iniquities blot out.*　The
desire implied in the anticipations of the two preceding verses now breaks
out into its proper form, that of direct petition.　*Hide thy face* from them,
so as not to see them, look no longer at them.　The same figure is applied, in an unfavourable sense, to God's apparent neglect of his suffering
servants, his refusal to behold them or to notice their condition.　See above,
on Ps. xiii. 2 (1), xliv. 25 (24).　*Blot out*, expunge, from thy account, or
from the book of thy remembrance, as in ver. 3 (1) above.　What he asks
as to his sins is that God will cancel and forget them.

12 (10.)　*A pure heart create for me, (O) God, and a fixed* (or *settled)
spirit renew within me.*　The petition in the first clause involves a confession of impurity, and of dependence on almighty power and sovereign grace
for its removal.　A pure heart is a familiar Scriptural figure for affections
free from the taint of sin.　See above, on Ps. xxiv. 4, and below, on Ps.
lxxiii. 1, and compare Mat. v. 8, Acts xv. 9.　While the use of the
word *create* implies the necessity of an almighty intervention, the additional
phrase *to* (or *for*) *me* suggests the idea of a gift which is often expressed
elsewhere in the same connection.　See Jer. xxiv. 7, Ezek. xi. 19, xxxvi.
26, and compare 1 Sam. x. 9.　The gift demanded in the last clause is that
of a firm, unwavering spirit, as opposed both to fickleness and cowardice,
Compare the use of the same adjective or participle in Ps. lvii. 8 (7),
lxxviii. 37, cxii. 7.　The word *renew* implies a previous possession of it,
derived not from nature but from grace, and interrrupted by his yielding
to temptation.　Though his faith and love could not utterly fail, his fixed-
ness of purpose was destroyed for the time, and could only be recovered
by a new conversion, as in the case of Peter (Luke xxii. 32).　*Within me, in
the midst* (or *in the inside*) *of me.*　The same Hebrew noun is repeatedly used
elsewhere, to denote the inward dispositions and affections, as distinguished

from a mere profession or appearance. See above, on Ps. v. 10 (9), xlix. 12 (11).

13 (11). *Cast me not away from thy presence, and thy Holy Spirit take not from me.* As indispensable prerequisites and means to the possession of such a heart and spirit as he had just prayed for, he recognises intimate communion with God, and the active influences of his Spirit. This prayer, unless we arbitrarily supply *again* or *for ever*, seems to imply that David was in actual possession of these blessings and afraid of losing them. There may be an intentional allusion to his own reception of the Spirit and to Saul's privation of it, as recorded in 1 Sam. xvi. 1, 7, 13. Compare 1 Sam. x. 6, 10, Isa. xi. 2.

14 (12). *Restore to me the joy of thy salvation, and* (with) *a willing spirit uphold me.* The first verb is a causative in Hebrew, meaning *make to return*, implying previous possession. The next phrase may be explained, according to a very common Hebrew idiom, *thy joy of salvation*, thy saving joy. See above, on Ps. ii. 6. But the obvious construction seems to yield the best sense, namely, that of joy occasioned by salvation, or relating to it as its subject. This joy was of course incompatible with any interruption of God's presence and the assurance of his favour. The word translated *willing* means spontaneous, prompt, forward to act without coercion ; then liberal, generous, noble. See above, on Ps. xlvii. 10 (9). It may be taken as an epithet of the Holy Spirit ; but the omission of the pronoun (*thy*) which determines it in the foregoing verse, and the repeated use of *spirit* in the context to denote his own heart, makes it more probable that this is the sense here likewise. By such a spirit of spontaneous conformity to God's will he desires and hopes to be *held up*, *i. e.* preserved from falling as he fell before.

15 (13). (Then) *will I teach transgressrs thy ways, and sinners unto thee shall return.* Here begins the expression of his thankfulness, or rather a description of the way in which he is determined to express it. The word supplied at the beginning points out the connection of the verses. " Then, when these petitions have been answered, I will teach," &c. The form of the Hebrew verb denotes a strong desire and a settled purpose, as if he had said, " I am resolved to teach." *Transgressors*, rebels, traitors, apostates. See above, on ver. 5 (3). *Thy ways*, as well the ways in which thou walkest as the ways in which thou requirest us to walk, the course of providence and the course of duty. See above, on Ps. xviii. 22, 31 (21, 30). In both these senses, he might naturally wish to " vindicate the ways of God to man." Of this resolution a partial fulfilment is recorded in Ps. xxxii. 8, 9. The effect of such instructions is recorded in the last clause of the verse before us. The Hebrew verb there used is not a passive (*shall be converted*), but an active form, *shall turn* or *return* to the Lord, perhaps with an allusion to the great original apostasy, in which the whole race is involved. See above, on Ps. xxii. 28 (27). To this verse there seems to be particular allusion in our Saviour's words to Peter, Luke xxii. 32.

16 (14). *Free me from blood, O God, God of my salvation,* (and) *my tongue shall celebrate thy righteousness.* The first clause contains the condition of the second, and the whole is equivalent to saying " If thou wilt save me, I will praise thee." *Blood*, literally *bloods*, the plural being idiomatically used when there is reference to murder. See above, on Ps. v. 7 (6). There may be an allusion to the frequent personification of the victim's blood, as crying out for vengeance on the murderer or pursuing him (Gen. iv. 10, ix. 5, 6). The verb translated *free* is applied to deliver-

ance from enemies in Ps. vii. 2 (1), and from sins (as here) in Ps.
xxxix. 9 (8).   The strength of the desire here expressed may derive some
illustration from the threatening in 2 Sam. xii. 9, 10.   *Celebrate*, applaud
by shout or song.   See above, on Ps. v. 12 (11), xx. 6 (5), xxxii. 11,
xxxiii. 1.

17 (15).   *Lord, my lips thou wilt open, and my mouth shall declare . thy
praise.*   The relation of the clauses to each other is the same as in the
foregoing verse.   "If thou wilt open my lips, my mouth," &c.   The first
clause therefore really includes a petition that his lips may be opened ; but
it also includes more, to wit, a confident anticipation that his prayer will
be granted.   The sense is therefore only partially expressed by rendering
the future as an imperative (*open thou my lips*).   The exact form as well
as the sense of the original is given in the Prayer-Book Version (*thou shalt
open my lips, O Lord*).   *Open my lips, i. e.* enable me to praise thee by
affording an occasion, and empower me to praise thee, by removing this
oppressive sense of guilt, which condemns me to perpetual silence.   Compare Isa. vi. 5–7.   *Declare*, tell, utter, or proclaim.   See above, Ps.
xix. 2 (1).

18 (16).   *For thou desirest not sacrifice, else would I give* (*it*), (*in*) *burnt-
offering thou delightest not.*   He now assigns the reason why he is determined to requite God's favour by becoming praise.   The literal translation
of the first clause is, *thou wilt not desire sacrifice, and I will give* (*it*), *i. e.*
but if thou dost desire it, I will give it.   By sacrifice we must here understand the mere material oblation, apart from the penitent and thankful
spirit, of which it was the required expression.   See above, on Ps. xl.
7. (6).   The parallel terms, *sacrifice* and *burnt-offering*, are commonly regarded as generic and specific expressions of the same idea.   But some
interpreters deny that they are ever confounded or promiscuously used, and
give the first the sense of *thank-offerings*, which are then joined with expiatory offerings, as a general description of all animal oblations.

19 (17).   *The sacrifices of God* (*are*) *a broken spirit ; a heart broken and
crushed,* (*O*) *God, thou wilt not despise.*   These are natural and perfectly
intelligible figures for profound and submissive sorrow on account of sin.
There is great significance and beauty in what seems at first to be a solecism in the language of the first clause.   *The sacrifice of God is a broken
spirit* might seem to be a more correct expression ; but it would have failed
to suggest the striking and important thought, that one such heart or spirit
is equivalent to all the various and complicated sacrifices of the ritual.   *The
sacrifices of God* are those which he requires and is willing to accept.   The
use of the word *contrite* in the English versions mars the beauty of the
metaphor, because that term is confined to the dialect of theology, whereas
the Latin *contritum*, from which it was borrowed, as well as the original
expression, exactly corresponds to *broken*, both in its literal and figurative
usage.   *Thou wilt not despise*, when it is offered, and especially when I
present it, as the solemn expression of my thanks for this deliverance.   The
substitution of the present for the future would both weaken and obscure
the sentence, and the same consideration might be urged in favour of a
strict translation in the verse preceding.   So far is a habitual sorrow for
sin from being inconsistent with the joy of God's salvation, that David here
engages to present it as a perpetual thank-offering.   Compare the language
of Hezekiah, Isa. xxxviii. 15.

20 (18).   *Do good, in thy favour, to Zion ; thou wilt build the walls of
Jerusalem.*   From his own personal necessities his mind now passes to

those of the whole church, of which he was the visible head and representative, thereby implying that his sense of guilt and danger had been aggravated by the thought of his official relation to God's people, who must have shared in his disgrace and punishment. See above, on Ps. iii. 4 (3), iv. 3 (2). The change of construction from the imperative to the future marks a natural transition from importunate desire to confident anticipation. See above, on ver. 9–11 (7–9). This delicate transition there is surely no need of obliterating by a gratuitous assimilation of the moods and tenses. The building of the walls is a poetical parallel to doing good or shewing favour, and the opposite of dismantling in Ps. lxxxix. 41 (40).

21 (19). *Then shalt thou be pleased with sacrifices of righteousness, burnt-offering and holocaust ; then shall they offer on thine altar bullocks.* Then *i. e.* when thou hast done good to Zion and fortified Jerusalem. *Sacrifices of righteousness*, righteous or right sacrifices. See above, on Ps. iv. 6 (5). Some have inferred from this verse, that the psalm was written in the Babylonish exile, when the temple was in ruins and the ceremonial law suspended, and that the Psalmist here anticipates the time when both should he restored. But this is forbidden by his saying, in ver. 18 (16), that if God desired burnt-offerings he would give them, plainly implying the continued observance of the sacrificial system. There is no ground, therefore, for disputing either the correctness of the title, which ascribes the psalm to David, or the genuineness of the last two verses, which some have rejected as an addition by a later hand. These verses are not only appropriate but necessary as a conclusion to the psalm, and every difficulty is removed by giving them their natural but figurative meaning, as an expression of desire and hope that God would favour his own people and graciously accept their service. *Holocaust* is here used to translate a single Hebrew word, meaning a sacrifice entirely consumed upon the altar. It does not describe something wholly distinct from the burnt-offering, but the burnt-offering itself considered as a complete and unreserved oblation. See 1 Sam. vii. 9. Bullocks are mentioned as the choicest victims in point of species, size, and age. By a slight change of construction we obtain the bold and striking declaration that the bullocks shall themselves ascend the altar, *i. e.* as a living and spontaneous sacrifice. Compare Isa. lx. 7.

Psalm 52

THIS psalm, besides the title, ver. 1, 2, contains three stanzas of three verses each. In the first, the Psalmist expostulates with an arrogant, cruel, and deceitful enemy, ver. 3–5 (1–3). In the second, he foretells the destruction of his enemy by the divine judgments, and the contempt to be excited by his folly, ver. 6–8 (4–6). In the third, he contrasts this fatal fruit of unbelief with the happy effects of his own trust in God, ver. 9–11 (7–9). The two *Selahs* in ver. 5, 7 (3, 5), have reference not so much to the form of the psalm as to the feelings of the Psalmist, and are therefore placed irregularly. See above, on Ps. iii. 3 (2). The variation of the English and the Hebrew Bible, in numbering the verses of this psalm, is the same, and arises from the same cause, as in the fifty-first.

1. *To the Chief Musician. Maschil. By David.* The psalm is expressly designated as a *Maschil* or didactic psalm, because its adaptation to this purpose might very easily be overlooked in consequence of its avowed

relation to a particular event in David's history. See above, on Ps. xxxii. 1, xlii. 1, xlv. 1. Though occasioned by this incident, however, it was written for the permanent and public use of the ancient church, and is therefore inscribed *to* (or *for*) *the Chief Musician*. See above, on Ps. iv. 1, li. 1.

2. *When Doeg the Edomite came and told Saul, and said unto him, David is come to the house of Ahimelech.* This is merely the beginning of the story, which is supposed to be familiar to the reader of the psalm, and which is given at length in 1 Sam. xxii. Doeg is mentioned only as the witness or informer, by whose means the matter came to Saul's knowledge. *When he came*, literally *in his coming*, the same form of expression as in Ps. li. 2.

3 (1). *Why wilt thou boast thyself in evil, mighty (man)? The mercy of the Almighty (is) all the day.* The future form of the verb suggests the idea of obstinate persistency. *Boast thyself in evil*, exult or triumph in the injury of others. The *mighty man* is not Doeg but Saul, who, of all the characters in sacred history, approaches nearest to the classical idea of a hero. There is something, therefore, of respect and admiration implied in the address, as if he had said " How can one who might have been so eminent in well-doing, glory in his shame or boast himself in evil ?" In the last clause there is an obvious antithesis between the malice of this mighty man and the unfailing goodness of the mighty God. The particular divine name here used therefore is peculiarly significant. See above, on Ps. v. 5 (4), l. 1. As if he had said, " Mighty and malicious as thou art, the might and mercy of Jehovah are still greater." *All the day, i. e.* perpetual, unceasing. See above, on Ps. xlii. 11 (10).

4 (2). *Mischiefs will thy tongue devise, like a razor whetted, working deceitfully.* The first word means calamitous events, brought on one man by the malice of another. See above, on Ps. v. 10 (9), xxxviii. 13 (12), and below, on Ps. lvii. 2 (1). The distinctive meaning of the future is the same as in ver. 3 (1). The *tongue* is here said to meditate or devise mischief, because it is personified, or poetically substituted for the speaker. The allusion is to Saul's cutting words when he accused Ahimelech and David of conspiracy against him (1 Sam. xxii. 13). This false charge, or the tongue which uttered it, is likened to a razor, not merely sharp but sharpened, whetted, for the purpose or occasion. See above, on Ps. xlv. 6 (5). Similar comparisons occur in Ps. lv. 22 (21), lvii. 5 (4), lix. 8 (7), lxiv. 4 (3), Jer. ix. 2, 7 (3, 8). *Working deceitfully*, literally *deceit* or *fraud*. These words may be grammatically referred to the speaker or his tongue as practising deceit; but it yields a more striking sense to understand them of the razor, as working deceitfully, *i. e.* moving silently and smoothly, when it cuts most keenly.

5 (3). *Thou hast loved evil (more) than good, falsehood (more) than speaking righteousness.* The past tense, like the futures in the foregoing verses, includes the idea of the present; but unlike them, it represents the love of sin as already long-continued and habitual. Compare the form of expression with that in Ps. xlv. 8 (7). *Righteousness* includes *truth* or *veracity*, as the genus comprehends the species. The particular unrighteousness here meant is falsehood, as appears from the antithesis. The *selah* tacitly suggests the writer's abhorrence of that which he describes.

6 (4). *Thou hast loved all devouring words, tongue of fraud.* This is not so much a continuation of the foregoing discourse, as a resumption or recapitulation for the purpose of drawing a conclusion from it. In periodic

style, the connection of the ideas might be thus exhibited: " Since then thou lovest, &c., therefore God will," &c. *Devouring words*, literally *words of swallowing* or deglutition. The second noun occurs only here; but the verb to *swallow up* is continually used in Hebrew to express the idea of complete destruction. See above, on Ps. xxi. 10 (9), xxxv. 25. *Tongue of deceit* or *deceitful tongue*. This phrase may be governed by the verb, *thou hast loved all devouring words (and* or *even) a deceitful tongue.* But it adds to the strength of the expression, and agrees better with the form of the context, to make it an apostrophe or direct address to the deceitful tongue itself.

7 (5). *(So) likewise shall God destroy thee for ever; he shall take thee away, and pluck thee out of (thy) tent, and root thee out of the land of life. Selah.* The particle at the beginning, *also, likewise,* shews the dependence of this verse upon the one before it, which is really conditional though not in form. " As thou, on thy part, lovest all devouring words, so likewise God, on his part, will destroy thee." No exact translation can convey the full force of the verbs in this verse, which suggests a variety of striking figures for destruction or extermination. The first denotes properly the act of pulling down or demolishing a house (Lev. xiv. 45), and this would also seem to be the primary meaning of the third (Prov. xv. 25), although some suppose it to denote the act of pulling up, and to be the opposite of *plant*, as the first verb is of *build*. The second verb, in every other place where it occurs, has reference to the handling and carrying of fire or coals. See Prov. vi. 27, xxv. 22, Isa. xxx. 14. To a Hebrew reader, therefore, it would almost necessarily suggest, not the general idea of removal merely, but the specific one of removing or taking away like fire, *i. e.* as coals are swept out from a hearth, or otherwise extinguished. The remaining verb adds to these figures that of violent eradication, and is well represented by its English equivalent. The *land of life*, or, as it is commonly translated, *and of the living*, is a poetical description of life itself, or the present state of existence, under the figure of a country. See above, on Ps. xxvii. 13. The quick recurrence of the pause implies excited feeling, and invites attention to the threatening which immediately precedes.

8 (6). *And the righteous shall see, and they shall fear, and at him they shall laugh.* The fear meant is that religious awe produced by any clear manifestation of God's presence and his power. In Ps. lxiv. 9, 10 (8, 9), it is assumed to be compatible with joy, and here with laughter at the wicked, not a selfish exultation in his sufferings, which is explicitly condemned in the Old Testament (Prov. xxiv. 17, Job xxxi. 29), but that sense of the absurdity of sin, which must be strongest in the purest minds, and cannot, therefore, be incompatible with pity, the rather as it is ascribed to God himself (Ps. ii. 4). The paronomasia of the verbs translated *see* and *fear* is the same as in Ps. xl. 4 (3). *Shall see, i. e.* the destruction threatened in ver. 7 (6). *At him*, the person thus destroyed, the same who is addressed directly in the foregoing context. The *enallage personœ* may be avoided by exchanging *at him* for *at it, i. e.* the destruction itself; but this is not so agreeable to Hebrew usage, which always prefers personal to abstract forms of speech.

9 (7). *Behold the man* (who) *will not make God his strength, but will trust in the increase of his wealth,* (and) *will be strong in his wickedness.* This may be regarded as the language of the laughers mentioned in ver. 8 (6). *Behold the man, see* to what he is reduced. The effect of the *behold* is similar to that of the interrogation in Isa. xiv. 16. The word translated

man is not one of the usual terms, but one implying strength or power, so
that its use here gives a kind of sarcastic import to the passage. See the
analogous use of an opposite expression in Ps. viii. 5 '(4), x. 18. The
future expresses fixed determination and anticipated perseverance in refusing.
Make, literally *place* or *set*. See above, on Ps. xl. 5 (4). *His strength*, or
more exactly, his *stronghold* or fortress. See above, on Ps. xxvii. 1,
xxxvii. 39, xliii. 2. *Increase*, or simply abundance, greatness. See above,
on Ps. v. 8 (7), li. 3 (1). The word translated *wickedness* is the singular
of that translated *mischiefs* in ver. 4 (2) above. It seems to signify particularly an inclination to malicious mischief.

10 (8). *And I (am) like a green olive-tree in the house of God, I have
trusted in the mercy of God (to) eternity and perpetuity.* He expects not
only the destruction of the wicked but his own salvation. To express the
connection of the verses clearly, our idiom would require an' adversative
particle at the beginning, *but I*. See above, on Ps. ii. 6. A verdant fruitful tree is a favourite emblem of prosperity. See above, on Ps. i. 3. The
olive is here specified, as palms and cedars are in Ps. xcii. 13, 14 (12, 13).
The imagery of the verse before us is copied in Jer. xi. 16. *The house of
God*, the tabernacle, considered as his earthly residence, in which he enter-
tains his friends and provides for his own household. See above, on Ps.
xv. 1, xxii. 6, xxvii. 4, 5, xxxvi. 9 (8). The mixed metaphors only shew
that the whole description is a figurative one, and should be so interpreted.
I have (already) *trusted*, which includes his present trust, but also includes
more, to wit, that it is not a new or sudden impulse, but a settled habit of
his soul. The two nouns, *eternity* and *perpetuity*, are combined in the
adverbial sense of *for ever and ever*. See above, on Ps. x. 16, xxi. 5 (4),
xlv. 7 (6), xlviii. 15 (14). This qualifying phrase relates, not to the act,
but to the object, of his trust. His meaning is not, " I will trust for ever
in God's mercy," which would have required a future verb ; but, " I have
already trusted, and do still trust, in his mercy, as a mercy that will last
for ever."

11 (9). *I will thank thee to eternity because thou hast done (it), and will
hope (in) thy name—because it is good—before thy saints.* The common
version of the first verb (*praise*) is not sufficiently specific, as it properly
denotes a particular kind of praise, namely, that for benefits received. See
above, on Ps. vi. 6 (5), vii. 18 (17), xlix. 19 (18). The object of the verb
hast done is to be supplied from the context. See above, on Ps. xxii. 32
(31), xxxvii. 5, xxxix. 10 (9). *Thy name*, the manifestation of thy nature.
See above, on Ps. v. 12 (11), xx. 2 (1), xxiii. 3, xlviii. 11 (10). To expect
God's name, or wait for it, is to trust in the future exercise and exhibition
of the same divine perfections which have been exhibited already. The
common version, *I will wait on thy name*, is not so happy as the one in the
Prayer Book, *I will hope in thy name*. Here again, as in ver. 10 (8), the
epexegetical clause, *for it is good*, relates not to the act of expectation, but
its object. He does not mean, " because it is good to hope in thy name,"
but " because thy name is good, and is therefore to be hoped in." This is
clear from the analogy of Ps. liv. 8 (6), lxix. 17 (16), cix. 21, which also
shews that the concluding words, *before thy saints*, are to be construed neither
with what follows, *it is good before thy saints, i. e.* in their estimation, nor
with the remoter antecedent, *I will thank thee*, but with the neare antecedent, *I will wait for thy name before thy saints, i. e.* I will profess my trust
in thy mercy, not in private merely, but in the presence of thy people, of
the church. Compare Ps. xxii. 23 (22). *For it is good* must then be read

as a parenthesis. *Thy saints*, the merciful objects of thy mercy. See above, on Ps. iv. 4 (3), l. 5. It is here used simply as a general designation or description of God's people.

Psalm 53

A SECOND edition of the fourteenth psalm, with variations, more or less important, in each verse. That either of these compositions is an incorrect copy of the other is highly improbable, because two such copies of the same psalm would not have been retained in the collection, and because the variations are too uniform, consistent, and significant, to be the work of chance or mere traditional corruption. That the changes were deliberately made by a later writer is improbable, because such a liberty would hardly have been taken with a psalm of David, and because the later form, in that case, would either have been excluded from the Psalter, or substituted for the first form, or immediately connected with it. The only satisfactory hypothesis is, that the original author afterwards re-wrote it, with such modifications as were necessary to bring out certain points distinctly, but without any intention to supersede the use of the original composition, which therefore still retains its place in the collection. This supposition is confirmed by the titles, which ascribe both psalms to David. Of this kind of *retractatio*, which is not unknown to the practice of uninspired hymnologists, we have already met with a remarkable example in the case of David. See above, the concluding note on Ps. xviii. p. 87. As a general fact, it may be stated, that the variations in the psalm before us are such as render the expression stronger, bolder, and in one or two cases more obscure and difficult. To these variations the remarks which follow will be restricted. For the exposition of the parts which are common to both psalms, the reader is referred to that of Ps. xiv.

1. *To the Chief Musician—upon Mahalath—Maschil—by David.* Between the inscription to the Chief Musician and the name of David, which are also found at the beginning of Ps. xiv., we have here two additional expressions. The first of these is by some regarded as the name or description of an instrument; but as it is so used nowhere else, and as forms almost identical occur more than once in the sense of sickness or disease (Exod. xv. 26, Prov. xviii. 14, 2 Chron. xxi. 15), it seems most natural to take the phrase as an enigmatical enunciation of the subject of the psalm, which is in strict accordance both with general usage and with that of David in particular. See above, on Ps. v. 1, xxii. 1, xlv. 1. By *disease* we may then understand the spiritual malady with which mankind are all infected, and which is really the theme or subject of the composition. In the only other title where it reappears (Ps. lxxxviii. 1), it denotes corporeal disease. The other addition (*maschil*) describes the psalm as a didactic one. See above, on Ps. lii. 1.

2 (1). *The fool hath said in his heart, There is no God. They have done corruptly, they have done abominable wickedness, there is none doing good.* See above, on Ps. xiv. 1. The only variation in this verse is the substitution of (עָוֶל) *iniquity* for (עֲלִילָה) *deed* or *act*. Instead of saying, *they have made* (their) *conduct abominable*, the Psalmist uses the stronger expression, *they have made iniquity abominable*, or *done abominably* (in their) *wickedness*.

3 (2). *God from heaven has looked down on the sons of man, to see if there is* (any) *acting wisely, seeking God.* See above, on Ps. xiv. 2. The only

difference in the Hebrew of these verses is that the name *Elohim* is here substituted for *Jehovah*. The same change occurs below, in ver. 5, 6, 7 (4, 5, 6). The name *Jehovah* is not used at all in the psalm before us, but occurs four times in Ps. xiv., and *Elohim* thrice. This difference seems to mark Ps. liii. as the later composition, in which the writer aimed at an external uniformity, which did not occur to him at first. This is a much more natural supposition than that he afterwards varied what was uniform at first. The attempts which have been made to account, still more particularly, for the use of the divine names in these two psalms, have entirely failed.

4 (3). *All of it has apostatised; together they have putrefied; there is none doing good; there is not even one.* See above, on Ps. xiv. 3. For *all of it* we there have *the whole*, *i. e.* the whole human race. The same thing seems to be intended by the more obscure phrase, *all of it*, in which the pronoun may refer to *man*, in the collective sense of *mankind* or the human race. The idea of departure from God, apostasy, is expressed in the parallel places by two verbs almost identical in form (סר and סג), the one of which means properly to turn aside and the other to turn back.

5 (4). *Do they not know—(these) workers of iniquity—eating my people (as) they eat bread—(and on) God call not?* See above, on Ps. xiv. 4. The only variation here, besides the change of the divine name which has been already mentioned, is the omission of the *all* before *workers of iniquity*. This has been noted by some critics as the only case in which the language of the fourteenth psalm is stronger than the parallel expression of the fifty-third.

6 (5). *There have they feared a fear, because God hath scattered the bones of thy besieger; thou hast put (them) to shame, because God hath rejected them.* See above, on Ps. xiv. 5, 6. The design to strengthen the expression is particularly clear in this case, where two verses are compresed into one, and the other changes all enhance the emphasis. Thus, instead of a general assurance of divine protection, *God is in the righteous generation*, we have here a description of their enemies' destruction, in the most poetical and striking terms, *God hath scattered the bones of thy besieger*, literally *thy encamper*, him that encampeth against thee. So, too, instead of the complaint, that the wicked treat the faith of pious sufferers with contempt—*the counsel of the sufferer ye will shame, because Jehovah is his refuge*—we have here the tables turned upon the scoffers by the scorn both of God and man—*thou hast put to shame* (the individuals included in the collective phrase *thy besieger*), *because God has rejected them*, an act implying both abhorrence and contempt. In this, which is by far the most considerable variation of the two editions, the existence of design is so apparent, that the supposition of an inadvertent or fortuitous corruption seems preposterous. So far are the two psalms from being contradictory. or even inconsistent, that they might be sung together, by alternate or responsive choirs, with the happiest effect. Nothing can be more natural, therefore, than the supposition that David gave the psalm this new shape, to express the same essential feelings in a higher degree, and a more emphatic form.

7 (6). *Who will give out of Zion salvations (to) Israel—in God's returning (to) the captivity of his people—let Jacob exult, let Israel joy!* See above, on Ps. xiv. 7. The only variations are the change of *Jehovah* to *Elohim*, and of the singular *salvation* to its plural, denoting variety and fulness. See above, on Ps. xviii. 51 (50). The exact translation is *salvations of Israel*, and the meaning of the next clause, " when God revisits (or in God's revisiting) his captive people."

Psalm 54

1. *To the Chief Musician. With* (or *on*) *stringed instruments. A didactic psalm. By David.* This is the title of Ps. iv., but with a change of the generic term *mizmor* to the specific one *maschil.* See above, on Ps. liii. 1. According to some modern interpreters, the plural *neginoth* does not denote a plurality of stringed instruments, but simply that kind of music, with its complex variety of tones. The psalm consists of a prayer for deliverance from wicked enemies, ver. 3–5 (1-3), with a confident anticipation of success, and a promise of thanksgiving, ver. 6-9 (4–7). As to the numbering of the verses, see above, on Ps. li. 1, lii. 1.

2. *In the coming of the Ziphites, and they said to Saul,* (*Is*) *not David hiding himself with us ?* The verse gives the historical occasion of the composition, in the same form as in the titles of Ps. li. and lii. Such an occurrence is twice recorded in the history, 1 Sam. xxiii. 19, xxvi. 1. The verbal coincidence is greater in the first case. The words of the Ziphites seem to have been remembered on account of some peculiarity in the expression, perhaps the use of the reflexive participle (מִסְתַּתֵּר), which remains unchanged in all three places, the earliest of which is probably the one before us. The interrogation implies surprise that Saul should be ignorant of what was so notorious. *Hiding himself,* now engaged in doing so, not merely wont to do so, or already hidden. *With us,* among us, or in our land, *i. e.* the wilderness or pasture ground of Ziph (1 Sam. xxiii. 14, 15), in or near which was a town of the same name (Josh. xv. 55, 2 Chron. xi. 8), the ruins of which are thought to be still visible, not far from what the natives call *Tell Ziph,* or the Hill of Ziph. (Robinson's Palestine, II. 191.)

3 (1). *O God, by thy name save me, and by thy might thou wilt judge me.* The insensible transition from the imperative to the future shews the confidence with which the prayer is offered. *By thy name, i. e.* the exercise of those perfections which have been already manifested. See above, on Ps. lii. 11 (9). That it is not a mere periphrasis for God himself, is clear from the parallel expression, *might* or *power. Judge me,* do me justice, vindicate my innocence, by saving me from spiteful enemies and false accusers. See above, on Ps. vii. 9 (8), xxvi. 1.

4 (2). *O God, hear my prayer, give ear to the sayings of my mouth.* See above, on Ps. iv. 2 (1), v. 2 (1).

5 (3). *For strangers are risen up against me, and oppressors seek my soul* (or *life*); *they have not set God before them. Selah.* To the earnest petitions in the two preceding verses he now adds a particular description of his danger. *Strangers,* not foreigners, but aliens in spirit, both to him and to Jehovah, with special reference to Saul. See below, on Ps. cxx. 5. *Oppressors,* persecutors, tyrants. The original expression implies the possession of power, and its lawless exercise. See above, on Ps. xxxvii. 35. Not to set God before them is to act as if they did not remember or believe in his existence and his presence. The *Selah* indicates a pause of indignation and abhorrence. See above, on Ps. lii. 5 (3).

6 (4). *Behold, God* (*is*) *a helper for me ; the Lord is among the upholders of my soul.* From the party of his enemies he looks to that of his defenders, and joyfully recognises God, not merely *with,* but *in* (the midst of) *them,* among them. The *behold* is expressive of surprise, and at the same time of a perspicacious faith. With the form of expression in the first clause, compare Ps. xxx. 11 (10); with the second Ps. cxviii. 7, Judges

xi. 35. The upholders of his soul are the defenders of his life against those who seek it. See above, ver. 5 (3). *Adhonai*, the divine name properly translated *Lord*, because expressive of God's sovereignty. It is peculiarly appropriate here, where he is claiming God as his protector.

7 (5). *The evil shall return to my enemies; in thy truth destroy them.* The future here runs into the imperative, as the imperative does into the future in ver. 3 (1), above. The imperative in this case is only a stronger form of prediction. *The evil*, which they mean to do me. *Return to*, or upon, them, *i.e.* shall befall themselves. See above, on Ps. vii. 17 (16), This is the sense required by the reading in the text (יָשׁוּב), which the modern critics commonly regard as the most ancient. The marginal or masoretic reading (יָשִׁיב) must be rendered, *he will cause to return*, repay, requite. *Thy truth*, the truth of thy promises and threatenings, thy veracity. See above, on Ps. xxx. 10 (9). The certain foresight of the doom of the wicked, which is expressed in the first clause, makes the prayer (if such it be considered) in the first clause a mere iteration of the previous threatening. A prayer that God will do what we are certain that he will do can be little more than an expression of that certainty. See above, on Ps. v. 11 (10).

8 (6). *With a free-will offering will I sacrifice unto thee; I will praise thy name, Jehovah, for it is good.* In the confident assurance of a favourable answer to his prayer, he promises a suitable acknowledgment. See above, on Ps. v. 8 (7). A *free-will* or *voluntary offering*, as opposed to one prescribed by law, not to one rendered obligatory by a vow, for then a voluntary offering would in this case be impossible. The Hebrew word is the technical term applied to such an offering in the law. See Lev. vii. 16, xxii. 23, and compare Exod. xxv. 2, xxxv. 29, Num. xv. 3. With the last clause compare Ps. lii. 11 (9).

9 (7). *For out of all distress he hath delivered me, and on my enemies my eye has looked.* In his confident assurance of a favourable issue, he speaks of it, though future, as already past. The sudden change of person, may be avoided by translating the first verb, *it (i. e.* thy name) *has delivered me*, according to the prayer in ver. 3 (1). *My eye has looked* or *gazed*, with an implication of delight, or at least of acquiescence, which is commonly conveyed by this construction. See above, on Ps. l. 23. This kind of satisfaction in the execution of God's threatenings is sinful only when combined with selfish malignity. Apart from this corrupt admixture, it is inseparable from conformity of will and coincidence of judgment with God. The same kind and degree of acquiescence which is felt by holy angels in heaven may surely be expressed by saints on earth, especially in their collective capacity as a church, in whose name the Psalmist is here speaking, and not merely in his own or that of any other individual.

Psalm 55

1. *To the Chief Musician. With* (or *on*) *stringed instruments   A didactic psalm. By David.* The psalm is designated as a *Maschil*, because it might at first sight seem to have relation merely to a case of personal maltreatment and distress, whereas it is a general description of the sufferings of God's people, or the righteous as a class, at the hands of false friends and malignant enemies. Although there seem to be allusions to the writer's own experience, in the times both of Saul and Absalom, the

whole description can be applied exclusively to neither. The only natural division of the psalm is the one suggested by the fact, that in the first part the sufferer complains of his enemies in general, ver. 2–12 (1–11); in the second, he singles out the case of one who had seemed to be his friend, but treacherously turned against him, ver. 13–16 (12–15); in the third, he confidently anticipates his own deliverance and the destruction of his enemies, ver. 17–26 (16–25).

2 (1.) *Give ear, O God, to my prayer, and hide not thyself from my supplication.* This is the general introductory petition, which is afterwards amplified and rendered more specific. The last word strictly means a cry or prayer for mercy. See above, on Ps. vi. 10 (9). To hide one's self is an expression used in the law to describe the act of wilfully withholding aid from one who needs it. See Deut. xxii. 1–4, and compare Isa. lviii. 7.

3 (2). *Hearken to me and answer me; I will give loose to my thought, and I will make a noise.* The first verb means to *attend*, especially to one speaking, to listen, to hearken. See above, on Ps. v. 3 (2), x. 17, xvii. 1. *Answer* or *hear*, in the sense of receiving a prayer favourably. See above, on Ps. iii. 5 (4), xxxviii. 16 (15). The literal translation of the next words is, *I will suffer to wander iu my thinking, i. e.* I will let my mind wander, or my thoughts rove as they will. He is resolved not only to think freely but to express his thoughts aloud. The same use of the Hebrew verb occurs in Micah ii. 12. The thinking or meditation here meant is reflection on his sufferings, to which the Hebrew verb is specially applied. With the whole verse, and with this clause in particular, compare Job vii. 11.

4 (3). *From the voice of the enemy, from before the persecution of the wicked; for they will shake over me iniquity, and in wrath will oppose me.* He now declares from what his distress arises. The preposition, in Hebrew as in English, has a causal meaning, or at lest suggests a relation of cause and effect. *From the voice, i. e.* because of it. *From before* or *from the face* conveys the same idea still more strongly, by a kind of personification of the evil dreaded. *Persecution of the wicked :* compare the *oppression of the enemy*, in Ps. xlii. 10 (9). *Shake over me*, or cause to slide upon me, a striking figure for the wilful infliction of evil on another. *Iniquity* may here be put, as it sometimes is, for active wickedness towards others, the cause of suffering rather than suffering itself. With this clause compare Ps. xli. 9 (8). *Oppose me*, be my adversaries, whether in the way of resistance or assault. The Hebrew verb is a cognate form to that from which comes *Satan* or the *Adversary*.

5 (4). *My heart writhes in the midst of me, and terrors of death have fallen upon me.* The future form of the first verb implies an apprehension that the pain will continue and be permanent. *In the midst of me*, inside of me, within me. He is not merely involved in outward troubles, but pained at heart. *Terrors of death* might be strictly understood as meaning fear or dread of death; but it agrees better with the strong figurative language of the first clause, to take it in the sense of deadly, mortal terrors. An analogous expression is *death-shade* or shadow of death. See above, on Ps. xxiii. 4, xliv. 20 (19). The figure of falling necessarily suggests the idea of infliction by a superior power.

6 (5). *Fear and trembling enter into me, and horror hath covered me.* The future in the first clause represents the action as not yet completed, and might be rendered, they are entering or about to enter. The Hebrew verb with this preposition denotes more than *come upon;* it describes the terror as not only on him but within him. The word translated *horror* is a

stronger synonyme of *trembling*, and might be translated *shuddering* or *a shudder*. *Covered me, i. e.* overspread or overwhelmed me.

7 (6). *And I said, who will give me a pinion like the dove ? I will fly away and be at rest.* This is equivalent to saying, if I had the pinions of a dove, I would fly away, &c. *Who will give* is an idiomatic optative expression, tantamount to saying, *Oh that I had*, &c. See above, on Ps. xiv. 7. The word translated *pinion* properly denotes the *penna major* or flag-feather of a bird's wing, and is here put poetically for the wings themselves. The two last verbs are in the paragogic or augmented form, expressing strong desire or settled purpose. See above, on Ps. ii. 3. The last verb usually means *to dwell*, but has either the primary or secondary sense of reposing, resting. See above, on Ps. xxxvii. 3. The first verb is immediately dependent on the last of the preceding verse, a grammatical relation which may be expressed thus in our idiom : " horror hath covered me so that I say," &c.

8 (7). *Lo, I will wander far, I will lodge in the wilderness. Selah.* The *lo* or *behold* is tantamount to pointing with the finger, or to saying *there ! see there !* The next phrase is highly idiomatic and literally means, " I will make remote to wander." To *lodge* is here to take up one's abode, to dwell, as in Ps. xxv. 13. *The wilderness*, not necessarily a barren desert, but an uninhabited region, the essential idea here being that of separation from human society, a strong though indirect mode of affirming its extreme corruption. The strength of the feeling which prompted this desire is indicated by a solemn pause.

9 (8). *I will hasten my escape from rushing wind, from tempest.* Another construction of the first clause makes the verb intransitive and the noun a local one, as indicated by its form, *I will hasten (to) my refuge.* It is better, however, to give the hiphil verb its proper meaning, and nouns of the form here used denote not only the place of action but the act itself. *My escape*, literally *an escape for me* or *for myself*. The preposition in the last clause, though it properly means *from*, is constantly employed in Hebrew to denote or indicate comparison. If thus explained in this case, it would make the clause descriptive of the speed with which he wishes to escape, *more than the rushing wind and tempest*. This sense is preferred by some interpreters; but the other is more obvious and simple, and is also recommended by the frequent representation of calamity under the figure of a storm or tempest, which would hardly have been joined with that of wind, if the only idea meant to be conveyed had been that of great velocity.

10 (9). *Destroy, O Lord, divide their tongue ; for I have seen violence and strife in the city.* The first word properly means *swallow up*. See above, on Ps. xxi. 10 (9). The object to be supplied is not *their tongue* but *themselves*. *Divide their tongue, i. e.* confound their speech or make it unintelligible, and as a necessary consequence confound their counsels. There is obvious reference to the confusion of tongues at Babel (Gen. xi. 7-9), as a great historical example of the way in which God is accustomed and determined to defeat the purposes of wicked men and execute his own. The word translated *cruelty* denotes violent injustice, or injustice accompanied by violence. See above, on Ps. vii. 17 (16). *In the city* is supposed by some to mean nothing more than among men, in human society ; but the words could hardly fail to suggest to any Hebrew reader the idea of the holy city, as the place directly meant, although the words themselves may be applied to any other place where the same state of things exist.

11 (10). *Day and night they will surround her on her wall; and iniquity*

and trouble will be in the midst of her. The Violence and Strife of the preceding verse are here personified as a besieging enemy. At the same time the interior is occupied by Iniquity and Trouble, no less formidable enemies. *Her walls,* those of *the city* mentioned in the foregoing verse. Iniquity and trouble are here, and often elsewhere, put together as cause and effect, the last denoting the distress or trouble which the wickedness of one man brings upon another. See above, on Ps. vii. 15 (14),

12 (11). *Mischiefs (are) in the midst of her, and from her street will not depart oppression and deceit,* The first word in Hebrew necessarily suggests the two ideas of *calamities* and *crimes, i. e.* calamities occasioned by the crimes of others. See above, on Ps. v. 10 (9), xxxviii. 13 (12), lii. 4, 9 (2, 7). The word translated *street* denotes a wide place, and is specially applied to the square or open space surrounding the gates of oriental cities, and used both for markets and for courts of justice. See Neh. viii. 1, 3, 16. The word therefore very nearly corresponds to the Greek *agora* and the Latin *forum,* and may be here used to suggest the idea both of legal and commercial malfeasance. Neither their markets nor their courts are ever free from these two forms of gross injustice, namely, fraud and violence.

13 (12). *For (it is) not an enemy (that) will revile me, else would I bear it ; (it is) not one hating me (that) has magnified (himself) against me, else would I hide myself from him.* The Hebrew word answering to *else,* is, in both these cases, the usual copulative particle, and the original construction seems to be, *and* (if it is) *I will bear it, and* (if it is) *I will hide myself.* See above, on Ps. li. 18 (16). The act of reviling here includes both calumny and insult. The future in the first clause suggests the idea of an indignity or injury about to be endured. As if he had said, "when I go forth among my neighbours, it is not my open enemy that will malign me." But that such treatment had already been experienced, is intimated by the preterite of the last clause. The verb to *magnify* is here used reflexively or absolutely, as in Ps. xxxv. 26, xxxviii. 15 (16). There is no need therefore of supposing an ellipsis, or identifying this form of expression with the one in Ps. xli. 10 (9). *Hide myself,* literally *be hidden ;* but the passive forms in Hebrew not unfrequently imply a reflex act, like the middle voice in Greek. The negation in this verse is of course not absolute but relative, and must be qualified by due regard to the circumstances of the case. That he was reproached and threatened by avowed enemies, is not only a frequent subject of complaint elsewhere, but sufficiently implied in ver. 4 (3) above. The true solution of this seeming contradiction is, that he here passes from a general description of the prevalent iniquity to a particular case, in which his feelings were personally interested. In this particular case, it was not an open enemy that slandered or insulted him. It is therefore as if he had said, "But it is not of this open and unblushing wickedness that I especially complain, but rather of the perfidy of false friends." Thus understood, the verse, instead of contradicting ver. 4 (3), presupposes what is there affirmed.

14 (13). *But thou, a man mine equal, my associate, my acquaintance.* It is a striking illustration of the difference between the Hebrew and English idiom, that the former uses *and* at the beginning of this sentence, where in English *but* is absolutely indispensable. The word for man is that denoting frailty and mortality. See above, on Ps. viii. 5 (4), ix. 20, 21 (19, 20), x. 18. But it seems to be used here without any emphasis, in simple apposition with what follows, or as a vocative, *thou, O man, mine equal.* This

last expression is in Hebrew, *according to my valuation*, the noun being a
technical term of the Mosaic Law, denoting the official estimation of the
priest, in certain cases of redemption or pecuniary penalty. See Lev.
v. 15, 18, xxvii. 12. The whole phrase here employed is understood by
some to mean *one whom I value, i. e.* highly, or more specifically, *one whom
I value as myself.* More probably, however, it means one who is (or may
be) estimated at the same rate with myself, which is precisely the idea
conveyed by the common version, *my equal*, one of my own rank and circle,
my associate. This last is the sense put by the modern interpreters on the
next word in Hebrew. The old translation (*guide*) rests on a doubtful
etymology, and the authority of the ancient versions. (LXX ἡγεμών. Vulg.
dux). *Acquaintance* seems to be a weaker expression than the others; but
the Hebrew word always implies very intimate association. See above, Ps.
xxxi. 12 (11), and below, Ps. lxxxviii. 9, 19 (8, 18).

15 (14). (*With*) *whom we take sweet counsel ; in the house of God we march
with noise.* The future forms can only be accounted for by supposing that
he here anticipates a violation of the laws of friendship which had not yet
visibly occurred. The false friend, of whom he is complaining, seems to
be one with whom he is still intimate, but whose defection he clearly fore-
saw. As if he had said, " With this man I must still continue to be associated, although he is eventually to betray me." In this particular, the
case described resembles that of our Lord and Judas Iscariot, which may
indeed be considered as included in the general description. The form of
the first clause is idiomatic and peculiar : *who* (or *as to whom*) *together we
will sweeten counsel*, or rather confidential intercourse. See above, on Ps.
xxv. 14. The other clause may possibly mean, *we march to the house of
God.* But the strict sense of the particle may be retained and the whole
referred to solemn processions within the sacred enclosure or court of the
tabernacle. *With noise, i. e.* with festive tumult. See above, on Ps.
xlii. 5 (4).

16 (15) *Desolations* (*are*) *upon them! They shall go down to Sheol alive!
For evils are in their dwellings, in their heart.* The optative form given to
this sentence in most versions is entirely gratuitous. All that the Hebrew
words express is a confident anticipation. The common version of the first
words (*let death seize upon them*) is founded on the masoretic reading (יַשִּׁיא
מָוֶת) ; but the best critics now prefer the older reading in the text
(יַשִּׁימוֹת), which, instead of a verb and a singular noun, exhibits one noun
in the plural number, meaning *desolations*, and agreeing with the substantive verb understood. *Upon them*, hovering or impending over them.
Sheol, the grave, the state of the dead, the wide old English sense of *hell*.
See above, on Ps. vi. 6 (5). There is an obvious allusion to another great
historical type of God's retributory judgments, the destruction of Korah
and his company, who *went down alive into the pit*, Num. xvi. 33. The
word *quick*, in the common English version of this sentence, is an adjective synonymous with *living* or *alive*, and not an adverb meaning *soon* or
swiftly. *Evils, i. e.* evil deeds and evil thoughts. *In their heart*, or inside,
inner part, as in Ps. v. 10 (9), xlix. 12 (11). This is a much better sense
than *in the midst of them*, among them.

17 (16). *I to God will call, and Jehovah will save me.* The pronoun is
emphatic, I on my part. While they are brought to desolation and to
death, I, on the contrary, will call to God. If the use of two divine names
has any significance beyond the requisitions of the parallelism, the meaning

may be, " I will call to God, and as the covenant God of Israel he will save me." Compare Ps. xviii. 4 (3).

18 (17). *Evening and morning and noon I will muse and murmur—and he has heard my voice.* The first clause is supposed by some to prove that the observance of three stated hours of prayer was as old as David; others suppose the observance to have been suggested by the clause itself. But the natural and obvious division of the day here mentioned may have given occasion both to the clause and the observance. *Muse and murmur* is a combination descriptive of prayer, both as mentally conceived and audibly expressed. *Murmur* is perhaps not strong enough to convey the full sense of the Hebrew verb, which elsewhere means to make a loud noise. See above, on Ps. xlii. 6, 12 (5, 11), xlvi. 4, 7 (3, 6). The assimilation or confusion of the tenses in this verse by some translators is not only arbitrary but injurious to the sense. What is mentioned in the first clause as still future is recorded in the last clause as already past. As if he had said, " Thus did I resolve to pray, and now my prayer has been already made and answered." Such transitions are among the characteristic beauties of the Psalter, and ought not to be gratuitously sacrificed, still less at the expense of violating usage and the rules of grammar.

19 (18). *He redeemed in peace my soul from the war against me, for many were with me.* *In peace*, or *with peace*, as the result of this redemption. *Against me*, literally *to me*, the war that was to me, that I had. The last clause, to an English ear, conveys the idea that his friends or champions were many, but the meaning of the Hebrew is directly opposite, *with me* being used in such connections to denote a relation of hostility, as we speak of fighting, quarrelling, contending *with* one. In either case, the particle expresses really no more than joint or simultaneous action, the idea of enmity or opposition being gathered from the context. The literal translation of the last clause is, *in many were (those) with me, i. e.* consisting in many. The adverse party was composed of many individuals. This usage of the *in* is strictly appropriate only to numerals. See Deut. x. 22, xxviii. 62.

20 (19). *God will hear and answer them, and* (He) *inhabiting antiquity* (will hear and answer those) *to whom there are no changes, and* (who) *fear not God.* As he has heard me in mercy, so will he hear them in wrath. As he has answered my prayer in the way described above, ver 19 (18), so will he answer them in the way described below, ver. 24 (23). In this case, what is heard and answered is not prayer, but *the voice of the enemy*, ver. 4 (3), and his malignant slanders, ver. 13 (12). *Inhabiting antiquity*, or as the English Bible phrases it, *he that abideth of old.* The first Hebrew verb, however, could not fail to suggest its primary meaning, which is to *sit*, and more especially to *sit enthroned*, as a sovereign and a judge. See above, on Ps. ix. 5, 12 (4, 11). The phrase may therefore be said to represent God as having been a king and a judge from the remotest antiquity. The last clause is by some supposed to mean, that the persons here referred to undergo no moral change, but still persist in their refusal to fear God ; by others, that they undergo no outward changes, no vicissitudes of fortune, and for that reason will not fear him. But as the word translated *changes* is repeatedly employed by Job in a military sense, to signify either an alternate service, as, for instance, in relieving guard, or a succession in the service, as when one corps is disbanded and another takes its place, some of the best interpreters suppose this clause to mean that those enlisted in this evil warfare have no such reliefs or discharges to expect, but must continue in the unremitting service of sin, and as a neces-

sary consequence cannot fear God. The grammatical structure of the whole verse is peculiar, and can be made intelligible only by supplying the ellipsis.

21 (20). *He has stretched out his hands against his allies: he has profaned his covenant.* This might seem at first sight to refer to God ; but such a reference, if not forbidden by the nature of the acts alleged, would be at variance with the subsequent context, where the subject is undoubtedly the wicked enemy. The sudden change of number is in strict accordance with the usage of the Psalmists in speaking of their enemies, or in this case may arise from the same cause as in ver. 13 (12) above. See above, on Ps. x. 10. The word translated *allies* is the plural of one meaning *peace,* but seems to be poetically used here to denote those at peace with him, his friends or allies. Compare the analogous expressions in Ps. vii. 5 (4), xli. 10 (9). To *profane a covenant* is to treat it as no longer sacred, and by implication to break it. Compare Isa. xxxiii. 8. This is a varied repetition, under military figures, of the description in ver. 13–15 (12–14).

22 (21) *Smooth are the butterings of his mouth, and* (yet) *war* (is in) *his heart*; *soft are his words, more than oil, and* (yet even) *they are drawn* (*swords*). To the charge of violence he adds that of treacherous hypocrisy, thus amplifying the laconic phrase *oppression and deceit,* in ver. 12 (11) above. The English Bible, following some older versions, assimilates the clauses by making both comparative, *smoother than butter, softer than oil.* But in order to sustain this construction of the first clause, it is necessary to change the pointing of one Hebrew word, and to supply another as the nominative of the plural verb, which cannot without violence agree with *mouth.* The letter prefixed to the first noun is a part of it, and not a particle meaning *than* or *more than,* and the whole word denotes preparations of butter, cream, or rather curdled milk, which is the meaning of the primitive noun. As to the adversative use of *and* in both these clauses, see above, on ver. 14 (13). *War* (is in) *his heart,* or still more simply, because not requiring the insertion of the particle, *war* (*is*) *his heart, i. e.* his cherished wish and purpose. The word translated *war* is a poetical term, the same that is employed above in ver. 19 (18). In the last clause, *even* is supplied as well as *yet,* in order to convey, as far as possible, the emphasis of the Hebrew pronoun. *And they themselves, i. e.* the very oily words just mentioned, are drawn swords. This last expression is in Hebrew properly an adjective or participial form, but is specifically used in application to the sword, as *brandished* is in English, and so comes to be employed absolutely or as a substantive, expressing the entire complex idea of *drawn swords,* as weapons of attack, ready for use or on the point of being used forthwith.

23 (22). *Cast upon Jehovah* (what) *he gives thee, and he will sustain thee ; he will never suffer the righteous to be moved.* What he gives thee to endure, what he lays upon thee, cast thou upon him, by trusting in him. The phrase *he gives thee* (or *has given thee*) may also be explained as a noun with a possessive pronoun, *thy gift,* not in the active sense of *what thou givest,* but in the passive sense of *what is given to thee. Sustain* does not here mean to hold up or support under the burden, but to nourish or sustain life by administering food and other necessaries, to provide for. Compare the primitive use of the Hebrew verb in Gen. xlv. 11, xlvii. 12, l. 21. The common version of the last clause above given is a correct paraphrase of the original, the form of which is highly idiomatic. A literal translation would be, *he will not give for ever moving* (or *movement*) *to the righteous.* The verb *to give* is often used in Hebrew in the sense of allowing or per-

mitting. The word translated *moving* is the one so often used to signify the violent disturbance of a person in the midst of his prosperity. See above, on Ps. x. 6, xvi. 8, &c.

24 (23). *And thou, God, wilt bring them down to the pit of corruption ; men of blood and fraud shall not live out half their days.* The first verb is a causative, and as such may be rendered, *thou wilt cause them to descend.* The word translated *pit* is the common term in Hebrew for a *well*, but is here used in a wide sense, including all such excavations. The next word is (שַׁחַת), a derivative of the verb (שָׁחַת) to corrupt or destroy. The sense of *pit*, as if derived from the verb (שׁוּחַ) to *sink*, would convert the phrase into a weak tautology. See above, on Ps. xvi. 10. Men of *bloods and deceit, i. e.* bloody (or murderous) and deceitful men, as in Ps. v. 7 (6) above. The literal translation of the last words is, *they shall not halve their days*, a form of expression copied in the margin of the English Bible, as well as in the Septuagint (ἡμισεύσωσι) and Vulgate (*dimidiabunt*). The meaning of course is, that they shall not live half so long as they might have lived, but for their bloody and deceitful acts. This is not asserted as a general fact, but uttered as a threatening to the murderers and traitors whom the Psalmist had directly in his eye.

Psalm 56

AFTER the title, ver. 1, comes a general petition for deliverance from persecution and oppression, ver. 2, 3 (1, 2), followed by a strong expression of trust in God, ver. 4, 5 (3, 4), a description of the malice of the enemy, ver. 6, 7 (5, 6), and a confident anticipation of his punishment, ver. 8–10 (7–9), founded on faith in the divine promise, ver. 11, 12 (10, 11), and a vow or resolution to make due acknowledgment of the mercy experienced, ver. 12, 13 (11, 12).

1. *To the Chief Musician. Upon Jonath-elem-rehokim. By David. Michtam. When the Philistines took him in Gath.* The last clause of this inscription seems to refer to the incident recorded in 1 Sam. xxi. See above, on Ps. xxxiv. 1. An enigmatical allusion to the same event seems to be latent in the obscure phrase, *Jonath-elem-rehokim*, in which the first word means a *dove*, a favourite emblem of suffering innocence ; the second means *silence*, dumbness, sometimes put for uncomplaining submission ; and the third means *distant* or *remote*, agreeing with places or persons, probably the latter, in which sense it is applicable to the Philistines, as aliens in blood and religion. Compare Ps. xxxviii. 14 (13), lvi. 2 (1), lxv. 6 (5), lxxiv. 19. Thus understood, the whole is an enigmatical description of David as an innocent and uncomplaining sufferer among strangers. For the most probable etymology and sense of *Michtam*, see above, on Ps. xvi. 1.

2 (1). *Be merciful unto me, O God, for man pants for me* (or *is gaping after me) ; all the day, he devouring* (or *the devourer) is pressing on me.* The word for *man* is that denoting human frailty and implying the unreasonableness of such rage in one so impotent. See above, on Ps. ix. 20, 21 (19, 20), x. 18. The image here presented is that of a devouring monster or voracious beast. Instead of *pants* or *gapes*, some suppose the second verb to mean *snorts* or *snaps*, as an animal expression of rage. For the meaning of the word translated *devouring*, see above, on Ps. xxxv. 1. *Pressing on me*, or pressing me. See Num. xxii. 25.

3 (2). *My enemies have gaped upon me all the day; for* (there are) *many devourers to me, O most High.* The word translated *enemies* is that supposed by some to mean spies or watchers. See above, on Ps. xxvii. 11, liv. 7 (5). Having first spoken of his enemy in the singular number, he now substitutes the plural, to explain which seems to be the object of the last clause. " I say enemies, because my devourers are many." The last word in the verse strictly means a high place, and particularly heaven, but is sometimes applied to God himself. See below, on Ps. xcii. 9 (8). Some interpreters, however, understand it as an abstract noun meaning loftiness or pride, and then used as an adverb in the sense of arrogantly, proudly. Compare Ps. lxxiii. 8.

4 (3). *The day I am afraid, unto thee will I confide.* The complaint is followed, as in many other cases, by an expression of his confidence in God. *The day I am afraid* is an unusual expression, meaning simply *when I am afraid*, and probably belonging to the dialect of poetry. *Unto thee* suggests the act of turning and looking towards the quarter from which help is expected. The same form of expression occurs above, Ps. iv. 6 (5), xxxi. 7 (6).

5 (4). *In God I will praise his word, in God I have trusted; I will not fear; what can flesh do unto me?* The meaning of the first clause seems to be, that in the general praise of God he will include a particular acknowledgment of his gracious word or promise upon this occasion. The construction of the last clause in the English Bible, *I will not fear what flesh can do unto me*, gives substantially the same sense, but does not agree so well with the masoretic interpunction of the sentence. *Flesh*, humanity, as opposed to deity. See below, on Ps. lxv. 3 (2), and compare Isa. xxxi. 3, xl. 6.

6 (5). *All the day my words they wrest; against me* (are) *all their thoughts for evil.* The word translated *wrest* means strictly *vex* or *pain*, but is here used in the sense of twisting or distorting language by putting false constructions on it. *Thoughts*, purposes, designs. *For evil*, tending to my injury.

7 (6). *They will gather, they will hide—they, my supplanters, will watch, as they have* (already) *waited for my soul.* They will gather or combine against me. They will hide (themselves or their devices), they will plot, or lie in wait, for my destruction. The common explanation of the next phrase, *they mark my steps* or *my heels*, does not account for the emphatic pronoun *they*. The Hebrew word has probably the same sense as in Ps. xlix. 6 (5) above. *Waited for my soul* or *life, i. e.* waited to destroy it.

8 (7). *By iniquity* (there is) *escape to them ; in anger bring down nations, O God!* The first clause is obscure, but may mean either that they have hitherto escaped by their iniquity, or that they now depend, rely upon it for deliverance. The interrogative construction commonly adopted ought not to be assumed, in the absence of an interrogative particle, without a decided exegetical necessity. The Hebrew particle at the beginning sometimes indicates the means or instrument, with the additional idea of dependence or reliance, as in the English phrase to live *on* bread and water. See Gen. xxvii. 40.

9 (8). *My wanderings thou hast told ; put thou my tears into thy bottle ; are they not in thy book?* The Hebrew words for *wanderings* and *tears* are both in the singular number. See above, on Ps. vi. 7 (6), xxxix. 13 (12). The first of these words suggests the ideas of flight and exile, and may contain an allusion to the wanderings of Cain in a country designated by this very word, *The Land of Nod*, Gen. iv. 16, although this phrase may really

mean nothing more than *the land of (his) banishment* or *exile*. The English word *told* is here retained because the Hebrew one is equally ambiguous. In this case the primary idea is to count or number. See above, Ps. xxii. 17 (16), xl. 5 (4), xlviii. 13 (12). The act of counting implies particular attention. The idea of recollection is expressed by the strong figure which follows, *put my tears into thy bottle*, *i. e.* preserve them in thy memory. This singular metaphor is thought by some to have been suggested by the word for *wandering* (נֹד or נוֹד), which is almost identical with that for *bottle* (נֹאד). The latter strictly means a skin or leathern bottle, such as is still used in the East. See below, on Ps. cxix. 83. The interrogation in the last clause has the force of a direct assertion. *Thy book*, the book of thy remembrance, another figurative expression for the memory itself. Compare Mal. iii. 16.

10 (9). *Then shall my enemies turn back, in the day I call; this I know, that God is for me.* The particle of time at the beginning of the verse has reference to what follows, *in the day I call*, but as this was to be connected closely with the last clause, the natural order of the sentence was inverted. *Turn back*, be repulsed, defeated, disappointed. See above, on Ps. vii. 12 (11), ix. 4 (3). *In the day (that) I shall call:* the ellipsis of the relative is equally common in Hebrew and in English. *Call* may mean simply *call for help* or *pray;* but some connect it with the last clause thus : *in the day that I shall call* (or cry as follows) *" this I know,"* &c. There is also an ambiguity in the phrase *this I know*, which may either mean, "I know that my enemies shall thus turn back, because God is for me," or, "my enemies shall turn back when they hear me cry. This much I know, to wit, that God is for me." The last phrase may be also rendered *to me*, he belongs to me, he is my God, which of course includes the idea of his favour or his being on the speaker's side.

11 (10). *In God I will praise* (this) *word; in Jehovah I will praise* (this) *word.* This unusual form of speech must have the same sense as in ver. 5 (4) above. Some understand it to mean *by God's help*, others, *in union with God*, I will praise (his) *word.* But on the whole, the most natural explanation still seems to be, " what I shall particularly praise in God, both as God, and as the tutelary God of Israel and my own, is the word of promise, which he has uttered and fulfilled in this case."

12 (11). *In God have I trusted; I will not fear; what can man do unto me?* As the foregoing verse is a resumption and emphatic iteration of the first clause of ver. 5 (4), so this seems to bear the same relation to the last clause of that same verse. The only variation in the form of expression is the substitution of the literal term *man* (or *mankind*) for the more obscure term *flesh*. See above, on ver. 5 (4). Here again it is a possible construction, although not so agreeable to the masoretic accents, to make the interrogation an oblique one. " I will not fear what man can do unto me."

13 (12). *Upon me, O God, (are) thy vows; I will pay thanksgiving unto thee.* The first clause represents his vows or voluntary obligations as incumbent on himself and due to God, and he resolves to discharge them by thanksgivings, not merely verbal acknowledgments, but sacrificial tokens of his gratitude, such as were familiar to the ancient saints and recognised in the Law of Moses.

14 (13). *For thou hast delivered my soul from death;* (wilt thou) *not (deliver) my feet from falling, to walk before God in the light of life?* The ellipsis in the second clause may also be supplied as follows, *hast thou not delivered?* as the only terms expressed are those of interrogation and nega-

tion. The word translated *falling* is a very strong one, and means thrusting,
casting down.   The verbal root occurs above, in Ps. xxxv. 5, xxxvi. 13 (12).
To walk before God is to live in the enjoyment of his favour and protection.
The *light of life* is opposed to the darkness of death.   It may also be and
usually is translated, *in the light of the living, i e.* the light which living
men enjoy.   See above, on Ps. xxvii. 13.

Psalm 57

IN the first part of this psalm a sufferer describes his own afflictions,
occasioned by the malice of his enemies, and earnestly prays to be delivered
from them, ver. 2–5 (1–4).   In the second he anticipates a favourable
answer to his prayer, and praises God for it, ver. 6–12 (5–11).

1. *To the Chief Musician. Destroy not. By David. A Secret. When
he fled from before Saul in the cave.*   The enigmatical inscription, *Al-tashheth, destroy not,* reappears in the titles of the next two psalms, and of the
seventy-fifth.   As in other cases of the same kind, some interpreters regard
it as a musical expression, others as the first words of a well-known poem,
to the air of which this was to be sung.   The best explanation is the one
suggested by the Chaldee Paraphrase, to wit, that the psalms which bear this
title belong to that period of David's history, when he was under the perpetual necessity of saying *Destroy not,* and are therefore suited to all
similar emergencies of other ˙saints.   It is not at all impossible, that this
was a favourite saying of David in real life, the rather as it is borrowed
from the prayer of Moses in Deut. ix. 26, of which it may be said to be an
abbreviated citation, not unlike the Latin designations, *De Profundis,
Miserere, Venite Exsultemus, Non Nobis Domine, Te Deum,* &c.   The explanation above given is corroborated by the obvious allusion in these three
psalms (lvii.–lix.) to the Sauline persecution.   The very expression may be
traced in 1 Sam. xxvi. 9, where David utters, as a command to his followers, what he so often had occasion to utter as a prayer in his own behalf.
This psalm is described as a *michtam,* mystery, or secret, on account of the
extraordinary consolation and support which he experienced, enabling him
to triumph even in the midst of enemies and dangers.   See above, on Ps.
xvi. 1.   *In the cave* of Adullam (1 Sam. xxii. 1), or of Engedi (1 Sam.
xvi. 1–3), or more indefinitely *in the cave,* equivalent to saying *in caves,* as
a generic description of the mode of life which he then led (Heb. xi. 38),
not without some reference to the subterranean cavern, as an emblem of
solitude and darkness.   Hence the absence of any more specific allusion to
particular incidents which occurred in caves, such as that recorded in
1 Sam. xxiv., and the obvious reference to the whole period of the Sauline
persecution, as a time of wandering, danger, and distress.   Hence, too, the
striking similiarity, in sentiment and form, between this psalm and the one
before it.

2 (1). *Be merciful unto me, O God, be merciful unto me, for in thee has
my soul sought refuge, and in the shadow of thy wings will I seek refuge,
until* (these) *calamities be overpast.*   The repetition of the prayer for mercy
shews the intensity of his desire.   *Sought refuge* from the persecutions mentioned in Ps. lvi. 2 (1).   *The soul* is mentioned as the object of pursuit.
See above, on Ps. liv. 5 (4), lvi. 7 (6), and compare 1 Sam. xxiv. 12 (11).
The shadow of thy wings : the same beautiful figure for protection is pre-

sented in Ps. xvii. 8, xxxvi. 8 (7). *Calamities*, occasioned by the crimes of others. See above, on Ps. lii. 4, 9, (2, 7).

3 (2). *I will cry unto God Most High, unto the Almighty, finishing for me, i. e.* perfecting what he has begun. Compare Phil. i. 6. This verse assigns two reasons for his crying unto God. The first is the supremacy and omnipotence of God himself, the second is the previous experience of his faithfulness in fully performing whatever he has promised. See below, on Ps. cxxxviii. 8.

4 (3). *He will send from heaven and save me*—(when or whom) *the devourer reviles, Selah!—God will send his mercy and his truth.* The first verb may govern *hand*, as in Ps. cxliv. 7, or *help*, as in Ps. xx. 3 (2), or be used absolutely, as in Ps. xviii. 17 (16). *The devourer*, literally the one gaping after me, snorting with rage against me, or panting for my destruction. See above, on Ps. lvi. 2, 3 (1, 2). Without supplying anything, this clause may be taken as a short independent proposition—*the devourer has reviled*—interposed between the two principal members of the sentence. See above, on Ps. xxvii. 8, xlv. 6 (5). In the last clause, Mercy and Truth seem to be personified, like Integrity and Uprightness in Ps. xxv. 21, Violence and Strife in Ps. lv. 10 (9). With this clause compare Ps. xliii. 3.

5 (4). *My soul (is) in the midst of lions; I will lie down (among) burning ones, sons of man, (whose) teeth (are) spears and arrows, and their tongue a sharp sword.* By his soul he means himself, or rather his endangered life. *Lions*, as often elsewhere, means ferocious enemies. See above, on Ps. vii. 3 (2), xxii. 13, 14 (12, 13). The form of the verb which follows is the one denoting fixed determination. " Though surrounded by lions I will fearlessly lie down," &c. *Among* or *upon* them. *Burning* may possibly refer to *lions* and mean *raging;* but the indefinite application is more natural. *Sons of man* is added to shew that what precedes is to be figuratively understood; but in the very next clause, the writer relapses into language still more highly metaphorical. In likening their teeth to swords he presents the double image of a wild beast and a warrior. The mention of the tongue has reference, no doubt, to the slander and abuse, which entered so largely into the Sauline persecutions. These had already been referred to in the middle clause of ver. 4 (3), of which this may be regarded as an amplification.

6 (5). *Be high above the heavens, O God, above all the earth thy glory!* Some, in the last clause, read *on all the earth*, and then explain *on the heavens* to mean nothing more than *in heaven*. The whole verse then is the expression of a wish that God may be exalted both in heaven and earth. But this is far less natural than the usual construction, which supposes a comparison, and makes the verse exalt God above all his works. Compare Ps. viii. 2 (1).

7 (6). *A net they prepared for my steps; he pressed down my soul; they digged before me a pit; they fell into the midst of it. Selah.* This verse assigns the reason or occasion of the praise ascribed to God in that before it. The image here presented is the same as in Ps. vii. 16 (15), ix. 16 (15). The sudden change of number is particularly common in the Psalms when speaking of an ideal person, representing many real individuals. See above, on Ps. lvi. 3 (2). The phrase *pressed down* is borrowed from the Prayer-Book version, and is well suited to convey the idea of an animal caught and held down by a trap or snare. That version is also more correct than the English Bible in giving to the verb an active meaning; of the neuter or passive there is no example elsewhere. *Before me*, in my path,

where am I walking. The *Selah* at the close is almost equivalent to an *Amen*, as expressing acquiescence in God's righteous retributions.

8 (7). *Fixed (is) my heart, O God, fixed (is) my heart; I will sing and play.* The repetition adds solemnity and force to the declaration. *Fixed, i. e.* firmly resolved and proof against all fear. See above, on Ps. li. 12 (10), and below on Ps. cxii. 7. The two verbs in the last clause are properly descriptive of the two kinds of music, vocal and instrumental; but in the usage of the Psalms they always have reference to the praise of God.

9 (8.) *Awake, my glory! awake, lute and harp! I will awaken morning.* The same idea is now expressed in the form of a poetical apostrophe. By *glory* most interpreters understand the *soul*, as the glory of the whole man, but some the *tongue*, as the glory of the body. See above, on Ps. vii. 6 (5), xvi. 9, xxx. 13, and below, on Ps. cviii. 2 (1). It is possible, however, that it here means that in which he gloried, his inspiration as a sacred poet, and which he personifies, as the heathen poets invoked the muse. *Lute and harp* is the translation in the Prayer Book. Any other combination, denoting two familiar instruments, such as *harp and lyre*, would be here appropriate. The verb in the last clause is a causative of that in the first, and is related to it as the English verb *awaken* to *awake*. Strictly translated, this clause contains a bold but beautiful poetical conception, that of awakening the dawn instead of being awakened by it, in other words, preventing or anticipating it by early praises. In like manner, Ovid says the crowing of the cock *evocat auroram*. We thus obtain the same sense, in a far more striking form than is expressed by the inexact and prosaic version, *I will awake early.* The intransitive sense given to the verb, and the adverbial sense given to the noun, are both without sufficient authority in usage. From this verse some have inferred, that the psalm was expressly designed to be an even-song; but he does not say, I will do thus to-morrow. The meaning rather is that he will do it daily. See above, on Ps. xvii. 15. The summons to the harp and lyre, may be understood as implying, that they have long slept without occasion for such praise as they are now to utter.

10 (9). *I will thank thee among the nations, Lord; I will praise thee among the peoples.* The divine interposition to be celebrated is so great and glorious as to be entitled to the praises of the whole world. See above, on Ps. xviii. 50 (49.)

11 (10). *For great unto the heavens (is) thy mercy, and unto the clouds thy truth.* By a natural and favourite hyperbole, God's goodness is described as reaching from earth to heaven. See above, on Ps. xxxvi. 6 (5), and compare Jer. li. 9.

12 (11). *Be thou high above the heavens, O God, above all the earth thy glory!* The strophe ends as it began in ver. 6 (5) above. In the last clause the verb of the first may be repeated, *be thy glory high;* or the substantive verb alone may be supplied, *let thy glory be above all the earth!*

Psalm 58

1. *To the Chief Musician. Al-tashheth. By David. Michtam.* See above, on Ps. lvii. 1. The Psalmist complains of unjust, spiteful, hardened enemies, ver. 2–6 (1–5), and prays that their power may be broken, ver. 7–12 (6–11). The contents of the psalm agree with its title in shewing that it belongs to the period of Saul's persecutions, when David had to

contend with unjust rulers, who were at the same time his personal enemies. But although suggested by his own experience, the psalm was
designed for permanent and public use, and is therefore inscribed *to the
Chief Musician.*

2 (1). *Are ye indeed dumb* (when) *ye* (should) *speak righteousness* (and)
judge equitably, sons of man? The first words are exceedingly obscure.
One of them (אֵלֶם), not expressed in English and the ancient versions,
means *dumbness,* as in Ps. lvi. 1, and seems to be here used as a strong
expression for *entirely speechless.* In what respect they were thus dumb,
is indicated by the verb which follows, but the connection can be made
clear in English only by a circumlocution. The interrogation, *are ye indeed,* expresses wonder, as at something scarcely credible. Can it be so?
is it possible? are you really silent, you whose very office is to speak for
God and against the sins of men? See Deut. i. 16, 17. That the speaking here meant is judicial speaking, appears from the more specific parallel
expression. The word translated *equitably* is a plural noun meaning *equities*
or *rectitudes.* See above, on Ps. xvii. 2. Strictly understood, it is not a
qualifying term, but the object of the verb *judge,* as in the other clause *righteousness* is governed directly by the verb *speak.* The address to them as
sons of man reminds them of their own dependence and responsibility.

3 (2). *Nay, in heart, iniquities ye practise; in the land, the violence of
your hands ye weigh.* The particle at the beginning is, as usual, emphatic,
meaning not only this but something more. See above, Ps. xviii. 49 (48),
xliv. 10 (9). Not contented with neglecting their official functions, they
were guilty of positive injustice. The Hebrew for *iniquities* is the plural of
a word used in Ps. xxxvii. 1, xliii. 1, and denotes various acts of injustice. The
future forms (*ye will do, ye will weigh*) implies an obstinate persistency in
evil. To do or practise wickedness in heart may mean to plan or contrive
it, as in Micah. ii. 1, leaving the execution to be inferred as a matter of course.
Or the phrase may be translated *with the heart, i. e.* cordially, *ex animo,
con amore,* or to use an idiomatic English expression *with a will.* The
first words of the last clause, *in the land,* may seem, from their position, to
be in contrast with the phrase *in heart;* but the antithesis, if any, is between the *heart* and *hands,* and *in the land* suggests the aggravating circumstance, that all this was practised by persons in authority under the theocracy, among the chosen people. *Violence,* violent injustice. See above,
on Ps. lv. 10 (9). The last verb in this sentence means to *level* or *make
even,* and in that sense is repeatedly applied to paths. See Isa. xxvi. 7,
Prov. iv. 26, v. 6, 21. But as the derivative noun (פֶּלֶס) means a balance (Prov. xvi. 11, Isa. xl. 12), the verb may here denote the act of
weighing, levelling the balance, rendering it even, which some, without necessity, ascribe to it in several of the places above cited, where its constant
combination with a way or path seems to exclude the idea of weighing as
incongruous, and to require that of smoothing or levelling as peculiarly
appropriate. This last might be retained even here, and the metaphor be
understood to mean that they facilitated or promoted violence (*q. d.* levelled
or prepared its way); but the sense of weighing is equally appropriate,
and agrees well with the favourite idea of the scales of justice, which is found
not only in the classics but in Scripture. See Job xxxi. 6. The meaning
then is, that these wicked rulers, instead of weighing out justice to their
subjects, weighed out, administered, dispensed, the most violent injustice,
and that, too, devised and practised by themselves.

4 (3). *Estranged are the wicked from the womb ; they go astray from*
(their) *birth, speaking lies.* The first verb in Hebrew is not a passive but
a neuter form, denoting the condition of estrangement, alienation, from God
and from all goodness. *The wicked* thus described are the whole class,
of which his persecutors formed a part. The preterite tense is used in
the original (*were estranged, went astray*) on account of the retrospective
reference to the beginning of life. The verb translated *go astray* is one
frequently applied to moral aberrations. *From their birth*, literally *from
the belly.* See above, Ps. xxii. 11 (10). *Speaking lies,* or with closer
adherence to the form of the original, *speakers of falsehood, i. e.* habitual
liars. The other version seems to mean that they begin to lie as soon as
they are born, a hyperbolical expression, of which some interpreters relieve
the sentence by making this the subject of the proposition and parallel to
wicked in the other clause. *Speakers of falsehood go astray from* (their)
birth. In this description of the wicked there is nothing inconsistent with
the doctrine of universal depravity, as recognised in Ps. xiv. 1, li. 7 (5)
above, and in Gen. viii. 21, Job xiv. 4, because the holiness of some men
is a mere exception to the general rule, produced by the distinguishing grace
of God, which frees them from the paramount influence of that corruption
to which others still continue subject.

5; 6 (4, 5). *There is poison to them like the poison of a serpent, as a deaf
adder stops its ear, which will not hearken to the voice of enchanters, of* (*one*)
charming charms, (*of one*) *most wise.* The first words are equivalent to the
English construction, *they have poison,* The Hebrew noun originally signifies *heat,* and especially the heat of anger, in which sense it repeatedly occurs
above, Ps. vi. 2 (1), xxxvii. 8, xxxviii. 2 (1). The same sense is retained
here by the ancient versions (θυμός, *furor*), and agrees well with the popular
idea of vindictive spite, as a natural instinct of this class of animals. But
most interpreters explain the word, here and in Deut xxxii. 24, as meaning
venom, animal poison, so called from its inflammatory effects upon the
person bitten. The Hebrew phrase translated *like* means strictly *after* (or
according to) *the likeness of.* Compare its use in Gen. i. 26. It may be
here employed, instead of the simple particle of comparison, for the sake of
emphasis, as we say *like,* but more emphatically *just like.* As to the species
of serpent mentioned in the second clause of ver. 5 (4), all that is necessary
to a correct interpretation of the verse is to understand it as denoting a
variety regarded as peculiarly malignant, and therefore resisting the incan-
tations by which other species were subdued, especially in Egypt. See the
allusions to this practice in Eccles. x. 11, Jer. viii. 17. This clause admits
of a different construction, *like the deaf adder he stops his ear,* which some
interpreters prefer because an adder cannot stop its ears, and need not stop
them if naturally deaf, whereas it is by stopping his that the wicked man
becomes like a deaf adder. The word translated *enchanters* properly means
whisperers or *mutterers,* in allusion to familiar practices of the ancient
wizards. *Charming charms,* laying spells, or as the Hebrew words are
commonly supposed to signify originally, *tying knots* with a magical design.
The last word in ver. 6 (5), is a passive participle, analogous to our word
learned, and here meaning *skilful.* The English versions and the Vulgate
make it an adverb (*sapienter, never so wisely*) *;* but the Septuagint and
Jerome give it its proper meaning as an adjective, in which case it is probably in apposition with the nouns preceding, and connected in like manner
with the *voice* of the first clause. The general idea of the verse, however
construed, is that the malice of his enemies is stubborn and inexorable.

7 (6). *O God, crush their teeth in their mouth; the grinders of the young lions shatter, O Jehovah!* The complaint is now followed by a prayer, that these ferocious enemies may be disarmed and disabled. This idea is expressed by the use of the same figure as in Ps. iii. 8 (7), that of wild beasts rendered harmless by the breaking of their teeth. Compare Job xxix. 17. Hence in the last clause they are expressly called lions. See above, Ps. lvii. 5 (4). *Young lions*, not mere whelps, from which they are distinguished in Ezek. xix. 2, 3, but full-grown lions, in the first maturity of their strength, and therefore more to be dreaded than when older or younger. See above, Ps. xvii. 12, xxxiv. 11 (10), xxxv. 17. The Hebrew verbs in this verse are peculiarly expressive, and, though wholly unconnected with each other, are both used elsewhere to express the ideas of violently breaking, breaking down, breaking out, breaking off, and breaking through. See Exod. xv. 7, xix. 21, Lev. xiv. 45, Judges vi. 30, 1 Kings xviii. 30.

8 (7). *Let them melt away as waters, let them go their way; let him bend his arrows, as if they were cut off.* The optative meaning of these features seems to be determined by the imperatives in ver. 7 (6). There is nothing ungrammatical, however, in retaining the strict future sense, and regarding the verse as an expression of strong confidence as to the event. The first verb elsewhere has the sense of being rejected with contempt, and is so used in Ps. xv. 9; but as two of its radical letters coincide with those of a verb meaning to be melted, most interpreters prefer this sense. The other might, however, be retained, and the phrase explained to mean that they should be cast aside as water, and especially as filthy water, is rejected. *Go their way*, literally *go to them* or to themselves. Some understand it to mean *for themselves*, *i. e.* for their own benefit, their destruction being represented, by a sort of irony, as all that they have gained by their hostility. Compare the use of the same phrase in Ps. lxiv. 6 (5), lxvi. 7 (6). In the next clause, most interpreters assume a sudden change of number, such as frequently occurs in speaking of an ideal person representing a plurality of real individuals. See above, on Ps. lvii. 4, 7 (3, 6). *He* (*i. e. the enemy*) *shall bend his arrows*, literally *tread them*, *i. e.* bend by treading on them. This expression is applicable strictly to the bow, and it is so applied repeatedly above. See Ps. vii. 13 (12), xi. 2, xxxvii. 14. Having thus acquired the secondary sense of fitting, making ready, it is transferred from the bow to the arrows, not only here but in Ps. lxiv. 4 (3), below. If the last verb be construed with the arrows as its subject, they would seem to be described as blunted or deprived of their points, and the meaning of the clause is, that the weapons of the enemy take no effect. The whole clause, however, will admit of a different construction, which refers the singular verb and pronoun to God/himself, and the plural verb to these rebellious sinners. Let him bend his arrows, as if they were cut off, *i. e.* so that they may be cut off. Notwithstanding the obscurity of this clause, the connection is preserved unbroken by the obvious meaning of the other.

9 (8). *As a snail melts, let him go;* (like) *the untimely birth of a woman, they have not beheld the sun.* The idea of speedy and entire disappearance is still more strongly expressed here. The meaning of the word translated *snail* rests upon rabbinical tradition and a doubtful etymology. The point of comparison may relate to some popular belief or to some apparent idiosyncrasy in this class of animals, perhaps to the idea of its losing a portion of its body by locomotion. The next noun primarily signifies what falls from the tree, unripe fruit, and is then transferred to animal abortions. The past tense in the last clause seems to mark it as a kind of reflection

introduced into the midst of the prayer. " So far from living too long, as I feared, they seem scarcely to have lived at all."

10 (9). *Before your pots can feel the thorn, whether raw or done, he will blow him away.* This is one of the obscurest and most difficult verses in the book, and yet the general idea is sufficiently clear. The *he* in the last clause relates to God, the *him* to his wicked enemy. The verb translated *blow away* means properly to *storm away*, or carry away with (or like) a tempest. The rapidity of this movement is expressed by a familiar comparison. *Your pots*, your vessels used in cooking. The address seems to be to the sinners, afterwards referred to as a single person. *Feel*, perceive the heat. Compare Job vi. 30. *The thorn*, used as fuel, kindles quickly and immediately burns out, so that this comparison suggests the idea of a very sudden change. The singular expression which follows literally means *as* (well) *living as heat ;* but as the adjective is elsewhere used to signify *raw*, not cooked (1 Sam. ii. 15), the noun joined with it may be taken in the opposite sense of *cooked* or *done*. This may be a proverbial expression, borrowed from the dialect of common life, to convey the idea of a sudden change, which waits for nothing, but carries men away in the midst of their employments. This, though still an unusual form of speech, will seem less unnatural if we suppose the process of cooking to be here used as a figure for the plots and devices of the enemy, a metaphor by no means far-fetched or unknown to other writers. The idea, then, is that while these devices, so to speak, are cooking, the cooks are snatched away by a superior power, without caring whether the operation is complete or not. " Before the seething pot of your contrivances begins to feel the quickly kindled heat which you apply to it, the tempest of divine wrath carries you away, whether your mess be cooked or raw."

11 (10). *Rejoice shall the righteous, because he has seen vengeance ; his steps he shall bathe in the blood of the wicked.* The vengeance in which he shall rejoice is not his own, but God's, in the vindication of whose righteousness and honour all holy beings must rejoice for ever, although not in the suffering of those who perish. The same idea is expressed more strongly in the last clause by a martial figure. To bathe his feet (or rather his steps) in the blood of others is to walk where their blood is flowing, to tread the battle-field where they have fallen, to gain a sanguinary triumph over them, or rather it is to partake in the triumph of another. Thus one of the old commentators says that David washed his feet in Saul's blood, Elijah in Ahab's, Hezekiah in Sennacherib's, without any agency or share in their destruction, and without any selfish or malignant exultation in their ruin. Let it also be observed that in this, as in many like cases, the act is ascribed to an ideal person, and is therefore no example for our imitation.

12 (11). *And man shall say, Yes, there is fruit to the righteous ; yes, there is a God judging in the earth.* This shall be said, not by *a man*, nor by any particular man, but by men in general, by man as opposed to God. The particle translated *yes* really means *only*, and denotes that this and nothing else is true. See above, on Ps. xxxix. 12 (11). *There is fruit to the righteous*, or, in our idiom, *he has fruit, i. e.* he reaps what he has sown. Compare Isa. iii. 10, 11. The very power that destroys his enemies is his protector. The idea of existence is expressed in the last clause, contrary to usage, and is therefore emphatic. THERE IS, notwithstanding all denials, doubts, and false appearances, THERE IS a God judging in the earth. Another unusual circumstance in this clause is, that not only the divine name,

but the participle agreeing with it, is in the plural number. The same thing occurs in Josh. xxiv. 19, 1 Sam. xvii. 26. In this case it may possibly be intended to suggest the idea, that although these earthly representatives of God are so unfaithful, there are, nevertheless, gods judging in the earth, *i.e.* one God, who possesses in himself the source of all the justice exercised by other beings. See above, on Ps. xi. 7.

Psalm 59

THIS psalm consists of two parallel parts, in both which the succession of ideas is substantially the same. A sufferer complains of treacherous and cruel enemies, ver. 2–5 (1–4), prays to be delivered from them, ver. 6 (5), and confidently anticipates their ruin, ver. 7–12 (6–11). In the second part we have again, in the same order, the complaint, ver. 13 (12), the prayer, ver. 14 (13), and the anticipation, ver. 15–18 (14–17).

1. *To the Chief Musician. Al-tashheth. By David. Michtam. When Saul sent, and they watched the house to kill him.* This remarkable incident in David's life, which was the beginning of his long and painful wanderings, is recorded, almost in the same words, 1 Sam. xix. 11. The title or inscription is the same as in the two preceding psalms.

2 (1). *Free me from my enemies, my God, from those rising up* (against) *me thou wilt raise me, i. e.* place me beyond their reach. Here, as often elsewhere, the tone of supplication is insensibly exchanged for that of confident anticipation. But the change is momentary, and the form of supplication is immediately resumed. *My insurgents* or assailants ; see above, on Ps. xvii. 7. The idea and expression at the close are the same as in Ps. xx. 2 (1). Compare Ps. xviii. 49 (48).

3 (2). *Free me from workers of iniquity, and from men of blood save me.* The same words and phrases have occurred repeatedly before. See above, Ps. v. 6 (5), vi. 9 (8), xiv. 4, xxvi. 9, xxviii. 3. This verse and the one before it constitute the general introductory petition, the ground and reason of which are afterwards assigned.

4 (3). (This I ask) *because* (such enemies as I have just described) *have laid wait for my soul* (or life)*; there assemble against me strong ones, not* (for) *my transgression, and not* (for) *my sin, Jehovah !* Or, (it is) *not my fault nor my sin, Jehovah.*

5 (4). *Without iniquity* (on my part, to excuse or even to provoke them) *they run and set themselves* (against me). Both these are military terms, and seem to denote strictly the scaling of a wall. See above, on Ps. xviii. 30 (29). *Awake* (arouse thyself from this apparent inactivity) *to meet me* (to respond to my petition), *and see* (my danger, and the malice of my enemies).

6 (5). *And thou, Jehovah, God,* (Lord of) *Hosts, God of Israel, awake to visit all the nations; spare not all traitors of iniquity. Selah.* The accumulation of divine names is not unmeaning, but suggestive of reasons why the prayer should be answered, to wit, because He to whom it was addressed was not only the Eternal, Self-existent God, the Sovereign of the Universe, but the God of Israel, and therefore bound by covenant to save his people. *All the nations, i. e.* such as are the enemies of God and of his people; and if whole nations are thus dealt with, how much more may Jehovah be expected to destroy his individual enemies ? *Traitors of iniquity,* wicked traitors. The depth of the feeling here expressed is further indicated by the *Selah.*

7 (6). *Let them return at evening, let them howl like the dog, and go around the city.* The verbs may also be rendered as simple futures, expressive of a confident anticipation: *they shall return,* &c. In either case, the verse contains a metaphorical description of the disappointment of the enemy, who are here compared to the gregarious untamed dogs by which the oriental cities are infested. As these dogs prowl about the streets in search of food, and howl for want of it, so let (or so shall) my wicked enemies. Others, with equal probability, explain this verse as a description of their present fierceness and avidity.

8 (7). *Lo, they pour out with their mouths; swords* (are) *in their lips; for who* (is) *hearing?* He here reverts to his description and complaint of his enemies. The first verb is expressive of a constant flow or gush. See above, on Ps. xix. 3 (2). What it is that they thus pour out, although not expressed, may be readily gathered from the context, namely, slanders and reproaches. The *swords in their lips* are significant of sharp and cutting speeches. See above, on Ps. lv. 22 (21), and compare Ps. lii. 4 (3). The English version, by supplying " *say they,*" makes the last clause the language of these wicked foes, who are then to be understood as denying God's omniscience or his justice. See above, on Ps. x. 11, 13, and compare Ps. xiv. 1, xlii. 11 (10). But a still more striking sense may be obtained by making this clause the complaint of the Psalmist himself, as if he had said: no wonder that they thus pour out their bitter words; for who is there to observe and punish them? The question implies that God himself had ceased to notice their offences, and the participial form, that this neglect had now become habitual.

9 (8). *And thou, Jehovah, wilt laugh at them; thou wilt mock at all nations.* The resistance of whole nations, or of all collectively, is but an object of contempt to thee; how much more that of even the most potent individuals. See above, on Ps. ii. 4, xxxvii. 13. The connection between this verse and the one before it depends upon the meaning of the question with which ver. 8 (7) closes. If that be regarded as the language of the enemy, the thought to be supplied is, " But although they thus imagine that thou dost not hear, thou wilt soon undeceive them by deriding them." On the other supposition it is this: " Although I am continually tempted to say, who doth hear? I am, nevertheless, persuaded that thou dost hear and despise their impotent malignity."

10 (9). *His strength unto thee will I keep, for God is my high place.* The first clause is so obscure that some interpreters have thought it necessary to change the text (עֻזִּי for עֻזּוֹ), and read *my strength,* i. e. thou who art my strength, *for thee will I watch* or *wait.* Some who retain the common text suppose a sudden change of person, (as for) *his strength,* i. e. God's, *I will watch for thee,* O God! But this is much less natural than the common version (*because of*) *his strength,* i. e. the enemy's, *will I wait upon thee.* According to the first translation above given, the meaning of the clause is, I will reserve the strength and violence of the enemy, to be dealt with and disposed of by Jehovah. *My high place,* beyond the reach of enemies and dangers. See above, on Ps. ix. 10 (9), xviii. 3 (2), xlvi. 8, 12 (7, 11).

11 (10). *My God* (with) *his mercy will meet me; God will make me to gaze upon my enemies.* This translation of the first clause follows the reading in the text of the Hebrew Bible. The common version exhibits the marginal or masoretic emendation, *the God of my mercy,* i. e. my merciful God, or the God who shews me mercy, *shall prevent me,* in the primrary

and proper sense of coming before me. The idea here is that of coming to meet one in a friendly manner. See above, on Ps. xxi. 4 (3), and compare the unfavourable meaning of the same verb in Ps. xvii. 13, xviii. 6 (5), 19 (18). *To gaze, i. e.* with joy and triumph. See above, on Ps. liv. 9 (7). This is equivalent to saying, he will give me the victory. The word for *enemies* is the same as in Ps. v. 9 (8).

12 (11). *Slay them not, lest my people forget; make them wander by thy power and bring them down, our shield, O Lord !* The meaning of the first clause, as appears from the context, is, destroy them not utterly, or once for all. *My people, i. e.* Israel, the chosen race. *Make them wander,* like Cain and like Israel in the wilderness, to both which cases the same verb is applied, Gen. iv. 12, Num. xxxii. 13. These are tacitly referred to, as familiar examples of this kind of punishment, inflicted both on individuals and nations. *Bring them down,* cause them to descend, from their present high position, humble them, and make their humiliation an example and a warning to all others. This was signally fulfilled in the case of Saul and his household, as well as in that of the nations which resisted the divine will and oppressed the chosen people, to both which cases the expressions of this psalm are designedly appropriate. *Our shield,* our protector ; not only *mine* but *ours;* not only David's but all Israel's. The figure of a shield is a favourite one with David. See above, on Ps. iii. 4 (3), xviii. 3 (2), xxviii. 7. It is not only striking and expressive, but historically associated with the origin of the nation in the calling of Abraham and the patriarchal promises. See Gen. xv. 1.

13 (12.) *The sin of their mouth—the word of their lips—and they shall be taken in their pride—and from cursing and falsehood they will tell.* This is a close translation of this very obscure verse, that is to say, obscure in its particular expressions, though its general sense is obvious enough. The construction given in the English versions, (for) *the sin of their mouth* (and) *the word of their lips they shall be taken,* either overlooks the copulative particle before the verb or makes it unmeaning, *they shall even be taken.* The latest interpreters prefer to render it, *the sin of their mouth* (*is*) *the word of their lips, i. e.* the word of their lips is the sin of their mouth ; whatever they speak is spoken sinfully ; they cannot speak without committing sin. *They shall be taken,* caught, surprised, as they have sought to surprise others. See above, Ps. ix. 16 (15), xxxv. 8. It may also be read as an expression of desire, *may they be taken ! In their pride,* not merely on account of it, although this is included, but in the midst of it, in the act of indulging it. *From* cursing represents their capture as *arising* (or *proceeding*) *from* their cursing, and may therefore be translated *for,* as in the English Bible. *Cursing,* or rather *swearing* in attestation of a falsehood. See above, on Ps. x. 7. The phrase to *tell a falsehood* is common to both idioms. Most interpreters supply a relative, (*which*) *they tell,* or *will tell.* Otherwise, *from* must be understood as meaning *of, concerning.*

14 (13.) *Consume in wrath, consume* (*them*), *and let them be no more, and let them know that God* (*is*) *ruling in Jacob, unto the ends of the earth.* The first verb strictly means to cause to cease, to finish, to destroy so that nothing is left. *Let them be no more,* let them cease to be. By itself, the Hebrew phrase would seem to mean, *and they are not,* but the tense, which is not expressed in the original, must be determined by the prayer preceding. The last clause might at first sight seem to mean, let my enemies know that God rules not only in Israel, but throughout the earth. But this is forbidden by the prayer that they may cease to be, and would require a

connecting particle of some sort after *Jacob*. The true construction, indicated by the accents, is, *and let them* (*i. e.* men in general) *know to the ends of the earth, that God* (*is*) *ruling* (*i. e.* habitually rules) *in Jacob*. This description of the whole world as witnessing and interested in God's dealings with his chosen people, is in strict accordance with the very end for which he chose them, and is particularly characteristic of David. See above, on Ps. xviii. 50 (49), lvii. 6, 10, 12 (5, 9, 11), and compare his language to Goliath, 1 Sam. xvii. 46 : "This day will Jehovah deliver thee into my hand, and I will smite thee . . . that all the earth may know that there is a God in Israel."

15 (14). *Then let them return at evening, howl like the dog, and go around the city.* The first word in Hebrew is a simple copulative, meaning *and ;* but the connection seems to be, since God is my protector and these enemies are doomed to destruction, let them threaten as they will, I shall not fear them. It is equally grammatical, though not so natural, to understand the verse as a prediction or confident anticipation of the miserable state to which these enemies should be reduced, like a herd of oriental dogs without a master or a home, prowling about in search of food, and howling with hunger, but remaining still unsatisfied. See above, on ver. 7 (6).

16 (15). *They shall wander* (in quest of something) *to eat,* (and) *if they are not satisfied, remain all night.* This sentence is obscure, whether it be understood as a defiance or a threatening, though the latter construction is recommended by the emphatic pronoun at the beginning. *They themselves*, the very persons who now threaten me, shall roam about in search of food, &c. The most probable meaning of the last clause is : and not being satisfied, not finding what they seek, they must continue seeking it by night as well as by day. The conversive particle before the last word seems to be here equivalent to *then* or *still* after a conditional clause—" if they are not satisfied, *then* they shall remain all night"—or "though they be not satisfied, *yet* must they remain all night."

17 (16). *And I will sing thy strength, and celebrate in the morning thy mercy ; for thou hast been a high place to me, a refuge in my distress.* The pronoun at the beginning is emphatic, I, on my part, as contrasted with these wretches. *Thy strength* or *power*, thus exerted in my behalf. *In the morning*, or *at break of day*, which is the primary meaning of the term. The phrase is in obvious antithesis to *at evening* in ver. 15 (14). There may also be allusion to the frequent use of night and morning, as emblems of suffering and relief. Compare the words of David in 2 Sam. xxiii. 4. *A height*, high place, or place of safety, as in ver. 10 (9) above. *In my distress*, or retaining the original construction, *in distress to me*. The form of expression is the same as in Ps. xviii. 7 (6).

18 (17). *My strength, unto thee will I sing ; for God is my high place, the God of my mercy.* The most natural construction of the first phrase is that which makes it a direct address to God, as the author of his strength. But as the structure of the clause is precisely similar to that at the beginning of ver. 10 (9), some adopt a similar construction, *my strength will I sing unto thee*. I will praise my strength to thee, because I shall thereby praise thyself. This is equivalent to saying, I will celebrate thee as my strength. *High place*, place of safety, refuge, or asylum, as in ver. 10, 17 (9, 16). *God of my mercy*, my merciful God, or the God who shews me mercy. See above, on ver. 11 (10).

Psalm 60

1. *To the Chief Musician. On the Lily of Testimony. A Mystery. By David. To be Learnt.* The *lily* is probably, in this case, as in Ps. xlv. 1, an emblem of beauty or loveliness. The *testimony* is a name given to the Law, as God's testimony against sin. See above, on Ps. xix. 8 (7), and compare 2 Kings xi. 12, where the term is applied absolutely to the Law, considered as a book or writing. This enigmatical inscription, therefore, may be understood as representing the theme or subject of the psalm to be the beauty of the law, or something lovely in it, with reference most probably to the gracious promise cited from it. At the same time, there seems to be an allusion to the precept in Deut. xxxi. 19, "Now therefore write ye this song for you, and TEACH it the children of Israel; put it in their mouths, that this song may be a WITNESS for me against the children of Israel." To this verse there seems to be a double allusion in the one before us; first in the word *testimony*, which is a cognate form to that translated *witness*, and then in the concluding words, *to teach*, where the verb is the same with that in Deuteronomy. The title before us, therefore, seems to say, this song is like the song of Moses, which was to be taught to the people, as a witness or testimony against them, in case of unbelief or disobedience. *To teach* then means *to be taught* or *to be learned* by heart, committed to memory. Compare 2 Sam. i. 18, where the English version incorrectly supplies (*use of*) *the bow*, instead of (*song of*) *the bow*, meaning the elegy on Saul and Jonathan which immediately follows, so called, according to an ancient custom, from the mention of Jonathan's favourite weapon in ver. 22. See above, on Ps. ix. 1. From this enigmatical allusion, and the disguised form under which the truth is here revealed, the psalm is justly represented as a *Michtam*, mystery, or secret. See above, on the titles of the four preceding psalms. The body of the psalm, apart from the additional title or historical inscription in ver. 2, may be divided into three equal stanzas or strophes, each consisting of four verses. In the first, the Psalmist takes occasion from God's seeming desertion of his people, to recall his former interventions in their favour, ver. 3–6 (1–4). In the second, he pleads an express promise, as a ground of present hope, ver. 7–10 (5–8). In the third, he expresses his confidence of safety and success, in the proposed expedition against Edom, ver. 11–14 (9–12). Throughout the psalm the ideal speaker is Israel, considered as the chosen people.

2. *When he conquered Aram Naharaim and Aram Zobah, and Joab returned and smote Edom in the Valley of Salt, twelve thousand men.* The common version of the first verb (*strove with*) seems too weak, as a victory is clearly presupposed, and the idea of contention is conveyed by a cognate form of the same verb. The name *Aram* corresponds to *Syria* in its widest and vaguest sense, and is joined with other names to designate particular parts of that large country. It even includes Mesopotamia, which is a term of physical rather than political geography, and denotes the space between the Tigris and Euphrates, corresponding to *Aram-Naharaim*, or *Syria of the Two Rivers*, in the verse before us. The king of this country was tributary to the king of Aram Zobah, as appears from the account of David's second Aramean war (2 Sam. x. 16, 19). It was after the return of the victorious army from this war, that Joab marched against Edom and achieved the victory here ascribed to him, as the leader of the army, but in

1 Chron. xviii. 12, to his brother Abishai, who probably commanded under him, as he did in a subsequent campaign (2 Sam. x. 10), and in 2 Sam. viii. 13, to David himself as the sovereign whom they both represented. The *Valley of Salt* has been identified by modern travellers with a valley south of the Dead Sea, on the ancient confines of Israel and Edom. See Robinson's Palestine, vol. ii. p. 483. The number killed on this occasion is stated in 2 Sam. viii. 13, and 1 Chron. xviii. 12, at eighteen thousand. But this diversity might easily arise from different modes of computation, and seems at least to shew that the writer of the verse before us did not blindly copy the historical books, while the smaller number which he gives evinces his exemption from all disposition to embellish or exaggerate.

3 (1). *O God, thou hast cast us off; thou hast broken us; thou hast been angry; thou wilt restore to us* (thy favour or our previous prosperity). Clear as the marks of thy displeasure have been, we still confidently look for thy returning favour. This may refer to disasters experienced in the former part of the campaign. *Cast us off*, with abhorrence and contempt, as in Ps. xliii. 2, xliv. 10, 24 (9, 23). *Broken us*, or made a breach in us, which appears to be a military figure, and a favourite with David in real life. See 2 Sam. v. 20, vi. 8, and compare Judges xxi. 15, Job xvi. 14, xxx. 14. The last verb means to restore, as in Ps. xix. 8 (7), xxiii. 3, but in application to a different object. Compare Isa. lviii. 12.

4 (2). *Thou hast made the earth quake, thou hast riven it; heal its breaches, for it moves.* The idea of social disaster and calamity is here expressed by the figure of an earthquake and its natural effects, to which God is besought to put an end by the removal of the cause.

5 (3). *Thou hast made thy people see* (what is) *hard; thou hast made us drink wine of staggering* (or *reeling*). The meaning of the first clause is, that God had made them experience hardship. See a similar expression in Ps. lxxi. 20. *Wine of staggering*, wine that causes men to reel or stagger, here used as a figure for confusion, weakness, and distress. The same image reappears in Ps. lxxv. 9 (8), Isa. li. 17, 22, Jer. xxv. 15, xlix. 12. See above, on Ps. xi. 6.

6 (4). *Thou hast given to those fearing thee a banner to be lifted because of* (thy) *truth. Selah.* In the sight of thy discomfited and downcast people, thou hast set up a signal, as a rallying point, and an assurance of the truth of thy engagements. The word (נֵם) translated *banner* means anything elevated as a signal, being derived from the following verb, which, in the form here used, means properly to *raise itself*, as in Zech. ix. 16. The word for *truth* is not the one commonly so rendered, but has the same meaning in Prov. xxii. 21, and in the Aramaic dialects. See Dan. ii. 47, iv. 34. *Because of*, literally *from before* or *from the face of*, an expression indicating, as the cause of the effect described, the truth or veracity of God himself. The translation of the last clause in the ancient versions and some modern ones, *to flee from before the bow*, gives an unauthorised meaning both to the verb and noun.

7 (5). *In order that thy beloved ones may be delivered, save* (with) *thy right hand and hear* (or *answer*) *us.* This is a prayer naturally prompted by the previous experience of God's favour, as recorded in the foregoing verse. *Thy beloved*, an epithet applied to Benjamin in Deut. xxxiii. 12, and forming a part of Solomon's additional name *Jedidiah*, 2 Sam. xii. 25. See also Ps. xlv. 1. The common version of the last words (*hear me*) rests upon the marginal reading or Keri.

8 (6). *God hath spoken in his holiness; I will triumph; I will divide*

Shechem, and the Valley of Succoth I will measure. As a further ground for his petition, the Psalmist, speaking in the name of Israel, appeals to the promise of Jehovah, that his people should possess the entire land of Canaan. The reference is not to any insulated promise, but to that pervading the whole Law. There *God had spoken*, uttered his promise, *in his holiness, i. e.* as a holy God, and as such incapable of failing to perform it. See the similar expressions in Ps. lxxxix. 36 (35), Amos iv. 2. Some understand what follows as the words which God had spoken; but as ver. 11 (9) is confessedly the language of the people or their representative, and as no intermediate point of transition can be well assumed, it seems better to explain these also as the words of David or of Israel. " God hath spoken in his holiness (and therefore) I will triumph." Because he has promised me victorious possession of the land, I exult in confident anticipation of it. This idea of triumphant occupation is expressed in terms appropriate to the times of the original conquest, when the land was measured and distributed among the tribes. See Josh. xiii. 7, xviii. 5. The two great divisions of the country, east and west of Jordan, are denoted by Shechem and Succoth, the places where Jacob pitched his tent on his return from exile, as if to claim the Land of Promise as his heritage. See Gen. xxxiii. 17, 19.

9 (7). *To me* (belongs) *Gilead and to me Manasseh, and Ephraim the strength of my head, Judah my lawgiver.* The idea still is that the whole of Canaan rightfully belongs to Israel. The form of expression is analogous to that in the preceding verse, but with a beautiful variation. As the two great divisions of the country, east and west of Jordan, are there represented by detached points, Shechem and Succoth, so here by the names of extensive districts, Judah and Ephraim, the two largest territories on the west, Bashan and Gilead on the east, the latter called by its own name, the former by that of the tribe which occupied the greater part of it. See Deut. iii. 12, 13. The last clause does due honour to the military strength of Ephraim (Gen. xlviii. 19, Deut. xxxiii. 17), but asserts the civil supremacy of Judah (Gen. xlix. 10). The phrase translated *strength of my head* might seem to mean *my chief strength;* but that would require the terms to be inverted, *head of my strength.* Compare Gen. xlix. 3. It rather means the protection of my head, as *strength of my life* in Ps. xxvii. 1 means that which protects my life, the head being mentioned as the vital part peculiarly exposed. Compare Ps. lxviii. 22 (21), cx. 6. Some suppose the figure to be that of a helmet, which is too specific. In the last clause there is obvious allusion to the prophecy in Gen. xlix. 10. *Lawgiver* has its proper sense of ruler, sovereign. That of rod or sceptre, which some give it, rests upon a doubtful explanation of Num. xxi. 18.

10 (8). *Moab (is) my wash-pot; at Edom will I throw my shoe; at me, Philistia, shout aloud!* The three hostile powers, with which Israel was most frequently at war, are here put together, as the objects of a contemptuous address. Moab is likened to the humblest household utensil, the vessel in which slaves were wont to wash their master's feet. Edom is likened to the slave himself, to whom or at whom the master throws his shoe when about to bathe his feet. Compare Mat. iii. 11, Acts xiii. 25. This is much better suited to the context than the allusion, which some assume, to the practice mentioned in Ruth iv. 7, where the removal of the shoe is a symbol of renunciation, and could not be here used to express the opposite idea of seizure or triumphant occupation. *Shout aloud,* or *make a noise,* is by some explained as an expression of triumph, and the whole

clause treated as ironical. Others understand it of the acclamation or shout of welcome and applause by which subjects recognise and hail their sovereign. See above, on Ps. ii. 11, where the exhortation to *rejoice with trembling* is, by the same interpreters, explained in the same manner. In either case, the clause implies superiority in him who speaks, and willing or compulsory subjection on the part of those whom he addresses.

11 (9). *Who will bring me (to) the fenced city? Who has led me up to Edom?* In reliance on God's promise, and in the possession of the hope and courage just expressed, his people are ready to go forward, and only waiting, as it were, for some one to conduct them into the enemy's country, nay, into his very citadel. The *fenced city*, literally, *city of defence*, or *fortification*, a phrase already used in Ps. xxxi. 22 (21), is Petra, the famous capital of Idumea, hewn in the rock, and almost perfectly impregnable. See Robinson's Palestine, vol. ii. pp. 573–580. The past tense in the last clause represents the question as already answered. *Up to*, even to, as far as, implying not mere motion or direction, but actual arrival.

12 (10). (Is it) *not thou, O God,* (who) *hast cast us off and will not go forth with our hosts?* A simpler construction of the first clause would be, *hast thou not cast us off?* But it seems better to explain the verse as an indirect answer to the question in the one preceding. Who has brought us into Edom, if not he who had rejected us ? The terms are borrowed from Ps. xliv. 10 (9), which seems to have been written in the midst of the distress here spoken of as past. " Wilt not thou, of whom we lately were compelled to say, thou hast forsaken us and wilt not go forth with our hosts ? " Compare 2 Sam. v. 24.

13 (11). *Give us help from trouble* (or *from the enemy*); *and* (the rather because) *vain* (*is*) *the salvation of man, i. e.* the deliverance which man affords. The causal particle, *for, because*, which seems necessary to connect the clauses, is implied but not expressed in Hebrew. The second noun (צר) may either mean *distress*, as in Ps. iv. 2 (1), xviii. 7 (6), or one who gives distress, a persecuting or oppressing enemy, as in Ps. iii. 2 (1), xiii. 5 (4), xxvii. 2, 12, xliv. 6, 8, 11 (5, 7, 10). Either sense would be appropriate, but the latter is strongly recommended by its occurrence in the next verse.

14 (12). *In God we will make* (*i. e.* gain or gather) *strength, and he will tread down* (or *trample on*) *our adversaries* (persecutors or oppressors). The prayer is followed by the confident anticipation of the answer. *In God, i. e.* in union with him, in possession of him. See above, on Ps. xviii. 30 (29). The common version of the next phrase (*shall do valiantly*) is vague and dubious, being inadmissible in several of the cases where the phrase occurs, whereas they all admit of the translation *make* or *gather strength*, in reference to the acquisition or recovery of force by those who had before been in a state of weakness. See below, on Ps. cviii. 14 (13), cxviii. 15, 16, and compare Ezek. xxviii. 4, Ruth iv. 11, Deut. viii. 17, 18, Num. xxiv. 18, to the last of which places there is obvious allusion here, as relating to the very same enemies. *Treading* or *trampling*, as an emblem of violent subjection, occurs above in a contemporaneous passage, Ps. xliv. 6 (5). The last eight verses reappear as a part of Ps. cviii., in the exposition of which the points of difference and the general relation of the passages will be considered.

Psalm 61

1. *To the Chief Musician—on a stringed instrument* (or with an instrumental accompaniment)—*of David*. The peculiar form of the original construction (נְגִינַת לְדָוִד) cannot be reproduced in English, but seems to connect the name of David both with the Hebrew word preceding, as the owner or conductor of the music, and with the psalm itself as the author. That is to say, the words are so combined as to convey both these ideas— *a stringed instrumeut of David*—and *a psalm of David*. The musical term (*neginath*) is the same as in the titles of Ps. iv., vi., liv., lv., but in the singular number and the construct form. The psalm itself consists of a prayer with an expression of strong confidence, ver. 2–5 (1–4), and an appeal to the divine promise, as the ground and object of that confidence, ver. 6–9 (5–8).

2 (1). *Hear, O God, my cry; attend unto my prayer!* The psalm opens with an introductory petition to be heard. See above, on Ps. v. 2, 3 (1, 2), xvii. 1, lv. 2 (1), and compare Ps. xxxix. 13 (12). The word translated *cry*, which sometimes means a joyful shout or thankful song—Ps. xxx. 6 (5), xlii. 5 (4), xlvii. 2 (1)—is here determined by the parallelism and the context to denote a cry for help or mercy.

3 (2). *From the end of the earth unto thee will I call, in the covering of my heart* (when it is covered, *i. e.* overwhelmed, or covered with darkness). *To a rock* (that) *is high from me* (*i. e.* higher than I, or too high for me), *thou wilt lead me*. To the saints of the Old Testament exclusion or involuntary distance from the sanctuary seemed equivalent to exile in the remotest countries, sometimes called the *end of the earth* (Deut. xxviii. 64), sometimes the *end of heaven* (Deut. iv. 32), although this last phrase may be understood to mean the sensible horizon or boundary of vision (Isa. xiii. 5). *A rock*, often mentioned as a place of refuge. See above, on Ps. xviii. 3 (2), xl. 3 (2). *Too high for me* to reach without assistance. In the last clause an earnest prayer is latent under the form of a confident anticipation. The feelings here expressed, and the terms used to express them, are peculiarly appropriate to David's situation during Absalom's rebellion. See above, on Ps. iii. 1, xlii. 1.

4 (3). *For thou hast been a refuge to me, a tower of strength* (or strong tower), *from before* (from the face or presence of) *the enemy*. He appeals to former mercies as a ground for his present expectation. The verb of existence is here emphatic, and cannot, without a violation of usage, be translated as a present, which is almost invariably suppressed in Hebrew. The *enemy* is a collective term, or one denoting an ideal person, including many real individuals.

5 (4). *I will sojourn* (or *abide*) *in thy tent* (or *tabernacle*) *ages* (or *eternities*, *i. e.* for ever); *I will trust* (take refuge or find shelter) *in the shadow of thy wings*. The first verb is in the paragogic form, expressing strong desire or fixed determination. See above, on Ps. ii. 3. To dwell in God's tent or house is to be a member of his family, to enjoy his bounty and protection, and to live in intimate communion with him. See above, on Ps. xv. 1, xxiii. 6, xxvii. 4, 5. David here tacitly appeals to the promise recorded in 2 Sam. vii. See above, on Ps. xxi. 5 (4). The beautiful figure for protection in the last clause is the same as in Ps. xvii. 8, xxxvi. 8 (7).

6 (5). *For thou, O God, hast heard* (or *hearkened to*) *my vows* (and the

prayers which they accompanied); *thou hast given* me *the heritage of those fearing* (or *the fearers of*) *thy name, i. e.* the reverential worshippers of thy revealed perfections. See above, on Ps. liv. 3 (1). The heritage here mentioned is participation in the honours and privileges of the chosen people, with particular though tacit reference to the vicarious royalty conferred on David, and ensured to his posterity in answer to his prayers. See above, on Ps. xxi. 3–5 (2–4), and compare 2 Sam. vii. 16.

7 (6). *Days to the days of the king thou wilt add ; his years* (shall be, or, thou wilt multiply) *like generation and generation.* The preposition in the first clause strictly means *upon*, and suggests the idea not of mere addition but accumulation, which would also be conveyed in English by the literal translation, *days upon days.* His use of the third person shews that he does not mean himself alone, but the king of Israel as an ideal or collective person, comprehending his posterity. The life of this ideal person would of course not be restricted to a single generation, but continued through many, which is the meaning of the idiomatic expression in the last clause.

8 (7). *He shall sit* (enthroned) *to eternity before God ; mercy and truth do thou provide ; let them preserve him* (or *they shall preserve him*). The first verb suggests the two ideas of continuance or permanence and regal exaltation. See above, on Ps. lv. 20 (19), and compare 2 Sam. vii. 29. *Before God*, in his presence and under his protection. See above, on Ps. lvi. 14 (13). *Provide*, prepare, afford, or have in readiness. Mercy and Truth are personified, as in Ps. xl. 12 (11), lvii. 4 (3). Compare Ps. xliii. 3. They seem to be here represented as God's messengers or agents in preserving his Anointed.

9 (8). *So will I celebrate thy name for ever, that I may pay my vows day* (*by*) *day.* The *so* at the beginning may mean, on this condition, when this prayer is granted ; or more probably, in this assurance, in the confident expectation of this issue. *Celebrate* musically, both with instrument and voice. See above, on Ps. lvii. 8 (7), and compare Ps. lix. 18 (17). *That I may pay*, literally *to* (or *for*) *my paying*, or, as some explain it, *by my paying*, which, however, is a rare and dubious use of the infinitive. *Day* (*by*) *day* or *day* (*and*) *day, i. e.* one day with or after another, implying not only frequency but regularity. The Vulgate version of this idiomatic phrase is *de die in diem.*

Psalm 62

1. *To the Chief Musician over Jeduthun. A psalm by David.* Jeduthun seems here to mean the family or choir so called from the Chief Musician of that name. See above, on Ps. xxxix. 1. The psalm consists of three equal stanzas or strophes, each beginning with the particle (אַךְ) *only*, and the first and second ending with *selah.* In all these parts, the theme or burden is the same, to wit, a contrast between God and man, as objects of confidence.

2 (1). *Only to God* (is) *my soul silent ; from him* (is) *my salvation.* The frequent repetition of the first word (אַךְ) is characteristic of the psalm before us. In all these cases it is to be taken in its strict exclusive sense of *only.* See above, on Ps. lviii. 12 (11). Only in looking towards God as my Saviour, is my soul *silent*, literally *silence.* See above, on Ps. xxii. 3 (2), xxxix. 3 (2). This trust, and this alone, can set his mind at rest, and free him from the natural disquietude of man when alienated from his God.

3 (2). *Only He* (is) *my rock and my salvation, my height* (high place, refuge, or asylum) ; *I shall not be shaken* (moved from my firm position) *much* (or *greatly*). The adverbial use of *much* is the same in Hebrew and in English. This qualified expression seems to be intended to suggest, that he does not hope to escape all disaster and calamity, but only such as would be ruinous. See above, on Ps. xxxvii. 24. As to the figures in the first clause, see above, on Ps. ix. 10 (9), xviii. 3 (2). *He only,* God and no one else, can be such a protector.

4 (3). *Until when* (how long) *will ye break loose upon* (or *against*) *a man, will ye murder* (*i. e.* seek to murder him) *all of you* (combined against a single person, who is consequently) *like a wall inclined* (or bent by violence), *a fence* (or hedge) *crushed* (broken down ?) That the last clause relates to himself and not his enemies, is clear from the continuation of the same description in the next verse.

5 (4). *Only from his elevation they consult to thrust* (him, and as a means to this end) *they delight in falsehood ; with his mouth,* (*i.e.* with their mouths) *they will bless, and in their inside* (inwardly, or with their heart) *they will curse. Selah.* The sudden change of number in the middle of the verse, and indeed the whole description, are like those in Ps. v. 10 (9).

6 (5). *Only to God be still my soul, for from him* (is) *my hope.* The view just taken of his fellow-men drives him back to God, and he exhorts himself to cherish the same confidence which he had before expressed. *Be still,* silent, trusting, and submissive. See above, on ver. 2 (1), and compare Ps. xxxvii. 7. The meaning of the last clause is, from him proceeds whatever I desire or hope for.

7 (6). *Only he is my rock* (the foundation of my hope) *and my salvation* (*i. e.* its source and author)—*my high place* (refuge or asylum)—*I shall not be moved* (or *shaken*). This more absolute expression, as compared with ver. 3 (2), seems to indicate a stronger faith, derived from the previous comparison of God and man as objects of trust and affection.

8 (7). *Upon God* (*i. e.* dependent, founded on him) *is my salvation, and my honour* (both official and personal) ; *the rock of my strength* (my strong rock, or the basis upon which my own strength rests) ; *my hiding-place* (my refuge) is *in God.* It is in his presence, favour, and protection, that I hide myself from all my enemies and all my dangers. See above, on Ps. vii. 11 (10), lxi. 4 (3).

9 (8). *Trust in him at every time, O people, pour out before him your heart ; God* (is) *a refuge for us. Selah.* The faith which he cherishes himself he recommends to others also. *At every time,* not merely in prosperity, but even in the sorest trials and the worst extremities. *People,* not merely men or persons, but people of God, his chosen people. To pour out the heart is a natural and lively figure for a full disclosure of the thoughts and feelings. See above, on Ps. xlii. 5 (4), and below, on Ps. cxlii. 3 (2), and compare 1 Sam. i. 15, Lam. ii. 19. The last clause gives the reason of the exhortation, and indicates its earnestness by a solemn pause.

10 (9). *Only vanity* (are) *sons of Adam, a falsehood sons of man ; in the scales* (they are sure) *to go up ; they are of vanity* (or *less than vanity*) *together.* As to the supposed antithesis between men of high and low degree in the first clause, see above, on Ps. iv. 3 (2), xlix. 3 (2). *Only vanity,* see above, on Ps. xxxix. 6 (5). *A falsehood,* something that deceives expectation, a false confidence. See above, on Ps. iv. 3 (2). *Of vanity,* composed of it, containing nothing else ; or giving the particle its frequent comparative sense, (*less*) *than vanity,* or (*vainer*) *than vanity* (*itself*). The

same doubt exists as to the meaning of the similar expressions in Isa. xl. 17, xli. 24.

11 (10). *Trust not in oppression, and in robbery become not vain;* (on) *wealth, when it grows, set not* (your) *heart.* The first two nouns are used together in Lev. v. 23 (vi. 4) to signify that which is acquired by violence. They are not therefore to be taken as distinct grounds of confidence, but as different parts or different descriptions of the same. *Become not vain,* by being assimilated to the vain, unsatisfying objects of your love and hope. See 2 Kings xvii. 15, and compare Jer. ii. 5, Job xxvii. 12. The word translated *wealth* means strictly *strength* or *power,* but is applied to pecuniary as well as military force. See above, on Ps. xlix. 7 (6). *Grows,* literally *sprouts,* or springs up of its own accord, perhaps with an antithetical allusion to wealth gained by violence. Even when lawfully or accidentally acquired, set not your heart upon it. This phrase in Hebrew sometimes means nothing more than to apply the mind or give attention, and so some understand it here, "when wealth increases, take no notice, think not of it;" but the stronger sense of fixing the affections on it, loving it, and trusting it, is better in itself and better suited to the context.

12, 13 (11, 12). *One* (thing) *hath God spoken, these two* (things) *have I heard, that strength* (belongeth) *unto God, and* (that) *unto thee, O Lord,* (belongeth) *mercy,* (but) *that thou wilt render to a man according to his deed* (or *doing*). There are really three attributes of God here mentioned, his power, his mercy, and his justice; but as the last is only introduced to qualify the second, by a kind of after-thought, they may still be reckoned as but two. The construction given in the English and many other versions separates the sentences, and makes the first refer to a repeated utterance or revelation of the one truth there propounded, namely, *that power belongeth unto God.* Instead of *one thing, two things,* we must then read *once* and *twice.* But this, though favoured by the imitation of the verse before us in Job xxxiii. 14, xl. 5, is not the most obvious construction here. It is evident that *one* and *two,* when absolutely or elliptically used, may sometimes mean *one time,* (*i. e.* once) and *two times,* (*i. e.* twice); but it does not follow that the same words, in a different connection, may not mean *one word* or *thing, two words* or *things.* It is also a familiar practice of the sacred writers to borrow one another's words, or to repeat their own, with some slight change of sense or application. The pronoun (זו) in ver. 12 (11) may be either a demonstrative or relative, and on the latter supposition we may read, (there are) *two* (things) *which I have heard;* but the other is a simpler and more obvious construction. The apostrophe or sudden change of person in ver. 13 (12) is a figure of speech common in the psalms of David, and indicates a growing warmth of feeling, so that He who had just been calmly spoken of as absent, is abruptly addressed as if seen to be personally present.

Psalm 63

1. *A Psalm by David, in his being* (when he was) *in the wilderness of Judah.* This is the wilderness along the eastern frontier of the tribe of Judah. It is frequently mentioned in the history of Absalom's rebellion and of David's flight before him. See 2 Sam. xv. 23, 28, xvi. 2, 14, xvii. 16. In that history we also meet with several of the very same expressions that are here used, which, together with the strong internal

similarity of this psalm to some others having reference to Absalom's rebellion, such as Ps. iii., iv., xlii., lxi., suffice to shew that it belongs to the same period, and not to that of Saul's persecution, which is indeed forbidden by the mention of the king in ver. 12 (11). The psalm consists of two parts, each exhibiting essentially the same succession of ideas, but with the variation usual in all such cases. Both begin with the expression of intense desire for God's presence and communion with him, and end with a confident anticipation of his mercy; but in the first, ver. 2–9 (1–8), this is supposed to be displayed in the deliverance of the Psalmist from his sufferings; in the second, ver. 7–12 (6–11), it is viewed as securing the destruction of his enemies.

2 (1). *O God, my God (art) thou; I will seek thee early ; for thee thirsts my soul; for thee longs my flesh, in a dry land, weary without water.* The second divine name is the one denoting power, and might be translated here, *my Mighty (One).* The very use of it involves a direct appeal to God's omnipotence. The verb in the first clause is connected in its etymology with a noun meaning the dawn of day, which occurs above, Ps. lvii. 9 (8). The modern lexicographers exclude the sense of *early*, and suppose the verb to mean nothing more than *seek* in English, or at most to seek with eagerness. But that the notion of time is really included seems to follow from the antithesis in Isa. xxvi. 9. The act of seeking a thing early implies impatience or importunate desire. The soul and the flesh together mean the whole man. See above, on Ps. xvi. 9. There is evident allusion to the actual privations experienced by David in the wilderness of Judah. See the places cited in the note upon ver. 1, to which add 2 Sam. xvii. 2. The Hebrew word for *weary* is there applied to David himself, which requires or allows the same application in the case before us, especially as the form of the adjective is masculine, and *land* is feminine. The strict grammatical concord is perhaps with *flesh*, which is a masculine in Hebrew.

3 (2). *To see thy power and thy glory, so (as) I have beheld thee in the sanctuary.* The first clause states the object of the strong desire expressed in the preceding verse. To make this connection clear, the clauses are transposed in the common version, which is here retained, as being, on the whole, the best among the many which have been proposed. One of the latest makes the verse an acknowledgment that he had actually found a sanctuary in the desert, because it is always to be found where God is pleased to manifest his presence. But however sound and scriptural this sentiment may be, it can hardly be extracted from the verse before us without violence.

4 (3). *Because thy favour is better than life, my lips shall praise thee.* A simpler construction, and perhaps more agreeable to Hebrew usage, is that which makes the first clause give a reason for the strong desire expressed in the foregoing verses, *for thy favour is better than life*, and the last clause merely add a pledge of thankful acknowledgment, *my lips shall praise thee. Better than life*, not merely than the life I now live, which was scarcely entitled to be so considered, but better than any life I could live, destitute of God's favour, which is therefore more than a sufficient substitute or compensation.

5 (4). *So will I bless thee in my life, in thy name will I raise my hands. So*, that is, according to the gift bestowed. *Bless, i. e.* praise and thank thee. See above, on Ps. xvi. 7, xxxiv. 2 (1). *In my life* may either mean *as long as I live*, which is the obvious and usual interpretation, or *when*

restored to life, from this state of living death, which is the sense preferred by some of the best interpreters, on account of the supposed allusion to *better than life* in the preceding verse; but it is far from being the most natural construction. *In thy name,* invoking thee as the object of my worship, and particularly of my thankful praise. *Lift up my hands* in prayer, and more specifically here, in thanksgiving. See above, on Ps. xxviii. 3 (2).

6 (5). *As* (with) *marrow and fatness shall my soul be satisfied, and* (with) *lips of rejoicing shall my mouth praise* (thee). He continues the expression of his joyful confidence and hope. *Marrow* and *fatness* are used to represent two Hebrew words, both meaning animal fat, here put for rich food, and that for abundant supplies of every kind. *Lips of rejoicings* may denote either joyful lips, or lips by which rejoicings are uttered. The unconditional engagement to praise God implies, as usual, a firm belief that he will have occasion so to do. See above, on Ps. v. 8 (7).

7 (6). *When I remember thee upon my bed, in the watches I will meditate upon thee.* The first word in Hebrew is the one commonly translated *if;* but the condition indicated by it is sometimes specifically that of time. There seems to be reference in this verse to the old division of the night, for municipal and military purposes, into three watches, the first (Lam. ii. 19), the middle (Judges vii. 19), and the morning watch (Exod. xiv. 24, 1 Sam. xi. 11). See below, on Ps. xc. 4. *I will meditate of thee,* or more literally *in thee,* implying an entire absorption of his powers and affections in the object. See above, on Ps. i. 2.

8 (7). *For thou hast been a help to me, and in the shadow of thy wings will I rejoice.* The protection which he has experienced already he is sure of still enjoying in the time to come. The translation of the first verb as a present (*thou art my help*) not only weakens the antithesis but violates a constant usage. See above, on Ps. lix. 17 (16), lxi. 4 (3). The image presented in the last clause is the same as that in Ps. xvii. 8, xxxvi. 8 (7), lvii. 2 (1), lxi. 5 (4).

9 (8). *My soul cleaves after thee, thy right hand holds me.* This is a strong metaphorical description of the mutual relation between God and the believer; a relation of trustful dependence on the one hand, and of constant favour and protection on the other. *Cleaves after* is a frequent phrase for *follows cleaving to thee.* The right hand is the constant symbol of strength. See above, on Ps. xviii. 36 (35), xliv. 4 (3), lx. 6 (5).

10 (9). *And they to* (their) *ruin are seeking my soul; they shall go into the depths of the earth.* The phrase *to ruin* has precisely the same sense as in Ps. xxxv. 8, namely, to their own destruction. *Are seeking,* will seek; the idea suggested by the future is, that if they still persist in seeking it, they will do so to their own destruction. Some obtain the same sense by a different construction, *they* (shall come) *to ruin* (who) *are seeking my soul;* but this supposes two ellipses, which are not to be assumed without necessity. Still less satisfactory is the construction which regards the whole verse as a single proposition : *they* (who) *seek my soul to ruin* (or destroy it) *shall go,* &c. To seek the soul implies a purpose of destruction, without any qualifying adjunct, even in prose. See 2 Sam. xvi. 11. The *depths of the earth,* literally its lower or lowest parts, which may simply mean the grave (as we say *under ground*), or contain an allusion to the fate of Korah and his company (Num. xvi. 31–34). See above, on Ps. lv. 16 (15).

11 (10). *They shall be abandoned to the power of the sword, the prey of jackals shall they be.* The literal translation of the first clause is, *they shall*

pour him out upon the hands of the sword, where the use of the plural verb in an indefinite or passive sense, and the sudden alternation of the singular and plural form in speaking of the enemy, together with the bold and idiomatic figures of a sword with hands and men poured on them, present such a concurrence of apparent solecisms as can be made intelligible only by a paraphrase. The word translated *prey* means properly a *share* or *portion;* it occurs above, Ps. xi. 6, xvi. 5. The other noun in this clause is the common Hebrew word for *foxes*, but is used with so much latitude as to include the jackal, which sense must be here preferred, as the fox does not prey upon dead men, unless the clause be understood to mean nothing more than that they shall be left lying in the desert, where these creatures have their home, which is a good sense, but much weaker than the one just put upon the words.

12 (11). *And the king shall rejoice in God;* (in him) *shall every one boast* (or *glory*) *that swears by him, because the mouth of those speaking falsehood shall be shut* (or stopped). Instead of the personal pronoun he inserts his official title, *the king, i. e.* I as king. *Rejoice in God, i. e.* in union with him and in the experience of his favour. *Boast* or *praise himself, i.e.* felicitate himself on the possession of these glorious distinctions and advantages. *Swearing by him, i.e.* as some suppose, by the king here mentioned, according to the old Egyptian custom (Gen. xlii. 15, 16), of which we find some traces even in Israel (1 Sam. xvii. 55, xxv. 26, 2 Sam. xi. 11). If this were the true grammatical construction we might perhaps explain the phrase to mean *swearing to him, i. e.* swearing fealty or allegiance, doing homage to him as a rightful sovereign. But there is, in fact, no sufficient reason for departing from the obvious construction which refers the pronoun to the nearest antecedent, *God.* The last clause assigns the immediate occasion of the joy and triumph here predicted, namely, the defeat of false and treacherous insurgents. See above, on Ps. lxii. 5 (4), and compare 2 Sam. xviii. 7, 8.

Psalm 64

1. *To the Chief Musician. A Psalm by David.* The correctness of this title is abundantly established by the marked internal similarity between this and other psalms of David. Its very structure is Davidic, exhibiting the two familiar elements of a prayer for deliverance from wicked enemies, ver. 2–6 (1–5), and a confident anticipation of a favourable answer, ver. 7–11 (6–10).

2 (1). *Hear, O God, my voice in my complaint; from fear of the enemy thou wilt preserve my life.* Here, as in Ps. liv. 3 (1), the expression of confidence insinuates itself into the prayer itself. *Complaint*, literally musing, meditation, but with special reference to suffering and danger. See above, on Ps. lv. 3 (2). *Fear of the enemy*, that which I have reason to fear from him.

3 (2). *Thou wilt hide me from the secret of evil doers, from the tumult of the workers of iniquity.* By *secret* we are here to understand their confidential consultations and the devices there matured. See above, on Ps. xxv. 14. The participle *doing evil*, used as a noun (*evil doers*) to describe the whole class of wicked men, is a favourite expression of David's. See above, Ps. xxii. 17 (16), xxvi. 5, xxvii. 2, xxxvii. 1, 9. As *secrecy* belongs to the formation of the plot, so does *noise* or *tumult* to its execution. The same figures are combined, but in a very different application, Ps. lv. 15 (14).

4 (3). *Who have sharpened, like the sword, their tongue, have strung their
arrow, bitter speech.* The figure in the first clause is a favourite with David.
See above, on Ps. lii. 4 (2), lvii. 5 (4), lix. 8 (7). *Strung their arrow,*
literally *trod* (*i. e. bent*) *it,* which must either be explained as an ellipsis—
bent their (bow to shoot their) arrow—or as a poetical transfer to the arrow
of what is strictly applicable only to the bow. See above, on Ps. lviii. 8
(7). The figure of an arrow is peculiarly appropriate to the poignant pain
produced by insult and calumny, which is also well expressed by the epithet
bitter. Compare Deut. xxxii. 24, 1 Sam. xv. 32.

5 (4). *To shoot in secret places* (*at*) *the perfect ; suddenly they will shoot
him, and will not fear.* With the first clause compare Ps. x. 8, xi. 2. The
perfect, the sincere and upright servant of God, who is free from all fatal
and essential defect of character. See above, on Ps. xv. 2, xviii. 24 (23),
vii. 9 (8), xxv. 21, xxvi. 1, 11, xxxvii. 37, in the last of which places the
Hebrew adjective has the same form as in the case before us. *And will
not fear, i.e.* without being deterred by the fear of God or man. See above,
on Ps. lv. 20 (19).

6 (5). *They will strengthen for themselves an evil word; they will tell about
hiding snares ; they have said, who will see to them?* To *strengthen* is to
make strong, to construct so as to be strong. *An evil word* is an idiomatic
phrase for a malignant plot, so called because it is the fruit of mutual discourse and consultation. See above, on Ps. xli. 9 (8). *Tell about,* count
and recount their various devices, past and present. See above, on Ps. lix.
13 (12). The interrogation in the last clause is an indirect one ; the equivalent direct form would be, *who will see to us, i.e.* regard us ? Compare
Ps. x. 11, lix. 8 (7).

7 (6). *They search out iniquities;* (they say) *We are ready—a consum-
mate plan! and the inward thought and heart of* (*every*) *man* (*is*) *deep.*
They rack their invention and ransack their memory for modes of doing
mischief. *We are ready,* literally *finished,* just as we might say in English,
we are done. The next phrase consists of a passive participle, derived from
the verb at the beginning of the sentence, and a cognate noun. The participle here corresponds to *exquisite, recherché,* something not to be had
without laborious search, and the noun describes the product of the search
itself. The last clause is added to enhance the danger, by representing the
device as springing, not from shallow, superficial, but profound contrivance.
Inward thought, literally *inside,* an equivalent to *heart,* often used by David.
See above, on Ps. v. 10 (9), xlix. 12 (11), lv. 16 (15), lxii. 5 (4).

8 (7). *But God has shot them—with an arrow—suddenly—the wounds
are theirs.* By an abrupt but beautiful transition he describes the tables as
completely turned upon the enemy. The antithesis is rendered very striking by the repetition of the verb, noun, and adverb used in ver. 4, 5 (3, 4).
Just as they are about to shoot an arrow suddenly at the righteous, God
shoots an arrow suddenly at them. The wounds which they intended to
inflict on others have become (וַיִּהְיוּ) their own. When they thought to
strike others, they were struck themselves. The general idea is the same
as in Ps. vii. 12–17 (11–16), liii. 6 (5), lvii. 7 (6). The adversative particle at the beginning is substituted for the simple copulative of the Hebrew,
to make the transition or antithesis more obvious in English. See above,
on Ps. lii. 10 (8), lv. 14 (13).

9 (8). *And he has cast them down; upon them* (*comes*) *their own tongue; all
shall flee gazing at them.* *Cast down,* literally *made to fall or stumble.* See
the use of the same verb in historical prose, 2 Chron. xxv. 8, and compare

the original of 2 Chron. xxvii. 23. The construction is indefinite, as in Ps. lxiii. 11 (10), *they have cast him down, i.e.* he is cast down, meaning the enemy as an ideal person, who, according to the usage of these psalms, is immediately afterwards referred to in the plural number. *Their tongue, i.e.* the consequences of their false, malignant speeches, and their mischievous deliberations. The verb in the last clause is an intensive form of the one used in Ps. xxxi. 12 (11), lv. 8 (7). *Gazing at them,* not simply seeing them, but seeing with emotion, whether that of wonder, joy, or terror. See above, on Ps. liv. 9 (7), lix. 11 (10). The clause seems to contain an allusion to the flight of the people, when the earth opened to devour Korah and his company, Num. xvi. 34.

10 (9). *And all men fear, and pronounce* (*it*) *God's doing, and his work they understand.* The conversive futures shew the dependence of the sentence upon that which goes before it, and describe the action, not as actually past, but as directly consequent upon the great catastrophe described in the preceding context. *And declared the work of God, i.e.* pronounced it to be such. Compare Exod. viii. 19. *His work they understand, i.e.* no longer foolishly ascribe it to mere chance or human agency.

11 (10). *Glad shall the righteous be in Jehovah, and shall trust in him ; and* (in him) *shall boast* (or *glory*) *all the upright in heart.* Having described the effect of the divine interposition on the wicked, and on men in general, he now shews how it will affect the righteous. *In Jehovah* means, as usual, in union with him and possession of him. The word translated *trust* is that which seems originally to denote the act of seeking shelter under an overshadowing object. See above, on Ps. lxiii. 8 (7). With the last clause compare Ps. lviii. 11 (10), lxiii. 12 (11).

Psalm 65

1. *To the Chief Musician. A Psalm. By David. A Song, i.e.* a song of praise. See above, on Ps. xlviii. 1, xlii. 9 (8). God is first praised in general, as a God of mercy and benevolence to all men, ver. 2–9 (1–8), and then in particular, as the giver of fruitful seasons and abundance, ver. 10–14 (9–13).

2 (1). *To thee* (belongeth) *silence, praise, O God, in Zion, and to thee shall be paid the vow.* The two words, *silence-praise,* form a kind of compound term, like *humility-righteousness* in Ps. xlv. 5 (4), meaning, as some suppose, *silent praise,* but this is hardly consistent with the fact that the praise here offered is vocal. More probably it means such praise as is accompanied by a cessation of all tumultuous and passionate excitement. See above, on Ps. lxii. 2, 6 (1, 5). *In Zion,* as the appointed place of prayer and praise under the old economy. The last clause implies that fresh occasion was continually given for thankful vows and their fulfilment, by the constant repetition of God's providential favours.

3 (2). *Hearer of prayer, up to thee shall all flesh come.* The first word in Hebrew is a participle, *hearing,* thou who habitually hearest prayer. This is mentioned as one of the divine characters or attributes. *Up to thee,* even to thee, implying actual arrival, and therefore a stronger expression than *unto thee.* *All flesh* sometimes means all animals, all living creatures (Gen. vi. 17, 19), but is here used in its narrower sense of all mankind (Gen. vi. 3, 12). To thee they shall come, *i.e.* must come, for the supply of their necessities, the forgiveness of their sins, and in short, for **every**

good and perfect gift (James i. 17), both of a temporal and spiritual nature.

4 (3). *Words of iniquities are too strong for me ;* (as for) *our transgressions, thou wilt expiate them,* or forgive them for the sake of an atonement. *Words of iniquities* is by some regarded as a pleonastic paraphrase for iniquities themselves. More probably, however, the phrase means the charge or accusation of iniquity. See above, on Ps. vii. 1, xli. 9 (8), and below, on Ps. cv. 27. *Too strong for me,* more than I am able to account for or endure. See above, on Ps. xl. 13 (12), and below, on Ps. cxxx. 3. The last clause contains the encouragement suited to the alarming situation mentioned in the first.

5 (4). *Happy* (he whom) *thou wilt choose and bring* (him) *near, i. e.* admit him to thy presence and to intimate communion with thee, (so that) *he shall inhabit thy courts ; we shall be sated,* satisfied or filled, *with the good, i. e.* the pleasure, the enjoyment, *of thy house, the holy* (place) *thy temple,* or thy holy temple, thy sanctuary, an expression used both of the tabernacle and the temple properly so called. See above, on Ps. v. 8 (7). The privilege described is not merely that of public worship at the place of God's appointment, but of residence in his family and participation in the privileges of his household. See above, on Ps. xv. 1, xxiii. 6. The change from the third person singular to the first plural shews that the former was only an individualization of the church or chosen people.

6 (5). *Fearful things in righteousness thou wilt answer us, O God of our salvation, the confidence of all the ends of the land and sea*—(even) *the furthest.* Thou wilt give us fearful answers to our prayers, *i. e.* such as are suited to excite religious reverence and awe. *The confidence,* the object of their trust. *Earth* (or *land*) and *sea* are put together to describe the whole world, and the *ends* of both for the remotest countries, which idea is then expressed directly, by the word at the end of the sentence. The superlative cannot be expressed in Hebrew, but is here suggested by the context. The sense is not that all men actually feel this trust in God, but that whether they feel it or not, they are really dependent upon him alone. Compare Isa. xlii. 4.

7 (6). *Fixing the mountains by his strength, girded with power.* This verse accounts for the dependence of all creatures upon God by a reference to his almighty power, which is not described in general terms, but by one of its effects or acts, the settling of the mountains, as the most solid and immovable portions of the earth. He is then metaphorically represented as *girded* or invested with power. See below, on ver. 13 (12).

8 (7). *Stilling the roar of seas, the roar of their waves, the tumult of nations.* The sentence is continued from the foregoing verse. God not only formed the material universe at first, but still controls it. There is here a beautiful transition from the literal to the figurative use of the same language. It is true, in the strict sense, that God stills the raging of the seas ; but it is also true that he subdues the commotion of human societies and states, of which the sea is a natural and common emblem. See above, on Ps. xlvi. 3, 4 (2, 3). Hence he adds in express terms, *the tumult of nations.*

9 (8). *Then were afraid those inhabiting the ends* (or most distant parts) *of thy signs ; the outgoings of morning and evening thou wilt make to shout* (or *sing*). *Then* is not expressed in Hebrew, but employed in the translation to shew the dependence of the verb on that of the preceding sentence. The sense is, that whenever God thus stills the tumult of the nations, even

the remotest are affected by *his signs*, *i. e.* the sensible indications of his presence and immediate agency. *Outgoings* is a local noun in Hebrew, and denotes the places where the evening and the morning come forth or begin, *i. e.* the points at which the sun sets and rises, the east and west, here put for eastern and western lands, and these for their inhabitants. That the fear mentioned in the first clause is not mere slavish dread, but an affection perfectly compatible with joy, is clear from the remainder of the sentence.

10 (9). *Thou hast visited the earth and drenched it ; thou wilt much enrich it ; the river of God is full of water ; thou wilt prepare their corn, for thus thou dost prepare it, i. e.* the earth, for this very purpose. God is said to *visit* his creatures when he manifests his presence with them, whether in the way of judgment or of mercy. See above, on Ps. viii. 5 (4). *Drenched*, soaked, or made to overflow. The word translated *much* is the same as in Ps. lxii. 3 (2). *The river of God*, as opposed to earthly streams. However these may fail, the divine resources are exhaustless. *Their corn*, that required for men's subsistence. See above on Ps. iv. 8 (7). The meaning of the last clause seems to be that he who provides rain to fertilize the earth, may be expected to provide the fruit itself.

11 (10). *Its furrows drench, its ridges beat down: with showers thou wilt soften it ; its vegetation thou wilt bless.* The first verb means to water abundantly, the second to lower or beat down, implying a great violence of rain. The word translated *showers*, according to its etymology and usage, denotes frequent and abundant rains. *Soften*, dissolve, or loosen it. The Hebrew verb is a derivative of that in Ps. xlvi. 7 (6). *Vegetation*, germination, that which sprouts or springs up from the seed when sown. Some make the verbs in the first clause infinitives, determined by the finite tenses which precede and follow. But their form permits them to be taken as imperatives, from which the transition to the future is entirely natural and in accordance with the usage of David's psalms, whenever an expression of confident anticipation is to be immediately subjoined to one of strong desire. See above, on Ps. liv. 3 (1).

12 (11). *Thou hast crowned the year of thy goodness, and thy paths drop fatness.* The first clause may either mean, thou hast crowned the year *with* thy goodness, or, as some prefer to construe it, thou hast crowned the year of thy goodness, the year distinguished by thy goodness, with particular instances and proofs of that goodness. The obvious meaning of the strong but beautiful figure in the last clause is, that wherever he appears his movements are attended by a rich and fertilizing influence. *Fatness* is as usual a figure for rich food, and that for general abundance,

13 (12). *They drop—the pastures of the wilderness, and* (with) *joy the hills are girt.* The word translated *pastures* properly means *dwellings*, but is specially applied to folds and pastures, as the places to which flocks resort. See above, on Ps. xxiii. 1. The word translated *wilderness*, according to its most probable etymology, originally signifies, not a barren desert, but a tract of country neither tilled nor thickly peopled, though perhaps luxuriant and abundant as a pasture ground. The general metaphor of clothing which occurs in the next verse, is here anticipated by the specific one of a girdle, as that which surrounds the body and confines the dress. See above, on Ps. xviii. 33 (32).

14 (13). *The pastures are clothed with flocks, and the vales shall be robed in grain; they shall shout* (for joy), *yea, they shall sing.* Some translate the first clause, *the flocks are clothed with lambs*, denying that the first noun in Hebrew ever means pastures. But see above, on Ps. xxxvii. 20. The

image presented in the first translation is certainly more natural and beautiful. It also makes the parallelism more complete, the fields being covered by the waving crops in the same sense that the meadows are covered by the grazing flocks. In the last clause the pastures and valleys, by a beautiful personification, are described as breaking forth into shouts of joy and songs of praise. See above, on Ps. lx. 10 (8).

Psalm 66

1. *To the Chief Musician. A Song. A Psalm. Shout unto God, all the earth !* The second clause of the inscription represents it as a psalm of praise. See above, on Ps. lxv. 1. This is confirmed by the contents and structure of the psalm itself, in which we have, first, a general celebration of God's wonderful dealings with his people in all ages, ver. 1–7 ; then a similar acknowledgment of what he had done in a particular case, ver. 8–12 ; and lastly, a pledge or promise of thanksgiving, ver. 13–20. The resemblance to the forty-sixth psalm has led some to suppose that this psalm was occasioned by the same event, or composed in imitation of the other, for the use of the church in similar emergencies. The verb *shout* is plural in its form, which shews that *earth* has a collective sense.

2. *Sing the honour of his name ; give* (him) *honour,* (give) *him praise.* The *honour* or *glory of his name* is that due to his manifested excellence. See above, on Ps. xxix. 2. *Give,* literally *place* or *put,* the verbs expressing these ideas being often interchanged in Hebrew. The same phrase that is here used occurs also in Josh. vii. 19, Isa. xlii. 12, and is clearly equivalent to *give honour* in Ps. xxix. 1, 2, lxviii. 35 (34), Jer. xiii. 16. The form of the last clause is peculiar, *give honour (as* or *to) his praise.*

3. *How fearful are thy doings ! In the greatness of thy strength shall thine enemies lie to ˌthee.* Here begin, as some interpreters suppose, the words in which the required praise is to be rendered to Jehovah ; an admissible, though not by any means a necessary supposition. The first clause may likewise be translated, *how fearful* (art thou in) *thy doings,* after the analogy of ver. 5 below, the ellipsis of the pronoun being similar to that in Ps. lxviii. 36 (35). *In the greatness of thy strength, i. e.* because of it, or rather in the knowledge and belief of it. See above, on Ps. v. 8 (7). *Lie to thee,* make false professions of allegiance, yield a feigned obedience, through the influence of fear. See above, on Ps. xviii. 45 (44).

4. *All the earth shall worship thee and sing to thee ; they shall sing thy name. Selah.* Here again the verbs are plural, shewing that *all the earth* is to be taken in a collective sense, as meaning *all lands,* or all the dwellers upon earth. See above, on ver. 1. *Worship thee,* bow or prostrate themselves before thee, as an act both of civil and religious homage. See above, on Ps. v. 8 (7). They shall not only sing to thee, but sing thy name, *i. e.* not only celebrate thy being but thy manifested nature, the attributes revealed by thy previous works. This anticipation of universal homage to Jehovah is in strict accordance with the whole spirit and design of the Mosaic dispensation.

5. *Go, see the works of God, fearful (in) action on the sons of man.* The verb *go* is often used in Hebrew, as a formula of invitation or of challenge, where in English we say *come.* See below, ver. 16, and compare Isa. ii. 3, 5. In this case, however, *go* may be intended to express something more than would have been expressed by *come.* The meaning may be, if

you do not believe these general declarations of God's power and dominion, go and see for yourselves the proofs already given in the history of mankind, and more especially in that of Israel: go to Egypt, to the Red Sea, to the Wilderness, to Jordan, and in the wonders there performed and still repeated in the experience of the church, see the evidence that God is indeed possessed of a tremendous power to control and influence mankind. With the first clause compare Ps. xlvi. 9 (8), the only other place where the word מִפְעֲלוֹת occurs.

6. *He turned the sea into the dry (land); through the river they shall pass on foot; there will we rejoice in him.* There is an obvious allusion to the crossing of the Red Sea and the Jordan, not as mere historical events, but as types or samples of God's extraordinary interpositions on behalf of Israel, such as might be realized again in their experience. Hence the promiscuous use of preterite and future forms, as if to say, the God of Israel will again turn the Red Sea into dry land for the passage of his people; if need be, they shall again cross the Jordan dry shod; there, on the scene of these miraculous events, shall we again rejoice in him. The combination of sea and river seems to shew that by the latter we must understand Jordan, and not, as some interpreters suppose, the Euphrates, which is commonly so called. But see Isa. xi. 15, 16, Zech. x. 11.

7. *Ruling by his might for ever; his eyes over* (or *among*) *the nations watch; let not the rebels exalt themselves. Selah.* The participle in the first clause is expressive of habitual action, "he [constantly, habitually rules." See above, Ps. xxii. 29 (28). *By his might,* with which he was before described as girded. See above, Ps. lxv. 7 (6). The noun *eternity* is used adverbially to mean *for ever.* The divine inspection here described implies that man can no more evade God's power than resist it. The last clause may be either a prayer to God or an admonition to his enemies. *Exalt themselves:* the Keri or marginal reading is, *be high for them* (or *for themselves*); the Kethib or textual reading, *lift* (or *raise*) *for themselves,* in which case *horn* may be supplied from Ps. lxxv. 5, 6 (4, 5), or *head* from Ps. cx. 7. The rebels, *i. e.* against God, his stubborn and incorrigible enemies.

8. *Bless, O ye nations, our God, cause to be heard the voice of his praise!* To the general description of God's gracious dispensations towards his people there seems now to be added the commemoration of a particular event of this kind; not one of merely local interest, however, but of such importance, that the nations are invited to unite in praising God for it. See above, on Ps. xviii. 50 (49), xxii. 28 (27).

9. *The (one) putting,* who puts, *our soul in life, and has not given* (up) *to removal our foot,* has not allowed it to move or slip. The unusual expression in the first clause seems to mean restoration to life, a figure for relief from great distress, which is not unfrequently described as death. See above, on Ps. xxx. 4 (3), xlix. 16 (15). To *set in life* is not unlike the phrase to *set in safety,* Ps. xii. 6 (5). The form of expression in the last clause is analogous to that in Ps. lv. 23 (22) above, and identical with that in Ps. cxxi. 3 below. *Given up to removal,* suffered to be moved from its firm position or its place of safety.

10. *For thou hast tried us, O God, thou hast purged* (or *assayed*) *us like the purging of silver,* as silver is purged, with particular reference, as some suppose, to the long-continued and repeated process of refinement necessary in the case of silver. See above, on Ps. xii. 7 (6), xxvi. 2, and compare Isa. i. 25, xlviii. 10, Zech. xiii. 9, 1 Pet. i. 7. The general idea here is

that of affliction, as a means both of trial and purgation, and is carried out in the following verses.

11. *Thou hast caused us to come into the net; thou hast put pressure on our loins.* The first clause is descriptive of complicated difficulties and embarrassments, the second of suffering and weakness. The word translated *net* occurs above in the very different sense of a *tower* or fortress, Ps. xviii. 3 (2). But even when so used, it strictly means a *hunting tower, i. e.* a post of observation and of safety used by hunters, and from the same root (צוד, to hunt) may be deduced the sense of *net* or *snare*, as a customary implement of hunting, in which sense it is certainly employed by Ezekiel (xii. 13). The word translated *pressure* occurs only here, but its essential meaning is clear from its etymological affinities. Compare the cognate form in Ps. lv. 4 (3). Some suppose the idea to be that of a superincumbent pressure, load, or burden, corresponding to the verb as used in Amos ii. 13. Others make *pressure* mean contraction, stricture, and by necessary implication, pain or anguish. The loins are mentioned as the seat of strength (Deut. xxxiii. 11), an injury to which implies both pain and weakness. See below, on Ps. lxix. 24 (23).

12. *Thou hast caused* (or *suffered*) *men to ride at our head, we came into the fire and into the waters, and* (now) *thou he t caused us to come forth to abundance*, overflow, *i. e.* of enjoyment. *Man*, frail or mortal man, whose tyranny is therefore the more insupportable. See above, on Ps. viii. 5 (4). This first clause is ambiguous, in Hebrew as in English. *To ride at our head*, though an exact translation, suggests only the idea of command or guidance, whereas some kind of suffering is required by the context. The common version, *to ride over our heads*, presents the image of horsemen trampling on their conquered enemies. Some suppose the idea to be that of *riding on us*, as a man controls and guides the horse that carries him. The *head* must then be mentioned only as the noblest part, without implying that the rider actually sits upon it. But this very circumstance makes the interpretation an unnatural and forced one. *Fire* and *water*, as the two great destroying elements, are common figures for distress and danger. Compare Isa. xliii. 2. The last Hebrew word in the verse occurs only here and in Ps. xxiii. 5.

13. *I will come* (to) *thy house with burnt-offerings; I will pay to thee my vows, i. e.* the offerings thus promised. His acknowledgments shall not be merely verbal or mental, but ceremonial, *i. e.* expressed in the symbolical form required by the dispensation under which he lived. The reference is neither to internal feelings nor to outward rites exclusively, but to both together. See above, on Ps. xl. 7 (6), l. 8, li. 18 (16). With the last clause, compare Ps. lxv. 2 (1). The sudden change of number, from the plural to the singular, shews that what follows is the words of an ideal speaker, representing the same persons who had spoken in the foregoing context, if not identical with them.

14. *Which my lips uttered and my mouth spake in my distress.* The first verb is a very strong and expressive one, in this connection not unlike our familiar phrases, *bolted, blurted out*, implying that he spoke from some irresistible impulse, and thus suggesting what is afterwards explicitly affirmed, that the vows in question were occasioned by extreme distress. The Hebrew verb originally means to open or distend the lips, whether as a gesture of mockery (Lam. ii. 16), or menace (Ps. xxii. 14), or for the purpose of articulate speech (Job xxxv. 16). That its absolute use, in special reference to vows spontaneously and hastily uttered, was familiar to the ancients,

may be seen from Judges xi. 35, 36. *In my distress ;* the original expression is, *in the distress to me.* See above, on Ps. xviii. 7 (6).

15. *Burnt-offerings of fatlings will I offer to thee, with incense of rams ; I will make* (an oblation of) *cattle with he-goats. Selah.* The word translated *fatlings* is especially applied to lambs, Isa. v. 17. The verb is the first clause in the one from which the noun rendered *burnt-offering* is derived, and strictly means *I will cause to ascend, i. e.* upon the altar, or in vapour from it. *Incense* may here be taken in its etymological sense of something *burnt* sacrificially, although in usage limited to aromatic fumigations, which is also the case with the Hebrew word in every place but this, where it seems to mean the sacrificial fat that was burned upon the altar. The verb to *make* is absolutely used, as a technical term of the Mosaic Law, to denote the act of sacrifice. See Exod. xxix. 36, Lev. ix. 7, and compare Judges vi. 19, 1 Kings xviii. 23, 26. The different species of victims are enumerated here, to convey the idea of a regular and perfect sacrifice, implying more than ordinary thankfulness.

16. *Go* (or in our idiom, *come*), *hear, all ye fearers of* (ye that fear) *God, and I will tell you what he hath done to* (or for) *my soul.* The fearers of Jehovah is a common description of believers or the people of God. See Ps. lx. 6 (4), lxi. 6 (5). The invitation is like that in Ps. xxii. 24 (23). *Tell,* in the primary sense of counting or numbering, and the secondary one of recounting or relating. *To my soul, i.e.* to me, whose life or soul was threatened. *To me* as the object of the act alluded to, or *for me,* as the person to be benefited. This address prepares the way for the ensuing declaration, founded on his own experience, that it is only by sincere submission and devotion to God that his protection is to be secured.

17. *To him* (with) *my mouth I called, and high pruise* (exaltation) *was under my tongue.* By a slight change in the pointing, or by supposing an irregularity of punctuation, the last clause may be rendered, *he was extolled under my tongue, i. e.* by means of it as an instrument of praise. But as a corresponding plural form occurs below, Ps. cxlix. 6, the Hebrew word (רוֹמַם) is probably a noun, meaning lofty praise, or exaltation by means of praise. *Under my tongue* may be simply equivalent to *on* or *with my tongue,* or it may be intended to suggest the additional idea of a store or deposit of such praises still in reserve, to be employed hereafter, which some suppose to be the meaning of the phrase in Ps. x. 7.

18. *Iniquity if I have seen in my heart, the Lord will not hear.* If I had any wicked end in view, God would not hear my prayer. The same idea is expressed in Prov. xv. 29, Isa. i. 15, lix. 2, John ix. 31, 1 John iii. 22. It is here stated as the ground on which he means to argue his own innocence of any such corrupt design, and actually does so in the next verse.

19. (But) *verily God hath heard ; he hath attended to the voice of my prayer.* The Hebrew particle at the beginning is strictly not adversative but affirmative. See above, on Ps. xxxi. 23 (22). It is equivalent in force to our expressions, *whereas, really, in fact,* &c. The doubt subjected in the foregoing verse had been removed in his case by the application of the test there mentioned. God had already heard his prayer and thereby borne witness that he was not guilty of the duplicity in question.

20. *Blessed* (be) *God who hath not put away my prayer* (from him) *and his mercy from me.* Here as elsewhere, when applied to God, *blessed* can only mean *praised* or entitled to be praised. The double application of the verb in the last clause cannot well be imitated in translation. The same

word in Hebrew may be used to express the act of *rejecting* a petition, and
that of *withdrawing* or withholding favour.

Psalm 67

1. *To the Chief Musician. With* (or on) *stringed instruments. A Psalm.
a Song, i. e.* a psalm of praise. See above, on Ps. lxvi. 1. For the meaning of the second clause of this inscription, see above, on Ps. lv. 1, and
compare Ps. lxi. 1. The psalm before us, like the sixty-fifth, seems to
have special reference to the manifestation of God's goodness in the gift of
fruitful seasons and abundant harvests. See below, on ver. 7 (6), and
above, on Ps. lxv. 1. But from this the Psalmist, or the church, of which
he is the spokesman, takes occasion to anticipate the extension of God's
covenanted gifts, both temporal and spiritual, to all the nations of the earth.
This expectation is indeed the burden of the psalm, its immediate occasion
being only mentioned incidentally near the close, yet not so obscurely as to
make it doubtful. Any formal division of this short and simple composition can only tend to mar its beauty.

2 (1). *God be merciful unto us and bless us, and cause his face to shine
upon us !* The form of expression is evidently borrowed from the sacerdotal benediction, Num. vi. 24, 25, but with a substitution of the first
person plural for the second singular, so as to convert the authoritative
blessing upon others into an expression of desire for themselves. The
optative meaning of the sentence is determined by the form of the second
verb in Hebrew. *Upon us,* literally *with us,* a form of speech probably
intended to suggest the idea of the divine presence and communion. As to
the figure in the last clause, see above, on Ps. iv. 7 (6), xxxi. 17 (16).

3 (2). *That thy way may be known in the earth, in all nations thy salvation.* The original construction of the first clause is, *to know in the earth
thy way ;* but the sense can only be made clear in English by a passive
form. *Thy way, i. e.* thy mode of dealing with thy people, referring more
particularly here to providential favours, the knowledge of which he hopes
to see extended to all nations, as a means to the promotion of still higher
ends. The pleonastic phrase, *saving health,* retained in the authorised version
from an older one, has nothing corresponding to it in the Hebrew but the
single word which always means *salvation,* and is commonly so rendered.

4 (3). *The nations shall acknowledge thee, O God, the nations shall
acknowledge thee—all of them.* The common version of the verb here twice
used (*praise*) is too wide. As it is commonly applied to the acknowledgment of benefits, a nearer equivalent is *thank.* See above, on Ps. lvii. 10 (9).

5 (4). *Nations shall joy and triumph, because thou shalt judge peoples* (in)
rectitude, and nations in the earth—thou shalt guide them. The divine
guidance implies protection and control. Compare Isa. lviii. 11. The
anticipation of universal happiness, as springing from the judicial acts of
the Messiah, is not unusual in prophecy. See below, on Ps. lxii. 12–14,
and compare Isa. ii. 3. The word translated *rectitude* occurs above, Ps.
xlv. 7 (6).

6 (5). *The nations shall acknowledge thee, O God, the nations shall
acknowledge thee—all of them.* This repetition shews the anticipation here
expressed to be the principal though not the primary subject of the psalm.
The position of the universal terms, at the close of this verse and ver. 4 (3),
is highly emphatic, and precludes, in the most explicit manner, all restriciton

7 (6). *The earth* (or *land*) *has yielded her produce; God will bless us,* (even) *our God.* The translation of the first verb as a future is entirely gratuitous, and therefore ungrammatical. Correctly rendered, it affords a hint of the immediate occasion of the psalm itself. The mutual relation of the clauses is that of a thankful acknowledgment for gifts received already to a joyful and believing expectation of the same hereafter. God has blessed us, and since he is our own God, he will bless us still.

8 (7). *God will bless us, and all the ends of the earth shall fear him.* The God who has bestowed this harvest on us will continue to afford us tokens of his covenant love and faithfulness; and the day is coming when the intimate relation which we now sustain to him will be extended to all nations. *Ends of the earth,* even the remotest countries, but of course without excluding those at hand. It is really tantamount to saying, *all lands* or *the whole earth.* See above, on Ps. ii. 8.

Psalm 68

1. *To the Chief Musician. By David. A Psalm of Praise.* Literally, *a psalm, a song,* but see above, on Ps. lxv. 1, lxvi. 1, lxvii. 1. This psalm, like the eighteenth, which it very much resembles, is a triumphal song, occasioned by some signal victory or success in war, perhaps that recorded in 2 Samuel xii. 26–31, which closed the last important war of David's reign. The psalm opens with a general praise of God as the deliverer of the righteous and destroyer of the wicked, ver. 2–7 (1–6). This is then illustrated and confirmed by a reference to certain periods in the history of Israel, and first to the march through the wilderness, ver. 8–11 (7–10). Then comes the period of the judges, ver. 12–15 (11–14). Then the erection of the monarchy on Zion, and its confirmation by the victory just achieved, ver. 16–20 (15–19). This is then represented as a part of the general plan of Jehovah's dealings with his people, ver. 21–24 (20–23). The triumphal procession is described, ver. 25–28 (24–27). All this, however, is but a specimen or foretaste of a universal conquest yet to come, ver. 29–32 (28–31). In anticipation of this revolution, the nations are summoned to unite in the praises of Jehovah, ver. 33–36 (32–35). The resemblence of this last part to the corresponding parts of the two preceding psalms may account for the position of the one before us.

2 (1.) *God shall arise, his enemies shall scatter; those hating him shall flee before him.* This verse propounds, as the theme of the whole psalm, a fact continually verified in history. There is also an obvious allusion to the form of speech uttered by Moses at the removal of the ark, the symbol of God's presence. See Num. x. 35. The wish there expressed is here said to be realised. Hence the change of the imperative (קוּמָה) into a future (וְקָם), shewing that this verse has not an optative meaning (*let God arise*), but is declaratory of what certainly will be hereafter, as it has been already, in the case which gave occasion to the psalm. The present time is not excluded, but involved in the general proposition, that it must and will be so. *Shall scatter* is a more exact translation of the Hebrew verb than *be scattered,* although the idea is undoubtedly that of involuntary violent dispersion. *Before him,* from his face, or from his presence. See above, on Ps. ix 4 (3), lxi. 4 (3).

3 (2). *As smoke is driven, thou wilt drive* (them); *as wax is melted before*

fire, the wicked shall perish before God.   The form of expression is the same
as in the preceding verse, *from the face of fire, from the face* (or *presence*) *of
God.*   The verb in the first clause is the same with that in Ps. i. 4, where
the wind, implied here, is expressly mentioned, as the driving or propelling
agent.   The comparison with wax is a common one in Scripture, and occurs
above, in Ps. xxii. 15 (14).   With the last clause compare the conclusion
of the Song of Deborah (Judges v. 31), of which there are various imitations,
or at least reminiscences, in this psalm.

4 (3). *And the righteous shall be glad; they shall triumph before God,
and shall joy with gladness.*   This is true not only of righteous individuals
but of righteous nations, and especially of Israel, as such considered,
although many of its members were unrighteous.   But these are not considered as really belonging to the church or chosen people, but are classed
among the wicked enemies of God.   *Before God* shall the righteous rejoice,
as the wicked flee *before him.*

5 (4). *Sing unto God, celebrate his name, cast up* (a highway) *for the
(one) riding through the deserts, by his name Jah, and exult before him.*
The second clause alludes to the opening of roads for kings and armies.
See above, on Ps. l. 23, and compare Isa. xl. 3, Mal. iii. 1.   The common
version of the verb (*extol*) conveys an idea wholly foreign from the usage of
the Hebrew word.   *Riding, i. e.* journeying, or giving it a military application, *marching.*   The common version of the next noun (*heavens*) is
entirely unauthorised by usage.   The Hebrew word is one still applied by
the Arabs to the region over which the Israelites wandered forty years.
The idea here suggested is more fully carried out in ver. 8–10 (7–9).   *By
his name Jah, i. e.* in the character denoted by this name, which is an
abbreviation of *Jehovah,* peculiar to the song of Moses (Exod. xv. 2) and the
later imitations of it.   See my notes on Isa. xii. 2, xxxviii. 11.   The
people are summoned to prepare for the reception of this glorious visitor.

6 (5). *Father of orphans and judge of widows* (is) *God in his abode of
holiness.*   One of the most glorious divine characters is that of a protector
of the innocent and helpless.   *Judge,* vindicator, patron, one who does
them justice.   His *abode of holiness* cannot in this connection denote
heaven, but must be referred to his peculiar residence among his chosen
people.   It was there that, both by the provisions of this law and the dispensations of his providence, he asserted his right to the exalted character
here claimed for him.

7 (6). *God makes the lonely dwell in houses, makes the captives come forth
into enjoyments ; only rebels* (still) *inhabit a dry land* (or *desert*).   This,
though a general proposition, seems to have a special reference to the
change in the condition of the Israelites, when brought out of the wilderness into possession of the promised land.   The participles in the original
(*settling, bringing out*) express habitual or customary acts.   *In houses,*
literally *in a house,* or still more closely *to a house,* the idea of removal
being really implied.   The word might also be translated *homewards* or *at
home.*   The last word in this clause occurs nowhere else, and has been
variously explained to mean *in chains, by force,* and *into pleasures* or enjoyments, which last is now preferred by most interpreters.

8 (7). *O God, in thy going out before thy people, in thy marching through
the wilderness. Selah.*   The sentence is completed in the next verse, being
here divided by a pause of solemn and admiring recollection.   The general
description of the foregoing verses is now confirmed and illustrated by
a reference to the exodus from Egypt, and the journey through the wilder-

ness. *Before thy people*, in the pillar of cloud, as their guide and their commander. *Thy marching*, literally *thy stepping*, *treading*, or more exactly still, *thy step* or *tread*. To make the allusion still more pointed, the word for *wilderness* is not the one commonly so rendered, but one borrowed from Deut. xxxii. 10.

9 (8). *The earth shook, nay, the heavens dropped, this Sinai, at the presence of God, the God of Israel.* *Dropped*, discharged drops, rained. This is mentioned as a natural and usual accompaniment of a thunderstorm. *This Sinai* probably means, *this (was at) Sinai*, and should be read as a parenthesis. The usual construction not only requires a verb to be repeated or supplied, but yields an obscure and doubtful sense, as no reason can be given why Sinai should be called *this Sinai*, and the version *Sinai itself* is unauthorised by usage. The first clause is descriptive of the grand and terrible phenomena attending the theopany at Sinai. See Exod. xix. 16–18.

10 (9). *A rain of free gifts thou pourest down, O God ; thine inheritance and (that) exhausted, thou dost confirm* (or *strengthen*) *it.* The first clause probably refers to the abundant and refreshing gifts (of which rain is a natural and common emblem) bestowed upon the people in the wilderness, including manna, quails, and water. The future tense is like those in Ps. xviii. 7 (6). *Pour down*, literally *shake* or shake out. *Thine inheritance*, thy people. The construction is that of an absolute nominative, (*as to*) *thine inheritance*. The next clause heightens the description by suggesting that the gift came precisely when it was most needed.

11 (10). *Thy flock hath dwelt therein ; thou wilt provide, in thy goodness, for the wretched.* The first noun strictly means an animal, and more especially a beast, but was probably employed as a collective to denote a herd or flock, in which sense it was figuratively applied in David's time to a company or troop of men, (2 Sam xxiii. 11, 13). *Therein*, *i. e.* in the land of promise, which was present to the writer's mind, though not expressly mentioned in the context. See below, ver. 15 (14), and compare Isa. viii. 21. *Thou wilt provide*, indefinitely, whatsoever may be needed ; or more specifically, *wilt prepare*, *i. e.* prepare a home, a resting place. The future tense describes it as a customary method of proceeding upon God's part, but specially exemplified in the case of Israel, who, until his settlement in Canaan, might well be called a sufferer, a wretched or afflicted one.

12 (11). *The Lord will give the word ; the (women) publishing (it) are a great host.* As to the future, see above, on ver. 10, 11 (9, 10). *Word* here means tidings, news, and, as the whole connection shews, good news, which is also suggested by the word translated *publishing*, but in usage constantly applied to joyful tidings. See above, on Ps. xl. 10 (9). There is obvious allusion to the ancient oriental custom of women celebrating victories with song and dance. See Exod. xv. 20, 1 Sam. xviii. 6, 7. The reference is not to any one occasion, but to an ideal choir chanting all the victories of some great period, perhaps that of the Judges.

13 (12). *Kings of armies shall flee, shall flee, and she that tarrieth at home shall divide the spoil.* The flight described is not that of kings alone, but of kings at the head of armies. The repetition of the verb denotes the certainty and completeness of the rout. The *dweller in the house* is by some literally understood to mean the woman who takes no part in the battle. But others regard it as a figure for the chosen people, dwelling quietly at home, after the disappearance of their enemies, when " the land had rest," Judges v. 31, viii. 28.

14 (13). *When ye lie down between the borders,* (ye shall be like) *the wings of a dove covered with silver and her pinions with yellow gold.* The general idea seems to be that when "the land had rest," her condition was one of peaceful prosperity. The common version of the first clause (*though ye have lien among the pots*) is justified neither by rabbinical tradition nor the ancient versions. The Hebrew noun occurs only here and in Ezekel xl. 43, where it is equally obscure, and the cognate forms in Gen. xlix. 14, Judges v. 16, are scarcely less so. The only meaning, besides those already mentioned, which has any probability, is that of *folds* or *sheep-cotes,* lying among which might be viewed as a poetical figure for rural or pastoral repose, thus amounting to the same thing with the first translation, which describes the people as residing quietly *between the borders, i. e.* within the boundaries or frontiers of their territory, now once more forsaken by the enemy. The beautiful allusion in the last clause to the changeable colours of a dove's plumage seems intended to suggest the idea of a peaceful but splendid prosperity.

15 (14). *When the Almighty scatters kings therein, it snows in Zalmon.* The change from war to peace is likened to the dazzling whiteness of snow in the midst of blackness or darkness. This last idea is conveyed by *Zalmon,* an unimportant eminence near Shechem, partly perhaps in reference to the dark forests which covered it (Judges ix. 48), but chiefly to the meaning of the name itself, to wit, *shade* or *shadow.* The parallel term, *snow,* suggests the idea of the brightest light. See Ps. li. 9 (7), Isa. i. 18, Mark ix. 3, Mat. xxviii. 3, Rev. i. 14, and compare Mat. xvii. 2. Some, with far less probability, explain the verse as meaning that the land was whitened with the slain, as Zalmon was with snow; but this ascribes too great an altitude to Zalmon. The Hebrew construction in the first clause is, *in the Almighty's scattering kings, i.e.* at the time of his so doing. The divine name here used is not the one so frequently translated *Mighty* in the Psalms, but the patriarchal title mentioned in Exod. vi. 3. Compare Gen. xvii. 1, xxviii. 3. It is here introduced because the events in question were remarkable exertions and displays of God's omnipotence. *Scattered* here means routed, put to flight. See above, ver. 13 (12), and compare the use of the same Hebrew verb in Zech. ii. 10 (6).

16 (15). *A mount of God (is) mount Bashan, a mount of peaks* (or *ridges) is mount Bashan.* The first phrase means a mountain shewing forth the creative power of God by its vastness. See above, on Ps. xxxvi. 7 (6). *Mount Bashan,* not a single eminence, but the lofty range of Antilibanus, also called *Hermon,* and by other races, *Sion* and *Sirion.* See Deut. iii. 9, iv. 48, Ps. xlii. 7 (6), Ps. lxxxix. 13 (12). The last two names would be apt to suggest, by a fortuitous resemblance, that of the holy hill of Zion. A mount of peaks or ridges, *i. e.* not a detached mountain, but a chain with many lofty summits, forming the northern boundary of Bashan. At the same time, the expression of this verse would necessarily suggest the idea of great states or kingdoms, of which mountains are the standing symbols. See above, on Ps. xlvi. 3 (2), lxv. 7 (6).

17 (16). *Why will ye watch, (ye) hills, (ye) ridges, the hill God hath desired for his dwelling? Yea, Jehovah will inhabit (it) for ever.* The interrogative form implies disapprobation and contempt. See above, on Ps. ii. 1. The verb occurs nowhere else in the Old Testament, but its meaning has been preserved in Arabic, namely, to watch as an enemy, to lie in wait, or, as some allege, to view with envy. Common to both is the idea of hostility or ill-will. The translation of this verb in the English Bible (*leap*)

and in the Prayer-Book version (*hop*) seems to rest on mere conjecture. The two nouns, *hills* and *ridges*, are by some supposed to form a sort of compound, *ridge-hills*, *i. e.* high or rugged hills. Compare the phrase *wine-reeling*, Ps. lx. 5 (3). The plural form may denote the several peaks, or the whole class which this range of mountains merely represented. Zion is here described as an object of hostility or envy to the mountains of the heathen world, on account of the honour put upon it by its being chosen as the earthly residence of God. Having first poetically said that he *desired* it, *i. e.* preferred and chose it, to preclude all doubt as to the event, the Psalmist adds, not only so, but he does and will dwell there for ever. The verbs of the second and third clause, although synonymous, are not identical in Hebrew. There is evident significance in the choice of the divine names here employed. Not only did he choose it, as Elohim, for his dwelling, but he actually dwells there as Jehovah, as the God of revelation and the covenanted God of Israel.

18 (17). *The chariots of God (are) two myriads, multiplied thousands; the Lord is among them, Sinai in the sanctuary.* As David's most formidable foes were particularly strong in chariots of war (2 Sam. viii. 4, x. 18), so here God's power of protection is expressed by an innumerable multitude of chariots. The same mode of representation occurs in the history of Elisha, 2 Kings vi. 17. *Two myriads* is a closer version than *twenty thousand*, because the Hebrew word is the dual of one used both in the vague sense of a multitude, and in the precise sense of a myriad. See above, on Ps. iii. 7 (6), where the plural of the same word occurs. The next phrase strictly means *thousands of repetition* or *reduplication*, *i. e.* thousands upon thousands. Compare Dan. vii. 10. There is no mention of *angels* in the text, although interpreters in every age have supposed their presence to be necessarily implied, as the conductors of God's chariots, if not as the chariots themselves, which is the sense put upon the Hebrew phrase by both the English versions (*even thousands of angels*). There is also an obvious allusion to the giving of the law at Sinai, as described in Deut. xxxiii. 2, 3, the presence of angels at which appears to be assumed in the New Testament, Gal. iii. 19, Heb. ii. 2. It is not, however, the mere number, even of these heavenly hosts, that constitutes the safety of the holy place, but the personal presence of the Lord (*Adhonai*) among them, which is therefore asserted in the next clause· The last words of the verse are obscure, but seem most probably to mean that the same glorious theophany which once took place on Sinai is now renewed on Zion, with particular reference, as some imagine, to the presence of the ark and the tables of stone in the one case, as a perpetual memorial, and even a perpetual renewal, of the legislation in the other. This fine poetical identification of the two mountains hallowed by God's presence may have been in the mind of the apostle when he drew that sublime contrast or parallel between them, Heb. xii. 18–24. Under the law Sinai was renewed in Zion. Under the gospel Zion superseded Sinai.

19 (18). *Thou hast gone up to the high-place; thou hast captured a captivity; thou hast taken gifts among mankind, and* (even among) *rebels,* (so as) *to dwell* (here), *Lord, God!* In order to carry out his choice and resolution, as recorded in ver. 17 (16) above, *i. e.* in order to establish Zion as his earthly dwelling-place, God has encountered all opposing powers, vanquished them, and forced them to pay tribute, even the stoutest and most stubborn. The sign of the conquest being finished is the conqueror's return to his throne, whether upon earth or in heaven. See above, on Ps.

vii. 8 (7), and compare Ps. xviii. 17 (16), xciii. 4, cii. 20 (19). *Captured a captivity*, *i.e.* taken captive a multitude of enemies. The *gifts* meant are the forced gifts of the conquered. *Among men*, *i. e.* while present among them as their conqueror, and by implication *from* them. *Even rebels*, even the most rebellious, are compelled to submit. In other words, the conquest is complete. According to the military figures here used, it would seem to be implied that the gifts thus extorted by the conqueror are distributed among his followers. To *receive gifts* on the one hand, and *bestow gifts* on the other, are correlative ideas and expressions, so that Paul, in applying this description of a theocratic triumph to the conquests of our Saviour, substitutes one of these expressions for the other (Eph. iv. 9). He also, in his comment on the passage, justly represents the ascension there described as necessarily implying a previous descent. In other words, victory presupposes conflict. The last clause obviously refers back to the corresponding clause of ver. 17 (16). *Lord God*, literally *Jah, God !* See above, on ver. 5 (4).

20 (19). *Blessed be the Lord, day* (by) *day ;* (whoever) *lays a load upon us, the Mighty* (God is) *our salvation. Selah.* The second clause, which is obscure from brevity, also admits of this translation : (man) may lay a load upon us, (but) God is our salvation. *Lay a load upon us*, literally *load to us*, or *as to us*. According to both these constructions, loading means oppression. It is possible, however, to attach to it the sense of benefits or favours, put upon it in the English versions, but with a very different construction of the whole clause. *The Mighty (God) will heap upon us our salvation*, or, *will load us with salvation*. The depth of feeling and the strength of faith, on which this anticipation rests, are indicated or betrayed by the meditative pause which follows.

21 (20). *God is for us a God of salvation, and to Jehovah the Lord* (belong) *issues from death*. A more exact translation of the verse, retaining the peculiar idioms, would be this : *the Almighty* (is) *for us an Almighty for salvation, and to Jehovah the Lord* (belong)*, as to death, outgoings* or *escapes*. This is only an amplification of the last clause of the verse preceding, *God is our salvation*, or according to the other construction, *God loads us with salvation*.

22 (21). *Surely God will crush the head of his enemies, the hairy scalp going on in his trespasses.* The first word properly means *only*, and is here used to denote that this and not the contrary is true, a purpose which in our idiom may be answered by a particle of strong asseveration, such as *certainly* or *surely*. See above, ver. 7 (6), and compare Ps. xxxix. 12 (11), lviii. 12 (11). *Crush the head*, a strong figure for violent and complete destruction. See below, on ver. 24 (23), and compare Gen. iii. 15, Ps. cx. 6, Num. xxiv. 8, 17. The *hairy scalp*, or *crown of hair*, is merely a poetical equivalent or parallel to *head*. The words that follow seem to be applied to it by a kind of personification. Compare Prov. xvi. 31. But this figure, if too bold, may be avoided by supplying *of one* or *of the man* before *going*. This last word does not necessarily mean *going on*, but according to its usage elsewhere may be rendered *going about*, *i. e.* habitually acting, in a sinful manner. See above, on Ps. xii. 9 (8), xx. 7 (6), xxvi. 3, xxxv. 14, xxxix. 7 (6), xliii. 2 (1).

23 (22). *The Lord hath said, From Bashan I will bring* (them) *back, I will bring* (them) *back from the depths of the sea.* Some suppose the object of the verbs in this verse to be *Israel* or *my people*, as in Isa. xlix. 12 (compare Gen. xiv. 14). But as the enemy is still the subject of the fol-

lowing verses, it is better to understand the one before us as threatening
to bring them back for punishment and destruction, even when they seemed
to have withdrawn in triumph. Here, as in verse 15 (14), *Bashan* is
mentioned as a frontier province of the Holy Land. In the last clause
there is an obvious climax. I will bring them back, not from Bashan
merely, but if need be, from the bottom of the ocean. Compare Ps.
cxxxix. 9, and especially Amos ix. 2, 3.

24 (23). *In order that thou mayest crush* (them)—*thy foot in blood*—
(and) *the tongue of thy dogs* (in blood) *from the enemies* (even) *from him.*
The general import of this verse is clear, but its construction doubtful
and obscure. The first verb cannot mean to *dip* or *wash* without an arbitrary change of text by reading תרחץ as in Ps. lviii. 11 (10). The original
verb (תמחץ) must have the same sense as in ver. 22 (21), and may have
the same object, namely, the enemies of God and of his people. The next
words may then be taken as a parenthetical and qualifying clause, like
sword in hand, and other such forms in English. *Thy foot in blood, i. e.*
with thy foot in their blood, or so that thy foot shall tread in their blood.
The last word in Hebrew (מנהו) is by some understood as a noun with a
suffix meaning *its portion, i. e.* the share of the tongue ; but for this there
is no authority in usage. Others translate the phrase, *of it, i. e.* of the
blood, and the whole clause, *the tongue of thy dogs (shall receive) of it from
the enemies.* According to the first version given above, the last phrase is
a mere specification of the one before it ; *from the enemies,* (even) *from
him,* referring to some real or ideal representative of the entire class.

25 (24). *They saw thy goings, O God, the goings of my God, my king,
in the holy place.* The subject of the first verb may be either men in general, or the spectators, those who took no part in the triumphal pageant here
described. *The holy place,* not in the restricted sense, but in that of the
Greek *ἱερόν,* meaning the whole of the sacred enclosure, as distinguished
from *ναός,* the sacred edifice. Into this enclosure the procession seems to
be described as entering, for the purpose of bringing back the ark.

26 (25). *Before went singers, behind players, in the midst of damsels
drumming,* playing upon timbrels, which is still an oriental custom. Some
suppose the order mentioned in the first clause to denote the precedence
or priority of vocal above instrumental music, as a rational or reasonable
service. The English version of the last clause, *among (them were) the
damsels,* inverts the true sense by needlessly supplying two words, a construction forbidden by the masoretic pointing. The true sense is, that the
singers and performers were themselves surrounded by these players upon
timbrels.

27 (26). *In assemblies bless ye God, the Lord, from the fountain of
Israel.* Not only individually, or in triumphal marches, but in the stated
convocations of the people at the sanctuary. See above, on Ps. xxvi. 12, the
only other place where the Hebrew word occurs, except as a proper name
(Num. xxxiii. 25), and where it evidently has the same sense. The only satisfactory explanation of the last words, *from the fountain of Israel,* is that
afforded by supplying *ye who are* before it, and applying the whole clause
as a description of the chosen people, under the figure of a stream derived
or flowing from a fountain. Compare the similar ideas and expression in
Isa. xlviii. 1, li. 1.

28 (27.) *There is little Benjamin, subduing them ; the chiefs of Judah,
stoning them ; the chiefs of Zebulon ; the chiefs of Naphtali.* These are
named as representatives of all the tribes supposed to be *there, i. e.* in the

triumphal march. They seem to be selected, partly with reference to their
local habitation, as the northern and southern extremities of Israel ; partly
because the most remarkable exploits, from the time of Moses to the time of
David, were performed by these tribes. See Judges v. 18, 1 Sam. xviii. 7.
Little Benjamin, so called in allusion to Jacob's partial fondness for his
youngest son. See Gen. xliii. 33, and compare 1 Sam. ix. 21. *Their
conqueror,* or *subduing them* as Saul did the surrounding nations. See
1 Sam. xiv. 47, 48. *Stoning them,* literally *their stoning,* from a verb which
invariably means to *stone.* The allusion may be to their skill as slingers,
or more specifically to the means by which David killed Goliath (1 Sam.
xvii. 49, 50). The suffix refers to the enemy, as in the clause preceding.
Some interpreters have noted, as an observable coincidence, that our Lord
and several of his apostles were of Judah, Paul was of Benjamin (Phil.
iii. 5), and the remaining apostles of Galilee, in which lay the domain of
Zebulon and Naphtali (Mat. iv. 13).

29 (28). *Thy God* (O Israel) *hath ordained thy strength; be thou strong,
O God, who hast wrought* (it) *for us.* Ordained, provided and secured by
his omnipotence. *Be strong, i. e.* shew thy strength by exerting it in our
behalf, hereafter as thou hast done heretofore. *Wrought for us,* indefinitely
and in general, or *wrought (it, for us, i. e.* this deliverance which we have
been celebrating. See above, on Ps. xxii. 32 (31), and compare Isa.
xxvi. 12.

30 (29). *Because of thy temple above Jerusalem, to thee shall kings bring
tribute.* The first word properly means *from ;* but as the local sense would
here be inadmissible, *from* may be understood as in the phrase *arising from,
proceeding from,* in which the idea is that of an effect or consequence. As
the word translated *temple* originally means a *palace,* it is applicable both
to the Mosaic sanctuary and to Solomon's temple which succeeded it. See
above, on Ps. v. 8 (7), xlviii. 10 (9), lxv. 5 (4). *Above Jerusalem,* both in
a physical and moral sense, as Zion and Moriah overhung the city, and as
the presence of the sanctuary was at once its protection and its crowning
glory. The last word in Hebrew occurs only here and in passages founded
upon this. See below, Ps. lxxvi. 12 (11), and compare Isa. xviii. 7.

31 (30). *Rebuke thou the beasts of the reeds, the crowd of strong* (bulls)
*with the calves of the nations, crouching with pieces of silver ; he has scattered
nations* (that) *in wars delight.* What he confidently anticipates is prayed
for in the first clause, and in the last described as already realized, both
common modes of indirect prediction. The word for *beasts* is that translated *flock* in ver. 11 (10) above ; but here both senses seem to be suggested,
as they may be by the use of the plural in English. The *beast of the reeds*
has been variously explained to be the lion (Jer. xlix. 19, l. 44, Zech. xi. 3),
the crocodile (Ezek. xxix. 3, xxxii. 2), and the hippopotamus, the Hebrew
name of which is plural in its form (*Behemoth*) and therefore analogous to
the collective term here used. This animal is also represented elsewhere
as lying *in the covert of the reed* (Job xl. 21). Either the crocodile or hippopotamus would necessarily suggest the idea of Egypt, here referred to as
the most powerful of heathen states, and therefore a fit emblem of the
heathen world. The adjective *strong* is a poetical description of *wild bulls,*
as in Ps. xxii. 13 (12). These may represent the leaders of the nations,
and the *calves* their subjects. The participle *crouching* is a singular in
Hebrew, *prostrating himself,* the many being suddenly transformed into an
ideal individual. See above, on Ps. x. 10. *With pieces of silver,* silver
coins, offered as tribute to their conquerors. See above, on ver. 19 (18),

and compare Isa. lx. 9. In the close of the verse he sees the warlike
enemies of Israel already scattered by the hand of God.

32 (31). *Princes shall come out of Egypt ; Ethiopia shall soon stretch out
her hands unto God.* Egypt is again named as the representative of the
Gentile world, but in conjunction with the neighbouring state of Cush or
Ethiopia, often referred to by the prophets as a powerful and splendid
empire. See Isa. xviii. 7, xlv. 14, Zeph. iii. 10. The word translated
princes means originally *fat ones*, elsewhere put for prosperous and potent
men. See above, on Ps. xxii. 30 (29). From this word is supposed to be
derived the name *Hasmonean, which was* given to the Maccabees or Jewish
princes in the interval between the Old and New Testaments. *Soon stretch
out* is not a version but a paraphrase of the original expression, which means
strictly, *make its hands to run,* and may perhaps denote the eagerness with
which the action is performed.

33 (32). *Kingdoms of the earth, sing unto God ; praise* (or *celebrate*) *the
Lord ! Selah.* In view of the conquests here foreseen, the whole world is
summoned to acknowledge the God of Israel as the universal sovereign.
Compare Rev. xi. 15.

34 (33). (*Sing*) *to the* (one) *riding in the heavens of heavens of old ; lo,
he utters his voice, a voice of strength.* This verse is designed to magnify
the object of the praise enjoined. *Riding,* as a conqueror in triumph. See
above, on ver. 5 (4). *The heavens of heavens* are the highest heavens, the
heaven of that which is heaven to us. See 1 Kings viii. 27, and compare
Deut. x. 14, xxxiii. 26. *Of old* does not qualify *riding,* as it may seem to
do in English, but the nouns immediately preceding, *the heavens of antiquity*
or *ancient heavens.* See above, on Ps. lv. 20 (19). In the last clause, he
seems to hear an audible response from heaven itself. The *lo,* as usual,
implies that something suddenly assails the senses. *Utters his voice,* literally *gives* (forth a sound) *with his voice,* as in Ps. lxvi. 7 (6).

35 (34). *Give strength to God ! Over Israel* (is) *his mdjesty, and his
strength in the clouds.* To *give,* in such connections, is of course to ascribe.
See above, on Ps. xxix. 1, 2. The remainder of the verse contains the
ground of this injunction. God is entitled to the praise of power, because
his greatness is displayed in the protection which he extends over Israel.
As the sanctuary was above Jerusalem, so God was above the chosen people,
their chief and their protector. See above, on ver. 30 (29). At the same
time his power is displayed throughout the universe, especially those extraordinary dispensations, in which he appears to speak from heaven or the
clouds. See above, on Ps. xxvi. 6 (5).

36 (35). *Terrible* (art thou), *O God, out of thy holy places ; the Mighty*
(*God*) *of Israel—he is* (a God) *giving strength and forces to the people.
Blessed* (be) *God !* The winding up is like that of the twenty-ninth psalm.
Out of thy sanctuaries, as displayed thence, in blessings bestowed upon thy
people. He is not only mighty in himself, but the giver of might to others.
Compare Isa. xl. 29, 31.

Psalm 69

A SUFFERER describes his own condition, ver. 2–5 (1–4). He represents
himself as suffering for God's sake, ver. 6–13 (5–12). He therefore prays
to be delivered, ver. 14–19 (13–18). He again describes his suffering, but
with more explicit reference to its cause, the malice of his enemies, ver.

20–22 (19–21). He therefore prays that they may be destroyed, ver. 23–29 (22–28). He anticipates a favourable answer to his prayers and the happiest effect upon his brethren, ver. 30–34 (29–33). Nay, he expects to see the same mercy exercised towards the church or chosen people, ver. 35–37 (34–36).

1. *To the Chief Musician. Upon lilies. By David.* The *lilies* probably refers to the delightful consolations and deliverances experienced or hoped for. See above, on Ps. xlv. 1, lx. 1. The subject of the psalm is an ideal person, representing the whole class of righteous sufferers. The only individual in whom the various traits meet in Christ. That he is not, however, the exclusive or even the immediate subject, is clear from the confession in ver. 6 (5). There is no psalm, except the twenty-second, more distinctly applied to him in the New Testament.

2 (1). *Save me, O God, for the waters are come in, even to my soul,* i. e. so as to endanger my life. See Jer. iv. 10, Jonah ii. 6. The figure for extreme distress is the same as in Ps. xl. 3 (2).

3 (2). *I have sunk in the mire of the depth* (or *deep place*) (where) *there is no standing ; I have come into depths of water, and the flood has overwhelmed me.* The image is that of one sunk in the bottom. of a sea or river. *Mire of depth* is not merely deep mire, but the mire found in a deep place.

4 (3). *I am weary of my crying ; parched is my throat ; my eyes fail, waiting for my God.* The literal meaning of the first clause is, *I am weary in my crying,* i. e. have grown weary in the act of calling upon God for help. See above, on Ps. vi. 7 (6). *Parched,* dried, by excessive exertion of the voice, or giving the Hebrew verb the stronger sense which properly belongs to it, *inflamed.* His eyes are represented as exhausted, worn out, by continued looking for God. See below, Ps. cxix. 82, and compare Lam. iv. 17. The participle *waiting* does not agree with *eyes,* as it might seem to do in English, but with the person to whom they belong, and may be construed absolutely, *I waiting* (*me expectante*), *i. e.* while I wait.

5 (4). *More than the hairs of my head* (are) *those hating me without cause ; strong are my destroyers, my false enemies ; what I did not rob, then must I restore.* With the first clause compare Ps. xl. 13 (12); with the second, Ps. xxxv. 9, xxxviii. 20 (19); with the third, Ps. xxxv. 11, 2 Sam. xvi. 8. *False enemies,* literally *enemies of falsehood,* which may either mean in general perfidious, treacherous, or more specifically, using calumny and falsehood as a means for the attainment of their wicked ends. *Then* or afterwards, in reference to the previous innocence which he asserts. Though he took nothing at first, yet afterwards he must restore.

6 (5). *O God, thou knowest of* (or *as to*) *my foolishness, and my trespasses from thee have not been hid.* He does not deny his own demerit in the sight of God, but nevertheless prays to be delivered from destruction. See above, on Ps. vi. 2 (1), xxxviii. 4–6 (3–5), xl. 13 (12), xli. 15 (14). As if he had said, "True, I am a sinner; it is vain to deny it; thou, God, knowest it; but nevertheless," &c.

7 (6). *Let not them be ashamed in me that wait for thee, Lord, Jehovah, of Hosts ; let not them be disgraced in me that seek thee, God of Israel !* He prays that the principle laid down in Ps. xxv. 3 may not be falsified. *In me,* not merely *by me,* or *because of me,* but *in me,* as the representative of the whole class. *Ashamed,* disappointed and defeated in their hopes. *Wait for thee,* for thine appearance and the fulfilment of thy promises. *Seek thee, i. e.* seek to know thee, and enjoy thy favour.

8 (7). *Because for thee* (or *thy sake*) *I have borne reproach, disgrace hath covered my face.* In his disgrace all God's servants must participate, because he is one of them, and as such suffers. With the first clause compare Ps. xliv. 23 (22), Jer. xv. 15, with the last, Ps. xliv. 16 (15).

9 (8). *I am become a stranger unto my brethren, and an alien unto the sons of my mother.* The literal meaning of the first clause is, *I have been estranged to* (or *as to*) *my brothers.* There may be an allusion to the envious treatment of David by the other sons of Jesse. See 1 Sam. xvii. 28. The loss or alienation of the nearest friends is spoken of as one of the severest trials in Ps. xxvii. 10.

10 (9). *For the zeal of thine house,* jealous regard for the honour of the sanctuary, as the visible centre of the true religion, *has consumed me,* implying an extreme intensity of feeling ; and in consequence of this zeal, *the revilings of thy revilers have fallen upon me.* That such revilers did exist in David's time, we learn from 2 Sam. xii. 14. The first clause of the verse before us is applied to Christ in John ii. 17, and the second in Rom. xv. 3.

11 (10). *And I wept* (*away*) *my soul,* or wept myself away, *in fasting, and* (even that) *was for revilings to me,* even that became a subject of malignant mockery against me. That weeping and fasting, as natural concomitants, were not unknown to David's experience in real life, appears from 2 Sam. xii. 16, 21, 22. The first clause likewise admits of this construction : *and I wept, my soul* (was) *in fasting, i. e.* fasted. But this, though it agrees well with the Hebrew usage which represents fasting as a mortification of the soul (see above, on Ps. xxxv. 13), is neither so natural nor so striking as the ¦first construction above given, which is found in an anonymous translation of the Psalms, published by Bagster, London, 1830.

12 (11). *And I gave,* put on (as) *my clothing, sackcloth, and was to them, in consequence, for a comparison,* a proverb, by-word, or *became a by-word to them.* See above, on Ps. xxxv. 13, and xliv. 15 (14). The context makes it probable that the mourning described in this and the preceding verse was not in reference to his own sufferings merely, but to the sins of the whole people.

13 (12). *They think of me,* imagine things against me, *they who sit in the gate;* (they imagine) *songs,* lampoons or satires, *they who drink strong drink.* The *gate* meant is that of the city, where the oriental courts and markets were held. Hence some suppose the sense to be, that even in the place of serious business, they indulged their spiteful mirth at my expense. But it seems more natural to make the sitters in the gate mean simply those frequenting public places. See above, on Ps. lv. 12 (11, and compare Josh. xx. 4, Ruth iv. 1, 2, Lam. v. 14.

14 (13). *And I,* but as for me, in contradistinction from these mockers, *my prayer* (is) *to thee,* I pray to thee in spite of their derision, *O Jehovah ;* (let there come or let there be) *a time of acceptance, in the abundance of thy mercy; answer me,* grant my petition, *in the truth of thy salvation,* or thy truth of salvation, in the exercise of that fidelity which secures the salvation of all who trust it. Compare Isa. xlix. 8, lxi. 2.

15 (14). *Deliver me from the mire, and let me not sink ; let me be delivered from my haters, from the depths of water.* He here returns to the figures in ver. 2 (1), where profound suffering is described as submersion under water and in mire. The meaning of the figure is explained in the last clause of the verse before us by the addition of a literal expression.

16 (15). *Let not the flood overwhelm me, and let not the deep swallow*

me, and let not the well (or pit) *shut its mouth upon me.* In the earnestness of his entreaty, he passes from the figure of a sea or stream to that of
a well or cistern, the idea common to both being that of deep water.

17 (16) *Answer me,* grant my prayer, *Jehovah ; for good* (or as we
should say, great) is *thy mercy ; according to the multitude of thy compassions, turn to me,* or towards me, implying that his looks were before
averted. See above, on Ps. iv. 7 (6), xiii. 2 (1).

18 (17.) *And hide not thy face from thy servant, for* (there is) *distress to
me,* I am distressed, *make haste, answer me, i. e.* grant me what I ask without delay,

19 (18). *Draw nigh unto my soul,* to me whose soul or life is threatened,
ransom it, rescue it from ruin ; *because* (or *for the sake*) *of my enemies,
redeem me,* so that they may not triumph in my fall. See above, on Ps.
xiii. 5 (4), and with the first clause compare Ps. xxii. 2 (1).

20 (19). *Thou knowest,* literally *hast known,* as a thing of long standing,
my reproach, the contempt of which I am the object, *and my shame and
my disgrace ; before thee,* in thy sight and known to thee, (*are*) *all my
adversaries,* persecutors or oppressors, not their persons merely, or their
conduct in general, but their treatment of me. The conviction that God
knows all involves a persuasion that he will do justice to both parties. See
above, on Ps. i. 6.

21 (20). *Reproach,* including calumny and insult, *hath broken my heart,*
a common figure for extreme distress, *and I am sick,* sick at heart or sick
in spirit, but without excluding the idea of corporeal suffering, as the effect,
or as a part, of his distress ; *and I have waited for pity,* literally mourning,
i. e. sympathy, condolence, on the part of my cruel enemies, *and it is not,*
or *there is none, and for comforters,* (those) comforting, *and have not found*
(them). With the phrase, *I am sick,* compare Ps. vi. 3 (2).

22 (21). *And,* so far from pitying me they have aggravated my distress,
for *they have given in my food,* or *as my food, gall,* here put for the extreme
of bitterness, *and for my thirst, i. e.* to slake it, or *at* (the time of) *my
thirst,* in my thirst, when I thirst, *they give me vinegar to drink.* Gall
and vinegar are here put together to denote the most unpalatable forms of
food and drink. The passion of our Lord was providentially so ordered
as to furnish a remarkable coincidence with this verse. The Romans were
accustomed to give sour wine with an infusion of myrrh to convicts on the
cross, for the purpose of deadening the pain. This practice was adhered
to in our Saviour's case (Mark xv. 23). Though in itself not cruel, but the
contrary, it formed part of the great process of murderous persecution.
On the part of the Roman soldiery it may have been an act of kindness ;
but considered as an act of the unbelieving Jews, it was giving *gall and
vinegar* to one already overwhelmed with anguish. And so Matthew, in
accordance with his general method, represents it as a verification of this
passage (Mat. xxvii. 34). He does not contradict Mark's account before
referred to, but merely intimates, that the wine and myrrh thus offered were
to be regarded as identical with the gall and vinegar of this prediction.
And in order to prevent the coincidence from being overlooked, our Lord,
before he died, complained of thirst and vinegar was administered. (Mat.
xxvii. 48, John xix. 28). The word translated *food* in the first clause
occurs only here, and its verbal root only in the history of David (2 Sam.
xii. 17, xiii. 6, 10).

23 (22). *Let their table before them,* at which they eat and where they
are accustomed to enjoy themselves, *be for* (or *become*) *a snare,* an occasion

of unexpected danger, *and to those secure*, thinking themselves safe, (let it be for, or become) *a trap.* The first word in the last clause is the plural of one meaning *peace*, but seems to be here used, as in Ps. lv. 21 (20), for those who are at peace, at ease, tranquil and secure. Compare 1 Thess. v. 3. The ancient versions give it the equally appropriate sense of *for requitals*, *i. e.* in recompence of their transgressions. But although this sense may be deduced from the verbal root (שָׁלַם), and belongs to several collateral derivatives (שִׁלֵּם, שָׁלָם, שִׁלֵּם), it has no existence in the usage of the one before us (שְׁלוֹמִים). The circuitous construction in the English version is not only forced, but wholly unnecessary. The imprecations in this verse and those following it are revolting only when considered as the expression of malignant selfishness. If uttered by God, they shock no reader's sensibilities, nor should they, when considered as the language of an ideal person, representing the whole class of righteous sufferers, and particularly Him who, though he prayed for his murderers while dying (Luke xxiii. 34), had before applied the words of this very passage to the unbelieving Jews (Mat. xxiii. 38), as Paul did afterwards (Rom. xi. 9, 10). The general doctrine of providential retribution, far from being confined to tke Old Testament, is distinctly taught in many of our Saviour's parables. See Mat. xxi. 41, xxii. 7, xxiv. 51.

24 (23). *Let their eyes darken, i. e.* be or grow dark, *from seeing*, so as not to see, *and their loins do thou cause to bend*, give way, or swerve, *i. e.* paralyse their strength. See above, on Ps. lxvi. 10 (9). The first clause probably does not refer to blindness, but either to the dimness of the eyes in death, or to darkness as a figure for calamity in general.

25 (24). *Pour upon them thine anger, and let the heat of thy wrath*, thy hot wrath, *overtake them*, reach them after they have long seemed to escape it and expected to escape it still.

26 (25). *Let their home be desolated, in their tents may there be no one dwelling*, or *let no one dwell.* The word translated *home* seems properly to mean an *enclosure*, with special reference, perhaps, to an encampment or collection of tents (Gen. xxv. 16, Num. xxi. 10). The translation *castle* in the English version of the places just referred to, and that of *palace* in the margin of the one before us, seem entirely conjectural. The Septuagint here has a Greek word (ἔπαυλις), meaning a place to pass the night in, especially for flocks and herds, and thence transferred to farm or country houses. This expression is retained in Acts i. 20, where the verse before us is quoted, in connection with Ps. cix. 8, and applied to Judas Iscariot, not as an individual merely, but as a type and representative of the Jewish people, in their malignant and perfidious enmity to Christ. This does not prove our Lord to be the exclusive subject of the whole psalm, a conclusion forbidden by the confession of sin in ver. 6 (5) above ; but it does shew that He is not only one, but the chief member, nay the great type and representative, of the whole class of innocent sufferers at the hands of wicked enemies. See also Mat. xxiii. 38.

27 (26). *For (those) whom thou hast smitten they persecute*, have persecuted heretofore and do so still; *and as to the grief of thy wounded, they tell* or talk. The pronoun in the first clause is emphatic, " thou and not man, or man only as thy blind unconscious instrument." Compare 2 Sam. xvi. 11, 12, Job xix. 21, 22. The same persons are described as *thy wounded*, the original expression having commonly the sense of mortally wounded, and being therefore often rendered *slain.* See Isa. lxvi. 16, Jer.

xxv. 33. The preposition before *grief* denotes the theme or subject, as it does with the same verb in Ps. ii. 7. To tell about it or talk of it is to make it the subject of unfeeling or derisive comment. See above, on Ps. xli. 9 (8).

28 (27). *Give* (or *place*) *iniquity upon iniquity, and let them not come into thy righteousness.* Luther and others understand the first clause as a prayer that sin may be made the punishment of sin (Rom. i. 28). But there seems to be rather an allusion to the double sense of the equivocal term (עָוֹן), which properly denotes sin as such or in itself considered, but some-

times seems to mean sin considered in its consequences or effects. Thus understood, it is a prayer that sin may be followed by the natural effects of sin. The *righteousness* of God is that which he bestows by the judicial act of justification, including pardon. To *come into* it is to come into posses-sion or enjoyment of it, to become a sharer in it.

29 (28). *Let them be blotted from the book of life* (or *of the living*), *and with the righteous let them not be written*, registered, enrolled. The *book* is not here a figure for the memory, as in Ps. lvi. 9 (8), but for the divine decree. The primary idea is that of a register containing the names of those who are to live or be preserved alive. The figure is Mosaic, being evidently borrowed from Exod. xxxii. 32. The translation *living*, which is given in the ancient versions, is favoured by the parallel expression *righteous* (*men*), if not by the analogy of Ps. xxvii. 13, lii. 7 (5). But the abstract version *life* is equally appropriate, and is recommended by the use of the phrase *book of life* in the New Testament with reference to the future state. See Philip. iv. 3, Rev. xx. 15.

30 (29). *And I* (*am*) *afflicted and suffering ; let thy salvation, O God, set me on high*, beyond the reach of danger, which is tantamount to saying, in a place of safety. See above, on Ps. xx. 2 (1), lix. 2 (1). The verb might also be translated as a future proper, expressive of a confident anti-cipation, *thy salvation will secure me.* But it seems more natural to under-stand it as a prayer for himself, subjoined to the foregoing series of prayers for the destruction of his enemies. As if he had said, " Remember, Lord, that I am suffering, and interpose for my deliverance, as well as for their punishment."

31 (30). *I will praise the name of God with song*, or in a song, *and will magnify him with thanksgiving.* Here, as in many other cases, the certainty of the event is indicated by an expressed determination to thank God for it. See above, on Ps. v. 8 (7).

32 (31). *And it shall be better to Jehovah*, this shall please him more, *than ox* (or) *bullock horned* (and) *hoofed.* The contrast is not between material and spiritual offerings, but between a legitimate offering of both kinds and the mere oblation of a beast, as an *opus operatum* of intrinsic virtue, or as if God could take delight in hoofs and horns, which are there-fore contemptuously specified. See above, on Ps. xl. 7 (6), l. 8, li. 18 (16). The last words are highly idiomatic, and scarcely susceptible of close trans-lation, the original forms being those of active participles, *horning, hoofing*, *i. e.* having or producing horns and hoofs.

33 (32). *The humble see and rejoice*, literally *have seen and will rejoice*, in my deliverance (even ye) *that seek God*, seekers of God, *and may your heart live !* May you be revived and cheered by witnessing this exhibition of God's power and goodness ! The wish that it may be so includes a promise that it shall be, as in Ps. xxii. 27 (26), where the form of expres-sion is the same.

34 (33). *For hearkening*, habitually listening, (*is*) *Jehovah to the poor*, *i. e.* the poor among his people, the righteous, pious, or believing poor ; *and his prisoners*, those imprisoned in affliction by himself, or by human oppressors for his sake, *he hath not despised*, and therefore never will. The general inference here drawn from the speaker's own experience is the same as in Ps. xxii. 25 (24) above.

35 (34). *Let heaven and earth praise him, seas and everything creeping in them*, *i. e.* moving with an animal or vital motion. In the particular mercy experienced by himself he sees a pledge of gifts deserving and demanding universal praise.

36 (35). *For God will save Zion, and will build the cities of Judah, and they shall dwell in them and possess them.* He who is thus faithful to the the individual believer must be faithful to the whole church. It is characteristic of the ancient saints to regard every personal mercy as a pledge of greater favours to the body of God's people. This is peculiarly appropriate in such a case as this, where the words are those of an ideal person representing a whole class, and that a class including, as its most conspicuous member, the Messiah himself. There is no need of supposing an allusion, either prophetical or historical, to the restoration of the Jews from Babylon, the rather as the temple is referred to in ver. 10 (9), as still standing. *They* in the last clause are *the poor* of ver. 34 (33), *i. e.* the righteous or God's people.

37 (36). *And the seed of his servants shall inherit it*, *i.e.* Judah or the land of promise, *and the lovers of his name*, of his revealed perfections, *shall dwell* (quietly and safely) *in it.* The foregoing promises are not restricted to a single generation, but extend to the remotest posterity. *Inherit it*, possess it by hereditary right from generation to generation. As temporal and spiritual blessings were inseparably blended in the old dispensation, the promise of perpetual possession and abode in Palestine is merely the costume in which that of everlasting favour to the church is clothed in the Old Testament.

Psalm 70

THE Fortieth Psalm, as we have seen (p. 177), consists of a thanksgiving for deliverances experienced already, ver. 2–14 (1–13), and of a prayer for fresh occasion of thanksgiving, ver. 15–18 (14–17). The latter portion is here repeated by itself, as a kind of appendix to the sixty-ninth and preface to the seventy-first, with both which it has several points of contrast and resemblance. The mutual relation of the two editions is the same as that between the fourteenth and the fifty-third. The supposition of an erroneous copy or an accidental repetition is forbidden by the fact that both are left on record, and by the appearance of an uniform design in the variations. In this case, as in that of the fifty-third Psalm, no comments will be made upon those expressions which are common to both forms and have therefore been explained already.

1. *To the Chief Musician. By David. To remind*, *i. e.* to remind God of the Psalmist's necessities. The same inscription is prefixed to Ps. xxxviii. The phrase *by David* represents him as the author, not of the fortieth Psalm merely, but of this abridgment. See above, on Ps. liii. 1, and compare p. 87.

2 (1). *O God, to deliver me, O Lord, to help me, hasten!* The first word

of Ps. xl. 14 (13), *be pleased*, is here omitted, for the purpose, as some suppose, of making the commencement more abrupt, and thereby marking the whole composition as a fragment. Another variation, which interpreters have laboured to account for as significant, is the sustitution of *Elohim* in the first clause for *Jehovah*, the only Divine name which appears in the fortieth ʿpsalm at all. It is quite as probable, to say the least, that the names were interchanged as *God* and *Lord* are often by ourselves, without special reason or design.

3 (2). *Ashamed and confounded shall be* (those) *seeking my soul; turned back and disgraced shall be* (those) *desiring* (or *delighting in*) *my hurt.* See above. on Ps. xl. 15 (14). The only variation consists in the omission of the words *together* and *to destroy it*, in accordance with the obvious design of condensation and abridgment.

4 (3). *They shall turn back on account of their shame, i. e.* retreat from their assault on me confounded and ashamed—*those saying, Aha, aha!* See above, on Ps. xl. 16 (15). For the strong expression, *they shall be desolate*, we have a milder one borrowed from Ps. vi. 11 (10). The only other variation consists in the omission of the unimportant phrase *to me*.

5 (4). *They shall rejoice and be glad in thee—all* (those) *seeking thee; and they shall say always, great be Jehovah—*(those) *loving thy salvation.* See above, on Ps. xl. 17 (16). The only variation here is the insertion of the copulative *and* at the beginning of the second clause.

6 (5). *And I am afflicted and poor—O God, hasten unto me! My help and my deliverer* (art) *thou—O Jehovah, linger not,* do not delay! See above, on Ps. xl. 18 (17). Instead of *God*, the parallel passage has *Jehovah*, and instead of *Jehovah*, in the second clause, *my God*. Another variation is that the significant expression, *he will think of me* (or *for me*), is exchanged for the petition *hasten to me*, thus bringing back the prayer to the point from which it started.

Psalm 71

A SUFFERER from the spite of wicked enemies prays for deliverance, ver. 1–3. He acknowledges God's goodness to him in early life, ver. 4–8, and prays that it may be continued in old age, ver. 9–13. He confidently anticipates an answer to his prayers, ver. 14–21, and promises a suitable return of praise, ver. 22–24.

This psalm bears a strong resemblance to the others in which the sufferings of the righteous are theʿgreat theme, such as the twenty-second, thirty-fifth, thirty-eighth, and fortieth, a portion of which last seems to have been prefixed to it, as a kind of text or theme, or for the purpose of connecting it with the whole class of compositions just referred to. This explains the absence of a title or inscription in the psalm before us, as in the case of the second, tenth, forty-third, and others.

1. *In thee, O Jehovah, have I trusted*, taken refuge; *let me not be shamed*, disappointed and confounded, *to eternity*, for ever. This verse and the next two are borrowed, with slight variations, from the beginning of Ps. xxxi.

2. *In thy righteousness thou wilt deliver me and cause me to escape; incline to me thine ear and save me.* See above, on Ps. xxxi. 2, 3 (1, 2), where the imperative form of the preceding clause is still retained, instead of being changed, as here, into the future. The verb *deliver me* there occurs in what

is here the second clause ; and the qualifying term, *haste* or *quickly,* is omitted in the case before us. The division of the sentences is also different, so that the verses do not exactly correspond.

3. *Be thou to me for a rock of habitation,* a rock where I may safely dwell and make my home, (whither I may be able) *to come always, i. e.* whenever it is necessary ; *thou hast commanded to save me,* my deliverance is decreed already ; *for my rock,* my hiding place, *and my fortress art thou.* The images presented and the terms used are similar to those in Ps. xviii. 3 (2). *Commanded to save me ;* see above, on Ps. xliv. 5 (4), lxviii. 29 (28). The imitation of Ps. xxx. here insensibly merges into a new and independent composition.

4. *My God, free me,* cause me to escape, *from the hand of* the wicked, *from the palm,* a poetical equivalent to *hand,* of the *perverse and corrupt doer.* The last word in Hebrew occurs only here, but from its form appears to be the particle of a verb that means to be (or become) sour, to ferment, to putrefy. The infinitive of the same verb is applied to moral evil in Isa. i. 17.

5. *For thou* (*art*) *my hope, O Lord, Jehovah, my confidence,* the object of my trust, *from my youth.* Compare the combination *Lord Jehovah* with those in Ps. lxviii. 21 (20), lxix. 7 (6), and the phrase *my confidence* with Ps. xl. 5 (4).

6. *Upon thee I leaned,* or by thee was held up, sustained, *from the womb ; from the bowels of my mother,* a synonymous expression, *thou* (*art*) *my bringing out,* the one that brought me out, a different expression of the same idea as in Ps. xxii. 11 (10). The meaning of the verb here used, both in its transitive and in transitive forms, may be gathered from Ps. xc. 10, Num. xi. 31. *In thee is my praise always ;* it originates, revolves, and ends in thee. Compare the analogous expression in Ps. xxii. 26 (25).

7. *As a prodigy,* or wonder, an object of contemptuous astonishment, *was I,* or have *I been to many,* on account of my extraordinary sufferings ; *but thou art my refuge of strength,* my strong refuge, at once my protector and my hiding place. With the first clause compare Deut. xxviii. 46, Isa. liii. 14, 1 Cor. iv. 9.

8. *Filled shall my mouth be* (*with*) *thy praise, and all the day* (*with*) *thy beauty,* or glory, as the subject of that praise. The sight of thine excellency now excites, and will excite for ever, my admiration and my praise.

9. *Cast me not off, at the time of old age ; as my strength fails,* literally according to the failure of my strength, *leave me not,* do thou not abandon or forsake me. He here prays that the grace which he experienced in youth, and which he has already acknowledged in the foregoing context, may be continued and extended to his old age. Compare Isa. xlvi. 3, 4.

10. *For my enemies have said* (*so*) *to me, i. e.* have told me that God would forsake or had forsaken me, and as a proof that they believe it, *the watchers of my soul,* those who watch and lie in wait for its destruction, *have consulted together, i. e.* against me, which they would not have done if they had really believed me to be under the Divine protection. Instead of *to me* in the first clause, we may read *of* (*i. e. concerning*) *me,* without any violation of usage or material change of meaning. See above, on Ps. iii. 3 (2).

11. *Saying, God hath forsaken him, pursue and seize him, for there is no deliverer,* literally none delivering. This verse is an amplification of the phrase *they say* (*so*) in the verse preceding. It gives the very words in which they say so. With the first clause compare Ps. iii. 3 (2), xli. 6 (5),

and the words of Ahithophel in 2 Sam. xvii. 1, 2, to which there may be
a direct allusion, as an actual instance of the thing ideally described in
David's own experience.   With the last clause compare Ps. vii. 3 (2).

12. *O God, be not far from me ; O my God, to* (or *for*) *my help hasten.*
Compare the similar expressions of Ps. xxii. 20 (19), xxxv. 22, xxxviii. 22,
23, (21, 22), xl. 14 (13), lxx. 2 (1).   The stronger expression *my God*, in
the second clause, urges his covenant relation to God, as a reason for expecting to be heard.

13. *They shall be shamed, they shall cease* (or *be consumed*)—*the adversaries of my soul ; they shall put on* (or *be clothed with*) *reproach or disgrace
—the seekers of my hurt*.   The verbs may also be translated as optatives,
let them be shamed, &c.   But this is really included in the strict sense of
the future.   Compare the parallel passages, Ps. xxxv. 4, 26, xl. 15 (14),
lxx. 3 (2).

14. *And I will always hope, and add to* (literally *add upon*, accumulate,
increase) *all thy praise*.   To all thy praise which I have uttered hitherto, I
will continue still to add.

15. *My mouth shall recount thy righteousness, all the day* (*long*) *thy salvation, for I know not numbers* (to express them), I cannot number them, they
are innumerable.   The *righteousnesss* or rectitude of God, including his
veracity or faithfulness, is here referred to as the cause of his *salvation*, the
salvation of which he is the source and author.

16. *I will come with the mighty deeds of the Lord Jehovah ; I will mention* (or *commemorate*) *thy righteousness, thine only*.   The first phrase may
also be translated, *I will enter into the mighty deeds*, &c., as we speak of
entering into the particulars of a subject.   But this is rather an English
than a Hebrew idiom.   The common version, *I will go in the strength of
the Lord God*, is at variance with the usage both of the verb and noun, as
the former does not mean to *go* absolutely, but either to *enter* or to *come* to
a particular place, expressed or understood.   The ellipsis here may be supplied from Ps. v. 8 (7) and lxvi. 13, in both which places the same verb
denotes the act of coming to God's house for the purpose of solemn praise,
and in the second passage cited is followed by the same preposition, *I will
come into thy house with burnt-offerings, i. e.* I will bring them thither.   This
sense agrees well with the vow to praise God in the two preceding verses,
and with the promise of commemoration in the other clause of this verse.
See above, on Ps. xx. 8 (7).   It also enables us to give the noun (גְּבוּרוֹת)
its usual sense of God's exploits or mighty deeds.   See below, Ps. cvi. 2,
and compare Deut. iii. 24.   *Thine only*, not my own or that of any creature.   See above, on Ps. xliv. 4, 7 (3, 6).

17. *O God, thou hast taught me* (to praise thee) *from my youth*, by thy
providential dealings with me, *i. e.* given me occasion to celebrate thy praise,
and until now I will declare, i. e. I am still declaring, still have reason to
declare, *thy wondrous works*.   See above, on Ps. ix. 2 (1), xxvi. 7, xl. 6 (5).

18. *And also* (or *even*) *unto old age and hoary hairs, O God, forsake me
not, till I declare thine arm, i. e.* the exertion of thy power, *to the* (next)
generation, (and) *to every one that is to come thy power*.   The last clause
determines the sense of the indefinite expression, *a generation*.   See above,
on Ps. xxii. 31 (30).   With the phrase *thy arm*, compare Ps. xliv. 4 (3).

19. *And thy righteousness, O God,* (reaches) *even to the height* (or *high
place*), *i. e.* heaven, (thou) *who hast done great things, O God, who is like
thee ?*   With the first clause compare Ps. xxxvi. 6 (5), lvii. 11 (10) ; with
the last, Exod. xv. 11, Deut. iii. 24, 2 Sam. vii. 22.

20. (Thou) *who hast shewed us,* made us see, *i. e.* caused us to experience, *distresses many and severe* (or *many distresses and evils*) *wilt return* (and) *make us live,* revive or quicken us, *and from the depths of the earth wilt return* (and) *bring us up,* make or cause us to ascend. The sudden change from the singular to the plural form, in reference to the same subject, led the authors of the masoretic punctuation to restore the singular in this verse also ; but the reading in the text is no doubt the original and true one. As the word translated *depths* is elsewhere invariably applied to water, some suppose an allusion to the deluge, as in Ps. xxix. 10, xxxii. 6, xxxvi. 7 (6). Compare Isa. viii. 7, 8. The verb *return,* twice used here, may, agreeably to Hebrew usage, merely qualify the verbs to which it is prefixed, *thou wilt quicken us again, thou wilt bring us again.* But the similar expression in the next verse makes it probable that the verb was meant to have an independent meaning, and to point out the dependence of the quickening and the restoration here expected on Jehovah's return to his forsaken people. See above, on Ps. xiv. 7.

21. *Thou wilt increase my greatness, and wilt turn* (and) *comfort me.* As the word translated *greatness* is elsewhere applied to the great things done by God for the protection and deliverance of his people (Ps. cxlv. 3, 2 Sam. vii. 23) *my greatness* may have here the objective sense of great things done to or for me. See above, on ver. 19, and compare Ps. xl. 6 (5).

22. *Also I will thank thee with a harp-instrument, i. e.* with a harp or lyre as the instrument of praise, (for) *thy truth,* or *as to thy truth,* veracity and faithfulness ; *I will play to thee,* make music to thee, praise or celebrate thee, *with a lyre,* (thou) *Holy* (*One*) *of Israel, i. e.* his peculiar God, possessed of all divine perfections. See above, on Ps. xxii. 4 (3). From this place the title has been borrowed by the prophets, and by none so frequently as by Isaiah.

23. *My lips shall sing when I play to thee, and my soul which thou hast redeemed.* The first clause, as above translated, seems to promise the combination of vocal and instrumental praise. But as the first verb usually means to shout or sing for joy, and sometimes simply to rejoice, and the second commonly conveys the idea, not of music merely, but of praise, the clause may be explained, *my lips shall rejoice, for I will sing to thee* (or *praise thee*), *and my soul* (shall also rejoice). With the last clause compare Ps. xxxiv. 23 (22).

24. *Also my tongue all the day shall muse of thy righteousness, because they are ashamed, they blush—the seekers of my hurt.* The verb in the first clause means to think aloud, to talk to one's self, and therefore suggests the idea both of thought and sound. It is here applied to the tongue, as the instrument by which one's thoughts are thus expressed, not to others but himself. See above, on Ps. i. 2, ii. 1, xxxv. 28, xxxvii. 30, xxxviii. 13 (12), lxiii. 7 (6), and below, on Ps. xc. 9. The position of the subject at the end of the last clause is emphatic, as in ver. 13 above. The preterite form of the verbs represents the effect as one already past, though really still future.

Psalm 72

A GLOWING description of the reign of the Messiah, as righteous, ver. 1–7, universal, ver. 8–11, beneficent, ver. 12–14, perpetual, ver. 15–17, to which are added a doxology, ver, 18, 19, and a postscript, ver. 20.

1. *By Solomon. O God, thy judgments to the king give, and thy righteousness to the king's son.* The form of expression in the first clause or title
is precisely the same as in the phrase so often rendered, *by David.* That
it designates the author, may be argued, not only from this usage, but from
the fact, that the imagery of the psalm is as evidently borrowed from the
peaceful and brilliant reign of Solomon, as that of the second from the
martial and triumphant reign of David. The prayer in this verse is virtually a prediction, as the Psalmist only asks what he knows that God will
give. The judicial power, under the theocracy, was exercised in God's
name and by his representatives. See Deut. i. 17, Exod. xxi. 6, xxii. 7, 8,
Prov. viii. 15, 2 Chron. xix. 6. The Messiah was therefore expected to exhibit this peculiar character in its perfection. See Isa. xi. 2, 3. By *the
king and the king's son* we are not to understand the descendants and successors of David indefinitely, but the last and greatest of them in particular.

2. *He shall judge thy people with righteousness, and thy afflicted (ones)
with judgment.* This is stated as the necessary consequence of the granting
of the prayer in the preceding verse. " Give him thy righteousness, and
then he shall judge," &c. There is no need, therefore, of putting an
optative sense upon the future, " Let them judge," &c., especially as it
would then be necessary to extend the same construction to the verses following, and so long a series of optative expressions is without example.

3. *(Then) shall the mountains bear peace for the people, and the hills, by
righteousness.* The effect of the divine gift asked at the beginning of the
psalm is still described in this verse, under the figure of a general growth
or harvest of peace, to spring up in the whole land. *Bear*, in the sense of
bringing forth, producing. *Mountains* and *hills* are mentioned as the salient
points or prominent features of the country. This was the more natural, as
the hills of Palestine were carefully tilled in ancient times, as appears from
the terraces still visible. See above, Ps. lxv. 13 (12), and below, Ps.
cxlvii. 8, and compare Deut. xxxiii. 15. *Peace*, as opposed to war and its
accompanying evils. This is often mentioned as a characteristic trait of the
Messiah's reign. See Isa. ii. 4, ix. 6, 7 (5, 6), xi. 9, lxv. 25, Micah iv. 3,
Zech. ix. 10. It was typified by the peaceful reign of Solomon (1 Kings
v. 4), whose very name suggests it. *The hills, i. e.* the hills shall bear
peace or produce it. The words *by righteousness* belong to both clauses,
and denote that the peace here promised was to be the fruit of righteous
government.

4. *He shall judge the afflicted of the people; he shall save* (or *bring salvation*) *to the sons of the needy, and shall crush* (or *break in pieces*) *the oppressor.*
To judge them is to do them justice, to redress their wrongs and vindicate
their rights. *The afflicted of the people*, those who suffer among the chosen
people. *The needy* or *the poor man* is an ideal person, representing the
whole class, whose individual members are described as his sons or children.

5. *They shall fear thee with the sun, and before the moon, generation of
generations.* The first verb may be construed with *the sons of the needy*, or
taken indefinitely, *men shall fear thee*, which is nearly equivalent to saying,
thou shalt be feared. The verb itself denotes religious reverence or awe,
and is here put for worship. The object of address, here and throughout
the psalm, is God, whose worship is described as one fruit of the righteous
reign predicted. *With the sun*, as long as they have the sun with them, *i. e.*
possess or enjoy him. *Before the moon*, in her presence, as long as she
continues to be visible, or to afford them light. This is one of the scriptural expressions for perpetual duration, an idea which is also expressed by

the idiomatic phrase, *generation of generations, i. e.* through all generations, or from one generation to another.

6. *He shall come down like rain upon mown (grass), like showers, the watering of the earth* (or *land*). This beautiful comparison suggests the idea of a gentle yet refreshing and fertilising influence, to be exerted by the king, whose reign is here foretold. The word translated *showers*, by its etymological affinities, suggests the idea of abundance or copiousness. The noun which follows occurs only here, but may be traced to verbal roots which mean to drop or to flow.

7. *In his days shall the righteous sprout*, spring up, or shoot forth, *and abundance of peace, till the failure* (or *cessation*) *of the moon*. The idea is the same as in ver. 3, 5, with a slight change in the form of the expression. By a lively figure, the righteous man is substituted for righteousness in the abstract, as the fruit of the earth and the productive cause of peace. The idea of perpetuity is again conveyed by repeating one of the comparisons in ver. 5.

8. *And he shall rule from sea to sea, and from the river to the ends of the earth.* There is here an obvious allusion to the limits of the land of promise, as defined in Exod. xxiii. 31; but that these are not directly intended in the case before us, is clear from the mention of foreign kings and nations in the following verses. The meaning rather is, that as the realm of the theocratic kings was bounded by the Mediterranean and the Euphrates, that of the Messiah, whom they represented, should extend from sea to sea, *i. e.* from any sea to any other, even the most distant, or from any sea around to the same point again, and from the river (Euphrates), or from any other river, as a *terminus a quo*, to the ends of the earth. In other words, it should be universal. The same mode of describing the extent of Christ's dominion is adopted by the prophets. See Zech. ix. 10, and compare Amos viii. 12, Micah vii. 12.

9. *Before him shall crouch wild (men), and his enemies the dust shall lick.* The first noun denotes dwellers in the wilderness, and is applied both to brutes (Isa. xiii. 21, xxxiv. 14, Jer. l. 39) and men (Ps. lxxiv. 14). The common version of the first verb (*bow*) is too weak in itself and in comparison with the parallel expression, *lick the dust*, implying the most unconditional and abject submission.

10. *The kings of Tarshish and the Islands an oblation shall send back; the kings of Sheba and Seba a reward shall bring near.* The last noun in the first clause, and the verb in the second, are technical terms of the Mosaic law, the first denoting specially a vegetable offering, and the other the solemn act of presentation in God's presence. The use of these expressions implies that what is here described is not the mere payment of tribute or the presentation of friendly gifts, but a religious offering. It is also worthy of remark, that the verb in the first clause, and the last noun in the second, both suggest the idea, not of a simple gift, but of a recompence or requital, perhaps in allusion to the benefits which Christ was to bestow upon the nations, and of which these gifts would be a thankful acknowledgment. The verb *return*, however, is used elsewhere to denote the simple act of paying tribute. See 2 Kings iii. 4, xvii. 3. The proper names in this verse are mere specimens or samples of the nations generally. *Tarshish* is mentioned, both as a well-known mart or source of wealth, and as a representative of the extreme west. *The Islands*, agreeably to Hebrew usage, include all distant sea-coasts, but particularly those of the Mediterranean. The distant south is represented, in like manner, by *Sheba*, a province of

Arabia Felix, and *Seba*, now commonly supposed to be Meroe, a part of ancient Ethiopia, both famous for their wealth and commerce. The obvious allusion to the Queen of Sheba's visit to Jerusalem (1 Kings x. 1–10) is another stroke in this prophetic picture evidently borrowed from the times of Solomon.

11. *And to him shall all kings bow* (or *prostrate themselves*), *all nations shall serve him*. That the preceding verse contains only a sample of the nations over whom the Messiah was to reign, is distinctly intimated by the universal and unqualified expressions of the verse before us. The act described in the first clause is one expressive both of civil homage and religious worship. The same thing is true of the verb in the last clause, which may be applied either to the civil service of a sovereign by his subjects, or to the religious service of a deity by his worshippers. In this case, as in ver. 10, both were meant to be included.

12. *For he will deliver the needy crying* (to him for help), *and the sufferer, and him that hath no helper.* The literal translation of the last clause is, *and there is no one helping him*, or, *and there is no helper to him*. By referring the pronoun to *the sufferer* mentioned just before, we may take this, not as the description of a third class, but as a further description of the second, *the sufferer to whom there is no helper.* The whole verse represents the king in question as the protector, not the oppressor, of his subjects, and assigns a reason for their tribute being represented as a requital of benefits received. See above, on ver. 10.

13. *He will have pity on* (or *spare*) *the poor and needy, and the souls* (or *lives*) *of the needy he will save.* In the first clause the adjectives are of the singular number, and properly denote *the poor* (*man*) *and the needy* (*man*). The change to the plural in the second clause, *needy* (*ones*) or *needy* (*people*), shews that the singular was not meant to denote a real individual, but rather an ideal person, representing a whole class, which is then directly designated by the plural.

14. *From oppression and from violence he will redeem their soul, and precious shall their blood be in his eyes* (or *sight*). This last is an idiomatic expression of the idea, that a person sets such a value on the life of another that he will not suffer it to be destroyed. See below, on Ps. cxvi. 15, and compare 1 Sam. xxvi. 21, 2 Kings i. 14.

15. *And he*, the poor man thus delivered, *shall live*, shall be preserved alive, *and*, in token of his gratitude and willing subjection to such a sovereign, *he shall give to him*, as tribute, *of the gold of Sheba*, one of the regions mentioned in ver. 10, and famous for its gold; *and he*, meaning still the grateful tributary, *shall pray for him continually, i. e.* for the progress and extension of Messiah's kingdom; *all the day* (*long*) *shall he bless him. i. e.* praise him, as well for what he is in himself, as for the gifts which he bestows. By some interpreters the meaning is reversed, and the sentence made to signify that the Messiah shall live again, or live for ever, and give precious gifts to the believer, and by his constant intercession secure to him the blessing of Jehovah. This is a good sense in itself, and appropriate to the context; but the dubious question of construction seems to be determined by the mention of the gold of Sheba, which, in this connection, far more probably denotes the tribute of the subject than the favour of the sovereign. See above, on ver. 10.

16. *Let there be* (but) *a handful of corn in the land, in the top of the mountains; its fruit shall wave* (or *shake*) *like Lebanon, and they shall flourish from the city like grass of the earth.* The first noun in Hebrew

occurs only here, and has been taken in senses directly opposite. The rabbinical tradition makes it mean *a handful*, the modern lexicographers *a plenty*, each relying on a doubtful etymology. According to the second explanation, the clause is a direct prediction of abundance, and should be translated, *there shall be plenty of corn in the land.* According to the other and more ancient view, the verse contains a beautiful antithesis between the small beginnings and the vast results of the Messiah's kingdom, not unlike that suggested by our Saviour's parable of the grain of mustard seed. This exegetical analogy, together with the striking character imparted to the verse by this interpretation, are sufficient to entitle it to the preference, even without regard to its antiquity and traditional authority. The apocopated future (יְהִי) may then be taken in its proper sense, as a concession or a wish, equivalent to saying, *though there be but a handful of corn in the land*, and that in the least favourable situation, *on the top of a mountain*, which though cultivated (see above, on ver. 3), must of course be colder and less fertile than the plains below. Neither *wave* nor *shake* conveys the full force of the Hebrew verb, which suggests the additional idea of a rushing noise, like that of the wind among the cedars of Lebanon. This comparison is certainly more natural and obvious than that which some interpreters assume with the grain-crops or harvest-fields of Lebanon itself. This would be merely likening one harvest to another, nor is any such allusion ever made elsewhere to the mountain, though its circumjacent plains and valleys were productive. See Hos. xiv. 5–7. The word translated *flourish* means originally to *shine* or *glitter* (Ps. cxxxii. 18), but is specially applied to the brilliancy of vegetation, and might therefore be translated *bloom* or *blossom.* See Num. xvii. 23 (8), and compare Ps. xc. 6, xcii. 8 (7), ciii. 15. *From the city* seems to mean from Jerusalem or Zion, as the centre of Messiah's kingdom and his royal residence, out of which this productive influence was to go forth. Compare the form of expression in this clause with Num. xxiv. 19, Job v. 25.

17. *His name shall be for ever ; in the presence of the sun, i.e.* as long as the sun shines, *his name shall propagate (itself) ; and by him shall they (i. e.* men in general) *bless themselves ; all nations shall felicitate him* (or pronounce him happy). The form of expression in the second clause is borrowed from the patriarchal promises (Gen. xii. 3, xviii. 18, xxviii. 14), and is intended to suggest the idea there expressed, that the Messiah should be not only blessed himself, but a source of blessing to all nations. As the happiness of the parent is bound up in that of the children, and the prosperity of the sovereign inseparable from that of the subjects, the one part of this prediction necessarily implies the other. If the head is blessed, so must be the members, the whole body. If all nations are to call Messiah blessed, it must be because he is the author and the giver of their own prosperity, nay more, of their salvation.

18, 19. *Blessed (be) Jehovah, God, the God of Israel, doing wonders alone, and blessed (be) his glorious name to eternity, aud filled with his glory be the whole earth. Amen and Amen.* This is commonly explained as a doxology belonging, not to this psalm, but to the second book, of which it marks the close. See above, on Ps. xli. 14 (13). But as the psalm would end somewhat abruptly with the foregoing verse, and as this addition carries out the idea there expressed, by giving, as it were, the very words in which the nations shall pronounce him blessed, we have reason to believe that the doxology was added by the author, and that this conclusion of the psalm was not the effect but the occasion of its being placed at the close of one of the traditional divisions of the psalter. The wish in the second clause ef ver. 19 is borrowed from the promise in Num. xiv. 21, of which this whole psalm is in fact a prolonged echo.

20. *Ended are the prayers of David, son of Jesse.* The position of this sentence after the doxology, and its prosaic form, shew that it forms no part of the psalm, but relates to the whole series preceding. It does not therefore prove, as some suppose, that Solomon was not the author of the seventy-second psalm, since this exception and a very few others could not prevent the collection being called the prayers of David. *A potiori fit denominatio.* In like manner, the whole Psalter is still called the Psalm of David by many who believe it to contain some psalms by other writers. That this is the conclusion of an original and separate collection is by no means probable, as there is no historical proof that such collections ever existed, and it would not be easy to account for the omission of so many psalms undoubtedly composed by David. On the whole, it is most probable that these words were added to the first great subdivision of the whole collection, as entirely composed of Psalms by David and his contemporaries, with a few added to them on account of some marked similarity in form or substance. The only remaining supposition is that these words are part of the original composition, and were added by Solomon to shew that what he here predicts would be the fulfilment of his father's wishes and the answer to his prayers. The objection to this, besides the form and position of the verse itself, is, that the verb is never used to denote fulfilment or accomplishment, except in the Hebrew of the later books. See Ezra i. 1, Dan. xii. 7.

Psalm 73

1. *A Psalm. By Asaph. Only good to Israel (is) God, to the pure of heart.* This last expression is added to limit or explain the application of the national name *Israel*, as here denoting not the race or nation, simply as such considered, but the true Israel, the sincere and spiritual members of the ancient church. To these God is good, and *only good*, *i. e.* never otherwise, never unmerciful, or even indifferent. This is the theme of the whole psalm, and the peculiar form in which it is propounded has reference to the previous conflicts and misgivings of the Psalmist, through which he had passed in reaching the conviction here expressed. As if he had said, " I once thought otherwise, but now I know that God is only good, and always good, to the true Israel, his real people." He then goes on to describe the conflicts thus tacitly referred to, first, by a statement of the facts out of which they sprang, ver. 2–11, then of the effect which these produced upon his mind, ver. 12–16, and then of the means by which he had been disabused, ver. 17–20, and under the influence of which he now condemns his own irrationality, ver. 21, 22, adores the grace by which he had been rescued from the consequences of his error, ver. 23, 24, and concludes with an expression of his hearty reliance upon that grace for his safety and happiness hereafter, ver. 25–28. There is not the slightest ground for doubting the correctness of the title, which ascribes the psalm to Asaph, the contemporary of David and his chief musician, and himself moreover an inspired psalmist. This last fact, which is matter of recorded history (see above, on Ps. l. 1), together with the fact that where only one name is mentioned

in the title of a psalm it is uniformly that of the writer, may suffice to set aside the supposition that Asaph is only named as the performer.

2. *And I* (or *as for me*), *my feet were almost gone, my steps had well nigh slipped.* The pronoun in the first clause is emphatic. I, who so confidently make this profession of my faith in God's unchanging goodness, am one whose feet were almost gone, literally *inclined* or *bent*, either from the straight course or from an erect position. See above, on Ps. lxii. 3 (2), where the same verb is applied to a wall inclined or bent by violence. The phrases rendered *almost* and *well nigh* strictly mean *like little* and *like nothing*, and imply that it wanted little or nothing of a fearful fall on his part, in other words, that he had narrowly escaped it. *Slipped*, literally *poured out*, which seems to be a figure both for weakness and divergence. Instead of pursuing a direct course, or remaining in a firm position, his steps were scattered and without effect, like water poured upon the ground. See above, on Ps. xxii. 15 (14).

3. *For I was envious at the proud ; the peace of wicked* (men) *I see* (and must see). He now proceeds to state more distinctly the nature of the fall from which he had so narrowly escaped. It was the sin and folly of denying the justice and fidelity of God because of providential inequalities and mysteries. *The proud* or *insolent*, a general description of the wicked, as in Ps. v. 5 (4). The common version in both places (*foolish*) is less probable, but does not materially change the sense. In the last clause, he reverts to his experience at an earlier date, and expresses himself as he might have done at that time. This relation of the clauses may be rendered clearer by supplying a word or phrase between them. " I was envious at the proud (and said), the peace," &c. *Peace*, as the negation and the opposite of all disturbing causes, really suggests the idea of prosperity in general. The future form of the verb has respect, not to the date of composition, but to that of the events recorded, when the Psalmist not only saw, but expected long to see, the undisturbed prosperity of sinners.

4. *For there are no bands at their death ; and fat, i. e.* healthy or robust, (*is*) *their strength.* Some understand the first clause to mean that they are not bound or forced to die like other men. The more obvious sense is, that when they do die, they are not in bonds or chains like other men, but free, common figures for distress or suffering and its opposite.

5. *In the labour of man they are not*, they are not partakers in the common troubles of humanity, *and with mankind they are not smitten* (or *afflicted*). The use of the future is precisely the same as in ver. 3. They are not, and to all appearance never will be, sharers in the common calamities of life.

6. *Therefore pride has enchained them, the garb of violence* (injustice or cruelty) *covers them.* The first verb strictly means to encircle or adorn the neck, perhaps with allusion to the carriage of that member as indicative of pride. See Isa. iii. 16, Job xv. 26.

7. *Their eyes stand out with fatness ; the imaginations of the heart pass* (out, come forth, or are disclosed). The common version of the last clause, *they have more than heart could wish*, assumes as the literal meaning of the words, *they surpass the desires of their heart.* According to the other construction above given, the meaning is that as their eyes stand out with fatness, so their hearts overflow with evil thoughts. Compare Mat. xii. 35, xv. 19, Mark vii. 21, Luke ii. 35, vi. 45.

8. *They mock and speak in wickedness* (or *malice*) *; oppression from on high they speak.* To speak oppression is to speak words tending to the

injury of others. *From on high*, proudly, with arrogant contempt of others. They speak as if from a superior position.

9. *They set their mouth in heaven, and their tongue goes on earth.* The idea in the first clause is the same as in the last clause of the foregoing verse. They speak as if they thought themselves superior beings, their mouth in heaven and their tongue on earth. *Goes*, runs, is actively employed.

10. *Therefore he brings back his people hither, and waters of fulness are wrung out to them* (or *drained by them*). This obscure verse admits of several interpretations, the most natural of which understands the sense to be, that God still suffers or requires his people to survey the painful spectacle and drain the bitter draught presented by the undisturbed prosperity of wicked men. According to the masoretic reading in the margin of the Hebrew Bible, the first verb is intransitive, *his people shall* (or *must*) *return hither*. See above, on Ps. xiv. 7, liii. 7 (6).

11. *And they say, how should God know, and* (how) *can there be knowledge in the Highest?* Some interpreters regard these as the words of the prosperous sinners whom he has been describing. But according to the sense just put upon the tenth verse, the eleventh must express the misgivings of God's people, with respect to the providential inequalities in question. When still brought back to the sight of these, they are constrained to ask how they can possibly be reconciled with the hypothesis of God's omniscience. This is much more natural than to suppose that the sinners themselves admit the being of a God, and yet gratuitously question his omniscience. In the latter case the *how* would be unmeaning; in the former, it is the most natural expression of the doubt supposed. An atheist, whether theoretical or practical, would hardly ask, how can God know? Even a wicked theist would be rather apt to say, he does not know. But nothing can be more appropriate in the mouth of a perplexed and tempted believer than the question, how can God know this and yet suffer it?

12. *Lo, these are wicked* (men), *and* (yet they are) *secure for ever, they increase strength* (or *substance*). These are still the words of the perplexed believer, expressing his surprise at the prosperity of sinners. See, these are wicked men, and yet instead of being wretched, or prospering only for a little while, they are *prosperers of eternity*, perpetually prospered and at ease, secure from change. See above, on Ps. xxx. 7. Instead of losing what they have, they still gain more, and go on adding to their wealth, and to the power which it gives them. See above, on Ps. lx. 14 (12).

13. *Only* (in) *vain have I cleansed my heart, and in innocence have washed my hands.* These may be taken either indefinitely as the words of any person in the painful situation just described, or more specifically as the words of the Psalmist, by whom the whole class was, in fact, represented. They contain the inference which would be naturally drawn in such a situation, even by a true believer, but one tempted to repine and doubt by the sight of providential enigmas. " Since, then, it is the wicked who enjoy God's favour, all my efforts to avoid sin and to do his will have been gratuitous and fruitless." With the first words of the verse compare Ps. xxxix. 6, 12 (5, 11).

14. *And I have been smitten all the day, and my chastisement* (has been inflicted) *every morning*, literally *at* (or *in*) *the mornings*. A similar form of expression occurs twice in Job vii. 18. *Smitten*, literally *touched*, *i. e.* by the hand of God, a common expression for affliction, and especially for bodily disease considered as a divine judgment. The same idea was meant to be

conveyed by the common version (*plagued.*) The psalmist here contrasts his own afflictions with the undisturbed enjoyments of his wicked neighbours. " While they, though wicked, still increase in wealth and seem secure for ever, I, who have faithfully endeavoured to avoid sin and to do the will of God, am subjected every day, and all day, to privation and distress."

15. *If I have said, I will declare thus, behold, the generation of thy sons I have perfidiously treated.* This is equivalent to saying, if I did say so, I should be acting falsely towards thy children. It is indeed the only Hebrew form in which such a hypothetical proposition could well be clothed. *Said*, *i.e.* to myself, proposed it, formed the purpose. *Thus declare, i. e.* publicly express my doubts and sceptical misgivings. This, as it has been well observed, the true believer never does, until he is able to announce his conflict and his victory together. *Behold*, or *lo*, is here equivalent to our idiomatic *why then*, meaning *in that case*, or *on that supposition*, and expressing at the same time some surprise at his own suggestion as a strange one. *The generation of thy sons*, the contemporary race of true believers, called the sons of God, not only as the objects of his love, but as partakers of his nature (2 Pet. i. 4). *Treated perfidiously*, proved false to them, by weakening the foundation of their hope, instead of strengthening their faith and allaying their misgivings. See above, on Ps. xxv. 3.

16. *And I meditated to know this ; a trouble (was) it in my eyes.* Although he abstained from openly expressing what he thought, he still did think, he pondered the whole matter, with a view to understand it, to discover some solution of the mystery, which not only puzzled but distressed him. The apparent inequality of God's providential dealings was a toil, a trouble, an unhappiness in his esteem.

17. *Until I come to the sanctuaries of God, I will consider* (or *observe*) *their end.* The futures have reference, as in ver. 3, 5, to the date of the anterior experience here recorded. " But I said to myself, I will wait till I come into God's presence and inquire of him, and then, or in the mean time, I will look at or attend to the end as well as the beginning and the progress of their lives." The plural form *holy places*, is the same as in Ps. lxviii. 36 (35). It denotes the sanctuary in its whole extent, as the earthly residence of God, and the place where he communed with his people. See above, on Ps. xxviii. 2.

18. *Only in slippery places thou wilt set them*, or art setting them, (and now) *thou hast let* (or made) *them fall into destruction.* However honourable and happy their position may appear to themselves, the Psalmist can see nothing but its danger, as implied in his use of the word *only*. *Smoothnesses*, smooth or slippery places, where their foothold is precarious and fall inevitable. He sees God, by his providential favours, placing them in this desired but fearful situation, and then allowing them to drop into destruction. The last word in Hebrew occurs only here and in the next psalm, where it means *ruins*. If this sense be adopted here, we must suppose a change of figure and an allusion to the fall, not of a man from a slippery precipice, but of a building crumbled by decay or violence.

19. *How are they* (brought) *to desolation as* (in) *a moment! They have ceased, they are consumed with terrors!* He here expresses his surprise at the abruptness and completeness of their ruin. The meaning of the last clause seems to be, that their very apprehensions were sufficient to destroy them, much more the actual experience of what they apprehended.

20. *As a dream on waking, Lord, in waking, their image thou wilt*

scorn. The word translated *image* means an appearance, as opposed to the substance or reality. See above, on Ps. xxxix. 7 (6). The present prosperity of wicked men will seem hereafter, and to God's eye now seems, like an empty dream, worthy only of contemptuous oblivion. The only dubious expression in the verse is that translated *waking* in the second clause, which is entirely different from the one so rendered in the first clause. The Hebrew phrase (בָעִיר) is used in more than fifty other places, and in all of them means *in the city.* See, for example, Ps. lv. 10 (9). This meaning is retained by some interpreters in the case before us. The reference will then be either to the holy city, as in Ps. lxxii. 16, or to the city where the previous scene is supposed to have been laid, as in Ps. xxxi. 22 (21). The old interpretation takes the word as an infinitive, from a verb which, however, is always transitive, and means to *awaken,* except, perhaps, in Job viii. 6, and in Ps. xxxv. 23 above. To this interpretation it is furthermore objected, that it supposes an unusual contraction (בָעִיר) for בְּהָעִיר), and that the sense which it conveys is an incongruous one. But that God should despise them *in the act of waking* is, to say the least, as intelligible as that he should despise them *in the city.* In either case, the general meaning of the sentence is too clear to be mistaken.

21. *For my heart is soured, and (in* or *as to) my reins I am pierced.* The Hebrew verbs are of the future form, although really relating to past time, which the psalmist's memory recalls as a state of things then likely to continue. See above on ver 3, 5. The verbs are also properly reflexives, *my heart exacerbates itself, I pierce myself,* and are perhaps intended to describe his sufferings as the fruit of his own sin and folly.

22. *And I* (am) *brutish and know not* (the true state of the case); *a beast have I been with thee.* The last noun is in the plural number (*beasts*), as if to signify a beast by way of eminence, in which sense it is literally applied to one of the wonders of the animal kingdom (Job xl. 15). With the first clause compare Prov. xxx. 2, and see above, on Ps. xlix. 11 (10). These strong expressions contain an acknowledgment of his own irrationality in questioning God's faithfulness and kindness. In this verse there is an insensible transition from the present to the past, from the ideal to the real time of the events in question. *With thee* suggests an aggravating circumstance, to wit, that this folly was committed in the presence of God, and as it were in his society. See above, on Ps. xviii. 26, 27 (25, 26).

23. *And* (yet) *I* (am) *still with thee ; thou hast held* (me) *by my right hand.* Notwithstanding his ungrateful and irrational conduct in God's presence, he had not been driven from it, as he justly might have been. The word translated *still* properly means *always,* and denotes that there had been no change or interruption in the previous relation of the parties. There is a perfectly analogous usage of the French *toujours.* In the last clause he seems to return to the metaphor with which he set out. As the fatal error which he had escaped is in ver. 2 represented as a fall, so here his preservation from it is ascribed to God's having held him up by his right hand. See above, on Ps. xvii. 5, xli. 13 (12), lxiii. 9 (8).

24. *In* (or *by) thy counsel thou wilt guide me, and after glory thou wilt take me.* The form of the original is such that it may either express consent or confident expectation ; but the latter in this case really includes the former. *By thy counsel,* thy instruction and advice, considered as a means of safety ; or *in thy counsel, i. e.* in the execution of thy plan or purpose, as the end to be accomplished. The last clause is obscure. To the com-

mon version (*and afterward receive me to glory*) it has been objected, that it takes the preposition *after* as an adverb, and assumes an unusual sense and construction of the verb, and also that it makes the guidance and the glory too distinct and successive. The construction which it is proposed to substitute is, *thou wilt take me after glory, i. e.* make me overtake it, cause me to attain it, bring me to it. The same construction may be made to yield another sense, to wit, after honouring me here thou wilt receive me to thyself, *after honour thou wilt take me.* This, it is true, is liable to some of the objections brought against the usual construction. But the choice at best is one of difficulties, and some of the objections spring entirely from the wish to exclude a reference to a future state, which, however, is as evident in this verse as it is in ver. 16, 19, if interpreted in any natural and reasonable manner.

25. *Whom have I in heaven? And with thee I have not desired* (any) *upon earth.* The literal translation of the first clause is, *who* (*is*) *to me in heaven, i. e.* what protector or provider ? The idea of another besides God may be supplied in this clause from the next, where *with thee* can denote either combination or comparison. I have desired none in addition or in preference to thee ; thou art alone and all-sufficient.

26. *Spent is my flesh and my heart ; the rock of my heart and my por-tion* (*is*) *God to eternity.* The first clause is by some understood as mean-ing *even if* or *even when* my flesh, &c. But the Psalmist rather assumes the actual occurrence of the extreme case here described, or places himself in it as an ideal situation. *Flesh and heart,* body and soul, the whole man, or the whole life, outward and inward, bodily and mental. *The rock of my heart,* the support of my life, that on which it rests as on a solid basis. The idea is not simply that of strength but of a strong foundation. See above, on Ps. xviii. 3 (2). *My portion,* the source of my subsistence and my happiness. See above, on Ps. xvi. 5, and with the whole verse com-pare Job xix. 25–27.

27. *For lo, those far from thee shall perish ; thou hast destroyed all* (or *every one*) *whoring from thee.* This verse assigns his reason for relying upon God and making him his portion. *Those far from thee,* literally, *thy far* (*ones*). They certainly will perish, for all such have perished heretofore. The union between God and his people being often represented by the figure of a conjugal relation, their violation of the covenant is spoken of as spiritual whoredom or adultery. See above on Ps. xlv. 1, and compare Lev. xx. 6, Num. xiv. 33. In the same sense our Saviour calls the unfaithful Israel of his day a wicked and adulterous generation. See Mat. xii. 39, xvi. 4, Mark viii. 38. The persons threatened with destruction here are not merely sinners in general, but the wicked members of the ancient church or chosen people in particular.

28. *And I,* or *as for me—the approach of God to me* (*is*) *good ; I have placed in the Lord Jehovah my trust, to declare all thy doings.* The absolute nominative at the beginning puts himself in strong contrast with the apos-tates of the foregoing verse. Compare the beginning of ver. 2, 23, above. The *nearness* or *approach of God* is an ambiguous expression, as in Isa. lviii. 2, where it may either mean God's drawing near to the people or their drawing near to him. In the case before us both may be implied, as in James iv. 8, both are expressed, *Draw nigh to God and he will draw nigh to you. To me* may be connected either with *approach,* as in Ps. xxvii. 2, or with *good,* as in ver. 1 above. *Good* is here to be taken in the absolute sense of the *sum num bonum* or chief good. The meaning is not merely

that nearness to God is a good thing in itself, or a useful thing to man, but that it comprehends whatever he can wish or hope for. " Let apostates wander far from God and perish ; I am resolved to seek my highest happiness in being near him." The *Lord Jehovah* is a combination expressive of God's sovereignty, self-existence, and covenant relation to his people. *My trust,* my hiding-place or refuge. See above, on Ps. xi. 1. The last clause shews that he wishes to be something more than a mere passive beneficiary. He desires not only to enjoy but to celebrate God's goodness. The word translated *doings* is applied both to acts and to affairs or business.

Psalm 74

THE church prays for deliverance from extreme distress, enforcing the petition, first by a description of the actual state of things, ver. 1–12, and then by an appeal to former mercies, ver. 13–23. The historical occasion is not given, but the terms of the description seem peculiarly appropriate to the state of Judah after the destruction of the temple and the holy city by the Babylonians, as described in Jer. lii. 12–34.

1. *Maschil. By Asaph. Why, O God, hast thou cast off for ever, smokes thy wrath at the flock of thy pasture?* The description of the psalm as a didactic one shews that it was not meant to be used in reference to its original occasion merely, but in every emergency resembling it. For this reason the question, what that occasion was, is of little exegetical importance, although not without interest in connection with the critical inquiry as to the date of composition. The state of things assumed, and indeed described, is so unlike that which existed in the time of David, that we must either make the psalm prophetical, which is arbitrary and without analogy, or no less arbitrarily reject the title as a spurious addition to the text, or understand by Asaph the descendants of David's Chief Musician, among whom the gift and office of their ancestors were hereditary. See above, on Ps. l. 1, and compare 2 Chron. xxxv. 15, Ezra ii. 41, iii. 10, Neh. vii. 44, xi. 22. That this title indicates the author, and not merely the performer, can only be inferred from the general fact, that where a single name is given it is usually that of the writer. See above, on Ps. xlii. 1, lxxii. 1. The interrogation in this verse does not involve a disavowal of guilt or ill-desert, but is rather a passionate expostulation and indirect petition for deliverance. *Cast off,* a verb implying abhorrence and disgust. See above, on Ps. xliii. 2, xliv. 10, 24 (9, 23), lx. 3, 12 (1, 10). As the object is easily supplied, namely, *us* or *thy people,* its omission adds to the strength of the expression. *Cast off for ever,* as it seems to us and others. Why hast thou cast us off with what appears to be a final and perpetual rejection ? See above, on Ps. xiii. 2 (1). The interrogation is continued throughout the sentence. (*Why*) *smokes* or *will smoke?* The future form suggests the same idea as the *for ever* in the other clause. "Why is thy wrath to continue smoking ? " The presence of smoke presupposes that of fire ; but the former is particularly mentioned, perhaps for the purpose of adding to the primary idea of distress or destruction the secondary one of gloom and terror. *At* or *against* thy people, literally *in, among them.* See below, on Ps. lxxx. 5 (4), and compare Deut. xxix. 19 (20). *The sheep* (or *flock*) *of thy pasture,* those who feed upon thy pasture, or are fed by thee, a favourite designation of the chosen people, as the occupants of the Land of Promise. The figurative form of the description was originally furnished by the pas-

toral experience of David, but from him was borrowed by other sacred writers. See below, Ps. lxxix. 13, c. 3.

2. *Remember thy congregation thou hast purchased of old*, (and) *redeem the rod of thine inheritance, this mount Zion thou hast dwelt in.* The ellipsis of the relative in both the clauses of this verse is common to the Hebrew and the English idiom. The word translated *congregation* is one of those applied in the Old Testament to Israel as an organised body and the people of Jehovah. See above, on Ps. i. 5. *Purchased*, acquired, made thine own. The word translated *of old* is an noun meaning *antiquity*, but here used as an adverb of time. The full phrase occurs below in ver. 12. The next verb contains a specification of the first, to wit, that he *purchased* by *redeeming* them from bondage, with particular reference to the exodus from Egypt. *The rod of thine inheritance* is a phrase which, to any Hebrew reader, would suggest the twofold idea of a chieftain's staff, the badge of authority in the several tribes, and that of a measuring rod, here put for the portion of land measured. The whole sense conveyed by these associations is that of a definite province, with its population, of which God is the possessor and the sovereign. The last clause applies what had been said of the people and the land still more specifically to the central point of the theocracy. *Mount Zion* may be understood as a description of the whole of Jerusalem, including the temple upon mount Moriah. *This mount Zion*, with which the speakers were familiar, and at or near which they are supposed to be speaking. The explanation of *this* as a relative is gratuitous, nor could the idea (*this mount Zion*) have been well expressed in any other form of Hebrew words. The grand distinction of mount Zion, in the wide sense just explained, was the inhabitation of Jehovah, which is therefore here expressly mentioned in the closing words.

3. *Lift thy steps to the perpetual ruins, all the enemy has ill done in the holy place.* The first phrase is a poetical expression meaning simply *advance, draw near*, for the purpose of inspection. The word translated *ruins* occurs only here and in Ps. lxxiii. 18. The whole phrase strictly means *ruins of perpetuity, i. e.* such as appears likely to continue for ever, and will certainly do so, unless God comply with this request to draw near. The construction of the second clause adopted by some writers, *the enemy has destroyed all* (or *every thing*) *in the holy place*, is scarcely grammatical. To express that idea, the word *all* would have the article, as in Ps. xiv. 3, or a suffix, as in Ps. xxix. 9, whereas its intimate connection here with the following verb in Hebrew is equivalent to a relative construction. *Ill done*, injured or destroyed, done mischief.

4. *Thine adversaries have roared in the midst of thine assembly; they have set their signs* (as) *signs.* The tumultuous violence of the destroyers is described in the first clause by a figure borrowed from the habits of wild beasts, and elsewhere used as an expression of extreme distress. See above, on Ps. xxii. 2 (1), xxxii. 3, xxxviii. 9 (8). The word translated *assembly* is not the same that is rendered *congregation* in ver. 2, but one that strictly means a meeting by mutual agreement or appointment, and is specially applied to the meeting between God and his people at the sanctuary, which was therefore designated in the law as the *tent of meeting* (אֹהֶל מוֹעֵד), not merely the tent where the people assembled, but the place where they met with God by previous appointment. See Exod. xxv. 8, xxix. 42, 43, 45, 46, Num. xvii. 19 (4). The ideas suggested by the etymology and usage of the Hebrew noun are those of previous appointment, the act of

meeting consequent upon it, the persons met, and the place where they
assemble. The full sense, therefore, of the phrase here used is, " In the
midst of thy people assembled at the appointed time and place to meet
thee." The exclusive local meaning put by some upon the words is quite
gratuitous. The plural form which some assume (*thine assemblies*) varies
the meaning only by suggesting the idea of repeated convocations, " In the
midst of thy people, whenever (or as often as) they meet thee thus," but
without at all conveying the idea of numerous or even different places. *Set*,
fixed, established ; or *set up*, exhibited, exposed to view. See above, on
Ps. xviii. 44 (43), xxxix. 9 (8), xliv. 14, 15 (13, 14). The common version of the last words, *ensigns for signs*, conveys a false impression of the
form of the original, in which the two nouns are identical. The word *signs*
does not necessarily denote either military or religious ensigns, but rather
signifies in general the insignia of sovereignty. For all that once marked
the presence and authority of God the impious enemy had substituted the
signs or tokens of their own ascendancy. In other words, they had usurped
God's place in his very sanctuary, the spot which he had chosen for his
earthly residence.

5. *He is known* (or *shall be known*) *as* (one) *raising on high, in the thicket
of the wood, axes*. The most probable sense of this obscure verse is as
follows : the ruthless enemy is known or recognised as dealing with the
sanctuary no more tenderly than a woodman with the forest which he fells.
On high seems to be added to suggest the force of the blow, and the sweep
of the arm which deals it. *The thicket* may be mentioned for the purpose
of contrasting the delicate and complicated wood-work of the temple with
the worthless undergrowth which the woodman cuts away without scruple
or discrimination. The word translated *wood* is often used as a collective,
meaning *trees*.

6. *And now the carvings thereof together* (or *at once*) *with sledge and ham-
mers they beat* (*down*). This completes the comparison begun in the preceding verse, with which the one before us is connected by the phrase *and now*,
i.e. in this case. As in the case supposed the woodman deals with trees
and thickets, so in the real case the spoiler deals with the costly fruits of
art and skill. The word translated *carvings* is expressly used in the description of the temple. See 1 Kings vi. 29, and compare Exod. xxviii. 11,
xxxix. 6. The suffix (*thereof*) has no grammatical antecedent in the sentence ; the form was probably determined by a word not expressed, though
present to the writer's mind. *At once* does not mean quickly, suddenly,
without delay, but all together, indiscriminately, in confusion.

7. *They have set on fire thy holy place ; to the earth they have profaned
the dwelling of thy name*. The literal translation of the first clause is, *they
have sent* (or *cast*) *into the fire thy holy place*. The construction in the last
clause is a pregnant one, *profaned to the earth, i. e.* profaned by casting to
the ground a sacred edifice. This form of expression would be inappropriate to mere profanation by defilement, without actual prostration of the
edifice itself.

8. *They have said in their heart, let us destroy them together* (or *at once*) ;
they have burned all the assemblies of God in the land, by burning the only
place where such assemblies could be held (Deut. xii. 5, 11). Others,
with less probability, suppose that the Hebrew word itself denotes the place
of assembly, and that *all* such places means the *only* such place. The
translation *synagogues* has no authority from Hebrew usage, or the ancient
versions (LXX. ἑορτάς Vulg. *dies festos*. Jer. *solennitates*), and has been

abused to prove that the psalm was written after the Babylonish exile, before which synagogues are commonly supposed to have had no existence.

9. *Our signs we see not ; there is no more* (any) *prophet, and* (there is) *not with us* (any one) *knowing until what time,* or *how long,* these things are to last. By *signs* we are here to understand the tokens of God's presence, and of Israel's peculiar relation to him. One of these is then specified, to wit, the gift of prophecy, which seemed to cease at the time of the Babylonian conquest, although afterwards renewed. Even Jeremiah's ministry may be considered as then closing. The complaint of this, as of a recent loss, shews that the period meant is not that of the persecutions under Antiochus Epiphanes, when the gift of prophecy had, been withdrawn for many generations.

10. *Till when, O God, shall the foe revile, the enemy contemn thy name for ever ?* By making the last clause a distinct interrogation (*shall the enemy despise thy name for ever ?*) we avoid the solecism of combining *how long* and *for ever ;* but this can occasion no more difficulty here than in ver. 1, and in Ps. xiii. 2 (1). The verb in the last clause means to treat contemptuously, to shew contempt by word or deed. *Blaspheme* expresses only one mode of doing this, and that too strongly.

11. *Why wilt thou withdraw thy hand and thy right hand ? From the midst of thy bosom* (draw it and) *consume* (them). The future here includes the present (*why dost thou withdraw thy hand?*) with the additional idea of continuance or perseverance in so doing. The hand, and especially the right hand, is the seat and symbol of strength. The *and* between them is equivalent to the English *even.* To make the hand return, or draw it back, is to cease from action, the continuance of which cessation is described as hiding it in the bosom.

12. *And God* (is) *my king of old, working salvations in the midst of the land.* Having pleaded the greatness of the danger and distress as a reason for imploring the divine interposition, the church now pleads her covenant relation to him as her Sovereign and her Saviour in former emergencies, with particular reference to the plagues of Egypt, which makes it probable that *land,* and not *earth,* is the true translation of the last word. The very form of expression is borrowed from the narrative of Moses. See Exod. viii. 18 (22). *Doing,* working, as opposed to a mere promise or prediction. The participle signifies continued action, and extends the description beyond the particular occasion specially referred to. God is described as He who, then and ever, works *salvations* or *deliverances,* the plural form implying fulness and variety. See above, on Ps. xviii. 51 (50), xxviii. 8, xlii. 6, 12 (5, 11), xliii. 5, liii. 7.

13. *Thou hast burst, with thy strength, the sea ; thou hast broken the heads of dragons on the water.* The word translated *dragons* is applied to the largest class of aquatic animals. Some suppose these to be here emblematic of Egypt and other hostile powers, as in Ezek. xxix. 3, 4, Isa. li. 9, 10. Others, with more probability, explain the verse as a description of God's power over nature, and particularly over the sea, as specially manifested in the passage of the Red Sea. The dragons or sea-monsters are then added merely to complete the picture. As if he had said, " Thou hast subdued and crushed the sea, and its most terrible inhabitants." This is described as taking place, not *in* or *under the waters,* the abode of the sea-monsters, but on the surface, where the contest becomes visible. The pronoun at the beginning is emphatic : " it is thou that hast done all this, and not another."

14. (It is) *thou* (that) *hast crushed the heads of Leviathan,* (that) *wilt give him* (as) *food to the people, to the wild men,* or the dwellers in the desert. See above, on Ps. lxxii. 9. *Leviathan,* according to its etymology, denotes a coiled or crooked serpent, but like *dragon* in ver. 13, is used as a generic term for huge aquatic animals. Having no plural form, it is here used in a collective sense, as appears from the expression *heads,* unless we understand this as denoting a many-headed monster, to which, however, there is no analogy in Scripture. In the last clause, *people* seems to mean *men* in general, and is then rendered definite by the use of the specific term which follows. By the people of the desert some understand the savage beasts, by whom the Egyptians were devoured after the overthrow of Pharaoh; others, with more probability, the wild men living on the shores of the Red Sea, and subsisting on its fish, and hence called by the Greeks the Ichthyophagi. The transition from the past tense to the future seems to represent the scene as actually passing, or the act as one that may be frequently repeated. " It is thou that hast done all this, and wilt do it again."

15. (It is) *thou* (that) *didst cleave fount and flood,* (that) *didst dry up rivers ever flowing.* Fountain and flood is a kind of proverbial expression for smaller and greater bodies of water. The primary historical allusion here is to the passage of the Jordan. The original construction of the last phrase is *streams of perpetuity,* perennial or unfailing streams, as distinguished from the winter torrents of the Holy Land, which disappear in summer. The common version, *rivers of strength* or *mighty rivers,* is not sustained by etymology or usage.

16. *To thee* (belongs) *day, yea, to thee night;* THOU *hast prepared light and sun.* From the mention of God's actual control over the elements, as exercised in certain memorable cases, the Psalmist here proceeds to assert his sovereignty by right of creation. Not only day but night, which seems to sense beyond the reach of government or regulation, is subject to God's power. *Thou,* and no other, as in the three preceding verses. *Prepared* for the place which they now fill and the work which they perform. *Light* and *sun* are related as the genus and the species, like *hand* and *right hand* in ver. 11, *signs* and *prophet* in ver. 9. *Light,* in the local sense of luminary, which the same Hebrew word has in Gen. i. 14–16.

17. THOU *hast set* (or *established*) *all the bounds of earth; summer and winter—thou hast formed them.* This is the seventh emphatic repetition of the pronoun *thou.* The bounds of earth are supposed by some to be the limits of the land, by which it is separated from the sea. See above, on Ps. xxiv. 2. The description of God's power over nature is completed by referring to it the revolution of the seasons as not only appointed but created by him. He is not only the ordainer of the change itself, but the author of the causes which produce it.

18. *Remember this; an enemy has reviled Jehovah, and a foolish people have contemned thy name.* For the meaning of the verbs see above on ver. 10, where the same facts are alleged, but are here recalled to God's remembrance as a reason for his interposition. *Jehovah* may also be construed as a vocative, which makes the parallelism more exact. *Foolish,* in the strong sense of that word, as used in Scripture, to denote the irrationality of sin. See above, on Ps. xiv. 1, and compare Deut. xxxii. 6, from which place the whole phrase is borrowed.

19. *Give not to the greedy herd thy turtle-dove: the herd of thy afflicted* (ones) *forget not for ever!* The general import of this prayer is obvious,

and the only doubtful point is the precise sense of the word (חַיַּת), twice
translated *herd* above. It usually means an *animal* or living thing, and
more especially a *wild beast*, as distinguished from domesticated cattle.
This would yield a good sense in the first clause (*greedy beast*), but is
inadmissible in the other. The same objection lies against the explanation
of the first as meaning *life*, and the last as meaning *flock*. The only meaning equally admissible in both parts of the sentence is the one just mentioned, that of *animal* collectively, and then a flock or herd of animals,
from which it is sometimes transferred to human subjects. See above, on
Ps. lxviii. 11 (10). *Greedy herd*, literally *herd of appetite*. See above, on
Ps. xxvii. 12, xli. 3 (2). The *turtle-dove* is here used as an emblem of
innocence and helplessness, as well as an expression of affectionate en-
dearment.

20. *Look to the covenant; for filled are the darknesses of earth with homes
of violence* (or *cruelty*). The prayer in the first clause is equivalent to
saying, Remember thy promise, fulfil thy covenant engagements. The
reason assigned is, that the existing state of things is such as to require
this fulfilment. The word translated *darknesses* has the form of a local
noun, and may therefore mean *dark places*, not in the sense of hiding
places, but in that of gloomy, dismal places. The same idea, of distress
and gloom, which is always included in the sense of the word elsewhere,
may be obtained by making it an obstract, *darkness*, or supposing the
plural form to be emphatic, *profound darkness*, not as an attribute of certain places, but of the whole earth. As if he had said, the darkness of the
earth, or this dark world, is filled with homes of cruelty. This word (חָמָס),
here as elsewhere, comprehends the two ideas of injustice and violence.
See above, on Ps. vii. 17 (16), xviii. 49 (48). The use of the word *homes* (or
habitations) indicates that violence or cruelty is there domesticated, permanently resident. See above, on Ps. xxv. 13. The meaning of the
whole verse thus explained is, that the permanent establishment and prevalence of "wrong and outrage" in the darkness of the world may be
urged as a reason for the fulfilment of God's promise, nay, his solemn oath,
that the whole earth shall be filled with his glory (Num. xiv. 21).

21. *Let not the oppressed turn back confounded; let the sufferer and the
poor (man) praise thy name.* The word translated *oppressed* means strictly
broken, bruised, or crushed. See above, on Ps. ix. 10 (9), x. 18. *Turn
back*, abandon his pursuit, retire in despair. *Confounded*, disappointed,
put to shame, by the frustration of his hopes and wishes. See above, on
Ps. xxxv. 4, xl. 15 (14), lxix. 7 (6), lxx. 3 (2).

22. *Arise, O God! Plead thine own cause! Remember thy reviling by
the fool all day!* The first prayer is the common one, that God would put
an end to his apparent inaction and indifference to the sufferings of his
servants. See above, on Ps. iii. 8 (7), vii. 7 (6), ix. 20 (19), x. 12,
xvii. 13, xxxv. 2, xliv. 27 (26). *Plead thine own cause*, literally *strive thy
strife*. See above, on Ps. xliii. 1. "Remember how thou art reviled by
the irrational transgressor, and arouse thyself to silence his reproaches."

23. *Forget not the voice of thy foes, the noise of thy assailants, ascending
always.* The voice and noise here meant are the clamorous revilings and
blasphemies of wicked men, continually going up into the ears of God, and
calling down his wrath upon them. This striking figure, representing
gross sin as a vocal and audible witness against him who commits it, is a
common one in Scripture, from the earliest books downwards. See Gen.

iv. 10, xviii. 21, xix. 13, and compare Jonah i. 2. *Thy assailants,* or more literally *thy insurgents,* those who rise up against thee, in the way not only of attack but of rebellion. See above, on Ps. iii. 2 (1), xviii. 40. 49 (39, 48), xliv. 6 (5), and compare Exod. xv. 7, Deut. xxxiii. 11, 2 Sam. xxii. 49. All this the Psalmist, or rather the Church, in whose behalf he speaks, recalls to the divine remembrance, as a ground or reason for immediate interference.

Psalm 75

1. *To the Chief Musician. Al-tashheth. A Psalm by Asaph. A song* (of praise). See above, on Ps. lxviii. 1. In this psalm the ancient church expresses a confident anticipation of divine assistance and deliverance from the domination of some great hostile power, the catastrophe of which is here foretold. The immediate historical occasion we have no direct means of determining ; but the one to which the psalm itself seems most appropriate is the destruction of the Assyrian host in the reign of Hezekiah. See above, on Ps. xlvi. 1, and below, on Ps. lxxvi. 1, and compare Isa. xxxvi. and xxxvii. That the psalm has reference to a period of imminent and extraordinary danger, is moreover indicated by the phrase *al-tashheth,* or *destroy not.* See above, on Ps. lvii. 1.

2 (1). *We give thanks to thee, O God, we give thanks ; and (near) is thy name ; they recount thy wonders.* The thanksgiving is in anticipation of some great event, and implies a strong faith in the certainty of its occurrence. *Thy name is near,* a signal manifestation of thine attributes is just at hand, so that men begin already to recount thy wondrous works, as if actually past. Or this may mean that they recount God's former dealings with them, as a reason for expecting like or greater things to come. Another construction of the last clause, perhaps still more natural, is that adopted in the English Bible : *thy name is near, thy wondrous works declare.* For the sense and usage of the last word in Hebrew, see above, on Ps. ix. 2 (1), xxvi. 7, xl. 6 (5), lxxi. 17.

3 (2). *For I will take a set time ; I will equitably judge.* The best interpreters are now in favour of explaining these as the words of God himself, containing the promise upon which was built the hope expressed in the preceding verse. *Take* then includes the two ideas of choosing and using for the end proposed. The word translated *set time* is the same that means *assembly* in Ps. lxxiv. 4, 8. The idea of constituted time, which is included even there, is here predominant. The same use of the word occurs in Ps. cii. 14 (13), Hab. ii. 3, Dan. viii. 19, xi. 27, 35. There is here an obvious allusion to the stated times at which justice is publicly administered. Compare Acts xix. 38. As if he had said, I will appoint a time, and when it comes, I will ascend the judgment-seat. The parties to be tried are the foes and oppressors of God's people. The pronoun is emphatic ; I, and no other, will be judge. See above, on Ps. l. 6. *Equitably,* literally *equities* or *rectitudes.* See above, on Ps. xvii. 2, lviii. 2 (1). The use of the plural, as an abstract, and that of the noun in an adverbial sense, are both familiar Hebrew idioms. The judging of the wicked at God's bar implies their condemnation, and, as a necessary consequence, the deliverance of those whom they oppress or injure.

4 (3). *Melted (are) the earth and all dwelling on it ; I have weighed the pillars of it. Selah.* Dissolved with fear, enfeebled, or reduced to nothing.

See above, on Ps. xlvi. 7 (6). The figure in the last clause is obscure. The act of weighing may be intended to suggest that of raising, bearing up. Compare Isa. xl. 12, 13, 15. Some suppose, however, that it means to measure, estimate, or value, and implies not only perfect knowledge but creative power. As a part of the promise or encouraging assurance begun in the preceding verse, the one before us must mean that God himself will prevent or rectify the evils caused or threatened by his enemies.

5 (4). *I said to the boasters, Boast not, and to the wicked, Lift not up the horn !* Some regard these as the words of the psalmist, speaking again in the person of the church. The sense will then be that, encouraged by God's promise of protection and deliverance, his people warn their adversaries not to triumph. It seems more natural, however, to explain them as a continuation of the words of God himself, whose very assurance of protection to his people was in fact a warning of destruction to his enemies. The objection, that what follows must then be referred to the same speaker, is of little weight, as the transition from one person to another, in the psalms of a dramatic structure, is not commonly a marked one, and is often quite insensible. The concluding metaphor is borrowed from the habits of horned animals, and nearly equivalent to the act of holding the head high, as a sign of human pride. For a different application of the figure, see above, on Ps. xviii. 3 (2).

6 (5). *Do not raise on high your horn* (and) *speak with a proud neck*, or *speak with* (outstretched) *neck proudly.* The last word is an adjective meaning insolent or arrogant. See above, on Ps. xxxi. 19 (18). It may either agree with *neck*, and signify a position and carriage of the neck indicative of pride (Ps. lxxiii. 6), or constitute the object of the verb, in which case *with the neck* may mean *with* outstretched or prolonged neck, not projecting forwards but inclining backwards. See Isa. iii. 16, and compare Job xv. 26 in Hebrew. For a similar ellipsis, see below, Ps. lxxvii. 16 (15).

7 (6). *For not from east, and* (not) *from west, and not from the wilderness of mountains*, is the judgment on these sinners to proceed, but from a very different quarter. The word translated *east* means properly the *sunrise*, or rather the place of his coming forth ; the parallel term the *sunset*, or the place of evening. A third point of the compass is denoted by the *wilderness*, the great Arabian desert lying to the south of Palestine. The last word in Hebrew (הָרִים) admits of two entirely different explanations. One of these, given in the English Bible, makes it the infinitive of the verb translated *raise* in ver. 5, 6 (4, 5), and supposes it to mean the act of raising, or a state of exaltation. The sense will then be that promotion cometh not from any quarter upon earth, but from God and God alone. Others object that the question here is not one of promotion but of judgment, as appears from the foregoing and the following context. They accordingly adhere to the ancient versions in making (הָרִים) the plural of the common Hebrew word for *hill* or *mountain*, and explain the whole phrase to mean a *hilly desert* or a *wilderness of mountains*, a description eminently applicable to Idumæa and Arabia Petræa. The essential idea is still that of the *south*, here added to the *east* and *west*, as a general description of the countries contiguous to Palestine. The south is mentioned last, perhaps for the sake of an emphatic reference to Egypt, as the foreign power, on which the Jews were supposed by the Assyrians to rely with special confidence. Compare Isa. xxxvi. 4–6. The omission of the *north* may either be fortuitous or (as some suppose) intended to suggest that this

was the quarter from which the hostile incursion had proceeded, as it was in fact, invaders even from the furthest east commonly entering the country from that side. The meaning of the whole verse then is, that the danger which impended from one quarter could not be averted by mere human aid from any other, but only by the means referred to in the next verse.

8 (7). *For God* (is) *judge* (or actually *judging*); *this* (one) *he will humble, and this* (one) *will exalt.* The *for* at the beginning introduces the reason of the negative statement in the verse preceding. It is not man, *for* it is God, who can perform this. The same relation of the sentences is commonly expressed in our idiom by *but.* The act of judging, or the office of a judge, here implies absolute sovereignty. *This and this* is the idiomatic Hebrew phrase answering to *one and another* in English. See above, on Ps. xx. 8 (7).

9 (8). *For a cup* (is) *in the hand of Jehovah, and the wine ferments, and it is full of mixture, and he pours out from this* (cup); *only its dregs shall they wring* (or *suck*) *out, shall they drink—all the wicked of the earth* (or *land*). This is a common figure in the Scriptures for the wrath of God. See above, on Ps. xi. 6. The cup contains the prescribed or allotted portion of the sinner to whom it is administered. *Ferments* or *has fermented*, implying that it is real wine and strong wine. The translation *it is red* is now supposed to rest upon a doubtful etymology. Some interpreters explain the phrase, *it foams with wine*; but this construction is not only in itself less simple, but puts a sense upon the verb not entirely authorised by usage, and requires the noun (כּוֹס) *cup*, which is elsewhere feminine, to be construed as a masculine. *It* (the wine) *is full of mixture, i. e.* mixed with spices to increase its strength and stimulating power. *Only its dregs* is an idiomatic Hebrew phrase, which does not mean, as it may seem to do in English, that they shall drink nothing but the dregs. The meaning rather is, that they shall have nothing left for it, no resource, or no alternative, except to drain the cup to the very dregs, *i. e.* to suffer God's wrath to the uttermost (1 Thess. ii. 16). The position given to the subject of the sentence at its close makes it more emphatic. See above on Ps. xl. 15 (14).

10 (9.) *And I will declare for ever, I will sing praise to the God of Jacob.* The emphatic pronoun puts him in opposition to *the wicked of the earth* or *land.* " While they are thus destroyed, I will declare," &c. The object of the verb in the first clause is determined by the second. *Sing praise*, make music, as a means of celebrating the divine praise. See above, on Ps. ix. 12 (11), xxx. 5 (4), xlvii. 7 (6), lxvi. 4. *To the God of Jacob*, to him who has proved himself to be such, by fulfilling the promise made of old to Israel. The personal name of the patriarch is poetically substituted for the one which properly belonged to him as founder of the nation. See above, on Ps. xxiv. 6.

11 (10). *And all horns of wicked ones will I cut off; lifted up shall be the horns of the righteous.* The same noun and verb, that were used in ver. 5, 6 (4, 5), to denote the self-exaltation of the wicked, are here used in a good sense to denote God's gracious exaltation of the righteous. Compare Mat. xxiii. 12, Luke xiv. 11, xviii. 14. In the first clause, to the simple correlative idea of humiliation is superadded that of violent destruction. While the horns of the righteous are to be exalted, those of the wicked are not only to be lowered but cut off. The change from the plural (wicked men) to the singular (a righteous man), if meant to be significant at all, may have reference to the speaker as an ideal individual. The construction of these words as those of God himself is a gratuitous and harsh one. They are

rather uttered by the Church, as representing him, or acting in his strength and under his authority.

Psalm 76

1. *To the Chief Musician. With* (or *on*) *stringed instruments. A Psalm by Asaph. A song* (of praise). The resemblance of this title to that of the preceding psalm, their juxtaposition in the Psalter, and their internal similarity, all favour the opinion that they had respect originally to the same historical occasion, with this difference, that the first is rather an anticipation of the great deliverance as certain but still future, and the other a commemoration of the same as actually past or really experienced. In this, as in the other case, the event is ascribed to a wonderful divine interposition, and described as one affecting the whole world or the nations generally, which was emphatically true of the great stroke, by which the power of Assyria was broken.

2 (1). *Known in Judah* (is) *God; in Israel great* (is) *his name.* Known as God, and as the God of Israel, his chosen people, which, after the great schism in the time of Rehoboam, continued to exist in the kingdom of Judah. · It was only in the ancient church that his name was fully known, his perfection clearly manifested.

3 (2). *And in Salem was his tabernacle. and his home in Zion.* This is explanatory of the first verse. He was best known there because it was his chosen earthly residence. *Salem* is evidently used poetically for *Jerusalem.* The former name means peaceful and secure, and some suppose it to be one of the elements of which the other name is composed, so as to signify a peaceful or secure possession. The same interpreters identify the *Salem* of Gen. xiv. 18 with *Jerusalem.* The word translated *tabernacle* properly means a *booth* or *shed* composed of leaves and branches, in allusion to the moveable and temporary form of the first sanctuary.

4 (3). *Thither he shattered the bolts of the bow—buckler and sword and battle. Selah.* Some translate the first word *there,* but there is no clear instance of the Hebrew adverb being so used, and the best interpreters suppose the sense to be that he destroyed them on their way there, while in motion towards the Holy City. The word (שִׁבַּר) translated *shattered* is an intensive species of the common verb (שָׁבַר) to *break.* Both forms occur together in Ps. xxix. 5. See also Ps. iii. 8 (7). The ambiguous word *bolts* is used to represent a Hebrew one, which properly means thunderbolts or flashes of lightning, but is here applied to the flight of arrows, with or without allusion to the practice of igniting them (Eph. vi. 16). To the shield and sword, as the most important pieces of offensive and defensive armour, he adds, by a bold and striking figure, war itself, perhaps as a residuary aggregate of all other arms and weapons.

5 (4). *Bright* (art) *thou, glorious, more than the mountains of prey.* The object of address is God, who had been previously spoken of, in the third person. The first word in Hebrew is a participle, meaning illuminated, made to shine, and therefore bearing some affinity to our word *illustrious.* The other epithet means grand, glorious, sublime. See above, on Ps. viii. 1. The common version (*excellent*) seems to restrict the praise to moral qualities. As mountains are standing symbols of states and kingdoms, *mountains of prey, i. e.* mountains occupied by robbers, may

denote oppressive powers, such as that of Assyria, to which the prophets apply similar descriptions. See Nah. ii. 11, 12, iii. 1. To all such hostile powers God is here represented as superior.

6 (5). *Spoiled are the stout. of heart ; they have slept their sleep ; and all the men of might have not found their hands.* The meaning of the first clause seems to be, that the spoilers are themselves spoiled, by a signal providential retribution. Some, however, explain the first word to mean *snatched away*, caused to disappear, or vanish. They have slept their own sleep, *i. e.* they, like others, in their turn, sleep the sleep of death. See above, on Ps. xiii. 4 (3), and compare Nah. iii. 18, 2 Kings xix. 35. *Stout of heart* suggests the two distinct ideas, courageous and hard-hearted. The same expression is used, in an unfavourable sense, by Isaiah (xlvi. 12). *All have not found* does not imply that some have found, but on the contrary, that none have found, or in other words that the negative proposition is true of all without exception. *Found their hands* is understood by some to mean *regained their strength*. But the direct sense of the word is, that they have not found the use of their hands, or been able to employ them with advantage.

7 (6). *At thy rebuke, O God of Jacob, put to sleep* (is) *both chariot and horse.* The particle at the beginning is both temporal and causal, *post hoc et propter hoc.* After and because of thy rebuke. This noun denotes not merely a verbal but a real or practical expression of the divine displeasure. See above, on Ps. ix. 6 (5), lxviii. 31 (30). *God of Jacob,* see above, on ver. 10 (9). *Put to sleep* is here used to translate a passive participle, denoting not a mere state or condition, but the violence by which it is produced. The sleep meant is of course the sleep of death. The application of this figure to the chariot as well as to the horse, is less paradoxical in Hebrew, where the noun used is sometimes a collective meaning cavalry. See my note on Isaiah xxi. 7. At the same time there is beauty in the figure, as suggesting that the noisy rattle of the wheels is hushed in death-like silence.

8 (7). *Thou* (art) *to be feared,* (even) *thou, and who shall stand before thee, when once thou art angry?* The Hebrew passive participle often has the force of the future passive or gerundive in Latin. See above, on Ps. xviii. 4 (3). The repetition of the pronoun mades it highly emphatic and even exclusive, thou and no other, thou and only thou. *Who shall stand?* includes the kindred question, *who may or can stand?* To stand before God means, in this connection, to stand one's ground in opposition to him, or in independence of him. See above, on Ps. i. 5. The common version of the last words, which is retained above, conveys correctly the idea, but without the peculiar form of the original, which is highly idiomatic, and not susceptible of literal translation. The last word strictly means *thy anger* and the one before it *from then* or *from that time.* The nearest approach to it in English would be *since thy anger,* a construction which is actually given in the latest German versions.

9 (8). *From heaven thou hast caused judgment to be heard ; the earth feared and rested,* or, *the earth was afraid and was still.* From his throne in heaven God had pronounced judgment on his wicked enemies, the sound of which had struck the dwellers upon earth with awe and calmed their tumult. The last Hebrew verb is especially applied to repose after the noise and agitation of war. See Josh. xiv. 15, Judges v. 31, Isa. xiv. 7.

10 (9). *In God's arising for the judgment, to save all the humble of the earth.* This completes the sentence begun in the preceding verse, by assign-

ing the date, and at the same time the cause, of the effect there recorded. The earth was awe-struck and reduced to silence when God arose to judgment, *i. e.* to act as judge or sovereign arbiter. In the last clause, as in many other places, the judgments of God upon his enemies are represented as occasions of deliverance to his people, here described by one of their characteristic qualities, not merely as the *meek* in temper, but as the *lowly* in spirit, the *humble* in the strong religious sense. See above, on Ps. ix. 13 (12), x. 12, 17, xxii. 27 (26), xxv. 9, xxxiv. 3 (2), xxxvii. 11, lxix. 33 (32). The last word in the verse has here a kind of double sense, since the promise made directly to *the humble of the land, i. e.* the spiritual Israel, was really intended to include *all the humble of the earth, i. e.* all the truly pious, whether Jews or Gentiles.

11 (10). *For the wrath of man shall praise thee* (or *acknowledge thee*); *the remainder of wraths thou shalt gird* (about thee). The very passions which excite men to rebel against God shall be used as instruments and means of coercion. See above, on Ps. xxxii. 9. And so complete shall be this process, that even the remnant of such passionate excitement, which might be expected to escape attention, will be nevertheless an instrument or weapon in the hands of God. This last idea is expressed by the figure of a girdle, here considered as a sword-belt. So too in other cases the verb *to gird* is absolutely used in the sense of girding on a sword, or the still more general one of arming one's self. See above, on Ps. xlv. 4 (3), and compare Judges xviii. 11, 1 Kings xx. 11, 2 Kings iii. 21. Others, with less probability, suppose the figure to denote the act of attaching to one's self, as in Ps. cix. 19, Isa. xi. 5, Jer. xiii. 11, and apply it to the future conversion of all remaining enemies. The plural in the last clause (*wraths or angers*) seems to be an emphatic designation of abundance or success. See above, on Ps. xviii. 51 (50).

12 (11). *Vow and pay unto Jehovah your God, all* (*ye that are*) *round about him; let them bring tribute to the Dread* (*One*). The first clause may be understood to mean, pay now what you have vowed before, *i. e.* before the great deliverance and during the impending danger. The addition of *your God* shews that the object of address is Israel. Compare Deut. xxiii. 22 (21). According to the masoretic interpunction, *all that are round about him* belongs to the first clause, and denotes the host of Israel, in the midst of whom Jehovah's tent was pitched (Num. ii. 2). The English Bible, following the ancient versions, throws these words into the last clause, as the subject of the verb that follows, *let all that are round about him bring presents*, or *they shall bring presents*. This last word in Hebrew denotes tribute from the conquered or dependent to the conqueror or sovereign. See above, on Ps. lxviii. 30 (29), and compare Isa. xviii. 7. This was literally verified in the case of Hezekiah's rescue from the power of Sennacherib. See 2 Chron. xxxii. 23. God is here called Fear or Terror, as an object to be reverenced or dreaded. Compare the similar expressions in Isaiah viii. 12, 13.

13 (12). *He cuts off the spirit of princes; he is feared* (or *to be feared*) *by the kings of earth.* The first verb is specially applied to the pruning or cutting of vines. See Jer. vi. 9, xxv. 30, xlix. 9, and compare Rev. xiv. 18, 19. Its future form includes a potential sense. He can do it when he will, and he will do it when he sees occasion. *Spirit* or *breath* is here put for the life or vital principle, to cut which is to kill. He who possesses this alarming power is or ought to be an object of religious fear, not only to ordinary men, or to certain great men in particular, but to all the kings

of the earth. Compare Mat. x. 28, Luke xii. 5. These expressions shew
that the historical occasion of the psalm was not an event of merely local
interest, but a great historical and national catastrophe, such as the blow
inflicted on the power of Assyria by the sudden destruction of Sennacherib's
host.

Psalm 77

1. *To the Chief Musician over* (the choir or family of) *Jeduthun. By
Asaph. A Psalm.* For the meaning of this title, see above, on Ps.
lxii. 1. The psalm before us contains a complaint and prayer of the ancient
church in times of deep distress. It consists of two parts. In the first,
the church describes her sad condition, and complains of God's desertion,
ver. 2–10 (1–9). In the second, she encourages herself by the remembrance of former deliverances, and especially of that from Egypt, ver. 11–21
(10–20). The particular historical occasion is not specified; but if, as
some suppose, it be the crisis of affairs in the reign of Josiah, the name
Asaph must be understood as a description of the family, and not of its progenitor. See above, on Ps. l. 1. There are several obvious imitations of
this psalm in the third chapter of Habakkuk.

2 (1). *My voice unto God* (I will raise) *and will cry; my voice unto God*
(I will raise), *and he will give ear to me.* Some make the last verb an imperative, *and* (when I raise my voice) *do thou give ear.* But besides the
sudden change of person, which, though common, is not to be assumed
without necessity, the form of the Hebrew verb is that of an infinitive, to
be determined by assimilation to the one before it. The last clause then
really assigns a reason for the purpose expressed in the first. He would
not pray if he despaired of being heard.

3 (2). *In the day of my distress the Lord I sought; my hand by night
was spread, and grew not numb; my soul refused to be comforted.* Day is
here put for time, but not without allusion to the mention of the night in
the clause following, so as to express the idea that he prayed day and night.
The verb translated *spread* means strictly spilt, poured out, scattered, but
seems to be here poetically applied to the spreading of the hands as a customary
gesture of entreaty. See above, on Ps. xliv. 21 (20). The common version, *my sore ran*, has no foundation in etymology or usage. For the
meaning of the next verb, see above, on Ps. xxxviii. 9 (8). Its form is
future, but the copulative particle, though separated from it by the negative, may be considered as exerting a conversive force.

4 (3). *I remember God and murmur; I muse, and overwhelmed is my
spirit. Selah.* The recollection of God's former kindness, as contrasted with
what seems to be his present desertion, extorts from the sufferer an expression
of disquietude. The second verb in Hebrew is the same with that in Ps.
xxxix. 7 (6), xlii. 6, 12 (5, 11), lv. 18 (17). *My spirit* is not simply
equivalent to *myself*, but suggests the additional idea of profound internal
agitation.

5 (4). *Thou hast held fast my eyes; I am smitten and cannot speak.*
The word here rendered *fast* is properly a passive participle, meaning
watched, kept, and here, from the connection, kept awake or open. This
circumstance is added to enhance the description of his miserable state.

6 (5). *I thought on days of old, years of antiquities* (or *perpetuities.*)
The contrast of the present with the past is again urged as an aggravating
circumstance in his condition.

7 (6). *I will remember my song in the night, with my heart will I muse, and my spirit inquires.* The futures of the first clause have reference to the time of actual suffering. The word translated *song* means strictly a *stringed instrument*, or that kind of music, but is here used more generally to denote the musical expression of thanksgiving. *In the night* qualifies the words immediately preceding (*my song*), not the remoter antecedent (*I remember*). *With my heart, i. e.* in communion with it, with myself. *My spirit inquires, i. e.* I, from the bottom of my heart, ask the questions recorded in the following verses.

8 (7). *For ever will the Lord reject, and will he no more favour ?* It was thus that the spirit of the sufferer made inquiry. *For ever*, literally *to eternities* or *ages*. *Reject*, with abhorrence and contempt. See above, on Ps. xliii. 2, xliv. 10, 24 (9, 23), lx. 3, 12 (2, 11), lxxiv. 1. The idiomatic form of the last clause is, *will he not add to favour again* (or *any longer*) *?*

9 (8). *Ceased for ever has his mercy, failed* (*his*) *word to generation and generation ?* The general term *word* here denotes specifically a word of promise. See above on Ps. xviii. 31 (30). *Generation and generation, i. e.* all generations in succession, are not mentioned as the objects of the pro-mise, to whom God's word was pledged, but as the period of its failure.

10 (9). *Has the Mighty* (*One*) *forgotten to be gracious, or closed in wrath his mercies ? Selah.* The use of the divine name *El* is here significant, as if it had been asked, does the goodness of God no longer bear proportion to his greatness ? The verb translated *closed* is one found only in poetical style. The original expression for *his mercies* suggests the idea of *his bowels*, according to the idiom which represents the viscera as the seat of the tenderest affections.

11 (10). *And I said, This is my affliction, the years of the right hand of the Highest.* This may be regarded as the turning point of the entire composition. After all the repinings and misgivings just described, I said, at length, what I might and should have said before. *My affliction*, literally *my sickness*, that specific form of suffering being put for suffering in general, as inflicted by the hand of God. The use of the word *years* seems to imply that the trial was one of long continuance. The divine name or description (*Most High*) suggests the duty and necessity of yielding to his sovereign pleasure.

12 (11). *I will commemorate the deeds of Jah ; for I will remember thy wonders of old.* The forms of the verb in the two clauses are different, though needlessly assimilated by the masoretic critics and the versions. The second is the primitive verb *remember ;* the first its derivative, cause to be remembered, commemorate, celebrate. The literal meaning of the last words is *from antiquity thy wonder*, a collective and abstract expression for *thy wondrous works*. For the origin and use of the divine name JAH, see above, on Ps. lxviii. 5 (4).

13 (12). *And I will meditate of all thy work, and of thy doings will I muse.* The original expression is not *of* but *in* them, as if implying a complete absorption of the thoughts and feeling in the object.

14 (13). *O God, in holiness is thy way. What Mighty* (*One*) *is great like God ?* The common version, *in the sanctuary*, yields a good sense ; but the other is entitled to the preference on account of Exod. xv. 11, to which place there is evident allusion. *Holiness* here means the divine perfection, all that distinguishes the Maker from his creatures. See above, on Ps. xxii. 4 (3). *Thy way, i. e.* thy mode of dealing with thy creatures, and particularly with thy people. The use of the name *El* is again significant. Who is there like God, even among the mightiest and most exalted beings ?

15 (14). *Thou (art) the Almighty doing wonders ; thou hast made known in the nations thy strength.* Thou art the true Almighty as distinguished from all counterfeits. *Doing, i. e.* habitually, characteristically, doing wonders. The next word has the singular form but a collective meaning, as in ver. 12 (11) above. *In the nations*, not only to them, but among them, in the midst of them, and in their own experience. The display of God's omnipotence had not been confined to his own people, but extended to surrounding nations, This is particularly mentioned in the history of the exodus from Egypt. See Exod. ix. 16, xv. 14.

16 (15). *Thou hast redeemed with the arm thy people, the sons of Jacob and Joseph.* Selah. The particular display of the divine strength just referred to is now specified. *Redeemed*, recovered from captivity or bondage. *With the arm, i.e.* by the exercise of power. See above, on Ps. xliv. 4 (3). *Joseph* is named as well as *Jacob*, in order to include the ten tribes in the statement, which might otherwise have been applied to Judah only, as the legitimate successor of the ancient Israel. In this clause some interpreters see a distinct allusion to the downfall of the kingdom of the ten tribes, as an event which had already taken place when the psalm was written.

17 (16). *The waters saw thee, God, the waters saw thee ; they shake, yea, the depths quake.* The historical reference is of course to the passage of the Red Sea, but at the same time with allusion to the symbolical use of seas in Scripture. See above, on Ps. xlvi. 3 (2). The transition from the past tense to the future or present shews that the writer suddenly transports himself into the midst of the events which he commemorates. The *yea* or *nay* (אף) in the last clause is emphatic. Not merely the surface of the water moves ; its very depths are agitated and convulsed.

18 (17). *The clouds poured water ; the skies gave a sound : yea, thine arrows fly.* These are natural phenomena of storms, here noted as betokening God's presence. See above, on Ps. xviii. 12–15 (11–14). *The skies*, the vapours constituting the visible heavens. See above, on Ps. lxviii. 35 (34). *Gave a sound*, uttered their voice, a beautifiul description of the thunder. The *yea* indicates a climax. There was not only rain and thunder but lightning, the flashes of which are poetically spoken of as arrows. See above, on Ps. xviii. 15 (14). The word translated *fly* is an intensive form of the verb to *go*, implying swiftness and perhaps diversity of direction, hither and thither, to and fro. See above, on Ps. xxvi. 3, xxxv. 14. With this verse compare Hab. iii. 11.

19 (18). *The voice of thy thunder (was) in the whirlwind ; lightnings made the world shine ; (then) shook and quaked the earth.* The word translated *whirlwind* usually means a *wheel*, but is sometimes applied to anything whirled or driven round before the wind. See below, on Ps. lxxxiii. 14 (13), and compare Isa. xvii. 13. Hence it may naturally be employed to designate the whirlwind itself as the cause of this rotary motion. This is surely more agreeable to usage than to make it descriptive of mere swiftness or velocity. The common version, *in the heaven*, if not entirely arbitrary, must rest upon a supposed allusion to the convex appearance of the heavens. *Made to shine*, illuminated, lighted up. There is, however, no affinity between the Hebrew word and that for *lightnings*. The whole description is remarkably like that of the theophany in Ps. xviii. See also Hab. iii. 14.

20 (19). *In the sea (was) thy way and thy paths in great (or many) waters,*

and thy footsteps were not known. This may be understood as a general description of the divine operations as inscrutable, in which case the verbs supplied should have the present form, *is thy way, are not known.* It is more agreeable, however, to the context, and in far better keeping with the vivid graphic character of this part of the psalm, to understand the verse, at least in the first instance, as referring to the exodus from Egypt, when it might indeed be said that the way of Jehovah, as the deliverer and conductor of his people, was *in the sea,* and that his footsteps and theirs could not be traced, because the waters instantly rolled over them. With this verse compare Hab. iii. 15.

21 (20). *Thou didst guide like a flock thy people, by the hand of Moses and Aaron.* Like a flock in perfect safety and with perfect ease. The comparison of Moses, at this juncture, to a shepherd, reappears in Isa. lxiii. 11–14. The conclusion of the psalm appears abrupt, but any devout Israelite could draw the inference for himself, that he who had so gloriously saved his people could deliver them again.

Psalm 78

THIS psalm appears to have been written after David's elevation to the throne, and perhaps before he was acknowledged by the whole race of Israel (2 Sam. v. 5). Its design is to impress upon the public mind the true grounds of the transfer which had taken place, of the pre-eminence in Israel, from the tribe of Ephraim to that of Judah, as the execution of a divine purpose long before disclosed, and at the same time a just judgment on the sins committed by the people under the predominant influence of Ephraim, from the time of Joshua to that of Eli. The internal character of the psalm determines its external form, which is simple, and admits of no minute division, beyond that afforded by the historical succession of events and the logical design of the composition, to prove that the Israelites under the ascendancy of Ephraim were similar in character to the elder generation which came out of Egypt.

1. *Maschil. By Asaph. Listen, my people, to my law; incline your ear to the sayings of my mouth.* This is eminently a didactic psalm, because it teaches the true meaning of events in the history of Israel which might otherwise seem to be mere matters of curiosity. For the same reason it was necessary that it should be so designated in the title or inscription. See above, on Ps. xxxii. 1, xlii. 1, lii. 1, &c. The Asaph meant, as we have seen, is probably the contemporary and chief musician of David, but also an inspired psalmist. See above, on Ps. l. 1. In this verse he invites attention, as if to something strange and unexpected. *My people,* fellow-members of the ancient church, not as individuals, however, but as an organised body. *My law,* my inspired instructions which, as such, have a binding authority and force.

2. *I will open, in a parable, my mouth ; I will utter riddles from antiquity.* By a *parable* we are here to understand an analogical illustration of divine truth. An exposition of the true design and meaning of the history of Israel was in this sense a *mashal* or parable. *Riddles,* enigmas, not the events themselves, but their latent import, which escaped a merely superficial observation. See above, on Ps. xlix. 5 (4). *Of old,* or from antiquity, *i. e.* belonging to the early period of our national existence. *Utter,* literally pour forth, cause to flow or gush. See above, on Ps. xix. 3 (2).

3. *Which we have heard, and have known them, and our fathers recounted to us.* Here, as often elsewhere, the knowledge of God's ancient dealings with his people is ascribed to that national tradition, which they were not only suffered but required to cherish and perpetuate (Exod. xii. 14, Deut. vi. 20), but which was not at all exclusive of a written and authoritative record.

4. *We will not hide (them) from their sons, to an after generation recounting the praises of Jehovah, and his strength, and his wonders which he did.* The psalmist here recognises the obligation resting on the individual parent, but above all on the church as such, to continue the transmission of this knowledge to the latest generations.

5. *And set up a testimony in Jacob, and a law established in Israel, which he commanded our fathers, to make them known unto their sons.* The essential idea here conveyed still is, that the traditional transmission of God's mighty deeds entered into the very end or purpose for which Israel existed as a nation.

6. *In order that the after generation might know, sons be born, arise, and tell (it) to their own sons.* This prolonged reiteration of the same thing seems intended to preclude the thought or feeling, that the things about to be recounted were mere relics of antiquity, without interest or use to the contemporary race.

7. *And might place in God their hope, and not forget the deeds of the Almighty, and his commandments might observe (or keep).* The construction is continued from the verse preceding. The recollection thus enjoined was not a mere historical or speculative exercise, but designed to have a practical effect, to wit, that of securing obedience.

8. *And might not be as their fathers, a generation stubborn and rebellious, a generation that did not prepare its heart, and whose spirit was not true to God.* A still more specific purpose is here mentioned, to wit, that of warning by means of bad examples. The *fathers* here meant are the elder race that came out of Egypt. The description *stubborn and rebellious* is borrowed from Deut. xxi. 18. To *prepare the heart* is to dispose or devote it to God's service. Compare 1 Sam. vii. 3, 2 Chron. xx. 33.

9. *The sons of Ephraim, armed bowmen, turned (back) in the day of battle.* The people, during the ascendancy of Ephraim, proved false to their great mission of subduing Canaan and destroying its inhabitants. This neglect is represented, in the history itself, as the source of all the national calamities that followed. As the bow among the ancients was one of the chief weapons of war, the description *armed bowmen* is equivalent to well armed soldiers, and is added to enhance the guilt and shame of those who thus betrayed their trust, in spite of every external advantage.

10. *They kept not the covenant of God, and in his law refused to walk.* They violated the condition of their national vocation, and refused to do the very thing for which they were brought out of Egypt.

11. *And forgot his deeds and his wonders which he shewed them.* The second generation forgot the proofs of God's presence and power, which, in the person of their fathers, they had seen when they came out of Egypt.

12. *Before their fathers he did a wonder, in the land of Egypt, in the field of Zoan.* Wonder has here the same collective sense as in Ps. lxxvii. 12, 15 (11, 14). *Zoan,* called by the Greeks *Tanis,* was the ancient capital of Lower Egypt. See Num. xiii. 22. The *field of Zoan* was the country immediately adjacent to it.

13. *He clave the sea, and let them pass, and made the waters stand as a*

heap. This last expression is derived from Exod. xv. 8. See above, on Ps. xxxiii. 7.

14. *And led them by the cloud by day, and all the night by light of fire.* See Exod. xiii. 21, 22. The original expression, *in the cloud,* may denote something more than instrumental agency, to wit, the personal presence of the Divine Angel in the cloud itself.

15. *He cleaves rocks in the wilderness, and gives them drink as a great deep.* This last is a hyperbolical description of an abundant flow of water in the desert. Some account for it by supposing an allusion to the flood, from the account of which (Gen. vii. 11) some of the expressions are borrowed. The verse has reference to both miraculous supplies of this kind, one in the first, and one in the last year of the error in the wilderness. See Exod. xvii. 6, Num. xx. 8.

16. *And brings out torrents from a rock, and brings down waters like the rivers.* This verse relates to the later miracle, recorded in the twentieth of Numbers.

17. *And they continued still to sin against him, to rebel against the Highest in the desert.* What ought to have been the effect of these divine interpositions, is clearly implied in this description of the actual effect. The very means which should have made them more obedient made them more rebellious. The last word in Hebrew means a desert, properly so called, a dry land, and may here be used to suggest the idea, that they foolishly and wickedly provoked God in the very situation where they were most dependent on him for protection and supplies. The extent of this dependence is implied in the use of a divine name signifying sovereignty, supremacy.

18. *And tempted God in their heart, to ask food for their soul.* To tempt God is to require unnecessary proof of what should be believed without it. Instead of trusting in his bounty to supply them, they anxiously demanded what they looked upon as necessary for their sustenance. *In their heart* describes the first conception of the sin, as distinguished from its outward commission in the next verse. *To ask,* by asking, or rather, so as to ask. Such was their impious distrust of God, that they actually asked, &c. *For their soul,* for themselves ; or, for their appetite, to gratify their inordinate desire of bodily indulgence ; or, for their life, as absolutely necessary to preserve it.

19. *And spake of God (and) said, Will the Almighty be able to set a table in the wilderness ?* This they not only said, but said it speaking of or against God. The unreasonableness of the doubt is aggravated by the use of a divine name which implies omnipotence. As if they had said, Can he do this who can do everything ?

20. *Lo, he smote the rock, and waters flow, and streams gush out;* (but) *can he also give bread or provide flesh for his people?* The same thing is now proved by an appeal to what he had done. The question is reduced to an absurdity by introducing as a kind of preamble, what ought to have prevented its being asked at all. The doubters are described in these two verses as virtually reasoning thus : God is almighty; but is he able to supply our wants ? He has given us water; but can he give us bread or meat ?

21. *Therefore Jehovah heard and was wroth, and fire was kindled in Jacob, and also anger came up in* (or *against*) *Israel.* The first clause exemplifies a common Hebrew idiom, equivalent to saying, therefore when he heard he was angry. *Heard,* not the rumour or report of their offence, but the

offence itself, which consisted externally in speaking against God. The second verb is a reflexive form of one that means to pass out or over, and properly denotes the act of letting one's self out or giving vent to the emotions. *Fire* seems to be a figure for this same wrath, with or without allusion to material fire as a destroying agent. Compare Num. xi. 1. *Came up*, in the mind. See 2 Sam. xi. 20. Or there may be an allusion to the visible ascent of smoke and flame, as in Ps. xviii. 9 (8).

22. *Because they believed not in God, and trusted not in his salvation.* Compare the terms of the history in Exod. xiv. 13, Num. xiv. 11.

23. *And he commanded the cloud above, and the doors of heaven he opened.* The connection of the sentences is correctly although freely given in the common version, *though he had commanded*, &c. *Above*, literally *from above*, but see on Ps. l. 4. The whole verse expresses the idea of a copious supply from heaven. In the last clause there seems to be a reference to the opening of the windows of heaven at the deluge. Compare Gen. vii. 11, and see above on ver. 15.

24. *And rained upon them manna to eat, and corn of heaven gave to them.* The expression *rained* is borrowed from the history, Exod. xvi. 4. The addition of the words *to eat* may have reference to the primary import of the word (מָן) *manna* as an interrogative or indefinite pronoun, meaning *what* or *somewhat*, so that the words here might also bear the sense of *something to eat*. See Exod. xvi. 15, 31. It is called *corn of heaven* as a miraculous substitute for bread, and also in allusion to its granular form and appearance, Exod. xvi. 31.

25. *Bread of the mighty (ones) did (each) man eat; victual he sent them to the full.* The first Hebrew word, as appears from the preceding verse, is used in its specific sense of *bread*, and not in the generic one of *food*, which is otherwise expressed in ver. 20. Some explain *bread of the mighty* to mean delicate or costly bread, like that used by the rich and noble. But to these the epithet is nowhere else applied, as a similar one is to the angels in Ps. ciii. 20, a circumstance which favours the old explanation given in the Targum and the Septuagint, according to which manna is called *angels' bread*, not as being their food, but as coming from the place where they reside. *Man* is not used generically in antithesis to angels, which would have required another Hebrew word (אָדָם), but distributively in the sense of *every one*, as it is in the history of this very miracle, Exod. xvi. 16. The idea then is that enough was sent for all without exception. The word translated *victual* denotes specially provision for a march or journey. See Exod. xii. 39. *To the full,* or *to satiety*, enough and more than enough to satisfy the appetite of every individual; another expression borrowed from the history. See Exod. xvi. 3.

26. *He rouses an east-wind in the heavens, and guides by his power a south-wind.* The first verb is a causative of that used in Num. xi. 31, which strictly means to strike a tent or break up an encampment, and then to set out upon a march or journey, but is there applied to the sudden rise of a particular wind. The east and south are here named as the points from which the strongest winds were known to blow in that part of the world. The history itself contains no such specification. *Guides*, directs it in the course required for this purpose.

27. *And he rained upon them, like dust, flesh, and like the sand of seas, winged fowl* (or *birds of wing*). Here, as in the miracle of water, two miraculous supplies of flesh are brought together. See Exod. xvi. 13, Num.

xi. 31, 32. To these two is transferred the figure of rain, which, in the history, is applied only to the manna.

28. *And let it fall in the midst of his camp, round about his dwellings.* The pronoun *his* refers to Israel as a body, and may be rendered clearer by the use of the plural *their*. Several of the terms here used are borrowed from the Mosaic narrative. See Exod. xvi. 13, Num. xi. 31.

29. *And they ate and were sated exceedingly, and* (thus) *their desire he brings to them.* The first clause is an amplification of the phrase *to the full* in ver. 25 above. Compare the history in Num. xi. 18–20. *Their desire, i. e.* the object of it, that which they had longed for.

30. *They were not* (yet) *estranged from their desire; still* (was) *their food in their mouth.* This is merely the protasis or conditional clause of the sentence completed in the next verse. The first clause does not mean that the food had not begun to pall upon their appetite, but, as the other clause explains it, that it was still in their possession, in their very mouths, when God smote them. Compare Num. xi. 33.

31. *And the wrath of God came up among them* (or *against them*), *and slew among their fat ones, and the chosen* (*youths*) *of Israel brought low.* The form of expression in the first clause is the same as in ver. 21 above. *Among their fat ones, i.e.* killed some or many of them. The parallel term, according to its etymology, means picked or chosen men, but its usage is applied to young men in their full strength and the flower of their age, and therefore fit for military service. Thus the youngest and strongest are described as unable to resist the exhibition of God's wrath against his people.

32. *For all this they sinned still, and believed not for his wonders.* Notwithstanding all these favours and extraordinary interpositions, the generation that came out of Egypt still persisted in their evil courses. The last clause does not charge them with denying the reality of the wonders which they witnessed, but with refusing to trust God on the strength of them. This appears from the history itself, Num. xiv. 11, to which there is obvious allusion.

33. *And* (therefore) *he wasted in vanity their days and their years in terror.* As the preceding verse relates to the refusal of the people to go up against the Canaanites in the first year of the exodus, so this relates to the forty years of error in the wilderness, by which that refusal was at once indulged and punished. The fruitless monotony of their existence during this long period, and their constant apprehension of some outbreak of divine wrath, are expressed here by the words translated *vanity* and *terror*. The meaning of the verb is that he suffered or caused their years to be thus unprofitably and miserably spent. Compare Ps. lxxiii. 19.

34. *If he slew them, then they sought him, and returned and inquired early after God.* Whenever, during this long interval, he punished them with more than usual severity, a temporary and apparent reformation was the immediate consequence. The verb in the last clause denotes eager and importunate solicitation. See above, on Ps. xliii. 2 (1).

35. *And remembered that God* (*was*) *their Rock, and the Mighty, the Most High, their Redeemer.* It was only at these times of peculiar suffering that the people, as a body, called to mind their national relation to Jehovah, as their founder, their protector, and their refuge. See above, on Ps. xviii. 3 (2), and compare Deut. xxxii. 4, 15, 18, 31.

36. *And* (yet) *they deceived him with their mouth, and with their tongue they lie to him.* Even these apparent reformations only led to hypocritical professions. The verb in the first clause does not describe the effect but

the intention. It may therefore be translated *flattered*, although this is not the strict sense of the Hebrew word.

37. *And their heart was not fixed* (or *constant*) *with him, and they were not true to* (or *faithful in*) *his covenant.* Their obedience was capricious and imperfect, and proceeded from no settled principle or genuine devotion to his service. They were false to the very end for which they existed as a nation. For the meaning of a *fixed* or *settled heart*, see above, on Ps. li. 12 (10), and compare Ps. lvii. 8 (7).

38. *And he, the Merciful, forgives iniquity, and does not* (ütterly) *destroy; and he often withdrew his anger, and would not arouse all his wrath.* The first clause relates rather to God's attributes, or to his method of proceeding in the general, than to his proceeding in this particular case, which is not brought forward till the last clause. There is obvious allusion to the description of God's mercy in Ex. xxxiv. 6, 7. *Forgives* is a very inadequate translation of the Hebrew word, which necessarily suggests the idea of expiation as the ground of pardon. *Often withdrew*, literally multiplied to withdraw his wrath, or cause it to return without accomplishing its object.

39. *And he remembered that they* (were but) *flesh, a breath departing and returning not.* Here, as elsewhere, the frailty and infirmity of man is assigned as a ground of the divine forbearance. Compare Ps. ciii. 14–16. *Flesh*, a common scriptural expression for humanity or human nature, as distinguished from superior beings, and especially from God. See above, on Ps. lvi. 5 (4), and compare Gen. vi. 3, Isa. xxxi. 3. The idea of fragility and brief duration is expressed still more strongly by the exquisite figure in the last clause. The melancholy thought with which it closes is rendered still more emphatic in Hebrew by the position of the verb and the irregular construction of the sentence, *a breath going and it shall not return.*

40. *How oft do they resist him in the wilderness* (and) *grieve him in the desert!* Many particular occurrences are summed up in this pregnant exclamation. The future form of the verbs seems to have reference to the ideal situation of the writer, looking forward in imagination to the error as still future, and saying as Moses might have said, if gifted with prophetic foresight of the sins of Israel, Notwithstanding all these favours and these high professions, how oft will they resist his authority and rouse his wrath!

41. *And they turned and tempted God, and* (on) *the Holy One of Israel set a mark.* Having described the conduct of the first generation in the wilderness, the Psalmist now proceeds to shew that the younger generation, after the death of Joshua (Josh. xxiv. 31), were *like their fathers* (ver. 57 below). The first verb may either have the independent meaning *turned away*, or *turned back* from his service, or qualify the next verb by denoting repetition of the action ; *and they tempted again*, or *still tempted*. They tempted God by doubting his supremacy, and practically challenging him to the proof of it. See above, on ver. 19. The last word in Hebrew is of doubtful meaning. Some explain it, by a Syriac analogy, and on the authority of the ancient versions, to mean *provoked* or *grieved*. In the only other place where the Hebrew word occurs (Ezek. ix. 4) it means to set a mark upon a person, which some apply here, in the figurative sense of stigmatising or insulting. A cognate verb is used by Moses (Num. xxxiv. 7, 8) to denote the act of laying off or marking out a boundary, which is probably the origin of the common version, *limited*, *i.e.* prescribed bounds to the power of Jehovah in their unbelief, *Holy One of Israel*, see above, on Ps. lxxi. 22)

42. *They remembered not his hand, the day that he redeemed them from*

distress (or *from the enemy*). The psalmist still confounds or identifies the several generations as one aggregate or national person. The younger race remembered not the miraculous favours experienced by their predecessors. *His hand*, the exertion of his power, a favourite Mosaic figure. See particularly Exod. vii. 5, xiii. 9, Deut. vii. 8. The last clause admits of two constructions. *The day* may be in apposition with *his hand*, and a collateral object to the verb, as in the common version; or it may be an adverbial expression qualifying what precedes. " They remembered not how his power was exerted in the day that he redeemed them from the enemy." The essential meaning is the same in either case.

43. (*He*) *who set in Egypt his signs and his wonders in the field of Zoan.* The miraculous interpositions at the exodus were *signs* of God's presence and immediate agency. To *set* these was to hold them up to view. See above, on Ps. lxxiv. 4. The description of Egypt in the last clause is repeated from ver. 12 above.

44. *And turned to blood their rivers, and their streams they cannot drink.* The general statement of the preceding verse is rendered more specific by the mention of several of the plagues in detail, beginning with the first. See Exod. vii. 18–20. The word translated *rivers* is the plural of one commonly applied to the Nile, and supposed to be of Egyptian origin. It may here be understood as denoting either the natural branches of the Nile, or the artificial channels by which its waters are employed in the irrigation of the country. In the last clause, by a very common trope, the writer speaks as he might have spoken at the time of the event.

45. *He sends among them* (or *against them*) *flies and they devour them, and frogs and they destroy them.* Two of the other plagues are here added, from the narrative in Exod. viii. The first noun in Hebrew was explained by the ancient writers as denoting a *mixture* of noxious animals ; but the best interpreters are now agreed that it means the Egyptian dog-fly, which Philo represents as feeding upon flesh and blood.

46. *And he gave* (*up*) *to the caterpillar their produce, and their labour to the locust.* Both the animal names in this verse are really designations of the locust, one meaning the *devourer*, and the other denoting the vast numbers of that insect. *Their labour, i. e.* its effect or fruit. Compare the narrative in Exod. x. 12–19.

47. *He kills with hail their vine and their sycamores with frost.* The destruction of the vines is not mentioned in the history (Exod. ix. 23–32), though it is in Ps. cv. 33. It has even been denied that the culture of the vine was known in ancient Egypt ; but the fact has been fully established by modern investigation and discovery. The last word of the sentence occurs nowhere else. Some of the moderns explain it, from an Arabic analogy, to mean an *ant ;* but the parallelism favours the usual interpretation which is derived from the ancient versions.

48. *And delivered their cattle to the hail and their herds to the flames.* The Hebrew verb strictly means *shut up*, and occurs elsewhere in the combination to *shut up in the hand, i. e.* abandon to the power, of another. See above, on Ps. xxxi. 9 (8), and compare 1 Sam. xxiii. 11. Here, as in Deut. xxxii. 30, the verb is used absolutely in the sense of the whole phrase. The word translated *flames* occurs above in Ps. lxxvi. 4 (3), and is here a poetical description of the lightning. The common version (*hot thunderbolts*) is striking and poetical, but perhaps too strong. This verse does not relate to a distinct plague, but to the effects of the hail-storm upon animals, as its effect upon plants was described in the preceding verse.

49. *He sends upon them the heat of his anger, wrath and indignation and anguish, a mission of angels of evil.* Before mentioning the last and greatest plague of all, he accumulates expressions to describe it as the effect of the divine displeasure. The slaughter of the first-born is ascribed in the history itself to a *destroyer* or destroying angel (Exod. xii. 23, Heb. xi. 28), which may be a collective as it seems to be in 1 Sam. xiii. 17, or denote the commander of a destroying host (Josh. v. 15), here called *a mission* or *commission of angels.* The destroying angel reappears in the history of David (2 Sam. xxiv. 16) and of Hezekiah (2 Kings xix. 35). The original construction in the case before us is peculiar, *angels of evil* (*ones*). This cannot mean *evil angels,* in the sense of fallen spirits, who are not described in the Old Testament as the executioners of God's decrees. The best explanation is perhaps to take the plural *evils* in an abstract sense, *angels of evil,* not moral but physical, *i. e.* authors of suffering or destruction.

50. *He levels a path for his anger ; and he did not withhold from death their soul, and their life to the plague gave up.* For the meaning of the first verb, see above, on Ps. lviii. 3 (2). The meaning of the figure seems to be, that he removes all hindrance to his anger and allows it free scope. Not content with having smitten their possessions and their persons, he now extends his stroke to their lives. The word translated *life* more usually means an *animal* or *animals* collectively. See above, on Ps. lxviii. 11, 31 (10, 30), lxxiv. 19. If we retain this meaning here, the verse may be referred to the death of the Egyptian cattle by the murrain (Exod. ix. 1–7). But the parallelism and the context rather favour the translation *life,* and the reference of the passage to the death of the first-born, which was probably occasioned by a pestilence (Exod. ix. 15) and is expressly mentioned in the next verse.

51. *And smote all the first-born in Egypt, the first-fruits of strength in the tents of Ham.* Compare the narrative in Exod. xii. 29, 30. The poetical description of the first-born in the last clause is derived from Gen. xlix. 3 (compare Deut. xxi. 17), and that of Egypt from Gen. x. 6.

52. *And brought out, like sheep, his people, and led them, like a flock in the wilderness.* For the precise meaning of the first verb, see above, on ver. 26, and compare Exod. xii. 37, xv. 22. The guidance in the wilderness·includes that on both sides of the Red Sea, as appears from Exod. xii. 37.

53. *And guided them in safety, and they did not fear, and their enemies the sea covered.* They did not fear, because he removed all ground of apprehension. This was especially the case at the passage of the Red Sea, Exod. xv. 19, to which there is clearly a particular allusion.

54. *And brought them to his holy border, this mountain* (which) *his right hand won.* The bound or border of his holiness, the frontier of the land which he had set apart as holy. *This mountain* may, agreeably to Hebrew usage, mean this hilly country, as it does in Deut. iii. 25. But there is no doubt a particular reference to mount Zion, in the wide sense, as the central point of the theocracy, designated as such long before the conquest of Canaan. See Gen. xxii. 14, and compare Exod. xv. 13, 17. *His right hand,* the exertion of his strength. *Won,* purchased, not in the restricted modern sense of buying, but in the old and wide sense of acquiring.

55. *And drove out before them nations, and assigned them by measure* (as) *a heritage, and caused to dwell in their tents the tribes of Israel. Before them,* literally from their face or presence. *Nations,* whole nations, not mere armies, much less individuals. *Assigned them,* literally made them fall, by

lot or otherwise, a common expression for the distribution and allotment of the land. See Num. xxxiv. 2. The pronoun (*them*) refers to the nations, put for their possessions, and especially their territory. The word translated *measure* means primarily a measuring line, but then the portion of land measured. Hence we may also read, *assigned them as* (or *for*) *a hereditary portion*. In the last clause, *their tents* means of course those of the Canaanites, not of the Israelites themselves, which would make the clause unmeaning.

56. *And they tempted and resisted God, Most High, and his testimonies did not keep.* Having brought down the narrative of God's dealings with the older race to the conquest of Canaan, the Psalmist now resumes his charge (against the following generations) of being no better than their fathers. To *tempt* God and *resist* him, or *rebel* against him, has the same sense as in ver. 18, 40. The divine title עֶלְיוֹן suggests that their rebellion was against the highest and the most legitimate of all authority. *His testimonies* against sin, contained in his commandments; hence the use of the verb *keep*. The form of expression, in both clauses of this verse, is borrowed from Deut. vi. 16, 17.

57. *And revolted and dealt falsely like their fathers; they were turned like a deceitful bow.* He here resumes the thread dropped at ver. 8, for the purpose of relating what *their fathers* did and were, *i. e.* the older generation who came out of Egypt. Having shewn this at great length, he now reiterates the charge that their descendants, after the days of Joshua, were no better, and proceeds to prove it. The first clause describes them both as rebels and traitors. *They were turned, i. e.* as some suppose, turned aside, swerved or twisted in the archer's hand, so as to give a wrong direction to the arrow. Others understand it to mean, *they were converted* (or *became*) *like a deceitful bow, i. e.* one which deceives the expectation, and fails to accomplish the design for which it is employed. By a similar trope, falsehood or lying is ascribed to waters which are not perennial, but fail precisely when most needed. See Isa. lviii. 11, Job vi. 15. The figure of a *deceitful bow* is borrowed from this passage by Hosea (vii. 16).

58. *And made him angry with their heights, and with their idols made him jealous.* Here, for the first time, idolatry is mentioned as the great national sin of Israel after the death of Joshua and the contemporary elders. This sin is intimately connected with the one described in ver. 9, since the failure to exterminate the Canaanites and gain complete possession of the country, with its necessary consequence, the continued residence of gross idolaters in the midst of Israel, could not fail to expose the chosen people to perpetual temptation, and afford occasion to their worst defections. In the last clause, *graven images* are put for the whole class of idols or created gods, of whom the true God must be jealous as his rivals, as well as indignant at the heights or high places, the hill-tops where these false gods were most usually worshipped. The whole form of expression is Mosaic. See Deut. xxxii. 16, 21, and compare Exod. xx. 5.

59. *God heard and was indignant, and rejected Israel exceedingly.* The same sin is followed by the same retribution as in ver. 21. *Abhorred* is an inadequate translation of the last verb, which denotes not merely an internal feeling, but the outward exhibition of it. It means not merely to abhor, but to reject with abhorrence. See above, on Ps. xv. 4. The addition of the intensive adverb, *very* or *exceedingly*, serves at the same time to enhance and to restrict the meaning of the verb which it qualifies. He abhorred them, not a little but exceedingly, and as a token of his doing so, rejected

them exceedingly, yet not utterly or altogether. As there is nothing to restrict the application of this statement, we must understand it in its widest sense, as meaning that the whole people was regarded with displeasure, and punished on account of its transgressions during the ascendancy of Ephraim.

60. *And forsook the dwelling-place of Shilo, the tent* (which) *he caused to dwell among men.* The punishment of Ephraim, not as the sole offender, but as the unfaithful leader of the chosen people, consisted in the transfer of the sanctuary, and the manifested presence of God in it, to the tribe which was intended from the first to have that honour (Gen. xlix. 10), but whose rights had been held in abeyance during the experimental chieftainship of Ephraim. The ark, after it was taken by the Philistines (1 Sam. iv. 17), never returned to Shiloh, but was deposited successively at Nob (1 Sam. xxi. 2) and at Gibeon (1 Kings iii. 4), until David pitched a tabernacle for it on mount Zion (2 Chron. xv. 1). See above, on Ps. xxiv. 1. *Caused to dwell* is an expression used in the very same connection in the history. See Josh. xviii. 1, and compare Deut. xii. 11, where the sanctuary is described as the place in which God caused his name to dwell. *Among men* implies that this was his only earthly residence, and hints at the true meaning of the sanctuary, as propounded in the law (Exod. xxv. 8).

61. *And gave up to captivity his strength, and his beauty into the foeman's hand.* This is a still more distinct allusion to the capture of the ark by the Philistines (1 Sam. iv. 17). The pronouns admit of two constructions, as they may be referred either to God or Israel. In the former case, the ark is called his strength, because it was the symbol of his saving presence and a pledge for the exertion of his power to protect and save his people. It is called his beauty or honour, as it marked the place where God was pleased to manifest his glory. At the same time it was Israel's strength, because it was considered as ensuring the divine protection (1 Sam. iv. 3), and his glory, because the possession of this symbol was his highest honour (1 Sam. iv. 21). Both these senses are so perfectly appropriate, that it is not easy to choose either, to the entire exclusion of the other.

62. *And abandoned to the sword his people, and at his heritage was wroth.* For the meaning of the first verb, see above on ver. 48, and for that of the second, on ver. 21. *To the sword*, to defeat and destruction in war, with particular reference to 1 Sam. iv. 10. The severity of these judgments is enhanced by their having been inflicted on *his people* and *his heritage*.

63. *His youths* (or *chosen ones*) *the fire devoured, and his maidens were not praised.* This may either mean that they attracted no attention on account of public troubles, or that they were not praised in nuptial songs, implying what is expressed in the text of the English Bible, to wit, that they *were not given to marriage*. The *fire* may be a figure for destructive war, as in Num. xxi. 28. The pronoun (*his*) refers to Israel as a whole or an ideal person.

64. *His priests by the sword fell, and his widows weep not.* The priests are particularly mentioned because, at the time specially referred to, the chief magistracy was vested in a sacerdotal family, and because Hophni and Phinehas, the sons of Eli, were among the first victims of the great calamity in question. See 1 Sam. iv. 11, 17. In the last clause there seems to be allusion to the death of Phinehas's wife, whose sorrow for her husband and herself was lost in sorrow for the departing glory of Israel (1 Sam. iv. 21). In a wider sense, the words may represent the whole class of Israelitish widows as not weeping for their husbands, either because they were engrossed by their own perils and personal sufferings, or, as

some interpreters suppose, because the bodies of the slain were absent, and there could not therefore be a formal mourning in accordance with the oriental usage. The last words of this verse are copied in Job xxvii. 15.

65. *Then awoke, as a sleeper, the Lord, as a hero rejoicing from wine.* His apparent connivance or indifference to what was passing was abruptly exchanged for new and terrible activity. *The Lord,* the sole and rightful sovereign, both of men in general and of Israel in particular. *A hero,* mighty man, or warrior. See above on Ps. xiv. 8. *From wine* is not to be construed with *awoke* or *awakes* understood, but with *rejoicing,* exhilarated, cheered by wine.

66. *And he struck his foes back* (and) *disgrace of eternity gave them.* The idea of driving his assailants back, repelling or repulsing them, is worthier in itself, and better suited to the context than the one expressed in the English Bible. *Perpetual dishonour* was in fact the doom of the Philistines from the time of the events in question. The successes particularly meant are those of Saul and David. *Gave them,* or *to them,* as their portion.

67. *And rejected the tent of Joseph, and the tribe of Ephraim did not choose.* This is the completion and specification of the statement in ver. 60. Even after the punishment of Israel, as a whole, had ceased, Ephraim, though still a member of the chosen people, was deprived of the ascendancy, of which he had proved himself unworthy, and by means of which he had betrayed the whole race into grievous sin. The *tent* or house of Joseph (the progenitor of Ephraim) is particularly mentioned, because the honour taken from that family was the honour of God's dwelling in the midst of them. The last clause might be rendered, *and the tribe of Ephraim no* (longer) *chose.* But the original contains a simple negative without qualification ; and according to the scriptural account, Ephraim never was the chosen tribe, but only allowed to act as such, for a particular purpose, just as the experimental reign of Saul afterwards preceded the commencement of the true theocratical monarchy in David.

68. *And chose the tribe of Judah, the Mount Zion which he loved.* He now assigned the visible pre-eminence to Judah, who had long enjoyed it in the divine purpose (Gen. xlix. 10). Zion is mentioned as the capital of Judah, the place of the sanctuary, and the seat of the theocratic monarchy. The name, as usual in this book, does not signify the single eminence so called, but the entire height on which Jerusalem was built.

69. *And built like high* (places) *his sanctuary, like the earth* (which) *he founded for ever.* Some give the adjective in the first clause the abstract sense of *heights,* which it never has in usage. Others supply *heavens,* but the construction most agreeable to usage is that which supplies *hills* or *mountains.* The sanctuary is then described as being, not externally but spiritually, lofty as mountains and enduring as the earth.

70. *And chose David* (as) *his servant, and took him from the sheep-folds.* Having spoken of the tribe and the particular locality preferred to Ephraim and Shiloh, he now brings into view the personal instrument or agent, by whom it pleased God that the theocratic kingdom should be founded. He did not choose David because he was his servant, *i. e.* a good man, but to be his servant, in the same pregnant and emphatic sense in which the title is applied to him in Ps. xviii. 1. The sovereignty of the choice is indicated by the humble occupation and condition from which he was promoted.

71. *From behind the suckling* (ewes) *he brought him, to feed Jacob his people and Israel his heritage.* From behind them, *i. e.* from following and

watching them with tender care, one of the chief duties of a shepherd. The next word in Hebrew is a participle, and means nursing, giving suck. The sense is incorrectly given in the common version of this place, and ambiguously in that of Isa. xl. 11. *To feed* expresses only one part of the meaning of the Hebrew verb, which signifies to do the work or exercise the office of a shepherd. See above, on Ps. xlix. 14 (13). The contrast presented is, that he who had spent his youth in tending sheep was now to be the shepherd of a nation, nay, of the chosen people, of the church, the heritage of God himself. To this passage, and those portions of the history on which it is founded (2 Sam. vii. 8, 1 Chron. xi. 2), may be traced the constant use of pastoral images, in the later Scriptures, to express the relation which subsists between the Church and Christ, as its Chief Shepherd, and his faithful ministers as his representatives and deputies.

72. *And he has fed them after his integrity of heart, and in the skill* (or *prudence*) *of his hands will lead them* (still). This is no sudden interruption of the psalm, but the conclusion to which all was tending from the first. At the same time it implies that when the psalm was written, David was still reigning and expected to reign longer. Besides the divine attestation here afforded to his theocratical fidelity, the verse may be regarded as a beautiful tribute to the good and great King from his chief musician and fellow-seer. To *lead*, in the last clause, is to lead or tend a flock, and, with the parallel term *feed*, makes up the full description of a shepherd.

Psalm 79

THIS psalm belongs to the same period with Ps. lxxiv., perhaps that of the Babylonish conquest, and contains a description of the sufferings of the chosen people, ver. 1-4, a prayer for deliverance, ver. 5–12, and a promise of thanksgiving, ver. 13.

1. *A Psalm. By Asaph. O God, gentiles have come into thy heritage ; they have defiled thy holy temple ; they have turned Jerusalem to heaps.* The intrusion of heathen into the sanctuary was its worst dishonour, They have placed Jerusalem for heaps, or as a heap of ruins. This includes the destruction of the temple. Compare Ps. lxxiv. 4.

2. *They have given the corpse of thy servants* (as) *food to the bird of the heavens, the flesh of thy saints to the* (*wild*) *beast of the earth.* A common description of extensive and promiscuous carnage. The words translated *corpse, bird, beast*, are all collectives. The last has here its most specific and distinctive sense as denoting beasts of prey. See above, on Ps. lxviii. 11 (10), lxxiv. 19.

3. *They have shed their blood like water round about Jerusalem, and there is none burying*, or none to bury them. There is no period in the history of ancient Israel to which these terms can be applied without extravagance, except that of the Babylonian conquest.

4. *We have been* (or *become*) *a contempt to our neighbours, a scorn and derision to those round about us.* See above, on Ps. xliv. 14 (13), where the very same expressions are employed.

5. *Unto what* (*point*), until when, how long, *Jehovah, wilt thou be angry for ever, will burn like fire thy zeal* (or *jealousy*) ? With the first clause compare Ps. xiii. 2 (1), lxxiv. 1, 10 ; with the second, Ex. xx. 5, Deut. xxix. 19 (20), Ps. lxxviii. 58.

6. *Pour out thy wrath against the nations which have not known thee,*

and upon kingdoms which thy name have not invoked. This is commonly explained as a prayer for divine judgments on the nations which combined for the destruction of Judah (2 Kings xxiv. 2). But it seems to be rather an expostulation and complaint that God had made no difference between his own people and the heathen. As if he had said, If thou must pour out thy wrath, let it rather be on those who neither know nor worship thee than on thine own peculiar people.

7. *For he hath devoured Jacob, and his dwelling* (or *his pasture-ground*) *they have laid waste.* The singular verb in the first cause relates to the chief enemy, the plural in the last to his confederates. The wide sense of *dwelling* and the narrower one of *pasture* are both authorised by usage. See above, on Ps. xxiii. 2, lxv. 13 (12), lxxiv. 20.

8. *Remember not against us the iniquities of former (generations) ; make haste, let thy compassions meet us, for we are reduced exceedingly.* Against us, literally as to us, respecting us, which, in this connection, must mean to our disadvantage or our condemnation. *Former iniquities* is scarcely a grammatical construction of the Hebrew words usually so translated. The adjective, when absolutely used, always refers to persons, and means ancestors or ancients. Personal and hereditary guilt are not exclusive but augmentative of one another. The sons merely fill up the iniquities of their fathers. The verb *hasten* (מַהֵר) may be either imperative or infinitive. If the latter, it qualifies the following verb, as in the English version, *let thy tender mercies speedily prevent us.* For the meaning of this last verb, see above, on Ps. xxi. 4 (3). *Reduced,* weakened, brought low, both in strength and condition. See above, on Ps. xl. 2 (1), where the cognate adjective is used. It was probably the verse before us that determined the position of this psalm, in close connection with Ps. lxxviii., the great theme of which is the iniquity of former generations.

9. *Help us, O God of our salvation, on account of the glory of thy name ; and set us free and pardon our sins for the sake of thy (own) name.* The title, *God of our salvation,* is expressive of a covenant obligation to protect his people, as well as of protection and deliverance experienced already. *On account,* literally *for the word,* or as we say in English, *for the sake,* which is used above, however, to translate a different Hebrew word. *The glory of thy name,* to maintain and vindicate the honour of thy attributes as heretofore revealed in act. See above, on Ps. v. 12 (11), xxiii. 3. *Set us free,* deliver us, from our present sufferings and the power of our enemies. *Pardon our sins,* literally make atonement for them, *i.e.* forgive them for the sake of the expiation which thou hast thyself provided. See above, on Ps. lxxviii. 38. It is characteristic of the ancient saints to ask God's favour, not for their own sake merely, but for the promotion of his glory.

10. *Wherefore should the nations say, Where (is) their God? Known among the nations, in our sight, be the avenging of the blood of thy servants, the (blood) poured out, (or shed),* as was described above, in ver. 3. This argument in favour of God's interposition, founded on the false conclusions which his enemies would draw from his refusal, is of frequent occurrence in the Pentateuch. See Exod. xxxii. 12, Num. xiv. 13-16, Deut. ix. 28, and compare Joel ii. 17, from which the words before us are directly borrowed. *Where is their God,* the invisible, spiritual being whom they worship, but who cannot save them from external dangers ? Or the meaning may be, Where is the proof of that almighty power, and that love for his own people, of which they have so often and so loudly boasted ? The English Bible makes the verb in the second clause agree with God (*let him be known*), and

supplies a preposition before vengeance (*by the revenging*). But the ancient versions, followed by the Prayer Book and the best modern interpreters, construe the verb and noun together (*known be the avenging*). The diversity of gender may be easily reduced to the general law of Hebrew syntax, that when the verb precedes its subject, and especially when separated from it, the former may assume the masculine form, not as such, but as the primitive and simplest form. *In our sight*, literally *to our eyes*, just as we say in English, *to our faces*. This aggravating circumstance is borrowed from Deut. vi. 22, and the idea of avenging blood from Deut. xxxii. 43.

11. *Let the sighing of the prisoner come before thee, according to the greatness of thine arm, suffer to survive the sons of death* (or of mortality). The nation is here viewed as an individual captive, not without reference to the literal captivity and exile occasioned by the Babylonian conquest, and with evident historical allusion to the bondage of Israel in Egypt, from the account of which (Exod. ii. 23–25) some of the expressions here are borrowed. *Come before thee*, reach thee, and attract thy notice. Compare the opposite expression in Isa. i. 23. The *arm*, as usual, is the symbol of exerted strength. See above, on Ps. x. 15, xxxvii. 17, xliv. 4 (3). The whole phrase is a Mosaic one. See Exod. xv. 16, and compare Num. xiv. 19, Deut. iii. 24. The last verb in the sentence means to *leave behind* or *over*, to cause or suffer to remain. See Exod. x. 15, xii. 10, Isa. i. 9. The last noun in Hebrew occurs only here, but is an obvious derivative from (מוּת) *death*, bearing perhaps the same relation to it that *mortalitas* sustains to *mors*. According to a well-known oriental idiom, the whole phrase denotes *dying men*, or those about to die, or more specifically, those condemned or doomed to death.

12. *And render to our neighbours sevenfold into their bosom their contempt* (*with*) *which they have contemned thee, Lord!* The first verb is a causative, and means to bring back or cause to return. See above, on Ps. lxxii. 10. The neighbours are those mentioned in ver. 4, and the allusion here at least includes the expression of contemptuous incredulity in ver. 10. *Sevenfold*, a common idiomatic term denoting frequent repetition or abundance. See above, on Ps. xii. 7 (6). *Into the bosom*, an expression which originally seems to have had reference to the practice of carrying and holding things in the lap or the front fold of the flowing oriental dress, has in usage the accessory sense of retribution or retaliation. See my note on Isa. lxv. 6, 7, and compare Jer. xxxii. 18, Luke vi. 38. The cognate noun and verb, translated *contempt* and *contemned*, denote not the mere internal feeling, but the oral expression of it by revilings, scoffs, and insults. See above, on Ps. xlii. 11 (10), lxix. 10 (9). The *Lord* at the conclusion is by no means a mere expletive, but aggravates the sin of these despisers by describing it as committed against their rightful sovereign.

13. *And we, thy people and flock of thy pasture, will give thanks to thee for ever, to generation and generation will we recount thy praise.* Some interpreters needlessly make two distinct propositions, *we* (are) *thy people* (and therefore) *will give thanks*, &c. *The flock of thy pasture*, that which thou feedest, that of which thou art the shepherd. See above, on Ps. lxxiv. 1, lxxviii. 70–72. *For ever*, literally *to eternity*. The following words, though thrown into the first clause by the masoretic interpunction, belong to the second, as appears from the parallel structure of the sentence.

Psalm 80

THIS psalm was probably occasioned by the overthrow and deportation of the ten tribes, and expresses the feelings of the ancient church in view of that event. Besides a title or inscription, ver. 1, it contains a lamentation or complaint, in reference to the strokes which had befallen Israel, ver. 2–8 (1–7) ; an exquisite picture of the vocation and original condition of the chosen race, under the image of a transplanted vine, ver. 9–14 (8–13) ; and an earnest prayer that God would again have mercy on his afflicted people, ver. 15–20 (14–19). The structure of the psalm is very regular, deriving a strophical character from the recurrence of a burden or *refrain* in ver. 4 (3), 8 (7), 20 (19). The disputed questions, as to the occasion and design of the composition, will be considered in the exposition of the several verses.

1. *To the Chief Musician. As to lilies. A Testimony. By Asaph. A Psalm.* The first and last of these inscriptions shew that the composition was intended to be used in public worship. The preposition before *lilies* indicates the theme or subject, as in Ps. v. 1. *Lilies,* as in Ps. xlv. 1, lx. 1, lxix. 1, probably means loveliness, delightfulness, as an attribute of the divine favour which is here implored. *Testimony* is a term commonly applied to the divine law, as a testimony against sin, and in such cases as the present indicates the divine authority under which the Psalmist writes. See above, on Ps. lx. 1.

2 (1). *Shepherd of Israel, give ear, leading Joseph like a flock, sitting (on) the cherubim, shine forth !* The description of Jehovah as the Shepherd of Israel is peculiarly appropriate in this connection, because borrowed from Jacob's blessing upon Joseph, Gen. xlviii. 15, xlix. 24. According to some interpreters, *Joseph* is simply a poetical equivalent to *Israel,* the son being put upon a level with the father in the usage of the language, on account of his historical pre-eminence and his being the progenitor of two of the twelve tribes. According to another view, *Joseph* denotes the ten tribes as distinguished from the kingdom of Judah, which is rendered more probable by the specification of certain tribes in the next verse. On this hypothesis, the verse before us is an invocation of Jehovah, as the patron and protector, not of Judah merely but of all Israel, including the posterity of Joseph and the tribes politically allied to them. *Dwelling* (between) *the Cherubim,* or *sitting* (enthroned upon) *the Cherubim,* a token of superiority to all his creatures. See above, on Ps. xviii. 11 (10).

3 (2). *Before Ephraim and Benjamin and Manasseh arouse thy strength and come to save us.* The first clause alludes to the encampment and march through the wilderness, in which these three tribes always went together, as the descendants of one mother (Gen. xliv. 20, Num. ii. 18–24, x. 22–24). It has commonly been inferred from 1 Kings xii. 21, that the tribe of Benjamin adhered to the kingdom of Judah. But Hengstenberg has made it highly probable, at least, that those words relate only to the dwellers in Jerusalem and the immediately circumjacent country; that the tribe, as such, was reckoned one of the ten tribes, among which Simeon was not included, because, in fulfilment of Jacob's prophecy (Gen. xlix. 7), they had no distinct or compact territory of their own, but certain towns within the boundary of Judah (Josh. xix. 1–9). Hence we are told expressly and repeatedly that in the great schism after the death of Solomon, but one tribe remained faithful to the house of David (1 Kings xi. 13, 32, 36, xii. 20), *i. e.* one

complete tribe, having a definite and independent share in the allotment of the land. That Benjamin should take part with Ephraim and Manasseh rather than with Judah, might have been expected from the near affinity and mutual affection of the sons of Rachel, and from the jealousy which must have been excited by the transfer of the crown from Saul, a Benjamite, to David, a Jew. The same thing incidentally appears from such passages as 2 Sam. xix. 21 (20), where Shimei, a Benjamite, speaks of himself as representing the whole house of Joseph. If this be admitted or assumed, the mention of Benjamin with Ephraim and Manasseh, in the verse before us, far from invalidating, seems to confirm the application of the passage to the kingdom of the Ten Tribes, and that of the whole psalm to their overthrow and deportation by the Assyrians. Thus understood, the verse before us is a prayer, that God would again march at the head of the "camp of Ephraim," as he did of old. *Arouse thy strength*, awake from thy present state of seeming inaction and indifference. See above, on Ps. xliv. 24 (23), lxxviii. 65. *Come*, literally *go*, which may mean go forth, march; but see above, on (Ps. xlvi. 9 (8). *To save us*, literally *for salvation to us*.

4 (3). *O God, restore us, and let thy face shine; and let us be saved!* The verb in the first clause would suggest two ideas to a Hebrew reader, both of which are here appropriate. The first is that of a literal bringing back from exile or captivity; the other that of restoration to a former state, without regard to change of place or other local circumstances. In the case before us, the general and figurative sense of restoration includes that of literal return. The church prays to be restored to her integrity and normal state, by the redemption of the part which had gone into captivity. This prayer was substantially fulfilled in the return of many members of the ten tribes with Judah from the Babylonish exile, while the tribes themselves, as organised bodies, and the apostate kingdom which they constituted, ceased to exist. The petition, *cause thy face to shine, i. e.* look upon us with a favourable countenance, is borrowed from the sacerdotal blessing, Num. vi. 25. See above, on Ps. iv. 7 (6), xxxi. 17 (16). The last verb in the verse may also be explained as an expression of strong confidence, *we shall be saved*, which really involves the subjunctive sense preferred by some interpreters, *that we may be saved*. This sentence, which is solemnly repeated at the close of ver. 4, 20 (3, 19), is thereby marked as the theme or key-note of the whole composition.

5 (4). *Jehovah, God, (God of) Hosts, how long dost thou smoke against the prayer of thy people?* The accumulation of divine names involves an appeal to the perfections which they indicate, as so many arguments or reasons why the prayer should be favourably heard and answered. See above, on Ps. l. 1, and for the meaning of the third title, on Ps. xxiv. 10. *How long*, literally *until when?* The verb is preterite in form (*hast thou smoked*), implying that the state of things complained of had already long existed. *Smoke* is here (as in Ps. lxxiv. 1) put for *fire*, the common emblem of divine wrath, for the sake of an allusion to the smoke from the altar of incense, the appointed symbol of the prayers of God's people. See Lev. xvi. 13, and compare Ps. cxli. 2, Isa. vi. 4, Rev. v. 8, viii. 3, 4. There is then a tacit antithesis between the two significations of the symbol. The smoke of God's wrath, and that of his people's prayers, are presented in a kind of conflict.

6 (5). *Thou hast made them eat tear-bread, and made them drink of tears a tierce (or measure).* The noun *tear* in Hebrew is commonly collective,

but the singular and plural forms are here combined. See above, on Ps. vi. 7 (6), xxxix. 13 (12), lvi. 9 (8). The same strong figure of tears as nourishment occurs above, Ps. xlii. 4 (3). The last word in Hebrew means a measure which is the third of another measure, thus corresponding to the old and wide sense of the English *tierce*. See my note on Isa. xl. 12. Measure here denotes abundance.

7 (6). *Thou makest us a strife unto our neighbours, and our enemies amuse themselves* (at our expense). The future verbs imply a probable continuance of this humiliating treatment unless God interpose to put an end to it, and thus suggest a reason for his doing so. *Makest us*, literally puttest, settest up. See above, on Ps. xliv. 14 (13). *A strife*, a subject of contention, perhaps in reference to the emulous desire of their neighbours to insult and aggravate their sufferings. Here, as in Ps. xliv. 14 (13), lxxix. 4, these neighbours are the circumjacent nations, who always triumphed in the time of Israel's calamities (Amos i. 9, 11, Obad. 12). The literal translation of the last words is *will mock* (or *scoff*) *for them*, *i. e.* for themselves, for their own gratification, and at their own discretion, as they will.

8 (7). *O God*, (God of) *Hosts, restore us, and let thy face shine, and let us be saved!* See above, on ver. 4 (3). The only variation in the case before us is the addition of a second divine title, implying God's supremacy above the hosts of heaven, both material and spiritual, and thus indirectly urging a new argument for being heard and answered. See above, on ver. 5 (4).

9 (8). *A vine out of Egypt thou transplantest, thou drivest out nations and plantest it.* There is a twofold usage of the first verb in Hebrew, which imparts peculiar force and beauty to the sentence. Its primary meaning, to pluck up, is strictly appropriate to the act of transplanting, while its secondary but more usual sense of moving an encampment, marching, is equally appropriate to the removal of the nation which the vine here represents, and is actually so applied in Ps. lxxviii. 52 above, as well as in the history itself, Exod. xii. 37, xv. 22. The next verb is also used in Ps. lxxviii. 55 and Exod. xxiii. 28, xxxiii. 2, xxxiv. 11. The figure of planting occurs above, in Ps. xliv. 3 (2), that of a vine in Isa. v. 1–7. The points of comparison are probably assiduous culture, luxuriant growth, and fruitfulness. The argument involved is that by forsaking Israel God would be undoing his own work. Compare Jer. xlv. 4.

10 (9). *Thou didst clear* (the way) *before it, and it took root and filled the land.* The first word means to clear by the removal of obstructions. See Gen. xxiv. 31, Lev. xiv. 36, and compare my notes on Isa. xl. 3, lvii. 14, lxii. 10. The sense may here be, *thou didst clear* (the ground), *i. e.* from weeds and stones (compare Isa. v. 2) *before it*, *i. e.* to make room for it or prepare a place for it. *Took root*, literally *rooted its roots*, the cognate verb and noun being combined by a common Hebrew idiom. See my note on Isa. xxvii. 6.

11 (10). *Covered were the mountains* (with) *its shadow, and with its branches the cedars of God.* This is an amplification and poetical exaggeration of the last words of ver. 10 (9). So completely did it fill the land that its shadow was cast upon the highest hill-tops, and its tendrils overran the loftiest trees. *Cedars of God*, *i. e.* in their kind the noblest products of his power, the attribute suggested by (אֵל) the divine name here used.

See above, on Ps. xxxvi. 7 (6). Some interpreters suppose the southern range of mountains west of Jordan, sometimes called *Mount Judah* or the

Highlands of Judah, to be here specifically meant and contrasted with the cedars of Lebanon, the northern frontier of the Land of Promise, just as Lebanon and Kadesh are contrasted in Ps. xxix. 5–8. That Lebanon, though not expressly mentioned, is referred to, appears probable from the analogy of Ps. xxix 5, xcii. 13, civ. 16. The literal fact conveyed by all these figures is the one prophetically stated in Gen. xxviii. 14, Deut. xi. 24, Joshua i. 4.

12 (11). *It sends forth its boughs to the sea, and to the river its shoots* (or *suckers*). Compare the description in Isa. xvi. 8. If the north and south are indicated in the preceding verse, the other cardinal points may here be represented by the Mediterranean and the Euphrates.

13 (12). *Why hast thou broken down its walls* (or *hedges*), *and all pluck it that pass by the way?* See below, on Ps. lxxxix. 41, 42 (40, 41), and compare Isa. v. 5. The last words are descriptive of the hostile powers of the heathen world, with particular reference to the *neighbours* of ver 6 (5).

14 (13). *The boar out of the wood doth waste it, and the beast of the field feeds upon it.* For the precise sense of the word translated *beast*, see above, on Ps. l. 11, the only other place where it occurs in such an application, being thus peculiar to the psalms which bear the name of Asaph. The essential idea conveyed by the figures of this verse is that of fierce and greedy enemies. If any more specific explanation be admissible, the wild boar may denote the Assyrian power, and the parallel term its allies and dependents. *Feeds upon it*, as a sheep upon its pasture. See above, on Ps. xxxvii. 3.

15 (14). *O God,* (God of) *Hosts, pray return, look from heaven and see and visit this vine.* The expostulation and complaint are followed by an earnest prayer. *Pray return* is used to represent (נָא) the Hebrew particle of entreaty, expressed in the English Bible by a circumlocution (*we beseech thee*). The prayer that God will return, implies that the evils just complained of were occasioned by his absence. *Visit,* manifest thy presence and thy favourable disposition. See above, on Ps. viii. 5 (4). *This vine,* Israel, the church or chosen people, which, though robbed of some of its luxuriant branches, still lives and is yet to bear abundant fruit.

16 (15). *And sustain what thy right hand has planted, and over the child thou hast roared for thyself* (do thou watch, or extend thy protection). The common version of the first words (*and the vineyard*) is countenanced neither by the ancient versions nor by Hebrew etymology and usage. By giving it, as a verbal form, the sense of covering, protecting (which belongs to some kindred roots), the *over* in the last clause may depend upon it, and no verb need in that case be supplied. *Thy right hand* implies an exertion of strength, and at the same time involves an allusion to the name of *Benjamin* (Son of the Right Hand), here perhaps representing the whole race, on account of the connection of that tribe with both the rival kingdoms, its central position, its possession of the sanctuary, and its historical relation to the infant-monarchy under Saul the Benjamite. To complete the allusion, the other element in the name (בֵּן, a son) is then introduced and metaphorically applied to the vine, which is still the Psalmist's theme, by an assimilation of animal and vegetable life common in all languages. *Reared*, literally strengthened, made strong, *i. e.* raised, brought up. See my note on Isa. xliv. 14. *For thyself,* not for its own sake, but as a means of promoting the divine praise and glory.

17 (16). (It is) *burnt with fire, cut* (*down* or *up*) *; at the rebuke of thy

countenance they perish. The prayer is interrupted for a moment by a new description of the evils which occasioned it. The first clause alludes to the destruction of vineyards by fire and steel in ancient warfare, here recognised, however, as a divine judgment. *At the rebuke, i. e.* at the time, and also as a consequence of it. Any expression of disapprobation and displeasure, whether by word or deed, is a rebuke. See above, on Ps. lxxvi. 7 (6). The rebuke is here supposed to be expressed in the countenance, a much more natural interpretation than that which makes *thy face* mean *thy presence.* They perish, those who had before been represented by the vine transplanted out of Egypt. The future form implies that it will always be so, when God utters his rebuke.

18 (17). *Let thy hand be on the man of thy right hand, on the son of man thou hast reared* (or *made strong) for thyself.* Here again the component parts of the name *Benjamin* are introduced as parallels, precisely as in ver. 16 (15). The *man of thy right hand* may either be the man whom thy power has raised up, or the man who occupies the post of honour at thy right hand. That the words were intended to suggest both ideas, is a supposition perfectly agreeable to Hebrew usage. A more doubtful question is that in reference to the first words of the sentence, *let thy hand be upon* him, whether this means in favour or in wrath. The only way in which both senses can be reconciled is by applying the words to the Messiah, as the ground of the faith and hope expressed. Let thy hand fall not on us but on our substitute. Compare the remarkably similar expressions in Acts v. 31.

19 (18). *And* (then) *we will not backslide from thee ; thou wilt quicken us, and on thy name will we call.* Forgiveness founded on atonement is the best security against relapses into sin. The first verb is the one used to describe the general apostasy in Ps. liii. 4 (3). *Quicken,* restore to life, or save alive, or simply make alive. Compare Ps. lxxi. 20. The meaning of the last clause is, *thee (alone) will we invoke,* as the object of our trust and worship, a profession involving the repudiation of all other gods.

20 (19). *Jehovah, God,* (God of) *Hosts, restore us, let thy face shine, and let us be saved !* While the prayer in this verse is identical with that in ver. 4 (3) and 8 (7), there is a kind of climax in the form of the address. In the first of the three places it is simply *God,* in the second *God of Hosts,* in the third and last *Jehovah God of Hosts,* as if to add to the general ideas of divinity and sovereignty those of self-existence, eternity, and covenant relation to his chosen people, as additional warrants for the hope and prayer, that he would turn them, smile upon them, save them.

Psalm 81

1. *To the Chief Musician. On* (or *according to) the Gittith. By Asaph.* For the probable meaning of *the Gittith,* see above on Ps. viii. 1. In the absence of any proof to the contrary, the Asaph of this title must be assumed to be the contemporary of David. See above, on Ps. l. 1. The psalm before us was probably intended to be sung at the Passover, as it consists of an exhortation to praise God for the deliverance of Israel from Egypt, ver. 2–8 (1–7), a complaint of their ingratitude, ver. 9–13 (8–12), and a glowing picture of the happy effects to be expected from obedience and fidelity, ver. 14–18 (13–17).

2 (1). *Sing aloud unto God our strength, make a joyful noise unto the God*

of Jacob ! The first verb is properly a causative meaning *make* or *let rejoice.* See above, on Ps. lxv. 9 (8), and compare Deut. xxxii. 43, in which place, and in this, it is commonly supposed to be intransitive. The parallel verb is a generic term, applied both to shouting and the sound of a trumpet. See above, on Ps. xli. 12 (11), xlvii. 2 (1). *God our strength,* our strong protector and deliverer, in which character he specially revealed himself in the deliverance of Israel from Egypt, the main theme or subject of this psalm, and thereby proved himself to be indeed the covenant or tutelary God of Jacob.

3 (2). *Raise the song, and beat the drum, the sweet harp with the lute* (or *lyre*). *Beat,* literally *give, i. e.* give forth its sound, or sound it. See above, on Ps. xlvi. 7 (6), lxviii. 34 (33), lxxvii. 18 (17). This is to be understood as a mutual exhortation of the musicians to each other during the actual performance.

4 (3). *Blow, in the month, the trumpet, at the full moon, on the day of our feast.* The month, by way of eminence, was the first month, in which the passover was celebrated (Exod. xii. 1, 2). Here, as in the Hebrew of Lev. xxiii. 5, the month is first named, then the particular part of it. That this last was no unessential circumstance, appears from the fact, that when an extraordinary passover was kept, it was on the same day of another month (Num. ix. 9–14), and that when Jeroboam changed the feast of tabernacles, he transferred it to the same day of the eighth month (1 Kings xii. 32). The time thus selected for religious observance seems to have been that of the full moon. Compare the original and marginal translation of Prov. vii. 20. *The day of our festival* or feast, *i. e.* the great day of the Passover. *Our feast,* if emphatic, is intended to describe it as a distinctive national solemnity. The continued use of instrumental music at this festival appears from 2 Chron. xxx. 21.

5 (4). *For a law to Israel* (*is*) *this, a right* (belonging) *to the God of Jacob.* The observance of this festival was not a mere matter of usage or conventional arrangement, but binding on the people and due to Jehovah as their God. The personal pronoun (*it*) at the end of the first clause is emphatic, and may be better expressed in English by a demonstrative. *A right, jus,* that to which he is rightfully entitled.

6 (5). (As) *a testimony in Joseph he set it, in his coming out over the land of Egypt. A speech I knew not I am hearing.* Besides the constant use of *testimony* in the sense of *law,* Ps. xix. 8 (7), lx. 1, lxxviii. 5, lxxx. 1, the word is appropriate, in its strict sense, to the Passover, as a perpetual memento or memorial of the exodus from Egypt. *Joseph* is here put for *Israel,* on account of his pre-eminence during the residence in Egypt (Gen. xlix. 26, Exod. i. 8). *He set it, i. e.* God instituted or ordained the festival. *In his coming,* at the time, or in the very act, of his departure. *Over the land of Egypt* includes the usual expression, *from* or *out of* it (Exod. xxxiv. 18), but suggests the additional ideas of publicity and triumph. Israel, at the exodus, passed over a considerable tract of the Egyptian territory, and at the same time, as it were, over the heads of the humbled and terrified Egyptians. Compare Exod. xiv. 8, Num. xxxiii. 3. *Speech,* literally *lip,* a common idiomatic expression for dialect or language. According to the version of this last clause above given, it refers to the words of God that follow, and describes the people as having then heard what they never heard before. Some interpreters, however, understand it as describing the condition of the people while in Egypt, by one of its most marked and painful circumstances, namely, that they there resided in the midst of

a foreign and by implication heathen race. This agrees better with the figurative usage of *lip* elsewhere, and is strongly favoured by the analogy of Deut. xxviii. 49, Jer. v. 15, Ps. cxiv. 1. Compare my note on Isa. xxxiii. 19. Thus understood, the clause may be translated, (where) *I heard a tongue I did not understand.* The future form of the first verb has reference to the actual time of the events, into which the speaker here transports himself.

7 (6). *I removed from the burden his shoulder ; his hands from the basket escape.* The first verb strictly means *I caused* (or *suffered*) *to depart.* The idea is borrowed from Exod. vi. 6, 7. The specific reference is no doubt to the carrying of bricks and mortar, and the pot or basket of the next clause is the vessel used for that purpose, the form of which has been found delineated in a burial-vault at Thebes. *Escape,* literally pass away.

8 (7). *In distress thou hast called and I have delivered thee ; I will (yet) answer thee in the secret place of thunder ; I will try thee at the waters of Strife.* The secret or hiding place of thunder is the dark cloud charged with tempest which overhung mount Sinai at the giving of the law (Exod. xx. 18). This is here anticipated or predicted, as well as the murmuring of the people at Meribah (Exod. xvii., Num. xx.) as a signal instance of their unbelief and disobedience. Thus understood, the verse continues the words of God himself, at the crisis of the exodus. According to the other exegetical hypothesis already mentioned, there is here a sudden change of speaker, and the future verbs in this verse are to be explained as historical presents.

9 (8). *Hear, my people, and I will testify against thee, Israel, if thou wilt hearken to me.* There is a strong resemblance between this verse and Ps. l. 7. The conditional particle (*if*) in the last clause is by some taken optatively, *Oh that thou wouldst hearken,* or, as we might say in English, *if thou wouldst but hearken.* As examples of this usage, Ps. xcv. 7, cxxxix. 19, Prov. xxiv. 11, are cited. Other interpreters deny its existence and regard this as an instance of aposiopesis, *if thou wilt hearken to me* (thou shalt do well), like those in Exod. xxxii. 32, Luke xix. 42. See above, on Ps. xxvii. 13. A simpler and more natural construction than either is to make this the condition of the statement in the first clause. " I will speak, if thou wilt hear me."

10 (9). *There shall not be in thee a strange god, and thou shalt not worship a foreign god.* The divine name here used is the one denoting power. " Thou shalt acknowledge no Almighty but the true one." The prohibitory futures have a stronger sense than that expressed in some translations, *let there be no strange god in thee, i. e.* in the midst of thee, among you. *A strange god,* a god who is an alien to Jehovah and to Israel. *Worship,* literally bow down or prostrate thyself. *A foreign god,* a god of strangeness, or belonging to foreign parts, in other words, a heathen deity. See above, on Ps. xviii. 45, 46 (44, 45). The specific reason here implied is that expressed in Deut. xxxii. 12. The general principle is the same that is propounded in the first commandment (Exod. xx. 3, Deut. v. 7).

11 (10). *I am Jehovah, thy God, who brought thee up out of the land of Egypt ; open thy mouth wide, and I will fill it.* The reason of the precept in the foregoing verse is now explicitly declared. *The* (one) *making thee ascend,* or causing thee to come up. *Open thy mouth wide,* literally *widen it.* The supply of food is here put for that of all necessities. The reason here suggested for adhering to Jehovah is, that He not only had delivered them from Egypt, but was abundantly able to provide for them in Canaan and the wilderness.

12 (11). *And my people did not hearken to my voice, and Israel did not consent unto me.* God having once been introduced as speaking, the description of the subsequent events is still ascribed to him. The phrase *my people* is designed to aggravate the guilt of their rebellion. *My voice* has special reference to the warning in ver. 7–11 (6–10), supposed to be uttered at the exodus from Egypt. Some interpreters, however, make the whole verse a general description. *Consent unto me*, acquiesce in my requirements, and. agree to do my will. The form of expression is like that in Deut. xiii. 9 (8).

13 (12). *And I gave them up to the corruption of their own heart; they go on in their own counsels.* The first verb strictly means *I sent them forth*, *i. e.* to walk in the corruption of their own heart. The word translated *corruption* occurs elsewhere only in Deut. xxix. 18, and in Jeremiah's imitations of it (Jer. iii. 17, vii. 24, ix. 13, xi. 8). According to a Syriac analogy, and the most probable Hebrew etymology, it properly means *hardness*, corresponding to the πώρωσις of the New Testament (Mark vii. 5, Rom. xi. 25, Eph. iv. 18). *In their own counsels*, in the execution of their own evil purposes and unwise plans. The verb in the last clause may be read as a concession or permission, by referring the words to an anterior point of time. " I gave them up, &c., (saying) let them go on in their own counsels." As to the fearful kind of retribution here denounced, see Prov. i. 30, 31, Rom. i. 24, 2 Thess. ii. 10, 11.

14 (13). *If my people would (but) hearken to me (and) Israel in my ways would walk.* The conditional particle at the beginning, although not the same with that in ver. 9 (8), is construed in the same way, but with a stronger optative meaning. To listen to God's teaching and commands implies a docile and obedient spirit. To walk in his ways is to act as he approves and has required.

15 (14). *Soon would I bow down their enemies, and on their foes bring back my hand.* The first Hebrew phrase strictly means *like a little*, but is used like the English *yet a little*, *i. e.* in a little while. See above, on Ps. ii. 12, and compare Ps. lxxiii. 2. *To draw back the hand*, in Ps. lxxiv. 11, means to withdraw or withhold it from action; but in this connection it conveys the opposite idea of bringing it again into action, with specific reference, as some suppose, to its use in former exigencies, ver. 8 (7). The phrase itself denotes mere action; the idea of hostile or destructive action is suggested by the context. See my note on Isa. i. 25.

16 (15). *The haters of Jehovah should lie to him, and their time should be for ever.* The first phrase is intended to suggest the consolatory thought that the foes of God's people are the foes of God himself. There is no need, therefore, of referring *him* *to Israel* or *my people*, as in Deut. xxxiii. 29, from which the clause is borrowed. The plurals before and after render this less natural, and as the interests of God and his people are identical, the meaning is the same in either case. To *lie* is here to yield a feigned obedience to a conqueror or superior enemy. See above, on Ps. xviii. 45 (44), lxvi. 3. *Their time*, *i. e.* the continued existence of Israel as the chosen people. Compare 2 Sam. vii. 24.

17 (16). *And he would feed him with the fat of wheat, and from the rock with honey sate him.* The first verb is a causative, and means *would let* (or *make) him eat*. The fat of wheat, its richest part or finest quality, another transfer of animal attributes to vegetable objects. See above, on Ps. lxxx. 16 (15). Honey from the rock, some suppose to mean wild honey ; others, with more probability, honey supplied by miracle, like the water from

the rock in the desert. All these strong expressions are borrowed from Deut. xxxii. 13, 14, and are imitated likewise in Ps. cxlvii. 14, Isa. xxxiv. 16. Wheat and honey, by a natural and primitive association, are here put for the necessaries and the luxuries of human sustenance, and these again for the highest enjoyment and prosperity. The English version refers these four verses all to past time, *had hearkened, had walked, should have subdued, should have submitted, should have endured, should have fed, should have satisfied.* This is in fact the true construction of the similar passage in Isa. xlviii. 18; but there the conditional or optative particle is construed with the preterite, and not with the future tense as here, which makes an essential difference of syntax. See Nordheimer's Hebrew Grammar, § 1078.

Psalm 82

A BRIEF but pregnant statement of the responsibilities attached to the judicial office under the Mosaic dispensation. After declaring the relation which the judges bore to God, ver. 1, he rebukes their malversation, ver. 2, and exhorts them to a better practice, ver. 3, 4, and in case of their persistency in evil, ver. 5, notwithstanding their acknowledged dignity, ver. 6, threatens them with condign punishment, ver. 7, to which the church responds by praying God himself to appear as the universal judge and sovereign, ver. 8.

1. *A Psalm. By Asaph. God stands in the assembly of the Mighty; in the midst of the gods he judges.* There is no reason for doubting that the Asaph mentioned in this title was the Asaph of the reign of David, in whose times the necessity for such a warning must already have existed, if not in the person of the king, who, perhaps on that account, is not particularly mentioned, yet in his chiefs or nobles, the exalted though inferior magistrates who executed justice under him. The judicial appearance of Jehovah here presented is like that in Ps. l. 1. *Stands*, or, as the participle strictly means, (*is*) *standing*, stationing himself, assuming his position. The word translated *assembly* is one commonly applied to the congregation of Israel, as an organised whole or body politic. See Exod. xii. 3, xvi. 1, Lev. iv. 15, Num. xxvii. 17. *Mighty* is singular, not plural, in Hebrew, being one of the divine names (אֵל), and qualifies the congregation or assembly as belonging to God himself, *i. e.* instituted by him, and held under his authority. The parallel expression, *in the midst of the gods*, superadds to this idea an allusion to a singular usage of the Pentateuch, according to which the theocratical magistrates, as mere representatives of God's judicial sovereignty, are expressly called *Elohim*, the plural form of which is peculiarly well suited to this double sense or application. See Exod. xxi. 6, xxii. 7, 8 (8, 9), and compare Deut. i. 17, xix. 17, 2 Chron. xix. 6. Even reverence to old age seems to be required on this principle (Lev. xix. 32), and obedience to parents in the fifth commandment (Exod. xx. 12), which really applies to all the offices and powers of the patriarchal system, a system founded upon natural relations, and originating in a simple extension of domestic or parental government, in which the human head represents the original and universal parent or progenitor. The remarkable use of the name *God* in Exodus, above referred to, is concealed from the reader of the English Bible, by the arbitrary use of the word *judges*, as a translation of the Hebrew, which of course it cannot be. *He judges*, will judge, is about to judge. The idea is, that as the judges were gods to other men, so he

would be a judge to them.   Compare Isa. iii. 13–15, Micah iii. 1–4, Jer. xxii. 1–4.

2. *How long will ye judge wrong, and the faces of wicked men accept?* *Selah.*   The question implies that they had done so long enough, nay, too long, since it was wrong from the beginning.   *Wrong*, in the strongest moral sense, injustice, wickedness.   *Wrong*, in Hebrew as in English, may be construed either as an adverb or a noun, or both, *i. e.* as a noun adverbially used to qualify the verb.   See the similar construction of its counterpart or converse, Ps. lviii. 2 (1).   The last clause exemplies one of the most peculiar Hebrew idioms.   The combination usually rendered *respect persons* in the English Bible, and applied to judicial partiality, means literally to *take* (or *take up*) *faces.*   Some suppose this to mean the raising of the countenance, or causing to look up from deep dejection.   But the highest philological authorities are now agreed, that the primary idea is that of accepting one man's face or person rather than another's, the precise form of expression, though obscure, being probably derived from the practice of admitting suitors to confer with governors or rulers face to face, a privilege which can sometimes only be obtained by bribes, especially though not exclusively in oriental courts.   The *Selah* commends the implied charge of official malversation to the serious reflection of the accused parties.

3. *Judge the weak and fatherless,* (*to*) *the sufferer and the poor do justice.* The indirect censure of their evil deeds is followed by a direct exhortation to do well.   Compare Isa. i. 16, 17.   The verb of the first clause is explained by that of the second, which is a technical forensic term, meaning to make innocent or righteous, *i. e.* to recognise or declare as such by a judicial act.   See Exod. xxiii. 7, Deut. xxv. 1, and compare 2 Sam. xv. 4, Isa. v. 23, 1. 8.   The word translated *weak* is applied to the defect of bodily strength and of property or substance.   See above, on Ps. xli. 2 (1).   It is used by Moses in the same connection, Exod. xxiii. 3.   The fatherless or orphans are continually spoken of, as proper objects both of mercy and of justice.   See above, on Ps. x. 14, lxviii. 6 (5), and compare Exod. xxii. 21 (22).   The word translated *poor* seems strictly to denote one who has grown poor or become impoverished.   See the verbal root in Ps. xxxiv. 11 (10).

4. *Deliver the weak and the needy* (*man*), *from the hand of wicked* (*men*) *free* (him).   The first verb means originally to suffer or cause to escape ; the second to extricate or disembarrass.   *From the hand* of the wicked implies from their power, as actually exercised for coercion.   The structure of the sentence may be made more regular by disregarding the pause-accent and attaching *the needy* to the last clause, *and the poor from the hand of the wicked set free.*

5. *They know not and they will not understand ; in darkness they will* (still) *walk ; shaken are all the foundations of earth.*   This is the Lord's complaint of their incorrigible ignorance and indocility, which rendered even his divine instructions unavailing.   The object of the first verbs is suggested by the context, as in Ps. xiv. 4.   What they did not know and would not understand was their judicial duty and responsibility, the end for which they were invested with authority.   *Darkness* is a figure both for ignorance and wickedness.   See Prov. ii. 13.   The denial or perversion of justice is described as disorganising society.   Compare the figures in Ps. xi. 3, lxxv. 4 (3).

6. *I have said, Gods* (*are*) *ye, and sons of the Highest all of you.*   Their sin did not consist in arrogating to themselves too high a dignity, but in

abusing it by malversation, and imagining that it relieved them from responsibility, whereas it really enhanced it. They were God's representatives, but for that very reason they were bound to be pre-eminently just and faithful. *I have said*, not merely to myself or in secret, but in my law; referring to the passages in Exodus already cited. See above, on ver 1. *Ye are gods*, or *God, i.e.* ye occupy his place and are entrusted with his honour as a just and holy God. The pregnant significancy of the plural form is here the same as in ver. 1 above. The parallel expression, *sons of the Most High*, denotes the closest and most intimate relation to Jehovah, as the Supreme or Sovereign God. See above, on Ps. ii. 7. This verse is cited by our Lord (John x. 34, 35), to shew that if the divine name had been applied by God to mere men, there could be neither blasphemy nor folly in its application to the incarnate Son of God himself.

7. (Yet) *verily like mankind shall ye die, and like one of the princes shall ye fall.* Our idiom requires an adversative particle at the beginning, to bring out the antithetical relation of the sentences. But the first word in Hebrew is properly a particle of strong asseveration, *certainly, assuredly.* See above, on Ps. xxxi. 23 (22), and compare my note on Isa. liii. 4. *Like mankind*, or *men* collectively, or like *a man* indefinitely, *i.e.* any other man. So in the other clause, *like one of the princes, i.e.* any other prince, or person holding an exalted station. The clauses constitute a climax. The first merely describes them as sharers in the general mortality of man. The second threatens them with death, *i.e.* violent or untimely death, as a special punishment. *Ye shall fall*, by the sword (Jer. xxxix. 18), or in some analogous manner. The verb is often absolutely used in this way to denote a violent and penal loss of life. See above, Ps. xx. 9 (8), and below, Ps. xci. 7, and compare Exod. xix. 21, Jer. viii. 12. The general meaning of this verse, when taken in connection with the one before it, is that notwithstanding their exalted dignity, bestowed and recognised by God himself, they were not thereby exempted from the common mortality of men, nor even from those signal and destructive strokes, with which God often visits men as highly favoured and exalted as themselves.

8. *Arise, O God, judge the earth; for thou art to possess all nations.* This is not, as some interpreters suppose, a mere wish that God would do what he had just threatened; for this would make the psalm end with a feeble anti-climax. It is rather a petition that, since the representative or delegated judges had proved so unfaithful, God would appear in person and reclaim the powers which had been so wickedly abused. And this he is besought to do, not only in Israel, where the proximate occasion of the prayer was furnished, but throughout the earth, over all whose nations he possessed, and was one day to make good, the same hereditary right, *i.e.* a right continuing unchanged through all successive generations.

Psalm 83

1. *A Song. A Psalm. By Asaph.* To the general description (*mizmôr*), there is here prefixed a more specific one (*shîr*), which designates the composition as a song of praise or triumph. The same combination occurs above, in the title of Ps. xlviii., a composition which, as we have there seen, was probably occasioned by the victory of Jehoshaphat over the Moabites, Ammonites, and their confederates, as described in 2 Chron. xx. This agrees well with the hypothesis, conclusively maintained by Hengstenberg,

that the psalm before us has relation to the same event, and that as the forty-seventh was probably sung upon the field of battle, and the forty-eighth after the triumphant return to Jerusalem, so the eighty-third was composed in confident anticipation of the victory. The points of agreement with the history will be indicated in the exposition of the several verses. After a general petition for divine help, ver. 2 (1), follows a description of the violence, craft, destructive purpose, and extensive combination of the enemies of Judah, ver. 3–9 (2–8), and then an earnest prayer for the renewal of God's ancient deeds in similar emergencies, ver. 10–15 (9–14), with a view to the promotion of his glory in the destruction of his irreconcilable enemies, ver. 16–19 (15–18). According to the view of the historical occasion above given, the *Asaph* of the title must denote some descendant of the ancient seer, as it seems to do in several of the preceding psalms. Now it happens, by a singular coincidence, that in the history (2 Chron. xx. 14), such a descendant is particularly mentioned, Jahaziel, upon whom the Spirit of the Lord came in the midst of the assembly, and prompted him to take a leading part in the preliminary movements which resulted in the triumph of Judah (*ib.* ver. 15–18). Compare the similar coincidence in reference to the Sons of Korah, as the authors of Ps. xlviii. p. 213.

2 (1). *O God, be not silent, hold not thy peace, and be not still, O Mighty (One) !* This is a general introductory petition, that God would not remain inactive and indifferent to the dangers which environed his own people. The peculiar form of expression in the first clause, *let there not (be) silence to thee,* is copied by Isaiah (lxii. 6, 7). The next phrase is one that has occurred repeatedly before. See Ps. xxviii. 1, xxxv. 22, xxxix. 13 (12). The third petition, *be not still* or *quiet, rest not,* has the same relation to act that the others have to word or speech. The use of this divine name (אֵל) involves an appeal to God's omnipotence, as furnishing a reason for his interference. Why should He who is Almighty remain silent and inactive, when his people are in danger and his enemies apparently triumphant ?

3 (2). *For lo, thine enemies roar, and thy haters raise the head.* The general prayer in the preceding verse is now enforced by a description of the danger, beginning with the violence and confidence of the assailants. The *lo* is equivalent to *see there,* and converts the passage into a description of a present scene. The enemies of Israel are, as usual, identified with those of God, as a reason why he should appear for their destruction. The first verb means to make a noise, and is applied to the roar of the sea in Ps. xlvi. 4 (3), as it is to the howl of dogs in Ps. lix. 7 (6), and to internal commotions in Ps. xxxix. 7 (6), xlii. 6, 12 (5, 11). *Lift up the head,* as a natural indication of confidence and triumph. Compare the description of a conquered people, Judges viii. 28.

4 (3). *Against thy people they take crafty counsel, and consult against thy hidden ones.* To the qualities of violence and arrogance, the description now adds that of treacherous cunning. The construction in the first clause is, *they make (their) consultation crafty.* For the meaning of the Hebrew noun see above, on Ps. xxv. 14, lv. 15 (14), lxiv. 3 (2). *Thy hidden ones,* those whom thou hast hidden for safe-keeping, the objects of thy merciful protection. See above, on Ps. xxvii. 5, xxxi. 21 (20).

5 (4). *They have said, Come and let us destroy them from (being) a nation, and let not the name of Israel be remembered any more.* Not only were they turbulent and confident and crafty, but malignant and determined to destroy. The past tense of the first verb represents the combination as already

formed. The idiomatic phrase, *from a nation,* is used more than once by Isaiah (vii. 8, xxiii. 1). The expression for complete extirpation in the last clause is borrowed from the curse on Amalek, Exod. xvii. 14. *Israel,* as the name of the chosen people, was rightfully claimed by Judah after the great schism, even while the rival kingdom still existed.

6 (5). *For they have consulted heartily together; against thee a covenant they ratify.* The word translated *heartily* is really a noun meaning *heart,* but here used to qualify the verb by adding the idea, *with the heart, ex animo,* cordially, heartily. The phrase rendered *one heart* in 1 Chron. xii. 38, is altogether different. For the meaning of the last verb, see above, on Ps. l. 5. The preterite and future tense represent the combination as already formed and still continued.

7 (6). *The tents of Edom and the Ishmaelites, Moab and the Hagarenes.* The use of the word *tents* does not necessarily imply a wandering mode of life, as it may mean military tents, or be a figure for dwellings. See above, on Ps. lxxviii. 67, and compare Judges vii. 8, 1 Kings xii. 16. The Ishmaelites inhabited a part of Desert Arabia (Gen. xxv. 18), as did also the Hagarenes or Hagarites, a people driven from their lands by the tribe of Simeon in the reign of Saul. See 1 Chron. v. 10, 19–22, and compare 1 Chron. xi. 38, xxvii. 31.

8 (7). *Gebal and Ammon and Amalek, Philistia with the inhabitants of Tyre.* Gebal was probably a part of Idumea. Ammon and Amalek are joined in the same manner, Judges iii. 13, as Philistia and Tyre are, Ezek. xxxviii. 13, and Philistia, Tyre, and Edom, Amos i. 6–10.

9 (8). *Also Assyria was joined with them.* (These) *were an arm to the Sons of Lot. Selah.* Assyria is put last, as the remotest and least interested in this combination against Judah. It had evidently not yet supplanted Babylonia as the dominant power of Western Asia. The last clause refers, not merely to Assyria, as the plural verb shews, but to all the confederates except the Sons of Lot, *i. e.* Moab and Ammon (Gen. xix. 37, 38), who are here referred to, as the authors and conductors of the expedition.

10 (9). *Do to them as* (thou didst) *to Midian, as* (to) *Sisera, as* (to) *Jabin, in the valley of the Kishon.* This is a prayer for such deliverances as Israel experienced of old. The examples here selected are the victory of Gideon over the Midianites (Judges vii. viii.), and that of Deborah and Barak over Jabin and Sisera (Judges iv. v.) Between the first of these and the event which the psalm before us was designed to celebrate, there was this remarkable resemblance, that the enemies of Israel were in both cases made to destroy each other (Judges vii. 22, 2 Chron. xx. 23). Compare the allusions to the same event in Isa. ix. 4 (3), Hab. iii. 7. The Kishon is repeatedly mentioned in the history of Deborah and Barak's triumph (Judges iv. 7, 13, v. 21).

11 (10). *They were destroyed at Endor, they were dung to the earth.* This refers to the second of the battles mentioned in the preceding verse. Endor is not expressly named in the history, but is known to have been in the vicinity of Tabor, which is repeatedly there mentioned (Judges iv. 6, 12, 14). The last clause derives illustration from the extraordinary fruitfulness of certain battle-fields in modern times, particularly that of Waterloo. Compare 2 Kings ix. 37, Jer. ix. 21 (22).

12 (11). *Make them,* (even) *their nobles, like Oreb and like Zeeb; and like Zebah and like Zalmunnah all their princes.* He asks not only that the masses of the enemy may fare like those of Midian, but that their chief men may be utterly destroyed as the kings and chiefs of Midian were by

Gideon. See Judges vii. 25, viii. 5–21. The appeal to the historical associations of the people is greatly strengthened by this recital of familiar names. The first word properly means *set* or *place them, i. e.* put them in the same condition.

13 (12). *Who have said, let us inherit for ourselves the dwellings* (or *pasture-grounds) of God.* This relates not to the former but to the present enemies of Israel, and assigns the reason why they should experience the same fate with their predecessors. The double meaning of the word translated *dwellings* makes it peculiarly descriptive of the Holy Land, where God dwelt with his people, and where he fed them as a shepherd. See above, on Ps. xxiii. 3, lxv. 13 (12), lxxiv. 20.

14 (13). *My God, make them like the whirling chaff before the wind.* Make them, literally place them, as in ver. 11. *Like the whirling chaff,* literally *like the whirl* (or *whirlwind), like the chaff.* See above, on Ps. lxxvii. 19 (18), and compare Isa. xvii. 13.

15 (14). *As fire consumes a forest, and as a flame kindles mountains.* The original construction is *like a fire* (which) *consumes, like a flame* (which) *kindles.* By *mountains* we are here to understand what covers them or grows upon them.

16 (15). *So wilt thou pursue them with thy storm, and with thy tempest scare them.* There is no need of translating these futures as imperatives. It is one of those cases, so frequent in Hebrew, and especially in this book, where the form of direct petition alternates with that of confident anticipation.

17 (16). *Fill their face with shame, and* (men) *will seek thy name, Jehovah !* With the first clause compare Ps. lxix. 8 (7), lxxxix. 46 (45). Some refer the last clause also to the enemies ; but their destruction is still anticipated in the next verse, and to *seek the name* of God can hardly be expressive of a compulsory humiliation. The word translated *shame* is very strong, and means contempt, disgrace, or ignominy.

18 (17). *They shall be shamed and terror-stricken to eternity, and blush and perish.* This no doubt includes a prayer or the expression of a wish, but it also includes a strong and confident anticipation. To discard the future form is therefore at the same time weakening to the sense and destructive of a characteristic feature of the language. With the first clause compare Ps. vi. 11 (10). The word translated *terror-stricken* is the same that was rendered *scared* in ver. 16 (15). See above, on Ps. ii. 5, vi. 4 (3), xlviii. 6 (5).

19 (18). *And* (men) *shall know that thou, whose name* (is) *Jehovah,* (art) *alone Most High over all the earth.* The reference here, as in ver. 17 (16), is not to the impression made upon the minds of those destroyed, but upon men in general considered as spectators of their fate. See above, on Ps. lix. 14 (13), and compare 1 Sam. xvii. 46, 2 Kings xix. 19, Isa. xxxvii. 16, 20. The original construction is peculiar : " they shall know that thou —thy name Jehovah—thou alone—art Most High over all the earth." The simple pronoun *thou* is explained and amplified by the addition of the words, *thy name Jehovah, i. e.* thou who hast revealed thyself already as the self-existent and eternal God, and as the covenant God of Israel.

Psalm 84

1. *To the Chief Musician. On* (or *according to) the Gittith. By* (or *for) the Sons of Korah.* The Psalmist celebrates the blessedness of intimate

communion with God, ver 2–8 (1–7), and prays that he may himself enjoy it, ver. 9–13 (8–12). The resemblance of this psalm, in subject, tone, and spirit, to Ps. xlii., is the more remarkable because each stands at the beginning of a series inscribed *to the Sons of Korah.* The experience here recorded is so evidently David's, that we must either understand the Sons of Korah to be mentioned merely as the musical performers, or suppose that they composed it to express the feelings of the king himself, a hypothesis which Hengstenberg illustrates by the case of David playing and singing before Saul, in order to alleviate his paroxysms of madness. For the arguments on both sides of the question, see above, on Ps. xlii. 1, and for the meaning of *the Gittith*, on Ps. viii. 1, lxxxi. 1.

2 (1). *How dear* (to me are) *thy dwellings, O Jehovah,* (God of) *Hosts!* The adjective is rendered by the English versions *amiable*, in the sense of the French *aimable*, lovely. But the usage of the Hebrew word requires it to be understood as meaning *dear, beloved*, which is exactly the idea here required by the context. See above, on Ps. xlv. 1. The plural *dwellings* has reference to the subdivisions and appurtenances of the sanctuary, and is applied to the tabernacle in Ps. xliii. 3. Compare Ps. lxviii. 36 (35). The divine titles are as usual significant. While one suggests the covenant relation between God and the petitioner, the other makes his sovereignty the ground of a prayer for his protection. The force of this impassioned exclamation is enhanced by the structure of the sentence, which consists of a single clause, like Ps. xviii. 2 (1). With the whole verse compare Ps. xxvii. 1–5.

3 (2.) *Longs and also faints my soul for the courts of Jehovah, my heart and my flesh ; they sing* (with joy) *unto the living God.* The first verb is expressive of intense desire, as in Ps. xvii. 12. Compare Gen. xxxi. 30. Instead of *and also* the English Bible has *yea even*, which is perhaps too strong, and indicates a climax not intended by the writer. *Faints*, fails, or is consumed with strong desire. The plural *courts, i. e.* enclosures, is to be explained like *dwellings* in ver. 2 (1). Solomon's temple had two courts ; but one was appropriated to the priests, 2 Chron. iv. 9. The courts of the tabernacle are mentioned as the place where God statedly communed with Israel. See above, on Ps. lxv. 5 (4), and below, on Ps. xcii. 14 (13). They are here mentioned merely as a sign of the communion itself, which might be enjoyed in any place whatever. See above, on Ps. xxvii. 4, xxxvi. 9. Soul, heart, and flesh, denote the whole man. See above, on Ps. lxiii. 2 (1). The Hebrew accents connect *heart and flesh* with the preceding words. A much more natural division is the common one, which construes them directly with the verb of the last clause. That verb elsewhere always denotes a joyful shout or song ; but the derivative noun (רִנָּה) is used to signify a cry for help or earnest prayer, which meaning some attach to the verb itself in this place, so as to make the clauses strictly parallel. If the usual meaning of the verb be here retained, the clause shews that the speaker had already experienced that for which he prays. The *living God*, really existing, and the giver of life to others. See above, on Ps. xlii. 3 (2).

4 (3). *Yes, the sparrow has found a home, and the swallow a nest,* (in) *which she lays her young, even thine altars, Jehovah,* (God) *of Hosts, my King and my God.* The first word properly means *also*, as in the preceding verse, and is by some translated *even*, as if he had said, " the very birds have nests in the sanctuary of God, while I am excluded from it." Compare Mat. viii. 20. But the fact thus alleged is highly improbable and nowhere recorded. A more natural interpretation is to make the spar-

row and the swallow (put for small and helpless birds in general) emblems of
the worshipper himself. As if he had said, yes, this wandering bird has at
last found a resting-place, or home, both for itself and for its young. That
this is perfectly in keeping with Davidic usage, is plain from 1 Sam. xxvi. 20,
Ps. xi. 1, lv. 7 (6), lvi. 1. The translation *even thine altars* supposes the
Hebrew particle (אֵת) to indicate the object of the verb, as it does before
the same noun in 1 Kings xix. 10, 14. It may, however, be a proposition
meaning *at* or *near*, and this sense is preferred by those interpreters who
suppose a literal nestling of the birds in the sanctuary to be here alluded
to. The *altars* meant are those of burnt-offering and of incense, as in
Num. iii. 31. They are particularly mentioned, because it was by means
of sacrifice and prayer that communion between God and man was possible.
Compare Ps. xxvi. 6. The young birds are introduced, not only to complete the picture, but to shew that the communion and divine protection,
which the Psalmist so highly valued, were not merely personal but domestic
and social privileges, which he desired both for himself and those dependent
on him. The address, *Jehovah* (God) *of Hosts*, has the same sense as in
ver. 2 (1). The same essential notions of supremacy and covenant relation
are conveyed by the parallel expression, *my King and my God*, a combination which occurs only here and in Ps. v. 3 (2).

5 (4). *Happy the dwellers in thy house*, (for) *still they praise thee* (or *will
praise thee*). The first phrase is the idiomatic one with which the book
begins, for the peculiar form and sense of which, see above on Ps. i. 1,
ii. 12, xxxii. 1, 2, xxxiii. 12, xli. 2 (1). *Dwellers in*, inhabitants of, thy
house, *i. e.* members of thy family, as the same words literally mean in
Jer. xx. 5. For the spiritual or figurative meaning, see above, on Ps.
xv. 1, xxiii. 6, xxiv. 3, xxvii. 4, lxi. 5 (4), lxv. 5 (4). The privilege thus
described might be enjoyed in any local situation ; but the outward sign of
it, under the old economy, was the frequenting of the sanctuary. As inmates, not mere visitors, they will still have occasion and opportunity of
doing what they do when first admitted into God's household. *They will
still praise*, because they will have renewed cause so to do. See above, on
Ps. v. 8 (7), l. 15, 23, lxxix. 13.

6 (5). *Happy the man who* (has) *strength in thee*, (who have) *highways in
their heart*. The original consists of several exclamations or ejaculations—
happy man !—(there is) *strength to him in thee !*—(there are) *highways in
their heart ?* This last unusual and obscure expression is supposed by
some to mean, in whose thoughts, (or affections) are the highways to
Jerusalem, *i. e.* who still think of going up to worship there. But another
explanation, which agrees far better, both with the immediate context and
with usage and analogy, supposes the figure to be identical with that in Ps.
l. 23, Prov. xvi. 17, Isa. xl. 3, 4, where the removal of all moral or
spiritual hindrances to God's revisiting his people and communing with
them, is poetically represented as the opening, levelling, and raising of a
causeway through a pathless wilderness or otherwise impracticable ground.
The word translated *highways* is determined, both by etymology and usage,
to denote not a mere beaten track or footpath, but a road artificially constructed, and raised above the level of the ground through which it passes.
The sudden change of number in the last clause shews that *man* is a generic or collective term.

7 (6). *Passing through the Vale of Tears, a spring they make it ; also
with blessings is the teacher clothed*. This is one of the obscurest verses in
the book. Interpreters, however, are now commonly agreed as to the first

clause. The explanation of *Baca,* as meaning the Valley of Mulberry or Baca-trees (2 Sam. v. 23, 24, 1 Chron. xiv. 13, 14), is now very commonly abandoned for the one given in the ancient versions, the Vale of Weeping or of Sorrow, a beautiful poetical description of the present life as one of suffering. To the *fons lacrymarum* is opposed the fountain of salvation or of joy, a figure so familiar in the Scriptures, as to be readily suggested by the one word *spring* or *fountain.* See above, on Ps. xxxvi. 10 (9), xlvi. 5 (4), and compare Isa. xii. 3. The meaning of the clause, as thus explained, is, that the persons pronounced happy in the foregoing verse are a source of happiness, and convert the very Vale of Tears into a fountain of delight. The meaning of the other clause is still disputed. As the first noun, by varying a single vowel-point, may mean either *pools* or *blessings,* and the next, though it commonly means *teacher* (2 Kings xvii. 28, Prov. v. 13, Isa. xxx. 20),¡has in one other place (Joel ii. 23) the sense of *rain,* or rather of the *early rain* in Palestine, the clause admits of several very different explanations. 1. The rain also covers the pools. 2. The teacher is clothed in blessings. 3. The rain covers it with blessings. In favour of the second is its close adherence to the usage of the three leading words. It is also found substantially in the ancient versions. The meaning then is, that this strange transforming power is exerted by the good man as a teacher of righteousness, in which sense one of the disputed words (מוֹרֶה) occurs in Joel ii. 23, which accounts for its being there repeated in the very same sentence, by a kind of paronomasia, in the sense of *early rain,* elsewhere denoted by a cognate form (יוֹרֶה). Compare the sentiment with that in Ps. li. 15 (13). For the neuter or intransitive meaning of the last verb, see Lev. xiii. 45, Mic. iii. 7, Jer. xliii. 12.

8 (7). *They shall go from strength to strength; he shall appear to God in Zion.* The change of number is the opposite of that in ver. 6 (5), but to be explained on the same principle. Or the singular verb in the last clause may refer to the Teacher in ver. 7 (6). The *strength* is that bestowed by God, in the experience of which they make continual advances. The form of expression in the last clause is one used in the Law to denote the stated appearance of the Israelites at the sanctuary. The meaning of the whole verse is, that they who answer to the previous description shall finally attain to the full fruition of that union with God in which their happiness resides.

9 (8). *Jehovah, God,* (Lord of) *Hosts, hear my prayer; give ear, O God of Jacob! Selah.* Here begins the second part of the psalm, containing the petition founded on the preceding view of the happiness arising from communion with God. The names applied to him suggest, as usual, the grounds of the petition, namely, his eternity, self-existence, sovereignty, and covenant relation to his people.

10 (9). (*Oh*) *our shield, see,* (*O*) *God, and behold the face of thine Anointed.* Some make the first noun the object of the verb that follows, *see our shield;* but in ver. 12 (11) God himself is so described, as well as in Ps. iii. 4 (3), Gen. xv. 1. Its position, as a vocative, is certainly unusual, but seems to be emphatic. *Behold the face, i. e.* behold it favourably, look upon it graciously. *Thine Anointed* (*One*), *i. e.* David, by whom, or in whose name, the psalm was written.

11 (10). *For better* (*is*) *a day in thy courts than a thousand; I have chosen to occupy the threshold in the house of my God, rather than dwell in tents of wickedness.* The comparison in both clauses is expressed, as usual

in Hebrew, by the preposition *from, away from.* " Good from, *i. e.* in comparison with, a thousand." " I choose from dwelling, *i. e.* rather than to dwell." The first clause of course means that one day in God's courts is better than a thousand elsewhere. *I have chosen*, and do still choose, a stronger expression than *I would choose* or *would rather*. The next verb occurs only here, and is evidently formed from the noun (סַף) *sill* or *threshold*.

To *be a door-keeper* (guard the threshold), and to *lie on the threshold*, are too specific, and appear to add something to the sense of the original. The idea perhaps is, that he would rather stand at the door of God's house and look in (which was all that the worshippers could do at the Mosaic sanctuary), than dwell in the interior of tents or houses where iniquity prevailed. The use of the word *tents* in this clause makes it still more probable that the tabernacle, not the temple, is meant by the parallel expression, *house of God.*

12 (11). *For a sun and a shield is Jehovah, God ; grace and glory will Jehovah give ; he will not refuse* (anything) *good to those walking in a perfect* (way). The *for* shews that this verse gives a reason for the preference expressed in that before it. God is here called a sun, as he is called a light in Ps. xxvii. 1. Both these figures represent him as a source of happiness ; that of a shield describes him as a source of safety, or a strong protector. *Grace* and *glory* (or *honour*) are related as the cause and the effect. The latter includes all the sensible fruits and manifestations of the divine favour. See above, on Ps. xlix. 17 (16). *In a perfect* is by some understood to mean *as a perfect* person, *i. e.* perfectly, uprightly. See above, on Ps. xv. 2, xviii. 24 (23), and compare Gen. xvii. 1.

13 (12). *Jehovah* (Lord of) *Hosts, happy the man trusting in thee.* The participle is expressive of habitual reliance. *Trusting in thee*, as I do.

Psalm 85

1. *To the Chief Musician. To* (or *by*) *the Sons of Korah. A Psalm.* On the ground of former benefits, the Church prays for deliverance from present evils, ver. 2–8 (1–7), and joyfully anticipates a favourable answer, ver. 9–14 (8–13). There is nothing in the title, or the psalm itself, to determine its date or confine its application to any particular historical occasion. It seems to be appropriate to every case in which the fulfilment of the promise (Lev. xxvi. 3–13) was suspended or withheld.

2 (1). *Thou wast gracious, O Jehovah, to thy land ; thou didst return* (to) *the captivity of Jacob.* Some interpreters refer these words to favours recently experienced ; *thou hast* (now) *been gracious*, &c. But it is clear from ver. 5–8 (4–7), that the people were actually suffering, and that the acknowledgments in ver. 2–4 (1–3) must relate to former instances of God's compassion. The idea, that the benefit acknowledged was deliverance from the Babylonish exile, has arisen from a false interpretation of the last clause, for the true sense of which see above, on Ps. xiv. 7. Captivity is a common figure for distress, and God's revisiting the captives for relief from it. It is also worthy of remark, that the favour shewn was to the *land, i. e.* to the people while in possession and actual occupation of it.

3 (2). *Thou didst take away the guilt of thy people ; thou didst cover all their sin. Selah.* The same form of expression occurs above, in Ps. xxxii. 1, 5. Both verbs suggest the idea of atonement as well as pardon.

4 (3). *Thou didst withdraw all thy wrath ; thou didst turn from the heat of thine anger.* There is probably an allusion here to the prayer of Moses in Exod. xxxii. 12. The Hebrew verb of the second clause corresponds strictly to the English verb in its transitive or causative sense. It is used, however, in the same way by Ezekiel (xviii. 30, 32), who, in one place (xiv. 6), has the phrase to *turn away the face,* of which the other.may be an abbreviation.

5 (4.) *Return to us, O God of our salvation, and cease thine anger towards us.* The recollection of former mercies is here followed by a prayer for their renewal. " As thou hast had pity on thy people heretofore, so have pity on them now." *Return to us,* revisit us again in mercy. See above, on ver. 2 (1), and on Ps. xiv. 7. The verb in the last clause means to annul or nullify, put an end to, cause to cease. It occurs above, Ps. xxxiii. 10. The word translated *anger* is one which properly expresses a mixed feeling of grief and indignation. See above, on Ps. vi. 7 (6).

6 (5). *For ever wilt thou be angry at us? Wilt thou draw out thine anger to generation and generation !* The first Hebrew word strictly means *to ages* or *eternities.* The verb to *draw out,* protract, continue, is used in a favourable sense, Ps. xxxvi. 11 (10). The idea here expressed is the opposite of that in Ps. xxx. 6 (5).

7 (6). *Wilt thou not return* (and) *quicken us,* (and) *shall* (not) *thy people rejoice in thee?* With the first clause compare Ps. lxxi. 20, lxxx. 19 (18), Deut. xxxii. 39, Hos. vi. 2. With the second compare Ps. v. 12 (11), ix. 3 (2), xl. 17 (16). " Wilt thou not revisit us in mercy, raise us from the dead or dying state in which we now are, and give us, as thy people, fresh occasion to rejoice in our relation to thee, and in our union and communion with thee ? " The construction which continues the interrogation through the sentence is much simpler and more natural than that which makes the second clause contingent and dependent on the first, *that thy people may rejoice in thee.* At the same time, the interrogative form expresses a more confident anticipation than a bare petition.

8 (7). *Let us see, O Lord, thy mercy; and thy salvation thou wilt give unto us.* The first petition is, that God would cause them to experience his mercy. In the last clause, as in many other places, the form of petition is insensibly exchanged for that of anticipation. As if he had said, " We can confidently ask thee to shew us thy mercy, for we know that thou wilt grant us thy salvation."

9 (8). *I will hear what the Mighty* (*God*), *Jehovah, will speak; for he will speak peace to his people and to his saints; and let them not return to folly.* The first clause expresses the people's willingness to hear and to abide by God's decision. The second gives the reason of this willingness, to wit, because they know that the response will be auspicious. The third assigns the necessary limitation to this confidence, by stating the condition of God's favourable answer. The failure to comply with this condition accounts for the partial fulfilment of the promise, both in the case of individuals and of the church at large. See above, on Ps. lxxx. 19 (18), and compare the promise in Lev. xxvi. 3–13. *His saints,* the objects of his mercy and subjects of his grace. See above, on Ps. iv. 4 (3). *And let them not turn* is equivalent to saying, *so* (or *therefore*) *let them not turn.* The real connection of the clauses might be brought out still more clearly in our idiom by the paraphrase, " provided they do not return to folly."

10 (9). *Only nigh to his fearers* (is) *his salvation, for glory to dwell in our land.* As the limitation of the promise to those fearing God is an

essential stroke in this description, there is no need of departing from the strict sense of (אַךְ) the particle with which the sentence opens. See above, on Ps. lxii. 10 (9), lxviii. 7 (6), and compare Ps. lviii. 12 (11), lxxiii. 1. The meaning then is, that salvation is provided by God's mercy for none but those who fear him. The last clause, which is literally rendered above, is equivalent to saying in our idiom, *that glory may dwell in our land.* Glory has the same sense as in Ps. lxxxiv. 12 (11). *Dwell*, reside permanently, long continue.

11 (10). *Mercy and truth have met (together); righteousness and peace have kissed (each other).* By *truth*, we are to understand the truth of God's promises, the divine veracity. See above, on Ps. xxv. 5. The same combination with grace or mercy occurs above, in Ps. xxv. 10, xl. 11 (10), lvii. 4 (3), lxi. 8 (7), and below, Ps. lxxxix. 15 (14). *Righteousness*, considered as the gift of God, justification, whether judicial or providential. *Peace*, immunity from all disturbing causes, which implies prosperity of every kind. See above, on Ps. lxxii. 3. *Have met*, in a peaceable and friendly manner, an idea still more strongly expressed by the kiss of reconciliation or affection in the last clause. A still more pointed and emphatic meaning may be put upon the sentence by supposing it to mean, that God's mercy or free favour to the undeserving is now seen to be consistent with his truth, which was pledged for their destruction, and their peace or safety with his righteousness or justice, which might otherwise have seemed to be wholly incompatible.

12 (11). *Truth from the earth is springing, and righteousness from heaven looks down.* The truth of God's promise may be seen, as it were, springing from the earth in its abundant fruits, and its rectitude, or faithfulness to his engagements, looking down from heaven in the rain and sunshine. By this bold and beautiful conception, the certainty of God's providential care is expressed more strongly than it could be by any mere didactic statement. The beauty of the image in the last clause is heightened by the use of a verb which originally means to lean or bend over, for the purpose of gazing down upon a lower object. See above, on Ps. xiv. 2, and compare Judges v. 28, 2 Sam. vi. 16.

13 (12). *Jehovah also will give the* (material or earthly) *good, and our land will give its produce* (or *increase*). In other words, the promise shall be verified that stands recorded in the Law (Lev. xxvi. 4), from which the form of the expression is borrowed, as it is in Ps. lxvii. 7 (6).

14 (13). *Righteousness before him shall march, and set* (us) *in the way of his steps.* The verb in the first clause is a poetical intensive form of one which means to walk or go. The idea here expressed seems to be that of public and solemn manifestation. The last clause is obscure, and of dubious construction. The latest interpreters understand it as meaning, *and set its steps for a way, i.e.* mark out by its own steps the way in which we are to walk. This yields, in the end, the same sense as the common version above given.

Psalm 86

1. *A Prayer. By David. Incline, O Jehovah, thine ear* (and) *answer me, for wretched and needy* (am) *I.* The whole psalm is called a prayer, because entirely made up, either of direct petitions, or of arguments intended to enforce them. The tone and substance of the composition are

well suited to David's situation in his days of suffering at the hands of Saul
or Absalom, more probably the latter, on account of the repeated allusions
to deliverance from former trials of the same kind. Some account for the
position of this psalm in the midst of a series inscribed to *the Sons of Korah*,
by supposing that the latter composed it in the person or the spirit of David.
See above, on Ps. lxxxiv. 1. The same hypothesis is used by these interpreters
to explain the many forms of expression borrowed from other psalms of
David, as,if the *Sons of Korah* meant to comfort him by the repetition of
his own consolatory words in other cases. Compare 2 Cor. i. 4. The
psalm admits of no minute or artificial subdivision. The only marked
diversity of the parts is, that in ver. 1-10, petition is combined with argument, whereas in ver. 11-17, it is more unmixed. The first ground or
reason is derived, in this verse, from the urgency of the necessity. At the
same time, there is a tacit claim to God's protection, on the ground that
he who asks it is one of his own people. According to the usage of the
psalms, the afflicted and the needy denote sufferers among God's people.
See above, on Ps. x. 2.

2. *Keep my soul, for a gracious one (am) I ; save thy servant, even thou,
my God, the* (servant) *trusting in thee.* He prays for the safe keeping of
his soul or life, because it was this that the enemy threatened. See below,
ver. 14. The grounds assigned are two, or rather one exhibited in two
forms. The first is, that he is a (חָסִיד) saint or gracious one, a merciful
object of God's mercy. See above, on Ps. lxxxv. 8 (7). The other is that,
as a servant of Jehovah, he believes and trusts in him alone. The original expression is not *in* but *to* or *towards* thee, as if implying that the believer turns or looks away from every other ground of confidence to God
alone. The same construction occurs twice above, in Ps. iv. 6 (5), xxxi.
7 (6).

3. *Be gracious unto me, O Lord, for unto thee will I cry all the day.*
The prayer is still substantially the same, but enforced by two additional
reasons : one implied in the divine name used, to wit, that God is his sovereign, and as such bound to protect his subject ; the other expressed,
namely, that his subject never ceases to invoke his aid. The future meaning of the verb includes the present, but suggests the additional idea of
determination to pursue the same, course till the blessing is obtained. Compare Gen. xxxii. 27 (26), Luke xviii. 1. *All the day* is a common idiomatic
phrase equivalent to *all the time* in English, and may therefore be considered as including, though it does not formally express, the idea of *every
day* or *daily.* See above, on Ps. xlii. 4, 11 (3, 10).

4. *Gladden the soul of thy servant, for unto thee, Lord, my soul do I
raise.* The first clause is not a mere periphrasis for " make me glad," or
" cause me to rejoice." It means " make me heartily rejoice, because I
am thy servant," thus suggesting a new ground of his petition, different in
form although substantially identical with that in the preceding verse. A
similar analogy exists between the second clause of that verse and the
second clause of.this, the form of which, however, is borrowed from Ps.
xxv. 1. Here, as there, to raise the soul to God is to regard him with
affection and strong confidence. See above, on Ps. xxiv. 4. At the same
time, there is an allusion to the strict sense of the Hebrew verb, as if he had
said, " make my soul rejoice, since I bring it up or raise it to thee for this
very purpose." The force of the future is the same as in ver. 4.

5. *For thou, Lord, art good and forgiving, and rich in mercy to all
(those) invoking thee.* God is not only the sovereign of his people, and as

such bound by covenant to protect them, but benevolent or good in his own nature ; and that not merely in the general, or in reference to all his creatures, but especially in reference to the undeserving and the ill-deserving; that is, to such of them as really desire his favour, and evince their willingness to have it by the act of asking for it. *Rich* (*in*) *mercy*, literally *great* (or much, abundant, plenteous, as to) *mercy*. This expression, and indeed the whole description, is borowed from Exod. xxxiv. 6.

6. *Give ear, Jehovah, to my prayer, and attend* (or *hearken*) *to the voice of my supplications.* The same verbs are used in a similar connection, Ps. v. 2, 3 (1, 2). The last word in Hebrew, according to its etymology, denotes specifically prayers for favour, grace, or mercy. See above, on Ps. xxviii. 6, xxxi. 23 (22). There is no new ground or argument suggested here, beyond what is implied in the use of the word just explained, and of the divine name in the first clause.

7. *In the day of my distress I will invoke thee, for thou wilt answer me.* The future includes the present, I do and will invoke thee, call thee to my aid, or call upon thee for assistance. The second clause assigns the reason, namely, his conviction that he shall not call in vain. The implied ground of this conviction is, that he never does and never did call, in the exercise of faith, without being favourably heard or answered.

8. *There is none like thee among the gods, O Lord, and nothing like thy works* (among their works). This last, which might seem to be needed to complete the sense and the parallelism, was suppressed perhaps in order to suggest the idea, that the gods have no works, even the Gentiles who worship them being creatures of Jehovah, as is expressly stated in the next verse. Even the full comparison, however, in the first clause, does not necessarily concede the personal existence of the gods themselves, but only that of their material images, or at most the belief of their besotted worshippers. Compare with this verse its Mosaic models, Exod. xv. 11, Deut. iii. 24, and the Davidic imitations of them, 2 Sam. vii. 22, Ps. xviii. 32 (31). The exclusive Godhead of Jehovah is here urged as a distinct ground or reason of importunate petition to him.

9. *All nations which thou hast made shall come and worship before thee, O Lord, and give honour to thy name.* The common relation of Jehovah to all men as their Maker, although now denied by most nations, shall be one day universally acknowledged, not in word merely, but in act, the most expressive act of worship, involving a believing recognition of the previous display of God's perfections, in the language of the Scriptures called his *name.* This prospective view of the conversion of the world to the belief and service of its Maker shews how far the Old Testament writers were from cherishing or countenancing the contracted nationality of the later and the less enlightened Jews. See above, on Ps. xxii. 28, 29 (27, 28), xlv. 13–17 (12–16), xlvii. 10 (9), and compare Jer. xvi. 19, Zeph. ii. 11, Zech. xiv. 9, 16.

10. *For great* (art) *thou and doing wonders, thou* (art) *God alone.* The only new idea here is the evidence afforded of Jehovah's sole divinity by his miraculous performances. The *for*, at the beginning of the verse, implies that these proofs of divinity must sooner or later have their full effect.

11. *Guide me, Jehovah,* (*in*) *thy way ; I will walk in thy truth ; unite my heart to fear thy name.* The common version of the first verb (*teach me*) is too vague, as it fails to bring out the peculiar suitableness of the term to express the kind of teaching here specifically meant. The original

meaning of the Hebrew word is to point out or mark the way. According to the usage of the Psalms, the *way* of God is here the course of his providential dealings, and his *truth* the truth of his promises, to *walk* in which is to assent to them, or acquiesce in them and trust them. See above, on Ps. xxv. 4, 5, xxvi. 3. That he may be enabled to do this without distraction or reserve, is the prayer of the last clause. The idea of a united heart is the opposite of a double heart. See above, on Ps. xii. 3 (2), and compare James iv. 8.

12. *I will thank thee, O Lord my God, with all my heart, and I will honour thy name for ever.* The first verb means not merely to praise in general, but to praise for benefits received. See above, on Ps. vi. 6 (5). This verse describes the effect that is to follow from the granting of the prayer at the close of the preceding verse. When his heart is once united to fear God, cordial and perpetual thanksgiving will follow as a necessary consequence.

13. *For thy mercy* (has been) *great towards me, and thou hast freed my soul from the lowest hell.* The most natural explanation of these words is that which makes them an appeal to former mercies as a reason for expecting new ones. If the psalm belongs to the period of Absalom's rebellion (see above, on ver. 1), the reference here may be to David's dangers and deliverances from Saul. *Towards me*, literally *on me*, with an implication of descent from above. *Hell*, in the wide sense of death or the state of the dead. See above, on Ps. vi. 6 (5). *Lowest*, or lower, lying under, subterraneous. The expression is derived from Deut. xxxii. 22. With this verse compare Ps. xviii. 6 (5), lvi. 14 (13).

14. *O God, proud* (men) *have arisen against me, and an assembly of violent* (men) *have sought my soul, and have not set thee before them.* Nearly the same words had been used by David in reference to the Sauline persecution, Ps. liv. 5 (3). But instead of *aliens*, he here speaks of *proud ones*, and before the parallel term *violent*, oppressive, or tyrannical (Ps. xxxvii. 35), inserts *congregation* or *assembly*, as if to imply organization, both which variations agree well with the hypothesis that this psalm relates to the revolt of Absalom.

15. *And thou, Lord,* (art) *a God merciful and gracious, long-suffering, and plenteous in mercy and truth.* He here appeals to God's description of himself as warranting his prayer for mercy. See Exod. xxxiv. 6, and the imitations or quotations of it by Joel (ii. 13) and Jonah (iv. 2). See also Ps. lxxxv. 11 (10).

16. *Turn towards me and be gracious to me ; give thy strength to thy servant, and grant salvation to the son of thy handmaid.* The first prayer.implies that God's face had previously been averted. *Give thy strength*, exercise it for his protection. *The son of thy handmaid* or female slave, *i. e.* a homeborn and hereditary servant, and as such entitled to defence and sustenance. The expression is borrowed from Exod. xxiii. 12, and reappears in Ps. cxvi. 16. The last verb is the common one meaning *to save*, but here connected with its object by the preposition *to*.

17. *Shew me a token for good, and* (then) *my haters shall see and be shamed, because thou, Jehovah, hast helped me and comforted me.* The phrase translated *shew me* strictly means *do with me*, and is here used because the *sign* or *token* asked is neither a verbal declaration nor a miracle, but a practical or providential indication of God's favour, furnished by his dealings *with him*. The word translated *good* is the one used in Ps. xvi. 2, where, as here, it has the sense of physical good, welfare, happiness. A

token for good is a pledge of its possession and enjoyment. The oblique construction, *that my haters may see*, is really included in the direct future. *Shamed*, surprised, disappointed, and confounded. The preterites in the last clause have reference to the time when this effect shall be produced upon the enemy, and when the divine help and consolation shall have been already granted.

Psalm 87

1. *To* (or *by*) *the Sons of Korah. A Psalm. A Song. His foundation* (*is*) *in the hills of holiness.* The first title decides nothing as to the date of composition. See above, on Ps. xlii. 1, xlvi. 1, xlvii. 1, xlviii. 1. It is not only a *psalm*, a religious lyric, but a *song*, *i.e.* a song of praise or triumph. See above, on Ps. lxxxiii. 1. This agrees well with the tone of the composition, which seems to indicate some great deliverance as its historical occasion. The only one that can be fixed upon with any great degree of probability is that of Hezekiah from the power of Assyria. See above, on Ps. xlvi. 1, lxxv. 1, lxxvi. 1. In view of some such signal intervention in behalf of Israel, the psalm celebrates the actual security of Zion, ver. 1–3, and anticipates its future honours as the spiritual birth-place of the nations, ver. 4–7. *His foundation*, that which he has founded, meaning his sanctuary and his theocratical kingdom. The plural expression, *hills of holiness*, means Zion in the wide sense, including all the heights on which Jerusalem was built. It was peculiarly appropriate in this case, if the psalm was written in the reign of Hezekiah, because at that time Zion, in the strict sense, was no longer the exclusive residence of God on earth. At the same time, there is particular reference to Zion as the citadel, in which the strength of the royal city was concentrated.

2. *Jehovah loves the gates of Zion more than all the dwellings of Jacob.* This description of Jehovah's choice of Zion as his dwelling-place is similar to that in Ps. lxxviii. 68. The gates of a walled city give access to it and power over it, and are therefore naturally here put for the whole. The Hebrew participle (*loving*) implies constant and habitual attachment.

3. *Glorious things* (have been) *spoken in thee, O City of God. Selah.* Glorious or honourable things, in the way of prophecy and promise, the fulfilment of which is here implied. As if he had said, the promises respecting thee are great, but they are or shall be fully verified. So too in the other clause the meaning is, thou art well called the city of God, for he is in thee, to protect and honour thee. See above, on Ps. xlvi. 5 (4), xlviii. 2, 9 (1, 8). Instead of *in thee* some read *of thee*, but the former is entitled to the preference: first, because it is the strict sense, and therefore not to be rejected without reason; then, because it really includes the other, but is not included in it; lastly, because it suggests the additional idea of the holy city as the scene, no less than the theme, of the prophetic visions.

4. *I will mention Rahab aad Babylon as knowing me. Lo, Philistia and Tyre with Ethiopia ! This* (*one*) *was born there.* Interpreters are commonly agreed, that these are the words of God himself, though not expressly so announced. The first verb in Hebrew is a causative, I will make to be remembered, celebrate, commemorate. See above, Ps. xx. 8 (7), xlv. 18 (17), lxxi. 16 (15), lxxvii. 12 (11). It here means to announce or proclaim. To know God is to love him and to be his servant. See above, on Ps. xxxvi. 11 (10), and compare Isa. xix. 21. Those knowing him in

this sense are his people. *As knowing me,* literally to those knowing me, *i. e.* belonging to their number. Or the sense may be, *for knowers of me,* I will recognise and reckon them for such. Compare the Hebrew of Exod. xxi. 2, *he shall go out free,* literally *for free, i.e.* as free. The nations thus announced as belonging to God's people are mere samples of the whole gentile world, those being chosen for the purpose, who were or had been most connected with the history of Israel, and were at the same time ruling powers of antiquity. *Rahab* is an enigmatical name given to Egypt by the Prophet Isaiah. See below, on Ps. lxxxix. 11 (10), and compare my notes on Isa. xxx. 7, li. 9. *Babylon* is named instead of *Assyria,* perhaps because in Hezekiah's reign the former began to supersede the latter as the dominant power of Western Asia. See my note on Isa, xxxix. 1. Compare the prophecy respecting Egypt and Assyria in Isa. xix. 23, 24. Philistia and Tyre are put together, as in Ps. lxxxiii. 8 (7). As to the latter, see above, on Ps. xlv. 13 (12), and compare Isa. xxiii. 18. The conversion of *Cush* or Ethiopia had already been foretold by David, Ps. lxviii. 32 (31), and by Solomon, Ps. lxxii. 10. The last words are obscure. but may be rendered clearer by supplying before them, *as to each of these it shall be said.* The pronoun (*this*) is then to be referred not to individual men, but to the nations as ideal persons. The idea of regeneration or spiritual birth, applied in the New Testament to individuals, is here applied to nations, who are represented as born again, when received into communion with the church or chosen people.

5. *And of Zion it shall be said,* (This) *man and* (that) *man was born in her, and He will establish her, the Highest.* The strict translation of the first words is *to Zion,* but the subsequent use of the third person (*in her*) shews that the act described is that of speaking of a person in his presence, yet not directly to him, or, as we sometimes say in English, talking *at him.* See above, on Ps. iii. 3 (2), lxxi. 10. The idiomatic phrase *man and man* means every one or each one severally. See the Hebrew of Esther i. 8, and compare that of Lev. xvii. 10, 13. The clause may then be understood as asserting of individuals what had just been said of whole communities, or as repeating the latter, in a more emphatic form, for the purpose of connecting it with an additional promise, namely, that the church thus enlarged by the accession of the Gentiles, shall be permanently established and secured. The pronoun is emphatic, and is rendered more so by the epithet attached to it. *He the Highest,* or *the Highest himself.* The protector of the church is neither man nor angel, but the supreme and sovereign God. See above, on Ps. xlvii. 3 (2), xlviii. 9 (8).

6. *Jehovah shall count, in enrolling the nations : This* (one) *was born there. Selah.* The theme or idea of the whole psalm, that Zion should yet be the birth-place of all nations, is again repeated, under a new figure, that of registration. Compare Ezek. xiii. 9. The meaning is that, as he counts the nations, he shall say of each, in turn or one by one, this one was also born there. *In enrolling,* literally *writing, i. e.* inscribing in a list or register. The common version (*when he writeth up the people*) not only fails to reproduce the plural form of the last word, or to shew in any way that more than a single nation is referred to, but ascribes the act of writing to the Lord himself, which, though not so inadmissible in a figurative passage as some writers think it, is not necessarily implied in the original, where the form of expression is *in the writing, i. e.* at the time or in the act of doing so, whether the act be that of God himself or merely done by his authority and under his direction.

7. *And singers as well as well as players* (shall be heard saying), *All my springs are in thee.* The construction in the first clause is peculiar, *singers as players.* See above, on Ps. xlviii. 6 (5). The image present to the Psalmist's mind seems to be that of a procession or triumphal march, composed of the nations on their way to Zion. At the head of this procession are the minstrels, who, as the spokesmen of the rest, acknowledge that the source of their happiness is henceforth to be sought in Zion, not as a mere locality, but as the place where God was pleased to manifest his gracious presence. It matters little, therefore, whether the closing words (*in thee*) be referred to God directly, or to Zion, as the channel through which he imparted spiritual blessings to the gentiles. Compare the figure of a spring or stream in Joel iv. 18 (iii. 18), Zech. xiii. 1, xiv. 8, Ezek. xlvii. 1, and see above, on Ps. lxxxiv. 7 (6). The word joined with singers admits of a twofold derivation, and may either mean *players upon instruments*, or still more definitely, *pipers*, as the players on stringed instruments are named in the same connection, Ps. lxviii. 26 (25); or as some of the latest interpreters prefer, it may mean *dancers*, as this indication of joy was commonly practised, in connection with singing, not only by women but by men. See above, on Ps. xxx. 12 (11), and below, on Ps. cl. 4. and compare Exod. xv. 20, 2 Sam. vi. 16. The *Selah* at the end of the preceding verse shews that the variations of the main theme are concluded, and separates the body of the psalm from this verse, which contains the words neither of the Psalmist nor the Church nor God himself, but of the converted Gentiles.

Psalm 88

1. *A Song. A Psalm. To* (or *by*) *the Sons of Korah. To the Chief Musician. Concerning afflictive sickness. A didactic Psalm. By Heman the Ezrahite.* The first word of this title elsewhere denotes a song of praise or triumph. See above, on Ps. xlii. 9 (8), lxxxiii. 1. It is here prefixed, however, to the most despondent psalm in the collection, in which the complaints and lamentations are relieved by no joyful anticipations or expressions of strong confidence. The only satisfactory explanation of these facts is afforded by the supposition, that Ps. lxxxviii. and lxxxix were intended to constitute a pair or double psalm, like the first and second, third and fourth, ninth and tenth, forty-second and forty-third, &c. The desponding lamentations of Ps. lxxxviii. are then merely introductory to the cheering expectations of Ps. lxxxix. This supposition also explains the unusual length of the inscription now before us, the first part of which may then be considered as belonging to both psalms, while the last clause corresponds to the title of Ps. lxxxix. *Afflictive sickness*, literally *sickness to afflict* or *humble.* For the figurative use of sickness, and the sense of this inscription, see above, on Ps. liii. 1. Heman the Ezrahite is mentioned, with Asaph and Ethan, as chief musicians in the reign of David, 1 Chron. vi. 18 (33), xv. 17, xvi. 41, 42. The Heman and Ethan, spoken of in 1 Chron. ii. 6 as Ezrahites (*i. e.* sons of Zerah), and in 1 Kings v. 11, as eminent for wisdom, are supposed by some to be different persons, because they were of the tribe of Judah, while others suppose that they were Levites adopted into that tribe. The Psalm before us neither requires nor admits of any minute or artificial subdivision.

2 (1). *Jehovah, God of my salvation,* (by) *day have I cried, and by night, before thee.* God of my salvation, the God in whom I trust to save me,

because he is a saving God, or God my Saviour. See above, on Ps. lxxxv. 5 (4). *Day* and *by night* are related to each other here, as *night* and *by day* are in Ps. lxxvii. 3 (2). *Before thee* implies that his cries were not mere instinctive expressions of distress, but prayers addressed to God. With the whole verse compare Ps. xxii. 3 (2).

3 (2). *Let my prayer come before thee ; incline thine ear unto my cry.* The first petition is that his prayer may attract the divine attention, which is varied in the last clause by the figure of one bending down to catch a faint or distant cry. See above, on Ps. xvii. 6, xxxi. 3 (2), lxxi. 2.

4 (3). *For sated with evils is my soul, and my life to the grave draws near.* *Evils,* sufferings, distresses. As *life* is plural in Hebrew, it can be construed regularly with the plural verb ; but as this is properly a causative, it may also be construed with *evils,* or with men indefinitely, *they have brought my life near to the grave.* The first construction is favoured by the analogy of Ps. cvii. 18. The *grave, sheol,* the state of the dead. See above, on Ps. vi. 6 (5).

5 (4). *I am reckoned with those going down to the pit ; I am* (or *am become*) *as a man witth no strength.* With the first clause compare Ps. xxviii. 1, cxliii. 7. *With no strength,* literally (to whom) *there is no strength.* The last word in Hebrew occurs only here, but a cognate form in Ps. xxii. 20 (19). There is in the original an antithesis, which cannot be conveyed by mere translation, arising from the fact that the first word for *man* is one implying strength.

6 (5). *With* (or *among*) *the dead, free, like the slain, lying in the grave, whom thou rememberest no more, and they by* (or *from*) *thy hand are cut off.* As to be God's servant is the highest privilege and honour (Ps. lxxxvi. 16), so to be free from his service (Job iii. 19) is to be miserable. The reference is not to death in general, but to death by violence and as a punishment. *The slain,* literally *the* (mortally) *wounded.* See above on Ps. lxix. 27 (26). The latter half of the verse contains a strong poetical description of the wicked, as no longer the objects of God's protecting care. Of the two translations, *from* and *by thy hand,* the first conveys the same idea with the foregoing words, while the second represents the destruction of God's enemies as the work of his own hands.

7 (6). *Thou hast placed me in a deep pit, in dark places, in abysses.* A deep pit, literally a pit of low or under places. See above, on Ps. lxiii. 10 (9), lxxxvi. 13, and compare Ezek. xxvi. 20. The *dark places* are those of the invisible and lower world. *Abysses,* deeps, or depths of water. See above, on Ps. lxix. 3 (2).

8 (7). *Upon me weighs thy wrath, and* (*with*) *all thy waves thou dost oppress me. Selah.* The word translated *waves* corresponds etymologically to *breakers.* See above, on Ps. xlii. 8 (7). With the first clause compare Ps. xxxviii. 3 (2). The verb to *oppress* or *afflict* is applied in historical prose to the oppression of Israel in Egypt, Gen. xv. 13, Exod. i. 12. The infinitive of the same verb occurs in the title of the psalm before us. The *Selah* indicates the depth of his distress, and the necessity of a pause before resuming the description.

9 (8). *Thou hast put far my acquaintances from me ; thou hast made me an abomination to them ;* (I am) *shut up and cannot come forth* The circumstance complained of in the first clause, is one often mentioned as an aggravation of distress. See above, on Ps. xxxi. 12 (11), xxxviii. 12 (11), lxix. 9 (8), and compare Ps. xxvii. 10. The next clause shews that he complains of something more than mere neglect. *Made me,* literally *put* or

placed me. See above, on Ps. xxxix. 9 (8). There may be an allusion to the statement in the history, that the Israelites were an abomination, an object of religious detestation and abhorrence, to their Egyptian masters. See Gen. xliii. 32, xlvi. 34. The last clause is by some understood to mean, I am encompassed by inextricable difficulties. Compare Lam. iii. 7, Job iii. 23. Others, with more probability, connect it with what goes before, and understand the sense to be, that he is not willing to expose himself to this unmerited hatred and contempt. See Job xxxi. 34, and compare Ps. xliv. 14 (13), lxxx. 7 (6).

10 (9). *My eye decays by reason of affliction; I invoke thee, O Jehovah, every day; I spread out unto thee my hands.* With the first clause compare Ps. vi. 8 (7), xxxi. 10 (9), xxxviii. 11 (10), lxix. 4 (3). With the last compare Ps. xliv. 21 (20). The first Hebrew verb is one of rare occurrence; a derivative noun is used by Moses, Deut. xxviii. 65. The preterites represent the suffering as no new thing, but one of long continuance.

11 (10). *Wilt thou to the dead do wonders, or shall ghosts arise* (and) *thank thee?* *Selah.* The argument implied is that the present life is the appropriate time for those favours which belong to it. See above, on Ps. vi. 6 (5). The word *Rephaim*, in the last clause, is the name of a Canaanitish race of giants, but is applied poetically to the gigantic shades or spectres of the dead. See my note on Isa. xiv. 9. *Do wonders*, literally *wonder*, as in Ps. lxxvii. 12 (11).

12 (11). *Shall thy mercy be recounted in the grave, thy faithfulness in destruction?* The last word (*Abaddon*) appears elsewhere in conjunction with the grave and death, as a poetical equivalent. See Prov. xv. 11, Job xxvi. 6, xxviii. 22.

13 (12). *Shall thy wonders be known in the dark, and thy righteousness in the land of forgetfulness?* These are varied metaphorical descriptions of the state of death, considered negatively as the privation or the opposite of life. *Darkness* is here opposed to the *light of life* or *of the living*, Ps. lvi. 14 (13). The land of forgetfulness, where men forget, Eccles. ix. 5, 6, 10, and are forgotten, Ps. xxxi. 13 (12).

14 (13). *And I unto thee, O Jehovah, have cried, and in the morning shall my prayer come before thee.* What he has done he is still resolved to do, as the only means of safety. Hence the alternation of the preterite and future. The first verb means to cry for help. See above, on Ps. xviii. 42 (41). With the last clause compare Ps. v. 4 (3), lvii. 9 (8), lix. 17 (16). The verb has its proper sense of coming before one or into his presence. See above, on Ps. xvii. 13, xviii. 6 (5), xxi. 4 (3).

15 (14). *Why, O Jehovah, wilt thou reject my soul, wilt thou hide thy face from me?* The first verb means to reject with abhorrence. See above, on Ps. xliii. 2, xliv. 10, 24 (9, 23), lx. 3, 12 (1, 10), lxxiv. 1, lxxvii. 8 (7). The question implies that such rejection would be inconsistent with God's faithfulness, and is therefore not expressive of entire despondence.

16 (15). *Wretched* (am) *I and expiring from childhood; I have borne thy terrors; I despair.* Expiring, ready to perish, at the point of death, a strong description of extreme distress. The *childhood* may be that of the individual sufferer, or of Israel as a nation (Hos. xi. 1). Both applications may have been intended.

17 (16). *Over me have passed thine indignations; thy terrors have destroyed me.* The image in the first clause is the same as in Ps. xlii. 8 (7). *Indignations*, literally heats or inflamations, but always applied to anger. The plural occurs only here. The unusual form of the last verb is supposed

by some to have been coined by the writer, for the sake of an allusion to Lev. xxv. 23.

18 (17). *They have surrounded me like waters all the day; they have encompassed me at once* (or *all together*). The figure of overwhelming waves is still continued. The subject of the verbs can only be the indignations and the terrors of ver. 17 (16).

19 (18). *Thou hast put far from me lover and friend; my acquaintances* (are) *darkness* (or a dark place). The first clause is a repetition of ver. 9 (8). The other is obscure, and is supposed by some to mean, my acquaintances vanish, disappear in darkness; by others, my acquaintances give way to darkness, are succeeded by it; my only friend is now the dark place, *i. e.* the grave or death. Thus understood, the sentiment is not unlike that in Job xvii. 14.

Psalm 89

1. *Maschil. By Ethan the Ezrahite.* From the fact that Ethan and Jeduthun are both named with Asaph and Heman, but never named together, it has been inferred that they are two names of the same person, or rather that *Ethan* is the personal name, and *Jeduthun* (derived from a verb which means to *praise*) the official title. Heman and Ethan are both described as Ezrahites, *i. e.* adopted sons of Zerah, 1 Chron. ii. 5, but by birth were no doubt both *Sons of Korah*, 1 Chron. vi. 18, 22 (33, 37). To the lamentations and complaints of Heman in the first part of this double psalm (Ps. lxxxviii.) is now added an appeal to the divine promise by Ethan in the psalm before us. The particular promise here insisted on is that in 2 Sam. vii., which constitutes the basis of all the Messianic psalms. The hypothesis of Hengstenberg and others, that the psalm was composed in the interval between the death of Josiah and the Babylonish exile, by the Korhites of that period, who merely assumed the name and breathed the spirit of their great progenitors, could be justified only by extreme exegetical necessity, which does not here exist, since nothing is more natural than to assume, that these psalms were nearly contemporaneous with the promise itself, and intended to anticipate misgivings and repinings, which, although they existed even then in germ, were not developed till the period of decline began, or rather till it was approaching its catastrophe. By far the larger part of this psalm is occupied in amplifying and expounding the great Messianic promise, ver. 2–38 (1–37), while the remainder, like Ps. lxxxviii., teaches the chosen people how to apply it, in their times of suffering and despondency, ver. 39–53 (38–52), a feature of the composition which fully warrants its description in the title as a *maschil* or didactic psalm.

2 (1). *The mercies of Jehovah for ever will I sing; to generation and generation will I make known thy faithfulness with my mouth.* The *mercies* particularly meant are the favours promised to David as the progenitor and type of the Messiah. The *faithfulness* mentioned in the other clause is that of God in the fulfilment of these promises. Compare my note on Isa. lv. 3, where the same idea is expressed by *the sure mercies of David*. *For ever*, literally *eternity*, the noun being used adverbially, as its plural is in Ps. lxi. 5 (4). The promise of perpetual commemoration shews that the Psalmist speaks not only for himself, but for the church of which he is the mouth or spokesman.

3 (2). *For I have said, For ever shall mercy be built up. The heavens—*

thou wilt fix thy faithfulness in them. The church will celebrate God's mercy and faithfulness for ever, because they will endure for ever. *I have said, i. e.* this is the view of the matter I have taken and expressed already. The scheme of God's gracious dispensations is conceived of as a building, already founded and hereafter to be carried up to its completion. The emphatic construction of *the heavens* as an absolute nominative (*as to the heavens, thou wilt fix, &c.*) is inadequately represented in the common version (*shalt thou establish in the very heavens*). For the proverbial use of the heavens and the heavenly bodies as a standard of permanence and immutability, see above, on Ps. lxxii. 5. The idea here is, thou shalt make thy faithfulness as fixed and stable as the frame of nature.

4 (3). *I have ratified a covenant with my chosen (one); I have sworn unto David my servant.* These are the words of God himself, though not expressly so described, as in ver. 20 (19) below. We have here a summary statement of the substance of the promise in 2 Sam. vii., upon which this and the other Messianic psalms are founded. *Ratified a covenant*, see above, on Ps. l. 5. *With my chosen*, literally *to my chosen*, as in the parallel expression, because what is here called a covenant was really a conditional promise or engagement upon God's part. *My servant, i. e.* my chosen and appointed instrument in executing my designs. See above, on Ps. xviii. 1, and compare Ps. lxxxvi. 16.

5 (4). *Unto eternity will I confirm thy seed, and build, to generation and generation, thy throne. Selah. Confirm thy seed*, establish thy descendants in the permanent possession of the royal dignity. The same two verbs which, in the foregoing verse, are applied to the divine grace and fidelity, are here applied directly to their objects, the throne and family of David.

6 (5). *And the heavens acknowledge thy wonders, Jehovah, likewise thy faithfulness* (is acknowledged) *in the assembly of holy (ones).* The promise just cited is entitled to men's confidence, because the omnipotence and faithfulness of Him who uttered it are thankfully acknowledged by superior beings. The parallelism of *heavens* and *holy ones* shews that the former are here put for their inhabitants. For the true meaning of the first verb, see above, on Ps. vi. 6 (5), and for that of the following noun, on Ps. lxxvii. 12 (11), lxxxviii. 11 (10.) *Wonders* or *miracles* are here referred to, as proofs of a mighty power. The *and, also*, at the beginning of the clauses, have the force of *even, yea*, in our idiom. The word translated *holy ones* is entirely different from that usually rendered *saints*. The latter is always applied to men, the former usually to superior beings, *i. e.* angels. See Deut. xxxiii. 2, 3, Dan. viii. 13, Zech. xiv. 5, Job. iv. 18, xv. 15.

7 (6). *For who, in the sky, can compare to Jehovah?* (Who) *is like and Jehovah among the Sons of the Mighty?* The question involves a strong negation, or an affirmation that there is none like him, even in the orders of existence superior to man. This is given as a reason for the adoring recognition of his power and veracity in ver. 6 (5). The word translated *sky* is elsewhere used in the plural to denote the *clouds* collectively. See above, on Ps. lxviii. 35 (34), lxxvii. 18 (17), lxxviii. 23. The singular form, in this sense, is peculiar to the psalm before us. See below, ver. 38 (37). The twofold usage of the English verb *compare*, as active and neuter, corresponds exactly to that of the original expression, for the primary and proper sense of which, see above on Ps. v. 4 (3), xl. 6 (5), l. 21. The *Sons of the Mighty or Almighty* are the angels. As to the peculiar form of the description, see above, on Ps. xxix. 1, from which it seems to be directly borrowed in the case before us.

8 (7). *A God to be dreaded in the secret council of (his) holy (ones) greatly, and to be feared above all (those) about him.* This is not a distinct proposition, but a further description of the Being pronounced in the foregoing verse to be incomparable. The divine name (אֵל) here used implies that what makes him so terrible is his infinite power. The angels are again called *holy ones*, but furthermore described as the privy council, the confidential intimates, of God himself. See above, on Ps. xxv. 14. lv. 15 (14), lxxxiii. 4 (3). Yet even to these, as being endlessly superior, he is and ought to be an object of adoring fear. The intensive adverb *greatly* is the same with that in Ps. lxii. 3, and like it is placed emphatically at the end of the clause. Compare Ps. xlviii. 2 (1), lxv. 10 (9). *Above* may either mean *more than*, or *by*, with an implication of his vast superiority as the cause or reason. *Those about him, i. e.* those immediately surrounding him, his heavenly attendants, the angels. See the same expression, in a somewhat different application, Ps. lxxvi. 12 (11).

9 (8.) *Jehovah, God of Hosts, who (is) like thee, mighty, Jah, and thy faithfulness (is) round about thee.* The infinite superiority of God to men and angels is here expressed, or rather indicated, by an accumulation of descriptive titles. We have here the full phrase, *Jehovah God of Hosts*, which occurs so frequently in an abbreviated form. See above, on Ps. xxiv. 10. The word translated *mighty* is used only here ; but its sense is clear from the analogy of cognate forms, confirmed by the testimony of the ancient versions. As to *Jah*, the pregnant abbreviation or concentration of *Jehovah*, see above, on Ps. lxviii. 5 (4). It may here be in apposition either with *Jehovah*, as a vocative, or with *Jah*, as a descriptive title. " Who is like thee, a mighty one, O Jah ? " Or, " who like thee is mighty, who like thee is Jah ? " *Faithfulness*, as elsewhere, is veracity or truth in the fulfilment of a promise. The word translated *round about* is the feminine or neuter form of that used in the preceding verse, and there applied to persons. The meaning of the whole clause is that God's fidelity is never absent from him, but appears wherever he does, the proofs of its existence being visible on all hands. The English Bible supplies a preposition and assumes a second question, " who is like thy faithfulness round about thee ? " But the other construction, which is that adopted in the ancient versions, is much simpler and more natural, the ellipsis of the preposition in such cases being rare, whereas that of the substantive verb is the general rule of Hebrew syntax, to which its insertion is a mere exception.

10 (9). *Thou rulest the swell of the sea ; in the rise of its waves thou stillest them.* The general declaration of God's power is now rendered more distinct by specifying one of the most striking forms in which it manifests itself. At the same time, there is no doubt an allusion to the scriptural usage of the sea as an emblem of the world and its conflicting powers. See above, on Ps. xlvi. 3, 4 (2, 3), lxv. 8 (7). The appropriateness of the words both to physical and moral changes affords an easy and beautiful transition to the latter in the next verse. The verbal form at the beginning is a participle, *thou (art) ruling, i. e.* habitually, constantly. The connective particle may be retained by rendering it *rulest over*. The first noun is applied elsewhere (Ps. xvii. 10) to the swelling or elation of the heart with pride ; but that this is only a derived and secondary meaning may be gathered from the use of the same word to denote the loftiness or majesty of God (Ps. xciii. 1), and also from the application of the verbal root to the rise of water in an inundation (Ezek. xlvii. 5). The parallel term is an

abbreviated infinitive used as a noun, and therefore well represented by the English *rise*, which is also both noun and verb.

11 (10). *Thou didst crush, like the slain, Rahab; with thine arm of strength thou didst scatter thy foes.* This relates wholly to the sea of nations, in which Egypt stands first, as the earliest national enemy of Israel, and also perhaps because the power of Pharaoh, at the exodus, was literally broken in the sea. The first verb means to shatter, crush, or break in pieces. See above, Ps. lxxii. 4. The pronoun is emphatic; (it was) *thou* (and none other that) *didst crush*, &c. The significant name *Rahab*, meaning pride or insolence, corresponds to the swelling of the sea, in the foregoing verse. See above, on Ps. lxxxvii. 4. *Like the slain*, like one mortally wounded, especially in battle. See above, on Ps. lxxxviii. 6 (5). The point of comparison is the sudden change from overbearing arrogance to helplessness and weakness. *Thine arm of strength*, or *strong arm*, the active exertion of thy power. See above, on Ps. x. 15, xxxvii. 17, xliv. 4 (3), lxxxiii. 9 (8). The last verb belongs to the dialect of poetry, and occurs above, in Ps. liii. 6 (5). See below, Ps. cxii. 9, cxli. 7. This verse relates only indirectly to the enemies of God in general. Even the last clause has specific reference to the enemies who perished in the Red Sea.

12 (11). *To thee* (belongs) *heaven, also to thee earth, the world and its fulness, thou didst found them.* The power of God is now described as universal and creative. *Heaven and earth* is the usual comprehensive phrase for the whole frame of nature or material universe. The last clause is evidently borrowed from Ps. xxiv. 1. *Its fulness*, that which occupies and fills it, its contents and its inhabitants. The verb to *found* suggests the two ideas of creation and sustentation. He not only called them into being, but made them permanent or lasting. See above, on Ps. lxxviii. 69, and below, on Ps. civ. 5. The *world*, the cultivated and productive earth, as opposed to the desolate and barren sea. The English Bible, following the masoretic accents, construes *the world and its fulness* as absolute nominatives. A simpler construction is to put them in apposition with *heaven* and *earth*, and refer the pronoun at the end to all these antecedents.

13 (12). *North and south, thou didst create them; Tabor and Hermon in thy name rejoice.* The pronoun at the end of the first clause is superfluous in English; the original construction requires *north and south* to be taken absolutely, (*as for*) *the north and south, thou hast created them.* The word for *north* originally means concealment; that for *south* the right hand. The east and west are represented by two mountains on either side of Jordan. As to Hermon, see above, on Ps. xlii. 7 (6). The points of the compass are here put, like heaven and earth in the preceding context, for the whole world, and described as rejoicing in God's name, *i. e.* praising his perfections by their very existence.

14 (13). *To thee* (is) *an arm with strength; strong is thy hand, high is thy right hand.* This is simply another declaration of the divine omnipotence, under the usual emblems, arms, hand, and right hand. See above, on ver. 11 (10).

15 (14). *Justice and judgment* (are) *the place of thy throne; mercy and truth shall go before thy face.* The word translated *place* may also have the more specific sense of dwelling-place. The meaning is that God reigns in the midst of perfect righteousness. See above, on ver. 9 (8). The verb in the last clause always means to *go* or *come before*, sometimes in the sense of coming into one's presence, sometimes in that of meeting or encountering, sometimes (as here) in that of being a forerunner. See above, on Ps. lxxxv. 14 (13).

16 (15). *Happy the people knowing joyful noise ; Jehovah, in the light of thy face they shall walk.* The unusual expression in the first clause seems to mean those who know how and have occasion to rejoice in the experience of God's favour. The last noun in Hebrew denotes any loud expression sf exultation, either by voice or instrument. See above, on Ps. xxvii. 6. The light of God's face is the cheering expression of his countenance as indicating favour or benignity. See above, on Ps. iv. 7 (6), xliii.* 3, xliv. 4 (3). To walk in this light is to live in the habitual enjoyment of it. This last clause gives the reason for their being pronounced happy in the first.

17 (16). *In thy name they shall rejoice all the day, and in thy righteousness shall be exalted.* In thy name, in the display of thy perfections. In thy righteousness, *i. e.* in the exercise of that essential rectitude which secures the performance of God's promise and thereby the salvation of his people.

18 (17). *For the beauty of their strength (art) thou, and in thy favour thou wilt lift up our horn.* God is at once their mighty ornament and their glorious protection. See above, on Ps. lxxviii. 61. *In thy favour*, at the time, and by the means, of thy experienced favour. *Lift our horn*, enable us to triumph in security. See above, on Ps. lxxv. 11 (10), and below, on Ps. xcii. 11 (10).

19 (18). *For unto Jehovah* (belongs) *our shield, and to the Holy One of Israel our king.* Our protectors are themselves protected by Jehovah. This construction is much simpler and more natural than that adopted in the English versions, which entirely overlooks the preposition in both clauses, or arbitrarily regards it as a sign of the nominative case. A better construction, although not precisely the true sense, is given in the margin of the English Bible.

20 (19). *Then thou spakest in vision to thy gracious one and saidst, I have laid help on a Mighty (Man) ; I have raised one chosen from* (among) *the people.* The Psalmist here returns to the vocation by David and the promise made to him. See 2 Sam. vii. 17 (compare 1 Chron. xvii. 9), where the divine communication made through Nathan to David is called a *vision. Thy saint* or *gracious one* may signify either of these persons. The ancient versions, followed by the Prayer-Book and some eminent interpreters, have the plural form instead of the singular, *thy saints*, meaning Israel at large, to whom the promise was truly addressed. See 2 Sam. vii. 10, 1 Chron. xvii. 9. *To lay help upon* one is to impart it to him, with a strong implication of descent from above. See above, on Ps. xxi. 6 (5). The gift in this case was not merely for himself, but for others through his agency. God helped him to help the people. *Chosen* has here its strict sense, but not without allusion to its specific use as signifying a young warrior. See above, on Ps. lxxviii. 31, 63.

21 (20). *I have found David my servant; with my holy oil have I anointed him.* This verse removes all doubt as to the person primarily intended in the following verse, but without excluding his successors, and especially the last and greatest of them, to whom the royal dignity was given in the unction of David. See 1 Sam. xvi. 13. This act denoted not only consecration to the divine service, but the spiritual gifts required in order to its right performance. See above, on Ps. ii. 2.

22 (21). *With whom my hand shall be ever present; also my arm shall strengthen him. Ever present*, literally established, permanently fixed. See below, ver. 38 (37), and above, Ps. lxxviii. 37. The hand and arm, as usual, are emblems of strength. See above, on ver. 11, 14 (10, 13).

23 (22). *The enemy shall not vex him, and the son of iniquity shall not*

afflict him. The verb in the first clause means specifically to annoy or persecute as a creditor his debtor. The second clause is copied almost word
for word, from 2 Sam. vii. 10. Compare 1 Chron. xvii. 9.

24 (23). *And I will crush before him his foes, and his haters I will smite.*
The last verb is especially applied to strokes inflicted by the hand of God.

25 (24). *And my faithfulness and my mercy* (shall be) *with him, and in
my name shall his horn be high.* See above, on ver. 17, 18 (16, 17). Faithfulness and mercy are combined, as in Ps. lxxxviii. 12 (11).

26 (25). *And I will set in the sea his hand, and in the floods his right
hand.* I will cause him to lay hands upon them, and exercise authority
over them, as his own possession and domain. *Hand and right hand*, as
in ver. 14 (13). *Sea and floods*, streams, or rivers, as in Ps. xxiv. 2. The
watery parts of the earth are here put for the whole. Compare 1 Chron. xiv. 17.

27 (26). *He shall call me* (or *cry unto me*), *Thou art my Father, my God,
and the rock of my salvation.* The emphatic pronouns in the original bring
out more clearly the mutual relation and reciprocal action of the parties.
With the first clause compare 2 Sam. vii. 14, 1 Chron. xxii. 10, Job.
xvii. 14. With the second compare Ps. xviii. 3 (2), xxxi. 3 (2). *The rock
of my salvation*, the rock that saves me, the hiding-place and stronghold
where my safety lies.

28 (27). *Also I* (as my) *first-born will give him, higher than kings of the
earth.* He shall be treated not only as the son but as the eldest son of God
himself. The same description is applied elsewhere to Israel (Exod. iv. 22),
to Ephraim (Jer. xxxi. 9), and to Christ (Heb. i. 6). The last clause is
borrowed, both in form and substance, from Deut. xxviii. 1 (compare
xxix. 16); but instead of *high above*, we have here *high as to*, in reference
to (or in comparison with) the kings of the earth.

29 (28). *For ever will I keep for him my mercy, and my covenant is sure
to him.* *For ever*, literally to eternity. *Keep, i. e.* keep it in reserve for
him. *My covenant*, or conditional promise. See above, on ver. 4 (3).
Sure, or more exactly, made sure, ratified, confirmed. Compare Isa. lv. 3.

30 (29). *And I will establish for ever his seed, and his throne as the days
of heaven.* See 2 Sam. vii. 12. The promise is now extended from David
to his posterity. *Establish*, literally set or place. The pronoun in the
second clause may refer either to David or his seed. In the latter case, it
might be rendered *its* or *their throne.* The question, however, is purely
grammatical, since the throne of David and the throne of his descendants
are identical. In the last clause the idea of duration is again expressed by
a reference to the stability of nature. See above, on Ps. lxxii. 5, 7, 17,
and compare Deut. xi. 21.

31–33 (30–32). *If his sons forsake my law, and in my judgments will
not walk; if my statutes they profane, and my commandments will not keep;
then will I visit with a rod their transgressions, and with stripes their guilt.*
The promise of perpetual favour to the house of David was not intended to
insure impunity to its unfaithful members. To *profane* God's statutes is
to deny in theory or practice their sacred obligation and divine authority.
The *and* at the commencement of the last verse is equivalent to *then* in
English after a conditional clause. The whole passage is an amplification
of 2 Sam. vii. 14.

34 (33). *And my mercy I will not withdraw from him, and will not
prove false* (or *deal falsely*) *in my faith.* Our idiom requires a *but* to render
clear the relation of this sentence to the foregoing context. The verb in
the first clause means to break or violate, but construed, as it here is, with

the preposition *from*, suggests the idea of breaking an engagement by withdrawing what was stipulated to be given and secured. *Faith* in the last clause means fidelity or truth, as in the phrases, *good faith, keep faith*, &c. See above, on Ps. xliv. 18 (17). The promise in this verse is not to *them* but *him*, not to the sinning individuals mentioned just before, but to the family or race as such, to David as still living in his natural descendants. Compare 1 Kings xi. 36, 2 Kings viii. 19, 2 Chron. vi. 42, Isa. xxxvii. 35.

35 (34). *1 will not profane my covenant, and the utterance of my lips 1 will not change.* In the first clause there is obvious allusion to ver. 32 (31). What God requires of them he renders to them. The engagement is reciprocal. As they are not to profane his covenant by breaking it, neither will He. The obligation is a sacred one on both sides. See below, on the next verse, and above, on Ps. lv. 21 (20). The *utterance* or *outgoing* of the lips is a technical expression of the Law, in reference to oral vows and other engagements. See Num. xxx. 13 (12), Deut. xxiii. 24 (23). It is a stronger expression than *that which I have said* or *promised*, although this is really the meaning here. *I will not change*, evade the execution of my promise by altering its terms or its conditions. Compare the form of expression in Ps. xv. 4.

36 (35). *One (thing) have I sworn in my holiness, I will not lie unto David.* The first word in Hebrew is not an adverb of time (ἅπαξ, *semel*, once), but a numeral adjective in the feminine form, used as the neuter is in Greek and Latin. See above, on Ps. xxvii. 4. " Whatever else may fail, there is one thing that cannot, for I have sworn that it shall come to pass." *In my holiness*, as a holy God, including all divine perfection, but with special reference to moral rectitude. See above, on Ps. lx. 8 (6). The last verb might be rendered, *1 cannot lie*. See Num. xxiii. 19, 1 Sam. xv. 29, and compare Heb. vi. 18, vii. 20, 21. The form of the original is highly idiomatic, *if I lie* unto David. Compare the Hebrew of 1 Sam. xxiv. 7 (6), 2 Sam. iii. 35.

37 (36). *His seed to eternity shall be ; and his throne as the sun before me.* See above, on ver. 30 (29), and compare Ps. xlv. 7 (6). *Shall be,* shall continue to exist. Or the whole phrase may mean, *shall be eternal. As the sun*, see above, on Ps. lxxii. 5, 17. *Before me*, in my sight and under my protection.

38 (37.) *As the moon is fixed eternally, and the witness in the sky is sure.* The verse thus translated, does not repeat the promise in the one before it, but merely confirms it by a further reference to the course of nature, as the customary standard of duration. It is equally grammatical, however, to translate, *as the moon it* (the throne) *shall be fixed for ever, and (as) the witness in heaven is sure.* In either case the witness is the moon. See above, on ver. 7 (6), 29 (28), and compare Ps. lxxii. 5.

39 (38). *And (yet) thou hast cast off and rejected ; thou art wroth with thine Anointed.* Having fully recited and expounded the great promise to the house of David, the psalm now contrasts it with the present reality, and seems to complain that it had not been verified. For a similar transition, see above, Ps. xliv. 10 (9). There is no need of confining this description to the last days of the kingdom of Judah, or to any other period of its history exclusively. If the psalm was really composed by Ethan, as we have no sufficient ground for doubting that it was, he may have designedly so framed it as to suit any season of distress and danger, in which the theocratic sovereign seemed to be forsaken of Jehovah. Both verbs in the first clause signify abhorrent and contemptuous

rejection. See above, on Ps. xv. 4, xliii. 2, xliv. 10 (9), lxxviii. 59, 67, lxxxviii. 15 (14).

40 (39.) *Thou hast broken the covenant of thy servant ; thou hast pro-faned to the earth his crown.* The first verb in Hebrew occurs only here and Lam. ii. 7. The usual explanation is conjectural, or founded on the ancient versions. A cognate verb in Arabic means to *abhor*, which would be appropriate in this place. *The covenant of thy servant, i.e.* thy covenant with thy servant. See above, on ver. 29, 35 (28, 34). The pregnant construction, *profaned to the ground, i.e.* profaned by casting to the ground, occurs above, Ps. lxxiv. 7. The theocratical crown was a sacred or reli-gious dignity, any contempt of which might therefore well be called a pro-fanation. Compare what is said of the priestly diadem. Exod. xxviii. 36, xxix. 6.

41 (40.) *Thou hast broken down all his walls; thou hast made his de-fences a ruin.* As the word translated *walls* is commonly used to denote the enclosures of vineyards, whether walls or hedges, this may be the figure here intended, which is then exchanged, in the last clause, for that of a walled town, with its *defences* or defensive works, its fortifications. See above, on Ps. lxxx. 13 (12). Some interpreters allege that the last word always has the sense of *terror ;* but it may be doubted whether it ever has, whereas that of *ruin* often occurs, particularly in the Book of Proverbs.

42 (41). *All spoil him that pass by the way ; he has become a contempt to his neighbours.* With the first clause compare Ps. lxxx. 13 (12) ; with the last, Ps. lxxx. 7 (6). These resemblances prove nothing as to the rela-tive antiquity of the two psalms, or the date of either. The figure is more fully carried out in Ps. lxxx, but this no more proves that to be the original than it proves it to be the copy. If any such conclusion were legitimate, it would be easier to account for the amplification of the hint here thrown out by a later writer, than for the omission, in the case before us, of so many fine strokes in that admirable apologue. *A contempt,* an object of supercilious pity and disdainful wonder.

43 (42). *Thou hast lifted the right hand of his foes, hast caused to triumph all his enemies.* As the hand, and especially the right hand, is the symbol of exerted strength, and a high hand that of triumphant superiority, espe-cially in war, so to raise the right hand in the first clause of the verse be-fore us, really means nothing more than the literal expression (*caused to triumph*) in the other. This seemed to be in direct contradiction to the promise in ver. 23, 24 (22, 23), as well as to the prayer in Ps. xxv. 2.

44 (43). *Also thou turnest the edge of his sword, and dost not allow him to stand in the battle.* The particle (אַף) at the beginning indicates a climax. Not only was his enemy superior, but himself delinquent and dis-graced. *Edge,* literally *rock, of his sword.* The idea suggested may be that of hardness, as a hard edge is essential to a serviceable weapon. See my note on Isa. xxvii. 1. Some interpreters, however, think it best to adhere to the ordinary usage of *rock* in Hebrew as an emblem of strength, and to un-derstand the whole phrase as meaning *the strength of his sword,* either in the strict sense or in that of *strong sword,* both of which are here appro-priate. See above, on ver. 27 (26). The construction in the last clause is ambiguous, as the pronoun may refer to *sword* or *rock,* no less grammatically than to its possessor. The general sense remains the same, however, as in the similar case above, ver. 30 (29).

45 (44). *Thou hast made (him) to cease from his brightness, and his throne to the earth cast down.* *Brightness* is in various languages a figure

for distinction, eminence, celebrity, or glory. Compare with the last clause what is said of the crown in ver. 40 (39), and of the throne itself in ver. 5 (4).

46 (45). *Thou hast shortened the days of his youth ; thou hast covered him with shame. Selah. His youth,* his youthful energy and vigour. See Job xxxiii. 25. Thou hast made him an object of contempt by cutting short his vigorous career and rendering him prematurely old. This may be said of certain individual kings, as well as of the kingdom when approaching its catastrophe. *Covered him with shame,* literally *covered shame upon him, i. e.* heaped it on him so as to cover him.

47 (46). *How long, Jehovah, wilt thou hide thyself for ever?* (How long) *shall burn, like fire, thy wrath?* On the doubtful construction of the first clause, and the meaning of the combination, *how long for ever,* see above, on Ps. xiii. 2 (1), lxxix. 5. *How long,* literally *until what, i. e.* until what point (*how far*), or until what time (*how long*)?

48 (47). *Remember what duration I have ; why (for) nought hast thou created all the sons of Man* (or *Adam*)? The construction in the first clause is obscure and broken, as if it consisted of incoherent exclamations. *O remember—I—what—duration.* For the meaning of the last word, see above, on Ps. xvii. 14, xxxix. 6 (5), and with the whole clause compare Ps. lxxviii. 39, cxix. 84, Job vii. 6, xiv. 1. The last clause is to be hypothetically understood. " Why hast thou made all men in vain, as must be the case if their short life is entirely filled with suffering ? " Or, " why dost thou give colour and occasion to the charge of having made men to no purpose ? *Why,* literally *on what* (account) or *for what* reason ? The next word in Hebrew (שָׁוְא) is a noun meaning vanity, nonentity, or nothing, here, and in Ps. cxxvii. 1, 2, used adverbially in the sense of vainly, to no purpose, or for nought.

49 (48). *What man shall live and not see death* (but) *rescue his soul from the hand of Sheol ? Selah.* An indirect assertion of the melancholy fact that all must die, rendered still more pointed by the use of a word for *man* implying strength. See above, on Ps. lxxxviii. 5 (4). As if he had said, what man is so strong as to live for ever and escape the common destiny of mortals ? This allusion cannot be preserved in any mere translation. *Rescue,* literally *cause to escape. His soul,* considered as his life or vital principle. *Hand* may be here, as often elsewhere, a figure for power ; or it may have its proper sense and denote the hand of *Sheol,* the *Grave, Mortality* or *Death,* as an ideal person. The *Selah* has the same force as in Ps. xxxix. 6, 12 (5, 11).

50 (49). *Where are thy former mercies, Lord, thou didst swear unto David in thy truth* or (*faithfulness*). The *first* or *former mercies* of the Lord are those which he promised of old, especially to David, as expressly mentioned in the other clause. See above, on ver. 4, 36 (3, 35). The inquiry where they are implies that they have vanished, or that the fulfilment has not become visible. The last clause may be closely united with the first by supplying a relative between them, as in the common version, *which thou swearest unto David.* A simpler and more emphatic syntax is to make it a distinct proposition : *thou didst swear unto David,* and thy oath cannot be broken. See above, on ver. 36 (35). This last idea is involved in the concluding words, *in thy veracity* or *faithfulness.* What God, as a God of truth, has sworn, not only will but must be executed.

51 (50). *Remember, Lord, the reproach of thy servants, my bearing in my bosom all the many nations.* The form of address is the same as in ver. 48

(47). *The reproach of thy servants*, the contempt and disgrace to which they are subjected. *Thy servants*, of whom I am one. Or the sudden transition to the first person singular may shew that the petitioner, in this whole context, is not an individual believer, but the Church at large. *In my bosom* may denote good measure or abundance. See above, on Ps. lxxix. 12. Or *bearing in my bosom* may mean *feeling in my heart, i. e.* intensely, exquisitely, in which case *nations* must be put for the contempt of nations. More probable than either is the figure of gestation, according to which Zion, although now despised or hated by the nations, is one day to be their spiritual mother or their spiritual birth-place. See above, on Ps. lxxxvii. 4, 6. The Hebrew adjective (רַבִּים) may mean either *great* or *many ;* but the latter sense is more agreeable to usage and the collocation of the words in this case. The idiomatic phrase, *all many nations*, is equivalent to saying, all the nations who are many in number. The word *all* might be used, however small the number of the nations. To express the whole idea, therefore, both words were required.

52 (51). *Wherewith thine enemies have reproached, Jehovah, wherewith they have reproached the footsteps of thine Anointed.* The connection indicated by the relative at the beginning is by no means clear. The common version, above given, makes *reproach* in ver. 51 (50) the antecedent. Some interpreters connect the relative with the verb at the beginning of that verse, and give it the force of a conjunction, " remember that (or how) thine enemies have reproached." Its proper meaning as a relative pronoun may be retained by referring it to different antecedents. " (I) whom thine enemies have reproached, (thine enemies) who have reproached the steps of thine Anointed." This last expression seems to mean that they had tracked or followed him, wherever he went, with calumny and insult.

53 (52). *Blessed (be) Jehovah to eternity. Amen, and Amen.* This is commonly regarded as no part of the psalm, but a doxology, marking the conclusion of the third book. See above, on Ps. xli. 14 (13), lxxii. 18–20, and compare the Preface, p. 5.

Psalm 90

THE Fourth Book, according to the ancient traditional division of the Psalter, opens with the oldest Psalm in the collection. Or rather the author of the present arrangement, who was probably no other than Ezra, placed this sublime composition by itself, between the two great divisions of the book, containing respectively the Earlier and Later Psalms. See the Preface, p. 6. It may therefore be regarded as the heart or centre of the whole collection, and indeed as the model upon which even David, "the sweet psalmist of Israel" (2 Sam. xxiii. 1), formed that glorious body of psalmodic literature or hymnology, which, with its later but inspired and authoritative imitations, constitutes the present Book of Psalms. The date of the composition, though uncertain because not recorded, may with most probability be fixed near the close of the Error in the Wilderness, when the dying out of the older generation on account of their transgressions, and the threatened exclusion of Moses himself from the Promised Land, were exactly suited to produce such views of man's mortality and sinfulness as are here presented, but without destroying the anticipation of a bright futurity, such as really ensued upon the death of Moses, and is prospectively disclosed in the conclusion of this psalm. Its great theme is the frailty and

brevity of human life, considered as the consequence of sin, and as a motive
to repentance and obedience. He first contrasts the eternity of God with
the mortality of man, ver. 1–6, which is then described as the effect of the
divine wrath on account of sin, ver. 7–11, and made the ground of a prayer,
with which the psalm concludes, for the speedy restoration of the divine
favour, ver. 12–17.

1. *A Prayer. By Moses, the Man of God. Lord, a home hast thou
been to us, in generation and generation.* The psalm is called *a prayer*,
because the petition at the close (ver. 12–17) contains the essence of the
composition, to which the rest is merely preparatory. For another case
precisely similar, see above, on Ps. lxxxvi. 1. The correctness of the title,
which ascribes the psalm to Moses, is confirmed by its unique simplicity
and grandeur ; its appropriateness to his times and circumstances, as
already stated ; its resemblance to the law in urging the connection between
sin and death ; its similarity of diction to the poetical portions of the Pentateuch, without the slightest trace of imitation or quotation ; its marked
unlikeness to the psalms of David, and still more to those of later date ;
and finally, the proved impossibility of plausibly assigning it to any other
age or author. The arguments against its authenticity have commonly been framed by a preposterous inversion of the evidence, converting into proofs of later date the very points of similarity which prove
that this was the original and model psalm, the primeval basis upon which
even David reared a noble superstructure of his own. The title *Man of
God* is given to Moses, in Deut. xxxiii. 1, Josh. xiv. 6, Ezra iii. 2. and is
often applied to later prophets, especially Elijah and Elisha. See 1 Sam.
ii. 27, 1 Kings xvii. 18, 24, xx. 28, 2 Kings i. 13, iv. 9, 21, 27, 42. It
is here significant, implying that Moses wrote the psalm in this capacity.
See above, on Ps. xviii. 1, xxxvi. 1, where David is in like manner called
the *Servant of Jehovah*, a title given to Moses himself in the account of his
death, Deut. xxxiv. 5, as David, on the other hand, is called the *Man of
God*, 2 Chron. viii. 14. Instead of *hast been* some read *art ;* but though
the preterite of other verbs may be used to express general truths, the present of the substantive verb is so commonly suppressed, that its form, when
inserted, must have some significance. The truth seems to be, that the
verse expresses only what God had been, but implies what he still was
and still would be. *A home,* a fixed or settled dwelling, even while they
wandered in the desert. The same noun is used by Moses, Deut. xxvi. 15,
and a kindred form, Deut. xxxiii. 27. *In generation and generation,* in all
successive generations. See above, on Ps. x. 6, xxxiii. 11, xlv. 18 (17),
xlix. 12 (11), lxi. 7 (6).

2. *Before mountains were born, and* (before) *thou hadst brought forth
earth and land, and* (indeed) *from eternity to eternity, thou* (art) *God.* The
mountains are first mentioned, according to a scriptural usage which describes them as the oldest portions of the earth. See Gen. xlix. 26, Num.
xxiii. 7, Deut. xxxiii. 15, Hab. iii. 6. By a strong but common and intelligible figure, creation is here described as generation. This is true not
only of the first verb but of the second, which is too vaguely rendered in
the common version (*thou hadst formed*). *Earth,* as opposed to heaven ;
land, as opposed to sea. These are separately mentioned, as in the account
of the creation. See Gen. i. 1, 9. The last clause may also be translated,
thou art, O God ! It then simply asserts his existence from eternity. According to the other and more usual construction, it likewise asserts his
omnipotence, the attribute denoted by the divine name here employed.

This is the fuller and more comprehensive sense; but in favour of the other may be urged, that it is simpler and agrees best with the proximate design of the Psalmist to contrast the eternal God with short-lived man.

3. *Thou turnest man even to dust, and sayest, Return, sons of Man* (or *Adam*)*!* The evident allusion to Gen. iii. 19, which is also found in Job x. 9, xxxiv. 15, and reappears in Ps. civ. 29 (compare Ps. ciii. 14), may serve to determine the meaning of the word translated *dust* in the first clause, but which is properly an adjective signifying *crushed*, broken to pieces, ground to powder, and is figuratively applied, in Ps. xxxiv. 19 (18), to brokenness of heart. Compare Isa. lvii. 15. The Hebrew preposition (עַד) is stronger than our *to*, and means as far as, even to. The full sense of the whole phrase is, even to the state of one completely crushed or ground to powder, even to a pulverised condition. The shortness and fragility of human life is thus brought into the strongest contrast with the eternity of God.

4. *For a thousand years in thine eyes (are) as yesterday when it is past and a watch in the night.* However long human life may appear to man himself, it is in God's sight evanescent and contemptible. Even the patriarchal measure, which so often approximated to a thousand years, was in God's sight like a single day in man's, or rather like a mere subdivision of it, a third part of the night, which was divided by the ancient Hebrews into three watches. See above, on Ps. lxiii. 7 (6). That this division was as old as Moses, may be seen from Exod. xiv. 24. *When it is past*, or *passing*. It might also be translated, *for it passes, i. e.* no less hastily and swiftly. This verse is quoted and amplified, but without any change of meaning, 2 Pet. iii. 8.

5. *Thou sweepest them away—a sleep are they—in the morning, like the grass, they pass away.* The first Hebrew verb has no equivalent in English ; it means to sweep away or carry off, as by a driving rain. The supposition of a reference to the flood is not necessary, though admissible. A derivative form of the same verb occurs above, Ps. lxxvii. 18 (17). The comparison of human life to a sleep or dream is common in all languages. The morning is mentioned as the time of waking, the time when we are most impressed with the unsubstantial nature of our dreams. See above, Ps. lxxiii. 20, and compare Ps. xxxix. 7 (6). The *grass* is an additional but obvious emblem of caducity. The last verb is not a plural form in Hebrew, but agrees with *sleep*, or rather with *man*, in the generic sense, whose life is here compared to sleep.

6. *In the morning it blooms and* (then) *passes away,* (for) *at evening he mows and it withers.* The mention of the morning, in ver. 5, as following the night, suggests the mention of the morning here, as followed by the evening. The first verb means not merely to flourish in the wide sense, but to bloom, as plants do. See above, on Ps. lxxii. 16, and compare Num. xvii. 23 (8), which proves it to be a Mosaic expression. The verbs may agree with *grass*, or with *man*, whom the grass represents, more probably the latter. The idea conveyed by supplying *then* is really involved in the grammatical relation of the Hebrew verbs, the second of which never means to grow or sprout, but always to pass or undergo a change. The third verb is active, but may be construed with an indefinite subject, and is then equivalent in meaning to a passive, *he is mown and withers.* The withering is not here referred to as the effect of natural decay but of violent excision. With the whole verse compare Ps. xxxvii. 2, ciii. 15, Job xiv. 2.

7. *For we fail in thine anger, and in thy wrath are we affrighted.* The natural decay or violent interruption of man's life is the effect of God's displeasure. The first verb means to waste away, decay, wear out, cease to exist. Compare its use in Ps. lxxi. 9, lxxiii. 26. The other verb is very inadequately represented by the English *troubled*. It means shocked, confounded, agitated, terror-stricken. See above, on Ps. ii. 5, vi. 3, 4 (2, 3), xlviii. 6 (5), lxxviii. 33, lxxxiii. 16 (15), and below, on Ps. civ. 29, and compare my note on Isa. lxv. 23. It here denotes the natural instinctive dread of death. There is here a very sensible progression in the thought. Thus far the Psalmist had insisted merely on the frailty and brevity of human life ; but now he proceeds further and propounds the fearful doctrine, that this sorrowful mortality is not an accident but an infliction, the direct effect of the divine wrath. Whatever instrumental agencies may be employed to kill us, our real destroyer is the anger of our Maker.

8. *Thou hast set our iniquities before thee, our secret (sins) in the light of thy countenance.* As man's mortality is the effect of God's wrath, so this wrath itself is the effect of sin. And this sin becomes the cause of death. See Gen. ii. 17, and compare Rom. v. 12. The verse before us represents God in the act of shortening man's life, and gives the necessary explanation of what might otherwise have seemed at variance with his infinite benevolence. The Bible, as an eminent interpreter has well said. throws the blame of death entirely on man himself. When God slays man, he puts his sins before him, looks directly at them ; not only those which are notorious, but those which are concealed from every eye but that of omniscience. See Jer. xvi. 17, Heb. iv. 14, and compare Ps. xix. 15 (14), 1 Cor. iv. 4, 5. Another reading in the last clause, and most probably the true one, makes *secret* or *concealed* a singular and not a plural form, *our secret ;* but the reference is still to sin. The word translated *light* does not properly denote the element itself, but that from which it is derived, a *luminary,* just as we call a candle or a lamp *a light.* See above, on Ps. lxxiv. 16. The precise sense seems to be, that God holds our sins to the light of his own countenance, and therefore cannot fail to see them.

9. *For all our days are gone in thine anger ; we spend our years like a thought.* The *all* in the first clause is emphatic. What he says is true of our whole life. *Are gone,* literally *turned away,* as an act preparatory to departure. The word translated *anger,* though synonymous, is not identical with either of those used above in ver. 7. It occurs, however, in Ps. vii. 7 (6), and according to its derivation properly denotes an outbreak of angry feeling. *Spend,* not as a mere synonyme of *pass,* but in the strong sense of consuming, wasting, as in Job xxxvi. 11 (compare xxi. 13). The Hebrew verb is the causative of that translated *fail* in ver. 7. The use of *years* as a parallel to *days* gives the sentence a climacteric effect. The word translated *thought* is elsewhere applied to audible sound (Ezek. ii. 10, Job xxxvii. 2), but only as the natural spontaneous expression of the thoughts and feelings, not to others but one's self. See above, on Ps. lxiii. 7 (6), lxxvii. 13 (12). By some strange misapprehension the Septuagint and Vulgate make it mean a *spider,* and the English versions have the singular periphrasis, *a tale that is told.*

10. *The days of our years !* *In them* (are contained) *seventy years, and if with strength eighty years, and their pride (is) trouble and mischief, for he drives* (us) *fast and we fly away.* The parallelism of *days* and *years* in the preceding verse suggests their combination here, a combination used by Moses elsewhere in describing the long lives of the patriarchal history. See

Gen. xxv. 7, xlvii. 8 (9). The words may here be taken simply as an absolute nominative, (*as for*) *the days of our years*, *in them*, *&c.* See above, on Ps. lxxxix. 3 (2). But it adds to their significance, as well as to the beauty of the sentence, to explain them as a kind of wondering exclamation, as if such a term scarcely deserved to be computed. *In them are seventy years*, this is what they comprise or comprehend, it is to this that they amount. The life of Moses was much longer (Deut. xxxiv. 7), but even in the history appears to be recorded as a signal exception to the general rule. *If with strength*, if accompanied with strength, or, as some prefer to construe it, if (the person be endued) with (more than usual) strength. The plural (*strengths*) may be an idiomatic form of speech, simply equivalent to the singular, or an intensive term denoting extraordinary strength. See above on Ps. xviii. 51 (50). *Their pride*, the best part of our days or years, the part in which we are most confident or most contented. The words translated *trouble and mischief* are in usage both applied to suffering at the hands or through the fault of others. The common version of the next verb (*it is cut off*) rests upon a doubtful etymology. In the only other place where the Hebrew verb certainly occurs (Num. xi. 31), it is applied to the driving of the quails by a strong wind over the camp of Israel. It may here agree with God himself, or with a subject undefined, *one drives* (us), which is tantamount to saying, *we are driven*. *Fast*, literally (*in*) *haste* or *hastily*. *And*, as a necessary consequence *we fly* before the propellent power.

11. *Who knows the power of thine anger and, according to thy fear, thy wrath?* The separation of the clauses as distinct propositions makes the last unmeaning. The whole is one interrogation, implying strong negation, as if he had said, no one knows the power of thine anger. See above, on Ps. xiv. 4, liii. 5 (4). The sense is not that no one can, but that no one will know it, as he might and ought. *Knows*, literally *knowing*, *i. e.* habitually. See above, on Ps. i. 6. *The power of thine anger*, its degree and the extent to which it operates. *According to thy fear*, as true piety or reverence for God demands. *Thy wrath*, the same word that is used in the first clause of ver. 9 above.

12. *To number our days thus make us know, and we will bring a heart of wisdom.* The verb translated *make us know* is the causative of that in the preceding verse, to which there is an obvious allusion. It is therefore probable that they were meant to govern the same object. " Who knows the power of thine anger ?" " So make us know (the power of thine anger)." The first words of the verse before us are then not immediately dependent on the phrase *make* (*us*) *know*, but merely indicate the end for which the knowledge was desired. " In order that we may number our days, *i. e.* know and feel how few they are, thus make us know, *i. e.* give us this knowledge of the connection between God's wrath and our own mortality." The common version of the last clause (*that we may apply our hearts unto wisdom*) is forced and ungrammatical, without an arbitrary change of pointing. The only admissible construction of the masoretic text is that first given, which may either mean, as some of the rabbinical interpreters suppose, " we will bring into ourselves (*i. e.* acquire) a heart of wisdom," or " we will bring (as an offering to thee) a heart of wisdom," with allusion to Gen. iv. 3, 4, where the same verb is absolutely used of Cain and Abel's offerings.

13. *Return, Jehovah ! How long* (wilt thou forsake us) ?—*And repent as to thy servants*. To the prayer that the people may understand the causes of God's wrath is now added a prayer for its removal. The loss of

God's favour is, as usual, represented as his absence. The aposiopesis in the question (*how long ?*) is like that in Ps. vi. 4 (3), xiii. 2 (1). This clause being parenthetical, what follows is connected by the copulative particle with the imperative at the beginning. The meaning of the last clause is, so change thy dealing with thy servants as if thou hadst repented of afflicting them. The same bold form of speech is used by Moses elsewhere. See Exod. xxxii. 12, Deut. xxxii. 36, and compare the imitations in Judges ii. 18, Jer. xv. 6, Joel ii. 13, Jonah iv. 2, Ps. cxxxv. 14.

14. *Satisfy us, in the morning, with thy mercy, and* (then) *we shall rejoice and be glad through all our days.* God's grace is here presented as the food required for the sustenance of his people. *Satisfy* or *sate us, i. e.* fill us, abundantly supply us. *In the morning*, early, speedily, perhaps with an allusion to the night as a common figure for affliction. See above, on Ps. v. 4 (3), xlvi. 6 (5), xlix. 15 (14), lix. 17 (16), lxxxviii. 14 (13). The oblique construction of the last clause, *that we may rejoice, &c.*, is really involved in the direct one, which is much more pointed and emphatic. *In* or *through all our days, i. e.* throughout the remainder of our lives. The English idiom allows the suppression of the particle, as in the common version.

15. *Make us glad according to the days thou hast afflicted us, the years we have seen evil. According to*, literally *as* or *like*. The meaning is, compensate all our sufferings by proportionate enjoyments. The ellipsis of the relative is common in both idioms. The English Bible, by supplying it, enfeebles the expression without making the sense clearer. *Days* and *years*, as in ver. 9. The plural forms in the Hebrew are unusual and borrowed from Deut. xxxii. 7, a Mosaic feature of the psalm which cannot possibly be reproduced in any version.

16. *Let appear unto thy servants thy doing, and thy glory on their sons* (or *children*). He prays that even to the elder generation there may be vouchsafed a *token for good* (Ps. lxxxvi. 17), *i. e.* some assurance of the favours to be actually bestowed upon their children. Thus understood, the use of the two prepositions, *to* and *on*, is not unmeaning or fortuitous. God's *work* or *doing* is the course of his providential dealings, as in Ps. xcii. 5 (4) below; his *glory*, the manifestation of his divine perfections in external act. See above, on Ps. viii. 6 (5) xlv. 4 (3). This was to appear not only *to* but *on* the younger race, *i. e.* in their own experience.

17. *And let the beauty of Jehovah our God be upon us, and the work of our hands establish upon us, and the work of our hands, establish thou it.* While the glory of Jehovah is expected to be fully revealed only in his dealings with the next generation, he is still besought to grant their fathers the experimental knowledge of his *beauty*, loveliness, or all that renders him an object of affection. See above, on Ps. xxvii. 4. The work of our hands is a favourite Mosaic phrase for all that we do or undertake, all our affairs and interests. See Deut. xiv. 29, xvi. 15, xxiv. 19, xxviii. 12, xxx. 9. To *establish* or *confirm* it is to prosper and succeed it, to bring it to a favourable issue. The expression *on us*, as before, suggests the idea of an influence exerted and a favour granted from above. The *yea* of the common version is substituted for the idiomatic repetition of the copulative *and* in the original.

Psalm 91

AN amplification of the theme, that God is the dwelling-place and refuge of his people. This and other points of contact with the Prayer of Moses seem to mark it as an imitation of that psalm, and thereby account for its position in the Psalter. The most remarkable peculiarity of form in the psalm before us is the frequent change and alternation of the persons. The only division which can well be made is that into two stanzas or strophes, supposed to be marked by the recurrence in ver. 9 to the theme propounded in ver. 1.

1. *Sitting* (or *dwelling*) *in the secret place of the Most High, in the shadow of the Almighty he is lodged.* The common version seems to make this an identical proposition, amounting really to this, that he whom God protects is protected by him. To avoid this, some make the whole verse a mere description of the person speaking in the next verse, and as this seems to be forbidden by the use of the first person there, they either make an arbitrary change of pointing (אֹמֵר) for (אָמַר), or suppose a sudden change of person, as in other parts of this same psalm. Better than either of these constructions is a third, which makes the parallel clauses of this first verse descriptive of an ideal person, with whom the speaker is then tacitly identified. As if he had said, " happy the man who dwells," &c., and then added, " such is my condition ; I can say," &c. For the figure of a secret place or covert, see above, on Ps. xxvii. 5, xxxi. 21 (20), xxxii. 7 ; for that of a shadow, on Ps. xvii. 8, xxxvi. 8 (7), lvii. 2 (1). The divine titles, *Highest* and *Almighty*, suggest the reason of this perfect safety. The latter is the patriarchal title mentioned in Exod. vi. 3, where it is combined with (אֵל) a more familiar name denoting the same attribute. The last verb is strictly a reflective, and as such means to take up one's lodgings, to domesticate one's self, implying a voluntary choice more clearly than the primitive verb, as used above, in Ps. xxv. 13, xxx. 6 (5), xlix. 13 (12).

2. *I will say to Jehovah, My refuge and my fortress, my God, I will trust in him.* The first verb, while it expresses purpose or determination, includes both a present and potential meaning. *I can say,* I have reason and a right to say ; and *I do* (habitually) *say.* In order to avoid another change of person, the common version and some others read *of the Lord*, which is admissible but needless. See above, on Ps. iii. 3 (2). Compare the other figures here used to denote divine protection with those in Ps. xviii. 3 (2), lxxi. 7. In the last clause, *I will trust in him*, there may seem to be another sudden change of person ; but these words are really equivalent to a relative construction, *in whom I trust*, and may therefore be used even in a direct address.

3. *For lo, he will free thee from the fowler's snare, from the plague of mischiefs.* The confiding soul is now addressed directly in the tone of promise. The supposition of responsive choirs is a gratuitous refinement. The *fowler's snare* is a figure for insidious and complicated dangers. See above, on Ps. xviii. 6 (5), and below, on Ps. cxxiv. 7, and compare 2 Tim. ii. 26. The parallelism requires *plague* or *pestilence* to be taken as a metaphor, no less than *snare*. Both probably denote dangers arising from the craft of wicked enemies, to which the word translated *mischiefs* is peculiarly appropriate. See above, on Ps. v. 10 (9), lii. 4, 9 (2, 7), lvii. 2 (1).

4. *With his pinion he will cover thee, and under his wings thou shalt find*

shelter ; shield and buckler (is) his truth. Compare the figure of an eagle, Deut. xxxii. 11. For the meaning of the first noun, see above, on Ps. lxviii. 14 (13). *Cover thee,* literally *cover* (or *provide a covering*) *for thee.* Find *shelter* or *take refuge,* see above on Ps. ii. 12. The word translated *buckler* is properly a participle, and means *surrounding.* See above, on Ps. xxxv. 2.

5. *Thou shalt not be afraid for the terror by night, for the arrow* (that) *flies by day.* Shalt not fear, *i. e.* shalt have no reason for alarm. *Terror by night,* literally *of night, i. e.* nightly or nocturnal terror. There is no need of restricting this expression to any particular form of danger or distress, since all are usually aggravated by their occurrence in the night. Should any specific sense be put upon the figure of an arrow, from analogy and usage, it would be that of human enmity. See above, on Ps. lviii. 8 (7). The Hebrew preposition, in both clauses, properly means *from, i. e.* arising or proceeding from, occasioned by, in consequence of, something else.

6. *For the plague* (that) *in darkness walks, for the pestilence* (that) *wastes at noon.* Here the words are to be taken in their proper sense, and not as in ver. 3, where they are figures for a different kind of danger, or for danger in the general.

7. *There shall fall at thy side a thousand, and a myriad at thy right hand; to thee it shall not come nigh.* This is equivalent to saying in our idiom, *though a thousand fall, &c.,* which, however, would not be an exact translation, as it substitutes a hypothetical for an affirmative proposition. For the double sense and usage of the word translated *myriad,* see above, on Ps. iii. 7 (6), and compare the cognate form, Ps. lxviii. 18 (17). *Myriad* represents the original term better than *ten thousand,* because it is wholly different, in form and etymology, from that translated *thousand.*

8. *Only with thine eyes shalt thou behold, and the recompence of wicked* (*men*) *see.* The *only* puts mere sight in opposition to experience or participation. Compare Deut. xxxii. 35, 41. As usual in such cases, it is implied that the destruction of the wicked and deliverance of the righteous will be coincident and simultaneous. See below, on Ps. xcii. 12 (11).

9. *For thou, Jehovah,* (*art*) *my refuge. The Most High hast thou made thy home* (or *habitation*). The construction adopted in the English Bible is a forced one, only assumed in order to avoid the *enallage* or sudden change of person, which, however, is characteristic of this psalm. Equally needless and objectionable is the supposition of responsive choirs.

10. *There shall not happen to thee* (*any*) *evil, and a stroke shall not approach into thy tent.* The first verb is a causative passive, and strictly means, shall not be suffered or allowed to happen. *Evil, i. e.* natural evil, suffering or distress. The word translated *stroke* is very commonly applied to God's strokes or afflictive judgments. See above, on Ps. xxxviii. 12 (11), xxxix. 11 (10). *Into thy tent* is an expression apparently intended to qualify the promise, which might otherwise have seemed too absolute and inconsistent with the context, from which we learn that danger was to draw nigh, even to the righteous, but not so as actually to enter his tent, and take up its abode with him.

11. *For his angels he will charge concerning thee, to keep thee in all thy ways.* The plural *angels* shews that there is no allusion to a guardian spirit attending the individual believer, but merely to the angels collectively, as ministering spirits, the instrumental agents of God's providential care over his people. See Heb. i. 14. The promise here given does not extend to dangers rashly incurred or presumptuously sought, and was therefore no justification of the act to which our Lord was tempted by the devil, Mat.

iv. 6.   That the mere omission of the phrase *in all thy ways* was a part of
the temptation, seems to be a gratuitous refinement, as our Lord himself
makes no such charge ; as the first words of the sentence would of course
suggest the rest ; and as *ways*, in the usage of the Psalms, does not mean
ways of duty, but the ways in which a man is led by providence.   Neither
the tempter's argument nor our Lord's reply to it would be at all affected
by the introduction of the words suppressed.

12. *Upon* (their) *hands shall they bear thee, lest thou strike against the stone
thy foot.*   The dual form, denoting *both hands*, might be regarded as emphatic
and suggestive of peculiar care ; but the Hebrew noun has no other plural
form in common use.   A smooth path and unimpeded walk is a common
figure for prosperity and safety.   Compare Prov. iii. 23.

13. *On lion and adder thou shalt tread ; thou shalt trample young lion and
dragon.*   These are commonly supposed to be strong figures for the two
kinds of danger from which men need protection, open violence and secret
treachery.   The last word denotes a serpent, as in Exod. vii. 9.   The
specific meaning of the parallel term is unimportant.   The young lion
(not the lion's whelp) is mentioned as peculiarly fierce and greedy.   See
above, on Ps. xvii. 12, xxxiv. 11, xxxv. 17.   From this verse our Lord
derived the terms in which he promised protection to his followers, Luke
x. 19.

14. *For he has set his love upon me, and I will rescue him ; I will set him
on high because he knows my name.*   The first verb is a very strong expression for the warmest and most violent attachment, corresponding in part
with our idiomatic phrase *to fall in love*, and followed by a kindred preposition.   It seems to be here used to describe God as an object of supreme
devotion to the true believer.   *Rescue him*, cause him to escape.   *Set him
on high, i.e.* beyond the reach of danger.   See above, on Ps. xviii. 3 (2),
49 (48), xx. 2 (1), lix. 2 (1), lxix. 30 (29).   *Knows my name*, has already
experienced my goodness and seen the evidence of my perfections.   See
above, on Ps. v. 12 (11), ix. 11 (10).

15. *He shall call me and I will answer him.   With him* (am) *I in trouble.
I will deliver him and honour him.*   The meaning of the first clause is essentially the same as if he had said, *when he calls I will answer*, but with much
more directness and force in the expression.   *Calls me* to his aid, invokes
me, prays to me.   *Answer him* by granting his request, the idea commonly
conveyed by the Hebrew verb here used.   See above, on Ps. iii. 5 (4).   The
futures have their proper sense, as this is a direct and formal promise.   *I
will be with him* would have been expressed in the same manner ; but *I am
with him* is still stronger, for it describes God as already present for the
protection and deliverance of his people.   *Deliver him*, extricate him from
his embarrassments and dangers ; and lest the promise should be thought
to ensure mere safety, it is added, *I will honour him*, procure for him the
respect of others by shewing that I favour him myself.

16. (With) *length of days will I satisfy him, and will shew him my salvation.*   With the first clause compare Exod. xx. 12, Deut. v. 16, Ps. xxiii. 6.
Satisfy or *satiate, i.e.* abundantly supply and fully gratify his largest wishes.
With the last clause compare Ps. l. 23, where we have the same idiomatic
construction of the verb to *see* with the preposition *in*, meaning to behold
with strong emotion, and especially, emotion of a pleasurable kind.   For a
different application of the same phrase, see above, on Ps. xxxvii. 34.   In
the last three verses, God is himself the speaker, although not expressly so
announced.   See above, on Ps. xlvi. 11 (10), lxxv. 3, 4 (2, 3), lxxxvii. 4.

Psalm 92

1. *A Psalm. A Song. For the Sabbath-Day.* The second title designates the psalm as one of praise, in strict conformity to its contents. The
immediate subject of the praise is the exhibition of God's power and wisdom
in his providential dealings, both with the wicked and the righteous. As
one main design of the Sabbath was to afford an opportunity for the admiring
contemplation of God's works or doings, the psalm before us was peculiarly
appropriate at such a time, and the third clause of the inscription is evidently
correct.

2 (1). *Good* (is it) *to give thanks unto Jehovah, and to make music to thy
name, Most High !* The duty about to be performed is here described as
not only right but pleasant. For the meaning of the two verbs, see above,
on Ps. vii. 18 (17).

3 (2). *To declare in the morning thy mercy, and thy faithfulness in the
nights.* The sentence is continued from the preceding verse, the infinitive
with which this opens being governed by the phrase *it is good. In the
morning*, taken by itself, implies eagerness and promptness, and with the
parallel phrase *(in the nights)* unremitting diligence and constancy. See
above, on Ps. xvi. 7, xlii. 9 (8), lxxvii. 7 (6), lxxxviii. 14 (13), xc. 14 (13).
Faithfulness in the fulfilment of promises. Faithfulness and mercy are
here combined like truth and mercy in Ps. lxxxix. 15 (14).

4 (3). *On decachord and on lyre, on meditation with a harp.* The first
word in Hebrew means a decade, a group or set of ten, and then an instrument of ten strings. See above, on Ps. xxxiii. 2. In the last clause, by a
bold but intelligible figure, *meditation* is referred to as an instrument, precisely as the lyre and harp are, the latter being joined with it as a mere
accompaniment.

5 (4). *For thou hast gladdened me, Jehovah, with thy work ; in the doings
of thy hands I will rejoice.* This verse introduces the theme or subject of
the praise proposed, to wit, the work and doings of the Lord, *i. e.* his providential dealings. See above, on Ps. xc. 16, 17. The last verb denotes
properly the vocal expression of an inward joy.

6 (5). *How great are thy doings, Jehovah,* (how) *exceedingly deep thy
thoughts !* Thoughts and doings are correlative expressions, signifying plan
and execution. *Deep*, not mysterious, but vast, immense, and inexhaus-
tible, corresponding to *great* in the other clause. With this verse, compare
Ps. xl. 6 (5), Isa. lv. 9, Rom. xi. 23.

7 (6). *A man-brute will not know, and a fool will not understand this.*
The compound term at the beginning means a man who is no better than
a brute, *i. e.* equally irrational. See above, on Ps. xl. 21 (20), lxxiii. 22,
and below, on Ps. xciv. 8. *Will not*, cannot, or does not know. *This,*
i. e. what has just been said as to the depth of God's providential plans and
purposes.

8 (7). *In the springing up of wicked* (men) *like grass, and* (when) *all the
doers of iniquity bloom, (it is) that they may be destroyed for ever.* The infinitive, as well as the future, indicates the time of action. The literal
translation of the last words is, *for them to be destroyed until eternity.*

9 (8). *And thou* (art) *Most High to eternity, Jehovah !* This brief but
pregnant proposition is the centre of the psalm, and at the same time a
summary of its contents. The superlative expression *Most High* is here
used to translate a single Hebrew word which strictly means a height or

high place, but here denotes that which holds the highest place in the scale
of being.   For other applications of the same word, see above, on Ps. vii.
8 (7), x. 5, xviii. 17 (16).

10 (9). *For lo, thine enemies, Jehovah—for lo, thine enemies shall perish ;
dispersed shall be all the doers of iniquity.*   Jehovah must be the Most High,
because his enemies not only yield to him, but perish in his presence.   Here,
as in Ps. lxxxix. 11, 52 (10, 51), the enemies of God and of his people are
identified.   The last verb is properly a reflective, and may be translated,
they shall scatter (or *disperse*) *themselves*, implying more activity and eagerness than the simple passive, *shall be scattered*.   Compare Job iv. 11.

11 (10). *And thou hast raised, like the unicorn's, my horn ; I am anointed
with fresh oil.*   He now contrasts his own experience with that of his enemies and God's.   With the figure of the first clause compare Ps. xviii.
3 (2), lxxv. 5, 6, 11 (4, 5, 10), lxxxix. 18, 25 (17, 24).   *I am anointed*
or *I anoint* (my head), the Hebrew verb being elsewhere always active.
The figure is borrowed from the ancient custom of anointing the head on
festive occasions.   See above, on Ps. xxiii. 5.   *Fresh oil*, literally *green*,
i. e. verdant, a quality properly belonging to the tree being here transferred
to its most valuable product.

12 (11). *And my eye has looked upon my enemies ; of those rising up
against me, evil-doers, my ears shall hear.*   The sense is that he sees and
hears what is become of them.   Their destruction is implied, though not
expressed.   The word translated *enemies* occurs only here.   According to
the most probable etymology it means *watchers*, liers in wait or ambush.
See above, on Ps. xxvii. 11, liv. 7 (5), lvi. 3 (2), lix. 11 (10), where a cognate form occurs.   *My insurgents*, or those rising up against me, expresses
the accessory idea of rebellion against rightful authority.   See above, on
Ps. iii. 2 (1), liv. 5 (3), lxxxvi. 14.   The addition of *malefactors*, evil-doers,
shews that it is not merely as his enemies, but on account of their transgressions against God, that he expects his foes to perish.

13 (12). *A righteous* (man) *like a palm-tree shall sprout, like a cedar in
Lebanon shall grow.*   Some suppose an allusion to the fact that these trees
thrive even in the most unfavourable situations.   All that it is necessary to
assume, however, is that as trees in general are natural and common emblems of a prosperous existence, so the same idea is conveyed with still
more emphasis by the noblest species.   The supposition of a reference to
the decorations of the temple is gratuitous and far-fetched.

14 (13). *Planted in the house of Jehovah, in the courts of our God they
shall bloom* (or *flourish*).   See above, on Ps. lii. 10 (8), where the same
image is presented, in a still more specific form, the olive-tree being there
particularly mentioned.

15 (14.) *Still shall they bear fruit in old age ; fat and green shall they be.*
In old age, literally in grey or hoary hair.   Of the epithets in the last clause
one properly denotes an animal, the other a vegetable quality.   The essential idea is that of the foregoing verse carried out into detail.

16 (15). *To declare that Jehovah is just—my Rock—and no unrighteousness in Him.*   See above on Ps. xviii. 3 (2), and compare Deut. xxxii. 4.
The epithet *just* denotes the essential rectitude of God, including his veracity and faithfulness to his engagements.   See above, on Ps. xxv. 8.   *My
Rock* may be simply in apposition with Jehovah, *Jehovah my Rock is just*,
or a second predicate, *Jehovah is just* (and) *my Rock.*

Psalm 93

THE theme of this psalm is God's superiority to all opposing powers, and the consequent safety of his church and people. There are strong reasons for believing that it was designed, with the one before it, to form a pair or double psalm. Besides those drawn from the number of verses and of the divine names, this whole psalm may be described as an amplification of the laconic dictum in Ps. xcii. 9 (8). There is nothing to determine its precise date ; but there seem to be expressions in it, which imply the existence of imminent danger to the theocracy from some great hostile power.

1. *Jehovah reigns ;* (with) *majesty he clothes himself ; Jehovah clothes himself with strength* (and) *girds himself; also established is the world, it shall not be moved.* The first clause does not simply affirm Jehovah's sovereignty as a general truth, but announces the fact that he has just become king or begun to reign, *i. e.* manifested himself anew in his regal character. The same form of the verb is used in reference to the accession of earthly monarchs, 2 Sam. xv. 10, 1 Kings i. 11, 13, 2 Kings ix. 13. The word translated *majesty* is the one applied in Ps. lxxxix. 11 (10) to the swelling of the sea. Its use here may be intended to suggest the superiority of God to the powers of this world. *Clothes himself with*, literally puts on, wears. The other verb is reflective in form. The *also* introduces the consequence of this exaltation. See below, Ps. xcvi. 10, xcvii. 1, xcix. 1, and compare Isa. xxiv. 23, Obad. 21, Zech. xiv. 9, Rev. xi. 17, xix. 6.

2. *Fixed (is) thy throne of old ; from eternity (art) thou.* *Fixed*, firmly established, permanently settled. Compare 2 Sam. vii. 13, 16, 1 Kings ii. 45. *Of old*, literally *from then*, as in the margin of the English Bible. Compare Prov. viii. 22, Isa. xlviii. 3, v. 7. With the last clause compare Ps. xc. 2, and with the whole verse Rev. i. 17.

3. *The floods have raised, Jehovah, the floods have raised their voice ; the floods will raise their crash*, or crashing noise. The last Hebrew word occurs only here, but its etymology is obvious and perfectly analogous to that of waves or *breakers* in the next verse. The idea here conveyed is that of the noise made by the dashing of waves against each other or upon the shore. The preterite and future forms include the present, but suggest the additional idea of what has been heretofore and may be expected to continue hereafter. The emphatic repetition of the verb is like that in ver. 1, and reappears in this whole series (Ps. xci.–c.) as a characteristic feature.

4. *More than the voices of waters—many—mighty—sea-billows—mighty in the high-place (is) Jehovah.* *More than*, literally *from, away from*, the particle by which comparison is commonly expressed in Hebrew. The common version of the next clause, *mighty waves of the sea*, is scarcely grammatical, as the adjective, according to analogy and usage, cannot agree with the noun following, but must be in apposition with the adjective before it, and agree with the same object. The word translated *mighty* corresponds, in part, to our epithets, *sublime* and *grand*. See above, on Ps. viii. 1. *Sea-billows*, literally *breakers of the sea*. Compare Ps. xlii. 8 (7), lxxxviii. 8 (7), Jonah ii. 4 (3). That the comparison was meant to be between the noise of the sea and that of thunder considered as the voice of God, is an admissible but not a necessary supposition. See above, on Ps. xxix. 5.

5. *Thy testimonies are sure, very (sure) ; to thy house suits* (or *is becoming*) *holiness, Jehovah, unto length of days.* The testimonies of God are all

the provisions of his Law, as in Ps. xix. 8 (7), xxv. 10, but with special reference, in this as in several other cases, to its promises. See above, on Ps. lx. 1, lxxx. 1. The verb here used is a passive, meaning strictly to be founded, settled, or secured. From this clause is borrowed the form of expression in Rev. xix. 9, xxi. 5, xxii. 6. The intensive adverb *very* or *exceedingly* has the same effect as when in English we use an epithet and add *extremely so* or *very much so*. The verb translated *suits* (or *is becoming*) is the root of the adjective used in Ps. xxxiii. 1. Compare my note on Isa. lii. 7. *Holiness* is by some understood to mean *sacredness*, immunity from profanation, and of course from violent intrusion. See above, on Ps. lxxiv. 3. The house of God is here referred to, as the place where he dwelt with his people, and they with him. *To length of days*, see Ps. xxiii. 6.

Psalm 94

THIS psalm may be divided into two parts, in the first of which the ancient church complains of Jehovah's absence and apparent desertion, and of the consequent triumph of his enemies, ver. 1–11, while in the second she asks and confidently looks for his return and their destruction, ver. 12–23. There is nothing to determine the precise date of the composition, much less to restrict it to any particular historical occasion. Though some things in it seem peculiarly appropriate to the state of Judah on the eve of the Babylonish conquest, it is so constructed as to be a vehicle of pious feeling to the church in various emergencies.

1. *God of revenges, Jehovah, God of revenges, shine forth!* Some interpreters, following the ancient versions, make the last Hebrew word a finite verb, as it certainly is in Deut. xxxiii. 2, Ps. l. 2, lxxx. 2 (1). The meaning then is, *he has shined* or *shines*, and the psalm opens with a confident anticipation of God's intervention, as in Ps. xciii. 1, xcvii. 1, xcix. 1. In this case, however, the tone of confidence does not reappear until ver. 12, and the imperatives in ver 2 make the similar construction of the verb in this case much more natural, though less agreeable to usage, than the other. The terms of this verse are borrowed from Deut. xxxii. 35, xxxiii. 2. See above, on Ps. l. 2. The plural form (*revenges*) denotes fulness and variety. See above, on Ps. xviii. 51 (50). This expression, with the two divine names (*El* and *Jehovah*) recognise God as almighty, eternal, self-existent, bound by covenant to his people, and alone entitled to take vengeance.

2. *Raise thyself, Judge of the Earth, return a recompence upon the proud.* The first verb is equivalent in meaning to the more familiar term, *arise, i.e.* arouse thyself from inactivity, address thyself to action. See above, on Ps. iii. 8 (7). The specific sense, which some interpreters assume, " Ascend the judgment-seat," is not expressed by this verb, but suggested by the context. The word translated *recompence* strictly means the treatment of one person by another, to return which is to retaliate or recompense it. See above, on Ps. vii. 5 (4), and compare Ps. lxxix. 12. The use of the particle *upon* implies the inequality of the parties or the superiority of the avenger, from whom the recompence, as it were, comes down upon the guilty.

3. *How long shall wicked* (men), *Jehovah, how long shall wicked* (men) *triumph?* The question, as usual in such cases, implies that they have already triumphed long enough or too long, and therefore really involves a prayer that they may triumph no longer. The interruption and resumption of the sentence is like that in ver. 1, and in Ps. xcii. 9 (8), xciii. 1, 3.

4. (How long) *shall they pour forth, utter insolence, talk of themselves—all the workers of iniquity?* This is usually taken as an independent proposition, *they pour forth*, &c. But it seems a more natural construction to continue the interrogation from the other sentence. *Pour forth* is a figure for excessive and unadvised speech. See above, on Ps. lix. 8 (7), and compare Ps. xix. 3 (2). *Utter* in words, speak, talk. *Insolence*, arrogance, as in Ps. lxxv. 6 (5). The last verb is a reflexive form of the verb (אמר) to say, occurring only here. According to the general analogy of those forms, it may mean to talk to one's self, or of one's self, or with each other. The second agrees best with what is said just before of their insolent or arrogant discourse.

5. *Thy people, Jehovah, they grind* (or *crush*), *and thy inheritance they humble* (or *afflict*). The first verb means to bruise, break in pieces, or reduce to powder. The *people* and *heritage* of God are synonymous expressions, the people being so called because they belonged to him, and were possessed by him, from generation to generation. The terms of this verse seem to point out foreign persecutors or oppressors as the subject of complaint.

6. *Widow and stranger they kill, and orphans they murder.* The strongest description of injustice and violence is given by saying, that they not only wrong but murder the very classes of sufferers, who in the Law are constantly exhibited as objects of compassion. See Ex. xxii. 20–23 (21–24), Deut. x. 18.

7. *And they say, Jah will not see, and the God of Jacob will not attend.* The same impious presumption is expressed in Ps. x. 11, 13, xiv. 1, lix. 8 (7). The divine names are, as usual, significant. That the self-existent and eternal God should not see, is a palpable absurdity; and scarcely less so, that the God of Israel should suffer his own people to be slaughtered without even observing it. The last verb means to mark, note, notice.

8. *Attend, ye brutish among the people; and ye fools, when will ye act wisely?* See above, on Ps. lxxiii. 22, xcii. 7 (6). The first verb is the same with that at the end of the preceding verse. It is stronger than the English word *attend*, implying in all cases an intelligent attention, so that it may be rendered, as it is by many, *understand*. The word translated *brutish* is a participle, denoting habitual conduct or a permanent condition. The question in the last clause is a virtual exhortation to being at once. The verb in this clause has its usual active meaning. See above, on Ps. ii. 10. xiv. 2, xli. 2 (1). *In* (or *among*) *the people* no doubt means in Israel itself, as in Judges v. 9, where the form of expression is the same.

9. *Shall the planter of the ear—shall he not hear? Or the former of the eye, shall he not see?* The words translated *planter* and *former* are active participles, and denote something continually going on. The figure of planting suggests the two ideas of formation and insertion. By a similar figure we might speak in English of *implanting* the faculty or sense of hearing. The act denoted by the parallel Hebrew word is that of shaping, moulding. The participle here used, when employed as a noun, means a *potter*. See above, Ps. ii. 9. The peculiar form of the translation of the first clause is intended to represent that of the original, in which the interrogative but not the negative particle is repeated. This may be reckoned as another instance of the reduplicated forms by which this series of psalms is characterised.

10. *Shall the reprover of nations—shall he not chastise—he that teaches*

mankind knowledge? The antithesis is not between Israel and the Gentiles, but between whole nations or all mankind and individual offenders. *Reprover*, the one reproving or accustomed to reprove, warn, or admonish. See above, on Ps. ii. 10, xvi. 7. The parallel term is nearly synonymous, and means to correct by word or deed. The structure of the first clause is the same as in the verse preceding. In the last clause, by an aposiopesis not uncommon in the Hebrew idiom, the parallelism is left to be completed by the reader. The full sense seems to be, is he who teaches all mankind not competent to teach men individually ? *He that teaches*, literally *the (one) teaching.*

11. *Jehovah knows the thoughts of mankind, that they (are) vanity.* The verbal form is still that of a participle, *knowing*, habitually knowing, what they are and what they deserve. Such knowledge carries with it, as a necessary consequence, condemnation and punishment. See above, on Ps. i. 6. *Thoughts*, purposes, designs. See above, on Ps. xl. 5 (4). Instead of *that*, some give the particle its usual sense of *for, because*, without a material change of meaning. The pronoun *they* seems in English to relate necessarily to *thoughts;* but in Hebrew the more natural antecedent is *man* as a generic or collective term, because the pronoun is masculine and *thoughts* feminine ; because the same thing is predicated, in the same form, of men themselves, Ps. xxxix, 6, 12 (5, 11); and because this idea is better suited to the context here.

12. *Happy the man whom thou warnest, Jah, and from thy law teachest him.* This is the turning point, at which the tone of the composition becomes more encouraging. The word for *man* is the one implying strength, and here suggesting the idea, that he is truly fortunate whose strength arises from the divine counsel and control. *Warnest* and wilt warn, or admonish, the same verb that occurs in the first clause of ver. 10. *From thy law* may be partitively understood, as meaning something of thy law, a part or portion of it. But it more probably means *out of, from, thy law*, as the source of consolation and instruction. See above, on Ps. xxii. 26 (25).

13. *To give him rest from days of evil, until a pit be digged for the wicked.* Compare Ps. xlix. 6 (5), cxii. 8. The first verb is a causative, *to make him rest.* *From days of evil* does not mean merely after them, but so as to escape them. The last clause ensures the safety of the righteous even during the prosperity and triumph of the wicked.

14. *For Jehovah will not forsake his people, and his inheritance he will not leave.* The reason why they are happy who confide in and obey the divine instructions is that God can never utterly forsake those who thus trust him, although he may leave them for a time when they leave him. See Deut. xxxii. 15, Judges vi. 13, Isa. ii. 6.

15. *For unto righteousness shall judgment turn, and after it* (shall go) *all the upright in heart.* The apparent disturbance of the divine administration is to cease, and justice to return to its accustomed channels. In the last clause the righteous are described as following in its train or attending its triumphal march.

16. *Who will arise for me with evil doers? Who will stand up for me with workers of iniquity?* Arise, address himself to action. See above, on Ps. iii. 8 (7). *For me*, for my support in my defence. *With*, in conflict or contention with. *Stand up*, take a stand, assume a position. See above, on Ps. ii. 2. *Evil-doers*, as in Ps. xcii. 12 (11). *Workers of Iniquity*, as in ver. 4 above. The interrogation in this verse prepares the way for the expression of confidence in that which follows.

17. *Unless Jehovah were a help for me, soon would my soul inhabit silence.*
The phrase *a help for me* occurs above, Ps. lxiii. 8 (7), and a similar one,
Ps. xliv. 27 (26). For the meaning of the phrase translated *soon*, see
above, on Ps. ii. 12, lxxxi. 15 (14). To *dwell in* (or *inhabit*) *silence* is to
be constantly surrounded by the silence of the grave or of death. See
above, Ps. xxxi. 18 (17), and below, Ps. cxv. 17.

18. *If I say, My foot slips, thy mercy, O Jehovah, holds me up.* If at
any time my hope of safety from the Lord's protection yields to fear, his
grace sustains and reinvigorates it. The preterites in the Hebrew of the
first clause imply that such lapses or temptations have occurred in his experience, when his foot seemed to have swerved or slipped already ; while
the future at the close represents the act of sustentation as one which he
expects to be continued or renewed hereafter.

19. *In the multitude of my cares within me, thy comforts cheer my soul.*
The second noun, which is of rare occurrence, 'does not mean thoughts in
general, but uneasy, anxious thoughts, solicitudes, or cares. The addition
of *within me* renders still more prominent the idea that it was not mere
external troubles that disturbed his peace. *Thy comforts*, the consolations
of thy word. See above, on ver. 13. *Cheer* or *shall cheer*, gladden, or
exhilarate. *My soul* not only completes the parallelism, but suggests the
idea of a cordial genuine exhilaration. See above, on Ps. iii. 3 (2).

20. *Shall the throne of iniquity have fellowship with thee, which frameth
mischief by a law.* This, which is the version in the English Bible, yields
a good sense, and the one preferred by some of the best interpreters.
Others explain the last clause, *framing mischief against law.* In either
case, *framing* means contriving, plotting. The first verb in Hebrew is
supposed by some to be a passive form, *shall it be associated or allied (with)
thee*, the connective particle being omitted by a common poetic licence, for
another instance of which see above, Ps. v. 5 (4). Others explain it as an
active verb corresponding with the dubious English verb *to fellowship* a
person. *Iniquity*, or more exactly, *crimes.* See above, on Ps. v. 10 (9),
xxxviii. 13 (12), lii. 4, 9 (2, 7), lv. 12 (11), lvii. 2 (1), xci. 3. Both this
word and its parallel translated *mischief* are applied in usage to the sufferings brought upon one person by the misconduct of another. With respect
to the second term (עָמָל), see above, on Ps. vii. 17 (16).

21. *They crowd upon the soul of the righteous, and innocent blood they
condemn.* The first verb means to rush in crowds or troops, and may
therefore be expressed in English by the verbs, *to crowd, to troop. Condemn*, literally make guilty, *i. e.* recognise and treat as such. The futures,
as usual, suggest the probable continuance of the evil in question.

22. *And* (yet) *Jehovah has been to me for a high place, and my God for
the rock of my refuge.* Our idiom would require *but* at the beginning of
this sentence. The verb *to be* followed by *for*, is sometimes used in Hebrew to express the meaning of our verb *become*, which may here be considered as at least included. *A high place*, beyond the reach of danger.
My rock of refuge, the rock where I take refuge from my enemies. See
above, on Ps. ix. 10 (9), xviii. 3 (2), xlvi. 8, 12 (7, 11), xlviii. 4 (3),
lix. 10, 18 (9, 17).

23. *And he returns upon them their iniquity, and in their wickedness he
will destroy them,* (yes) *destroy them will Jehovah our God.* The first verb
denotes retaliation or requital. The preposition *upon* suggests the idea of
infliction by a superior power. *Iniquity* expresses their misconduct towards

others, *wickedness* the general depravity which prompted it. *In their wickedness, i. e.* in the midst of it, and by implication on account of it. The verb *destroy* is the one used in Ps. liv. 7 (5), lxix. 5 (4), ci. 5. The repetition of the last verb with its object is like that in Ps. xc. 17. Compare Ps. xcii. 8 (7), xciii. 4, xciv. 1. The force of this emphatic repetition may be partially secured in English by a particle of affirmation, *yea* or *yes*.

Psalm 95

This psalm contains, first, an exhortation from the Psalmist to praise God as the creator and the sovereign of the earth, ver. 1–8, and then, a warning from God himself to his people not to imitate the obstinate unbelief of their fathers in the wilderness, ver. 9–11. The psalm is quoted in the New Testament (Heb. iv. 7) as what God said *in David*, which may either mean the Book of Psalms, so called from its chief author, or this particular psalm, as actually written by him. The latter supposition, although not necessary, is entirely admissible, because, however suitable the psalm may seem to particular junctures long posterior to David, the very generality of its expressions makes it probable that it was not composed in the midst of the events, but long beforehand.

1. *Come, let us sing unto Jehovah, let us shout unto the rock of our salvation.* The first verb properly means *go*, but is constantly used like *come* in other languages, as a formula of invitation, in summoning others to participate in some act of the speaker. The two verbs in this verse are those commonly applied to the vocal expression of joy and triumph. *The rock of our salvation*, the strong ground of our confidence, the basis upon which our hope of safety rests. See above, on Ps. xviii. 3 (2), and compare Ps. lxii. 8 (7), xcii. 16 (15), xciv. 22.

2. *Let us come before his face with thanksgiving, and in songs let us shout unto him.* The first verb is here used in its primary and proper sense. See above, on Ps. xvii. 13. That of surprising, or taking by surprise, upon which some interpreters insist, is neither intelligible in itself, nor suited to the context, nor justified by usage. To *shout in songs* is to sing aloud and with a voice of triumph.

3. *For a great God* (*is*) *Jehovah, and a great King above all gods.* This is not inconsistent with the doctrine elsewhere taught, that other gods have no real existence. See below, Ps. xcvi. 4, 5, where both truths are asserted together. The very name of God used in the first clause is expressive of omnipotence.

4. *In whose hand are the depths of the earth, and the strength of the hills* (belongs) *to him.* God's possession of the whole earth is so asserted as to leave no room for other gods. The word translated *depths* means, according to its etymology, places to be searched into, *i. e.* requiring search to find them, inmost recesses. The word translated *strength* is plural in Hebrew, and seems properly to mean fatiguing exertions, from which some derive the idea of strength, others that of extreme height, which can only be reached by exhausting effort.

5. *To whom* (belongs) *the sea, and he made it, and the dry land his hands did form.* The land and water are here put together, as the depths and heights are in ver. 4, to describe the earth in its whole extent as subject to Jehovah, by virtue of his right as its creator.

6. *Come, let us bow down and bend, let us kneel before Jehovah our Maker*
The *come* at the beginning of this verse is not a mere particle of exhortation,
as in ver. 1, but an invitation to God's presence. The Hebrew verb is one
that strictly means to *come*, and sometimes to *enter*. See above, on Ps.
lxxi. 16. This verse requires the external indication of devout emotion,
and not the mere internal feeling, although the latter is the most essential,
as appears from what follows.

7. *For He* (*is*) *our God, and we* (*are*) *the people of his pasture, and the
sheep of his hand, to-day, if to his voice ye will hearken.* The people of his
pasture are those fed and nurtured by him. The sheep of his hand are
those led and guarded by him. See above, on Ps. xxiii. 3, 4, lxxiv. 1,
lxxx. 13 (12). We not only have been so, but are so now, *to-day,* provided
we obey him. The last clause contains the condition of the first, precisely
as in Ps. lxxxi. 9 (8). In both cases this construction is more natural and
satisfactory than either of the others among which interpreters have been
divided ; some making *if* an optative particle, " if ye would only hear !"—
some supplying an apodosis, as in Exod. xxiii. 21, 22, to which there
seems to be an obvious allusion ;—some continuing the sentence into the
next verse, which is forbidden by the change of person there. This last
construction is adopted in the Septuagint, as quoted in Heb. iii. 9 ; but
this decides nothing as to the Hebrew syntax. To hear (or hearken to)
God's voice is a common Hebrew phrase for obeying his commands.

8. *Harden not your heart like Meribah, like the day of Massah in the
wilderness.* Be not wilfully and obstinately insensible. *Your heart,* in the
singlar number, because the people are addressed as an ideal person. *Like
Meribah, i. e.* as your fathers did at Meribah. *Like the day of Massah,* as
they did at that period of your national history associated with the name
of Massah. The reference is to Exod. xvii. 7. The incident there recorded
is here specified, for the sake of the significant names given to the place,
Meribah (strife) and *Massah* (temptation). God himself is here abruptly
introduced as speaking. See above, on Ps. xlvi. 11 (10), lxxv. 3, 4 (2, 3),
lxxxvii. 4, xci. 14.

9. *When* (or *where*) *your fathers tempted me ; they proved me* (and) *also
saw my work.* The first word in Hebrew is the relative pronoun, *which* for
in which, as in Ps. lxxxiv. 4 (3). This may either mean in which place
(where), or at which time (when), more probably the former, as the preceding verse is full of local nouns. *Tempted me,* see above, on Ps. lxxviii.
18, 41. *Proved me,* put me to the proof of my existence, presence, and
power, by requiring me to work, *i. e.* to act in an extraordinary manner.
And this desire, unreasonable as it was, I gratified. They not only demanded but they likewise (□ֲ) saw *my work, i. e.* what I could do. Some
restrict these last words to the previous displays of God's almighty power,
especially the plagues of Egypt. " They proved me, or put me to the
proof, although they had seen my work." But neither the sense thus put
upon the *likewise,* nor the pluperfect meaning of the verb, should be assumed without a greater necessity than here exists.

10. *Forty years I am vexed with a* (wicked) *generation, and say, A people
of wanderers in heart* (are) *they, and they do not know my ways.* The first
verb strictly means to be sick of, or disgusted with, a thing or person.
The future form expresses more distinctly the idea of protracted trial and
annoyance. *A generation,* or contemporary race, as distinguished from
mere individuals. This expression is the more appropriate because the
threatening was fulfilled, with scarcely an exception, in the whole genera

tion that came out of Egypt. The qualifying epithet supplied in the translation is derived from Deut i. 35 (compare Deut. ii. 14). *I say* or *said,*
i. e. I had occasion or good cause to say, I could have said with truth, or
I was compelled to say. The next clause contains an allusion to their
twofold wandering or error. They were not only wanderers in body but in
heart, *i. e.* they erred from the path of duty, truth, and safety. This
allusion seems to be continued in the last clause. They were not more
bewildered in the mazes of the trackless waste, than ignorant of God's ways,
i.e. of the meaning and design of his providential dealings with them.
Compare Deut. xxix. 3.

11. *Unto whom I sware in my wrath, If they shall come into my rest* (or
resting-place). Here again the first word is a relative pronoun, and may
either be a dative, as in the common version of the first clause above given ;
or an adverb of time or place (*when* or *where*), as in ver. 9 above ; or a conjunction (*so that*), as the latest interpreters prefer. The conditional clause,
with which the sentence closes, is the strongest form of negation, being
that employed in the most solemn oaths. See above, on Ps. lxxxix. 36 (35).
It is here equivalent to saying, *they shall not come, &c.* The form of speech
is that actually used in the original threatening, as recorded by Moses,
Num. xiv. 23, 30, Deut. i. 35. The word for *rest* is not an abstract but a
local term, as indicated by its form. It is here applied to the Promised
Land, as in Deut. xii. 9. There is something unusual and abrupt in the
conclusion of this psalm, without any cheering prospect to relieve the
threatening. This may be best explained by assuming, that it was not
meant to stand alone, but to form one of a series.

Psalm 96

A JOYOUS celebration of the universal spread of the true religion and
conversion of the Gentiles. The structure of the psalm is perfectly simple,
and all attempts at artificial subdivision and arrangement are either wholly
arbitrary or founded upon dubious hypotheses. The marked resemblance
of the diction to that of Isaiah in his later prophecies, has been thought to fix
the date of the composition as posterior to that prophet. This seems indeed to be forbidden by the fact that in 1 Chron. xvi., as commonly interpreted, this psalm, with portions of others, is said to have been sung at the
dedication of the tabernacle on mount Zion in the time of David. But
according to Hengstenberg, the true sense of that passage is, that David
instituted the musical service of the sanctuary, of which samples are then
given, taken not from the most ancient psalms, but from those most familiar to the people when the history was written. See below, the prefatory
note to Ps. cv. and cvi. The psalm before us seem to form a pair or double
psalm with that preceding, the Jews and Gentiles being then successively
addressed, as in Isa. ii. 3–5, but in an inverted order.

1. *Sing unto Jehovah a new song ; sing unto Jehovah all the earth.* A
new song implies fresh occasion to praise God, not for the mere repetition
of his former favours, but for some new dispensation of his grace. See
above, on Ps. xxxiii. 3, xl. 3 (2). The one here meant is the extension of
his favour to the nations, who are therefore summoned in the last clause to
celebrate his praise themselves. Compare Isa. xlii. 10, Rev. v. 9, 10.

2. *Sing unto Jehovah, bless his name, proclaim from day to day his sal-*
vation. To bless his name is to praise him for the manifestation of his

attributes. The verb translated *proclaim* is constantly applied to joyful tidings. See above, on Ps. xl. 10 (9), lxviii. 12 (11), and compare Isa. lx. 9, lii. 7, lx. 6. The phrase *from day to day* implies that the occasion of the praise required is not a transient one but permanent and perpetual. *His salvation*, that which he hast wrought, provided and revealed, not for the Jews only but for the Gentiles also. With this and the preceding verse compare 1 Chron. xvi. 23.

3. *Recount among the nations his glory, among all the peoples his wonders.* The use of *glory*, to denote the special manifestation of God's attributes, is a characteristic feature of Isaiah's later prophecies. To preclude all doubt as to the extent of the invitation, the ambiguous expression *all the earth*, in ver. 1, is here explained to mean *the nations*, and then still more absolutely *all the peoples*. The only variation of the parallel passage (1 Chron. xvi. 24) is the insertion of the objective particle (אֵת) in the first clause.

4. *For great (is) Jehovah, and to be praised exceedingly ; to be feared (is) He above all gods.* He is not a mere local deity, as the heathen were disposed to imagine, even in reference to their own divinities. With this verse compare Ps. xlvii. 3 (2), xlviii. 2 (1), lxxvii. 14 (13), lxxxvi. 8, xcv. 3, xcvii. 8, xcix. 2.

5. *For all the gods of the nations are nothings, and Jehovah the heavens did make.* *Nothings*, nonentities, a favourite description of idols in Isaiah's later prophecies. See *e. g.* Isa. xli. 24, and compare Lev. xix. 4, xxvi. 1, 1 Cor. viii. 4–6, x. 19. A less probable etymology of the Hebrew word makes it a diminutive of (אֵל) *El*, analogous to *godlings*, as an expression of contempt. The contrast intended is extreme and absolute. He called the world into existence ; they do not even exist themselves. See above, Ps. xcv. 4.

6. *Honour and majesty (are) before him, strength and beauty in his holy place.* The first combination occurs above, Ps. xlv. 4 (3). *Before him*, as his constant attendants or forerunners. *Beauty*, all that is lovely and admirable. See above, on Ps. lxxi. 8. *His holy place*, his earthly residence, regarded as a radiating centre even to the Gentiles ; or the place where God reveals himself, whatever it may be.

7. *Give to Jehovah, ye families of nations, give to Jehovah glory and strength.* Compare Ps. xxix. 1. Here, as there, to *give* is to ascribe or recognise as belonging to him. The expression *families of nations* is Mosaic. See Gen. xii. 3. The parallel passage (1 Chron. xvi. 27) has, *strength and joy (are) in his place.*

8. *Give unto Jehovah the glory of his name ; take an offering and come to his courts.* With the first clause compare Ps. xxix. 2. The verb translated *take* includes the ideas of taking up and carrying. See above, on Ps. lxviii. 30 (29), lxxii. 10, lxxvi. 12, and compare 2 Sam. viii. 2. The word *offering* is the one used to denote the bloodless or vegetable oblation of the Mosaic ritual. *His courts*, see above, on Ps. lxv. 5 (4), lxxxiv. 3 (2), xcii. 14 (13). The parallel passage (1 Chron. xvi. 29) has *before him.*

9. *Bow down to Jehovah in beauty of holiness ; tremble before him, all the earth ?* The first verb denotes the act of bowing to the ground, as practised in the East. For the meaning of the next phrase, *beauty of holiness*, see above, on Ps. xxix. 2, from which place it is borrowed here. The last clause enjoins the reverential awe due to the exhibition of the divine majesty. Compare Ps. ii. 11. The plural form of the verb (*tremble ye*) shews that *the earth* is put for its inhabitants. *Before him*, literally *from his face.* The parallel passage (1 Chron. xvi. 30) has a double preposition, a He-

brew idiom which cannot be reproduced in English, and which does not in
the least affect the sense. We also find there added to the verse before us
the middle clause or member of the next verse.

10. *Say ye among the nations, Jehovah reigns; likewise fixed is the
world, it shall not be moved ; He will judge the peoples in rectitude.* The
object of address can only be the nations themselves, as in the foregoing
context. They are therefore summoned to announce the joyful news to one
another. *Jehovah reigns,* has begun to reign, *i. e.* visibly. See above, on
Ps. xciii. 1, and compare Isa. xxiv. 23, lii. 7. As in Ps. xciii. 1, the con-
servation of the world is ascribed to God's power, so here to his justice.
Compare Ps. lxxv. 4 (3). *He will judge the nations;* see above, on Ps.
vii. 9 (8), lxxii. 2, 4, and compare Isa. xi. 4. *In equities,* see above, on
Ps. lxxv. 3 (2). It may here mean *impartiality,* without distinction between Jew and Gentile. This last clause is omitted in the parallel passage
(1 Chron. xvi. 31) which also has instead of *say ye, they shall say,* and
joins it to what is here the next verse.

11. *Let the heavens rejoice and the earth exult ; let the sea roar and its
fulness.* The optative form of the second verb determines the meaning of
the other futures, which, however, really include a prediction, or what here
amounts to the same thing, a confident anticipation. *Its fulness,* that which
fills it, its contents. This verse does not necessarily imply a participation
of inferior creatures in God's favour to his people (Rom. viii. 21), but may
be understood as a strong poetical description of events so joyous that even
the inanimate creation breaks forth into singing. Compare Isa. xliv. 23,
lv. 12. The verb translated *roar* is a cognate form of that which means to
thunder, Ps. xxix. 3.

12. *Let the field exult, and all that* (*is*) *in it ; then shall sing for joy all
trees of the wood* (or *forest*). The strict sense of the future, which was
latent in the preceding verse, here, by a beautiful transition, reasserts
itself. See below, on Ps. cxxvi. 2, and compare Isa. xxxv. 5, 6. *The
field* is the cultivated and productive portion of the earth. *All that is in it,*
with particular reference to its productions. *Sing for joy* is the translation of a single verb in Hebrew. See above, on Ps. xcv. 1. The parallel
passage (1 Chron. xvi. 32, 33) has precisely the same sense, but with two
slight variations in the words, a less familiar form being substituted in one
case, and a more familiar form in the other.

13. *Before Jehovah, for he cometh, for he cometh to judge the earth; he shall
judge the world in righteousness, and nations in his truth* (or *faithfulness*).
The rejoicing described in the preceding verse is to take place in the presence (literally to the face) of God when he assumes his universal sovereignty, the judicial function of which is here made prominent, in order to
suggest the moral perfection of his reign. *In righteousness,* not merely in
a righteous manner, but in the exercise of his inherent and essential justice.
The use of the word *people,* in the common version of the last clause, obscures the sense, by seeming to apply the verse to Israel, whereas it is
expressly applied in the original to the nations generally. Even the *truth*
or *faithfulness* of God, which commonly denotes his veracity in fulfilling
his promises to the chosen people, has here a wider sense, as opposed to
the dishonesty or partiality of human judges. In the parallel passage
(1 Chron. xvi. 33) the emphatic repetition in the first clause, and the
whole of the last clause, are omitted, perhaps because so striking and sonorous a conclusion would not have been appropriate, when another psalm
was to be added.

Psalm 97

ANOTHER exhibition of Jehovah's universal sovereignty, in which his judicial functions are again made prominent, but with special reference to the condemnation and destruction of the unbelieving nations. The structure of the psalm is remarkably like that of the second, consisting of four stanzas of three verses each. The first describes the Lord's appearing as the Judge of the Nations, ver. 1–3. The second, its effects upon inanimate creation, ver. 4–6. The third, its effects upon idolaters and Israel respectively, ver. 7–9. The fourth applies it as a present warning and encouragement to true believers, ver. 10–12. The characteristic feature of the psalm is its frequent citation of older scriptures, all anterior to the Babylonish exile, from which Hengstenberg infers, not only the date of this composition, but the fact that all the sacred writings of the ancient Hebrews are now extant in the Bible.

1. *Jehovah reigneth, let the earth exult ; glad be the many islands !* For the meaning of the first clause, see above, on Ps. xciii. 1, xcvi. 10; for that of the second, on Ps. xcvi. 11. The manifestation of the divine royalty is often represented as a cause for universal joy, even when attended by direct advantage only to the chosen people, and by fearful judgments to mankind at large. See above, on Ps. xviii. 50 (49), xlvii. 2 (1), and compare Deut. xxxii. 43. The last clause bears a strong resemblance to Isa. xlii. 10, 12, the use of the word *isles* in both, to designate the Gentiles, being founded upon Gen. x. 5. See also Ps. lxxii. 10. *The many islands,* see above, on Ps. lxxxix. 51 (50).

2. *Vapour and gloom (are) round him ; righteousness and judgment (are) the place of his throne.* The images and terms in the first clause are borrowed from Deut. v. 22. Compare Exod. xix. 16, 18, and see above, on Ps. xviii. 10, 12 (9, 11). With the last clause compare Ps. lxxxix. 15 (14). Righteousness and judgment seem to be here related as the attribute and act. The word translated *place* has, from its very derivation, the specific sense of a permanent or fixed place, and especially a dwelling-place. Compare 1 Kings viii. 13. The figures in the first clause are expressive of concealment or mystery, but only as a source of solemn awe, as in the great theophany on Sinai.

3. *Fire before him goes, and burns up around (him) his foes.* With the first clause compare Ps. l. 3 ; with the last, Isa. xlii. 25. See also Ps. lxxxiii. 15 (14). The future form is used because the verb describes not what the wrath of God is doing or has actually done, but what it will do when provoked by obstinate resistance.

4. *His lightnings made the world shine* ; (then) *saw and trembled the earth.* Compare Ps. lxxvii. 17, 19 (16, 18). Here begins the second stanza, in which, as in most cases of the same sort, inanimate creation is described as sharing in the powerful effects of the divine epiphany. See above, on Ps. xviii. 8 (7), xcvi. 11, 12, and compare Judges v. 4, Nahum i. 5, Hab. iii. 6. Isa. lxiv. 1.

5. *Mountains like wax are melted from before Jehovah, from before the Lord of all the earth.* Compare Micah i. 4, iv. 13. As in all such cases, while mountains are mentioned as the salient points of the earth, they suggest, at the same time, the idea of great states and kingdoms, of which they are a standing symbol. See above, on Ps. xxx. 8 (7), xlvi. 3 (2).

6. *The heavens declare his righteousness, and all the nations see his glory.*

With the first clause compare Ps. l. 6, and with the last Isa. xl. 5, lxvi. 18.
See also Isa. xxxv. 2, lix. 19. The manifestation of Jehovah's glory to the
Gentiles is a favourite conception of Isaiah, and particularly frequent in his
later prophecies.

7. *Shamed shall be all serving a graven image and boasting themselves of
idols. Bow down to him, all ye gods!* The first word means not merely
ashamed, but disappointed, defeated, and confounded. *All serving* or *all
servers* (*i. e.* worshippers) *of a graven image. Boasting themselves*, exulting
in the knowledge and possession and imagined favour of material images.
Idols, nothings or nonentities, as in Ps. xcvi. 5. The use of this word shews
that in the following clause the false gods are invested with existence only
to be treated with the more contempt. Compare Exod. xii. 12, Num.
xxxiii. 4, Isa. xix. 1, xlii. 17, xliv. 9. The verb in this clause might be
taken as a preterite, *worship* or *have worshipped;* but the imperative construction seems to be required by the analogy of Ps. xcvi. 9. These words are
not applied to Christ directly in Heb. i. 6. It is merely said that when
God sends his Son into the world, he may be understood as saying again
(πάλιν) of him, what is here said of himself, to wit, that even the false gods
are required to worship him, much more the angels who have real existence.
The passage was no doubt suggested to the mind of the New Testament
writer by the fact that the Septuagint renders *gods* by *angels*, though he
does not copy this erroneous version.

8. *Zion hears and rejoices, and glad are the daughters of Judah, because
of thy judgments, Jehovah!* While the heathen are confounded, the people
of God rejoice. The terms of the verse are borrowed from Ps. xlviii.
12 (11), in the note upon which the ambiguous phrase, *daughters of Judah*,
is explained. The judgments here particularly meant are those inflicted on
the unbelieving Gentiles.

9. *For thou, Jehovah, (art) Most High above all the earth; greatly art
thou exalted above all gods.* Jehovah's infinite superiority to idols and their
worshippers is once more solemnly asserted. With the first clause compare
Ps. lxxxiii. 19 (18); with the second, Ps. xlvii. 10 (9). It is remarkable
that two psalms are here put together in quotation, which there is strong
internal reason for supposing to have been occasioned by a victory of
Jehoshaphat.

10. *Lovers of Jehovah, hate evil! He keeps the souls of his gracious ones;
from the hand of wicked (men) he will set them free.* The people of God are
now exhorted not to do evil in the hope of thereby being safer. *Evil*, in
the moral sense of wickedness, and more especially injustice. See above,
on Ps. vii. 10 (9), xxxiv. 14, 15. With the first words of the verse compare Ps. v. 12 (11). *He keeps*, or rather, *he (is) keeping, i. e.* habitually,
constantly preserving. The danger, against which they particularly need
protection, is distinctly mentioned in the last clause, namely, that arising
from the enmity of wicked men. *Gracious ones*, objects of God's mercy,
subjects of his grace, a favourite description of the righteous or true believers,
as a class. See above, on Ps. iv. 4 (3).

11. *Light (is) sown for the just (man), and for right-hearted (men) joy.*
The figurative term *light* is explained by the literal one *joy* or *gladness*. Its
being *sown* suggests the two ideas of diffusion and productiveness. Compare the similar and parallel expression, Ps. cxii. 4. The alternation of
the singular and plural number shews that the just man of the first clause
is an ideal person, representing a whole class.

12. *Rejoice, ye righteous, in Jehovah, and give thanks to the memory of his*

holiness. Since joy is the portion of the righteous, let them accept it and make use of it, but only in the Lord, *i. e.* in reference to the possession and enjoyment of his favour, as the reason and the warrant for rejoicing. At the same time let them testify their gratitude to that divine perfection which is treasured in their memory and suggested by the name of God. See above, on Ps. xxx. 5 (4), xxxii. 11, from which the language of this verse is borrowed.

Psalm 98

THIS psalm is similar, in tone and structure, to the one before it, containing three stanzas of three verses each. The first propounds the subject of the praise to which the whole world is exhorted, ver. 1–3. The second prescribes the form in which it shall be rendered, ver. 4–6. The third determines its extent, or in other words, requires it to be universal, ver. 7–9.

1. *A Psalm   Sing ye to Jehovah a new song, for wonders he has done; his right hand has wrought salvation for him, and his holy arm.* This is the only case in which the word *psalm* (מִזְמוֹר) stands by itself as a complete inscription. This fact has been ingeniously explained by supposing that the word was intended to distinguish this, as a purely lyrical composition, from the one before it, which has more of the prophetic character and style. The first clause after this inscription is like Ps. xcvi. 1, where the words have been explained already. *Wonders*, or wondrous deeds, things wonderfully done, as in Ps. xcvi. 3. *Wrought salvation*, literally *saved for him, i. e.* enabled him to save his people. The idea and expression are both found in Isa. lix. 16, lxiii. 5, as the expression *arm of holiness* (or *holy arm*) is in Isa. lii. 10. This is one of the cases in which *holiness* has the wide sense of divine perfection, as opposed to what is finite or belongs to the creature. See above, on Ps. xxii. 4 (3). With the whole verse compare Judges vii. 2. The allusion to Isaiah, or quotations from him, shew that the *wonders* to be celebrated are like those which constitute the theme of his later prophecies, namely, Jehovah's interpositions for the deliverance and protection of his people.

2. *Jehovah hath made known his salvation, to the eyes of the nations he hath revealed his righteousness.* He hath shewn the world his power and his willingness to save his own people according to his promise, with respect to which *his righteousness* and *his salvation* are related to each other as cause and effect. With this verse compare Isa. lii. 10.

3. *He hath remembered his mercy and his truth for the house of Israel; all the ends of the earth have seen the salvation of our God.* The common version connects *to the house of Israel* with what immediately precedes, the mercy and truth which he formerly exercised towards the house of Israel. But according to the Hebrew idiom and the usage of the psalms, the preposition is dependent on the leading verb: "He has called to mind his mercy and truth for the present benefit of the house of Israel." *Truth*, fidelity to his engagements. See the same combination in Ps. xcii. 3. The last clause is another citation from Isa. lii. 10, which shews that the salvation primarily meant is that of Israel. This, however, is closely connected in prophecy with that of the Gentiles.

4. *Shout to Jehovah, all the earth! Burst forth, and sing, and play!* The second stanza prescribes the form or manner of the praise. This verse

accumulates the verbs denoting joyful noise, whether inarticulate, or instrumental. The first clause differs from Ps. xcvi. 1, only by substituting one
divine name for another. See also Ps. xlvii. 2 (1). The verb (פצח) to
burst forth (into praise or singing) is almost peculiar to Isaiah (xiv. 7,
xliv. 23, xlix. 12, liv. 1). This very combination with the verb *to sing*
occurs in Isa. lii. 9.

5. *Make music to Jehovah with a harp, with a harp and a musical voice!*
The first verb is the one translated *play* in the preceding verse. Its repetition is like that in Ps. xlvii. 2 (1). It is strictly applied to instrumental
music, but often extended to any musical expression, especially of praise to
God. A *musical voice*, or a voice of singing, as distinguished from the voice
of speech. The phrase occurs in Isa. li. 3. The repeated introduction of
the verb זמר or its derivatives is supposed by some to be the reason of the
title מזמור. See above, on ver. 1.

6. *With trumpets and sound of cornet, shout before the King, Jehovah!*
The first noun is supposed to denote the long straight trumpet, the other
the cornet or curved horn of ancient music. These are named as the accompaniments of the act described in the other clause, where the verb may
therefore have the sense of shouting, which it has most generally in these
psalms. The act described is the joyful acclamation at the accession or
public recognition of a sovereign. *King Jehovah* is a combination found in
Isa. vi. 5. Compare Ps. xcv. 3, xcvi. 10, xcvii. 1. The whole is equivalent to saying, hail him who has now become your king!

7. *Let the sea thunder and what fills it—the land and those dwelling on it.*
The last stanza represents the praise as universal. For the meaning of the
first clause see above, on Ps. xcvi. 11; for that of the second, on Ps.
xxiv. 1. The word there translated *world* is here used in opposition to *sea*,
and therefore rendered *land*. See above, on Ps. xc. 2.

8. *Let rivers clap the hand; together let mountains sing* (or shout for joy)!
This bold but beautiful personification is also found in Isa. lv. 12, the only
other place where the clapping of the hands is ascribed to lifeless objects.
This was a customary sign of joy, especially when joined with acclamation
in honour of a sovereign, as it is not only here, and in Ps. xlvii. 2 (1), in
highly figurative poetry, but also in historical prose, *e. g.* the account of the
coronation of Joash, 2 Kings xi. 12. *Together*, not merely with each other,
but at the same time and in concert with the applauses of the floods or
rivers.

9. *Before Jehovah, for he cometh to judge the earth; he will judge the
world in righteousness and nations in equity.* The acclamations must be
uttered to Jehovah, not only as a sovereign king, but as a righteous judge.
The first clause is like Ps. xcvi. 13, except that it omits the emphatic repetition, which is also the case in 1 Chron. xvi. 33. The first verb might,
in all these cases, be more exactly and emphatically rendered, *he is come.*
In equity, literally *equities* or *rectitudes*, the plural form denoting fulness and
perfection. See above, on Ps. xcvi. 10.

Psalm 99

THE theme of this psalm, as of those immediately preceding, is the kingship
of Jehovah, ver. 1. The remainder falls into two stanzas of four verses each.
In the first, Jehovah's goodness to his people is propounded as a subject of
applause to all mankind, ver. 2–5. In the second, the same duty is en-

forced by an appeal to historical examples, ver. 6–9. The strophical arrangement is marked by the resemblance of ver. 5 and 9. The psalm is related in the closest manner to those before and after it, as forming one connected series. See below, on Ps. c.

1. *Jehovah reigns, the nations tremble; sitting on* (or *dwelling between*) *the cherubim* (he reigns), *the earth quakes.* The second member of each clause describes the effect produced by the disclosure of the fact that God has begun to reign, is actually reigning. For the meaning of the phrase *sitting on* (or *dwelling between*) *the cherubim*, see above, on Ps. lxxx. 2 (1). As used in history, it always presupposes the presence of the ark as symbolising that of God himself. See 1 Sam. iv. 4, 2 Sam. vi. 2, 2 Kings xix. 15. Its use here, therefore, shews that the psalm before us, and by necessary consequence, the series to which it belongs (Ps. xci.–c.), and by parity of reasoning, the later prophecies of Isaiah, were all composed before the Babylonian conquest, when the temple was destroyed and the ark lost sight of. The futures have their strict sense, as this is a prediction. If they were optative (*let the nations tremble*, &c.) one of the verbs at least would have that form.

2. *Jehovah in Zion* (*is*) *great, and high* (*is*) *he above all nations.* Compare Ps. xlviii. 2 (1), xcv. 3, xcvi. 4, xcvii. 9. The addition of the qualifying phrase *in Zion* shews that the reference is not to God's absolute essential greatness, but to some signal manifestation of his greatness to his people. The word translated *high* is originally a participle, and may be likened to our English *towering*.

3. *They shall acknowledge thy name, great and terrible : Holy* (*is*) *He!* The subject of the first verb is *the nations* mentioned in ver. 2. See above, Ps. xcvi. 9, xcvii. 7, xcviii. 1, 4. The verb itself means to acknowledge thankfully, to thank, to praise for benefits received. See above, on Ps. vi. 5 (4). *Thy name*, the evidence already furnished of thine infinite perfection. *Great* and *feared*, or *to be feared*, epithets derived from Deut. x. 17, xxviii. 58. In the last clause some would read, *Holy* (*is*) *it, i. e.* thy name. But the sense is determined by the analogy of ver. 5, 9, and the obvious allusion to Isa. vi. 3. This allusion is by some supposed to be the reason of the sudden change of person, *He* instead of *Thou.* But this may be still more readily accounted for, by making these the very words in which God is acknowledged by the nations : (saying) *Holy is he! Holy*, in the wide sense which it has in the Old Testament, and more particularly in the Psalms. See above, on Ps. xxii. 4 (3).

4. *And the king's strength loves judgment ; thou hast established equity : judgment and justice in Jacob thou hast done.* Some continue the construction from the preceding sentence ; *they shall acknowledge thy name and the king's strength loving judgment.* But as sentences of this length are unusual in Hebrew, and as אָהֵב is not elsewhere a participle or verbal adjective, the best construction is the old one, which makes this an independent proposition. The meaning of the first clause seems to be, that God's power is controlled in its exercise by his love of justice. To *establish equity* is to give it permanence by a habitually pure administration of justice. The terms of the last clause are the same by which the history describes the judicial fidelity of David, 2 Sam. viii. 15, as if to indicate that it was a mere type of God's more perfect and infallible administration of impartial justice.

5. *Exalt ye Jehovah our God, and prostrate yourselves to his footstool. Holy* (*is*) *He!* With the first clause compare Ps. xxx. 2 (1), xxxiv. 4 (3); with the second, Ps. xcvi. 9, xcvii. 7. As in those cases, the address is to

the nations. *Bow down* (or *prostrate*) *yourselves*, as an act of worship.
Not *at his footstool*, as the mere place of worship, but *to it*, as the object,
this name being constantly given to the ark, 1 Chron. xxviii. 2, Lam. ii. 1,
Ps. cxxxii. 7, Isa. lx. 13. Even in Isa. lxvi. 1, there is allusion to the
ordinary usage of the terms. The ark is here represented as the object of
worship, just as Zion is in Isa. xlv. 14, both being put for the God who
was present in them.

6. *Moses and Aaron among his priests, and Samuel among those calling
on his name—calling to Jehovah, and he answers them.* The structure of
the sentence is elliptical, and may be completed either by supplying *are* or
were before *among*, or by making the participle *calling* mean *are calling*,
call. In explaining the sentence due regard must be had to its parallel
structure. As Moses and Aaron are evidently meant to be included among
those who called upon the name of the Lord, so Samuel must be comprehended *among his priests*. Moses and Samuel are so described because
they were theocratic mediators between God and the people, and as such
performed occasionally what were strictly sacerdotal functions. See Lev.
viii. 15–30, 1 Sam. ix. 13. The prayers here referred to are their inter-
cessions for the people. See Exod. xviii. 19, xxxii. 11–30, Num. xi. 2,
xiv. 9, xxi. 7, Deut. v. 5, ix. 18, 19, 1 Sam. vii. 9, xii. 23, Ps. cvi. 23.
The connection of this verse with the foregoing context is obscure, but the
idea seems to be, that as even the chiefs of the theocracy were under the
necessity of seeking the divine favour, such prayer must, to say the least,
be equally necessary in the case of others.

7. *In a pillar of cloud he speaks to them. They kept his testimonies and
the statute he gave unto them.* The first clause may be figuratively understood as denoting any special divine communication, or what was literally
true of Moses and Aaron (Exod. xxxiii. 9, Num. xii. 5, Deut. xxxi. 15)
may be here applied to all three indiscriminately. The verse contains a
second lesson drawn from the history of the theocracy, to wit, the necessity
of obedience no less than of prayer. It was true, God spoke to these men
in an extraordinary manner ; but it was for the purpose of making known
his will, and that will they obeyed. For the meaning of *testimonies*, see
above, on Ps. xciii. 5. The last clause may be construed as an independent
proposition, *and he gave a statute to them, i. e.* he rewarded their obedience
by revealing to them new laws. But the sense thus obtained is not so clear
or natural as that afforded by the relative construction, *and the statute*
(*which*) *he gave them*.

8. *Jehovah our God, thou didst answer them ; a forgiving God wast thou
to them, and* (a God) *taking vengeance on their crimes.* The apostrophe to
God himself adds solemnity and tenderness to the discourse. The pronoun
is emphatic, they called and thou didst hear or answer. The following
description is borrowed from Exod. xxxiv. 7. The divine name (אֵל),
implies that he had infinite power to destroy, and yet forgave them. The
last Hebrew word in the verse is used of God in a good sense, and of man
always in a bad one. See above, on Ps. ix. 12 (11), xiv. 1, lxxvii. 13 (12).
There is here a beautiful transition from the representatives of the people
to the people themselves. The pronoun in the first clause (*them*) can refer
only to Moses, Aaron, and Samuel ; in the second, it is applicable both to
them and to the people ; in the third, it relates to the latter exclusively.

9. *Exalt ye Jehovah our God, and bow down to his holy hill ; for holy*
(*is*) *Jehovah our God.* See above, on ver. 5, from which this differs only

in the substitution of the holy hill for the equivalent expression *footstool*, and in the more distinct assertion of God's holiness as a reason for the worship thus required.

Psalm 100

THIS psalm is related to the ninety-ninth as the ninety-eighth is to the ninety-seventh. The prophecy there latent is here clothed in a genuine lyrical form. There is also the same likeness as to structure and arrangement. The theme, propounded in ver. 1, is amplified in two short stanzas, of two verses each. In both these an exhortation to praise God is followed by a reason for so doing. Men ought to praise him as their creator and preserver, ver. 2, 3. They ought also to praise him for his infinite goodness, constancy, and faithfulness, ver. 4, 5. Besides completing the foregoing psalm, it closes the whole series or cycle of harmonious addresses to the nations or the world at large.

1. *A Psalm. For thanksgiving. Shout unto Jehovah, all the earth!* The title resembles that of Ps. xcvii., but is rendered more specific by the addition *for thanksgiving*. The version *praise* is too restricted. See above, on Ps. xcix. 3. The rest of the verse is identical with Ps. xcviii. 4. See also Ps. ii. 11, lxvi. 1.

2. *Serve Jehovah with joy, come before him with singing!* Since he is the king of the nations, they are his subjects, and as such bound to serve him. What they are required to do in Ps. ii. 11 with fear and trembling, as repentant rebels, they are here invited to do with joy and gladness, as his willing subjects.

3. *Know ye that Jehovah is God; (it is) He (that) made us, and not we (ourselves), his people, and the sheep of his pasture.* This is the first reason given for acknowledging Jehovah's sovereignty, to wit, that he has made his people what they are. With the first clause compare Ps. xlvi. 11 (10). Instead of *and not we ourselves*, the keri or masoretic reading in the margin of the Hebrew Bible has, *and his we are*. These phrases, though so unlike in English, differ only in a single letter, *and not* (לֹא) *we, and to him* (לוֹ) *we*. The first is adopted by the Septuagint and Vulgate, the second by the Targum and Jerome. In favour of the latter is the similar construction of the pronoun (אֲנַחְנוּ) *we* with (עַמּוֹ) *his people* in Ps. lxxix. 13. xcv. 7. In favour of the other is its antiquity, and its greater significancy and appropriateness to the context. Some who adopt it read, *it is he that has made us* (to be) *his people the sheep*, &c. But besides the violence of this construction, *he made us* has no doubt the same sense as in Ps. xcv. 6, and *his people* must mean *us who are his people. Sheep* (or *flock*) *of his pasture*, as in Ps. lxxiv. 1, lxxix. 13, xcv. 7.

4. *Enter his gates with thanksgiving and his courts with praise; give thanks unto him, bless his name!* Compare Ps. lxxxiv. 3 (2), xcii. 14 (13), xcv. 2, xcvi. 2, 8, xcvii. 12. The substance of the exhortation is, join in the worship of his people. That the reference to the sanctuary at Jerusalem is merely typical or metaphorical, is clear from the analogy of Isa. lxvi. 23, where all mankind are required to come up every sabbath, a command which, if literally understood, is perfectly impracticable. The combination of the verb to *thank* (הוֹדוּ) with its derivative noun (תּוֹדָה) may throw some light upon the title, *a psalm for thanksgiving* (לְתוֹדָה).

5. *For good* (*is*) *Jehovah, to eternity his mercy, and even to generation and generation his faithfulness* (or *truth*). This verse assigns a second reason for the invitation to praise Jehovah, namely, the goodness, truth, and constancy of the divine nature. With the first clause compare Ps. xxv. 8, xxxiv. 9 (8), lxxxvi. 5; with the second, Isa. liv. 8, 10; with the third, Ps. lxxxix. 2 (1), xcii. 3 (2).

Here ends what Hengstenberg describes as a decalogue of Psalms (xci.–c.), all intended to exhibit the relation between Israel and the world at large; all of a cheering and triumphant character, without the slightest intermixture of complaint or lamentation; all crowded with citations from the older Scriptures, or allusions to them; almost all pointing to a glorious theophany still future; and almost all distinguished by emphatic repetitions, and the frequent use of musical terms, especially the names of instruments. That these psalms are not thrown together at random, is apparent from the fact that the series begins with a general assurance of divine protection (Ps. xci.), and of God's power both to save the righteous and destroy the wicked (Ps. xcii.), followed by variations on the grand theme that THE LORD REIGNETH (Ps. xciii.–xcix.), and closing with an earnest exhortation to the whole world to receive him as their sovereign (Ps. c). The mutual relation of the several psalms has been already indicated in the exposition. According to Hengstenberg, these ten psalms are in Psalmody what the later chapters of Isaiah (xl.–lxvi.) are in Prophecy; and as the former are undoubtedly anterior to the exile, they confirm the genuineness of the latter.

Psalm 101

AFTER propounding as his theme the mercy and justice of the Lord, ver. 1, the Psalmist announces his determination to be blameless in his own walk, ver. 2–4, and so to exercise his power over others as to favour the godly and drive out the wicked, ver. 5–8.

1. *By David. A Psalm. Mercy and judgment will I sing; to thee, Jehovah, will I play* (or *make music*). As such a declaration of a present purpose in the Psalms is always followed by its execution, the older interpreters suppose *mercy and judgment* to be those which David meant to practise, as he states more fully in the remainder of the psalm. But besides that, he says nothing in what follows of his *mercy*, there is no usage of the Psalms more settled than that *mercy and justice* are combined to denote divine not human attributes, and that *to sing and make music to Jehovah* never means to praise something else in an address to him, but always to sing praises to himself. See above, Ps. ix. 12 (11), xiii. 6 (5), xviii. 50 (49), xxx. 5 (4), 13 (12), xxxiii. 2, lxviii. 5 (4), lxxi. 22, 23, in all which cases the form of expression seems to be derived from Judges v. 3. But the psalm before us contains no such celebration of God's mercy and justice beyond this first verse. The best solution of this fact appears to be the one proposed by Hengstenberg, according to which the execution of the purpose here avowed is contained in Ps. ciii., which then, together with the one before us, and of course the intervening one, compose a *trilogy* or series of three psalms, all by David, each complete in itself, and yet designed to be connected with the others and interpreted by them. Supposing this to be the case, we must regard them all as psalms of David, whose name is prefixed to the third and the one before us, in which he lays down

a rule, as it were, for his own government, and that of his successors in the regal office. The impression made by these inspired instructions on the first of those successors may account for the remarkable coincidences of expression between this psalm and the Book of Proverbs.

2. *I will act wisely in a perfect way. When wilt thou come to me? I will walk in the integrity of my heart within my house.* As to the first verb, see above, on Ps. ii. 10, xiv. 2. Its form here is one expressing fixed determination. *A perfect way*, as in Ps. xviii. 31, 33 (30, 32). This and other figurative expressions of the same kind, Ps. xviii. 24, 26 (23, 25), xv. 2, are founded upon Gen. xvii. 1. *When wilt thou come to me*, and bless me, in fulfilment of thy promise? Exod. xx. 21. This interrogative ejaculation implies a sense of his dependence on divine aid for the execution of his purpose. *Integrity* (*integritas*, completeness) *of my heart* is an expression borrowed from Gen. xx. 5, 6. See above, on Ps. lxxviii. 72, and compare 1 Kings iii. 14, Prov. xx. 7. *Way* and *walk* are familiar figures for habitual conduct. *Within*, literally *in the midst* (or *inside*) *of my house*, *i. e.* at home, in private life, as distinguished from the house of God and his official conduct there, to which he afterwards adverts.

3. *I will not set before my eyes a word of Belial; the doing of apostasies I hate, it shall not cleave to me.* The positive terms of the preceding verse are now exchanged for negatives. Having said what he will do, he now says what he will not do. See a similar transition, but in the inverse order, Ps. i. 1, 2. *Set before my eyes*, as a model to be copied, or as an object of approving contemplation. *A word of Belial*, as in Ps. xli. 9 (8), except that *word*, which there most probably relates to slander or false accusation, may here denote a proposition, and the whole phrase a worthless (*i. e.* wicked) plan or purpose. *Apostasies*, departures, deviations from the right course. See the verbal root as used in Ps. xl. 5 (4), and a cognate verb in Num. v. 12, 19. Some make the word here used a participle or verbal noun, as in the English Bible, *the work of them that turn aside.* But its form and the analogy of Hos. v. 2, entitle the other construction to the preference. *It shall not cleave to me*, I will not be concerned or implicated in it; or more emphatically still, it shall not cleave to me as a reproach or stigma. In favour of the former sense is the analogy of Deut. xiii. 18 (17), from which the expression seems to have been borrowed.

4. *A crooked heart shall depart from me; evil I will not know. Crooked*, froward, or perverse, as in Ps. xviii. 27 (26). Compare Prov. xi. 20, xvii. 20. The whole phrase might be understood to mean a person having such a heart, and the whole clause that the Psalmist would have no intercourse with such. The parallel term *evil* would then mean *a wicked person*, as translated in the English Bible. On the ground, however, that the person of the sinner seems to be reserved for the latter part of the psalm, the best interpreters take *evil* in the abstract sense of moral evil, wickedness, as in Ps. xxxiv. 17, lii. 5 (3). The first clause will then naturally mean, my own heart shall not be perverse or froward.

5. (One) *slandering in secret his fellow—him I will destroy;* (one) *lofty of eyes and wide of heart—him I will not bear.* Having declared what his own course of life should be, he now describes the conduct which he should require in his confidential servants. Here again the statement is both negative and positive, but in this case beginning with the former. See above, on ver. 3. It is not an improbable conjecture that in specifying slander, David had reference to his sufferings from that cause in the days of Saul. See above, on Ps. xviii. 1, lii. 4–7 (2–5), and compare Ps.

xv. 3. The verb translared *slandering* occurs, in any of its forms, only here and Prov. xxx. 10. *Wide of heart* means neither magnanimous nor greedy, but proud, self-confident, as appears from Prov. xxviii. 25. Both figurative phrases here used are combined again in Prov. xxi. 4. The last verb in the sentence usually means *to be able*, but is here used absolutely, as in Isa. i. 13.

6. *My eyes (are) on the faithful of the land, to dwell with me.* (One) *walking in a perfect way—he shall serve me.* On the faithful, literally *in* or *with* them. See above, on Ps. xxxiv. 16, 17 (15, 16)), and compare Ps. xxxii. 8 (7). *My eyes are on them* is equivalent to saying, I will seek them out to dwell with me and serve me. The word translated *faithful* is properly a passive participle meaning *trusted*, relied upon, confided in. Another passive participle from the same root is commonly supposed to be used in the same sense, Ps. xii. 2 (1), xxxi. 24 (23). In the first words of the last clause there is manifest allusion to the form of expression in ver. 2 above. This clause is to be understood exclusively, such a person and no other. *Shall serve ne*, be employed by me, clothed with responsible and honourable offices.

7. *Not in the inside of my house shall dwell* (one) *practising fraud, telling lies ; not settled shall he be before my eyes.* Here again the form of expression corresponds to that in the first part of the psalm. Compare *in the midst of my house* with ver. 2, and *before my eyes* with ver. 3. *Shall not dwell*, or still more strongly, *shall not* (even) *sit*, which is the primary meaning of the Hebrew verb. The corresponding verb in the last clause means to be established, permanently settled, as opposed to a mere temporary, transient presence. As if he had said, though they should even gain admission to my house, they shall not take up their abode there.

8. *In the morning will I destroy all the wicked of the land,* (so as) *to cut off from the city of Jehovah all workers of iniquity.* The first phrase literally means *at the mornings*, and may be intended to suggest the twofold idea of early and constantly, in the morning and every morning. See above, on Ps. lxxiii. 14, and compare Jer. xxi. 12. The last clause serves to shew, or to remind the reader, that this rigour was not simply prudential or political, but religious. It had reference not merely to Jerusalem as a city, but as the city of Jehovah, his earthly residence, the centre of the theocracy, the temporary seat of the true religion. See above, on Ps. xlvi. 5 (4), xlviii. 2 (1), lxxxvii. 3. Under the peculiar institutions of the old economy, the safety of the theocratic state required peculiar vigilance and rigour, in exercising even those powers which are common to all governments.

Psalm 102

1. *A Prayer. By a Sufferer, when he is troubled, and before Jehovah pours out his complaint.* The psalm is called a *prayer*, because petition constitutes its substance. See above, on Ps. xc. 1. The translation *for the sufferer* (or *afflicted*) would also be grammatical, and perfectly consistent with the real design of the composition. But phrases of this kind, in the titles of the psalms, so constantly indicate the author or performer, and when only one occurs, the former, that a departure from this usage here is highly improbable, and the assumption of it altogether arbitrary. At the same time, the indefinite expression, *a sufferer*, or *an afflicted person*, seems to be intentionally used for the purpose of giving the psalm an unrestricted application,

though the primary reference is no doubt to the suffering kings of Israel, in whom the sufferings of the people were concentrated and represented. The other terms of the inscription all occur in psalms of David : *troubled* (or *overwhelmed*) in Ps. lxi. 3 (2) ; *complaint* (or *moaning*) in Ps. lv. 3 (2), lxiv. 2 (1) ; and *pouring out the soul* in Ps. lxii. 9 (8). This agrees with the general Davidic character of the composition, and favours Hengstenberg's hypothesis, not otherwise demonstrable, nor even very probable, that this psalm forms the connecting link between the pious resolutions of Ps. ci. and the joyful acknowledgments of Ps. ciii., and was composed in prophetic foresight of the straits to which the theocratical state should be reduced, and in which the sufferings of David, here immediately described, should, as it were, be realised anew. The psalm may be divided into two parts, in the first of which the tone of lamentation or complaint predominates, ver. 2–12 (1–11), while in the second it is tempered and controlled by the contemplation of God's attributes, and confident anticipation of his favour, ver. 13–29 (12-28).

2 (1). *Jehovah, hear my prayer, and let my cry* (for help) *unto thee come.* With this verse compare Ps. iv. 2 (1), xvii. 1, xviii. 7 (6), liv. 4 (2). There is no more reason for regarding these resemblances as imitations by a later writer in the case before us than in any of the others. And if not such, they may serve to shew, that David only asks, for the future or for others, that favour which he has himself sought and experienced already.

3 (2). *Hide not thy face from me ; in the day* (there is) *distress to me, incline to me thine ear ; in the day I call, make haste* (and) *answer me* Compare Ps. x. 1, xiii. 1, xvii. 6, xviii. 7 (6), xxvii. 9, xxxi. 3 (2), lvi. 10 (9), lxvi. 14 (13), lxxi. 2. We find here accumulated nearly all the phrases used by David to express the same ideas elsewhere. This is not unnatural if we suppose him to have been preparing a form of complaint and supplication for the use of his successors in their worst distresses.

4 (3). *For wasted in smoke are my days, and my bones like a burning are kindled.* With the first clause compare Ps. xxxvii. 20. The bones are mentioned as the seat of strength. See above, on Ps. vi. 3 (2), xxxi. 11 (10), xxxv. 10, xlii. 11 (10). This description, although strictly applicable to the case of individual sufferers, may also be applied to the decline of the theocratic monarchy and the approach of its catastrophe.

5 (4). *Smitten like grass and withered is my heart, for I have forgotten to eat my bread.* The first verb is used to describe the effect of the sun on plants, Ps. cxxi. 6, Isa. xlix. 10. (Compare Jonah iv. 7.) The heart is mentioned as the seat of life. The common version of the last clause (*so that I forget*) is ungrammatical. The failure of the strength is rather described as immediately occasioned by the want of food (1 Sam. xxviii. 20), and this by loss of appetite from extreme distress. See below, on Ps. cvii. 18, and compare 1 Sam. i. 7, **xx.** 34, 1 Kings xxi. 4. *Forgotten to eat*, literally *forgotten from eating*, so as not to eat, a common idiomatic use of the preposition *from* in Hebrew.

6 (5). *From the voice of my groaning, my bone cleaves to my flesh.* The word *voice* implies an audible and loud expression of distress. The first clause means, in consequence of the agony which makes me groan. *My bone* may signify each of my bones, or be used collectively for the whole skeleton or framework of the body. The only natural explanation of this clause is that it describes emaciation, as a consequence and symptom of extreme distress. See above, on Ps. **xxii.** 15, 18 (14, 17).

7 (6). *I resemble a pelican of the wilderness ; I am become like an owl*

(haunting) *ruins*. The simple idea conveyed by these figures is that of extreme loneliness and desolation. Beyond the fact that they inhabit solitudes, the natural history of the birds mentioned is of no exegetical importance.

8 (7). *I have watched, and have been like a sparrow dwelling alone upon a house-top.* The first words suggest the idea of a solitary vigil. As to the word translated *sparrow*, see above, on Ps. lxxxiv. 4 (3). The word *dwelling* is supplied in the translation of the last clause, in order to retain the form of the original expression, which is that of an active participle. Some suppose the idea to be that of a bird, deprived of its mate or of its young.

9 (8). *All the day my enemies have taunted me, my infuriated* (foes) *swear by me.* The verb in the first clause suggests the ideas of contempt and hatred, calumny and insult. See above, on Ps. xlii. 11 (10). The first word of the last clause is a passive participle, *my enraged* (or *maddened*) *ones*, those who are mad (*i. e.* insane with enmity) against me. The last phrase does not mean *swear at me, i. e.* vent their rage by oaths and curses, nor *are sworn against me*, neither of which is justified by Hebrew usage ; but *swear by me. i. e.* use me as a formula of execration, imprecating upon others misery like mine. Compare Isa. lxv. 15, Jer. xxix. 22. The preterite forms imply a long previous continuance of this furious persecution, as *all the day* does its constant, unremitted raging.

10 (9). *For ashes like bread have I eaten, and my drink with weeping have mixed.* The ashes, in which he sat, or with which he was covered, as a sign of mourning, became mingled with his food, and his tears fell into his *drink*. This last word is, in Hebrew, of the plural number, *drinks* or *beverages*, analogous to *victuals* as a simple synonyme of *food*. As an opposite example of the same idiomatic difference, the word translated *ashes* is a singular in Hebrew. The whole verse is a strong poetical description of constant and extreme distress.

11 (10). *Because of thine indignation and thy wrath ; for thou hast taken me up and cast me away.* The first clause describes his suffering as the fruit of God's displeasure. See above, on Ps. xc. 7. The antithesis presented in the common version of the last clause (*lifted me up and cast me down*) does not seem to be the sense of the original, in which there is probably allusion to the figure of a storm or whirlwind catching things up and blowing them away. The Prayer Book version of the first verb (*taken me up*) is more exact.

12 (11). *My days* (are) *like a shadow inclined, and I* (*myself*) *like the grass wither.* An *inclined shadow* is an unusual and obscure expression, but seems to mean a shadow verging towards its disappearance, ready to vanish away. The double or reflexive pronoun (*I myself*) in the translation of the last clause is necessary to convey the full force of the Hebrew pronoun, which is seldom expressed, except when it is meant to be emphatic, *I wither*, am withering, or about to wither.

13 (12). *And thou Jehovah, to eternity shall sit, and thy memory* (shall endure) *to generation and generation* Here again the pronoun is emphatic, and exhibits a strong contrast between God's eternity and human frailty. While I wither like the grass, thou endurest for ever, and not only so, but reignest, sittest on the throne. See above, on Ps. ix. 8 (7), xxix. 10, lv. 20 (19). The word *memory* seems here to be employed for the sake of the antithesis which it implies. While I perish and am utterly forgotten, thy existence and thy memory shall last for ever. It may, however, have

the same sense as in Ps. xxx. 5 (4), namely, the divine perfection, associated in our memory with the name of God. Thou shalt not only reign for ever, but be worthy, as an infinitely perfect being, so to do.

14 (13). *Thou wilt arise, wilt have mercy upon Zion, when* (it is) *time to favour her, when the set time is come.* The pronoun is again emphatic. Thou, the God, thus glorious and immutable, wilt certainly arise from this apparent inaction, and have mercy or compassion on thy people, when the time fixed in thy eternal purpose is arrived. The sense of *when*, thus given to the Hebrew particle (כִּי), although less usual, is sometimes absolutely necessary, and is therefore admissible in this case, where it suits the sense much better than the ordinary sense of *for.* Or the one may be resolved into the other, by explaining the whole thus : thou wilt certainly arise and have compassion upon Zion, at the proper time, FOR there is a time fixed at which thou dost design to favour her. For the meaning of the word translated *set time*, see above on Ps. lxxv. 3 (2).

15 (14). *When thy servants love her stones, and her dust regard with favour.* Both verbs in Hebrew mean to favour, or more strongly to delight in, to take pleasure in. See above, Ps. lxii. 5 (4), lxxxv. 2 (1). *Stones* and *dust* are here put for ruins or rubbish, as in Neh. iii. 34 (iv. 2), iv. 4 (10). The verse may be understood as a condition or a premonition of her restoration, that before it takes place, God will fill his servants with affectionate concern for her desolate condition. The same sense may be obtained without departing from the usual sense of the particle. Thou wilt have mercy upon Zion, FOR thy servants already look with interest and strong desire on her ruins, a sure sign of the approaching restoration.

16 (15). *And nations shall fear the name of Jehovah, and all kings of the earth thy glory.* The impression of awe, unavoidably produced by these exhibitions of Jehovah's attributes, shall not be limited to Israel, but extend to other nations, and even kings shall vie with each other in their reverential admiration of his regal honours. Compare the similar expressions of Isaih (lix. 19).

17 (16). *Because Jehovah has built Zion ; he has been seen in his glory.* These are not *præterita prophetica*, describing future events as past ; nor are they to be taken as mere presents, but as denoting a relative past, dependent on the futures of the verse preceding. The nations and their kings are to fear because Jehovah has built (*i. e.* will then have built) Zion. Still another construction may seem possible, viz. "when Jehovah has built Zion he shall be seen in his glory." But in this case, Hebrew usage would require the last verb, if not both, to have the future form.

18 (17). *He has turned unto the prayer of the destitute, and has not despised their prayer.* This verse continues to assign the reason why the nations and their kings will be struck with awe, viz., because this great and glorious God has turned round, as it were, and listened to the prayer of the destitute and granted their petition. The word translated *destitute* occurs only here and in Jer. xvii. 6 ; but from its etymological affinities and its intensive form, appears to mean stark naked, and then figuratively, stripped of everything, impoverished, entirely destitute.

19 (18). *This shall be written for an after generation, and a people* (yet to be) *created shall praise Jah.* This fulfilment of God's promise and illustration of his attributes is left on record for the learning or instruction of posterity. Compare 1 Cor. x. 11. *An after generation,* as in Ps. xlviii. 14 (13), lxxviii. 4. Equivalent in meaning, but abridged in form, is the expression in the passage upon which these are founded, Ps. xxii. 31

(30). See also Ps. lxxi. 18. *Created* may have the force of a gerundive, as the passive particle often has in Hebrew ; or it may mean *(then) created (but not now)*. See above, on Ps. xxii. 32 (31). As the verb (בָּרָא) *create* is applied only to divine acts, its use here seems to indicate that what is meant is not merely a future generation, a race yet to come into existence, but a *people* in the strict sense, an organised body to be formed hereafter by sovereign authority and almighty power. *Shall praise Jah*, recognise Jehovah as possessing and as being all that is denoted by his name.

20 (19). *For he has leaned from the high place of his holiness ! Jehovah from heaven to earth has looked.* The first word may also be translated *that*, and the verse be understood as an amplification of the pronoun *this* at the beginning of ver. 19 (18). This is what shall be written for a future generation ; this is what they shall praise Jah for ; viz. that he has looked, &c. To avoid the repetition of the English verb, as well as to add life to the description, the Hebrew verb is here represented by what seems to be its primary meaning. See above, on Ps. xiv. 2, lxxxv. 12 (11), and compare Deut. xxvi. 15.

21 (20). *To hear the groaning of the prisoner, to loose the sons of mortality.* The construction is continued from the foregoing verse, and the design of God's thus looking down is stated. The word translated *groaning* is almost peculiar to the Psalms of David, and according to its etymology properly denotes suffocation. To *loose*, literally to *open*, sometimes applied to the opening of a dress for the purpose of removing it, as in Ps. xxx. 12 (11) ; then to the loosening of chains, as in Ps. cxvi. 16 ; then to the deliverance of the prisoner himself. *Sons of mortality* or *death, i. e.* those doomed to die. See above, on Ps. lxxix. 11.

22 (21). *To recount in Zion the name of Jehovah, and his praise in Jerusalem.* This, according to the laws of Hebrew syntax, does not necessarily denote an act of God himself, as the similar construction in the preceding verse does, but may have a vaguer sense equivalent to saying *that his name may be declared in Zion.* To recount God's name is to recount the mighty deeds which constitute it, and the celebration of which constitutes his praise. Zion is still represented as the great scene of Jehovah's triumphs, not, however, as the capital of Israel or Judah merely, but as the radiating centre of religious light and influence to all the earth.

23 (22). *In the gathering of peoples together, and kingdoms to serve Jehovah.* This verse is necessary to complete and qualify the sense of that before it. God has looked down from heaven to deliver his people and receive their praise, not in their secluded, insulated state, but in their glorious reunion with the converted nations. The first verb is a passive infinitive in Hebrew, *in their being gathered.* The preposition *in* relates both to the time and to the act of convocation. *To serve Jehovah*, not only as a King, but as a God, to be both his subject and his worshipper. Compare Ps. ii. 11.

24 (23). *He has humbled in the way his strength ; he has. shortened my days.* The Psalmist here resumes the tone of complaint, but only for a moment, and as an introduction to what follows. *Humbled*, weakened, or afflicted. *In or by the way* of his providential guidance, as distinguished from the glorious end to which it led. *His strength* and *my days* seem clearly to refer to the same person. To avoid this harsh enallage, the masoretic critics changed a single letter, and for (כֹּחוֹ) *his strength* read (כֹּחִי) *my strength*, which, though adopted in most versions, is an obvious

evasion of a supposed difficulty. With the last clause compare Ps. lxxxix. 46 (45). See also Ps. lv. 24 (23).

25 (24). *I will say, O my God, take me not up in the half of my days; through generation of generations* (are) *thy years.* *Take up,* cause to ascend, *i. e.* as some suppose, like smoke, which is very forced and far-fetched. Others make it simply mean to take away, which gives a good sense, but is not sufficiently sustained by usage. Better than either is the supposition that death or removal out of life is here described by a figure corresponding to the actual departure of Enoch and Elijah. See Gen. v. 24, 2 Kings ii. 1, 3, 5, 10, 11. *In the half* (or *midst*) *of my days;* see above, on Ps. lv. 24 (23), and compare Isa. xxxviii. 10. *Generation of generations, i. e.* all generations, as in Ps. lxxii. 5, Isa. li. 8. He prays that God, whose years are endless, would not, as it were, grudge the few days granted to his creatures. See above, on Ps. xxxix. 6 (5).

26 (25). *At first thou the earth didst found, and the work of thy hands* (are) *the heavens.* The phrase at the beginning means originally *to the face,* and then *before,* as an adverb both of time and place ; but this would be ambiguous here, since it might be understood as a conjunction, *before thou didst found the earth,* expressing the same idea as in Ps. xc. 2. It here means long ago, of old, in the beginning. With the last clause compare Ps. viii. 4 (3), xix. 2 (1), xxxiii. 6. God's creative power is here added to his eternity, in order to enhance the contrast between his infinity and man's littleness, as a reason for compassion to the latter.

27 (26). *They shall perish and thou shalt stand, and all of them like a garment shall wear out, like a dress shalt thou change them and they shall change.* The contrast is brought out as pointedly as possible in Hebrew, by the insertion of the pronouns *they* and *thou,* neither of which is grammatically necessary to the expression of the meaning. *Stand,* stand fast, endure, remain, continue. *All of them,* without exception, even the noblest of God's works, shall at least lose their present form, and in that sense perish, a sense which may be still more readily put upon the parallel verb *pass away* or *change.* The twofold usage of the English verb, as active and neuter, or transitive and intransitive, makes it an appropriate representative of the primitive and derivative forms of the Hebrew verb (חלף). The corresponding verb, in the second member of the sentence, means not only to *wax old,* but, as the necessary consequence, to *wear out.* See above, on Ps. xxxii. 3, and compare Ps. xlix. 15 (14).

28 (27). *And Thou* (art) *He—and thy years shall not be finished.* The construction of the first clause is disputed. Some read it, *Thou thyself and thy years shall not end.* Others, *Thou art the same,* giving הוא the same sense with the Greek ὁ αὐτός, which is actually used here to translate it in the Septuagint. In favour of the version first above given, is its agreement with the usage of the Hebrew words, with the analogy of Deut. xxxii. 39, and Isa. xliii. 10, and with the context here. The meaning then is, Thou art the Unchangeable One just described. Or, it is Thou, and nothing else, that shall thus endure. *Be finished,* spent, consumed, as the Hebrew word invariably means. What is elsewhere literally said of the violent destruction of human life is here transferred to the lapse of time.

29 (28). *The sons of thy servants shall abide, and their seed before thee shall be established.* This might also be translated as a prayer, *let the sons of thy servants continue,* which is really included even in the prediction. *Before thee,* as in Gen. xvii. 1, Ps. lxxxix. 37 (36). *Be established,* as in Ps.

lxxxix. 38 (37), ci. 7. With this conclusion of the whole psalm compare
Ps. lxix. 36, 37 (35, 36), xc. 16, 17.

Psalm 103

The Psalmist calls upon himself to praise God for personal favours
already experienced, ver. 1–5. From these he rises, in the body of the
psalm, to the contemplation of God's attributes, in themselves considered
and as manifested in his dealings with his people, ver. 6–19. He concludes
as he began, with an exhortation to bless God, no longer addressed merely
to himself, but to all creatures, ver. 20–22. According to the exegetical
hypothesis already mentioned, this is the song of *mercy and judgment* promised in Ps. ci. 1. The arguments in favour of this theory have been
already stated. The principal objection to it, and that by no means a conclusive one, is the want of unison and even concord, as to tone and spirit,
between the psalm before us and the two preceding it. Be this as it may,
the psalm before us is a complete and finished composition, being one of
the most simple and yet regular in structure that the book contains. This
has contributed, with other obvious peculiarities, to make it a favourite
vehicle of thankful praise among the pious of all ages.

1. *By David. Bless, O my soul, Jehovah, and all within me* (bless) *his
holy name !* The attempts which have been made by modern critics to
discredit the inscription in the first clause chiefly consist in representing
the many imitations and allusions to this⸱noble composition in the later
scriptures as a cento of citations from those scriptures by the writer of the
psalm itself, a preposterous inversion of the laws of evidence to which the
neological critics are especially addicted, and by which anything and everything can be disproved or proved at pleasure. *Bless*, when applied to God,
means to praise, but with a strong implication of devout affection. By
calling on his soul to do this, he acknowledges his own obligation, not only
to praise God, but to praise him cordially, *with all the heart*, according to
the solemn requisition of the law (Deut. vi. 5), to which there is perhaps a
reference in all such cases. See above on Ps. iii. 3 (2). The parallel
expression, *all within me*, is the plural form of one repeatedly used elsewhere, and denoting the *inside* of anything, and more especially of man,
his mind or heart, as distinguished from his mere professions or external
acts. See above, on Ps. v. 10 (9), xlix. 12 (11). The literal translation
of the form here used is *my insides* or *inner parts*, the strong and comprehensive meaning of the plural being further enhanced by the addition of *all*,
as if to preclude exception and reserve, and comprehend within the scope
of the address all the powers and affections. *His name of holiness* (or *holy
name*), *i. e.* the revelation of his infinite perfections. See above, on Ps.
v. 12 (11), xxii. 4 (3).

2. *Bless, O my soul, Jehovah, and forget not all his dealings.* The
positive exhortation is repeated as a kind of foil to the negative one following, in which there seems to be allusion to the frequent admonition in the
Law to Israel, not to forget the Lord who brought him up out of the land of
Egypt. See Deut. vi. 12, viii. 11, 14. The last word in the verse before
us is the passive participle of a verb which means to *treat*, and commonly to
treat well. See above, on Ps. vii. 5 (4). The idea here conveyed is that
of *treatment*, determined by the context to be kind and gracious treatment.
The latitude of meaning and the plural form are both represented in the

English word *dealings*, which, though susceptible of either application can, in this connection, only have a good one.

3. *Forgiving all thy guilt, healing all thy sicknesses*. The participles are to be grammatically construed with *Jehovah* as the object of the praise required, and assign a reason for the requisition, furnished by the personal experience of the soul itself. The original expression is still more definite, each participle having the article prefixed, *the (one) forgiving, the (one) healing*. See a similar construction carried out still further in Ps. xviii. 33–35 (32–34), 48–51 (47–50). The last word in the verse is an unusual one borrowed from Deut. xxix. 21, where *sicknesses* are joined with *plagues* or *strokes*, to signify calamities considered as penal inflictions. The same idea is expressed in other words, Exod. xvi. 26. The relation of the clauses, in the verse before us, may be that of cause and effect. Forgiving all thy guilt and thereby removing all the misery occasioned by it.

4. *Redeeming from the grave thy life, crowning thee (with) mercy and compassions*. The combination of the article and participle is the same as in ver. 3, *the (one) redeeming, the (one) crowning*. The continuation of the sentence in this form keeps the attention fixed upon the reasons for which, or the characters in which, the Lord is to be praised. As if he had said, Bless him as the one forgiving thee and healing thee, redeeming thee and crowning thee. *Redeeming* means delivering, but with a strong implication of cost and risk. For the twofold sense of (שַׁחַת) the word translated *grave*, see above, on Ps. xvi. 10, and compare Ps. xxx. 10 (9). The peculiar form of the possessive pronoun, in this verse and the one before it, has been represented as a proof of later date, but really belongs to the dialect of poetry, from which, in all languages, certain expressions are continually passing into that of common life, so that what in one age is poetical is in the next colloquial, and seems therefore to belong to the later period and to shew the recent date of any composition in which it occurs. The familiar use of such words as *oftentimes, perchance*, &c., in our own day may thus be used hereafter to prove the writings of our older poets spurious. The figure of *crowning*, which occurs above in Ps. lxv. 12 (11), suggests the idea of dignity and beauty, while the absence of merit in the object, and the sovereign freeness of the gift, are indicated by making the crown itself a crown of *mercy and compassion*. The last word in Hebrew is expressive of the warmest and tenderest affections. See above, on Ps. xviii. 2 (1), xxv. 6, xl. 12 (11).

5. *Filling with good thy soul—(then) is renewed, like the eagle, thy youth*. The peculiar construction of the two preceding verses is continued through the first clause of the one before us, and then suddenly abandoned. *Filling, the (one) filling*, in the sense of satisfying or abundantly supplying, but without the accessory notion of satiety. See above, on Ps. lxxxi. 17 (16), xci. 16. *With good*, literally *the good*, by way of eminence, the chief good or the real good. *Thy soul* is not a literal translation of the Hebrew term, which, in every other case where it occurs, means *ornament* or *decoration*. See, for example, Ps. xxxii. 9 (8). The translations *mouth, life*, &c., are gratuitous conjectures from the context. The best explanations is that furnished by the analogous word (כָּבוֹד) *honour, glory*, which is sometimes applied to the soul as the nobler part of man. See above, on Ps. xvi. 9. This explanation is confirmed by the frequent combination of the noun *soul* and the verb to *satisfy*. See above, Ps. lxiii. 6 (5), and below, Ps. cvii. 9, and compare Isa. lviii. 11. It is also sanctioned by the ancient

versions; for although the Targum makes it mean *old age*, a palpable conjecture, the Septuagint and Vulgate have *desire* (ἐπιθυμίαν, *desiderium*), a
frequent sense of (נֶפֶשׁ) *soul* in Hebrew, and Jerome translates it literally,
ornamentum. The word *then* is introduced into the translation of the second
clause, in order to retain the Hebrew collocation, which is not without its
emphasis. *Is renewed*, or retaining the reflective form of the original,
renews itself. The supposed allusion in this clause to a fabulous or real
renovation of the eagle in its old age, rests upon a misconception of the
language, as the only point of comparison with the eagle is its strength and
vigour, as in 2 Sam. i. 23, Isa. xl. 31, and the whole verse may be paraphrased as follows : " So completely does his bounty feed thy strength, that
even in old age thou growest young again, and soarest like an eagle."

6. *Doing righteousnesses* (is) *Jehovah, and judgments for all oppressed.*
Thus far the reasons urged for praising God were personal, *i. e.* derived
from individual experience. With these, from the very constitution of our
nature, all our grateful exercises must begin. But if genuine they do not
stop there, as the Psalmist, at this point, ascends from private causes of
thanksgiving to more general views of God's administration, as a basis for
the universal call with which the psalm concludes. The connection here
may thus be stated : " Such have been the Lord's compassions to myself,
but these are only samples of his goodness. He is not only merciful to me,
but to all who are oppressed, and to deliver whom he executes his judgments." There is no contrast here intended between mercy and justice,
with respect to different objects of the Lord's compassion. The meaning
is, that man's injustice is redressed by God's mercy. The redemption of
his people is often represented as coincident with the condign punishment
of their oppressors. Compare my note on Isa. i. 27. *Doing*, i. e. *practising* in general, and *executing* in particular cases. The participle (*doing*)
signifies habitual and constant action; the plural form (*righteousnesses*) completeness and variety, adapted to all possible emergencies. *Judgments*, as
usual, denotes judicial acts, as distinguished from mere attributes or
principles.

7. *He makes known his ways to Moses, to the children of Israel his* (mighty)
deeds. The general statement of the fact in the preceding verse is now followed by the great historical example furnished in Jehovah's dealings with
his people. This serves, not only to illustrate what was said before, but to
shew that it was not a mere vague declaration of what God will do to all
men, but a definite assertion of his purpose and his practice with respect
to his own people. *All the oppressed*, to whom he grants or promises deliverance, are not mankind in general, without distinction or exception, but
his own people when in that condition. The first clause contains an obvious allusion to the prayer of Moses, as recorded by himself, Exod. xxxiii.
13, from which passage it appears that the ways of God, which he desired
to know, were his modes of dealing with his people, or the course of his
dispensations towards them. See above, on Ps. xxv. 4, lxvii. 3 (2). The
knowledge thus imparted was experimental or afforded by experience. The
parallelism between *Moses* and the *Children of Israel* shews that the latter
were represented by the former. The last Hebrew word is one constantly applied to God's exploits or mighty deeds in behalf of Israel. See above, on
Ps. ix. 12 (11), lxxviii. 11.

8. *Compassionate and gracious* (is) *Jehovah, slow to anger, and rich in
mercy.* See above, on Ps. lxxvii. 10 (9), lxxviii. 38, lxxxvi. 15, in all
which cases, as in this, the terms of the description are borrowed from

Exod. xxxiv. 6. There is here an evident progression in the thought. Not only is God good to me, but to all his people in distress ; not only did he prove this to Moses and to Israel by saving them from Pharaoh and their other enemies, but by bearing with their own offences. The previous context might have seemed to concede innocence, if not merit, to God's people, as the object of his kind regard ; but they are here exhibited as sinners, needing his forbearance and forgiveness.

9. *Not to perpetuity will he strive, and not to eternity retain* (his anger). This, of course, implies that he is sometimes angry, even with his people, and sometimes strives in opposition to their strivings against him. But as he is always in the right, and they are always in the wrong, it is a signal proof of the divine compassion, that he does not strive and is not wroth for ever. The first clause is closely copied by Isaiah (lvii. 16). The second is itself derived from Lev. xix. 18, where we find a verb meaning to *retain* or *reserve* used absolutely in the sense of harbouring a grudge or cherishing a secret spite. This remarkable form of expression is copied, in the case before us, and in Nah. i. 2, Jer. iii. 5, 12. The original passage is a prohibition, in obeying which the Lord, as it were, here sets his people an example. Compare Mat. v. 48, 1 Cor. xi. 1, Eph. v. 1.

10. *Not according to our sins has he done to us, and not according to our iniquities has he dealt with us.* That the people stood in need of the divine forbearance, is now still more distinctly intimated. The last verb is the one of which the participle occurs in ver. 2, and might here be rendered, with still closer adherence to the strict sense of the Hebrew preposition, *has he bestowed upon us.* See the same construction in the Hebrew of Ps. xiii. 6, cxvi. 7, cxlii. 8 (7). The past tense has reference to the previous history of Israel as a nation, but involves the statement of a general truth. At the end of the verse, we may suppose it to be tacitly added: as he might have done, not only in strict justice, but in execution of his express threatening, Lev. xxvi. 21.

11. *For as the heavens are high above the earth, mighty is his mercy above those that fear him.* The Hebrew preposition is the same in both clauses, and cannot be varied in translation without weakening the sentence. In the last clause it suggests the ideas of descent from above, superior power, and protection, in addition to that of mere relation or direction, which is all that is conveyed by the translation *to* or *towards.* The force of the original is likewise impaired by substituting *great* for *strong* or *mighty.* The idea meant to be conveyed is not that of mere extent but of efficiency. The literal meaning of the first words is, *like the height of the heavens,* or *like their being high. His fearers,* or *those fearing him,* is a common description of the righteous, or God's people, who are more particularly characterised in ver. 18.

12. *As far as the east is from the west, he hath put far from us our trangressions.* The form of expression at the beginning is the same as in ver. 11, *like the distance of the east,* or *like its being far.* The Hebrew words for *east* and *west,* according to their etymology, denote the place of sunrise and the place of evening. *Put far from us,* as no longer having anything to do with us, a figure which suggests the idea both of pardon and renewal, justification and sanctification.

13. *As a father has compassion on* (his) *children, Jehovah has compassion on his fearers.* The compound phrase, *has compassion,* is here substituted for the simple verb *pity,* in order to retain the preposition *on,* which follows it in Hebrew, and also because the plural form, *compassions,* was neces-

sarily employed in ver. 4 to translate the cognate noun. The Hebrew verb is peculiarly appropriate in speaking of parental love. See above, on Ps. xviii. 2 (1). The preterite forms represent the fact alleged as one already known and well attested by experience.

14. *For he knows our frame, mindful that dust (are) we.* The fragility of man is here again assigned as a ground of the divine compassion. See above, on Ps. lxxviii. 39, lxxxix. 48 (47). *Frame*, formation, constitution, or as we say familiarly in English, *our make, our build.* The Hebrew noun is derived from the verb used in Ps. xciv. 9, and may therefore be intended to suggest the same idea that is there expressed. He who formed us knows of course how we are formed. The same noun is applied to the moral constitution, Gen. vi. 5, viii. 21, Deut. xxxi. 21. The word translated *mindful* is, in form, a passive participle, (זָכוּר) meaning *remembered*, but equivalent in use to the active, *remembering*, or the verbal adjective *mindful*, just as the like form (בָּטֻחַ) *trusted* is equivalent to *trusting*, Ps. cxii. 7, the English *rejoiced* to *rejoicing*, &c. *We are dust,* i. e. made of it, and tending to it. Compare Gen. ii. 7, iii. 19, Ps. xc. 3.

15. (As for) *man, his days (are) like the grass; like the blossom of the field, so he blossoms.* As the preceding verse expresses the fragility of man by referring to his origin and end, so this verse does the same by a familiar but beautiful comparison, borrowed from Ps. xc. 6, and repeated in Isa. xl. 6–8, Job xiv. 2. The very name here given to the race is one denoting frailty and infirmity. See above, on Ps. viii. 5 (4).

16. *For a breath passes over him and he is not, and no more shall his place know him.* The pronouns may with equal grammatical correctness, be referred to the grass and rendered *it, its.* The primary meaning of the first noun (*breath*) is, in this connection, stronger than the secondary (*wind*). The wind may be a whirlwind ; but to say that a mere breath is sufficient to destroy one is the strongest possible expression of fragility. That the wind is called the breath of God, as the thunder is his voice, is a striking and poetical but needless supposition. *He is not* or *no more*, there is none of him, no such thing or person. See above, on Ps. xxxvii. 10. With the first clause compare Isa. xl. 7; with the second, Job vii. 10. The last verb means to *recognise* or know again, as in Ps. cxlii. 5 (4), and the whole clause, that death makes men strangers to the objects with which they have been most familiar.

17. *And the mercy of Jehovah (is) from eternity even to eternity upon those fearing him, and his righteousness to children's children.* Having carried the description of man's frailty to the furthest point, the Psalmist suddenly contrasts with it God's everlasting mercy. The use of the simple copulative *and*, in such a marked antithesis, where *but* might to us seem indispensable, is one of the most striking and familiar Hebrew idioms. *Upon those fearing him* suggests the idea of a gift from above. *To children's children* simply means given (or belonging) to them. Unless we make the last clause a threatening of hereditary vengeance to the wicked *his righteousness* can only mean his rectitude, including his veracity and faithfulness in exercising covenanted mercy. *Children's children*, literally *sons of sons.*

18. *To the keepers of his covenant, and to the rememberers of his laws, to do them.* This is the necessary qualification of a promise which might otherwise have seemed too absolute. Even to the descendants of those fearing him the promise availed nothing, unless they themselves were faithful to his covenant and obedient to his law. The last words (*to do them*)

shew that the remembrance of the law required was not merely intellectual but practical and tending to obedience.

19. *Jehovah in the heavens has fixed his throne, and his kingdom over all rules.* Not only is he infinitely merciful and faithful, but a universal and almighty sovereign, no less able than willing to fulfil his promises and execute his purposes of mercy. The word translated *fixed*, like its English representative, suggests the two ideas of preparing and establishing. The same combination with *throne* occurs above, Ps. ix. 8 (7). See also Ps. xi. 4, xlvii. 9 (8). *Over all ;* the original expression is still stronger, *over the whole*, the universe, τὸ πᾶν. The same phrase is applied to the entire human race, Ps. xiv. 3. The past tense of the last verb represents this unlimited dominion as already established or revealed. The future would have made its ulterior continuance the prominent idea.

20. *Bless Jehovah, ye his angels, mighty in strength, doing his word,* (so as) *to listen to the voice of his word.* Having finished his assertion of God's claims to universal praise, the Psalmist resumes the tone of exhortation with which he began. His appeal, however, is no longer to his own soul, but to the hosts of heaven, the noblest of God's creatures, the highest order of finite intelligences. *Mighty in strength*, more exactly *mighty (ones) of strength*, or, as the first word is applied as a substantive to warriors or conquerors, *heroes of strength* or *mighty heroes.* See above, on Ps. xxiv. 8, lxxviii. 25. The construction in the last clause is obscure. The infinitive may here have the force of a gerund, *audiendo, auscultando,* by listening to the voice of his word, or, as in Ps. lxxviii. 18, it may denote the extent or the effect of their obedience, *so as to hearken,* or *so that they hearken, i. e.* listen for the faintest intimation of his will. The expression *hearken to his voice,* as thus applied, is a Mosaic one. See Deut. xxvi. 17, xxx. 20.

21. *Bless Jehovah, ye his hosts, his ministers, the doers of his will.* As the word *hosts* is applied both to the angels and the heavenly bodies (see above, on Ps. xxiv. 10), some interpreters, in order to relieve this verse of a tautology, suppose it to relate to the heavenly hosts in one sense, as the preceding verse does in another. In the same way they account for the change of expression in the last clause. Only intelligent creatures can be literally said to listen for God's word and to obey it; but even the inanimate creation may be said, without a metaphor, to execute his will. This last phrase occurs also in Ps. xl. 9 (8).

22. *Bless ye Jehovah, all his works, in all places of his realm ; bless thou, O my soul, Jehovah !* The angels and heavenly bodies, with men and every other creature, are now summed up in the comprehensive phrase, *all his works, i. e.* all that he has made, all creatures, and invited to bless God, which invitation the Psalmist then addresses once more to himself, and thus, by a beautiful transition, brings us back to the point from which we started.

Psalm 104

WE have here another of those psalms, in which the hopes of God's people are excited and their faith strengthened by a view of the authority and providential care which he exercises over the creation. The sum of the whole psalm is contained in the first verse, and its application indicated in the last. Here, as in Ps. viii., xix., xxix., lxv., the description of God's glory, as exhibited in nature, is entirely subservient to a moral and religious purpose, and the psalm is therefore fully entitled to a place in the collection, and adapted to the permanent use of the church.   The arrangement of the psalm is founded on the history of the creation, but with such variations as were suited to the writer's purpose.   After a general statement of this purpose, ver. 1, the Psalmist traces the creative and providential agency of God in the works of the first and second day, ver. 2–5, then in that of the third, ver. 6–18, then in that of the fourth, ver. 19–23, then in that of the fifth, ver. 24–26, with an allusion to the rest of the seventh day in ver. 31.   The psalm closes with a summary statement of the dependence of all living creatures upon God's care and bounty, ver. 27–32, a resolution to glorify him accordingly, ver. 33, 34, and a pregnant inference, that they who are under such protection have nothing to fear from human enemies, ver. 35.   According to Hengstenberg, this and the two next psalms compose a trilogy added to the Davidic one immediately preceding (Ps. ci.–ciii.) about the time of the Babylonish exile.   This hypothesis, he thinks, accounts for the occurrence of Davidic psalms in this part of the Psalter, which would otherwise have found their place among the Psalms of David in the first division of the book.   But having been made the basis or the nucleus of later compositions, they were naturally placed with these in their proper chronological position.

1. *Bless, O my soul, Jehovah! O Jehovah, my God, thou art great exceedingly; honour and majesty hast thou put on.*   The resemblance of the first clause to Ps. ciii. 1 shews the designed connection of the two psalms. The remainder of the verse is a kind of response to this invocation, and contains, as it were, the words in which his soul does actually bless God. At the same time it exhibits in advance the sum and substance of the whole composition, the design of which is to describe the glories of creation and providence as the royal robe of the divine sovereign.   Compare Ps. xlv. 4 (3), xciii. 1, xcvi. 6, Job xl. 10, Isa. li. 9.

2. *Wearing light like a robe, spreading heaven like a curtain.*   In carrying out the idea summarily stated in the first verse, he begins where the cosmogony in Genesis begins, with the light and the firmament, not the act of their creation, but their use, as the Creator's robe and curtain.   It follows of course that *light* and *heaven* must be taken in their popular and ordinary sense, and not as denoting the heaven of heavens and the light inaccessible in which he is elsewhere represented as dwelling.   The definite forms of the original, *the robe, the curtain*, as contrasted with the vaguer forms, *light, heaven*, may be intended to suggest the idea of the robe and curtain known and used in common life, which man puts on and stretches out with perfect ease, but not more easily than God puts on the light and stretches out the sky.   Compare Gen. i. 6, Isa. xl. 22, Job ix. 8.

3. *Framing with water his halls; making clouds his conveyance; moving on wings of the wind.*   The first word means laying beams or rafters.   The next phrase may either mean *in* or *with water*.   The first is more obvious, the last more striking, as it represents a solid building, made of a liquid or fluid material.   In the other case the waters meant are those above the firmament.   See Gen. i. 6, 7, Ps. xviii. 12 (11), where the clouds and the wings of the wind are also mentioned in the same connection.   The word translated *halls* denotes the highest room of an oriental house, which is frequently the largest.   Hence the frequent mention, in the New Testament, of the ὑπερῷον as a place of assembly.   *Making*, literally setting, placing. *Chariot* is too specific a translation of the Hebrew word, which means any-

thing on which a person rides. The preposterous figure of *walking on wings* belongs entirely to the versions, ancient and modern. The Hebrew word, though often so applied, is a generic one, denoting all progressive movement, and nearly equivalent to our word *going*, which is not so agreeable, however, in this place, to English usage, as the more general and poetical term *moving*. See above on Ps. xviii. 11 (10).

4. *Making his angels winds, his ministers flaming fire.* According to the simplest and most obvious construction of this verse, it can only mean that God makes his angels or ministering spirits swift and ardent in his service. But such a statement would be wholly out of place in a psalm, the rest of which relates exclusively to the material creation. The best interpreters are therefore of opinion that *angels* and *ministers* are predicates, not subjects, or in other words, that the idea meant to be conveyed is, that he makes the winds his messengers or angels, and the flaming fire his minister or servant. This agrees exactly with the previous declaration that he makes the clouds his chariot or conveyance, and moves upon the wings of the wind. It may seem, however, to be inconsistent with the use made of the passage in Heb. i. 7, as a proof that the angels are inferior to the Son of God. But how could this inferiority be proved by the fact that the angels are spirits, or even wind and fire ? The latter cannot be literally true, and if metaphorical, can only mean that they are swift and ardent in God's service, which they might be and yet equal to the Son in nature, who, considered as a messenger or agent of the Father, exhibits precisely the same qualities. The truth is, that the passage, as thus understood, is perfectly irrelevant and useless to the argument, and therefore that this mode of explaining it is not entitled to the preference, whatever difficulties may attend the other. Let it be observed, too, that the Septuagint version, which is quoted in Heb. i. 7, is an exact transcript of the Hebrew, both as to the sense and collocation of the words, so that if the original admits of a different construction, it may be extended to the version likewise. The most satisfactory conclusion is, that the words are not quoted as an argument or proof of the inferiority of angels, but merely as a striking yet familiar form of words in which to clothe the writer's own idea, which is this, that angels are mere messengers and ministers, and as such may be classed with the material agencies which God employs in execution of his purpose. The wind and the lightning are God's angels and his ministers, and are expressly so described in the Old Testament ; but they are never called his sons, much less addressed directly as the sovereign, eternal, righteous, ever-blessed God. Nor are the ministering spirits, who share with these material agencies the character of messengers and servants, ever so described or so addressed. By thus supplying the suppressed links of the chain of argument, the verse before us, in the only sense of which the context really admits, will be found not only as appropriate as the other to the purpose for which it is quoted in the New Testament, but incomparably more so.

5. *He founded the earth on its bases ; it shall not be moved for ever and ever.* The idea of *bases* is rather suggested by the context, and especially the verb *founded*, than expressed by the Hebrew noun itself, which properly means *places*, or more specifically, fixed and settled places. See above, on Ps. lxxxix. 15 (14), xcvii. 2, and with the whole verse compare Ps. lxxviii. 69, lxxxix. 12 (11), cii. 26 (25).

6. *(With) the deep, like a garment, thou didst cover it ; above the mountains stand the waters.* Next in importance to the separation of the land and water in the beginning (Gen. i. 9, 10), was the temporary confounding

of the two in the universal deluge (Gen. vii. 19, 20), which the Psalmist therefore here connects with the creation, as equally demonstrative of almighty power, and also for the purpose of founding on this seeming violation of the promise in the last clause of ver. 5, a still more solemn repetition of it. The grammatical objection that the pronoun in the phrase *didst cover it* is masculine, and cannot therefore refer to *earth* which is feminine, is easily removed by a reference to the general licence of the Hebrew syntax with respect to genders, and the idiomatic tendency to use the masculine,not as a distinctive but as a generic form, in cases where the subject is sufficiently indicated by the context. There are, moreover, several clear examples of the masculine construction of this very noun (אֶרֶץ) besides those in which *earth* or *land* is put for its inhabitants. See *e. g.* Gen. xiii. 6, Isa. ix. 18. The allusion in the last clause to Gen. vii. 19, 20, is too plain to be mistaken.

7. *At thy rebuke they flee, at the voice of thy thunder they hasten away.* The same power that produced the deluge put an end to it. The verbs agree with *waters* in ver. 6. The divine command that they should cease or disappear is poetically spoken of as a *rebuke.* See above, on Ps. xviii. 16 (15), lxxvi. 7 (6), and compare Isa. l. 2. The Hebrew particle means *from,* denoting both the time and cause of the effect described. The last verb is a passive meaning strictly to be panic-struck, or to flee in consequence of being panic-struck. See above, on Ps. xxxi. 23 (22), xlviii. 6 (5). The *voice of thy thunder* may be literally understood to mean the sound of thunder, or according to a well-known Hebrew idiom, thy voice of thunder, or thy thundering voice.

8. *They go up mountains, they go down valleys, to this place thou hast founded for them.* The first clause is a beautiful description of the fluctuations which attend the subsidence of swollen waters, not only in the case of Noah's flood (Gen. viii. 4, 5) to which the words relate in the first instance, but in all other cases, where the same rule still holds good, so that the verse, by an insensible transition, founds the statement of a general truth on that of a particular event. The use of the demonstrative (*this*) is highly idiomatic. The original construction is, *to a place, this (which) thou hast founded for them.* This form of expression is equivalent to pointing with the hand, and therefore adds not a little to the graphic vividness of the description.

9. *A bound thou didst set, they shall not pass over, they shall not return to cover the earth.* This grand exception to the law which governs the relations between land and water is the only one to be permitted or expected. The limits broken were renewed with an assurance that henceforth they should be inviolable. See Gen. ix. 15. Besides the immediate reference to the flood, the verse contains the statement of a general fact in the economy of nature, and thus furnishes a natural transition to the similar statements of the next verse.

10. *Sending springs into the valleys ; between hills they go.* The participial construction, interrupted by the parenthetical account of the flood, is here resumed, the participle, like the others, agreeing directly with Jehovah understood, as *the (one) sending,* which is the precise form of the original. See above, on Ps. ciii. 3–6. *Springs* or *fountains,* not in the restricted sense, but comprehending both the source and stream, as in Joel iv. 18 (iii. 18). The word translated *valleys* is restricted in usage to such as have streams flowing through them. The last word is the one translated *walketh* by the English Bible in ver. 3 above, but here *run,* although *walk* is given

in the margin, as a more precise and literal translation, while Jerome inserts it in his text, *ut inter medios montes ambulent.*

11. *They water every beast of the field ;* (at them) *wild asses quench their thirst.* The subject of the first verb is still the *waters.* The verb itself means to *water,* in the sense of giving drink to animals, though sometimes metaphorically applied to irrigation. See Gen. ii. 10. The form of the parallelism in this verse is peculiar, although not uncommon in Hebrew poetry, the last clause containing a specification of the general statement in the first. What is first said of animals, or wild ones in the general, is then said of the wild ass in particular. *Quench,* literally *break, i. e.* subdue, assuage. A derivative noun is applied in Hebrew to corn or grain, as that which *breaks* or assuages hunger, although most interpreters and lexicographers suppose a reference to the literal breaking or grinding of the corn itself.

12. *Above them the birds of heaven dwell, from between the branches they give voice.* The poetical character of the composition is in nothing more obvious than in these minute strokes of exquisite painting, superadded to the more essential parts of the description. At the same time these are not to be regarded as mere lavish or gratuitous embellishments, since the Psalmist's purpose is to celebrate God's wonderful and bountiful provision for his living creatures, and the running brooks would fail to answer one of their most valuable ends, if there were no birds to *give voice* or sing among the branches of the overhanging trees. The word translated *birds* is a collective answering to the old English *fowl,* not as used in the version of this psalm, where it is plural, but in that of Gen. i. 20, 22, 26, 28. That passage furnishes an explanation of the phrase *fowl* (or *birds) of heaven,* in the fuller description (Gen. i. 20), *fowl that may fly above the earth in the open firmament of heaven, i. e.* through the air, across the face of the expanse or visible heaven.

13. *Watering mountains from his upper rooms—from the fruit of thy works is the earth filled.* He still returns to God as the author of these merciful provisions, and represents him by a beautiful figure, as pouring this abundant supply of water from his *upper rooms,* the same word that was rendered *halls* in ver. 3 ; but here the connection seems to require that its precise etymological import should be prominent. *The fruit of thy works,* the result or product of thy creative energy. *Filled,* not in the sense of being occupied, which would require a different Hebrew verb, but in that of being abundantly supplied or saturated. See above, on Ps. ciii. 5. The sudden apostrophe to God himself enhances the poetical effect.

14. *Causing grass to grow for the cattle and herb for the culture of man,* (so as) *to bring forth bread from the earth.* In this verse there is a transition from God's care of the inferior animals to his care of man. The word translated *herb* denotes any green plant or vegetable, and is here applied to such as constitute or furnish human food. The common version of the next words, *for the service of man,* can only mean for his benefit or use, a sense not belonging to the Hebrew word, which, as well as its verbal root, is applied to man's servitude or bondage as a tiller of the ground (Gen. iii. 17–19), and has here the sense of husbandry or cultivation, as in Exod. i. 14, Lev. xxv. 39, it has that of compulsory or servile labour. The infinitive in the last clause indicates the object for which labour is imposed on man.

15. *And wine gladdens the heart of man—*(so as) *to make his face shine*

more than oil—and bread the heart of man sustains. The general expression at the end of ver. 14 is now rendered more specific by distinctly mentioning the great staples of production and subsistence in the Holy Land. The only doubt is whether two or three are mentioned. The text of the English Bible makes *oil* a distinct item in the catalogue, *and oil to make his face to shine.* But this is an impossible construction of the Hebrew, in which the infinitive (*to make shine*) bears the same relation to what goes before as the infinitive (*to bring forth*) in the verse preceding, and is therefore expressive, not of a distinct cause and effect, but of a consequence resulting from the one just mentioned. The true construction is given in the margin of the English Bible, *to make his face shine with oil* or *more than oil.* To the first of these alternative translations it may be objected that wine cannot make men's faces shine with oil, unless there is allusion to the festive unctions of the ancients, which, however, were restricted to the head. The other, therefore, seems to be the true sense, in which oil is merely mentioned as a shining substance. The description of food as sustaining the heart is very ancient. See Gen. xviii. 5, Judges xix. 8.

16. *Full are the trees of Jehovah ; the cedars of Lebanon which he planted.* Full, *i. e.* abundantly supplied, saturated, as in ver. 13. The English versions supply *sap ;* but the idea suggested by the context is the more general one of moisture, irrigation. The mutual relation of the clauses is the same as in ver. 11. What is first said of trees, or of the noblest trees in general, is then said of the cedars in particular. The *trees of Jehovah,* like the *cedars of God* in Ps. lxxx. 11 (10), are those which he has planted (Num. xxiv. 6), those which, by their loftiness or fruitfulness or beauty, bear the strongest impress of their Maker's hand. The *cedars of Lebanon* are often mentioned as the noblest and most famous of their kind. See above, on Ps. xxix. 5, xcii. 13 (12).

17. *Where the (small) birds nestle ; (as to) the stork, the cypresses (are) her house* He again recurs to the provision made for birds which is here connected with the trees, as it is in ver. 12. The word translated *birds* is not the one there used, but the same with that in Ps. lxxxiv. 4 (3), cii. 7, where it is commonly translated *sparrow,* though supposed to be a general term for small birds, so called from their chirping, twittering noise. Here it may represent the smaller, and the stork the larger class of birds. The Hebrew name of the stork means *merciful* or *pious,* and is supposed to have reference to the natural kindness of that bird, both to its parents and its young. *Nestle* or *build their nests.* The choice between the old translation, *fir-trees,* and the new one, *cypresses,* is exegetically unimportant.

18. *Mountains, the high (ones), are for the wild goats—rocks (are) a refuge for the conies.* The idea seems to be, that even the wildest situations, and the most inaccessible to man, afford shelter and subsistence to some form of life, and are therefore proofs of the divine benevolence and wisdom. Of the names of animals here mentioned, the first occurs also in the book of Job (xxxix. 1) ; the second in the list of unclean beasts, Lev. xi. 5, Deut. xiv. 7 ; and both in the writings of Solomon, Prov. v. 19, xxx. 26. Of the second, various explanations have been given, but none of them more probable than that derived from the rabbinical tradition. Nor is the question of the slightest exegetical importance, since the only peculiarities involved are those suggested by the text itself, to wit, that the animals intended must be such as inhabit rocks and mountains. Some supply *a refuge* in the first clause from the second ; but a better sense is yielded by the simpler construction, *they belong to* (or *are intended for*) *the wild goats,*

which agrees exactly with the drift of the whole psalm, to shew that all parts of the inanimate creation contribute something to the comfort of the living sentient creature.

19. *He made the moon for seasons; the sun knows his setting.* Even the heavenly bodies have a reference to man's advantage. The moon is a measure of time, and the sun defines the period of active labour. The word translated *seasons* is the plural of the one translated *set time* in Ps. lxxv. 3 (2), cii. 14, and the same that means *assemblies* in Ps. lxxiv. 4, 8. It is here put for all divisions of time, including the succession of day and night, to which there is perhaps a special reference, as in the other clause, where the meaning seems to be, that the sun knows when and where to set, and does not make the day, with its attendant toils, perpetual. This is a strong poetical description of an obvious and familiar fact, and no more presupposes a particular theory or system of astronomy than the similar language of uninspired poets among ourselves.

20. *Thou makest darkness and it is night ; in it begins to move every beast of the forest.* The first verb in Hebrew means to *set* or *place*, but is used precisely as a word of the same meaning is in ver. 3. Its abbreviated form does not indicate an optative meaning, but is substituted for the full form by poetic licence. *It is night*, or night is, night begins to be. The same inceptive meaning is expressed in the translation of the third verb which denotes animal motion, but is specially applied to that of reptiles. The idea of a secret, stealthy motion, as suggested by the common version (*do creep forth*), can hardly be intended, as the context shews the main idea of the passage to be this, that as the day affords a time for active motion to mankind and to domestic animals, the night affords a like time for the wilder beasts, or *beasts of the forest*, an expression which occurs above, in Ps. l. 10.

21. *The young lions roaring for the prey, and to seek from God their food.* By translating the participle and infinitive both as presents, the common version makes this a distinct proposition. But in Hebrew it forms part of the preceding sentence, and contains a specification of the general statement there made. When night comes on, all the beasts of the forest are aroused, and among the rest the lion, roaring for his prey, (is roused) to seek his food from God. This last expression implies no such purpose on the lion's part, but merely that he seeks what can only be bestowed by an almighty being, which idea is suggested by the name of God here used.

22. *The sun rises—they are gathered—and in their dens lie down.* The first clause may also be translated, *let the sun rise, they are gathered*, or paraphrased in more accordance with our idiom, *when the sun rises they are gathered;* but neither of these constructions is so striking and poetical as the exact version first above given. *Gathered, i. e.* called in from their wanderings and dispersions. The word translated *dens* means *abodes* or *homes*, and is a cognate form to that in Ps. xc. 1 ; but the form here used is specially applied to the lairs or resting-places of wild beasts, not only here but in Amos iii. 4. The last verb is also one appropriated to the lying down of animals. See above, on Ps. xxiii. 2. The construction is a pregnant one : *they lie down to* (or) *into their dens, i.e.* go into them and lie down.

23. *Forth goes man to his work, and to his labour until evening.* This verse presents the day-scene corresponding to the night-scene of the two preceding verses. When night comes on, the beasts of the forest are in motion ; when the sun appears, they gather to their lairs, and man comes

forth to labour *until evening*, when the scene is shifted as before.   Leaving out of view all higher claims to admiration and respect, the poetical
merit of this whole description is of the highest order.   The word translated *labour* is the same that was translated *culture* in ver. 14.

24. *How manifold are thy works, Jehovah ; all of them in wisdom hast
thou wrought; full is the earth of thy riches.*   The first verb in Hebrew
strictly means *are many*, but as the context has respect to the variety,
and not to the mere number, of God's works, the sense is well conveyed by
the term used in the English version (*manifold*).   *Works* and *wrought* represent a cognate verb and noun in Hebrew, a combination which adds
point and animation to the sentence.   The last word in the verse is
derived from a verb which means to acquire, either by creation or by
purchase.   While the noun, therefore, strictly denotes acquisitions or
possessions, its etymological affinities would instantly suggest to every
Hebrew reader the idea of creation, as the ultimate source of these possessions, a modification of the thought which cannot be conveyed by any
mere translation.

25. *Here is the sea, great and wide on all hands ; there are moving
things and without number, small animals with great.*   The exclamation
or reflection in the preceding verse affords a transition to the survey of
other parts of the creation, not included in the catalogue before recited,
yet no less striking in themselvess, and as proofs or illustrations of the
Maker's wisdom.   *Such is the sea*, or *here, for instance, is the sea*, are the
phrases which would probably be used in our idiom, to introduce the first
example.   The same thing was probably intended by the Hebrew phrase,
this (is) the sea, as if the speaker at the same time pointed to it.   See
above, on ver. 8.   *Wide of both hands* is another idiomatic phrase used
also by Moses (Gen. xxxiv. 21), and Isaiah (xxxiii. 21).   It obviously means
stretching out in all directions.   The sense of *hand* as thus used, is the
same as in the English phrase *on all hands*, and is probably derived from
the use of the right and left hand to distinguish position or direction.
Moving things is here used to translate a single Hebrew word (רֶמֶשׂ) the
cognate noun of the verb employed in ver. 20 to denote animal motion.   It
is applied to marine animals, as here in Gen. i. 9, Ps. lxix. 35 (34).   The
use of the word *beasts*, in the common version of the last clause, is not consistent with its modern usage, which restricts it to terrestrial quadrupeds.

26. *There the ships go—Leviathan—this (that) thou hast formed to play
therein.*   While the ships connect the sea with man's activity and interests,
Leviathan, the standing representative of aquatic monsters, may be here put
for the population of the sea itself.   *To play therein*, as in his native element.
Compare Job xl. 20.   The idiomatic use of *this* is like that in ver. 25.   The
word translated *go*, in the common version of the first clause, is the same
that was rendered *walk* in ver. 3, and *run* in ver. 10.

27. *All of them on thee rely, to give their food in its season.*   The *all of
them* obviously relates to all the living creatures previously mentioned, and
not to any one or more exclusively, the proposition being no less true of
men than brutes, or of brutes than men.   *On thee rely* is not an exact
translation of the Hebrew, which indeed does not admit of one, because it
combines a verb and preposition which cannot be combined in English.
The form of the original is, *to thee wait, expect*, or *hope*, the verb expressing
confidence, the particle the act of looking towards the object thus confided
in.   The description of the animals as thus expecting their supplies from
God, is merely the poetical costume in which the Psalmist clothes the fact

that they are really, although unconsciously, dependent on him.   In precisely the same manner, other poets represent the earth, in time of drought, as parched with thirst and longing for the rain, which expressions no sane man would either charge with falsehood, or consider as implying a belief in the conscious personality of Earth.   Compare my note on Isa. xlii. 4.   *In its season, i. e.* when they need it.

28. *Thou givest to them, they gather ; thou openest thy hand, they are filled (with) food.*   The point of the significant antithesis is this, that God as easily bestows as they receive.   He has only to give, they have only to gather.   He has but to open his hand, and they are instantly provided, even to satiety.   *Filled,* satisfied, abundantly supplied, as in ver. 13.   The verb rendered *gather* means to pick up or collect from the ground.   It is used in the history of the manna (Exod. xvi. 1, 5, 16), to which there is obvious allusion.   The act of gathering from the ground seems to presuppose a previous throwing down from heaven.   The common version, *that* (meaning *what*) *thou givest them they gather,* weakens the sentence, if it does not render it unmeaning.

29. *Thou hidest thy face, they are confounded ; thou withdrawest their breath, they expire, and to their dust return.*   The hiding of God's face is the opposite of looking with a favourable aspect.   See above, on Ps. xiii. 2 (1).   It here means the suspension or withdrawing of the various benefits before described.   *They are troubled* is, in every case, a feeble version of one of the strongest words in the language, which has been already more than once explained.   Even *confounded,* though much stronger, does not perfectly convey the idea, which is that of being agitated, terror-stricken, or convulsed.   See above, on Ps. ii. 5, lxxviii. 33, xc. 7.   *Their breath,* the vital principle imparted by the Spirit of God (Gen. ii. 7), who is the God of the spirits of all flesh, *i. e.* the author of all life whatever.   See Num. xvi. 22, xxvii. 16, and compare Heb. xii. 9.   The verb *expire* is used in the account of the destruction of all living creatures by the flood, Gen. vii. 21, 22, to which there is no doubt allusion, as there is in the next clause to Gen. iii. 19.   Compare Ps. xc. 3, ciii. 14, Eccles. xii. 7.   *Their dust,* their own, their native dust, to which they belong, and from which they sprang.

30. *Thou sendest thy breath, they are created, and thou renewest the face of the earth.*   The absolute power of God over the life of his creatures is expressed by representing him as annihilating and creating the whole race at pleasure, by a breath.   With equal correctness we might read *thy spirit,* but *thy breath* is more poetical, and therefore better suited to the context as the primary meaning, though the spirit be really intended.   *They are created* refers the effect more directly to God's power than *they live* or *they revive* would do.   In the last clause there is evident allusion to the renovation of the earth desolated by the flood, and the joyous change of its face or aspect when re-peopled.

31. *Let the glory of Jehovah be for ever ; let Jehovah rejoice in his works.*   The optative form of the first verb here determines the meaning of the other.   It would also be grammatical, though much less natural in this connection, to regard the abbreviated form of the first verb as a mere poetic licence, and explain both as futures proper.   *The glory of Jehovah shall be to eternity ; Jehovah shall rejoice in his works.*   The grammatical question is of less importance, because one of these senses really implies the other.   The wish is not for something doubtful but infallibly certain, and the prediction is in strict accordance with the wish of him who utters it.   In this

verse some interpreters suppose an allusion to God's satisfaction in his own work of creation when he rested from it on the seventh day. See Gen. ii. 1, 2.

32. *He that looks at the earth and it quakes, touches the hills and they smoke.* There is something in the form of this verse similar to that of ver. 28. God has only to look at the earth to make it quake. He has only to touch the mountains and they smoke. His controlling and terrifying acts are as prompt and easy as his acts of grace. There seems to be a reference to the words of Moses in describing the effects of the theophany at Sinai, when its summit smoked, and its very roots or bases were on fire. See Exod. xix. 18, Deut. xxxii. 22. To those familiar with the constant use of mountains as a symbol of great monarchies, this verse would necessarily suggest the thought, that God's power over states is no less absolute than that which he exercises over individuals, or over the inanimate creation.

33. *I will sing to Jehovah while I live, I will make music to my God while I still (exist).* This is the Psalmist's conclusion from the view which he has taken, with respect to his own interest and duty. If the Lord be such a God to all his creatures, then I can do no better than expend the remainder of my life in praising him. The two verbs are those continually joined to denote vocal and instrumental praise. The closing words of each clause, and especially the second, have a highly idiomatic character. The phrase translated *while I live* means literally *in my life* or *lives*. The corresponding one can scarcely be translated, as it is composed of the preposition *in*, the adverb *yet* or *still*, and the pronoun of the first person, *in my yet*, *i. e. in my (being) yet*, while I still am, or continue to exist.

34. *Sweet shall be of him my meditation; I will rejoice in Jehovah.* The ancient versions and the Prayer Book, with some of the best interpreters, put an optative sense upon the first clause, *may my thought (or speech) be acceptable to him*. In favour of this interpretation is the fact that a synonymous verb, followed by the same preposition (עַל), means to be pleasing to a person, in Ps. xvi. 6. In favour of the other is want of anything to indicate a wish, and the parallelism of the second clause, which relates to the expression of his own feelings towards Jehovah, not to the dispositions of Jehovah towards himself. Thus understood, the whole verse completes the Psalmist's practical conclusion from the view which he has taken of God's power, wisdom, and goodness, namely, that the knowledge and possession of this God is happiness.

35. *Consumed are sinners from the earth, and (as for) wicked men, they are no more. Bless, O my soul, Jehovah. Hallelujah!* This verse has no perceptible connection, either with the verse immediately before it, or with the general drift of the whole psalm, except upon the supposition, that the whole psalm was intended to derive, from the view of God's authoritative care over his works, an encouraging assurance that his people must be safe; that he who feeds and shelters the inferior animals, and makes provision for the physical necessities of men in general, cannot fail to provide for the security and happiness of those whom he has set apart for himself, or to free them from the malice of those sinners who are equally the enemies of God and of his people. The psalm, like the one before it, closes with the same words which began it. The last word, *Hallelujah (praise ye Jah)*, occurs here for the first time, and is supposed by some to form no part of the original composition, but to have been added for the purpose of adapting it to some public service at a later date.

Psalm 105

THIS, like the Seventy-Eighth, is a historical psalm, recounting God's ancient dealings with his people, especially in Egypt. The practical design of the commemoration is not to bring the people to repentance, as in the case referred to, but to excite their hopes of an analogous deliverance. According to a theory already mentioned, this is the second member of a trilogy, added to one of older date (Ps. ci.–ciii.) during the time of the captivity. It differs from the psalm before it in deriving from history the same consolation which is there derived from nature. After the introduction, ver. 1–7, the arrangement is simply chronological, beginning with the promise to Abraham, and ending with the conquest of Canaan, ver. 8–44. The first fifteen verses of this psalm are found in 1 Chron. xvi., combined with Ps. xcvi. and three verses of Ps. cvi. See above, on Ps. xcvi. 1.

1. *Give thanks unto Jehovah, call upon his name, make known among the nations his exploits.* The original meaning of the second phrase is, *call (him) by his name, i. e.* give him the descriptive title most expressive of his divine perfections; or more specifically, call him by his name Jehovah, *i. e.* ascribe to him the attributes which it denotes, to wit, eternity and self-existence, together with that covenant relation to his people, which, though not denoted by the name, was constantly associated with it, and therefore necessarily suggested by it. The meaning of the next phrase is obscured, if not entirely concealed, in the common version, *among the people.* The plural form and sense of the original expression are essential to the writer's purpose, which is to glorify the God of Israel among all nations. See above, on Ps. xviii. 50 (49), lvii. 10 (9). For the meaning of the last word, see above on Ps. ciii. 7.

2. *Sing to him, play to him, muse on all his wondrous deeds.* The exhortation seems to be addressed to the Gentiles, who are called upon to join in the praises and to share the blessings of the chosen people. For the meaning of the last verb, see above, on Ps. civ. 34.

3. *Glory in his holy name! Glad shall be the heart of those who seek Jehovah.* Congratulate yourselves that you possess a right and interest in the favour of so glorious a Being. The last clause presents as an inducement, that to seek the favour of this God is a source, and by implication the only source, of joy and happiness. Compare Ps. xxxiv. 3 (2), xl. 17 (16), lxix. 7 (6).

4. *Seek Jehovah and his strength, seek his face evermore.* The Hebrew verbs, although synonymous, are not identical. *And his strength,* the protection secured by his almighty power. Seek him, not as a finite being, but as the omnipotent Jehovah, the source, as well as the possessor, of all strength. *Seek his face,* not merely his presence, but his countenance, his favourable look or aspect. With the several expressions of this verse compare Ps. ix. 11 (10), x. 4, xiv. 2, xxiv. 6, xxxiv. 5 (4), lxi. 4 (3), lxii. 8 (7), lxiii. 3 (2), lxviii. 35 (34), xcvi. 7.

5. *Remember his wondrous deeds which he did, his miracles and the judgments of his mouth.* They are exhorted not to forget them, as Israel is charged with doing, Ps. lxxviii. 11. *Miracles,* prodigies or wonders, proofs of divine power. There is no need of identifying these with the *judgments of his mouth,* which include his laws and the sentences pronounced upon his enemies. The latter is probably the prominent idea, as best suited to this context.

6. *Ye seed of Abraham his servant, ye sons of Jacob, his chosen (ones).*
Descendants of the patriarchs, and therefore heirs of the patriarchal promises.   The common version of the last phrase (*his chosen*), though exact,
conveys a wrong idea, as it seems to make *chosen* an epithet of *Jacob*, which
would also seem to be required by the parallelism ; but the Hebrew word is
plural, and describes the object of address as the church or chosen people.
Compare Isa. lxv. 9.   Abraham is called the servant of God, in an emphatic
sense, as being his chosen instrument and confidential agent.   See above,
on Ps. xviii. 1, and compare Ps. xc. 1.   The parallel passage (1 Chron.
xvi. 13) has *Israel his servant.*

7. *He is Jehovah our God ; in all the earth (are) his judgments.*   His
covenant relations are with us the seed of Abraham ; but the proofs of his
existence and vindicatory justice are common to all nations.   This whole
introduction seems intended to dispose both Jews and Gentiles to the praise
of God.

8. *He remembered for ever his covenant, the word he commanded for a
thousand generations.*   There is here a kind of antithetical allusion to the
exhortation in ver. 5.   They should remember what he did, since he remembers what he promised.   What he has done involves a pledge of what he
will do.   He has remembered (and will remember) his covenant to eternity.
The word is the word of promise.   He is said to have commanded it, partly
because his promise is conditional and annexed to his commandment, and
for that reason called a covenant ; partly because all that God says must of
necessity be said with authority, so that even his promises partake of the
nature of commands.   The last phrase, *a thousand generations*, is Mosaic.
See Deut. vii. 9, and compare Exod. xx. 6.

9. *Which he ratified with Abraham, and his oath to Isaac.*   The sentence
is continued from the foregoing verse.   *Ratified*, literally *cut ;* see above,
on Ps. l. 5.   *His oath* (which he sware) *to Isaac*, or, *his oath for* (the benefit
of) *Isaac.*   The distinction, if any be intended, is that the covenant was
formally made only with Abraham, and merely sanctioned or confirmed by
oath to his successors.   See Gen. xv. 18, xxvi. 3, xxviii. 13.   *His oath* is
governed by *remembered* in ver. 8.   Compare Ps. lxxxix. 28, 34 (27, 33).

10. *And confirmed it to Jacob for a statute, to Israel (for) an everlasting covenant.*   *Confirmed it*, literally made (or let) it stand, instead of suffering it
to expire with the person to whom it was originally given.   *A statute*, in
the wide sense of a permanent arrangement, a perpetual constitution, or as
it is called in the last clause, *a compact of eternity*, an everlasting covenant.
See Gen. xxviii. 13, xxxv. 12.

11. *Saying, To thee will I give the land of Canaan, as the portion of your
heritage.*   The subject or substance of the promise is now more distinctly
stated.   The word translated *portion* primarily means a *line*, especially a
measuring line, and then what is measured by it, to wit, a piece of land, a
lot of ground.   This was not to be given to the patriarchs in person, but to
their descendants, as the portion of their heritage or their hereditary portion.   The plural *your* may refer, however, to the patriarchs themselves, as
the promise was repeated to Abraham, Isaac, and Jacob.

12. *When as yet they could be numbered—very few, and strangers in it.*
The first clause involves an antithetical allusion to the promise, afterwards
fulfilled, that they should be innumerable as the stars, or as the sand upon
the shore, Gen. xxii. 17.   The form of the original is highly idiomatic, *in
their being men of number, like a little*, or like littleness itself.   See above,
on Ps. lxxiii. 2, and compare Isa. i. 9.   *Strangers*, sojourners, living on the

lands of others, at their will, or by their sufferance. See above, on Ps.
xxxix. 13 (12). *In it,* the land of Canaan, mentioned in the preceding
verse. The whole verse qualifies the previous account of the patriarchal
covenant, which was not made with Israel when already a great nation, but
with their ancestors when few in number and without a settled home. The
parallel passage (1 Chron. xvi. 19) has *when ye were.* See Gen. xxxiv. 30,
and compare Deut. xxxiii. 6, Isa. x. 19.

13. *And they went about from nation to nation, from kingdom to another
people.* This may be regarded as in contrast with ver. 12, *and (yet) they
went about,* notwithstanding their small number and their being strangers.
Or ver. 12, 13, may be the protasis of the sentence, and ver. 14 its apodosis. " When they were few and strangers, and went from nation to nation,
he let no man," &c. This verse describes the characteristic feature in the
condition of the chosen people, during the patriarchal period of their history, namely, their migratory intercourse with various nations. These are
mentioned in the first clause as distinct races, in the last as distinct states
or bodies politic. Where we might have expected *from kingdom to kingdom,*
the ear is somewhat disappointed by the phrase *from kingdom to another
people,* which may have been intended to distinguish the Egyptian and
other monarchies from the more democratical or patriarchal institutions of
the Arabians and other nations. *They went about* seems to be the force of
the reflexive or frequentative verb, as distinguished from that of the primitive, *they went.* See above, on Ps. xxvi. 3, xxxv. 14, ci. 2, and compare
Gen. v. 22, xvii. 1, xxiv. 6, 9, 40, xlviii. 15.

14. *He suffered no man to oppress them, and reproved, for their sake,
kings.* The precise sense of the first clause is, he suffered not man (or
men in general) to oppress them. The protection of the patriarchs is certainly one of the most striking facts in sacred history. The kings mentioned in the last clause are the kings of Egypt and Gerar (Gen. xii. 17,
xx. 3), not without reference perhaps to those mentioned in Gen. xiv. 1.

15. *Touch not mine anointed ones, and to my prophets do no harm.* These
are the words of God himself, and are designated as such in the English
Bible, by supplying the word *saying,* which is expressed in the analogous
case, ver. 11. *Touch not,* as in Gen. xxvi. 11, 29. In the Old Testament,
unction is the symbol of spiritual gifts, and especially of those imparted to
the great theocratical offices. See above, on Ps. ii. 2. From the case of
Elisha (1 Kings xix. 16) it would seem that prophets were anointed when
inducted into office. The patriarchs are here called *prophets* in the proper
sense of the term, as denoting men inspired of God, and admitted to confidential intercourse with him. The allusion here is to Gen. xx. 7, where
God says to Abimelech of Abraham, " Restore the man his wife, for he is
a prophet, and he will pray for thee, and thou shalt live."

16. *And he called (for) a famine on the land ; every staff of bread he brake.*
The Psalmist now passes from the Patriarchal to the Egyptian period of
the history, by stating the occasion of Israel's migration into Egypt. The
meaning of the first clause seems to be, that he summoned famine, as his
instrument or servant, to come down upon the land, as sent from above,
that is to say, from himself. The meaning of the last clause is, that the
people were deprived of every customary means and source of subsistence.
The figure of a staff or stay is a Mosaic one. See Lev. xxvi. 26, and compare Isa. iii. 1. It is near akin to the description of food as staying or
sustaining the heart. See above, on Ps. civ. 15. The historical reference
in the verse before us is to Gen. xli. 54.

17. *He sent before them a man ; sold for a slave was Joseph.* The same providential purpose is assigned to Joseph's bondage by himself, Gen. xlv. 5. With the last clause compare Gen. xxxvii. 36. Some interpreters, assuming, as we have already seen, that this psalm was composed in the time of the captivity, suppose a parallel, in this verse, between Joseph and Daniel, both of whom, in addition to their personal qualities, were sent into captivity before the body of their brethren ; both gained the royal favour, and were exalted to high station in the land of their captivity ; and both employed the influence thus gained for the advantage of their countrymen. To the Jews in exile such a parallel must have been not only interesting, in a historical or poetical point of view, but consolatory and encouraging as *a token for good*, a sign that God was about to renew the exodus from Egypt in an exodus from Babylon.

18. *They hurt, with the fetter, his feet; into iron came his soul.* That Joseph was actually chained or fettered is included in the true sense of the word *bound*, applied to him in the history. See Gen. xl. 3, and compare Gen. xxxix. 20, 22. *They*, the Egyptians, or his gaolers ; or the verb may be indefinitely construed, as if it had been said, *his feet were hurt*. The verb means elsewhere to humble or mortify, but is here used in its strict sense of afflicting, causing to suffer. The Prayer Book version of the last clause, *the iron entered into his soul*, is ungrammatical, the word for *iron* being masculine, while that for *soul* is, like the verb, feminine. The general sense is given in the text of the English Bible, and the exact form in the margin. The mention of the soul, as in many other cases, is of course not meant to be exclusive of the body, but to suggest the idea of intimate and heartfelt suffering. See above, on Ps. iii. 3 (2), xi. 1, &c.

19. *Until the time that his word came* (to pass), *the saying of Jehovah tried him.* The last verb properly denotes the assaying of metals, but is figuratively applied to moral trial and purgation. See above, on Ps. xii. 7 (6), xvii. 3. xviii. 31 (30), xxvi. 2. The most probable meaning of the verse is, that during the two years which intervened between his explanation of the prisoners' dreams, and the favourable issue to which it ultimately led, his faith in the divine promise both to himself and to his people, was severely but favourably tried. Compare the history in Gen. xl. xli.

20. *The King sent and loosed him—the ruler of nations, and set him free.* Both verbs strictly apply to the removal of his fetters, the first meaning properly to knock off (Isa. lviii. 6), the other to open for the purpose of removing. See above, on Ps. xxx. 12 (11). The king of Egypt is called a *ruler of peoples*, either in reference to the tribes or nomes of Egypt itself, or because there were other nations tributary to him.

21. *He made him Lord of his house and ruler of all his wealth.* The literal meaning of the first clause is, *he placed him lord to his house.* See Gen. xli. 40, 41, 43, xlv. 8. For the meaning of the last word in the sentence, see above, on Ps. civ. 24 It is one of the points of resemblance which are thought to identify the two psalms as the work of the same author.

22. *To bind his chiefs at his pleasure, and his elders to make wise.* The words translated *chiefs* and *elders* are those commonly applied to the heads of tribes and families, the hereditary magistrates under the patriarchal system. The application of the second word to Egypt is found also in the history, Gen. l. 7. *At his pleasure*, literally *with his soul*, which some explain as a bold metaphor, describing Joseph's mind or soul as the cord

or chain with which he bound the Egyptians, *i. e.* forced them to perform his will. But see Ps. xvii. 9, xxvii. 12, xli. 3 (2).

23. *And* (so) *Israel entered Egypt, and Jacob sojourned in the land of Ham.* This was the main event, to which those just recited were preparatory. *Israel* and *Jacob* are the names both of the individual patriarch and of his descendants as a nation. In this case both the applications are admissible, or rather requisite, in order to exhaust the writer's meaning. The patriarch himself came into Egypt, but his sons literally came with him, and all his descendants figuratively in him. *The land of Ham,* from whom *Mizraim* was descended. See above, on Ps. lxxviii. 51.

24. *And he increased his people greatly, and made them stronger than their enemies.* Increased, literally rendered fruitful. The same verb is used in the promise to Abraham and Jacob (Gen. xvii. 6, xxviii. 2), and in the history of Israel in Egypt, Exod. i. 7. The word here used for enemies is one implying persecution and oppression. The singular pronouns in the Hebrew, *made him stronger than his enemies,* are in strict grammatical agreement with the collective noun *people.*

25. *He turned their heart to hate his people, to deal craftily with his servants.* The first clause asserts God's sovereign control even of the free acts of his sinful creatures, a truth repeatedly affirmed in the history which this psalm recapitulates. See Exod. iv. 21, vii. 3, and compare 1 Sam. xxvi. 9, 2 Sam xvi. 10, xxiv. 1. The last verb occurs only in the history of Joseph, Gen. xxxvii. 18. The corresponding term in Exodus (i. 10) is *let us deal wisely,* or more exactly, *let us make ourselves wise,* as the verb in this case may be rendered, *let us make ourselves subtle* or *crafty,* both being reflexive forms. The historical allusion is of course to the murderous policy, which preceded the violent oppression of the Hebrews.

26. *He sent Moses his servant* (and) *Aaron whom he chose.* The meaning is not *Moses* (who was) *his servant,* or (because he was) *his servant,* but (to be) *his servant,* his instrument in the great work of delivering his people. See above, on ver. 6, and on Ps. xviii. 1, xxxvi. 1, lxxviii. 70.

27. *They placed among them the words of his signs and wonders in the land of Ham.* The first phrase seems to mean nothing more than *set before them,* or *exhibited to them.* *Words of signs* is by some understood to mean *matters* (or *affairs*) *of signs,* and to be either a pleonastic phrase for *signs* alone, or an emphatic phrase denoting *all the signs.* See above, on Ps. lxv. 4 (3). The first is a gratuitous assumption, the last a forced interpretation. Better than either is the explanation which gives to *words* its proper meaning, and supposes stress to be intentionally laid on the divine word of Jehovah, and the prophetic word of Moses and Aaron, in the way of threatening and command, as well as on the physical effects which followed these denunciations. Compare the use of *words* in Ps. vii. 1, and the explanation there given. *Signs, i. e.* tokens of God's presence and activity, and indications of his will. *Wonders,* prodigies, miracles, the same word that occurs above in ver. 5.

28. *He sent darkness and made it dark, and they did not resist his words,* or according to the marginal reading, *his word.* This is by some understood to mean the plague of darkness, which immediately preceded the slaughter of the first-born, Exod. x. 22. But to this explanation there are two objections : first, that it entirely disturbs the order of the plagues, which is otherwise observed with great exactness, the only deviation being very trivial compared with this ; secondly, because it would then be necessary to apply the last clause to Moses and Aaron, or to Israel in general, there-

by making it unmeaning, or else to admit a contradiction of the history, which expressly says that the Egyptians did resist the word of God even after the plague of darkness, Exod. x. 27. The only remaining explanation is, that darkness, in the verse before us, as in many other cases, is a figure for calamity in general, and applied not to one plague in particular, but to the whole series, of which a more detailed account is then subjoined.

29. *He turned their waters to blood and killed their fish.* Here begins the more particular enumeration of the plagues of Egypt. Compare Ps. lxxviii. 44, where the inconvenience specified is that they could not drink the water, whereas here it is the loss of their accustomed food. This last word is used as a collective in both languages.

30. *Their land teemed with frogs—in the chambers of their kings.* That even these were not safe from the hateful intruders, is an aggravating circumstance, particularly mentioned in the original threatening, and implied in the narrative of its execution. See Exod. viii. 3, 9. The first verb means to bring forth in abundance, and is so used in the history of the creation, with particular reference to the genesis of animals, Gen. i. 20.

31. *He said, and the fly came and gnats* (or *lice*) *in all their border.* See above, on Ps. lxxviii. 45, where the gnats or lice are omitted, and the flies precede the frogs. So here, the flies precede the lice, a slight departure from the order of the history. See Exod. viii. 5, 16. *He said, i. e.* he said so, which is tantamount to saying, *he commanded. In all their border, i. e.* every where within it, throughout the land. This expression is borrowed from the history. See Exod. viii. 2 (vii. 27).

32. *He gave them hail for rain* (and) *flaming fire in their land.* This, which is the common version, represents the sense correctly, but with a deviation from the form of the original, which is highly idiomatic. A bald translation is, *he gave their rains hail, fire of flames in their land.* The terms are chosen for the sake of an allusion to the promise in Lev. xxvi. 4, *I will give your rains in their season.* Instead of these he gave the Egyptians a destructive hail-storm. Compare Ps. lxxviii. 48.

33. *And smote their vine and their fig-tree, and shattered the trees of their border.* Compare Ps. lxxviii. 47, where sycamores are particularly mentioned. The history says nothing of the vines, but speaks of the breaking of the trees, using the same intensive verb as here. See Exod. ix. 25. *Their border,* as before, means their land or territory in its whole extent, just as *the ends of the earth* is put for all its parts. See above, on Ps. ii. 8.

34. *He said, and the arbeh came, and the yelek, and* (that) *without number.* The two Hebrew words, here retained, denote varieties of the locust, and have no equivalents in English. See above, on Ps. lxxviii. 46, where the first word here stands second, and the place of the other is supplied by *hasil,* another distinctive term of the same kind. *Without number,* literally *there is no number.* See the same expression, Ps. civ. 25.

35. *And devoured every herb in their land, and devoured the fruit of their ground.* The verb, though varied in the common version, is the same in both clauses of the Hebrew. See above, on Ps. xlviii. 46, and compare the original narrative, Exod. x. 5, 15.

36. *And he smote all the first-born in their land, the first-fruits of all their strength.* For the meaning the last clause, see above, on Ps. lxxviii. 51, and compare Exod. xii. 29, 30.

37. *And he brought them out with silver and with gold, and there was not in his tribes a totterer* (or *stumbler*). The first clause relates to the spoiling

of the Egyptians, Exod. xii. 35, 36. The last word denotes a person unfit for military service. Compare Isa. v. 27.

38. *Glad was Egypt at their going forth, for their fear had fallen upon them.* This panic terror, which followed the last plague and facilitated the escape of Israel (Exod. xi. 1, xii. 31–33), accounts for the readiness with which the Egyptians gave whatever was demanded, and completely vindicates the children of Israel from the charge of borrowing what they never meant to pay. The terms used in the history denote the acts of asking and giving, not those of borrowing and lending. The terms of the last clause are derived from Exod. xv. 16, Deut. xi. 25.

39. *He spread a cloud for a covering, and fire to give light by night.* See above, on Ps. lxxviii. 14. The poetical description of the cloud as covering the host is derived from the statement that " the cloud of Jehovah was over (or above) them by day," Num. x. 34. Compare Num. ix. 16, Neh. ix. 12, Isa. iv. 5, 6.

40. (The people) *asked and he made quails come—and bread of heaven satisfied them.* See above, on Ps. lxxviii. 25–27, and compare Exod. xvi. 4–13, Num. xi. 31. As to the alternation of the singular and plural forms, see above, on ver. 24. *Bread* may be either the subject of the verb, as given above, or a qualifying term, (*with*) *bread.*

41. *He opened a rock and forth gushed waters ; they ran in the wastes, a river.* See above, on Ps. lxxviii. 16, 20. The word translated *wastes* means, according to its etymology, dry places.

42. *Because he remembered his holy word with Abraham his servant.* This brings us back to the statement in ver. 8, 9, in proof of which this long array of facts has been presented. Nothing of all this would have taken place if God had been forgetful of his covenant. This covenant is here meant by *his holy word*, which is therefore followed by the preposition *with*, as in Exod. ix. 24, where the covenant is expressly mentioned.

43. *And brought out his people in joy, in triumph his chosen (ones).* He remembered his promise, and in execution of it brought out his people, &c. The parallelism of *people* and *chosen* throws light upon the latter term, as used in ver. 6.

44. *And gave to them nations' lands, and peoples' labour they inherit.* The prominent idea is not that of *gentiles* or *heathen*, in the religious sense, but that of other nations, and whole nations, to whose place and possessions they succeeded. *Labour* is put for its result or product, as a synonymous Hebrew word is in Ps. lxxviii. 46.

45. *To the end that they might keep his statutes and his laws observe. Hallelujah !* The emphatic phrase at the beginning, corresponding to our phrases, to the end, for the purpose, or in order that, points this out as the qualification or condition of the promise which had been so gloriously verified. The same condition is expressed or implied elsewhere. See above, on Ps. lxxviii. 7, and compare Gen. xviii. 19, Deut. iv. 40, xxvi. 17. *Hallelujah (praise ye Jah)*, as above, in Ps. civ. 35.

Psalm 106

AFTER an introduction, praising the divine goodness, and expressing the hope of a participation in it, ver. 1-5, this psalm contains a solemn confession of the sins of Israel through all the periods of his history : in Egypt, ver. 6-12 ; in the wilderness, ver. 13-33 ; in Canaan, ver. 34-43 ;

and a prayer, founded on encouraging tokens of the Lord's compassion, that
he will save his people from the punishment incurred by their unfaithfulness,
ver. 44–48. According to Hengstenberg's hypothesis already mentioned,
this is the third psalm of the trilogy added to Ps. ci.–ciii., in the times of
the captivity, and a direct continuation of the series, since the moral condition of God's covenant, propounded at the close of Ps. cv., is here acknowledged to have been violated by his people, who are also represented as
actually suffering the punishment of this violation, but encouraged by
returning tokens of a favourable change, to hope and pray for the forgiveness
of their sins and the removal of the judgments which they have so well
deserved. The first verse and the two last form a part of the mixed composition in First Chronicles, which has been already mentioned. See
above, on Ps. xcvi. 1. But a still more interesting parallel to this psalm
is the prayer or confession in the ninth chapter of Daniel, which resembles
it so much in subject, tone, and diction, that although not otherwise
demonstrable, it would not be absurd to regard the psalm before us as a
lyrical paraphrase of that confession, prepared for permanent and public use
by Daniel himself or some contemporary writer.

1. *Hallelujah! Give thanks unto Jehovah, for (he is) good, for unto
eternity (is) his mercy.* The *Hallelujah (praise ye Jah!)* which concludes
the two preceding psalms, stands both at the beginning and the close of
this. The exhortation to *give thanks unto Jehovah* is also found at the
beginning of Ps. cv. The reason here assigned, *that he is good, and his
mercy endures for ever*, is expressed in the same words, Ps. c. 5.

2. *Who shall tell the mighty deeds of Jehovah ?* (Who) *shall utter all his
praise ?* The potential meaning (*who can tell ?*) is here included in the
simple future. *Mighty deeds* answers to a single word in Hebrew meaning
strengths or *powers*. The expression is borrowed from Deut. iii. 24, where
the English Bible has the singular form *might*. The verb translated *utter*
is a causative, who shall cause to hear or to be heard ? See above, on Ps.
xxvi. 7. The interrogation involves a negative assertion, namely, that they
cannot be fully expressed or duly celebrated.

3. *Happy the keepers of judgment, the doer of righteousness at every time.*
The form of expression at the beginning is the same as in Ps. i. 1. The
keepers of judgment are those who observe justice as the rule of their conduct, the same idea that is afterwards expressed in other words, *the doer*
(or *practiser*) *of righteousness*, not occasionally merely but at all times. The
change from the plural to the singular is common, where the latter denotes
an ideal individual, the representative of a whole class. The condition
here propounded is identical with that in Ps. cv. 45, ciii. 18, Dan. ix. 4.

4. *Remember me, Jehovah, with the favour of thy people ; visit me with
thy salvation.* The speaker is the Church or chosen people, and therefore
prays to be remembered with the kindness due to her as such. *Visit me,*
manifest thy favourable presence. See above, on Ps. viii. 5 (4). Such a
prayer, uttered by the church itself, implies that the tokens of God's
favourable presence had been interrupted or withdrawn.

5. *To witness the welfare of thy chosen (ones), to rejoice in the joy of thy
nation, to glory with thy heritage.* Our idiom requires the subject of the
verb to be more distinctly indicated. The meaning evidently is, *that I may
witness, that I may rejoice, that I may glory*. The phrase translated *witness
the welfare* literally means *to see in the good*, i. e. to look on, to be a spectator, when thy chosen ones are in possession or enjoyment of good. *Thy
nation* is here used instead of the customary phrase *thy people*, perhaps

because the meaning is, the nation which is thy chosen people. The general meaning of the whole verse is, that I may once more be recognised and treated as thy people.

6. *We have sinned with our fathers, we have done perversely, we have done wickedly.* The connection with the foregoing context may be made clear by supplying a few intermediate thoughts. "True, we have no right to expect this, much less to demand it. We have not performed the condition of thy covenant ; we have not kept thy statutes or observed thy laws ; we have not kept judgment or done righteousness." The national confession here begun is nearly co-extensive with the psalm itself. The terms of this verse are borrowed, here as well as in Dan ix. 5, from that great model of ecclesiastical and national devotion furnished by Solomon, in his prayer at the dedication of the temple, 1 Kings viii. 47. Compare Isa. lix. 12. *With our fathers*, not merely like them, but as sharing their responsibility and guilt. Of the three verbs used in this confession, the first denotes failure to discharge one's obligations, the second wilful perversion or distortion, the third disorderly or turbulent transgression. See above, on Ps. i. 1.

7. *Our fathers in Egypt did not understand thy wondrous works, they did not remember the abundance of thy mercies, and rebelled upon the sea, at the Red Sea.* The general confession in ver. 6 is now followed by a more detailed acknowledgment, beginning with the exodus from Egypt. The *wondrous works* of God, the things done wonderfully by him, then and there, for the deliverance of his people, the great body of them did not understand. Even those who referred them to their true source and author, did not fully appreciate the end for which they were performed, or enter into the majestic plan, in executing which they were permitted to be God's co-workers. The truth of this charge is abundantly established by the narrow, grovelling, selfish views and feelings so repeatedly betrayed by the generation which came out of Egypt, shewing clearly that they did not *practically understand* God's dealings with them. This is probably the idea meant to be conveyed by the Hebrew verb, which usually means to *act wisely*, but is here modified by governing a noun directly. See above, on Ps. ii. 10, xiv. 2. The twofold local designation, *on the sea, at the Red Sea*, was probably suggested by the parallelism in Exod. xv. 4. The variation of the particle seems merely a poetical embellishment; the difference in meaning is no greater than in our *on* and *at*. The *Sea of Sea-weed* was the name given by the Hebrews and Egyptians to that bay or gulf of the Indian Ocean, which was called the Red Sea by the Greek geographers.

8. *And he saved them for his name's sake, to make known his might.* This is an answer to a tacit objection, namely, that their conduct had been sanctioned by God's saving them. True, he did save them, because they were necessary to his purpose. He saved them not for their sake but his own, to accomplish his own ends, and exhibit his own power.

9. *And he rebuked the Red Sea and it dried up, and he made them go through the deeps like the desert.* This is merely a specification of the general statement in the preceding verse. The divine intervention here commemorated was the more remarkable because it took place on the very spot where they first rebelled, as mentioned in ver. 7. Though they disobeyed him at the Red Sea, he nevertheless dried the Red Sea, *i. e.* as much of it as was required to furnish them a passage. *Rebuked*, as in Ps. civ. 7. *Like the desert*, as in the desert, *i. e.* in a level and extensive plain, without obstruction or unevenness. See my note on Isa. lxiii. 13, where the same comparison is used.

10. *And he saved them from the hand of the hater, and redeemed them from the hand of the enemy.* Both epithets are intended to apply to Pharaoh, not only as a personal oppressor of the Israelites, but as the representative of Egypt, all of which now feared and hated the occasion of its multiplied and aggravated sufferings.

11. *And the waters covered their adversaries; not one of them was left.* The Psalmist dwells upon the completeness of the overthrow and destruction experienced by Pharaoh and his host, in order to aggravate the previous and subsequent ingratitude of Israel, as well as to enhance the free grace of Jehovah, and the fidelity with which he executed his engagements, even to the faithless.

12. *And they believe his words, they sing his praise.* Then (and not till then) do they believe. This is not an encomium on their faith, but a confession of their unbelief. It was not till the promise was fulfilled that they believed it. With the first clause compare Exod. xiv. 31; with the second, Exod. xv. 1.

13. *They made haste, they forgot his deeds, they did not wait for his counsel.* Their propensity to evil was so strong that they are said to have hastened to forget what God had done for them, which means much more than that they soon forgot it. They did not even wait for the promise to be verified by the event. The expression in the first clause is borrowed from Exod. xxxii. 8. The works or deeds of God are not in this case, as in Ps. ciii. 22, civ. 24, the works of nature, but the plagues of Egypt. See Deut. xi. 3, and compare Dan. ix. 4.

14. *And they lusted a lust in the wilderness and tempted God in the desert.* The confession now passes from their sins in Egypt to their sins in the wilderness. The strong expression in the first clause relates to their wanton craving of animal food. See Num. xi. 4, 34. With the last clause compare Ps. lxxviii. 18. The two words for wilderness and desert are the same as those in Ps. lxxviii. 40. See also Ps. lxviii. 8 (7).

15. *And he gave them their request and sent (them) leanness in their soul.* The last phrase is by some translated *against*, by others *into their soul;* but it is really a qualifying phrase, designed to shew that the emaciation or decay which was sent upon them was not bodily but spiritual. See Num. xi. 18, and compare Ps. lxxviii. 10, 18.

16. *And they were envious at Moses in the camp, at Aaron, the Holy One of Jehovah.* This is another of their wilderness sins. See Num. chap. xvi. Aaron is not called the *Saint of the Lord* in reference to his personal holiness, which does not seem to have been eminent, but his *Holy* (or *Consecrated) One*, in reference to his sacerdotal dignity.

17. (Then) *opens the earth and swallows Dathan, and covers over the company of Abiram.* This relates to the destruction of those followers of Korah who were not Levites. See Num. xvi. 32, 33, and compare Deut. xi. 6. From the first of these passages some interpreters supply *her mouth* after *opens;* but the absolute use of the verb is perfectly consistent with our idiom.

18. *And a fire devours their company, a flame consumes* (those) *wicked* (men). This relates to the destruction of Korah himself and his Levitical followers. See Num. xvi. 35, xxvi. 10.

19. *They make a calf in Horeb, and bow down to a molten image.* This was a third sin committed in the wilderness. See Exod. xxxii. 1–6, and compare Exod. xxxiv. 4. The golden calf appears to have been an imperfect and diminutive copy of the bull Apis, worshipped in Egypt.

20. *And exchange their glory for the likeness of an ox eating grass.* This must be read in the closest connection with ver. 19, in order to complete it. Their folly consisted in exchanging the true God, whose worship and whose favour was their highest honour, for the mere likeness of an irrational brute. *Eating grass,* not in the act, but in the habit, of so doing. Although the golden calf at Horeb, and the golden calves at Dan and Beersheba, were all regarded as representatives of Jehovah himself, their worship was uniformly treated as idolatry, and as a virtual though not a formal or avowed renunciation of his service. Compare Jer. ii. 10–13.

21. *They forgot God that saved them, that did great* (things) *in Egypt. That saved, that did,* literally saving, doing.

22. *Wonderful* (things) *in the land of Ham, terrible* (things) *on the Red Sea. Wonderful,* literally (things) made wonderful or strangely done. *Terrible,* literally to be dreaded. Compare Ps. cv. 23, 27.

23. *And he said he would destroy them—unless Moses his elect had stood in the breach before him, to turn back his wrath from destroying.* The first and last verbs are different in Hebrew, but have only one exact equivalent in English. The second clause is not a part of what God said, but a historical statement of what really prevented the execution of his threatening. He said he would destroy them, and he would have done so, had not Moses, &c. Moses is called the Elect or Chosen of Jehovah, as having been selected and set apart to be God's instrument in the great work of deliverance and legislation. The plural is elsewhere applied to the whole nation as the chosen people. See above, ver. 5, and Ps. cv. 43. *Stood in the breach* is a military figure, drawn from the desperate defence of a besieged town or fortress. Compare Jer. xv. 1, Ezek. xiii. 5, xxii. 30. The historical reference is to Exod. xxxii. 11–14, Deut. ix. 18, 19. *To turn back his wrath* is to prevent its accomplishing its object. See above, on Ps. lxxviii. 38, and compare Num. xxv. 11.

24. *And they rejected the pleasant land, they did not believe his word.* This refers to the refusal of the people to invade the land of Canaan in the first year of their exodus from Egypt, and to their believing the report of the ten spies in preference to God himself. See above, on Ps. lxxviii. 22, 32, and compare Num. xiv. 31. *The land of desire,* the desired or desirable land, is a name also found in Jer. iii. 19.

25. *And they murmured in their tents ; they did not hearken to the voice of Jehovah.* The form of expression in the first clause is borrowed from Deut. i. 27 ; in the second from Num. xiv. 22.

26. *And he lifted his hand to them, to make them fall in the wilderness.* The first phrase does not mean, he raised his hand against them, or to strike them, but as the ancient gesture of swearing. See Num. xiv. 28, 30, Deut. i. 34, ii. 14. The last clause contains the oath itself, or what he swore, to wit, that he would make them fall, slay them, in the wilderness. See Num. xiv. 29, 32.

27. *And to make their seed fall in the nations, and to scatter them in the lands.* As the appointed punishment of the older generation was to die in the wilderness, so that of their descendants was to die in dispersion and captivity among the Gentiles. See Lev. xxvi. 33, 38, and compare Deut. xxviii. 32, 36, 64, 68. The recollection of this threatening must have been peculiarly affecting to the Jews in Babylon.

28. *And they joined themselves to Baal Peor, and ate the sacrifices of the dead.* He now adds a sin committed near the end of the long error, and on the very borders of the Promised Land. The first verb is properly pas-

sive, *they were joined*, but this of course does not mean by others but themselves, and thus the simple passive comes to have a reflexive meaning. Baal Peor is the name given to Baal, or the supreme god of the Tyrians and Moabites, as he was worshipped, with licentious rites, at Peor, a mountain in the land of Moab. See Num. xxv. 1–3. *The dead*, not dead men, in allusion to necromantic superstitions, but the dumb or lifeless gods whom they worshipped. See below, on Ps. cxv. 4–7, and compare 1 Cor. xii. 2.

29. *And they provoked him by their crimes, and the plague broke out among them.* The first verb means to excite both grief and indignation. Compare the use of the cognate noun in Ps. vi. 8 (7), and of the verb itself in Ps. lxxviii. 58. The word translated *plague*, like its English equivalent, has both a generic and specific meaning; that of a divine stroke or infliction in general, and that of a pestilential disease in particular. See Num. xxv. 18, 19.

30. *Then stood up Phinehas and judged, and (so) was stayed the plague.* He *stood* (or *rose*) *up* from among the rest, presented himself before the people. He *judged, i. e.* assumed the office and discharged the duty, from which the regular official judges seemed to shrink. The verb includes the act both of pronouncing and of executing judgment. See the narrative in Num. xxv. The form of expression in the last clause is borrowed from Num. xvii. 13 (xvi. 48).

31. *And it was reckoned to him for righteousness, to generation and generation, even to eternity.* The form of expression is borrowed from Gen. xv. 6; but what is here meant is evidently not a justifying act by which Phinehas was saved, but a praiseworthy act for which he, a justified or righteous man already, received the divine commendation and a perpetual memorial of his faithfulness. Compare Deut. vi. 25, xxiv. 13. The particular reward promised (Num. xxv. 13), that of a perpetual priesthood, is not here mentioned, but was familiar to the mind of every Hebrew reader.

32. *And they angered* (him) *at the waters of Strife, and it went ill with Moses, on their account.* See above, on Ps. lxxxi. 8 (7), xcv. 8, xcix. 8. The Hebrew word for *strife* is the name given to the place, *Meribah.* The object of the first verb is *Jehovah*, as in ver. 29. *It went ill with Moses*, or, more literally, *it was bad for Moses.*

33. *For they resisted his spirit, and he spake unadvisedly with his lips.* *His spirit* may grammatically signify either that of God or that of Moses. The latest writers are in favour of the first construction, which is not without analogies in other parts of Scripture (Isa. lxiii. 10, Eph. iv. 30), but the other seems entitled to the preference in this connection, because the first clause then contains the ground or reason of the other. It was because the mind of Moses was excited by their opposition, that he spake unadvisedly with his lips. The last verb is one used in the law to denote a precipitate inconsiderate engagement, Lev. v. 4.

34. *They did not destroy the nations which the Lord said to them.* The confession now passes from the sins of the wilderness to those of Canaan. The neglect to destroy the Canaanites completely was not only a direct violation of God's precept, but the source of nearly all the public evils that ensued. There is no need of giving to the last verb a rare and dubious sense (*commanded*). The meaning of the clause is, *which Jehovah said to them* (must be destroyed).

35. *And they mixed themselves with the nations and learned their doings.* The reflexive verb at the beginning indicates an active and deliberate amal-

gamation, as distinguished from a passive and involuntary one. *The nations* of the Canaanites, and those which inhabited surrounding countries. The primary idea is not that of *gentiles* or *heathen*, in the religious sense. *Learned their doings* or *practices*, learned to do as they did. With the first clause compare Josh. xxiii. 12, 13, Judges iii. 6 ; with the second, Deut. xviii. 9, xx. 18.

36. *And served their idols, and they were to them for a snare.* The word translated *idols*, by its etymological affinities, suggests the idea of vexations, pains. See above, on Ps. xvi. 4. *A snare, i. e.* a temptation to idolatry. Compare Deut. vii. 16.

37. *And they sacrificed their sons and their daughters to the demons.* This last is the Septuagint version, and, if not directly sanctioned, is at least referred to in the New Testament (1 Cor. x. 20). That the worship of idols was connected with that of fallen spirits, is neither improbable in itself nor contradictory to Scripture. According to the modern etymologists, the Hebrew word means *lords* or *masters*, and is a poetical equivalent to Baalim, which means the same thing. Compare Deut. xxxii. 17, and the χύριοι of 1 Cor. viii. 5. The word translated *devils* in Lev. xvii. 7 is entirely different.

38. *And they shed innocent blood, the blood of their sons and daughters, which they sacrificed to the idols of Canaan ; and defiled was the land with bloods.* The first verb means to pour out, and here implies a copious or abundant bloodshed, corresponding to the next verb, which is an intensive form of that used in ver. 37. *Blood*, in the singular, is used in a physical sense ; the plural *bloods*, in a moral one, always implying guilt, and especially the guilt of murder. See above, on Ps. v. 7 (6), xxvi. 9, li. 16 (14), lv. 24 (23). The first three members of the sentence have respect to the prohibitions in Deut. xii. 31, xviii. 10, xix. 10. With the last clause compare Num. xxxv. 33.

39. *And they were polluted by their own doings, and went a whoring by their own crimes.* They defiled not only the land of promise but them-selves. Or rather, this verse is explanatory of the last clause of ver. 38, and shews that the pollution of the land was nothing more nor less than that of its inhabitants. The figure of spiritual whoredom or adultery is often used to signify the violation, by the chosen people, of their covenant with God, which is constantly described as a conjugal relation. See above, on Ps. xlv., and compare Ps. lxxiii. 27. This is not stated as an additional offence, but as an aggravating circumstance attending the iniquities already mentioned.

40. *And the anger of Jehovah was enkindled at his people, and he abhorred his heritage.* This is the strongest form in which his detestation of their sins could be expressed, but does not necessarily imply the abroga-tion of his covenant with them. The feeling described is like that of a parent towards his wicked children, or of husbands and wives, who do not cease to love each other, though grieved and indignant at each other's sins. The word *heritage* adds great point to the sentence. He abhorred the very people whom he had chosen to be his, not merely for a single generation, but for many. See above, on Ps. lxxviii. 59, 62.

41. *And he gave them into the hand of nations, and over them ruled their haters.* The same nations whom they had rebelliously spared, with others of like spirit,—the same nations who had led them into sin,—were used as instruments of punishment. Compare Lev. xxvi. 17, Judges ii. 14.

42. *And their enemies oppressed them, and they were bowed down under*

their hand. They not only governed them, but governed them tyrannically, so that they were not only under coercion and constraint, but humbled and degraded from the rank of an independent state to that of tributaries and bondsmen. With the terms of this verse compare Judges i. 34, iii. 30, iv. 3, viii. 28.

43. *Many times he frees them, and they resist* (him) *by their counsel, and are brought low by their guilt.* Having given in the preceding verses a brief but lively summary of the Book of Judges, the Psalmist now passes, by an almost insensible transition, to the later periods of the history, and indeed to its catastrophe; for the meaning of the last clause seems to be, that after all their fluctuations, they at length sink or fall into a ruinous condition, as the ultimate fruit of their rebellions. The meaning of the first clause is, that by their self-willed plans and projects they continually come into collision with the will of God, and with that great providential purpose, in promoting which it was their duty, and would have been their happiness, to co-operate. With the last clause compare Lev. xxvi. 39, Ezek. xxxii. 10.

44. *And he has looked at their distress when he heard them cry.* The idiomatic form of the original may thus be represented by a bald translation, *and he saw in the distress to them in his hearing their cry.* As this follows the brief statement of their downfall, there is much probability in the opinion, that it relates to the "tokens for good," which were granted to the exiled Jews in Babylon long before their actual restoration. With the first clause compare Exod. ii. 25, iv. 31, Deut. iv. 30, Ps. xviii. 7, cii. 3.

45. *And he has remembered for them his covenant, and repented according to the abundance of his mercy.* For them, *i. e.* in their favour, for their benefit. It does not qualify *covenant*, but *remembered*. With the first clause compare Lev. xxvi. 42, 45, Ps. cv. 8, 42; with the second, Num. xiv. 19, Ps. v. 8 (7), lxix. 14 (13), Neh. xiii. 22. The common version of the last word (*mercies*) rests upon the marginal or masoretic reading; the more ancient text is *mercy*.

46. *And has given them favour before all their captors.* The literal translation of the first clause is, *and has given them for mercies or compassions.* This remarkable expression is borrowed from 1 Kings viii. 50 (compare 2 Chron. xxx. 9), not only here but in the history of Daniel and his fellow-captives (Dan. i. 9), which makes it not at all improbable, that what is there recorded is among the indications of returning divine favour here referred to by the Psalmist.

47. *Save us, Jehovah, our God, and gather us from the nations, to give thanks unto thy holy name, to glory in thy praise.* Encouraged by these tokens of returning favour, the church prays that the hopes thus raised may not be disappointed, but abundantly fulfilled in the restoration of the exiles to their own land, in return for which she indirectly engages to render praise and thanksgiving to Jehovah as her liberator. We are thus brought back to the beginning of the psalm, and the voice of confession is again lost in that of anticipated praise. Instead of *our God*, the parallel passage (1 Chron. xvi. 36) has *God of our Salvation.* The word translated *glory* occurs only in that passage and the one before us. It is synonymous, however, with the one used in Ps. cv. 3, and often elsewhere, both meaning properly to praise one's self. With the second clause compare Ps. xxx. 5 (4).

48. *Blessed* (be) *Jehovah, God of Israel, from eternity even to eternity. And all the people says Amen. Hallelujah!* Some interpreters regard the psalm as closing with the preceding verse, and the one before us as a doxo-

logy added to mark the conclusion of the Fourth Book. But here, as in Ps. lxxii. 19, it is far more probable that this doxology was the occasion of the psalm's being reckoned as the last of a Book, notwithstanding its intimate connection with the one that follows. This probability is strengthened, in the case before us, by the addition of the words, *and all the people says Amen*, which would be unmeaning, unless the doxology formed part of the psalm itself. The additional words are borrowed from Deut. xxvii. 15–26. The parallel passage (1 Chron. xvi. 36) has, *And all the people said Amen and give praise* (or *gave praise*) *to Jehovah*, which last words are represented, in the verse before us, by the *Hallelujah* (*Praise ye Jah!*)

Psalm 107

AFTER propounding as his theme the goodness of God in delivering his people, and especially in bringing them back from their dispersions, ver. 1–3, the Psalmist celebrates this great event, under the various figures of safe conduct through a desert and arrival in a populous city, ver. 4–9 ; emancipation from imprisonment, ver. 10–16 ; recovery from deadly sickness, ver. 17–22 ; deliverance from the dangers of the sea, ver. 23–32 ; then describes, in more direct terms, the fall of the oppressor, the restoration of Israel, and his happy prospects, ver. 33–42 ; ending, as he began, with an earnest exhortation to remember and commemorate Jehovah's goodness, ver. 43. The psalm is so constructed as to admit of being readily applied, either literally or figuratively, to various emergencies : but its primary reference to the return from exile seems to be determined by ver. 2, 3. According to Hengstenberg's hypothesis, this psalm was added to the double trilogy by which it is preceded (Ps. ci.–cvi.), immediately after the return from exile, when the holy city was re-peopled, and the first harvest had been gathered, but the rebuilding of the temple had not yet begun. The whole seven then compose one series or system, intended to be used together in the public worship of the ancient church.

1. *Give thanks unto Jehovah, for he* (*is*) *good, for unto eternity* (*is*) *his mercy.* The repetition of the first words of the foregoing psalm, as the beginning of the one before us, strongly favours the opinion, that the latter was designed to be a kind of supplement or appendix to the former.

2. (*So*) *say the Redeemed of Jehovah, whom he has redeemed from the hand of distress* (or *of the enemy*). What they are to say is not the exhortation in the first clause, but the reason for it in the last clause, of the foregoing verse. Let them acknowledge his unceasing mercy, who have just experienced so remarkable a proof of it. The ambiguous word (צר) should probably be taken in the same sense which it elsewhere has throughout this psalm. See below, ver. 6, 13, 19, 28, and compare Ps. cvi. 44. Indeed, the two senses may be reconciled by simply supposing the distress to be personified. Compare the unambiguous expression in Ps. cvi. 10. The *Redeemed of the Lord* is a favourite expression of Isaiah (xxxv. 9, 10, lxii. 12, lxiii. 3).

3. *And from the lands has gathered them, from the east and from the west, from the north and from the sea.* The Babylonish exile is continually spoken of as a dispersion, either because it is considered as including other minor deportations, or because the migration of the great mass of the people into Babylonia was unavoidably accompanied, followed, or preceded, by a less extensive and more scattering migration of many individuals and

families to other quarters. On the false assumption of a perfect parallelism
as indispensable, some have supposed that *sea* is here put for the *south*.
But this is not the only case in which the enumeration of the cardinal
points is complete only in number. See Isa. xlix. 12, and compare Isa.
xliii. 5, 6, lvi. 8. The mention of the sea instead of the south may perhaps
have reference to the prophecy in Deut. xxviii. 68. The verse before us
records the answer to the prayer in Ps. cvi. 47, and thus affords another
indication, that the writer of the later composition had the earlier in his
eye, and wrote with some intention to illustrate or complete it.

4. *They wandered in the wilderness, in a desert way; a city of habitation
found they not.* Here begins the first metaphorical account of the Captivity
and Restoration, in which the exiles are described as wanderers in a *desert
way, i. e.* as some suppose a pathless desert, which sense, however, can
scarcely be extracted from the Hebrew words. Others understand the
phrase to mean a way, *i. e.* a course, a region to be traversed, which is
desert ; but this supposes *way* to be the subject and *desert* the qualifying
term, as they would be in English, but in Hebrew the precise sense is a
desert of way, or a *way-desert*, which some interpreters explain· to mean a
desert in reference to its ways or paths, thus arriving, by a different course,
at the meaning first suggested, namely that of a pathless wilderness. *City
of habitation* may mean a habitable or inhabited city in general, or a city
for them to inhabit in particular. The latter is more probable, because the
word translated *habitation* is not an abstract but a local noun, meaning the
place where men sit or dwell, according to the primary and secondary
meaning of the verbal root. See above, on Ps. i. 1. It may here be either
governed by *city*, as above, or in apposition with it, *a city, a dwelling-place,
i. e.* a city in which they might dwell. There is obvious allusion to Jerusalem, as well as to the great Arabian wilderness, although the contrast of
the city and the desert suggests the idea of suffering and relief, by a natural
as well as a historical association. See Ezek. xxix. 5, and compare Job xii. 24.

5. *Hungry—also thirsty—their soul in them shrouds itself.* This verse
continues the description of the wanderers in the desert. To avoid the
ambiguity of an exact version, in which *hungry* and *thirsty* might seem to
agree with soul, the substantive verb may be supplied in the first clause,
(*they are*) *hungry, also thirsty*. The primary sense of the reflexive verb at
the end of the sentence seems to be that of covering one's self with darkness, or sinking overwhelmed beneath some great calamity. See above,
on Ps. lxxvii. 4 (3), and compare the cognate forms in Ps. lxi. 3 (2), lxv.
14 (13), cii. 1, Isa. lvii. 16.

6. *And they cried to Jehovah in their distress ; from their straits he frees
them.* Both the nouns, according to their etymology, convey the idea of
pressure, compression, painful restraint. *In their distress*, literally *in the
distress to them*, that which they had or suffered. See above, on Ps. cvi. 44,
and compare Deut. iv. 30. The change from the past tense to the future
seems intended merely to describe the act denoted by the second or more
recent.

7. *And he led them in a straight course, to go to a city of habitation.* No
exact version can preserve or imitate the paronomasia arising from the
etymological affinity of the first verb and noun, analogous to that between
the English *walk* and *to walk*, though the Hebrew forms are only similar
and not identical. The idea of physical rectitude or straightness necessarily
suggests that of moral rectitude or honesty, commonly denoted by the
Hebrew word.

8. *Let* (such) *give thanks to Jehovah* (*for*) *his mercy, and his wonderful works to the sons of man.* Some interpreters make this the close of a long sentence, beginning with ver. 4, and adopt, in all the intervening verses, a relative construction, as if he had said, let such as wandered in the wilderness, whose soul fainted in them, who cried unto the Lord, whom he led, &c., let such give thanks unto his name. But although this is certainly the logical connection of the passage, its involution and complexity of form are as far as possible removed from the simplicity of Hebrew syntax, which prefers a distinct enunciation of particulars to all such artificial combinations. This verse constitutes the burden or chorus of the psalm.

9. *For he has satisfied the craving soul, and the hungry soul has filled with good.* This is merely the conclusion of the first scene or picture, with a change of figure but a very slight one, as the want of food is one of the most painful and familiar hardships of a journey through a desert, and as such would necessarily occur to every Israelite who knew the story of the error in the wilderness. The first verb has the same sense as in Ps. civ. 13; the last noun the same sense as in Ps. ciii. 4, civ. 28. The unusual word translated *craving* is borrowed from Isa. xxix. 8.

10. *Dwelling in darkness and death-shade, bound in affliction and iron.* Here begins the second picture, which exhibits the same sufferers, no longer as wanderers in the desert, but as closely confined prisoners. The *darkness* primarily meant is that of the dungeon, but not without reference to the frequent use of darkness in general as an emblem of misery. See above, on Ps. lxviii. 7 (6). The idea of darkness is then expressed in a still stronger form by the striking compound *death-shade* or shadow of death, a bold but beautiful description of the most profound obscurity. See above, on Ps. xxiii. 4. The leading words of the two clauses might, in one respect, be more exactly rendered, *inhabitants of darkness, prisoners of affliction.* See above, on Ps. lxxviii. 61. There is no mixture of literal and figurative terms in the last clause, but only the addition of a specific to a general term. The *affliction* particularly meant is that produced by *iron, i.e.* chains or fetters. See above, on Ps. cv. 18, and with the verse before us compare Isa. xlii. 7, xlix. 9, Job xxxvi. 8, Luke xiii. 16.

11. *Because they resisted the words of the Mightiest, and the counsel of the Highest contemned.* This verse introduces what was wanting in the first scene, the fact that these were not innocent sufferers. However cruel or unjust their sufferings at the hands of men, they were but condign punishments as sent by God. This is a point of contact and resemblance with the preceding psalm, which is not without importance. *Resisted,* rebelled against, a favourite expression in these psalms. See above, on Ps. cv. 28, cvi. 7, 33, 43. *Words* or *sayings,* commonly applied to promises, and even here combining that idea with the sense of command, because the command which they resisted or rebelled against had reference to the plan or *counsel* of the Lord for the deliverance of his people. The word translated *mightiest* is (אֵל) one of the divine names, here represented by an English superlative, in order to preserve the antithesis with *Most High* in the other clause.

12. *And he brought down, with trouble, their heart; they stumbled and there was no helper.* The remedial design and effect of their punishment are beautifully set forth in the first clause. The word translated *trouble* means originally work or labour, then the pain attending it or flowing from it. *Stumbled* may here be put for *fell,* or have the milder sense of tottering or stumbling, as distinguished from a total fall. *No helper,* or *none helping,*

except God, as intimated in the next verse ; or against God, when he chose
to punish them.

13. *And they cried to Jehovah in their distress; out of their straits he saves
them.* An exact repetition of ver. 6, except that the first verb is exchanged
for a cognate one, differing only in a single letter, and the last verb for a
synonyme still more familiar. As to the consecution of the tenses, see
above, on ver. 6.

14. *He brings them out from darkness and deathshade, and their bonds he
severs.* The terms used in describing the deliverance are studiously made
to correspond with the account of the captivity in ver. 10. It is more
remarkable, though possibly fortuitous, that the words of the second clause
are the same which David puts into the mouth of the revolted nations, Ps.
ii. 3. The English word *severs* is here used instead of *breaks*, in order to
represent the more uncommon and poetical term used in Hebrew.

15, 16. *Let* (such) *give thanks unto Jehovah (for) his mercy, and his
wonderful works to the sons of man, because he has broken doors of brass, and
bars of iron has cut asunder.* The burden in ver. 15 is in all respects identical
with ver. 8, but the supplementary verse differs, according to the prominent
figures in the two scenes or pictures. As the idea of famine was selected,
in ver. 9, from among the hardships of the wilderness, so here the fasten-
ings of the prison are presented in precisely the same manner. In this
striking regularity of form, combined with vividness and beauty of conception, there is evidence of art and skill as well as genius. The verb in the
first clause of ver. 16 is an intensive form of the verb to *break*, and might
here be rendered *shattered, shivered*, or the like. The corresponding verb
in the last clause is a similar intensive of the verb to *cut*. The whole verse
is copied from Isa. xlv. 2, where we find the promise, of which this is the
fulfilment.

17. *Fools by their course of transgression, and by their crimes, afflict themselves.* Here begins the third scene or picture, at the very opening of which
the charge of folly is added to the previous one of guilt. The reflexive
meaning of the verb is essential, and cannot be diluted into a mere passive
without weakening the whole sentence, the very point of which consists in
making them the guilty authors of their own distresses. The word for
transgression is the one that originally means revolt from God, apostasy.
See above on Ps. xxxvi. 2 (1). *Course*, literally way or path. *By*, literally
from, as when we speak of an effect as arising or proceeding from a cause.

18. *All food their soul abhors, and they draw near to the very gates of
death.* This verse abruptly brings before us the same persons whom we
lately beheld wandering in the desert, and then chained in a dark dungeon,
now suffering from disease, such as not only mars their pleasures, but
threatens to abbreviate their lives. Compare Ps. cii. 3, Job xxxiii. 20.
The expression *very gates*, in the translation of the last clause, is intended
to convey the full force of the Hebrew preposition (עַד) which is stronger
than (אֶל) *to*. See above, on Ps. lvii. 11 (10). With the last clause compare Ps. ix. 14, lxxxviii. 4 (3), Job xxxiii. 22, Isa. xxxviii. 9.

19. *And they cry to Jehovah in their distress; out of their straits he saves
them.* See above on ver. 6, 13, with the last of which this agrees exactly.

20. *He sends his word and heals them, and makes them escape from their
destructions, i. e.* those which threatened them, and from which escape
appeared impossible. *He sends his word*, he issues his command, exerts
his sovereign power and authority. The last word in the Hebrew occurs

only here and once in Lamentations (iv. 20). The modern interpreters have *pits* or *graves ;* but such a derivation from the verbal root is without example or analogy. See above, on Ps. xvi. 10. With the first clause compare Ps. xxx. 3 (2), xxxiii. 9, Isa. lvii. 18; with the last Ps. ciii. 4.

21, 22. *Let* (such) *give thanks unto Jehovah,* (for) *his mercy and his wonderful works to tke sons of man; and let them sacrifice sacrifices of thanksgiving, and recount his deeds with (joyful) singing.* The freedom from technical and artificial rules of rhetoric or versification, even in those parts of the composition which exhibit most of art and skill, is peculiarly observable in this verse, where, instead of adding to the uniform chorus or refrain some particular image from the scene just closing, as in ver. 9, 16, the Psalmist continues and completes the sentence by repeating the exhortation to give thanks, in another but still figurative form, derived from the musical and sacrificial customs of the temple worship. They must not only utter thanks but offer them in sacrifice. They must not only offer them in sacrifice, but sing them. With the first clause compare Ps. l. 14.

23. *Going down the sea in ships, doing business in the many waters.* Here again the scene is shifted, and the exiles pass before us, not as wanderers in the desert, or as captives in the dungeon, or as suffering from sickness, but as mariners engaged in an adventurous voyage. *Descending, going down,* seems to be an idiomatic phrase, borrowed from Isa. xlii. 10, and equivalent to *going out* to sea in English. The expression may have reference to the general elevation of the land above the water (see above, on Ps. xxiv. 2), but is directly opposite to our phrase, *the high seas,* and to the classical usage of *ascending* ships, *i. e.* embarking, and *descending, i. e.* landing. *Doing business* has its ordinary sense, as applied to trade or traffic. The last words may also be translated *great* or *mighty* waters; but the usage of the Psalms is in favour of the version *many waters,* which, moreover, forms a beautiful poetical equivalent to *sea* or *ocean.* This image could not fail to suggest, however, indirectly, the idea of the world with its commotions, of which the constant emblem is the sea. See above, on Ps. xlvi. 4 (3), lxv. 8 (7), lxxxix. 10 (9), xciii. 3, 4, and compare Mat. viii. 23–26, Mark iv. 36–41, Luke viii. 22–25.

24. THEY *saw the works of Jehovah, and his wonders in the deep.* The pronoun at the beginning is emphatic, (it is) *they* (that) *see* (or *saw*) *the works of the Lord,* as if others could lay claim to no such privilege or honour. Both the senses of the phrase *God's works* are appropriate in this connection, his works of creation and his works of providence. The last word is another poetical equivalent to *sea* or *ocean.* See above, on Ps. lxix. 3 (2).

25. *And he said—and there arose a stormy wind, and it lifted up his waves.* He now parenthetically specifies some of the divine *works* which he had just mentioned in the general. The form of expression at the beginning, as in all like cases, involves an allusion to the history of the creation, where each creative act is preceded by God's saying, *let it be.* So here the full sense is, *and God said* (let a stormy wind arise) *and a stormy wind arose.* See above, on Ps. xxxiii. 9. *Arose,* literally stood, stood up, as in Ps. cvi. 30. A *stormy wind,* literally a wind of storm or tempest. Instead of *his waves* we may read *its waves,* and refer the pronoun to the remoter antecedent (*sea*) in ver. 23. *Deep,* in ver. 24, is of a different gender. It is equally correct, however, and more natural, to refer it to Jehovah, as the maker of the sea and the ruler of its waves. Compare the expression *thy waves and thy billows* in Ps. xlii. 8. See also Isa. li. 15, Jer. xxxi. 35.

26. *They rise (to) the heavens; they sink (to) the depths; their soul with
evil dissolves itself.* That the verbs in the first clause relate not to the waves
but to the mariners, is evident from the last clause. The words *rise* and
sink are used instead of *ascend, descend,* or *go up, go down,* because the
Hebrew verbs have no etymological affinity, nor even a single letter common
to their roots. The ellipsis of the preposition *to* is frequent, or rather verbs
of motion in Hebrew may be construed directly with a noun, where our
idiom requires the intervention of a particle. *Evil* in the last clause may
denote their evil state or painful situation, with all the circumstances comprehended in it; or, more specifically, their distress and painful feelings.
Compare Gen. xli. 29. The reflexive form of the last verb is not essential
to the meaning of the sentence, as in ver. 17, and may therefore be explained as an intensive or emphatic passage, *it is melted.* See above, on
Ps. xxii. 15 (14). With the whole verse compare Ps. civ. 8.

27. *They reel and stagger like a drunken (man), and all their wisdom is
confounded.* By *wisdom* we are here to understand reason, common sense,
that which makes men rational and raises them above the brutes. This is
plain from the comparison with drunkenness, the only point of which must
be the loss of reason. The reeling and staggering may relate to the irregular and violent motion of a vessel in a storm, or, as the last clause does,
to the mariners themselves. The last verb literally means *is swallowed up,*
or retaining the reflexive form, still more strongly, *swallows itself up.* But
see above, on the last word of ver. 26.

28. *And they cried to Jehovah in their distress, and out of their straits
he brings them forth.* The consecution of the tenses corresponds to the
relation of the acts which they denote, as viewed by a spectator. "Now
they have cried to the Lord, and now he is bringing them forth." The verse
differs from ver. 13, 19, in the first verb, which agrees with ver. 6, and in
the last verb, which is unlike both.

29. *He stills the storm to a calm, and silent are their waves.* This is an
amplification of the last phrase in ver. 28, and shews how it is that *he
brings them forth.* The first verb strictly means *he makes it stand,* but in
a sense directly opposite to that of a synonymous though different verb in
ver. 25. *Calm,* literally silence, stillness. *Their waves,* the waves from
which they suffer, by which they are buffeted. Compare *his waves,* in
ver, 25.

30. *And they are glad that they are quiet, and he guides them to their
desired haven.* The connection might be rendered clearer by translating
with the English Bible, *then are they glad, &c.* The last word in the verse
occurs only here, and is by some translated *shore,* by others *goal :* but it is
safer to retain the old interpretation, which affords a perfectly good sense,
and rests upon the joint authority of the Rabbinical tradition and the Septuagint version.

31, 32. *Let* (such) *give thanks to Jehovah (for) his mercy, and his wonderful works to the sons of man ; and let them exalt him in the congregation
of the people, and in the session of the elders praise him.* Here again we
have a striking instance of variety combined with uniformity. The burden
or chorus, as in ver. 22, is followed by a solemn exhortation to connect the
required thanksgiving with the forms of public worship. But instead of
the temple with its sacrifices and its chants, the reference in this case, it
should seem, is to the spiritual worship of the synagogue. The word
translated *congregation* is one constantly applied to Israel, as actually
gathered at the place of worship. See above, on Ps. xxii. 23 (22). The

word *session* is employed in the translation of the last clause, not for the sake of a verbal coincidence with Presbyterian institutions, a coincidence, however, which is not to be denied, but because it adequately represents the Hebrew (מוֹשַׁב) in its double acceptation, as denoting both the act and the place cf sitting, and especially of sitting together. See above, on ver. 4. The *elders*, here as elsewhere, are the heads of tribes and families, the hereditary chiefs and representatives of Israel.

33. *He turns streams into a wilderness, and springs of water to a thirsty place.* As the shifting of the scene is not renewed in the remainder of the psalm, which, on the other hand, if viewed as a distinct and independent portion of the poem, mars its symmetry of structure, it seems best to regard these verses as an episode belonging to the last scene and containing the praises of the people and their elders. The figures in this verse are often used, particularly by Isaiah, to denote an entire revolution, whether physical or moral, social or political. Compare Isa. xliv. 26, 27, l. 2, Jer. l. 38, li. 36. It thus prepares the way for the subsequent rejoicings in the downfall of Babylon and the restoration of the exiled Jews.

34. *A fruitful land to saltness, for the wickedness of those dwelling in it.* The sentence is continued from the foregoing verse, the nouns being governed by the verb *he turns*. The first phrase literally means a *land of fruit.* The next noun may be taken either in the abstract sense of *saltness* or the concrete one of a *saline soil* or *region*, and by implication barren. *For,* literally *from,* as in ver. 17 above. Compare the threatening in Isa. xiii. 19, and the great historical type of all such judgments, the destruction of Sodom and Gomorrah.

35. *He turns a desert to a pool of water, and a dry land into springs of water.* This is the reverse of the description in ver. 33, to which the terms are studiously conformed. In both cases the first verb literally means *he sets* or *puts,* and the noun translated *springs* means issues or places where the waters issue. Compare Isa. xxxv. 7, xli. 18, xliii. 20.

36. *And has settled there famished (men), and they have established a city to dwell in.* There is no need of assuming, that the desert thus transformed is Palestine or Canaan. It is better to adhere to the general import of the figures, which is change for the better. *Settled,* literally caused to dwell. The primary meaning of the last clause is that those once homeless have a home ; but there is of course a reference to the repossession and rebuilding of Jerusalem. The last phrase in Hebrew is the same with that translated *city of habitation* in ver. 4.

37. *And have sowed fields, and planted vineyards, and made fruits of increase.* The form of all these verbs requires them to be understood, like those of ver. 36, as referring to time actually past, from which some have inferred that the date of the psalm itself lay between the first ingathering of the fruits by the returned Jews and the founding of the temple, to which there is here no allusion. The word translated *increase* is applied elsewhere to the annual productions of the earth. See Lev. xxv. 16. To *make* these is to gain or acquire them by cultivation, as we speak of *making* money, but of *raising* corn. See above, on Ps. lx. 14 (12).

38. *And he has blessed them, and they have increased greatly, and (even) their cattle he does not diminish. Increased,* not in numbers merely, but in wealth, strength and prosperity. See Deut. xxx. 16. The verb to *diminish* is borrowed from Lev. xxvi. 22. The negation may be understood as a *meiosis,* meaning to increase or multiply. The whole of this description

agrees well with the encouraging appearances, by which the Restoration was attended and immediately followed, before the colony experienced reverses or had lost the fresh impression of their recent sufferings and privations, which are mentioned in the next verse.

39. *And they were diminished and brought low, from oppression, suffering, and grief.* The only grammatical construction of the verbs is that which refers them to a former time, *i. e.* to the condition of the people under Babylonian oppression. The sense is therefore quite mistaken in the English, though correctly given in the ancient versions. The contrast is intended to enhance the joy and thankfulness of the restored exiles. These, now so prosperous, are the very men who lately were in abject misery.

40. *Pouring contempt on princes—and he has made them wander in a waste* (where there is) *no way.* From the exiles he reverts to their Deliverer, and describes him as spurning the most lordly of their persecutors—nay, as making them take the place of those whom they oppressed, which idea is conveyed by the figure before used of wanderers in a pathless desert. See above, on ver. 4, and compare Job xii. 21, 24. The word for *waste* or *void* is one of those used in Gen. i. 2, to describe the original condition of the earth.

41. *And has raised the poor from affliction, and made like a flock families.* The first verb suggests the twofold idea of elevation from a wretched state, and security from future danger. For its ordinary sense, see above, on Ps. xx. 2 (1), xci. 14. The last clause simply means, he has increased the people who were so reduced in strength and numbers.

42. *The righteous shall see and rejoice, and all iniquity stop her mouth.* The righteous are the true Israel, as in Ps. xxxiii. 1, Num. xxiii. 10, Dan. xi. 17. With the last clause compare Job v. 16, Isa. lii. 15.

43. *Who* (is) *wise and will observe these things, and attentively consider the mercies of Jehovah?* The change of number in the Hebrew does not affect the meaning. *Whoever is* wise will observe these things, and *all who are* wise will consider them. With this conclusion compare Hosea xiv. 10, Isa. xlii. 23, Jer. ix. 11.

Psalm 108

1. *A Song. A Psalm. By David.* This is not an original or independent composition, but a compilation from two other psalms, which have already been explained. The introduction, ver. 2–6 (1–5), is substantially identical with Ps. lvii. 8–12 (7–11); the body of the psalm, ver. 7–13 (6–12), with Ps. lx. 7–14 (5–12). The supposition of erroneous copies, or of later corruptions, is still more improbable in this case than in those of Ps. xviii., liii., lxx. The best solution which has been proposed is, that David himself combined these passages to be the basis of a trilogy (Ps. cviii.–cx.), adapted to the use of the church at a period posterior to the date of Ps. lvii. and lx. The comments here will be confined to the variations, as in Ps. liii. and lxx.

2 (1). *Fixed is my heart, O God, fixed is my heart; I will sing and play —also my glory.* See above, on Ps. lvii. 8 (7). The words here added, *also my glory*, correspond to the first clause of the next verse in that psalm, *awake my glory!*

3 (2). *Awake lute and harp! I will awaken the dawn* (or *morning*). See above, on Ps. lvii. 9 (8). The only variation is the one already mentioned,

the omission here of the words *awake my glory*, for which the last clause of ver. 2 (1) is a substitute.

4 (3). *I will thank thee among the nations, O Jehovah, I will praise thee among the peoples.* See above, on Ps. lvii. 10 (9). The only variation is the substitution of the name *Jehovah* for *Adhonai*, a change scarcely perceptible in the English versions.

5 (4). *For great from above the heavens (is) thy mercy, and unto the clouds thy truth.* See above, on Ps. lvii. 11 (10). The only variation is the change of (עַד) *unto* into (מֵעַל) *from above*, apparently intended to suggest the idea of God's mercy as descending upon man.

6 (5). *Be thou high above the heavens, O God, and above all the earth thy glory.* See above, on Ps. lvii. 12 (11). The only variation is the introduction of the copulative *and* at the beginning of the second clause.

7 (6). *In order that thy beloved (ones) may be delivered, save with thy right hand, and hear* (or *answer*) *us.* See above, on Ps. lx. 7 (5), with which this verse agrees in all points, not excepting the keri or various reading in the last word (*me* for *us*).

8 (7). *God hath spoken in his holiness* (and therefore) *I will triumph, I will divide Shechem, and the valley of Succoth I will measure.* See above, on Ps. lx. 8 (6), with which this verse agrees exactly.

9 (8). *To me* (belongs) *Gilead, to me Manasseh, and Ephraim the strength of my head, Judah my lawgiver.* See above, on Ps. lx. 9 (7). The only variation is the omission, in the verse before us, of the *and* after *Gilead.*

10 (9). *Moab (is) my wash-pot ; at Edom will I throw my shoe ; over Philistia will I shout aloud.* See above, on Ps. lx. 10 (8). At the end of this verse is the most material variation in the whole psalm, which, however, is evidently not fortuitous or by a later hand, but intentional and made by the original writer. *I will shout aloud*, as an expression of triumph over a conquered enemy.

11 (10). *Who will bring me (to) the fortified city ! Who leads* (or *has led*) *me up to Edom ?* See above, on Ps. lx. 11 (9). The only variation is the change of one synonymous word for another, to express the idea of a fortified city.

12 (11). (Is it) *not God who has cast us off, and wilt not go forth with our hosts?* See above, on Ps. lx. 12 (10). The only variation consists in the omission of the emphatic pronoun *thou*, which is expressed in the parallel passage, and only implied in the one before us. Some interpreters suppose a sudden change of construction from the third to the second person. *Is it not God*—(even thou who) *didst cast us off*, &c.

13 (12). *Give us help from the enemy* (or from distress); *and* (the rather because) *vain is the salvation of man*, meaning that which he affords. See above, on Ps. lx. 13 (11), which agrees with this exactly.

14 (13). *In God we will make (i. e.* gain or gather) *strength, and he will tread down* (or *trample on*) *our adversaries* (persecutors or oppressors). See above, on Ps. lx. 14 (12), between which and the verse before us there is not the slightest difference.

Psalm 109

THIS psalm consists of three parts ; a complaint of slanderous and malignant enemies, ver. 1–5 ; a prayer for the punishment of such, ver. 6–20 ;

and a prayer for the sufferer's own deliverance, with a promise of thanksgiving, ver. 21–31. According to the theory repeatedly referred to, this is the second psalm of a Davidic trilogy. See above, on Ps. cviii. This psalm is remarkable on two accounts: first, as containing the most striking instances of what are called the imprecations of the psalms; and then, as having been applied in the most explicit manner to the sufferings of our Saviour from the treachery of Judas, and to the miserable fate of the latter. These two peculiarities are perhaps more closely connected than they may at first sight seem. Perhaps the best solution of the first is that afforded by the second, or at least by the hypothesis, that the Psalmist, under the direction of the Spirit, viewed the sufferings of Israel, which furnished the occasion of the psalm, as a historical type of the Messiah's sufferings from the treachery of Judas, representing that of Judah, and that with this view he expresses his abhorrence of the crime, and acquiesces in the justice of its punishment, in stronger terms than would have been, or are elsewhere, employed in reference to ordinary criminals.

1. *To the Chief Musician. By David. A Psalm. God of my praise, be not silent.* The first inscription was particularly necessary here, because the psalm might otherwise have seemed to be a mere expression of strong personal feeling. See above, on Ps. li. 1. *God of my praise, i. e.* the object of it, whom I delight, or am accustomed, or have cause, to praise. *Be not silent* means not merely *do not refuse to answer,* but amidst the threats and railings of my enemies, let thy voice be heard also. See above, on Ps. xxviii. 1, xxxv. 22, xxxix. 13 (12).

2. *For a wicked mouth and a mouth of deceit they have opened; they have spoken against me with a tongue of falsehood.* Compare Ps. xxxv. 11, lv. 4 (3). The subject of the first verb is his enemies, and not the nouns preceding, as the verb translated *open* is elsewhere always active. *Against me,* literally *with me,* implying that they charged him falsely to his face, a circumstance remarkably fulfilled in Christ. See Mat. xxvi. 59.

3. *And with words of hatred they have compassed me, and have fought against me without cause.* See above, on Ps. xxxv. 20, xxxvi. 4 (3.)

4. *In return for my love they are my adversaries—and I (am) prayer.* The first word in Hebrew strictly means *instead* or *in lieu of.* The unusual expression at the end can only mean, I am all prayer, I do nothing but pray, which some understand to signify, I bear their persecution meekly and continue my devotions undisturbed by their calumnies and insults. But as the whole context is descriptive, not of the sufferer's behaviour but of his enemies', a more probable sense is, I am forced to be continually praying for protection against them and deliverance from them.

5. *They lay upon me evil instead of good, and hatred instead of love.* The first verb literally means *they set* or *place. Instead of* the good and the love which they owed me, or *in return* for my kindness and love to them, as in ver. 4.

6. *Appoint thou over him a wicked one, and let an adversary stand upon his right hand.* The first verb in Hebrew means to place one in authority or charge over another. See Gen. xxxix. 5, xli. 34, Num. i. 50, and compare Lev. xxvi. 16, Jer. xv. 3. *Wicked one* and *adversary (Satan),* although here used as appellatives or common nouns, are the very terms applied, in the later scripture to the Evil Spirit, or the Devil. See Job i. 6, ii. 1, 1 Chron. xxi. 1, Zech. iii. 1, 2. In the place last cited he stands too at the right hand of the sinner to accuse him. The change of number in the verse before us might, in conformity with usage, be explained as a mere

difference of form, the ideal person denoted by the singular being really the type and representative of the whole class denoted by the plural. But the constancy with which the change, in this case, is adhered to, rather favours the conclusion, that a real individual is meant, to whom the Psalmist turns from the promiscuous crowd of his oppressors. For a similar transition, see above, on Ps. lv. 13 (12).

7. *When he is tried he shall go forth guilty; and his prayer shall be for sin.* The future meaning of the second verb is determined by the form of the third, which is not apocopated, as in ver. 12, 13. *When he is tried,* literally, in his being tried. The next phrase simply means that he shall be condemned ; the last clause, that his very prayer for mercy shall be reckoned as a new offence, a strong description of extreme judicial rigour and inexorable justice.

8. *Let his days be few—his office let another take.* The word translated *office* is a collateral derivative of the verb at the beginning of ver. 6, and means commission, charge. This expression makes it still more probable that a real individual is referred to, as the possession of a charge or office could not be common to the whole class of malignant enemies. The Septuagint version is ἐπισκοπήν, oversight or supervision, corresponding exactly to the meaning of the Hebrew verb in ver. 6. This translation is retained in Acts i. 20, where the verse before us is expressly quoted by Peter as " written in the book of Psalms," and applied to the case of Judas Iscariot.

9. *Let his sons be orphans and his wife a widow.* He here passes from the person of the criminal to the sufferings of those dependent on him, See Exod. xx. 5.

10. *And wander—wander—let his sons and beg, and seek* (their food) *from* (among) *their ruins.* The emphatic repetition of the first verb is expressed in the English Bible, by a paraphrase, *let his children be continually vagabonds.* The last clause is extremely graphic, representing them as creeping forth in search of food from amidst the ruins of their habitations.

11. *Let a creditor entrap all he has, and strangers plunder* (the fruit of) *his labour.* The first noun originally means a lender, but in usage has the accessory sense of a hard creditor, an extortioner. The verb means to *lay a snare for,* as in Ps. xxxviii. 13 (12.) *Strangers,* not his natural heirs, not members of his family. See Deut. xxv. 5.

12. *Let there be no one to him extending mercy, and let there be no one shewing favour to his orphans.* The verb translated *extend* literally means *draw out, prolong,* and is applied to the continued indulgence both of hostile and amicable feelings. See above, on Ps. xxviii. 3, xxxvi. 11 (10), lxxxv. 6 (5). *Shewing favour,* exercising mercy, as in Ps xxxvii. 21.

13. *Let his posterity be cut off; in the next generation, blotted out be their name.* The word for posterity strictly means futurity, after part, or latter end. See above, Ps. xxxvii. 37, 38. *Cut off,* literally for cutting off. *The next* or *after generation,* as in Ps. xlviii. 14 (13). The plural pronoun *their* refers to the collective noun *posterity.*

14. *Let the guilt of his fathers be remembered by Jehovah, and his mother's sin not blotted out.* This is perhaps the most fearful imprecation in the psalm, as it extends the consequences of transgression, not merely to the children, who might naturally be expected to partake of them, but to the parents. It is not to be forgotten, however, that in all such cases, the personal guilt of the implicated parties is presupposed, and not inferred from their connection with the principals. *Remembered by* (literally *to*)

Jehovah, which may possibly mean brought to his remembrance, recalled to mind by another, perhaps by the accuser before mentioned.

15. *Let them be before Jehovah always, and let him cut off from the earth their memory.* The subject of the first clause is the *guilt* and *sin* mentioned in the verse preceding. *Before Jehovah*, in his sight, an object of attention to him. See above, Ps. xc. 8. With the last clause compare Ps. ix. 7, (6), xxxiv. 17 (16).

16. *Because that he did not remember to do mercy, and persecuted an afflicted and poor man, and one smitten in heart, to kill (him).* There is an antithesis between the *remember* of this verse and the *remembered* of ver. 14. Though he did not remember mercy, God remembers guilt. The last phrase, *to kill*, denotes both the design and the extent of the malignant persecution which was deadly or to death. The object of the persecution is the psalmist himself, or the ideal person whom he represents. See ver. 22.

17. *And he loved a curse, and it has come (upon) him ; and he delighted not in blessing, and it has removed far from him.* This verse contemplates the event as actually past. The optative meaning, given to the verbs in the English Bible, is as inconsistent with the form of the original as the future meaning given in the Prayer Book and the ancient versions.

18. *And he has put on cursing as his garment, and it has come like water into his inside, and like oil into his bones.* There is an obvious climax in this verse. That which is first described as the man's exterior covering, is then said to be within him, first as water, then as oil or fat, first in the vessels of his body, then in his very bones. The general idea is that the curse, which he denounced and endeavoured to inflict on others, has taken possession of himself, both within and without. Compare Num. v. 22, 24, 27. The first clause admits of a different construction, which would make it descriptive of the crime and not the punishment. He put on cursing as his garment, and (now) it has come, &c. This construction introduces an antithesis, and thereby adds to the point of the sentence, and is also recommended by the analogy of ver. 17.

19. *Let it be to him as a garment* (that) *he wears, and for a belt let him always gird it.* This is not a mere reiteration of the figure in the first clause of ver. 18, but conveys the additional idea of a habitual and constant presence. The word *belt* is used in the translation of the last clause, because the Hebrew word to which it corresponds is not the usual derivative of the verb that follows, but etymologically unconnected with it.

20. *(Be) this the wages of my adversaries from Jehovah, and of those speaking evil against my soul.* The pronoun *this* in the first clause refers to the whole preceding series of denunciations. The word translated *wages* means originally *work*, and secondarily the price or recompence of work or labour, and is so used in the law of Moses. See Lev. xix. 13. It is here peculiarly appropriate, because it represents the misfortunes of his enemies as the direct fruit of their own misconduct. No single word in English can express this double meaning of the Hebrew. Such is their *work* and such their *wages*. The word translated *adversaries* is a cognate form to that used in ver. 6, and might suggest the idea of *my Satans ;* but this would probably convey too much. *From Jehovah*, their reward or recompence to be expected from him, or already bestowed by him. The description in the last clause includes insult, slander, and malicious plotting.

21. *And thou, Jehovah, Lord, do with me for thy name's sake, because good is thy mercy set me free.* The emphatic *thou* at the beginning indi-

cates a contrast between God and his oppressors. *Do with me* is a common English phrase meaning *deal with me, dispose of me ;* but no such idiom exists in Hebrew, and the best authorities regard the construction as elliptical, and make it mean, *do kindness* (or *shew mercy*) *to me.* With the last clause compare Ps. lxiii. 4 (3), lxix. 17 (16).

22. *For afflicted and poor* (*am*) *I, and my heart is wounded within me.* This, though indefinite in form, is equivalent to saying, I am the afflicted and poor man whom the malignant adversary persecuted, as was said, in ver. 16. The word translated *wounded* strictly means pierced or perforated, a stronger expression than the one in ver. 16. With the first clause compare Ps. xl. 18 (17), lxix. 30 (29).

23. *Like a shadow at its turning I am gone; I am driven away like the locust.* The first comparison is the same with that in Ps. cii. 12. Our idiom enables us to imitate the phrase *I am gone*, a passive which in Hebrew occurs only here. The other verb is rare, but its meaning is sufficiently determined by usage. The allusion here is to the violence with which a cloud of locusts in the east is scattered by the wind. Compare Exod. x. 19, Joel ii. 20, Nah. iii. 17.

24. *My knees totter from fasting, and my flesh fails from fatness.* The last phrase is obscure, but seems to mean *from being fat*, so that it is not fat ; the privative usage of the preposition being very common. The sense thus put upon the verb is justified by the analogy of Isa. lviii. 11, where an equivalent expression is applied to failing waters. Some interpreters, however, insist upon retaining the strict sense both of verb and noun, and understand the clause to mean, my flesh lies or deceives the eye, by no longer appearing as it once did, or by seeming to exist when it is gone, *from oil, i. e.* from want of oil, because no longer taken care of and anointed. But no construction could well be more forced and far-fetched. It may also be objected that the external use of oil was to anoint the head on festive occasions, not to fatten the person or preserve the flesh.

25. *And I have been a reproach to them, they see me, they shake their head.* A *reproach*, an object of contempt, as in Ps. xxii. 7 (6), xxxi. 12 (11). As to the meaning of the gesture mentioned in the last clause, see above, on Ps. xxii. 8 (7).

26. *Help me, Jehovah, my God, save me, according to thy mercy.* The renewed description of his sufferings, in ver. 22–25, is followed by a renewed petition for deliverance, corresponding to that in ver. 21. *According to thy mercy, i. e.* in proportion to its greatness and the freeness with which it is exercised.

27. *And they shall know that this* (*is*) *thy hand ; thou, Jehovah, hast done it.* The optative construction, *let them know*, and the subjunctive one, *that they may know*, are really involved in the more exact translation, *they shall know.* The subject of the verb may be men in general, or the persecuting adversaries in particular, more probably the latter, because they are referred to both before and after. *This is thy hand, i. e.* this deliverance is the product of thy power. Compare Ps. lix. 14 (13).

28. *They will curse, and thou wilt bless ; they have risen up, and shall be shamed, and thy servant shall be glad.* The first clause, expressed in our idiom, would be, *they may curse, but thou wilt bless. Risen up, i. e.* against me, a favourite expression in the Psalms. *Shamed*, in the pregnant sense of being disappointed, defeated, confounded. *Thy servant, i. e.* I, as such, in that capacity or character.

29. *Clothed shall my adversaries be with confusion, and dressed, as a robe,*

in their shame. This is not the mere expression of a wish, like that in ver. 18, which would here be out of place, but a confident anticipation, with which he concludes the psalm. Compare Ps. lxxi. 13. The word tran- slated *robe* denotes a garment reaching to the feet, and expresses therefore still more strongly the idea that his foes shall be completely covered with confusion.

30. *I will thank Jehovah greatly with my mouth, and in the midst of many will I praise him.* He vows that his thanksgiving shall not be merely mental or domestic, but audible and public. With the last clause compare Ps. xxii. 23 (22).

31. *For he will stand at the right hand of a poor (man), to save (him) from the judges of his soul.* This assigns the special reason of his promised praise. The verse is in strong contrast to ver. 6 above, especially if *Satan* be there taken as a proper name. The right hand here is not the place of honour but of protection. *A poor man*, as in ver. 16, means *this poor man*, *i. e.* me a poor man. Compare Ps. xxxiv. 7 (6). The last clause is correctly paraphrased in the common version, *those that condemn his soul.*

Psalm 110

THIS is the counterpart of the Second Psalm, completing the prophetic picture of the conquering Messiah. The progressive development of the Messianic doctrine lies in this, that the Kingship of Messiah, there alleged and confirmed by a divine decree, is here assumed at the beginning, and then shewn to be connected with his Priesthood, which is also solemnly proclaimed, and its perpetuity ensured by a divine oath. This constitutes the centre of the psalm, ver. 4, to which all the rest is either introductory, ver. 1–3, or supplementary, ver. 5–7. The repeated, explicit, and emphatic application of this psalm, in the New Testament, to Jesus Christ, is so far from being arbitrary or at variance with the obvious import of the psalm itself, that any other application is ridiculous. The chief peculiarity of form is a frequent change of person, not unlike that in Ps. xci.

1. *By David. A Psalm. Thus saith Jehovah to my Lord, Sit thou at my right hand, until I make thine enemies thy footstool.* The ascription of the psalm to David is not only uncontradicted by external evidence, but corroborated by the internal character of the composition, its laconic energy, its martial tone, its triumphant confidence, and its resemblance to other undisputed psalms of David. In addition to all this, we have the authority of Christ himself, who not only speaks of it as David's, but founds an argument upon it, the whole force of which depends upon its having been composed by him. See Mat. xxii. 43, Mark xii. 36, Luke xx. 42, and compare Acts ii. 34. As a further confirmation of the truth of this inscription, some allege the obvious relation of this psalm to those before it, as forming with them a Davidic trilogy. See above, on Ps. cviii. 1. *Thus saith Jehovah*, or more exactly, *a dictum* (or *saying*) *of Jehovah*. For the origin and usage of this formula, used only in prophetic declara- tions, see above on Ps. xxxvi. 2 (1). *My Lord, i. e.* David's, as our Saviour explicitly declares in the passages already cited, yet not of David merely as a private person, nor even as an individual king, but as repre- senting his own royal race and the house of Israel over which it reigned. The person thus described as the superior and sovereign of David and his

house, and of all Israel, could not possibly be David himself, nor any of his sons and successors except one, who, by virtue of his twofold nature, was at once his sovereign and his son. See Rom. i. 3, 4. That the Lord here meant was universally identified with the Messiah by the ancient Jews, is clear, not only from their own traditions, but from Christ's assuming this interpretation as the basis of his argument to prove the Messiah's super-human nature, and from the fact that his opponents, far from questioning this fact, were unable to answer him a word, and afraid to interrogate him further (Mat. xxii. 46). The original form of expression, in the phrase *Sit at my right hand*, is the same as in Ps. cix. 31. A seat at the right hand of a king is mentioned in the Scriptures as a place of honour, not arbitrarily, but as implying a participation in his power, of which the right hand is a constant symbol. See above, on Ps. xlv. 10 (9), and compare Mat. xix. 28. The sitting posture is appropriate to kings, who are frequently described as sitting on their thrones. See above, on Ps. xxix. 10. In this case, however, the posture is of less moment than the position. Hence Stephen sees Christ *standing* at the right hand of God (Acts vii. 55, 56), and Paul simply says he *is* there (Rom. viii. 34). The participation in the divine power, thus ascribed to the Messiah, is a special and extraordinary one, having reference to the total subjugation of his enemies. This idea is expressed by the figure of their being made his footstool, perhaps with allusion to the ancient practice spoken of in Josh. x. 24. This figure itself, however, presupposes the act of sitting on a throne. It does not imply inactivity, as some suppose, or mean that Jehovah would conquer his foes for him, without any intervention of his own. The idea running through the whole psalm is, that it is in and through him that Jehovah acts for the destruction of his enemies, and that for this very end he is invested with almighty power, as denoted by his session at the right hand of God. This session is to last until the total subjugation of his enemies, that is to say, this special and extraordinary power of the Messiah is then to terminate, a representation which agrees exactly with that of Paul in 1 Cor. xv. 24–28, where the verse before us is distinctly referred to, although not expressly quoted. It is therefore needless, though grammatical, to give the *until* an inclusive meaning, namely, until then and afterwards, as in Ps. cxii. 8 below. This verse, it has been said, is more frequently quoted or referred to, in the New Testament, than any other in the Hebrew Bible. Besides the passages already cited, it lies at the foundation of all those which represent Christ as sitting at the right hand of the Father. See Mat. xxvi. 64, 1 Cor. xv. 25, Eph. i. 20–22, Phil. ii. 9–11, Heb. i. 3, 14, viii. 1, x. 12, 13, 1 Pet. iii. 22, and compare Rev. iii. 21.

2. *The rod of thy strength will Jehovah send forth from Zion; rule thou in the midst of thine enemies.* The Psalmist now addresses the Messiah directly. The idea latent in the figures of the first verb, namely that of power, is here expressed. The word (מַטֶּה) translated *rod* never means a *sceptre*, as the synonymous term (שֵׁבֶט) sometimes does, from which it is distinguished by Ezekiel (xix. 11), but a rod of correction and of chastisement. See Jer. xlviii. 12, and compare Isa. ix. 3 (4), x. 5, 15, xiv. 4, 5, Ezek. vii. 10, 11. It is here named as the instrument with which the foes are to be subdued. Compare Ps. ii. 9. There may be an allusion to the rod of Moses. See Exod. xiv. 16, 21, and compare Isa. x. 24, 26. The *rod of thy strength*, or thy rod of strength, thy strong rod, or rather the rod by means of which thine own strength is to be exerted. As

this strength is not human but divine, it is said to be sent forth by Jehovah out of Zion, considered as his earthly residence, the seat of the theocracy. See above, on Ps. xx. 3 (2). The verb translated *rule* is not applied in usage to a peaceful reign, but to coercive or compulsory dominion over conquered enemies. See above, on Ps. xlix. 15 (14), and compare Num. xxiv. 19. The imperative here involves prediction in its strongest form. As if he had said, All is ready for the conquest; there is no resistance; there can be no doubt of the result; rule, therefore, in the midst thine enemies, *i. e.* over the very enemies by whom thou art surrounded, and who threatened to dethrone thee.

3. *Thy people* (are) *free-will-offerings in the day of thy power, in holy decorations, from the womb of the dawn, to thee* (*is*) *the dew of thy youth.* Every member of this very obscure verse has been a subject of dispute and of conflicting explanations. The common version of the first words (*thy people shall be willing*) is entirely inadmissible as an exact translation, since the word translated *willing* is a plural substantive of the feminine gender, and not an adjective agreeing with the masculine singular noun *people*. The idea, however, is the same, but expressed with far more strength and beauty. The plural noun just mentioned is the one used to denote spontaneous gifts, or free-will-offerings, under the law of Moses. See above, on Ps. liv. 8 (7), and compare Exod. xxv. 2, xxxv. 29, xxxvi. 3, Lev. xxii. 23. By supplying the correlative verb, which may be considered as latent in the noun, we obtain the sense, *thy people* (offer) *voluntary gifts*. But by supplying the substantive verb, which is far more natural and common, we obtain the still more striking sense, thy people are themselves such gifts, *i. e.* they freely consecrate themselves to God. In this sense of voluntary self-dedication, the reflexive form of the verbal root is used even in historical prose (1 Chron. xxix. 14, 17), especially in reference to military service (Judges v. 2, 9, 2 Chron. xvii. 16). *The day of thy power*, the day in which it is exerted and displayed in the subjugation of thine enemies. The next phrase literally means, *in beauties* (or *ornaments*) *of holiness*, which may either have its obvious spiritual sense, as in Ps. xxix. 2, or that of *holy decorations*, with allusion to the sacerdotal dress, which is expressly called *garments of holiness*, Lev. xvi. 4. The last is the sense put by the modern interpreters upon the phrase, which then means that the people, when they make this solemn offering of themselves to God, appear clothed in sacerdotal vestments, as the servants of a priestly king (ver. 4 below), and themselves a "kingdom of priests" (Exod. xix. 6). *The womb of the dawn* (or *daybreak*) is a very strong poetical description of the origin or source of the *dew* which immediately follows, and the sense of which must determine that of the whole clause. The most probable opinions as to this point are the following. Some suppose the clause to be descriptive of the multitude of warriors who devote themselves to the Messiah, and who are then described as no less numerous than the drops of dew born from the womb of morning. The objection to this is, that it lays too much stress upon mere members, and expresess that idea by a figure neither common nor altogether natural. Another explanation makes the point of the comparison with dew, not numbers, but beauty, brilliancy thus corresponding to the holy decorations of the other clause. Here again the comparison selected is by no means obvious, much less familiar. Lovely or beautiful as dew is not a combination likely to occur to the mind of any writer. In the two interpretations which have now been given, *youth* must be taken in the sense of *young men*, like the Latin *pubes* and *juventus*, when applied to a youthful soldiery, or

made to qualify the noun before it *youthful dew*, still meaning the young warriors. But of such a figure there is not a trace in Hebrew usage, and in the only other place where the word (יַלְדוּת) occurs, it evidently means *youth*, as a period of human life (Eccles. xi. 9, 10). Free from all these objections is the supposition, that the clause relates not to the numbers or the beauty of Messiah's people, but to their perpetual succession, expressed by a fine poetical comparison with dew, engendered afresh daily from the womb of the morning. *Youth* will then have its proper sense, as denoting the perpetual youth of the Messiah, whose body is thus constantly renewed by the successive generations of his people. This construction also enables us to divine the clause more equally than in the masoretic interpunction, which, at all events, is either incorrect or rather musical than logical.

4. *Sworn hath Jehovah, and will not repent, Thou (shalt be) a priest for ever, after the order of Melchizedek.* The declaration in the last clause of ver. 3 is here repeated in another form, and with a statement of the ground or reason upon which it rests. What was there poetically represented as the perpetual youth of the Messiah is here more solemnly described as a perpetual priesthood, indissolubly blended with a perpetual kingship, both secured by the oath of God himself. *He will not repent*, there is no fear or even possibility of his breaking or retracting this engagement, for such it is, and not a mere declaratory attestation of the present fact or general truth, as it might seem to be from the common version, not only here but in Heb. v. 6, vii. 17, 21, in every one of which places the Greek conforms exactly to the Septuagint version and the Hebrew text, the *art* being constantly supplied by the translators. That the clause is a promise, and as such relates directly to the future, is clear from the whole tenor of the psalm as a prophetic one, as well as from the oath, which is not used in Scripture to attest mere matters of fact, but to confirm the divine promise and threatenings. The indefinite expression, *a priest*, is intended to describe the office in itself considered, without reference to temporary distinctions and gradations. It therefore comprehends whatever appertained to the office of the High Priest, as the head and representative of all the rest. *After the order*, *i. e.* according to the manner, character, or institution. It is remarkable that this phrase (like יַלְדוּת in ver. 3) is almost peculiar to this psalm and the book of Ecclesiastes, being found besides in only one place (Job v. 8). In all the direct quotations of the verse in Hebrews, the Septuagint version of this word (τάξιν) is retained. But in one of the more indirect citations (Heb. vii. 15) another word (ὁμοιότητα) is substituted, shewing that the essential idea is that of likeness or resemblance. This likeness consists primarily in the union of the regal and sacerdotal offices. See Gen. xiv. 18. The meaning of the verse in its original connection is, that this royal conqueror is also a priest, who makes atonement for the sins of his people, and thus enables and disposes them to make the dedication of themselves described in the preceding verse. The perpetuity of this relation, and its confirmation by the oath of God, are attendant circumstances but essential, and as such insisted on by the apostle, Heb. vii. 20–24. The coincidences founded on the meaning of the names Melchizedek and Salem (Heb. vii. 2), and on the want of hierarchical succession in both cases (Heb. vii. 3), are perfectly legitimate, but not essential to the understanding of the verse in its original connection. The inspired commentary on this sentence, which occupies the whole seventh chapter of Hebrews, is not intended merely to explain its meaning, but also to make use of its terms, and the

associations coupled with them, as a vehicle of other kindred truths, belonging to the Christian revelation, and not necessarily suggested by the psalm to its original readers.

5. *The Lord on thy right hand has smitten, in the day of his anger, kings.* Some suppose this to be addressed to Jehovah, and *the Lord* to mean Messiah, on the ground that they could not each be on the right hand of the other. See above, ver. 1. That they could be so, however, only shews that the whole description is a figurative one, and that the principal figure has a twofold meaning. *On the right hand* has precisely the same meaning here as in Ps. cix. 31, where it denotes the place of protection or assistance, the figure being probably derived from the usages of war, in which one who succours or protects another may be said to strengthen his right hand, as the member which he uses in his own defence. In one sense, therefore, the Lord is at the right hand of Jehovah ; in another sense, Jehovah is at his. This assistance, far from excluding, presupposes his own action, or rather, what Jehovah is described as doing for him he does through him. See above, on ver. 1. The word translated *smite* is very strong and has repeatedly occurred before. See above, on Ps. xviii. 39 (38), lxviii. 22, 24 (21, 23). The day of Jehovah's wrath is coincident with that of the Lord's strength in ver. 3. The strength of the Messiah, as a conqueror, is to be exerted in giving effect to Jehovah's wrath against his enemies. The position of the word *kings* at the end of the sentence, although harsh and almost ungrammatical in English, is retained in the translation for the sake of its effect upon the emphasis and point of the description. The objects of Jehovah's wrath and the Messiah's strokes are not to be mere ordinary men, but kings, if they continue to oppose themselves. See above, on Ps. ii. 2, 10. The tense of the verb may be regarded as an instance of *præteritum phropheticum*, describing what is certainly to happen as already past.

6. *He will judge among the nations—he has filled (them) with corpses—he has smitten the head over much land* (or *over the wide earth*). By another sudden change of form, the Messiah is again spoken of as a third person. The judgment here ascribed to him is only another name and figure for the conquest just described. The form of expression in the last clause is unusual and obscure. The common version makes both *head* and *land* collectives, *the heads over many countries*. Some interpreters explain the second word in this way, but the first more strictly, as denoting a single ruler over many countries. Others invert the terms, and understand by *head* the various chiefs of nations, but by *earth* the whole earth with its qualifying epithet of *great* or *wide*. Amidst these questions of construction or minute interpretation, the general idea is clear enough, to wit, that of universal conquest on the part of the Messiah, and extending to all earthly principalities and powers.

7. *From the brook in the way he will drink, therefore will he raise the head.* According to the masoretic interpunction, *in the way* does not qualify *the brook* but *he will drink*, a distinction of little exegetical importance. Unlike the foregoing verse, the one before us is perfectly clear in its particular expressions, but obscure in its general import and relation to the context. The most probable meaning of thr first clause is, that he shall not be exhausted like those wandering in the desert (Ps. cii. 24, cvii. 4, 5) but refreshed and strengthened, with a reference, as some suppose, to the relief experienced by Samson (Judges xv. 18, 19). The raising of the head, in the last clause, is an obvious and intelligible figure for exhilaration, or relief from dejection and depression, which is naturally indicated by the

hanging of the head. The only question is whether this effect is here supposed to be produced in the conqueror himself or in others. In favour of the former explanation is the parallel clause, which represents him as assuaging his own thirst. In favour of the other is the analogy of Ps. iii. 4 (3), xxvii. 6, where God is said to raise the head of man. As in other doubtful cases, where the senses are not incompatible or exclusive of each other, it is safe, if not entirely satisfactory, to leave them side by side, the rather as the words could probably not fail to suggest both ideas to the Hebrew reader.

Psalm 111

THIS is an alphabetical psalm, in which the Hebrew letters mark the beginning not of verses but of clauses. The first eight verses contain each two clauses; the last two consists of three. The psalm begins with an invitation to the public praise of God, ver. 1, then assigns, as the ground and object of this praise, his dealings with his people, ver. 2–9, and ends with the conclusion, that the fear of the Lord is the beginning of wisdom, ver. 10. There is nothing in the psalm itself to determine its date or its historical occasion. According to Hengstenberg, it is the first psalm of a trilogy, added to the ancient one preceding (Ps. cviii.–cx.) after the return from exile.

1. *Hallelujah! I will thank Jehovah with a whole heart, in the company of the upright and in the congregation.* The *Hallelujah* (*praise ye Jah*) marks the designation of the latter psalms for permanent use in public worship, as the inscription *to the chief musician* does that of the older ones. *With a whole heart*, or *with all* (*my*) *heart*, as it is fully expressed in Ps. lxxxvi. 12. Compare Ps. cxix. 2. The word translated *company* means properly a circle of confidential friends. See above, on Ps. xxv. 14, lv. 15 (14), lxiv. 3 (2), lxxxiii. 4 (3). It is here applied to the church or chosen people, as constituting such a company or circle, in opposition to the world without. It is not, therefore, really distinct from the *congregation* mentioned in the last clause, but another name for it. The *upright* (or *straightforward*) is a title given to the true Israel, from the days of Balaam downwards. See Num. xxiv. 10.

2. *Great are the works of Jehovah, sought (according) to all their desires.* The common version of the last phrase, *all them that have pleasure therein*, supposes the text to be differently pointed, as in Ps. xl. 15 (14), lxx. 3 (2). The received text can only mean *to* (*for* or *according to*) *all their wishes*. The antecedent of the pronoun (*their*) seems to be *the upright* in ver. 1. For a similar construction of the same pronoun, see below, on ver. 10. The clause, thus construed, is obscure, but may be understood to mean, that when the works of God are *sought out*, investigated, or explored, their greatness fully satisfies the hopes and wishes of his people. Another possible sense is, that they are *sought for*, *i. e.* the experience or knowledge of them eagerly desired, *with* (literally *as to*) *all their wishes*, *i. e.* with avidity, or, as it is expressed in the preceding verse, *with all the heart.*

3. *Honour and majesty* (*is*) *his work—and his righteousness standing for ever.* In the first clause, *work* is the subject of the proposition, *honour and majesty* the predicate. *His work is honour and majesty*, *i.e.* all that he does is noble and majestic, worthy of the great King, to whom these epithets are often applied elsewhere. See above, on Ps. civ. 1. *His work* means

specifically here what he does for the protection and deliverance of his people. In the last clause, as in many other places, this work is referred to his *righteousness*, not his *justice*, in the technical and strict sense, but his *rectitude*, including his fidelity to his engagements, and securing the exercise of his covenanted mercy. This seems more natural than to explain it as meaning the practical justification of his people by his providential care of them. *Standing to eternity* (or *perpetuity*), not fitful or capricious, not confined or temporary, but perpetual and constant.

4. *A memory has he made for his wonderful works; gracious and compassionate* (*is*) *Jehovah*. The first clause, though not exactly rendered, is correctly paraphrased in the English Bible, *he hath made his wonderful works to be remembered*, and still more freely in the Prayer-Book version. The last clause shews that the *wonderful works* of the first are not the wonders of creation, nor those of providence in general, but those wrought for the benefit of Israel. The terms of this clause are borrowed from Exod. xxxiv. 6. See above, on Ps. ciii. 8.

5. *Prey hath he given to those fearing him; he will remember to eternity his covenant*. The first word properly denotes the food of wild beasts, and may here be either a poetical equivalent to *food, provision*, as in Prov. xxxi. 15, Mal. iii. 10, or intended to suggest the additional idea of food obtained at the expense of enemies. In either case there seems to be no reason for restricting the clause to the supply of Israel in the desert, although that would necessarily occur to every reader, as the great historical example of the general fact alleged, and in the last clause represented as a proof of God's fidelity to covenant engagements.

6. *The power of his works he has declared to his people*, (so as) *to give to them a heritage of nations*. He has shewn them what powerful things he can do, by favouring them so far as to drive out nations from their seats, and make his people their successors and, as it were, their heirs. This refers to the conquest of Canaan, as the first in a long series of such dispossessions, including all the territories gained in war from the surrounding nations, till the death of David. The construction of *to give* as a gerund (*by giving*) is not a Hebrew idiom, and restricts the meaning of the clause unduly. See above, on Ps. lxxviii. 18.

7. *The works of his hands are truth and judgment; sure* (*are*) *all his precepts*. The second clause is not an iteration of the first, but an inference from it. If what God does himself is always done in faithfulness and justice to his people, then what he requires them to do must certainly be right and best, and his requisitions therefore may be trusted and confided in, the true sense of the adjective or participle here employed.

8. *Settled for ever and ever, done in truth and right*. The subjects are the same as in ver. 7, but presented in an inverse order, the first clause relating to the *precepts*, the last to the *works*, of God. The former are *settled*, firmly supported, founded, or established, not capricious and precarious. The latter, by which they are recommended and attested (see above, on ver. 9), and works of faithfulness and rectitude. The last word in Hebrew is an adjective used as a neuter or abstract noun, in which respect the English *right* resembles it.

9. *Redemption he has sent to his people; he has ordained to eternity his covenant; holy and fearful is his name*. That this verse was intended to consist of three clauses, is clear from the fact that it contains three letters of the alphabet in regular succession. The same thing is true of the remaining verse. The first clause relates mainly, not exclusively, to the

deliverance from Egypt. As in ver. 5, the second clause affirms a general truth, attested and exemplified by the particular fact mentioned in the first. *Fearful*, not merely to his foes but to his people, who can never cease to worship him with holy awe.

10. *The beginning of wisdom is the fear of Jehovah ; a good understanding (is) to all (those) doing them ; his praise endureth for ever.* This is the conclusion drawn from all that goes before. Since all God's dealings with his people are in faithfulness and truth, and his commands not only are but must be right, then the first step in wisdom, its first principle or element, is reverence for such a Being, proved by obedience to his will. The same sentiment occurs in Prov. i. 7, ix. 10, Job xxviii. 28. The intimate connection of the verse, notwithstanding its proverbial or aphoristic form, with the foregoing context, is apparent from the reference of the pronoun *them* to the plural nouns of the preceding verses. *Endureth for ever*, literally (*is*) *standing to eternity*. This is eqvivalent to saying that he will and must be praised for ever, corresponding to the *Halleujah* at the beginning of the psalm.

Psalm 112

ANOTHER alphabetical psalm of precisely the same character, coinciding with the one before it, even in the number of verses, and the number of clauses in each verse. This formal agreement shews the intimate connection of the two compositions, and makes it highly probable that they belong not only to the same age but to the same author, and were meant to form parts of one continued series or system. This psalm begins precisely where the one before it ends, *i. e.* with the happiness arising from the fear of God, ver. 1, the blessed effects of which are then recounted under several particulars, ver. 2–9, and finally contrasted with the fate of the ungodly, ver. 10.

1. *Happy the man fearing Jehovah, in his commandments delighting greatly.* There is here not only an obvious connection with the close of the preceding psalm, but an obvious advance upon it or progression of ideas. As the fear of the Lord is there declared to be the principle of all true wisdom, so here it is declared to be the source of all true happiness. The second clause defines the meaning of the first, by shewing that the fear there mentioned is a fear consistent with, or rather necessarily involving, a complacent acquiescence in God's will, thus entirely excluding a mere slavish dread, which is incompatible with such a disposition.

ι 2. *Mighty in the earth shall be his seed ; the race of the upright shall be blessed.* The first phrase is borrowed from Gen. x. 8, and would at once suggest to every Hebrew reader the idea of a mighty man like Nimrod and the other ancient heroes. Now a promise of personal heroism is perhaps without analogy, especially as given to the son, to the exclusion of the father. This anomaly can be avoided only by assuming, what is probable enough in itself, that the ideal person here described represents the chosen people, the *upright* of the other clause, each successive generation of whom might be expected to excel its predecessors in heroic eminence.

3. *Wealth and riches (are) in his house, and his righteousness endureth for ever.* Not only in his dwelling but in his family, so that his wealth or prosperity might have been said to endure for ever as well as his righteousness, *i. e.* his recognition and reception as a righteous person, his justification. *Endureth*, literally (*is*) *standing*, the same expression that is used in

Ps. cxi. 3 of God himself.   There is also an analogy, at least in form, between the *majesty and honour* of the righteous God and the *wealth and
riches* of the righteous man.

4. *There arises in the darkness light to the upright—kind, and compassionate, and righteous.*   The figure in the first clause is a natural and common one, denoting relief from deep distress.   See above, on Ps. xcvii. 11.
In the last clause we have another instance of the singular way in which
terms applied to God in the preceding psalm are copied and applied to man
in this.   The first two epithets in this clause are employed above in Ps.
cxi. 4.   The principle involved may be the same as in Luke vi. 36. " Be ye
therefore merciful, as your Father also is merciful."   Compare Matt. v. 48.
To these two epithets is added that of *righteous*, in the wide sense including
both the others.   The construction of the sentence is unusual and doubtful;
but most probably the second clause sustains the same relation to the other,
as in ver. 1 ; that is to say, it limits and defines the general description
upright, by confining it to such as have the qualities expressed by the three
adjectives that follow.   The alternation of the numbers is familiar where the
singular denotes an ideal individual including many real ones.

5. *Happy the man shewing favour and lending ; he shall sustain his affairs
by justice.*   The first word in Hebrew, which means *good*, is here descriptive not of character but of condition, and denotes good fortune.   It is used
in the same sense by Isaiah (iii. 10) and Jeremiah (xliv. 17).   The common version (*a good man*) is forbidden by the Hebrew collocation.   *Lending*,
not as a financial or commercial operation, but as an act of charity, lending
to the poor.   The verb in the last clause strictly means to provide for or
sustain, especially with food.   See above, on Ps. lv. 23 (22).   It is here
applied to the control and management of all one's interests.   *Affairs*,
literally *words*, but in the wider sense of that which words denote, namely
things, affairs, in which sense it is sometimes applied to causes or suits at
law.   The last word is commonly translated *judgment*, not in the sense of
discretion, given in the English versions, but in that of practical justice,
righteous conduct.   He shall best secure his own interests by treating those
of others justly and generously.

6. *For to eternity he shall not be moved ; to the memory of eternity he shall
be righteous.*   The *for* assigns the reason for his being pronounced happy.
Moved, *i. e.* from his prosperous condition, or from his position as a righteous
man.   The construction of the last clause in the English versions (*the
righteous shall be in everlasting remembrance*) is grammatical, and yields a
good sense ; but the latest interpreters prefer another, which makes *to everlasting remembrance* mean the same as *to eternity*.   As long as he shall be
remembered, he shall be remembered as a righteous man.   This construction
has the advantage of making the parallelism more exact.

7. *From evil tidings he shall not fear ; fixed is his heart, trusting in
Jehovah.*   The first Hebrew noun is in the singular number, and is properly
a participle passive meaning *heard*, used absolutely as a noun denoting what
is heard, a rumour or report, news or tidings.   The common version (*he
shall not be afraid of evil tidings*) seems to confine the negation to the mere
apprehension or anticipation of bad news, whereas the original expression
comprehends, and indeed more properly denotes, being frightened when the
evil tidings are heard.   A *fixed heart* is the negation both of fickleness and
cowardice.   See above, on Ps. li. 12 (10), lvii. 8 (7), cviii. 1.   Instead of
the active participle *trusting*, the Hebrew has the passive *trusted*, analogous
to that in Ps. ciii. 14.

8. *Settled (is) his heart, he shall not fear, until he look upon his foes* (with triumph). The first word is another expression borrowed from the foregoing psalm, but applied in a manner altogether different. See Ps. cxi. 8, where the plural of the same participle is applied to God's commandments. The construction in the last clause is the idiomatic one of the verb *see* with the preposition *in*, which usually means to see with strong emotion, and especially with joy or triumph. See above, on Ps. l. 23, liv. 9 (7). *Until* does not imply that he shall then fear, but that there will then be no occasion so to do. See above, on Ps. cx. 1.

9. *He has scattered, he has given to the poor, his righteousness endureth for ever, his horn shall be high with honour.* The first verb denotes profuse munificence, as in Prov. xi. 34. This is alleged not as the cause but the effect, and therefore as the evidence of his being righteous. The next clause is the same as the last of ver. 3. With the last clause compare Ps. lxxv. 5 (4), lxxxix. 18 (17).

10. *The wicked shall see and fret; his teeth he shall gnash, and shall melt away; the desire of the wicked shall perish.* He shall see, but not with triumph or delight, like the righteous in ver. 8. The word translated *fret* means both to grieve and be angry, and has no exact equivalent in English. See above, on Ps. vi. 8 (7), x. 14, xxxi. 10 (9). *Gnash with his teeth*, a strong expression of impotent malignity. See above, on Ps. xxxv. 16, xxxvii. 12. *Melt away*, literally be melted, *i. e.* waste or decay. See above, on Ps. xxii. 15 (14), lxviii. 3 (2). *The desire of the wicked* is his wish to see the righteous perish. Compare Prov. x. 24, 28, Job viii. 13, and the contrary promise to the humble, Ps. ix. 19 (18).

Psalm 113

THE Psalmist celebrates the majesty of God, ver. 1–5, in contrast with his gracious condescension to his suffering creatures, ver. 6–9. According to a Jewish usage, which appears to have existed even in the time of Christ, the six psalms beginning with this one constitute the *Greater Hallel*, sung at the annual festivals, especially the Passover and the Feast of Tabernacles. According to Hengstenberg's arrangement, this psalm closes a second trilogy, added to the Davidic one (Ps. cviii.–cx.) after the return from Babylon.

1. *Hallelujah! Praise, O ye servants of Jehovah, praise the name of Jehovah!* As the title, *Servant of Jehovah*, is applied to eminent leaders of the chosen people (Ps. xviii. 1, xxxvi. 1, xc. 1, cv. 6), so the plural, *Servants of Jehovah*, designates his chosen people itself. See above, Ps. xxxiv. 23 (22), lxix. 37 (36), and below, Ps. cxxxvi. 22, and compare Ezra v. 11, Neh. i. 10, from which last places it appears, that this was a familiar form of speech with the returned exiles.

2. *Be the name of Jehovah blessed, from now and even to eternity.* In this as well as the preceding verse, the *name of Jehovah* involves the usual allusion to the manifestation of his nature in his former acts. See above, on Ps. v. 12 (11). The wish expressed in this verse implies a perpetual continuation or renewal of the evidence already furnished.

3. *From the rising of the sun even to its setting, (to be) praised (is the) name of Jehovah.* With the first clause compare Ps. l. 1. The last clause might be grammatically construed as a wish, like that in the preceding verse, *praised (be the) name of Jehovah.* It is more probable, however,

that the passive participle (*laudatus*) was meant to have the force of a gerundive (*laudandus*). See above, on Ps. xviii. 4 (3).

4. *High above all nations* (*is*) *Jehovah ; above the heavens* (*is*) *his* (*glory*). The two clauses are declaratory of his infinite superiority, both to the animate and inanimate creation, each being represented by its noblest part ; the former by mankind, and that considered not as individuals but nations ; the latter by the heavens. This is certainly more natural, and yields a better sense, than to give the preposition (עַל) a different meaning in the two clauses, in the first that of *above*, in the second that of *on*, in which case it is necessary to explain *on heaven* as meaning *in heaven*, just as *on the earth* and *in the earth* are convertible expressions. See above, on Ps. lvii. 6 (5).

5. *Who is like Jehovah, our God, the* (*one*) *dwelling high?* The verb denotes not merely *dwelling*, but *sitting enthroned*, sitting as a king. The original construction of the last clause is peculiar, *the* (*one*) *making high to sit* (or *dwell*).

6. *The one seeing deep—in heaven and in earth.* The construction of the first clause is precisely the same with that of the last clause in ver. 5, and must be explained in the same manner. As *making high to dwell* means *dwelling high*, so *making low* (or *deep*) *to see* must mean *seeing deep*, *i. e.* far below. It also follows from the exact correspondence of these clauses, that the remaining words of ver. 6 are to be connected with the first words of ver. 5. *Who is like Jehovah, our God . . . in heaven and in earth?* The rest will then be read as a parenthesis. This construction is confirmed by the analogy of Deut. iii. 24.

7. *Raising from the dust the poor—from the dunghill he will lift the needy.* The mention of God's seeing far below him suggests the idea of his conde- scension to the humblest objects which he thus beholds. The word trans- lated *poor* is one of wide signification, meaning sometimes poor in flesh and sometimes poor in purse. See above, on Ps. xli. 2 (1). The parallel term means *poor* in the strict sense, *i. e.* needy, destitute. *Dust* and *dunghill*, common figures in all languages for a degraded social state. The terms are borrowed from the prayer of Hannah, 1 Sam. ii. 8. Compare Ps. xliv. 26 (25).

8. *To make him sit with nobles, with the nobles of his people.* Not merely *to dwell*, which is too vague, but *to sit* with them, as their equal and asso- ciate. There is also a climax in the last clause. He not only raises the poor to an equality with nobles in general, but with the nobles of his people, *i. e.* with the noblest of mankind. See again, 1 Sam. ii. 8.

9. *Making the barren* (*one*) *of the house to sit a joyful mother of children. Hallelujah!* The common version (*to keep house*) is founded upon Ps. lxviii. 7 (6), but is here at variance both with Hebrew usage and the masoretic accents, which require (עֲקֶרֶת) *barren* and (הַבַּיִת) *the house* to be closely united in construction, as above. The form of expression is like one in Ps. lxviii. 13 (12). *To sit* might be rendered *to dwell* without any material change of sense ; but the former keeps up the uniformity with ver. 5, 8, where the same Hebrew word is used. The historical allusion is to Hannah who, with other long childless mothers mentioned in the sacred history, was a type of the Church in its low estate, and more especially in exile. Compare Isa. liv. 1.

Psalm 114

As the preceding psalm encouraged the people of God, in a time of trial, by reminding them that, although infinitely exalted, he condescends to notice and relieve the sufferings of his creatures, so the one before us is intended to produce the same effect, by bringing to their recollection what he actually did for Israel in the period of the exodus from Egypt. By that deliverance he acknowledged Israel as his chosen people, ver. 1, 2, and attested the acknowledgment by miracle, ver. 3, 4. Nature herself, whose course was interrupted, is appealed to as a witness, ver. 5, 6, that she is subject to the God of Israel, ver. 7, 8. There is no improbability in the opinion that this psalm, with those which immediately follow, was intended to continue the series begun in the two preceding trilogies (Ps. cviii.–cx., cxi.–cxiii.), and intended to sustain the hopes of the Jewish Church after its return from Babylon.

1. *In the coming forth of Israel from Egypt, of the house of Jacob from a people of strange language.* The first phrase is not to be restricted to the very act or moment of the exodus, but comprehends the whole Mosaic period, of which this was the characteristic and critical event. The *house of Jacob* is a phrase peculiarly appropriate to those who entered Egypt as a family, and left it as a nation. *Of strange language* is a paraphrase of one Hebrew word, apparently a participle and occurring only here ; but according to its obvious etymological affinities, it probably means *stammering*, and then, by an association common in antiquity, *speaking barbarously i. e.* in a foreign language. All such expressions may perhaps involve an allusion to the pre-eminence of Hebrew, as the primitive and sacred language. It was no small part of the humiliation to which Israel was subjected in Egypt, that the people of God should sustain for ages a relation of dependence to a nation who did not even speak the sacred language, much less profess the true religion, so inseparably blended with it. See above, on Ps. lxxxi. 6 (5), and compare my note on Isa. xxxiii. 19.

2. *Judah became his sanctuary, Israel his dominion.* Judah is put as an equivalent to Israel, not only because it had really become so, when the psalm was written, but because it was destined to become so from the first. See Gen. xlix. 10. *Became*, literally *was for*, which might mean nothing more than *served as* or *was treated as ;* but this construction of the verb *to be* with *to* or *for* is the only representative in Hebrew of our word *become*. The sense thus obtained is entirely consistent with the calling of Abraham, because what is here meant is that Israel, as a nation, was now publicly declared to be the chosen or peculiar people, an idea expressed by the phrase *his sanctuary* or *holy thing, i. e.* something set apart exclusively to his use and service. The parallel word in the original is plural, *dominions* or *domains*, in reference, as some suppose, to the plurality of tribes, but according to others, in contrast with the lordships and dominions of the world, to all which Israel is described as more than equipollent, just as the infinite superiority of the true God to all false gods is expressed or suggested by the plural name *Elohim*. Here, as in Ps. lxxxvii. 1, the pronouns are without an antecedent in the sentence. The reference to God is so self-evident, that the only question has respect to the unusual form, which some explain by supposing that the psalm was originally part of the preceding one, or at least designed to be always read or sung directly after it. The latest interpreters prefer the explanation, that the name of God

was designedly suppressed, in order that the questions in ver. 5, 6, might appear more natural and yet more striking.

3. *The sea saw and fled—the Jordan turns back.* By supposing the conversive prefix to affect both verbs, we may render the last also as a preterite, *turned back.* The historical allusion is to Exod. xiv. 21, Josh. iii. 14–17. At the same time, as seas and rivers are familiar emblems of the world and its nations, the reminiscence is adapted to suggest the hope, that other seas and other rivers may be yet controlled by the same power. See above, on Ps. lxxvii. 17 (16), xciii. 3, cvii. 23.

4. *The mountains skipped like rams, (the) hills like the young of sheep.* As the Psalmist is reciting actual events, to be used as symbols and pledges of others, this cannot be explained as a poetical figure, but must be understood as referring to the concussion of Sinai, with its various peaks and neighbouring mountains. See Exod. xix. 18, Judges v. 4, Ps. lxviii. 9 (8), xcvii. 4, 5, Hab. iii. 6. Here again the familiar use of mountains to denote states and empires is suggestive of the same consolation as in ver. 3.

5. *What aileth thee, O sea, that thou fleest—O Jordan (that) thou turnest back?* By a fine poetical apostrophe, the Psalmist, instead of simply stating the cause of these effects, puts the question to the natural objects which thus witnessed and attested the divine presence. The first phrase literally means, *what (is) to thee*, the nearest approach that the Semitic dialects can make to our expression, *what have you*, which in some languages, the French for instance, is the usual equivalent to *what ails you?*

6. *Ye mountains, (that) ye skip like rams—ye hills, like the young of sheep?* The sentence is continued from the foregoing verse, being still dependent on the question there asked. In this interrogation the terms of ver. 3, 4, are studiously repeated. *The young of sheep*, literally *sons of the flock.*

7. *From before the Lord tremble, O earth, from before the God of Jacob.* As in other cases of rhetorical interrogation, the writer or speaker answers his own question. The imperative mood is here peculiarly significant, including both a recollection and prediction; as if he had said, the earth might well tremble at the presence of the Lord, and may well tremble at it still. *From before* is better than *at the presence of*, because the very form of the expression necessarily suggests the ideas of recoil and flight. *Before* is itself a compound term in Hebrew, meaning *to the face of.* The word translated *Lord* is the simple or primitive form of *Adhonai*, and is applied both to God and man, in the sense of lord or master. See Exod. xxiii. 17, Mal. iii. 1.

8. *Turning the rock* (into) *a pool of water, the flint to springs of water.* This refers to the miraculous supply of water in the desert. See above, on Ps. cvii. 35, and compare Exod. xvii. 6, Num. xx. 11, Deut. viii. 15, xxxii. 13, Isa. xli. 18. The connection with the preceding verse is still more marked in the original, the first words of which strictly mean *the (one) turning*, &c. The reader is left to draw for himself the natural and obvious conclusion, that the God, who thus drew water from a flinty rock for the supply of Israel, can still educe the richest blessings from what seem to be the hardest and most inauspicious situations. When this thought is supplied, the psalm no longer seems unfinished or abrupt in its conclusion.

Psalm 115

God is entreated by his people to vindicate not their honour but his own, ver. 1, 2, which is contrasted with the impotence of idols and their worshippers, ver. 3–8, and urged as a reason why his people should trust in him, for a large increase, ver. 9–15, and a fulfilment of his purpose to glorify himself by the praises of the living, not the dead, ver. 16–17, in the promotion of which end the church declares her resolution to co-operate for ever, ver. 18. The general tenor of the psalm, thus stated, and its particular contents, make it perfectly well suited to the state of things in which the series is supposed to have been written, namely, that succeeding the return from exile, but before the actual rebuilding of the temple.

1. *Not unto us, Jehovah, not unto us, but to thy name give glory, for thy mercy, for thy truth.* The glory meant is not that of former but of future deeds. The implied petition is, that God would interpose for the deliverance of his people, not to do them honour, but to glorify himself, and especially to vindicate his mercy and fidelity, which seemed to be dishonoured by his desertion of the chosen people. See above, on Ps. lxxix. 9, and compare Num. xiv. 15, Isa. xliii. 7, 25, xlviii. 9, 11, Dan. ix. 18. The favour sought is the completion of the work of restoration, still imperfect, though auspiciously begun.

2. *Why should the nations say, Where now is their God?* Why should they have occasion so to ask? The form of expression is borrowed from Ps. lxxix. 10, with the addition of (נָא) *now*, which is not a particle of time, but of entreaty, or, in this connection, of triumphant demand. *Where, pray, is their God?* This verse is explanatory of the one before it, by shewing that there really was need of something to silence the reproaches of the heathen, a description exactly corresponding to the state of the Jews at the Restoration.

3. *And our God (is) in heaven; all that he pleased he has done.* The *and*, though foreign from our idiom, adds sensibly to the force of the expression. They ask thus, as if our God were absent or had no existence; and yet all the while our God is in heaven, in his glorious and exalted dwelling-place. Compare Ps. ii. 4, xi. 4, ciii. 19. The same phrase, but in the future tense, is used by Solomon (Eccles. viii. 3). The same idea is expressed in other words, Gen. xviii. 14, Job xxiii. 13.

4. *Their idols (are) silver and gold, the work of the hands of man.* Here begins the contrast between the true God and all others. *Their idols*, those of the Gentiles, who reproach us with the absence or indifference of our God. For the associations coupled with the word for *idols*, see above, on Ps. cvi. 38. *Hands of man*, not of *a man*, but of *mankind, i. e.* human hands. With this whole passage compare Isa. xl. 18–20, xli. 7, xliv. 9–20, xlvi. 5–7, Jer. ii. 28, x. 3–15.

5. *They have a mouth and speak not; they have eyes and see not.* As the verb *to have* is wanting in the Hebrew and its cognate languages (see above, on Ps. cxiv. 5), it is not a literal translation of the original expression, (there is) *a mouth to them*, (there are) *eyes to them*. The future includes not only a simple affirmation, *they speak not, they see not*, but the future and potential sense, they never will or can speak or see.

6. *They have ears and hear not, they have a nose and smell not.* The antithesis is that expressed in Ps. xciv. 9, that God is the former of the eye and the planter of the ear in man; much more than can he see and hear himself.

7. *They have hands, and feel not; they have feet, and walk not; they do not mutter in their throat.* The sameness of this long enumeration, the force of which is logical and not poetical, is partially relieved by a change in the form of the original, which cannot well be imitated in translation.

Their hands, and they feel not ; their feet, and they walk not. Some make
the first words in each clause nominatives absolute ; *their hands—they feel
not ; their feet—they walk not.* But in the preceding parts of the description, the verbs relate not to the particular members, but to the whole person. It is better, therefore, to supply a verb—*their hands* (are there), *and*
(yet) *they feel not—their feet* (are there), *and* (yet) *they go not.* The English *feel* is to be taken in its physical and outward sense, corresponding to
the Latin *palpo,* here used by the Vulgate and Jerome. A less equivocal
translation would be *touch.* The other verb denotes all progressive movements of the body, comprehended in the English *go.* See above, on Ps.
civ. 3. The meaning of the last clause is, that they cannot even make the
faintest and most inarticulate guttural noise, like the lower animals ; much
less speak as men do. See above, on Ps. xxxv. 28, lxxi. 24.

8. *Like them shall be those who made them, every one who trusts in them.*
The last clause forbids the application of the first to the mere artificers, as
such, and fastens it on those who trust in idols, whether made by them or
by others for them. However formidable now, they shall hereafter be as
powerless and senseless as the gods they worship. The translation *are* is
contrary to Hebrew usage, which requires the present tense of the substantive verb to be suppressed.

9. *O Israel, trust thou in Jehovah ; their help and their shield* (is) *He.*
This is the practical application of the contrast just presented. Since idols
are impotent and God almighty, it is folly to fear them or their servants ;
it is worse than folly not to trust in Him. The last clause is borrowed
from Ps. xxxiii. 20. After addressing Israel directly in the first clause, he
resumes the third person in the second, and, as if speaking to himself,
assigns the reason for the exhortation. The first clause is, as it were,
uttered in a loud voice, and the second in a low one.

10. *O house of Aaron, trust ye in Jehovah : their help and their shield*
(is) *He.* Before the exile this particular address to the priests would have
been surprising. It is perfectly natural, however, after the return from
Babylon, when the priests bore so large a proportion, not only to the other
Levites, but to the whole nation, and naturally exercised a paramount
influence in its affairs.

11. *Fearers of Jehovah, trust ye in Jehovah ; their help and their shield*
(is) *He.* He turns again to the people at large, who are here described as
fearers of Jehovah, not in reference to the actual character of all the individual members, but to the high vocation of the body. See above, Ps.
xxii. 24 (23), cxi. 5.

12. *Jehovah hath remembered us ; he will bless, he will bless the house of
Israel ; he will bless the house of Aaron.* The exhortation to confide in God
does not imply that he has yet done nothing. He has already shewn
his gracious recollection of us by beginning to bless us, and he will still go
on to bless us ; an idea simply but beautifully expressed by the repetition
of the verb, the effect of which is spoiled in the common version by needlessly supplying *us.*

13. *He will bless the fearers of Jehovah, the small with the great.* There
is no need of explaining *the great* to be the priests and *the small* the laity.
It is much more natural to understand this as an instance of a common
Hebrew idiom, which combines *small* and *great* in the sense of *all,* just as
neither good nor evil means neither one thing nor another, *i. e. nothing.*
Compare 2 Kings, xviii. 24, Jer. xvi. 6, Rev. xiii. 16, xix. 6.

14. *May Jehovah add to you, to you and to your children !* This implies

a previous diminution of the people, such as really took place in the Babylonish exile. The optative meaning of the verb, both here and in Gen. xxx. 24, is clear from Deut. i. 11, 2 Sam. xxiv. 3. The Hebrew preposition strictly means *upon* you, and conveys the idea of accumulation much more strongly. See above, on Ps. lxxi. 14, where we have an example of the same construction.

15. *Blessed are ye of Jehovah, Maker of heaven and earth.* Ye are the people blessed of old in the person of your father Abraham, by Melchizedek, priest of the Most High God, saying, " Blessed be Abraham of the Most High God, creator of heaven and earth," Gen. xiv. 19. *Of Jehovah,* literally *to Jehovah,* as an object of benediction to him. Or the Hebrew preposition, as in many other cases, may be simply equivalent to our *by.* The creative character of God is mentioned, as ensuring his ability, no less than his willingness, to bless his people.

16. *The heavens* (are) *heavens for Jehovah, and the earth he has given to the sons of man.* This verse suggests another reason why God would increase them, namely, that although he reserved heaven for himself, he designed the earth to be filled and occupied by man, and hence in the primeval blessing on mankind, as originally uttered, and as repeated after the flood (Gen. i. 28, ix. 1), the command to increase is coupled with that to fill the earth. Now if it is not God's will that the race should be diminished and reduced to nothing, much less can such be his intention with respect to his own people. The form of expression in the first clause is unusual. The construction given in the English Bible (*the heaven, even the heavens, are the Lord's*) is entirely gratuitous, the distinction of numbers (*heaven, heavens*), and the emphatic *even,* being both supplied by the translators. The Hebrew word is plural in both cases, and is indeed used only in that number.

17. (It is) *not the dead* (that) *are to praise Jah, and not all* (those) *going down in silence.* This may be regarded as a further reason for expecting the divine protection. God has chosen a people, from among the nations of the earth, to praise him, not when dead but living, not in the silence of the grave, but with their voices in the present life. Thus understood, the verse teaches nothing as to the employments of the disembodied spirit, or of soul and body in the future state. All that is affirmed here (and perhaps in other places like it) is that the praises of the chosen people, as such, must be limited to this life. See above, on Ps. vi. 6 (5), xxx. 10 (9) lxxxviii. 11–13 (10–12), and compare Isa. xxxviii. 18. *Silence,* a poetical description of the grave or the unseen world, as in Ps. xciv. 17.

18. *And* (therefore) *we will bless Jah from now even to eternity. Hallelujah !* As it is not the dead who are to do it, and as we are still preserved alive, let us answer our vocation and the very end of our existence. The insensible transition from temporal to eternal praise is altogether natural. The *hallelujah* refers back to the expression *praise Jah (yehallelujah)* in ver. 17. As if he had said, Let us do what the dead can not, shout Hallelujah !

Psalm 116

THE Church declares her resolution to praise Jehovah for the deliverance which she has experienced, ver. 1, 2, and which is then described with some particularity, ver. 3–10, followed by a declaration of the way in which the Church means to express her gratitude, ver. 11-19. The Septuagint and Vulgate, which combine the two preceding psalms as one, divide the one before us into two, with as little reason in the one case as the other. The state of things referred to in this psalm, as one of mingled joy and grief, and its peculiarities of language, all combine to fix its date immediately after the return from Babylon.

1. *I love—because Jehovah hears my voice, my supplications.* The common version gives the sense correctly, but by a transposition of *Jehovah*, avoids the singular peculiarity of form in the original. The object of the verb *I love* is easily supplied from the remainder of the sentence. Compare Ps. xviii. 2 (1), Deut. vi. 5. Both verbs may be translated in the present, though of different tenses in the Hebrew. The preterite form of the first (*I have loved*) implies that the occasion had already been afforded; the future form of the second (*he will hear*), that it was continued and would be continued. The last word, according to its etymology, means prayers for grace or favour.

2. *For he has inclined his ear to me, and in my days I will call (upon him).* The original idea of the figure in the first clause seems to be that of leaning forward to catch a sound otherwise too faint to be distinctly audible. See above, on Ps. xxxi. 3 (2), and compare Ps. xvii. 6, lxxi. 2, lxxviii. 1, cii. 3. *In my days* is commonly understood to mean through all the days of my life, or as long as I live. Compare Isa. xxxix. 8, and see above, on Ps. civ. 33. *I will call* might be understood to mean, I will still pray to him who has hitherto answered my petitions. But *to call upon God* is applied not only to prayer but to thanksgiving, as appears from ver. 13 below, where indeed we have the execution of the purpose here avowed.

3. *The bands of death enclosed me, and the pangs of hell found me ; distress and grief I find.* Here begins the description of the sufferings from which God had delivered him. The expressions are borrowed from Ps. xviii. 5, 6 (4, 5). The twofold use of the verb *find* in this verse is analogous to that of the synonymous verbs *catch* and *seize* in English, when a man is said to catch a disease, and the disease is said to seize the man. Compare Ps. cxix. 143 with Prov. vi. 33. *Hell*, in the wide sense corresponding to *sheol*, the grave, death, or the state of the dead. See above, on Ps. vi. 6 (5).

4. *And on the name of Jehovah I call; ah now, Jehovah, deliver my soul !* The future in the first clause may be strictly translated (*I will call*) as expressing the determination which he formed in the midst of his distress. See above on Ps. xviii. 5, 7 (4, 6). *Ah now* corresponds exactly, both in origin and meaning, to the intensive particle of entreaty (אָנָּה for אָנָּא from אָה and נָא), which the common version paraphrases, *I beseech thee.* One of the elements of which it is compounded occurs above, Ps. cxv. 2.

5. *Gracious (is) Jehovah and righteous, and our God shews pity.* With the first clause compare Ps. cxi. 4, cxii. 4. The last word in Hebrew is the active participle of the verb to *pity*, to *compassionate*, and is here used to denote a habit as distinguished from a momentary feeling.

6. *A preserver of the simple (is) Jehovah ; I was brought low, and to me he brought salvation.* Here again the first word is an active participle, *keeping the simple, i. e.* habitually watching over them. For the meaning of *the simple*, see above, on Ps. xix. 8 (7). The word *brought*, twice used in translating this verse, has nothing distinctly corresponding to it in the

Hebrew, but by a fortuitous coincidence, enters into two English phrases, by which the original verbs may best be represented. The verb translated *brought low* means to be reduced, in person, strength, or circumstances. See above, on Ps. lxxix. 8, and compare the cognate adjective in Ps. xli. 2 (1). The other is the common Hebrew verb *to save*, here expressed by a circumlocution, for the purpose of retaining the original construction with the preposition *to*, which also occurs above, Ps. lxxii. 4, lxxxvi. 16.

7. *Return, O my soul, unto thy rest, for Jehovah hath bestowed upon thee* (favour). By calling on his soul, which had been agitated and alarmed, to return to its repose, he implies the cessation of the danger. *Rest*, literally *rests* or *resting-places*, implying fulness or completeness of repose. See above, on Ps. xxiii. 2. For the sense and usage of (גָּמַל) the last verb, see above, on Ps. xiii. 6 (5), and compare Ps. vii. 5 (4), ciii. 10. The unusual grammatical forms in this verse are similar to those in Ps. ciii. 2, 5.

8. *For thou hast delivered my soul from death, my eye from weeping, my foot from falling.* By a sudden apostrophe, God is now addressed directly. The first and last members of the sentence are borrowed from Ps. lvi. 14 (13). The second bears some resemblance to Ps. lvi. 9 (8) and Jer. xxxi. 16.

9. *I will walk before Jehovah in the land of life* (or *of the living*). This is also borrowed from Ps. lvi. 14 (13), with the substitution of *land* (literally *lands*) for *light*. Compare Ps. xxvii. 13. The hope here expressed is in contrast with Ps. cxv. 17.

10. *I believed, for* (thus) *I speak; I was afflicted greatly.* I must have exercised faith, or I could not thus have spoken. The Septuagint version, retained in the New Testament (2 Cor. iv. 13), clothes the same essential meaning in a different form, *I believed, therefore have I spoken.* It was because his faith enabled him to speak, so that his speaking was a proof of faith.

11. *I said in my terror, All mankind* (are) *false.* The form of expression in the first clause is borrowed from Ps. xxxi. 23 (22). But instead of being a confession of error it is here rather a profession of faith. Even in the midst of his excitement, terror, panic, he could turn away from all human aid and trust in God alone. The proposition, *all mankind are false,* i. e. not to be trusted or relied upon, implies as its complement or converse, therefore God alone is to be trusted. See the same contrast stated more explicitly in Ps. cxviii. 8, and compare Ps. lxii. 9, 10 (8, 9), cviii. 13 (12), cxlvi. 3, 4.

12. *How shall I requite to Jehovah all his bestowments upon me.* Between this verse and that before it, we must supply the thought that his faith was rewarded and justified by the event. This is indeed implied in the interrogation now before us. *How*, literally *what, i. e.* (in) *what* (*way*), or (*by*) *what* (*means*)? See Gen. xliv. 16. The unusual word *bestowments* is here used to represent a Hebrew one occurring only here, but evidently formed from the verb (גָּמַל) to confer or bestow upon, employed in ver. 7 above. The peculiar form both of the noun and pronoun (תַּגְמוּלוֹהִי) is regarded by the highest philological authorities as fixing the date of the composition after the Captivity.

13. *The cup of salvations I will take up, and on the name of Jehovah will call.* This is commonly explained by a reference to the Jewish tradition of a cup of thanksgiving which accompanied or followed the thank-

offerings. But we read of no such cup in Scripture, and its origin may probably be traced to the rabbinical interpretation of this very passage, Interpreted by Scriptural analogies, it simply means, I will accept the portion God allots me. For this figurative use of *cup*, see above, on Ps. xi. 6, xvi. 5. The plural form, *salvations*, denotes fulness or completeness, as in Ps. xviii. 52 (51), liii. 7 (6). *Take up*, as if from the table where the hand of God has placed it; or *lift up*, towards heaven as a gesture of acknowledgment.

14. *My vows to Jehovah will I pay—in the presence of all his people.* The word *now*, in the common version, misleads the English reader, who can scarcely fail to understand it as an adverb of time, meaning *at present*, *immediately*, *without delay*, whereas it is the particle of entreaty (נָא) used in Ps. cxv. 2, and here employed to modify the bold avowal of a purpose, by making it dependent on divine permission. As if he had said : my vows to Jehovah I will pay—let me do it in the presence (I entreat) of all his people. The same meaning is attached by some to the augmented or paragogic form of the word translated *presence*, and which strictly means the front or forepart. Both these peculiarities are reckoned among the indications of a later age of Hebrew composition.

15. *Precious in the eyes of Jehovah* (is) *the death of his gracious ones* (or *saints*). The idea and expression are borrowed from Ps. lxxii. 14, where the same thing is said of their blood. The word for *death* has the same peculiarity of form as that for *presence* in ver. 14, and is construed in the same way with the preposition *to*, *the death to his saints*, *i. e.* the death belonging to them, which they die. These are regarded by the critics as additional tokens of the age in which the psalm was written. The verse assigns the reason for the preceding vow, to wit, that God counts the death of his people too costly to be lightly or gratuitously suffered.

16. *Ah now, Jehovah—for I* (am) *thy servant, I* (am) *thy servant, the son of thy handmaid ; thou hast loosed my bonds.* The expression of entreaty at the beginning has reference to some thing not expressed, though easily supplied, namely permission thus to testify his gratitude. Ah now, Lord (suffer me thus to do) for I am thy servant, &c. The additional phrase, *son of thy handmaid*, is much stronger than *thy servant*, and describes him as a home-born slave. See above, on Ps. lxxxvi. 16. In the last clause we have another instance of a preposition (לְ) interposed between the active verb and its object, in a way unknown to the older Hebrew. It is possible, however, to translate the words, *thou hast freed* (me) *as to* (*i. e.* from) *my bonds.*

17. *To thee will I sacrifice a sacrifice of thanks, and on the name of Jehovah will I call.* The sense is not, I will offer thanks instead of an oblation, but an oblation really expressive of thanksgiving and appointed for that purpose.

18. *My vows to Jehovah will I pay in the presence* (I entreat) *of all his people.* An exact repetition of ver. 14, with all its singularities of form.

19. *In the courts of the house of Jehovah, in the midst of thee, Jerusalem. Hallelujah !* This verse completes the one before it, and explains the phrase, *before all his people.* Some regard it as a proof that the psalm was composed after the actual rebuilding of the temple. But in Ezra ii. 68, iii. 8, we find the designation *house of God* applied to the consecrated site. The use of the word *courts* is still more natural, because it originally means *enclosures*, which might be and no doubt were defined, long before the temple was rebuilt. This explanation seems to be confirmed by the

addition of the last clause. In the courts of the Lord's house, that is, on the consecrated spot in the midst of thee, O Jerusalem, the Holy City.

Psalm 117

THIS, which is the shortest psalm in the collection, has evidently no independent character or even meaning of its own, but was designed to be a chorus or doxology to a longer composition. Its position is sufficiently accounted for by the assumption, that it was primarily meant to serve the purpose just described with reference to the psalm or to the trilogy immediately preceding; while its being separately written as an independent psalm may have arisen from the purpose to use it sometimes in a different connection, with which view it would naturally be left moveable, like the doxologies in our modern books, which may be attached to any psalm or hymn, at the discretion of the person who conducts the service.

1. *Praise Jehovah, all ye nations; laud him, all ye peoples.* The last word is a different plural from that in Gen. xxv. 16, Num. xxv. 15, and belongs, no doubt, to the later Hebrew. Here, as in Ps. xlvii. 2 (1), lxvi. 8, xcviii. 4, the whole world is invited to praise God for his favours shewn to Israel.

2. *For mighty over us has been his mercy, and the truth of Jehovah (is) to eternity. Hallelujah!* The verb at the beginning means not merely to be great, but to be strong or powerful. See above, on Ps. ciii. 11. The preposition *over* suggests the idea of protection, or, if translated *on*, that of favour descending from above.

Psalm 118

AFTER an invitation to praise God for his goodness to his people, ver. 1–4, the occasion of this praise is more particularly stated, namely, that he has delivered Israel from great distress, and thereby proved himself worthy of their highest confidence, ver. 5–14. After another statement of the favour just experienced, ver. 15–18, the people are described as entering the sanctuary, there to give thanks and implore the divine blessing on the enterprise in which they are engaged, ver. 19–29. The ideal speaker, throughout the psalm, is Israel, as the Church or chosen people. The deliverance celebrated cannot be identified with any one so naturally as with that from the Babylonish exile. Some, on account of supposed allusions to the temple as already built, refer the psalm to the times of Nehemiah. Others, with more probability, though not with absolute conclusiveness, infer from the tone of lively joy and thankfulness pervading the whole composition, that it was written and originally sung soon after the return; and from the allusions in ver. 22, 25, that it has reference to the founding of the second temple, and is the very psalm, or one of the psalms mentioned in the history, Ezra iii. 10, 11, where its first and last words are recited. The mention of David in that passage is accounted for by the assumption that this psalm was sung only as a part of the whole series, which opens with a Davidic trilogy, Ps. cviii.–cx.

1. *Give thanks unto Jehovah, for (he is) good, for unto eternity (is) his mercy.* The opening formula is common to this psalm with Ps. cvi. and cvii. Its elements are also found, combined with others, in Ps. c. 4, 5. With the second member of the sentence compare Ps. xxv. 8, lxxiii. 1.

2. *Oh that Israel would say—for unto eternity (is) his mercy.* The first clause of this translation is a paraphrase of the original, to which the particle of entreaty (נָא) gives a strong optative meaning. Here, as in Ps. cxvi. 14, 18, the common version (*now*) is equivocal. That version also has *that* instead of *for*, in the last clause of this and the two next verses. This translation is perfectly grammatical, and makes the sentence more complete in itself. But besides that it breaks the studied uniformity of the context by varying the version of the particle (כִּי), the dependence of the clause on the preceding verse, required and denoted by the use of the word *for*, is really essential to the writer's object. It is as if he had said, the reason for thus urging man to praise Jehovah is because his mercy endureth for ever, and oh that Israel would join in affirming this reason. *Oh that Israel would say* (I will give thanks), *for his mercy endureth for ever.*

3, 4. *Oh that the house of Aaron would say—'for unto eternity (is) his mercy.' Oh that the fearers of Jehovah would say—'for unto eternity (is) his mercy.'* The succession of Israel, the house of Aaron, and the fearers of Jehovah, in this and the following verses, is the same as in Ps. cxv. 9–11. This and the trine repetitions in ver. 10–12, 15, 16, compared with that in Ps. cxv. 12, 13, are corroborations of the assumed affinity between the psalms of this whole series, both in origin and purpose.

5. *Out of anguish I invoked Jah ; heard me in a wide place Jah.* The first noun is a rare one, common to this place and Ps. cxvi. 3, another indication of affinity. *Heard*, in the pregnant sense of heard favourably, heard and answered. See above, on Ps. xxii. 22 (21). As the word translated *anguish* originally means pressure, confinement, the appropriate figure for relief from it is a wide room, ample space, enlargement. See above, on Ps. iv. 2 (1). To *answer in a wide place* is to grant his prayer by bringing him forth into such a place.

6. *Jehovah (is) for me ; I will not fear ; what can man do to me?* Instead of *for me, i. e.* in my favour, on my side, the Hebrew (לִי) may also be translated *to me, i. e.* is or belongs to me, is mine. See above, on Ps. lvi. 5, 10, 12 (4, 9, 11). *Man* does not here mean *a man*, but *mankind*, or Man as opposed to God.

7. *Jehovah is for me, among my helpers, and I shall look upon my haters.* Here again, the first clause may be rendered, *Jehovah is to me (or I have Jehovah) among* or *with my helpers.* With this last expression compare Ps. xlv. 10 (9), xcix. 6. The construction in the last clause is the idiomatic one meaning to see with joy or triumph, or to see their punishment and subjugation. See above, on Ps. liv. 9 (7), and with the whole verse compare Ps. liv. 6 (4). As the ideal speaker is the ancient church or chosen people, the haters or enemies here meant are primarily heathen persecutors and oppressors.

8. *It is good to confide in Jehovah* (more) *than to trust in man.* This and the next verse affirm clearly and fully what is more obscurely intimated in Ps. cxvi. 11. As the Hebrew has no distinct form of comparison, this is the nearest possible approach to saying, *it is better. Than*, literally *from, away from*, implying difference, and then comparison, but not expressing it. The verb *confide* is the expressive one originally meaning to take refuge or find shelter. See above, on Ps. ii. 12.

9. *It is good to confide in Jehovah* (more) *than to trust in nobles.* This merely strengthens the foregoing declaration, by rendering it more specific and emphatic. The Lord is more to be confided in, not merely than the

mass of men, but than their chiefs. *Nobles* is a better translation than
princes, because it keeps up the association with the adjective sense *noble*,
generous, liberal, spontaneous, which is otherwise lost sight of. See
above, on Ps. li. 14 (12). Even the Persian patrons and protectors of the
Jews had not entirely deserved their confidence; nor at all, in comparison
with Jehovah their covenanted God.

10. *All the nations surround me; in the name of Jehovah—that I will
cut them off.* The hyperbolical expression, *all the nations*, is less strange
than it might otherwise appear, because (בּוֹיִם) *nations* had now begun to be
familiarly applied to the gentiles or heathen, not as organized bodies merely,
but as individuals, especially when numerous. There is nothing unnatural,
therefore, in the use of this expression to describe the heathen adversaries
of the Jews at the period of the Restoration, not excepting the Samaritans,
who, though they claimed to be a mixed race, were really heathen, both in
origin and character. Another way in which the hyperbole may be explained, or rather done away, is by supposing the first clause to be substantially although not formally conditional. *Should all nations* (or *thoug
all nations should*) *surround me.* The strongest sense may then be put
upon the words *all nations*, as the act ascribed to them is merely hypothetical. The construction of the last clause is unusual and doubtful. Some
arbitrarily make the כִּי a particle of affirmation, yea, yes, verily, &c.
Others gain the same sense by explaining the whole phrase to mean, (it is
true, or it is certain) *that I will cut them off.* The same use of the particle
is thought to be exemplified in Isa. vii. 9. Perhaps the best solution is the
one afforded by the Hebrew usage of suppressing the principal verb in oaths
or solemn affirmations. If this may be omitted even when there is nothing
to denote the character of the expression, and when the form of the expression itself is liable to misconstruction, as for instance in the formula with
if, much more may it be omitted where the sense of the expression is quite
clear, and its juratory or imprecatory character denoted by accompanying
words. The sense will then be, *in the name of Jehovah* (I swear or
solemnly affirm) *that I will cut them off.* This last verb always means *to
cut*, and except in Ps. xc. 6, where one of its derived forms is used, *to
circumcise.* It was here used, as some suppose, to suggest that the uncir-
cumcised enemies of Israel, as they are often called, should be cut or cut
off in another sense. Compare the play upon the corresponding Greek
words in Phil. iii. 2, 3.

11. *They surround me, yea they surround me; in the name of Jehovah*
(I declare) *that I will cut them off.* The same sentence is repeated with a
slight variation, which consists in the omission of the subject and the
iteration of the verb, rendered more emphatic by a change of form. The
word translated *yea* means *also, likewise*, but cannot be so used in the
English idiom. The climax indicated may be, that the act described is no
longer hypothetical but actual. They surround me; yes, they really, in
fact, surround me.

12. *They surround me like bees; they are quenched as a fire of thorns; in
the name of Jehovah* (I declare) *that I will cut them off.* This completes the
trine repetition so characteristic of these psalms. The point of comparison
with bees is their swarming multitude and irritating stings. Compare Deut.
i. 44. That with thorns is the rapidity and ease with which they are both
kindled and extinguished. See above, on Ps. lviii. 10 (9).

13. *Thou didst thrust, thrust at me, to* (make me) *fall, and Jehovah*

helped me. By a lively apostrophe the enemy is here addressed directly, that is, the hostile heathen power, from whose oppression Israel had just been rescued. See above, on ver. 7. The verb *to thrust* or *strike at* is the root of the noun translated *falling* in Ps. lvi. 14 (13), cxvi. 8.

14. *My strength and song (is) Jah, and he has become my salvation.* These words are from Exod. xv. 2. The first clause is also borrowed by Isaiah (xii. 2). *My strength and song,* my protection or deliverer, and as such the object of my praise. *Become my salvation,* literally *has been to me for salvation,* a stronger though synonymous expression for *my saviour.*

15. *The voice of joy and salvation in the tents of the righteous—the right hand of Jehovah has made strength.* The word translated *joy* means properly the audible expression of it by shout or song, and is sometimes applied even to a cry of distress. Compare Ps. xxx. 6 (5), xlii. 5 (4), xlvii. 2 (1), with Ps. xvii. 1, lxi. 2 (1). *Joy and salvation* are related as cause and effect, joy occasioned by salvation. *Tents,* a poetical expression for dwellings. See above, on Ps. xci. 10. *The righteous,* the true Israel, the people of God, as such considered. See above, on Ps. xxxiii. 1. The substantive verb (*is*) may be supplied in this verse, so as to make it a complete proposition ; or it may be a kind of exclamation, as if he had said, Hark ! the voice of joy, &c. Compare Isa. xl. 3, 6. The last clause may then be understood as containing the words uttered by the voice. The idiomatic phrase at the end may either mean that God has acquired or exerted strength. See above, on Ps. lx. 14 (12), cviii. 14.

16. *The right hand of Jehovah is raised, the right hand of Jehovah makes strength.* This, with the last clause of ver. 15, makes another of the triplets or trine repetitions, which are characteristic of these psalms. See above, on ver. 2–4, 10–12. Instead of *is raised* some read *raises* or *exalts,* which is equally grammatical, as the active and passive forms in this case are coincident. The meaning then is, that his right hand raises or exalts his people, as the other clause says that his right hand gains or exercises strength in their behalf. It seems more natural, however, to explain it as an instance of a common figure which describes God's hand as raised, when he exerts his power.

17. *I shall not die but live, and recount the works of Jah.* The existence thus to be preserved is that of Israel, and the last clause describes the final cause of that existence, which is here stated as a ground of confidence, and is elsewhere urged as an argument in prayer. See above, on Ps. cxv. 17, cxvi. 9, 15, and compare Ps. lxxi. 20. The original construction of the first clause is, *I shall not die, for I shall live.*

18. *Surely has Jah chastened me, but to death did not give me.* This verse, though simple in its structure and transparent in its meaning, is highly idiomatic in its form. The adverb used in the translation represents the emphatic repetition of the verb in Hebrew, which is sometimes imitated in the English Bible (*chastening has Jah chastened me*), but seldom so as to convey the whole idea. Of such a repetition we have had an instance in ver. 13. Another unavoidable departure from the original form consists in using *but* for *and,* at the beginning of the second clause. Did not *give,* give up, give over or abandon. The chastisement here mentioned must be the calamity from which the people had been recently delivered, and in which we have already seen good grounds to recognise the Babylonish conquest, domination and captivity.

19. *Open ye to me the gates of righteousness, I will come in by them, I will thank Jah.* This may have been intended to accompany the entrance of

the priests and people into the sacred enclosure, for the purpose of laying the foundation of the temple, as when David pitched the tabernacle on Mount Zion. See above, on Ps. xxiv.

20. *This (is) the gate* (that belongs) *to Jehovah ; the righteous shall come in by it.* Or the meaning may be, since this is the Lord's gate, let the righteous (and no others) enter at it. Many interpreters find obvious indications here of double or responsive choirs, by which the psalm was to be sung. But this, though possible, is not a necessary supposition, nor is there any certain trace of such a usage or arrangement elsewhere in the book of Psalms. See above, pp. 109, 110, 112.

21. *I will thank thee, for thou hast answered me, and hast become my salvation.* This verse assigns the reason for their entrance. *Answered,* in the specific sense of answering or granting prayer. See above, on ver. 5. The last clause is from ver. 14.

22. *The stone* (which) *the builders rejected has become the head of the corner.* This is a proverbial expression, and as such applicable to any case, in which what seemed to be contemptible has come to honour. This mode of expressing the idea was most probably suggested by the founding of the temple. There is no need, however, of supposing any actual dispute among the Jewish builders in relation to the corner stone of the sacred edifice. The sight of the stone, or the act of laying it, would be sufficient to suggest the proverb and its application to the happy change experienced by Israel, so lately blotted from the list of nations, and regarded by the heathen as unworthy even of an humble place in the proud fabric of consolidated empire, but now restored not only to a place, but to the highest place among the nations, not in point of power, wealth, or worldly glory, but as the chosen and peculiar people of the Most High God. As this psalm was sung by the people at the last Jewish festival attended by our Saviour, he applied this proverb to himself, as one rejected by the Jews and by their rulers, yet before long to be recognised as their Messiah whom they had denied and murdered, but whom God had exalted as a Prince and a Saviour, to give repentance to Israel and remission of sins (Acts v. 31). This, though really another application of the proverb in its general meaning, has a certain affinity with its original application in the verse before us, because the fortunes of the ancient Israel, especially in reference to great conjunctures, bore a designed resemblance to the history of Christ himself, by a kind of sympathy between the Body and the Head. Even the temple, which suggested the original expression, did but teach the doctrine of divine inhabitation, and was therefore superseded by the advent of the Son himself. *The head of the corner* means the chief or corner-stone of the foundation, even in Zech. iv. 7, where it is translated *head stone.* The application of the verse before us made by Christ himself (Matt. xxi. 42) is renewed by Peter (Acts. iv. 11.)

23. *From Jehovah is this ; it is wonderfully done in our eyes.* This signal revolution in the condition of the chosen people is not the work of man but of God. *From the Lord, i. e.* proceeding from him as its author. *Is this,* literally *has been, i. e.* happened, come to pass. In the last clause it is said to be not merely *wonderful,* but *wonderfully done,* the Hebrew word being a passive participle, which strictly means distinguished, made to differ, made strange, strangely done. Its plural is continually used as a noun in application to God's wondrous works or doings. This, no less than the proverb to which it is attached, was as appropriate to the case of the Messiah as to that of his people, and is accordingly applied in the same manner by himself (Matt. xxi. 42).

24. *This is the day Jehovah has made, we will rejoice and triumph in it.* By the day we are here to understand the happier times which Israel, through God's grace, was permitted to enjoy. This day he is said, as the author of this blessed revolution, to have made, created. Some understand by *day* the festival or celebration, at which the psalm was intended to be sung. The *day*, in this sense, God is said to have *made* or instituted, not so much by positive appointment as by having providentially afforded the occasion for it. In a still higher sense, the words may be applied to the new dispensation, as a glorious change in the condition of the church, compared with which the restoration from captivity was nothing, except as a preliminary to it and a preparation for it. There is no allusion to the weekly Sabbath, except so far as it was meant to be a type of the rest of the church from the heavy burdens of the old dispensation.

25. *Ah now, Jehovah, save, we beseech thee! Ah now, Jehovah, prosper, we beseech thee!* The circumlocution, *we beseech thee,* is the only form in which the force of the supplicatory particle (נָא) can be expressed, without the risk of its being mistaken for an adverb of time. The whole phrase (הוֹשִׁיעָה נָּא) *save, we pray,* became a standing formula of supplication with reference to great public interests or undertakings, and reappears in the New Testament under the form *Hosanna.* See Matt. xxi. 9, where we find it, in the acclamations of the multitude, combined with other expressions from this same psalm which, as we have seen, they were accustomed to sing at their great festivals. See above, on ver. 22.

26. *Blessed be he that cometh in the name of Jehovah! We bless you from the house of Jehovah.* According to the accents, the construction of the first clause is, *blessed, in the name of Jehovah, be he that cometh.* This agrees exactly with the frequent mention of blessing in the name of Jehovah. See below, Ps. cxxix. 8, and compare Num. vi. 27, Deut. xxi. 5, 2 Sam. vi. 18. *He that cometh* is commonly and not improbably supposed to have meant primarily the people or their representatives, to whom, as they approach the sacred spot, these words were to be uttered. There were other thoughts, however, which the words could hardly fail to suggest, for example that of Israel coming back from exile, that of God coming back to his forsaken people, and at least in the most enlightened minds, that of the great Deliverer, to whose coming all the rest was but preparatory, to whom the name הַבָּא or ὁ ἐρχόμενος was afterwards given as a standing appellation, in allusion either to this passage or to Mal. iii. 1, or to both, and to whom this very sentence was applied by the multitude who witnessed and attended Christ's triumphal entrance into the Holy City. See Matt. xxi. 9.

27. *Mighty (is) Jehovah and hath given light to us. Bind the sacrifice with cords as far as the horns of the altar.* The first word does not express the general idea of divinity, but that of divine power, which is no doubt essential to the writer's purpose. It was the power of Jehovah which had turned the night of Israel to day, and illumined the darkness of their sore distress with the light of his returning favour. The figure is borrowed from the pillar of fire, the token of Jehovah's presence with his people in the wilderness. See Exod. xiii. 21, xiv. 20, Neh. ix. 12. The last clause has been the subject of a good deal of dispute. It is commonly admitted that (חַג) a Hebrew word, which properly denotes a periodical or stated festival, is here put for the victim offered at it, as in Exod. xxiii. 18, *the fat of my sacrifice* is in Hebrew the fat of my festival (חַגִּי), and in 2 Chron. xxx. 22, another word for festival (מוֹעֵד) is used in precisely the same way, being governed by the verb to *eat*, although this singular expression is avoided in the English Bible, by the use of the word " throughout." Those who agree in this, however, are at variance in relation to the act required. As the word translated *cords* is sometimes applied to the thick boughs or branches of a tree (Ezek. xix. 11, xxxi. 3, 10, 14), some understand the sense to be, Bind the sacrifice with branches, sacrificial wreaths. But this practice, and the meaning put upon the Hebrew word, are both denied by others who allege, moreover, the repeated combination of the same verb and noun in the sense of tying, making fast, with cords. See Judges xv. 13, xvi. 11, Ezek. iii. 25. The English Bible makes the clause refer to the fastening of the victim to the altar. To this it is objected that the preposition (עַד) means *as far as*, and implies a verb of motion, expressed or understood. To avoid this difficulty, some of the latest writers understand the words to signify the conducting of the victim bound until it reaches the altar as the place of sacrifice. Hold fast the sacrifice with cords, until it comes to the horns of the altar, poetically put for the altar itself, not only as its prominent or salient points, but as the parts to which the blood, the essential vehicle of expiation, was applied. Thus understood the clause is merely an invitation to fulfil the vow recorded in Ps. cxvi. 14, 17, 18.

28. *My God art thou, and I will thank thee; my God, I will exalt thee.* The Hebrew words for *God* are not the same. The second is that commonly so rendered, while the first is that used in ver. 27, and denoting the divine omnipotence.

29. *Give thanks unto Jehovah, for (He is) good, for unto eternity (is) his mercy.* In these words we are brought back to the point from which we started, and the circle of praise returns into itself.

Psalm 119

THERE is no psalm in the whole collection which has more the appearance of having been exclusively designed for practical and personal improvement, without any reference to national or even to ecclesiastical relations, than the one before us, which is wholly occupied with praises of God's word or written revelation, as the only source of spiritual strength and comfort, and with prayers for grace to make a profitable use of it. The prominence of this one theme is sufficiently apparent from the fact, to which the Masora directs attention, that there is only one verse which does not contain some title or description of the word of God. But notwithstanding this peculiar character, the position of the psalm in the collection, and especially its juxtaposition with respect to Ps. cviii.–cxviii., its kindred tone of mingled gratitude and sadness, and a great variety of minor verbal correspondences, have led some of the best interpreters to look upon it as the conclusion of the whole series or system of psalms, supposed to have been written for the use of the returned Jews, at or near the time of the founding of the second temple. The opinion, held by some of the same writers, that the ideal speaker, throughout this psalm, is Israel, considered as the church or chosen people, will never commend itself as natural or likely to the mass of readers, and is scarcely consistent with such passages as ver. 63, 74, 79, and others, where the speaker expressly distinguishes himself as an individual from the body of the people. The same difficulty, in a less degree, attends the national interpretation of the psalms immediately preceding. Perhaps the best mode of reconciling the two views is by supposing that this psalm was intended as a manual of pious and instructive thoughts, designed for popular improvement, and especially for that of the younger generation after the return from exile, and that the person speaking is the individual believer, not as an isolated personality, but as a member of the general body, with which he identifies himself so far, that many expressions of the psalm are strictly applicable only to the whole as such considered, while others are appropriate only to certain persons or to certain classes in the ancient Israel. To this design of popular instruction, and especially to that of constant repetition and reflection, the psalm is admirably suited by its form and structure. The alphabetical arrangement, of which it is at once the most extended and most perfect specimen, and the aphoristic character, common to all alphabetic psalms, are both adapted to assist the memory, as well as to give point to the immediate impression. It follows, of course, that the psalm was rather meant to be a store-house of materials for pious meditation than a discourse for continuous perusal. At the same time, the fact of its existence in the Psalter is presumptive proof that it was used in public worship, either as a whole, or in one or more of the twenty-two stanzas into which it is divided, corresponding to the letters of the Hebrew alphabet, all the eight verses of each paragraph beginning with the same Hebrew letter.

1. *Happy the perfect of way,* i. e. blameless in their course of life, *those walking in the law of Jehovah.* There seems to be allusion to the precept in Lev. xviii. 4. The common version of the second Hebrew word (*undefiled*) is derived from the Vulgate (*immaculati*), which is itself too confined a version of the Septuagint (ἄμωμοι). The essential idea is that of completeness or perfection. The form and construction of the first word are the same as in Ps. i. 1.

2. *Happy the keepers of his testimonies* (who) *with a whole heart seek him.* *Keepers,* observers, those obeying. *Testimonies,* the divine precepts, which bear witness against sin and in behalf of holiness. *With all the heart,* undivided affection. See above, Ps. cxi. 1, and compare 2 Kings xxiii. 3. *Seek him,* the knowledge of his will and the enjoyment of his favour.

3. (Who) *also do not practise wrong,* (but) *in his ways walk.* This verse both limits and completes the one before it, by shewing that no zeal in seeking God can be acceptable, if coupled with a wicked life. *In his ways,* not in those of his enemies, nor even in their own.

4. *Thou hast commanded thy precepts, to be kept strictly.* *Commanded,* given them in charge, entrusted others with them. The literal meaning of the last clause is, *to keep very* (*much*), i. e. not formally or superficially, but really and thoroughly. Compare the use of (מְאֹד) as a noun in Deut. vi. 5.

5. *O that my ways were settled, to observe thy statutes!* The optative particle at the beginning occurs only here and, with a slight difference of pointing, 2 Kings v. 3. *My ways,* my customary modes of acting, my habits. *Settled,* fixed, confirmed, established, in opposition to capricious vacillation and unsteadiness. *To observe,* to watch for the purpose of obeying. The word translated *statutes,* according to its etymology, means definite and permanent enactments.

6. *Then shall I not be shamed, in my looking unto all thy commandments.* The *then* at the beginning has respect to the time mentioned in the last clause. *Shamed,* put to shame, defeated, frustrated, disappointed in one's

highest hopes. *In my looking* suggests the idea both of time and of causation, *when I look* and *because I look*. The act itself is that of looking towards a mark to be attained, or towards a model, rule, or standard, to be followed and conformed to.

7. *I will thank thee with rectitude of heart, in my learning the judgments of thy righteousness.* It is only my experience of thy righteous judgments that enables me to praise thee as I ought ; a sentiment peculiarly appropriate to the period of some great deliverance, for instance that of the return from exile, when the righteousness of God had been so signally displayed in the destruction of his enemies, and in the fulfilment of his promise to his people. Here again, *in my learning* does not mean merely *after I have learned*, but in the very act and in consequence of learning.

8. *Thy statutes I will keep ; Oh forsake me not utterly.* The fixed resolution to obey is intimately blended with a consciousness of incapacity to do so, unless aided by divine grace. *Utterly*, unto extremity, or still more literally, *until very (much)*. The initial words of this first stanza are all different, except that ver. 1, 2, both begin with (אשְׁרֵי) *happiness* or *happy.*

9. *By what* (means) *can a youth cleanse his path,* (so) *as to keep* (it) *according to thy word?* To *cleanse* is here to keep clean or pure from the stain of sin. Most interpreters regard the last clause as an answer to the question in the first. But this requires the infinitive to be construed as a gerund (*by keeping*), a construction too rare and doubtful to be anywhere assumed without necessity. See above, on Ps. lxxviii. 18, cxi. 6. It is much more simple and agreeable to usage to regard the whole as one interrogation, and the second clause as supplementary to the first. *To keep* may then mean to adhere to it, or rather, in accordance with the figure of the first clause, to preserve it clear or pure as God requires. The answer is suppressed, or rather left to be inferred from the whole tenor of the psalm, which is, that men, and especially the young, whose passions and temptations are strong in proportion to their inexperience, can do nothing of themselves but are dependent on the grace of God. The omission of an an answer, which is thus suggested by the whole psalm, rather strengthens than impairs the impression on the reader.

10. *With my whole heart have I sought thee; let me not err from thy commandments.* While the first clause alleges his sincerity in seeking God, the second and third owns his dependence on him for success and safety.

11. *In my heart have I hid thy saying, that I may not sin against thee.* The first phrase means *within me,* as opposed to a mere outward and corporeal possession of the written word. Not in my house, or in my hand, but in myself, my mind, with special reference, in this case, to the memory. *Hid*, not for concealment, but for preservation. The word *saying,* elsewhere used to signify God's promise, here denotes his precept, as it does in ver. 67 below. *Against thee*, literally *as to, with respect to thee.* See above, on Ps. li. 6 (4).

12. *Blessed (be) thou, Jehovah ! Teach me thy statutes !* The doxology seems designed to break the uniformity of this series of aphorisms, by an occasional expression of strong feeling. At the same time, it furnishes a kind of ground for the petition in the last clause. Since thou art the blessed and eternal God, have pity on my weakness, and instruct me in the knowledge of thy will.

13. *With my lips have I recounted all the judgments of thy mouth.* I have not confined the knowledge of thy precepts to my own mind, but im-

parted it to others. See above, on Ps. xl. 10, 11 (9, 10). *Judgments*, judicial decisions, determinations as to what is right and binding, a description perfectly appropriate to the divine precepts. *Of thy mouth*, which thou hast uttered. There seems to be allusion to the phrase *with my lips* in the first clause.

14. *In the way of thy testimonies I rejoice as over all wealth.* Not merely in the knowledge of God's will, but in the doing of it, in treading the path which he prescribes for us. *Over* may be simply equivalent to *in*, or intended to suggest the additional idea of superiority, *above*, (or *more than*) *all wealth*. *As over*, as I do over all the wealth I have, or as I should do over all wealth if I had it.

15. *In thy precepts will I meditate, and look* (at) *thy paths.* Not only *of* thy precepts or concerning them, but *in* them, while engaged in doing them. *Look* has the same sense as in ver. 6.

16. *In thy statutes I will delight myself; I will not forget thy word.* Delight or enjoy myself, seek my pleasure, find my happiness. Here ends the second stanza, in which all the verses except one (ver. 12) begin not only with the same letter but the same word, the preposition (בְּ) *in*.

17. *Grant to thy servant* (that) *I may live, and I will keep thy word.* *Grant to*, bestow upon, thy servant this favour. See above, on Ps. xiii. 6 (5). There may be an allusion to the way in which the law connects life and obedience. See Lev. xviii. 5, Deut. vi. 24.

18. *Uncover my eyes and I will look—wonders out of thy law!* The last clause is a kind of exclamation after his eyes have been uncovered. This figure is often used to denote inspiration, or a special divine communication. *Out of thy law*, *i. e.* brought out to view, as if from a place of concealment.

19. *A stranger* (am) *I in the earth* ; *hide not from me thy commandments.* A stranger, an exile, one without friends or home, a poetical description of calamity in general, not without allusion to the captivity both in Babylon and Egypt, and to the consequent mention of strangers in the Law as objects of compassion. The prayer in the last clause is, that God will not withhold from him the knowledge of his will.

20. *My soul breaketh with longing for thy judgments at every time.* The Hebrew verb occurs only here, but its meaning is determined by the cognate dialects. The word translated *longing* belongs also to the later Hebrew. Its verbal root occurs below in ver. 40, 174. *Judgments* includes God's precepts mentioned in ver. 19, and his penal inflictions on the wicked mentioned in ver. 21.

21. *Thou hast rebuked the proud, the accursed, those wandering from thy commandments.* Compare Ps. ix. 6 (5). Rebuked, not merely by word but by deed, *i. e.* punished.

22. *Roll from off me reproach and contempt, for thy testimonies I have kept.* The first verse coincides in form with that at the beginning of ver. 18, but is from a different root. There is an obvious allusion to the rolling off of the reproach of Egypt, Joshua v. 9.

23. *Also princes sat and at me talked together, and thy servant muses of thy statutes.* This is one of the expressions in the psalm not literally applicable to the individual believer, and regarded therefore as a proof of its national design and import. The princes are then the chiefs of the surrounding nations. The *also* (גַּם) seems to be inserted merely on account of the alphabetical arrangement which requires the letter gimel.

24. *Also thy testimonies* (are) *my delights, the men of my counsel.* He

calls them his counsellors, in opposition to the malignant counsels of the enemy. *Delights*, enjoyments, happiness, the plural form denoting fulness and completeness. Two of the verses in the stanza ending here begin with (גם) *also*, and two with (גל), though in different senses.

25. *My soul cleaveth unto the dust; quicken thou me according to thy word.* The first clause seems intended to suggest two consistent but distinct ideas, that of deep degradation, as in Ps. xliv. 26 (25), and that of death, as in Ps. xxii. 30 (29). The first would be more obvious in itself, and in connection with the parallel referred to ; but the other seems to be indicated as the prominent idea by the correlative petition in the last clause. *Quicken*, *i. e.* save me alive, or restore me to life, the Hebrew word being a causative of the verb *to live*. See above, on Ps. xxx. 4 (3). *Thy word*, the promise annexed to thy commandment, as in ver. 28 below.

26. *My ways have I recounted, and thou hast answered me ; teach me thy statutes.* The first clause is not to be restricted to a confession of sin, though that may be included, but extended to a statement of his cares, anxieties, and affairs in general. Hence the correlative expression, *thou hast answered me*, the Hebrew verb being specially appropriated to the hearing or answering of prayer, *i. e.* granting what it asks. The last clause expresses a desire to testify his gratitude for God's compassion by obeying his commandments, with the usual acknowledgment that these cannot be executed without divine assistance, or even known without divine instruction.

27. *The way of thy precepts make me understand, and I will muse of thy wonders.* The first clause expresses the same wish, arising from the same consciousness of weakness, as in ver. 26. The verb in the last clause is one of those in the usage of which the ideas of speech and meditation run continually into one another. See above, on Ps. lv. 18 (17), lxix. 13 (12), lxxiv. 4, 7 (3, 6), cv. 2.

28. *My soul weeps from sorrow ; raise me up according to thy word.* The meaning of the first verb seems to be determined by Job xvi. 20, where the same thing is predicated of the eye. The oldest versions make it mean *to slumber* (LXX. ἐνύσταξεν. Vulg. *dormitavit*), which would make the clause remarkably coincident with Luke xxii. 45.

29. *The way of falsehood remove from me, and thy law grant unto me graciously.* The way mentioned in the first clause is that of unfaithfulness to God's covenant, or of apostasy from it. See above, ver. 21. *Remove*, a causative in Hebrew, meaning *make to depart*. The common version of the last verb, as above given, is a correct paraphrase of the Hebrew verb (וחנני) to be gracious, to act graciously, and here still more specifically, to give graciously, to bestow as a free favour. To give the law is still, as in the preceding verses, to make it known by a divine illumination.

30. *The way of truth have I chosen ; thy judgments have I set* (before me). *Truth*, in the sense of faithfulness, fidelity to obligations, the opposite of the *falsehood* mentioned in ver. 29. His own choice coincides with the divine requisitions. *Judgments*, as in ver. 7, 13, above. *I have set, i. e.* before me, as an end to be aimed at, and a rule to be followed. The Hebrew verb occurs above, Ps. xviii. 34 (33), xxi. 6 (5), lxxxix. 20 (19), and the full phrase, Ps. xvi. 8. The Septuagint renders it here, *I have not forgotten*.

31. *I have cleaved unto thy testimonies, O Jehovah, put me not to shame.* The first verb is the same with that in ver. 25. *Unto*, literally *in*, as if implying a complete absorption in the object. See above, on Ps. i. 2. *Testi-*

monies, precepts, as in ver. 2.   *Shame me not*, suffer not my hopes to be disappointed and confounded.   The Hebrew verb is a causative of that in ver. 6.

32. *The way of thy commandments will I run, for thou wilt enlarge my heart.*   The verb to *run* expresses a more zealous obedience than the usual expression *walk*.   To *enlarge* is sometimes to relieve from confinement. See above on Ps. cxviii. 5.   But the whole phrase, *to enlarge the heart*, seems, especially in this connection, to denote a change in the affections leading to more prompt obedience.   Of the eight verses in this stanza five begin with the noun (דֶּרֶךְ) *way* or its plural, and two with the verb (דָּבַק) *to cleave*.

33. *Guide me, Jehovah*, (in) *the way of thy statutes, and I will keep it* (to the) *end*.   The first verb is here used in its primary sense of shewing or pointing out the way, from which is deduced the secondary one of teaching. *Keep it*, observe it, adhere to it, keep in it.   The last word in Hebrew, which occurs above, in different senses and connections, Ps. xix. 12 (11), xl. 16 (15), lxx. 4 (3), is used adverbially here and in ver. 112 below.

34. *Make me understand* (it) *and I will keep thy law, and will observe it with a whole heart.*   The first verb is too vaguely rendered in the English versions (*give me understanding*).   It has here the same sense as in ver. 27, and the object is to be supplied from the next member of the sentence. The form of the last verb is one expressing strong desire and fixed determination.   *With a whole heart*, or *with all* (*my*) *heart*, as in ver. 2.

35. *Make me tread in the path of thy commandments, for in it do I delight.* The first verb is the causative of that used in Ps. vii. 13 (12), xi. 2, xxxvii. 14, xci. 13.   *I delight*, have delighted, not at present merely but in time past.

36. *Incline my heart unto thy testimonies, and not to gain.*   Here again the sense of absolute dependence or divine influence is strongly implied. *Testimonies*, as in ver 31.   *Gain*, profit, lucre, as in Ps. xxx. 10 (9), but here put for overweening love of it, supreme devotion to it.

37. *Turn away my eyes from seeing falsehood; in thy ways quicken me.* The first verb strictly means to *cause to pass* (or *turn*) *away*.   *Falsehood* is not the word so rendered in ver. 29, but the negative term (שָׁוְא) meaning *vanity*, nonentity, and here applied to all objects of religious trust besides God.   These the Psalmist desires not even to see, much less to gaze at with delight and confidence.   See above, Ps. xxxi. 7 (6), xl. 5 (4), lx. 13 (11), lxii. 10 (9).   *Quicken me*, save me or make me alive, as in ver. 25. *In thy ways*, by leading me in the way of thy commandments.

38. *Make good to thy servant thy word which* (thou hast spoken) *to thy fearers.*   The first verb means to cause to stand, to set up, to establish, to confirm, and in this connection to fulfil or verify.   *To thy servant*, not merely *to me*, but *to me who am thy servant*, in a special and emphatic sense, which is applicable either to the chosen people as a whole, or to its individual members.   *Thy word*, as in ver. 25, 28.   *To thy fearers*, literally *to thy fear*, the abstract being put for the concrete term : or it might be rendered *for thy fear*, that thou mayest be feared.   See below, on Ps. cxxx. 4.

39. *Turn away my disgrace which I dread, for thy judgments (are) good.* The first word is the same with that in ver. 37, meaning *make* (or *cause*) *to pass away*.   In this connection it might either mean to remove or to avert ; but the latter agrees better with the next phrase, *which I dread*.   The

original is not the common Hebrew word for *fear*, but one used by Moses in precisely the same sense as here. See Deut. ix. 19, xxviii. 60, and compare Job ix. 28. *Thy judgments are good, i. e.* prompted and controlled by infinite goodness, and should therefore fall upon the wicked, not the righteous.

40. *Behold, I long for thy precepts ; in thy righteousness quicken me.* The first word is equivalent to *see* (or *thou seest*) that it is so, and involves an appeal to the divine omniscience. The first verb is the root of the noun *longing* in ver. 20. To long for God's precepts is to long for the knowledge of them and for grace to obey them. The last clause prays that since God's judgments are good (ver. 39), instead of killing they may make alive. See above, on ver. 17, 25, 37. In the stanza closing with this verse, only one initial word is repeated, namely (הַעֲבֵר) *cause to pass* or *turn away.*

41. *And let thy mercies come (unto) me, O Jehovah, thy salvation, according to thy word.* That the stanzas were not meant to be regarded as distinct and independent compositions, is clear from the copulative (*and*) at the beginning of this verse. *Mercies,* suited to my various necessities. *Come to me,* or *upon me,* or *into me,* which are the ideas commonly expressed by this verb when construed directly with a noun. See above, Ps. xxxv. 8, xxxvi. 12 (11), c. 4. *Salvation* is in apposition with *mercies,* being that in which all other gifts and favours are summed up and comprehended. With the last words compare ver. 38 above.

42. *And* (then) *I will answer my reviler a word ; for I trust in thy word.* The best answer to the calumnies and insults of his enemies is that afforded by his manifest experience of God's favour, and the practical vindication thereby afforded. The addition of *word,* which in our idiom is superfluous, may have some reference to its use in the corresponding clause. As if he had said, Only let thy word be fulfilled, and I shall have a word to say in answer to my enemies.

43. *And take not out of my mouth* (this) *word of truth utterly, for in thy judgments do I hope.* Deprive me not of this conclusive answer to my enemies, by withholding that providential vindication of my character and practical attestation of thy favour towards me, which I confidently look for. The first verb is used in its primary sense (Gen. xxxii. 12), from which comes the usual but secondary one of snatching out of danger, extricating, saving. For the literal meaning of the Hebrew phrase translated *utterly,* see above, on ver. 8. The last phrase in the verse means, *for thy judgments I have waited, i. e.* confidently looked for their appearance.

44. *And I will observe thy law always, unto eternity and perpetuity.* Not merely for a time, or for the purpose of securing this triumph over his enemies, but for ever, to express which idea the three strongest terms afforded by the language are combined. As the keeping of the law, so often mentioned in this psalm, has evident reference to the present life, the strong promise of perpetual obedience, in the verse before us, is considered by some writers as a proof that the ideal speaker is not an individual believer, but the church or chosen people.

45. *And I will walk in a wide place, for thy precepts have I sought.* Free from the pressure and confinement to which he had been previously subject. See above, on Ps. cxviii. 5. *Sought thy precepts, i. e.* sought to know them and to do them. Compare the combination, *keep and seek,* in 1 Chron. xxviii. 8.

46. *And I will speak of thy testimonies before kings, and will not be ashamed.*

Here again some eminent interpreters have found an indication of the national design and meaning of the whole psalm, as the individual believer could not be expected to bear witness to the truth in such a presence. He might, however, do so, as one of the component parts of the whole body. But the words are really expressive only of a readiness to declare the divine testimony against sin, in any presence, even the most august, if it should be necessary. This passage seems to have been present to our Saviour's mind when he uttered the prediction in Mat. x. 18. *Ashamed* has here its strict sense, as denoting a painful feeling of humiliation.

47. *And I will delight myself in thy commandments which I love.* I will not obey them merely from a selfish dread of punishment or painful sense of obligation, but because I love them and derive my highest happiness from doing them. See above, on Ps. xix. 12 (11). The first verb has the same sense as in ver. 16. The past tense of the last verb (*I have loved*) represents his love to God's commandments as no new-born and capricious passion, but a settled habit and affection of his soul.

48. *And I will raise my hands to thy commandments which I love, and I will muse of thy statutes.* The raising of the hands is a symbol of the raising of the heart or the affections to some elevated object. See above, on Ps. xxviii. 2. *Which I love*, or *have loved*, as in ver. 47, the terms of which are studiously repeated with a fine rhetorical effect, which is further heightened by the *and* at the beginning, throwing both verses, as it were, into one sentence. As if he had said, I will derive my happiness from thy commandments, which I love and have loved, and to these commandments, which I love and have loved, I will lift up my hands and heart together. For the meaning of the last clause, see above, on ver. 27. The connective force of the conjunction *and* must not be urged in this verse, as it was needed to supply the initial *vau*, a letter with which scarcely any Hebrew words begin.

49. *Remember* (thy) *word to thy servant, because thou hast made me to hope.* The obvious meaning of the first clause is, *remember the word* (spoken) *to thy servant.* But Hebrew usage makes it probable, that the first and last words of the clause are to be construed together, so as to mean *remember for thy servant*, i. e. for his benefit, as in Ps. xcviii. 3, cvi. 45. *Word* is then absolutely put for promise, as in Ps. lvi. 11 (10), and the meaning of the whole clause is, remember thy promise in compassion to thy servant. The common version of the last clause (*upon which, &c.*) is forbidden by the facts, that the Hebrew verb is never construed elsewhere with the preposition *on*, and that Hebrew usage would require a different combination (אשר עליו) to convey the sense supposed. That the one here used (על אשר) may mean *because*, is clear from Deut. xxix. 24, 2 Sam. iii. 30. The same verb that means *to hope* in ver. 43 is used as a causative, *to make hope*, here and in Ezek. xiii. 6.

50. *This* (is) *my comfort in my suffering, and thy word quickens me.* The reference to continued suffering in the first clause, and to its partial cessation in the second, agrees well with the condition of the chosen people when restored from exile. The terms, however, are so chosen as to be equally appropriate to personal afflictions, restorations, and deliverances. The word for *comfort* occurs elsewhere only in Job vi. 10, where it has precisely the same form. *Thy word* includes thy decree or order and thy promise. *Quickens*, saves alive, or restores to life, according to the prayer in ver. 25, 37, 40. The past tense (*has quickened*) implies that the con-

servative or restorative effect has already been experienced, though not yet perfected.

51. *Proud (ones) deride me greatly ; from thy law I swerve not.* Both verbs are in the past tense, which would seem to indicate that the derision here complained of, although recent, had now ceased or been abated. The clause agrees well with the scorn excited in the heathen neighbours of the restored Jews by what seemed to be their mad attempt to build the temple. The omission of a connective makes the antithesis more pointed. *Swerved*, declined, or turned aside. See above, on Ps. xliv. 19 (18), and compare Ps. xl. 5 (4). The first word in the verse is one commonly applied to presumptuous high-handed sinners. See above, on Ps. xix. 14 (13).

52. *I have remembered thy judgments from eternity, Jehovah, and consoled myself.* His faith and hope under present trials are sustained by recollection of the past. *Thy judgments*, not merely the punishments inflicted on thy enemies, but all the exhibitions of thy righteousness in outward act, including the deliverances of thy people. *From eternity*, or from an indefinite antiquity, which is the primary meaning of the Hebrew word. There is no reason for discarding the reflexive form of the last verb, as some versions do, especially as it suggests the idea, not of a mere passive reception of the comfort, but of an active effort to obtain it.

53. *Rage has seized me from wicked (men) abandoning thy law.* No English word is strong enough to represent the first one in the Hebrew of this verse except rage or fury. See above, on Ps. xi. 6. It here denotes the highest pitch of indignant disapproval. *From, i. e.* arising or proceeding-from, because of. *Forsaking thy law*, not only refusing in practice to obey it, but avowedly abjuring its authority.

54. *Songs for me have been thy statutes in the house of my sojournings.* Instead of abjuring them as presumptuous sinners do, I make them the subject of my thankful and triumphant songs (Isa. xxiv. 16), even while I sojourn as a pilgrim and a stranger in a strange land. *The house of my sojournings, i. e.* the house where I sojourn, is an imitation of the phrase, *land of sojournings*, which occurs so often in the patriarchal history. See Gen. xvii. 8, xxviii. 4, xxxvi. 7, xxxvii. 1. *Pilgrimage* is less exact, because it suggests the idea of locomotion rather than of rest. The statutes of God are thus rejoiced in, not as mere requisitions, but as necessarily including promises.

55. *I remember in the night thy name, Jehovah, and observe thy law.* The night is mentioned as the natural and customary season of reflection and self-recollection, and also as the time when pains of every kind are usually most acute. See above, on Ps. xci. 5. With this clause and the verse preceding compare Job xxxv. 10. *Thy name, i. e.* all that is denoted by thy names, and more especially by the one here mentioned, thy eternal self-existence and thy covenant relation to thy people.

56. *This has been to me, for thy precepts I have kept.* The usual interpretations, *this I had because I kept thy precepts*, and *this I have* (namely) *that I keep thy precepts*, are almost unmeaning. When taken in connection with the one before it, the true sense of the verse appears to be, that what he was thus wont to promise or resolve, he had performed. The substantive verb is to be taken in the sense which it so often has in history. This has happened to me, come to pass, been verified in my experience. In the stanza which here ends, three verses begin with some form of the verb (זָכַר) *to remember*, and two with the pronoun (זֹאת) *this*.

57. *My portion, O Jehovah, I have said, (is) to keep thy words.* This construction is rejected by Hengstenberg and others, as forbidden by the accents and the analogy of Ps. xvi. 5, lxxiii. 26. But as the same words may either express the sense here given or *my portion (is) Jehovah*, we are at liberty to choose the one best suited to the context, even in opposition to the accents, which cannot be regarded as an ultimate authority. In favour of the sense first given is its perfect agreement with the close of the preceding stanza. In reference to the resolution there recorded and described as having been fulfilled, he here adds, thus have I said (declared my purpose), O Lord, to obey thy words.

58. *I have sought thy favour with all* (my) *heart; be gracious unto me according to thy word.* In the first clause, we have a repetition of the singular and striking idiom used in Ps. xlv. 13 (12), and explained by some as meaning strictly to soothe or stroke the face, and by others to soften or subdue it, *i. e.* the hostility or opposition expressed by it. *With all* (my) *heart*, or *with a whole heart*, as in ver. 2, 34, above. *Thy word* or *saying*, *i. e.* thy promise. The original expression is not (דבר), the one so constantly employed in this psalm, but (אמרה), that used in ver. 10, 41, and derived from the verb (אמר) *to say*.

59. *I have thought on my ways, and turned back my feet to thy testimonies.* The first verb here means *thought over*, pondered, as in Ps. lxxvii. 6 (5). *My ways, i.e.* as appears from the last clause, my departures from thy testimonies or commandments. See above, on ver. 2, 14, 31, 36, 46. The common version of the last verb (*turned*), although correct, is not sufficient to convey the full force of the Hebrew word, which is a causative, meaning to bring back or make to return, and implying previous departure, whereas the primitive verb *turn* carries with it no such implication. While this verse is exactly descriptive of the process of personal conviction and conversion, it is also strikingly appropriate to the effects of the captivity on Israel, as a church and nation.

60. *I hastened, and delayed not, to observe thy commandments.* This continues the account of his conversion, begun in the preceding verse. The first clause exemplifies the idiomatic combination of a positive and negative expression of the same idea. The second verb is peculiarly expressive, and seems to be applied, in the most ancient Hebrew books, to a trifling and unreasonable tarrying in great emergencies. See Gen. xix. 16, xliii. 10, Exod. xii. 39. In this respect, as well as in relation to its singular reduplicated form, the Hebrew verb bears some analogy to certain familiar terms in English, which are colloquially used in the same manner.

61. *The bands of wicked men environed me,* (but) *thy law I did not forget.* As descriptive of personal experience, this may be translated in the present (*environ me, forget not*) ; but in order to include a reference to the Babylonish exile, and the preservation of the people from apostasy at that eventful crisis, the preterite forms of the original must be preserved. The figure of the first clause is borrowed from Ps. xviii. 5, 6 (4, 5), but with the substitution of a verbal form used only here, and represented by the word *environed*. The relation of the clauses, to denote which in English *but* has been supplied, is the same as in ver. 51 above.

62. *At midnight I will rise to give thanks unto thee on* (account of) *the judgments of thy righteousness.* The first phrase, which literally means *the half* (or *halving*) *of the night*, is borrowed from the history of the midnight massacre in Egypt, Exod. xi. 4, xii. 29, to which there is also a historical allusion, as a signal instance of divine interposition and miraculous deliverance. A similar allusion may be traced in Job xxxiv. 20. *The judgments of thy righteousness,* thy judgments of righteousness, thy righteous judgments, cannot be altogether different in meaning from the very same words in ver. 7, as supposed by some interpreters, who there explain the phrase to mean God's precepts or his requisitions, here his penal inflictions. The solution of the difficulty lies in this, that the words mean neither of these things specifically, but something which comprehends them both, viz., the actual manifestations of God's righteousness, in word or deed, by precept or by punishment.

63. *A fellow (am) I to all who fear thee, and to the keepers of thy precepts.* Not merely a *companion* or frequenter of their company, but an associate, a congenial spirit, one of the same character. Compare the use of the same Hebrew word in Ps. xlv. 8 (7), where the plural is translated *fellows* in the English Bible. The verse before us is one of those which it seems most difficult to understand of Israel as a whole; for in what sense was the church or chosen people a companion of those fearing God and keeping his commandments, when all the people in the world of that description were embraced within her own communion? The force of this objection is so great that Hengstenberg applies the description to the pious ancestors of the returned Jews, and refers to Mal. iii. 24 (iv. 6). The necessity of such a forced construction goes far to confirm the exegetical hypothesis, already stated as most probably the true one, that the psalm was intended to express the feelings of an individual believer, but that some of its terms are, from parity of circumstances, equally descriptive of what had been experienced by the house of Israel as a church and nation.

64. *Of thy mercy, O Jehovah, full is the earth; thy statutes teach me.* Since thy mercy fills the whole earth, let it reach to me, enabling me to understand thy will and to obey it. The relation of the clauses is not unlike that in ver. 12. The stanza closing with this verse is the first in which the initial words of all the verses are entirely different. See above, on ver. 8, 16, 24, 32, 40, 48, 56.

65. *Good hast thou done to thy servant, O Jehovah, according to thy word* The common version of the first clause (*thou hast dealt well with thy servant*) is equally correct, and has the advantage of retaining the preposition *with,* which may be used in English after *deal,* but not after *do.* The sense expressed by both translations is the same, to wit, thou hast treated him graciously or kindly. *According to thy word, i. e.* the promise annexed to thy commandments, as in ver. 25, 28 (compare ver. 41, 58). This verse is equally appropriate as a personal thanksgiving, and an acknowledgment of national deliverances, such as that from Babylon.

66. *Goodness of judgment and knowledge teach me, for in thy commandments I believe.* The first word in Hebrew is not (טוֹב) the adjective *good,* as in ver. 65, but (טוּב) the corresponding abstract noun meaning *goodness,* as in Ps. xxv. 7, xxvii. 13, xxxi. 20 (19). That it here denotes not moral but intellectual excellence, is determined by the addition of (מַעַם) a word originally meaning *taste,* and then transferred to reason, judgment, understanding. See above, on Ps. xxxiv. 1. *Teach me good judgment, i. e.* impart it by divine instruction. Judgment and knowledge may be here distinguished as in common parlance, the one denoting the faculty employed, the other the result of its exertion. The *knowledge* meant is that continually prayed for in this psalm, to wit, the knowledge of God's will. The connection of the clauses seems to be, that he has faith and would fain have

knowledge ; he takes God's precepts upon trust, but then prays that he may understand them. To believe in God's commandments is to believe that they are his, and therefore right and binding.

67. *Before I suffered I* (*was*) *going astray, and now thy saying I observe.* Going astray, wandering, erring, *i. e.* habitually, ever straying. *And now* (on the contrary), where our idiom would require a *but*. The *saying* of God is what he says, including both commands and promises, which indeed are represented in the Old Testament, and especially in this psalm, as inseparable. *Observe*, attend to, keep in view, according to the nature of the object, trusting the promise, obeying the command. The last verb strictly means *I have observed*, implying that the salutary fruit of the affliction was already realised and still continued. The sentiment of this verse has been echoed, and its very words repeated, by the godly sufferers of every age, a strong proof that it was meant to be so used. At the same time it furnishes an exquisite description of the effect produced upon the Jews, as a body, by the Babylonish exile, and especially the end which it for ever put to their continual lapses into idolatry, by which their early history was characterised, and with respect to which the whole race might well have said, Before I suffered I was (ever) straying.

68. *Good* (*art*) *thou and doing good—teach me thy statutes!* Good, both essentially and actively or practically ; good in thyself and good to others. The participle, as in ver. 67, denotes habitual, constant action, (*ever*) *doing good.* It is characteristic of this psalm, that the petition founded on the goodness of God's nature, on his beneficence, and even on his infinite perfection, is still, *teach me thy statutes !* Make me acquainted with thy will, and shew me how to do it ! See above, on ver. 12, 64.

69. *Proud* (*men*) *have forged a lie against me ; I, with all* (*my*) *heart, will keep thy precepts.* Proud, presumptuous, overbearing sinners, as in ver. 51. *Forged* expresses the essential meaning of the Hebrew word, but not its figurative form, which seems to be that of sewing, analogous to that of weaving, as applied to the same thing, both in Hebrew and in other languages. We may also compare our figurative phrase, *to patch up*, which, however, is not so much suggestive of artifice or skill as of the want of it. The connection of the clauses is, that all the craft and malice of his enemies should only lead him to obey God with a more undivided heart than ever. See above, on ver. 58. With the same surprising skill and wisdom as in many other cases which have been already mentioned, this verse is so framed as to be equally well suited to such national and public evils as those described in the fourth chapter of Ezra, and to the sufferings of the pious individual, arising from the pride and spite of wicked enemies.

70. *Fat as grease* (*is*) *their heart. I* (*in*) *thy law delight.* The connection of the clauses lies in the figurative use of fat to denote insensibility. See above, on Ps. xvii. 10, lxxiii. 7. While they are utterly insensible to spiritual pleasures, and especially to those springing from the knowledge of thy law, I find therein my highest happiness. The verb in the last clause is a cognate form to that in ver. 16, 47, and identical with that in Isa. xi. 8, where it means to play, sport, or enjoy one's self.

71. (It is) *good for me that I was made to suffer, to the end that I might learn thy statutes.* The prayer so frequently repeated, *teach me thy statutes*, is now proved to be sincere by a hearty acquiescence in the painful discipline by which it had been partially fulfilled already. *Good for me*, and therefore good on God's part. The idea of compulsory subjection to this salutary process is suggested by the passive causative form of the verb

used in ver. 67. *To the end* or *intent*, a phrase corresponding, both in form and meaning, to the Hebrew.

72. *Good for me is the law of thy mouth, (more) than thousands of gold and silver.* *For me*, for my use as well as in my estimation. *The law of thy mouth*, that which thou hast uttered. See above, on ver. 13. *Than*, literally *from*, away from, as distinguished from, as compared with, which is just the meaning of the English *than*. The combination *good than*, or good *from*, is the nearest approach of which the Hebrew idiom admits, to *better than*. The indefinite term *thousands* may refer to weight or number, to coin or bullion; to coins in general, or to shekels or talents in particular. While this verse primarily expresses the changed estimate which Israel learned in exile to put upon the law, it is equally expressive of the feeling cherished by all true believers, in their best estate, as to the value of the word of God. Here ends the ninth stanza, of which five verses begin with the word (טוֹב) *good.*

73. *Thy hands made me and fashioned me; make me understand and let me learn thy commandments.* As I owe my existence to thy power, so too I rely upon thy grace for spiritual illumination. Compere Deut. xxxii. 6. *Fashioned*, literally fixed, established, *i. e.* framed my constitution as it is.

74. *Thy fearers shall see me and rejoice; for in thy word have I hoped.* Compare Ps. v. 12 (11), xxxiv. 3 (2). They shall rejoice in my case, as a new proof that they who trust in God cannot be disappointed. The literal meaning of the last clause is, because for thy word I have waited, *i. e.* patiently and trustfully awaited its fulfilment.

75. *I know, Jehovah, that righteouness are thy judgments, and* (in) *faithfulness thou hast afflicted me* (or *made me suffer*). *Thy judgments*, thy sovereign decisions and their execution, *are righteousness* itself, *i. e.* perfectly righteous. So in the next clause, for *in faithfulnes* we may read *as faithfulness itself*, as one absolutely faithful to his promise and engagements. This confession would be untrue, if those who made it were not conscious of their guilt and ill-desert. Compare Deut. xxxii. 4.

76. *Oh that thy mercy might be for my comfort, according to thy saying to thy servant.* The optative expression, *oh that*, is here used to represent the Hebrew particle of entreaty (נָא), correctly paraphrased in the English Bible, *I pray thee.* *For my comfort*, literally *to comfort* (or *console*) *me.* *Thy saying*, that which thou hast said or promised. *To thy servant*, to me as thy servant, and as such in covenant with thee. This description is equally appropriate to the body and its members.

77. *Let thy compassions come unto me* (or *upon me*), *and I shall live, for thy law (is) my delights.* The construction in the first clause is like that in ver. 41. *And I shall live*, or as we might express it, *that I may live.* See above, on ver. 17. He pleads what he has received already as a ground for asking more. The plural *(delights)* expresses fulness and completeness, or perhaps implies that this joy is equal or superior to all others, or includes them all. The Hebrew noun is derived from the verb in ver. 16, 47, 70.

78. *Shamed be the proud, for falsely have they wronged me; I will muse of thy precepts.* *Falsely*, literally *falsehood*, *i. e.* in or by it. *Wronged*, literally bent, perverted. With the last clause compare ver. 27, 48.

79. *Let them return to me that fear thee and know thy testimonies.* Let thy servants who have looked upon me as abandoned by thee now restore to me their confidence. The various reading in the last clause (יֵדְעוּ and

יֵדְעוּ) does not affect the meaning of the sentence, except that the reading in the text may be included in the wish, *let them know thy testimonies, i. e.* let them learn from my experience to understand thy precepts better.

80. *Let my heart be perfect in thy statutes, to the end that I may not be ashamed.* *In thy statutes,* in the knowledge and the practice of them, or as it is expressed in Ps. xix. 12 (11), *in keeping them.* *Shamed,* put to shame by the frustration of my highest hopes. See above, on ver. 6. Two of the verses in this stanza begin with the same Hebrew word (יְהִי).

81. *For thy salvation faints my soul ; for thy word do I wait.* Both verbs are in the preterite, implying that it is so and has been so. *Faints,* is spent or wasted. This strong expression for intense desire is borrowed from Ps. lxxxiv. 3 (2). With the last clause compare ver. 74.

82. *My eyes fail for thy saying, so that I say, when wilt thou comfort me ?* The first verb in Hebrew is the same with the first in the preceding verse. *Thy saying,* the fulfilment of thy promise. The Hebrew noun is derived from the following verb, *to say,* so as to say, so that I say. It might also be translated, but with less exactness, *while I say.*

83. *For I have been like a bottle in the smoke ; thy statutes I have not forgotten.* The bottle meant is one of skin, still common in the east. The comparison is not entirely clear. Some suppose that the blackening and shrivelling effect of the smoke upon the skin is simply used as a figure for distress. Others understand the words as conveying the additional idea, that as wine-skins are not meant to be involved in smoke, so distress is not the normal or natural condition of God's people. Others, assuming that the skins were intentionally smoked by way of seasoning, suppose the principal idea to be that of painful but salutary discipline. There can be no doubt that the clause relates, in some way, to the afflictions, either of the chosen people, or of individual believers, or of both. The meaning of the last clause is that, notwithstanding these afflictions, the sufferer has not forgotten God's commandments.

84. *How many are the days of thy servant ? When wilt thou execute upon my persecutors judgment ?* The shortness of life is indirectly urged as an argument for speedy action. See above, on Ps. xxxix. 5, 14 (4, 13), lxxviii. 39, lxxxix. 48, 49 (47, 48). *Execute judgment,* or *do justice,* as in Ps. ix. 5 (4).

85. *Proud (men) dig for me pits, which (are) not according to thy law.* The presumptuous sinners (ver. 51, 69, 78) who are his enemies use the most treacherous means for his destruction, without regard to the divine command or prohibition. See above, on Ps. vii. 16 (15), lvii. 7 (6).

86. *All thy commandments (are) faithfulness ; falsely do they persecute me ; help thou me.* The promises annexed to God's commandments are infallible. *Falsely,* as in ver. 78, *falsehood, i. e.* in falsehood, without right or reason, or *with* (by means of) *falsehood,* as their instrument. The verb agrees with the remoter antecedent (*persecutors*) in ver. 84. '

87. *They almost consumed me in the land, and I did not forsake thy precepts.* The verb *consumed* or *destroyed* (כִּלּוּ) and the phrase *in the land* both occur in reference to the Canaanites, 2 Chron. viii. 8. The translation *in the earth* (ver. 19) is admissible, but less significant and less in keeping with the national import of the psalm. The second clause, as usual in such cases, declares that notwithstanding his afflictions, he still sought to know and do the will of God.

88. *According to thy mercy quicken me, and I will keep the testimony of thy mouth.* Restore me to life, or save me alive, as in ver. 25, 37, 40. *Of thy mouth,* as in ver. 11, 72. This closes the eleventh stanza and the first half of the psalm. Two of these eight verses begin with different forms of the verb (כלה) *to fail* or *faint,* and three (including ver. 84) with the particle (כ) *as* or *like.*

89. *To eternity, Jehovah, thy word is settled in heaven.* The translation, *eternal* (art thou), *Lord,* is contrary to usage, which requires the pronoun, in that case, to be expressed. *Settled,* literally made to stand, *i. e.* unalterably fixed. *In heaven,* beyond the reach of all disturbing causes. See above, Ps. lxxxix. 3 (2).

90. *To generation and generation (is) thy faithfulness ; thou hast fixed the earth and it stands.* Resolved into our idiom, the meaning of this verse is, that the truth of God's promises, or his fidelity to his engagements, is secured by the same divine perfection, which brought the world at first into existence, and has ever since preserved it. The verb translated *fixed* is not the one employed in ver. 89, but that used in Ps. vii. 10 (9), ix. 8 (7), xl. 3 (2), xlviii. 9 (8), lxviii. 10 (9), xc. 17, xcix. 4, cvii. 36. The sense *prepared* is rare and doubtful, and too feeble for this context.

91. *For thy judgments they stand to-day, for all are thy servants.* The subject of the first verb, though obscure, is probably the heavens and the earth, mentioned in the two preceding verses. These stand, continue to exist, for the execution of God's judgments, with reference, perhaps, to the destruction wrought by fire from heaven, by the opening of the earth, &c. *All,* literally *the whole,* τὸ πᾶν, the universe ; but the construction of this with the plural *servants* would be harsh in English. The same expression is applied in Ps. xiv. 3 to all mankind, but here to the material universe. *Thy servants,* the instruments employed to execute thy will.

92. *Unless thy law were my delights, then should I perish in my affliction.* The verse admits also of the construction in the English Bible, which refers it to a remoter past, and represents the danger as escaped, whereas the first construction implies a continued state of suffering. The law of God, as usual in this psalm, is here viewed, not as a body of mere requisitions, but as a covenant, a law accompanied by promises.

93. *To eternity I will not forget thy precepts, for in them hast thou quickened me.* *In them,* or *by them,* which is really included in the other, meaning in the practice of them and by means of them. *Quickened,* as in ver. 17, 25, 37, 40, 50.

94. *Thine am I—save me—for thy precepts I have sought.* The original form of the first clause is, *to thee (am) I.* *Sought,* as in ver. 2, 10, 45.

95. *For me have wicked (men) waited, to destroy me ; thy testimonies will I understand.* With the first clause compare Ps. lvi. 7 (6). *Consider,* though correct, is an inadequate translation of the last verb, which denotes a fixed and intelligent attention. The only effect of his enemies' malignant plots is a still more serious contemplation of God's precepts.

96. *To all perfection I have seen an end,* (but) *wide is thy command exceedingly.* By *end* we are not to understand the end of its existence, but the limit or boundary of its extent. To all other perfection (so called) I can see an end, but that required and embodied in thy law is boundless. All the verses of this stanza except one (ver. 92) begin with the preposition (ל) *to* or *for,* as all those of the second do with (כ) *in.*

97. *How I love thy law! All the day it is my meditation, i. e.* the subject of my solitary musing. This continual representation of God's law, not as a mere rule, but as an object of affection and a subject of perpetual reflection, is characteristic of the Psalms, and appears at the very threshold of the whole collection. See above, on Ps. i. 2.

98. (More) *than my enemies do thy commandments make me wise ; for to eternity it is mine* (or *to me*). This is the construction of the first clause preferred by the latest interpreters, although it requires a singular verb to be construed with a plural noun. But as the same irregularity exists in the construction of the pronoun in the second clause, however the first may be explained, it is best to explain both anomalies alike, *i. e.* partly by the relative position of the words, and partly by the aggregate sense in which *commandments* is here used as equivalent to *law*, and which, agreeably to general usage, may sufficiently account for its construction with a verb and pronoun in the singular. As analogous cases have been cited, 2 Sam. xxii. 23—"(as for) his statutes, I depart not from it "—and 2 Kings xvii. 22 —" the sins of Jeroboam which he did, they departed not from it." As the sins of Jeroboam were concentrated in one, so the statutes of Jehovah might be viewed as one great comprehensive precept. The meaning of the last clause is not merely, *it is ever with me*, but *it is for ever to me, i. e.* mine, my inalienable, indefeasible possession. See above, ver. 94.

99. (More) *than all my teachers I act wisely, for thy testimonies (are) a meditation to me.* My teachers, my superiors in natural and worldly wisdom. As the Hebrew verb has always elsewhere an active meaning, it is better to retain it here, the rather as it indicates more clearly that the wisdom which he boasts was practical, experimental. See above, on Ps. ii. 10, xiv. 2, xxxii. 8 (7), xli. 2 (1) lxiv. 10 (9), ci. 2. The essential meaning of the last clause is the same with that of ver. 97, but the use of the expression (לִי) suggests the same idea of possession that is expressed in ver. 98. Thy testimonies are mine, belong to me, as an object of incessant contemplation.

100. (More) *than old men I understand, because thy precepts I have kept.* The first verb is the same, and has the same sense as in ver. 95. The ambiguous Hebrew word (זְקֵנִים) cannot be expressed by any one in modern English, as it may mean either *old men* in the proper sense, whose greater experience entitled them to be considered wiser than their juniors; or the *ancients*, those of former generations, who are popularly looked upon as wiser than their children and successors. One of these senses suits the personal, the other the national design and application of the psalm. In either case, there is really no boast of superior intelligence, as a distinguishing endowment, but merely an assertion, in a striking form, that the highest wisdom is to do the will of God. See above, on Ps. cxi. 10.

101. *From every evil path I refrain my feet, to the intent that I may keep thy word.* Of the two ideas conveyed by *word*, that of command is here predominant, but not exclusive of the other. To keep God's word is primarily to obey his precept, but secondarily to verify his promise. This verse teaches clearly that the keeping of God's word is something incompatible with treading any evil path.

102. *From thy judgments I do not depart, because thou guidest me.* We have here another word of comprehensive meaning, in which sometimes one phrase of the essential idea is presented prominently, sometimes another. The divine *judgments*, in this psalm, are always the external exhibitions of the divine righteousness, in word or deed, by precept or by punishment.

Here, of course, the former are especially intended. The figure of a way, though not expressed, is still indicated by the verbs *depart* and *guide*. As to the latter, see above, on ver. 33. From this verse it is doubly clear that he claims nothing as belonging to himself, or as accomplished in his own strength, but ascribes all to the power and grace of God. The preterite forms, in this and the preceding verse, merely make the past more prominent than the future, as an accessory idea to the present.

103. *How sweet to my palate are thy sayings, sweeter than honey to my mouth !* As the Hebrew verb occurs only here, it is better to follow the rabbinical tradition and the ancient versions, which make the idea to be that of sweetness, than the uncertain etymological deductions of the lexicons, which make it to be that of *smoothness*. The passive form may possibly denote that the Psalmist's relish for God's word was not a native but acquired taste. Some interpreters unreasonably give to *word* the sense of law, excluding that of promise altogether, whereas both must unavoidably have been suggested to a Hebrew reader. The original word means neither more nor less than that which God has said. The figures of this verse are borrowed from Ps. xix. 11 (10).

104. *From thy precepts I get understanding; therefore I hate every path of falsehood.* The common version of the first verb comes as near to the exact sense of the original as any other English word or phrase. The Hebrew verb is the same that occurs above, ver. 95, 100. As he knows no wisdom independent of the truth, he hates falsehood as the height of folly, and regulates his life accordingly. All the verses of this stanza begin either with the exclamation (מָה) *how*, or with the preposition (מִן) *from, than*.

105. *A lantern for my foot is thy word, and a light for my path.* To the figure of a path, so frequently presented in this psalm already, is now added that of a light, to make it plain amidst surrounding darkness. The parallelism is completed by adding the generic term, *light*, to the specific one, *lamp* or *lantern*. *For my foot, i. e.* to guide it. *For my path, i. e.* to shew it.

106. *I have sworn, and will perform* (my oath), *to observe the judgments of thy righteousness.* The second verb occurs above, ver. 28, in its primary sense of raising up, or causing to stand upright. In the later books, particularly that of Esther, it occurs very often in the sense of ratifying or confirming, and might here be rendered, *l confirm* (my oath already made). In either case, it merely strengthens the expression which precedes it. *Observe*, keep, or obey, as in ver. 4, 5, 8, &c. *Thy righteous judgments*, as in ver. 7, 62. Considered as the language of the whole church or nation, this verse may have reference to the covenant entered into at mount Sinai and renewed in the plains of Moab, while as a personal profession, it has its counterpart in the experience of every true believer.

107. *I am afflicted even to extremity; Jehovah, quicken me according to thy word.* That the first clause does not relate merely to past sufferings (*I was afflicted*), seems to follow from the prayer in the last clause, which may, however, be understood as a petition for deliverance from the deadening effects of a calamity already past, such as the Babylonish exile, the enfeebling influence of which, notwithstanding incidental benefits, continued to be felt for ages. The first verb in Hebrew, with the idea of suffering, always suggests that of humiliation. *Even to extremity*, the same words that occur above, in ver. 8, 43, 51. The meaning of the last clause is, be-

stow upon me that life which is promised in the Law to those who keep it.
See Lev. xviii. 5, Deut. vi. 24.

108. *The free-will offerings of my mouth accept, I pray thee, O Jehovah,
and thy judgments teach me,* For the meaning of the first Hebrew word see
above, on Ps. cx. 8. It is here a figure for prayers and praises, as appears
from the addition of *my mouth.* The verb *accept* is one continually used in
the Law, with respect to sacrificial offerings. See above, on Ps. li. 18 (16),
and compare Ps. l. 14. The recurrence of the prayer, *thy judgments teach
me,* shews that the writer's object was to make everything tend to this conclusion, and that however a sentence may begin, it cannot be complete
without a repetition of this favourite idea.

109. *My soul is in my hand always, and* (yet) *thy law I have not forgotten.*
The sense of the strong figure in the first clause is clear from Judges
xii. 13, 1 Sam. xix. 5, xxviii. 21, where he who risks or jeopards his own
life, in war or otherwise, is said to put his soul into his hand, as if to have
it ready to give up or throw away at any moment. The same expression
reappears in Job xiii. 14. The meaning of the whole verse is, that even
amidst the deadly perils which environed him, he still remembered the
divine law, as an object of supreme affection.

110. *Wicked* (men) *have laid a snare for me, and* (yet) *from thy precepts
I have not strayed. Laid for me,* literally *given to me,* as we might speak
of a snare as *presented* to a person, *i. e.* set before him. The devices and
temptations of the wicked were as powerless as all the other causes previously mentioned, in leading him away from the path of truth and safety.

111. *I inherit thy testimonies to eternity, for the joy of my heart are they.*
The first verb means to take as a possession or inheritance, and is here
used in allusion to those places of the Pentateuch where it is applied to the
possession of the promised land. See for example Exod. xxiii. 30.

112. *I incline my heart to do thy statutes to eternity,* (even to) *the end.*
The preterite form of the first verb represents the effort as already made,
but still continued. For the meaning of the last word, see above, on
ver. 33. This stanza, like the eighth, has a different initial word in every
verse.

113. *Waverers I hate, and thy law I love.* The first word in Hebrew
occurs only here. According to the most probable etymology, it means
men of divided and unstable minds. See above, on Ps. xii. 3 (2), and
compare James i. 8.

114. *My hiding-place and my shield* (art) *thou—for thy word I wait, i.e.*
for the fulfilment of thy promise. See above, on ver. 81. The first word
in the verse means properly a secret or a secret place. See above, on Ps.
xxvii. 5, xxxii. 7, lxi. 5 (4), xci. 1. The shield is a favourite figure for
protection. See above, on Ps. iii. 4 (3), vii. 11 (10), xviii. 3, 31, (2, 30).

115. *Depart from me, evil doers, and I will keep the commandments of God.*
The first clause is borrowed from Ps. vi. 9 (8). The meaning in both cases
seems to be, that he has no fear of their enmity. The reason given in this
case is, because he is resolved to do the will of God, and is therefore sure
of his protection.

116. *Uphold me according to thy promise, and let me live, and let me not
be ashamed of my hope.* Promise, literally saying, that which thou hast
said, as in ver. 82. *Let me live* might also be translated *and I shall live,*
or paraphrased *that I may live.* See above, on ver. 17. *Of my hope,*
literally *from my hope,* which some understand in a privative sense *away*

from, deprived of, without my hope, *i. e.* without having it fulfilled. *Ashamed of my hope* 'does not convey the sense so fully as *shamed in my hope*, frustrated, disappointed, in my expectations.

117. *Sustain me and I shall be saved, and I will look to thy statutes always.* The first verb is nearly synonymous with that at the beginning of ver. 116, and the same that occurs above, Ps. xx. 3 (2), xli. 4 (3), xciv. 18, civ. 15. *I shall be saved*, or *let me be saved*, or *that I may be saved*, precisely as in the preceding verse. The strict future sense is here to be preferred, as the verb is not both preceded and followed by a prayer, as in the other case. *Look to*, have respect to, regard, as the rule of my conduct. The construction of the verb and proposition is the same as in Exod. v. 9.

118. *Thou despisest all (those) straying from thy statutes, for a lie (is) their deceit.* They are objects not only of disapprobation but of scorn, because in attempting to deceive others they deceive themselves. Their deception of others is a lie to themselves.

119. *(As) dross hast thou made to cease all the wicked of the earth ; therefore I love thy testimonies.* The purifying tendency of God's judgments is itself a reason for delighting in them. The verb in the first clause, which occurs in its primary sense in Ps. viii. 3 (2), is applied to the purging out of leaven at the passover (Exod. xii. 15), and to the extirpation of wild beasts (Lev. xxvi. 6).

120. *My flesh shudders from dread of thee, and of thy judgments I am afraid.* The first verb in Hebrew occurs only here, but is universally admitted to denote some bodily effect of fear, such as trembling, shuddering, or the instinctive creeping of the flesh. *Afraid of*, in the last clause, does not fully represent the Hebrew phrase, which denotes not mere apprehension of something still future or absent, but terror in view of something actually present. *Judgments* has its usual wide sense, but with special reference, in this case, to God's penal visitations. Here ends the fifteenth stanza, in which, as in the one before it, every verse has a distinct initial word.

121. *I do justice and righteousness ; leave me not to my oppressors.* The first verb is in the past tense, I have done and I still do. *Do justice*, not in the restricted or forensic sense of redressing wrong judicially, but in the wide sense of executing justice or reducing it to practice.

122. *Be surety for thy servant for good ; let not the proud oppress me.* The sense and construction of the first verb are precisely the same as in Gen. xliii. 9, xliv. 32. Compare Job xvii. 3, and see my note on Isa. xxxviii. 14. It means not merely take me under thy protection, but become answerable for me, stand between me and those who, under any pretext, even that of legal right, may seek to oppress me. *For good, i. e.* for my good, for my safety or deliverance. Compare Deut. vi. 24, x. 13, xxx. 9. This is noted in the masora as the only verse in which the word of God, or some equivalent expression, is not found.

123. *My eyes fail for thy salvation, and for the word of thy righteousness.* With the first clause compare ver. 82. The word of thy righteousness, thy word of righteousness, thy righteous word, the promise of a righteous God who cannot lie.

124. *Deal with thy servant according to thy mercy, and thy statutes teach me.* The first words strictly mean *do with thy servant*, which may be an ellipsis for *do good to him*, or deal kindly with him, as in ver. 65. See above, on Ps. cix. 21.

125. *Thy servant (am) I ; make me understand and let me know thy testi-*

monies. That *thy servant* is not a mere periphrasis for *I* or *me* in ver. 122
and elsewhere, appears from the first clause of the verse before us, where it
constitutes the predicate of the proposition. In the second clause, we have
the same choice of constructions as in ver. 116, 117. *Let me know*, or
(*then*) *I shall know*, or *that I may know*, all implying one another, and
amounting to the same thing.

126. (It is) *time for Jehovah to do—they break thy law.* The absolute
use of *do*, without an object, or leaving it to be suggested by the context, is a
peculiar Hebrew idiom. See above, on Ps. 22 (21). We may here supply
justice from ver. 121 (compare ver. 84); or more indefinitely, whatever
should be done ; or more indefinitely still, *it is time to do* (something), *i. e.*
to act, which is substantially the meaning of the common version (*time to
work*). Retaining the order of the Hebrew words, the sense would seem to
be, *it is time to do* (something) *for Jehovah, i. e.* for his people to do it.
But the direct address to God in the last clause, and the whole tenor of the
context, make it more probable that God himself is here entreated to do
something for the vindication of his broken law. The verb in the last clause
is to be construed indefinitely ; *they, i. e.* men in general, or the wicked in
particular. With this clause compare Isa. xxiv. 5.

127. *Therefore I love thy commandments* (*more*) *than gold and* (*more*)
than fine gold. The first word refers not to the immediately preceding verse
but to the whole previous description of the excellence of God's commandments. The comparison in the last clause, like that in ver. 103, is borrowed from Ps. xix. 11 (10).

128. *Therefore all* (thy) *precepts* (as to) *all* (things) *I think right ; every
way of falsehood do I hate.* The *therefore* is co-ordinate with that in
the preceding verse, and to be explained in the same manner. Both
were probably occasioned by the alphabetical arrangement here requiring
an initial *ayin.* *Precepts* of course mean those of God, as *word* means
his word in ver. 49. The construction here is very foreign from our
idiom, and by no means easily translated into it. The literal meaning
of the words is, *all precepts of all*, which some understand to mean *of all
kinds*, as in ver. 14 and Ps. cxviii. 10. But others deny that *all* has
this sense, even in the places cited, and explain it here to mean *concerning
all*, on all subjects. The clause is then condemnatory of all partial distinctions between God's commandments, which may be the *way of falsehood*
specially intended in the last clause. Compare Mat. v. 17–19. The verb
in the first clause always elsewhere means to make straight, to go straight,
or to direct aright ; but the best interpreters agree in making it here mean,
to think right or approve. It is worthy of remark, that as to all these points,
the true sense of this difficult clause seems to be given in the English Bible.
With the last clause compare ver. 104. In the sixteenth stanza, which here
closes, two of the verses begin with (עַל־כֵּן) *therefore*, and two with different
forms of the verb (עָשָׂה) *to do.*

129. *Wonderful* (are) *thy testimonies ; therefore my soul keepeth them.*
The first word in Hebrew is a plural form of that in Ps. lxxvii. 12, 15
(11, 14), lxxviii. 12, lxxxviii. 11 (10), and properly means *wonders, i. e.*
miracles or prodigies of moral excellence. *My soul*, not merely I, but I
with all my heart or soul.

130. *The opening of thy words enlightens, making the simple understand.*
The common version of the first word (*entrance*) is inaccurate, and the one

here given, though exact, is ambiguous. The clause does not refer to the mechanical opening of the book by the reader, but to the spiritual opening of its true sense, by divine illumination, to the mind which naturally cannot discern it. For the Scriptural usage of the word translated *simple*, see above, on Ps. xix. 8 (7), cxvi. 6.

131. *My mouth I stretch and pant, because for thy commandments I long.* The first verb usually means to *gape* or *yawn*, but these verbs are intransitive in English, and cannot be construed with the noun directly. For the meaning of the next verb, see above, on Ps. lvi. 2, 3 (1, 2), lvii. 4 (3). Both are figurative expressions of the idea conveyed directly by the third verb, which occurs nowhere else, but differs only in a single letter from the verb of the same meaning used in ver. 40, 174, which also is peculiar to this psalm.

132. *Turn to me, and be gracious to me, as* (is) *due to the lovers of thy name.* The first verb does not mean to *return* or come back, but to turn round to or towards an object from which the looks have been averted. See above, on Ps. cii. 18 (17). *Be gracious or merciful*, shew favour to or favour me. *As is due to*, or *according to the right of*, the lovers, &c. The Hebrew word (מִשְׁפָּט) has here the meaning of the Latin *jus*, as in Ps. lxxxi. 5 (4). For the meaning of *the lovers of thy name*, see above, on Ps. v. 12 (11).

133. *My steps establish by thy word, and let not any iniquity rule over me.* Establish, *i. e.* make firm, cause me to walk safely. See above, on Ps. xl. 3 (2). *By thy word* or *saying*, what thou hast said, *i. e.* by the fulfilment of thy promise. The last clause might seem to be a prayer against the power of his own corruption ; but the frequent use of the Hebrew noun to denote the mutual injustice of men, together with the language of the next verse, seems to shew that this too is a prayer against oppression. The verb in this clause is applied by Nehemiah (v. 15), to the oppression suffered by the restored Jews. The Arabic verb of the same form is the root of the royal title *Sultan.*

134. *Redeem me from the oppression of man, and I will keep thy precepts.* These two verses are peculiarly appropriate to the trials and temptations of the Jews at the time of the Restoration. The form of the last verb denotes strong desire and determination.

135. *Let thy face shine upon thy servant, and teach me thy statutes.* The prayer of the first clause is the same as that which forms the burden of Ps. lxxx. (4, 8, 20). *Thy servant, i. e.* me who am thy servant ; hence the first person is immediately resumed.

136. *Streams of water run down my eyes, for* (that) *they do not keep thy law.* In the Hebrew of the first clause, *eye* is the subject, not the object, of the verb. See the same or similar idiomatic constructions, Jer. ix. 17, xiii. 17, Lam. i. 16, iii. 48, Ezek. vii. 17. The preposition in the last clause is to be construed with the relative understood, in the sense of *for that*, forasmuch as, because. The complete phrase occurs above, ver. 49. *They do not, i. e.* men indefinitely, others. Here ends the seventeenth stanza, all the verses of which begin with different Hebrew words.

137. *Righteous* (art) *thou, O Jehovah, and just thy judgments.* The English and the ancient versions make the second adjective agree with *judgments*, although different in number. This might be justified by making (יָשָׁר) *just* a neuter adjective or substantive, as in Ps. cxi. 8. It is much

more simple and agreeable to usage to apply the epithet to God himself, as in Deut. xxxii. 4, and explain *thy judgments* as a kind of adverbial or qualifying phrase, very common in Hebrew, but in our idiom requiring the insertion of a preposition, *upright (in* or *as to) thy judgments.*

138. *Thou hast commanded righteousness thy testimonies, and faithfulness —exceedingly.* This is another elliptical construction, wholly foreign from our idiom. Some resolve it by supplying *to* or *to be :* thou hast commanded thy testimonies to (or to be) righteousness, *i. e.* hast made them righteous. It is simpler, however, and more like the syntax of the verse preceding, to supply *in* or *with :* thou hast commanded (in) righteousness thy testimonies, &c. The *very* or *exceedingly* may belong to *faithfulness* alone, or to the whole proposition. The mention of faithfulness shews that the idea of God's promise is included in his testimony. With this verse compare ver. 86, and Ps. xciii. 5.

139. *My zeal consumes me, because my adversaries forget thy word.* The verbs strictly mean, *has consumed, have forgotten,* but without excluding the present, as they might seem to do, if rendered literally into English. *Zeal,* jealous regard for God's authority and honour. See above, on Ps. lxix. 10 (9). The first Hebrew verb occurs above, Ps. lxxxviii. 17 (16). The last clause gives the reason or occasion of his jealousy. *Adversaries,* persecutors or oppressors. *Thy word,* includes thy promise to me and thy command to them.

140. *Pure (is) thy word—exceedingly, and thy servant loves it.* Pure, literally purged, tried, assayed, refined, like precious metal. See above, on Ps. xviii. 31 (30). *Saying,* as elsewhere in this psalm, alternates with *word,* and has the same comprehensive meaning. *Thy servant,* I as thy servant, and because I am so. *Loves* and has long loved.

141. *Little (am) I and despised,* (but) *thy precepts do I not forget.* However proudly or however justly I may be despised, I can still lay claim to one distinction, that I have not, like my despisers, forgotten God's commandments. These words are peculiarly appropriate to Israel, as a body, at the Restoration.

142. *Thy righteousness (is) right for ever, and thy law (is) truth.* Right is here used as a noun, in order to vary the expression in English as in Hebrew, where two cognate forms (צדקה and צדק) are employed. With the first clause compare Ps. ciii. 17, cxi. 3. The idea here is, that God's rectitude is not capricious or mutable, as might be inferred from the afflictions of his people, but unchangeable and *to eternity. Thy law,* both in its precepts and its promises, is true, is truth itself.

143. *Distress and anguish seize* (or *seized) me ; thy commandments (are) my delight.* Even in the midst of suffering, thy commandments not only solace me but make me happy. *Seize,* literally *find,* as in Ps. cxvi. 3. *Delight,* literally *delights,* a succedaneum for all other pleasures. See above, on ver. 24.

144. *Right (are) thy testimonies to eternity ; make me understand, and I shall live. Right,* righteousness, the second of the nouns used in ver. 142. *Make me understand* (them), *i. e.* these thy testimonies. *And (then) I shall live,* which includes *let me live* and *that I may live.* See above, on ver. 17, 116. Three of the verses in this stanza begin with derivatives of the root צדק.

145. *I invoke (thee) with a whole heart—answer me, Jehovah—thy statutes will I keep.* I have invoked thy favour with a heartfelt sense of its neces-

sity; grant it to me, according to my prayer, and I am fully resolved to keep thy statutes.

146. *I invoke thee—save me—and I will observe thy testimonies.* The pronoun implied in the preceding verse is here expressed. The augmented form of the last verb is emphatic or intensive. *I* WILL observe thy testimonies, *i. e.* obey thy precepts and believe thy promises.

147. *I come before (thee) in the (morning) twilight, and I cry to (thee) ; for thy words do I wait.* The first verb has the same sense as in Ps. xcv. 2. Compare Ps. lxxxviii. 14 (13). Early prayer implies importunate desire. The *twilight* meant is that of morning, as in 1 Sam. xxx. 17, Job vii. 4. The second verb means to cry for help. Its augmented form is common in verbs of speaking, and supposed by some grammarians to denote motion or direction towards the object of address, like the local or directive ח in nouns. See Judges vi. 10, 1 Sam. xxviii. 15, Neh. v. 7, xiii. 11, 17, 21, Dan. ix. 4.

148. *My eyes anticipate the watches, to muse of thy promise.* Before the stated hours of vigil he is awake and ready for devout meditation. *To muse,* that I may muse or meditate. See above, on ver. 62, and compare Ps. lxiii. 7 (6), lxxvii. 5 (4), Lam. ii. 19.

149. *My voice hear according to thy mercy, O Jehovah, according to thy judgments quicken me.* According to the promises annexed to thy commandments.

150. *Near are those pursuing crime; from thy law they are far off. Pursuing,* eagerly devising and attempting. *Crime,* malicious mischief, as in Ps. xxvi. 10. In the last clause there is a kind of play upon the words *far* and *near,* as if he had said, the nearer they are to harming me, the further are they from obeying thee.

151. *Near (art) thou, Jehovah, and all thy commandments are truth.* The *lusus verborum* may be said to be continued. As they are near to injure, thou art near to save, and all thy promises to those who do thy will are true, are truth itself.

152. *Long have I known from thy testimonies (themselves) that thou unto eternity hast founded them.* The first word in Hebrew is a noun used adverbially, as in Ps. lv. 20 (19). The precepts of the law describe themselves as everlasting. See Exod. xxvii. 21, xxviii. 43, xxxvi. 21, Lev. iii. 17, vi. 11, vii. 36, Num. x. 8. This concludes the nineteenth stanza, two of the initial words in which are derivatives of קרא, two of קרב, three of קדם.

153. *See my suffering and deliver me ; for thy law I forget not.* The first petition, in the same words, occurs above, Ps. ix. 14 (13). The first verb originally signifies to extricate or disembarrass. *I forget not,* and have not forgotten, both of which ideas would be necessarily suggested to a Hebrew reader.

154. *Strive my strife and redeem me ; as to thy word, quicken me.* With the first clause compare Ps. xliii. 1, lxix. 19 (18). *As to,* according to, in fulfilment of, *thy saying,* that which thou hast said, thy promise. See above, ver. 41.

155. *Far from the wicked (is) salvation : because thy statutes they seek not.* The first word in Hebrew is a masculine adjective, and does not agree regularly with *salvation,* which is feminine, but is construed as a neuter, *something far,* as the first word in ver. 72 means *a good thing. Seek not,* and have not sought, *i. e.* desired either to know or do thy will. See above, on ver. 45.

156. *Many* (or *manifold are*) *thy compassions, O Jehovah, according to thy judgments quicken me.* That the first word means *many*, not *great*, in this connection, seems clear from the next verse. *According to thy judgments*, as in ver. 149.

157. *Many* (are) *my persecutors and oppressors ; from thy testimonies I decline not.* The second noun is often rendered *adversaries*, as in ver. 139, but it may here be taken in its primary sense, which is near akin to that of the preceding word. *I decline not*, and have not declined, deviated, swerved.

158. *I see traitors and am sickened*—(*those*) *who thy saying keep not.* The wicked are called traitors against God, their rightful sovereign, as in Ps. xxv. 8. The first verb is the reflexive form of that in Ps. xcv. 10, *I sicken* (or *disgust*) *myself.* The common version of the relative (*because*) conveys an idea not expressed but understood. There is no need of departing from the strict sense of the pronoun. *See* and have seen, *keep* and have kept.

159. *See how I love thy precepts, Jehovah ; according to thy mercy, quicken me.* *See how*, literally *see that*, which is tantamount to saying, *thou seest that*,

160. *The head of thy word* (*is*) *truth, and to eternity* (*is*) *every judgment of thy righteousness.* *Head* is by some explained as meaning the sum total, by others as synonymous with the cognate form (רֵאשִׁית) in Ps. cxi. 10. *Every judgment of thy righteousness*, every one of thy righteous judgments. Three verses of the twentieth stanza begin with some form of the verb (רָאה) *to see.*

161. *Princes persecute me without cause*—*and at thy words my heart is awed.* Both Hebrew verbs are in the past tense. The first verb, like its representative, originally means to follow after, to pursue, but is commonly employed in a hostile sense. *Without cause* answers to a single Hebrew word (חִנָּם) an adverb related to the noun (חֵן) *favour*, as *gratis* is to *gratia* in Latin. So in modern English, the idea here might be expressed by the one word *gratuitously*. *At thy words*, literally *from them*, *i. e.* because or on account of them. The last verb is not a passive in Hebrew, but a less usual synonym of (יָרֵא) *to fear*, correctly paraphrased in the English versions (*standeth in awe*). The masoretic reading is *thy word* in the singular, but, as in most other cases, the best critics now prefer the reading in the text.

162. *Rejoicing* (*am*) *I over thy saying, like* (*one*) *finding much spoil.* The participle indicates continued and habitual rejoicing. *Thy saying*, that which thou hast said, thy law with its attendant promises.

163. *Falsehood I hate and abhor; thy law I love.* Hate and have hated, love and have loved. *Falsehood* or *lying*, as in ver. 29. The second verb has the same augmented and intensive form that occurs above, ver. 147, 158.

164. *Seven times in the day I praise thee, for the judgments of thy righteousness.* Seven times is a proverbial idiom for often or repeatedly. The use of this form of expression here is not the effect but the occasion of the observance of canonical hours. See above, on Ps. lv. 18 (17). *Praise thee*, and have been accustomed so to do. With the last clause compare ver. 160.

165. (*There is*) *much peace to the lovers of thy law, and there is to them no stumbling-block.* Peace, in opposition to the disquietude inseparable from a course of sin. A stumbling-block is a common scriptural figure for an occasion of unbelief or sin. The idea here is, that the best preservative against temptation is a love to God's commandments. The Prayer-Book version (*they are not offended at it*) and that in the text of the English

Bible (*nothing shall offend them*) convey a very different meaning from the true one to a modern reader. The latter indeed seems directly contradictory to ver. 53, 158. The correct sense is intelligibly given in the margin of the common version.

166. *I hope for thy salvation, O Jehovah, and thy commandments I do.* *I hope* and have hoped, *do* and have done. In the mean time, while expecting thy salvation, I am careful to perform thy will.

167. *My soul observes thy testimonies, and I love them greatly* (or *exceedingly*). I observe them, pay particular regard to them, in regulating my behaviour, not with a mere external conformity, but from or with my soul, because I love them greatly.

168. *I observe thy precepts and thy testimonies, because all my ways are before thee.* He does not affect to be prompted by a love exclusive of all fear, but only of a slavish dread. He stands in awe of God's omniscience, and is influenced by dread of his disapprobation to obey his precepts, as well as by attachment to the law itself. *My ways*, my courses of conduct, mode of life, behaviour. *Before thee*, open to God's infallible inspection, and subjected to his judgment. Two of the verses in this stanza begin with forms of the verb (שָׁמַר) *to observe* or *keep*. It is also worthy of remark that שׂ and שׁ are treated as one letter, three of the verses beginning with the former, namely, the two first and the sixth.

169. *Let my cry come near before thee, O Jehovah ; according to thy word, make me understand.* The first noun denotes an audible expression of strong feeling, whether sorrowful or joyful. See above, on Ps. xvii. 1, xxx. 6 (5). *Come near before thee*, not only near enough to be heard, but into thy presence, so that he who utters it may be seen. *According to thy word*, thy commandment which requires, and thy promise which secures, the understanding of thy will. See above, ver. 25, 65, 107, and compare Deut. xxx. 6.

170. *Let my supplication come before thee; according to thy promise, free me* (or *deliver me*). The first noun, according to its etymology, denotes a prayer for grace or favour. See above, Ps. vi. 10 (9), lv. 2 (1). In this and the preceding verse, the prayer for deliverance from outward troubles is subjoined, and as it were subordinated, to that for grace to do the will of God. The same connection may be traced in Ps. xc. 11–17.

171. *My lips shall pour forth praise ; for thou wilt teach me thy statutes.* The first verb means to cause to gush or flow, and is the same with that in Ps. xix. 3 (2), lxxviii. 2. It here denotes eager, abundant, and unceasing praise. The last clause expresses the confident expectation of the blessing so often and importunately asked throughout the psalm. As if he had said, Now shall my lips praise, for I am about to receive what I had prayed for ; thou wilt, indeed, teach me thy statutes. The translation *when thou hast taught me* (or *shalt teach me*) is less exact, less forcible, and really included in the other.

172. *Let my tongue answer thy saying—that all thy commandments are right.* The verb which usually means to answer prayer (see above, ver. 26, 145) is here used in the sense of responding to a precept or a promise by the language of praise and acquiescence. Compare ver. 42. There is no need of treating the optative form of the verb as a poetic licence. The strict sense agrees well with the prayer in the next verse. What is here asked is occasion thus to praise God. As the last clause seems to assign no pertinent reason for the prayer in the first, it may be regarded as the

response itself. Let my tongue say in answer to all thy requisitions, that all thy commandments are right, or righteousness itself, as in ver. 142, 144.

173. *Let thy hand be* (near) *to help me; for thy precepts do I choose.* The word supplied in this translation is not necessary to the sense, but is introduced for the purpose of retaining the original construction, *be to help me, i. e.* be my help, or simply help me. The reason given in the last clause is, that as he voluntarily makes choice of God's will as his rule of conduct, he thereby renounces all other protection. The Hebrew verb is a preterite; *I choose*, and have already chosen.

174. *I long for thy salvation, O Jehovah, and thy law (is) my delights.* I long and have longed. With the first clause compare ver. 40, 81, 131; with the second, ver. 24, 77, 92.

175. *Let my soul live and praise thee; and let thy judgments help me.* This verse sums up in conclusion the petitions of the whole psalm. Save me, and thereby give me cause to praise thee, for the blessings which I have derived from the promises and precepts of the law. *Let my soul live*, because it is that which is in danger. *Judgments*, as in ver. 149, 156.

176. *I wander like a lost sheep—seek thy servant—for thy commandments I do not forget.* The English versions of the first clause (*I have gone astray*), although they adhere strictly to the form of the original, seem to make the primary idea that of sin, which is really included, but only as the cause of that which is directly intended, namely, misery, represented by the wandering of a lost and helpless sheep. Compare Jer. l. 6. *Seek thy servant*, deliver from this wretched state one who is still thy servant, and as such remembers thy commandments, even in the midst of his worst sufferings. As the preceding verse sums up the petitions of the psalm, so this sums up its complaints in the first clause and its professions in the last, connected by the short prayer (*seek thy servant*) as by a single link. The predominant use of the past tense, even to the end, shews how deeply the entire psalm is founded upon actual and previous experience. In this last stanza, the only initial word repeated is (תְּהִי) the verb of existence.

Psalm 120

1. *A Song of the Ascents. To Jehovah, in my distress, I called, and he answered me.* This is the first of fifteen psalms (cxx.–cxxxiv.), all bearing the inscription, *song of ascents* or *upgoings, i. e.* sung during the periodical journeys or pilgrimages to Jerusalem at the times of the great yearly festivals. On these occasions the people are said, even in historical prose, to *go up* to Jerusalem, in reference both to its physical and moral elevation. See Exod. xxxiv. 24, 1 Kings xii. 27, 28. The Hebrew verb (עָלָה) employed in such connections is the root of the noun (מַעֲלוֹת) *ascents* in these inscriptions. This explanation of the title is much more satisfactory than any other which has been proposed. A rabbinical tradition represents these psalms as having been sung by the people, as they ascended the fifteen steps (in Hebrew מַעֲלוֹת), seven on one side and eight on the other, repeatedly mentioned by Ezekiel (xl. 6, 22, 26, 31, 34, 37). But apart from the intrinsic improbability of this tradition, some psalms in the series were evidently not meant to be sung at the temple. No less improbable than this very ancient explanation is the modern one, that the inscription has

reference to a peculiarity of structure, the repetition of a phrase or clause of one sentence in the next with an addition, forming a kind of climax or progression in the terms as well as the ideas. But even admitting that this peculiarity of form might be described by (מַעֲלוֹת) the Hebrew word in question, this word could not have been prefixed to each of the fifteen psalms, when the examples of the fact alleged are confined almost exclusively to one or two of them. Much nearer to the truth is the opinion, that these psalms were intended to be sung during the return from Babylon, which is called an *ascent* (מַעֲלָה) by Ezra (vii. 9). But this can only be maintained by arbitrarily denying the genuineness of the titles, which ascribe four of the psalms (cxxii., cxxiv., cxxxi., cxxxiii.) to David, and one (cxxvii.) to Solomon. The position assigned to these, and the difference of tone between them and the rest, are ingeniously accounted for by Hengstenberg's hypothesis, that these five ancient psalms, sung by the people, as they went up to Jerusalem before the captivity, were made the basis of a whole series or system, designed for the same use by an inspired writer after the Restoration, who not only added ten psalms of his own, as appears from the identity of tone and diction, but joined them to the old ones in a studied and artificial manner, entirely inconsistent with the supposition of fortuitous or random combination. The one psalm by Solomon stands in the centre of the series or system and divides it into two equal parts, in each of which we find two psalms of David and five anonymous or new ones, the former being separated and surrounded by the latter, an additional and strong proof of intended adaptation to the times when the later psalms were written, to which Hengstenberg still further adds the number and distribution of the divine names in the whole series and its subdivisions. The psalm immediately before is anonymous, but its tone and diction mark it as belonging to the period of the Restoration. It begins with an acknowledgment of that great mercy, ver. 1, followed by a prayer for deliverance from treacherous and spiteful enemies, ver. 2, and a confident anticipation of their punishment, ver. 3, 4, but closes with a further lamentation and complaint of present sufferings, ver. 5-7. In this, as in all the other psalms of the series, the ideal speaker is Israel or Judah, considered as the church or chosen people. This first verse, although general in its terms, is perfectly appropriate to the Captivity, as the *distress* out of which the sufferer cried to God, and to the Restoration, as the *answer* to his prayer. *In my distress*, literally *in distress to me*, an expression like that in Ps. xviii. 7 (6). The augmented form of the Hebrew noun is like that in Ps. iii. 3 (2).

2. *O Jehovah, free my soul from lip of falsehood, from tongue of fraud.* The soul is particularly mentioned as usual when the life or the existence is in danger. The last two nouns in Hebrew are not in construction but in apposition, *a tongue (which is) fraud*, equivalent in meaning to the same English words in an inverted order, *fraud-tongues*. See a somewhat similar combination, Ps. xlv. 5 (4), lx. 5 (4). The terms of the description are too strong to be applied to mere delusive promises, and necessarily suggest the idea of calumnious falsehood, as in Ps. xxxi. 19 (18), cxix. 69, 78. The reality answering to this description in the case of the restored Jews is the spiteful misrepresentation, by which the Samaritans retarded the rebuilding of the temple, as recorded in the fourth chapter of Ezra.

3. *What will he give to thee, and what will he add to thee, thou tongue of fraud?* Having complained to God of the false tongue, the ideal speaker turns to it as actually present, and addresses it directly, speaking of God in

the third person. The meaning of the question is, what recompence can
you expect from an infinitely righteous God for these malignant calumnies ?
The peculiar form of the interrogation is derived from that of an ancient
oath, *The Lord do so to me and more also*, literally *and so add*, *i. e.* further do, or in addition to the thing in question. See 1 Sam. iii. 17,
xiv. 44. As explained by this allusion, the words have a new force. What
good or evil may be imprecated on thee, as the consequence of these malicious falsehoods.

4. *Arrows of a warrior sharpened*, *(together)* *with coals of juniper.* The
general idea of severe and painful punishment is here expressed by the
obvious and intelligible figures of keen arrows and hot coals. The *arrows
of a mighty man*, warrior, or hero, are those used in battle, perhaps with
an allusion to the fact, that one of the races mentioned in the next verse
excelled in archery. See Isa. xxi. 17. The word which the rabbinical
tradition explains to mean the juniper, is by modern lexicographers identified with the Arabic name of a species of broom-plant, which is thought, on
account of its inflammatory quality, to make the best charcoal. See Robinson's Palestine, vol. i. p. 299. With the figures of the verse before us
compare Ps. vii. 14 (13), xviii. 13, 14 (12, 13), cxl. 11 (10).

5. *Alas for me, that I sojourn (with) Meshech*, *(and) dwell near the tents of
Kedar !* The first verb seems elsewhere, in the same construction, to denote the act of dwelling with one, Ps. v. 5 (4). The Hebrew preposition
in the last clause properly means *with*, and denotes association and proximity. The English Bible, by twice employing our preposition *in*, obscures
the meaning of both clauses, which is not that the people were in the power or
even in the midst of the enemies here mentioned, but compelled to reside
near them and to suffer from their neighbourhood. *Meshech* is the name
given in Gen. x. 2 to the Moschi, a barbarous people inhabiting the mountains between Colchis, Armenia, and Iberia. *Kedar* was one of the sons
of Ishmael (Gen. xxv. 13), whose name is sometimes used to designate an
Arabian tribe (Isa. xxi. 16, xlii. 11), and in later Hebrew the Arabians
generally. As these races, dwelling far off, in the north and south, were
never in immediate or continued contact with the Israelites, they are probably named as types and representatives of warlike barbarism, just as the
names Goths, Vandals, Huns, Turks, Tartars, Cossacks, have at different
times been used proverbially in English, to describe those supposed to exhibit the same character, however unconnected or remote in genealogy and
local habitation. A slight approach to the same usage was produced
among ourselves by the revolutionary war, in reference to the national
names, British and Hessian. In the case before us, it is evident from ver.
6, that *Meshech* and *Kedar* are mere types and representatives of those who
hate peace and delight in war. Compare Ezek. xxxviii. 2, where Meshech
appears as a chief leader under Gog, the great prophetic representative of
heathendom.

6. *My soul has dwelt too long for her with* (one) *hating peace.* The
substitution of *my soul* for *I* implies the intimate conviction and the painful sense of what is here asserted. *Too long*, literally *much* or *too much*.
As to this peculiar idiom, see above, on Ps. lxv. 10 (9). *For her*, may be
an idiomatic pleonasm, adding nothing to the meaning of the verb, with
which it must be read in close connection ; or it may have the meaning
which the corresponding phrase would naturally seem to have in English,
for her good or *for her interest*. See above, on Ps. lviii. 8 (7). *Hating
peace* is clearly a collective or aggregate expression, comprehending all de-

noted by the Meshech and Kedar of the preceding verse, as an ideal individual.

7. *I am peace, and when I speak, they (go) to war.* The first phrase resembles *I am prayer* in Ps. cix. 4, and seems to mean, I am all peace, nothing but peace, peace itself, *i. e.* entirely peaceful or pacific. *Speak* may be an ellipsis for *speak peace*, a phrase repeatedly occurring in the Psalms. See above, Ps. xxxv. 20, lxxxv. 9 (8), and below, Ps. cxxii. 8. The sense will then be, whenever I desire or propose peace. If the verb be absolutely understood, the sense is that every word he utters is made an occasion of attack or conflict. The double *for*, in the common version of this sentence, is as incorrect as the double *in* of ver. 5, and more enfeebling to the sense. I am not only *for peace*, but am peace itself. They are not only *for war*, but arise, proceed, or address themselves to it.

Psalm 121

1. *A Song for the Ascents. I raise my eyes to the mountains. Whence cometh my help?* The title differs from that of the preceding psalm only in the use of the preposition *for*, instead of the simple genitive construction. This variation, though without effect upon the sense, is favourable to the explanation which has been already given of these titles, as *a song for the ascents* or pilgrimages to Jerusalem is certainly more intelligible than *a song for the steps* of the temple, and still more so than *a song for the returns* from exile, while the modern theory of climacteric resumptions fails altogether to account for the expression here used. The whole psalm is a description of Jehovah as the guardian or protector of his people. The only material distinction of the parts is that arising from the alternate use of the first and second person, as in Ps. xci., which has led some to assume without necessity, that the psalm was intended to be sung by alternate or responsive choirs. The phrase, to lift the eyes, though sometimes used to signify the mere act of directing them to an object, has its strict and full sense when a higher object is particularly mentioned, such as hills or heavens. The mountains here meant, are the heights on which Jerusalem is built. It is not improbable that this psalm was intended to be sung when the pilgrims came in sight of the Holy City. Some suppose, moreover, that it was meant to be an evening song, and used when they halted for the last night's rest before they reached Jerusalem. The relative construction of the last clause yields a good sense, but is not in perfect keeping with the usage of the compound particle (מֵאַיִן), which is elsewhere always interrogative.

2. *My help is from Jehovah, Maker of heaven and earth.* The creative power of Jehovah is particularly mentioned, to demonstrate his ability to help his people. Compare Ps. cxv. 15.

3. *May he not suffer to be moved thy foot; may he not slumber—thy keeper.* This is the expression of a wish, the only sense consistent with the form of the orignal. *Let him not give up to moving thy foot.* See above, Ps. xxxviii. 17 (16), lxvi. 9 (8). The figure is peculiarly appropriate in the mouth of pilgrims, making their way among the hills and rocks of Palestine. The same thing is true of the figures in the subsequent verses.

4. *Lo, he shall not slumber, and he shall not sleep—the keeper of Israel.* What is desired in the third verse, is affirmed in this. The position of the subject at the end of the sentence, in both cases, is emphatic. Most inter-

preters assume a gradation in the meaning of the two verbs, as if one denoted lighter and the other deep sleep; but they differ on the question which is the stronger of the two expressions. The latest writers say the first. See above, on Ps. iv. 9 (8).

5. *Jehovah is thy keeper; Jehovah is thy shade upon thy right hand.* The keeper or protector of Israel, who had twice been mentioned by that title, is now named. A shade or shadow is a common figure for protector, and the right hand often mentioned as the place of a protector. See above, on Ps. cix. 6, cx. 5, and compare Num. xiv. 9.

6. *By day the sun shall not smite thee, and the moon by night.* The last clause does not necessarily refer to injurious effects produced directly by the moon, but may be understood as a poetical description of all noxious influences operating in the night, over which the moon was constituted ruler at the time of its creation. See Gen. i. 16, xxxi. 40, Jer. xxxvi. 30.

7. *Jehovah will keep thee from all evil; he will keep thy soul.* The protection which had been repeatedly promised to Israel on the part of God, is now described as extending to all evils and to the very life and soul.

8. *Jehovah will keep thy going out and thy coming in from now even to eternity.* This is the third repetition of the phrase, *Jehovah will keep, i. e.* keep safe, protect, preserve, as if to silence the misgivings of a weak or tempted faith, by the reiterated declaration of this cheering truth. *Going out and coming in* is a proverbial Hebrew phrase for all the occupations and affairs of life. See Deut. xxviii. 6, 1 Sam. xxix. 6. The original reference is to man's going out to labour in the morning and returning home to rest at night. See above, on Ps. civ. 23. With the last clause compare Ps. cxiii. 2, cxvi. 18, cxxv. 2. The promise of eternal preservation is addressed directly to the church as such; but that it involves the blessed immortality of individual believers, is admitted even by those least disposed to find allusions to the future state in the Book of Psalms.

Psalm 122

1. *A Song of the Ascents. By David. I rejoice in* (those) *saying to me, To the house of Jehovah we will go.* This psalm, though so much older than the two before it, was probably placed third in the series, because it was intended to be sung, and was actually sung, at the entrance of the Holy City, whereas the others were used at the commencement of the march, and on coming in sight of Jerusalem. The ideal speaker represents the church or chosen people. After the introduction, ver. 1, 2, comes a panegyric on Jerusalem, as the royal and holy city, ver. 3–5, followed by a prayer for her prosperity as such, ver. 6–9. *The Ascents*, or upward journeys of the people to the sanctuary, as in Ps. cxx. 1, cxxi. 1. To *rejoice in those saying* is to rejoice because they say. On the last clause is founded Isa. ii. 3, where the gentiles are described as joining in the words here uttered by the Jews.

2. *Standing are our feet in thy gates, O Jerusalem !* The common version (*shall stand*) is entirely ungrammatical. The past tense of the substantive verb with the participle means strictly *have been standing, i. e.* have begun to stand, or are already standing.

3. *Jerusalem, the* (one) *built like a city which is joined to itself together.* This seems to be a continuation of the address in the preceding verse. The unusual expressions in the last clause are intended to describe the city

as substantially and strongly built. The sense is correctly given in the English Bible, *a city that is compact together*. This seems to imply that Jerusalem had recently assumed this character, and may therefore help to determine the period in the reign of David, when the psalm was written. See 2 Sam. v. 9. The abbreviated relative (שֶׁחֻבְּרָה) has by some been made a proof of later date; but it no doubt belonged from the beginning to the dialect of common life, though not commonly employed in writing till a later date. It occurs in the song of Deborah, Judges v. 7, and elsewhere in the Book of Judges (vi. 17, vii. 12. viii. 26).

4. *Where the tribes go up, the tribes of Jah (as) a testimony to Israel, to give thanks to the name of Jehovah.* There is obvious reference to the requisition in Exod. xxiii. 17, xxxiv. 23, Deut. xvi. 16, which is called a testimony, not merely as the law in general is (Ps. xciii. 5), but as a constant memorial of God's goodness to his people. The mention of the tribes seems to point to the period of the undivided monarchy.

5. *For there sit thrones for judgment, thrones for the house of David.* This means simply that Jerusalem was a civil as well as a religious capital. *There*, literally *thither*, implying that the singers were themselves in motion towards these thrones. *Sit*, or as we should say in English, *stand*. See below, Ps. cxxv. 1.

6. *Pray for the peace of Jerusalem; may they have peace that love thee!* Peace, in both clauses, includes all prosperity. There is obvious allusion to the meaning of the name *Jerusalem*. See above, on Ps. lxxvi. 3 (2).

7. *Peace be within thy rampart, and repose within thy palaces.* Peace and repose from all distracting causes, of whatever nature. *Rampart*, breast-work, circumvallation. Rampart and palaces are put for the outer and inner masses of building. Compare Ps. xlviii. 14.

8. *For the sake of my brethren and my friends, let me speak, Peace (be) within thee.* By brethren and friends we are to understand the whole body of the chosen people. *For their sake* may include the sense of *in their behalf.* The last clause admits of a different construction, *Let me speak peace to thee*, literally *in thee*. See above, on Ps. lxxxv. 9 (8). The optative meaning of the verb is determined by the particle (נָא), the use of which here seems to be imitated in Ps. cxv. 2, cxvi. 4.

9. *For the sake of the house of Jehovah our God, I will seek thy good.* The house of God is here the sanctuary and all the interests of which it was the local centre. *Jehovah our God*, our patron and protector, our peculiar covenant God. *Seek* includes every form of effort to promote it; but the prominent idea is that of intercession.

Psalm 123

1. *A Song of the Ascents. Unto thee do I raise my eyes, the (one) sitting in the heavens.* This psalm contains an expression of solicitous desire for divine help, ver. 1, 2, a direct prayer for mercy, ver. 3, and a statement of the circumstances which occasioned it. With the first clause compare Ps. cxxi. 1, with the second, Ps. ii. 4, xi. 4, ciii. 19, cxiii. 3, 5.

2. *Behold, as the eyes of servants (are turned) to the hand of their masters, as the eyes of a maid to the hand of her mistress, so our eyes (are turned) to Jehovah our God, until he have mercy upon us.* The *behold as*, at the beginning, is equivalent to *see how* in English. Some suppose the act of

looking towards the hand of a superior to denote desire of protection; others an appeal to his bounty, as in Ps. civ. 27, 28, cxlv. 15, 16; others an implied prayer that punishment may cease. Compare Gen. xvi. 6, 8, 9. Perhaps all these explanations err in being too specific, and the sense of the comparison is simply that they look with deference and trust to the superior power which controls them.

3. *Have mercy upon us, O Jehovah, have mercy upon us; for greatly are we sated with contempt.* This petition forms the centre of the psalm, to which what goes before is introductory, and what follows supplementary. The contempt is that of heathen neighbours, and especially that of the Samaritans, which is expressly mentioned in the history. See Neh. i. 3, ii. 19.

4. *Much sated in itself is our soul with the scorning of the secure, the contempt of the proud.* In itself, literally *to* or *for itself*, as in Ps. cxxii. 3. *Secure (sinners)*, those at ease, indifferent to the sufferings of others, and without apprehension of their own. Compare Ps. lxxiii. 12.

Psalm 124

1. *A Song of the Ascents. By David. If (it had) not (been) Jehovah who was for us—Oh let Israel say.* This psalm consists of two parts, an acknowledgment of God as the deliverer of Israel, ver. 1–5, and a consequent determination to trust in him exclusively for future favours, ver. 6–9. The verse before us propounds the theme of the whole composition, in a conditional and imperfect, but for that very reason a more striking form. It is tantamount to saying, what if the Lord had not been for us?—leaving the answer to the imagination of the reader. *For us*, in our favour, on our side; or *to us*, belonging to us, ours, which really includes the other. See above, on Ps. lvi. 10 (9). *Oh that* in the last clause represents (נָא) the particle of entreaty. The common version (*now*) conveys the very different idea, *at length*, after all that we have suffered, let Israel so say. The mistake is rendered more natural or rather unavoidable, to mere English readers, by the seeming antithesis between the *now* of this verse and the *then* of ver. 3, 4, 5, of which there is not the slightest trace in the original.

2. *If (it had) not (been) Jehovah who was for us, in the rising up of man against us.* What was left unfinished in the first verse, as a mere suggestion of the Psalmist's theme, is now repeated, for the purpose of being carried out. This is one of the rhetorical resumptions, which some modern critics hold to be the (מַעֲלוֹת) *degrees*, from which these fifteen psalms derived their common designation. With this verse compare Ps. lvi. 12 (11).

3. *Then alive would they have swallowed us, in the kindling of their wrath against us.* With respect to the *then* at the beginning of this verse, there is danger of an error just the opposite of that already pointed out in reference to the *now* of ver. 1. As the English reader would be almost sure to take that for a particle of time, which it is not, he would be equally certain to mistake this for a term of logic, meaning in that case, upon that supposition, or the like; whereas it really means *at that time*, the well remembered time of our extremity, when God so wonderfully interposed for our deliverance. The Hebrew particle occurs in this form only here, and is consequently no more a proof of recent than of early date. Another word liable to misconstruction in the English versions of this clause is

quick, here used in its primary sense of *living* or *alive*, from which may be easily deduced its secondary sense of *swift*, implying lively motion. The historical allusion, in this and other like passages, is no doubt to the fate of Korah and his company. Compare Num. xvi. 32, 33, where the same verb and adjective occur together. See above, on Ps. lv. 16 (15). The plural pronoun *their* refers to the collective *man* in the preceding verse.

4. *Then the waters would have overwhelmed us* (and) *a stream passed over our soul.* The common version (*had overwhelmed us*) is entirely correct, and more poetical in form than that here given, but at the same time ambiguous, as the sentence, taken by itself, would seem to mean, that before the time signified by *then*, the waters had actually overwhelmed them, which was not the case. The figures are the same as in Ps. xviii. 5, 17 (4, 16), cxliv. 7.

5. *Then had passed over our soul the waters, the proud* (*waters*). The waters are so described, partly because of the ideas suggested by their swelling (Ps. lxxxix. 10), partly because they represent dangers arising from the selfish pride of human enemies. Some, without necessity, recur to the primary meaning of the root, and explain the adjective to mean boiling, effervescing.

6. *Blessed* (*be*) *Jehovah, who did not give us* (*as*) *prey to their teeth.* By one of those rhetorical transitions which are constantly occurring in the figurative diction of the psalms, the enemies and dangers, which had just been represented as an overwhelming flood or torrent, are suddenly transformed into devouring beasts. See above, on Ps. iii. 8 (7), lviii. 7 (6). With the benediction or doxology, *blessed* (*be*) *Jehovah*, compare Ps. xxviii. 6, xxxi. 22 (21).

7. *Our soul is escaped, like a bird, from the snare of the fowlers ; the snare is broken and we are escaped.* We have here a second transition and a third comparison, to wit, that of the enemies to fowlers, and of their devices to snares or traps used in catching birds. In the second clause there is an obvious climax. Not only is the bird gone, but the snare is broken. This is peculiarly appropriate to the restoration of the Jews from Babylon, which was occasioned by the fall of Babylon itself. With the figures of this verse compare Ps. xviii. 5 (4), xci. 3. The English phrase *is escaped*, denoting a change of state, and not, like *has escaped*, a single act, is well suited to represent the Hebrew verb, which though active in meaning, has the passive form.

8. *Our help is in the name of Jehovah, maker of heaven and earth.* The conclusion drawn from the experience here recorded is, that he who had helped them must help them still. *Our help* for the future no less than the past. *In the name of Jehovah*, the manifested attributes, which constitute his *name*, in the peculiar dialect of Scripture, and especially of this book. See above, on Ps. v. 12 (11), xx. 2 (1). With this verse compare also Ps. xxxiii. 22, cxxi. 2.

Psalm 125

1. *A Song of the Ascents. Those trusting in Jehovah* (*are*) *like mount Zion,* (*which*) *is not moved* (*but*) *stands for ever.* This psalm contains an expression of strong confidence in the divine protection, ver. 1, 2, especially against wicked enemies, ver. 3, with a prayer that this confidence may not go unrewarded, ver. 4, and a prophetic anticipation of the fate of the

ungodly, ver. 5. The condition of the chosen people, here described or presupposed, as suffering from the spite of heathen enemies, not in captivity or exile, but at home in their own land, and internally divided into two great parties, the sincere and hypocritical, agrees exactly with the period of the Restoration, and especially that part of it in which the building of the temple was suspended, as known to us from history and prophecy. The psalm before us was well suited to alarm and warn the false Israel, as well as to encourage and support the true. According to Hengstenberg, it was intended, with the psalms before and after it, to form a trilogy, consisting of one ancient and two later compositions. *Those trusting in Jehovah* is a characteristic designation of the true church, the spiritual Israel, the chosen people. The meaning is, not merely that they individually exercise this faith, but that collectively, or as a body, they are built upon it, and have no security except in the divine protection. *Mount Zion*, not as a figure for the church, which would then be compared with itself, but simply as a mountain, and like other mountains solid and enduring, here selected as a sample or an emblem of these qualities, because it had also a religious pre-eminence, as the earthly seat and centre of the true religion. It *is not* (and shall not be) *moved*, shaken from its firm position. See above, on Ps. xlvi. 6 (5). *Stands for ever*, literally *sits to eternity*, the Hebrew idiom using one of these postures as we use the other, or rather using both as we use only one, to denote the opposite of vacillation and prostration. See above, on Ps. cxxii. 5.

2. *Jerusalem* (has) *hills about her, and* (so) *Jehovah* (is) *about his people, from now even to eternity.* The site of Jerusalem, with its peculiar features, furnishes the Psalmist with a striking image of the divine protection. As in ver. 1, the permanent security of the church itself is likened to the firmness of mount Zion on its base, so here the protecting care, which causes this security, is likened to the heights by which the city is surrounded upon all sides. The verb *has*, supplied in the translation of the first clause, is really a violation of the Hebrew idiom, to which, as well as to the kindred tongues, the verb *to have* is utterly unknown. In our own idiom, however, it expresses the precise idea, and enables us to retain the Hebrew collocation, which assigns *Jerusalem* the first place in the sentence. The Hebrew corresponding to *about* is a compound phrase, consisting of a local adverb and a preposition, *around as to*. *His people*, meaning *those who trust him* (ver. 1), to the exclusion of all hypocrites and unbelievers.

3. *For not to rest is the rod of wickedness over the lot of the righteous, to the intent that the righteous may not put forth to iniquity their hands.* This unusually long verse clearly shews the actual condition of the chosen people, here assumed or presupposed, as well-known to the writer and original readers of the psalm. The present ascendancy of wicked men is not inconsistent with the truth just stated, because it is to be brought to an end, lest the faith and patience of God's people should fail, and they should be tempted to renounce his service as unprofitable, nay, as ruinous. Compare Ps. lxxiii. 13, 14. *To rest*, not merely to remain, but to continue undisturbed. The *rod* or *staff* is here a symbol of authority, and might be rendered *sceptre*, if the subject of discourse were kings. See above, on Ps. ii. 9, xlv. 7 (6). *The lot of the righteous*, their share of the inheritance of the chosen people, at first distributed by lot. *To the intent* indicates the reason why this undeserved superiority is not to last. The reason is founded not merely on the ill desert of the wicked, but on the interest and welfare of the righteous. *Put forth*, or stretch out, literally *send into*. See the

same construction, Gen. xxxvii. 22, Exod. xxii. 7, 10 (8, 11). To touch iniquity is here to meddle with it, not, as some suppose, in the shape of revenge merely, but in all its degrees and forms, by which the righteous can be tempted.

4. *Do good, O Jehovah, to the good, and to (those) upright in their hearts.* These are additional descriptions of the true church, or spiritual Israel, to whom alone the promise of divine favour and protection had been given. *Upright,* literally *straight,* straightforward, as opposed to all moral obliquity whatever. See above, on Ps. vii. 11 (10). The prayer involves a prophetic declaration, that to such and such only, God will do good or act kindly in the highest sense. See above, on Ps. lxxiii. 1.

5. *And,* (as to) *those turning aside* (in) *their crooked* (ways), *Jehovah will let them go with the doers of iniquity. Peace* (be) *upon Israel!* The participle in the first clause is properly a transitive and means *causing to turn aside,* but has here the sense of *going aside,* or *turning* in the intransitive sense, the English verb having precisely the same double usage. This construction of the Hebrew verb, which occurs also in Isa. xxx 11, Job xxiii. 11, may be resolved into the usual one, by supposing an ellipsis of *their feet* or *steps.* The adjective translated *crooked* occurs only here and in Judges v. 6, where the noun (*ways* or *paths*) is expressed. It denotes the by-ways of corrupt inclination and transgression, by which men deviate from the straight and narrow highway of God's commandments. Compare Deut. ix. 16, Mal. ii. 8, 9. The *workers of iniquity* are not a different class from these wanderers, but that to which they belong, and the doom of which they would gladly escape; but the Lord will let them go on still with those whom they resemble in character, and as they have been like them by the way, they shall be like them in the end. Compare Ps. xxvi. 9, xxviii. 3. Having thus excluded hypocritical pretenders from the object of the benediction, he concludes by wishing or invoking *peace upon* (the true or spiritual) *Israel.* Compare Isa. lvii. 19, 21.

Psalm 126

1. *A Song of the Ascents. In Jehovah's turning (to) the turning of Zion, we were like* (men) *dreaming.* The church acknowledges the good work of deliverance as joyfully begun, ver. 1–3, and prays that it may be completed, ver. 4–6. For the meaning and construction of the first verb see above, on Ps. xiv. 7, lxxxvi. 5 (4), and compare my note on Isa. lii. 8. Instead of the usual combination (שְׁבוּת שׁוּב) *return to the captivity,* we have here one resembling it in form (שִׁיבַת שׁוּב), but meaning to *return to the return* or meet those returning, as it were, half-way. Compare Deut. xxx. 2, 3, James iv. 8. The Hebrew noun denotes *conversion,* in its spiritual sense, and the verb God's gracious condescension in accepting or responding to it. The great historical example of this condescension, which the Psalmist had immediately in view, was the deliverance from Babylon; but the terms are so selected as to be appropriate to the most intimate personal experience of the same kind. *Zion* is here put for the church or chosen people, of which it was the local seat or centre. *Like the dreamers,* or *those dreaming, i. e.* out of our ordinary normal state, and in an ecstasy or trance, arising from excess of joy. The idea of incredulity may be included, but must not be suffered to exclude all others.

2. *Then was filled with laughter our mouth, and our tongue with singing;*
then said they among the nations, Jehovah hath done great things to these
(*people*). The particle (אָז) *then* is followed by the future in the sense of
the preterite, in prose as well as poetry. See Exod. xv. 1, Deut. iv. 41,
Josh. x. 12. There is no need therefore of supposing that the writer
simply retained the future forms of the passage from which this was copied,
namely, Job viii. 21. *Laughter* and *singing*, both as signs of joy. *Done*
great things, literally *magnified to do*, an idiomatic phrase borrowed from
Joel ii. 21. *To these*, literally *with these, i. e.* in his associations and trans-
actions with them.

3. *Jehovah has done great things to us. We are joyful.* This last is not
a mere appendage to the first clause, we are glad that he has done great
things for us, but an independent proposition, containing the proof of that
by which it is preceded. He has indeed done much for us, for whereas we
were lately wretched, we are now rejoicing, or more closely rendered, have
become joyful.

4. *Turn, O Jehovah, to our captivity, like the streams in the south.* The
prayer is that God will return to, or revisit his people in their bondage or
distress, and by necessary implication set them free from it. See above,
on ver. 1. where we have a studied variation of this favourite expression.
According to the usual interpretation (*bring back our captivity*), this verse is
either inconsistent with the first, or a proof that the restoration is not mentioned there as past already. *Like the streams in the south*, as the temporary
torrents in the dry southern district of Palestine reappear in the rainy
season, after having ceased to flow in the preceding drought.

5. *Those sowing with weeping with singing shall reap. Those sowing*,
literally *the sowing, i. e.* the (same persons or the very persons) sowing.
With weeping, or in tears ; the Hebrew noun is a singular collective. See
above, on Ps. vi. 7 (6), xxxix. 13 (12), lvi. 9 (8). *Singing*, as a vocal expression of joy. See above, on ver. 2. The figures are natural and common ones for means and end, or for the beginning and the issue of any
undertaking. They may have been suggested here by the mention of the
parched and thirsty south, where the fears of the husbandman are often
disappointed by abundant rains and the sudden reappearance of the vanished
streams.

6. *He may go forth, he may go forth, and weep, bearing (his) load of seed.*
He shall come, he shall come with singing, bearing sheaves. The emphatic
combination of the finite tense with the infinitive is altogether foreign from
our idiom, and very imperfectly represented, in the ancient and some
modern versions, by the active participle (*venientes venient*, coming they
shall come), which conveys neither the peculiar form nor the precise sense
of the Hebrew phrase. The best approximation to the force of the original
is Luther's repetition of the finite tense, *he shall come, he shall come*, because in all such cases the infinitive is really defined or determined by the
term which follows, and in sense, though not in form, assimilated to it.
Load of seed, literally *drawing* or *draught of seed*, an obscure phrase, probably denoting that from which the sower draws forth seed to sow, or perhaps the seed itself thus drawn forth. The only analogous expression is in
Amos ix. 13, where the sower is called (מֹשֵׁךְ הַזָּרַע) *a drawer* (*forth of*)
seed. The common version (*precious seed*) has no foundation either in etymology or usage. The contrast so beautifully painted in this verse was
realised in the experience of Israel, when " the priests and the Levites, and

the rest of the children of the captivity, kept the dedication of the house of God with joy " (Ezra vi. 16), " and kept the feast of unleavened bread seven days with joy, because the Lord had made them joyful, and turned the heart of the king of Assyria unto them, to strengthen their hands in the work of the house of God, the God of Israel " (Ezra vi. 22). See also Nehemiah xii. 43.

Psalm 127

1. *A Song of the Ascents. By Solomon. If Jehovah will not build a house, in vain toil its builders in it. If Jehovah will not keep a city, in vain watches (its) keeper.* This is the central psalm of the series, having seven before and seven after it. This position it may owe to its being the only psalm of Solomon, whereas four are by David, and the remaining ten probably by one and the same author. See above, on Ps. cxx. 1. The admission of this psalm among the Songs of Pilgrimage was probably occasioned by its opening words, which, though admitting of a general application, were peculiarly appropriate to the building both of the first and second temple. It was perfectly natural, apart from all particular divine direction, that the rebuilders of the temple should rejoice to appropriate the words of Solomon, their great exemplar. The correctness of the title, which ascribes the psalm to him, is not only free from any plausible objection, but abundantly confirmed by its internal character, its allusion to a state of high prosperity, and its resemblance to the Book of Proverbs, where the sentiment here uttered is frequently reiterated. See for example Prov. x. 22. The general principle, that human care and toil are unavailing without God's blessing, is applied successively to several of the most familiar interests of real life. Beyond this the plan admits of no subdivision. The first specification has respect to human dwellings, both on a small and on a large scale. The futures, *will not build, will not keep,* may also be explained as presents, *builds not, keeps not.* The phrase (בּוֹ) *in it* or *on it* is to be connected with the verb, and not with *builders. Watches,* wakes, remains awake, but always with a view to the exercise of vigilance. See above, on Ps. cii. 8, and compare Prov. viii. 34. The last word in Hebrew is properly the participle of the verb translated *keep.*

2. *It is in vain for you, rising up early, sitting down late, eating the bread of cares* (or *troubles*). *So he giveth his beloved sleep.* The first phrase means, you labour in vain. *Rising up,* not merely from sleep, but to labour, addressing yourselves to work. *Sitting down,* to rest when the work is done. The contrast is sufficiently maintained by the common version, *sitting up late ;* but it is objected that the Hebrews did not work in a sitting posture. Both these phrases are peculiar in their form—*making early* (or *hastening*) *to rise*—*making late* (or *delaying*) *to sit. Bread of cares* (or *troubles*) is bread earned by hard toil and consumed amidst it. There is obvious allusion to Gen. iii. 17, 19. The last clause is exceedingly obscure. Some understand it to mean that while others labour, God's beloved sleeps. But this is contradicted by notorious facts and inconsistent with the doctrine of the Bible, and especially the Book of Proverbs, with respect to idleness and diligence. See Prov. vi. 9, 10, xxxi. 27. Another possible interpretation is that God gives his beloved refreshing sleep after their labour, but this cannot be said of such exclusively. The latest writers understand the clause to mean, that what others hope to gain

exclusively by labour, but in vain, the Lord bestows upon his people while they sleep, they know not how. According to this view of the passage, it must be translated, so, *i. e.* such, namely, what they thus seek, *he gives to his beloved one (in) sleep.* This, which is not a very obvious construction, derives some additional colour from the seeming allusion to Solomon's name Jedidiah (2 Sam. xii. 25), *the Beloved of the Lord*, and to the promise of prosperity communicated to him in a dream (1 Kings iii. 5, 15).

3. *Lo, a heritage from Jehovah (are) children; a reward (is) the fruit of the womb.* What is true of dwellings and the means of subsistence is no less true of those from whom these advantages are commonly provided. *An inheritance* or *heritage, i. e.* a valuable possession derived from a father. *Children*, literally *sons*, a term very often used indefinitely. *A reward* or *hire*, the expression used by Leah, in naming her son Issachar, Gen. xxx. 18. In the same chapter (Gen. xxx. 2) children are called the *fruit of the womb*, and represented as the gift of God. See also Deut. vii. 13.

4. *As arrows in the hand of a warrior, so are the sons of youth.* The first clause describes them as defenders of their parents. *A warrior*, literally *a strong* or *(mighty) one. Sons of youth, i. e.* born while their parents are still young. See Gen. xxxvii. 3, Isa. liv. 6. The allusion is not only to the vigour (Gen. xlix. 3), but to the value of their aid to the parent in declining age.

5. *Happy the man who has filled his quiver with them—they shall not be put to shame—they shall speak with adversaries in the gate.* The first clause carries out the figure of arrows in the verse preceding. The mention of the gate, in the last clause, as the place both of commercial and judicial business, seems to mark a transition from martial to forensic conflict, and to shew that the enemies or adversaries here meant are adverse parties in litigation. See above, on Ps. lxix. 13 (12). For a striking contrast to this picture, see Job v. 4. This last example, although perfectly in keeping with the views of the ancient Israelites in general, seems peculiarly natural and life-like in a psalm of Solomon.

Psalm 128

1. *A Song of Ascents. Happy is every fearer of Jehovah, the (one) walking in his ways.* This psalm seems intended to assure the tempted and discouraged people of Judah, under the most adverse circumstances, that devotion to his service cannot lose its reward. As if he had said, however things may now seem to an eye of sense, it is still a certain truth that the truly happy man is he who fears Jehovah, not in mere profession, but who testifies his fear of him by walking in his ways or doing his commandments.

2. *The labour of thy hands when thou shalt eat, happy thou and well with thee.* The promise implied is the opposite of the threatening in Deut. xxviii. 33, Lev. xxvi. 16. What the enemies of Israel are there described as doing, it is here said that Israel shall do himself. *Well with thee*, literally *good for thee.* The conjunction (כִּי) in the first clause is not to be construed as in Ps. cxviii. 10, but as a particle of time. *Happy thou*, or oh thy *happiness*, is an expression borrowed from Deut. xxxiii. 29.

3. *Thy wife, as a fruitful vine at the sides of thy house; thy sons, as olive-plants around thy table.* The word translated *sides* always means the edge or border, and, according to some, the innermost part. See above, on Ps.

xlviii. 3 (2). *Sons*, as usual, represent the children of both sexes. The olive-plants are emblems of luxuriance and fruitfulness. See above, on Ps. lii. 10 (8), and compare Jer. xi. 16. The Hebrew for *around* or *about* is the same as in Ps. cxxv. 2.

4. *See—for so shall be blessed the man fearing Jehovah.* The *lo* or *behold* at the beginning is equivalent to saying, Look upon this picture, for it re-presents the state of one who truly fears the Lord. Although such a con-nection between goodness and prosperity was far from uniform and constant under the Old Testament than now, it is not to be supposed that these pro-mises were actually verified in the experience of every godly Israelite. This has led some of the most eminent interpreters to the conclusion, that the promises of this psalm are not personal at all, but addressed to an ideal person representing the whole class of true believers, the true Israel.

5. *Jehovah bless thee out of Zion, and look thou upon the welfare of Jerusalem.* The consecution of the future and imperative is the same as in Ps. cx. 2. The latter might, therefore, be translated as a promise, *the Lord shall bless thee*, but the optative meaning seems more natural in this connection. In either case, the imperative conveys substantially the same idea. See above, on Ps. xxxvii. 3, 4, 27. *From Zion*, as his earthly resi-dence, the seat of the theocracy. See above, on Ps. xx. 3 (2). *Look upon*, with joy and triumph. See above, on Ps. xxii. 18 (17), xxxvii. 14, liv. 9 (8). *Welfare*, literally *goodness*, not of character but of condition, good for-tune. The Hebrew word occurs above, Ps. cxix. 66.

6. *And see thou sons to thy sons. Peace* (be) *upon Israel !* The first clause is a virtual promise of long life—*thou shalt see thy children's children.* An interesting parallel is furnished by Zech. viii. 4, the whole of which chapter is, indeed, a prophetic commentary on this psalm. For the mean-ing of the last clause see above, on Ps. cxxv. 5.

Psalm 129

1. *A Song of the Ascents. Many* (a time) *have they distressed me from my youth—oh let Israel say !* On the recollection of deliverances in times past, ver. 1–4, rests the hope of others in time to come, ver. 5–8. The first word after the inscription properly means *much* or *too much*. See above, on Ps. cxx. 6, cxxiii. 4. But most interpreters agree in referring it to time, as in the English version, *many a time* or *often*. The *youth* of Israel, as a nation, was the period of his residence in Egypt. See Hosea ii. 17, Jer. ii. 2, xxii. 21, Ezek. xxiii. 3. For the optative meaning of the last clause, and the true sense of the Hebrew particle (נָא), see above, on Ps. cxviii. 2, cxxiv. 1. *Distressed*, persecuted or oppressed me. Compare the use of the participle in Ps. vi. 8 (7), vii. 5 (4), xxiii. 5.

2. *Many* (a time) *have they distressed me from my youth; yet have they not prevailed against me.* The statement in the first verse is repeated, for the sake of being joined with one of a more cheering character. *Yet*, literally *also*. As if he had said; it is true that they have so done, but it is *also* true, &c. *Prevailed against me*, literally *been able* (as) *to me, i.e.* able to accomplish their designs respecting me. See Gen. xxxii. 26 (25), and com-pare Ps. xiii. 5 (4).

3. *Upon my back ploughed ploughers; they made long their furrows.* The expression *on my back* seems to shew that the allusion is to wounds pro-

duced by stripes. As if he had said, my back was furrowed by their whips
or scourges. We have here then an example of the image of an image.
The ploughing is a figure for scourging, and the scourging a figure for the
manifold sufferings inflicted upon Israel by his cruel enemies.

4. *Jehovah (is) righteous; he cut the cord of the wicked.* He is righteous,
and therefore faithful to his promise, and to his covenant engagements to
his people. The *cord* (not *cords*) is that which fastened the ox to the
plough. This continuation of the figure in ver. 3 is much more natural
than the assumption of a new one, that of confinement by the tying of the
limbs, as in Ps. ii. 3. According to the first translation above given, the
meaning of the clause is, that Jehovah put an end to their inflictions by a
violent separation from their victim.

5. *Shamed and turned back are* (and shall be) *all haters of* Zion. What
Jehovah has already done for Zion, as recorded in ver. 4, creates and justifies the confident belief that he will do still more. This language was peculiarly appropriate to Israel at the Restoration, when the main deliverance
had already been accomplished, but others were still needed to complete
the happy revolution. With the first clause compare Ps. vi. 11 (10),
xxxv. 4 (3), xl. 14 (13).

6. *They shall be like the grass of the house-tops, which, before one pulls
(it) withers.* The flat roofs of the oriental houses being often covered with
earth, grass and weeds readily spring up, but having no depth of root soon
wither. Compare my note on Isa. xxxvii. 27, from which place the figure
is here borrowed. The common version (*afore it groweth up*) is founded on
Jerome's (*statim ut viruerit*). The other is supported by the Septuagint
and Vulgate (πρὸ τοῦ ἐκσπασθῆναι, *priusquam evellatur*), and by the usage of
the verb (שָׁלַף) in the sense of drawing (a sword), drawing off (a shoe), &c.

7. (With) *which the reaper fills not his hand and his bosom,* (when) *binding sheaves.* The ephemeral and worthless vegetation of the house-top is
contrasted still further with the useful products of the earth, in order to
contrast still more strongly the end of the righteous and the wicked. The
last Hebrew word is translated above strictly as a participle of the verb (עָמַר)
to bind or gather sheaves, and may agree with (קוֹצֵר) *reaper* in the first
clause. Since the latter, however, is itself a participle used as a noun,
most interpreters put the same construction on the other word, and suppose
it to denote a different person from the reaper. *With which the reaper fills
not his hand nor his bosom the sheaf-binder.* The word translated *bosom* is
explained by lexicographers to mean the front fold of the oriental robe, in
which things are carried. It might also be translated *lap.* Hengstenberg's
version is *his arm.* Compare my note on Isa. xlix. 22.

8. *Nor do the passers by say, The blessing of Jehovah* (come) *unto you,
we bless you in the name of Jehovah.* The negative description is still carried
out, with unusual distinctness and particularity. This verse affords an
interesting glimpse of ancient harvest usages, confirmed by the historical
statement in Ruth ii. 4, from the analogy of which place it is altogether
probable, although denied by some, that there is here allusion to the alternate or responsive salutations in common use among the people. We may
then supply in thought before the last clause, *nor receive the customary
answer.* As the Hebrew preposition before *you* does not mean *on* but *to*
or *unto*, it seems better to supply *come* than *be.* With this verse compare
Ps. cxviii. 26.

Psalm 130

1. *A Song of Ascents. Out of the depths do I invoke thee, O Jehovah!* This is the penitential psalm of the series, in which the guilt of the chosen people is distinctly acknowledged, as the cause of its calamities, but not as an occasion of despair. After an introductory petition to be heard, ver. 1, 2, comes the indirect confession of sin, ver. 3, 4, then an expression of strong confidence, ver. 5, 6, and an exhortation to Israel to indulge the same, ver. 7, 8. The distinction made in this last stanza, between Israel at large and the penitent who utters the previous confession, would seem to shew, that the latter is to be conceived of as an individual, and not as representing the whole people. But the best interpreters are of opinion, that the distinction is entirely formal, and that the object of address in the last stanza is identical with the person speaking in the others. See above, on Ps. lxix. 3, 15 (2, 14), and compare Isa. li. 10, in all which places the word translated *depths* occurs, and in the same sense, as a figure for extreme dejection and distress. The figure itself is also used in Ps. xl. 3 (2), Ezek. xxvii. 34.

2. *Lord, hearken to my voice ; let thine ears be attentive to the voice of my supplications.* The first word in Hebrew is (אֲדֹנָי) the one strictly meaning *Lord*, and shewing that the prayer is offered to a sovereign God. The common verb (שָׁמַע) *to hear* is here construed with a preposition (בְּ), thus resembling, in its syntax, our verbs *hearken, listen.* The adjective *attentive* is peculiar to the later Hebrew, though its verbal root is of frequent occurrence in the psalms. *Supplications*, prayers for grace or mercy. See above, on Ps. xxviii. 6, xxxi. 23 (22).

3. *If iniquities thou mark, O Jah—O Lord, who shall stand?* This interrogation clearly implies consciousness of guilt, and is therefore an indirect confession of it. To *mark* is to note, take notice of, observe. The Hebrew verb is used in precisely the same manner, Job x. 14, xiv. 16. To *stand* is to stand one's ground, maintain one's innocence, and perhaps in this case, to endure one's sentence. See above, on Ps. i. 6, and compare Nah. i. 6, Mal. iii. 2. The question is equivalent to a strong negation, or an affirmation that none can stand.

4. *For with thee (there is) forgiveness, to the intent that thou mayest be feared.* The *for* has reference to a thought suppressed but easily supplied. Since none can stand, O Lord, forgive, *for* with thee, &c. Or, since none can stand, our only hope is in free forgiveness, *for* with thee, &c. *With thee*, belonging to thee, exercised by thee. The word rendered *forgiveness* is peculiar to the later Hebrew; its plural form occurs in Neh. ix. 17. *The forgiveness* that we need, *the* (only) *forgiveness* that is available or attainable. *To the intent*, for this very purpose, not merely *so that*, as an incidental consequence. *Fear* or godly reverence is here represented as one fruit and evidence of pardoned sin.

5. *I wait for Jehovah—my soul waits—and in his word do I hope.* The last verb also means *to wait for* his word, *i. e.* the fulfilment of his promise, as in Ps. cxix. 74, 81, 82, 114, 147. *My soul waits*, I wait with all my soul or heart. My powers and affections are absorbed in this earnest expectation.

6. *My soul* (waits) *for the Lord more than* (those) *watching for the morning—watching for the morning.* There is something beautiful and touching

in this simple repetition, though it is not easy to account for its effect, which is sensibly impaired by the attempt made in the English version to relieve the baldness of the iteration, *I say more than they that watch for the morning.* The comparison suggested is between the impatience of nocturnal watchers for the break of day and that of sufferers for relief, or of convicted sinners for forgiveness.

7. *Hope thou, Israel, in Jehovah ; for with Jehovah* (is) *mercy and abundantly with him redemption.* The third person used in the English Bible (*let Israel hope in the Lord*) is an inaccuracy the more remarkable because not found in the Prayer Book Version (*O Israel, trust in the Lord*). In Jehovah, literally to him, *i.e.* look to him with confident expectation, as in Isa. li. 5. The construction in the last clause is idiomatic, and not susceptible of close translation. The word corresponding to *abundantly* is the infinitive of a verb meaning to increase or multiply, but is often used adverbially in the sense of much, greatly, or abundantly. See above, on Ps. li. 4 (2). *Redemption,* deliverance, especially from bondage, that of Babylon in Ps. cxi. 9, that of sin or condemnation in the case before us.

8. *And He will redeem Israel from all his iniquities.* The pronoun is emphatic ; only trust him for redemption, and he will himself redeem thee. As the first clause shews by whom Israel is to be redeemed, to wit, by God alone, so the second shews from what, to wit, from sin, as the cause of his sufferings. This is a very significant variation of the older passage, Ps. xxv. 22, where the sufferings alone are expressly mentioned.

Psalm 131

1. *A Song of Ascents. By David. O Jehovah, not haughty is my heart, and not lofty are my eyes, and I meddle not with great* (*things*) *and* (with things) *too wonderful for me.* This short psalm is perfectly in David's manner, as well as his spirit, displaying in a high degree that childlike royalty, in which he is resembled by no other even of the sacred writers. *Haughty,* literally *high,* but with particular reference to *hauteur* or loftiness of spirit. Lofty eyes are mentioned elsewhere by David himself as a sign of pride. See Ps. xviii. 28 (27), ci. 5. The elation here described is elsewhere represented as the natural fruit of undisturbed prosperity. See Deut. xxxii. 15, 2 Chron. xxvi. 16, xxxii. 25. This confirms the Davidic origin of the psalm, and shews that it was only adapted by the later writer to his own purpose, when the original conception would have been almost impossible. *Meddle,* literally *walk* or *walk about* , *i. e.* employ or (as the English versions have it) exercise myself. *Too wonderful for me,* wonderfully done (more) than I (can comprehend). The great and wonderful things meant are God's secret purposes and sovereign means for their accomplishment, in which man is not called to co-operate but to acquiesce. As David practised this forbearance by his patient expectation of the kingdom, both before and after the death of Saul, so he here describes it as a characteristic of the chosen people.

2. (God knows) *if I have not soothed and quieted my soul, as a weaned* (child leans) *upon his mother; as a weaned* (child leans) *on me my soul.* The first clause contains a strong asseveration, in the idiomatic form of an ancient oath, very feebly represented by our adverb *surely.* See above, on Ps. lxxxix. 36 (35). The word translated *soothed* means rather *smoothed,* levelled, as in Isa. xxviii. 25. *Quieted,* stilled, hushed, reduced to silence.

The repeated use of the preposition *on* in this connection is so marked and striking, that it seems to make it necessary to supply a verb with which it may be construed. This is certainly better than to give it a different meaning in the two clauses, or in both one which does not belong to it. In the version above given, the comparison suggested is between a weaned child, quietly reposing on its mother's breast, without desiring to be suckled as of old, and the soul of the Psalmist, by a bold conception represented as his child, and acting in like manner. Hengstenberg denies that there is any reference to the mother's milk, or that *weaned* has any other meaning here than that of infant or young child, as in Isa. xi. 8, xxviii. 9. The comparison is then coincident with that in Mat. xviii. 3, 4. But the use of the word *weaned*, which was here required by no parallelism as in Isaiah, and the singular aptness of the figure suggested by the word when strictly understood, have led most interpreters, and will probably lead most readers, to prefer the obvious and strict interpretation.

3. *Hope thou, Israel, in Jehovah from now even to eternity.* This is the opposite of the feeling disavowed in the preceding verses. From the first clause that of Ps. cxxx. 7 was no doubt borrowed by the later writer, who prefixed that psalm to the one before us. With the last clause compare Ps. cxxi. 8.

Psalm 132

1. *A Song of Ascents. Remember, O Jehovah, for David, all his affliction.* This psalm contains a commemoration of David's zeal for the house of God, ver. 1–9, and a prayer that it may be rewarded by the fulfilment of the promise to him and to his house, ver. 10–18. The common version (*remember David and all his afflictions*) omits a preposition and inserts a conjunction, both without necessity. The same verb and preposition (זכר ל) are combined elsewhere, in the sense of remembering something in a person's favour, to his advantage, for his benefit. See above, on Ps. xcviii. 3, cvi. 45, cxix. 49. So here : remember, in behalf of David how he was distressed. The common version of this last phrase (*all his afflictions*) supposes the Hebrew word (עֻנּוֹת) to be a plural noun, whereas it is the infinitive of the passive verb (עֻנָּה) to be afflicted or distressed (Ps. cxix. 71), and is therefore more correctly rendered in the Prayer Book (*all his trouble*). The precise sense is, *his being afflicted.* The distress referred to is the great anxiety which David felt, first to reunite the ark and tabernacle, and then to build a more permanent sanctuary. This zeal for the house of God is one of the most characteristic features in the history of David, and for this he was rewarded, not only with a promise that his son should execute his favourite design, but also with a promise that God would build a house for him, by granting a perpetual succession in his family upon the throne of Judah. This promise seemed to be forgotten at the time of the Captivity, and even after the first Restoration, when the house of David was reduced so low, that its hereditary representative, Zerubbabel, never even bore the royal title. The form of the petition in this verse is copied from that of Solomon, at the dedication of the temple, as recorded in 2 Chron. vi. 42.

2. *Who swore to Jehovah, vowed to the Mighty One of Jacob.* This last expression is borrowed, both here and in Isa. i. 24, from Jacob himself. See Gen. xlix. 24.

3. *If I go into the tent* (which is) *my house, if I go upon the bed* (which is) *my couch.* The elliptical form of swearing here used is equivalent to saying, *I will not go.* See above, on Ps. cxxxi. 2. *The tent my house, the couch my bed,* are mere poetical expressions for the house where I dwell, the couch where I lie. Instead of being in apposition, however, they may be in regimen *the tent of my house, the couch of my bed, i.e.* the dwelling place of my house, the resting-place of my bed.

4. *If I give sleep to my eyes, to my eylids slumber.* This is a part of the sentence begun in ver. 3 and completed in ver. 5. The promise is, of course, not to be absolutely understood, but as meaning, that he would not sleep at ease, or abandon himself to undisturbed repose, till the condition was complied with.

5. *Until I find a place for Jehovah, dwellings for the Mighty One of Jacob.* The implication in the first clause, that Jehovah was without a place on earth, may remind us of Christ's memorable saying, Mat. viii. 20, Luke ix. 58. The word translated *dwellings* is peculiarly expressive, because, although strictly a generic term, it is specially applied in usage to the sanctuary with its enclosures and appendages. See above, on Ps. lxxxiv. 2 (1).

6. *Lo, we heard it in Ephrathah; we found it in the fields of the wood.* These are most probably the words of David and his contemporaries, with respect to the recovery of the ark. *We heard it,* or heard of it, *i. e.* of the ark, implying that they did not see it, that it was out of public view. *In Ephrathah* has been variously explained. Some suppose it to mean Ephraim, as *Ephrathi* means an Ephraimite, and apply the words to Shiloh, where the ark was long deposited. But *Ephrathah* itself is never so used elsewhere, and the ark, while at Shiloh, was as much in public view as at Jerusalem. Others, because *Bethlehem Ephrathah* and *Bethlehem Judah* are convertible expressions (1 Sam. xvi. 12, Micah v. 1), make Ephrathah another name for Judah, which it never is, however, when it stands by itself. The only explanation, equally agreeable to usage and the context, is that which makes Ephrathah the ancient name of Bethlehem (Gen. xlviii. 7), here mentioned as the place where David spent his youth, and where he used to hear of the ark, although he never saw it till long afterwards, when he found it in the fields of the wood, or in the neighbournood of *Kirjath-jearim,* which name means Forest-town or City of the Woods. Compare 1 Sam. vii. 1 with 2 Sam. vi. 3, 4.

7. *Let us come to his dwellings; let us bow down to his footstool.* Another step is here taken in reviewing the history of the sanctuary and of David's zeal for it. These are such words as might have been spoken at the public and solemn introduction of the ark into Jerusalem. As if it had been said, the ark of God has long been lost or out of sight, but now that a dwelling is provided for it on mount Zion, let us come, &c. Without any material change of sense, the future form may be retained, and the paragogic augment understood to express a strong determination. Now that the ark is established on mount Zion, we will come, &c. With respect to the representation of the ark as the footstool of Jehovah, and the act of bowing down to it, see above on Ps. xcix. 5.

8. *Arise, Jehovah, to thy resting-place, thou and the ark of thy strength.* Here again the form of expression is borrowed from the words of Solomon at the dedication of the temple, as recorded in 2 Chron. vi. 41. This shews that the Psalmist regarded Solomon as merely carrying out his father's plan, or acting as the executor of his will, which is in fact the mutual relation of these personages as they appear in sacred history. A more remote allusion may be traced to Num. x. 35. See above, on Ps. lxviii. 2 (1). The word translated *resting-place*, has here its proper meaning as a local noun. The last clause shews the true import of the ark in the Mosaic system, as a pledge and token of Jehovah's presence, so that its solemn entrance into Zion was the entrance of the Lord himself, and to bow down to it was to worship him. *The ark of thy strength* is by some, in accordance with a common Hebrew idiom, resolved into *thy ark of strength*, and that into *thy strong* (or *mighty*) *ark*. It is simpler, however, and in this case yields a better meaning, to retain the original expression in its obvious sense, the ark which assures us of the presence and exertion of thy power for our protection.

9. *Let thy priests be clothed with righteousness, and let thy saints shout (or sing)*. This is the conclusion of the sentence quoted from 2 Chron. vi. 41. Instead of *righteousness* we there read *salvation*, which has led some to explain the two words as synonymous, while others understand by *righteousness* the practical justification which salvation carries with it. Another possible construction is to take the righteousness as that of God, which is displayed in the salvation of his people, and in which his priests, who officially declared it, might be said to clothe themselves. See the same figure in Job xxix. 14. *Saints*, gracious ones, or true believers. The parallel passage has, *rejoice in good* or *goodness*.

10. *For the sake of David thy servant, turn not away the face of thine Anointed*. The most obvious construction of this verse is that which makes it intercede, on the ground of the divine partiality to David, for another person, supposed by some to be one or more of his successors in the kingly office, by others Israel at large. A comparison, however, of the place from which the words are borrowed (2 Chron. vi. 42) and of ver. 17 below, makes it highly probable that both clauses relate to David himself. This may be rendered clearer and more natural by making the first clause an elliptical petition, entirely distinct from the second. *For the sake of David thy servant* (grant these requests which are really his); *turn not away* (his face which is) *the face of thine Anointed*. The frequency with which God is urged to hear and answer prayer *for David's sake* (1 Kings xi. 12, 13, xv. 4, 2 Kings viii. 19, &c.), is not to be explained by making *David* mean the promise to David, nor from the personal favour of which he was the object, but from his historical position, as the great theocratical model, in whom it pleased God that the old economy should reach its culminating point, and who is always held up as the type and representative of the Messiah, so that all the intervening kings are mere connecting links, and their reigns mere repetitions and continuations of the reign of David, with more or less resemblance as they happened to be good or bad. Hence the frequency with which his name appears in the later Scriptures, compared with even the best of his successors, and the otherwise inexplicable transfer of that name to the Messiah himself. It is in this unique character and office, as the Servant of the Lord, that David is here mentioned, first by his own name, and then as the Anointed King of Israel, whose face Jehovah is entreated not to turn away, a figure for refusing him an audience, or at least denying his petition, which we know to have been used in David's times. See the Hebrew of 1 Kings ii. 16, 17, 20.

11. *Sworn hath Jehovah to David* (in) *truth, he will not turn back from it : Of the fruit of thy body I will place on the throne for thee*. See above, on Ps. lxxxix. 4, 36 (3, 35), and compare 2 Sam. vii. 28. *Turn back,*

recede from his engagement, or fail to perform it. *Of the fruit*, from among thy posterity or offspring. *On the throne*, literally *to* or *for* it. See above, on Ps. ix. 5 (4). *For thee*, in thy place, as thy representatives, or (*belonging*) *to thee*, *i. e.* thy throne.

12. *If thy sons will observe my covenant and my testimonies which I teach them*, (then) *likewise their sons unto perpetuity shall sit upon the throne for thee*. This is the condition of the promise, the breach of which accounts for the apparent violation of the promise itself. Such a suspension of the promise was not only just in itself, but foreseen and provided for (2 Sam. vii. 14, 15), as something perfectly consistent with the perpetuity of the engagement. *I teach you* refers not only to external legislation, but to spiritual guidance and illumination.

13. *For Jehovah has chosen Zion, has desired* (*it*) *for a dwelling for him.* Besides the oath and promise made directly to David, the petition of the psalm is here enforced by the divine choice of Zion, which was inseparably connected with the exaltation of the family of David. See the same thing asserted or implied, Ps. xliii. 2 (1), lxv. 2 (1), cxxv. 2. As in ver. 11, 12, the last words in Hebrew (לו) may be also rendered *to him*, belonging to him, *his dwelling*.

14. *This is my resting-place to perpetuity ; here will I dwell, because I have desired it.* These are the words of God, though not expressly so described. See above, on Ps. lxxxvii. 4, lxxxix. 4, 5 (3, 4). The word translated *dwell* means originally to *sit*, and especially to sit enthroned, so that this idea would be necessarily suggested with the other to a Hebrew reader. See above, on Ps. xxix. 10, lv. 20 (19), cii. 13 (12), cxxiii. 1.

15. *Her provision I will bless, I will bless ; her poor I will satisfy* (with) *bread.* The repetition of the verb may express either certainty or fulness. *I will surely bless*, or *I will bless abundantly.* See above, on Ps. cxxvi. 6. The word translated *provision* is a cognate form to that in Ps. lxxviii. 25. *Satisfy*, amply or abundantly supply.

16. *And her priests I will clothe with salvation ; and her saints shall shout, shall shout* (for joy). This is the promise corresponding to the prayer in ver. 9. The word *salvation*, for which *righteousness* was substituted there, is here restored from the original passage, 2 Chron. vi. 41. The last verb in Hebrew means to express joy by shouting or singing. As to the emphatic repetition, see above, on ver. 15.

17. *There will I make to bud a horn for David ; I have trimmed a lamp for mine Anointed.* These are common figures in the Scripture for strength and prosperity. See above, on Ps. xviii. 11 (10), 29 (28), lxxxix. 18 (17), xcii. 11, and compare 1 Sam. ii. 1, 2 Sam. xxi. 17, Ezek. xxix. 21. The last clause contains an allusion to the law, which cannot be preserved in any version. The word translated *lamp* is used to designate the several burners of the golden candlestick (Exod. xxv. 37, xxxv. 14, xxxvii. 23, xxxix. 37), and the verb here joined with it is the one applied to the ordering or tending of the sacred lights by the priests (Exod. xxvii. 21, Lev. xxiv. 3). The meaning of the whole verse is, that the promises of old made to David and to Zion should be yet fulfilled, however dark and inauspicious present appearances.

18. *His enemies I will clothe with shame, and on him shall bloom his crown.* The pronouns refer to David, as the Lord's Anointed, mentioned in ver. 17. The figure in the first clause is the converse or counterpart of that in ver. 9, 16, and the same with that in Ps. xxxv. 26, cix. 29. With the last clause compare Ps. lxxxix. 40 (39). The verb to *bloom* or *blossom* agrees

well with the idea of a wreath or chaplet. Compare the ἀμαράντινον στέφανον of 1 Pet. v. 4. Some prefer, however, to retain what they regard as the original meaning of the Hebrew verb; *on him shall his crown shine* (or glitter). See above, on Ps. lxxii. 16.

Psalm 133

1. *A Song of Ascents. By David. Behold, how good and how pleasant (is) the dwelling of brethren also together.* This psalm is an effusion of holy joy occasioned by the sight of the gathering of Israel as one great household at the yearly feasts. It is distinguished from the later compositions of this series by the absence of complaint or lamentation, while its freshness and vivacity and antique phraseology confirm the title which ascribes it to David. The idiomatic use of (גַּם) *also* in the last clause is not easily transferred to any other language. The meaning may be, that although the children of Israel were *brethren* even when divided and dispersed, it was only in these great convocations that, besides being thus related to each other, they *also* actually dwelt together. There might likewise be allusion, in the first instance, to the previous jealousies and alienations in the family of Israel, which seemed to be exchanged for mutual concord and affection, on David's accession to the throne of the whole nation.

2. *Like the oil, the good (oil), on the head, running down upon the beard, the beard of Aaron, which runs down to the edge of his robes.* The joyous character of this great family meeting suggests the "oil of joy" (Isa. lxi. 3), the standing symbol of festivity, to which a more specific and religious character is then imparted by a beautiful transition to the *good oil* (*i.e.* sweet and costly), with which Aaron was anointed (Exod. xxix. 7, xxx. 22, xl. 13), as a sign of consecration and of spiritual influences. See above, on Ps. ii. 2. As we read of the anointing of no subsequent High Priest, except prospectively (Lev. xxi. 10, Num. xxxv. 25), the reference here may be confined to Aaron himself. This is alleged to have differed from the unction of the other priests, by adding to the simple application of the oil to certain parts of the body, a copious affusion on the head, extending to the beard and even to the sacerdotal vestments. Some interpreters apply the last clause to the beard itself as reaching down to the mouth (פִּי) or opening at the neck of the official tunic. But the repetition of the verb (יֹרֵד), and the strong improbability that so much stress would have been laid upon the length of the beard, to which nothing is compared and which illustrates nothing, seem decisive in favour of the other explanation.

3. *Like the dew of Hermon, which comes down upon the mountains of Zion; for there has Jehovah commanded the blessing, even life for evermore.* The comparison with oil is now exchanged for one with dew, suggesting the idea of a refreshing, fertilizing influence. As the general comparison with *oil* is rendered more specific by the mention of the kind most highly valued, because made under the divine direction and applied to a most sacred use, so the general term *dew* is specified in like manner as the dew of Hermon, the dew falling on the lofty heights of Antilibanus. See above, on Ps. lxxxix. 13 (12). How this dew could be said to fall upon the mountains of Zion, is a question which has much divided and perplexed interpreters. Some have assumed a peculiar theory or system of physics on the writer's part.

Others suppose *dew of Hermon* to be merely descriptive of the quality, irre-
spective of the actual place of the deposit.   Simpler and more natural than
either of these, although not without difficulties of its own, is the interpretation which restricts the comparison itself to the first few words, and
includes all that follows in the application.   *Like the dew of Hermon* (is
the influence) *which descends upon the hills of Zion, for there,* &c., the last
clause then explaining what this influence was.   Whether this be the true
solution of the question as to form or not, it is no doubt the essential
meaning of the passage, upon any exegetical hypothesis whatever.   The
dew of Hermon was mere moisture, but the dew of Zion was the promise
of eternal life, there made and verified.   *Even life for evermore,* literally
life even to eternity.

Psalm 134

1. *A Song of Ascents.   Behold! bless Jehovah, all ye servants of Jehovah,
those standing in the house of Jehovah by night.*   The whole series of pilgrimage songs closes, in the most appropriate manner, with a summons to
bless the Lord, addressed by the people on arriving at the sanctuary to the
priests there in attendance, ver. 1, 2, and indirectly answered by a priestly
blessing on the worshippers themselves, ver. 3.   The *lo* or *behold* at the
beginning is equivalent to saying, *See, we are here,* or *we are come.*   To
bless God, as in all other cases, is to praise him in a reverential and adoring manner.   The *servants of the Lord* here meant are not his people indiscriminately, but his official servants, and most probably the priests, as will
appear from ver. 3 below.   *The (ones) standing,* the appropriate posture of
attendants, even in the courts of earthly monarchs.   *By night,* literally *in
the nights,* which does not, however, necessarily mean *all night* (1 Chron.
ix. 33), as appears from Ps. xcii. 3, where it stands opposed to *in the
morning,* and may therefore denote simply *in the evening,* with specific reference, as some suppose, to the *evening sacrifice,* with which the daily service
of the priests concluded.   We may then assume, although we cannot prove,
that the pilgrims were accustomed to reach the sanctuary at that hour,
singing this last " song of ascents."
2. *Raise your hands to the holy place, and bless Jehovah !*   The gesture
mentioned in the first clause symbolized the raising of the heart to God.
See above, on Ps. xxviii. 2, lxiii. 5 (4).   The word for *holy place* or *sanctuary* is the same in form with that so frequently translated as an abstract,
holiness.   For its local meaning, see above, on Ps. xx. 3 (2).   It here denotes the temple or its site, as distinguished from the courts around it.
As to the act of praying *to* or *towards it,* see above, on Ps v. 8 (7), xcix. 5.
3. *Jehovah bless thee out of Zion, Maker of heaven and earth.*   As the
priests were called upon to bless God in behalf of the people, so here they
bless the people in behalf of God.   Between the verses we may suppose the
previous request to be complied with.   The priests, having blessed God,
turn and bless the people.   The obvious allusion to the sacerdotal blessing, Num. vi. 23–27, favours the optative construction of this verse, which
really includes a prediction (*the Lord will bless thee*).   *Out of Zion,* as in
Ps. cxxviii. 5.   *Maker of heaven and earth,* and therefore infinitely able to
fulfil this prayer.   See above, on Ps. cxv. 15, cxxi. 2, cxxiv. 8.

Psalm 135

THE people of Jehovah are exhorted to praise him as their peculiar God, ver. 1–4, as the God of nature, ver. 5–7, as the deliverer of Israel from Egypt and in Canaan, ver. 8–12, as their hope also for the future, ver. 13, 14, rendered more glorious by contrast with the impotence of idols, ver. 15–18, after which the psalm concludes as it began, with an exhortation to praise God, ver. 19–21. According to Hengstenberg's arrangement and distribution, this is the first of a series of twelve psalms (cxxxv.–cxlvi.), sung at the completion of the second temple, and consisting of eight Davidic psalms (cxxxviii.–cxlv.), preceded by three (cxxxv.–cxxxvii.), and followed by one (cxlvi.) of later date. In this way he accounts for the omission of these ancient psalms in the former part of the collection, because they were no longer looked upon as independent compositions, but as inseparable parts of the series or systems into which they had been introduced.

1. *Hallelujah! Praise the name of Jehovah. Praise (it), ye servants of Jehovah!* The close of the psalm shews that although the priests are included (ver. 19) among the *servants of Jehovah,* they are not exclusively intended, as in Ps. cxxxiv. 1. Even there, however, the priests are representatives of Israel at large.

2. *Who (are) standing in the house of Jehovah, in the courts of the house of our God.* The participle indicates continued action. The mention of the courts confirms what has been already said, as to the objects of address in ver. 1.

3. *Hallelujah* (praise ye Jah!) *for good (is) Jehovah. Make music to his name, for it is lovely.* The last words may also be translated, *he is lovely, i. e.* an object worthy of supreme attachment.

4. *For Jacob did Jah choose for himself, Israel for his own possession.* They are particularly bound to praise him, as his chosen and peculiar people. The last word in Hebrew means a possession of peculiar value, set apart and distinguished from all others. See Exod. xix. 5, Deut. vii. 6, xiv. 2, xxvi. 18.

5. *For I know that great is Jehovah, and our Lord (more) than all gods.* However ignorant the world may be of his superiority, I, the representative of Israel, and as such speaking in his name, know and am assured of the truth from my own observation and experience.

6. *All that Jehovah will he does in the heavens and in the earth, in the seas and all depths.* Compare Ps. cxv. 3, Eccles. viii. 3, Jonah i. 14, Isa. xlvi. 10, 11. It is not merely as their own peculiar God that they are bound to praise him, but as the universal sovereign. Heaven, earth, and sea, are put for the whole frame of nature, as in Exod. xx. 4.

7. *Causing vapours to ascend from the end of the earth—lightnings for the rain he makes—bringing out the wind from his treasures.* As certain portions of the world are specified in ver. 6 to define the extent of his dominion, so here certain natural phenomena are mentioned as the product of his power. Compare Jer. x. 13, li. 16. *From the end of the earth, i. e.* from all parts of it, not excepting the most remote. See above, on Ps. lxi. 3 (2). The second clause is by some explained to mean, *turning lightnings into rain, i. e.* causing the thunder-cloud to dissolve in rain. But this is not so natural as the common version, *he maketh lightnings for the rain, i. e.* to accompany it, or according to the paraphrase in the Prayer

Book, *sendeth forth lightnings with the rain.* With the last clause compare Job xxxviii. 22.

8. *Who smote the first-born of Egypt, from man even to beast.* From the proofs of God's supremacy in nature, he now proceeds to those in history, and especially the history of his dealings with his people and their enemies. This is precisely the relation between Ps. civ. and cv. The first example chosen here is the last and greatest of the plagues of Egypt. *From man to beast,* including both; in other words, both man and beast.

9. *Sent signs and wonders into the midst of thee, O Egypt, upon Pharaoh and on all his servants. Signs and wonders, i. e.* miracles, to wit, those which preceded and accompanied the exodus. See above, on Ps. lxxviii. 43. *In the midst of thee, O Egypt,* an expression similar to that in Ps. cxvi. 19, *in the midst of thee, O Jerusalem! Upon Pharaoh,* literally in Pharaoh and in all his servants.

10. *Who smote many nations and slew mighty kings.* To the miracles of Egypt and the Exode are now added those of Canaan and the Conquest.

11. *Sihon king of the Amorites, and Og king of Bashan, and all the kingdoms of Canaan.* Each of these three particulars is preceded in Hebrew by the preposition (לְ) *to* or *for;* and that this is not an inadvertence or an accident, appears from its repetition in the next psalm (cxxxvi. 19, 20). Though not in accordance with the usage of the verb (הָרַג) which is construed elsewhere with the verb directly, the particle must be regarded here as an objective sign, as in Ps. cxix. 3, unless we suppose the sense to be, that what had just been said in general is true in particular *as to Sihon, as to Og,* and *as to the kingdoms* (here put for the kings) *of Canaan.*

12. *And gave their land* (as) *a heritage, a heritage to Israel his people.* The land of Canaan was an inheritance to Israel, not as the heirs of the Canaanites, but because it was to be transmitted from father to son, by hereditary right and succession. See above, on Ps. cv. 44, cxi. 6.

13. *Jehovah, thy name* (is) *to eternity. Jehovah, thy memory is to generation and generation. Name* and *memory* are here equivalent expressions, meaning that by which God is remembered or commemorated, namely, his perfections as exhibited in act. The perpetuity of this implies continued or repeated acts of goodness.

14. *For Jehovah will judge his people, and for the sake of his servants will repent.* He will fulfil the promise in Deut. xxxii. 36. *He will judge* (*i.e.* do justice to) *his people.* See above, on Ps. lxxii. 2. For the sense in which repentance is ascribed to God, see above, on Ps. xc. 13.

15. *The idols of the nations* (are) *silver and gold, works of the hands of man.* The divine perfection of the Lord is now exhibited in contrast with the impotence and nullity of idols. The terms of the comparison are borrowed, with several variations, from Ps. cxv. 4–8.

16. (There is) *a mouth to them, and* (yet) *they speak not;* (there are) *eyes to them, and* (yet) *they see not.* See above, on Ps. cxv. 5, which agrees exactly with the verse before us.

17. (There are) *ears to them, and* (yet) *they hear not; likewise there is no breath in their mouth.* See above, on Ps. cxv. 6. This verse contains the most considerable variation of the passages. The second clause in both begins with the same Hebrew word (אַף ; but in the one case it is a noun, meaning the *nose,* in the other an adverb, meaning *likewise.* This kind of

variation, in which the form is retained but with a change of meaning, is
perfectly agreeable to Hebrew usage.

18. *Like them shall be those making them, every one who (is) trusting in
them.* See above, on Ps. cxv. 8, with which this verse agrees exactly. If
the meaning had been simply, those who make them *are* like them, Hebrew
usage would have required the verb to be suppressed. Its insertion, therefore, in the future form (יִהְיוּ) requires it to be rendered strictly *shall be*,
i. e. in fate as well as character. Idolaters shall perish with their perishable idols. Compare Isa. i. 31.

19. *O house of Israel, bless Jehovah! O house of Aaron, bless Jehovah!*
Having shewn what God is, in himself and in comparison with idols, he
repeats the exhortation which this description was intended to explain and
justify. With this and the next verse compare Ps. cxv. 9–11, cxviii. 2–4.
Instead of *trust* we have here *bless*, as at the beginning of the Psalm. Compare Ps. cxxxiv. 1.

20. *O house of Levi, bless Jehovah! Fearers of Jehovah, bless Jehovah!*
The Levites are not particularly mentioned in the parallel passages.

21. *Blessed (be) Jehovah from Zion—inhabiting Jerusalem—Hallelujah!*
There is here an allusion to Ps. cxxxiv. 3. As Jehovah blesses out of
Zion, so also he is blessed out of Zion, by the diffusion of his praise, as
from a radiating centre. This is said to be the only place in which Jeru-
salem is put for Zion, as the earthly residence of God. But see above, on
Ps. lxxvi. 3 (2), and compare Ps. cxxv. 1, 2.

Psalm 136

IN theme and structure, this psalm resembles that before it, a resemblance
rendered still more striking by particular coincidences of expression. In
this case also, the people are invited to praise Jehovah, ver. 1–3, as the
God of nature, ver. 4–9, as the deliverer of Israel from Egypt, ver. 10–15,
his guide in the wilderness, ver. 16, the conqueror of his enemies, ver.
17–24, the provider of all creatures, ver. 25, and the God of heaven, to
whom, in conclusion, praise is again declared to be due, ver. 26. The
grand peculiarity of form in this psalm, by which it is distinguished from
all others, is the regular recurrence, at the close of every verse, of a burden
or *refrain*, like the responses in the Litany, but carried through with still
more perfect uniformity. The text or theme, which thus forms the second
clause of every verse, is one which has repeatedly occurred already, in Ps.
cvi. 1, cvii. 1, cxviii. 1–4, 29. Compare 1 Chron. xvii. 34. It has been
a favourite idea with interpreters, that such repetitions necessarily imply
alternate or responsive choirs. But the other indications of this usage in
the Psalter are extremely doubtful, and every exegetical condition may be
satisfied by simply supposing that the singers, in some cases, answered
their own questions, and that in others, as in that before us, the people
united in the burden or chorus, as they were wont to do in the Amen. See
above, on Ps. cvi. 48.

1. *Give thanks unto Jehovah—for unto eternity (is) his mercy.* This
introductory sentence is identical with those already cited from Ps. cvi.,
cvii., cxviii.

2. *Give thanks unto the God of gods—for unto eternity (is) his mercy.*
The divine title or description, both in this verse and the next, is borrowed

from Deut. x. 17. *Gods* does not here mean false gods, but is a superlative plural qualifying that before it. See above, on Ps. lxxvii. 14 (13), cxxxv. 5.

3. *Give thanks unto the Lord of lords—for unto eternity (is) his mercy.* The *Lord of lords*, i. e. the supreme Lord, the Lord by way of excellence, as in the English phrase *heart of hearts* for inmost heart.

4. *To (him) doing wondrous (things), great (things), alone—for unto eternity (is) his mercy.* Compare the expression *doing wonders*, Exod. xv. 11. *Alone*, not merely more than others, but to their exclusion. The *for*, in this and the following verses, has reference, not to what immediately precedes, but to the verb *give thanks*, to be supplied at the beginning of the sentence.

5. *To him that made the heavens in wisdom—for unto eternity (is) his mercy.* That *made*, literally *making*, perhaps in reference to the continued exercise of God's creative power. *In wisdom*, or with *understanding*. See above, on Ps. civ. 24, and compare Prov. iii. 19.

6. *To him that spread the earth above the waters—for unto eternity (is) his mercy.* That *spread*, literally *spreading*, as in ver. 5. *Above* (not upon, but higher than) *the waters*. See above, on Ps. xxiv. 2.

7. *To him that made great lights—for unto eternity (is) his mercy.* The plural *lights* (אוֹרִים) occurs only here, but is cognate and synonymous with the one used in Gen. i. 14, 16.

8. *The sun to rule by day—for unto eternity (is) his mercy.* The musical design of the composition is especially observable where the burden or chorus is interposed between inseparable parts of the same sentence, as in this one, the substance of which is borrowed from Gen. i. 16, but with some change both in the words and the construction.

9. *The moon and stars to rule by night—for unto eternity (is) his mercy.* To rule, literally *for rules* or *dominions*, perhaps because the stars are here made sharers with the moon in the dominion of the night.

10. *To him that smote Egypt in their first-born—for unto eternity (is) his mercy.* We have here the transition from nature to history, as in Ps. cxxxv. 8. *Him that smote* (or *the smiter of*) *Egypt*, i. e. the Egyptians. Hence the plural pronoun, *their first-born*.

11. *And brought out Israel from the midst of them—for unto eternity (is) his mercy.* Here for the first time we have a finite tense (the future conversive), interrupting the long series of participles, all agreeing with *Jehovah* understood.

12. *With a high hand and with an arm outstretched—for unto eternity is his mercy.* These are favourite Mosaic figures for the active and energetic exercise of power. See Exod. iii. 19, vi. 1, 6, xiii. 9, xv. 12, Deut. iv. 34, v. 15, vii. 19, xi. 2, xxvi. 8.

13. *To him that parted the Red Sea into parts—for unto eternity (is) his mercy.* *Parted* and *parts* have the same relation to each other as the Hebrew verb and noun.

14. *And made Israel to pass through the midst of it—for unto eternity (is) his mercy.* Here again we have a finite tense, not the conversive future, as in ver. 11, but the preterite. *Through the midst of it*, between the parts into which it was divided. Some suppose an allusion to the covenant transaction in Gen. xv. 17, where the word translated *parts* is the one used in ver. 13 above.

15. *And cast Pharaoh and his host into the Red Sea—for unto eternity (is) his mercy.* The first verb strictly means *knocked off* or *shook off*,

and is borrowed from Exod. xiv. 27. A passive form of it occurs above, Ps. cix. 23.

16. *To him that led his people in the wilderness—for unto eternity (is) his mercy.* Led, literally, caused to go. See above, Ps. cxx. 5. The participial construction is again resumed.

17. *To him that smote great kings—for unto eternity (is) his mercy.* Compare the parallel passage, Ps. cxxxv. 10, which is here divided by the theme or chorus. See above, on ver. 8.

18. *And slew mighty kings—for unto eternity (is) his mercy.* The first clause answers to the latter half of Ps. cxxxv. 10, with the substitution of another Hebrew word for *mighty.*

19. *Sihon king of the Amorite—for unto eternity (is) his mercy.* Literally *to, for,* or *as to* Sihon, &c. See above, on Ps. cxxxv. 11.

20. *And Og king of Bashan—for unto eternity (is) his mercy.* To, for, or as to, Og king of Bashan.

21. *And gave their land as a heritage—for unto eternity (is) his mercy. As a heritage,* literally for it. See above, on Ps. cxxxv. 12.

22. *A heritage to Israel·his servant—for unto eternity (is) his mercy.* This is the latter half of Ps. cxxxv. 12, divided from the first half by the theme or chorus.

23. *Who in our low estate remembered us—for unto eternity (is) his mercy.* In our low estate, in our humiliation, in our being humbled or reduced. Remembered us, or for us, for our benefit, as in Ps. cxxxii. 1. From the analogy of Ps. cvii. 16, 18, 26, cxv. 12, we learn that this relates to the captivity in Babylon, which is also the subject of the next psalm.

24. *And snatched us from our adversaries—for unto eternity (is) his mercy.* The first verb always denotes violent action. See above, on Ps. vii. 3 (2). It here means to snatch or tear away, as in Lam. v. 8, and has reference to the great catastrophe by which the Babylonian power was broken and the Jews set free.

25. *Giving bread to all flesh—for unto eternity (is) his mercy.* Here the description passes suddenly from God's acts of mercy towards his people to his general beneficence towards all that lives, perhaps with a design to intimate that he who thus cares for men in general and even for the lower animals, will not and cannot let his people perish. See Matt. vi. 30.

26. *Give thanks unto the God of heaven, for unto eternity (is) his mercy.* The God of heaven is a new description as to form, but substantially equivalent to that in Ps. vii. 8 (7), xi. 4, xiv. 2, xxxiii. 13, 14.

Psalm 137

THIS is the most direct and striking reminiscence of the Babylonish Exile in the whole collection, and could scarcely have been written but by one who had partaken of its trials. The first part of the psalm recalls the treatment of the Jews in Babylonia, ver. 1–6 ; the second anticipates the punishment of Edom and of Babylon, as persecuting enemies of Israel, ver. 7–9.

1. *By the rivers of Babylon, there we sat down, yea we wept when we remembered Zion.* The first word sometimes means *along,* and especially along the course of streams, as in Ps. xxiii. 2. *Babel* or *Babylon* is here put for the whole country which we call Babylonia. Its rivers are the Tigris, the Euphrates, the Chaboras, and the Ulai, with their tributary

branches. Various explanations have been given of the exiles being represented as sitting by the rivers; but none of them are so satisfactory as the
obvious and simple supposition, that the rivers are mentioned as a characteristic feature of the country, just as we might speak of the mountains of
Switzerland or the plains of Tartary, meaning Switzerland or Tartary itself.
There is emphatic; there, even in that distant heathen country. *Sat* or *sat
down*, if significant at all, may mean that they sat upon the ground as mourners.
Yea, literally *also ;* we not only sat but *also wept. When we remembered,*
literally in our remembering, *i. e.* at the time, and as the effect of our so
doing. *Zion*, not merely as the mother country or its capital, but as the
seat of the theocracy and earthly centre of the true religion.

2. *On willows in the midst of it we hung our harps.* It has been objected
that the willow is unknown in the region once called Babylonia, which is
said to produce nothing but the palm tree. Some avoid this difficulty by
explaining the whole verse as metaphorical, hanging up the harps being a
figure for renouncing music, and willows being suggested by the mention of
streams, perhaps with some allusion to associations connected with this
particular tree. It may also be observed that extraordinary changes have
taken place in the vegetable products, and especially the trees, of certain
countries. Thus the palm-tree, so frequently referred to in the Scriptures,
and so common once that cities were called after it, is now almost unknown
in Palestine.

3. *For there our captors asked of us the words of a song, and our spoilers
mirth,* (saying) *Sing to us from a song of Zion. Words of a song* may either
be an idiomatic pleonasm meaning simply song itself, or denote, as in English, the words sung as distinguished from the music. *Our spoilers* is by
some taken in a passive sense, our spoiled or plundered ones; but the
usual explanation is favoured by tradition and analogy. *One of the Songs*
can hardly be the meaning of the Hebrew phrase, in which the noun is
singular. The literal translation above given yields a perfectly good sense.
A Song of Zion is a psalm, a religious lyric, such as many of the heathen
knew to be employed in the temple worship at Jerusalem. Many interpreters suppose the object of this request to be contempt or ridicule; but the
words themselves necessarily suggest nothing more than curiosity.

4. *How shall we sing the song of Jehovah on a foreign soil ?* These are
the words with which the invitation was or might have been rejected at the
time. The question implies a moral impossibility. The idea is not that
the psalms themselves would be profaned by being sung there, but that the
expression of religious joy would be misplaced and incongruous, implying an
oblivion of the sanctuary and its forfeited advantages. *A foreign soil*, a
ground or land of strangeness. See above, on Ps. xviii. 45, 46 (44, 45).

5. *If I forget thee, O Jerusalem, let my right hand forget (its skill).* This
is a disavowal of the forgetfulness which would have been implied in yielding to the wishes of their captors. *Jerusalem* is here used precisely as
Zion is in ver. 1, 3. The object of the verb in the last clause is supposed
by some to be *me ;* let my right hand forget me, *i. e.* let me be forgotten
by myself. But most interpreters concur in the correctness of the common
version, in which *cunning* has its old English sense of *skill*. The only question
then is, whether this is to be understood indefinitely of all that the right hand
can do, and is wont to do, for the convenience of the person, or whether it
is to be understood specifically of its use in playing on an instrument. The
former is the more comprehensive meaning, but the latter is more pointed
and better suited to this context. The sense will then be : if I so far for-

get thee as to strike the harp while in this condition, let my right hand lose the power so to do.

5. *Let my tongue cleave to my palate if I do not remember thee, if I do not raise Jerusalem above the head of my rejoicing.* What he had first wished as to his power of instrumental performance, he now wishes with respect to his vocal organs. If I forget thee, let my hand for ever cease to strike the harp, and my tongue to utter sound! The most natural meaning of the last clause is the one paraphrastically given in the English version, *if I prefer not Jerusalem above my chief joy.*

7. *Remember, O Jehovah, against the sons of Edom, the day of Jerusalem,* (against) *those saying, Make bare, make bare, to the very foundation in it.* Most interpreters regard this as a kind of comment by the Psalmist on the preceding recollection of the Captivity. But the transition then seems too abrupt and unaccountable. The best explanation is, that these are still the real or supposed words of the captives, in reply to the request of their oppressors, far from granting which they break forth in a prayer for the destruction of those who had destroyed Jerusalem. As if they had said : No ; instead of singing psalms to gratify your idle or malignant curiosity, we will rather pray God to avenge the insults offered to his holy city. This interpretation is moreover recommended by its rendering the strong terms that follow more natural than if uttered in cold blood and in calm deliberation at a later period. *Remember against,* literally *for* or *with respect to.* See above, on Ps. cxxxii. 1, cxxxvi. 23, where the same idiomatic phrase is used in a favourable sense. The *day of Jerusalem* is the day of its calamity or great catastrophe. Compare Obad. 11–13, where the same crime is charged upon Edom, namely that of concurring and rejoicing in the downfall of his kinsman Israel. See also Jer. xlix. 7–22, Lam. iv. 21, 22, Ezek. xxv. 12–14.

8. *Daughter of Babylon, the desolated ! Happy (he) who shall repay to thee thy treatment wherewith thou hast treated us.* The daughter of Babylon (or virgin Babylon) is the people or kingdom of Babylonia, personified as a woman. See above, on Ps. ix. 14 (13). *The wasted* or *desolated* is the epithet belonging to her by way of eminence in prophecy and history. There is no need therefore of distinguishing between a partial and total desolation, or between that of the city and the kingdom at large. The last clause may mean nothing more than that such a revolution is at hand that he will be esteemed a fortunate man who treats thee as thou hast treated us. For the true sense of the last verb, see above, on Ps. xiii. 6 (5, 6).

9. *Happy he (who) shall seize and dash thy little ones against the stones.* This revolting act was not uncommon in ancient warfare. See 2 Kings viii. 12, Hosea xiv. 1, Nah. iii. 10, Isa. xiii. 16, 18. The more revolting, the stronger the description of the change awaiting Babylon. The day is coming when he shall be deemed fortunate who, according to the usages of war, requites thy own sanguinary cruelties. The word translated *dash* means really to dash in pieces, as in Ps. ii. 9. The act here meant is commonly expressed by (רטשׁ) a different Hebrew verb. *Taketh and dasheth* is equivocal, the first of these verbs being used in familiar English as a kind of auxiliary, whereas the corresponding verb in Hebrew denotes a distinct and independent act.

Psalm 138

THIS is the first of a series of eight psalms (cxxxviii.–cxlv.), probably the last composed by David, a kind of commentary on the great Messianic promise in 2 Sam. vii. They are found in this part of the Psalter, in consequence of having been made the basis, or rather the body, of a system or series (cxxxv.–cxlvi.), by a later writer. See above, on Ps. cxxxv. 1. The psalm before us contains an acknowledgment of God's goodness as experienced already, ver. 1-3, an anticipation of his universal recognition by the nations, ver. 4, 5, and in the mean time of additional favours to the Psalmist, or to the church of which he was the temporary head, ver. 6–8. Such a psalm was of course well suited to sustain the faith and revive the hopes of a later generation.

1. *By David.* *I will thank thee with all my heart; before gods I will praise thee.* The Davidic style and tone of composition are acknowledged even by the sceptical interpreters. *With all my heart* implies the greatness of the gift to be acknowledged, which was no doubt the promise of Messiah contained in 2 Sam. vii. See above, on Ps. ix. 2 (1). *Before gods, i. e.* in the presence, to the face, and in contempt of all imaginary rival deities. The translation *before God* is grammatical, but confounds the second and third person in a single clause. The Septuagint and Vulgate have *before angels,* which is inconsistent with the usage of the Hebrew word. *Thank thee,* in the strict sense of praising for benefits received ; or in a wider sense, *acknowledge thee* as God. *Praise thee,* make music, sing and play to thee. With this verse compare Ps. vii. 18 (17), xviii. 50 (49), liv. 8 (7), lvii. 10 (9), ci. 1.

2. *I will bow down to thy holy temple, and will thank thy name, for thy mercy and for thy truth ; for thou hast made great, above all thy name, thy promise.* With the first clause compare Ps. v. 8 (7). *Bow down,* or prostrate myself, as an act of worship. *Mercy* in promising, *truth* in performing. See above, on Ps. xxv. 10. *Above all thy name, i. e.* all the previous manifestations of thy nature. *Thy word,* literally *thy saying,* that which thou hast said, but applied specifically to the divine promise. See above, on Ps. xviii. 31 (30), cxix. 38, 50, 103, 140. The transcendent promise here referred to is that of the Messiah in 2 Sam. vii., which is there described as unique by David himself, and which forms the basis of many psalms, but especially of Ps. xviii., xxi., lxi., ci., cii., ciii., and the one before us.

3. *In the day I called and thou didst answer me, thou makest me brave in my soul (with) strength.* This may be connected with what goes before, thou didst magnify thy word in the day when I called, &c. The promise in 2 Sam. vii. was an answer to his prayer for a perpetual succession. See above, on Ps. xxi. 3, 5 (2, 4), lxi. 6 (5). The common version of the last clause (*strengthenedst me with strength in my soul*), contains a paronomasia not in the original, where the verb and noun have not even a letter in common. The verb is by some translated *made me proud, i. e.* elated me, not with a vain or selfish pride, but with a lofty and exhilarating hope. *In my soul,* as opposed to a mere outward influence. *Strength, i. e.* strength of faith and confidence in God.

4. *Jehovah, all kings of the earth shall acknowledge thee, when they have heard the sayings of thy mouth.* Not merely one king, though that king be David, shall acknowledge, thank, and praise thee, but all others who receive

the true religion, when they know what thou hast promised, and especially when they compare the promise and fulfilment, with particular reference to the promise of Messiah, which is described in Scripture as a grand means for the conversion of the nations and the chiefs which represent them. See above, on Ps. lxviii. 30, 32 (29, 31), cii. 16 (15).

5. *And they shall sing in the ways of Jehovah, for great* (shall be) *the glory of Jehovah.* The kings of the earth, representing its nations, shall join in the praise of the true God, walking in his ways, *i. e.* as converts to the true religion. Compare Micah iv. 2, Isa. iv. 3. Instead of *for* we may read *when,* as in ver. 4 ; when the glory of Jehovah has been duly exalted and diffused by the extension of the true religion. Some make this clause the theme or subject of the praise—they shall sing that the glory of Jehovah is great—a less natural construction, but one which yields an equally good sense.

6. *For lofty is Jehovah—and the low he sees—and the haughty from afar he knows.* The first two clauses may be in antithesis, *and yet he looks upon the low,* or simply co-ordinate, *and therefore he looks upon the low, i. e.* the lowly, who shall be exalted, while the opposite end of the proud is implied in the concluding declaration. Even from afar, from the distant heaven where he seems to behold nothing, he knows precisely what the proud man is, what he deserves, and what is actually to befall him. See above, on Ps. i. 1.

7. *If I go through the midst of distress, thou wilt save* (or *make*) *me alive ; upon the wrath of my enemies thou wilt stretch forth thy hand, and save me* (*with*) *thy right hand.* The first clause resembles that of Ps. xxiii. 4. *Go through* or *walk in the midst of trouble.* To *quicken* or *revive,* as in Ps. xxx. 4 (3), lxxi. 20. *Upon the wrath,* implying motion from above, which is more significant and graphic than *against.* The common version of the last words (*and thy right hand shall save me*) is equally grammatical, and found in all the ancient versions ; but the other is recommended by its ascribing the deliverance directly to God, and by the analogy of Ps. lx. 7 (5), where *hand* is adverbially construed with the same verb. See also Ps. xvii. 14.

8. *Jehovah will complete for me* (what he has begun) ; *Jehovah, thy mercy* (*is*) *for ever ; the works of thy hands do not forsake.* The work begun and yet to be completed was the whole series of God's gracious dispensations towards David and his seed, beginning with the first choice of the former and ending in the Messiah. With the first clause compare Ps. lvii. 3 (2), Phil. i. 6. The second member of the sentence might be read, *let thy mercy be for ever* or *unto eternity.* But it is more probably an affirmation, similar to that in Ps. ciii. 17, and the clause contains an appeal to the promise of eternal favour, 2 Sam. vii. 13, 26, or perhaps to the eternity of God's compassions, as a reason why he should not and could not abandon what had been so graciously begun.

Psalm 139

THE Psalmist describes God's omnipresence and omniscience, ver. 1–12, as attributes necessarily belonging to him as the Creator, ver. 13–18, and appeals to them in attestation of his own aversion to the wicked, ver. 19–24. From its collocation it is probable that this psalm records David's exercises under the powerful impressions of the great Messianic promises in 2 Sam.

vii., and is therefore to be regarded as a confession and profession made not merely for himself but for his successors on the throne of Israel, and intended both to warn them and console them by this grand view of Jehovah's constant and infallible inspection.

1. *To the Chief Musician. By David. A Psalm. Jehovah, thou hast searched me and knowest.* As a later writer could have no motive for prefixing the title *to the Chief Musician*, it affords an incidental proof of antiquity and genuineness. *Thou hast searched me*, or continually *searchest me*. The Hebrew verb originally means to *dig*, and is applied to the search for precious metals (Job xxviii. 3), but metaphorically to a moral inquisition into guilt. See above, on Ps. xliv. 22 (21), and compare Job xiii. 9. It is here used in the intermediate sense of full investigation. *Thou hast known* or *knowest* all that can result from such a scrutiny, not only my corruptions and infirmities but my cares and sorrows. The object is not expressed in this verse, which is a summary of the whole psalm, because the very object of what follows is to state it in detail.

2. *Thou knowest my sitting and my rising; thou understandest as to my thought from afar.* Sitting and rising or standing represent rest and motion, or all the various conditions of the living, waking man. See above, on Ps. i. 1, xxvii. 2. In every posture, state, and occupation, thou knowest me. The next phrase does not merely signify, thou perceivest the meaning of my thought, but thou knowest all about it, its origin, its tendency, its moral quality; *thou understandest* (every thing) *respecting it. From afar*, unimpeded by local distance, by which men are prone to imagine the divine omniscience to be circumscribed. See Job xxii. 12–14, and compare with this verse Ps. cxxxviii. 6, Jer. xxiii. 23.

3. *My path and my lair thou siftest, and with all my ways art acquainted.* Path is here put for going, lair for lying, and these, like the terms of the preceding verse, for motion and rest, or the active and passive parts of human life. The poetical word *lair* is used to represent a Hebrew one, occurring only here, but the verbal root of which is used by Moses, Lev. xviii. 23, xx. 16. The last verb means to be accustomed (Num. xxii. 30), and then by a natural association, acquainted or familiar (Job xxii. 21). *My ways*, my condition and my conduct, what I do and what I suffer.

4. *For there is not a word in my tongue,* (but) *lo, Jehovah, thou knowest all of it.* The relation of the clauses may be also expressed thus in English, *which, O Lord, thou knowest not, all of it* (or *altogether*). *In my tongue*, in its power, or, as it were, in its possession. This verse merely applies to his words specifically what was said before of all his actions. The *lo* or *behold* is equivalent to *see there*, or to the act of pointing at the words as objects of sight and as actually present.

5. *Behind and before thou dost beset me, and layest upon me thy hand.* There is here an insensible transition from God's omniscience to his omnipresence, out of which the Scriptures represent it as arising. *Behind and before, i. e.* on all sides. The idea of *above* and *below* is suggested by the last clause. *Beset*, besiege, hem in, or closely surround. *Thy hand*, or the palm of thy hand, as the Hebrew word strictly denotes.

6. *Such knowledge is too wonderful for me; it is exalted, I cannot* (attain) *to it.* The literal meaning of the Hebrew word is, *wonderful knowledge away from me*, or *more than I* (can comprehend); *it is exalted, I cannot* (do anything) *as to it.* With the word *wonderful* compare the use of the cognate verb, Deut. xxx. 11, Prov. xxx. 18. The knowledge meant is man's finite knowledge of the infinite.

7. *Whither shall I go from thy Spirit, and whither from thy face shall I flee?* The interrogation involves a denial of all possible escape from God's inspection, when a guilty conscience prompts to seek one. Compare Amos ix. 2.

8. *If I scale the heavens, there* (art) *thou; and if I spread the grave, lo thou* (art there). The word *scale* is used to represent a Hebrew verb occurring only here, and no doubt belonging to the dialect of poetry. The verb translated *spread* means specifically to spread a couch or make a bed. *If I make sheol my bed, i.e.* lie down in the grave or hell, in the wide old English sense. See above, on Ps. vi. 6 (5).

9. *I will raise the wings of day-break. I will dwell in the end of the sea.* By supplying *if,* although the sense is not materially changed, the form of expression becomes much less striking. The conditional construction is forbidden also, or at least rendered highly improbable, by the form of the second verb, expressing strong desire and resolution. The truth is, that we have here a bold transition. After speaking of guilty flight from God himself, the Psalmist now speaks of anxious flight from other enemies, and as if visibly surrounded by them, here resolves to escape from them. This, which is Hengstenberg's interpretation, is strongly favoured by the unconditional construction, although he himself retains the other. The same writer objects to the translation *raise the wings*, that before one can raise wings he must have them. But for that very reason the possession of them may be presupposed, or considered as implied in the act expressed. The same combination is employed by Ezekiel (x. 16, 19), in a way that admits of only one translation. The Hebrew word (שַׁחַר) is not the common one for morning, but one denoting day-break or the dawn. See above, on Ps. lvii. 9 (8). The point of comparison appears to be the incalculable velocity of light. The *extremity* (or *end*) *of the sea*, is added to heaven and hell, in order to convey the idea of the most remote points.

10. *Even there thy hand guides me, and thy right hand holds me.* From the use of similar expressions to denote a friendly guidance and support, in Ps. xviii. 17 (16), lv. 7–9 (6–8), v. 9 (8), xxiii. 3, xxvii. 11, lxxiii. 24, and other places, Hengstenberg infers that this must mean, when I fly to the ends of the earth before my enemies, thou art still there to protect me, and that the psalm was therefore meant not merely to alarm but to console.

11. *And I say, only darkness overwhelms me, night is the light become around me.* The ideal situation is the same as in ver. 9, one of danger and terror, in which he is constrained to say, nothing but darkness comes upon me, smites me, and the very light is turned to darkness round about me. According to this view of the passage, darkness, as in many other places, is a figure for calamity and danger. See Isa. l. 10, Ps. cxxxviii. 7. According to the usual interpretation, it denotes concealment from the eye of God.

12. *Even darkness does not make* (it) *dark to him, and night like day shines; as the darkness, so the light.* The interpretation given of the foregoing verse does not necessarily affect the sense of this, which still means that nothing can prevent God's seeing either sin or suffering, either the danger of his people or the malice of their enemies. *Make dark*, as in Ps. cv. 28. *To thee,* literally *from thee, i. e.* so as to conceal from thee.

13. *For thou possessest my reins; thou coverest me in my mother's womb.* The meaning of the first clause seems to be : thou hast in thy power and at thy control the very seat of my strongest sensibilities, my pains and plea-

sures ; and this subjection is coeval with my being, for even before birth I
was under thy protection and command, as I am now. The sense of *weaving*, which is given to the last verb by some modern writers, rests on a mere
etymological deduction, and has no foundation either in tradition or in usage.
The *for* at the beginning of this verse marks the transition from the fact of
God's omniscience to its origin or reason in his creative character and
rights. As a logical particle, the *for* relates, not to the immediately
preceding verse, but to the whole preceding context. God is omnipresent
and omniscient, *for* he is the maker of the universe.

14. *I thank thee, because fearfully I am distinguished ; wonderful (are)
thy works, and (that) my soul knoweth right (well).* He makes it a subject
of grateful acknowledgment, that God has distinguished him or made him
to differ from inferior creatures, both in constitution and in destiny. *Because*
is in Hebrew a compound particle (עַל כִּי) like *for that, forasmuch as.*
Fearfully, literally *fearful (things)*, but used adverbially, as in Ps. lxv. 6 (5).
It might here be rendered *(by) fearful (things)*. The words corresponding
to *distinguished* and *wonderful* are in Hebrew passive forms from cognate
roots (פלה and פלא). The particular statement of the first clause is resolved
by the last into the general one, of which it is a mere specification. The
concluding words express a strong and, as it were, experimental conviction
of the truth.

15. *Not hid was my frame from thee, when I was made in secret, embroidered in depths of the earth.* The *not hid* is a meiosis, implying that
God saw it clearly, and fully understood it, inasmuch as he himself created
it. *Frame*, literally *strength*, as in Deut. viii. 17, but applied to the bones
and sinews as the strength and framework of the body. See above, on
Ps. vi. 3 (2), and compare Job x. 11. The common Hebrew word for
bone differs only in the pointing. The word translated *when* is (אֲשֶׁר)
the relative pronoun, and may here retain its proper meaning, although then
not easily translated, as its antecedent is latent in the phrase *my frame*,
which may be thus resolved, *the frame of me who was made*, &c. *In secret*,
i. e. in the womb. *Embroidered*, which is the invariable meaning of the
Hebrew verb, is a bold but beautiful expression for the complicated tissue
of the human frame, in which so many and such various threads are curi-
ously interwoven. *Depths of the earth* can only be explained as a comparative expression, corresponding to *in secret* and denoting the same thing,
which it describes as no less dark and hidden from the view of men than
subterraneous caverns, or as some suppose *sheol*, the invisible world. See
above on Ps. lxiii. 10 (9), and compare Job i. 21, where the figure is inverted, and the grave is confounded with the womb.

16. *My unformed substance did thine eyes see, and in thy book all of
them are written, days are formed, and there is not one among them.* This
is one of the most obscure and doubtful verses in the book of Psalms. Its
difficulty to our own translators may be gathered from the fact, that
substance yet being unperfect answers to a single Hebrew word, and that
my members is a gratuitous addition to the text. The first word in Hebrew occurs only here, but is clearly derived from a verb which means to
roll or *roll up* (2 Kings ii. 8), and may therefore be supposed itself to signify
something rolled up or rolled together, and from this may be deduced the
sense of something shapeless or unformed, or more specifically that of an
embryo or fœtus. The next difficulty lies in the expression *all of them*,
evaded in the English Bible by changing it to *all my members*, and then

making this the subject of the plurals following. The best interpreters are now disposed to construe *all of them* with *days* by a grammatical prolepsis. In thy book all of them are written, namely, all my days, as they were planned, projected, or decreed, before as yet one of them had really existed. *Written* and *formed* are then parallel expressions. *All of them are written, days are delineated* or *depicted.* By *days* (translated in our Bible *in continuance*) we are then to understand not merely the length but the events and vicissitudes of life. See Job xiv. 5, Ps. lvi. 9 (8). This is one of those cases in which the difficulty lies in the particular expressions, while the general import of the passage is clearly determined by the context. Instead of (לֹא) *not*, the keri or marginal reading in the Hebrew Bible has (לוֹ) *to him*, a variation to which no one has succeeded in attaching a coherent sense. Precisely the same difference of text exists in Ps. c. 3.

17. *And to me how precious are thy thoughts, O God! How great is the sum of them!* Having presented this impressive view of God's omniscience, he now tells how he is himself affected by it. So far from thinking it a hardship to be subject to this scrutiny, he counts it a most valuable privilege. However others may regard this truth, *to me*, my judgment and my feelings, *how costly*, valuable, *are thy thoughts*, *i. e.* thy perpetual attention to me. For the true sense of *precious*, see above, on Ps. xxxvi. 8 (7), xlv. 10 (9). *Great is the sum*, literally *strong* (or *many*) *are their sums*, an expression which can hardly be retained in our idiom.

18. *I will count them*—(but no)—*more than sand they are many—I awake and still I* (*am*) *with thee.* The first clause is equivalent to a conditional proposition, *If I would count them*, &c., but far more striking and poetical in form. See above, on Ps. xl. 6 (5). *I am still with thee* has the same essential meaning with the similar expression in Ps. lxxiii. 23, namely, I am still in the society or company. But there the reference is chiefly to divine protection, here to meditation on the divine attributes. Thou art still before me as an object of adoring wonder, not by day only, but by night; not merely in the *watches* of the night, but even in my sleep. See above, on Ps. i. 2, xvi. 7, lxiii. 7 (6).

19. *If thou wilt slay, O God, the wicked* (*man*)*! And ye men of blood, depart from me?* The first clause is in fact, though not in form, the expression of a wish. If thou wouldst but slay! In form, there is no aposiopesis, which may be variously supplied by adding, I will praise thee, I will rejoice, it will be just, or the like. *Men of bloods*, murderers or murderous men. See above, on Ps. v. 7 (6), xxvi. 9, lv. 24 (23). *Depart from me* is the same expression as in Ps. vi. 9 (8), cxix. 15, but the main idea here is that of disavowal or repudiation. Oh that God would slay them, and until he does, I desire to have no communion with them. Compare Job xxi. 14, Mat. vii. 23.

20. *Who speak of thee for wickedness and take in vain—thy foes.* Speak of thee, or name thee, use thy name, for the accomplishment of wicked ends. The other clause will then be strictly parallel, *and take* (thy name) *in vain*, as in Exod. xx. 7. For the meaning of this difficult expression, see above, on Ps. xxiv. 4. The subject of the proposition is placed emphatically at the end.

21. *Thy haters, O Jehovah, shall not I hate, and with thine assailants be disgusted?* The simple future in the first clause comprehends several distinct shades of meaning. Do I not, may I not, must I not, hate those hating thee? Hate them, not as man hates, but as God hates. See above, on Ps. v. 6 (5). The construction of the verb and preposition in

the last clause is the same in Hebrew and in English. *Be disgusted*, literally sicken or disgust myself, abhor, or loathe. *Thine assailants*, those rising up against thee, as rebellious enemies. The Hebrew word is a noun formed from the participle used above, Ps. xvii. 7, lix. 2 (1).

22. *(With) perfection of hatred do I hate them, as enemies they are to me.* Literally *they are for enemies, i. e.* I so esteem them. As enemies of God, they must be mine.

23. *Search me, God, and know my heart; try me, and know my thoughts.* The last expression is emphatic, meaning even my most anxious and disturbed thoughts, into which corruption might most easily find entrance. See above, on Ps. xciv. 19, the only other place where the Hebrew word occurs. In this verse, he again appeals to the divine omniscience for the purity of his intentions, and thus comes back to the point from which he started.

24. *And see if a way of pain be in me, and guide me in a way of eternity.* In the first clause some translate, *the way of an idol*, an idolatrous way. But the meaning *idol* is not justified by usage. A way of pain is one that leads to suffering and misery hereafter. The opposite of this is *a way of eternity*, by which some understand an everlasting way, as distinguished from the perishable way of sinners, Ps. i. 6. Others, more probably, the way that leads to everlasting life. Usage, however, is in favour of a third and very different interpretation, which gives the Hebrew phrase (דֶּרֶךְ עוֹלָם) the same sense with a kindred one (נְתִיבוֹת עוֹלָם) used by Jeremiah (vi. 16), to wit, that of *old or ancient way*, the one pursued by prophets, patriarchs, and saints of old. Similar expressions are found in Jer. xviii. 15, Job xxii. 15, applied, in a bad sense, to the course pursued by ancient sinners. The prayer, however, still amounts to the same thing, to wit, that God would lead him in the good old way, which is itself the way to everlasting life.

Psalm 140

1. *To the Chief Musician. A Psalm. By David.* We find ourselves, in this psalm, carried back not only to the times of David, but to those of the Sauline persecution, from which the images are evidently borrowed. Besides the warlike tone, the vigorous conciseness, the verbal agreements with Davidic psalms, combined with eminent originality, the very structure is Davidic, and exhibits the familiar sequence of complaint, ver. 2–6 (1–5), prayer, ver. 7–9 (6–8), and confident anticipation, ver. 10–14 (9–13). So clearly do these features of the composition mark its origin, even independently of the inscription, that nothing can account for its position here but the hypothesis already stated, that these ancient psalms were incorporated into a series of later date, and placed in the collection, not according to their individual antiquity, but according to the date of the whole set or system, into which they had been made to enter. Like the psalms immediately preceding, this was probably composed by David after the reception of the great Messianic promise, and with immediate reference to it.

2 (1). *Deliver me, Jehovah, from the bad man; from the man of violences thou wilt preserve me.* This is one of those pictures so abundant in the genuine Davidic psalms, of which Saul seems to have furnished the

original. Compare Ps. lii. The first *man* is the generic term (אָדָם), the other the individual designation (אִישׁ), which seem, however, to be used here as equivalents. The insensible transition from direct prayer to confident anticipation is characteristic of the psalms of David. *Man of violence* is another favourite expression. See above, on Ps. xviii. 49 (48), and compare the parallel passage, 2 Sam. xxii. 49, where the plural form (*violences*) is used, as in the verse before us.

3 (2). *Who imagine evils in (their) hearts ; all the day they gather (for) battles.* That the preceding verse, notwithstanding the reference to Saul, is the description of a whole class, is clear from the plural forms in this verse. *Think*, meditate, devise, imagine. *Evils*, particularly such as are inflicted on others, well expressed in the common versions, *mischiefs*. Another construction of the last clause, preferred by some interpreters, is, *all the day they dwell with wars* (or *in wars*), *i. e.* are constantly involved in them and busied with them. This use of the verb (גּוּר) is justified by Ps. v. 5 (4), cv. 23, cxxv. 5. But the analogy of Ps. lvi. 7 (6), lix. 4 (3), is decisive in favour of the other explanation. Compare Ps. xxxi. 14 (13), xxxv. 15, Isa. liv. 15.

4 (3). *They sharpen their tongue as a serpent; the poison of an adder (is) under their lips, Selah.* Not *as a serpent (does)*, but (spiteful or venomous) *as a serpent.* See above, on Ps. lxiv. 4 (3). With the last clause compare Ps. x. 7, lviii. 5 (4). The word for *asp* or *adder* occurs only here. The only point of exegetical importance is, that it means a poisonous serpent, and is thus a specification of the general expression in the other clause.

5 (4). *Keep me, Jehovah, from the hands of the wicked (man); from the man of violences thou wilt preserve me, who have thought to subvert my steps.* A varied repetition of the prayer in ver. 1. With the last clause compare Ps. xxxv. 5, xxxvi. 13 (12), lvi. 14 (13), cxviii. 13.

6 (5). *High (ones) have hid a snare for me, and cords—they have spread out a net by the side of the road—traps have they laid for me, Selah.* This is little more than an accumulation of the various terms in which David elsewhere clothes one of his favourite figures, as if he saw his own perils reappearing in the future. *High ones, i. e.* proud or haughty men. *By the side*, literally *the hand*, as we say on either hand. The word translated *road*, according to its etymology, denotes a waggon-road, a track worn by wheels.

7, (6). *I have said to Jehovah, My God (art) thou ; give ear, Jehovah, (to) the voice of my supplications.* All the component parts of this verse are of constant occurrence in the psalms of David. With the first clause compare Ps. xvi. 2, xxxi. 15 (14). With the second, Ps. v. 2, 3 (1, 2), xvii. 1, xxviii. 2, 6 (1, 5), xxxi. 23 (22), xxxix. 13 (12), liii. 4 (3).

8 (7). *Jehovah, Lord, the strength of my salvation ; thou hast covered my head in the day of battle.* My covenant God and sovereign, whose power saves me. *Head* is preceded by a preposition (לְ), *thou hast been a covering* (or *afforded shelter*) *to* (or *for*) *my head.* The day of battle, literally of armour or of weapons, *i. e.* the day when they are used. With this verse compare Ps. v. 12 (11), lx. 9 (7), lxii. 2, 12 (1, 11), cxxxix. 13, 1 Sam. xxviii. 2.

9 (8). *Grant not, Jehovah, the desires of the wicked man—his device succeed not—they will be exalted.* Succeed not, suffer not to prosper ; literally, draw not out, *i. e.* to a successful issue. The last clause states

what would be the effect of their success; they would be elated, or exalt themselves. With this verse compare Ps. xxvii. 12, xxxi. 14 (13), xxxvii. 12, lxvi. 7 (6), Deut. xxxii. 27.

10 (9). *The head of those surrounding me—the mischief of their lips shall cover them.* The nominative absolute refers back to the covering of the Psalmist's head in ver. 8 (7). While my head is covered by the divine protection, the head of those by whom I am beset shall be covered with the consequences or the punishment of the mischief occasioned by their calumnies and insults. Or the trouble, which their lips have caused to others, shall return upon themselves. Compare Ps. vii. 17 (16). *Those surrounding me*, or, as a noun, *my surroundings*, as in 2 Kings xxiii. 5. The participle would, according to analogy and usage, mean *causing me to turn back* or *retreat* (Jer. xxi. 4), which yields a good sense here. The head of those who once drove me back shall be covered, &c.

11 (10). *Coals shall be cast upon them; into the fire he shall make them fall, and into deep waters, (whence) they shall not rise.* The first noun in Hebrew always means burning or live coals. See above, on Ps. xviii. 13, 14 (12, 13). *Shall be cast* is the keri or marginal reading, no doubt intended to relieve the harshness and obscurity of the reading in the text, *they shall cast* or *shake*, an indefinite or impersonal construction, really equivalent in meaning to the passive. In the second member of the sentence the action is ascribed to God himself. *Deep waters* answers to a single Hebrew word occurring only here, and by some supposed to mean *deep pits* or excavations. The first sense above given is founded on an Arabic analogy.

12 (11). *A man of tongue shall not be established in the land, (nor) a man of violence, a bad (man)—he shall hunt him to destruction.* A man of a calumnious unbridled tongue (James i. 26) shall not be permanently seated in a prosperous condition. See above, on Ps. ci. 7, cii. 29 (28). The next words may be variously construed; *a man of wicked violence*, or, disregarding the accents, *a man of violence, evil shall hunt him, &c.* According to the other constructions, God is the subject of the verb, as of the second in ver. 11 (10). *To destructions*, the plural form denoting fulness and completeness. Others render it *by strokes*, i. e. successive strokes; others again, *in haste*, which agrees well with the usage of the verbal root. See 2 Chron. xxvi. 20, Esth. iii. 15, vi. 12, viii. 14.

13 (12). *I know that Jehovah will do justice to the sufferer, and judgment for the poor.* Compare Ps. ix. 5, 17 (4, 16). Literally, *the right of the sufferer, the judgment of the poor.*

14 (13). *Only the righteous shall give thanks unto thy name, the upright shall sit in thy presence.* Only the righteous shall have occasion for thanksgiving. There is no need therefore of departing from the proper sense of (אַךְ) the Hebrew particle. See above, on Ps. lxxiii. 1. *Sit in thy presence,* as thy friends or guests or favoured servants. Perhaps it may mean *sit (enthroned) before thee.* Compare Mat. xix. 28. Some understand the sense to be, *shall dwell* (in the land) *before thee,* i. e. under thy protection and inspection. Compare Ps. xxi. 7 (6), xli. 13 (12), lvi. 14 (13).

Psalm 141

AFTER an introductory petition for a favourable hearing, ver. 1, 2, the Psalmist prays to be delivered from the power of temptation, ver. 3, 4, comforts himself under his afflictions as paternal chastisements, ver. 5, 6, anticipates the ruin of his enemies, ver. 7, and prays for deliverance from them in the mean time, ver. 8–10. This psalm, like the one before it, is distinguished by a pregnant brevity and the use of rare expressions, while at the same time it is full of verbal and real coincidences with the psalms of David. These indications are so clear and undeniable, that a sceptical critic of great eminence (De Wette) pronounces it one of the oldest psalms in the collection. With respect to its position in the Psalter, see the prefactory notes to Ps. cxxxv., cxl.

1. *A Psalm. By David. Jehovah, I invoke thee; hasten to me; give ear to my voice in my calling to thee.* This verse is entirely made up of phrases frequently occurring in the psalms of David. *I invoke thee,* Ps. xvii. 6. *Hasten to me,* Ps. xxii. 20 (19), lxx. 2 (1), lxxi. 12. *Hear my voice,* Ps. cxl. 7 (6). *In my calling,* Ps. iv. 2 (1).

2. *Let my prayer continue (as) incense before thee, the offering of my hands (as) the evening oblation. Continue,* literally *be established,* as in Ps. cxl. 12 (11). He prays not only for acceptance, but for constant or perpetual acceptance, as the offerings referred to were the stated daily services of the Mosaic ritual. *Incense* is in Scripture the symbol of prayer. In the books posterior to the Pentateuch it is commonly mentioned as an evening oblation (1 Kings xviii. 29, 36, 2 Kings xvi. 15, Dan. ix. 21, Ezra ix. 4, 5), perhaps because in the evening it was reckoned the main offering, whereas in the morning it was merely an appendage to the animal sacrifice. *Lifting up* is not the meaning of the Hebrew word (מַשְׂאַת) in any other place, whereas it often means a gift, and especially a portion of food (Gen. xliii. 34, 2 Sam. xi. 8), in which sense it might naturally be applied to the vegetable offerings of the Law.

3. *Set, O Jehovah, a guard at my mouth; watch over the door of my lips.* The prayer, for which he had bespoken audience and acceptance, was a prayer against the power of temptation, and first with reference to sins of speech. See above, on Ps. xxxix. 2 (1). The words translated *watch* and *door* are forms occurring only here, but etymologically near akin to others which are in common use.

4. *Incline not my heart to an evil word, to practise practices in wickedness with men* (who are) *workers of iniquity, and let me not eat of their dainties.* An *evil word* may be strictly understood, as referring still to sins of the tongue, or be taken in the idiomatic sense of an *evil matter,* which last is preferred by most interpreters. The assonance in *practise practices* is copied from the Hebrew, where the cognate verb and noun are combined in the same manner. *Practices in wickedness,* or wicked practices. The last words seem to be a prayer, that he might not be tempted, by the luxurious prosperity of wicked men, to follow their example. See above, on Ps. lxxiii. 3–7, 12.

5. *Let the righteous smite me (in) mercy and chasten me—oil for the head let not my head refuse—for* (it is) *still* (to come)—*and my prayer* (must still ascend) *in their injuries.* This verse is so obscure as to be almost unintelligible. According to the English versions, it expresses his willingness to be rebuked by good men for his benefit. But this sense is not only hard to be extracted from the words, but foreign from the context. Of the many contradictory interpretations which have been proposed, the most probable is that which makes the sentence mean, that the sufferings endured by the good man, even at the hand of the wicked, are chastisements inflicted by a righteous God in justice and in mercy, and as such may be likened to a festive ointment, which the head of the sufferer should not refuse, as he will

still have need of consolation and occasion to invoke God, in the midst of trials and of mischiefs yet to be experienced.

6. *Thrown down among the rocks are their judges ; and* (then) *they hear my words, for they are sweet.* When the judgments in reserve for the leaders of my enemies shall come upon them, they will perceive too late how reasonable are my words, and wish that they had hearkened to them sooner. *Thrown down*, originally *let go*, here used as in 2 Kings ix. 33. *Among the rocks*, literally *in* (or *into*) *the hands of the rock.* Some understand this to mean *into its power* (see ver. 9 below); others, *against its sides* (see Ps. cxl. 6); but the simplest explanation is that which supposes the rock to be personified and represented as standing below and holding out its hands to catch the person or thing falling. Some in the last clause read, *that they are sweet.* Then, when it is too late, they shall perceive how sweet my words are.

7. *Like* (one) *ploughing and cleaving the earth—scattered are our bones at the grave's mouth* (or *the mouth of hell*). There are only two plausible interpretations of this obscure comparison. As the first Hebrew verb (פלח), in its derivative forms, has the general sense of *cleaving*, and the second (בקע) is expressly used (Eccles. x. 9) in that of *splitting wood*, some interpreters give both verbs that specific meaning here, and suppose the verse to be simply a description of mortality or carnage, the effect of which is, that human bones lie about the opening of the grave, or the devouring jaws of hell (Isa. v. 14), as numerous and as little heeded as so many logs or sticks of wood. To this it is objected, that the phrase *in* (or *on*) *the earth* is then unmeaning, or at least superfluous, and that the verse, if thus explained, does not cohere with the ensuing context, which supposes the contents of this verse to be cheering and consolatory. The other interpretation avoids these objections, by explaining the first clause not of cleaving wood but ploughing, to which the first verb is applied in Arabic. *Like* (one) *ploughing and cleaving* (making furrows) *in the earth*, not for the sake of mangling its surface, but to make it fruitful and productive, (so) *our bones are scattered at the mouth of hell*, as the necessary means of a glorious resurrection.

8. *For unto thee, Jehovah, Lord, (are) my eyes—in thee have I confided —pour not out my soul.* The *for* refers to the consolatory import of the verse preceding. The one before us contains several favourite Davidic phrases. *My eyes are unto thee*, Ps. xxv. 15. *In thee have I confided* (or *sought refuge*), Ps. ii. 12, xxxi. 2 (1). In the last clause the soul or life is confounded with its vehicle. See Gen. ix. 4, Lev. xvii. 11, 14. The same remarkable expression is applied by Isaiah (liii. 12) to the voluntary death of the Messiah. That the verb literally means to *pour out*, is clear from Gen. xxiv. 20, Isa. xxxii. 15. This verse resembles Ps. cxl. 8 (7), in two points, the combination *Jehovah Adhonai*, and the supernumerary ה in סכּוֹתה and בּכּה.

9. *Keep me from the hands of the snare which they have netted for me, and the nets of the doers of iniquity.* The word *hands* is entirely omitted both in the English Bible and the Prayer Book version. It is put, by a favourite personification, for power or possession. The use of the expression here was probably occasioned by its previous use in Ps. cxl. 4. The verb *netted* is here employed to represent the cognate verb and noun in Hebrew.

10. *Let the wicked fall into their own traps, while I at the same time escape.* Compare Ps. vii. 16 (15). The combination of the singular and plural in the first clause—*wicked* (men) and *his snares*—shews that the singular denotes not a real but ideal person, representing a whole class. The

best construction of the last clause is that given in the English Bible and
retained above, with the single change of *withal* to the synonymous but less
ambiguous expression, *at the same time.* The transpositions of this clause
are unusual, even in Hebrew—*at the same time 1 until* (or *while*) *I pass,*
i. e. pass by uninjured or escape.

Psalm 142

1. *Maschil. By David, when he was in the cave. A prayer.* It is
called a *maschil* or didactic psalm, because it might otherwise have seemed
to contain matter wholly personal to David. See above, on Ps. xxxii. 1.
When he was, literally *in his being,* which does not refer exclusively to time,
but suggests the occasion or exciting cause. The reference may be either
to the cave of Adullam (1 Sam. xxii. 1), or to that of Engedi (1 Sam.
xxiv. 3), or to that period and mode of life in general, when David was
obliged to seek refuge in caves, and which, he might expect to see reproduced, under other forms, in the experience of his successors, for whose
guidance and encouragement this psalm was written. See above, on Ps.
lvii. 1. It is called a *prayer,* because the complaint or description of the
danger, ver. 2–5 (1–4), is merely introductory to the petition for deliverance, ver. 6–8 (5–7). See above, on Ps. xvii. 1, lxxxvi. 1, xc. 1, cii. 1.

2 (1). (*With*) *my voice to Jehovah I cry ;* (*with*) *my voice to Jehovah 1*
make supplication. With the first clause compare Ps. iii. 5 (4) ; with the
second, Ps. xxx. 9 (8). There are also coincidences of expression with Ps.
xxii. 6 (5). lxxvii. 2 (1), cxl. 7 (6). cxli. 1. *With my voice, i. e.* audibly,
aloud, as opposed to a mere mental prayer. The word translated *supplica-*
tion means, according to its etymology, a prayer for grace or mercy.

3 (2). *I pour out before him my care; my trouble before him I tell.* With
the first clause compare Ps. xlii. 5 (4), lxii. 9 (8), 1 Sam. i. 15, Lam.
ii. 19. The word translated *care* means properly reflection, meditation,
musing, especially such as is anxious and sad. See above, on Ps. lxiv. 2 (1).

4 (3). *Because my spirit is overwhelmed within me—and thou knowest my*
path—in the way that I go, they have hid a snare for me. The literal translation of the first words is, *in my spirit's being overwhelmed,* which may
indicate either the time or the cause of his distress. See above, on ver. 1.
Some adopt this construction : when my spirit is overwhelmed (then) thou
knowest my path. Others suppose two reasons to be given for his calling
upon God, his distress and his trust in the divine omniscience. Because
my spirit is overwhelmed, and (because) thou knowest my path. But as
the form of the two phrases is entirely different in Hebrew, the simplest
and safest construction is to treat the second clause as parenthetical.
Within me, literally *upon me;* see above, on Ps. xlii. 5–7 (4–6). *In the*
way that I go, i. e. along my path. See above, on Ps. cxl. 5 (4). The
words may mean, however, as in Ps. cxliii. 8, *in the way that I should go,*
i. e. in the path of duty. Without my fault they hid a snare for me. With
the first clause of this verse compare Ps. xlii. 5 (4), lxi. 3 (2), lxxvii. 4 (3),
and with the last, Ps. cxl. 6 (5), cxli. 9, cxliii. 8.

5 (4). *Look to the right and see—and there is no one knowing me—refuge*
has failed me—there is no one caring for my soul. The first two verbs must
be translated as imperatives, as in the margin of the English Bible. The
right hand is mentioned as the post of a protector. See above, on Ps.
cix. 6, cx. 5, cxxi. 5. The *and* at the beginning of the second clause is

foreign from our idiom, which would seem to require *that* or *for*. We might however say, look to the right and see, and (you will find that) there is not one, &c. *Knowing*, recognising, willing to acknowledge, much less to defend. *There is none to me, i. e.* I have none. Far from having a protector at my right hand, I have not even one who will acknowledge that he knows me. *Caring*, literally *seeking*, asking, or inquiring after it, in order to assist or save it. Nearly the same form of speech is used to express the very opposite idea, that of *seeking one's soul* to destroy it. See above, on Ps. xxxv. 4.

6 (5). *I have cried unto thee, Jehovah. I have said, Thou (art) my refuge, my portion in the land of life.* I have cried and still cry; I have said and still say. With this last expression compare Ps. xxxi. 15 (14), xli. 5 (4). *Thou (art) my refuge,* as in Ps. lxii. 8 (7), lxxi. 7. *My portion,* as in Ps. xvi. 5, lxxiii. 26, cxix. 57. *Land of life* (or *of the living*), as in Ps. xxvii. 13, lii. 7 (5).

7 (6). *Hearken to my cry, for I am reduced greatly; free me from my persecutors, for they are mightier than I.* All these are favourite Davidic phrases. *Hearken to my cry,* as in Ps. xvii. 1, lxi. 2 (1). *I am reduced* (or *weakened*) *greatly,* as in Ps. lxxix. 8 (7), cxvi. 6. Compare Judges vi. 6. *Free me from my persecutors,* as in Ps. vii. 2 (1). *They are mightier than I,* as in Ps. xviii. 18 (17).

8. *Bring out from prison my soul, to thank thy name. Me shall the righteous surround when thou shalt bestow on me* (favour). With the first clause compare Ps. xxv. 17, cvii. 10, cxliii. 11. Some suppose an allusion to Joseph's imprisonment and liberation. See above, on Ps. cv. 17–20. *To thank* (or *praise*) *thy name,* although an exact translation, is restricted by the English idiom to the person mentioned just before, and can only mean in accordance with our usage, *that I may thank thy name;* whereas the Hebrew infinitive knows no such limitation, and in this case simply means, that some one (without defining who) may praise thy name; or, exchanging the active for the passive form, *that thy name may be praised;* or, retaining the indefiniteness of the original expression, *for the praising of thy name.* The agents here intended are probably *the righteous,* who are mentioned in the next clause. The verb *surround,* which has a hostile sense in Ps. xxii. 13, Hab. i. 4, here means to gather round one with a friendly curiosity and eagerness, which some suppose to be suggested by the construction with the preposition (ב), which cannot be expressed in English. This sympathy of the righteous in his joys and sorrows is a favourite idea with David. See above, on Ps. xxxv. 27, xl. 17 (16). For the meaning and construction of the last verb see above, on Ps. xiii. 6, ciii. 10, cxvi. 7.

Psalm 143

THIS psalm may be divided into two equal parts, separated by the Selah in ver. 6. The first contains a complaint, ver. 1–6; the second a prayer for mercy, ver. 7–12. It resembles the preceding psalm, not only in this relation of its parts, but in its whole tone and diction, its Davidic phraseology combined with an originality never exhibited by the mere imitator or compiler.

1. *A Psalm. By David. Jehovah, hear my prayer, give ear unto my cries for mercy; in thy faithfulness answer me (and) in thy righteousness.* The combination of faithfulness and righteousness is like that in Ps. xxxvi. 6, 7 (5, 6). They can hardly be regarded as distinct grounds of argument, but rather as modified statements of the same. The faithfulness

of God has direct reference to his promise or covenant engagements; his righteousness has reference to the claims of his own people, but claims which owe their existence to those same covenant engagements.

2. *And enter not into judgment with thy servant, for just before thee is no one living.* To enter into judgment is a forensic phrase meaning to go to law, to prosecute, to sue. See Job ix. 32, xxii. 4. The verb in the last clause is not a passive meaning to be justified, but a neuter meaning to be just or innocent, to be in the right or on the right side of the controverted question. The acknowledgment in this verse has caused the psalm to be reckoned among the penitential psalms. The verse is often imitated or referred to elsewhere. See Job ix. 2, xiv. 3, xv. 14, Rom. iii. 20, &c.

3. *For the enemy persecutes my soul, crushes to the earth my life, makes me dwell in dark places like the dead of old.* This verse assigns a reason for the preceding prayers, a connection indicated by the *for*. He prays that God will deal with him in mercy, not in justice, by abandoning him to the fate here described. Compare Ps. vii. 6 (5), but especially Ps. lxxxviii. 4–7 (3–6). See also Lam. iii. 6. The last words some understand to mean *for ever dead*.

4. *And overwhelmed within me is my spirit; in the midst of me desolated is my heart.* With the first clause compare Ps. cxlii. 4 (3); with the the second Ps. xl. 16 (15).

5. *I remember the days of old; I meditate of all thy doings, of the work of thy hands I muse.* He recalls and ponders them not as a source of comfort, as in Ps. xliv. 2–4 (1–3), but of sorrow, from their painful contrast with his actual condition. See above, on Ps. xxii. 4–6 (3–5), lxxvii. 6 (5), and with the last clause compare Ps. xcii. 5.

6. *I spread my hands unto thee; my soul is like a weary land to thee, i. e.* thirsts or longs for thee, as a dry or thirsty land for rain. See above, on Ps. lxiii. 2 (1). A *weary land* is an unusual expression, and one of the peculiar features of this psalm. With the first clause compare Ps. xliv. 21 (20). The close of the complaint or lamentation, and the strength of the feeling with which it is uttered, are both indicated by the *Selah*.

7. *Hasten, answer me, Jehovah—my spirit fails—hide not thy face from me—or I shall be confounded with (those) going down (to) the pit.* The meaning of the first clause is, hasten to grant my petition. *Fails,* is spent or exhausted. See above, on Ps. xxviii. 1, xxxix. 11 (10), lxix. 18 (17), cii. 3 (2). That he is in extremity, is urged as a reason why God cannot fail to hear and answer him. This verse begins the main prayer of the psalm, that in ver. 1, 2, being merely introductory to the complaint in ver. 3–6, which is itself introductory to the prayer that follows.

8. *Let me hear in the morning thy mercy; let me know the way that I must go, for unto thee I raise my soul.* All these are familiar thoughts and terms to the readers of the psalms of David, and may be severally found in Ps. xxv. 1–4, li. 10 (8), lix. 17 (16). *The way that I must go,* not merely to be right, but to be safe and happy; the way of safety as well as that of duty. See above, on Ps. cxlii. 7 (6).

9. *Free me from my enemies, Jehovah, with thee I hide myself.* With the first clause compare Ps. lix. 12 (11), cxlii. 7; with the second, Ps. xxvii. 5, xxxi. 21 (20). The form of expression here, however, is peculiar and original. The literal meaning is, *to thee I cover,* i. e. cover myself, the reflexive use of the Hebrew verb being clear from Gen. xxxviii. 14, Deut. xxii. 12, Jonah iii. 6. The force of the pregnant construction is well, though freely, given in the English version, *I flee unto thee to hide me.*

10. *Teach me to do thy will, for thou (art) my God. Thy spirit (is)*

good ; let it guide me in level ground. This is a prayer for external safety, and at the same time for that spiritual guidance without which it is un-attainable. Compare Ps. v. 9 (8), xxvi. 12, xxvii. 11, xl. 9 (8), cxxxix. 10, 24. Some make but two clauses, and instead of the short proposition in the middle, read, *let thy good spirit guide me, &c*, or *let thy spirit,* (which is) *good, guide me, &c. Level ground,* literally *earth* (or *land*) *of evenness* (or *straightness*). See above, on Ps. xxvi. 12.

11. *For thy name's sake, Jehovah, thou wilt quicken me; in thy righteous-ness thou wilt bring out of distress my soul.* Here again we have an accu-mulation of Davidic ideas and expressions. *For thy name's sake,* as in Ps. xxiii. 3, xxv. 12, xxxi. 4, cix. 21. *Thou wilt quicken me,* as in Ps. cxxxviii. 7. *In thy righteousness,* as in Ps. xxxi. 2. *Bring my soul out of trouble,* as in Ps. xxv. 15, xxxiv. 18 (17), cxlii. 8 (7).

12. *And in thy mercy thou wilt destroy my enemies and cause to perish all that vex my soul ; for I* (*am*) *thy servant.* With the first clause compare Ps. xxxi. 17 (16), xviii. 41 (40). Some find here an allusion to the pro-mise in Deut. vii. 24. *Vexers,* adversaries, persecutors of my soul. *Thy servant,* not merely a believer, but a chosen instrument ; not merely one of thy people, but their chief and representative, and as such entitled to deliverance both for their sake and my own. In these two verses, the form of direct petition is insensibly exchanged for that of confident anticipation.

Psalm 144

THIS is a kind of supplement or counterpart to Ps. xviii., in which the view there taken of David's personal experience is applied to the anticipated case of his successors. The design thus assumed accounts for the position of the psalm in the collection. That its being placed precisely here is not fortuitous, may be inferred from its furnishing a kind of link between the urgent entreaties of the preceding psalms and the triumphant praise of those which follow. The Davidic origin of this psalm is as marked as that of any in the psalter. The accumulation of Davidic phrases is confined to the first part, while the last is independent and original, a fact entirely in-consistent with the supposition of a later compilation. The Psalmist thanks God for his protection of himself and of mankind in general, ver. 1–4, prays for deliverance from present dangers, ver. 5–8, expresses his confident anticipation of a favourable answer, ver. 9, 10, renews his prayer, not only for himself but for the chosen people, ver. 11–14, and felicitates them that they are such, ver. 15.

1. *By David. Blessed be Jehovah, my Rock, the* (*one*) *training my hands for fight, my fingers for war.* See above, on Ps. xviii. 35, 47 (34, 46), where most of these expressions have already been explained. *Fight* and *war* are both verbs and nouns in English, but the Hebrew words are nouns with the article prefixed. David here begins by referring all the successes of himself and his successors to Jehovah.

2. *My mercy and my fortress, my high place, and a deliverer for me, my shield and* (*he*) *in whom I trust, the* (*one*) *subduing my people.* No less than five of these descriptive epithets are taken from a single verse of Ps. xviii., viz. ver. 3 (2). Peculiar to the place before us is *my mercy, i. e.* my God of mercy. See above, on Ps. lix. 18 (17). The benefit of these rela-tions to Jehovah David claims not merely for himself but for his royal race, which was closed and yet perpetuated in the Messiah. *He in whom I trust,*

literally *and in him I trust.* *My people,* in its widest sense, including Israel and the Gentiles who were to be added to the kingdom of David under the reign of the Messiah. Compare Ps. xviii. 44, 48 (43, 47) with the parallel passages in 2 Samuel.

3. *Jehovah, what (is) man, that thou shouldst know him, the son of man, that thou shouldst think of him ?* The greatness of God's goodness is enhanced by a view of man's insignificance and unworthiness. The original construction seems to be, *what is man ?* (nothing), *and* (yet) *thou knowest him,* &c. To know is here to recognise as being in existence, to take notice of. The first *man* is the generic term, the second one denoting weakness. See above, on Ps. viii. 5 (4), and compare 2 Sam. vii. 18.

4. *Man to vanity is like; his days (are) as a passing shadow.* He cannot therefore be a worthy object, in himself, of the divine regard and favour. With the first clause compare Ps. xxxix. 6, 7 (5, 6), lxii. 10 (9) ; with the second, Ps. cii. 12 (11), ciii. 15.

5. *Jehovah, bow thy heavens and come down ; touch the mountains and let them smoke.* With the first clause compare Ps. xviii. 10 (9). What God is there described as doing, he is here besought to do again. With the last clause compare Ps. civ. 32. *Mountains,* in all such connections, would necessarily suggest the idea of states and kingdoms. See above, on Ps. xlvi. 3, 4 (2, 3).

6. *Lighten lightning and scatter them ; send out thy arrows and confound them.* The first word in Hebrew is a verb occurring nowhere else, and composed of the same radicals with the common word for *lightning* which immediately follows. For the meaning of the other terms, see above, on Ps. xviii. 15 (14), and compare the parallel passage, 2 Sam. xxii. 15 (14), with which the writer of the psalm before us was certainly acquainted, as appears from his occasional use of its peculiar readings.

7. *Send thy hands from on high ; rid me and free me from* (the) *many waters, from the hand of aliens.* With the first clause compare Ps. xviii. 17 (16). For *hand* we have here the plural *hands,* and for the two verbs there used two substantially equivalent, the first of which has the sense here given to it only in this place and the cognate languages,. and is therefore well represented by the less usual English word *rid.* With the last clause, compare Ps. xviii. 45, 46 (44, 45), where the phrase *sons of strangeness* (or *of foreign parts*) has been explained already.

8. *Whose mouth speaks fraud, and their right hand (is) a right hand of falsehood.* The word translated *fraud* is properly a negative meaning vanity or emptiness, but applied to the want of moral goodness and especially of truth. See above on Ps. xxiv. 4. The right hand is mentioned in allusion either to the practice of swearing with uplifted hand (Ps. cvi. 26), or to that of striking hands in bargains (2 Kings x. 15). There seems to be reference, in this verse, to the feigned obedience of the enemy, Ps. xviii. 45 (44).

9. *O God, a new song I will sing to thee ; with a lyre of ten* (strings) *I will play* (or *make music*) *to thee.* See above, on Ps. xxxiii. 2, 3, where David exhorts others to do what he here resolves and vows to do himself. The new song still implies a new occasion for it, so that he here begins to anticipate the answer to his foregoing prayers.

10. *The (one) giving salvation to kings ; the (one) ridding David his servant from an evil sword.* This mode of connecting sentences, by a participle agreeing with a noun in the foregoing context, is a characteristic feature of Ps. xviii. See p. 82. The *kings* particularly meant are the theocratical sovereigns, the royal family of David. *Ridding,* the participle of the verb

so rendered in ver. 7. *David (as) his servant*, because he is his servant, in the sense repeatedly explained already. See above, on Ps. cxliii. 2, 12. David speaks of himself by name, not only here but in Ps. xviii. 51 (50), lxi. 7 (6), lxiii. 12 (11), 2 Sam. vii. 26. *An evil sword*, not only dangerous but wicked. Compare Ps. xxii. 21 (20).

11. *Rid me and free me from the hand of aliens, whose mouth speaks fraud and whose right hand (is) a right hand of falsehood.* In resuming the language of direct petition, the terms of ver. 7, 8, are studiously repeated, as if to shew that this prayer is parallel to that, and not an addition to it.

12. *So that our sons (may be) as plants grown large in their youth, our daughters as corner-stones hewn (for) the building of the temple.* The reminiscences or imitations of Ps. xviii. suddenly cease here, and are followed by a series of original, peculiar, and for the most part no doubt antique expressions. On the supposition that the title is correct in making David the author, this is natural enough. On any other supposition it is unaccountable, unless by the gratuitous assumption, that this is a fragment of an older composition, a mode of reasoning by which any thing may be either proved or disproved. The first word in Hebrew is the relative pronoun, and the literal meaning of the clause is, *(by) which* (or *in consequence of which*) *our sons*, &c. The *which* refers to the deliverance prayed for in the preceding verse. *Grown large*, literally *magnified* or *made great*. The common version (*grown up in their youth*) has a paradoxical appearance, arising from the ambiguity of our phrase *grown up*, which is applied (like the Greek ἡλικία) both to age and stature. The word translated *corner-stones* has the same sense in Zech. ix. 15. The corner-stones are mentioned as those which were hewn and polished with peculiar care. *Likeness* or *model* would agree better with the usage of the Hebrew word (תַּבְנִית), but its primary sense, as a derivative of the verb (בָּנָה) *to build*, is here still more appropriate. Most interpreters give the last word the vague sense of *a palace*, considered as a splendid building. There is something, however, far more striking in the translation *temple*, found in the Prayer-Book and the ancient versions. The omission of the article is a poetic licence of perpetual occurrence. The temple was the great architectural model and standard of comparison, and particularly remarkable for the great size and skilful elaboration of its foundation-stones, some of which, there is reason to believe, have remained undisturbed since the time of Solomon. See Robinson's Palestine, vol. i. pp. 422–426.

13. *Our garners full, affording from kind to kind ; our flocks bearing thousands, multiplied by myriads, in our streets.* From kind to kind seems to denote not only variety but regular succession, as expressed in Hengstenberg's version, *one kind after another*. Compare Ps. lxxxiv. 8 (7). The participles in the next clause are highly idiomatic and scarcely reproducible in any other language. A somewhat similar example occurs above, Ps. lxix. 32 (31). But there both forms are active, whereas here we have one active and one passive participle, formed directly from the Hebrew words denoting a thousand and a myriad, the last of which is a derivative of the verb *to increase* or *multiply*, and would therefore necessarily suggest that idea. See above, on Ps. iii. 7 (6), lxviii. 18 (17). *Streets*, though not incorrect, is an inadequate translation of the Hebrew word (חוּצוֹת), which means external spaces, streets as opposed to the inside of houses, fields or country as opposed to a whole town. Here it includes not only roads but fields.

14. *Our oxen loaded—no damage and no loss—and no complaint in our*

streets. The first particular implies abundance. For the use of oxen as beasts of burden, see 1 Chron. xii. 40. *Damage* and *loss*, literally *breach* and *going forth. Complaint*, literally *cry*, but especially for loss of the fruits of the earth. See Isa. xxiv. 11. Some give the sentence an entirely different meaning, by supposing the word translated *oxen* to mean *princes*, as it does in Zech. ix. 7, xii. 5, 6, and giving the participle joined with it the Chaldee sense of *raised erect* or *upright. Going out* then means going out to war, as in Amos v. 3, *breach* the incursion of an enemy, and *cry* a war-cry. But the first Hebrew word in question (אַלּוּף) is applied only to the chiefs of Edom (Gen. xxxvi. 15), except in the latest books of the Old Testament, such as Zechariah ; and we naturally look for oxen after sheep, as in Ps. viii. 8 (7).

15. *Happy the people (with) whom (it is) thus ! Happy the people whose God (is) Jehovah !* The clauses are not antithetical, but equivalent. *The people* means *the (chosen) people*, Israel, with whom, in prosperous times, it was thus, and was thus for the very reason that Jehovah was their God.

Psalm 145

THIS has been happily characterised as the " new song" promised in Ps. cxliv. 9. In other words, it is the song of praise, corresponding to the didactic, penitential, and supplicatory psalms of this series. In form it is an alphabetical psalm, and like others of that class (see p. 113), admits of no analysis, being made up of variations on a single theme, the righteousness and goodness of the Lord to men in general, to his own people in particular, and more especially to those who suffer. The letter *nun* is wanting, being omitted, as some suppose, for the sake of having three equal stanzas, each containing seven verses. The Septuagint supplies the omission, in a very inartificial manner, by anticipating ver. 17 before ver. 15, with a simple change of *righteous* (צַדִּיק) to *faithful* (נֶאֱמָן), as in Ps. cxi. 7.

1. *Praise. By David. I will exalt thee, my God, the King, and will bless thy name to eternity and perpetuity.* This is the only case in which the word *Praise* stands alone as the designation or description of a psalm. It evidently bears an antithetical relation to the title *Prayer* in Ps. cxlii. 1, the rather as the Hebrew words (תְּפִלָּה and תְּהִלָּה) are still more alike than their English equivalents differing only in a single letter. *I will exalt thee*, as in Ps. xxx. 2 (1), where the reason is expressed that is here implied, to wit, that God had exalted him. *The king*, the only true king, the king of kings, by whom they are put up and down, protected and punished. See above, on Ps. cxliv. 10, and compare Ps. v. 3 (2), xx. 10 (9), xxiv. 8, 10, xxix. 10, xciii. 1, xcv. 3, xcvi. 10, xcix. 1. The regal honours paid to himself by others David here transfers as due to God alone. *Bless thy name, i. e.* reverently praise it. See above, on Ps. v. 12 (11), xxxiv. 2 (1), ciii. 1. *For ever and ever*, in reference not merely to himself but to his royal race, which is to live for ever. See above, on Ps. cxxxviii. 8.

2. *Every day will I bless thee, and praise thy name to eternity and perpetuity.* Compare Ps. lxviii. 20 (19), lxix. 31 (30), xcii. 2, 3. *Every day* denotes constancy and regularity.

3. *Great (is) Jehovah, and to be praised exceedingly, and to his greatness there is no search, i. e.* it is unsearchable. The first clause is quoted in

Ps. xlviii. 2 (1). *Greatly to be praised*, as in Ps. xviii. 4 (3), xcvi. 4, cxiii. 3. *His greatness*, as displayed in act, his great performance or performances. See above, on Ps. lxxi. 21. With the last words of the verse compare Ps. xl. 6 (5).

4. *Generation to generation lauds thy deeds, and thy mighty doings they declare.* With the first clause compare Ps. xix. 3 (2). The verbs are of the future form, lauds and will laud, declare and will declare. The first verb is the one used in Ps. lxiii. 4 (3), cxvii. 1. *Mighty doings*, literally *mights* or *powers*, but always used, like *greatness*, in an active not an abstract sense. See above, on Ps. xx. 7 (6), cvi. 2. *They declare* may agree with men indefinitely, or with the double *generation* in the first clause, which, however, is there construed with a verb in the singular.

5. *(Of) the beauty of the honour of thy majesty, and the words of thy wonders, I will muse* (or *meditate*). The accumulation of synonymous expression in the first clause has been falsely represented as a proof of later date and a corupted taste, whereas it only proves intensity of admiration. For examples of the same thing in undisputed psalms of David, see above, Ps. xviii. 3 (2), lxii. 8 (7). *Beauty* and *majesty*, as in Ps. xlv. 4 (3). *Honour* or *glory*, as in Ps. xix. 1. *Words of thy wonders* are the wonders or wondrous deeds themselves, considered as subjects of discourse or celebration. See above, on Ps. lxv. 4 (3), cv. 27. *I will muse*, as in Ps. lxxvii. 13 (12), cxix. 15, 23, 27, 48, 78, 148.

6. *And the force of thy dread (deeds) they utter—and (as to) thy greatness, I will recount it.* *Dread*, literally *feared*, and then *to be feared*, as *praised* means *to be praised* in ver. 3 above. *Utter*, literally *say* precisely as in Ps. xl. 11 (10). *Greatness*, or according to the reading in the text of the Hebrew Bible, *greatnesses*, *i.e.* great deeds, as *mights* means *mighty deeds* in ver. 5.

7. *The memory of thy great goodnes they pour forth, and (of) thy righteousness they sing* (or *shout*). Memory, as in Ps. vi. 6 (5). *Great goodness* is the order of the words not only in English but in Hebrew, where it is unusual. See above, on Ps. lxxxix. 51 (50). *Pour forth*, as in Ps. xix. 3 (2), lxxviii. 2. Compare Ps. lix. 8 (7). *Thy righteousness*, as in Ps. xxxi. 2 (1), li. 16 (14), cxliii. 1. *Sing* or *shout* for joy. The construction is like that in Ps. li. 16 (14), lix. 17 (16).

8. *Gracious and compassionate (is) Jehovah, slow to anger and great (in) mercy.* Compare Ps. lxxxvi. 15 (14), ciii. 8, cxi. 4. Instead of the usual expression (רַב) *much* or *abundant*, we have here *great*, in allusion to its previous use in ver. 3, 6.

9. *Good (is) Jehovah to all, and his compassions (are) over all his works.* *All*, literally *the all*, the whole universe. See above, on Ps. cxix. 91. *Over* or *upon*, the first suggesting the idea of a covering, the second that of a descent from above. *His works*, the things which he has made, his creatures. See above, on Ps. ciii. 22. The argument implied is, how much more to his own people, the creatures of his grace. See above, on Ps. cxxxviii. 8.

10. *All thy creatures, O Jehovah, praise* (or *thank*) *thee, and thy saints bless thee.* The future forms, as usual, denote that it is so and will be so. The superfluous ה in the last word is an orthographical peculiarity like that in Ps. cxxxix. 3, cxl. 8, cxli. 8. As *saints* (or *gracious ones*) are more than *creatures*, so to *bless* is more than to *praise*. See above, on ver. 1.

11. *The glory of thy reign they utter, and thy might they speak.* Compare Ps. ciii. 19. *Thy reign* or *kingdom*, which is universal. The whole phrase may mean *thy royal dignity* or honour.

12. *To make known to the sons of man his mighty deeds, and the glory of*

the majesty of his reign (or *kingdom*). Some give the infinitive the force of a gerund, *by making known ;* but the true sense seems to be, *so as to* (or *so that they*) *make known.* See above, on Ps. lxxviii. 18.

13. *Thy reign is a reign of all eternities, and thy dominion in generation and generation.* These words are also found in Dan. iii. 33, iv. 31. The meaning of the last clause is, thy dominion still exists and shall exist in every successive generation.

14. *An upholder* (*is*) *Jehovah for all the falling, a lifter up for all the bowed down.* The first word in each clause is properly a participle, here used as a noun, and therefore followed by the preposition *to* or *for.* Translated in either way, the words necessarily suggest the idea of habitual action. With the first clause compare Ps. xxxvii. 17, 24, liv. 6 (4), cxix. 116.

15. *The eyes of all unto thee* (look and) *wait, and thou givest them their food in its season.* The verb in the first clause means to wait, expect, or hope, but is here construed with the preposition *to* or *towards,* which implies the act of turning or looking to the object confided in. *Givest,* literally *giving, i. e.* (*art habitually*) *giving.* See above, on Ps. civ. 27, where these words are quoted.

16. *Opening thy hand and satisfying to every living* (thing its) *desire,* or the desire of every living thing. Another construction, preferred by some interpreters, is, satisfying (giving satisfaction) to every living thing (in its) desire, viz. that which it desires. See the imitation of this verse in Ps. civ. 28, and compare Ps. ciii. 5, Acts xiv. 17. The words *satisfy* and *will* (or *desire*) are combined, as here, in Deut. xxxiii. 23.

17. *Righteous* (*is*) *Jehovah in all his ways and merciful in all his works.* Justice and mercy are not mentioned here as opposites, but rather as equivalents, the goodness of God being really included in the rectitude so frequently ascribed to him.

18. *Near* (*is*) *Jehovah to all calling upon him, to all calling upon him in truth, i. e.* sincerely, with importunate desire and strong confidence. With this verse compare Ps. xxxiv. 7, 19.

19. *The will of his fearers he will do, and their cry he will hear, and will save them.* He will do what they desire, or grant their prayer, especially their prayer for help in time of danger and distress, as intimated in the last clause. Compare Ps. xxxiv. 10, 16 (9, 15), xxxvii. 40.

20. *Jehovah keeps all that love him, and all the wicked will he destroy.* The *fearers* of ver. 19 and the *lovers* of this verse are identical, which shews that godly fear and love are not incompatible. *Keeps,* literally *keeping,* as in ver. 15, from all danger and distress, preserving.

21. *The praise of Jehovah shall my mouth speak, and all flesh shall bless his holy name for ever,* or retaining the idiomatic form of the original, *all flesh shall bless the name of his holiness* (or *his name of holiness*) *to eternity and perpetuity.* The use of the word *praise* connects this verse with the title or inscription in ver. 1, which is thereby justified or proved to be correct. *All flesh,* as in Ps. lxv. 3 (2). *His holy name,* as in Ps. xxxiii. 21.

Psalm 146

THIS psalm may be divided into two equal parts, the first of which describes the happiness of those who trust in God and not in man, ver. 1-5, while the second gives the reason, drawn from the divine perfections, ver. 6 10. The psalm is distinguished from the Davidic series which precedes it (cxxxviii.–cxlv.) by its whole internal character. At the same time its coincidences of expression with the one immediately before it shew that it was meant to be used in connection with it, and may therefore be regarded as the closing psalm of the whole series beginning with Ps. cxxxv., and belonging to the time of Haggai and Zechariah, to which the psalm before us is expressly referred in the Septuagint Version.

1. *Hallelujah ! Praise, O my soul, Jehovah !* See above, Ps. ciii. 1, 22, civ. 1, 35. The *Hallelujah* never appears in any psalm which bears the name of David, and is, indeed, as characteristic of the later psalms as the *Selah* is of the more ancient.

2. *I will praise Jehovah while I live ; I will make music to my God while I still* (exist). For the literal meaning of these words, see above, on Ps. civ. 33, from which they are borrowed, with the unimportant change of *sing* to *praise*.

3. *Trust ye not in princes, in the son of man, to whom there is no salvation,* who cannot save either himself or others, but is wholly dependent upon God. Compare Ps. xl. 5 (4), lxxv. 7, 8 (6, 7), cviii. 13, cxvi. 11, cxliv. 10. This may be regarded as an exhortation to men in general from Israel, an exhortation founded on his own experience.

4. *Forth goes his spirit, he returns to his earth ; in that very day his thoughts perish.* For the meaning of the first clause, see above, on Ps. civ. 29. The primary idea of *breath* and the secondary one of *spirit* run into each other in the usage of the Hebrew word (רוּחַ), so that either may be expressed in the translation, without entirely excluding the other. *His thoughts,* his vain notions or ambitious schemes.

5. *Happy he whose help is the God of Jacob,* (and) *his reliance on Jehovah his God.* *Whose help,* literally *in whose help, i. e.* engaged, employed in it, or more probably *among whose helpers.* Compare Ps. xlv. 10 (9), liv. 6 (4), xcix. 6, cxviii. 7. The divine name (אֵל) here used suggests the idea of almighty power, as opposed to that of human weakness. *Reliance,* literally *expectation, hope ;* but the first idea is necessarily suggested by the preposition *on.*

6. *Who made heaven and earth, the sea, and all that* (is) *in them—the* (one) *keeping truth for ever.* Two reasons are here given for thus relying upon God ; his almighty power, as exercised and proved in the creation of the world, and his unchangeable fidelity. See above, Ps. xxv. 5. *Who made,* literally *making,* with the usual reference to God's creative power as still exerted in the sustentation of the universe. See above, on Ps. lxv. 7 (6), cxxi. 2, cxliv. 2.

7. *Doing justice to the oppressed—giving bread to the hungry—Jehovah, freeing* (or *the liberator of*) *the bound.* He is not only able but accustomed to relieve those in distress, of whom several distinct classes are here specified as samples. Compare Ps. xxxvii. 19, lxviii. 6, 7 (5, 6), cvii. 5, 9, 10, cxlv. 14. Hunger and captivity are both familiar figures for spiritual evils, as well as literal designations of external ones, both which may here be considered as included.

8. *Jehovah opens* (the eyes of) *the blind ; Jehovah raises up the bowed down ; Jehovah loves the righteous.* The ellipsis in the first clause is not so harsh in Hebrew as in English, because the verb (פָּקַח) is almost confined, in usage, to the eyes, and would at once suggest them to a Hebrew reader. All the verbs are of the participial form, *opening, raising, loving, i. e.* continually doing so. The first clause is applicable both to bodily and

mental blindness. Compare Deut. xxviii. 29, Isa. lix. 10, Job. xii. 25. The second clause is borrowed from Ps. cxlv. 14.

9. *Jehovah preserves strangers ; orphan and widow he relieves ; and the way of wicked men makes crooked.* The stranger, the orphan, and the widow are constantly presented in the Law as objects of compassion and beneficence. See above, on Ps. lxviii. 6, 7 (5, 6). *Relieves,* restores, raises up from their low condition. As a straight path is an emblem of prosperity, to render one's path crooked is to involve him in calamity. The same verb is applied, in a moral sense, to the perverse conduct of the wicked, Ps. cxix. 78.

10. *Jehovah* (reigns and) *shall reign to eternity ; thy God, O Zion, to generation and generation. Hallelujah* (praise ye Jah) ! The psalm closes with a grand sentence from the song of Moses, Exod. xv. 18, to which a parallel clause is added, and a concluding *Hallelujah,* winding up the whole series of psalms, supposed to have been sung at the completion of the second temple.

Psalm 147

A SONG of praise to Jehovah on account of his goodness to his creatures generally, and to his church or chosen people in particular. Both these themes run through the psalm ; but one is predominant in the first part, ver. 1–11 ; the other in the second, ver. 12–20. The four remaining psalms (cxlvii.–cl.), connected together, and distinguished from what goes before, by the *Hallelujah* with which they all begin and end ; by their joyous tone, unmixed with lamentation or complaint ; by their frequent allusions to some great deliverance recently experienced ; and by the peculiar way in which they bring together the exhibitions of God's glory in the works of nature and in his dealings with the church ; have not improbably been represented as a series, intended to commemorate the completion of the walls of Jerusalem by Nehemiah, an event described in the history itself, as putting an end to the reproach of Israel, and restoring the Holy City to its proper rank. See Neh. i. 3, ii. 5, 17; vi. 6, 7, 15, 16, vii. 4, ix. 6, 13, 14, x. 29, xii. 27, 35, 41, 43.

1. *Hallelujah* (praise ye Jah), *for it is good to celebrate our God, for it is sweet (and) praise becoming.* This is made up of the beginnings of three other psalms. See above, Ps. xcii. 2 (1), cxxxv. 3, xxxiii. 1. *Celebrate,* make music to, with voice and instrument. See above, on Ps. vii. 18 (17). Instead of *it is sweet* some read *he is lovely, i. e.* a worthy object of supreme affection, as in Ps. cxxxv. 3. But even there the construction is a doubtful one, and here the first proposed above is recommended by the fact that the epithets before and after relate not to God himself but to his praise.

2. *Building Jerusalem (is) Jehovah ; the outcasts of Israel he gathers.* The rebuilding of the walls in the days of Nehemiah, may be said to have completed the fulfilment of the promise in Isa. xi. 12, lvi. 8. Compare Ps. cvii. 3.

3. *The (one) healing the broken-hearted and binding up their wounds.* This was true as a general description, and specially exemplified in the deliverance which Israel had experienced. See above, on Ps. xxxiv. 19 (18), ciii. 3, and compare Isa. lxi. 1.

4. *Telling the number of the stars—to all of them names he calls.* The God who thus provides for Israel is the God of nature no less than of grace. *Telling,* counting, reckoning, estimating. Not determining beforehand, but

simply doing what man cannot.   See Gen. xv. 5, and compare Gen. xiii. 16,
Num. xxiii. 10, Isa. lxv. 12.   He not only counts but names them, *calling
them all by name.*   The verse is borrowed from Isa. xl. 26, where, as here,
God's knowledge and control of nature is presented as a source of consolation to his people.

5. *Great is our Lord and of much power ; to his understanding there is
no number, i. e.* it is incalculable and immense.   Compare Isa. xl. 26, 28.
Of much power, or abundant in strength.

6. *Raising up the humble* (is) *Jehovah, casting down the wicked to the very
earth.*   See above, Ps. cxlvi. 8, 9.   *To the very earth,* literally even to the earth.

7. *Respond to Jehovah with thanksgiving ; make music to our God with a
harp.*   The first verb has its proper sense of answering or responding, as
in Ps. cxix. 172.   It may be doubted whether it ever has that of simply
singing.   *Respond, i. e.* to his manifold favours.

8. *The* (one) *covering the heavens with clouds—the* (one) *providing for
the earth rain—the* (one) *causing the mountains to put forth grass.*   The
grass as produced by means of the rain, and the rain by means of the clouds.
See above, on Ps. civ. 13.

9. *Giving to the cattle its food—to the young ravens which cry.*   The first
noun may also be translated *beast,* but still with reference to domestic animals, with which is contrasted in the other clause the raven, as a wild
bird, unconnected with mankind, and as some suppose with allusion to its
harsh and piercing cry.   See above, on Ps. civ. 21, cxlv. 15, and compare
Job xxxviii. 41.   *Young ravens,* literally *sons of the raven.*

10. *Not in the strength of a horse does hè delight ; not with the legs of a
man is he pleased.*   The best explanation of the singular expressions in the
last clause is, that the whole verse was intended to describe horse and foot,
or cavalry and infantry, as forming the military strength of armies.   It is
not to those who trust in these that God is disposed to extend favour, nor
do these advantages at all attract him.

11. *Pleased* (is) *Jehovah with those fearing him, with those hoping for
his mercy.*   This implies the want of secular advantages, or at least an
absence of reliance on them, and a sense of dependence upon God alone.

12. *Laud, O Jerusalem, Jehovah ! Praise thy God, O Zion !*   Here
begins the second division of the psalm, in which the goodness of God to
his people is the theme, and the people itself the object of address.

13. *For he hath strengthened the bars of thy gates ; he hath blessed thy
sons in the midst of thee.*   Although the first clause admits of a general
figurative application, it seems to contain an evident allusion to the historical occasion of the psalm, or at least to favour the opinion, that it was
designed to celebrate the renewed fortifications of the Holy City.

14. (*It is*) *he that makes thy border peace,* (and with) *the fat of wheat
he satisfies thee.   He that makes,* literally *the* (one) *placing.   Border* is
put for all that it contains or bounds, thy territory or domain.   To make
it peace is to make it peaceful or to give it peace.   See Isa. liv. 12.   With
the last clause compare Ps. lxxxi. 17, Deut. xxxii. 14.

15. *He that sendeth his commandment* (upon) *earth very swiftly runs his
word.*   The construction is like that in the preceding verse.   *He that
sendeth,* the (one) sending.   *Commandment,* literally *saying,* what he says.
Very swiftly, literally *even to swiftness.*   The authoritative word of God is
here personified as his messenger or agent, whose swift running signifies the
prompt execution of the divine will.

16. *He that gives snow like wool, hoar-frost like ashes sprinkles.*   As

easily as a man scatters wool or ashes, does God cover the earth with snow or frost. The selection of phenomena peculiar to winter may have reference to the season when the psalm was written or originally sung. At the same time they were probably designed to serve as emblems of the long distress, to which the Restoration put an end, as spring does to winter. The comparisons in this verse are less striking to us than to the people of countries where snow and frost are less familiar.

17. *He that sendeth his ice like crumbs. Before his cold who can stand ?* The second noun means scraps or morsels, but in usage is specially applied to food. See Gen. xviii. 5, Judges xix. 5. This seems to be descriptive of hail, which God sends upon the earth as easily and freely as man scatters crumbs or throws away the refuse of his food. The allusion to the feeding of domesticated animals, which some assume, is needless, though admissible.

18. *He sends his word and melts them—he makes his wind blow—waters flow. Sends his word,* utters his command. The plural pronoun (*them*) refers to snow, frost and ice, in ver. 16, 17. The winds meant are the warm winds of the spring, attended by a general thaw.

19. *Declaring his word to Jacob, his statutes and his judgments to Israel.* The God of Nature is the God of Revelation. He who thus controls the elements and seasons is the God of Israel, and will work spiritual changes corresponding to these natural phenomena, for the benefit of the people whom he has entrusted with the revelation of his will.

20. *He has not done so to every nation—and* (as for) *judgments, they know nothing of them.* This revelation to Israel is peculiar and exclusive. *Every nation,* and by implication, *any one.* This is, indeed, the only form in which that idea could be expressed in Hebrew. The last clause declares the other nations ignorant not only of *his laws* or *judgments,* but of any that deserve the name.

Psalm 148

THE universe, in all its parts, is summoned to praise God as its maker, and as infinitely worthy of its adoration. The invitation is addressed, in the first instance, to heaven and its inhabitants, exhorting them to praise God as their maker and preserver, ver. 1–6. It is then addressed to the earth and its inhabitants, exhorting them to praise him for his infinite perfection, as displayed in his works, but especially in his dealings with his chosen people, ver. 7–14. Even the most sceptical critics are constrained to acknowledge that this psalm and the two which follow are admirably suited to their purpose.

1. *Hallelujah ! Praise ye Jehovah from the heavens ! Praise him in the heights !* This verse designates the place, or part of the creation, from which the praise is to proceed. *Heights,* or high-places, is a simple equivalent to *heavens,* the plural form of which it takes by assimilation. Compare the singular in Ps. xviii. 17 (16). The preposition *from* denotes the direction of the sound, the preposition *in* the place where it is uttered.

2. *Praise ye him, all his angels ! Praise ye him, all his hosts !* As this last expression is applied both to the angels and the heavenly bodies, it here affords a natural transition from the one to the other. See above, on Ps. xxiv. 10, xxix. 1, ciii. 21.

3. *Praise ye him, sun and moon ! Praise him, all ye stars of light !* This is a specification of the general term, *his hosts,* in ver. 2. *Stars of light* is a beautiful poetical expression for bright or shining stars.

4. *Praise him, ye heavens of heavens, and ye waters which are above the heavens!* The object of address in the first clause is the highest heaven, the heaven of that which is heaven to us. See above, on Ps. lxviii. 34 (33), and compare Deut. x. 14, 1 Kings viii. 27, 2 Cor. xii. 2. The *waters* meant are the watery clouds above the lower heavens, as in Gen. i. 7. See above, on Ps. civ. 3.

5. *Let them praise the name of Jehovah, for he commanded and they were created.* The direct invitation to the heavens is followed by a statement of the reason why they should comply with it, expressed in the third person, as if addressed to others. The pronoun *he* is emphatic. (It was) *he* (that) *commanded* (and no other). See above, on Ps. xxxiii. 9, and compare Gen. i. 3.

6. *And made them stand to perpetuity and eternity; a limit he gave (them) and they cannot pass (it).* The immutability ascribed to the frame of nature, Ps. lxxii. 5, lxxxix. 3, 37 (2, 36), is not absolute but relative to the will of the Creator. All that is required by the context in such cases is, that they cannot change in opposition to his will or independently of it. See Ps. cii. 27. The first word in the second clause is here used in its primary sense of a definite boundary or limit, from which may be readily deduced the usual one of statute or permanent enactment. See above, on Ps. ii. 7. As the last verb is in the singular number, the most obvious construction is the one given in the English Bible, *a decree which shall not pass.* Compare Matt. v. 18. But the highest authorities appear to be agreed that the analogy of Job xiv. 5, Ps. civ. 9, Jer. v. 22, requires the verb to be taken in the sense of transcending or transgressing, and construed with the aggregate of the heavenly bodies.

7. *Praise Jehovah from the earth, ye dragons and all depths.* Here begins the second part, in which the address is to the earth and its inhabitants. *From the earth* is in antithesis to *from the heavens* in ver. 1. *Earth* here includes land and water; hence the last clause makes exclusive mention of the latter, as the word translated dragons is applied to huge aquatic animals (Ps. lxxiv. 13), and the one translated *depths* to large bodies of water (Ps. xxxiii. 7). As the first, however, sometimes means serpents (Ps. xci. 13), it may here be the connecting link between land and water.

8. *Fire and hail, snow and vapour, stormy wind doing his word.* The address here passes to the inanimate and unconscious agencies of nature. *Fire and hail,* as in Ps. cv. 32. The fire meant is commonly supposed to be lightning; but according to Hengstenberg the word is to be taken in its ordinary sense, and is separated from its natural attendant *smoke* (for such is the meaning of the Hebrew word elsewhere, *e. g.* Ps. cxix. 83) only for the purpose of contrasting hot and cold, white and black, which seems a little fanciful and far-fetched. The *storm-wind* (or *stormy wind*) is mentioned as a natural agent the least likely to be under control, and it is expressly described as doing God's word, *i. e.* executing his command. See above, on Ps. ciii. 20, civ. 4.

9. *The mountains and all hills, fruit-trees and all cedars.* Not *fruitful* trees, as distinguished from barren trees, but *fruit-trees* (literally *tree of fruit*), as distinguished from forest-trees, here represented by the cedar, which is usually spoken of in Scripture as the noblest species, and therefore called the *cedar of God,* Ps. lxxx. 11 (10).

10. *The wild (beast) and all cattle, creeping thing and flying fowl.* The contrast in the first clause is analogous to that between fruit-trees and cedars in ver. 9. The Hebrew word (רֶמֶשׂ) translated *creeping thing* has no exact equivalent in English. It seems strictly to denote animal or vital

motion, or as a concrete term whatever so moves, and is even applied to
aquatic animals, Ps. civ. 25. But when used distinctively, it denotes the
smaller classes of terrestrial animals, including insects, reptiles, and the
smallest quadrupeds. It is here added simply to complete the expression
of the general idea, all animals whatever. *Flying fowl,* literally *bird of wing.*
The first of the Hebrew words is specially applied to the smaller birds, and
sometimes specifically to the sparrow. See above, on Ps. xi. 1, lxxxiv. 4
(3), civ. 17, cxxiv. 7. This and the preceding item in the catalogue, suggesting the idea of the smallest animals, may possibly have been used to
denote the universality of the call here made upon all creatures, from the
greatest to the smallest, to praise God their maker.

11. *Kings of the earth and all nations, chiefs and all judges of the earth.*
He here passes from the lower animals to man. *Kings* and the nations
whom they represent. *Princes* is not an exact translation of the Hebrew
(שָׂרִים), which is especially, though not exclusively, applied to military
leaders of various rank, and may therefore be represented by the English
chiefs or *chieftains.*

12. *Young men and also maidens, old men with children.* The obvious
meaning of this verse is, all men, without distinction of sex or age. There
is no need, therefore, of refining on the several particulars, or undertaking
to explain why old men and young men are both mentioned, since neither
of them could have been omitted without failing to accomplish the design
of the enumeration. For the etymology and primary meaning of the first
word in Hebrew see above, on Ps. lxxviii. 63, where it stands in precisely
the same combination. The two nouns in the last clause may be considered
as of common gender.

13. *Let* (all these) *praise the name of Jehovah, for exalted is his name alone,
his glory is above earth and heaven.* The mention of earth and heaven
shews that the first verb relates not merely to that which immediately precedes, but to the whole enumeration of God's creatures with which the
psalm is occupied. See above, on Ps. civ. 27. *Exalted is his name,* as in
Isa. xii. 4. *His glory* or *majesty,* a Hebrew word especially applied to
royal dignity. See above, on Ps. xxi. 6 (5), xlv. 4 (3), xcvi. 6, civ. 1,
cxi. 3. *Above earth and heaven, i. e.* superior to their mere material splendour, or *on earth and heaven, i. e.* placed upon them as a crown. See
above, on Ps. viii. 2 (1), lvii. 6 (5).

14. *And he has raised up a horn for his people—praise for all his saints
—for the children of Israel—a people near to him. Hallelujah!* While
all the creatures before mentioned have abundant cause to praise God for
his infinite perfection and his goodness to themselves, a peculiar obligation
is incumbent on his people : first, for his distinguishing favour through all
periods of their history ; and then, for a special mercy recently experienced,
namely, the restoration from captivity, now completed by the renewal of
the temple and the reconstruction of the city walls. This restoration is
described, by a favourite Davidic figure, as exalting or lifting up the horn
of Israel. See above, on Ps. lxxv. 6, 7 (5, 6), xcii. 11 (10). The previous condition of the chosen people might be well represented by the opposite figure used in Job xvi. 15. *Raised a horn for his people* seems to be
only another way of saying *raised the horn of his people.* The first form of
expression may have been here used for the purpose of assimilating this
clause to the next, where *praise* is still dependent on the verb at the beginning, and to *raise up praise for his people* is to give them fresh occasion of
still higher praise than they had ever yet been called to utter. The ancient

church is here described in a fourfold manner : first, simply as *his people ;*
then, as *his saints* or *gracious ones*, the objects of his mercy and the subjects
of his grace ; then, by their national title, as *the sons* (or *descendants*) *of Israel;*
and lastly, as the *people near him, i. e.* nearer to him than all others, sustaining a more intimate relation to him, The same expression which is
elsewhere applied to the priests (Lev. x. 3, Ezek. xlii. 13) is here applied
to Israel as " a kingdom of priests and a holy nation" (Exod. xix. 6).

Psalm 149

This may be regarded as the special song of praise required of Israel at
the close of the preceding psalm : first, on account of mercies already
experienced by the chosen people, ver. 1–5 ; and then, in the hope of future
triumphs over all heathen and hostile powers, ver. 6–9. Nothing could
well be more appropriate to the state of things under Nehemiah, when the
city and nation had again been put into a posture of defence and resistance.

1. *Hallelujah ! Sing unto Jehovah a new song, his praise in the congregation of saints.* Compare Ps. xl. 4 (3), xcvi. 1, cxi. 1, cxlviii. 14, to
which last there is an obvious allusion, connecting the two psalms in the
closest manner.

2. *Let Israel rejoice in his Maker ! Let the sons of Zion triumph in their
King !* Not merely the creator of individuals, but of the church and nation
as such, and that not only at first, but by a kind of new creation, in the
restoration of the people from captivity. They are summoned to rejoice in
him, not only as their founder and restorer, but their sovereign. See above,
on Ps. xcv. 6, c. 3, cxlv. 1, and compare Isa. xliii. 1, xliv. 2, xlv. 13.

3. *Let them praise his name in the dance ; with timbrel and harp let
them play* (or *make music*) *to him.* The usual modes of expressing joy are
here combined. As to the dance, see above, on Ps. xxx. 12 (11).

4. *For Jehovah is pleased with his people ; he beautifies the humble with
salvation.* The first clause suggests the idea of a previous alienation, and
of his having been appeased or reconciled. See above, on Ps. lxxxv. 2 (1).
The verb is one applied in the Law to God's acceptance of the sacrifices,
and might therefore awaken here associations with atonement and forgiveness. See above, on Ps. xix. 15 (14), li. 22 (20). The verb occurs in
its general sense of being pleased or satisfied, Ps. cxlvii. 10, 11. With the
last clause compare Isa. lxi. 3.

5. *Let the saints exult in glory ; let them sing (for joy) upon their beds.*
The word translated *saints* is the same that occurs in Ps. cxlviii. 14, and is
there explained. *In glory* (or *honour*), *i. e.* the glorious or honourable
state into which Jehovah has now brought them. The glory is not that
which belongs to God, Ps. xxix. 9, xcvi. 7, but that which he bestows, Ps.
lxxxiv. 12 (11), lxxxv. 10 (9), The very phrase, *in honour*, occurs above,
Ps. cxii. 9. *Sing* or *shout*, as audible expressions of strong feeling, and
especially of joy. *On their beds*, where they have been accustomed to
lament their previous degradation, or what Nehemiah calls their " affliction
and reproach." See Neh. i. 3, iii. 36 (iv. 4).

6. *Praises of God in their throat, and a two-edged sword in their hand.*
A striking coincidence has been observed between this verse and Neh.
iv. 11, 12 (17, 18). As then they worked with one hand and brandished
the sword with the other, so now they might be said at the same time to
praise God and defy their enemies. This singular mixture of devotional and

martial spirit is characteristic of the psalm, and furnishes a valuable index to the date of composition. The conclusion thus reached is corroborated by the account of the military and religious pomp, with which the walls were dedicated, as described by Nehemiah (xii. 31–47).

7. *To execute vengeance among the nations, punishments among the peoples.* Not their own vengeance, but that of God, to whom alone it appertains. See above, on Ps. xviii. 48 (47), xciv. 1, and compare Deut. xxxii. 35, Rom. xii. 19, Heb. x. 30. This is really nothing more than a prediction, that God would use his people as his instruments in punishing the nations by whom they had themselves been persecuted and oppressed. This was partially fulfilled in the successes of the Maccabees, but under a new and unexpected form, in the spiritual triumphs of the true religion, and its actual or prospective subjugation of the world.

8. *To bind their kings with chains, their nobles with fetters of iron.* The word translated *nobles* is properly a participle, meaning *honoured (ones)*. The verse simply carries out the idea of the one before it, that of the subjugation of the gentiles by the true religion. The objection to this, as a spiritualising explanation of the text, springs from a narrow and erroneous view of the very end for which Israel existed as a nation. Those promises to Israel, which are not still available for us, were but of temporary local value.

9. *To execute among them the judgment written. An honour is that for all his saints.* This last phrase occurs also at the close of the preceding psalm (cxlviii. 14). As *written* may mean written in the book of God's decrees, there is no need of supposing a reference to any part of Scripture. If there be such reference, however, it is no doubt to the threatening in Deut. xxxii. 41–43. To act as God's instruments in this great judicial process, so far from being a disgrace or hardship, is an honour reserved for all the objects of his mercy and subjects of his grace. The psalm ends as it began, with *Hallelujah !*

Psalm 150

THIS is the closing Hallelujah or Doxology, which marks the conclusion of the last series or cycle (Ps. cxlvii.–cl.), of the Fifth Book (Ps. cvii.–cl.), and of the whole Psalter. In form and structure it is perfectly simple, merely reciting, in an animated manner, the place (ver. 1), the theme (ver. 2), the mode (ver. 3–5), and the extent (ver. 6) of the praise due to Jehovah.

1. *Hallelujah ! Praise God in his sanctuary ! Praise him in the firmament of his power !* The essential meaning of the verse is, praise him both in earth and heaven. The particulars detailed in Ps. cxlviii. are here condensed into a pregnant summary. The *sanctuary* is the earthly one, and as such stands opposed to the *firmament* or *heaven*, called the *firmament of his power*, as being one of the most glorious proofs and products of its exercise, and still the scene of its most striking exhibitions. The phrase is to be understood as comprehending the *hosts of heaven*, both inanimate and living, both material and spiritual. The parallelism is rendered still more perfect by the correspondence between *power* in the last clause and (אֵל) the divine name in the first.

2. *Praise him for his mighty acts ! Praise him according to his plenitude of greatness !* His *mighty acts*, literally *his mights* or *powers*. See above, on Ps. cxlv. 4. *For*, literally *in* them, *i. e.* praise him as exhibited and viewed in these. The corresponding particle means like, in accordance

with, in proportion to, in a manner worthy of his greatness. The last phrase in Hebrew is peculiarly expressive, consisting of the two strongest terms denoting magnitude, the abstract forms of *much* and *great*, which might be rendered, if our usage suffered it, *muchness of greatness.*

3. *Praise him with blast of trumpet ! Praise him with harp and lyre !* Here begins an enumeration of the instruments employed in public worship, and therefore necessarily associated with the idea of divine praise. The trumpet was used to assemble the people, and would therefore excite many of the same associations with our church-bells. The other instruments were used as actual accompaniments of the psalms performed in public worship.

4. *Praise him with timbrel and dance ! Praise him with strings and pipe !* The three great classes of instruments are here distinctly mentioned, namely, wind, stringed, and pulsatile. The last, represented by the drum or timbrel, still called by a kindred name in Arabic, is here accompanied by its inseparable adjunct *dancing*, which might seem misplaced in a list of instruments, and those employed in sacred music, but for the peculiar usages and notions of the ancient Hebrews, with respect to this external sign of joy. See above, on Ps. xxx. 12 (11), cxlix. 3. The common version of the last word (*organ*) is derived through the Vulgate from the Septuagint, where it denotes a system or combination of pipes. The Hebrew word, according to the Jewish tradition, means a simple pipe, and is so rendered in the Prayer Book version. It here represents the whole class of wind-instruments. See above, on Ps. lxviii. 26 (25), and compare 2 Sam. vi. 5.

5. *Praise him with cymbals of loud sound ! Praise him with cymbals of joyful noise !* The dominant idea, that of audibly expressed joy, is sustained to the last, where the cymbals are mentioned in both clauses, as an instrument peculiarly appropriated to occasions of unusual rejoicing. See 2 Sam. vi. 5, Ezra iii. 10, Neh. xii. 27. The effect is still further heightened by the qualifying epithets, the first of which strictly denotes *hearing* or the thing heard, *i. e.* sound, and here by implication, loud sound. To this idea the parallel term adds that of joyful sound, to which it is constantly applied in usage. See above, on Ps. xxvii. 6, lxxxix. 16 (15), and compare Num. xxiii. 21. The distinction, here assumed by some interpreters, between cymbals of a larger and a smaller size, is wholly unnecessary.

6. *Let all breath praise Jah ! Hallelujah !* The very ambiguity of *all breath* gives extraordinary richness of meaning to this closing sentence. From the simple idea of wind instruments, mentioned in the context, it leads us, by a beautiful transition, to that of vocal, articulate, intelligent praise, uttered by the breath of living men, as distinguished from mere lifeless instruments. See above, on Ps. lxviii. 26 (25). Then lastly, by a natural association, we ascend to the idea expressed in the common version, *everything that hath breath*, not merely all that lives, but all that has a voice to praise God. There is nothing in the Psalter more majestic or more beautiful than this brief but most significant *finale*, in which solemnity of tone predominates, without, however, in the least disturbing the exhilaration which the close of the Psalter seems intended to produce, as if in emblematical allusion to the triumph which awaits the church and all its members, when through much tribulation they shall enter into rest.

Classic Commentaries for Bible Study

STUDIES IN LEVITICUS   Samuel H. Kellogg

(Foreword by Cyril J. Barber.) Kellogg staunchly defends Mosaic authorship and ably treats Jewish ceremonial law in all its practical aspects. A classic study of the "law of the priests," the typology of the tabernacle, and the laws governing the daily lives of God's people.

0-8254-3041-0	574 pp.	paperback
0-8254-3043-7	574 pp.	deluxe hardcover

COMMENTARY ON THE PSALMS   J. J. Stewart Perowne

(Two volumes in one; Foreword by Walter C. Kaiser, Jr.) A classic exegetical work which highlights the sheer beauty and grace of language in the book of Psalms. Perowne provides a complete background for every Psalm along with detailed exegesis and commentary. Includes notes on the Hebrew text, the ancient versions, and other English translations. The best of evangelical scholarship is combined with profound spiritual perception to offer Bible students a trustworthy storehouse of insights into the Psalter.

0-8254-3485-8	1144 pp.	paperback
0-8254-3486-6	1144 pp.	deluxe hardcover

COMMENTARY ON EZEKIEL   Patrick Fairbairn

(Foreword by Peter M. Masters.) One of the most valuable works on this important Old Testament book. Fairbairn discusses the person, position, and circumstances of Ezekiel as well as looking at some of the more distinctive features of his prophetic character. This verse-by-verse commentary is a welcome addition to Old Testament studies.

0-8254-2627-8	512 pp.	paperback
0-8254-2630-8	512 pp.	deluxe hardcover

COMMENTARY ON ZECHARIAH: HIS VISIONS AND PROPHECIES   David Baron

(Foreword by Walter C. Kaiser, Jr.) W. H. Griffith Thomas called this ". . . the best available book on Zechariah." A thorough exposition of this prophetic book.

0-8254-2277-9	566 pp.	paperback
0-8254-2216-7	566 pp.	deluxe hardcover

COMMENTARY ON MATTHEW   John A. Broadus

One of the finest volumes ever produced on the Gospel of Matthew. John A. Broadus, perhaps one of America's greatest biblical scholars, offers a balanced commentary which contains a straightforward exegesis of the text. In addition, a gold mine of practical insights will provide the reader with a deeper understanding and application of this "gospel of the King!"

0-8254-2283-3	610 pp.	paperback
0-8254-2284-1	610 pp.	deluxe hardcover

COMMENTARY ON ROMANS   Robert Haldane

(Foreword by D. Martyn Lloyd-Jones.) One of the most authoritative expositions ever to appear on this Epistle. It offers exhaustive exegesis on every sentence in Romans, emphasizing scholarship, theological reflection, and spiritual insight. Special attention is given to the glorious doctrine of justification by faith. Clearly refutes critical attacks on the words and doctrines communicated by Paul.

0-8254-2865-3	754 pp.	paperback
0-8254-2862-9	754 pp.	deluxe hardcover

THE EPISTLE OF JAMES   Joseph B. Mayor

A monumental work on this often neglected portion of the New Testament which provides detailed analysis on such important aspects of the epistle as: authorship, evidence for authenticity, its relationship to the other New Testament books and earlier first century writings, its date, and its grammar and style. Mayor offers a detailed word-by-word commentary on James. This work offers an in-depth understanding of the epistle's background, message, and practical insights for application.

0-8254-3255-3	624 pp.	paperback
0-8254-3256-1	624 pp.	deluxe hardcover

COMMENTARY ON JUDE   Thomas Manton

(Foreword by Peter M. Masters.) An exhaustive, classic exposition. Manton's organization is excellent and his practical observations are valuable. "Manton's work is most commendable." - Spurgeon

0-8254-3239-1	384 pp.	paperback
0-8254-3240-5	384 pp.	deluxe hardcover